ROGET'S THESAURUS

OF
SYNONYMS
AND
ANTONYMS

BY

PETER MARK ROGET, M.D., F.R.S.

ENLARGED BY

JOHN LEWIS ROGET, M.A.

NEW EDITION REVISED AND ENLARGED BY

SAMUEL ROMILLY ROGET, M.A.

GALLEY PRESS
London, England

PLAN OF CLASSIFICATION

TABULAR SYNOPSIS OF CATEGORIES

Class I. ABSTRACT RELATIONS

I. EXISTENCE

1°. ABSTRACT...........	1. Existence.	2. Inexistence.
2°. CONCRETE..........	3. Substantiality.	4. Unsubstantiality.
3°. FORMAL............	*Internal.* 5. Intrinsicality.	*External.* 6. Extrinsicality.
4°. MODAL.............	*Absolute.* 7. State.	*Relative.* 8. Circumstance.

II. RELATION

1°. ABSOLUTE..........	9. Relation. 11. Consanguinity. 12. Correlation. 13. Identity. 15. Difference.	10. Irrelation. 14. Contrariety.
2°. CONTINUOUS........	16. Uniformity.	16a. Non-uniformity.
3°. PARTIAL...........	17. Similarity. 19. Imitation. 20a. Variation. 21. Copy.	18. Dissimilarity. 20. Non-imitation. 22. Prototype.
4°. GENERAL...........	23. Agreement.	24. Disagreement.

III. QUANTITY

1°. SIMPLE............	*Absolute.* 25. Quantity. 27. Equality.	*Relative.* 26. Degree. 28. Inequality.
2°. COMPARATIVE.......	29. Mean. 30. Compensation. *By Comparison with a Standard.* 31. Greatness. *By Comparison with a similar Object.* 33. Superiority. *Changes in Quantity.* 35. Increase.	32. Smallness. 34. Inferiority. 36. Decrease.
3°. CONJUNCTIVE.......	37. Addition. 39. Adjunct. 41. Mixture. 43. Junction. 45. Vinculum. 46. Coherence. 48. Combination.	38. {Non-addition. Subduction. 40. Remainder. 40a. Decrement. 42. Simpleness. 44. Disjunction. 47. Incoherence. 49. Decomposition.

SYNOPSIS OF CATEGORIES

2°. SENSATION

(1) General . . . .
- 375. Sensibility.
- 376. Insensibility.
- 377. Pleasure.
- 378. Pain.

(2) Special

1. Touch . .
- 379. Touch.
- 380. { Sensations of Touch.
- 381. Numbness.

2. Heat . . .
- 382. Heat.
- 383. Cold.
- 384. Calefaction.
- 385. Refrigeration.
- 386. Furnace.
- 387. Refrigeratory.
- 388. Fuel.
- 389. Thermometer.

3. Taste . . .
- 390. Taste.
- 391. Insipidity.
- 392. Pungency.
- 393. Condiment.
- 394. Savouriness.
- 395. Unsavouriness.
- 396. Sweetness.
- 397. Sourness.

4. Odor . .
- 398. Odor.
- 399. Inodorousness.
- 400. Fragrance.
- 401. Fœtor.

5. Sound . .

(i.) *Sound in General.*
- 402. Sound.
- 403. Silence.
- 404. Loudness.
- 405. Faintness.

(ii.) *Specific Sounds.*
- 406. Snap.
- 407. Roll.
- 408. Resonance.
- 408a. Non-resonance.
- 409. Sibilation.
- 410. Stridor.
- 411. Cry.
- 412. Ululation.

(iii.) *Musical Sounds.*
- 413. { Melody. Concord.
- 414. Discord.
- 415. Music.
- 416. Musician.
- 417. Musical Instruments.

(iv.) *Perception of Sound.*
- 418. Hearing.
- 419. Deafness.

6. Light . . .

(i.) *Light in General.*
- 420. Light.
- 421. Darkness.
- 422. Dimness.
- 423. Luminary.
- 424. Shade.
- 425. Transparency.
- 426. Opacity.
- 427. Semitransparency.

(ii.) *Specific Light.*
- 428. Color.
- 429. Achromatism.
- 430. Whiteness.
- 431. Blackness.
- 432. Gray.
- 433. Brown.
- 434. Redness.
- 435. Greenness.
- 436. Yellowness.
- 437. Purple.
- 438. Blueness.
- 439. Orange.
- 440. Variegation.

(iii.) *Perceptions of Light.*
- 441. Vision.
- 442. Blindness.
- 443. Dimsightedness.
- 444. Spectator.
- 445. Optical Instruments.
- 446. Visibility.
- 447. Invisibility.
- 448. Appearance.
- 449. Disappearance.

SYNOPSIS OF CATEGORIES

CLASS IV. INTELLECT

Division (I.). FORMATION OF IDEAS

I. OPERATIONS OF INTELLECT IN GENERAL.....

450. Intellect.   450a. Absence of Intellect.
451. Thought.   452. Incogitancy.
453. Idea.   454. Topic.
455. Curiosity.   456. Incuriosity.
457. Attention.   458. Inattention.
459. Care.   460. Neglect.

II. PRECURSORY CONDITIONS AND OPERATIONS......

461. Inquiry.   462. Answer.
463. Experiment.
464. Comparison.
465. Discrimination.   465a. Indiscrimination.
466. Measurement.
467. Evidence.   468. Counter-evidence.
469. Qualification.

III. MATERIALS FOR REASONING..........

Degrees of Evidence.
470. Possibility.   471. Impossibility.
472. Probability.   473. Improbability.
474. Certainty.   475. Uncertainty.

IV. REASONING PROCESSES

476. Reasoning.   477. { Intuition. Sophistry.
478. Demonstration.   479. Confutation.
480. Judgement.   481. Misjudgement.
480a. Discovery.
482. Over-estimation.   483. Under-estimation.

V. RESULTS OF REASONING

484. Belief.   485. { Unbelief. Doubt.
486. Credulity.   487. Incredulity.
488. Assent.   489. Dissent.
490. Knowledge.   491. Ignorance.
492. Scholar.   493. Ignoramus.
494. Truth.   495. Error.
496. Maxim.   497. Absurdity.

Faculties.
498. { Intelligence. Wisdom.   499. { Imbecility. Folly.
500. Sage.   501. Fool.
502. Sanity.   503. Insanity.
    504. Madman.

VI. EXTENSION OF THOUGHT

1°. *To the Past*...

505. Memory.   506. Oblivion.
507. Expectation.   508. Inexpectation.
    509. Disappointment.

2°. *To the Future.*

510. Foresight.
511. Prediction.
512. Omen.
513. Oracle.

VII. CREATIVE THOUGHT...

514. Supposition.
515. Imagination.

SYNOPSIS OF CATEGORIES
Division (II.). COMMUNICATION OF IDEAS

I. NATURE OF IDEAS COMMUNICATED......

516. Meaning.   517. Unmeaningness.
518. Intelligibility.   519. Unintelligibility
520. Equivocalness.
521. Metaphor.
522. Interpretation.   523. Misinterpretatic
524. Interpreter.
525. Manifestation.   526. Latency.
527. Information.   528. Concealment.
529. Disclosure.   530. Ambush.
531. Publication.
532. News.   533. Secret.
534. Messenger.
535. Affirmation.   536. Negation.

II. MODES OF COMMUNICATION..............

537. Teaching.   538. Misteaching.
   539. Learning.
540. Teacher.   541. Learner.
542. School.
543. Veracity.   544. Falsehood.
   545. Deception.
   546. Untruth.
547. Dupe.   548. Deceiver.
   549. Exaggeration.

III. MEANS OF COMMUNICATION

1°. Natural Means.......

550. Indication.
551. Record.   552. Obliteration.
553. Recorder.
554. Representation.   555. Misrepresentati
556. Painting.
557. Sculpture.
558. Engraving.
559. Artist.
560. Language.
561. Letter.
562. Word.   563. Neology.
564. Nomenclature.   565. Misnomer.
566. Phrase.
567. Grammar.   568. Solecism.

2°. Conventional Means

1. Language generally

569. Style.

Qualities of Style.
570. Perspicuity.   571. Obscurity.
572. Conciseness.   573. Diffuseness.
574. Vigour.   575. Feebleness.
576. Plainness.   577. Ornament.
578. Elegance.   579. Inelegance.

2. Spoken Language

580. Voice.   581. Aphony.
582. Speech.   583. Stammering.
584. Loquacity.   585. Taciturnity.
586. Allocution.   587. Response.
588. Interlocution.   589. Soliloquy.

3. Written Language

590. Writing.   591. Printing.
592. Correspondence.   593. Book.
594. Description.
595. Dissertation.
596. Compendium.
597. Poetry.   598. Prose.
599. The Drama.

Class V. VOLITION

Division (I.). Individual Volition

I. VOLITION IN GENERAL

1°. Acts....

600. Will.	601. Necessity.
602. Willingness.	603. Unwillingness.
604. Resolution.	605. Irresolution.
604a. Perseverance. ⎫	
606. Obstinacy. ⎭	607. Tergiversation.
	608. Caprice.
609. Choice.	⎰609a. Absence of Choice.
	⎱610. Rejection.
611. Predetermination.	612. Impulse.
613. Habit.	614. Desuetude.

2°. Causes..

615. Motive.	⎰615a. Absence of Motive.
	⎱616. Dissuasion.

3°. Objects..

617. Plea.	
618. Good.	619. Evil.
620. Intention.	621. Chance.
622. Pursuit.	623. Avoidance.
	624. Relinquishment.

II. PROSPECTIVE VOLITION........

1°. Conceptional..

625. Business.	
626. Plan.	
627. Method.	
628. Mid-Course.	629. Circuit.
630. Requirement.	

2°. Subservience to Ends...

1. Actual Subservience.

631. Instrumentality.
632. Means.
633. Instrument.
634. Substitute.
635. Materials.
636. Store.

637. Provision.	638. Waste.

639. Sufficiency.

641. Redundance.	640. Insufficiency.

2. Degree of Subservience.

642. Importance.	643. Unimportance.
644. Utility.	645. Inutility.
646. Expedience.	647. Inexpedience.
648. Goodness.	649. Badness.
650. Perfection.	651. Imperfection.
652. Cleanness.	653. Uncleanness.
654. Health.	655. Disease.
656. Salubrity.	657. Insalubrity.
658. Improvement.	659. Deterioration.
660. Restoration.	661. Relapse.
662. Remedy.	663. Bane.

3. Contingent Subservience.

664. Safety.	665. Danger.
666. Refuge.	667. Pitfall.
668. Warning.	
669. Alarm.	
670. Preservation.	
671. Escape.	
672. Deliverance.	

SYNOPSIS OF CATEGORIES

II. Prospective Volition—*cont.*	3°. *Precursory Measures*	673. Preparation.	674. Non-preparation.
		675. Essay.	
		676. Undertaking.	
		677. Use.	678. Disuse.
			679. Misuse.

III. Action

1°. *Simple*...
680. Action. — 681. Inaction.
682. Activity. — 683. Inactivity.
684. Haste. — 685. Leisure.
686. Exertion. — 687. Repose.
688. Fatigue. — 689. Refreshment.

2°. *Complex*.
690. Agent.
691. Workshop.
692. Conduct.
693. Direction.
694. Director.
695. Advice.
696. Council.
697. Precept.
698. Skill. — 699. Unskilfulness.
700. Proficient. — 701. Bungler.
702. Cunning. — 703. Artlessness.

IV. Antagonism

1°. *Conditional*....
704. Difficulty. — 705. Facility.

2°. *Active*....
706. Hindrance. — 707. Aid.
708. Opposition. — 709. Co-operation.
710. Opponent. — 711. Auxiliary.
712. Party.
713. Discord. — 714. Concord.
715. Defiance.
716. Attack. — 717. Defence.
718. Retaliation. — 719. Resistance.
720. Contention. — 721. Peace.
722. Warfare. — 723. Pacification.
724. Meditation.
725. Submission.
726. Combatant.
727. Arms.
728. Arena.

V. Results of Action.....
729. Completion. — 730. Non-completion.
731. Success. — 732. Failure.
733. Trophy.
734. Prosperity. — 735. Adversity.
736. Mediocrity.

Division (II.). Intersocial Volition

I. General.............
737. Authority. — 738. Laxity.
739. Severity. — 740. Lenity.
741. Command.
742. Disobedience. — 743. Obedience.
744. Compulsion.
745. Master. — 746. Servant.
747. Sceptre.
748. Freedom. — 749. Subjection.
750. Liberation. — 751. Restraint.
752. Prison.
753. Keeper. — 754. Prisoner.
755. Commission. — 756. Abrogation.
757. Resignation.
758. Consignee.
759. Deputy.

CLASS VI. AFFECTIONS

II. PERSONAL

1°. PASSIVE

827. Pleasure.	828. Pain.
829. Pleasureableness.	830. Painfulness.
831. Content.	{ 832. Discontent.
	{ 833. Regret.
834. Relief.	835. Aggravation.
836. Cheerfulness.	837. Dejection.
838. Rejoicing.	839. Lamentation.
840. Amusement.	841. Weariness.
842. Wit.	843. Dulness.
844. Humorist.	
845. Beauty.	846. Ugliness.
847. Ornament.	848. Blemish.
	849. Simplicity.
850. Taste.	851. Vulgarity.

2°. DISCRIMINATIVE

852. Fashion.	
	853. Ridiculousness.
	854. Fop.
	855. Affection.
	856. Ridicule.
	857. Laughing-stock.

3°. PROSPECTIVE

858. Hope.	{ 859. Hopelessness.
	{ 860. Fear.
861. Courage.	862. Cowardice.
863. Rashness.	864. Caution.
865. Desire.	867. Dislike.
866. Indifference.	
	868. Fastidiousness.
	869. Satiety.

4°. CONTEMPLATIVE

870. Wonder.	871. Expectance.
872. Prodigy.	
873. Repute.	874. Disrepute.
875. Nobility.	876. Commonalty.
877. Title.	
878. Pride.	879. Humility.

5°. EXTRINSIC

880. Vanity.	881. Modesty.
882. Ostentation.	
883. Celebration.	
884. Boasting.	
885. Insolence.	886. Servility.
887. Blusterer.	

III. SYMPATHETIC

1°. SOCIAL

888. Friendship.	889. Enmity.
890. Friend.	891. Enemy.
892. Sociality.	893. Seclusion.
894. Courtesy.	895. Discourtesy.
896. Congratulation.	
897. Love.	898. Hate.
899. Favorite.	
	900. Resentment.
	901. Irascibility.
	901a. Sullenness.
902. Endearment.	
903. Marriage.	{ 904. Celibacy.
	{ 905. Divorce.

2°. DIFFUSIVE	906. Benevolence.	907. Malevolence.
		908. Malediction.
		909. Threat.
	910. Philanthropy.	911. Misanthropy.
	912. Benefactor.	913. Evil doer.
3°. SPECIAL	914. Pity.	914a. Pitilessness.
	915. Condolence.	
	916. Gratitude.	917. Ingratitude.
4°. RETROSPECTIVE	918. Forgiveness.	919. Revenge.
		920. Jealousy.
		921. Envy.

IV. MORAL

1°. OBLIGATIONS	922. Right.	923. Wrong.
	924. Dueness.	925. Undueness.
	926. Duty.	927. Dereliction.
		927a. Exemption.
	928. Respect.	929. Disrespect.
		930. Contempt.
2°. SENTIMENTS	931. Approbation.	932. Disapprobation.
	933. Flattery.	934. Detraction.
	935. Flatterer.	936. Detractor.
	937. Vindication.	938. Accusation.
	939. Probity.	940. Improbity.
		941. Knave.
	942. Disinterestedness.	943. Selfishness.
3°. CONDITIONS	944. Virtue.	945. Vice.
	946. Innocence.	947. Guilt.
	948. Good Man.	949. Bad Man.
	950. Penitence.	951. Impenitence.
	952. Atonement.	
	953. Temperance.	954. Intemperance.
		954a. Sensualist.
4°. PRACTICE	955. Asceticism.	
	956. Fasting.	957. Gluttony.
	958. Sobriety.	959. Drunkenness.
	960. Purity.	961. Impurity.
		962. Libertine.
	963. Legality.	964. Illegality.
	965. Jurisprudence.	
	966. Tribunal.	
	967. Judge.	
	968. Lawyer.	
5°. INSTITUTIONS	969. Lawsuit.	
	970. Acquittal.	971. Condemnation.
	973. Reward.	972. Punishment.
		974. Penalty.
		975. Scourge.

V. RELIGIOUS

1°. SUPERHUMAN BE-INGS AND REGIONS	976. Deity.	
	977. Angel.	978. Satan:
	979. Jupiter.	980. Demon.
	981. Heaven.	982. Hell.
2°. DOCTRINES	983. Theology.	
	983a. Orthodoxy.	984. Heterodoxy.
	985. Revelation.	986. Pseudo-revelation.
3°. SENTIMENTS	987. Piety.	988. Impiety.
		989. Irreligion.

SYNOPSIS OF CATEGORIES

ABBREVIATIONS, &c.

Adj.	adj.	Adjectives, Participles, and Words having the power of Adjectives.
Adv.	adv.	Adverbs and Adverbial Expressions.
Int.	int.	Interjections.
Phr.	phr.	Phrases.
V.	v.	Verbs.

The numbers are those of the headings, or Categories.

Words in italics within parentheses are not intended to explain the meanings of the words which precede them, but to indicate the nature of allied group of words under the numbers which follow them.

THESAURUS

OF

ENGLISH WORDS AND PHRASES

1. Existence.—N. existence, being, entity, *ens, esse,* subsistence, quiddity.

reality, realness, actuality; positiveness etc. *adj.*; fact, matter of fact, sober reality; truth etc. 494; actual existence.

presence etc. (*existence in space*) 186; coexistence etc. 120.

stubborn fact; not a -dream etc. 515; no joke.

substance, essence, prime constituent, hypostatis. [Science of existence], ontology.

V. exist, be; have -being etc. *n.*; subsist, live, breathe, stand, obtain, be the case; occur etc. (*event*) 151; have place, rank, prevail; find oneself, pass the time, vegetate.

consist in, lie in, reside in, inhere in.

come into -existence etc. *n.*; arise etc. (*begin*) 66; come forth etc. (*appear*) 446.

become etc. (*be converted*) 144; bring into existence etc. 161; coexist, preexist, endure etc. 141.

Adj. existing etc. *v.*; existent, subsistent, under the sun; in -existence etc, *n.*; extant; afloat, on foot, current, prevalent, rife, in force, -vogue; un-destroyed.

real, actual, positive, absolute; true etc. 494; substan-tial, -tive; self-existing, -ent.

well-founded, -grounded; un-ideal, -imagined; not -potential etc. 2.

Adv. actually etc. *adj.*; in -fact, − point of fact, − reality; indeed; *de* −, *ipso-facto.*

2. Nonexistence.—N. nonexistence; inexistence, -subsistence; nonentity, *nil*; negativeness etc. *adj.*; nullity; nihil-ity, -ism; *tabula rasa*, blank; abeyance; absence etc. 187; no such thing etc. 4; nothingness, oblivion, *non esse.*

annihilation; extinction etc. (*destruction*) 162.

V. not -exist etc. 1; have no -existence etc. 1; be null and void; cease to -exist etc. 1; pass away, perish; be −, become-extinct etc. *adj.*; die out; disappear etc. 449; melt away, dissolve, leave not a rack behind, leave no trace; go, be no more; die etc. 360.

annihilate, render null, nullify; abrogate etc. 756; destroy etc. 162; take away; remove etc. (*displace*) 185.

Adj. inexistent, non-existent etc. 1; negative, blank, null and void; missing, omitted; absent etc. 187; visionary etc. 515.

unreal, potential, virtual; baseless, *in nubibus*; unsubstantial etc. 4; vain.

un-born, -created, -begotten, -conceived, produced, -made.

perished, annihilated etc. *v.*; extinct, exhausted, gone, lost, departed; defunct etc. (*dead*) 360; fabulous, ideal etc. (*imaginary*) 515; supposititious etc. 514.

Adv. negatively, virtually, etc. *adj.*

3. Substantiality.—N. substantiality, *hypostasis*; person, thing, object, article; something, a being, an existence; creature, body, substance, flesh and blood, stuff, *substratum*; matter etc. 316; physical nature.

[Totality of existences], world etc. 318; *plenum.*

Adj. substan-tive, -tial, concrete; hypostatic; personal, bodily; tangible etc. (*material*) 316; real, corporeal, evident.

Adv. substantially etc. *adj.*; bodily, essentially.

4. Unsubstantiality.—N. un-, in-substantiality; nothingness, nihility.

nothing, naught, *nil*, nullity, zero, cipher, no one, nobody; never −, ne'er -a one; no such thing, none in the world; nothing -whatever, − at all, − on earth; not a -particle etc. (*smallness*) 32; all -talk, − moonshine, − stuff and nonsense, matter of no import.

thing of naught, man of straw, John Doe and Richard Roe; *nominis umbra*, nonentity, figurehead, lay figure; flash in the pan, *vox et praeterea nihil.*

shadow; phantasm, phantom etc. (*fallacy of vision*) 443; dream etc. (*imagination*) 515; *ignis fatuus* etc. (*luminary*) 423; 'such stuff as dreams are made of;' air, thin air; bubble etc. 353; 'baseless fabric of a vision;' mockery.

hollowness, blank; vacuity, void etc. (*absence*) 187.

inanity, fool's paradise, fatuity, stupidity, emptiness of mind.

V. vanish, evaporate, fade, sink, fly −, die −, melt- away, dissolve, disappear etc. 449; become extinct, become invisible.

Adj. unsubstantial; fleeting; base-, ground-less; ungrounded; without −, having no- foundation.

visionary etc. (*imaginary*) 515; immaterial etc. 317; spectral etc. 980; dreamy; shadowy; ethereal, airy, imponderable, tenuous, vague.

vacant, vacuous; empty etc. 187; eviscerated; blank, hollow; nominal; null; inane.

Phr. there's nothing in it.

1

5. Intrinsicality.—N. intrinsicality, inbeing, inherence, inhesion, immanence; subjectiveness; *ego*; essence; essentialness etc. *adj.*; essential part, essential stuff, substance, quintessence, incarnation, quiddity, gist, pith, core, kernel, marrow, sap, life-blood, backbone, heart, soul, life, flower; important part etc. (*importance*) 642.

principle, nature, constitution, character, ethos, type, quality, crasis, *diathesis*.

habit; temper, -ament; spirit, humor, grain, disposition, streak, tendency etc. 176.

endowment, capacity; capability etc. (*power*) 157; moods, declensions, features, aspects; peculiarities etc. (*specialty*) 79; idiosyncrasy; idiocrasy; diagnostics.

V. be —, run- in the blood; be born so; be -intrinsic etc. *adj.*

Adj. derived from within, subjective; idiocratic, idiosyncratic, intrin-sic, -sical; fundamental, cardinal, normal, inherent, essential, natural; in-nate, -born, -bred, -dwelling, -grained; -wrought; radical, incarnate, thoroughbred, hereditary, inherited, immanent; congen-ital, -ite; connate, running in the blood; coeval with birth, genetic, ingenerate, -genite; indigenous; in the -grain etc. *n.*; bred in the bone, instinctive; inward, internal etc. 221; to the manner born; virtual.

characteristic etc. (*special*) 79, (*indicative*) 550; invariable, incurable, ineradicable, fixed, settled, constant, unchanging.

Adv. intrinsically. etc. *adj.*; at bottom, in the main, in effect, essentially, practically, virtually, substantially, *au fond*; fairly.

6. Extrinsicality.—N. ' extrinsicality, objectiveness, *non ego;* extraneousness etc. 57; accident; letter of the law.

Adj. derived from without; objective; extrinsic, -sical; extraneous etc. (*foreign*) 57; modal, adventitious, additional, supervenient, fortuitous; a-, ad-scititious; incidental, casual, accidental, unessential, non-essential, accessory.

implanted; ingrafted; instilled, inculcated.

outward etc. (*external*) 220.

Adv. extrinsically etc. *adj.*

7. State.—N. state, condition, category, estate, lot, case, trim, mood, pickle, plight etc. 704; temper; aspect etc. (*appearance*) 448.

constitution, habitude, *diathesis;* frame, fabric etc. 329; stamp, set, fit, mold.

mode, modality, schesis; fettle; form etc. (*shape*) 240.

tone, tenor, turn; trim, guise, fashion, light, complexion, style, character.

V. be in —, possess —, enjoy —, labor under- a -state etc. *n.;* be on a footing, do, fare; come to pass.

Adj. conditional, modal, formal; structural, organic.

Adv. conditionally etc. *adj.;* as -the matter stands, — things are; such being the case etc. 8.

8. Circumstance.—N. circumstance, situation, phase, position, posture, attitude, place, point; terms; *régime;* footing, standing, status.

occasion, juncture, conjuncture; contingency etc. (*event*) 151.

predicament; emergen-ce, -cy; exigency, crisis, pinch, pass, push; turning point; crossroads.

bearings, how the land lies.

Adj. circumstantial; given, conditional, provisional; critical; modal; contingent, incidental; adventitious etc. (*extrinsic*) 6.

Adv. in the circumstances etc. *n.,* under the conditions etc. 7; thus, in such wise.

accordingly; that —, such- being the case; that being so, since, seeing that.

as matters stand; as -things, — times- go.

conditionally, provided, if, in case; if -so, — so be, — it be so; if it so -happen, — turn out; in the event of; in such a -contingency, — case, — event; provisionally, unless, without.

according to -circumstances, — the occasion; as it may -happen, — turn out, — be; as the -case may be, — wind blows; *pro re natâ.*

9. Relation.—N. relation, bearing, reference, connection, apposition, interconnection, concern, cognation; applicability, appositeness; correlation etc. 12; analogy; similarity etc. 17; affinity, intimacy, friendship; homology, alliance, homogeneity, association, rapport; approximation etc. (*nearness*) 197; filiation etc. (*consanguinity*) 11; interest; relevancy etc. 23; relationship, relative position; relativity; interrelation etc. 12.

comparison etc. 464; ratio, proportion.

link, tie, bond, bond of union.

V. be-related etc. *adj.;* have a relation etc. *n.;* relate —, refer- to; bear upon, regard, concern, touch, affect, have to do with; pertain —, belong —, appertain- to; have respect to; answer to; interest.

bring -into relation with, — to bear upon; connect, associate, draw a parallel; link etc. 43.

Adj. relative; correlative etc. 12; cognate; relating to etc. *v.;* relative to, in relation with, referable *or* referrible to; belonging to etc. *v.;* appurtenant to, in common with.

related, connected; implicated, associated, affiliated, akin, allied to; collateral, cognate, congenial, kindred, affinitive, *en rapport*, in touch with.

approxima-tive, -ting; approaching; proportion-al, -ate, -able; allusive, comparable.

in the same -category etc. 75; like etc. 17; relevant etc. (*apt*) 23.

Adv. relatively etc. *adj.;* pertinently etc. 23.

thereof; as -to, — for, — respects, — re-gards; about; concerning etc. *v.;* anent; relating —, as relates- to; with -relation, — reference, — respect, — regard-to; in respect of; while speaking —, *à propos*-of; in connection with; by the -way, — by; whereas; for —, in -as much as; in point of, as far as; on the -part, — score- of; *quoad hoc; pro re natâ;* under the -head etc. (*class*) 75- of; in the matter of, *in re.*

Phr. 'thereby hangs a tale.'

10. Irrelation. [Want, or absence of relation.]—**N.** irrelation, dissociation; inapplicability; inconnection; multifariousness; disconnection etc. (*disjunction*) 44; inconsequence, independence; incommensurability; irreconcilableness etc. (*disagreement*) 24; heterogeneity;

unconformity etc. 83; irrelevancy, impertinence, *nihil ad rem;* intrusion etc. 24.

V. have no -relation etc. 9 to, — bearing upon, — concern etc. 9 with, — business with; not -concern etc. 9; have -nothing to do with, — no business there; intrude, etc. 24.

bring —, drag —, haul —, lug- in head and shoulders.

Adj. irrelative, irrespective, unrelated, irrelated; arbitrary; independent, unallied; un-, dis-connected; adrift, isolated, insular; extraneous, strange, alien, foreign, outlandish, exotic.

not comparable, incommensurable, heterogeneous; unconformable etc. 83.

irrelevant; rambling etc. 279; inapplicable; not -pertinent, — to the purpose; impertinent, inapposite, beside the mark, *à propos de bottes;* away from —, foreign to —, beside- the -purpose, — question, — transaction, — point; misplaced etc. (*intrusive*) 24.

remote, far fetched, out of the way, forced, neither here nor there, quite another thing; detached, segregated, segregate.

multifarious; discordant etc. 24.

incidental, parenthetical, *obiter dictum,* episodic.

Adv. parenthetically etc. *adj.;* by the -way, — by; *en passant,* incidentally; irrespecitively etc. *adj.;* without reference, — regard- to; in the abstract etc. 87; *a se.*

11. Consanguinity. [Relations of kindred.]—N. consanguinity, relationship, kindred, blood; parentage etc. (*paternity*) 166; filiation, affiliation; lineage, agnation, connection, cognation, alliance; family -connection, — tie; ties of blood; blood relationship; nepotism.

kins-man, -folk; people; kith and kin; relation, -tive; connection; sib; next of kin; uncle, aunt, nephew, niece; cousin, -german; first —, second- cousin; cousin -once, — twice etc.- removed; near —, distant-relation; brother, sister, one's own flesh and blood.

family, patriarch, matriarch; fraternity; brother-, sister-, cousin-hood.

race, stock, generation; sept etc. 166 ; stirps, side; strain; breed, clan, tribe.

V. be -related etc. *adj.* — to; claim -relationship etc. *n.*- with.

Adj. related, akin, consanguineous, matrilinear, patrilineal, of the blood, family, allied, collateral; cog-, ag-, con-nate; kindred; affiliated, affine; fraternal, avuncular.

intimately —, nearly —, closely —, remotely —, distantly- related, — allied; german.

12. Correlation. [Double or reciprocal relation.]—N. reciprocalness etc. *adj.;* recipro-city, -cality, -cation; mutuality, correlation, correspondence, interdependence; interchange etc. 148; exchange, barter; interrelation, interconnection; alternation, see-saw.

V. reciprocate, alternate; interchange etc. 148; exchange; counterchange; interact, correspond, mutualize, give and take.

Adj. reciprocal, mutual, commutual, correlative; alternate; interchangeable; international; correspondent, complementary, analogous.

Adv. *mutatis mutandis; vice versâ;* each other; by turns etc. 148; reciprocally etc. *adj.;* to and fro etc. 314.

13. Identity.—N. identity, sameness, oneness, ditto, homogeneity; unity, coincidence, coalescence; convertibility; equality etc. 27; self-ness, self, oneself; identification.

monotony, tautology etc. (*repetition*) 104.

synonym.

fac-simile etc. (*copy*) 21; *alter ego* etc. (*similar*) 17; *ipsissima verba* etc. (*exactness*) 494; same; self —, very —, one and the same; very —, actual-thing, no other.

V. be -identical etc. *adj.;* match, coincide, coalesce.

treat as —, render--the same , —identical; identify; recognize the identity of.

Adj. identical; self, ilk; the -same etc. *n.;* self same; synonymous; one and the same.

coincid-ent, coalesc-ent, -ing; indistinguishable; one; equivalent etc. (*equal*) 27; much -the same, — of a muchness; unaltered.

Adv. identically etc. *adj.;* on all fours; ibid-, -em.

14. Contrariety. [Non-coincidence.]—N. contrariety, contrast, foil, antithesis, oppositeness; counterpole; contradiction; antagonism etc. (*opposition*) 708; counteraction etc. 179.

inversion etc. 218; the -opposite, — reverse, — inverse, — converse, — antipodes, — other extreme etc. 237.

antonym.

V. be -contrary etc. *adj.;* contrast with, oppose; differ *toto coelo.*

invert, reverse, turn the tables etc. 218.

contra-dict, -vene; antagonize etc. 708.

Adj. contrar-y, -ious, -iant; opposite, counter, dead against; ad-, con-, reverse; opposed, antithetical, contrasted, antipodean, antagonistic, opposing; conflicting, inconsistent, contradictory, at cross purposes; negative; hostile etc. 708.

differing *toto coelo;* diametrically opposite; as opposite as -black and white, — light and darkness, — fire and water, — the poles, as different as chalk from cheese; 'Hyperion to a satyr;' quite the -contrary, — reverse; no such thing, just the other way, *tout au contraire.*

Adv. contrarily etc. *adj.; contra,* contrariwise, *per contra,* on the contrary, nay rather; topsyturvy; *vice versâ;* on the other hand etc. (*in compensation*) 30.

15. Difference.—N. difference, unlikeness; heterogeneity; vari-ance, -ation, -ety; diversity, dissimilarity etc. 18; disagreement etc. 24; disparity etc. (*inequality*) 28; distinction, contra-distinction; distinctness; discrepancy, divergence, contrast etc. 18; nonconformity, incompatibility, antithesis.

discord etc. 713.

modification, moods and tenses.

nice —, fine —, delicate —, subtle- distinction; shade of difference, *nuance;* discrimination etc. 465; *differentia.*

different thing, something else, variant, apple

off another tree, horse of another color, another pair of shoes; this that or the other.

V. be -different etc. *adj.;* differ, vary, ablude, mismatch, contrast; diverge —, depart —, deviate- -from; divaricate; differ -*toto coelo,* — *longo intervallo.*

disagree etc. 713.

vary, modify etc. (*change*) 140.

discriminate etc. 465.

Adj. differing etc. *v.;* different, diverse, divided, heterogeneous; distinguishable; varied, modified; divergent, incongruous, diversified, various; discrepant, dissentient, differential; divers, all manner of; variform etc. 81; discordant etc. 713.

other, another, not the same; unequal etc. 28; unmatched; widely apart.

distinctive, characteristic; discriminative; distinghishing.

Adv. differently etc. *adj.*

Phr. *il y a fagots et fagots; tot nomines tot sententiae;* one man's meat is another man's poison.

16. Uniformity.—N. uniformity; homogeneity, -ousness; continuity, stability, consistency; connatural-ity. -ness; homology; accordance; conformity etc. 82; agreement etc. 23.

regularity, constancy, even tenor, routine; monotony, evenness, sameness, dead level; steadiness, equability, unity.

V. be -uniform etc. *adj.;* accord with etc. 23; run through.

become -uniform etc. *adj.;* conform to etc. 82.

render uniform etc. *adj.;* assimilate, level, smooth, dress.

Adj. uniform; homo-geneous, -logous; of a piece, consistent, steady; connatural; monotonous, changeless, dreary, even, invariable, equable, level, regular, stereotyped, unchanged, unvarying; methodical etc. 60; habitual etc. 613.

Adv. uniformly etc. *adj.;* uniformly with etc. (*conformably*) 82; in harmony with etc. (*agreeing*) 23; in a -rut, — groove.

always, ever etc. 112; invariably, without exception, never otherwise; by clock-work; endlessly etc. 112.

Phr. *ab uno disce omnes.*

16a. Non-uniformity. [Absence or want of uniformity.]– **N.** diversity, irregularity, unevenness; multiformity etc. 81; unconformity etc. 83; roughness etc. 256; heterogeneity, heteromorphism.

Adj. diversified, varied, irregular, uneven, rough etc. 256; multifarious; multiform etc. 81; of various kinds; all -manner, — sorts, — kinds-of.

Adv. in all manner of ways, here there and everywhere.

17. Similarity.—N. similarity, resemblance, likeness, similitude, semblance; affinity, approximation, parallelism; parity; agreement etc. 23; ana-logy, -logicalness; correspondence, equality etc.

connatural-ness, -ity; brotherhood, family likeness.

alliteration, rhyme, pun.

repetition etc. 104; sameness etc. (*identity*) 13; uniformity etc. 16.

analogue; the like; match, *pendant,* fellow, companion, pair, mate, twin, double, counterpart, brother, sister; one's second self, *alter ego,* chip of the old block, *par nobile fratrum, Arcades ambo,* birds of a feather, *et hoc genus omne.*

parallel; simile; type etc. (*metaphor*) 521; image etc. (*representation*) 554; photograph; close —, striking —, speaking —, faithful etc *adj.* — likeness, — resemblance.

V. be -similar etc. *adj.;* look like, resemble, bear resemblance, favor; savor —, smack- of; approximate; parallel, match, rhyme with; take after; imitate etc. 19; run in pairs.

Adj. similar; resembling etc. *v.;* like, alike, twin.

analog-ous, -ical; parallel, of a piece; such as, so.

connatural, congeneric, allied to; corresponding, cognate; akin to etc. (*consanguineous*) 11.

approximate, much the same, near, close, something like, such like; a show of; mock, *pseudo,* simulating, representing.

exact etc. (*true*) 494; lifelike, faithful, realistic; true to -nature, — the life; the -very image — pic ure- of; for all the world like, *comme deux gouttes d'eau;* as like as -two peas, — it can stare; *instar omnium,* case in the same mold, ridiculously like.

Adv. as if, so to speak; as —, as if- it were; *quasi,* just as, *veluti in speculum.*

18. Dissimilarity.—N. dissimil-arity, -itude; unlikeness, diversity, disparity, dissemblance; divergence, inequality, difference etc. 15; novelty; variation, variety, originality, disguise.

V. be -unlike etc. *adj.;* vary etc. (*differ*) 15; bear no resemblance to, differ *toto coelo.*

render -unlike etc. *adj.;* vary etc. (*diversify*) 140.

Adj. dissimilar, unlike, disparate; of a different kind etc. (*class*) 75; unmatched, unique; new, novel; unprecedented etc. 83; original.

nothing of the kind; no such —, quite anotherthing; far from it, other than, cast in a different mold, *tertium quid,* as like a dock as a daisy, 'very like a whale;' as different as -chalk from cheese, — Macedon and Monmouth; *lucus a non lucendo.*

diversified etc. 16a.

Adv. otherwise, *alias.*

19. Imitation.—N. imitation; copying etc. *v.;* transcription; repetition, mimeograph, mimeotype, duplication, reduplication; quotation; reproduction.

mockery, mimicry, mime, simulation, personation; representation etc. 554; semblance, pretence; copy etc. 21; assimilation.

paraphrase, parody etc. 21.

plagiarism; forgery etc. (*falsehood*) 544.

imitator; echo, cuckoo, parrot, ape, monkey, mocking-bird, mimic, impersonator, copyist.

V. imitate, copy, mirror, reflect, reproduce, repeat, borrow; do like, echo, re-echo, catch; transcribe; match, parallel.

mock, take off, mimic, ape, simulate, personate, impersonate; forge; act etc. (drama) 599; represent etc. 554; counterfeit, duplicate; portray, parody, travesty, caricature, burlesque.

follow –, tread- in the- -steps, – footsteps, – wake- of; pattern after, take pattern by; follow - suit, – the example of; walk in the shoes of, take a leaf out of another's book, strike in with; take –, model -after; emulate.

Adj. imitated etc. v.; mock, mimic; counterfeit, false, pseudo; modelled after, molded on, paraphrastic; literal; imitative, apish; secondhand; imitable; sham etc. 545.

Adv. literally, to the letter, strictly, precisely, verbatim, literatim, sic, totidem verbis, word for word, mot à mot.

Phr. like master like man.

20. Non-Imitation.—N. no imitation, genuineness, originality; creativeness.

Adj. unimitated, uncopied; unmatched, unparalleled; inimitable etc. 33; unique, original, primordial, primary, pristine, underived, firsthand, archetypal, prototypal.

20a. Variation.—N. variation; alteration etc. (change) 140. modification, moods and tenses; modulation.

divergency etc. 291; deviation etc. 279; aberration; innovation.

V. vary etc. (change) 140; deviate etc. 279; diverge etc. 291.

Adj. varied etc. v.; modified; dissimilar etc. 18; diversified etc. 16a.

21. Copy. [Result of imitation.]—N. copy, facsimile, counterpart, effigies, effigy, symbol, image, form, likeness, similitude, semblance, resemblance, cast, electrotype, stereotype, tracing, ectype; imitation etc. 19; model, representation, adumbration, study; counterfeit presentment, portrait etc. (representment) 554.

duplicate; transcript, -ion; reflex, -ion; shadow, echo; chip of the old block; reprint, reproduction, casting, engraving, replica; transfer; second edition etc. (repetition) 104; réchauffé apograph, fair copy; revise.

parody, caricature, cartoon, burlesque, travesty, paraphrase.

servile -copy, – imitation; counterfeit etc. (deception) 545; pasticcio.

Adj. faithful; lifelike etc. (similar) 17

22. Prototype. [Thing copied.]—N. prototype, original, model, pattern, founding, precedent, standard, scantling, type, arche-, anti-type; protoplast, copy-book, module, exemplar, example, ensample, specimen; paradigm; guide; templet; lay-figure.

text, copy, manuscript, MS., design; fugleman, keynote.

die, mold; matrix, engraving, last, plasm; pro-, proto-plasm; mint; seal, punch, intaglio, negative, stamp.

V. be –, set- an example; set a copy; standardize.

23. Agreement.—N. agreement; ac-cord, -cordance; unison, harmony, concord etc. 714; concordance, concert, understanding, convention, entente -cordiale, consortium, consensus of opinion, pact, mutual understanding, unanimity.

conformity etc. 82; conformance; uniformity etc. 16; consonance, consentaneousness, consistency; congruity, -ence; keeping; congeniality; correspondence, concinnity, parallelism, apposition, union.

fitness, aptness etc. adj.; relevancy; pertinence, -cy; sortance; case in point; aptitude, propriety, applicability, admissibility, commensurability, compatibility, suitability; cognation etc (relation) 9.

adaptation, adjustment, arrangement, graduation, accommodation; reconcil-iation - ement; assimilation; attunement.

consent etc. (assent) 448; concurrence etc. 178; co-operation etc. 709.

right man in the right place, very thing; quite – just- the thing.

be -accordant etc. adj.; agree, accord, harmonize; correspond, tally, respond; meet, suit, fit, befit, do, adapt itself to; fall in –, chime in –, square –, quadrate –, consort –, comport- with; dovetail, assimilate; fit like a glove; fit to a -tittle, – T; match etc. 17; become one.

consent etc. (assent) 488.

render -accordant etc. adj.; fit, suit, adapt, accommodate; graduate; adjust etc. (render equal) 27; dress, regulate, readjust; accord, harmonize, reconcile; fadge, dovetail, square.

Adj. agreeing, suiting etc. v.; in accord, accordant, concordant, consonant, congruous, consentaneous, correspondent, corresponding, homologous, congenial; becoming; harmonious, reconcilable, conformable; in -accordance, – harminy, – keeping. – unison, etc. n.;-with; at one with, of one mind, of a piece; consistent, compatible, proportionate, answerable; commensurate; on all fours.

. apt, apposite, pertinent, pat; to the -point, – -purpose; happy, felicitous, germane, ad rem, in point, bearing upon, applicable, relevant, admissible.

fit, adapted, in loco, à propos, appropriate, seasonable; sortable, suitable, idoneous, deft; meet etc. (expedient) 646.

at home, in one's proper element.

Adv. à propos of; pertinently etc. adj.; pro rata.

Phr. rem acu tetigisti, the cap fits.

24. Disagreement.—N. disagreement, discord, -cordance; disunion, dissonance, dissidence, discrepancy; unconformity etc. 83; incongru-ity, -ence; discongruity, mésalliance, oxymoron; jarring etc. v.; clash, collision, dissension etc. 713; conflict etc. (opposition) 708; controversy etc. 720; falling out, wrangle, argument.

disparity, mismatch, misfit, disproportion; disproportionateness etc. adj.; variance, divergence, repugnance.

unfitness etc. adj.; inaptitude, impropriety; inapplicability etc. adj.; inconsistency, inconcinnity; irrelevancy etc. (irrelation) 10.

misjoin-ing, -der; syncretism, intrusion, interference; *concordia discors.*

fish out of water.

V. disagree; clash, quarrel, jar etc. (*discord*) 713; interfere, intrude, come amiss; not concern etc. 10; mismatch; *hymano capiti cervicem jungere equinam.*

Adj. disagreeing etc. *v.*; discordant, discrepant; at -variance, − war; hostile, antagonistic, repugnant, factious, contradictory, dissentious, incompatible, irreconcilable, inconsistent with; unconformable, exceptional etc. 83; intrusive, incongruous; disproportionate, -ed; unharmonious; unconsonant; divergent, repugnant to.

inapt, unapt, inappropriate, inept, infelicitous, improper; unsuit-ed, -able; inapplicable; un-fit, -fitting, -befitting; unbecoming; ill-timed, ill-adapted, unseasonable, *mal à propos,* inadmissible; inapposite etc. (*irrelevant*) 10.

uncongenial; ill-assorted, -sorted, -matched; mis-matched, -mated, -joined, -placed; unaccommodating, irreducible, uncommensurable, unsympathetic.

out of -character, − keeping, − proportion, − joint, − tune, − place, − season, − its element; at -odds, − variance with.

Adv. in -defiance, − contempt, − spite-of; discordantly etc. *adj.*; *à tort et à travers.*

25. Quantity. [Absolute quantity.]—N. quantity, magnitude; size etc. ((*dimensions*) 192; amplitude, mass, amount, *quantum,* measure, measurement, substance, strength.

[Science of quantity.] Mathematics, Mathesis.

[Definite or finite quantity] arm-, hand-, mouth-, spoon-, thimble-, capful; stock, batch, lot, dose, ration, quotum, quota, pittance, driblet, part, portion etc. 51.

Adj. quantitative, some, any, more or less.

Adv. to the tune of.

26. Degree. [Relative quantity.]—N. degree, grade, extent, measure, proportion, amount, ratio, stint, standard, height, pitch; reach, amplitude, range, scope, size, caliber; gradation, shade; tenor, compass; sphere, station, rank, standing; rate, way, sort.

point, mark, step, stage etc. (*term*) 71; intensity, strength etc. (*greatness*) 31.

V. compare, graduate, calibrate, measure.

Adj. comparative; gradual, shading off, gradational; within the bounds etc. (*limit*), 233.

Adv. by degrees, gradually, inasmuch, *pro tanto*; how-ever, -soever; step by step, bit by bit, little by little, inch by inch, drop by drop, gradatim; by -inches, − slow degrees, − little and little; in some -degree, − measure; to some extent; just a bit.

27. Equality. [Sameness of quantity or degree.]—N. equality, parity, co-extension, symmetry, balance, poise; evenness, monotony, level.

equivalence; equi-pollence, -poise, -librium, -ponderance; par, quits; not a pin to choose; distinction without a difference, six of one and half a dozen of the other; identity etc. 13; similarity etc. 17; isotropism; coequality.

equalization, equation, equilibration, co-ordination, adjustment, readjustment.

drawn -game, -battle, draw, stalemate; neck and neck race; tie, dead heat.

match, peer, compeer, equal, mate, fellow, brother; equivalent.

V. be -equal etc. *adj.*; equal, match, reach, keep pace with, run abreast; come −, amount −, come upto; be −, lie- on a level with; balance; cope with; come to the same thing; level off.

render -equal etc. *adj.*; equalize, level, dress, balance, equate, handicap, give points, trim, adjust, poise; fit, accommodate; adapt etc. (*render accordant*) 23; strike a balance; establish −, restore- equality, − equilibrium; readjust; stretch on the bed of Procrustes.

Adj. equal, even, level, monotonous, coequal, symmetrical, coordinate; on a -par, − level, − footing- with; up to the mark; equiparent.

equivalent, tantamount; quits; homologous; synonymous etc. 522; resolvable into, convertible, much at one, as broad as long, neither more nor less; much the same −, the same thing −, as good- as; all -one, — the same; equi-pollent, -ponderant, -ponderous, -balanced; equalized etc. *v.*; drawn; half and half; isochronous; isoperimetrical.

Adv. equally etc. *adj.*; *pari passu, ad eundem, caeteris paribus; in equilibrio;* to all intents and purposes.

Phr. it -comes, -adds up, − amounts- to the same thing.

28. Inequality. [Difference of quantity or degree.]—N. inequality; dis-, im-parity; odds; difference etc. 15; ill-balanced; unevenness; inclination of the balance, partiality; shortcoming; casting −make− weight; superiority etc. 33; inferiority etc. 34.

V. be -unequal etc. *adj.*; countervail; have −, give- the advantage; turn the scale; kick the beam; topple, -over; over-match etc. 33; not come up to etc. 34.

Adj. unequal, uneven, disparate, partial; un-, over-balanced; top-heavy, lop-sided.

Adv. *haud passibus aequis.*

29. Mean.—N. mean, medium, intermedium, average, run of the mill, normal, balance; mediocrity, generality, rule, ordinary -run, -ruck; golden mean etc. (*mid-course*) 628; middle etc. 68; compromise etc. 774; neutrality; middle point, middle course.

V. split the difference; take the -average etc. *n.*; reduce to a -mean etc. *n.*; strike a balance, pair off.

Adj. mean, intermediate; medial; middle etc. 68; average, normal, standard, neutral; middling, moderate.

médiocre, middle-class; *bourgeois,* commonplace etc. (*unimportant*) 643.

Adv. on an average, in the long run; taking - one with another, − all things together, − it for all in all; *communibus annis,* in round numbers.

30. Compensation.—N. compensation, equation; commutation; indemnification; compromise etc. 774; neutralization, nullification; counteraction etc. 179; reaction; measure for measure; retaliation etc. 718; equalization etc. 27; redemption, recoupment, recompense.

set-off, offset; make- casting-weight; counterpoise, equipoise, ballast; indemnity, reparation etc. 790; equivalent, *quid pro quo;* bribe, hushmoney, tribute etc. 784; amends etc. (*atonement*) 952; counterclaim, counterbalance, equiponderance, countervail, cross demand.

V. make -amends, — compensation; compensate, -pense; indemnify; counter-act, -vail, - poise; equiponderate; balance; out-, over-, counterbalance; set off, offset, cancel; hedge, square, give and take; make up -for, — lee way; cover, fill up, neutralize, nullify; equalize etc. 27; make good; redeem etc. (*atone*) 952; recoup, pay etc. 973.

Adj. compensat-ing, -ory; amendatory, reparative, countervailing etc. *v.;* in the opposite scale; equivalent etc. (*equal*) 27.

Adv. in -return, — consideration; but, however, yet, still, notwithstanding; neverthe-, nathless; although, though; al-, how-beit; in spite of, despite; mauger; at -all events, — any rate; be that as it may, for all that, even so, on the other hand, at the same time, *quoad minus, quand même,* however that may be; after all, — is said and done; taking one thing with another etc. (*average*) 29.

31. Greatness.— N. greatness etc. *adj.;* magnitude; size etc. (*dimensions*) 192; multitude etc. (*number*) 102; immensity, enormity, infinity etc. 105; might, strength, intensity, fulness; importance etc. 642; fame etc. 873.

great quantity, quantity, deal, power, sight, pot, volume, world; mass, heap etc. (*assemblage*) 72; stock etc. (*store*) 636; peck, bushel, load, cargo; cart —, wagon —, car —, truck —, shipload; flood, spring tide; abundance etc. (*sufficiency*) 639.

principal —, chief —, main —, greater —, major —, best —, essential- part; bulk, mass etc. (*whole*) 50.

V. be -great etc. *adj.;* run high, soar, loom up, tower, bulk large, transcend; rise —, carry- to a great height; know no bounds; scale, overtop, ascend.

enlarge etc. (*increase*) 35, (*expand*) 194.

Adj. great; greater etc. 33; large, considerable, fair, above par; big, massive, huge etc. (*large in size*) 192; ample; abundant etc. (*enough*) 639; Herculean etc. 159; full, intense, strong, sound, passing, heavy, plenary, deep, high; signal, at its height, in the zenith.

world-wide, wide-spread, extensive; wholesale; many etc. 102.

goodly, noble, precious, mighty; sad, grave, serious; far gone, arrant, downright; utter, -most; crass, gross, arch, profound, intense, consummate; rank, unmitigated, red-hot, desperate; glaring, flagrant, stark staring; thorough-paced, - going; roaring, thumping, thundering, strapping, whacking; extraordinary; .important etc. 642; unsurpassed etc. (*supreme*) 33; complete etc. 52.

vast, immense, enormous, extreme; inordinate, excessive, extravagant, exorbitant, outrageous, preposterous, unconscionable, swinging, monstrous, over-grown; towering, stupendous, prodigious, astonishing, incredible; terrific, frightful; marvelous etc. (*wonder*) 870; grand.

unlimited etc. (*infinite*) 105; unapproachable,

unutterable, indescribable, ineffable, unspeakable, inexpressible, beyond expression, fabulous.

un-diminished, -abated, -reduced, -restricted.

absolute, positive, stark, decided, unequivocal, essential, perfect, finished.

remarkable, of mark, marked, pointed, veriest; noticeable, uncommon, noteworthy, eminent etc. 873.

Adv. [in a positive degree] truly etc. (*truth*) 494; decidedly, unequivocally, purely, absolutely, seriously, essentially, fundamentally, radically, downright, in all conscience; for the most part, in the main.

[in a .complete degree] entirely etc. (*completely*) 52; abundantly, etc. (*sufficiently*) 639; widely, far and wide.

[in a great or high degree] greatly etc. *adj.;* much, muckle, well, indeed, very, very much, a deal, no end of, most not a little; pretty, — well; enough, in a great measure, passing richly; to a - large, — great, — gigantic- extent; on a large scale; so; never —, ever- so; ever so much; by wholesale; mightily, mighty, powerfully; with a witness, *ultra,* in the extreme, extremely, exceedingly, intensely, exquisitely, acutely, indefinitely, immeasurably; beyond -compare, — comparison, — measure, — all bounds; incalculably, infinitely.

[in a supreme degree] pre-eminently, superlatively etc. (*superiority*) 33.

[in a too great degree] immoderately, unduly, monstrously, grossly, preposterously, inordinately, exorbitantly, excessively, enormously, out of all proportion, with a vengeance.

[in a marked degree] particularly, remarkably, singularly, curiously, uncommonly, unusually, peculiarly, notably, signally, strikingly, pointedly, mainly, chiefly; famously, egregiously, prominently, glaringly, emphatically, strangely, wonderfully, amazingly, surprisingly, astonishingly, incredibly, marvelously, awfully, stupendously.

[in an exceptional degree] peculiarly etc. (*unconformity*) 83.

[in a violent degree] furiously etc. (*violence*) 173; severely, desperately, tremendously, extravagantly, confoundedly, deucedly, devilishly, with a vengeance; *à —, à toute- outrance.*

[in a painful degree] painfully, sadly, grossly, sorely, bitterly, piteously, grievously, miserably, cruelly, woefully, lamentably, shockingly, frightfully, dreadfully, fearfully, terribly, horribly, distressingly, balefully.

32. Smallness.—N. smallness etc. *adj.;* littleness etc. (*small size*) 193; tenuity; paucity; fewness etc. (*small number*) 103; meanness, insignificance etc. (*unimportance*) 643; mediocrity, moderation.

small quantity, *modicum, minimum;* vanishing point; material point, electron, atom, particle, molecule, corpuscle, point, dab, fleck, speck, dot, mote, jot, iota, ace; *minutiae,* details; look, thought, idea, *soupçon,* whit, tittle, shade, shadow; spark, *scintilla,* gleam; touch, cast; grain, scruple, granule, globule, minim, sup, sip, sop, spice, drop, droplet, sprinkling, dash, smack, tinge, tincture; inch, patch, scantling, dole; scrap, shred, tag, splinter, rag, tatter, cantlet, flitter, gobbet, mite, bit, morsel, crumb, seed, fritter, shive; snip, -pet; snick, snack, snatch, slip, scrag; chip, -ping; shiver, sliver, driblet, clipping, paring, shaving, hair.

nutshell; thimble-, spoon-, hand-, cap-, mouthful; fragment; fraction etc. (*part*)51; drop in the ocean, drop in the bucket.

animalcule etc. 193.

trifle etc. (*unimportant thing*) 643; mere −, next to- nothing; hardly anything; just enough to swear by; the shadow of a shade.

finiteness, finite quantity.

V. be -shall etc. *adj.;* lie in a nutshell.

diminish etc. (*decrease*) 36, (*contract*) 195.

Adj. small, little, tiny, weeny; diminutive etc. (*small in size*) 193; minute; minikin, fine, inconsiderable, dribbling, paltry etc. (*unimportant*) 643; faint etc. (*weak*) 160; slender, light, slight, scanty, scant, limited; meager etc. (*insufficient*) 640; sparing; few etc. 103; low, so-so, middling, tolerable, no great shakes; below −, under-par, − the mark; at a low ebb; halfway; moderate, modest; tender, subtle; petty, shallow, skin-deep.

inappreciable, evanescent, infinite-simal, homeopathic, very small, atomic, molecular, ultra-, -microscopic.

petty, shallow etc. 499.

mere, simple, sheer, stark, bare; near run.

Adv. [in a small degree] to a small extent, on a small scale; a -little, − wee, − tiny bit; slightly etc. *adj.;* imperceptibly; miserably, wretchedly; insufficiently etc. 640; imperfectly; faintly etc. 160; passably, pretty well, well enough.

[in a certain or limited degree] partially, in part; in −, to a certain degree; to a certain extent; comparatively; some, rather; in some -degree, -measure; some-thing, -what; simply, only, purely, merely; at −, at the- -least, − most; ever so little, as little as may be, *tant soit peu,* in ever so small a degree; thus far, *pro tanto;* within bounds, in a manner, after a fashion.

almost, nearly, well nigh, short of, not quite, all but; near −, close- upon; *peu s'en faut,* near the mark; within an -ace, − inch- of; on the brink of; scarcely, hardly, barely, only just, no more than.

[in an uncertain degree] about, therabouts, somewhere about, nearly, say; be the same - more, − little more- or less.

[in no degree] no- ways, − wise; not -at all, − in the least, − a bit, − a bit of it, − a whit, − a jot, − a shadow; in no -wise, − respect; by no - means, − manner of means; on no account, at no hand.

33. Superiority.—N. superiority, supremacy, majority; greatness etc. 31; advantage, odds, pull; preponderance, -ation; predominance, vantage ground, coign of vantage, prevalence, partiality; personal superiority; sovereignty etc. 737; nobility etc. (*rank*) 875; Triton among the minnows, *primus inter pares, nulli secundus,* super-man; captain etc. 475.

supremacy, pre-eminence; primacy, lead, *maximum;* record; climax, crest, top; culmination etc. (*summit*) 210; transcendence; *ne plus ultra;* lion's share, Benjamin's mess; excess; bisque, surplus etc. (*remainder*) 40, (*redundance*) 641.

V. be -superior etc. *adj.;* exceed, excel, transcend; out-do, -balance, -weigh, -rival, -Herod, outrank, pass, surpass, surmount, get ahead of; over-top, -ride, -pass, -balance, -weigh, -match; top, o'er-top, cap, beat, win out, cut out; beat hollow; outstrip etc. 303; eclipse, throw into the shade, take the shine out of, put one's nose out of joint; have the -upper hand, − whip hand of, − advantage; turn the scale, play first fiddle etc. (*importance*) 642; preponderate, predominate, prevail; precede, take .precedence, come first; come to a head, culminate; beat etc. all others, bear the palm; break the record, take the cake.

become −, render- -larger, etc. (*increase*) 35, (*expand*) 194.

Adj. superior, greater, major, higher; exceeding etc. *v.;* great etc. 31; distinguished, *ultra;* vaulting; more than a match for.

supreme, greatest, maximal, maximum, utmost, paramount, pre-eminent, foremost, crowning; first-rate etc. (*important*) 642, (*excellent*) 648; unrivalled; peer-, match-less; none such, second to none, *sans pareil;* un-paragoned, -paralleled, -equalled, -approached, -surpassed; superlative, inimitable, *facile princeps,* incomparable, sovereign, without parallel, *nulli secundus, ne plus ultra;* beyond -compare, − comparison; culminating etc. (*topmost*) 210; transcendent, -ental; *plus royaliste que le Roi.*

increased etc. (*added to*) 35; enlarged etc. (*expanded*) 194.

Adv. beyond, more, over; over −, above- the mark; above par; upwards −, in advance- of; over and above; at the top of the scale, on the crest, at it height.

[in a superior or supreme degree] eminently, egregiously, pre-eminently, surpassing, prominently, superlatively, supremely, above all, of all things, the most, to crown all, *par excellence,* principally, especially, particularly, peculiarly, *a fortiori,* even, yea, still more.

Phr. 'we shall not look upon his like again.'

34. Inferiority.—N. inferiority, minority, subordinancy; shortcoming, deficiency; handicap; *minimum;* smallness etc. 32; imperfection, shabbiness.

[personal inferiority] commonalty etc. 876; subordinate, substitute, sub.

V. be -inferior etc. *adj.;* fall −, come- short of; not -pass, − .come up to; want.

become −, render- smaller etc. (*decrease*) 36, (*contract*) 195; hide its diminished head, retire into the shade, yield the palm, play second fiddle, take a back seat; bow.

Adj. inferior, smaller; small etc. 32; minor, less, lesser, deficient, minus, lower, subordinate, secondary; second-rate etc. (*imperfect*) 651; sub, subaltern; thrown into the shade; weighed in the balance and found wanting; not fit to hold a candle to.

least, smallest etc. (*see* little, small etc. 193); lowest.

diminished etc. (*decreased*) 36; reduced etc. (*contracted*) 195; unimportant etc. 643.

Adv. less; under −, below- -the mark, − par; at -the bottom of the scale, − a low ebb, − a disadvantage; short of, under.

35. Increase.—N. increase; augmentation, addition, enlargement, extension; dilatation etc. (*expansion*) 194; multiplication; increment, accretion; accession etc. 37; production etc. 161; development, growth; aggrandizement, aggravation, intensification; rise; ascent etc. 305; anabasis; ex-aggeration, -acerbation; spread etc. (*dispersion*) 73; flood-, spring-, -tide; gain, produce, profit etc. 618; booty, plunder etc. 793.

V. increase, augment, add to, enlarge; dilate etc. (*expand*) 194; grow, wax, mount, swell, get ahead, gain strength; advance; run —, shoot- up; rise; ascend etc. 305; sprout etc. 194.

aggrandize; raise; exalt; deepen, heighten; lengthen; thicken; strengthen; intensify, enhance, inflate, magnify, double, redouble; multiply; aggravate, exaggerate; ex-asperate, -acerbate; add fuel to the flame, *oleum addere camino*, superadd etc. (*add*) 37; spread etc. (*disperse*) 73.

Adj. increased etc. *v.;* on the increase, undiminished, additional etc. (*added*) 37; increasing etc. *v.;* growing, crescent, intensive, cumulative.

Adv. *crescendo*, increasingly.

Phr. *vires acquirit eundo.*

36. Non-Increase, Decrease.—N. decrease, diminution, lessening etc. *v.;* subtraction etc. 38; reduction, abatement, declension; shrinkage etc. (*contraction*) 195; coarctation; abridgment etc. (*shortening*) 201; extenuation.

subsidence, catabasis, wane, ebb-, neap-tide, decline; descent etc. 306; decrement, reflux, depreciation; erosion, wear and tear, deterioration etc. 659; anticlimax; mitigation etc. (*moderation*) 174.

V. decrease, diminish, lessen; abridge etc. (*shorten*) 201; shrink etc. (*contract*) 195; drop —, fall —, tail- off; fall away, waste, wear, erode; wane, ebb, decline; descent etc. 306; subside; deliquesce, melt —, die -away; retire into the shade, hide its diminished head, fall to a low ebb, run low, languish, decay, crumble, consume away.

bate, abate, dequantitate; discount; depreciate; extenuate, lower, weaken, attenuate, fritter away; mitigate etc.(*moderate*) 174; belittle, minimize; dwarf; throw into the shade; keep down, reduce etc. 195; shorten etc. 201; subtract etc. 38.

Adj. unincreased etc. (*see* increase etc. 35); decreased etc. *v.;* decreasing etc. *v.;* on the -wane etc. *n.;* deliquescent.

Adv. *diminuendo, decrescendo,* decreasingly.

37. Addition.—N. addition, annexation, adjection; junction etc. 43; super-position, -addition, -junction, -fetation; accession, reinforcement; increase etc. 35; increment, supplement; accompaniment etc. 88; interposition etc. 228; insertion etc. 300; summation etc. 85; adjunct etc. 39.

V. add, annex, adject, affix, attach, superadd; subjoin, superpose; clap —, saddle- on; tack to, postfix, append, tag; ingraft; saddle with; sprinkle; introduce etc. (*interpose*) 228; insert etc. 300.

become added, accrue; ad-, supervene; add up etc. 85.

reinforce, strengthen, swell the ranks of; augment etc. 35.

Adj. added etc. *v.;* additional; supplement, -al, -ary; suppletory, subjunctive; adjec-, adsci-, ascititious; additive, extra, spare, further, fresh, more, new, ulterior, other, auxiliary, supernumerary, accessory.

Adv. in addition, more, plus, extra; and, also, likewise, too, furthermore, further, item; and - also, — eke; else, besides, to boot, *et cetera;* etc.; and so -on, — forth; into the bargain, *cum multis aliis*, over and above, moreover.

with, withal; including, inclusive, as well as, not to mention, let alone; together —, along —, coupled —, in conjunction- with; conjointly; jointly etc. 43.

38. Non-Addition. Subduction.—N. sub-traction, -duction; deduction, retrenchment; removal; ab-, sub-lation; abstraction etc. (*taking*) 789; garbling etc. *v.;* mutilation, detruncation; amputation, severance; abs-, ex-, re-cision; curtailment etc. 201; minuend, subtrahend; decrease etc. 36; abrasion.

V. sub-tract, -duct; rebate, de-duct, — duce; bate, retrench; remove, withdraw; take — from, — away; detract.

garble, mutilate, amputate, sever, detruncate; cut -off, — away, — out; expurgate; abscind, excise; pare, thin, prune, decimate; abrade, scrape, file; geld, castrate, emasculate, unman, spay, caponize; eliminate.

diminish etc. 36; curtail etc. (*shorten*) 201; deprive of etc. (*take*) 789; weaken.

Adj. subtracted etc. *v.;* subtractive.

tailless, acaudal.

Adv. in -deduction etc. *n.;* less; short of; minus, without, except, excepting, with the exception of, barring, bar, save, exclusive of, save and except, with a reservation.

39. Adjunct. [Thing added.]—N. adjunct, addit-ion, -ament; *additum;* affix, appendage, annex; augment, -ation; increment, reinforcement, supernumerary, accessory, item; garnish, sauce; accompaniment etc. 88; adjective, *addendum,* accession, complement, supplement; continuation; extension, subscript, tag, appendix, postscript, interlineation, interpolation, insertion.

rider, codicil, off-shoot, episode, side issue, corollary; piece; flap, lapel, label, tab, strip, fold, lappet, apron, skirt, embroidery, trappings, *cortège;* tail, suffix etc. (*sequel*) 65; wing.

Adj. additional etc. 37.

Adv. in addition etc. 37.

40. Remainder. [Thing remaining.]—N. remainder, residue; remains, *remanet*, remnant, rest, relic, relict; leavings, heel-tap, odds and ends, cheese-parings, candle ends, orts; *residuum;* dottle, dregs, etc. (*dirt*) 653; refuse etc. (*useless*) 645; stubble, result, educt; fag-end, stub; ruins, wreck, skeleton, stump; *alluvium.*

surplus, overplus, excess; balance, complement; superfluity etc. (*redundance*) 641; survival, -ance; afterglow.

V. remain; be -left etc. *adj.;* exceed, survive; leave.

Adj. remaining, left; left -behind, — over;

residu-al, -ary; over, odd; unconsumed, sedimentary; surviving; net; exceeding, over and above; outlying, -standing; cast off etc. 782; superfluous etc. (*redundant*) 641.

V. remain; be -left; left -behind, — over; redidual, -ary; over, odd; unconsumed, sedimentary; surviving; net; exceeding, over and above; outlying, -standing; cast off etc. 782; superfluous etc. (*redundant*) 641.

40a. Decrement. [Thing deducted.]—N. decrement, discount, rebate, defect, loss, deduction, eduction, tare; drawback; waste, wastage; reprise.

41. Mixture. [Forming a whole without coherence.]—N. mix-, admix-, commix-ture, -tion, mingling; commixion, immixture, interfusion, intermixture, alloyage, matrimony; junction etc. 43; combination etc. 48; entanglement, interlacing; miscegenation, interbreeding.

impregnation; in-, dif-, suf-, transfusion; infiltration; seasoning, sprinkling, interlarding; interpolation etc. 228; adulteration, sophistication.

[Thing mixed] tinge, tincture, touch, dash, smack, sprinkling, spice, seasoning, infusion, *soupçon*.

[Compound resulting from mixture] alloy, brass, bronze, pewter etc.; amalgam, *magma*, blend, half-and-half, *mélange, tertium, quid*, -miscellany, *ambigu*, medley, mess, hash, hotchpotch, hodgepodge, *pasticcio*, patchwork, odds and ends, all sorts; jumble etc. (*disorder*) 59; salad, sauce, mash, *omnium gatherum*, gallimaufry, ragout, *olla podrida, olio*, salmagundi, *potpourri*, Noah's ark; texture, mingled yarn; mosaic etc. (*variegation*) 440.

half-blood, -caste, -breed, Eurasian; mulatto; terc-, quart-, quinteron etc.; quad-, octo-roon; *griffo, zambo;* cross, hybrid, mongrel etc. 83.

V. mix; join etc. 43; combine etc. 48; com-, im-, inter-mix; mix up with, mingle; com-, inter-, bemingle; shuffle etc. (*derange*) 61; pound together; hash —, stir- up; knead, brew; impregnate with; interlard etc. (*interpolate*) 228; intertwine, -weave etc. 219; associate with, miscegenate, interbreed.

be mixed etc.; get among, be entangled with.

instil, imbue; in-, suf-, trans-fuse; infiltrate, dash, tinge, tincture, season, sprinkle, besprinkle, attemper, medicate, blend, cross; alloy, amalgamate, compound, adulterate, sophisticate, infect.

Adj. mixed etc. *v.;* implex, composite, half-and-half, linsey-wolsey, hybrid, mongrel, heterogeneous; motley etc. (*variegated*) 440; miscellaneous, promiscuous, indiscriminate; miscible.

Adv. among, amongst, amid, amidst, with; in the midst of, in the crowd.

42. Simpleness [Freedom from mixture.]—N. simpleness etc. *adj.;* purity, homogeneity.

elimination; sifting etc. *v.;* purification etc. (*cleanness*) 652.

V. render -simple etc. *adj.;* simplify.

sift, winnow, bolt, eliminate; narrow down; get rid of, exclude etc. 55; clear; purify etc. (*clean*) 652; disentangle etc. (*disjoin*) 44.

Adj. simple, uniform, of a piece, homogeneous, single, pure, clear, sheer, neat; Attic.

un-mixed, -mingled, -blended, -combined, -compounded; elementary, undecomposed; unadulterated, -sophisticated, -alloyed, -tinged, -fortified; pure and simple.

free —, exempt- from; exclusive.

Adv. simply etc. *adj.;* only.

43. Junction.—N. junction; joining etc. *v.;* joinder, union; con-nection, -junction, -jugation, compendency, annex-ion, -ation, -ment; coalition; astriction, attachment, compagination, vincture, ligation, alligation; accouplement; marriage etc. (*wedlock*) 903; infibulation, inosculation, symphysis, anastomosis, confluence, communication, concatenation; concurrence, meeting, reunion; assemblage etc. 72.

copulation, coition, intercourse.

joint, joining, juncture, chiasma, pivot, hinge, articulation, commissure, seam, suture, gusset, stitch, splice; link etc. 45; miter, mortise.

closeness, tightness etc. *adj.;* coherence etc. 46; combination etc. 48.

V. join, unite; con-join, -nect; associate; put —, lay —, clap —, hang —, lump —, hold —, piece —, tack —, fix —, bind up- together; embody, re-embody; roll into one.

attach, fix, affix, saddle on, fasten, bind, secure, clinch, twist, make -fast etc. *adj.;* tie, pinion, string, strap, sew, lace, stitch, tack, paste, knit, button, buckle, hitch, lash, truss, bandage; braid, splice, swathe, gird, tether, moor, picket, harness, chain; fetter etc. (*restrain*) 751; lock, latch, belay, brace, hook, grapple, leash, couple, accouple, link, yoke, bracket; marry etc. (*wed*) 903; bridge over, span.

pin, nail, bolt, hasp, clasp, clamp, screw, rivet; impact, solder, braze, cement, set; weld —, fuse-together; wedge, rabbet, mortise, miter, jam, dovetail, enchase; graft, ingraft, inosculate; en-, in-twine; inter-link, -lace, -twine, -twist, -weave; entangle; twine round, belay; tighten; trice —, screw-up.

be -joined etc.; hang —, hold- together; cohere etc. 46.

Adj. joined etc. *v.;* joint; con-joint, -junct; corporate, compact; hand in hand.

firm, fast, close, tight, taut, taught, tense, secure, set, intervolved; in-separable, -dissoluble, -secable, -severable.

Adv. jointly etc. *adj.;* in conjunction with etc. (*in addition to*) 37; fast, firmly etc. *adj.;* intimately.

44. Disjunction.—N. dis-junction, -connection, -unity, -union, -association, -engagement, -sociation; discontinuity etc. 70; inconnection; abstraction, -edness; isolation; insul-arity, -ation; oasis; separateness etc. *adj.;* severalty; *disjecta membra;* dispersion etc. 73; apportionment etc. 786.

separation; parting etc. *v.;* detachment, segregation; divorce, sejunction, seposition, diduction, diremption, discerption; elision; *caesura*, division, subdivision, break, fracture, rupture; compartition; dis-memberment, -integration, -location; luxation; sever-, dis-severance; scission; re-, ab-scission; circumcision;

lacer-, dilacer-ation; dis-, ab-ruption; avulsion, divulsion; section, resection, cleavage; fission; separability; separatism.

fissure, breach, rent, split, rift, crack, slit, slot, incision.

dissection, anatomy; decomposition etc. 49; cutting instrument etc. (sharpness) 253; saw.

V. be -disjoined etc.; come −, fall- -off, − to pieces; peel off; get loose.

dis-join, -connect, -engage, -unite, -sociate, -pair; divorce, part, dispart, detach, uncouple, separate, cut off, rescind, segregate; set −, keep-apart; insulate, isolate; throw out of gear; cut adrift; loose; un-loose, -do, -bind, -tie, -hitch, -chain, -lock etc. (fix) 43, -pack, -ravel; disentangle; set free etc. (liberate) 750.

sunder, divide, subdivide, sectionalize, sever, dissever, abscind; cut; segment; in-cide, -cise; circumcise; saw, snip, nib, nip, cleave, rive, rend, slit, split, splinter, chip, crack, snap, break, tear, burst; rend etc. -asunder, − in twain; wrench, rupture, shatter, shiver, cranch, crunch, craunch, chop; rip up; hack, hew, slash; whittle; haggle, hackle, discind, lacerate, scamble, mangle, gash, hash, slice.

cut up, carve, quarter, dissect, anatomize; take −, pull −, pick −, tear- to pieces; tear to tatters, − piecemeal; divellicate; skin etc. 226; dis-integrate, -member, -branch, -band; disperse etc. 73; dis-locate, -joint; break up; mince; comminute etc. (pulverize) 330; distribute, apportion etc. 786.

part, − company; separate, leave; alienate, estrange.

Adj. disjoined etc. v.; discontinuous etc. 70; bipartite, multipartite, abstract; digitate; disjunctive; isolated etc. v.; insular, separate, disparate, discrete, apart, asunder, far between, loose, free; unattached, -annexed, -associated, -connected; distinct; adrift; straggling; rift, reft, cleft, split.

[capable of being divided] scissile, partible, divisible, separable, severable, detachable.

Adv. separately etc. adj.; one by one, severally, apart; adrift, asunder, in twain; in the abstract, abstractedly.

45. Vinculum. [Connecting medium.]—N. vinculum, link, nexus; connec-tive, -tion; junction etc. 43; bond of union, copula, intermedium, hyphen; bracket; bridge, stepping-stone, isthmus.

bond, tendon, tendril; fiber; cord, -age; riband, ribbon, rope, guy, cable, line, halser, hawser, painter, moorings, wire, chain; string etc. (filament) 205.

fastening, tie; liga-ment, -ture; strap; bowline, halliard, tackle, lanyard, rigging, shrouds; standing −, running- rigging; traces, harness; yoke; band, -age; brace, roller, fillet, inkle; with, withe, withy; thong, braid; girder, tie-beam; girt, cinch, girth, girdle, cestus, garter, braces, suspenders, halter, noose, lasso, lariat, surcingle, knot, hitch, running knot, frog.

pin, corking pin, nail, brad, tack, skewer, staple, cleat, clamp; cramp; screw, button, buckle, clasp, hasp, hinge; hank, catch, latch, bolt, ring, latchet, pawl, tag; tooth; stud; hook, − and eye; morse, lock, holdfast, padlock, rivet; anchor, grappling-iron, drawbar, coupler, draw-

head, coupling, treenail, trennel, stake, pale, pile, post, bollard.

cement, glue, gum, paste, size, wafer, solder, lute, putty, bird-lime, mortar, stucco, plaster, grout.

shackle, rein etc. (means of restraint) 752; suspender etc. 214; prop etc. (support) 215.

V. bridge over, span; connect etc. 43; hang etc. 214.

46. Coherence.—N. co-, ad-herence, -hesion, -hesiveness; concretion, accretion; con-, agglutination, -glomeration; aggregation; consolidation, set, cementation; sticking, soldering etc. v.; connection.

tenacity, toughness; stickiness etc. 352; insepara-bility, -bleness; bur, remora.

conglomerate, concrete etc. (density) 321.

V. cohere, adhere, stick, cling, cleave, hold, take hold of, hold fast, close with, embrace, clasp, hug; grow −, hang-together; twine round etc. (join) 43.

stick like -a leech, − wax; stick close; cling like -ivy, − a bur; adhere like -a remora, − Dejanira's shirt.

glue; ag-, con-glutinate; cement, lute, paste, gum; solder, weld; cake, coagulate, consolidate etc. (solidify) 321; agglomerate.

Adj. co-, ad-hesive, -hering etc. v.; tenacious, tough; sticky etc. 352.

united, unseparated, sessile, inseparable, inextricable, infrangible; compact etc. (dense) 321.

47. Incoherence. [Want of adhesion, non-adhesion, immiscibility.]—N. non-adhesion; immiscibility; incoherence; looseness etc. adj.; laxity; relaxation; loosening etc. v.; freedom; disjunction etc. 44; rope of sand.

V. make -loose etc. adj.; loosen, slacken, relax; un-glue etc. 46; detach etc. (disjoin) 44.

Adj. non-adhesive, immiscible; incoherent, detached, loose, slack, baggy, lax, relaxed, flapping, streaming; dishevelled; segregated, like grains of sand; un-consolidated etc. 321; -combined etc. 48; non-cohesive.

48. Combination.—N. combination; mixture etc. 41; alloy; junction etc. 43; union, unification, synthesis, incorporation, amalgamation, embodiment, coalescence, crasis, fusion, blend, blending, absorption, centralization, federation.

compound, amalgam, composition, tertium quid; resultant, impregnation.

V. combine, unite, incorporate, alloy, intertwine etc. 41; amalgamate, embody, absorb, re-embody, blend, merge, fuse, melt into one, consolidate, coalesce, centralize, impregnate; put −, lump- together; federate, associate; fraternize; cement a union, marry, wed, couple, pair, ally.

Adj. combined etc. v.; conjunctive, conjugate, conjoint, allied, confederate; impregnated with, ingrained, inoculated.

49. Decomposition.—N. decomposition, analysis, diaeresis dissection, resolution, catalysis, electrolysis, hydrolysis, photolysis, dissolution; dispersion etc. 73; disjunction etc. 44;

putrescence, caries, necrosis, corruption etc. (*uncleanness*) 653.

V. decom-pose, -pound; analyze, disembody, dissolve; resolve −, separate- into its elements; electrolyze; dissect, decentralize, break up; disintegrate; disperse etc. 73; unravel etc. (*unroll*) 313; crumble into dust; decay etc. *n.;* deteriorate etc. 659.

Adj. decomposed etc. *v.;* catalytic, analytical.

50. Whole. [Principal part.]—N. whole, totality, integrity; totalness etc. *adj.;* entirety, *ensemble,* collectiveness; unity etc. 87; completeness etc. 52; indivisibility, indiscerptibility; integration, embodiment; integer, integral.

all, the whole, total, aggregate, one and all, gross amount, sum, sum-total, *tout ensemble,* length and breadth of, Alpha and Omega, 'be all and end all,' lock, stock and barrel.

bulk, mass, lump, tissue, staple, body, torso, *compages;* truck, bole, hull, hulk, skeleton; greater −, major −, best −, principal −, mainpart; essential part etc. (*importance*) 642; lion's share, Benjamin's mess; the long and the short; nearly −, almost- all.

V. form −, constitute- a whole; integrate, embody, amass; aggregate etc. (*assemble*) 72; amount to, come to.

Adj. whole, total, integral, entire; complete etc. 52; one, individual.

un-broken, -cut, -divided, -severed, -clipped, -cropped, -shorn; seamless; undiminished; undemolished, -dissolved, -destroyed, -bruised.

in-divisible, -dissoluble, -dissolvable, -discerptible.

wholesale, sweeping, comprehensive.

Adv. wholly, altogether; totally etc. (*completely*) 52; entirely, all; all in all, considering all things, in a body, collectively, all put together; in the -aggregate, − lump; − mass, − gross, − main, − long run; *en masse,* on the whole, as a whole, bodily, *en bloc, in extenso,* throughout, every inch; substantially.

51. Part.—N. part, portion; dose; item, particular; aught, any; division, ward; subdivision, section; chapter, verse; article, clause, count, paragraph, passage; phrase; number, volume, book, fascicule; sector, segment; fraction, fragment; cantle, -t; frustum; detachment, parcel, unit, class etc. 75.

piece, lump, bit; cut, -ting; chip, chunk, collop, slice, scale, shard; lamina etc. 204; moiety; small part; morsel, scrap, crumb; particle etc. (*smallness*) 32; instalment, dividend; share etc. (*allotment*) 786.

débris, odds and ends, oddments, *detritus;* excerpta; member, limb, lobe, lobule, arm, wing, scion, branch, bough, joint, link, offshoot, ramification, twig, stipule, tendril, bush, spray, sprig; runner; leaf, -let; stump; constituent, ingredient, component part etc. 56.

compartment; department etc. (*class*) 75; county etc. (*region*) 181.

V. part, divide, break etc. (*disjoin*) 44; partition etc. (*apportion*) 786.

Adj. fractional, fragmentary; sectional, aliquot; divided etc. *v.;* in compartments, multifid, incomplete, partial, divided etc. 44.

Adv. partly, in part, partially; piecemeal, part by part; by -instalments, − snatches, − inches, − driblets; bit by bit, inch by inch, foot by foot, drop by drop; in -detail, − lots.

52. Completeness.—N. completeness etc. *adj.;* completion etc. 729; integration; integrality.

entirety; universality; totality; perfection etc. 650; solid-ity, -arity; unity; all; *ne plus ultra,* ideal, limit.

complement, supplement, make-weight; filling up etc. *v.*

impletion; satur-ation, -ity; high water; high −, flood −, spring- tide; fill, load, bumper, belly-ful; brimmer; sufficiency etc. 639.

V. be -complete etc. *adj.;* come to a head.

render -complete etc. *adj.;* complete etc. (*accomplish*) 729; fill, charge, load, replenish; make-up, − good; piece −, eke- out; supply deficiencies; fill -up, − in, − to the brim, − the measure of; saturate etc. 869.

go the whole -hog, − length, go all lengths.

Adj. complete, entire; whole etc. 50; perfect etc. 650; full, good, absolute, thorough, plenary; solid, undivided; with all its parts.

exhaustive, radical, sweeping, thorough-going; dead.

regular, consummate, unmitigated, sheer, unqualified, unconditional, free; abundant etc. (*sufficient*) 639.

brimming; brim-, top-ful; chock −, choke-full; as full as- an egg is of meat, − a vetch, − a tick; saturated, crammed; replete etc. (*redundant*) 641; fraught, laden; full-laden, -fraught, -charged; heavy laden.

completing etc. *v.;* supplement-al, -ary; ascititious.

Adv. completely etc. *adj.;* altogether, outright, wholly, totally, *in toto,* quite; over head and ears; effectually, for good and all, nicely, fully, through thick and thin, head and shoulders; neck and -heel, − crop; all out; in -all respects, − every respect; at all points, out and out, to all intents and purposes; *toto coelo;* utterly, clean, − as a whistle; to the -full, − utmost, − backbone; hollow, stark; heart and soul, root and branch; down to the ground.

to the top of one's bent, as far as possible. *à outrance.*

throughout; from -first to last, − beginning to end, − end to end, − one end to the other, −Dan to Beersheba, − head to foot, − head to heels, − top to toe, − top to bottom; *de fond en comble; à fond, a capite ad calcem, ab ovo usque ad mala,* fore and aft; every -whit, − inch; *cap-à-pie,* to the end of the chapter; up to the -brim, − ears, − eyes; as ... as can be.

on all accounts; *sous tous les rapports;* with a -vengeance, − witness.

53. Incompleteness.—N. incompleteness etc. *adj.;* deficiency, short -measure, − wieght; shortcoming etc. 304; insufficiency etc. 640; imperfection etc. 651; immaturity etc. (*nonpreparation*) 674; half measures.

[part wanting] defect, deficit, shortage, ullage, defalcation, omission, *caret;* interval etc. 198; break etc. (*discontinuity*) 70; non-completion etc. 730; missing link.

V. be -incomplete etc. *adj.;* fall short of etc.
304; lack etc. (*be insufficient*) 640; neglect etc.
460.

Adj. incomplete; imperfect etc. 651; unfinished; uncompleted etc. (*see* complete etc.
729); defective, deficient, wanting; failing; in -de-
fault, – arrear; short, – of; hollow, meagre,
lame, half-and-half, perfunctory, sketchy; crude
etc. (*unprepared*) 674.

mutilated, garbled, mangled, docked, lopped,
truncated; bobtailed, cropped, bobbed, shingled.

in -progress, – hand; going on, proceeding.

Adv. incompletely etc. *adj.;* by halves.

Phr. *caetera desunt; caret.*

54. Composition.—N. composition, constitution, crasis, synthesis; make-up; combination etc. 48; inclusion, admission,
comprehension, reception; embodiment, formation, conformation, production.

compilation etc. 72. (*musical*) composition etc.
415; painting etc. 556; writing etc. 590;
typography etc. 591.

V. be -composed, – made, – formed, – made
up- of; consist of, be resolved into.

include etc. (*in a class*) 76; subsume; syn-
thesize; contain, hold, comprehend, take in,
admit, embrace, embody; involve; implicate,
drag into.

compose, constitute, form, make; make –, fill
–, build- up; weave, construct, fabricate; compile; write; draw; set up (*printing*); enter into the
composition of etc. (*be a component*) 56.

Adj. containing, constituting etc. *v.*

55. Exclusion.—N. exclusion, non-admission,
omission, exception, rejection, repudiation; exile
etc. (*seclusion*) 893; preclusion, lock out, ostracism, prohibition; disbarment, expulsion, ban.

separation, segregation, seposition, elimination, coffer-dam.

V. be excluded from etc.

exclude, bar, ban; leave –, shut –, thrust –,
bar- out; reject, repudiate, spurn, blackball;
ostracize, boycott; lay –, put –, set-apart, –
aside; relegate, segregate; throw overboard;
strike -off, – out; neglect etc. 460; banish etc.
(*seclude*) 893; separate etc. (*disjoin*) 44.

pass over, omit; garble; eliminate, weed,
winnow.

Adj. excluding etc. *v.;* exclusive.

excluded etc. *v.;* unrecounted, not included in;
inadmissible; preventive, interdictive.

Adv. exclusive of, barring, except; with the
exception of; save, bating.

56. Component.—N. component; component
–, integral –, integrant-part; element, constituent, ingredient, leaven; part and parcel; contents; appurtenance; feature; member etc. (*part*)
51; personnel.

V. enter into, – the composition of; be a -
component etc. *n.;* be –, form- part of; merge –,
be merged- in; be implicated in; share in etc.
(*participate*) 778; belong –, appertain- to.

form, make, constitute, compose.

Adj. forming etc. *v.;* inclusive; inherent etc. 5.

57. Extraneousness.—N. extraneousness etc.
adj.; extrinsicality etc. 6; exteriority etc. 220;
alienism.

foreign -body, – substance, – element; alien,
stranger, intruder, interloper, foreigner, tramontane, *novus homo,* new comer, immi-, emi-grant;
creole, Afrikander; outsider, outlander, tenderfoot.

Adj. extraneous, foreign, alien, ulterior; exterior, external, outside, outlandish; oversea; tra-
ultra-montane.

excluded etc. 55; inadmissible; exceptional.

Adv. in foreign -parts, – lands; abroad, beyond seas, overseas.

58. Order.—N. order, regularity etc. 80; uniformity, symmetry, *lucidus ordo;* harmony,
music of the spheres.

gradation, progression; series etc. (*continuity*)
69.

subordination; course, even tenor, routine;
method, disposition, arrangement, array,
system, economy, discipline; orderliness etc. *adj.*

rank, place etc. (*term*) 71.

V. be –, become- in order etc. *adj.;* form, fall
in, draw up; arrange –, range –, place- itself;
adjust; fall into –, take- -one's place, – rank;
rally round; arrange etc. 60.

Adj. orderly, regular; in -order, – trim, – its
apple-pie order, according to Cocker, – its
proper place, neat, neat as a pin, tidy, *en règle,*
well regulated, correct, methodical, uniform,
symmetrical, ship-shape, business-like, systematic; habitual; unconfused etc. (*see* confuse etc.
61) arranged etc. 60.

Adv. in order; methodically etc. *adj.;* in -turn,
– its turn; step by step; by regular -steps, –
gradations, – stages, – intervals; *seriatim,* sys-
tematically, by clockwork, *gradatim;* at stated
periods etc. (*periodically*)138.

59. Disorder. [Absence, or want of Order,
etc.]—N. disorder; derangement etc. 61;
irregularity; anomaly etc. (*unconformity*) 83;
anar-chy; -chism; want of method; dishevel-
ment, untidiness etc. *adj.;* disunion; discord etc.
24.

confusion; confusedness etc. *adj.;* disarray,
jumble, mix-up, huddle, litter, lumber; *cahotage;*
farrago; mess, muss, mash, muddle, hash; hotchpotch; *imbroglio,* chaos, *omnium gatherum,*
medley; mere -mixture etc. 41; fortuitous con-
course of atoms, *disjecta membra, rudis indigestaque moles.*

complexity; complexness etc. *adj.;* com-, implication; intri-cacy, -cation; perplexity; network, maze, labyrinth, wilderness, jungle;
involution, ravelling, entanglement; coil etc.
(*convolution*) 248; sleave, tangled skein, knot,
Gordian know, kink, web; wheels within wheels.

turmoil; ferment, etc. (*agitation*) 315; to do,
trouble, pudder, pother, row, disturbance,
convulsion, tumult, pandemonium, uproar, riot,
rumpus, stour, scramble, *fracas,* embroilment,
mêlée, spill and pelt, rough and tumble; whirlwind etc. 349; bear garden, Babel, Saturnalia,
Donnybrook Fair, confusion worse confounded,
most admired disorder, *concordia discors;*
Bedlam –, hell- broke loose; bull in a china shop;

all the fat in the fire, *diable à quatre*, Devil to pay; pretty kettle of fish; pretty piece of -work, — business.

slattern, slut, sloven; draggle-tail.

V. be -disorderly etc. *adj.*; ferment, play at cross purposes.

put out of order; derange etc. 61; ravel etc. 219; ruffle, rumple; bungle, botch.

Adj. disorderly, orderless; out of -order; — place, — gear, — whack; irregular, desultory; anomalous etc. (*unconformable*) 83; acephalous, disorganized, straggling; un-, im-methodical; unsymmetric; unsystematic; untidy, slovenly, bedraggled, messy; dislocated; out of sorts; promiscuous, indiscriminate; chaotic, anarchical, lawless; unarranged etc. 60; confused, tumultuous, turbulent, tempestuous; deranged etc. 61; topsy turvy etc. (*inverted*) 218; shapeless etc. 241; disjointed, out of joint.

com-plex, -plexed; intricate, complicated, perplexed, involved, ravelled, entangled, knotted, tangled, inextricable; irreducible.

troublous; riotous etc. (*violent*) 173.

Adv. irregularly etc. *adj.*; by fits and -snatches, — starts; pell-mell; higgledy-piggledy; helterskelter, harum-scarum; in a ferment; at -sixes and sevens, — cross purposes; upside down etc. 218.

Phr. the cart before the horse, chaos is come again.

60. Arrangement. [Reduction to Order.]—**N.** arrangement; plan etc. 626; preparation etc. 673; dispos-al, -ition; col-, al-location; disbribution; sorting etc. *v.*; assortment, allotment; grouping; apportionment, *taxis*, taxonomy, *syn-taxis*, graduation, organization, grading; re-organization, rationalization.

analysis, classification, division, digestion; systematism.

[Result of arrangement] order, orderliness, form, array; digest, synopsis etc. (compendi -um) 596; *syntagma*, table, atlas; register etc. (*record*) 551; score etc. 415; cosmos, organism, architecture.

[Instrument for sorting] sieve etc. 260; file, card index.

V. reduce to — , bring into- order; introduce order into; rally.

arrange, dispose, place, form; put —, set —, place- in order; straighten up, tidy up; set out, collocate, allocate, pack, marshal, range, size, rank, array, group, parcel out, allot, space, distribute, deal; cast —, assign- the parts; dispose of, assign places to; assort, sort; sift, riddle; put —, set- -to rights, — into shape, — in trim, — in array.

class, -ify; divide; file, string together, thread; register etc. (*record*) 551; list, catalogue, tabulate, index, alphabeticize, graduate, digest, grade, codify; orchestrate, score.

methodize, regulate, systematize, standardize, co-ordinate, organize, settle, fix.

unravel, disentangle, ravel, card; disembroil.

Adj. arranged etc. *v.*; embattled, in battle array; cut and dried; methodical, orderly, regular, systematic, tabular.

61. Derangement. [Subversion of Order; bringing into disorder.]—**N.** derangement etc. *v.*; dis-

order etc. 59; evection, discomposure, disturbance; dis-, de-organization; involvement; dislocation; perturbation, interruption; shuffling etc. *v.*; inversion etc. 218; corrugation etc. (*fold*) 258; insanity etc. 503.

V. derange; dis-, mis-arrange; dis-, mis-place; mislay, discompose, disorder, de-, dis-organize; embroil, unsettle, disturb, confuse, trouble, perturb, jumble, tumble; huddle, shuffle, muddle, toss, hustle, fumble, riot; bring —, put —, throw-into -disorder etc. 59; break the ranks, disconcert, convulse; break in upon.

unhinge, dislocate, put out of joint, throw out of gear.

turn topsy-turvy etc. (*invert*) 218; bedevil; complicate, involve, perplex, confound; im-, embrangle; tangle, en-tangle, ravel, tousle, dishevel, ruffle, rumple etc. (*fold*) 258; dement.

litter, scatter; mix etc. 41.

Adj. deranged etc. *v.*; syncre-tic, -tistic.

62. Precedence.—**N.** precedence; coining before etc. *v.*; the lead, *le pas*; superiority etc. 33; importance etc. 642; anteced-ence, -ency; anteriority etc. (*front*) 234; precursor etc. 64; priority etc. 116; precession etc. 280; anteposition, preference.

V. precede; come -before, — first; forerun, head, lead, take the lead; lead the -way, — dance; introduce, usher in; have the *pas*; set the fashion etc. (*influence*) 175; lead off, kick off, open the ball; take —, have- precedence; outrank; have the start etc. (*get before*) 280.

place before; prefix; premise, prelude, preface.

Adj. preceding etc. *v.*; pre-, antecedent; anterior, prior etc. 116; before; former, foregoing; before-, above-mentioned; aforesaid, said; precurs-ory, -ive; prevenient, preliminary, prefatory, introductory; prelus-ive, -ory; proemial, preparatory.

Adv. before; in advance etc. (*precession*) 280.

Phr. *seniores priores*.

63. Sequence.—**N.** sequence, coming after; going after etc. (*following*) 281; consecution, succession; posteriority etc. 117.

continuation; prolongation, order of succussion; successiveness; Elijah's mantle.

secondariness; subordinancy etc. (*inferiority*) 34.

V. succeed; come -after, — on, — next; follow, ensue, step into the shoes of; alternate.

place after, suffix, append.

Adj. succeeding etc. *v.*; sequent; sub-, consequent; sequacious, proximate, next; consecutive etc. (*continuity*) 69; alternate, amoebaean.

latter; posterior etc. 117.

Adv. after, subsequently; behind etc. (*rear*) 235.

64. Precursor.—**N.** precursor, antecedent, precedent, predecessor; forerunner, van-courier, *avant-coureur*, pioneer, prodrome, *prodromos*, outrider; leader, bell-wether; herald, harbinger; dawn.

prelude, preamble, preface, prologue, foreword, *avant-propos*, *protasis*, prolusion, proem, *prolepsis*, *prolegomena*, prefix, introduction;

lead, heading, frontispiece, groundwork; preparation etc. 673; overture, voluntary, *exordium*, symphony, *ritornello;* premises.

prefigurement etc. 511; omen etc. 512.

Adj. precursory; prelu-sive, -sory, -dious; pro-emial, introductory, prefatory, prodromous, inaugural, preliminary; precedent etc. (*prior*) 116.

65. Sequel.—N. sequel, suffix, successor; tail, *queue*, train, wake, trail, rear; retinue, suite; appendix, postscript, subscript; epilogue; conclusion; peroration; codicil; continuation, *sequela;* appendage etc. 39; tail –, heel-piece; tag, more last words; *colophon*.

follower, after-glow, -growth, -crop, -taste, -math.

after-part, -piece, -course, -thought, -game; *arrière pensee*. second thoughts.

66. Beginning.—N. beginning, commencement, opening, outset, incipience, inception, inchoation; introduction etc. (*precursor*) 64; *alpha;* initial; foundation; inauguration, *début, le premier pas*, embarcation, rising of the curtain; zero hour; exordium, curtain raiser; maiden speech; prelude; outbreak, onset, brunt; initiative, move, first move; gambit, narrow –, thin- end of the wedge; fresh start, new departure; forefront.

origin etc. (*cause*) 153; source, rise; bud, germ etc. 153; egg, rudiment; genesis, birth, nativity, cradle, infancy, incunabula; start, starting-point etc. 293; dawn etc. (*morning*) 125.

title-page; head, -ing, caption; van etc. (*front*) 234.

en-trance, -try; inlet, orifice, mouth, chops, lips, porch, portal, portico, *propylon*, door; gate, -way; postern, wicket, threshold, vestibule; skirts, border etc. (*edge*) 231; tee.

first -stage, – blush, – glance, – impression, – sight.

rudiments, elements, outlines, *principia*, grammar, *protasis;* alphabet, ABC.

V. begin, commence, inchoate. rise, arise, originate, institute, conceive, initiate, open. dawn, set in, take its rise, enter upon, start; enter; set out etc. (*depart*) 293; embark in.

usher in; lead -off, – the way; take the -lead, – initiative; inaugurate, head; stand -at the head, – first, – for; lay the foundations etc. (*prepare*) 673; found etc. (*cause*) 153; set -up, – on foot, – agoing, – abroach, – the ball in motion; apply the match to a train; launch, broach; open -up, – the door to; set -about, – to work; make a -beginning, – start; handsel; take the first step, lay the first stone, cut the first turf; break -ground, – the ice, – cover; pass –, cross- the Rubicon; open -fire, – the ball; ventilate, air; undertake etc. 676.

come into -existence, – the world; make one's *début*, take birth; burst forth, break out; spring –, crop- up.

begin -at the beginning, – *ab ovo*, – again, – *de novo;* start afresh, make a fresh start, shuffle the cards, resume, recommence.

Adj. beginning etc. *v.;* initi-al, -atory, -ative; inceptive, introductory, incipient; proemial, inaugural; incho-ate,. -ative; embryonic, rudimental; primogenial; primeval etc. (*old*) 124; rudimentary, aboriginal; natal, nascent.

first, foremost, front, leading, head; maiden. begun etc. *v.;* just -begun etc. *v.*

Adv. at –, in- the beginning etc. *n.;* first, in the first place, *imprimis*, first and foremost; *in limine;* in -the bud, – embryo, – its infancy; from -the beginning, – its birth; *ab -initio*, – *ovo*, – *incunabilis*, primarily, originally.

67. End.—N. end, close, termination; desinence, conclusion, *finis, finale*, period, term, *terminus*, last, *omega;* extreme, -tremity; gable –, butt –, fagend; tip, nib, point; tail etc. (*rear*) 235; verge etc. (*edge*) 231; tag, epilogue, peroration; *bonne bouche*, bitter end, tail end; terminal; *apodosis;* appendix.

consummation, *dénouement;* finish etc. (*completion*) 729; fate; doom, -sday; crack of doom, day of Judgment, fall of the curtain, wind-up; goal, destination; limit, stoppage, end all, determination; expiration, expiry; death etc. 360; end of all things; finality; eschatology.

break up, *commencement de la fin*, last stage, turning point; *coup de grâce*, death-blow; knock-out.

V. end, close, finish, terminate, conclude, be all over; expire; die etc. 360; come –, draw- to a -close etc. *n.;* have run its course; run out, pass away.

bring to an -end etc. *n.;* put an end to, make an end of; determine; get through; achieve etc. (*complete*) 729; stop etc. (*make to cease*) 142; shut up shop.

Adj. ending etc. *v.;* final, terminal, definitive, conclusive; crowning etc. (*completing*) 729; last, ultimate; hindermost; rear etc. 235; caudal.

contermin-ate, -ous, -able.

ended etc. *v.;* at an end; settled, decided, over, played out, set at rest.

penultimate; last but -one, – two, etc.

unbegun, uncommenced; fresh.

Adv. finally etc. *adj ;* in fine; at the last; once for all.

68. Middle.—N. middle, midst, mediety; mean etc. 29; medium, middle term; center etc. 222; mid-course etc. 628; *mezzo termine; juste milieu* etc. 628; half-way house, nave, navel, omphalos; nucle-us, -olus.

equidistance, bisection, half-distance; equator, diaphragm, midriff; interjacence etc. 228.

Adj. middle, medial, mesial, mean, mid; middle-, mid-most; middling; mediate; intermediate etc. (*interjacent*) 228; equidistant; central etc. 222; mediterranean, equatorial.

Adv. in the middle; in the thick; mid-, half-way; midships, *in medias res*.

69. Continuity. [Uninterrupted sequence.]—**N.** continuity; consecu-tion,, -tiveness etc. *adj.;* succession, round, suite, progression, series, train, chain; cat-, concat-enation; catena; scale; gradation, course, constant flow, perpetuity.

procession, column; retinue, *cortège*, cavalcade, rank and file, line of battle, array.

pedigree, genealogy, lineage, race etc. 166.

rank, file, line, row, range, tier, string, thread; team; suit; colonnade.

V. follow in –, form- a series etc. *n.;* fall in.

arrange in a -series etc. *n.;* string together, catenate, file, thread, graduate, tabulate.

Adj. continu-ous. -ed; consecutive; progressive, gradual; serial, successive; immediate, unbroken, entire; linear; in a -line, — row etc. *n.;* uninter-rupted, -mitting; unremitting; perennial, evergreen; constant.

Adv. continuously etc. *adj.; seriatim;* in a -line etc. *n.;* in -succession, — turn; running, gradually, step by step; *gradatim,* at a stretch; in -file, — column, — single file, — Indian file.

70. Discontinuity. [Interrupted sequence.]—N. discontinuity; disjunction etc. 44; anacoluthon; interruption, break, fracture, flaw, fault, split, crack, cut; gap etc. (*interval*) 198; solution of continuity, *caesura;* broken thread; parenthesis, episode; rhapsody, patchwork; intermission; alternation etc. (*periodicity*) 138; dropping fire.

V. be -discontinuous etc. *adj.;* alternate, intermit.

discontinue, pause, interrupt; intervene; break, — in upon; interpose etc. 228; break —, snap- the thread; disconnect etc. (*disjoin*) 44.

Adj. discontinuous, unsuccessive, broken, interrupted, *décousu;* dis-, un-connected, discrete, disjunctive; fitful etc. (*irregular*) 139; spasmodic, desultory, intermit-ting etc. *v.;* -tent; alternate; recurrent etc. (*periodic*) 138; few and far between.

Adv. at intervals; by -snatches, — jerks, — skips, — catches, — fits and starts; skippingly, *per saltum; longo intervallo.*

71. Term.—N. term, rank, station, stage, step; degree etc. 26; scale, remove, grade, link, peg, round —, rung- of the ladder, *status,* position, place, point, mark, *pas,* period, pitch; stand, - ing; footing, range.

V. hold —, occupy —, fall into- a place etc. *n.*

72. Assemblage.—N. assemblage; col-lection, location, -ligation; compilation, levy, gathering, ingathering, mobilization, meet, foregathering, muster, *attroupement;* con-course, -flux, - gregation, -tesseration, -vergence etc. 290; meeting, *levée, réunion,* drawing room, at home; conversazione etc. (*social gathering*) 892; assembly, congress, eisteddfod; conven-tion, -ticle; gemote; conclave, etc. (*council*) 696; posse, *posse comitatus;* Noah's ark.

miscellany, *collectanea,* symposium; museum, menagerie, etc. (*store*) 636.

crowd, throng, multitude; flood, rush, deluge; rout, rabble, mob, press, crush, *cohue,* jam, horde, body, tribe; crew, gang, knot, squad, band, party; swarm, shoal, school, covey, flock, herd, drove, kennel; array, bevy, galaxy; *corps,* company, troop, *troupe;* army, force, regiment, etc. (*combatants*) 726; host etc. (*multitude*) 102; populousness.

clan, brotherhood, association etc. (*party*) 712.

volley, shower, storm, cloud.

group, cluster, Pleiades, clump, pencil; set, batch, lot, pack; budget, *dossier,* assortment, bunch; parcel; pack-et, -age; bundle, *fasciculus,* fascine, bale; ser-on, oon; faggot, wisp, truss,

tuft; shock, rick, fardel, stack, sheaf, swath, gavel, haycock, stook.

accumulation etc. (*store*) 636; congeries, heap, lump, pile, *rouleau,* tissue, mass, pyramid; drift; snow-ball, -drift; acervation, cumulation; amassment, glom-, agglom-eration; conglobation; conglomeration, -ate; coacervation, coagmentation, aggregation, concentration, congestion, *omnium gatherum, spicilegium,* black hole of Calcutta; quantity etc. (*greatness*) 31.

collector, gatherer; whip, -per in.

V. [be or come together] assemble, collect, muster; meet, unite, join, rejoin; cluster, flock, swarm, surge, stream, herd, crowd, throng, associate; con-gregate, -glomerate, -centrate; center round, *rendezvous,* resort; come —, flock —, get —, pig- together; forgather; huddle; reassemble.

[get or bring together] assemble, muster, mobilize; bring —, get —, put —, draw —, scrape —, lump- together; col-lect, -locate, -ligate; get —, whip- in; gather; hold a meeting; con-vene, -voke, -vocate; rake up, dredge; heap, mass, pile; pack, put up, truss, cram; acervate; ag-glomerate, -gregate; compile; group, aggroup, concentrate, unite; collect —, bring- into a focus; amass, accumulate etc. (*store*) 636; collect in a drag-net; heap Ossa upon Pelion.

Adj. assembled etc. *v.;* closely packed, dense, serried, crowded to suffocation, teeming, swarming, populous; as thick as hops; all of a heap, fasciculated; cumulative.

Phr. the plot thickens.

73. Non-assemblage. Dispersion.—N. dispersion; disjunction etc. 44; divergence etc. 291; scattering etc. *v.;* dissemination, broadcasting, diffusion, dissipation, distribution; apportionment etc. 786; spread, respersion, circumfusion, interspersion, spargefaction.

waifs and estrays, flotsam and jetsam, *disjecta membra.*

V. disperse, scatter, sow, disseminate, radiate, diffuse, shed, spread, ted, bestrew, overspread, dispense, disband, disembody, demobilize, dismember, distribute; apportion etc. 786; blow off, let out, dispel, cast forth, draught off; strew, straw, strow; spirtle, cast, sprinkle, shatter; issue, deal out, retail; utter; re-, inter-sperse; set abroach, circumfuse.

turn —, cast- adrift; scatter to the winds; sow broadcast.

spread like wildfire, disperse themselves.

Adj. unassembled etc. (*see* assemble etc. 72); dispersed etc. *v.;* sparse, dispread, broadcast, sporadic, widespread; far-flung; epidemic etc. (*general*) 78; adrift, stray; dishevelled, streaming.

Adv. *sparsim,* here and there, *passim.*

74. Focus. [Place of meeting.]—N. focus; point of- convergence etc. 290; corradiation; center etc. 222; gathering-place, resort; haunt; retreat; *venue, rendezvous;* rallying point, head-quarters, home, club; *dépôt* etc. (*store*) 636; tryst, trysting-place; place of -meeting, — resort, — assignation; *point de —, lieu de- réunion;* issue.

V. bring to- a point, — a focus, — an issue; focus.

75. Class.—N. class, category, *categorema,* head, order, section; division, subdivision; department, province, domain, sphere.

kind, sort, genus, species, variety, branch, family, race, tribe, caste, sept, clan, breed; *clique, coterie;* type, kit, sect, set; assortment; feather, kidney; suit; range; gender, sex, kin.

manner, description, denomination, persuasion, connection, designation, character, stamp; predicament; conviction etc. 484.

similarity etc. 17.

76. Inclusion. [Comprehension under, or reference to a class.]—N. inclusion, admission, incorporation, comprehension, reception.

composition etc. (*inclusion in a compound*) 54.

V. be -included in etc.; come −, fall −, range- under; belong −, pertain- to; range with; merge in.

include, compromise, comprehend, contain, admit, embrace, receive; enclose etc. (*circum-scribe*) 229; incorporate, cover, embody, en- circle.

reckon −, enumerate −, number- among; refer to; place −, arrange-under, − with; take into account.

Adj. includ-ed; -ing etc. *v.;* inclusive; com- prehensive, all-embracing; congen-er, -erous; of the same -class etc. 75.

Phr. *et hoc genus omne,* etc.; *et caetera.*

77. Exclusion.*—N. exclusion etc. 55.

* The same set of words is used to express *Exclusion from a class* and *Exclusion from a compound.* Reference is therefore made to the former at 55. This identity does not occur with regard to *Inclusion,* which therefore con- stitutes a separate category.

78. Generality.—N. general-ity, -ization; un- iversality; catholic-ity, -ism; miscel-lany, - laneousness; drag-net.

every-one, -body; all hands, all the world and his wife; any body, N or M, all sorts; *tout le monde.*

prevalence, run.

V. be -general etc. *adj.;* prevail, obtain, be going about, stalk abroad.

render -general etc. *adj.;* generalize; spread, broadcast.

Adj. general, usual, current, generic, collec- tive; broad, comprehensive, sweeping; ency- clopedical, panoramic, widespread etc. (*dis- persed*) 73.

universal; catho-lic, -lical; common, world- wide; e-cumenical; transcendental; prevalent, prevailing, rife, epidemic, besetting; all over, covered with.

every, all; indeterminate, indefinite, un- specified, impersonal.

customary etc. (*habitual*) 613.

Adv. what-ever, -soever; to a man, one and all, without exception.

generally etc. *adj.;* always, for better for worse; in general, generally speaking; speaking generally; for the most part; in the long run etc. (*on an average*) 29.

79. Speciality.—N. speciality, *spécialité;* individ-uality, -uity; particularity, peculiairity;

idiocrasy etc. (*tendency*) 176; personality, characteristic, mannerism, idiosyncrasy, at- tribute specificness etc. *adj.;* singularity etc. (*un- conformity*) 83; reading, version, lection; state; *trait;* distinctive feature; technicality; *differ- entia.*

particulars, details, minutiae, items, counts.

I, self, I myself, *ego;* my-, him-, her-, it-self.

V. specify, particularize, individualize, realize, specialize, designate, differentiate, determine, define, denote, indicate, itemize, detail.

descend to particulars, enter into detail, come to the point.

Adj. special, particular, individual, specific, proper, personal, intimate, original, private, respective, definite, concrete, determinate, es- pecial, certain, esoteric, endemic, partial, party, peculiar, marked, appropriate, several, char- acteristic, diagnistic, exact, exclusive; singular etc. (*exceptional*) 83; idiomatic; typical, rep- resentative, distinctive.

this, that; yon, -der.

Adv. specially etc. *adj.;* in particular, *in propriâ personâ; ad hominem;* for my part.

each, apiece, one by one; severally, respective- ly, each to each; *seriatim,* in detail, bit by bit; *pro hac vice,* − *re natâ.*

namely, that is to say, *videlicet,* viz.; to wit.

80. Rule.—N. regularity, uniformity etc. 16; clock-work precision; punctuality etc. (*exact- ness*) 494; routine etc. (*custom*) 613; formula; system; rut; canon, convention, maxim; rule etc. (*form, regulation*) 697; key-note, standard, model; precedent etc. (*prototype*) 22; conformity etc. 82.

nature, principle; law; order of things; normal −, natural −, ordinary −, model- -state, − con- dition; standing -dish, − order; normality; Pro- crustean law; law of the Medes and Persians; hard and fast rule.

Adj. regular, uniform, symmetrical, constant, steady; according to rule etc. (*conformable*) 82; customary etc. 613; orderly etc. 58.

81. Multiformity.—N. multi-, omniformity; variety, diversity; multifariousness etc. *adj.*

Adj. multi-form, -fold, -farious, -generous; multiplex, variform, manifold, many-sided; multiplicate; omni-form, -genous, -farious; poly- morphic; protean; heterogeneous, motley, mosaic; epicene, indiscriminate, desultory, irre- gular, diversified, different, divers; all manner of; of -every description, − all sorts and kinds; *et hoc genus omne;* and what not? *de omnibus rebus et quibusdam aliis.*

82. Conformity.—N. conform-ity, -ance; observance.

naturalization; conventionality etc. (*custom*) 613; agreement etc. 23.

example, instance, specimen, sample, quo- tation; exemplification, illustration, case in point; object lesson.

conventionalist, formalist, Philistine.

pattern etc. (*prototype*) 22.

V. conform to, − rule; accommodate −, adapt- oneself to; rub off corners.

be -regular etc. *adj.;* move in a groove; follow −, observe −, go by −, bend to −, obey- -rules, − precedents; comply −, tally −, chime in −, fall in-with; be -guided, − regulated- by; fall into a -custom, − usage; follow the -fashion, − multitude; pass muster, do as others do, *hurler aves les loups;* do at Rome as the Romans do; go −, swim- with the -stream, − current, − tide; tread the beaten track, etc. *(habit)* 613; rubber-stamp; keep one in countenance.

exemplify, illustrate, cite, quote, put a case; produce an- instance etc. *n.*

Adj. conformable to rule, adaptable, compliant, consistent, agreeable; regular etc. 80; according to -regulation, − rule, − Cocker; *en règle, selon les règles,* well regulated, orderly; symmetric etc. 242.

conventional commonplace etc. *(customary)* 613; of -daily, − every day- occurrence; in the natural order of things; ordinary, common, − or garden, prosaic, habitual, usual.

in the order of the day; naturalized.

typical, normal, formal; canonical, orthodox, sound, strict, rigid, positive, uncompromising, Procrustean; point device.

secundum artem, ship-shape, technical.

exemplary, illustrative, in point.

Adv. conformably etc. *adj.;* by rule; agreeably to; in -conformity, − accordance, − keeping-with; according to; consistently with; as usual, *ad instar, instar omnium; more -solito,* − *majorum.*

for the sake of conformity; of −, as a matter of- course; *pro formâ,* for form's sake, by the card; according to plan.

invariably etc. *(uniformly)* 16.

for -example, − instance; *exempli gratiâ; e.g., inter alia.*

Phr. *cela va sans dire, ex pede Herculem, noscitur a sociis.*

83. Unconformity.—**N.** non-conformity etc. 82; un-, dis-conformity; unconventionality, informality, abnormity, anomaly; anomalousness etc. *adj.;* exception, peculiarity, etc. 79; infraction −, breach −, violation −, infringement- of -law, − custom, − usage; eccentricity, *bizarrerie,* oddity, *je ne sais quoi,* monstrosity, rarity; freak of Nature.

individuality, idiosyncrasy, singularity, oritinality, mannerism.

aberration; irregularity; variety; singularity; exemption; salvo etc. *(qualification)* 469.

nonconformist; nondescript, character, original, nonsuch, monster, prodigy, wonder, miracle, curiosity, missing link, flying fish, black swan, *lusus naturae, rara avis,* queer fish; mongrel; half-caste, -blood, -breed; *métis,* cross breed, hybrid, mule, mulatto, sacatra, marabou; *tertium quid,* hermaphrodite, gynander, androgyn.

phoenix, chimera, hydra, sphinx, minotaur; griff-in, -on; centaur; hippogriff, -centaur; sagittary; kraken; cockatrice, wyvern, roc, liver, dragon, sea-serpent; mermaid; unicorn; Cyclops, 'men whose heads do grown beneath their shoulders;. Teratolgy.

fish out of water; neither -one thing nor another, − fish flesh nor fowl nor good red her-

ring; one in a -way, − thousand; out-cast, -law; Ishmael, pariah; oasis.

V. be -unconformable etc. *adj.;* leave the beaten -track, − path; infringe −, break −, violate- a -law, − habit, − usage, − custom; drive a coach and six through; stretch a point; have no business there; baffle −, beggar- all description.

Adj. unconformable, exceptional; abnorm-al, -ous; anomal-ous, -istic; out of -order, − place, − keeping, − tune, − one's element; irregular, arbitrary; lawless, informal, aberrant, stray, wandering, wanton; peculiar, exclusive, unnatural, eccentric, crotchety, egregious; out of the -beaten track, − common, − common run, − pale of; misplaced; funny.

un-usual, -accustomed, -customary, -wonted, -common; rare, singular, *unique,* curious, odd, extraordinary, strange, monstrous; wonderful etc. 870; unexpected, unaccountable; *outré,* out of the way, remarkable, noteworthy; queer, quaint, nondescript, none such, *sui generis;* original, unconventional, Bohemian, unfashionable; un-described, -precedented, -paralleled, -exampled, -heard of, -familiar; fantastic, newfangled, grotesque, *bizarre;* outlandish, exotic, *tombé de nues,* preternatural; denaturalized.

heterogeneious, heteroclite, amorphous, mongrel, amphibious, epicene, half-blood, hybrid; androgyn-ous, -al; unsymmetric etc. 243.

qualified etc. 469.

Adv. unconformably etc. *adj.;* except, unless, save, barring, beside, without, save and except, let alone.

however, yet, but.

Int. what -on earth! − in the world!

Phr. never was -seen, − heard, − known- the like.

84. Number.—**N.** number, symbol, numeral, figure, cipher, digit, integer; counter; round number; formula; function; series.

sum, total, aggregate, difference, complement, subtrahend; product; multipli-cand, -er, -cator; coefficient, multiple; dividend, divisor, factor, quotient, sub-multiple, fraction; mixed number; numerator, denominator; decimal, circulating decimal, repetend; common measure, aliquot part; reciprocal; prime number; totitive, totient.

permutation, combination, variation; election.

ratio, proportion; progression; arithmetical −, geometrical −, harmonical- progression; percentage.

figurate −, pyramidal −, polygonal- numbers.

power, root, exponent, index, logarithm, anti-logarithm; modulus.

differential, integral, fluxion, fluent.

Adj. numeral, complementary, divisible, aliquot, reciprocal, prime, fractional, decimal, figurate, incommensurable.

proportional, exponential, logarithmic, logo-metric, differential, fluxional, integral.

positive, negative; rational, irrational; surd, radical, real, imaginary, impossible.

85. Numeration.—**N.** numeration, numbering etc. *v.;* pagination; tale, tally, recension, enumeration, summation, reckoning, computation, supputation; calcu-lation, -lus; algorithm, rhabdology, dactylonomy; measurement etc. 466; statistics.

arithmetic, analysis, algebra, fluxions; differential —, integral —, infinitesimal-calculus; calculus of differences.

[Statistics] dead reckoning, muster, poll, census, capitation, roll-call, recapitulation; account etc. (*list*) 86.

[Operations] notation, addition, subtraction, multiplication, division, proportion, rule of three, practice, equations, extraction of roots, reduction, involution, evolution, approximation, interpolation, differentiation, integration.

[Instruments] abacus, swan-pan, logometer, sliding —, slide- rule, tallies, Napier's bones, calculating —, adding- machine, difference engine; cash register.

arithmetician, calculator, abacist; mathematician, actuary, statistician, surveyor, geodesist.

V. number, count, tell; call —, run- over, take an account of, enumerate, call the roll, muster, poll, recite, recapitulate; sum; sum —, cast- up; tell off, score, cipher, compute, calculate, set a price, reckon, — up, estimate; suppute, add, subtract, multiply, divide, extract roots.

check, prove, demonstrate, balance, audit, overhaul, take stock; affix numbers to, page, foliate, paginate.

amount —, come- to.

Adj. numer-al, -ical; arithmetical, analytic, algebraic, statistical, numerable, computable, calculable; commensur-able, -ate; incommensur-able, -ate.

86. List.—N. list, catalogue, enumeration, inventory, schedule; register etc. (*record*) 551; account; bill, — of costs, syllabus; terrier, tally, file; almanac, calendar, index, table, atlas, contents, card index; rota, ticket; book, ledger; synopsis, *catalogue raisonné; tableau*, scroll, manifest, invoice, bill of lading; prospectus, *programme;* bill of fare, *menu, carte;* score, census, statistics, returns; Red —, Blue —, Domesday- book; *cadaster;* directory, gazetteer, dictionary, glossary, lexicon, thesaurus, gradus.

roll; check —, chequer —, bead- roll, — of honor; muster -roll, — book; roster, panel; cartulary, diptych.

V. list, enrol, schedule, register etc. *n.;* indent, post, docket; matriculate.

Adj. cadastral, listed etc. *v.*

87. Unity.—N. unity; oneness etc. *adj.;* individuality; solitude etc. (*seclusion*) 893; isolation etc. (*disjunction*) 44; unification etc. 48.

one, unit, ace; item; individual; solo, none else, no other, naught beside.

V. be -one, — alone etc. *adj.;* dine with Duke Humphrey.

isolate etc. (*disjoin*) 44.

render one; unite etc. (*join*) 43, (*combine*) 48.

Adj. one, sole, single, solitary, only- begotten; individual, apart, alone; kithless.

un-accompanied, -attended; *solus,* singlehanded; singular, odd, unique, unrepeated, azygous, first and last; isolated etc. (*disjoined*) 44; insular; unitary.

lone; lone-ly, -some; desolate, dreary.

in-secable, -severable, -discerptible; compact, irresolvable.

Adv. singly etc. *adj.;* alone, by itself, *per se,* only, apart, in the singular number, in the abstract; one -by one, — at a time; simply; one and a half, *sesqui-.*

Phr. *natura il fece, e poi roppe la stampa.*

88. Accompaniment.—N. accompaniment; appurtenance, adjunct etc. 39; context.

coexistence, concomitance, company, association, companionship; part-, copart-nership; coefficiency.

concomitant, accessory, coefficient; companion, attendant, fellow, associate, consort, spouse, colleague, *fidus Achates;* part-, co-partner; satellite, hanger on, shadow; escort, *entourage,* suite, *cortège;* convoy, follower etc. 65; attribute.

V. accompany, coexist, attend, convoy, chaperon; hang —, wait- on; go hand in hand with; synchronize etc. 120; bear —, keep- company; row in the same boat; bring in its train, associate —, couple- with.

Adj. accompanying etc. *v.;* concomitant, fellow, twin, joint; associated —, coupled- with; accessory, attendant, *obbligato.*

Adv. with, withal; together —, along —, in company- with; hand in hand, side by side; cheek by -jowl, — jole; arm in arm; there-, here-with; and etc. (*addition*) 37.

together, in a body, collectively.

89. Duality.—N. dual-ity, -ism; duplicity; biplicity, -formity; span, polarity.

two, deuce, couple, couplet, doublet, brace, pair, cheeks, twins, Castor and Pollus, *gemini.* Siamese twins; fellows; yoke, conjugation, dyad, distich.

V. [unite in pairs] pair, couple, bracket, yoke; conduplicate, mate.

Adj. two, twain; dual, -istic; binary, binomial; twin, biparous; dyadic; conduplicate; duplex etc. 90; *tête-à-tête;* paired; dihedral.

coupled etc. *v.;* conjugate.

both, — the one and the other.

90. Duplication.—N. duplication, doubling etc. *v.;* gemi-, ingemi-nation; reduplication; iteration etc. (*repetition*) 104; renewal.

V. double; re-double, -duplicate; geminate; repeat etc. 104; renew etc. 660; duplicate, copy etc. 21.

Adj. double; doubled etc. *v.;* bicameral, bicapital, bi-fold, -form, -lateral, -farious, -facial; two-fold, -sided, -headed, -edged etc.; duplex; double-faced; twin, duplicate, ingeminate; second; dual etc. 29.

Adv. twice, once more; over again etc. (*repeatedly*) 104; as much again; twofold.

secondly, in the second place, again.

91. Bisection. [Division into two parts.]—N. bi-section, -partition; di-, subdi-chotomy; halving etc. *v.;* dimidiation; *hendiadis.*

bifurcation, forking, branching, furcation, ramification, divarication; fork, prong; fold.

half, moiety.

V. bisect, halve, divide, split, cut in two, cleave, dimidiate, dichotomize, divaricate.

go halves, divide with.

separate, fork, bifurcate; branch -off, − out; ramify.

Adj. bisected etc. v.; cloven, cleft; bipartite, biconjugate, bicuspid, bifid; bifur-cous, -cate, -cated; semi-, demi- hemi-

92. Triality.—N. triality, trinity,* triplicity.

three, triad, triplet, trey, trio, ternion, trinomial, leash; tierce; triennium; trefoil, triangle, trident, tripod, triumvirate, *troika*.

third power, cube.

Adj. three; tri-form, -nal, -nomial; tertiary; triune.

*Trinity is hardly ever used except in a theological sense; see Deity 976.

93. Triplication.—N. tripli-cation, -city; trebleness, trine, trilogy.

V. treble, triple, triplicate, cube.

Adj. treble, triple; tern, -ary; triplex, triplicate, threefold, trilogistic; third; trinal; trihedral.

Adv. three -times, − fold; thrice, in the third place, thirdly; trebly etc. *adj.*

94. Trisection. [Division into three parts.]—N. tri-section, -partition, -chotomy; third, − part.

V. trisect, divide into three parts, trifurcate.

Adj. trifid; trisected etc. v.; tripartite, -chotomous, -sulcate.

95. Quaternity.—N. quaternity, four, tetrad, quartet, quaternion, square, quadrature, quarter, quadruplet; quadrilateral, quadrangle, quatrefoil; *quadriga*.

V. reduce to a square, square.

Adj. four; quat-ernary, -ernal; quadratic; quartile, quartic, tetractic, tetrad, tetrahedral; quadrennial; quadrivalent.

96. Quadruplication.—N. quadruplication.

V. multiply by four, quadruplicate, biquadrate.

Adj. fourfold; quad-ruple, -ruplicate, -rible; quadruplex; fourth.

Adv. four times; in the fourth place, fourthly.

97. Quadrisection. [Division into four parts.]—N. quadri-section, -partition; quartering etc. v.; fourth; quart, -er, -ern; farthing (*i.e.* fourthing); quarto.

V. quarter, divide into four parts, quadrisect.

Adj. quartered etc. v.; quadri-fid, -partite.

98. Five, etc.—N. five, cinque, quint, quincunx, quintuplet, quintet, pentagon, pentameter, Pentateuch; six, half-a-dozen; sextet, hexagon, hexameter; seven, Heptarchy; eight, octet, octagon, octave; nine, three times three; ten, decade; eleven; twelve, dozen; thirteen; long −, baker's-dozen.

twenty, score; twenty-four, four and twenty, two dozen; twenty-five, five and twenty, quarter

of a hundred; forty, two score; fifty, half a hundred; sixty, three score, sexagenarian; seventy, three score and ten, septuagenarian; eighty, four score, octogenarian; ninety, four score and ten, nonagenarian.

hundred, centenary, hecatomb, century; hundredweight, cwt.; one hundred and forty-four, gross; bicentenary, tercentenary etc.

thousand, chiliad; myriad, millennium, ·ten thousand; lac, lakh, one hundred thousand, plum; million; thousand million, *milliard*.

billion, trillion etc.

V. centuriate.

Adj. five, quinary, quintuple; fifth; senary, sextuple; sixth; seventh; octuple; eighth; ninefold, ninth; tenfold, decimal, denary, decuple, tenth; eleventh; duo-denary, -denal; twelfth; in one's 'teens, thirteenth.

vices-, viges-imal; twentieth; twenty-fourth etc. *n.*

cent-uple, -uplicate, -ennial, -enary, -urial; secular, hundredth; thousandth; millenary etc.

99. Quinquesection, etc.—N. division by -five etc. 98; quinquesection etc.; fifth etc.; decimation.

V. decimate, quinquesect.

Adj. quinque-fid, -partite; quinquarticular; octifid; decimal, tenth, tithe, teind; duodecimal, twelfth; sexagesimal, -genary; hundredth, centesimal; millesimal etc.

100. Plurality. [More than one.]—N. plurality; a -number, − certain number; one or two, two or three etc.; a few, several; multitude etc. 102.

Adj. plural, more than one, upwards of, some, certain; not -alone etc. 87.

Adv. *et cetera, etc.,* etc.

Phr. *non deficit alter.*

100a. Fraction [Less than one.]—N. fraction, fractional part, fragment; part etc. 51.

Adj. fractional, fragmentary, partial.

101. Zero.—N. zero, nothing, naught, nought, duck's egg, goose egg; cipher, none, nobody; not a soul; *âme qui vive*; absence etc. 187; unsubstantiality etc. 4.

Adj. not -one, − any.

102. Multitude.—N. multitude; numerousness etc. *adj.*; numer-osity, -ality; multiplicity; profusion etc. (*plenty*) 639; legion, host; great −, large −, round −, enormous- number; a quantity, numbers, array, sight, army, sea, galaxy; scores, peck, bushel, school, shoal, swarm, draft, bevy, cloud, flock, herd, drove, flight, covey, hive, brood, litter, farrow, fry, nest; mob, crowd etc. (*assemblage*) 72; lots, loads, heaps; all the world and his wife.

[Increase of number] greater number, majority; multiplication, multiple.

V. be -numerous etc. *adj.*; swarm −, teem −, crawl −, creep -with; crowd, swarm, come thick upon; outnumber, multiply; people; swarm like -locusts, − bees.

Adj. many, several, sundry, divers, various,

not a few; a -hundred, − thousand, − myriad, − million, − thousand and one; some -ten or a dozen, − forty or fifty etc.; half a -dozen, − hundred etc.; very −, full −, ever so- many; numer-ous, -ose; profuse, in profusion; manifold, multiplied, multitudinous, multiferous, multiple, multinomial, teeming, crawling, populous, peopled, crowded, thick, studded; galore.

thick coming, many more, more than one can tell, a world of; no end -of, − to; *cum multis aliis*; thick as -hops, − hail; plenty as blackberries; numerous as the -stars in the firmament, − sands on the sea-shore, − hairs on the head; and -what not, − heaven knows what; endless etc. (*infinite*) 105.

Phr. their name is 'Legion.'

103. Fewness.—**N.** fewness etc. *adj.*; paucity, small number; small quantity etc. 32; scarcity, sparsity; rarity; infrequency etc. 137; handfull; maniple; minority; exiguity.

[Diminution of number] reduction; weeding etc. *v.*; elimination, sarculation, decimation.

V. be -few etc. *adj.*

render -few etc. *adj.*; reduce, diminish the number, weed; eliminate, thin, decimate.

Adj. few; scarce; scant, -y; thin, rare, thinly scattered, few and far between; exiguous; infrequent etc. 137; *rari nantes*; hardly −, scarcely-any; to be counted on one's fingers; reduced etc. *v.*; unrepeated.

Adv. here and there.

104. Repetition.—**N.** repetition, iteration, reiteration, duplication, ding-dong, alliteration; *epistrophe;* harping, recurrence, succession, run; batto-, tauto-logy; monotony, tautophony; rhythm etc. 138; pleonasm, redundancy, diffuseness.

chimes, repetend, echo, *ritornello,* burden of a song, *refrain;* rehearsal; encore; *réchauffé, rifacimento,* recapitulation.

cuckoo etc. (*imitation*) 19; reverberation etc. 408; drumming etc. (*roll*) 407; renewal etc. (*restoration*) 660.

twice-told tale; old -story, − song, chestnut; second −, new- edition; reprint, new impression; return game, return match, reappearance, reproduction; periodicity etc. 138.

V. repeat, iterate, reiterate, reproduce, parrot, echo, re-echo, drum, harp upon, battologize, hammer, redouble.

recur, revert, return, reappear; renew etc. (*restore*) 660.

rehearse; do ¯−, say- over again; ring the changes on; harp on the same string; din −, drum- in the ear; conjugate in all its moods, tenses and inflexions, begin again, go over the same ground, go the same round, never hear the last of; resume, return to, recapitulate, reword.

Adj. repeated etc. *v.*; repetition-al, -ary; recurrent, -ring; ever recurring, thick coming; frequent, incessant, redundant, pleonastic, tautological.

monotonous, harping, iterative; mocking, chiming; retold; aforesaid, -named; above-mentioned, said; habitual etc. 613; another.

Adv. repeatedly, often, again, afresh, anew,

over again, once more; ditto, *encore, de novo, bis, da capo.*

again and again; over and over, − again; many times over; time- and again, − after time; year after year; day by day etc.; many −, several −, a number of- times; many −, full many- a time; times out of number, year in and year out, morning, noon and night; frequently etc. 136.

Phr. *ecce iterum Crispinus, toujours perdrix,* cut and come again; 'tomorrow and tomorrow.'

105. Infinity.—**N.** infini-ty, -tude, -teness etc. *adj.;* perpetuity etc. 112.

V. be -infinite etc. *adj.;* know −, have- no - limits, − bounds; go on for ever.

Adj. infinite, immense; number-, count-, sum-, measure-less; innumer-, immeasur-, incalcul-, illimit-, intermin-, unfathom-, unapproach-able; exhaustless, inexhaustible, indefinite; without - number, − measure, − limit, − end; incomprehensible; limit-, end-, bound-, termless; un-told, - numbered, -measured, -bounded, -limited; il-limited; perpetual etc. 112.

Adv. infinitely etc. *adj.; ad infinitum.*

106. Time.—**N.** time, duration; period, term, stage, space, span, spell, season; the whole -time, − period; course etc. 109.

intermediate, time, while, *interim,* interval, bit, pendency; inter-vention, -mission, -mittence, -regnum, -lude; respite.

era, epoch, eon, cycle; time of life, age, year, date; decade etc. (*period*) 108; moment, etc. (*instant*) 113; reign etc. 737.

glass −, ravages −, whirligig −, noiseless foot- of time; scythe.

V. continue, last, endure, go on, hold out, remain, stay, persist, abide, run; intervene; elapse etc. 109.

take −, take up −, fill −, occupy- time.

pass −, pass away −, spend −, while away −, consume −, talk against −, kill- time; tide over; use −, employ- time; tarry etc. 110; seize an opportunity etc. 134; waste time etc. (*be in-active*) 683.

Adj. continuing etc. *v.;* on foot; permanent etc. (*durable*) 110.

Adv. while, whilst, during, pending; during the -time, − interval; in the course of; for the time being, day by day; in the time of, when; mean-time, -while; in the -meantime, − interim; ad interim, pendente lite; de die in diem; from -day to day, − hour to hour etc.; hourly, always; for a -time, − season; till, until, up to, yet; the whole −, all the- time; all along; throughout etc. (*completely*) 52; for good etc. (*diuturnity*) 110.

here-, there-, where-upon; then; *anno, − Domini;* A.D.; *ante Christum;* A.C.; before Christ; B.C.; *anno urbis conditae;* A.U.C.; *anno regni,* A.R.; once upon a time, one fine morning.

Phr. time -runs, − runs against; *tempus fugit.*

107. Neverness.—**N.** 'neverness;' absence of time, no time; *dies non;* Tib's eve; Greek Kalends.

Adv. never; at no -time, − period; on no occasion, never in all one's born days, nevermore, *sine die.*

108. Period. [Definite duration, or portion of time.]—N. period; second, minute, hour, day, week, sennight, octave, month, moon, quarter, semester, year, *lustrum, quinquennium,* decade, *decennium,* indiction, lifetime, generation, epoch, era, cycle.

century, age, *millennium; annus magnus.*

Adj. horary; hourly, annual etc. (*periodical*) 138.

108a. Contingent Duration.—Adv. during - pleasure, — good behavior; *quamdiu se bene gesserit.*

109. Course. [Indefinite duration.]—N. course —, progress —, process —, succession —, lapse —, flow —, flux —, effluxion, stream —, tract —, current —, sweep —, tide —, march —, step —, flight- of time; duration etc. 106.

[Indefinite time] aorist.

V. elapse, lapse, flow, run, proceed, advance, pass; roll —, wear —, press —, drag- on; flit, fly, slip, slide, glide, crawl; run -its course.

out; expire; go —, pass- by; be -past etc. 122.

Adj. elapsing etc. *v.;* aoristic; progressive, transient etc. 111.

Adv. in due -time, — season; in -course, — process, — the fulness- of time; in time.

Phr. *labitur et labetur; truditur dies die; fugaces labuntur anni;* 'tomorrow and tomorrow and tomorrow creeps in this petty pace from day to day.'

110. Diuturnity. [Long duration.]—N. diuturnity; a -long —, length of -time; an age, a century, an eternity, aeons; slowness etc. 275; perpetuity etc. 112; blue moon.

dura-bleness, -bility; persistence, lastingness etc. *adj.;* continuance, assiduity, endurance, standing; permanence etc. (*stability*) 150; survival, -vance; longevity etc. (*age*) 128; distance of time.

protraction —, prolongation —, extension- of time; delay etc. (*lateness*) 133.

V. last, endure, stand, remain, abide, continue, brave a thousand years.

tarry etc. (*be late*) 133; drag -on, — its slow length along, — a lengthening chain; protract, prolong; spin —, eke —, draw —, lengthen- out; temporize; gain —, make —, talk against- time.

out-last, -live; survive; live to fight again.

Adj. durable; perdurable; lasting etc. *v.;* of long -duration, — standing; permanent, chronic, long-standing; intransi-ent, -tive; intransmutable, persistent; life-, live-long; longeval, long-lived, macrobiotic, diuturnal, sempervirent, evergreen, perennial; unin-, ter-, unremitting; perpetual etc. 112.

lingering, protracted, prolonged, spun out etc. *v.;* long-pending, -winded; slow etc. 275.

Adv. long; for -a long time, — an age, — ages, — ever so long, — many a long day; long ago etc. (*in a past time*) 122; *longo intervallo.*

all the -day long, — year round; the livelong day, as the day is long, morning, noon and night; hour after hour, day after day, etc.; for good; permanently etc. *adj.*

111. Transientness. [Short duration.]—N. transientness etc. *adj.;* evanescence, impermanence, fugacity, transitoriness, volatility, caducity, mortality, span; flash in the pan, nine days' wonder, bubble, May-fly; spurt; temporary arrangement, interregnum.

velocity etc. 274; suddenness etc. 113; changeableness etc. 149.

V. be -transient etc. *adj.;* flit, pass away, fly, gallop, vanish, fade, fleet, melt away, evaporate; pass away like a -cloud, — summer cloud, — shadow, — dream.

Adj. transi-ent, -tory, -tive; passing, evanescent, fleeting; flying etc. *v.;* fug-acious, -itive; shifting, slippery; spasmodic.

tempor-al, -ary; provis-ional, -ory; cursory, short-lived, ephemeral, deciduous; perishable, mortal, precarious; impermanent.

brief, quick, brisk; cometary, meteoric, extemporaneous, summary; pressed for time etc. (*haste*) 684; sudden, momentary etc. (*instantaneous*) 113.

Adv. temporarily etc. *adj.; pro tempore;* for - the moment, — a time; awhile, *en passant, in transitu;* in a short time; soon etc. (*early*) 132; briefly etc. *adj.;* at short notice; on the -point, — eve -of; *in articulo;* between cup and lip.

Phr. one's days are numbered; the time is up; her to-day and gone tomorrow; *non semper erit aestas; eheu! fugaces labuntur anni; sic transit gloria mundi.*

112. Perpetuity. [Endless duration.]—N. perpetuity, eternity, timelessness; everness, aye, sempiternity, immortality, athanasia; everlastingness etc. *adj.;* perpetuation; infinite duration.

V. last —, endure —, go on- for ever; have no end.

eternize, eternify, perpetuate, immortalize.

Adj. perpetual, eternal, eterne; everlasting, -living, -flowing; continual, constant, sempiternal; co-eternal; endless, unending; ceaseless, incessant, uninterrupted, indesinent, unceasing; interminable, having no end; unfading, evergreen, amaranthine; neverending, -dying, -fading; deathless, immortal, undying, imperishable.

Adv. perpetually etc. *adj.;* always, ever, evermore, aye; for -ever, — aye, — evermore, — ever and a day, —, ever and ever; in all ages, from age to age; without end; world —, time- without end; *in saecula saeculorum;* to the -end of time, — crack of doom, — 'last syllable of recorded time;' till doomsday; constantly etc. (*very frequently*) 136.

Phr. *esto perpetuum; labitur et labetur in omne volubilis aevum.*

113. Instantaneity. [Point of time.]—N. instantane-ity, -ousness; sudden-, abrupt-ness.

moment, instant, second, minute; twinkling, trice, flash, breath, crack, jiffy, *coup,* burst, flash of lightning, stroke of time.

epoch, time; time of -day, — night; hour, minute; very -minute etc., — time, — hours; present —, right —, true —, exact —, correct-time.

V. be -instantaneous etc. *adj.;* twinkle, flash.

Adi. instantaneous. momentarv. extempore. sudden, instant, abrupt; subitaneous, hasty; quick as- thought,* — lightning. — a flash; rapid as electricity.

Adv. instantaneously etc. *adj.*; in — in less than-no time; *presto, subito, instanter,* suddenly, at a stroke, like- a shot, — greased lightning; in a trice, in a moment etc. n.; eftsoons, in the twinkling of - ar eye, — a bed post; at one jump, in the same breath, *per saltum, uno saltu;* at —, all at- once; in one's tracks; plump, slap; 'at one fell swoop;' at the same -instant etc. n.; immediately etc. (*early*) 132; *ex tempore,* on the -spot, — spur of the moment, — dot; just then; slap- dash etc. (*haste*) 684; before you could -turn round, — say -knife, — Jack Robinson.
Phr. touch and go; no sooner said than done.
*See note on 264.

114. Chronometry. [Estimation, meas-urement, and record of time.]— **N.** chrono-, horo-metry, -logy; date, epoch; style, era.
almanac, calendar, ephemeris; register, -try; chronicle, annals, journal, diary, chronogram.
[Instruments for the measurement of time] clock, watch; chrono-meter, -scope, -graph; repeater, alarum; time-keeper, -piece; dial, sun-dial, *gnomon, pendule,* horologe, pendulum, hourglass, water clock, clepsydra.
mean —, Greenwich —, solar —, sidereal —, local —, summer- time; daylight saving.
chrono-grapher, -loger, -logist; annalist.
V. fix —, mark- the time; date, register, chronicle; measure —, beat —, mark- time; bear date.
Adj. chrono-logical, -metrical, -grammatical; isochronal.
Adv. o'clock; *a.m., p.m.*

115. Anachronism. [False estimate of time.]— **N.** ana-, meta-, para-, prochronism; *prolepsis,* misdate; anticipation, antichronism.
disregard —, neglect —, oblivion- of time.
intempestivity etc. 135.
V. mis-, ante-, post-, over-date; anticipate; take no note of time.
Adj. misdated etc. *v.;* undated; overdue; out of date; anachronous etc. *n.*

116. Priority.— N. priority, antecedence, anteriority, pre-existence,- precedence etc. 62; precession etc. 280; precursor etc. 64; the past etc. 122; premises.
V. precede, come before; forerun; antecede, go before etc. (*lead*) 280; pre-exist; dawn; premise, presage etc. 511.
be -beforehand etc. (*be early*) 132; steal a march upon, anticipate, forestall; have —, gain-the start.
Adj. prior, previous; preced-ing, -ent; anterior, antecedent; pre-existing, -existent; foresighted; former,·foregoing; afore —, before-, above-men-tioned; aforesaid, said; introductory etc. (*precur-sory*) 64; pre-war.
Adv. before, prior to; earlier; previously etc. *adj.;* afore, ere, theretofore, erewhile, ere —, before- -then, — now; erewhile, already, yet, beforehand; aforetime; on the eve of, in anti-cipation.

117. Posteriority.— N. posteriority; succes-sion, sequence; following etc. 281; subsequence,

supervention; futurity etc. 121; successor; sequel etc. 65; remainder, reversion.
V. follow etc. 281 —, come —, go- after; ensue, result; succeed, supervene; step into the shoes of.
Adj. subsequent, posterior, following, after, later, succeeding, postliminious, postnate; successive etc. 63; postdiluvial, -an; *puisné;* posthumous; post-war, future etc. 121.
Adv. subsequently, after, afterwards, since, later; at a -subsequent, — later- period; next, in the sequel, close upon, thereafter. thereupon, upon which, eftsoons; from that -time, — mo-ment; after a -while, — time; in process of time. postcenal, postcibal, postprandial, after-dinner.

118. The Present Time.— N. the present -time, — day, — moment, — juncture, — occasion; the times, existing time, time being; twentieth cen-tury; nonce, crisis, epoch, day, hour.
age, time of life.
Adj. present, actual, instant, current, latest, existing, that is.
Adv. at this -time, — moment etc. 113; at the - present time etc. *n.;* now, at present.
at this time of day, to-day, now-adays; al-ready; even —, but —, just-now; on the present occasion; for the -time being, — nonce; *pro hâc vice;* on the -nail, — spot; on the spur of the -mo-ment, — occasion.
until now; to -this, — the present day.

119. Different Time. [Time different from the present.]— **N.** different —, other- time.
[Indefinite time] aorist.
Adj. aoristic.
Adv. at that —, at which- -time, — moment, — instant; then, on that occasion, upon.
when; when-ever, -soever; upon which, on which occasion; at -another, — a different, — some other, — any - time; at various times; some —, one- -of these days, — fine morning, — day; sooner or later; some time or other; once upon a time, once.

120. Synchronism.— N. synchronism; coex-istence, coincidence; simultaneousness etc. *adj.;* concurrence, concomitance, unity of time, interim.
[Having equal times] isochronism, syntony.
contemporary, coetanian.
V. coexist, concur, accompany, go hand in hand, keep pace with; synchronize, isochronize.
Adj. synchron-ous, -al, -ical, -istical; simul-taneous, coexisting, coincident, concomitant, concurrent; coev-al, -ous; contempora-ry, - neous; coetaneous; coterminous, coeternal; isochronous.
Adv. at the same time; simultaneously etc. *adj.;* together, in concert; during the same time; in the same breath; *pari passu;* in the interim.
at the -very moment etc. 113; just as, as soon as; meanwhile etc. (*while*) 106.

121. Futurity. [Prospective time.]— **N.** futur-ity, -ition; future, hereafter, time to come; approaching —, coming —, after- -time, — age, — days, — hours, — years, — ages, — life;

morrow, to-morrow, by and by; millennium, doomsday, day of judgment, crack of doom, remote future.

approach of time, advent, time drawing on, womb of time; destiny etc. 152; eventuality.

heritage, heirs, posterity, descendants.

prospect etc. (*expectation*) 507; foresight etc. 510.

V. look forwards; anticipate etc. (*expect*) 507, (*foresee*) 510; forestall etc. (*be early*) 132.'

come −, draw- on; draw near; approach, await, threaten; impend etc. (*be destined*) 152.

Adj. future, to come; coming etc. (*impending*) 152; next, near; near −, close- at hand; eventual, ulterior; expectant, prospective, in prospect etc. (*expectation*) 507.

Adv. prospectively, hereafter, on the knees of the gods, in future; to-morrow, the day after to-morrow; in -course, − process, − the fulness- of time; eventually, ultimately, sooner or later; *proximo; paulo post futurum;* in after time; one of these days; after a -time, − while.

from this time; hence-forth, -forwards; thence; thence-forth, -forward; whereupon, upon which.

soon etc. (*early*) 132; on the -eve, − point, − brink- of; about to; close upon.

122. Preterition. [Retrospective time.]—N. preterition, priority etc. 116; the past, past time; days −, times- -of yore, − of old, − past, − gone by; bygone days, good old days; old −, ancient −, former -times; fore time; yesterdays; the olden −, good old- time; auld lang syne; eld.

antiquity, antiqueness, *status quo;* time immemorial; distance of time; remote -age, − time; ancient history; remote past; rust of antiquity; ancientness.

pale-ontology, -ography, -ology; palaetiology,* archaeology; archaism, antiquarianism, mediaevalism, pre- Raphaelitism; retrospection, looking back, memory etc. 505.

laudator temporis acti; mediaevalist, pre-Raphaelite; antiqu-ary, -arian; archaeologist etc.; Oldbuck, Dryasdust.

ancestry etc. (*paternity*) 166.

V. be -past etc. *adj.;* have -expired etc. *adj.;* − run its course, − had its day; pass; pass −, go- - by, − away, − off; lapse, blow over.

look −, trace −, cast the eyes- back; exhume.

Adj. past, gone, gone by, over, passed away, bygone, foregone; elapsed, lapsed, preterlapsed, expired, no more, run out, blown over, that has been, whilom, extinct, never to return, exploded, forgotten, irrecoverable; obsolete etc. (*old*) 124; extinct as the dodo.

former, pristine, *quondam, ci-devant,* late; ancestral.

foregoing; last, latter; recent, overnight; past, preterite, preter-perfect, -pluperfect, past perfect.

looking back etc. *v.;* retro-spective, -active; archaelogical etc. *n.*

Adv. formerly; of -old, −yore; erst, whilom, erewhile, time was, ago, over; in -the olden time etc. *n.;* anciently, long -ago, − since; a long - while, − time- ago; years −, ages-ago; some time -ago, − since, − back.

yesterday, the day before yesterday; last -year, − season, − month etc.; *ultimo,* lately etc. (*newly*) 123.

retrospectively; ere −, before −, till- now; hitherto, heretofore; no longer; once, − upon a time; from time immemorial; in the memory of man; time out of mind; already, yet, up to this time; *ex post facto.*

Phr. time was; the time -has, − hath- been. **Whewell.*

123. Newness.—N. newness etc. *adj.;* neologism, neoterism; novelty, recency; immaturity; youth etc. 127; gloss of novelty.

innovation; renovation etc. (*restoration*) 660.

modernist, neologist, neoteric.

modernism, modernity; mushroom; latest fashion, *dernier cri.*

upstart, *parvenu, nouveau riche.*

V. renew etc. (*restore*) 660; modernize.

Adj. new, novel, recent, fresh, green; young etc. 127; evergreen; raw, immature; virgin; untried, -handseled, -used, -trodden, -beaten; fledgling.

late, modern, neoteric; new-born, -fashioned, -fangled, -fledged; of yesterday; just out, brand −, span-new, up to date, topical; vernal, renovated; innovatory.

fresh as -a rose, − a daisy, − paint; spick and span.

Adv. newly etc. *adj.;* afresh, anew, lately, just now, only yesterday, the other day; latterly, of late.

not long −, a short time- ago.

124. Oldness.—N. oldness etc. *adj.;* age, antiquity; cobwebs of antiquity.

maturity, ripeness; decline, decay; senility etc. 128.

seniority, eldership, primogeniture.

archaism etc. (*the past*) 122; thing −, relic- of the past; megatherium.

tradition, prescription, custom, folklore, immemorial usage, common law.

V. be -old etc. *adj.;* have -had, − seen- its day; become -old etc. *adj.;* age, fade.

Adj. old, olden, ancient, antique; of long standing, time-honored, venerable; eld-er, -est; first-born.

prime; prim-itive, -eval, -igenous; primordi-al, -nate; aboriginal etc. (*beginning*) 66; diluvian, antediluvian; pre-historic; patriarchal, preadamite; paleocrystic; fossil, paleozoic, pre-glacial, ante-mundane; archaic, classic, mediaeval, pre-Raphaelite, ancestral, black-letter.

immemorial, traditional, prescriptive, customary, whereof the memory of man runneth not to the contrary; inveterate, rooted.

antiquated, of other times, rococo, of the old school, after-age, obsolete; fusty, moth-eaten; out of -date, − fashion; stale, old-fashioned, behind the -age, − times; exploded; gone out, − by; *passé,* outworn, run out; disused; senile etc. 128; time-worn; crumbling etc. (*deteriorated*) 659; second-hand.

old as -the hills, − Methuselah, − Adam, − history.

Adv. since the -world was made, − year one, − days of Methuselah.

125. Morning. [Noon.]—N. morning, morn, matins, forenoon, *a.m.*, prime, dawn, daybreak, daylight, sun-up, peep −, break- of day; aurora,

Eos; first blush —, prime- of the morning; twilight, crepuscule, sunrise, cockcrow.

spring; vernal equinox.

noon; mid-, noon-day; noontide, meridian, prime.

summer, midsummer; summer solstice.

Adj. matin, matutinal; vernal, aestival.

Adv. at -sunrise etc. *n.*; with the lark, when the morning dawns.

126. Evening. [Midnight.]—**N.** evening, eve; decline —, fall —, close- of day; eventide, evensong, vespers; candlelight; nightfall, curfew, dusk, twilight, blind man's holiday; eleventh hour; sun-set, -down; going down of the sun, cock-shut, dewy eve, gloaming, bed-time.

afternoon, *post meridiem, p.m.*

autumn; fall, — of the leaf; autumnal equinox, Indian summer, harvest-time.

midnight; dead —, witching time- of night; winter, — solstice.

Adj. vespertine, autumnal, nocturnal, wintry, brumal, hiemal.

127. Youth.—**N.** youth; juven- -ility, -escence; juniority; infancy; baby-, child-, boy-, girl-, youth-hood; *incunabula;* minority, immaturity, nonage, teens, tender age, bloom.

cradle, nursery, leading-strings, pupilage, puberty, *pucelage.*

prime —, flower —, spring-tide —, seedtime —, golden season - of life; heyday of youth, school days; rising generation, younger generation.

Adj. young, youthful, juvenile, green, callow, budding, sappy, *puisné,* beardless, unfledged, unripe, under age, in one's teens; *in statu pupillari;* younger, junior.

128. Age.—**N.** age; oldness etc. *adj.;* old —, advanced- age; sen-ility, -escence; years, anility, grey hairs, climacteric, grand climacteric, declining years, decrepitude, hoary age, caducity, superannuation; second childhood, -ishness; dotage; vale of years, decline of life, 'sear and yellow leaf;' three-score years and ten; green old age, ripe old age; longevity; time of life.

seniority, eldership; elders etc. (*veteran*) 130; firstling; *doyen,* dean, father; primogeniture; nostology.

V. be -aged etc. *adj.;* grow —, get- old etc. *adj.;* age; decline, wane.

Adj. aged; old etc. 124; elderly, senile; matronly, anile; in years; ripe, mellow, run to seed, declining, waning, past one's prime; grey, -headed; hoar, -y; venerable, time-worn, antiquated, *passé,* effete, doddering, decrepit, superannuated; advanced in -life, — years; stricken in years; wrinkled, marked with the crow's foot; having one foot in the grave; doting etc. (*imbecile*) 499.

old-, eld-er, -est; senior; first-born.

turned of, years old; of a certain age, no chicken, old as Methuselah; gerontic; ancestral; patriarchal etc. (*ancient*) 124.

129. Infant.—**N.** infant, babe, baby; nurse-, suck-, year-, wean-ling; *papoose, bambino.*

child, bairn, little- one, — tot, — mite, chick, brat, chit, pickaninny, kid, urchin; bant-, bratling; elf.

youth, boy, lad, slip, sprig, stripling, youngster, cub, unlicked cub, younker, callant, whipster, whipper-snapper, schoolboy, hobbledehoy, hopeful, cadet, minor, master.

scion; sap-, seed-ling; tendril, olive branch, nestling, chicken, duckling; larva, caterpillar, chrysalis, cocoon; tadpole, whelp, cub, pullet; fry, callow; codlin, -g; *foetus,* calf, colt, pup, foal, kitten; lamb, -kin.

girl; lass, -ie; wench, miss, damsel, *demoiselle, damozel;* maid, -en; virgin; nymph; colleen; minx, baggage, school-girl; tomboy, flapper, hoyden.

Adj. infant-ine, -ile; puerile; boy-, girl-, child-, baby-, kitten-ish; baby; new-born, unfledged, new-fledged, callow.

in -the cradle, — swaddling clothes, — long clothes, — arms, — leading strings; at the breast; in one's teens; young etc. 127.

130. Veteran.—**N.** veteran, old man, seer, patriarch, greybeard, dugout, grand-father, -sire; grandam, beldam; gaffer, gammer; hag, crone; pantaloon; sexage-, octoge-, nonage-, cente-narian; old stager; dotard etc. 501.

preadamite, Methuselah, Nestor, Rip van Winkle, old Parr; elders; forefathers etc. (*paternity*) 166.

131. Adolescence.—**N.** adolescence, pubescence, majority; adultness etc. *adj.;* manhood, virility, maturity; flower of age; prime —, meridian- of life.

man etc. 373; woman etc. 374; adult, no chicken.

V. come -of age, — to man's estate, — to years of discretion; attain majority, assume the *toga virilis;* have -cut one's eye-teeth, — sown one's wild oats, settle down.

Adj. adolescent, pubescent, of age; of -full, — ripe- age; out of one's teens, grown up, mature, full- blown, — grown, in one's prime, in full bloom, manly, virile, adult; womanly, matronly; marriageable, nubile.

132. Earliness.—**N.** earliness etc. *adj.;* morning etc. 125.

punctuality; promptitude etc. (*activity*) 682; haste etc. (*velocity*) 274; suddenness etc. (*instantaneity*) 113.

prematurity, precocity, precipitation, anticipation; prevenience, a stitch in time.

V. be -early etc. *adj.;* — beforehand etc. *adv.;* keep time, take time by the forelock, anticipate, forestall; have —, gain- the start; steal a march upon; gain time, draw on futurity; bespeak, secure, engage, pre-engage.

accelerate; expedite etc. (*quicken*) 274; make haste etc. (*hurry*) 684.

Adj. early, prime, timely, in time, punctual, forward; prompt etc. (*active*) 682; summary.

premature, precipitate, precocious; prevenient, anticipatory; rathe.

sudden etc. (*instantaneous*) 113; unexpected etc. 508; impending, imminent; near, — at hand; immediate.

Adv. early, soon, anon, betimes, rathe; eft, - soons; ere −, before- long; punctually etc. *adj.;* to the minute; in time; in -good, − military, − pudding, − due- time; time enough.

beforehand; prematurely etc. *adj.;* precipitately etc. (*hastily*) 684; too soon; before -its, − one's- time; in anticipation; unexpectedly etc. 508.

suddenly etc. (*instantaneously*) 113; before one can say 'Jack Robinson,' at short notice, extempore; on the spur of the -moment, − occasion; at once; on the -spot, − instant; at sight; off −, out of -hand; *à vue d'oeil;* straight, - way, -forth; forthwith, incontinently, summarily, instanter, immediately, briefly, shortly, quickly, speedily, apace, before the ink is dry, almost immediately, presently, at the first opportunity, in no long time, by and by, in a while, directly.

Phr. touch and go, no sooner said than done.

133. Lateness.—**N.** lateness etc. *adj.;* tardiness etc. (*slowness*) 275.

de-lay, -lation; cunctation, procrastination; detention; deferring etc. *v.;* filibuster, postponement, adjournment, prorogation, retardation, respite, reprieve, stay; protraction, prolongation, moratorium; contango; demurrage; remand; Fabian policy, *médecine expectante,* chancery suit; leeway; high time.

V. be -late etc. *adj.;* tarry, wait, stay, bide, take time; dawdle etc. (*be inactive*) 683; linger, loiter, saunter, lag behind; bide −, take- one's time; hang -about, − around, − back, − in the balance; gain time; hang fire; stand −, lie-over.

put off, defer, delay, lay over, suspend; shift −, stave- off; waive, retard, remand, postpone, adjourn; procrastinate; dally; prolong, protract; spin −, draw −, lengthen- out; prorogue; keep back; tide over; push −, drive- to the last; let the matter stand over; reserve etc. (*store*) 636; temporize; consult one's pillow, sleep upon it.

shelve, table, lay on the table.

lose an opportunity etc. 135; be kept waiting, dance attendance; kick −, cool- one's heels; *faire antichambre;* wait impatiently; await etc. (*expect*) 507; sit up, − at night.

Adj. late, tardy, slow, behindhand, belated, postliminious, posthumous, backward, unpunctual; dilatory etc. (*slow*), overdue 275; delayed etc. *v.;* in abeyance.

Adv. late; late-, back-ward; late in the day; at - sunset, − the eleventh hour, − length, − last, − long; ultimately; after −, behind- time; too late; too late for etc. 135.

slowly, leisurely, deliberately, at one's leisure; *ex post facto; sine die.*

Phr. *nonum prematur in annum.*

134. Occasion.—**N.** occasion, opportunity, opening, room, scope, field; suitable −, proper- - time, − season; high time; opportuneness etc. *adj.;* tempestivity.

crisis, turn, juncture, emergency, conjuncture; turning point; given time.

nick of time; golden −, well-timed −, fine −, favorable- opportunity; clear stage, fair field; *mollia tempora; fata Morgana;* spare time etc. (*leisure*) 685.

V. seize etc. (*take*) 789 −, use etc. 677 −, give etc. 784- an -opportunity, − occasion; improve the occasion.

suit the occasion etc. (*be expedient*) 646.

strike the iron while it is hot, *battre le fer sur l'enclume,* make hay while the sun shines, take time by the forelock, *prendre la balle au bond.*

Adj. opportune, timely, well-timed, timeous, timeful, seasonable.

providential, lucky, fortunate, happy, favorable, propitious, auspicious, critical; suitable etc. 23; *obiter dicta.*

Adv. opportunely etc. *adj.* ; in -proper, − due- -time, − course, − season; for the nonce; in the - nick, − fulness- of time; all in good time; just in time, at the eleventh hour, now or never.

by the -way, − by; *en passant, à propos; pro - re natâ,* − *hac vice; par parenthèse,* parenthetically, by way of parenthesis; while -speaking of, − on this subject; *ex tempore;* on the spur of the -moment, − occasion; on the spot etc. (*early*) 132.

Phr. *carpe diem; occasionem cognosce;* one's hour is come, the time is up; that reminds me.

135. Intempestivity.—**N.** intempestivity; un- seasonableness; unsuitable −, improper-time; unreasonableness etc. *adj.;* evil hour; *contretemps;* intrusion; anachronism etc. 115.

V. be -ill timed etc. *adj.;* mistime, intrude, come amiss, break in upon; have other fish to fry; be -busy, − engaged, − tied up, − occupied.

lose −, throw away −, waste −, neglect etc. 460- an opportunity; allow −, suffer- the - opportunity, − occasion- to -pass, − slip, − go by, − escape, − lapse; waste time etc. (*be inactive*) 683; let slip through the fingers, lock the stable door when the steed is stolen.

Adj. ill-, mis-timed; untimely, intrusive, un- seasonable; out of -date, − season; inopportune, timeless, untoward, *mal à propos,* unlucky, inauspicious, unpropitious, unfortunate, un- favorable; unsuited etc. 24; inexpedient etc. 647.

unpunctual etc. (*late*) 133; too late for; premature etc. (*early*) 132; too soon for; wise after the event.

Adv. inopportunely etc. *adj.;* as ill luck would have it, in an evil hour, the time having gone by, a day after the fair.

Phr. after meat mustard, after death the doctor.

136. Frequency.—**N.** frequency, oftness; repetition, etc. 104.

V. recur etc. 104; do nothing but; keep, − on.

Adj. frequent, many times, not rare, thickcoming, incessant, perpetual, continual, constant, recurrent, repeated etc. 104; habitual etc. 613; hourly, etc. 138.

Adv. often, often to be met with, oft; oft-, often-times; frequently; repeatedly etc. 104; un- seldom, not unfrequently; in -quick, − rapid- succession; many a time and oft; daily, hourly etc.; every -day, − hour, − moment etc.

perpetually, continually, constantly, in- cessantly, without ceasing, at all times, daily and hourly, night and day, day and night, day after day, morning, noon and night, ever and anon.

most often; commonly etc. (*habitually*) 613.

sometimes, occasionally, at times, now and then, from time to time, there being times when, *toties quoties*, often enough, again and again etc. 104.

137. Infrequency. —N. infrequency, infrequence, rareness, rarity; fewness etc. 103; seldomness, uncommonness.
V. be -rare etc. *adj.*
Adj. un-, in-frequent; uncommon, sporadic, rare, — as a blue diamond; few etc. 103; scarce; almost unheard of, unprecedented, which has not occurred within the memory of the oldest inhabitant, not within one's previous experience.
Adv. seldom, rarely, scarcely, hardly; not often, unfrequently, infrequently, unoften; scarcely —, hardly- ever; once in a blue moon.
once; once -for all, — in a way; *pro hac vice;* like angels' visits, few and far between.

138. Regularity of recurrence. **Periodicity.**—N. periodicity, intermittence; beat; oscillation etc. 314; pulse, pulsation; rhythm; alternation, -nateness, -nativeness, -nity.
bout, round, revolution, rotation, turn.
anniversary, birthday, jubilee, centenary, bi-, ter-centenary.
[Regularity of return] rota, cycle, period, stated time, routine; days of the week; Sunday, Monday etc.; months of the year; January etc.; feast, fast, saint's day etc.; Christmas, Easter, New Year's Day etc. 998; quarter-, Lady-, Midsummer-, Michaelmas-day; May Day, the King's Birthday; leap year, seasons.
punctuality, regularity, steadiness.
V. recur in regular -order, — succession; return, revolve, rotate; come -again, — in its turn; come round, — again; beat, pulsate; alternate; intermit.
Adj. periodic, -al; serial, recurrent, cyclic-, -al, rhythmic-, -al, even; recurring etc. *V.;* inter-, remittent; alternate, every other.
hourly; diurnal, daily; quotidian, tertian, weekly; hebdomad-al, -ary; bi-weekly, fortnightly; monthly, menstrual, catamenial; yearly, annual; biennial, triennial, etc.; bissextile; centennial, secular; paschal, lenten, etc.
regular, steady, punctual, constant, methodical, regular as clockwork.
Adv. periodically etc. *adj.;* at -regular intervals; — stated times; at -fixed, — established-periods; punctually etc. *adj.; de die in diem;* from day to day, day by day.
by turns, in -turn, — rotation; alternately, every other day, off and on, ride and tie, round and round.

139. Irregularity of recurrence.—N. irregularity, uncertainty, unpunctuality; fitfulness etc. *adj.*
Adj. irregular, uneven, uncertain, unpunctual, capricious, erratic, desultory, fitful, flickering; rambling, rhapsodical; spasmodic, unsystematic, unequal, variable, halting.
Adv. irregularly etc. *adj.;* by fits and starts etc. (*discontinuously*) 70.

140. Change. [Difference at different times.]—N. change, alteration, mutation, permutation, variation, modification, modulation, inflexion, mood, qualification, innovation, *metastasis,* deviation, shift, turn; diversion; break.
transformation, transfiguration; metamorphosis; metabolism; transmutation; transsubstantiation; metagenesis, transanimation, transmigration, metempsychosis; version, metathesis, transmogrification; catalysis; *avatar;* alterative.
conversion etc. (*gradual change*) 144; revolution etc. (*sudden or radical change*) 146; inversion etc. (*reversal*) 218; displacement etc. 185; transference etc. 270.
changeableness etc. 149; tergiversation etc. (*change of mind*) 607.
V. change, alter, vary, wax and wane; modulate, diversify, qualify, tamper with; turn, shift, veer, jibe, tack, chop, shuffle, swerve, dodge, warp, deviate, turn aside, evert, intervert; pass to, take a turn, turn the corner, resume.
work a change, modify, vamp, revamp, superinduce; trans-form, —mute, -ume, -figure etc. *n.;* metamorphose, ring the changes; convert, resolve; revolutionize; chop and change; patch, re-shape.
innovate, introduce new blood, shuffle the cards, spin the wheel; give a -turn, — color- to; influence, turn the scale; shift the scene, turn over a new leaf.
recast etc. 146; reverse etc. 218; disturb etc. 61; convert into etc. 144.
Adj. changed etc. *v.;* new-fangled; changeable etc. 149; transitional; modifiable; alterative.
Adv. *mutatis mutandis.*
Int. *quantum mutatus!*
Phr. 'a change came o'er the spirit of my dream;' *nous avons changé tout cela; tempora mutantur et nos mutamur in illis; non sum qualis eram.*

141. Permanence. [Absence of change.]—N. stability etc. 150; quiescence etc. 265; obstinacy etc. 606.
permanence, -cy, persistence, fixity, fixity of purpose, endurance, durability; standing, *status quo;* maintenance, preservation, conservation; conservatism; *laissez-faire;* law of the Medes and Persians; standing dish.
V. let -alone, — be; persist, remain, stay, tarry, rest; hold, — on; last, endure, bide, abide, aby, dwell, maintain, keep; stand, — still, — fast; subsist, live, outlive, survive; hold —, keep- one's ground, — footing; hold good.
Adj. stable etc. 150; persisting etc. *v.;* permanent; established, fixed; durable; unchanged etc. (change etc. 140); unrenewed; intact, inviolate; persistent; monotonous, uncheckered; unfailing.
un-destroyed, -repealed, -suppressed; conservative, *qualis ab incepto;* prescriptive etc. (*old*) 124; stationary etc. 265.
Adv. *in statu quo;* for good, finally; at a stand, - still; *uti possidetis;* without a shadow of turning.
Phr. as you were!; *j'y suis j'y reste; esto perpetua; nolumus leges Angliae mutari;* let sleeping dogs lie.

142. Cessation. [Change from action to

rest.]—N. cessation, discontinuance, desistance, desinence.

inter-, re-mission; sus-pense, -pension, interruption, hitch; hartal; stop; stopping etc. v.; closure, stoppage, halt; arrival etc. 292.

pause, rest, lull, respite, truce, armistice, drop; interregnum, abeyance.

closure etc. 261.

dead -stop, — stand, — lock; checkmate; comma, colon, semicolon, period, full stop; end etc. 67; death etc. 360; caesura.

V. cease, discontinue, desist, stay; break —, leave- off; hold, stop, pull up, stall, stop short, check; stick, deadlock, hand fire; halt; pause, rest.

have done with, give over, surcease, shut up shop; give up etc. (relinquish) 624.

hold —, stay- one's hand; rest on one's oars, repose on one's laurels.

come to a -stand, — standstill, — dead lock, — full stop; arrive etc. 292; go out, die away, peter out; wear -away, — off; pass away etc. (be past) 122; be at an end.

intromit, interrupt, suspend, interpel; inter-, re-mit; put -an end, — a stop, — a period- to; bring to a stand, -still; stop, cut out, cut short, arrest, avast; stem the -tide, — torrent; pull the check string; switch off.

Int. halt! hold! stop! enough! avast! have done! a truce to! soft! leave off! shut up! give over! chuck it!

143. Continuance in action.—N.continu-ance, -ation; run; extension, prolongation; maintenance, perpetuation; persistence etc. (perseverance) 604a; repetition etc. 104.

V. continue, persist; go —, jog —, keep —, carry —, run — hold- on; abide, keep, pursue, stick to; endure; take —, maintain- its course; keep up.

sustain, uphold, hold up, keep on foot; follow up, perpetuate, prolong; maintain; preserve etc. 604a; harp upon etc. (repeat)104.

keep -going, — alive, — at it, — the pot boiling, — the ball rolling, — up the ball; plod-, plug-along; slog on; die in harness; hold on —, pursue-the even tenor of one's way.

let be; stare super antiquas vias; quieta non movere; let things take their course.

Adj. continuing etc. v.; uninterrupted, unintermitting, unremitting, unvarying, unshifting; unreversed, unstopped, unrevoked, unvaried; sustained; undying etc. (perpetual) 112; inconvertible.

follow-up.

Int. carry on! right away!

Phr. vestigia nulla retrorsum,· labitur et labetur.

144. Conversion. [Gradual change to something different.]—N. conversion, reduction, transmutation, transformation, development, resolution, assimilation; assumption; naturalization.

chemistry, alchemy; progress, growth, lapse, flux.

passage; transit, -ion; transmigration, shifting etc. v.; conjugation; convertibility.

crucible, alembic, caldron, retort, test tube etc.

convert, neophyte, proselyte, pervert, renegade, deserter, apostate, turncoat.

V. be converted into; become, get, wax; come —, turn--to, — into; turn out, lapse, shift; run —, fall —, pass —, slide —, glide —, grow —, ripen —, open —, resolve itself —, settle —, merge- into; melt, grow, come round to, mature, mellow; assume the -form, — shape, — state. — nature, — character- of; illapse; assume a new phase, undergo a change.

convert —, resolve- into; make, render; mold, form etc. 240; remodel, new model, refound, reform, reorganize; assimilate —, bring — reduce- to; transform.

Adj. converted into etc. v.; convertible, resolvable into; transitional; naturalized.

Adv. gradually etc. (slowly) 275; in transitu etc. (transference) 270.

145. Reversion.—N. reversion, return; revulsion; reaction.

turning point, turn of the tide; status quo ante bellum; calm before a storm.

alternation etc. (periodicity) 138; inversion etc. 219; recoil etc. 277; regression etc. 283; restoration etc. 660; relapse etc. 661; vicinism, atavism, throwback.

V. revert, turn back, return; relapse etc. 661; recoil etc. 277; retreat etc. 283; restore etc. 660; undo, unmake; turn the -tide, — scale; escheat.

Adj. reverting etc. v.; revulsive, reactionary.

Adv. à rebours, wrong side out.

146. Revolution. [Sudden or violent change.]—N. revolution, bouleversement, subversion, break up; destruction etc. 162; sudden —, radical —, sweeping —, organic- change; clean sweep, coup d'état, overthrow, débâcle; counter-revolution, rebellion etc. 742.

transilience, jump, leap, plunge, jerk, start; explosion; spasm, convulsion, throe, revulsion; storm, earthquake, eruption, upheaval, cataclysm.

legerdemain etc. (trick) 545.

V. revolutionize; new model, remodel, recast; strike out something new, break with the past; change the face of, unsex; revert etc. 742.

Adj. unrecognizable.

Revolutionary, Bolshevik etc. 742.

147. Substitution. [Change of one thing for another.]—N. substitution, subrogation, commutation; supplanting etc. v.; supersession, metonymy etc. (figure of speech) 521.

[Thing substituted.] substitute, succedaneum, make-shift, temporary expedient, shift, pis aller, stop-gap, jury-mast, locum tenens, warming-pan, dummy, goat, scape-goat; double; changeling; quid pro quo, alternative; remount; representative etc. (deputy) 759; palimpsest.

price, purchase-money, consideration, equivalent.

V. substitute, put in the place of, change for; make way for, give place to; supply —, take- the place of; supplant, supersede, replace, cut out, serve as a substitute; step into —, stand in- the shoes of; make a shift —, put up- with; borrow of Peter to pay Paul; commute, redeem, compound for.

Adj. substituted etc. v.; vicarious, subditit-
ious; substitutional.
Adv. instead; in -place, − lieu, − the stead, −
the room- of; faute de mieux.

148. Interchange. [Double or mutual
change.]—N. inter-, ex-change; com-, per-, inter-
mutation; reciprocation, transposal, transposition, shuffling; reciprocity, castling [at chess];
hocus-pocus.
interchange-ableness, -ability.
barter etc. 794; tit for tat etc. (retaliation) 718;
cross fire, battledore and shuttlecock; quid pro
quo.
V. inter-, ex-, counter-change; bandy, transpose, shuffle, change hands, swap, trade, per-
mute, reciprocate, commute; give and take,
return the compliment; play at -puss in the
corner, − battledore and shuttlecock; retaliate
etc. 718; barter etc. 794.
Adj. interchanged etc. v.; reciprocal, mutual,
commutative, interchanged etc. v.; interchangeable, intercurrent.
Adv. in exchange, vice versâ, mutatis mutandis, backwards and forwards, by turns, turn
and turn about, turn about; each −, every one- in
his turn.

149. Changeableness.—N. changeableness etc.
adj.; mutability, inconstancy; versatility, mobility; instability, unstable equilibrium; vacillation etc. (irresolution) 605; fluctuation, vicissi-
tude; alternation etc. (oscillation) 314.
  restlessness etc. adj.; fidgets, disquiet; dis-, inquietude; unrest; agitation etc. 315.
moon, Proteus, chameleon, kaleidoscope,
quicksilver, shifting sands, weathercock, harlequin, Cynthia of the minute, April showers;
wheel of Fortune; transientness etc. 111.
V. fluctuate, vary, waver, flounder, flicker,
flitter, flit, flutter, shift, shuffle, shake, totter,
tremble, vacillate, wamble, turn and turn about,
ring , the changes; sway −, shift- to and fro;
change and change about; oscillate etc. 314;
vibrate −, oscillate- between two extremes; alternate; have as many phases as the moon.
Adj. change-able, -ful; changing etc. 140;
mutable, variable, checkered, ever changing,
kaleidoscopic, prote-an, -iform; versatile.
unstaid, inconstant; un-steady, -stable, -fixed,
-settled; fluctuating etc. v.; restless; mercurial;
agitated etc. 315; erratic, fickle; irresolute etc.
605; capricious etc. 608; touch-and-go; inconsonant, fitful, spasmodic; vibratory; afloat;
alternating; alterable, plastic, mobile; fleeting,
transient etc. 111.
Adv. see-saw etc. (oscillation) 314; off and on.

150. Stability.—N. stability; immutability etc.
adj.; unchangeableness etc. adj.; constancy;
stable equilibrium, immobility, soundness,
vitality, stabiliment, stabilization, stiffness,
ankylosis, solidity, aplomb.
  establishment, fixture; rock, pillar, tower,
foundation, leopard's spots, Ethiopian's skin,
law of the Medes and Persians.
stabilimeter, stabilizator.

permanence etc. 141; obstinacy etc. 606.
V. be -firm etc. adj.; stick fast; stand −, keep
−, remain- firm; weather the storm.
settle, establish, stablish, ascertain, fix, set,
stabilitate, stabilize; retain, stet, keep hold; make
-good, − sure; fasten etc. (join) 43; set on its legs,
float; perpetuate.
settle down; strike −, take- root; take up one's
abode etc. 184; build one's house on a rock.
Adj. unchangeable, immutable; unalter-ed, -
able; not to be changed, constant; permanent etc.
141; invariable, undeviating; stable, durable; perennial etc. (diuturnal) 110.
fixed, steadfast, firm, fast, steady, balanced;
confirmed, valid, fiducial, immovable, irremovable, riveted, rooted; settled, established etc. v.;
vested; incontrovertible, stereotyped, indeclinable.
tethered, anchored, moored, at anchor, on a
rock, firm as a rock; firmly -seated, − established etc. v.; deep-rooted, ineradicable; inveterate;
obstinate etc. 606.
transfixed, stuck fast, aground, high and dry,
stranded.
indefeasible, irretrievable, intransmutable,
incommutable, irresoluble, irrevocable, irreversible, reverseless, inextinguishable, irreducible;
indissol-uble, -vable; indestructible, undying, imperishable, indelible, indeciduous; insusceptible,
− of change.
Int. stet.

151. Eventuality.—N. eventuality, event, occurrence, incident, affair, transaction, proceeding, fact; matter of −, naked- fact; phenomenon;
advent.
business, concern; circumstance, particular,
casualty, happening, accident, adventure,
passage, crisis, pass, emergency, contingency,
consequence etc. 154.
the world, life, things, doings, affairs, matters; things −, affairs- in general; the times, state
of affairs, order of the day; course −, tide −,
stream −, current −, run −, march- of -things, −
events; ups and downs of life; chapter of
accidents etc. (chance) 156; situation etc. (circumstances) 8.
V. happen, occur; take -place, − effect; come,
become of; come -off, − about, − round, − into
existence, − forth, − to pass, − on; pass, present itself; fall; fall −, turn- out; run, be on foot,
fall in; be-fall, -tide, -chance; prove, eventuate,
draw on; turn −, crop −, spring −, cast- up;
super-, sur-vene; issue, emanate, arrive, ensue,
arise, start, hold, take its course; pass off etc. (be
past) 122.
meet with; experience; fall to the lot of; be
one's -chance, − fortune, − lot; find; encounter,
undergo; pass −, go- through; endure etc. (feel)
821.
Adj. happening etc. v.; going on, doing, current; in the wind, afloat; on -foot, − the tapis; at
issue, in question; incidental.
eventful, momentous, signal; stirring, bustling,
full of incident.
Adv. eventually, ultimately, in -the event of, −
case; in the course of things; in the -natural, −
ordinary- course of things; as -things, − times-
go; as the world -goes, − wags; as the -tree falls,
− cat jumps; as it may -turn out, − happen.
Phr. the plot thickens.

152. Destiny.—N. destiny etc. (*necessity*) 601;
hereafter, future —, post- existence; future state,
next world, world to come, after life; futurity etc.
121; everlasting -life, — death; prospect etc. (*expectation*) 507.

V. impend; hang —, lie —, hover- over;
threaten, loom, await, come on, approach, stare
one in the face; fore-, pre-ordain; predestine,
doom, foredoom, foreshadow, have in store for.

Adj. impending etc. *v.;* destined; about to -be,
— happen; coming, in store, to come, going to
happen, instant, at hand, near; near —, close- at
hand; overhanging, hanging over one's head, imminent; brewing, preparing, forthcoming; in the
wind, on the cards, in reserve; that -will, — is to-
be; in prospect etc. (*expected*) 507; looming in
the -distance, — horizon, — future; unborn, in
embryo; in the womb of -time; — futurity; on the
knees of the gods; pregnant etc. (*producing*) 161.

Adv. in -time, — the long run; all in good time;
eventually etc. 151; whatever may happen etc.
(*certainly*) 474; as -chance etc. 156- would have
it.

153. Cause. [Constant antecedent.]—N. cause,
origin, source, principle, element; occasioner,
prime mover, engine, turbine, motor, *primum
mobile; vera causa;* author etc. (*producer*) 164;
main-spring, agent; dynamo, generator, battery
(electric); leaven; groundwork, foundation etc.
(*support*) 215.

spring, fountain, well, font; fountain —,
spring- head; *fons et origo,* genesis; descent etc.
(*paternity*) 166; remote cause; influence.

pivot, hinge, turning-point, lever; key; kernel,
core; proximate cause, *causa causans;* last straw
that breaks the camel's back.

ground; reason, — why; why and wherefore,
rationale, occasion, derivation; final cause etc.
(*intention*) 620; *le dessous des cartes;* undercur-
rents.

rudiment, egg, germ, embryo, fetus, bud, root,
radix, radical, etymon, nucleus, seed, stem, stalk,
stock, *stirps,* trunk, tap-root; latent organism.

nest, cradle, nursery, womb, *nidus,* birth-,
breeding-place, hot-bed.

caus-ality, -ation; origination; production etc.
161.

V. be the -cause etc. *n.*- of; originate; give -
origin, — rise, — occasion- to; cause, occasion,
sow the seeds of, kindle, suscitate; bring -on, —
to pass, — about; produce; create etc. 161; set -
up, — afloat, — on foot; found, broach, institute,
lay the foundation of, inaugurate; lie at the root
of.

procure, induce, draw down, open the door to,
superinduce, evoke, entail, operate; elicit, provoke.

conduce to etc. (*tend to*) 176; contribute; promote; have a -hand in, — finger in- the pie; determine, decide, turn the scale, give the casting vote;
have a common origin; derive its origin etc.
(*effect*) 154.

Adj. caused etc. *v.;* causal, original; prim-ary, -
itive, -ordial; aboriginal; radical; inceptive,
embry-onic, -otic; *in -embryo,* — *ovo;* seminal,
germinal; formative, productive etc. 168; at the
bottom of; connate, having a common origin.

Adv. because etc. 155; behind the scenes.

154. Effect. [Constant sequent.]—N. effect,

consequence, sequela; derivative, -tion; result;
result-ant, -ance; upshot, issue, *dénouement;* out-
come; termination, end etc. 67; development,
outgrowth, fruit, crop, harvest, product, bud,
blossom, florescence, ear.

production, produce, product, finished product, work, handiwork, fabric, performance;
creature, creation; offspring, -shoot; first-fruits, -
lings; *prémices.*

V. be the -effect etc. *n.*- of; be -due, — owing-
to; originate -in, — from; rise —, arise —, take its
rise —, spring —, proceed —, emanate —, come
—, grow —, bud —, sprout —, germinate —, issue
—, flow —, result —, follow —, derive its origin
—, accrue- from; come -:to, — of, — out of;
depend —, hand —, hinge —, turn- upon.

take the consequences, sow the wind and reap
the whirlwind.

Adj. owing to; resulting from etc. *v.;* resultant;
derivable from; due to; caused etc. by, 153;
dependent upon; derived —, evolved- from;
derivative; hereditary.

Adv. of course, it follows that, naturally, consequently; as a —, in- consequence; through all,
all along of, necessarily, eventually.

Phr. *cela va sans dire,* thereby hangs a tale.

155. Attribution. [Assignment of cause.]—N.
attribution, theory, etiology, ascription, reference to, rationale; accounting for etc. *v.;* imputation, derivation from.

fil-, affil-iation; pedigree etc. (*paternity*) 166.
explanation etc. (*interpretation*) 522; reason
why etc. (*cause*) 153.

V. attribute —, ascribe —, impute —, refer —,
lay —, point —, trace —, bring home- to; put —,
set- down- to; charge —, ground- on; invest with,
assign as cause, charge with, blame, lay at the
door of, father upon; saddle with; affiliate; ac-
count-for, derive from, point out the -reason etc.
153; theorize; tell how it comes; put the saddle on
the right horse.

Adj. attributed etc. *v.;* attributable etc. *v.;*
refer-able, -rible; due to, derivable from; owing
to etc. (*effect*) 154; putative.

Adv. hence, thence, therefore, for, since, on
account of, because, owing to; on that account;
from -this, — that- cause; thanks to, forasmuch
as; whence, *propter hoc.*

why? wherefore? whence? how -comes, — is, —
happens- it? how does it happen?

in -some, — some such- way; somehow, — or
other.

Phr. that is why; *hinc illae lachrymae; cher-
chez la femme.*

156. Chance.† [Absence of assignable
cause.]—N. chance, indetermination, accident,
fortune, hazard, hap, haphazard, chance-med-
ley, random, luck, *raccroc,* casualty, fortuity, con-
tingence, coincidence, adventure, hit; fate etc.
(*necessity*) 601; equal chance; lottery, raffle, tombola, sweepstake; toss up etc. 621; turn of the -
table, — cards; hazard of the die, chapter of accidents; cast —, throw- of the dice; heads or tails,
wheel of Fortune, whirligig of chance; *sortes;* —
Virgilianae.

probability, possibility, contingency, odds,
long odds, run of luck; main- chance.

theory of -probabilities, − chances; book-making; assurance; speculation, gamble, gaming etc. 621.
V. chance, hap, turn up; fall to one's lot; be one's -fate etc. 601; stumble on, light −, blunder −, hit- upon; take one's chance etc. 621.
Adj. casual, fortuitous, accidental, haphazard, random, stray, adventitious, adventive, causeless, incidental. contingent, uncaused, undetermined, indeterminate; possible etc. 470; unintentional etc. 621.
Adv. by -chance, − accident; casually; perchance etc. (possibly) 470; for aught one knows; as -good, − bad, − ill-luck etc. n.- would have it; as it may -be, − chance, − turn up, − happen; as the case may be.

†The word Chance has two distinct meanings: the first, the absence of assignable cause, as above; and the second, the absence of design—for the latter see 621.

157. Power.—N. power; poten-cy, -tiality; puissance, might, force; energy etc. 171; dint; right -hand, − arm; ascendency, sway, control; pre-potency, -pollence; almightiness, omnipotence; authority etc. 737; strength etc. 159.
ability; ableness etc. adj.; competency; efficiency, -cacy; validity, cogency; enablement; vantage ground; influence etc. 175; horse power; dynamometer.
pressure; elasticity; gravity; attraction, repulsion; vis -inertiae, − mortua, − viva; friction, suction.
electricity, magnetism, galvanism, voltaic electricity, voltaism, electro-magnetism, electrostatics, electrification; electric − current, − power; potential −, dynamic −, kinetic −, electrical −, chemical −, atomic- energe; electric field, circuit, charge, discharge, shock, polarity, pole; amperage, voltage, wattage, resistance, conduction, induction, electrification, electrolysis.
electronics, radionics, electron physics, electrophysics, avionics, radiometry, photoelectronics; electron, negatron, positron, photoelectron, thermion, barytron; electronic effect; electron emission; electron −, cathode −, anode −, positive − ray; electron − current, − flow − stream, − beam, − volt; electronic circuit; conductance; electron tube, tube, vacuum tube, photoelectric tube, call; transistor.
capability, capacity; quid valeant humeri quid ferre recusent; faculty, quality, attribute, endowment, virtue, gift, property, qualification, susceptibility.
V. be -powerful etc. adj.; gain -power etc. n. belong −, pertain- to; lie −, be- in one's power; can.
electrify, generate, magnetize.
give −, confer −, exercise- power etc. n.; empower, enable, invest; in-, en-due; endow, arm; strengthen etc. 159; compel etc. 744.
Adj. powerful, puissant; potent, -ial; capable, able; equal −, up- to; cogent, valid; effect-ive, -ual; efficient, efficacious, adequate, competent; multi-, pleni-, omni-, armi- potent; mighty, ascendent; almighty.
electric, electrical, electronic etc.
forcible etc. adj. (energetic) 171; influential etc. 175; productive etc. 168.

Adv. powerfully etc. adj.; by -virtue, − dint-of.

158. Impotence.—N. impotence; in-, dis-ability; disablement, impuissance, imbecility, caducity; incapa-city, -bility; inapt-, inept-itude; indocility; invalidity, inefficiency, incompetence, disqualification.
telum imbelle, brutum fulmen, blank cartridge, flash in the pan, vox et praeterea nihil, dead letter, bit of waste paper, dummy; scrap of paper.
inefficacy etc. (inutility) 645; failure etc. 732.
helplessness etc. adj.; prostration, paralysis, palsy, ataxia, apoplexy, syncope, sideration, deliquium, collapse, exhaustion, softening of the brain, e nasculation, inanition, senility etc. 128; castrato, eunuch.
cripple, old woman, muff, molly-coddle, milksop.
V. be -impotent etc. adj.; not have a leg to stand on.
vouloir -rompre l'anguille au genou, − prendre la lune avec les dents.
collapse, faint, swoon, fall into a swoon, drop; go by the board; end in smoke etc. (fail) 732.
render -powerless etc. adj.; deprive of power; decontrol; dis-able, -enable; disarm, incapacitate, disqualify, ynfit, invalidate, undermine, deaden, cramp, tie the hands; double up, prostrate, paralyze, muzzle, cripple, becripple, maim, lame, hamstring, draw the teeth of; throttle, strangle, garrotte; ratten, silence, sprain, clip the wings of, render hors de combat, spike the guns; take the wind out of one's sails, scotch the snake, put a spoke in one's wheel; break the -neck, − back; un-hinge, -fit; put out of gear.
unman, unnerve, devitalize, attenuate, enervate; emasculate, spay, caponize, castrate, geld; effeminize.
shatter, exhaust; weaken etc. 160.
Adj. powerless, impotent, unable, incapable, incompetent; ineff-icient, -ective; inept; un-fit, -fitted; un-, dis-qualified; unendowed; in-, un-apt; crippled, decrepit; disabled etc. v.; armless.
harmless, unarmed, weaponless, defenceless, sine ictu, unfortified, indefensible, vincible, pregnable, untenable.
para-lytic, -lyzed; palsied, imbecile; nerve-, sinew-, marrow-, pith-, lust-less; emasculate, disjointed, out of -joint, − gear; un-nerved, -hinged; water-logged, on one's beam ends, rudderless; laid on one's back; done up, dead beat, exhausted, shattered, demoralized; gravelled etc. (in difficulty) 704; helpless, unfriended, fatherless; without a leg to stand on, hors de combat, laid on the shelf.
null and void, nugatory, imoperative, good for nothing; dud; invertebrate; ineffectual etc. (failing) 732; inadequate etc. 640; inefficacious etc. (useless) 645.

159. Strength. (Degree of power.]—N. strength; power etc. 157; energy etc. 171; vigor, force; main −, physical −, brute- force; spring, elasticity, tone, tension, tonicity.
stoutness etc. adj.; lustihood, stamina, nerve,

muscle, sinew, thews and sinews, *physique;* pith, - iness; virility, vitality.

athlet-ics, -icism; gymnastics, feats of strength.

adamant, steel, iron, oak, heart of oak; iron grip; grit, bone.

athlete, gymnast, tumbler, acrobat; Atlas, Hercules, Antaeus, Samson, Cyclops, Goliath, Titan; tower of strength; giant refreshed.

strengthening etc. *v.;* invigoration, refreshment, refocillation.

[Science of forces] dynamics, statics.

V. be -strong etc. *adj.,* − stronger; overmatch.

render -strong etc. *adj.;* give -strength etc. *n.;* strengthen, invigorate, brace, nerve, fortify, buttress, sustain, harden, case-harden, steel; gird; screw −, wind −, set- up; gird −, brace- up one's loins; recruit, set on one's legs; vivify; refresh etc. 689; refect; reinforce etc. *(restore)* 660.

Adj. strong, mighty, vigorous, forcible, hard, adamantine, stout, robust, sturdy, hardy, powerful, potent, puissant, valid.

resistless, irresistible, invincible, proof against, impregnable, unconquerable, indomitable, inextinguishable, unquenchable; incontestable; more than a match for; over-powering, - whelming; all-powerful; sovereign.

able-bodied; athletic, gymnastic; Herculean, Cyclopean, Atlantean; muscular, husky, brawny, wiry, well-knit, broad-shouldered, sinewy, strapping, stalwart, gigantic.

man-ly, -like, -ful; masculine, male, virile, in the prime of manhood.

un-weakened, -allayed, -withered, -shaken, - worn, -exhausted; in full -force, − swing; in the plenitude of power.

stubborn, thick-ribbed, made of iron, deeprooted; strong as -a lion, − a horse, − brandy; sound as a roach; in -fine, − high- feather; in fine fettle; like a giant refreshed.

Adv. strongly etc. *adj.;* by -force etc. *n.;* by main force etc. *(by compulsion)* 744.

Phr. 'our withers are unwrung.'

160. Weakness.—N. weakness etc. *adj.;* debility, atony, relaxation, languor, enervation; impotence etc. 158; infirmity; effeminacy, feminality; fragility, flaccidity; inactivity etc. 683.

declension −, loss −, failure- of strength; delicacy, invalidation, decrepitude, asthenia, adynamy, cachexy, *cachexia,* anemia, bloodlessness, sprain, strain.

reed, thread, rope of sand, broken reed, house -of cards, − built on sand.

soft-, weak-ling; infant etc. 129; youth etc. 127.

V. be -weak etc. *adj.;* drop, crumble, give way, totter, tremble, shake, halt, limp, fade, languish, decline, flag, fail, have one foot in the grave.

render -weak etc. *adj.;* weaken, enfeeble, debilitate, shake, deprive of strength, relax, enervate; un-brace, -nerve; cripple, unman, etc. *(render powerless)* 158; cramp, reduce, sprain, strain, blunt the edge of; dilute, impoverish; decimate; extenuate; reduce -in strength, − the strength of; invalidate; *mettre de l'eau dans son vin.*

Adj. weak, feeble, debile; impotent etc. 158; relaxed, unnerved etc. *v.;* sap-, strength-, powerless; weakly, unstrung, flaccid, adynamic, asthenic; nervous.

soft, effeminate, feminate, womanish.

frail, fragile, shattery, frangible, brittle etc. 328; flimsy, unsubstantial, gimcrack, gingerbread; rickety, cranky; creachy; drooping, tottering etc. *v.;* broken, lame, halt, game, withered, shattered, shaken, crazy, shaky, tumble-down; palsied etc. 158; decrepit; C3.

lanquid, poor, poorly, infirm; faint, -ish; sickly etc. *(disease)* 655; dull, slack, evanid, spent, short-winded, effete; weatherbeaten; decayed, rotten, worn, seedy, languishing, wasted, washy, wishy-washy, laid low, pulled down, the worse for wear.

un-strengthened etc. 159, -supported, -aided, -assisted; aidless, defenceless etc. 158.

on its last legs; weak as a -child, − baby, − chicken, − cat, − rat; weak as -water, − water gruel, − gingerbread, − milk and water; colorless etc. 429.

Phr. *non sum qualis eram.*

161. Production.—N. production, creation, construction, formation, fabrication, manufacture; building, architecture, erection, edification; coinage; organization; *nisus formativus;* putting togeher etc. *v.;* establishment; workmanship, performance;- achievement etc. *(completion)* 729; effect etc. 154.

flowering, fructification fruition.

bringing forth etc. *v.;* parturition, birth, birththroe, child-birth, delivery, confinement, *accouchement,* travail, labour, midwifery, obstetrics; geniture; gestation etc. *(maturation)* 673; evolution, development, growth; genesis, fertilization, breeding, conception, germination, generation, *epigenesis,* pro-creation, -generation, -pagation; fecundation, impregnation; spontaneous generation; *arche-genesis, -biosis; bio-, abio-, homo-, xeno-genesis.*

authorship, publication; works, *oeuvre, opus.*

edifice, building, structure, fabric, erection, pile, tower, flower, fruit.

V. produce, perform, operate, do, make, gar, form, construct, fabricate, frame, contrive, manufacture; weave, forge, coin, carve, chisel; build, raise, edify, rear, erect, put together; set −, run- up; establish, constitute, compose, organize, institute, get up; achieve, accomplish etc. *(complete)* 729.

flower, sprout, blossom, burgeon, bear fruit, fructify, spawn, teem, ean, yean, farrow, drop, calf, pup, whelp, kitten, kindle; bear, lay, bring forth, give birth to, lie in, be brought to bed of, evolve, pullulate, usher into the world.

make productive etc. 168; create; beget, conceive, get, generate, fecundate, impregnate; procreate, -generate, -pagate; engender; bring −, call- into -being, − existence; breed, hatch, develop, bring up.

induce, superinduce; suscitate; cause etc. 153; acquire etc. 775.

Adj. produc-ed, -ing etc. *v.;* productive of; prolific etc. 168; creative; formative; gen-etic, - ial, -ital; fertile, pregnant; *enceinte,* big −, fraught-with; with child, in the family way,

teeming, parturient, in the straw, brought to bed of; puerper-al, -ous.
architectonic; constructive.

162. Destruction. [Non-production.]—N. destruction; waste, dissolution, breaking up; di-, dis-ruption; consumption; disorganization.

fall, downfall, ruin, perdition, crash, smash, havoc, *délabrement, débâcle;* break -down, — up; prostration; desolation, *bouleversement,* wreck, crack-up, crash, wrack, shipwreck, cataclysm; Caudine Forks, Sedan.

extinction, annihilation; destruction of life etc. 361; knock-out, knock-down blow; doom, crack of doom.

destroying etc. *v.;* demo-lition, -lishment; biblioclasm; overthrow, subversion, suppression; abolition etc. (*abrogation*) 756; sacrifice; ravage, devastation, *sabotage, razzia;* incendiarism; revolution etc. 146; extirpation etc. (*extraction*) 301; *commencement de la fin,* road to ruin; dilapidation etc. (*deterioration*) 659.

V. be -destroyed etc.; perish; fall, — to the ground; tumble, topple; go —, fall- to pieces; break up; crumble, — to dust; go to -the dogs, — the wall, — smash, — shivers, — wreck, — pot, — wrack and ruin; go -by the board, — all to smash, — to pieces, — under; be all -over, — up- with; totter to its fall.

destroy; do —, make- away with; nullify; annul etc. 756; sacrifice, demolish; tear up; over-turn, -throw, -whelm; upset, subvert, put an end to; seal the doom of, do for, dish, undo; break -, cut- up; break —, cut —, pull, —, mow —, blow —, beat-down; suppress, quash, put down; cut short, take off, blot out; dispel, dissipate, dissolve; consume.

smash, — to smithereens, quell, squash, squelch, crumple up, shatter, shiver; batter; tear —, crush —, cut —, shake —, pull —, pick- to pieces; nip; tear to -rags, — tatters; crush —, knock- to atoms; pulverize; ruin; strike out; throw —, knock- -down, — over; lay by the heels; fell, sink, swamp, scuttle, wreck, crash, ship-wreck, engulf, submerge; lay in -ashes, — ruins; sweep away, erase, expunge, strike out, delete, efface, raze; level, — with the -ground, — dust.

deal destruction, lay waste, ravage, gut; dis-organize; dismantle etc. (*render useless*) 645; devour, swallow up, desolate, devastate, sap, mine, blast, confound; exterminate, extinguish, quench, annihilate; snuff —, put —, stamp —, trample- out; lay —, trample- in the dust; prostrate; tread —, crush —, trample- under foot; lay the axe to the root of; make -short work, — a clean sweep, — mincemeat- of; cut up root and branch; fling —, scatter- to the winds; throw overboard; strike at the root of, sap the foundations of, spring a mine, blow up; ravage with fire and sword; cast to the dogs; eradicate etc. 301.

Adj. destroyed etc. *v.;* perishing etc. *v.;* trembling —, nodding —, tottering- to its fall; in course of destruction etc. *n.;* extinct.

destructive, subversive, ruinous, incendiary, deletory; destroying etc. *v.;* suicidal; deadly etc. (*killing*) 361.

Adv. with -crushing effect, — a sledge-hammer.

Phr. *delenda est Carthago.*

163. Reproduction.—N. reproduction, renovation; restoration etc. 660; renewal; new edition, reprint etc. 21; revival, regeneration, palingenesia, revivification; apotheosis; resuscitation, reanimation, resurrection, resurgence, reappearance, atavism; Phoenix; reincarnation.

generation etc. (*production*) 161; multiplication.

V. reproduce; restore etc. 660; revive, renovate, renew, regenerate, revivify, resuscitate, reanimate, refashion, stir the embers, put into the crucible; multiply, repeat, resurge.

crop up, spring up like mushrooms.

Adj. reproduced etc. *v.;* renascent, reappearing; reproductive; resurgent; progenitive; Hydra-headed.

164. Producer.—N. producer, creator, deviser, designer, originator, inventor, author, founder, generator, mover, architect; grower, constructor, maker etc. (*agent*) 690.

165. Destroyer.—N. destroyer etc. (destroy etc. 162); cankerworm etc. (*bane*) 663; iconoclast; assassin etc. (*killer*) 361; executioner etc. (*punish*) 975; Hun, Vandal, nihilist, anarchist.

166. Paternity.—N. paternity; parentage; fatherhood; consanguinity etc. 11.

parent, father, sire, dad, daddy, papa, governor, *pater, paterfamilias, abba;* genitor, pro-genitor, procreator, begetter; ancestor; grand-sire, -father; great-grandfather.

house, stem, truck, tree, stock, *stirps,* pedigree, lineage, line, family, tribe, sept, race, clan; genealogy, descent, extraction, birth, ancestry; forefathers, forbears, patriarchs.

motherhood, maternity; mother, dam, mamma, *materfamilias;* grand-mother; matriarch.

Adj. paternal, parental; maternal; family, ancestral, linear, matrilineal, patrilineal, patriarchal.

167. Posterity.—N. posterity, progeny, breed, issue, offspring, brood, litter, seed, farrow, spawn, spat; family, children, grandchildren, heirs; great-grandchild.

child, son, daughter; kid; infant etc. 129; bantling, scion; shoot, sprout, olive branch, sprit; branch; off-shoot, -set; ramification; descendant; heir, -ess; heir -apparent, — presumptive; chip of the old block; heredity; rising generation.

straight descent, sonship, line, lineage, filiation, promogeniture.

Adj. filial.

168. Productiveness.—N. productiveness etc. *adj.,* fecundity, fertility, luxuriance, uberty.

pregnancy, pullulation, fructification, multiplication, propagation, procreation; superfetation.

milch cow, rabbit, hydra, warren, seed-plot, land flowing with milk and honey; second crop, after-crop, -growth, -math; fertilization.

V. make -productive etc. *adj.;* fructify; pro-create, generate, fertilize, spermatize, impregnate; fecund-ate, -ify; teem, pullulate, multiply; produce etc. 161; conceive.

Adj. productive, prolific; teem-ing, -ful; fertile, fruitful, frugiferous, fruit-bearing; fructiferous; fecund, luxuriant; pregnant, uberous.

procre-ant, -ative; generative, life-giving, spermatic; originative; multiparous; omnific; propagable.

parturient etc. (*producing*) 161; profitable etc. (*useful*) 644.

169. Unproductiveness.—N. unproductiveness etc. *adj.;* infertility, steril; ity, infecundity; impotence etc. 158- unprofitableness etc. (*inutility*) 645.

waste, desert, Sahara, wild, wilderness, howling wilderness.

V. be -unproductive etc. *adj.;* hang fire, flash in the pan, come to nothing.

Adj. unproductive, inoperative, barren, addle, unfertile, unprolific, arid, sterile, unfruitful, acarpous, infecund; *sine prole;* fallow; teem-, issue-, fruitless; unprofitable etc. (*useless*) 645; null and void, of no effect.

170. Agency.—N. agency, operation, force, working, strain, function, office, maintenance, exercise, work, swing, play; inter-working, -action, procuration, procurement.

causation etc. 153; instrumentality etc. 631; influence etc. 175; action etc. (*voluntary*) 680; *modus operandi* etc. 627.

quickening —, maintaining- power; home stroke.

V. be -in action etc. *adj.;* operate, work; act, — upon; perform, play, support, sustain, strain, maintain, take effect, quicken, strike.

come —, bring- into -operation, — play; have - play, — free play; bring to bear upon.

Adj. operative, efficient, efficacious, practical, effectual.

at work, on foot; acting etc. (*doing*) 680; in -operation, — force, — action, — play, — exercise; acted —, wrought- upon.

Adv. by the -agency etc. *n.-* of; through etc. (*instrumentality*) 631; by means of etc. 632.

171. Physical Energy.—N. energy, physical energy, force; keenness etc. *adj.;* intensity, vigor, strength, elasticity; go; pep, live wire, high pressure; backbone, mettle, fire, vim.

acri-mony, -tude, -dity; causticity, virulence, poignancy; harshness etc. *adj.;* severity, edge, point; pungency etc. 392.

cantharides; Spanish fly; seasoning etc. (*condiment*) 393, stimulant, excitant.

activity, agitation, effervescence; ferment, -ation; ebullition, splutter, perturbation, stir, bustle; voluntary energy etc. 682; quicksilver.

resolution etc. (*mental energy*) 604; exertion etc. (*effort*) 686; excitation etc. (*mental*) 824.

V. give -energy etc. *n.;* energize, stimulate, kindle, excite, activate, exert; sharpen, pep up, intensify; inflame etc. (*render violent*) 173; wind up etc. (*strengthen*) 159.

strike, — into, — hard, — home; make an impression.

Adj. strong, energetic, forcible, active; strenuous, forceful, mettlesome, enterprising, go ahead; intense, deep-dyed, severe, keen, vivid, sharp, acute, incisive, trenchant, brisk, vigorous, live.

rousing, irritating; poignant; virulent, caustic, corrosive, mordant, harsh, stringent; double-edged, — shotted, — distilled; drastic, escharotic; racy etc. (*pungent*) 392; sarcastic etc. 932.

potent etc. (*powerful*) 157; radio-active.

Adv. strongly etc. *adj.;* *fortiter in re;* with telling effect.

Phr. the steam is up; *vires acquirit eundo.*

172. Physical Inertness.—N. inertness, dulness etc. *adj.;* inertia, *vis inertiae,* inertion, inactivity, torpor, languor; dormancy, quiescence etc. 265; latency, inaction, passivity.

mental inertness; sloth etc. (*inactivity*) 683; inexcitability etc. 826; irresolution etc. 605; obstinacy etc. 606; permanence etc. 141.

V. be -inert etc. *adj.;* hang fire, smoulder.

Adj. inert, inactive, passive, pacific; torpid etc. 683; sluggish, stagnant, dull, heavy, flat, slack, tame, slow, blunt; lifeless, dead, uninfluential.

latent, dormant, smouldering, unexerted.

Adv. inactively etc. *adj.;* in -suspense, -abeyance.

173. Violence.—N. violence, inclemency, vehemence, might, impetuosity; boisterousness etc.; *adj.;* effervescence, ebullition; turbulence, bluster; uproar, riot, row, rumpus, *le diable à quatre,* devil to pay, all the fat in the fire.

severity etc. 739; ferocity, rage, berserk, fury; exacerbation, exasperation, malignity; fit, paroxysm, orgasm; force, brute force; outrage; *coup de main;* strain, shock, shog; spasm, convulsion, 'throe; hysterics, passion etc. (*state of excitability*) 825.

out-break, -burst; burst, bounce, dissilience, discharge, volley, explosion, blow up, blast, detonation, rush, eruption, displosion, torrent.

turmoil etc. (*disorder*) 59; ferment etc. (*agitation*) 315; storm, tempest, rough weather; squall etc. (*wind*) 349; earthquake, volcano, thunderstorm.

fury, dragon, demon, tiger, beldame, Tisiphone, Megaera, Alecto, madcap, wild beast; fire-eater etc. (*blusterer*) 887.

V. be -violent etc. *adj.;* run high; ferment, effervesce; romp, rampage; run -wild, — riot; break the peace; rush, tear; rush head-long, -foremost; run amuck, raise a storm, make a riot; make —, kick up- a row, — a fuss; bluster, rage, roar, riot, storm; boil, — over; fume, foam, come in like a lion, wreak, bear down, ride roughshod, out-Herod Herod; spread like wildfire.

break —, fly —, burst- out; bounce, shock, strain; break-, pry-, force-, prize- open.

render -violent etc. *adj.;* sharpen, stir up, quicken, excite, incite, urge, lash, stimulate; irritate, inflame, exacerbate, kindle, suscitate, foment; accelerate, aggravate, exasperate, convulse, infuriate, madden, lash into fury; fan —, add fuel to- the flame; *oleum addere camino.*

explode, go off, displode, fly, detonate, thunder, blow up, flash, flare, erupt, burst; let - off, − fly; discharge, detonize, fulminate.

Adj. violent, vehement, forcible; warm; acute, sharp; rough, rude, ungentle, bluff, boisterous, wild, vicious; brusque, abrupt, waspish; impetuous; rampant.

turbulent; disorderly; blustering, raging etc. v.; troublous, riotous; tumultu-ary, -ous; obstreperous, uproarious; extravagant; unmitigated; ravening, tameless; frenzied etc. (insane) 503; desperate etc. (rash) 863; infuriate, towering, furious, outrageous, frantic, hysteric, in hysterics.

fiery, flaming, scorching, hot, red-hot, ebullient.

savage, fierce, ferocious, fierce as a tiger.

excited etc. v.; un-quelled, -quenched, -extinguished, -repressed, -bridled, -ruly; headstrong; un-governable, -appeasable, -mitigable; un-, in-controllable; insup-, irre-pressible.

spasmodic, convulsive, explosive; detonating etc. v.; volcanic, meteoric; stormy etc. (wind) 349.

Adv. violently etc. adj.; amain; by -storm, − force, − main force; with might and main; tooth and nail, vi et armis, at the point of the -sword, − bayonet; at one fell swoop; with a high hand, through thick and thin; in desperation, with a vengeance; à −, à touteoutrance; head-long, -foremost, -first; like a bull at a gate.

174. Moderation.—N. moderation; lenity etc. 740; temperance, temperateness, gentleness etc. adj.; sobriety; quiet; mental calmness etc. (inexcitability) 826.

moderating etc. v.; relaxation, remission, mitigation etc. 834; tranquilization, alleviation, assuagement, appeasement, contemporation, pacification.

measure, juste milieu, golden mean etc. 29.

moderator; lullaby, sedative, lenitive, demulcent, rose-water, balm, soothing syrup, poppy, opiate, anodyne, milk, opium, laudanum, 'poppy or mandragora;' wet blanket; palliative, calmative.

V. be -moderate etc. adj.; keep within -bounds, − compass; sober −, settle- down; keep the pease, remit, relent; take in sail.

moderate, soften, mitigate, temper, accoy; at-, con-temper; mollify, lenify, dull, take off the edge, blunt, obtund, sheathe, subdue, chasten; sober −, tone −, smooth- down; censor, blue-pencil, weaken etc. 160; lessen etc. (decrease) 36; check; palliate.

tranquilize, assuage, appease, dulcify, swage, lull, soothe, compose, still, calm, cool, quiet, hush, quell, sober, pacify, tame, damp, lay, allay, rebate, slacken, smooth, alleviate, rock to sleep, deaden, smother; throw -cold water on, − a wet blanket over; slake; curb etc. (restrain) 751; tame etc. (subjugate) 749; smooth over; pour oil on the -waves, − troubled waters; pour balm into, mettre de l'eau dans son vin.

go out like a lamb, 'roar you as gently as any sucking dove.'

Adj. moderate; lenient etc. 740; gentle, mild; cool, sober, temperate, reasonable, measured; tempered etc. v.; calm, unruffled, quiet, tranquil,

still; slow, smooth, untroubled; tame; peaceful, -able; pacific, halcyon.

un-exciting, -irritating; soft, bland, oily, demulcent, lenitive, anodyne; hypnotic etc. 683; sedative; assuaging.

mild as mother's milk; milk and water; gentle as a lamb.

Adv. moderately etc. adj.; gingerly; piano; under easy sail, at half speed; within -bounds, − compass; in reason.

Phr. est modus in rebus.

175. Influence.—N. influence; importance etc. 642; weight, pressure, preponderance, prevalence, sway, pull; predomi-nance, -nancy; ascendency; control, dominance, reign; authority etc. 737; capability etc. (power) 157; interest; spell, magic, magnetism.

footing; purchase etc. (support) 215; play, leverage, vantage ground.

tower of strength, host in himself; protection, patronage, auspices.

V. have -influence etc. n.; be -influential etc. adj.; carry weight, actuate, sway, bias, weigh, tell; have a hold upon, magnetize, bear upon, gain a footing, work upon; take -root, − hold; strike root in.

run through, pervade, prevail, dominate, predominate, subject; out-, over-weigh; over-ride, -bear, − come; gain head; rage; be -rife etc. adj.; spread like wildfire; have −, get −, gain- -the upper hand, − full play.

be -recognized, − listened to; make one's voice heard, gain a hearing; play a -part, − leading part- in; lead, control, rule, master; get the mastery over; make one's influence felt, cut ice with; take the lead, pull the strings; turn −, throw one's weight into- the scale; set the fashion, lead the dance.

Adj. influential; important etc. 642; weighty; prevailing etc. v.; prevalent, rife, rampant; dominant, regnant, predominant, in the ascendant, hegemonical; authoritative, recognized, telling, with authority.

Adv. with telling effect.

175a. Absence of Influence.—N. impotence etc. 158; inertness etc. 172; irrelevancy etc. 10.

V. have no -influence etc. 175.

Adj. uninfluential; unconduc-ing, -ive, -ting to; powerless etc. 158; irrelevant etc. 10.

176. Tendency.—N. tendency; apt-ness, -itude; proneness, proclivity, bent, turn, tone, bias, set, warp, leaning to, predisposition, inclination, conatus, propensity, susceptibility; liability etc. 177; quality, nature, temperament; characteristic, idio-crasy, -syncrasy; cast, vein, grain; humor, mood; drift etc. (direction) 278; conduciveness, -ducement; applicability etc. (utility) 644; subservience etc. (instrumentality) 631.

V. tend, contribute, conduce, lead, dispose, incline, verge, bend to, warp, turn, trend, affect, carry, redound to, bid fair to, gravitate towards; promote etc. (aid) 707.

Adj. tending etc. v.; conducive, working to-

wards, in a fair way to, calculated to; liable etc. 177; subservient etc. (*instrumental*) 631; useful etc. 644; subsidiary etc. (*helping*) 707.
Adv. for, whither.

177. Liability.—N. lia-bility, -bleness; possibility, contingency; suscepti-vity, -bility.
V. be -liable etc. *adj.;* incur, lay oneself open to; run the −, stand a- chance; lie under, expose oneself to, open a door to.
Adj. liable, subject; in danger etc. 665; open −, exposed −, obnoxious- to; answerable, responsible, accountable, amenable; unexempt from; apt to; dependent on; incident to.
contingent, incidental, possible, on the cards, within range of, at the mercy of.

178. Concurrence.—N. concurrence, co-operation, coagency; coincidence, consilience; union; agreement etc. 23; consent etc. (*assent*) 488; alliance; concert etc. 709; partnership etc. 712; collaboration, conformity.
V. con-cur, -duce, -spire, -tribute; agree, unite, harmonize; hang −, pull- together etc. (*co-operate*) 709; help to etc. (*aid*) 707.
keep pace with, run parallel to; go −, go along −, go hand in hand- with.
Adj. concurring etc. *v.;* concurrent, conformable, joint, co-operative, concordant, coincident, concomitant, harmonious; in alliance with, banded together, of one mind, at one with; parallel.
Adv. with one consent.

179. Counteraction.—N. counteraction, opposition; contrariety etc. 14; antagonism, polarity; clashing etc. *v.;* collision, interference, resistance, renitency, friction; reaction; retroaction; repercussion etc. (*recoil*) 277; counterblast; neutralization etc. (*compensation*) 30; *vis inertiae;* check etc. (*hindrance*) 706.
voluntary -opposition etc. 708; − resistance etc. 719; repression etc. (*restraint*) 751.
V. counteract; run counter, clash, cross; interfere −, conflict- with; jostle; go −, run −, beat −, militate- against; stultify; antagonize, frustrate, oppose etc. 708; withstand etc. (*resist*) 719; hinder etc. 706; repress etc. (*restrain*) 751; react etc. (*recoil*) 277.
undo, neutralize, cancel; counterpoise etc. (*compensate*) 30; overpoise.
Adj. counteracting etc. *v.;* antagonistic, conflicting, retroactive, renitent, reactionary; contrary etc. 14.
Adv. although etc. 30; in spite of etc. 708; *malgré;* against.

180. Space. [Indefinite space.]—N. space, extension, extent, superficial extent, expanse, stretch; capacity, volume, room, accommodation; scope, range, latitude, field, way, expansion, compass, sweep, play, swing, spread.
dimension, fourth dimension; relativity, geometry.

spare −, elbow −, house- room; stowage, roomage, margin; opening, sphere, arena; lee-, sea-, head-way.
open −, free- space; wide open spaces, void etc. (*absence*) 187; waste; wild-, wilder-ness; up-, bottom-, moor -land; *campagna, veldt,* prairie, steppe.
abyss etc. (*interval*) 198; unlimited space; infinity etc. 105; world, wide world; ubiquity etc. (*presence*) 186; length and breadth of the land.
proportions, acreage; acres, − roods and perches; square -inches, − yards etc.
V. reach, extend, stretch, sweep, spread, range, cover, thrust out, reach forth.
Adj. spacious, roomy, extensive, expansive, capacious, ample; wide-spread, vast, world-wide, uncircumscribed; boundless etc. (*infinite*) 105; shore-, track-, path-less; large etc. 192.
spatial, dimensional, proportional; two-, three-, four-dimensional; stereoscopic.
Adv. extensively etc. *adj.;* wherever; everywhere; far and -near, − wide; right and left, all over, all the world over; throughout the -world, − length and breadth of the land; under the sun, in every quarter; in all -quarters, − lands; here, there and everywhere; from -pole to pole, − China to Peru, − Indus to the pole, − Dan to Beersheba, − end to end; on the face of the earth, in the wide world, from all points of the compass; to the -four winds, − uttermost parts of the earth.

180a. Inextension.—N. in-, non-extension; point; atom etc. (*smallness*) 32; pinprick; limitation etc. 229.

181. Region. [Definite space.]—N. region, sphere, sphere of influence, corridor, ground, soil, area, realm, hemisphere, quarter district, beat, orb, orbit, zone, belt, circuit, circle; pale etc. (*limit*) 233; com-, department; domain, tract, territory, terrain, country, canton, county, shire, province, *arrondissement,* diocese, parish, township, borough, constituency, *commune,* ward, wapentake, hundred, riding, lathe, garth, soke, tithing, bailiwick; empire, kingdom, principality, duchy, grand −, arch- duchy, palatinate, republic, commonwealth, dominion, colony, state, island.
arena, precincts, *enceinte,* walk, march; patch, plot, enclosure, etc. 232; close, *enclave,* field, court; street etc. (*abode*) 189.
clime, climate, zone, meridian, latitude.
Adj. territorial, local, parochial, provincial, insular.

182. Place. [Limited space.]—N. place, lieu, spot, point, dot; niche, nook, etc. (*corner*) 244; hole; pigeonhole etc. (*receptacle*) 191; compartment; premises, precinct, station, confine; area, court, yard, quadrangle, square, compound; abode etc. 189; locality etc. (*situation*) 183.
ins and outs; every hole and corner.
Adv. somewhere, in some place, wherever it may be, here and there, in various places, *passim.*

183. Situation.—N. situation, position, locality, *locale, status,* latitude and longitude; footing, standing, standpoint, post; stage, aspect; attitude, posture, *pose.*

place, site, base, station, seat, *venue,* whereabouts, environment, neighborhood; bearings etc. (*direction*) 278; spot etc. (*limited space*) 182.

top-, ge-, chor-ography; map etc. 554.

V. be -situated, − situate; lie; have its seat in.

Adj. situ-ate, -ated; local, topical, topographical etc. *n.*

Adv. in -situ. − *loco;* here and there, *passim;* here-, there-, whereabouts; in place, here, there.

in −, amidst- such and such- -surroundings, − *environs.* − *entourage.*

184. Location.—N. loca-tion, -lization; lodgement; de-, re-position; stow-, pack-age; collocation; packing, lading; establishment, settlement, installation; fixation; insertion etc. 300.

anchorage, roadstead, mooring, mooring mast, encampment, camp, bivouac.

plantation, colony, settlement, cantonment, encampment, reservation; colonization, domestication, situation; habitation etc. (*abode*) 189; cohabitation; 'a local habitation and a name;' indenization, naturalization.

. V. place, situate, locate, localize, make a place for, put, lay, set, seat, station, lodge, quarter, post, install; storehouse, stow; extablish, fix, pin, root; graft; plant etc. (*insert*) 300; shelve, pitch, camp, lay down, deposit, reposit; cradle; moor, tether, picket; pack, tuck in; embed; vest, invest in.

billet on, quarter upon, saddle with; load, lade, freight; pocket, put up, bag.

inhabit etc. (*be present*) 186; domesticate, colonize, populate, people; take −, strike-root; anchor; cast −, come to an- anchor; sit −, settle-down; settle; take up one's -abode, − quarters; plant −, establish −, locate- oneself; squat, perch, hive, *se nicher,* bivouac, burrow, get a footing; encamp, pitch one's tent; put up -at, − one's horses at; keep house.

indenizen, naturalize, adopt.

put back, replace etc. (*restore*) 660.

Adj. placed etc. *v.;* situate, posited, ensconced, embedded, embosomed. rooted; domesticated; vested in unremoved; settled, stationed, established.

moored etc. *v.;* at anchor.

185. Displacement.—N. displacement, elocation, transposition.

ejectment etc. 297; exile etc. '(*banishment*) 893; removal etc. (*transference*) 270; unshipment.

misplacement, dislocation etc. 61; fish out of water.

V. dis-place, -plant, -lodge, -nest, -establish; misplace, unseat, disturb; exile etc. (*seclude*) 893; ablegate, set aside, rèmove; take −, cart- away; take −, draft- off; lade etc. 184, unship.

unload, empty etc. (*eject*) 297; transfer etc. 270; dispel.

vacate; depart etc. 293.

Adj. displaced etc. *v.;* un-placed, -housed, - harbored, -established, -settled; house-, home-less; out of -place, − a situation.

misplaced, out of its element.

186. Presence.—N. presence; occupancy, - ation; attendance; whereness.

permeation, pervasion; diffusion etc. (*dispersion*) 73.

ubi-ety, -quity, -quitariness; omnipresence.

bystander etc. (*spectator*) 444.

V. exist in space, be -present etc. *adj.;* assist at; make one -of, − at; look on, attend, remain; find −, present- oneself; show one's face; fall in the way of, occur in a place; lie, stand; occupy.

people; inhabit, dwell, reside, stay, sojourn, live, room, abide, bunk, lodge, nestle, roost, perch; take up one's abode etc. (*be located*) 184; tenant, occupy.

resort to, frequent, haunt; revisit.

fill, pervade, permeate; be -diffused, − disseminated- through; over-spread, -run; run through; meet one at every turn.

Adj. present; occupying, inhabiting etc. *v.;* moored etc. 184; residential, resi-ant, -dent, - dentiary; domiciled.

ubiquit-ous, -ary; omnipresent.

peopled, populous, full of people, inhabited.

Adv. here; there, where, everywhere, aboard, on board, at home, afield; on the spot; here, there and everywhere etc. (*space*) 180; in presence of, before; under the -eyes, −nose- of; in the face of; *in propriâ personâ.*

187. Absence. [Nullibiety.]—N. absence; inexistence etc. 2; non-residence, absenteeism; non-attendance, *alibi.*

emptiness etc. *adj.;* void, *vacuum;* vac-uity, - ancy; *tabula rasa;* exemption; *hiatus* etc. (*interval*) 198; no man's land.

truant, absentee.

nobody; nobody -present, − on earth; no one; not a soul; *âme qui vive.*

V. be -absent etc. *adj.;* keep -away, − out of the way; play truant, absent oneself, stay away, withdraw, make oneself scarce, vacate; go away, slip out, slip away, retreat etc. 293.

Adj. absent, not present, away, nonresident, gone, from home; missing; lost; wanted, wanting; omitted; nowhere to be found; inexistent etc. 2.

empty, void; blank, vac-ant, -uous; unten-anted, -occupied, -inhabited; tenantless; desert, - ed; devoid; un-, uninhabitable.

exempt from, not having.

Adv. without, - *minus,* nowhere; elsewhere; neither here nor there; in default of; *sans;* behind one's back.

Phr. the bird has flown, *non est inventus.*

188. Inhabitant.—N. inhabitant; habitant, resident, -iary; dweller, in-dweller; occup-ier, - ant, farmer, planter; householder, lodger, boarder, paying guest; inmate, tenant, renter, incumbent, sojourner, *locum tenens,* commorant; settler, squatter, backwoodsman, colonist; islander; denizen, citizen; burgher, oppidan, cockney, cit, townsman, burgess; villager; cottager, -tier, -ter; compatriot.

native, indigene, aboriginal, aborigines, autochthones; Briton, Englishman, John Bull; new comer etc. (*stranger*) 57.

garrison, crew; population; people etc. (*mankind*) 372; colony, settlement; household.

V. inhabit etc. (*be present*) 186; indenizen etc. (*locate oneself*) 184.

Adj. indigenous; enchorial; national, nat-ive, -al; autochthonous; British, English; colonial; domestic, domiciliated, -ed; naturalized, vernacular, domesticated; domiciliary.

in the occupation of; garrisoned —, occupied-by.

189. Abode. [Place of habitation, or resort.]—**N.** abode, dwelling, lodging, -s; diggings, domicile, residence, address, habitation, where one's lot is cast, local habitation, berth, seat, lap, sojourn, housing, quarters, headquarters, resiance, tabernacle, throne, ark.

home, fatherland, mother country, country etc. 181; home-stead, -stall; fireside, chimney corner; hearth, — stone; household gods, *lares et penates*, roof, household, housing, *dulce domum*, paternal domicile; native -soil, — land, blighty.

nest, *nidus*, snuggery; arbor, bower etc. 191; lair, den, cave, hole, hidingplace, cell, *sanctum sanctorum*, aerie, eyry, rookery, hive; *habitat*.

haunt, covert, resort, retreat, perch, roost; nidification.

bivouac, camp, encampment, cantonment, castrametation; barrack, casemate, casern.

tent etc. (*covering*) 223; building etc. (*construction*) 161; chamber etc. (*receptacle*) 191.

tenement, messuage, farm, farmhouse, grange, *hacienda*.

cot, cabin, log cabin, shack, hut, *châlet*, croft, shed, booth, stall, hovel, bothy, shanty, igloo, tepee, wigwam; pen etc. (*inclosure*) 232; barn, bawn; kennel, sty, dog-hole, cote, coop, hutch, byre; cowhouse, -shed; stable, dove-cote, shippen.

house, mansion, place, villa, cottage, box, lodge, hermitage, *rus in urbe*, folly, rotunda, tower, *château*, castle, pavilion, hotel, court, manor-house, capital messuage, hall, palace, alcazar; country seat; kiosk, bungalow; temple etc. 1000; home of rest, alms-, poor-, work-house, asylum; boarding-, lodging-house; flat, maisonette, duplex, penthouse, suite of rooms, apartments, rooms, room building etc. 161; Mansion House, town hall, Capitol.

assembly-room, auditorium, coliseum, meeting-house, pump-room, spa, health resort, watering-place; club; theatre etc. 840; drill hall, gymnasium, church etc. 1000; Houses of Parliament etc. 696; school etc. 542; inn; hostel, -ry; hotel, tavern, caravansary, khan, hospice; public-, ale-, pot-, mug-house; gin-palace, gin mill; coffee-, eating-house; canteen, *restaurant*, *rotisserie*, cafeteria, grill-room, *buffet*, *cafe*, *estaminet*, *posada*, *bodega*; bar; saloon, speakeasy, shebeen.

hamlet, village, thorp, dorp, ham, kraal; borough, burgh, town, county-seat, — town, city, capital, metropolis; suburb, quarter, parish etc. 181; ghetto; province, country.

street, place, terrace, parade, esplanade, promenade, pier, embankment, road, villas, row, walk, lane, alley, court, quadrangle, quad, wynd, close, yard, passage, rents, mansions, buildings, mews.

square, polygon, circus, crescent, mall, *piazza*, arcade, colonnade, peristyle, cloister; gardens, grove, residences; block of buildings, market-place, *place*.

anchorage, roadstead, roads; dock, basin, wharf, quay, port; harbor; dry-, graving-, floating-dock.

garden, park, pleasure-ground, pleasance, demesne.

V. take up one's abode etc. (*locate oneself*) 184; inhabit etc. (*be present*) 186.

Adj. urban, oppidan, metropolitan; suburban; provincial, rural, rustic; countrified; regional, parochial, domestic; cosmopolitan; palatial.

190. Contents. [Things contained.]—**N.** contents; cargo, lading, freight, shipment, load, bale, burden; cart-, ship-load; cup —, basket —, etc. (*receptacle*) 191 - of; inside etc. 221; stuffing, ullage.

V. load, lade, ship, charge, fill, stuff.

191. Receptacle.—**N.** receptacle, container; inclosure etc. 232; recipient, receiver, reservatory.

compartment; cell, -ule; follicle; hole, corner, niche, recess, nook; crypt, stall, pigeon-hole, cove, oriel; cave etc. (*concavity*) 252.

capsule, vesicle, cyst, pod, calyx, *cancelli*, utricle, bladder, udder.

stomach, paunch, *venter*, abdomen, ventricle, crop, craw, ingluvies, maw, gizzard, bread-basket, belly, little Mary; mouth.

pocket, pouch, fob, sheath, scabbard, socket, bag, vanity bag, compact, sac, sack, saccule, despatch —, attaché-, tachy- case, wallet, scrip, card-, note-, case, billfold, poke, knit, knap-, haver-, ruck-sack, sachel, satchel, reticule, budget; net; ditty-, -box, -bag, kitbag; portfolio; saddlebags, holster; quiver etc. (*magazine*) 636.

chest, box, coffer, caddy, case, casket, pyx, pix, *caisson*, desk, *bureau*, reliquary, shrine; trunk, portmanteau, band-box, *valise*, suitcase, hand-, traveling-, overnight-, Gladstone-, carpet-bag, brief case; boot, imperial; *vache*; cage, manger, rack.

vessel, vase, bushel, barrel; canister, jar; pottle, basket, punnet, pannier, buck-basket, hopper, maund, creel, cran, crate, cradle, bassinet, wisket, whisket, *jardinière*, *corbeille*, hamper, wastepaper basket, dosser, dorser, tray, hod, scuttle, utensil, spittoon, cuspidor.

[For liquids] cistern etc. (*store*) 636; vat, caldron, barrel, cask, puncheon, keg, rundlet, tun, butt, firkin, hogshead, kilderkin, carboy, amphora, ampulla, bottle, jar, leather bottle, decanter, ewer, cruse, carafe, crock, kit, canteen, flagon; demijohn; flask, -et; stoup, noggin, vial, phial, ampoule, cruet, caster; gourd; urn, *épergne*, salver, *patella*, *tazza*, *patera*; pig-, big-gin; tea-, coffee-pot, percolator, *samovar*; tyg, nipperkin, pocket-pistol; tub, bucket, pail, skeel, pot, tankard, jug, pitcher, toby, mug, pipkin; gal-, gall-ipot, pannikin; matrass, receiver, retort, alembic, bolthead, can, kettle; bowl, basin, jorum, punch-bowl, cup, goblet, chalice, tumbler, glass, wineglass, rummer, beaker, tass, horn, saucepan, skillet, posnet, tureen, terrine, *casserole*, sauce-, gravy-boat.

plate, platter, paten, dish, vegetable —, *entrée*-dish, trencher, calabash, porringer, potager, saucer, pan, crucible.

shovel, trowel, spoon; table-, dessert-, tea-, egg-salt-spoon; spatula, ladle; dipper; baler; watch-glass, thimble.

closet, commode, cupboard, cellaret, *chiffonnière*, locker, bin, bunker, *buffet*, press, safe, sideboard, drawer, chest of drawers, till, *scrutoire*, *secrétaire*, *écritoire*, davenport, book-case, cabinet, canterbury; corner cupboard, wardrobe.

chamber, apartment, room, cabin; office, court, hall, atrium; suite of rooms, flat, story; saloon, *salon*, parlor; presence-chamber; sitting-, drawing-, reception-, state-, living-, work-room; gallery, cabinet, closet, cubicle; pew, box; *boudoir*; *adytum*, *sanctum*; bed-room, dormitory, dressing-room; refectory, dining-room, *salle-à-manger*; nursery, schoolroom; library, study; *studio*; billiard-, bath-, smoking-room; den, canteen, mess, officers' mess; gun-, ward-, mess-room.

attic, loft, garret, cockloft, clerestory; cellar, vault, hold, cockpit; *entre-sol*; mezzanine floor; ground-floor, *rez-de-chaussée*; basement, kitchen, cook-house, galley, pantry, scullery, offices; store-room etc. (*depository*) 636; lumber-room; dusthole, -bin; dairy, laundry, coachhouse; *garage*; *hangar*; out-, pent-house; lean-to.

portico, porch, piazza, verandah, lobby, court, hall, vestibule, corridor, passage; ante-room, chamber; lounge; *foyer*, *loggia*.

conservatory, green-house, glass-house, vinery, bower, arbor, summer-house, alcove, grotto, hermitage, pergola.

lodging etc. (*abode*) 189; bed etc. (*support*) 215; carriage etc. (*vehicle*) 272.

Adj. capsular; saccu-lar, -lated; recipient; ventricular, cystic, vascular, vesicular, cellular, camerated, locular, multilocular, poly-gastric; marsupial; siliqu-ose, -ous.

192. Size.—N. size, magnitude, dimension, bulk, volume; largeness etc. *adj.*; greatness etc. (*of quantity*) 31; expanse etc.. (*space*) 180; amplitude, mass; proportions.

capacity; ton-, tun-nage; caliber, scantling.

turgidity etc. (*expansion*) 194; corpulence, obesity; plumpness, etc. *adj.*; *embonpoint*, corporation, flesh and blood, lustihood.

hugeness etc. *adj.*; enormity, immensity, monstrosity.

giant, Brobdingnagian, Antaeus, Goliath, Gog and Magog, Gargantua, monster, mammoth, Cyclops; whale, porpoise, behemoth, leviathan, elephant, hippopotamus; colossus; tun, Jump, bulk, block, loaf, mass, clod, nugget, bushel, thumper, whopper, spanker, strapper; Triton among the minnows.

mountain, mound; heap etc. (*assemblage*) 72, largest portion etc. 50; full-, life-size.

V. ve- large etc. *adj.*; become -large etc. (*expand*) 194.

Adj. large, big; great etc. (*in quantity*) 31; considerable, bulky, voluminous, ample, massive, massy; capacious, comprehensive; spacious etc. 180; mighty, towering, fine, magnificent.

corpulent, stout, fat, plump, squab, full, lusty, strapping, bouncing; portly, burly, well-fed, full-grown; stalwart, brawny, fleshy; goodly; in good - case, - condition; in condition; chopping, jolly; chub-, chubby-faced.

lubberly, hulky, unwieldy, lumpish, gaunt, spanking, whacking, whopping, thumping, thundering, hulking; overgrown; puffy etc. (*swollen*) 194.

huge, immense, enormous, mighty; vast, -y; amplitudinous, stupendous; monst-er, -rous; gigantic, elephantine; giant, -like; colossal, Cyclopean, Brobdingnagian, Garguantuan, Titanic; infinite etc. 105.

large as life; plump as a dumpling, – partridge; fat as -a pig, – a quail, – butter, – brawn, – bacon.

193. Littleness.—N. littleness etc. *adj.*; smallness etc. (*of quantity*) 32; exiguity, inextension; parvi-tude, -ty; duodecimo; Elzevir edition, epitome, microcosm; rudiment; vanishing point; thinness etc. 203.

dwarf, pigmy, atomy, Liliputian, midget, chit, pigwidgeon, urchin, elf; doll, puppet; Tom Thumb, Hop-o'-my thumb, Humpty-dumpty; man-, mann-ikin; *homunculus*, dapperling, fingerling, dandiprat, cock-sparrow, scalawag.

animalcule, monad, mite, insect, emmet, fly, midge, gnat, shrimp, minnow, worm, maggot, entozoon; *bacillus*, microbe, micro-organism, *bacteria*; *infusoria*; microbe; grub; tit, tomtit, runt, mouse, small fry; millet-, mustard-seed; barleycorn; pebble, grain of sand; mole-hill, button, bubble.

point; atom etc. (*small quantity*) 32; fragment etc. (*small part*) 51; powder etc. 330; point of a pin, mathematical point; *minutiae* etc. (*unimportance*) 643.

micro-graphy, meter, -scope; vernier; scale.

V. be -little etc. *adj.*; lie in a nutshell; become small etc. (*decrease*) 36, (*contract*) 195.

Adj. little; small etc. (*in quantity*) 32; minute, diminutive, microscopic; inconsiderable etc. (*unimportant*) 643; exiguous, puny, tiny, wee, petty, minikin, miniature, pigmy, elfin; under sized; dwarf, -ed, -ish; spare, stunted, limited; cramp, -ed; pollard, Liliputian, dapper, pocket; port-ative, -able; duodecimo; dumpy, squat; compact, handy; short etc. 201.

impalpable, intangible, evanescent, imperceptible, invisible, inappreciable, infinitesimal, homeopathic; atomic, corpuscular, molecular; rudiment-ary, -al; embryonic.

weazen, scant, scraggy, scrubby; thin etc. (*narrow*) 203; granular etc. (*powdery*) 330; shrunk etc. 195.

Adv. in a -small compass, – nutshell; on a small scale.

194. Expansion.—N. expansion; increase etc. 35 -of size; enlargement, extension, augmentation; ampli-fication, -ation; aggrandizement, spread, increment, growth, development, pullulation, swell, dilation, dilatation, rarefaction; turg-escence, -idness, -idity; obesity etc. (*size*) 192; dropsy, tumefaction, intumescence, swelling, tumor, *diastole*, distension; puff-ing, -iness; inflation; pandiculation.

dilatability, expansibility.

germination, growth, upgrowth; accretion etc. 35.

over-growth, -distension; hypertrophy, tympany.

bulb etc. (*convexity*) 250; plumper; superiority of size.

V. become -larger etc. (large etc. 192); expand, widen, enlarge, extend, grow, increase, incrassate, swell, gather; fill out; deploy, take open order, dilate, stretch, spread; mantle, was; grow –, spring- up; bud, bourgeon, shoot, sprout, germinate, put forth, vegetate, pullulate, open, burst forth, flower, blow etc. 734; gain –, gather- flesh; outgrow; spread like wildfire, overrun.

be larger than; surpass etc. (*be superior*) 33.

render -larger etc. (large etc. 192); expand, spread, extend, aggrandize, distend, develop, amplify, spread out, widen, magnify, rarefy, inflate, puff, puff out, blow up, stuff, pad, cram; exaggerate; fatten.

Adj. expanded etc. *v.*; larger etc. (large etc. 192); swollen; expansive; wide-open, -spread; fan-shaped; flabelliform; overgrown exaggerated, bloated, fat, turgid, tumid, hypertrophied, dropsical; pot-, swag-bellied; edematous, obese, puffy, pursy; blowzy, distended; patulous; bulbous etc. (*convex*) 250; full-blown, -grown, -formed; big etc. 192.

195. Contraction.—N. contraction, reduction, diminution; decrease etc. 36- of size; defalcation, decrement; lessening, shrinkage; collapse, emaciation, attenuation, tabefaction, comsumption, marasmus, atrophy; systole, neck, hourglass.

condensation, compression, constraint, compactness; compendium etc. 596; squeezing etc. *v.* ; strangulation; corrugation; astringency, constringency; astringents, sclerotics; contractility, compressibility; coarctation.

inferiority in size.

V. become -small, – smaller; lessen, decrease etc. 36; grow less, dwindle, shrink, contract, narrow, shrivel, collapse, wither, lose flesh, wizen, fall away, waste, wane, ebb; decai etc. (*deteriorate*) 659.

be smaller than, fall short of; not come up to etc. (*be inferior*) 34.

render smaller, lessen, diminish, contract, draw in, shrink, shrivel, narrow, coarctate; constrict, constringe; condense, compress, boil down, deflate, exhaust, empty; squeeze, corrugate, crush, crumple up, warp, purse up, pack, stow; pinch, tighten, strangle; cramp; dwarf, bedwarf; shorten etc. 201; circumscribe etc. 229; restrain etc. 751; fold etc. 258.

pare, reduce, attenuate, rub down, scrape, file, grind, chip, shave, shear.

Adj. contracting etc. *v.*; astringent; shrunk, contracted etc. *v.*; strangulated, tabid, wizened, stunted, tabescent; marasmic; waning etc. *v.*; neap; compact; shriveled, preshrunk.

unexpanded etc. (expand etc. 194); inswept; contractile; compressible; smaller etc. small etc. 193).

196. Distance.—N. distance; space etc. 180; remoteness, farness; far- cry to; longinquity, elongation; offing, background; removedness; parallax; reach, span, stride; drift.

out-post, -skirt; horizon, sky-line; aphelion; foreign parts, *ultima Thule, ne plus ultra,* antipodes; long range, giant's stride.

dispersion etc. 73.

V. be -distant etc. *adj.*; extend –, stretch –, reach –, spread –, go –, get –, stretch away- to; range, outrange, outreach.

remain at a distance; keep –, stand- -away, – off, – aloof, – clear of.

Adj. distant; far -off, away; remote, telescopic, distal, wide of; stretching to etc. *v.*; yon, -der; ulterior; trans-marine, -pontine, -atlantic, -pacific, - continental, -polar, -equatorial, -alpine; tramontane; ultra-montane, -mundane; hyperborean, antihodean; inaccessible, out of the way; unapproached, -able; incontiguous.

Adv. far -off, – away; afar, -off; off; away; a - long, – great, – good- way off; wide away, aloof; wide –, clear- of; out of -the way. – reach; abroad, ' yonder, farther, further, beyond; *outre mer,* over the border, far and wide, over the hills and far away; from pole to pole etc. (*over great space*) 180; to the -uttermost parts, – ends- of the earth; out of -hearing, – range, nobody knows where, *à perte de vue,* out of the sphere of, wide of the mark; a far cry to.

apart, asunder; wide -apart, – asunder; *longo intervallo*; at arm's length.

197. Nearness.—N. nearness etc. *adj.*; proximity, propinquity; vicinity, -age; neighborhood, adjacency; contiguity etc. 199.

short -distance, – step, – cut; earshot, close quarters, brief span; stone's throw; bow –, gun –, pistol- shot; hair's breadth, span; close-up.

purlieus, neighborhood, vicinage, *environs, alentours,* suburbs, confines, *banlieue,* borderland; whereabouts.

bystander; neighbor, borderer.

approach etc. 286; convergence etc. 290; perihelion.

V. be -near etc. *adj.*; adjoin, hang about, trench on; border-, verge upon; stand by, approximate, tread on the heels of; cling to, clasp, hug; cuddle, huddle; hang about the skirts of, hover over; burn; abut.

bring –, draw- -near etc. 286; converge etc. 290; crowd etc. 72; place -side by side etc. *adv.*

Adj. near, nigh; close-, near- at hand; close, neighboring, propinquent, bordering upon; adjacent, adjoining, limitrophe; proxim-ate, -al; at hand, handy; near the mark, near run; home, intimate.

Adv. near, ' nigh; hard –, 'fast- by; close -to. upon, – up; at the point of; next door to; within - reach, – call, – hearing, – earshot, – range; within an ace of; but a step, not far from, at no great distance; on the -verge, – brink, – skirts- of; in the -environs etc. *n.*; at one's -door, – feet, – elbow, – finger's end, – side; on the tip of one's tongue; under one's nose; within a -stone's throw etc. *n.*; in -sight, – presence- of; at close quarters; cheek by -jole, – jowl; beside, alongside, side by side, *tête-à-tête*; in juxtaposition etc. (*touching*) 199; yard-arm to yard-arm; at the heels of; on the confines of, at the threshold, bordering upon, verging to; in the way.

about; here- there-abouts; roughly, in round

numbers; approxim- -ately. – atively; as good
as, well nigh.

198. Interval.—N. interval, interspace;
separation etc. 44; break gap, opening; hole etc.

260; chasm, *hiatus*, caesura; inter-ruption,-
regnum; interstice, *lacuna*, cleft, mesh, crevice,
chink, rime, creek, cranny, crack, chap, slit, slot,
fissure, scissure, rift, flaw, breach, fracture, rent,
gash, cut, leak, dike, ha-ha.

‘ gorge, defile, ravine, canon, *crevasse*, abyss,
abysm; gulf; inlet, frith, strait, gully, gulch, nullah;
pass; notch; furrow etc. 259; yawning gulf; *hiatus -
maxime*, – *valde- deflendus*; parenthesis etc. (*interjacence*) 228; void etc. (*absence*) 187; incompleteness etc. 530.

V. gape etc. (*open*) 260; part, remove.

Adj. with an interval, far between; separated;
spaced, split.

Adv. at intervals etc. (*discontinuously*) 70;
longo intervallo.

199. Contiguity.—N. contiguity, contact,
proximity, apposition, juxtaposition, touching etc.
v.; abutment, osculation; meeting, appulse, ap-
pulsion, *rencontre*, rencounter, syzygy, coincidence, conjunction, coexistence; adhesion etc.
46.

border-land; frontier etc. (*limit*) 233; tangent.

V. be -contiguous etc. *adj.*; join, adjoin, abut
on, march with, border; tick, graze, touch, meet,
osculate, kiss, come in contact; coincide; coexist;
adhere etc. 46.

Adj. contiguous; touching etc. *v.*; in -contact
etc. *n.*, conterminous, end to end, osculatory; per-
tingent; tangential.

hand to hand; close to etc. (*near*) 197; with no -
interval etc. 198.

200. Length.—N. length, longitude, span, extent, mileage.

line, bar, rule, stripe, streak, spoke, radius.

lengthening etc. *v.*; pro-longation, -duction, -
traction; ten-sion, -sure; extension.

[Measures of length] line, nail, inch, hand,
palm, foot, cubit, yard, ell, fathom, rod, pole,
perch, furlong, mile, league; chain, meter, kilo-,
centi-, milli- etc meter.

pedometer, perambulator, odometer, odograph,
speedometer, cyclometer, log, telemeter, range finder; scale etc. (*measurement*) 466.

V. be -long etc. *adj.*; stretch out, sprawl; extend –, reach –, stretch -to; make a long
arm, ‘drag its slow length along.’

render -long etc. *adj.*; lengthen, extend,
elongate; stretch; pro-long, -duce, -tract; let
–, pay –, draw –; spin- out; drawl.

enfilade, look along, view in perspective.

Adj. long, -some; lengthy, lank, wiredrawn, out-
stretched; stretched, drawn out, lengthened etc. *v.*;
sesquipedalian etc. (*words*) 577; interminable, no
end of.

line-ar, -al; longitudinal, oblong.

as long as -my arm, –to-day and to-morrow; un-
shortened etc. (shorten etc. 201).

Adv. lengthwise, at length, longitudinally, endlong, along; *tandem*; in a line etc. (*continuously*)
69; in perspective.

from -end to end; –stem to stern, –head to foot,
–the crown of the head to the sole of the foot, –
top to toe, –head to heels; fore and aft.

201. Shortness.—N. shortness etc. *adj.*; brevity;
littleness etc. 193; a span.

shortening etc. *v.*; abbrevia-tion, -ture;
abridgment, concision, retrenchment, curtailment,
decurtation; reduction etc. (*contraction*) 195;
epitome etc. (*compendium*) 596.

abridger, abstractor, epitomiser.

elision, ellipsis; conciseness etc. (*in style*) 572.

V. be -short etc. *adj.*; render -short etc. *adj.*;
shorten, curtail, abridge, abbreviate, take in,
reduce; compress etc. (*contract*) 195; epitomize
etc. 596.

retrench, cut short, obtruncate; scrimp, cut, chop
up, hack, hew; cut – , pare- down; clip, snip, dock,
lop, prune; shear, shave, mow, reap, crop; snub;
truncate, pollard, stunt, nip, nip in the bud, check
the growth of; [in drawing] foreshorten.

Adj. short, brief, curt; compendious, compact;
stubby, scrimp; shorn, stubbed; stumpy, thickset,
podgy, stocky, pug; squab, -by; squat, dumpy; little
etc. 193; curtailed of its fair proportions; short by;
oblate; concise etc. 572; summary.

Adv. shortly etc. *adj.*; in short etc. (*concisely*)
572.

202. Breadth. Thickness.—N. breadth, width,
latitude, amplitude; diameter, bore, calibre, radius;
superficial extent etc. (*space*) 180.

thickness, crassitude; corpulence etc. (*size*) 192;
dilatation etc. (*expansion*) 194.

V. be -broad etc. *adj.*; become – , render- -
broad etc. *adj.*; expand etc. 194; thicken, widen.

Adj. broad, wide, ample, extended; discous; fan-
like; out-spread, -stretched; wide as a church-door.

thick, dumpy, squab, squat, thickset, tubby; thick
as a rope, stubby etc. 201.

203. Narrowness. Thinness.—N. narrowness
etc. *adj.*; closeness, exility; exiguity etc. (*little*)
193.

line; hair’s – , finger’s -breadth; strip, streak,
vein.

thinness etc. *adj.*; tenuity; emaciation, slen-
derness, macilency, *marcor.*

shaving, slip etc. (*filament*) 205; threadpaper,
skeleton, shadow, scrag, anatomy, spindle-shanks,
barebones, lantern jaws, mere skin and bone.

middle construction, stricture, neck, waist, isthmus, wasp, hour-glass; ridge, *ghaut*, pass; ravine
etc. 198.

narrowing, coarctation, angustation, tapering;
contraction etc. 195.

V. be-narrow etc. *adj.*; narrow, taper, diminish,
contract etc. 195; render -narrow etc. *adj.*

Adj. narrow, close; slender, thin, fine; *svelte;*
thread-like etc. (*filament*) 205; finespun, taper,
slim, gracile, slight, slight-made; scant, -y; spare,
delicate, incapacious; contracted etc. 195; unexpanded etc. (expand etc. 194); slender as a thread,
capillary.

emaciated, lean, meager, gaunt, macilent; lank, -y; weedy, skinny, scrawny, scraggy; starv-ed, -eling; attenuated, shrivelled; wizened, pinched, peaky, skeletal, spindling, spindle- -legged, -shanked; extenuated, tabid, marcid, bare-bone, raw-boned; herring-gutted; worn to a shadow, lean as a rake; thin as a -lath,—whipping post,—wafer; hatchet-faced; lantern-jawed.

204. Layer.—N. layer, stratum, course, bed, zone, substratum,floor, flag, stage, story, tier, slab, escarpment, table, tablet, panel, plaque; board, plank; trencher, platter.

plate; lam-ina, -ella; sheet, flake, foil, wafer, scale, coat, peel, pellicle, ply, thickness, membrane, film, leaf, slice, shive, cut, rasher, shaving, integument etc. (covering) 223.

V. slice, shave, pare, peel; plate, coat, veneer; cover etc. 223.

Adj. lamell-ar, -ated, -iform; laminated, -iferous; micaceous; schist-ose, -ous; scaly; filmy, membranous, flaky, squamous; folia-ted, -ceous; stratified, -form; tabular, discoid, spathic.

205. Filament.—N. filament, line; fiber, fibril; funicle, vein, hair, capillament, cilium, tendril, gossamer; hair-stroke; harl.

wire, string, thread, packthread, cotton, sewing-silk, twine, twist, whip-cord, cord, rope, cable, yarn, hemp, oakum, jute, wool, worsted.

strip, shred, slip, spill, list, band, fillet, fascia, ribbon, riband, tape, roll, lath, slat, strake, splinter, shiver, shaving.

beard etc. (roughness) 256; ramification; strand.

Adj. fil-amentous, -aceous, -iform; fibr-ous, -illous; thread-like, wiry, stringy, ropy; capill-ary, -iform; funicular, wire-drawn; anguilliform; flagelliform; hairy etc. (rough) 256; ligulate.

206. Height.—N. height, altitude, elevation, ceiling; eminence, pitch; loftiness etc. adj.; sublimity.

tallness etc. adj.; stature, procerity; prominence etc. 250.

colossus etc. (size) 192; giant, grenadier, giraffe.

mount, -ain; hill, butte, monticle, fell, knap; cape; head-, fore-land; promontory; ridge, hog's back, dune; rising -, vantage- ground; down; moor, -land; Alp; up-, table-, high-lands; heights etc. (summit) 210; knoll, hummock, hillock, barrow, mound, mole, kopje; steeps, bluff, cliff, craig, tor, peak, pike, clough; escarpment, edge, ledge, brae; dizzy height.

tower, pillar, column, pylon, obelisk, monument, steeple, spire, minaret, campanile, belfry, turret, roof, dome, cupola, pagoda, pyramid; sky scraper; Eiffel tower.

pole, pikestaff, maypole, flagstaff; mast, top-, topgallant- mast.

ceiling etc. (covering) 223.

high water; high-, flood-, spring-tide.

altimetry etc. (angle) 244; altimeter, height-finder, hypsometer, barograph.

V. be -high etc. adj.; tower, soar, command;

hover; cap, culminate; overhang, hang over, impend, beetle; bestride, ride, mount; perch, surmount; cover etc. 233; overtop etc. (be superior) 33; stand on tiptoe.

become -high etc. adj.; grow, — higher, — taller; upgrow; rise etc. (ascend) 305.

render -high etc. adj.; heighten etc. (elevate) 307.

Adj. high, elevated, eminent, exalted, lofty, supernal; tall; gigantic etc. (big) 192; Patagonian; towering, beetling, soaring, hanging [gardens]; elevated etc. 307; upper; highest etc. (topmost) 210; monticulous, perching, hill-dwelling.

up-, moor-land; hilly, mountainous, alpine, sub-alpine, heaven-kissing; cloud-topt, -capt, -touching; aerial.

overhanging etc. v.; incumbent, overlying; super-incumbent, -natant, -imposed; prominent etc. 250.

tall as a -maypole, —poplar,—steeple; lanky etc. (thin) 203.

Adv. on high, high up, aloft, up, above, aloof, overhead; up—, above- stairs; in the clouds; on -tiptoe, —stilts,—the shoulders of; over head and ears; breast high.

over, upwards; from top to bottom etc. (completely) 52.

207. Lowness.—N. lowness etc. adj.; debasement, depression; prostration etc. (horizontal) 213; depression etc. (concave) 252.

molehill; lowlands; bottomlands; basement-ground-floor; rez de chaussee etc. 211; hold; feet, heels.

low water; low—, ebb—, neap—, spring- tide.

V. be -low etc. adj.; lie -low, —flat; underlie; crouch, slouch, wallow, grovel; lower etc. (depress) 308.

Adj. low, neap, debased; nether, -most; flat, level with the ground; lying low etc. v.; crouched, subjacent, squat, prostrate etc. (horizontal) 213.

Adv. under; be-, under-neath; below; down, -wards; adown, at the foot of; under-foot, -ground; down—, below-stairs; at a low ebb; below par.

208. Depth.—N. depth; deepness etc. adj.; profundity, depression etc. (concavity) 252.

hollow, pit, shaft, well, crater, abyss; gulf etc. 198; bowels of the earth, bottomless pit, hell.

soundings, sonar, depth of water, water, draught; submersion; plummet, sound, probe; sounding -rod, — line, — machine; lead; submarine, diving bell, bathysphere; diver.

V. be -deep etc. adj.; render -deep etc. adj.; deepen.

plunge etc. 310; sound, heave the lead, take soundings; dig etc. (excavate) 252.

Adj. deep, -seated; profound, sunk, buried; submerged etc. 310; sub-aqueous, -marine, -terranean, -terrene; underground.

bottom-, sound-, fathom-less; unfathom-ed, -able; abysmal; deep as a well, deep-sea.

knee-, ankle-deep.

Adv. beyond—, out of- one's depth; over head and ears, over one's head.

209. Shallowness.—N. shallowness etc. adj.; shoals; mere scratch; veneer, gloss, pinprick.

Adj. shallow, superficial; skin—, ankle—, knee-deep; just enough to wet one's feet; shoal, -y.
V. shallow, shoal, skim— over, —the surface, touch on.

210. Summit.—N. summit, -y; top, vertex, apex, zenith, pinnacle, acme, acropolis, culmination, meridian, utmost height, *ne plus ultra*, height, pitch, maximum, climax, apogee; culminating —, crowning —, turning- point; turn of the tide, fountain head; water-shed. -parting; sky, pole.

tip, -top; crest, crow's nest, cap, truck, peak, nib; end etc. 67; crown, brow; head, nob, noddle, pate, skull, cranium.

high places, heights.

top-, top-gallant mast, sky scraper; quarter —, hurricane- deck.

architrave, frieze, cornice, coping, coping-stone, zoophorus, capital, headpiece, capstone, epistyle, sconce, pediment, entablature; tympanum; ceiling etc. (*covering*) 223.

attic, loft, garret, house-top, upper story, roof. topping, icing, frosting.

V. culminate, cap, crown, top; overtop etc. (*be superior to*) 33.

Adj. highest etc. (high etc. 206); top; top-, upper-most; tip-top; culminating etc. *v.*; meridi-an, -onal; capital, head, polar, supreme, supernal, top-gallant.

Adv. a-top, at the top of — the tree, — the heap.

211. Base.—N. base, -ment; plinth, dado, wainscot, baseboard; foundation etc. (*support*) 215; substructure, sub · *stratum*, sump, ground, earth, pavement, floor, paving, flag, carpet, ground-floor, deck; footing, groundwork, basis; hold, bilge, orlop deck.

bottom, nadir, foot, sole, toe, hoof, keel, kelson, root.

Adj. bottom; under-, nether-most; fundamental; founded —, based —, grounded —, built- on.

212. Verticality.—N. verticality; erectness etc. *adj.*; perpendicularity; right angle, normal; azimuth circle.

wall, palisade, precipice, cliff, steep, bluff.

elevation, erection; square, plumb-line, plummet.

V. be -vertical etc. *adj.*; stand -up, — on end, — erect, — upright; stick —, cock-up.

render -vertical etc. *adj.*; set —, stick —, raise —, cock- up; erect, rear, raise, pitch, raise on its legs.

Adj. vertical, upright, erect, perpendicular, normal, plumb, straight, bolt upright; rampant; straight —, standing- up etc. *v.*; rectangular, orthogonal.

Adv. vertically etc. *adj.*; up, on end; up —, right- on end; *à plomb*, endwise; on one's legs; at right angles.

213. Horizontality.—N. horizontality; flatness; level, plane; stratum etc. 204; dead -level, — flat; level plane.

recumbency; lying down etc. *v.*; reclination, decumbence; de-, discumbency; proneness etc. *adj.*; accubation, supination, resupination, prostration; azimuth.

plain, floor, platform, bowling-green; cricket-ground; court; gridiron; base-ball diamond; hockey rink; tennis-, croquet-ground, — lawn; billiard table; terrace, estrade, esplanade, *parterre*, table-land, *plateau*, ledge.

spirit-, level; T-square.

V. be -horizontal etc. *adj.*; lie, recline, couch; lie -down, — flat, — prostrate; sprawl, loll;. sit down.

render -horizontal etc. *adj.*; lay, — down, — out; level, flatten, even, raze, equalize, smooth, align; prostrate, knock down, floor, fell, ground.

Adj. horizontal, level, even, plane; flat etc. 251; flat as a -billiard table, — bowling green; alluvial; calm, — as a mill-pond; smooth, —as glass.

re-, de-, pro-, ac-cumbent; lying etc. *v.*; prone, supine, couchant, jacent, prostrate. ♦

Adv. horizontally etc. *adj.*; on -one's back. —all fours, — its beam ends.

214. Pendency.—N. pend-, dependency; suspension, hanging etc. *v.*

pendant, drop, tippet, tassel, lobe, tail, train, flap, lappet, skirt, pig-tail, queue, pendulum; hanger, suspender, supporter.

peg, knob, button, hook, nail, stud, ring, staple, tenterhook; davit; fastening etc. 45; spar, horse. chande-, gase-, electro-lier.

V. be -pendent etc. *adj.*; hang, depend, swing, dangle, droop, sag; swag; daggle, flap, trail, flow. suspend, hang, sling, hook up, hitch, fasten to, append.

Adj. pend-ent, -ulous; pensile; hanging etc. *v.*; dependent; suspended etc. *v.*; lowering, overhanging, beetling, decumbent; loose, flowing.

having a -peduncle etc. *n.*; pedunculate, tailed, caudate.

215. Support.—N. support, backing, ground, foundation, base, basis; *terra firma*; bearing, fulcrum, *point d'appui*, caudex, purchase, footing, hold, -*locus standi*; landing, — stage, — place; stage, platform; block; rest, resting-place; ground-work, *substratum*, sustentation, subvention; floor etc. (*basement*) 211.

supporter; aid etc. 707; prop, stand, anvil, fulciment; hod, stay, shore, skid, rib, sprag, truss, bandage; sleeper; stirrup, stilts, shoe, sole, heel, splint, lap; bar, rod, boom, sprit, outrigger.

staff, stick, crutch, alpenstock, bourdon; *bâton*, maulstick, colstaff, cowlstaff, staddle; stalk, pedicel, -icle, — uncle.

post, pillar, shaft, column, pilaster; pediment, pedestal; plinth, shank, leg, socle, zocle; buttress, jamb, mullion, abutment; pile, baluster, banister, stanchion, king post; balustrade.

frame, -work, body, *chassis*, *fuselage*; scaffold, skeleton, beam, rafter, girder, lintel, joist, cantilever, travis, trave, corner-stone, summer, transom; rung, round, step, sill.

columella, back-bone; key-stone; axle, -tree; axis; arch, ogive, mainstay.

trunnion, pivot, rowlock; peg etc. (*pendency*)

214; tie-beam etc. (*fastening*) 45; thole pin.

board, ledge, shelf, hob, bracket, trevet, trivet, arbor, rack, hatrack; mantel, -piece, -shelf; slab, console; counter, dresser; flange, corbel; table, trestle, teapoy; shoulder; perch; horse; easel, desk; retable, predella.

seat, throne, dais; divan, musnud; chair, bench, form, stool, camp-stool, sofa, settee, davenport, stall, miserere, arm —, easy —, elbow —, rocking-chair; couch, day bed, *fauteuil*, woolsack, ottoman, settle, squab, bench, box, dicky; saddle, pannel, pillion; side —, pack- saddle; pommel.

bed, berth, pallet, tester, crib, cot, bassinet, hammock, shakedown, camp bed, bunk, truckle-bed, cradle, litter, stretcher, bedstead; four-poster, French bed; bedding, mattress, *paillasse;* pillow, bolster; mat, rug, cushion.

stool, footstool, hassock, faldstool, *prie-dieu;* tabouret; tripod.

Atlas, Persides, Atlantes, Caryatides, Hercules.

V. be -supported etc.; lie —, sit —, recline —, lean —, loll —, rest —, stand —, step —, repose —, abut —, beat —, be based etc.- on; have at one's back; be-stride, -straddle.

support, bear, carry, hold, sustain, shoulder; hold —, back —, bolster —, shore- up; up-hold, - bear; prop; under-prop,-pin, -set; bandage, etc. 43; brace, truss; cradle, pillow.

give —, furnish —, afford —, supply —, lend- - support, — foundations; bottom, found, base, ground, embed.

maintain, keep on foot; aid etc. 707.

Adj. support-ing, -ed, etc.*v.*; atlantean, columellar; sustentative, fundamental, basal.

Adv. astride on, astraddle; pick-a-back.

216. Parallelism.—N. parallelism; coextension, concentricity, collimation.

V. be —, lie- parallel to; collimate; equate, match.

Adj. parallel; coextensive, collateral, concentric, concurrent, abreast, aligned.

Adv. alongside, abreast etc. (*laterally*) 236.

·217. Obliquity.—N. obliquity, inclination, skew, slope, slant; crookedness etc. *adj.*; slopeness; leaning etc. *v.*; bevel, bezel, ramp, tilt; bias, list, twist, warp, swag, cant, lurch; distortion etc. 243; bend etc. (*curve*) 245; tower of Pisa.

acclivity, rise, ascent, grade, gradient, *glacis*, rising ground, hill, bank, declivity, downhill, dip, fall, devexity; gentle –, rapid- slope; easy -ascent, — descent; shelving beach; *talus; montagne Russe; facilis descensus Averni.*

steepness etc. *adj.*; cliff, precipice etc. (*vertical*) 212; escarpment, scarp.

[Measure of inclination]clinometer, theodolite, level, sextant, quadrant, protractor; angle, sine, cosine, tangent etc. hypothenuse.

diagonal; zigzag, chevron.

V. be -oblique etc. *adj.*; slope, slant, lean, incline, shelve, stoop, decline, descent, bend, heel, careen, sag, swag, seel, slouch, cant, sidle.

render -oblique etc. *adj.*; sway, bias; slope, slant; incline, bend, crook; cant, tilt; distort etc. 243.

Adj. oblique, inclined; sloping etc. *v.*; tilted etc.

v.; recumbent, clinal, skew, askew, slant, aslant, bias, plagiedral, indirect, wry, awry, ajee, crooked; knock-kneed etc. (*distorted*) 243; bevel, out of the perpendicular.

uphill, rising, ascending, acclivous; downhill, falling, descending; declining, declivous, devex, anticlinal; steep, abrupt, precipitous, breakneck.

diagonal; trans-verse, -versal; athwart, antiparallel; curved etc. 245.

Adv. obliquely etc. *adj.*; on —, all on- one side; askew, askant, askance, aslope, asquint, edgewise, at an angle; side-long, -ways; slope-, slant-wise; by a side wind.

218. Inversion.—N. in-, e-, sub-, re-, retro-, intro-version; contraposition etc. 237; contrariety etc. 14; reversal; turn of the tide.

overturn; upset, capsize; somer-sault, -set; summerset; *culbute*; revulsion; *pirouette.*

transposition, transposal, anastrophy, *metastasis, hyperbaton, anastrophe, hysteron--proteron,* hypallage, *synchysis, tmesis,·* parenthesis; *metathesis*; palindrome; Spoonerism.

pronation and supination.

V. be -inverted etc.; turn —, go —, wheel- -round, — about, — to the right about; turn —, go —, tilt —, topple-over; capsize, turn turtle.

in-, sub-, retro-, intro-vert; reverse; up-, overturn, -set; turn -topsy turvy etc. *adj.*; *culbuter*; transpose, put the cart before the horse, turn the tables.

Adj. inverted etc. *v.*; wrong side -out, — up; inside out, upside down; bottom —, keel- upwards; supine, on one's head, topsy turvy, *sens dessus sens dessous.*

inverse; reverse etc. (*contrary*) 14; opposite etc. 237.

topheavy, unstable.

Adv. inversely etc.*adj.*; hirdie-girdie; heels over head, head over heels.

219. Crossing.—N. crossing etc. *v.*; intersection, — lacement, — twinement, -digitation; decussation, transversion; convolution etc. 248.

reticulation, meshwork, network; ·inosculation, anastomosis, inter-texture, mortise.

net, *plexus*, web, mesh, twill, skein, sleeve, felt, lace; wicker; mat, ting; plait, trellis, wattle, lattice, grating, *grille*, gridiron, tracery, fretwork, filigree, reticle; tissue, netting, mokes.

cross, crucifix, rood, crisscross, crux; chain, wreath, braid, cat's cradle,knot; entanglement etc. (*disorder*) 59.

[woven fabrics] cloth, linen, muslin, cambric, drill, homespun, tweed, broadcloth etc.

V. cross, decussate; inter-sect, -lace, -twine, - twist, -weave, -digitate, -link.

twine, entwine, weave, inweave, twist, wreathe; anastomose, inosculate, dovetail, splice, link.

mat, plait, plat, braid, felt, twill; tangle, entangle, ravel; net, knot; dishevel, raddle.

Adj. crossing etc.*v.*; crossed, matted etc. *v.*; transverse.

cross, cruciform, crucial; reti-form, -cular, -culated; arcolar, cancellated, mullioned, latticed, grated, barred, streaked; textile, secant, plexal; interfretted.

Adv. across, thwart, athwart, transversely, crosswise.

220. Exteriority.—N. exteriority; outside, exterior; surface, superficies; skin etc. (*covering*) 223; *superstratum*; disk, disc; face, facet, external, the open.

excentricity; circumjacence etc. 227.

V. be -exterior etc. *adj.*; lie around etc. 227.

place -exteriorly, — outwardly, — outside; put —, turn- out.

Adj. exter-ior, -nal; extraneous, outer, -most; out-ward, -lying, -side, -door; round about etc. 227; extramural.

superficial; skin-deep; frontal, discoid.

extraregarding; eccentric; outstanding; extrinsic etc. 6.

Adv. externally etc. *adj.*; out, without, over, outwards, *ab extra*, out of doors; *extra muros*.

in the open air; *sub -Jove*, — *dio; à la belle étoile, al fresco.*

221. Interiority.—N. interiority; inside, -land, interior, endocrine; interspace, subsoil, *substratum*.

contents etc. 190; substance, pith, marrow; backbone etc. (*center*) 222; heart, bosom, breast, abdomen; vitals, viscera, entrails, bowels, belly, intestines, guts, chitterlings, womb, lap; gland, cell; internal organs, *penetralia*, recesses, innermost recesses; cave etc. (*concavity*) 252.

inhabitant etc. 188.

V. be -inside etc. *adj.*, — within etc. *adv.*

place —, keep- within; enclose etc. (*circumscribe*) 229; intern; embed etc. (*insert*) 300.

Adj. inter-ior, -nal; inner, inside, intimate, inward, intraregarding; in-, inner-most; deep-seated; visceral, intestine, -tinal; inland; subcutaneous; interstitial etc. (*interjacent*) 228; inwrought etc. (*intrinsic*) 5; enclosed etc. *v.*

home, domestic, indoor, intramural, vernacular; endemic.

Adv. internally etc. *adj.*; inwards, within, in, inly; here-, there-, where-in; *ab intra*, withinside; in —, within- doors; at home, in the bosom of one's family.

222. Centrality.—N. centrality, centricalness, center; middle etc. 68; focus etc. 74.

core, kernel; nucleus, nucleolus; heart, pole, axis, pivot, fulcrum, bull's eye; hub, nave, navel; *umbilicus*, spine, backbone, marrow, pith; hot-bed; concentration etc. (*convergence*) 290; centralization; symmetry.

center of -gravity, — pressure, — percussion, — oscillation, — buoyancy etc. metacenter.

V. be -central etc. *adj.*; converge etc. 290.

render central, centralize, concentrate; bring to a focus.

Adj. centr-al, -ical; middle etc. 68; axial, pivotal, focal, umbilical, concentric; middlemost, nuclear, centric, centraidal; spinal, vertebral.

Adv. middle; midst; centrally etc. *adj.*

223. Covering.—N. covering, cover; canopy, tilt, awning, baldachin, tent, marquee, *tente d'abri*, umbrella, parasol, sunshade; veil (*shade*) 424; shield etc. (*defense*) 717; hall.

roof, dome, cupola, mansard roof; ceiling; thatch, tile; pan-, pen-tile; tiling, shingles, slates, slating, leads; shed etc. (*abode*) 189.

top, lid, covercle, door, *operculum*, eyelid, blind, curtain.

bandage, plaster, lint, wrapping, dossil, finger stall.

coverlet, counterpane, sheet, quilt, comforter, eiderdown; tarpaulin, blanket, rug, drugget, linoleum, oilcloth; housing.

in-, tegument; skin, pellicle, fleece, fell, fur, ermine, miniver, sable, sealskin etc.; fabrikoid; leather, morocco, calf, pigskin, elk, kid, cowhide etc.; shagreen, hide; pelt, -ry; cuticle, *dermis*, scarfskin, *epidermis*.

clothing etc. 225; mask etc. (*concealment*) 530.

peel, crust, bark, rind, *cortex*, husk, shell, coat.

capsule; ferrule; sheath, -ing; pod, cod; casing, case, theca; *elytron; involucrum;* wrapp-ing, -er, cellophane; envelope, vesicle; dermatology, conchology.

armor, -plate, armoring; veneer, facing; pavement; scale etc. (*layer*) 204; coating, paint, stain; varnish etc. (*resin*) 356*a*; anointing etc. *v.*; inunction; incrustation, superposition, obduction; ground, enamel, whitewash, plaster, stucco, rough cast, pebble dash, compo; rendering; cerement; ointment etc. (*grease*) 356.

V. cover; super-pose, -impose; over-lay, -spread; wrap etc. 225; incase; face, case, veneer, pave, paper; tip, cap, bind, revet.

coat, paint, varnish, pay, incrust, stucco, cement, dab, plaster, tar; wash; be-, smear; be-, daub; anoint, do over; gild, plate, electroplate, japan, laquer, lacker, enamel, whitewash; lay it on thick.

over-lie, -arch; conceal etc. 528.

Adj. covering etc. *v.*; cutaneous, dermal, cortical, cuticular, tegumentary, skinny, scaly, squamous; covered etc. *v.*; imbricated, loricated, armor-plated, iron-clad; under cover, hooded, cloaked, cowled.

224. Lining.—N. lining, inner coating; coating etc. (*covering*) 223; stalactite, -agmite.

filling, stuffing, wadding, padding, bushing. wainscot, *parietes*, wall brattice.

V. line, stuff, incrust, wad, pad, fill.

Adj. lined etc. *v.*

225. Investment.—N. investment; covering etc. 223; dress, clothing, raiment, drapery, costume, attire, guise, toilet, *toilette,* trim; habiliment; vesture, -ment; garment, garb, palliament, apparel, wardrobe, wearing apparel, clothes, things.

array; tailoring, millinery; best bib and tucker; finery etc. (*ornament*) 847; full dress etc. (*show*) 882; garniture; theatrical properties.

outfit, equipment, *trousseau;* uniform, khaki, regimentals; academicals, canonicals etc. 999; livery, gear, harness, turn out, accoutrement, caparison, suit, rigging, trappings, traps, slops, togs, toggery; masquerade.

dishabille, morning dress, lounge suit, tea-gown, kimono, *négligé*, dressing-gown, *peignoir*, wrapper, undress; shooting-coat; smoking jacket, mufti; rags, tatters, old clothes; mourning, weeds; duds; slippers.

robe, tunic, dolman, *paletot*, habit, gown, coat, coatee, frock, blouse, *pelisse*, middy, sagum, *toga*, smock-frock; frock-, dress-, morning-, tail- coat; dress-suit, – clothes, swallow-tail coat, dinner-, Eton-jacket.

cloak, pall; mantle, mantlet, mantua, shawl, *pelisse*, veil, yashmak; cape, tippet, kirtle, plaid, muffler, comforter, Balaclava helmet, haik, huke, chlamys, mantilla, tabard, housing, horse-cloth, burnous, *roquelaure*, *houppelande*; sur-, top-, over-, great-coat; *surtout*, spencer, cardigan, sweater, blazer; mackintosh, waterproof, slicker, raincoat, oilskin, trench coat, ulster, monkey-, pea-pilot-jacket, redingote; wraprascal, poncho, cardinal, pelerine, talma.

jacket, jumper, vest, jerkin, waistcoat, doublet, *camisole*, gabardine; stays, *corsage*, corset, corselet, bodice; stomacher; skirt, petticoat, slip, farthingale, kilt, jupe, crinoline, bustle, hobble skirt, *panier*, apron, pinafore; loin cloth.

trousers; breeches, trews, pantaloons, un-mentionables, inexpressibles, overalls, pajamas, smalls, small-clothes; tights, pants, shorts, drawers; knickerbockers, knickers, plus fours, bloomers, divided skirt; phil-, fill-ibeg.

head-dress, -gear; cap, *béret*, tam o' shanter, glengarry, topee, sombrero; hat; cocked –, high –, tall –, top –, silk –, opera –, crush - hat, *gibus*, beaver, castor, bonnet, tile, wideawake, billy-cock; bowler; soft felt –, straw –, leghorn- hat, panama; toque; wimple; night-, mob-, skull-cap, biretta; hood, cowl, coif; capote, calach; scull-cap; kerchief, snood; head, *coiffure*; crown etc. (*circle*) 247; *chignon*, pelt, wig, front, peruke; periwig; caftan, turban, fez, *tarboosh*, taj, shako, csako, busby; *képi*, forage cap, bearskin; helmet etc. 717; mask, domino.

body clothes; linen; shirt, sark, smock, shift, *chemise*, *lingerie*; night-gown, -shirt; bed-gown, *sac de nuit*; jersey, guernsey; underclothing, -waistcoat.

neck-erchief, -cloth; tie, ruff, collar, cravat, stock, handkerchief, bandana, scarf; bib, tucker; dicky; boa; girdle etc. (*circle*) 247; cummerbund.

shoe, pump, brogue, boot, slipper, sandal, galoche, galoshes, arctics, rubber boots, overshoes, patten, clog, sabot; high-low; Blucher –, Wellington –, Hessian –, jack –, top- boot; Balmoral; legging, puttee, buskin, greave, galligaskin, moccasin, *gamache*, gambado, gaiter, spatter-dash, spat, antigropeles; stocking, hose, gaskins, trunk-hose, sock, hosiery.

glove, gauntlet, mitten, cuff, muffettee, wristband, sleeve.

swaddling cloth, baby-linen, *layette*; pocket-handkerchief.

shroud, etc. 363.

clothier, tailor, milliner, *costumier*, sempstress, seamstress, snip; dress-, habit-, breeches-, shoemaker; cordwainer, cobbler, Crispin, hosier, hatter; draper, linendraper, haberdasher, mercer.

V. invest; cover etc. 223; envelop, lap, involve; in-, en-wrap; wrap; fold –, wrap –, lap –, muffle-up; overlap; sheathe, swathe, swaddle, roll up in, shroud, circumvest.

vest, clothe, array, dress, dight, drape, robe, enrobe, attire, tire, garb, habilitate, apparel, accouter, rig, fit out; bedizen, deck etc. (*ornament*) 847; perk; equip, harness, caparison; dress up.

wear; don; put –, huddle –, slip- on; mantle.
Adj. invested etc. *v.*; habited; dight, -ed; clad, *costumé*, shod, *chaussé*; *en grande tenue* etc. (*show*) 882.
sartorial.

226. Divestment.—N. divestment; taking off, stripping, removal etc. *v.*
nudity; bareness etc. *adj.*; undress; dishabille etc. 225, altogether; nu-, denu-dation; decortication, depilation, excoriation, desquamation; molting; exfoliation.
baldness, alopecia, acomia.
V. divest; uncover etc. (*cover* etc. 223); denude, bare, strip; undress, unclothe, disrobe etc. (dress, enrobe, etc. 225); uncoif; dismantle; uncase; put –, take –, cast- off; shed, doff; husk, peel, pare, decorticate, desquamate; excoriate, skin, scalp, flay, bark, expose, lay open; exfoliate, molt, mew; cast the skin.
Adj. divested etc. *v.*; bare, naked, nude; undressed, -draped, -clad, -clothed, -appareled; exposed; in dishabille; *décolleté*; bald, threadbare, ragged, callow, roofless.
in -a state of nature, – nature's garb, – buff, – native buff, – birthday suit; *in puris naturalibus*; with nothing on, stark naked; bald as a coot, bare as the back of one's hand; out at elbows; barefoot; bareback; leaf-, nap-, hairless, shaved, clean shaven, tonsured, beardless, bald-headed, acomous.

227. Circumjacence.—N. circumjacence-ambience; environment, encompassment; atmosphere, medium; surroundings, *entourage*.
outpost; border etc. (*edge*) 231; girdle etc. (*circumference*) 230; outskirts, *boulevards*, suburbs, purlieus, precincts, *faubourgs*, environs, *banlieue*, neighborhood, vicinity.
V. lie -around etc. *adv.*; surround, beset, compass, encompass, environ, inclose, enclose, encircle, circle, embrace, circumvent, lap, gird; begird, girdle, engird; skirt, twine round; hem in etc. (*circumscribe*) 229; besiege, invest, blockade.
Adj. circum-jacent, -ambient, -fluent; ambient; surrounding etc. *v.*; circumferential, suburban.
Adv. around, about; without; on -every side, – all sides; right and left, all round, round about; in the neighborhood.

228. Interjacence.—N. inter-jacence, -currence, -venience, -location, -digitation, -penetration; permeation.
inter-jection, -polation, -lineation, -spersion, -calation; embolism.
inter-vention, -ference, -position; in-, ob-trusion; insinuation; insertion etc. 300; dovetailing; infiltration; intromission.
intermedi-um, -ary; go-between, agent, middleman, medium, bodkin, intruder, interloper; parenthesis, episode; fly-leaf.
partition, *septum*, diaphragm, mid-riff; party-wall, panel, vail, bulkhead, brattice, *cloison*; halfway house.
V. lie –, come –, get- between; intervene, slide in, interpenetrate, permeate.

put between, introduce, intromit, import; throw –, wedge –, edge –, jam –, worm –, foist –, run –, plough –, work- in; interpose, -ject, -calate. -polate, -line, -leave, -sperse, -weave, -lard, -digitate; let in, dovetail, splice, mortise; insinuate, smuggle; infiltrate, ingrain.

interfere, put in an oar, thrust one's nose in; intrude, obtrude; have a finger in the pie; introduce the thin end of the wedge; thrust in etc. (*insert*) 300.

Adj. inter-jacent, -current, -venient, -vening etc. *v.*, -mediate, -mediary, -calary, -sitital, -costal, -mural, -planetary, -stellar; embolismal.

parenthetical, episodic; mediterranean; intrusive; embosomed; merged, mean, middle, medium, median.

Adv. between, betwixt; 'twixt; among, -st; amid, st; 'mid, -st; in the thick of; betwixt and between; sandwich-wise; parenthetically, *obiter dictum*.

229. Circumscription.—N. circumscription, limitation, inclosure; confinement etc. (*restraint*) 751; circumvallation, encincture; envelope etc. 232.

V. circumscribe, limit, bound, confine, restrict, enclose; surround etc. 227; compass about; imprision etc. (*restrain*) 751; hedge –, wall –, rail-in; fence –, hedge- round; embar; picket, corral. enfold, bury, incase, pack up, enshrine, inclasp; wrap up etc. (*invest*) 225; embosom.

Adj. circumscribed etc. *v.*; begirt, lapt; circumambient; buried –, immersed- in; embosomed, in the bosom of, imbedded, encysted, mewed up; imprisoned etc. 751; land-locked, in a ring fence.

230. Outline.—N. outline, circumference; perimeter, -phery; ambit, circuit, lines, *tournure*, *contour*, profile, *silhouette*, lineaments; bounds, coastline.

zone, belt, girth, band, baldric, zodiac, girdle, tire, cingle, clasp, girt; *cordon* etc. (*inclosure*) 232; circlet etc. 247.

V. outline, delineate, *silhouette*, circumscribe etc. 229; profile, block out.

Adj. outlined etc. *v.*; circumferential, perimetric, peripheral.

231. Edge.—N. edge, verge, brink, brow, brim. margin, border, confines, skirt, rim, felloe, felly, flange, side, mouth; jaws, chops, chaps, *fauces*; lip, muzzle.

threshold, door, porch; portal etc. (*opening*) 260; coast, shore, strand, beach, bank, wharf, quay, dock.

frame, fringe, flounce, frill, list, trimming, edging, skirting, hem, selvedge, welt; furbelow, valance, exergue.

Adj. border, marginal, skirting; labial; labiated, marginated.

232. Inclosure.—N. inclosure, enclosure, envelope; package, box, crate, case etc. (*receptacle*) 191; wrapper; girdle etc. 230.

pen, fold, croft, sty; pen-, in-, sheep--fold; paddock, pound, corral, kraal; yard, compound; net, seine net.

wall; hedge, -row; *espalier*; fence etc. (*defence*) 717; pale, paling, balustrade, rail, railing, gunwale; quickset hedge, park paling, circumvallation, *enciente*, ring fence.

barrier, barricade; gate; -way; door, hatch, *cordon*; prison etc. 752.

dike, dyke, ditch, fosse, moat, trench.

V. inclose; circumscribe etc. 229.

233. Limit.—N. limit, boundary, bounds, confine, *enclave*, term, bourn, verge, kerb-stone, curbstone, but, pale; termin-ation, -us; stint, frontier, precinct, marches.

boundary line, landmark; line of -demarcation, – circumvallation; pillars of Hercules; Rubicon, turning-point; *ne plus ultra*; sluice, flood-gate.

V. limit, bound, confine, define, circumscribe, demarcate, delimit, encompass.

Adj. definite; contermin-ate, -able, terminable, limitable; terminal, frontier, border, bordering, boundary.

Adv. thus far, – and no further.

234. Front.—N. front; fore, – part; foreground; forefront, face, disk, disc, frontage, *façade*, *proscenium*, facia, frontispiece; priority, anteriority; obverse [of a medal].

fore –, front- rank, first line; van, -guard; advanced guard; outpost, scout.

brow, forehead, visage, physiognomy, phiz, features, countenance, map, mug; rostrum, beak, bow, stem, prow, prore, jib, bowsprit; forecastle. pioneer etc.(*precursor*) 64; metoposcopy.

V. be –, stand- in front etc. *adj.*; front, face, confront, breast, brave; bend forwards; come to the -front, – fore.

Adj. fore, forward, anterior, front, frontal, head-on, leading, first, primary.

Adv. before; in -front, – the van, – advance; ahead, right ahead; fore-, head-most; in the foreground; before one's -face, – eyes; face to face, / *vis-à-vis*.

235. Rear.—N. rear, back, posterior-ity; rear - rank, – guard; background, *hinterland*.

occiput, nape, scruff, chine; heels; tail, rump, croup, buttock, posteriors, bottom, seat, backside, scut, breech, *dorsum*, loin; dorsal –, lumbar-region; hind quarters.

stern poop, after-part, counter; postern, heel-, tail-piece, crupper.

wake; train etc. (*sequence*) 281.

reverse; other side of the shield.

V. be -behind etc. *adv.*; fall astern; bend backwards; bring up the rear; follow etc. 622; tail, shadow.

Adj. back, rear; hind, -er, -most, -ermost; postern, -erior; dorsal, after; caudal, lumbar; mizzen.

Adv. behind; in the -rear, – ruck, – background; behind one's back; at the -heels. — tail. — back- of; back to back.

after. -most. aft. abaft. astern. stern- most. aback. rear-. hind-. back-ward.

236. Laterality.—N. laterality; side, flank, beam, quarter, lee; hand; cheek, jowl, jole, wing; profile; temple, *parietes*, loin, haunch, hip.

gable. -end; broadside; lee side.

points of the compass; East, Orient, Levant; West, occident; orientation.

V. be -on one side etc. *adv.*; flank, outflank; sidle; skirt, border.

Adj. lateral, sidelong; collateral; parietal, flanking, skirting; flanked; sideling.

many-sided; multi-, bi-, tri-, quadri- lateral.

East-ern. -ward. -erly; orient. -al, auroral, Levantine; West-ern. -ward. -erly; occidental, Hesperian; equatorial.

Adv. side-ways. -long; broadside on; on one side, abreast, abeam, alongside, beside, aside; by, — the side of; side by side; cheek by jowl etc. (*near*) 197; to -windward, — leeward; laterally etc. *adj.*; right and left; on her beam ends.

237. Contraposition.—N. contraposition, opposition; polarity; inversion etc. 218; opposite side; antithesis; reverse, inverse; counterpart; antipodes; opposite poles, North and South.

V. be -opposite etc. *adj.*; subtend.

Adj. opposite; reverse, inverse; antipodal. subcontrary; fronting, facing, diametrically opposite.

Northern, Septentrional, Boreal, arctic; Southern, Austral, antarctic, polar.

Adv. over. — the way. — against; against; face to face, vis-à-vis; as poles asunder.

238. Dextrality.—N. dextrality; right, — hand; dexter. offside, starboard.

Adj. dextral, right-handed; ambidextral; dexterous. dextrorsal etc.

239. Sinistrality.—N. sinistrality; left, — hand; *sinister*, nearside, larboard, port.

Adj. sinistral, sinister. sinistrorsal etc., left-handed. sinistromanual, sinistrous.

240. Form.—N. form, figure, shape, physique; con-formation, -figuration; make., formation, frame, construction, design, cut, set, build, trim, cut of one's jib; stamp, type, cast, mold; fashion; contour etc. (*outline*) 230; structure etc. 329.

feature, lineament, outline, turn; phase etc. (*aspect*) 448; posture. attitude. *pose.*

[Science of form] morphology.

[Similarity of form] isomorphism.

forming etc. *v.*; form-, figur-, efform- ation; sculpture.

V. form. shape, figure, fashion, efform, carve, cut, chisel, hew, cast; rough-hew, -cast; sketch; block —. hammer- out; trim; lick —. put- into

shape; model, knead, work up into, set, mold, sculpture; cast, stamp; built etc. (*construct*) 161.

Adj. formed etc. *v.*

[Receiving form] plastic, fictile, full- fashioned etc.

[Giving form] plasmic, etc.

[Similar in form] isomorphous etc.

241. Amorphism. [Absence of form.]—N. amorphism, informity, uncouthness; unlicked cub, rough diamond; *rudis indigestaque moles*; disorder etc. 59; deformity etc. 243.

disfigure-, deface-ment, deformation; mutilation.

V. [Destroy form] deface, disfigure; deform, mutilate, truncate; derange etc. 61.

Adj. shapeless, amorphous, malformed, formless; un-formed, -hewn, -fashioned, -shapen; rough, rude, Gothic, barbarous, rugged, in the rough; misshapen etc. 243.

242. Symmetry. [Regularity of form.]—N. symmetry, shapeliness, finish; beauty etc. 845; proportion, eurythmy, eurythmic, uniformity, parallelism; bi-, tri-, multi-lateral symmetry; centrality etc. 222.

arborescence, branching, ramification.

Adj. symmetrical, shapely, well set, finished; beautiful etc. 845; classic, chaste, severe.

regular, uniform, balanced; equal etc. 27; parallel, coextensive.

arbor-escent, -iform; dendr-iform. -oid; branching; ramous, ramose.

243. Distortion. [Irregularity of form.]—N. dis-, de-, con-tortion; knot, mop, warp, buckle, screw, twist; crookedness etc. (*obliquity*) 217; grimmace; deformity; mal-, malcon-formation; monstrosity, misproportion, want of symmetry, *anamorphosis*; ugliness etc. 846; teratology.

V. distort, contort, twist, warp etc. *n.*; wrest, writhe, make faces, deform, misshape.

Adj. distorted etc. *v.*; out of shape, irregular, unsymmetric, awry, wry, askew, crooked, sinuous; anamorphous; not -true, — straight; on one side, crump, deformed -mis-shapen, -begotten; mis-, ill-proportioned; ill-made; grotesque, crooked as a ram's horn; hump-, hunch-, bunch-, crook-backed; bandy; bandy-, bow-legged; bow-, knock-kneed; splay-, club-footed; taliped; round-shouldered; snub-nosed; curtailed of one's fair proportions; scalene, stumpy etc. (*short*) 201; gaunt etc. (*thin*) 203; bloated etc. 194..

Adv. all manner of ways.

244. Angularity.—N. angular-ity. -ness; aduncity; angle, cusp, bend; fold etc. 258; notch etc. 257; fork, bifurcation.

elbow, knee, knuckle, ankle,. groin, crotch, crane, fluke, scythe, sickle, zigzag, kimbo.

corner, nook, recess, niche, oriel.

right angle etc. (*perpendicular*) 212; obliquity etc. 217; angle of 45 degrees, miter; acute —, obtuse —, salient —, re-entrant —, spherical — solid —, dihedral- angle.

angular -measurement, – elevation, – distance, – velocity; trigon-, goni-ometry; altimetry; clin-, graph-, goni-ometer; theodolite; transit circle; sextant, quadrant; dichotomy.

triangle, trigon, wedge; rectangle, square, lozenge, diamond; rhomb, -us; quadr-angle, -ilateral; parallelogram; quadrature; poly-, penta-, hexa-, hepta-, octa-, deca-gon.

Platonic bodies; cube, rhomboid; tetra-, penta-, hexa-, octa-, dodeca-, icosa-hedron; prism, pyramid; parallelopiped.

V. bend, fork, bifurcate, crinkle, divaricate, branch, ramify.

Adj. angular, bent, crooked, aduncous, uncinated, aquiline, jagged, serrated; falc-iform, -ated; furcular, furcated, forked, bifurcate, crotched; zigzag; dovetailed; knock-kneed, crinkled, akimbo, kimbo, geniculated; oblique etc. 217.

fusiform, wedge-shaped, cuneiform; tri-angular, -gonal, -lateral; quadr-angular, -ilateral; rectangular, square, foursquare, multilateral; polygonal etc. *n.*; cubical, rhomboidal, pyramidal.

245. Curvature.—N. curv-ature, -ity, -ation; incurv-ity, -ation; bend; flex- ure, -ion; conflexure; crook, hook, bought, bending; de-, inflexion; arcuation, devexity, turn; deviation, *détour*, sweep; curl, -ing; bough; recurv-ity, -ation; sinuosity etc. 248; aduncity.

curve, arc, arch, arcade, vault, dome, bow, crescent, *meniscus*, half-moon, lunule, horse-shoe, loop, crane-neck; para-, hyper-bola; catenary, festoon; conch-, cardi-oid; caustic, instep; tracery.

V. be -curved etc. *adj.*; sweep, swag, sag; deviate etc. 279; turn; re-enter.

render -curved etc. *adj.*; bend, curve, incurvate; de-, in-flect; crook; turn, round, arch, arcuate, arch over, loop the loop, concamerate; bow, coil, curl, recurve, frizzle.

Adj. curved etc. *v.*; curvi-form, -lineal, -linear, devex, devious; recurv-ed, -ous; *retroussé*; crump; bowed etc. *v.*; vaulted; hooked; falc-iform, -ated; semicircular, crescentic; lun-iform, -ular; semilunar, meniscal; conchoidal; cord-iform, -ated; cardioid; heart-, bell-, pear-, fig-shaped; reniform; lenti-form, -cular; bow-legged etc. (*distorted*) 243; oblique etc. 217; circular etc. 247.

246. Straightness.—N. straightness, rectilinearity, directness; inflexibility etc. (*stiffness*) 323; straight –, right –, direct-, bee- line; short cut.

V. be -straight etc. *adj*; have no turning; not -incline, – bend, – turn, – deviate- to either side; go straight; steer for etc. (*direction*) 278.

render straight, straighten, rectify; set –, put-straight; un-bend, -fold, -curl etc. 248, -ravel etc. 219, -wrap.

Adj. straight; rectiline-ar, -al; direct, even, right, true, in a line; unbent etc. *v.*; un-deviating, -turned, -distorted, -swerving; straight as an arrow etc. (*direct*) 278; inflexible etc. 323.

247. Circularity. [Simple circularity.]—N. circularity, roundness; rotundity etc. 249.

circle, circlet, ring, washer, areola, hoop, round-let, *annulus*, annulet, bracelet, armlet, armilla; ringlet; eye, loop, wheel; cycle, orb, orbit, rundle, zone, belt, *cordon*, band; sash, girdle, cestus, cincture, baldric, fillet, *fascia*, wreath, garland; crown, corona, coronet, chaplet, snood, necklace, collar; noose, lasso, lariat.

ellipse, oval, ovule; ellipsoid, cycloid; epicycloid, -cycle; semi-circle; quadrant, sextant, sector.

V. make -round etc. *adj.*; round. go round; encircle etc. 227; describe -a circle etc. 311.

Adj. round, rounded, circular, annular, orbicular; oval, ovate; elliptic, -al; ovoid, egg-shaped; pear-shaped etc. 245; cycloidal etc. *n.*; spherical etc. 249.

248. Convolution. [Complex circularity.]—N. winding etc. *v.*; con-, in-, circum-volution; wave, undulation, tortuosity, anfractuosity; sinu-osity, -ation, sinuousness; meandering, circuit, circumbendibus, twist, twirl, windings and turnings, *ambages*; torsion; inosculation; reticulation etc. (*crossing*) 219.

coil, roll; curl, buckle, spire, spiral, helix, corkscrew, worm, volute, whorl, rundle; tendril; scollop, scallop, escalop; kink.

serpent, snake, eel, maze, labyrinth.

V. be -convoluted etc. *adj.*; wind, twine, turn and twist, twirl; wave, undulate, meander; inosculate; entwine, intwine; twist, coil, roll; wrinkle, curl, crisp, twill; frizz, -le; crimp, crape, indent, scollop, scallop; wring, intort; contort; wreathe etc. (*cross*) 219.

Adj. convoluted; winding, twisted etc. *v.*; tortile, tortive; wavy; und-ated, -ulatory; circling, snaky, snake-like, serpentine; serpent-, anguill-, vermiform; vermicular; mazy, tortuous, anfractuous, sinuous, flexuous, wavy, sigmoidal.

involved, intricate, complicated, perplexed; labyrinth-ic, -ian, -ine; circuitous; peristaltic; daedalian, curly.

wreathy, frizzly, *crêpé*, buckled; ravelled etc. (*in disorder*) 59.

spiral, coiled, helical, turbinated.

Adv. in and out, round and round.

249. Rotundity.—N. rotundity; roundness etc. *adj.*; cyclindricity; spher-icity, -oidity; globosity.

cylin-der, -droid; barrel, drum; roll, -er; *rouleau*, column, rolling-pin, rundle; chimney-pot, drain-pipe.

cone, conoid; pear-, egg-, ball-shape.

sphere, globe, orb, orbit, ball, boulder, bowlder; spher-, ellips-, ge-, glob-oid, oblong –, oblate-spheroid; drop, spherule, globule, vesicle, bulb, bullet, pellet, *pelote*, clew, pill, marble, pea, knob, pommel, knot.

V. render -spherical etc. *adj.*; form into a sphere, sphere, roll into a ball; give -rotundity etc. *n.*; round.

Adj. rotund; round etc. (*circular*) 247; cylindric, ical; oid; columnar, lumbriciform; conic, -al; spher-ical, -oidal; glob-ular, -ated, -ous, -ose; egg-, bell-, pear-shaped; ov-oid, -iform; gibbous; campaniform, -ulate, -iliform; fungiform, bead-like, moniliform, pyriform, bulbous; *teres atque rotundus*; round as -an orange, — an apple, — a ball, — a billiard ball, — a cannon ball.

250. Convexity.—N. convexity, prominence, projection, swelling, gibbosity, bilge, bulge, protuberance, protrusion; excrescency, camber.

intumescence; tumor; tubercle, -osity; excrescence; hump, hunch, bunch, gnarl.

tooth, knob, elbow, process, *apophysis*, condyle, bulb, node, nodule, nodosity, tongue, *dorsum*, boss, embossment, bump, clump; sugar-loaf etc. (*sharpness*) 253; bow; mamelon.

pimple, wen, wheal, *papula*, postule, pock, proud flesh, growth, goiter, *sarcoma*, caruncle, corn, bunion, wart, furnuncle, polypus, adenoid, fungus, fungosity, *exostosis*, bleb, blister, blain; boil etc. (*disease*) 655; bubble, blob.

papilla, nipple, teat, pap, breast, dug, mammilla; proboscis, .ose, neb, beak, snout, nozzle, snozzle; Adam's apple; belly, paunch, corporation; withers, back, shoulder, lip, flange.

peg, button, stud, ridge, rib, jutty, trunnion, snag.

cupola, dome, bee-hive; arch, balcony, eaves; pilaster.

relief, relievo, *cameo*; *basso-*, *mezzo-*, *altorilievo*; low-, bas-, high-relief.

hill etc. (*height*) 206; cape, promontory, mull; fore-, head-land; point of land, naze, ness, mole, jetty, hummock, ledge, spur.

V. be -prominent etc. *adj.*; project, bulge, protrude, bag, belly, pout, bouge, bunch; jut —, stand —, stick —, poke- out; stick —, bristle —, start —, cock —, shoot- up; swell —, hang —, bend-over; beetle.

render -prominent etc. *adj.*; raise 307; emboss, chase.

Adj. convex, prominent, protuberant, underhung, undershot; projecting etc. *v.*; bossed, bossy, nodular, bunchy; clav-ate, -ated; hummocky, *moutonné*, mammiform; papul-ous, -ose; hemispheric, bulbous; bowed, arched; bold; bellied; tuber-ous, -culous; tumorous; cornute, knobby, odontoid; lenti-form, -cular; gibbous.

salient, in relief, raised, *repoussé*; bloated etc. (*expanded*) 194.

251. Flatness.—N. flatness etc. *adj.*; smoothness etc. 255.

plane; level etc. 213; plate, platter, table, tablet, slab.

V. render flat, flatten, squash; level etc. 213.

Adj. flat, plane, even, flush, scutiform, discoid; level etc. (*horizontal*) 213; smooth; flat as -a pancake, — a fluke, — a flounder, — a board, — my hand.

252. Concavity.—N. concavity, depression, dip; hollow, -ness; indentation, *intaglio*, cavity, antrum, dent, dint, dimple, follicle, pit, *sinus*, *alveolus*, *lacuna*; excavation, trench, shaft, sap, mine, tunnel, burrow; trough etc. (*furrow*) 259; honeycomb.

cup, basin, crater, punch-bowl; cell etc. (*receptacle*) 191; socket, faucet.

valley, vale, dale, dell, gap, dingle, combe, bottom, slade, strath, glade, grove, glen, cave, cavern, cove; grot, -to; alcove, *cul-de-sac*, blind alley; gully etc. 198; arch etc. (*curve*) 245; bay etc. (*of the sea*) 343.

excavator, sapper, miner.

V. be -concave etc. *adj.*; retire, cave in.

render -concave etc. *adj.*; depress, hollow; scoop, — out; gouge, dig, delve, excavate, dent, dint, mine, sap, undermine, burrow, tunnel, stave in.

Adj. depressed etc. *v.*; concave, hollow, stove in; dished; spoon-like; retiring; retreating; cavernous; porous etc. (*with holes*) 260; cellular, spongy, spongious; honeycombed, alveolar; infundibul-ar, -iform; funnel-, bell-shaped; campaniform, capsular; vaulted, arched.

253. Sharpness.—N. sharpness etc. *adj.*; acuity, acumination; spinosity.

point, spike, spine, *spiculum*, tine; needle, pin; tack, nail; prick, -le; spur, rowel, barb; spit, cusp; horn, antler; snag; tag; thorn, bristle.

nib, tooth, incisor, tusk; spoke, cog, ratchet.

crag, crest *arête*, cone, peak, sugar-loaf, pike, *aiguille*; spire, pyramid, steeple.

beard, *chevaux de frise*, porcupine, hedgehog, brier, bramble, thistle; comb, awn, bur.

wedge; knife-, cutting- edge; blade, edge-tool, cutlery, knife, penknife, whittle, razor; scalpel, bistoury, lancet; chisel; ploughshare, coulter; hatchet, axe, pick-axe, mattock, pick, adze, bill; billhook, cleaver, cutter; skiver; scythe, sickle, scissors, shears; sword etc. (*arms*) 727; bodkin etc. (*perforator*) 262.

sharpener, hone, strop; grind-, whet-stone, steel, emery.

V. be -sharp etc. *adj.*; taper to a point; bristle with.

render -sharp etc. *adj.*; sharpen, point, aculeate, acuminate, whet, barb, spiculate, set, strop, grind. cut etc. (*sunder*) 44.

Adj. sharp, keen; acute; aci-cular, -form; aculeated, -minated; pointed; tapering; conical, pyramidal; mucron-ate, -ated; spindle-, needleshaped; spiked, spiky, ensiform, peaked, salient, cusp-ed; -idate, -idated; corn-ute, -uted, -iculate; prickly; spiny, spinous; thorny, bristling, muricated, pectinated, studded, thistly, briery, craggy etc. (*rough*) 256; snaggy; digitated, twoedged, fusiform; denti-form, -culated; toothed; odontoid; star-like; stell-ated, -iform; arrowheaded; arrowy, barbed, spurred, sagittal; spearshaped, hastate; horned; conical.

cutting; sharp-, knife-edged; sharp —, keenas a razor; sharp as a needle; sharpened etc. *v.*; set.

254. Bluntness.—N. bluntness etc. *adj.*; abruptness, dullness.

V. be —, render- blunt etc. *adj.*; obtund, dull; take off the -point, — edge; turn.

Adj. blunt, obtuse, dull, bluff.

255. Smoothness.—N. smoothness etc. *adj.*; polish, gloss; lubric-ity, -ation.

down, velvet, silk, satin; slide; bowling green
etc. (level) 213; glass, ice; asphalt, pavement, flags.
  roller, steam-roller; iron, flat-iron, tailor's
goose; sand-, emery-paper; burnisher, turpentine
and bees-wax.
  V. smooth, -en; plane; file; mow, shave; level,
roll; macadamize; polish, burnish, planish,
levigate, calender, glaze; iron, hot-press, mangle;
lubricate etc. (oil) 332.
  Adj. smooth; polished etc. v.; even; level etc.
213; plane etc. (flat) 251; sleek, glossy; silken,
silky; lanate, downy, velvety; glabrous, slippery,
glassy, lubricous, oily, soft; unwrinkled; smooth as
-glass, – ice, – velvet, – oil; slippery as an eel;
wooly etc. (feathery) 256.

256. Roughness.—N. roughness etc. adj.;
tooth, grain, texture, ripple; asperity, rugosity,
salebrosity, corrugation, nodosity; arborescence
etc. 242.
  brush, hair, beard, shag, mane, whisker, mutton-
chops, moustache, mustachio, imperial, Van
Dyke, tress, lock, curl, ringlet, fimbriae, cilia,
villi; eye-lashes, eye-brows, love-lock.
  plum-age, -osity; plume, panache, crest; feather,
tuft, tussock, fringe, toupee.
  wool, velvet, plush, nap, pile, floss, fluff, fur,
down; byssus, moss, bur.
  V. be -rough etc. adj.; go against the grain.
  render -rough etc. adj.; roughen, rough cast,
knurl; ruffle, crisp, crumple, crinkle, corrugate,
engrail; set on edge, stroke –, rub- the wrong way,
rumple.
  Adj. rough, uneven; scabrous, knotted; nodular;
rug-ged, -ose, -ous; asperous, crisp, salebrous,
gnarled, unpolished, unsmooth, rough-hewn;
knurled, cross-grained, crag-gy, -ged; crankling,
scraggy, jagged, unkempt, prickly etc. (sharp) 253;
arborescent etc. 242; leafy, well-wooded; feathery;
plum-ose, -igerous; tufted, fimbriated, hairy,
bristly, ciliated, filamentous, hirsute; crin-ose, -ite;
bushy, hispid, villous, pappous, bearded, pilous,
shaggy, shagged; fringed, befringed; set-ous, -ose, -
aceous; 'like quills upon the fretful porcupine;'
rough as a -nutmeg grater, – bear.
  downy, velvety, flocculent, wolly; lan-ate, -ated;
lanugin-ous, ose; tomentous.
  Adv. against the grain, in the rough, on edge.

257. Notch.—N. notch, dent, nick, cut; indent,
-ation; serration; dimple.
  embrasure, battlement, machicolation; saw,
tooth, crenelle, scallop, scollop, vandyke.
  V. notch, nick, cut, pink, mill, score, dent, indent, jag, scarify, scotch, crimp, scollop, crenulate,
vandyke.
  Adj. notched etc. v.; crenate, -d; dentate, -d;
denticulate, -d; toothed, palmated, serrated.

258. Fold.—N. fold, plicature, pleat, plait, ply,
crease; tuck, gather; flexion, flexure, joint, elbow,
doubling, duplicature, wrinkle, rimple, crinkle,
crankle, crumple, rumple, rivel, ruck, ruffle, dog's
ear, corrugation, frounce, flounce, lapel; pucker,
crow's feet.

  V. fold, double, plicate, pleat, plait, crease,
wrinkle, crinkle, crankle, curl, smock, cockle up,
crocker, rimple, rumple, frizzle, frounce, rivel,
twill, corrugate, ruffle, crimple, crumple, pucker;
turn –, double- -down, – under; tuck, ruck, hem,
gather.
  Adj. folded etc. v.

259. Furrow.—N. furrow, groove, rut, sulcus,
scratch, streak, striae, crack, score, incision, slit;
chamfer, fluting.
  channel, gutter, trench, ditch, dike, dyke, moat,
fosse, trough, kennel; ravine etc. (interval) 198.
  V. furrow etc. n.; flute, groove,carve, corrugate,
plough; incise, chase, enchase, grave, engrave, etch,
bite in, cross-hatch.
  Adj. furrowed etc. v.; ribbed, straited, sulcated,
fluted, canaliculated; biscule-ous, -ate; trisulcate;
corduroy.

260. Opening.—N. hole, foramen; puncture,
blow-out, perforation; pin-, key-, loop-, port-,
peep-, mouse-, pigeon-hole; eye, – of a needle;
eyelet; slot.
  opening; apert-ure, -ness; hiation, yawning,
oscitancy, dehiscence, patefaction, pandiculation;
gap, chasm etc. (interval) 198.
  embrasure, window, casement, light; sky-, fan-
light; lattice; bay-, bow-window; oriel; dormer,
lantern.
  out-, in-let; vent, vomitory; embouchure; orifice,
mouth, sucker, muzzle, throat, gullet, placket,
weasand, wizen, nozzle, esophagus.
  portal, porch, gate, ostiary, postern, wicket, trap-
door, hatch, door; arcade; gate-, door-, hatch-,
gang-way; lych-gate.
  way, path etc. 627; thoroughfare; channel,
passage, tube, pipe; waterpipe etc. 350; air-pipe etc.
351; vessel, tubule, canal, gut, fistula; adjutage,
ajutage; chimney, smoke stack, flue, tap, funnel,
gully, tunnel, main; mine, pit, adit, shaft; gallery,
alley, aisle, glade, lane, vista.
  bore, caliber; pore; blind orifice.
  por-ousness, -osity; sieve, cullender, colander;
grater, shredder; cribble, riddle, screen;
honeycomb.
  apertion, perforation; piercing etc. v.;
terebration, empalement, pertusion, puncture,
acupuncture, penetration.
  opener, corkscrew, can opener, key, master-key,
passe-partout.
  V. open, ope, gape, dehisce, yawn, bilge; fly
open.
  perforate, pierce, empierce, tap, bore, drill; mine
etc. (scoop out) 252; tunnel; trans-pierce, -fix; enfilade, impale, spike, spear, gore, spit, stab, pink,
puncture, lance, trepan, trephine, stick, prick, riddle, punch; stave in.
  cut a passage through; make -way, – room- for.
  un-cover, -close, -rip; lay –, cut –, rip –, throw-
open.
  Adj. open; perforated etc. v.; perforate; wide
open, agape, ajar; un-closed, -stopped; oscitant,
gaping, yawning; patent.
  tubular, cannular, fistulous; per-vious, -meable;
foraminous; vesi-, vas-cular; porous, follicular.

cribriform, honeycombed, infundibular, riddled; tubul-ous, -ated, piped.

opening etc. *v.*; aperient.

Int. *open sesame!*

---

261. Closure.—N. closure, occlusion, blockade; shutting up etc. *v.*; obstruction etc. (*hindrance*) 706; gag; embolism; contraction etc. 195; infarction; con-, ob-stipation; blind -alley, — corner; *cul-de-sac*, *caecum*; imperforation, -viousness etc. *adj.*; -meability; stopper etc. 263; *operculum*.

V. close, occlude, plug; block —, stop —, fill —, bung —, cork —, button —, stuff —, shut —, damup, obturate; blockade; obstruct etc. (*hinder*) 706; bar, bolt, stop, seal, plumb; choke, throttle; ram down, tamp, dam, cram; trap, clinch; put to —, shut- the door; batten down the hatches.

Adj. closed etc. *v.*; shut, operculated; unopened.

unpierced, imporous, caecal; imperforate, - vious, -meable; impenetrable; un-, im-passable; invious; path-, way-less; untrodden.

unventilated; air-, water-tight; hermetically sealed; tight, snug.

---

262. Perforator.—N. perforator, piercer, borer, auger, gimlet, stylet, drill, wimble, awl, bradawl, scoop, terrier, corkscrew, dibble, trocar, trepan, trephine, probe, bodkin, needle, stiletto, broach, reamer, rimer, warder, lancet; punch, - eon; spikebit, gouge; spear etc. (*weapon*) 727.

---

263. Stopper.—N. stopper, stopple; plug, cork, bung, spike, spill, stop-cock, tap; rammer; ram, -rod; piston; stopgap; wadding, stuffing, padding, stopping, dossil, pledget, tompion, tourniquet, obturator; wad.

cover etc. 223; valve, slide valve; vent-peg, spigot.

janitor, door —, gate- keeper, porter, commissionaire, *concierge*, warder, beadle, Cerberus, usher, guard, sentry, sentinel; ostiary.

---

264. Motion. [Successive change of place. *] —N. motion, movement, move; motivity, motility, going etc. *v.*; unrest.

stream, current, flow, flux, run, course, stir; conduction, evolution; kinematics.

step, rate, pace, tread, stride, gait, clip, port, footfall, cadence, carriage, velocity, angular velocity; progress, locomotion; journey etc. 266; voyage etc. 267; transit etc. 270.

restlessness etc. (*changeableness*) 149; mobility; movableness, motive power; laws of motion; mobilization.

V. be -in motion etc. *adj.*; move, go, hie, gang, budge, stir, pass, flit; bowl round, — about; shift, slide, slither, glide; roll, — on; flow, stream, run, drift, sweep along; wander etc. (*deviate*) 279; walk etc. 266; change — , shift- one's -place, — quarters; dodge; keep -going, — moving.

put —, set- in motion; move; impel etc. 276; propel etc. 284; render movable, mobilize.

Adj. moving etc. *v.*; in motion; motile, transitional; motory, motive; shifting, movable, mobile, mercurial, unquiet; restless etc. (*changeable*) 149; nomadic etc. 266; erratic etc. 279.

Adv. under way; on the -move, — wing, — tramp, — march.

*A thing cannot be said to *move* from one place to another, unless it passes in succession through every intermediate place; hence motion is only such a change of place as is *successive*. 'Rapid, swift, etc., as thought' are therefore incorrect expressions.

---

265. Quiescence.—N. rest; stillness etc. *adj.*; quiescence; stag-nation, -nancy; fixity, immobility, catalepsy; indisturbance; quietism.

quiet, tranquillity, calm; repose etc. 687; peace; dead calm, anticyclone; statue-like repose; silence etc. 403; not a -breath of air, — mouse stirring; sleep etc. (*inactivity*) 683.

pause, lull etc. (*cessation*) 142; stand, — still; standing still etc. *v.*; lock; dead -lock, — stop, — stand; full stop; fix; embargo.

resting-place; bivouac; home etc. (*abode*) 189; pillow etc. (*support*) 215; haven etc. (*refuge*) 666; goal etc. (*arrival*) 292.

V. be -quiescent etc. *adj.*; stand — lie- still; keep quiet, repose, hold the breath.

remain, stay; stand, lie to, ride at anchor, remain *in situ*, mark time, tarry; bring —, heave —, lay- to; pull —, draw- up; hold, halt; stop, — short; rest, pause, anchor; cast —, come to an- anchor; rest on one's oars; repose on one's laurels, take breath; stop etc. (*discontinue*) 142.

stagnate, vegetate; *quieta non movere*; let - alone, — well alone; abide, rest and be thankful; keep within doors, stay at home, go to bed.

dwell etc. (*be present*) 186; settle etc. (*be located*) 184; alight etc. (*arrive*) 292.

stick, — fast; stand, — like a post; not stir a -peg, — step; be at a -stand etc. *n.*

quell, becalm, hush, stay, lull to sleep, lay an embargo on; put the brake on.

Adj. quiescent, still; motion-, move-less; fixed; stationary; at -rest, — a stand, — a stand-still, — anchor; stock-still; immotile; standing still etc. *v.*; sedentary, untravelled, stay-at-home; becalmed, stagnant, quiet; un-moved, -disturbed, -ruffled; calm, restful; cataleptic; immovable etc. (*stable*) 150; sleeping etc. (*inactive*) 683; silent etc. 403; still as a -statue; — a post, — a mouse, — death.

Adv. at a stand etc. *adj.*; *tout court*; at the halt.

Int. stop! stay! avast! halt! hold, — hard! whoa!

Phr. *requiescat in pace.*

---

266. Journey. [Locomotion by land.] —N. travel; traveling etc. *v.*; wayfaring, campaigning.

journey, excursion, expedition, tour, trip, grand tour, circuit, peregrination, discursion, ramble, pilgrimage, *trek*, course, ambulation, march, walk, hike, promenade, constitutional, stroll, saunter, tramp, jog-trot, turn, stalk, perambulation; noctambulation; somnambulism, sleep walking; outing, ride, drive, airing, jaunt.

equitation, horsemanship, riding, *manège*, ride and tie.

roving, vagrancy, pererration; marching and countermarching; nomadism; vagabond-ism, -age; gadding; flit, -ting; migration; e-, im-, de-, intermigration.

plan, itinerary, guide; hand-, road- book; Baedeker, Murray, Bradshaw, time table.

procession, parade, cavalcade, caravan, file, *cortège*, column.

[Organs and instruments of locomotion] vehicle etc. 272; locomotive etc. 271; legs, feet, pegs, pins, trotters.

traveler etc. 268.

V. travel, journey, course; tour; take —, go- a journey, take —, go out for- -a walk etc. *n.*; have a run; take the air.

flit, take wing; migrate, emigrate, *trek*; rove, prowl, roam, range, patrol, pace up and down, traverse; scour —, traverse- the country; peragrate; per-, circum-ambulate; nomadize, wander, ramble, stroll, saunter, hover, go one's rounds, straggle; gad; — about; expatiate.

walk, march, step, tread, pace, plod, wend; promenade; trudge, tramp; stalk, stride, straddle, strut, foot it, stump, bundle, bowl along, toddle; paddle; tread —, follow —, pursue- a path.

take horse, ride, drive, trot, amble, canter, prance, fisk, frisk, *caracoler*; gallop etc. (*move quickly*) 274; motor, cycle, taxi; go by -car, — train, — tram, — bus, — plane.

peg —, jog —, wag —, shuffle- on; stir one's stumps; bend one's -steps, — course; make —, find —, wend —, pick —, thread —, plough- one's way; coast, slide, glide, skim, skate, ski; march in procession, file off, defile.

go —, repair —, resort —, hie —, betake oneself-to.

Adj. traveling etc. *v.*; ambulatory, itinerant, peripatetic, perambulatory, roving, rambling, gadding, discursive, vagrant, migratory, nomadic; circumforane-an, -ous; somnambular, nocti-, mundivagant; locomotive, automotive, self-moving.

way-faring, -worn; travel-stained.

Adv. on -foot, — horseback, — Shanks's mare; by the Marrowbone stage; *in transitu* etc. 270; *en route* etc. 282.

Int. come along!

267. Navigation. [Locomotion by water, or air.]—**N.** navigation; aquatics; boating, cruising, yachting; ship etc. 273; oar, scull, sweep, punt pole, paddle, — wheel, screw, propeller, stern wheel, sail, canvas.

natation, swimming; fin, flipper, fish's tail.

aeronautics, aviation, flying, winging, cruising, gliding, ballooning; blind —, instrument — flying; avigation, take-off.

flight, trip, run; solo —, nolo (pilotless) —, supersonic —, test — flight; air -lift, -drop; shuttle, reconnaisence, mission, dry run (coll.), search mission, combat flight, sortie, air raid, bombing mission; air — support, — cover, — umbrella; formation flying, maneuvers, aerobatics, stunt flying (coll.), diving, rolling, barrel roll, spin, tail spin, loop, buzzing.

landing, instrument —, crash — landing.

angle, center, axis, stability, load, pressure, torsion, torque, thrust, propulsion, jet propulsion, pitch, lift, dray, yaw, resistance, drift, flow, wash.

course, heading, altitude; air -route, -lane.

voyage, sail, cruise, passage, circumnavigation, *periplus*; head-, stern-, lee-way.

astro-, cosmo- nautics; space —, interplanetary — travel; space — exploration, — flight.

mariner, aeronaut etc. 269.

V. sail; put to sea etc. (*depart*) 293; take ship, get under way; spread -sail, — canvas; gather way, have way on; make —, carry- sail; plough the - waves, — deep, — main, — ocean; walk the waters.

navigate, warp, luff, scud, boom, kedge; drift, course, cruise, coast; hug the -shore, — land; circumnavigate.

ply the oar, row, paddle, pull, scull, punt, steam.

swim, float; buffet the waves, ride the storm, skim, *effleurer*, dive, wade.

fly, pilot, copilot, astronavigate, solo, take off, taxi, ascend, climb, stunt, spin, loop, roll, dive, buzz, land, descend, level off, bail out, parachute.

Adj. sailing etc. *v.*; seafaring, nautical, maritime, naval; sea-going, coasting; afloat; navigable, aquatic, natatory.

volitant, volant, aerostatic, aerial, aeronautic; alar, alate, pennate.

Adv. under -way, — sail, — canvas, — steam; on the wing.

268. Traveler.—N. traveler, wayfarer, voyager, itinerant, passenger.

tourist, excursionist, globe-trotter; explorer, adventurer, mountaineer, Alpine Club; peregrinator, wanderer, rover, straggler, rambler; bird of passage; gad-about, -ling; vagrant, scatterling, landloper, waifs and estrays, wastrel, stray; loafer; tramp, -er, hobo, beachcomber, vagabond, nomad, Bohemian, gipsy, Arab, Wandering Jew, Hadji, pilgrim, palmer; peripatetic; somnambulist; sleep walker, noctambulist; emigrant, fugitive, refugee, *émigré*.

runner, courier, King's messenger; Mercury, Iris, Ariel, comet.

pedestrian, walker, foot-passenger; cyclist; wheelman.

rider, horseman, equestrian, cavalier, jockey, rough rider, trainer, breaker, huntsman.

driver, coachman, whip, Jehu, charioteer, postilion, post-boy, carter, wagoner, drayman, truckman; cab-man, -driver; *voiturier*, *vetturino*, *condottiere*; engine-driver; stoker, fireman, guard, brakeman, conductor; chauffeur, automobilist, motorist, motor —, truck —, taxi- driver.

269. Mariner.—N. sailor, mariner, navigator, argonaut; sea-man, -farer, -faring man; yachtsman; tar, jack tar, salt, gob, sea-dog, shellback, able seaman, A.B.; man-of-war's man, bluejacket, marine, jolly; midshipman, middy, reefer; captain, commander, master mariner, skipper, mate; ship-, boat-, ferry-, water-, lighter-, barge-, longshore-man, hoveller; bargee, gondolier; oar-, -sman; rower; boat-, cock-swain; coxswain; steersman, helmsman, pilot; crew; lascar.

aerial navigator, navigator; aero-, astro-, cosmonaut; balloonist, Icarus, aviator, pilot, flyer, copilot, spaceman; fighter —, bomber — pilot; bombardier, gunner; meteorologist; stewardess, aviatrix, aviatress; ground crew, aeromechanic, aeronautical engineer; parachutist, paratrooper.

270. Transference.—**N.** transfer; -ence; trans-, e-location; displacement; *meta-stasis*, *-thesis*; removal; re-, a-motion; relegation; de-, asportation; extradition, conveyance, draft; carrying, carriage; convection, -duction, -tagion, infection; transfusion; transfer etc. (*of property*) 783.

transit, transition; passage, ferry, gestation; portage, porterage, carting, cartage; shoveling etc. *v.*; vect-ion, -ure, -itation; shipment, freight, wafture; trans-mission, -port, -portation, -umption, -plantation, -lation; shift-, dodg-ing; dispersion etc. 73; transposition etc. (*interchange*) 148; traction etc. 285.

[Thing transferred] drift, alluvium, detritus, *moraine*; gift, legacy, bequest, lease; freight, mails, cargo, luggage, baggage, goods.

V. trans-fer, -mit, -port, -place, -plant; convey, assign, carry, bear, fetch and carry; carry —, ferry-over; hand, pass, forward; shift; conduct, convoy, bring, fetch, reach.

send, delegate, consign, mail post, relegate, turn over to, pass the buck, deliver; ship, embark; waft; switch, shunt; transpose etc. (*interchange*) 148; displace etc. 185; throw etc. 284; drag etc. 285.

shovel, lade, dip, ladle, bale, decant, draft off, transfuse.

Adj. transferred etc. *v.*; drifted; movable, portable, -ative; conductive; contagious, infectious.

transferable, assignable, conveyable, devisable, negotiable, transmissible.

Adv. from -hand to hand, — pillar to post. on —, by- the way; on the -road, — wing; as one goes; *in transitu, en route, chemin faisant, en passant*, in mid-progress.

271. Carrier.—**N.** carrier, porter, red cap, bearer, messenger, postman, tranter, conveyer; stevedore; coolie; conductor, locomotive, tractor, caterpillar tractor, motor.

beast of burden, cattle, horse steed, nag, palfrey, Arab, blood horse, thorough-bred, galloway, charger, courser, racer, hunter, jument, pony, filly, colt, foal, barb, roan, jade, hack, *bidet*, pad, cob, tit, punch, roadster, goer; race-, pack-, draft-, cart-, dray-, post-horse, mount; Shetland pony, sheltie; garran; jennet, genet, bayard, mare, stallion, gelding; stud.

Pegasus, Bucephalus, Rozinante.

ass, donkey, jackass, mule, hinny; sumpter-horse, — mule; reindeer; camel, dromedary, mehari, llama, elephant; carrier pigeon.

carriage etc. (*vehicle*) 272; ship etc. 273.

Adj. equine, asinine.

272. Vehicle.—**N.** vehicle, conveyance, carriage, car, caravan, van, furniture van, pantechnicon; wagon, wain, dray, cart, lorry.

carriole; sledge, sled, sleigh, bob-sleigh, toboggan, *luge*, truck, tram; limber, tumbrel, pontoon; barrow; wheel-, hand- -barrow, — cart, trolley; perambulator; Bath —, wheel —, sedan-chair, jinriksha, rickshaw; ekka; chaise; palankeen, -quin; litter, horse-litter, brancard, crate, hurdle, stretcher, ambulance; velocipede, hobbyhorse, coaster, scooter, go-cart; cycle; bi-, tri-, quadri-cycle; tandem, safety; skate, roller —, ice — skate; sled, sleigh; ski, snow-shoe.

equipage, turn-out; coach, chariot; *quadriga*, chaise, phaëton, break, brake, mail-phaëton, wagonette, drag, curricle, tilbury, whisky, landau, *barouche*, victoria, brougham, clarence, calash, *calèche*, britzska, *araba*, kibitka; berlin; sulky, *désobligeant*, sociable, *vis-à-vis, dormeuse*; jaunting —, outside- car; *tarantass*; runabout; shay.

post-chaise; diligence, stage; stage —, mail —, hackney —, glass- coach; stage-wagon; car, omnibus, bus, fly, *cabriolet*, cab, hansom, shofle, fourwheeler, growler, *droshki*, drosky.

dog-cart, trap, gig, whitechapel, buggy, four-in-hand, unicorn, random, tandem; shandredhan, *char-à-banc*.

automobile, motor-, auto-, touring-, racing-, cycle-, side-, steam-, electric- car; motor — cycle, — bike; motorized vehicle; bus, minibus; buggy, crate, tub, flivver, jalopy, wreck, clunker, dog, heap (all slang); coupe, coup, sedan, convertible, hard-top; camper, trailer, mobile home; limosine, landaulette, cabriolet, *coupé, voiturette*, runabout, electromobile, taxi, -cab.

train; passenger —, express —, freight —, subway —, special —, corridor —, parliamentary —, luggage —; goods- train, *train de luxe*; 1st-, 2nd-, 3rd- class- -train, — carriage, — compartment; Pullman —, sleeping-, club-, observation-, dining-, restaurant-car; mail-, luggage-, brake-van, coach, car, carriage; rolling stock; horse-box, cattle- truck.

273. Ship.—**N.** ship, vessel, sail; craft, bottom, navy, marine, fleet, flotilla, squadron; shipping, man of war etc. (*combatant*) 726; transport, tender, store-ship; merchant ship, merchantman; packet, liner; whaler, slaver, collier, coaster, tanker, freighter, freight steamer, cargo boat, lighter; fishing-, pilot- boat; trawler, drifter; cable ship; hulk; yacht; floating palace, ocean greyhound.

ship, bark, barque, brig, snow, hermaphrodite brig; brigantine, barquentine; schooner; topsail —, fore and aft —, three masted- schooner; *chassemarée*; sloop, cutter, corvette, clipper, foist, yawl, dandy, ketch, smack, lugger, barge, hoy, cat-, -boat, buss; sail-er, -ing vessel, wind jammer; steamer, -boat, -ship; mail—, paddle —, screw —, stern-wheel- steamer; tug; train-ferry; line of steamers etc.

boat, pinnace, launch, motor-boat, picket-boat; hydroplane; life-, long-, jolly-, bum-, fly-, cock-, ferry-, canal- boat, dory, dugout, galliot, shallop, gig, funny, skiff, dingy, scow, cockleshell, wherry, coble, punt, cog, lerret; eight-, four-, pair- oar; randan; out- rigger; float, raft, pontoon; prame, ice-yacht.

state barge, bucentaur.

catamaran, coracle, gondola, carvel, caravel; felucca, caique, canoe; trireme; galley, — foist; bilander, dogger, hooker, howker; argosy, carack; galliass, galleon; galliot, polacca, polacre, corsair, tartane, junk, lorcha, praam, proa, prahu, saick, sampan, xebec, dhow; dahabeah; nuggar, cayak, piroque; trireme.

submarine, submersible.

aircraft (*combatant*) etc. 726; flying machine, air mail, aero-, air-, mono-, bi-, tri-, hydro aeroplane, plane, cabin —, transport —, propeller — plane; *avion*, flying boat, glider; helicopter, rotor —, gyro-plane, whirlybird, autogyro, gyrodine; sea-, hydro-plane; amphibian; jet, — plane; turbo-, ram-, pulse-, subsonic —, supersonic —, strato- jet; rocket — plane, — ship,; space ship; war-, combat — plane; kamikaze, fleet, armada; trainer, fliight simulator; aerostat, dirigible, blimp (coll.), zeppelin; parachute, chute (coll.); kite.

rocket, flying —, ballistic —, guided — missile; projectile; rocket —, robot —, buzz-bomb; multistage —, step —, test — rocket; booster; satellite; flying saucer, unidentified flying object. (UFO).

nacelle, car, gondola, aileron; hangar, airport, landing field, airdrome; catwalk, controls, rudder, tail.

Adj. marine, maritime, naval, nautical, seafaring, sea-, ocean-going, sea-worthy.

aerial, aeronautical, air-worthy, flying etc. *n.*

Adv. afloat, aboard; on -board, — ship board, — board ship.

274. Velocity.—N. velocity, speed, celerity; swiftness etc. *adj.*; rapidity, eagle speed; expedition etc. (*activity*) 682; pernicity; acceleration; haste etc. 684.

spurt, rush, dash, race, steeplechase; smart —, lively —, swift etc. *adj.* —, rattling —, spanking —, strapping- -rate, — pace; round pace; flying, flight.

gallop, canter, trot, round trot, run, scamper; hand —, full- gallop; swoop.

lightning, light, electricity, wind; cannon-ball, rocket, arrow, dart, quicksilver; telegraph, express train; torrent; swallow flight.

eagle, antelope, courser, race-horse, gazelle; greyhound, hare, doe, squirrel.

Mercury, Ariel, Camilla, Harlequin.

[Measurement of velocity.] speedometer, log, -line, tachometer.

air speed, speed of sound, sonic —, subsonic —, supersonic —, ultrasonic —, hypersonic —, transonic — speed.

V. move quickly, trip, fisk; speed, hie, hasten, sprint, spurt, post, spank, scuttle; scud, -dle, scurry; scour, — the plain; scamper, sprint, dash, run, — like mad; fly, race, run a race, cut away, cut and run, shoot, tear, whisk, whiz, sweep, skim, brush; cut —, bowl- along; rush etc. (*be violent*) 173; dash -on, — off, — forward; bolt; trot, gallop, bound, flit, spring, dart, boom; march in -quick, - double-time; ride hard; et over the ground, scorch.

hurry etc. (*hasten*) 684; accelerate, put on; quicken; quicken —, mend- one's pace; clap spurs to one's horse; make-haste, — rapid strides, — forced marches, — the best of one's way; put one's best leg foremost, stir one's stumps, wing one's way, set off at a score; carry —, crowd- sail; go off like a shot, go ahead, gain ground; outstrip the wind, fly on the wings of the wind.

keep -up, — pace- with; outstrip etc. 303.

Adj. fast, speedy, swift, rapid, quick, fleet; nimble, agile, expeditious; express; active etc. 682; flying, galloping etc. *v.*; light- nimble-footed; winged; eagle-winged, mercurial, electric telegraphic; light-legged; light of heel; swift as -an arrow etc. *n.*; quick as -lightning etc. *n.*, — thought. *

Adv. swiftly etc. *adj.*; with -speed etc. *n.*; apace; at -a great rate, — full speed, — railway speed; full -drive, — gallop; post-haste, in full sail, tantivy; trippingly; instantaneously etc. 113; like a shot.

under press of -sale, — canvas, — sail and steam; *velis et remis*, on eagle's wing, in double quick time; with -rapid, — giant- strides; *à pas de géant*; in seven league boots; whip and spur; *ventre à terre*; as fast as one's -legs, — heels- will carry one; as fast on one can lay feet to the ground, at the top of one's speed; by leaps and bounds; with haste etc. 684; in- high — gear, — speed.

Phr. *vires acquirit eundo.*

*See note on 274.

275. Slowness.—N. slowness etc. *adj.*; languor etc. (*inactivity*) 683; drawl; creeping etc. *v.*, lentor.

retardation; slackening etc. *v.*; delay etc. (*lateness*) 133; claudication.

jog-, dog-trot, walk; mincing steps; slow -march, — time.

slow -goer, — coach, — back; lingerer, loiterer, sluggard, tortoise, snail; dawdle etc. (*inactive*) 683.

V. move -slowly, etc. *adv.*; creep, crawl, lag, slug, walk, drawl, linger, loiter, saunter; plod, trudge, stump along, lumber; trail; drag; dawdle etc. (*be inactive*) 683; grovel, worm one's way, steal along; jog —, rub —, bundle- on; toddle, waddle, wabble, shug; traipse, slouch, shuffle, halt, hobble, limp, claudicate, shamble; flag, falter. totter, stagger; mince, step short; march in -slow time, — funeral procession; take one's time; hang fire etc. (*be late*) 133.

retard, relax; slacken, check, moderate, rein in, curb; reef; strike —, shorten —, take in- sail; put on the drag, apply the brake; clip the wings; reduce the speed, decelerate; slacken -speed, — one's pace, lose ground; back -water, — pedal, put the engines astern, throttle down.

Adj. slow, slack; tardy; dilatory etc. (*inactive*) 683; gentle, easy; leisurely; deliberate, gradual; insensible, imperceptible; languid, sluggish, apathetic, phlegmatic, slow-paced, tardigrade, snail-like; creeping etc. *v.*

Adv. slowly etc. *adj.*; leisurely; *piano, adagio; largo, larghetto*; at half speed, under easy sail; at a -foot's, — snail's, — funeral- pace; slower than molasses in January; in slow time; with -mincing steps, — clipped wings; *haud passibus aequis*; inlow —, gear, — speed.

gradually etc. *adj.*; *gradatim*; by -degrees, — slow degrees, — inches, — little and little; step by step; inch by inch, bit by bit, little by little, *seriatim*; consecutively.

276. Impulse.—N. impulse, impulsion, impetus; momentum; push, pulsion, thrust, shove, jog, jolt, brunt, booming, boost, throw; explosion etc. (*violence*) 173; propulsion etc. 284, jet propulsion; firing, launching, projection, trajection.

percussion, concussion, collision, occursion, clash, encounter, cannon, *carambole*, appulse, shock, crash, bump; impact; *élan*; charge etc. (*attack*) 716; beating etc. (*punishment*) 972.

blow, dint, stroke, knock, tap, rap, slap, smack, pat, dab; fillip; slam, bang; hit, whack, thwack, clout; cuff etc. 972; squash, dowse, whap, swap, punch, thump, swipe, jab, pelt, kick, punce, calcitration; *ruade*; arietation; cut, thrust, lunge, yerk.

hammer, sledge-hammer, mall, maul, mallet, flail; ram, -mer; battering-ram, monkey, pile-driver, punch, bat, tamper, tamping iron; cudgel etc. (*weapon*) 727; axe etc. (*sharp*) 253.

[Science of mechanical forces] mechanics, dynamics etc.

V. give an -impetus etc. *n.*; impel, push; start, give a start to, set going; drive, urge, boom; thrust, prod, foin; cant; elbow, shoulder, jostle, justle, hustle, hurtle, shove, jog, jolt, bean, encounter; run –, bump –, butt- against; knock –, run- one's head against; impinge.

fire, launch, project, traject, propel, 284.

strike, knock, hit, bash, tap, rap, bat, slap, flap, dab, pat, thump, beat, bang, slam, dash; punch, thwack, whack; hit –, strike- hard; swap, batter, dowse, baste; pelt, patter, skelter, buffet, belabor, tamp; fetch one a blow, swat; poke at, pink, lunge, yerk; kick, calcitrate; butt; strike at etc. (*attack*) 716; whip etc. (*punish*) 972; propel etc. 284.

come –, enter into collision; collide; foul; fall –, run- foul of.

throw etc.

Adj. impelling etc. *v.*; im-pulsive, -pellent; booming; dynamic, -al; impelled etc. *v.*

277. Recoil.—N. recoil; re-, retro-action; revulsion; rebound, *ricochet*; re-percussion, - calcitration; kick, *contre-coup*; springing back etc. *v.*; elasticity etc. 325; reflexion, reflex, reflux; reverberation etc. (*resonance*) 408; rebuff, repulse; return.

ducks and drakes; boomerang; spring; reactionist, reactionary.

V. recoil, resile, react; spring –, fly –, bound-back; rebound, reverberate, repercuss, recalcitrate, echo, *ricochet*.

Adj. recoiling etc. *v.*; re-fluent, -percussive, - calcitrant, -actionary; retroactive.

Adv. on the -recoil etc. *n.*

278. Direction.—N. direction, bearing, course, set, drift, tenor; tendency etc. 176; incidence; bending, trending etc *v.*; dip, tack, aim, collimation; steer-ing, -age.

point of the compass, cardinal –, half –, quarter- points; North, East, South, West; N by E, ENE, NE by N, NE etc; rhumb, azimuth, line of collimation.

line, path, road, range, quarter, line of march; alignment; straight shot, bee-line.

course, bearing, heading, altitude, air -route, - lane, angle, center, axis, torsion, torque, pitch, lift, drift, flow, wash.

V. tend –, bend –, point- towards; conduct –, go- to; point -to, – at; bend, trend, verge, in-cline, dip, determine.

steer –, make- -for, – towards; aim –, level- at; take aim; keep –, hold- a course; be bound for; bend one's steps towards; direct –, steer –, bend –, shape- one's course; align –, align- one's march; go straight, – to the point; march -on, – on a point.

ascertain one's -direction etc. *n.*; *s'orienter*, see which way the wind blows; box the compass.

Adj. directed etc. *v.*, – towards; pointing towards etc. *v.*; bound for; aligned –, with; direct, straight; un-deviating, -swerving; straightforward; North, -ern, -erly, etc. *n.*

directable etc. *v.*

Adv. towards; on the -road, – high road- to; versus, to; hither, thither, whither; directly; straight, – forwards, – as an arrow; point blank; in a - direct, – straight- line -to, – for, – with; in a line with; full tilt at, as the crow flies.

before –, near –, close to –, against- the wind; windwards, in the wind's eye.

through, *via*, by way of; in all -directions, – manner of ways; *quaqua-versum*, from the four winds.

279. Deviation.—N. deviation; swerving etc. *v.*; obliquation, warp, refraction; flection, flexion; sweep; de-flection, -flexure; declination.

diversion, digression, departure from, aberration, drift, sheer; divergence etc. 291; zigzag; *détour* etc. (*circuit*) 629.

[Desultory motion] wandering etc. *v.*; vagrancy, evagation; by-paths and crooked ways.

[Motion sideways, oblique motion] sidling etc. *v.*; *échelon*, leeway; knight's move (at chess).

V. alter one's course, deviate, depart from, turn, trend; bend, curve, etc. 245; swerve, heel, bear off.

intervert; deflect; divert, – from its course; put on a new scent, shift, shunt, switch, wear, draw aside, crook, warp, short circuit.

stray, straggle; sidle, edge; diverge etc. 291; tralineate, digress, divagate, wander; wind, twist, meander, meander around Robin Hood's barn; veer, tack, sheer; turn -aside, – a corner, – away from; wheel, steer clear of; ramble, rove, drift; go -astray, – adrift; yaw, dodge; step aside, ease off, make way for, shy.

fly off at a tangent; glance off; turn, wheel –, face- about; turn –, face- to the right about; wabble etc. (*oscillate*) 314; go out of one's way etc. (*perform a circuit*) 629; lose one's way.

Adj. deviating etc. *v.*; aberrant, errant; ex-, dis-cursive; devious, desultory, loose; rambling; stray, erratic, vagrant, undirected; circuitous, in-direct, zigzag; crab-like.

Adv. astray from, round about, wide of the mark; to the right about; all manner of ways; cir-cuitously etc. 629.

obliquely, sideling, like the move of the knight on a chessboard.

280. Precession. [Going before.]**—N.** precession, leading, heading; precedence etc. 62; priority etc. 116; the lead, *le pas*; van etc. (*front*) 234; precursor etc. 64.

V. go -before, – ahead, – in the van, – in ad-vance; precede, forerun; usher in, introduce, herald, head, take the lead; lead, – the way, – the dance; get –, have- the start; steal a march; get -before, – ahead, – in front of; outstrip etc. 303; take precedence etc. (*first in order*) 62.

Adj. foremost, first, leading etc. *v.*

Adv. in advance, before, ahead, in the van; fore-head-most; in front.

Phr. *seniores priores*.

281. Sequence. [Going after.]—**N.** sequence, run; coming after etc. (*order*) 63; (*time*) 117; following; pursuit etc. 622.

follower, attendant, satellite, shadow, dangler, train.

V. follow; pursue etc. 622; go –, fly- after.

attend, beset, dance attendance on, dog, be-dog; tread -in the steps of, – close upon; be –, go –, follow- in the -wake, – trail, – rear- of; trail, follow as a shadow, hang on the skirts of; tread –, follow- on the heels of, tag- after.

lag, get behind.

Adj. following etc. *v.*

Adv. behind; in the -rear etc. 235, – train of, wake of; after etc. (*order*) 63, (*time*) 117.

282. Progression. [Motion forwards; progressive motion.]—**N.** progress, -ion, -iveness; advancing etc. *v.*; advance, -ment; ongoing; flood-tide, headway; march etc. 266; rise; improvement etc. 658.

V. advance; proceed, progress; get -on, – along, – over the ground; gain ground; jog –, rub –, wag- on; go with the stream; keep –, hold on-one's course; go –, move –, come –, get –, pass –, push –, press- -on, – forward, – forwards, – ahead; press onwards, step forward; make –, work –, carve –, push –, force –, edge –, elbow-one's way; make -progress, – head, – way, – headway, – advances, – strides, – rapid strides etc. (*velocity*) 274; go –, shoot- ahead; distance; make up leeway.

Adj. advancing etc. *v.*; pro-gressive, -fluent; advanced.

Adv. forward, onward; forth, on ahead, under way, *en route* for, on -one's way, – the way, – the road, – the high road- to; in -progress, – mid progress; *in transitu* etc. 270.

Phr. *vestigia nulla retrorsum.*

283. Regression. [Motion backwards.]—**N.** regress, -ion; retro-cession, -gression, -gradation, -action; *reculade*; retreat, withdrawal, retirement, remigration; recession etc. (*motion from*) 287; recess; crab-like motion.

re-fluence, -flux; backwater, regurgitation, ebb, return; resilience; reflexion (*recoil*) 277; *volte-face.*

counter -motion, – movement, – march; veering, tergiversation, recidivation, backsliding, fall, relapse; deterioration etc. 659.

turning point etc. (*reversion*) 145.

V. re-cede, -grade, -turn, -vert, -treat, -tire; retro-grade, -cede; back, – down, – out, crawl; withdraw; rebound etc. 277; go –, come –, turn –, hark –, draw –, fall –, get –, put –, run-back; lose ground; fall –, drop- astern; back water, put about; veer, – round; double, wheel, counter-march; ebb, regurgitate; *jib*, shrink, shy.

turn -tail, – round, – upon one's heel, – one's back upon; retrace one's steps, dance the back step; sound –, beat- a retreat; go home.

Adj. receding etc. *v.*; retro-grade, -gressive; re-gressive, -fluent, -flex, -cidivous, -silient; crab-like; reactionary etc. 277; counter-clockwise.

Adv. back, -wards; reflexively, to the right about; *à reculons, à rebours.*

Phr. *revenons à nos moutons,* as you were.

284. Propulsion. [Motion given to an object situated in front.]—**N.** pro-pulsion, -jection; *vis a tergo*; push etc. (*impulse*) 276; e-, jaculation; ejection etc. 297; throw, fling, toss, shot, discharge, shy.

[Science of propulsion] steam –, gas –, diesel –, jet –, rocket – propulsion, gunnery, ballistics, archery.

missile, projectile, ball, *discus*, javelin, hammer, quoit, brickbat, shot, bullet; arrow, shaft, gun etc. (*arms*) 727.

shooter, shot; gunner, gun-layer; archer, toxophilite; bow-, rifle-, marks- man; good –, crack- shot; sharpshooter etc. (*combatant*) 726.

V. propel, project, throw, fling, cast, pitch, chuck, toss, jerk, heave, shy, hurl; flirt, fillip.

dart, lance, tilt; e-, jaculate; fulminate, bolt, drive, sling, pitchfork.

send; send –, let –, fire- off; discharge, shoot; launch, send forth, let fly; dash.

put –, set- in motion; set agoing, start; give -a start, – an impulse- to; push, impel etc. 276; trun-dle etc. (*set in rotation*) 312; expel etc. 297.

carry one off one's legs; put to flight.

Adj. propelled etc. *v.*; propelling etc. *v.*; pro-pulsive, -jectile.

285. Traction. [Motion given to an object situated behind.]—**N.** traction; drawing etc. *v.*; draft, pull, tug, haul; rake; 'a long pull, a strong pull and a pull all together;' towage, haulage.

V. draw, pull, haul, lug, rake, drag, draggle, tug, tow, trail, trawl, train; take in tow.

wrench, jerk, twitch.

Adj. drawing etc. *v.*; tractive, tractile; ductile, pulling, hauling, tugging, towing.

286. Approach. Motion towards.]—**N.** ap-proach, approximation, appropinquation; access; appulse; afflux, -ion; advent etc. (*approach of time*) 121; pursuit etc. 622; convergence etc. 290.

V. approach, approximate; near; get –, go –, draw- near; come, – near, – to close quarters; move –, set in- towards; drift; make up to; gain upon; pursue etc. 622; tread on the heels of; bear up; make the land; hug the -shore, – land.

Adj. approaching etc. *v.*; approximative; con-vergent; affluent; impending, imminent etc. (*destined*) 152.

Adv. on the road.

Int. come hither! approach! here! come! come near!

287. Recession. [Motion from.]—**N.** recession, retirement, withdrawal; retreat; retrocession etc. 283; departure etc. 293; recoil etc. 277; flight etc. (*avoidance*) 623.

V. recede, go, move from, retire, ebb, withdraw, shrink; come –, move –, go –, get –, drift-away; depart etc. 293; retreat etc. 283; move –, stand –, sheer- off; swerve from; fall back, stand aside; run away etc. (*avoid*) 623.

remove, shunt, side track, switch off.

Adj. receding etc. *v.*

288. Attraction. [Motion towards, ac-tively.]—**N.** attract-ion, -iveness; pull; drawing to,

pulling towards, adduction, magnetism, gravity, attraction of gravitation; lure, bait, decoy.
lode-stone, -star; magnet, siderite, magnetite.
V. attract; draw −, pull −, drag- towards; adduce.
lure, bait, decoy.
Adj. attracting etc. *v.*; attrahent, attractive, adducent, adductive, alluring.

289. Repulsion. [Motion from, actively.]—**N.** repulsion;·driving from etc. *v.*; repulse; abduction.
V. repel; push −, drive − etc. 276; from; chase, dispel; retrude; abduce, abduct; send away, repulse, dismiss.
keep at arm's length, turn one's back upon, give the cold shoulder; send packing; send -off, − away- with a flea in one's ear, − about one's business.
Adj. repelling etc. *v.*; repellant, repulsive; abducent, abductive.

290. Convergence. [Motion nearer to.]—**N.** con-vergence, -fluence, -course, -flux, -gress, - currence, -centration; appulse, meeting; corradiation.
assemblage etc. 72; resort etc. (*focus*) 74; asymptote.
V. converge, concur; come together, unite, meet, fall in with; close -with, − in upon; center - round, − in; enter in; pour in.
gather together, unite, concentrate, bring into a focus.
Adj. converging etc. *v.*; con-vergent, -fluent, - current; centripetal; asymptotical.

291. Divergence. [Motion further off.]—**N.** diverg-ence, -ency; divarication, ramification, radiation; separation etc. (*disjunction*) 44; dispersion etc. 73; deviation etc. 279; aberration, declination.
V. diverge, divaricate, radiate; ramify; branch −, glance −, file- off; fly off, − at a tangent; spread, scatter, disperse etc. 73; deviate etc. 279; part etc. (*separate*) 44; splay apart.
Adj. diverging etc. *v.*; divergent, radiant, centrifugal; aberrant.

292. Arrival. [Terminal motion at.]—**N.** arrival, advent; landing; de-, disem-barkation; reception, welcome, *vin d'honneur.*
home, goal, bourn; landing-place, -stage; resting −, stopping -place; destination, harbor, haven, port; terminal, terminus, railway station, depot, airport; halt, halting -place, − ground; anchorage etc. (*refuge*) 666.
return, recursion, remigration; meeting; ren-, encounter.
completion etc. 729.
V. arrive; get to, come to; come; reach, attain; come up, − with, − to; overtake; make, fetch; complete etc. 729; join, rejoin.
light, alight, dismount; land, go ashore; debark, disembark; put -in, − into; visit, cast anchor, pitch

one's tent; sit down etc. (*be located*) 184; get to one's journey's end; make the land; be in at the death; come −, get- -back, − home; return; come in etc. (*ingress*) 294; make one's appearance etc. (*appear*) 446; drop in; detrain; outspan.
come to hand; come -at, − across; hit; come −, light −; pop −, bounce −, plump −, burst −, pitch- upon; meet; en- ren-counter; come in contact.
Adj. arriving etc. *v.*; homewardbound; terminal.
Adv. here, hither.
Int. welcome! hail! all hail! good- day, − morrow; greetings! hullo! well!

293. Departure. [Initial motion from.]—**N.** departure, decession, decampment; embarkation; take-off; outset, start; removal; exit etc. (*egress*) 295; exodus, Hejira, flight.
leave-taking, *congé*, valediction, valedictory, adieu, farewell, good-bye, stirrup-cup.
starting -point, − post; point −, place- of - departure; − embarkation; port of embarkation.
V. depart; go, − away; take one's departure, set out; set −, march −, put −, start −, be −, move −, get −, whip −, pack −, go −, take oneself-off; start, issue, march out, debouch; go −, sally-forth; sally, set forward; be gone.
leave a place, quit, vacate, evacuate, abandon; go off the stage, make ones' exit; retire, withdraw, remove; go -one's way, − along, − from home; take -flight, − wing; spring, fly, flit, wing one's flight; fly −, whip- away; take off, hop off; embark; go -on board, − aboard; set sail; put −, go-to sea; sail, take ship; hoist blue Peter; get under way, weigh anchor; strike tents, break camp, decamp; walk one's chalks, make tracks, cut one's stick; cut and run; take leave; say −, bid- -good-bye etc. *n.*; disappear etc. 449; abscond etc. (*avoid*) 623; entrain, embus, emplane; saddle −, harness −, hitch- up; inspan.
Adj. departing etc. *v.*; valedictory; outward bound.
Adv. whence, hence, thence; with a foot in the stirrup; on the -wing, − move.
Int. begone! etc. (*ejection*) 297; to horse! all aboard! farewell! adieu! good-bye, − day! *au revoir! auf wiedersehen!* fare you well! so long! God -bless you, − speed! *bon voyage!*

294. Ingress. [Motion into.]—**N.** ingress; entrance, entry; introgression; influx; intrusion, inroad, incursion, invasion, irruption; pene-, interpene- tration; illapse, import, importation, infiltration; immigration; admission etc. (*reception*) 296; insinuation etc. (*interjacence*) 228; insertion etc. 300.
inlet; way in; mouth, door etc. (*opening*) 260; path etc. (*way*) 627; conduit etc. 350; immigrant, visitor, incomer, newcomer, colonist.
V. have the *entrée*; enter; go −, come −, pour −, flow −, creep −, slip −, pop −, break −, burst- -into, − in; set foot on; burst −, break-in upon; invade, intrude, butt in, horn in, crash; insinuate itself; inter-, penetrate; infiltrate; find one's way −, wriggle −, worm oneself- into.
give entrance to etc. (*receive*) 296; insert etc. 300.

Adj. incoming, ingressive etc. *n.*; inward bound.
Adv. inward.

295. Egress. [Motion out of.]—**N.** egress, exit, issue; emer-sion, -gence; disemboguement; out-break, -burst; e-, pro-ruption; emanation; evacuation; ex, trans-udation; extravasation, per-spiration, sweating, leakage, percolation, distillation, oozing; gush etc. (*water in motion*) 348; outpour, -ing; effluence, effusion; efflux, -ion; drain; dribbling etc. *v.*; defluxion; drainage; out-come, -put; discharge etc. (*excretion*) 299.

export; expatriation; e-, re-migration; *débouche*; exodus etc. (*departure*) 293; emigrant, migrant, *émigré*, colonist.

outlet, vent, spout, tap, sluice, floodgate; pore; vomitory, out-gate, sally-port; way out; mouth, door etc. (*opening*) 260; path etc. (*way*) 627; con-duit etc. 350; air-pipe etc. 351.

V. emerge, emanate, issue; go –, come –, move –, pass –, pour –, flow- out of; pass off, evacuate; migrate.

ex-, trans-ude; leak; run, – out, – through; per-, trans-colate; seep; strain, distil; perspire, sweat, drain, ooze; filter, filtrate; dribble, gush, spout, flow out; well, – out; pour, trickle etc. (*water in motion*) 348; effuse, extravasate, disem-bogue, discharge itself, debouch; come –, break-forth; burst- out, – through; find vent, escape etc. 671.

Adj. effused etc. *v.*; outgoing, outward bound.
Adv. outward.

296. Reception. [Motion into, actively.]—**N.** reception; admission, admittance, *entrée*, im-portation; initiation; intro-duction, -mission, -ception; immission, ingestion, imbibition, ab-sorption, ingurgitation, inhalation; suction, sucking; eating, drinking etc. (*food*) 298; insertion etc. 300; interjection etc. 228.

V. give -entrance to, – admittance to, – the *entrée*; intro-duce, -mit; usher, admit, receive, im-port, initiate, bring in, open the door to, throw open, ingest, absorb, imbibe, inhale, infiltrate; let –, take –, suck- in; re-admit, -sorb, -absorb; snuff up; swallow, ingurgitate; enfuel, engorge; gulp; eat, drink etc. (*food*) 298.

Adj. admit-ting etc. *v.*, -ted etc. *v.*; admissible; absorbent; introductory, introceptive, intromittent, initiatory.

297. Ejection. [Motion out of, actively.]—**N.** ejection, emission, effusion, rejection, expulsion, eviction, extrusion, trajection; discharge.

egestion, evacuation, vomition, disgorgement, voidance, eruption, eruptiveness; ruc-, eruc-tation; blood-letting, venesection, phlebotomy, paracen-tesis; tapping, drainage; clear-ance, -age, voidance; vomiting, excretion etc. 299.

deportation; banishment etc. (*punishment*) 972; rogue's march; relegation, extradition; dislodgment.

V. give -exit, – vent- to; let –, give –, pour –, send- out; des-, dis-patch; exhale, excern, ex-crete, disembogue, secrete, secern; extravasate,

shed, void, evacuate, egest, emit; open the -sluices, – floodgates; turn on the tap; extrude, detrude; ef-fuse, spend, expend; pour forth; squirt, spirt, spill, slop; perspire etc. (*exude*) 295; breathe, blow etc. (*wind*) 349.

tap, draw off; bale –, lade- out; let blood, broach.

eject, reject; expel, discard; cut, send to Coven-try, boycott, ostracize; *chasser*; banish etc. (*punish*) 972; throw etc. 284 -out. – up, – off, – away, – aside; push etc. 276 -out, – off, – away, – aside; shovel –, sweep- -out, – away; brush –, whisk –, turn –, send- -off, – away; discharge; send –, turn –, cast- adrift; turn –, bundle- out; throw overboard; give the sack to; send -packing, – about one's business, – to the right about; strike off the roll etc. (*abrogate*) 756; turn out-neck and heels, – head and shoulders, – neck and crop; pack off; send away with a flea in the ear; send to Jericho; bow out, show the door to, dismiss; fire, sack.

turn out of -doors, – house and home; evict, oust; exorcise, un-house, -kennel; dislodge; un-, dis-people; depopulate; relegate, deport.

empty; drain, – to the dregs; sweep off; clear, – off, – out, – away; such, draw off, extract; clean out, make a clean sweep of, clear decks, purge.

em-, dis-, disem-bowel; eviscerate, gut; unearth, root -out, – up; averruncate; weed –, get out; eliminate, get rid of, do away with, shake off; exen-terate.

vomit, spew, puke, keck, retch; belch, – out, eruct, eructate; cast –, bring- up, disgorge; ex-pectorate, salivate, clear the throat, hawk, spit, sputter, splutter, slobber, drool, drivel, slaver, slab-ber.

unpack, unlade, unload, unship; break bulk.

be let out; ooze etc. (*emerge*) 295.

Adj. emitt-ing, -ed etc. *v.*

begone! get you gone! get –, go- away, – along, – along with you! go your way! away, – with! off with you! go, – about your business! be off! avaunt! aroynt! get out!

298. Food. [Eating.]—**N.** eating etc. *v.*; deglutition, gulp, epulation, mastication, man-ducation, rumination, gastronomy, gastrology; panto-, hippo-, ichthyo-phagy etc.; gluttony etc. 957; carnivorousness, vegetarianism.

mouth, jaws, mandible, mazard, chops.

drinking etc. *v.*; potation, draught, libation; carousal etc. (*amusement*) 840; drunkenness etc. 959.

food, *pabulum*; aliment, nourishment, nutriment, susten-ance, -tation; nurture, sub-sistence, provender, feed, fodder, provision, ration, keep, commons, board; commissariat etc. (*provision*) 637; prey, forage, pasture, pasturage; fare, cheer; diet, -ary; regimen; belly timber, staff of life; bread, -and cheese; proteins, carbohydrates, vitamines.

comestibles, eatables, victuals, edibles, *ingesta*, grub, prog, tack, hard tack; meat; bread, -stuffs; cereals; viands, cates, delicacy, dainty, creature comforts, contents of the larder, flesh-pots; festal board; ambrosia; good -cheer, – living.

hors-d'oeuvre; soup, pottage, *potage*, broth,

bouillon, consommé, purée, borsch, stock, skilly, gumbo; fish, − cakes, − pie; joint, *rôti, pièce de résistance, relevé,* hash, *réchauffé,* stew, *ragoût,* fricassee, mince, *salim, goulash, bouillabaisse,* remove, *entrée, croquette, rissole,* sausage, curry, bubble and squeak; haggis, collops, giblets; poultry, game etc.; biscuit, bun, scone, rusk, pancake, pie, pastry, pasty, patty, *patisseria,* tart, turnover, *vol-au-vent, soufflé,* dumpling, pudding, duff, *compote,* fritters, cake, napoleon, *blancmange,* custard, jelly, jam, sweets etc. 396; *entremet*; oatmeal, porridge, hasty pudding, gruel; eggs, omelet, cheese, matzoon, savory; vegetable, salad, *mayonnaise,* fruit; sauce, condiment etc. 393; kickshaws.

table, *cuisine,* bill of fare, *menu, table d'hôte,* ordinary, *à la carte*; cover.

meal, repast, feed, spread; mess; dish, plate, course, side dish; regale; regale-, refresh-, entertain-ment; refection, collation, picnic, feast, banquet, junket; breakfast; lunch, -eon, *déjeuner,* bever, tiffin, tea, dinner, supper, snack, whet, bait, dessert; pot-luck, *table d'hôte, déjeuner à la fourchette*; hearty −, square −, substantial −, full- - meal; blow out; light refreshment; pemmican.

mouthful, bolus, gobbet, tit-bit, morsel, sop, sippet.

drink, beverage, liquor, broth, soup; potion, dram, draft, drench, swill; nip, peg, sip, sup, gulp.

wine, champagne, spirits, *liqueur* beer, porter, stout, ale, malt liquor, julep, Sir John Barleycorn, stingo, heavy wet, bitter, lager- beer, cider; grog, toddy, flip, purl, punch, negus, cup, bishop, posset, wassail; bitters, *apéritif,* high-ball, cocktail; whisky, rum, absinthe; gin etc. (*intoxicating liquor*) 959; coffee, chocolate, cocoa, tea, *maté,* the cup that cheers but not inebriates.

eating-house etc. 189.

V. eat, feed, fare, devour, swallow, take; gulp, bolt, snap; fall to; despatch, dispatch; discuss; take −, get −, gulp-down; lay −, tuck- in; lick, pick, peck; gormandize etc. 957; bite, champ, munch, cranch, craunch, crunch, chew, masticate, nibble, gnaw, mumble.

live on; feed −, batten −, fatten −, feast- upon; browse, graze, crop, regale; carouse etc. (*make merry*) 840; eat heartily, do justice to, play a good knife and fork, banquet.

break -bread, − one's fast; breakfast; lunch, dine, take tea, sup.

drink, − in, − up, − one's fill; quaff, sip, sup; suck, − up; lap; swig; swill; tipple etc. (*be drunken*) 959; empty one's glass, drain the cup; toss -off, − one's glass; wash down, crack a bottle, wet one's whistle.

cater, purvey etc. 637.

Adj. eatable, edible, esculent, comestible, alimentary; cereal, cibarious; dietetic; culinary; nutri-tive, -tious; succulent; drinkable, pot-able, -ulent; bibulous.

omn-, carn-, herb-, frug-, gran-, gramin-, phytivorous; ichthyophagous.

prandial.

299. Excretion.—**N.** excretion, discharge, emanation; ejection etc. 297; exhalation, exudation, extrusion, secretion, effusion, extravasation, *ecchymosis,* evacuation, cacation, defecation, dysentery, dejection, *feces,* excrement;

perspiration, sweat; sub-, exud-ation; *diaphoresis*; sewage.

saliva, spittle, rheum; ptyalism, salivation, catarrh, distemper; diarrhea; *ejecta, egesta, sputum, sputa*; *excreta*; lava; *exuviae* etc. (*uncleanness*) 653.

hemorrhage, bleeding; catamenia, menses; outpouring etc. (*egress*) 295; leucorrhea.

V. excrete etc. (*eject*) 297; emanate etc. (*come out*) 295.

Adj. excretory, fecal, secretory; ejective, eliminant.

300. Insertion. [Forcible ingress.]—**N.** insertion, implantation, intercalation, embolism, introduction; interpolation, insinuation etc. (*intervention*) 228; planting etc. *v.*; injection, inoculation, importation, infusion; forcible -ingress etc. 294; immersion; submersion, -gence; dip, plunge; bath etc. (*water*) 337; interment etc. 363.

V. insert; intro-duce, -mit; put −, run- into; import; inject; interject etc. 228; infuse, instil, inoculate, impregnate, imbue, imbrue.

graft, ingraft, bud, plant, implant; dovetail.

obtrude; thrust −, stick −, ram −, stuff −, tuck −, press −, drive −, pop −, whip −, drop −, put- in; impact; empierce etc. (*make a hole*) 260.

embed; immerse, immerge, merge; bathe, soak etc. (*water*) 337; dip, plunge etc. 310.

bury etc. (*inter*) 363.

insert etc. itself; plunge *in medias res.*

Adj. inserted etc. *v.*

301. Extraction. [Forcible egress.]—**N.** extraction; extracting etc. *v.*; removal, elimination, extrication, eradication, evolution.

evulsion, avulsion; wrench; expression, squeezing; extirpation, extermination; ejection etc. 297; export etc. (*egress*) 295; distillation.

extractor, corkscrew, forceps, pliers.

V. extract, draw, pit; take −, draw −, pull −, tear −, pluck −, pick −, get- out; wring from, wrench; extort; root −, weed −, grub −, rakeup, − out; eradicate; pull −, pluck- up by the roots; averruncate; unroot; uproot, pull up, extirpate, dredge.

remove, educe, elicit; evolve, extricate; eliminate etc. (*eject*) 297; eviscerate etc. 297.

express, squeeze −, press- out; distil.

Adj. extracted etc. *v.*

302. Passage. [Motion through.]—**N.** passage, transmission; permeation; pene-, interpene-tration; transudation, infiltration; *osmosis,* osmose, endos-, exos-mose; intercurrence; ingress etc. 294; egress etc. 295; path etc. 627; conduit etc. 350; opening etc. 260; journey etc. 266; voyage etc. 267.

V. pass, − through; perforate etc. (*hole*) 260; penetrate, permeate, thread, thrid, enfilade; go through, − across; go −, pass- over; cut across; ford, cross; pass and repass, work; make −, thread −, worm −, force- one's way; make −, force- a passage; cut one's way through; find its -way. −

vent; transmit, make way, clear the course;
traverse, go over the ground.
Adj. passing etc. v.; intercurrent; osmotic etc. n.
Adv. en passant etc. (transit) 270.

303. Overstep. [Motion beyond.]—N. transcursion, -ilience, -gression; infraction, intrusion;
trespass; encroach-, infringe-ment; extravagation,
transcendence; redundance etc. 641; ingress etc.
294.
V. transgress, surpass, pass; go- beyond, — by;
show in —, come to the- front; shoot ahead of;
steal a march —, gain- upon.
over-step, -pass, -reach, -go, -ride- -leap, -jump, -
skip, -lap, -shoot the mark; out-strip, -leap, -jump,
-go, -step, -run, -ride, -rival, -do; beat, — hollow;
distance; leave in the -lurch, — rear; go one better,
throw into the shade; exceed, transcend, surmount;
soar etc. (rise) 305.
encroach, intrude, trespass, infringe, invade,
trench upon, intrench on; strain; stretch —, strain-
a point; pass the Rubicon.
Adj. surpassing etc. v.
Adv. beyond the mark, ahead.

304. Shortcoming. [Motion short of.]—N.
shortcoming, failure; delinquency; falling short etc.
v.; de-fault, -falcation; leeway; labor in vain, no
go.
incompleteness etc. 53; imperfection etc. 651;
insufficiency etc. 640; noncompletion etc. 730;
failure etc. 732.
V. come —, fall —, stop- -short, — short of; not
reach; want; keep within -bounds, — the mark, —
compass.
break down, stick in the mud, collapse, come to
nothing; fall -through, — to the ground, — down;
cave in, end in smoke, fizzle out, miss the mark,
fail; lose ground; miss stays, slump.
Adj. unreached; deficient; short, — of; minus;
out of depth; perfunctory etc. (neglect) 460.
Adv. within -the mark, — compass, — bounds;
behindhand; re infectâ; to no purpose; far from it.
Phr. the bubble burst.

305. Ascent. [Motion upwards.]—N. ascent,
ascension; rising etc. v.; rise, upgrowth; leap etc.
309; acclivity, hill etc. 217; stair, stairs, stair-case, -
way, flight of -steps, — stairs; ladder, companion,
— way; lift, elevator etc. 307.
rocket, lark; sky-rocket, -lark; Alpine Club.
V. ascend, rise, mount, arise, uprise; go —, get
—, work one's way —, start —, spring —, shoot-
up; zoom; aspire.
climb, clamber, ramp, scramble, swarm,
escalade, surmount; scale, — the heights.
tower, soar, hover, spire, plane, swim, float,
surge; leap etc. 309.
Adj. rising etc. v.; scandent, buoyant; super-
natant, -fluitant; excelsior.
Adv. uphill.

306. Descent. [Motion downwards.]—N.
descent, descension, declension, declination; fall;
falling etc. v.; drop, cadence; subsidence, lapse;
come-down, downfall, tumble, slip, tilt, trip, lurch;
cropper, culbute; titubation, stumble; fate of
Icarus; dive, nose-dive, volpané.
avalanche, débâcle, landslip, slide.
V. descend; go —, drop —; come-down; fall,
gravitate, drop, slip, slide, glissade, dive, plunge,
settle; decline, slump, set, sink, droop, come down
a peg.
dismount, alight, light, get down; swoop; stoop
etc. 308; fall prostrate, precipitate oneself; let fall
etc. 308.
tumble, trip, stumble, titubate, lurch, pitch,
swag, topple; topple —, tumble- -down, — over;
tilt, sprawl, plump down, come a cropper.
Adj. descending etc. v.; descendent, declivitous;
downcast; decur-rent, sive; labent, deciduous;
nodding to its fall.
Adv. down, -hill, -wards.

307. Elevation.—N. elevation; raising etc. v.;
erection, lift; sublevation, upheaval; sublimation,
exaltation; prominence etc. (convexity) 250.
lever etc. 633; crane, derrick, windlass, capstan,
winch, dredger, lift, elevator, escalator, dumb
waiter.
V. heighten, elevate, raise, lift, erect; set —,
stick —, perch —, perk —, tilt- up; rear, hoist,
heave; up-lift, -raise, -rear, -bear, -cast, -hoist, -
heave; buoy, weigh, mount, give a lift; exalt,
sublimate; place —, set- on a pedestal.
take —, drag —, fish- up; dredge.
stand —, rise —, get —, jump- up; spring to
one's feet; hold -oneself, — one's head- up; draw
oneself up to his full height.
Adj. elevated etc. v.; standing up; stilted, attollent, rampant.
Adv. on -stilts, — the shoulders of, — one's legs,
— one's hind legs.

308. Depression.—N. lowering etc. v.;
depression; dip etc. (concavity) 252; abasement;
detrusion; reduction.
over-throw, -set, -turn; upset; prostration, subversion, precipitation.
bow; courtesy, curtsy; genuflexion, kowtow,
obeisance, salaam.
V. depress, lower; let —, take- -down, — down
a peg; cast; let -drop, — fall; -sink, debase, bring
low, abase, slash, reduce, detrude, pitch,
precipitate.
over-throw, -turn, -set; upset, subvert, prostrate,
level, fell; cast —, take —, throw —, fling —, dash
—, pull —, cut —, knock —, hew- down; raze, —
to the ground; humiliate, trample in the dust, pull
about one's ears.
sit, — down; couch, squat, crouch, stoop, bend,
bow, courtesy, curtsy; bob, duck, dip, genuflect,
kneel; kowtow, salaam, make obeisance, prostrate
oneself; bend, bow- the -head, — knee; incline the
head; bow down; cower; recline etc. (be horizontal) 213.
Adj. depressed etc. v.; at a low ebb; prostrate
etc. (horizontal) 213; detrusive.

309. Leap.—N. leap, jump, hop, spring,
bound, vault, saltation.

dance, caper, gambol; curvet, caracole; *gambade, -bado*; capriole, demivolt; buck. – jump; hop, skip and jump.

kangaroo, jerboa, chamois, goat, frog, grasshopper, flea.

V. leap; jump -up, – over the moon; hop, spring, bound, vault, ramp, cut capers, gambol, trip, skip, dance, caper, curvet, *caracole*; foot it, bob, bounce, flounce, start, frisk etc. (*amusement*) 840; jump about etc. (*agitation*) 315; trip it on the light fantastic toe, dance oneself off one's legs.

Adj. leaping etc. *v.*; saltatory, frisky.

Adv. on the light fantastic toe.

310. Plunge.—N. plunge, dip, dive, header; ducking etc. *v.*; submergence, immersion, diver.

V. plunge, dip, souse, duck; dive, plump; take a -plunge, – header, make a plunge; bathe etc. (*water*) 337.

sub-merge, -merse; immerse, douse, sink, engulf, send to -the bottom, – Davy Jones' locker.

get out of one's depth; go -to the bottom, – down like a stone; founder, welter, wallow.

311. Circuition. [Curvilinear motion.]—**N.** circuition, circulation; turn, curvet; excursion; circum-vention, -navigation, -ambulation; north-west passage; ambit, gyre, lap, circuit etc. 629.

turning etc. *v.*; wrench; evolution; coil, helix, spiral; corkscrew.

V. turn, bend, wheel; go – , put- about; heel; go – , turn -round, – to the right about; turn on one's heel; make – , describe- a -circle. – complete circle; encircle; go – , pass- through -180°, – 360°

circum-navigate, -aviate, -ambulate, -vent; put a girdle round the earth, go the round, make the round of.

turn – , round- a corner; double a point.

wind, circulate, meander; whisk, twirl; twist etc. (*convolution*) 248; make a *détour* etc. (*circuit*) 629.

Adj. turning etc. *v.*; circuitous; circumforaneous, -fluent; devious, roundabout, circumambient, -flex, -navigable.

Adv. round about.

312. Rotation. [Motion in a continued circle.]—**N.** rotation, revolution, gyration, circulation, roll; circum-rotation, -volution, - gyration; volutation, circination, turbination, *pirouette*, convolution.

verticity; whir, whirl, swirl, eddy, vortex, whirlpool, gurge; cyclone, tornado; surge; *vertigo*, dizzy round; Maelstrom, Charybdis; Ixion; wheel of Fortune.

wheel, screw, propeller, whirligig, rolling stone, windmill; top, teetotum, merry-go-round; roller; cog-, fly-wheel, spit; jack; caster.

axis, axle, spindle, spool, pivot, pin, hinge, pole, swivel, gimbals, arbor, bobbin, mandrel, shaft.

[Science of rotatory motion] trochilics, gyrostatics.

V. rotate; roll, – along; revolve, spin; turn, – round; circumvolve; circulate; gyre, gyrate, wheel,

whirl, swirl, twirl, trundle, troll, bowl; slew round, roll up, furl; wallow, welter; box the compass; spin like a -top, – teetotum.

Adj. rotating etc. *v.*; rota-tory, -ry; circumrotatory, trochilic, vertiginous, gyratory; vortic-al, -ose.

Adv. head over heels, round and round, like a horse in a mill.

313. Evolution. [Motion in a reverse circle.]—**N.** evolution, unfolding, development; eversion etc. (*inversion*) 218.

V. evolve; un-fold, -roll, -wind, -coil, -twist, -furl, -twine, -ravel; disentangle; develop.

Adj. evolving etc. *v.*; evolved etc. *v.*

314. Oscillation. [Reciprocating motion, motion to and fro.]—**N.** oscillation; vibration, libration; motion of a pendulum; nutation; undulation; pulsation; pulse; throb; seismic disturbance.

alternation; coming and going etc. *v.*; ebb and flow, flux and reflux, ups and downs; wave, vibratiuncle, swing, beat, shake, wag, see-saw, dance, lurch, dodge; fluctuation; vacillation etc. (*irresolution*) 605.

seismometer, vibroscope, seismograph.

V. oscillate; vi-, li-brate; alternate, undulate, wave; sway, rock, swing; pulsate, beat; wag, -gle; nod, bob, courtesy, curtsy; tick; play; chatter, wamble, wabble; teeter, dangle, swag.

fluctuate, dance, curvet, reel, quake; quiver, quaver, shake, flicker; wriggle; roll, toss, pitch; flounder, stagger, totter, waddle; move – , bob- up and down etc. *adv.*; pass and repass, ebb and flow, come and go, shuttle; vacillate etc. 605.

brandish, shake, flourish.

Adj. oscillating etc. *v.*; oscill-, undul-, puls-, libr-atory; vibrat-ory, -ile; pendulous, shutterwise, seismic.

Adv. to and fro, up and down, backwards and forwards, see-saw, zigzag, wibble-wabble, in and out, from side to side, like buckets in a well.

315. Agitation. [Irregular motion.]—**N.** agitation, stir, tremor, shake, ripple, jog, jolt, jerk, shock, succession, trepidation, quiver, quaver, dance; jactit-ation, -ance; shuffling etc. *v.*; twitter, flicker, flutter.

disquiet, perturbation, commotion, turmoil, turbulence; tumult, -uation; hubbub, rout, bustle, fuss, racket, *subsultus*; staggers, megrims, epilepsy, fits, twitching, vellication, St. Vitus' dance.

spasm, throe, throb, palpitation, convulsion, paroxysm; tetanus.

disturbance etc. (*disorder*) 59; restlessness etc. (*changeableness*) 149.

ferment, -ation; ebullition, effervescence, hurly burly, *cahotage*; tempest, storm, ground swell, heavy sea, whirlpool, vortex etc. 312; whirlwind etc. (*wind*) 349.

V. be -agitated etc.; shake; tremble, – like an aspen leaf; quiver, quaver, quake, shiver, twitter, twire, dither, dodder; twitch, writhe, toss, shuffle, tumble, stagger, bob, reel, sway; wag, -gle, wiggle; wriggle, – like an eel; squirm; dance, stumble, shamble, flounder, totter, flounce, flop, curvet, prance.

throb, pulsate, beat, palpitate, go pit-a-pat; flutter, flitter, flicker, bicker; bustle.

ferment, effervesce, foam; boil, – over; bubble, – up; simmer.

toss –, jump- about; jump like a parched pea; shake like an aspen leaf; shake to its -center, – foundations; be the sport of the winds and waves; reel to and fro like a drunken man; move –, drive-from post to pillar and from pillar to post; keep between hawk and buzzard.

agitate, shake, convulse, toss, tumble, bandy, wield, brandish, flap, flourish, whisk, jerk, hitch, jolt; jog, -gle; hostle, buffet, hustle, disturb, stir, shake up, churn, jounce, wallop, whip, vellicate.

Adj. shaking etc. *v.*; agitated, tremulous; de-, sub-sultory; shambling; giddy-paced, saltatory, convulsive, jerky, unquiet, restless, all of a twitter.

Adv. by fits and starts; subsultorily etc. *adj.*; per saltum; hop, skip and jump; in -convulsions, – fits, pit-a-pat.

316. Materiality.—N. material-ity, -ness; materialization; corpor-eity, -ality; substantiality, material existence, incarnation, flesh and blood, *plenum*; physical condition.

matter, body, substance, brute matter, stuff, element, principle, protoplasm, plasma, *parenchyma*, material, *substratum*, hyle, *corpus*, *pabulum*; frame.

object, article, thing, something; still life; stocks and stones; materials etc. 635.

[Science of matter] physics; somatology, -ics; natural –, experimental- philosophy; physical science, *philosophie positive*, materialism, hylism; applied –, micro-, molecular –, nuclear – physics.

atomics, atomic science, nucleonics, quantum mechanics, radiology.

atom, radical, tracer, isotope, pleiad; atomic – nucleus, – cluster; nuclear particle, neutron, protron, shell, valence electron.

materialist, physicist, atomic scientist, radiologist.

V. materialize, incorporate, incarnate, substantiate, embody.

atomize, split –, smash – the atom; radioactivate.

Adj. material, bodily; corpor-eal, -al; physical; somat-ic, -oscopic; sensible, tangible, ponderable, palpable, substantial; fleshly, incarnate.

physical, bio-, electro-, geo-physical; atomic, nuclear, thermonuclear, radio-active.

objective, impersonal, neuter, unspiritual, materialistic.

317. Immateriality.—N. immaterial-ity, -ness; incorporeal, dematerialization, unsubstantiality, spirituality; inextension; astra! plane.

personality; I, myself, me; *ego*, spirit etc. (*soul*) 450; astral body; immaterialism; spiritual-ism, -ist; subliminal –, subconscious- self.

V. disembody, spiritualize, dematerialize.

Adj. immateri-al, -ate; incorpor-eal, -al; asomatous, unextended; un-, dis-embodied; extramundane, supersensible, unearthly;

pneumatoscopic; spiritual etc. (*psychical*) 450; aery.   ,

personal, subjective.

318. World.—N. world, creation, nature, universe; earth, globe, wide world; *cosmos*; terraqueous globe, sphere; macro-, mega-cosm; music of the spheres; strato-, tropo-sphere.

heavens, sky, welkin, empyrean; starry -heaven, – host; firmament; vault –, canopy- of heaven; celestial spaces.

heavenly bodies, stars, luminaries, nebulae; galaxy, milky way, galactic circle, *via lactea*.

sun, orb of day, Apollo, Phoebus; photo-, chromo-sphere; solar system; planet, -oid, asteroid; comet; satellite; moon, orb of night, Diana, Luna; aerolite, meteor; falling –, shooting-star; meteorite.

constellation, zodiac, signs of the zodiac, Charles's wain, Great Bear, Southern Cross, Orion's belt, Cassiopeia's chair, Pleiades etc.

colures, equator, ecliptic, orbit.

[Science of heavenly bodies] astronomy; uranography, -logy; cosmo-logy, -graphy, -gony; *eidouranion*, orrery; geography; geodesy etc. (*measurement*) 466; star-gazing, -gazer; astronomer; cosmogonist, geodesist, geographer; observatory.

Adj. cosmic, cosmical, mundane; terr-estrial, -estrious, -aqueous, -ene, -eous; telluric, earthly, geotic, geodetic, cosmogonal, under the sun; sublunary, -astral.

solar, heliacal; lunar; celestial, heavenly, empyreal, sphery; starry, stellar; sider-eal, -al; astral; nebular.

Adv. in all creation, on the face of the globe, here below, under the sun.

319. Gravity.—N. gravi-ty, -tation; weight; heaviness etc. *adj.*; specific gravity; ponderosity, pressure, load; bur-den, -then; ballast, counterpoise; lump –, mass –, weight- of.

lead, millstone, mountain, Ossa on Pelion.

weighing, ponderation, trutination; weights; avoirdupois –, troy –, apothecaries'- weight; grain, scruple, drachm, ounce, pound, lb., load, stone, hundredweight, cwt., ton, quintal, carat, pennyweight, tod, gram, kilogram etc.

[Weighing instrument] balance, scales, steelyard, beam, weighbridge, spring balance, weighing machine.

[Science of gravity] statics.

V. be -heavy etc. *adj.*; gravitate, weigh, press, cumber, load.

[Measure the weight of] weigh, poise.

Adj. weighty; weighing etc. *v.*; heavy, – as lead; ponder-ous, -able; lump-ish, -y; cumber-, burden-some; cumbrous, unwieldy, massive.

in-, superin-cumbent.

320. Levity.—N. levity; lightness etc. *adj.*; imponderability, imponderables, buoyancy, volatility.

feather, dust, mote, down, thistledown, flue, cobweb, gossamer, straw, cork, bubble; float, bouy; ether, air.

leaven, ferment, barm, yeast, enzyme.
V. be -light etc. *adj.*; float, swim, be buoyed up.
render -light etc. *adj.*; lighten, levitate; leaven.
Adj. light, subtile, subtle, airy; imponder-ous, -able; astatic, weightless, ethereal, sublimated; uncompressed, volatile; buoyant, floating etc. *v.*; barmy, frothy; portable.
light as -a feather, – thistle down, – air.
fermenting etc. *n.*

321. Density.—**N.** density, solidity; solidness etc. *adj.*; impenetra-, impermea-bility; incompressibility; imporosity; cohesion etc. 46; constipation, consistence, spissitude.
specific gravity; hydro-, areo-meter.
condensation; solid-ation, -ification; consolidation; concretion, caseation, coagulation; petrifaction etc. (*hardening*) 323; crystallization, precipitation; deposit, precipitate, silt; inspissation; thickening etc. *v.*
indivisibility, indiscerptibility, indissolvableness.
solid body, mass; block, knot, lump; con-cretion, -crete, -glomerate; cake, clot, stone, curd, coagulum, grume; bone, gristle, cartilage.
V. be -dense etc. *adj.*; become –, render- solid etc. *adj.*; solid-ify, -ate; concrete, set, take a set, consolidate, congeal, coagulate; curd, -le; fix, clot, cake, candy, precipitate, deposit, cohere, crystallize; petrify etc. (*harden*) 323.
condense, thicken, inspissate, incrassate; compress, squeeze, ram down, constipate.
Adj. dense, solid, solidified etc. *v.*; cohe-rent, -sive etc. 46; compact, close, serried, thickset; substantial, massive, lumpish; impenetrable, impermeable, imporous; incompressible; constipated; concrete etc. (*hard*) 323; knot-ted, -ty; gnarled; crystal-line, -lizable; thick, grumous, stuffy.
un-dissolved, -melted, -liquified, -thawed.
in-divisible, -discerptible, -frangible, dissolvable, -dissoluble, -soluble, -fusible.

322. Rarity.—**N.** rarity; tenuity; absence of -solidity etc. 321; subtility; sponginess, compressibility.
rarefaction, expansion, dilatation, inflation, subtilization.
ether etc. (*gas*) 334.
V. rarefy, expand, dilate, subtilize, attenuate, thin.
Adj. rare, subtile, thin, fine, tenuous, compressible, flimsy, slight; light etc. 320; cavernous, spongy etc. (*hollow*) 252.
rarefied etc. *v.*; unsubstantial; uncom-pact, -pressed.

323. Hardness.—**N.** hardness etc. *adj.*; rigidity, renitence, inflexibility, temper, callosity, durity.
induration, petrifaction; lapid-ification, -escence; vitri-, ossi-, corni-fication; crystallization.
stone, pebble, flint, marble, rock, fossil, crag, crystal, quartz, granite, adamant; bone, cartilage; heart of oak, block, board, deal board; iron, steel; cast –, wrought- iron; nail; brick, concrete; cement.

V. render -hard etc. *adj.*; harden, stiffen, indurate, petrify, temper, ossify, vitrify.
Adj. hard, rigid, stubborn, stiff, firm; starch, -ed; stark, unbending, unlimber, unyielding; inflexible, tense; indurate, -d; gritty, proof.
adamant-ine, -ean; concrete, stony, rocky, lithic, granitic, vitreous; crystalline; horny, corneous; bony; oss-eous, -ific; cartilaginous; hard as a -stone etc. *n.*; stiff as -buckram, – a poker.

324. Softness.—**N.** softness, pliableness etc. *adj.*; flexibility; pli-ancy, -ability; sequacity, malleability; flabbiness; duct-, tract-ility; extend-, extensibility; plasticity; inelasticity; flaccidity, laxity.
clay, wax, butter, dough, pudding; cushion, pillow, feather-bed, pad, down, padding, wadding.
mollification; softening etc. *v.*
V. render -soft etc. *adj.*; soften, mollify, mellow, relax, temper; mash, knead, squash, *massage*.
bend, yield, relent, relax, give.
Adj. soft, tender, supple; pli-ant, -able; flexible, -ile; lithe, -some; lissom, limber, plastic; ductile; tract-ile, -able; malleable, extensile, sequacious, inelastic, mollient.
yielding etc. *v.*; flabby, limp, flimsy.
flaccid, flocculent, downy; spongy, edematous, medullary, doughy, argillaceous, mellow.
soft as -butter, – down, – silk; yielding as wax; tender as a chicken.

325. Elasticity.—**N.** elasticity, springiness, spring, resilience, renitency, buoyancy.
india-rubber, caoutchouc, gutta-percha, whalebone, gum elastic.
V. be -elastic etc. *adj.*; spring back etc. (*recoil*) 227.
Adj. elastic, tensile, springy, ductile, resilient, renitent, buoyant.

326. Inelasticity.—**N.** want of –, absence of-elasticity etc. 325; inelasticity etc. (*softness*) 324.
Adj. inelastic etc. (*soft*) 324.

327. Tenacity.—**N.** tenacity, toughness, strength; cohesion etc. 46; sequacity; stubbornness etc. (*obstinacy*) 606; viscidity etc. 352.
leather; gristle, cartilage.
V. be -tenacious etc. *adj.*; resist fracture.
Adj. tenacious, tough, cohesive, adhesive, strong, resisting, sequacious, stringy, gristly, cartilaginous, leathery, coriaceous, tough as whit-leather; stubborn etc. (*obstinate*) 606.

328. Brittleness.—**N.** brittleness etc. *adj.*; frag-, friab-, frangib-, fiss-ility; frailty; house of -cards, – glass.
V. be -brittle etc. *adj.*; live in a glass house.
break, crack, snap, split, shiver, splinter, crumble, break short, burst, fly, give way; fall to pieces; crumble -to, – into- dust.

Adj. breakable, brittle, frangible, fragile, frail, friable, delicate, gimcrack, shivery, fissile; splitting etc. *v.*; lacerable, splintery, crisp, crimp, short, brittle as glass.

329. Texture. [Structure.]—**N.** structure, organization, anatomy, frame, mold, fabric, construction; frame-work, carcass, architecture; stratification, cleavage.

substance, stuff, *compages, parenchyma*; constitution, staple, organism.

[Science of structures]organ-, oste-, my- splanchn-. neur-, angi-. aden-ology; angi-. aden-ography.

texture; inter-, con-texture; tissue, grain, web, surface; warp and -woof, − weft; tooth, nap etc. (*roughness*) 256; fineness −, coarseness- of grain.

[Science of textures] histology.

Adj. structural, organic; anatomic, -al.

text-ural, -ile; fine-, coarse-grained; fine, delicate, subtile, gossamery, filmy; coarse; homespun; linsey-woolsey.

330. Pulverulence. [State of powder.]—**N.** pulverulence; sandiness etc. *adj.*; efflorescence; friability.

powder, dust, sand, shingle; sawdust; grit; attrition; meal, bran, flour, *farina*, spore, sporule; crumb, seed, grain; particle etc. (*smallness*) 32; thermion; limature, filings, *débris, detritus*, scobs, magistery, fine powder; *flocculi*.

smoke; cloud of -dust, − sand, − smoke; puff −, volume -of smoke; sand −, dust- storm.

[Reduction to powder] pulverization, comminution, attenuation, granulation; disintegration, subaction, contusion, trituration, levigation, abrasion, detrition, multure; limâtion; filing etc. *v.*

[Instruments for pulverization] mill, millstone, grater, rasp, file, pestle and mortar, nutmeg grater, teeth, molar, grinder, chopper, grindstone, kern, quern, muller.

V. come to dust; be -disintegrated, − reduced to powder etc.

reduce −, grind- to powder; pulverize, comminute, granulate, triturate, levigate; scrape, file, abrade, rub down, grind, grate, rasp, pound, bray, bruise; con-tuse, -tund; beat, crush, cranch, craunch, crunch, muller, scranch, crumble, disintegrate; attenuate etc. 195.

Adj. powdery, pulverulent, granular, mealy, floury, farinaceous, branny, furfuraceous,' flocculent, dusty, sandy, sabulous; aren-ose, -arious, -aceous; gritty; efflorescent, impalpable.

pulverizable; friable, crumbly, shivery; pulverized etc. *v.*; attrite; in pieces.

331. Friction.—**N.** friction, attrition; rubbing etc. *v.*; erasure; con-frication, -trition; affriction, abrasion, arrosion, limature, frication, rub; elbowgrease; rosin; *massage*.

V. rub, scratch, abrade, scrape, scrub, fray, rasp, graze, curry, scour, polish, rub out, erase, gnaw; file, grind etc. (*reduce to powder*) 330; *massage*.

set one's teeth on edge; rosin.

Adj. anâtriptic, abrasive.

332. Lubrication. [Absence of friction. Prevention of friction.]—**N.** smoothness etc. 255; unctuousness etc. 355.

lubri-cation, -fication; anointment; oiling etc. *v.* synovia; lubricant, graphite, glycerine, oil etc. 356; saliva; lather.

V. lubri-cate, -citate; oil, grease, lather, soap; wax.

Adj. lubricated etc. *v.*

333. Fluidity.—**N.** fluidity, liquidity; liquidness etc. *adj.*; gaseity etc. 334; liquefaction etc. 334.

fluid, inelastic fluid; liquid, liquor; lymph, humor, juice, sap, serum, blood, serosity, gravy, rheum, ichor, sanies.

solu-bility, -bleness.

[Science of liquids] hydro-logy, -statics, dynamics, hydraulics. etc.

V. be -fluid etc. *adj.*; flow etc. (*water in motion*) 348; liquefy etc. 335.

Adj. liquid, fluid, serous, juicy, succulent, sappy; fluent etc. (*flowing*) 348.

liquefied etc. 335; uncongealed; soluble, hydrostatic etc. *n.*

334. Gaseity.—**N.** gaseity, gaseousness, vapourousness etc. *adj.*; flatulence, -lency; volatility, aeration, gasification.

elastic fluid, gas, air, vapor, ether, steam, fume, reek, *effluvium, flatus*; cloud etc. 353.

[Science of elastic fluids] pneumat-ics, -ostatics; aero-statics, -dynamics etc.

gas-, gaso-meter.

V. gassify, aerate, aerify; emit vapor etc. 336.

Adj. gaseous, aeriform, ethereal, aerial, airy, vaporous, volatile, evaporable; flatulent; aerostatic etc. *n.*

335. Liquefaction.—**N.** liquefaction; liquescen-ce, -cy, deliquescence; melting etc. (*heat*) 384; colliqu-ation, -efaction; thaw; de-, liquation; lixiviation, dissolution.

solution, apozem, lixivium, infusion, decoction, flux.

solvent, diluent, menstruum, alkahest, *aqua fortis*.

V. render -liquid etc 333; liquefy, run, deliquesce; melt etc. (*heat*) 384; solve; dissolve, resolve; liquate; hold in solution; leach, lixiviate.

Adj. lique-fied etc. *v.*, -scent, -fiable; deliquescent, soluble, colliquative; solvent.

336. Vaporization.—**N.** vapor-, volatilization; gasification; e-, vaporation; distillation, cohobation, sublimation, exhalation; volatility.

vaporizer, still, retort, spray, atomizer; fumigation, steaming.

V. render -gaseous etc. 334; vaporize, volatilize; distil, sublime; evaporate, exhale, smoke, transpire; emit vapor, fume, reek, steam, fumigate.

Adj. volatilized etc. *v.*; reeking etc. *v.*; volatile; evaporable, vaporizable.

337. Water.—N. water; serum, serosity; lymph; rheum; diluent.

dilution, maceration, lotion; washing etc. *v.*; im-, mersion; humectation, infiltration, spargefaction, affusion, irrigation, *douche*, balneation, bath.

deluge etc. (*water in motion*) 348; high water, flood-, spring-tide.

V. be -watery etc. *adj.*; reek.

add water, water, wet; moisten etc. 339; dilute, dip, immerse; merge; im-, sub-merge; plunge, souse, duck, drown; soak, steep, macerate, pickle, wash, sprinkle, sparge, lave, bathe, affuse, splash, swash, douse, slosh, drench; dabble, slop, slobber, irrigate, inundate, deluge; syringe, inject, gargle; infiltrate, percolate.

Adj. watery, aqueous, aquatic, lymphatic; balneal, diluent; drenching etc. *v.*; diluted etc. *v.*; weak; wet etc. (*moist*) 339.

Phr. the waters are out.

338. Air.—N. air etc. (*gas*) 334; common –, atmospheric- air; atmosphere, stratosphere, isothermal layer, troposphere, Heaviside layer.

open, – air; sky, welkin; blue, – sky; cloud etc. 353.

weather, climate, rise and fall of the barometer, isobar.

[Science of air] pneumatics, aero-logy, -scopy, -graphy; meteorology, climatology; eudio-, baro-, aero-meter; aneroid, baro-graph, -scope; weather-gauge, -glass, -cock.

exposure to the -air, – weather; ventilation; aero-station; -nautics; -naut etc. 265 and 269.

V. air, ventilate; fan etc. (*wind*) 349.

Adj. containing air, flatulent, effervescent; windy etc. 349.

atmospheric, airy; aeri-al, -form; pneumatic; meteorological; weather-wise.

Adv. in the open air, out of doors, *à la belle étoile, al fresco*; *sub -Jove, – dio*.

339. Moisture.—N. moisture; moistness etc. *adj.*; hum-idity, -ectation; madefaction, dew; *serein*; marsh etc. 345; Hygromet-ry, -er.

V. moisten, wet; humect, -ate; sponge, damp, dampen, bedew; imbue, imbrue, infiltrate, saturate; seethe, sop; soak, drench etc. (*water*) 337.

be -moist etc. *adj.*; not have a dry thread; perspire etc. (*exude*) 295.

Adj. moist, damp; watery etc. 337; undried, humid, wet, dank, muggy, dewy; roric; roscid; juicy.

wringing wet; wet -through, – to the skin; saturated etc. *v.*

swashy, soggy, dabbled; reeking, seething, dripping, soaking, soft, sodden, sloppy, muddy; swampy etc. (*marshy*) 345; irriguous.

340. Dryness.—N. dryness etc. *adj.*; siccity, aridity, drought, ebb-, neap-tide, low water.

drying, ex-, de-siccation; evaporation; dehydration; arefaction, dephlegmation, drainage.

drier, desiccator.

V. be -dry etc. *adj.*; render -dry etc. *adj.*; dry;

dry –, soak- up; sponge, swab, wipe; ex-, desiccate, dehydrate, anhydrate; drain, parch.

be fine, hold up.

Adj. dry, anhydrous, arid, waterless; dried etc. *v.*; undamped; juice-, sap- less; sear; husky; rainless, without rain, fine; dry as -a bone, – dust, – a stick, – a mummy, – a biscuit; disiccated; dehydrated; water-proof, -tight.

341. Ocean.—N. sea, ocean, main, deep, brine, salt water, waters, waves, billows, high seas, offing, great waters, watery waste, 'vasty deep,' briny ocean, herring pond, steamer track, the seven seas; wave, tide etc. (*water in motion*) 348.

hydrograph-y, -er, oceanography; Neptune, Thetis, Triton, Naiad, Nereid; sea-nymph, Siren, mer-maid, -man; trident, dolphin.

Adj. oceanic; mar-ine, -itime; pleagic, -ian; sea-going, -worthy; hydrographic.

Adv. at –, on- sea; afloat, on the high seas.

342. Land.—N. land, earth, ground, dry land, *terra firma*.

continent, mainland, peninsula, delta; tongue –, neck- of land; isthmus; oasis; promontory etc. (*projection*) 250; highland etc. (*height*) 206.

coast, shore, scar, strand, beach; bank, lea; sea-board, -side, -shore, -bank, -coast, -beach; rock-, iron- bound coast; loom of the land; derelict; innings; *alluvium*, alluvion.

soil, glebe, clay, loam, marl, clodge, chalk, gravel, mold, subsoil, clod, clot; rock, crag, cliff.

acres; real estate etc. (*property*) 780; landsman, land-lubber, farmer.

geography etc. 318; agriculture etc. 371.

V. land, come to land; set foot on -the soil, – dry land; come –, go- ashore.

Adj. earthy; continental, midland; littoral, riparian, ripuarian; alluvial; terrene etc. (*world*) 318; landed, predial, territorial.

Adv. ashore; on -shore, – land.

343. Gulf. Lake.—N. land covered with water, gulf, gulph, bay, inlet, bight, estuary, arm of the sea, fiord, armlet; frith, firth, ostiary, mouth; lagune, lagoon; indraught; cove, creek; natural harbor; roads; strait, narrows; Euripus; sound, belt, gut, kyles.

lake, loch, lough, mere, tarn, plash, broad, pond, pool, lin, puddle, well, artesian well, tank, sump; standing –, dead –, sheet of- water; fish –, mill-pond; race; ditch, dike, dyke, dam; reservoir etc. (*store*) 636.

Adj. lacustrine; land locked.

344. Plain.—N. plain, table land, mesa, face of the country; open –, champaign-country; basin, downs, waste, weary waste, desert, tundra, wild, steppe, pampas, savanna, prairie, champaign, heath, common, wold, veld; moor, -land, uplands, fell; bush; *plateau* etc. (*level*) 213; *campagna*.

meadow, mead, haugh, pasturage, park, field,

lawn, green, plat, plot, grass-plat, greensward, sward, grass, turf, sod, heather; lea, ley, lay; grounds.
Adj. campestrian, champaign, alluvial.

345. Marsh.—N. marsh, swamp, morass, marish, moss, fen, bog, quagmire, slough, sump, wash; mud, squash, slush.
Adj. marsh, -y; swampy, boggy, plashy, poachy, quaggy, soft; muddy, sloppy, squashy, spongy; paludal; moor-ish, -y; fenny.

346. Island.—N. island, isle, islet, eyot, ait, holm, reef, atoll, breaker; archipelago; islander.
Adj. insular, sea-girt.

347. Stream. [Fluid in motion.]**—N.** stream etc. (of water) 348, (of air) 349.
V. flow etc. 348; blow etc. 349.

348. River. [Water in motion.]**—N.** running water.
jet, spirt, squirt, spout, splash, swash, rush, gush, jet d'eau; sluice, chute.
water-spout, -fall; fall, cascade, force, foss; lin, -n, ghyll, Niagara; cata-ract, -dupe, -clysm; débâcle, inundation, deluge.
rain, -fall; serein; shower, scud; downpour, cloud burst; driving –, pouring –, drenching-rain; hyeto-logy, -graphy; rainy season, monsoon; predominance of Aquarius, reigh of St. Swithin; mizzle, drizzle, stilliciduim, plash; dropping etc. v.
stream, course, flux, flow, profluence; effluence etc. (egress) 295; defluxion; flowing etc. v.; current, tide, race.
spring; fount, -ain; rill, rivulet, gill, gullet, rillet; stream-, brook-let; runnel, sike, burn, beck, brook, stream, river; reach; tributary.
body of water, torrent, rapids, flush, flood, swash, spate; spring –, high –, full-tide; bore; eagre, hugre; fresh, -et; undertow, indraught, reflux, undercurrent, eddy, vortex, gurge, whirlpool, Maelstrom, regurgitation, overflow; confluence, corrivation.
wave, billow, surge, swell, ripple; roller, ground swell, surf, breaker, white horses; comber, beach-comber; rough –, heavy –, cross –, long –, short –, chopping –, choppy- sea, choppiness; tidal wave.
[Science of fluids in motion] Hydrodynamics; Hydraul-ics etc.; raingauge etc.
water-bearer, – carrier, Aquarius.
irrigation etc. (water) 337; pump; watering-pot, – cart; hydrant, standpipe, hose, sprinkler, drencher; fire engine, squirt, syringe.
V. flow, run; meander; gush, pour, spout, roll, jet, well, issue; drop, drip, dribble, plash, squirt, spurt, spirtle, trill, trickle, distil, percolate; stream, overflow, inundate, deluge, flow over, splash, swash; guggle, murmur, babble, bubble, purl, gurgle, sputter, regurgitate; ooze, flow out etc. (egress) 295.

rain, – hard, – in torrents, – cats and dogs, – pitchforks; come down in sheets; pour with rain, drizzle, mizzle, spit, sprinkle, set in.
flow –, fall –, open –, drain- into; discharge itself, desembogue.
[Cause a flow] pour; pour out etc. (discharge) 297; shower down; irrigate, drench etc. (wet) 337; spill, splash.
[Stop a flow] stanch; dam, -up etc. (close).261; obstruct etc. 706.
Adj. fluent; dif-, pro-, af-fluent; tidal; flowing etc. v.; meand-ering, -ry, -rous; fluvi-al, -atile; streamy, showery, rainy, drizzly, drizzling, pluvial, pluviose, stillicidous.

349. Wind. [Air in motion.]**—N.** wind, draught, flatus, afflatus, air; breath, – of air; puff, whiff, zephyr; blow, drift; aura; stream, current; under-current.
gust, blast, breeze, squall, gale, half a gale, storm, tempest, hurricane, whirlwind, tornado, samiel, cyclone, typhoon; simoon; harmattan, monsoon, trade wind, sirocco, mistral, bise, föhn, tramontane, levanter; capful of wind; fresh –, stiff- breeze; keen blast; blizzard.
windiness etc. adj.; ventosity; rough –, dirty –, ugly –, stress of- weather; dirty-, windy-, mackerel- sky; mare's tail; thick –, black –, white- squall.
anemography, aerodynamics; windgauge, anemometer, weather-cock, vane.
suf-, insuf-, per-, in-, af-flation; blowing, fanning etc. v.; ventilation.
sneezing etc. v.; sternutation; hic-cup, -cough; catching of the breath; breathing etc.
Eolus, Eurus, Boreas, Zephyr, cave of Eolus.
air-pump, lungs, bellows, blow-pipe, fan, blower; pulmotor, ventilator, punkah, aspirator, exhauster, ejector.
V. blow, waft; blow -hard, – great guns, – a hurricane etc. n.; whistle, roar, howl, ring in the shrouds; stream, issue.
respire, breathe, in-, ex-hale, puff; whif, -fle; gasp, wheeze; snuff, -le; sniff, -le; sneeze, cough, belch.
fan, ventilate; in-, per-flate; blow –, pump- up.
Adj. blowing etc. v.; windy, airy, aeolian, flatulent; breezy, gusty, squally; stormy, tempestuous, blustering; boisterous etc. (violent) 173, pulmon-ic, -ary.

350. Conduit. [Channel for the passage of water.]**—N.** conduit, channel, duct, watercourse, race; head –, tail- race; adit, aqueduct, canal, trough, flume, gutter, pantile; dike, canyon, ravine, gorge, hollow, main, gully, moat, ditch, drain, sewer, culvert, cloaca, sough, kennel, siphon, piscina; pipe etc. (tube) 260; funnel; tunnel etc. (passage) 627; water –, waste- pipe; emunctory, gully-hole, artery, aorta, vein, blood vessel; lymphatic; throat, alimentary canal, intestine; pore, spout, scupper; ad-, a-jutage; hose; gar-, gurgoyle; penstock, weir; flood-, water-gate; sluice, lock, valve; rose; waterworks.
Adj. vascular etc. (with holes) 260.

351. Air-pipe. [Channel for the passage of air.]**—N.** air-pipe, – shaft, – way, – passage, –

tube; shaft, flue, chimney, funnel, vent, blow-hole, nostril, nozzle, throat, weasand, *trachea*; *bronchus*, *-ia*; larynx, tonsils, wind-pipe, spiracle; venti-duct, -lator; louvre, Venetian blinds; blow-pipe etc. (*wind*) 349; pipe etc. (*tube*) 260.

352. Semiliquidity.—N. semiliquidity; stickiness etc. *adj.*; visc-idity, -osity; gumm-, glutin-, muc-osity; spiss-, crass-itude; lentor; adhesiveness etc. (*cohesion*) 46.

inspiss-, incrass-ation; thickening, coagulation.

jelly, aspic, mucilage, gelatin, isinglass; colloid, mucus, phlegm; pituite, lava; glair, starch, gluten, albumen, milk, cream, protein; syrup, treacle; gum, size, glue, paste; wax, bee's-wax; emulsoid, emulsion, soup; squash, mud, slush, slime, ooze; moisture etc. 339; marsh etc. 345.

V. inspiss-, incrass-ate; coagulate, gelatinize, gelatinify, gel, jell, emulsify, thicken; mash, squash, churn, beat up.

Adj. semi-fluid, -liquid; half-melted, -frozen; milky, muddy etc. *n.*; lact-eal, -ean, -eous, -escent, -iferous; emulsive, curdled, thick, succulent, uliginous.

gelat-, album-, mucilag-, glut-inous; gelatine, mastic, amylaceous, ropy, clammy, clotted; vis-cid, -cous; sticky, tacky; slab, -by; lentous, pituitous; mu-cid, -culent, -cous.

353. Bubble. [Mixture of air and water.] [Cloud.]—**N.** bubble; foam, froth, head, fume, spume, lather, suds, spray, surf, yeast, barm, spin-drift.

cloud, vapor, fog, mist, haze, steam; scud, rack, *nimbus*; *cumulus*, woolpack, *cirrus*, *stratus*; *cirro-, cumulo-stratus*; *cirro-cumulus*; mackerel sky, mare's tail, dirty sky.

[Science of clouds] nephelognosy, nephology.

effervescence, fermentation; bubbling etc. *v.*

nebula; cloudiness etc. (*opacity*) 426; nebulosity etc. (*dimness*) 422.

V. bubble, boil, foam, froth, spume, mantle, sparkle, guggle, gurgle; effervesce, ferment, fizzle; aerate; cloud, overcast, befog.

Adj. bubbling etc. *v.*; frothy, nappy, ef-fervescent, sparkling, *mousseux*, up, fizzy, with a head on.

cloudy etc. *n.*; vaporous, nebulous, overcast; nubiferous, nephological; foggy, brumous.

354. Pulpiness.—N. pulpiness etc. *adj.*; pulp, paste, dough, sponge, curd, pap, rob, jam, pudding, mush, fool, poultice, grume.

Adj. pulpy etc. *n.*; pultaceous, grumous.

V. pulp, pulpify, mash.

355. Unctuousness.—N. unctuousness etc. *adj.*; unctuosity, lubricity; ointment etc. (*oil*) 356; anointment; lubrication etc. 332.

V. oil etc. (*lubricate*) 332.

Adj. unctuous, oily, oleaginous, adipose, sebaceous; fat, -ty; greasy, waxy, butyraceous, soapy, saponaceous, pinguid, lardaceous; slippery.

356. Oil.—N. oil, fat, butter, cream, grease, tallow, suet, lard, dripping, margarine, oleomargarine, exunge, blubber; glycerine, stearine, elaine, oleagine; soap; soft soap, wax, cerement; paraffin, spermaceti, adipocere; petroleum, mineral —, rock —, crystal- oil, kerosene, vegetable —, colza —, olive —, linseed —, cotton seed —, rape —, nut —, fusel- oil; animal —, neat's foot —, signal —, train- oil; oint-ment, unguent, liniment, salve, pomade, pomatum, brilliantine, spike —, nard.

356a. Resin.—N. resin, rosin, colophony; gum; lac, shellac, sealing-wax; amber, -gris; bitumen, pitch, tar, asphalt, -e, -um; varnish, copal, mastic, magilp, lacquer, japan.

V. varnish etc. (*overlay*) 223.

Adj. resinous, bituminous, pitchy, tarry.

357. Organization.—N. organized -world, — nature; living —, animated- nature; living beings; organic remains, organism; fossils; animal and vegetable kingdom, *fauna* and *flora*, biota.

prot-oplasm, -ein; albumen; structure etc. 329; organ-ization, -ism.

[Science of living beings] biology; natural history,* organic —, bio-chemistry, anatomy, physiology, embryology, morphology, evolution, Darwinism, Lamarkism, zoology etc. 368; botany etc. 369; naturalist, biologist etc.

Adj. organ-ic, -ized.

*The term *Natural History* is also used as relating to all the objects in Nature whether organic or inorganic, and in-cluding therefore *Mineralogy, Geology, Meteorology*, etc.

358. Inorganization.—N. mineral -world, — kingdom; unorganized —, inorganic —, brute —, inanimate- matter.

[Science of the mineral kingdom] mineralogy; geo-logy, -gnosy, -scopy; metall-urgy, -ography; lithology; orycto-logy, -graphy.

V. turn to dust, pulverize.

Adj. in-organic, -animate; unorganized; azoic; mineral.

359. Life.—N. life; vi-tality, -ability; animation; vital -spark, — flame, — force.

respiration, wind; breath -of life, — of one's nostrils; life-blood; Archeus; existence etc. 1.

vivification, vitalization; revivification etc. 163; Prometheus; life to come etc. (*destiny*) 152.

[Science of life] physiology, etiology, em-bryology, biology; animal economy.

nourishment, staff of life etc. (*food*) 298.

V. be -alive etc. *adj.*; live, breathe, respire; sub-sist etc. (*exist*) 1; walk the earth; strut and fret one's hour upon a stage; be spared.

see the light, be born, come into the world; fetch —, draw- -breath, — the breath of life; quicken; revive; come to, — life.

give birth to etc. (*produce*) 161; bring to life, put into life, vitalize; vivi-fy, -ficate; reanimate etc. (*restore*) 660; keep -alive, — body and soul together, — the wolf from the door; support life.

have nine lives like a cat.

Adj. living, alive; in -life, – the flesh, – the land of the living; on this side of the grave, above ground, breathing, quick, animated, viable; lively etc. (*active*) 682; alive and kicking; tenacious of life.

vital; vivi-fying; -fied etc. *v.*; Promethean.

Adv. *vivendi causâ.*

360. Death.—N. death, dying etc. *v.*; de-cease, -mise; dissolution, departure, *obit*, release, rest, *quietus*, fall; loss, bereavement.

end etc. 67 –, cessation etc. 142 –, loss –, extinction –, ebb- of -life etc. 359.

death-warrant, -watch, -rattle, -bed; stroke –, agonies –, shades –, valley of the shadow –, jaws –, hand- of death; last -breath, – gasp, – agonies; dying -day, – breath, – agonies; swan song, *chant du cygne*; *rigor mortis*; Stygian shore; crossing the bar, the great adventure.

King -of terrors, – Death; Death, Angel of Death; mortality; doom etc. (*necessity*) 601.

euthanasia; happy release; break up of the system; natural -death, – decay; sudden –, violent- death; untimely end, watery grave; suffocation, *asphyxia*; heart failure; fatal disease etc. (*disease*) 655; death-blow etc. (*killing*) 361.

necrology, bills of mortality, obituary; death-song etc. (*lamentation*) 839.

V. die, expire, perish; meet one's -death, – end; pass away, be taken; yield –, resign- one's breath; resign one's -being, – life; end one's -days, – life, – earthly career; breathe one's last; cease to -live, – breathe; depart this life; be -no more etc. *adj.*; go –, drop –, pop -off; lose –, lay down –, relinquish –, surrender- one's life; drop –, sink- into the grave; close one's eyes; fall –, drop- dead, – down dead; break one's neck; give –, yield- up the ghost; be all over with one.

pay the debt to nature, shuffle off this mortal coil, take one's last sleep; go the way of all flesh; join the -greater number, – majority, – choir invisible, to life immortal awake; come –, turn- to dust; cross the Stygian ferry; go to -one's long ac count, – one's last home, – Davy Jones's locker, – the wall; receive one's death warrant, make one's will, die a natural death, go out like the snuff of a candle; come to an untimely end; catch one's death; go off the hooks, kick the bucket, pet out; go West; hop the twig, turn up one's toes; die a violent death etc. (*be killed*) 361; make the supreme sacrifice.

Adj. dead, lifeless; deceased, demised, departed, defunct; late, gone, no more; ex-, in-animate; out of the world, taken off, released; departed this life etc. *v.*; dead and gone; bereft of life, stone dead, dead as -a door nail, – a door post, – mutton, – a herring, – nits; launched into eternity, gathered to one's fathers, numbered with the dead, gone to a better land, behind the veil, beyond the grave, – mortal ken.

dying etc. *v.*; mori-bund, -ent, Acherontic; hippocratic; *in -articulo*, – *extremis*; in the -jaws, – agony- of death; going, – off; *aux abois*; on one's -last legs, – death bed; at -the point of death, – death's door, – the last gasp; near one's end, given over, booked, fey; with one foot in –, tottering on the brink of- the grave.

still-born; mortuary; deadly etc. (*killing*) 361.

Adv. *post -obit, – mortem.*

Phr. life -ebbs, – fails, – hangs by a thread; one's -days are numbered, – hour is come, – race is run, – doom is sealed; Death -knocks at the door, – stares one in the face; the breath is out of the body; the grave closes over one; *sic itur ad astra.*

361. Killing. [Destruction of life; violent death.]—**N.** killing etc. *v.*; homicide, manslaughter, murder, assassination, trucidation, occision; lynching, effusion of blood; blood, -shed; gore, slaughter, carnage, butchery; *battue*, gladiatorial combat.

massacre; *fussillade, noyade, pogrom*; thuggism; racketeering.

death blow, finishing stroke, *coup de grâce*, *quietus*; execution etc. (*capital punishment*) 972; judicial murder; martyrdom.

butcher, slayer, murderer, Cain, assassin, cutthroat, garrotter, *bravo*, thug, racketeer, gunman, mobster, gangster, Moloch, *matador, sabreur; guet-à-pens*; gallows, executioner etc. (*punishment*) 975; man-eater.

regicide, parricide, fratricide, infanticide, aborticide etc.

suicide, *felo de se, suttee, hara kiri*, Juggernaut; immolation, holocaust.

suffocation, strangulation, *garrotte*; hanging etc. *v.*

deadly weapon etc. (*arms*) 727; Aceldama; the potter's field, the field of blood.

fatal accident, violent death, casualty.

[Destruction of animals] slaughtering; phthiozoics;* sport, -'ing; the chase, venery; hunting, coursing, shooting, fishing; pig-sticking; sports-, hunts-, fisher-man; hunter, Nimrod; slaughterer, knacker, slaughter-house, shambles, *abattoir.*

V. kill, put to death, slay, shed blood; murder, assassinate, butcher, slaughter; victimize, immolate; massacre; take away –, deprive of- life; make away with, put an end to; despatch, dispatch; burke settle, do, – to death, – for.

strangle, garrotte, hang, lynch, throttle, choke, stifle, suffocate, stop the breath, smother, asphyxiate, drown.

saber; cut -down, – to pieces, – the throat; jugulate; stab, run through the body, bayonet; put to the -sword, – edge of the sword.

shoot, – dead; blow one's brains out; brain, knock on the head; stone, lapidate; give –, deal- a death blow; give a -*quietus*, – *coup de grâce*.

behead, bowstring etc. (*execute*) 972.

hunt, shoot etc. *n.*

cut off, nip in the bud, launch into eternity, send to one's last account, bump off, rub out, sign one's death warrant, strike the death knell of.

give no quarter, pour out blood like water; decimate; run amuck, wade knee-deep –, imbrue one's hands- in blood.

die a violent death, welter in one's blood; dash –, blow- out one's brains; commit suicide; kill -make away with –, put an end to- oneself.

Adj. killing etc. *v.*; murd-, slaught-erous; sanguin-ary, -olent; blood-stained, -thirsty;

homicidal, red-handed; bloody, -minded; ensanguined, gory, sanguineous.
mortal fatal, lethal; dead-, death-ly; mort-, lethiferous; unhealthy etc. 657; internecine; suicidal.
sporting; piscator-ial, -y.
Adv. in at the death.
*Bentham, 'Chrestomathia.'

362. Corpse.—N. corpse, corse, carcass, bones, skeleton, dry-bones; defunct, relics, *relinquiae*, remains, mortal remains, dust, ashes, earth, clay; mummy; carrion; food for- worms, — fishes; tenement of clay, this mortal coil.
shade, ghost, *manes*, apparition etc. 980.
organic remains, fossils.
Adj. cadaverous, corpse-like; unburied etc. 363.

363. Interment.—N. interment, burial, inhumation, sepulture, entombment; in-, humation; obs-, ex-equies; funeral, wake, pyre, funeral pile; cremation.
funeral -rite, — solemnity; knell, passing bell; tolling; dirge etc. (*lamentation*) 839; cypress; *obit*, dead march, muffled drum; coroner, mortician, undertaker, mute, mourner, professional mourner, pallbearer; elegy; funeral -oration, — sermon; epitaph.
grave clothes, shroud; winding-sheet, cere-cloth; cerement.
coffin, shell, sarcophagus, urn, pall, bier, hearse, catafalque, cinerary urn.
grave, pit, sepulcher, tomb, vault, crypt, catacomb, mausoleum, *Golgotha*, house of death, narrow house, long home; cemetery, necropolis, boneyard; burial-place, -ground; grave-, churchyard; God's acre; mortuary, tope, cromlech, dolmen, menhir, barrow, tumulus, cairn; ossuary; bone-, charnel-, dead-house; *Morgue*; lich-gate; crematorium.
sexton, grave-digger.
monument, memorial, cenotaph, shrine; grave-, head-, tomb-stone; *memento mori*; hatchment, stone, cross.
exhumation, disinterment; necropsy, autopsy, *post mortem* examination.
V. inter, bury, lay in —, consign to- the -grave, — tomb; en-, in-tomb; inhume; lay out, prepare for burial, embalm, mummify; conduct a funeral, hold services; toll the knell; put to bed with a shovel.
exhume, disinter, unearth.
Adj. buried etc. *v.*; burial; fune-real, -brial; mortuary, sepulchral, cinerary; elegiac; necroscopic.
Adv. *in memoriam*; *post-obit*, *-mortem*; beneath —, under- the sod.
Phr. *hic jacet, ci-git, requiescat in pace*.

364. Animality.—N. animal life; anima-tion, -lity, -lization; breath.
flesh, — and blood; corporeal nature; *physique*; strength etc. 159.
V. animalize, incorporate.
Adj. fleshly, incarnate, carnal, corporeal, human.

365. Vegetability.—N. vegetable life; vegetation, -bility; herbage.

V. vegetate, germinate, sprout, shoot; cultivate.
Adj. vegetable etc. 367; rank, lush.

366. Animal.°**—N.** animal, — kingdom; *fauna*; brute creation.
beast, brute, creature, created being; creeping —, living- thing; dumb -animal, — creature.
flocks and herds, live stock; domestic —, wild-animals; game, *ferae naturae*; beasts of the fields, fowls of the air, denizens of the day.
vertebrate, bi-, quadru-ped, mammal, marsupial, bird, reptile, batrachian, amphibian, fish, crustacean, shell fish, articulate, mollusc, worm, insect, zoophyte; protozoon, animalcule etc. 193.
horse etc. (*beast of burden*) 271; cattle, kine, ox; bull, -ock; steer, stot; cow, milch-cow, calf, heifer, shorthorn; sheep; lamb, -kin; ewe —, pet-lamb; ewe, ram, tup; pig, swine, boar, hog, shoat, sow; tag, teg, wether.
dog, bitch, hound; pup, -py; whelp, cur, mutt, mongrel; house-, watch-, sheep-, shepherd's, sporting-, fancy-, lap-, toy-, bull-, badger-dog; mastiff; blood-, grey-, stag-, deer-, fox-, otter-, hound; harrier, beagle, spaniel, pointer, setter, retriever; Newfoundland; water -dog, — spaniel; pug, poodle; dachshund; Pinscher; turnspit; terrier; fox —, Skye- terrier; Dandie Dinmont; colley.
cat; puss,-y; kitten; grimalkin; gib-, tom-cat; mouser; fox, Reynard, vixen, stag, deer, hart, buck, doe, roe, antelope.
bird; poultry, fowl, cock, hen, chicken, chanticleer, partlet, rooster, dunghill cock, barn-door fowl; feathered -tribes, — songster; singing —, dicky- bird; canary; finch; auk, dodo, moa, roc, phoenix.
snake, serpent, viper, adder; newt, eft; asp, vermin.
Adj. animal, zoological.
equine, bovine, vaccine, canine, feline; fishy; piscator-y, -ial; molluscous, vermicular.
° *Extended lists of names of specific varieties of animals, vegetables, etc., are beyond the scope of this work.*

367. Vegetable.°**—N.** vegetable, — kingdom; *flora*, verdure.
plant; tree, shrub, bush; creeper; vine; herb, -age; grass.
annual; per-, bi-, tri-ennial; exotic.
timber; primeval —, virgin- forest; wood, -lands; hurst; frith, holt, weald, park, chase, greenwood, brake, grove, copse, coppice, *bocage*, *tope*, clump of trees, thicket, spinet, spinney; under-, brushwood; boscage, scrub; the oak and the ash and the bonny ivy tree.
bush, jungle, prairie; heath, -er; fern, bracken, furze, gorse, whin, broom; grass, turf, grassland, greensward, green, lawn, meadow; pas-ture, -turage; turbary; sedge, rush, weed; fungus, mushroom, toadstool; lichen, moss, conferva, mold; seaweed etc.; growth, crop.
foliage, leafage, branch, bough, ramage; spray etc. 51; leaf, frond, flag, petal, shoot, tendril.
flower, blossom, bud, bloom, bine; flowering plant; tree, sapling, pollard; timber-, fruit-tree; palm-, gum-tree; pulse, legume.
Adj. veget-able, -ous; herb-aceous, -al; botanic; sylvan, silvan; arbor- ary, -eous, -escent, -ical; den-

dritic, dendriform; woooy, grassy; ver-dant, -durous; floral, mossy; lign-ous, -eous; wooden, leguminous; end-, ex-ogenous.

*Extended lists of names of specific varieties of animals, vegetables, etc., are beyond the scope of this work.

368. Zoology. [The science of animals.]—N. zoo-logy, -nomy, -graphy, -tomy; anatomy; comparative anatomy; animal —, comparative-physiology; morphology.

anthrop-, ornith-, ichthy-, herpet-, ophi-, malac-, helminth-, entom-, oryct-, paleont-ology; ichthy- etc. -otomy; taxidermy.

zo- etc. -ologist.

Adj. zoological etc. n.

369. Botany. [The science of plants.]—N. botany; phyto-graphy, -logy, -tomy; vegetable physiology, herborization, dendr-, myc-, fung-, alg-ology; flora, pomona; botanist etc.; botanic garden etc. (garden) 371; hortus siccus, herbarium, herbal.

herb-ist, -arist, -alist, -orist, -arian etc.

V. botanize, herborize.

Adj. botanical etc. n.

370. Cicuration. [The economy or management of animals.]—N. taming etc. v.; cicuration, zoohygiantics; domestication, -ity; manège; veterinary art; breeding, pisciculture, apiculture etc.

menagery, vivarium, zoological garden, zoo; bear-pit; aviary, apiary, hive; aquarium, fishery, fish hatchery; duck-, fish-pond; stud-farm; stock farm, dairy.

[Destruction of animals] phthisozoics etc. (killing) 361.

neat-, cow-, shep-herd, shepherdess; grazier; drover, cowboy, cowkeeper; trainer, breeder, groom, ostler etc. 746; veterinary surgeon, vet, horse doctor; farrier; keeper; game keeper.

cage etc. (prison) 752; hen-coop, bird-cage, cauf; sheep-fold etc. (inclosure) 232.

V. tame, domesticate, acclimatize, breed, tend, break in, train, corral, round up; cage, bridle etc. (restrain) 751; ride etc. 266.

drive, yoke, harness, hitch; groom, curry-comb; milk; shear; hatch; incubate.

Adj. pastoral, bucolic; tame, domestic, domesticated, broken in, gentle, docile.

371. Agriculture. [The economy or management of plants.]—N. agriculture, cultivation, husbandry, farming; georgics, geoponics; tillage, tilth, agronomy, gardening, spade husbandry. vintage; hort-, arbor-, silv-, citr-, vit-, flor-iculture; intensive culture; landscape gardening; forestry, afforestation.

husbandman, horticulturist, citriculturist, gardener, florist; agricult-or, -urist; yeoman, farmer, cultivator, tiller of the soil, ploughman, sower, reaper; woodcutter, backwoodsman, forester; vine grower, vintager; Boer; Triptolemus.

field, meadow, garden; botanic —, winter —, or-

namental —, flower —, kitchen —, truck —, market —, hop- garden; nursery; green-, hot-, glass-house; conservatory, cucumber frame, cloche, bed, border, seed-plot; grass-plat, lawn; park etc. (pleasure ground) 840; partere, shrubbery, plantation, avenue, arboretum, pinery, pinetum, orchard, vineyard, vinery; orangery; farm etc. (abode) 189.

V. cultivate; till, — the soil; farm, garden; sow, plant; reap, mow, cut; manure, dress the ground, dig, delve, dibble, hoe, plough, plow, harrow, rake, weed, lop and top, force, transplant, thin out, bed out, prune, graft.

Adj. agr-icultural, -airan, -estic.

arable; predial, rural, rustic, country, bucolic, Boeotian; horticultural.

372. Mankind.—N. man, -kind; human -race, — species, — nature; humanity, mortality, flesh, generation.

[Science of man] anthropo-logy, -graphy, sophy; ethno-logy, -graphy; humanitarianism.

human being; person, -age; individual, creature, fellow creature, mortal, body, somebody, one; such a —, someone; soul, living soul; earthling; party, head, hand; dramatis personae.

people, persons, folk, public, society, world; community, — at large; general public; nation, -ality; state, realm; common-weal, -wealth; republic, body politic; million etc. (commonalty) 876; population etc. (inhabitant) 188.

cosmopolite; lords of the creation; ourselves.

Adj. human, mortal, personal, individual, national, civic, public, cosmopolitan; anthropoid.

373. Man.—N. man, male, he; manhood etc. (adolescence) 131; , gentleman, sir, master; yeoman, wight, swain, fellow, guy, blade, beau, chap, gaffer, good man; husband etc. (married man) 903; Mr., mister, monsieur, sahib, Herr, señor, signor; boy etc. (youth) 129; Adonis.

[Male animal] cock, drake, gander, dog, boar, stag, hart, buck, horse, entire horse, stallion; gib-, tom-cat; he-, Billy-goat; ram, tup; bull, -ock; capon, ox, gelding; steer, stot.

Adj. male, he, masculine; manly, virile; unwomanly, -feminine.

374. Woman.—N. woman, she, female, petticoat, skirt, moll, broad.

feminality, feminity, muliebrity; womanhood etc. (adolescence) 131; feminism; gynecology, gyniatrics, gynics.

womankind; the -sex, — fair; fair —, softer- sex; weaker vessel; the distaff side.

dame, madam, madame, mistress, Mrs., lady, mem-sahib, Frau, señora, signora, donna, belle, matron, dowager, goody, gammer; good -woman, — wife; squaw; wife etc. (marriage) 903; matronage, -hood.

Venus, nymph, wench, grisette; little bit of fluff; girl etc. (youth) 129.

inamorata (love) etc. 897; courtesan etc. 962. spinster, old maid, virgin, bachelor girl, new woman, amazon.

[Female animal] hen, slut, bitch, sow, doe, roe, mare; she-, Nanny-goat; ewe, cow; lioness, tigress; vixen.

gynecaeum, harem, *seraglio, zenana, purdah*.

Adj. female, she; feminine, womanly, ladylike, matronly, maidenly; womanish, effeminate, unmanly, gynecic.

375. Physical Sensibility.—N. sensibility; sensitiveness etc. *adj.*; physical sensibility, feeling, perceptivity, anaphylaxis, susceptibility, esthetics; moral sensibility etc. 882.

sensation, impression, effect; consciousness etc. (*knowledge*) 490.

external senses.

V. be -sensible etc. *adj.* -of; feel, perceive.

render, -sensible etc. *adj.*; excite, stir, sharpen, cultivate, tutor.

cause sensation, impress; excite –, produce- an impression.

Adj. sens-ible, -itive, -uous; esthetic, perceptive, sentient; conscious etc. (*aware*) 490; impressionable, responsive, alive to.

acute, sharp, keen, vivid, lively, impressive, thin-skinned.

Adv. to the quick.

376. Physical Insensibility.—N. insensibility, physical insensibility; obtuseness etc. *adj.*; palsy, paralysis, anesthesia, analgesia, narcosis, hypnosis, twilight sleep, stupor, coma, trance, catalepsy; sleep etc. (*inactivity*) 683; moral insensibility etc. 823; numbness etc. 381.

anesthetic agent, general –, local- anesthetic, opium, ether, chloroform, cocaine, novocaine, chloral; nitrous oxide, laughing gas; refrigeration.

V. be -insensible etc. *adj.*; have a -thick skin, – rhinoceros hide.

render -insensible etc. *adj.*; blunt, pall, obtund, benumb, deaden, paralyze; anesthetize, drug, dope; put under the influence of -chloroform etc. *n.*; hypnotize; stupefy, stun, narcotize.

Adj. insensible, unfeeling, senseless, comatose, dazed, impercipient, callous, thick-skinned, pachydermatous; hard, -ened; case-hardened; proof; obtuse, dull; anesthetic; paralytic, palsied, numb, dead.

377. Physical Pleasure.—N. pleasure; physical –, sensual –, sensuous- pleasure; bodily enjoyment, animal gratification, sensuality; hedonism, luxuriousness etc. *adj.*; dissipation, round of pleasure; titillation, *gusto*, creature comforts, comfort, ease; pillow etc. (*support*) 215; luxury, lap of luxury; purple and fine linen; bed of -down, – roses; velvet, clover; cup of Circe etc. (*intemperance*) 954.

treat; diversion, divertisement, entertainment; refreshment, regale; feast; *délice*; dainty etc. 394; *bonne bouche*.

source of pleasure etc. 829; happiness etc. (*mental enjoyment*) 827.

V. feel –, experience –, receive- pleasure; enjoy, relish; luxuriate –, revel –, riot –, bask –,

swim –, wallow- in; feast on; gloat -over, – on; smack the lips.

live -on the fat of the land, – in comfort etc. *adv.*; bask in the sunshine, *faire ses choux gras*.

give pleasure etc. 829.

Adj. enjoying etc. *v.*; luxurious, voluptuous, sensual, hedonistic, comfortable, cosy, snug, in comfort, at ease.

agreeable etc. 829; grateful, refreshing, comforting, cordial, genial; sensuous; palatable etc. 394; sweet etc. (*sugar*) 396; fragrant etc. 400; melodious etc. 413; lovely etc. (*beautiful*) 845.

Adv. in -comfort etc. *n.*; on -a bed of roses etc. *n.*; at one's ease.

378. Physical Pain.—N. pain; suffering, -ance; bodily – physical -pain, – suffering; mental suffering etc. 828; dolor, ache; aching etc. *v.*; smart; shoot, -ing; twinge, twitch, gripe, head-, ear-, toothache; *migraine*, neuralgia, neuritis, lumbago, gout, sciatica; hurt, cut; sore, -ness; discomfort, *malaise*; *tic douloureux*.

spasm, cramp; nightmare, *ephialtes*; crick, stitch, kink; thrill, convulsion, throe; throb etc. (*agitation*) 315; pang.

sharp –, piercing –, throbbing –, shooting – gnawing –, burning- pain; anguish, agony.

torment, torture; rack; cruci-ation, -fixion; martyrdom; martyr, toad under a harrow, vivisection.

V. feel –, experience –, suffer –, undergo-pain etc. *n.*; suffer, ache, smart, bleed; tingle, shoot; twinge, twitch, lancinate; writhe, wince, make a wry face; sit on -thorns, – pins and needles.

give –, inflict- pain; pain, hurt, chafe, sting, bite, gnaw, gripe, stab, grind; pinch, tweak; grate, gall, fret, prick, pierce, wring, convulse; torment, torture; rack, agonize; crucify; excruciate; break on the wheel, put to the rack; flag etc. (*punish*) 972; grate on the ear etc. (*harsh sound*) 410.

Adj. in -pain etc. *n.*; – a state of pain; pained etc. *v.*

painful; aching etc. *v.*; biting, poignant; sore, raw, tender, with exposed nerve.

379. Touch. [Sensation of pressure.] —**N.** touch; tact, -ion, -ility; feeling; palp-ation, -ability; manipulation; brush, tick, graze, contact etc. 199.

[Organ of touch] hand, finger, fore-finger, thumb, paw, teeler, *antenna*.

V. touch, feel, handle, finger, thumb, paw, fumble, grope, grabble; twiddle, tweedle; pass –, run-the fingers over, massage, rub, knead; palpate, stroke, manipulate, wield; throw out a feeler.

Adj. tact-ual, -ile; tangible, palpable; lambent.

380. Sensations of Touch.—N. itching etc. *v.*; titillation, formication, *aura*.

V. itch, tingle, creep, thrill, sting; prick, -le; tickle, titillate.

Adj. itching etc. *v.*

381. Numbness. [Insensibility to touch.] —**N.**

numbness etc. (*physical insensibility*) 376; pins and needles.

local anesthetic,cocaine novocaine etc.; morphia.

V. benumb etc. 376; freeze, dull, deaden.

Adj. numb; benumbed etc. *v.*; intangible, impalpable.

---

382. Heat.—N. heat, caloric; temperature, warmth, fervor, calidity; incal-, incand-, recal-, decal-escence; glow, flush, blush; fever, hectic.

phlogiston; fire, spark, scintillation, flash, flame, blaze; arc; bonfire; firework, pyrotechny; wild-fire; sheet of fire, lambent flame; devouring element; conflagration.

summer, dog-days, canicule; baking etc. 384 –, white –, tropical –, Afric –, Bengal –, summer –, blood- heat; heat wave, sirocco, simoon; broiling sun; isolation; warming etc. 384.

sun etc. (*luminary*) 423; fire worshipper etc. 991; furnace etc. 386.

geyser, hot spring, volcano.

: Science of heat. pyrology; thermology, -otics; thermometer etc. 389.

V. be -hot etc. *adj.*; glow, incandesce, flush, sweat, swelter, bask, smoke, reek, stew, simmer, seethe, boil, burn, singe, scorch, scald, grill, broil, blaze, flame; smoulder; parch, fume, pant.

heat etc. (*make hot*) 384; thaw, fuse, melt, give.

Adj. hot, heated, warm, mild, genial, tepid, lukewarm, unfrozen; therm-al, -ic; calorific; fervent, -id; ardent; aglow.

sunny, torrid, tropical, estival, canicular; close, sultry, stifling, stuffy, suffocating, oppressive; reeking etc. *v.*; baking etc. 384.

red –, white – -, smoking –, bruning etc. *v.* –, piping- hot; like -a furnace, – an oven; hot as -fire, – pepper; hot enough to roast an ox.

fiery; incand-, incal-escent; candent, ebullient, glowing, smoking; on fire; blazing etc. *v.*; in - flames, – a blaze; alight, afire, ablaze; unquenched, -extinguished; smouldering; in a -heat, – glow, – fever, – perspiration, – sweat; sudorific; swelter-ing, -ed; blood-hot, -warm; warm as -a toast, – wool; recalescent, thermogenic, pyrotechnic, feverish, febrile, inflamed.

volcanic, plutonic, igneous; isother-mal, -mic, -al.

Phr. Not a breath of air.

---

383. Cold.—N. cold, -ness etc. *adj.*; frigidity, gelidity, algidity, inclemency; *fresco.*.

winter; depth of –, hard- winter; Siberia, Nova Zembla; Ant-, arctic, North –, South- Pole.

ice; snow, – flake, – crystal – drift; sleet; hail, -stone; rime, frost; hoar –, white –, hard –, sharp- frost; icicle, thick-ribbed ice; fall of snow, snow storm, heavy fall, *avalanche*; ice-berg, -floe; floe, berg; *glacier*; *nevée*, *serac*.

[Sensation of cold] chilliness etc. *adj.*; chill shivering etc. *v.*; goose- skin, -flesh; *rigor*, horripilation, chattering of teeth; frostbite, chilblain.

V. be -cold etc. *adj.*; shiver, starve, quake, shake, tremble, shudder, didder, quiver; perish with cold; chill etc. (*render cold*) 385.

Adj. cold, cool; chill, -y; gelid, frigid, algid; fresh, keen, bleak, raw, inclement, bitter, biting,

niveous, cutting, nipping, piercing, pinching; clay-cold; starved etc. (*made cold*) 385; shivering etc. *v.*; aguish, *transi de froid*; frost- bitten, -bound, - nipped.

cold as -a stone, – marble, – lead, – iron, – a frog, – charity, – Christmas; cool as -a cucumber, – custard.

icy, glacial, frosty, freezing, wintry, brumal, hibernal, boreal, arctic, antarctic, polar, Siberian, hyemal; hyperbore-an, -al; ice-bound; frozen out, un-warmed, -thawed, -heated; isocheimal, - chimenal.

Adv. coldly, bitterly etc. *adj.*; *à pierre fendre.*

---

384. Calefaction.—N. increase of temperature; heating etc. *v.*; cale-, tepe-, torre-faction; melting, fusion; liquefaction etc. 335; burning etc. *v.*; kindling, combustion; in-, ac-cension; con-, cremation; scorification; cauter-y, -ization; ustulation, calcination; in-, cineration; cupellation; carbonization.

ignition, inflammation, adustion, flagration; de-, con-flagration; empyrosis, incendiarism; arson; *auto da fé*; suttee.

boiling etc. *v.*; coction, ebullition, estuation, elixation, decoction.

furnace etc. 386; blanket, flannel, fur, muffler, wrap; wadding etc. (*lining*) 224; clothing etc. 225.

match etc. (*fuel*) 388; incendiary, pryomaniac; *pétroleur, pétroleuse*; cauterant, caustic, lunar caustic, apozem, moxa.

sunstroke, *coup de soleil*; insolation, sunburn.

pottery, ceramics, crockery, porcelain, china; earthen-, stone-ware; pot, mug, *terra-cotta*, brick, clinker; cinder, ash, *scoriae*; embers, dross, slag, products of combustion, coke, carbon, charcoal.

inflamma-, combusti-bility.

[Transmission of heat] diathermancy, trans-calency, diathermy.

V. heat, warm, chafe, stive, foment; make -hot etc. 382; sun oneself, bask in the sun.

fire; set -fire to, – on fire; kindle, enkindle, light, ignite, strike a light; apply the -match, – torch- to; re-kindle, -lume; fan –, add fuel to- the flame; poke –, stir –, blow- the fire; make a bonfire of; burn at the stake.

melt, thaw, fuse; liquefy etc. 335.

burn, inflame, roast, toast, fry, grill, singe, parch, bake, torrefy, scorch; brand, cauterize, sear, burn in; corrode, char, carbonize, calcine, incinerate; smelt, cupel, scorify; reduce to ashes; burn to a cinder; commit –, consign- to the flames.

boil, digest, stew, cook, seethe, scald, parboil, simmer; do to rags.

take –, catch- fire; blaze etc. (*flame*) 382.

Adj. heated etc. *v.*; molten, sodden; réchauffe; heating etc. *v.*

inflammable, burnable, inflammatory, combustible; diatherm-al, -anous; burnt etc. *v.*; volcanic.

---

386. Refrigeration.—N. refrigeration, infrigidation, reduction of temperature; cooling etc. *v.*; con-gelation, -glaciation; ice etc. 383; solidification etc. (*density*) 321; refrigerator etc. 387.

extincteur; fire, – engine, – extinguisher, – annihilator, – brigade, – man; sprinkler, hose, hydrant, standpipe.

incombusti-bility, -bleness etc. *adj.*

V. cool, fan, refrigerate, refresh, ice; congeal, freeze, glaciate; benumb, starve, pinch, chill, petrify, chill to the marrow, nip, cut, pierce, bite, make one's teeth chatter; damp, slack; quench; put –, stamp- out; extinguish.

go –, burn- out.

Adj. cooled etc. *v.*; frozen out; cooling etc. *v.*; frigorific.

incombustible; un-, unin-flammable; fire-proof.

386. Furnace.—N. furnace, blast furnace, fire-box, stove, incinerator, destructor, crematorium, crematory, kiln, oven, oast-house; hot-, bake-, wash-house; laundry; conservatory; hearth, focus; athanor, hypocaust, reverberatory; volcano; forge, fiery furnace; *tuyère*, brasier, salamander, heater, warming-pan, foot-warmer, hot-water bottle; radiator; boiler, geyser, caldron, seething caldron, pot; urn, kettle; chafing-dish; retort, crucible, alembic, still; saggar.

fire-place, -dog, -irons; hearth, ingle, grate, range, kitchener; kitchen range; oil-, gas-, electric, -cooker, -stove; fireless cooker; fire; galley; ca-, cam-boose; poker, tongs, shovel, hob, trivet; and-, grid-iron; frying-, stew-pan etc.

hot –, Turkish –, Russian –, vapor –, shower –, warm- bath; *calidarium*, *tepidarium*, *sudatorium*, sudatory; *hammam*.

387. Refrigerator.—N. refrigerator, -y; *frigidarium*; cold storage; refrigerating-plant, – machine; ice-house, -pail, -bag, -chest, -pack; cooler, damper; wine-cooler, freezing mixture.

388. Fuel.—N. fuel, firing, combustible, coal, wallsend, anthracite, bituminous coal, slack, culm, cannel coal, lignite, briquette, coke, carbon, charcoal; turf, peat, fire-wood, bobbing, faggot, log, yule log, ember, cinder etc. (*products of combustion*) 384; kindling wood, tinder, touch-wood; fumigator, sulphur, brimstone; incense; port-fire; fire-barrel, -ball, -brand.

fuel oil, gas, gasoline, electricity.

brand, torch, fuse; wick; spill, match, safety match, light, lucifer, congreve, vesuvian, vesta, fusee, locofoco; linstock; illuminant.

candle etc. (*luminary*) 423; oil etc. (*grease*) 356; petrol, gasoline, methylated –, spirit; gas, acetylene.

Adj. carbonaceous; combustible, inflammable.

V. stoke, fire, feed, add fuel to the flames.

389. Thermometer.—N. thermo-meter, -scope, -stat, -pile, differential thermometer; pyro-, calorimeter; radio micrometer etc.

390. Taste.—N. taste, flavor, gust, *gusto*, relish, savor; sapor, sapidity; twang, smack, smatch; after-taste, tang.

tasting; de-, gustation.

palate, tongue, tooth, stomach.

V. taste, savor, smatch, smack, flavor, twang; tickle the palate etc. (*savory*) 394; smack the lips.

Adj. sapid, saporific; gusta-ble, -tory; strong; flavored, spiced, savory; palatable etc. 394

391. Insipidity.—N. insipidity; tastlessness etc. *adj.*

V. be -tasteless etc. *adj.*

Adj. void of -taste etc. 390; insipid; jejune; taste-, gust-, savor-less; ingustible, mawkish, milk ·and water, weak, stale, flat, vapid, *fade*, wishy-washy, mild; untasted.

392. Pungency.—N. pungency, piquancy, poignancy, *haut-goût*, strong taste, twang, race, tang.

sharpness etc. *adj.*; acrimony, acridity; roughness etc. (*sour*) 397; unsavoriness etc. 395.

niter, saltpeter; mustard, cayenne, caviar; seasoning etc. (*condiment*) 393; brine.

dram, cordial, nip, pick-me-up, bracer, potion, nicotine, tobacco, snuff, quid; segar; cigar, -ette, gasper, fag; cheroot; weed; fragrant –, Indian-weed; pipe, clay pipe, churchwarden, brier, meerschaum, hookah, hubble-bubble.

V. be -pungent etc. *adj.*; bite the tongue.

render -pungent etc. *adj.*; season, spice, salt, pepper, pickle, brine, devil, curry.

smoke, chew, take snuff.

Adj. pungent, strong; high-, full-flavored; high-tasted, -seasoned; gamy; sharp, stinging, rough, *piquant*, racy; biting, mordant; spicy; seasoned etc. *v.*; hot, – as pepper; peppery, vellicating, escharotic, meracious; acrid, acrimonious, bitter; rough etc. (*sour*) 397; unsavory etc. 395.

salt, saline, brackish, briny; salt as -brine, – a herring, – Lot's wife.

393. Condiment.—N. condiment, flavoring, salt, mustard, pepper, cayenne, curry, seasoning, sauce, spice, cinnamon, chillies, relish, *sauce piquante*, caviare, pot-herbs, onion, garlic, pickle, chutney, nutmeg etc.

V. season etc. (*render pungent*) 392.

394. Savoriness.—N. savoriness etc. *adj.*; relish, zest.

tit-bit, dainty, delicacy, ambrosia, nectar, *bonne bouche*; game, turtle, venison.

V. taste good, be -savory etc. *adj.*; tickle the -palate, – appetite; flatter the palate.

render -palatable etc. *adj.*

relish, like, smack the lips.

Adj. savory, well-tasted, to one's taste, tasty, good, palatable, nice, dainty, delectable; tooth-ful, -some; gustful, appetizing, lickerish, delicate, delicious, exquisite, rich, luscious, ambrosial.

Adv. *per amusare la bocca.*

Phr. *cela se laisse manger.*

395. Unsavoriness.—N. unsavoriness etc. *adj.*; amaritude; acri-mony, -tude; roughness etc. (*sour*) 397; acerbity, austerity; gall and worm-wood, rue, quassia, aloes; sickener.

V. be -unpalatable etc. *adj.*; sicken, disgust, nauseate, pall, turn the stomach.

Adj. un-savory, -palatable, -sweet; ill-flavored, un-appetizing, -eatable, inedible; bitter, — as gall; acrid, acrimonious; rough.

offensive, repulsive, nasty; sickening etc. *v.*; nauseous; loath-, ful-some; unpleasant etc. 830.

396. Sweetness.—N. sweetness, dulcitude, saccharinity.

sugar, cane-, beet-sugar; saccharine, glucose, syrup, treacle, molasses, honey, manna; confection, -ary; sweets, grocery, conserve, preserve, *confiture*, jam, marmalade, julep; sugar-candy, -plum; licorice, liquorice, plum, lollipop, *bon bon*, *jujube*, comfit, sweetmeat, caramel, toffee, butterscotch.

nectar; hydromel, mead, metheglin, honeysuckle, *liqueur*, sweet wine.

pastry, pie, tart, puff, pudding, cake.

dulc-ification, -oration.

V. be sweet etc. *adj.*

render -sweet etc. *adj.*; sugar, saccharize, sweeten; edulcorate; dulc-orate, -ify; candy; mull.

Adj. sweet, sugary; sacchar-ine, -iferous; dulcet, honied, candied, luscious, nectarious, melliferous; sweetened etc. *v.*

sweet as -a nut, — sugar, — honey.

397. Sourness.—N. sourness etc. *adj.*; acid, -ity; acetous fermentation; acerbity.

vinegar, verjuice, crab, alum.

V. be —, turn- -sour etc. *adj.*; set the teeth on edge.

render -sour etc. *adj.*; acid-ify, -ulate.

Adj. sour; acid, -ulous, -ulated; acerb; tart, crabbed; acet-ous, -ose; sour as vinegar, sourish, acescent, sub-acid; styptic, hard, rough; unripe, green.

398. Odor.—N. odor, smell, odorament, scent, effluvium; eman-, exhal-ation; fume, essence, trail, nidor, redolence.

sense of smell; scent; act of -smelling etc. *v.*

V. have an -odor etc. *n.*; smell, — of, — strong of; exhale; give out a -smell etc. *n.*; scent.

smell, scent; snuff, — up; sniff, nose, inhale.

Adj. odor-ous, -iferous; smelling, strong-scented; redolent, graveolent, nidorous, pungent.

[Relating to the sense of smell] olfactory, quick-scented..

399. Inodorousness.—N. inodorousness; absence —, want- of smell.

V. be -inodorous etc. *adj.*; not smell.

deodorize.

Adj. inodor-ous, -ate; scentless; without —, wanting- smell etc. 398.

deodoriz-ed, -ing.

400. Fragrance.—N. fragrance, aroma, redolence, perfume, *bouquet*; sweet smell, aromatic perfume.

perfumery; incense; musk, frankincense; pastil, -le; myrrh, perfumes of Arabia, chypre; otto, ottar, attar; bergamot, balm, civet, *pot-pourri*, pulvil; nosegay, *boutonnière*; scent, -bag; *sachet*, scent-bottle, smelling bottle, *vinaigrette*; toilet water, *eau de Cologne*; thurible, censer, thurification.

perfumer; incense bearer.

V. be -fragrant etc. *adj.*; have a -perfume etc. *n.*; smell sweet, scent, perfume, thurify, embalm.

Adj. fragrant, aromatic, redolent, spicy, balmy, scented; sweet-smelling, -scented; perfum-ed, -atory; thuriferous; fragrant as a rose, muscadine, ambrosial.

401. Fetor.—N. fetor, fetidness; bad etc. *adj.*; -smell, — odor; stench, stink; mephitis, foul —, mal- odor; *empyreuma*; mustiness etc. *adj.*; rancidity; foulness etc. (*uncleanness*) 653.

stoat, polecat, skunk; asafetida; fungus, garlic; stink-pot, -bomb.

V. have a -bad smell etc. *n.*; smell; stink, — in the nostrils, — like a polecat; smell -strong etc. *adj.*; — offensively.

Adj. fetid; strong-smelling; high, bad, strong, fulsome, offensive, noisome, rank, rancid, reasty, tainted, musty, fusty, frouzy; olid, -ous; nidorous; smelling, stinking; putrid etc. 653; suffocating, mephitic; empyreumatic.

402. Sound.—N. sound, noise, strain; accent, twang, intonation, tone, tune; cadence; sonority, sonorousness etc. *adj.*; audibility; resonance etc. 408; voice etc. 580.

[Science of sound] acou-, acu-stics; catacoustics; cataphonics; phon-ics, -etics, -ology, -ography; diacoustics, -phonics.

telephone, phonograph etc. 418.

V. produce sound; sound, make a noise; give out —, emit- sound; phonetize, phonate; resound etc. 408.

Adj. sounding; soniferous; sonorific; resonant, audible, acoustic, auditory, distinct; stertorous; phonic, sonant; phonetic.

403. Silence.—N. silence; stillness etc. (*quiet*) 265; peace, hush, lull, rest; muteness etc. 581; solemn —, awful —, dead —, deathlike-silence.

V. be -silent etc. *adj.*; hold one's tongue etc. (*not speak*) 585.

render -silent etc. *adj.*; silence, still, hush; stifle, muffle, gag, stop; muzzle, put to silence etc. (*render mute*) 581.

Adj. silent; still, -y; calm, quiet; noise-, sound-, speech-less; hushed etc. *v.*; mute etc. 581; aphonic.

soft, solemn, awful, deathlike, silent as the grave; inaudible etc. (*faint*) 405.

Adv. silently etc. *adj.*; *sub silentio*; in perfect silence.

Int. hush! 'sh! silence! soft! whist! tush! chut! tut! *pax!* mum's the word! hold your tongue! shut up! be

silent! be quiet! stop that noise! hold your row! dry
up! peace, be still!
Phr. one might hear a -feather, – pin- drop.

404. Loudness.—N. loudness, power; loud
noise, din; clang, -or; clatter, noise, bombilation,
roar, uproar, racket, static, grinders, hubbub,
fracas, *charivari*, trumpet blast, blare, flourish of
trumpets, fanfare, *tintamarre*, peal, swell, blast,
alarum, boom; resonance etc. 408.
vociferation; pandemonium, hullaballoo etc.
411; lungs; Stentor; megaphone; siren.
artillery, cannon, gunfire, shellburst, bomb;
thunder.
V. be -loud etc. *adj.*; peal, swell, clang, boom,
thunder, fulminate, roar; resound etc. 408; speak
up, shout etc. (*vociferate*) 411; bellow etc. (*cry as
an animal*) 412; give tongue.
rend the -air, – skies; fill the air; din –, ring
–, thunder- in the ear; pierce –, split –, rend-
the-ears, – head; deafen, stun; *faire le diable a
quatre*; make one's windows shake; awaken –
startle- the echoes; make the welkin ring.
Adj. loud, sonorous; high-, big- sounding;
blatant; deep, full, powerful, noisy, clangorous,
multisonous, *fortisimo*; thundering, deafening etc.
v.; trumpet-tongued; ear-splitting, -rending, -
deafening; piercing; obstreporous, rackety,
uproarious; enough to wake the -dead, – seven
sleepers.
shrill etc. 410; clamorous etc. (*vociferous*) 411;
stentor-ian, -ophonic.
Adv. loudly etc. *adj.*; aloud; at the top of one's
voice, lustily, in full cry.
Phr. the air rings with.

405. Faintness.—N. faintness etc. *adj.*; faint
sound, whisper, breath; under-tone, -breath; murmur, hum, rustle, buzz, purr; plash; sough, moan,
sigh, susurration; tinkle; 'still small voice.'
hoarseness etc. *adj.*; raucity.
silencer, soft pedal, damper, mute, *sourdine*.
V. whisper, breathe, murmur, purl, hum, gurgle,
ripple, babble, flow; tinkle; mutter etc. (*speak imperfectly*) 583.
steal on the ear; melt in –, float on- the air.
muffle, mute, deaden, damp, stifle.
Adj. inaudible; scarcely –, just- audible; low,
dull; stifled, muffled; hoarse, husky; gentle, soft,
faint; floating; purling, flowing etc. *v.*; whispered
etc. *v.*; liquid; soothing; dulcet etc. (*melodious*)
413. .
Adv. in a whisper, with bated breath, *sotto voce*,
between the teeth, aside; *pian-o, -issimo*; 'a la sourdine*; *con sourdine*; out of earshot, inaudibly etc.
adj.

406. Snap. [Sudden and violent sounds.]—N.
snap etc. *v.*; rapping etc. *v.*; de-, crepitation;
smack, clap, report; thud; burst, explosion,
discharge, detonation, blow-out, back-fire, firing,
salvo, volley, pistol-shot.
squib, cracker, gun, rifle, pop-gun.
V. rap, snap, tap, knock; click; clash; crack, -

le; crash; pop; slam, bang, clap, thump, plump;
toot; back-fire, explode, burst on the ear.
Adj. rapping etc. *v.*
Int. crash! bang!

407. Roll. [Repeated and protracted
sounds.]—N. roll etc. *v.*; drumming etc. *v.*; tattoo; ding-dong; tantara; rataplan; whirr; rat-a-
tat; rub-a-dub; pit-a-pat; quaver, clutter,
charivari, racket; cuckoo; repetition etc. 104; peal
of bells, devil's tattoo; reverberation etc. 408.
drumfire, barrage.
machine gun.
V. roll, drum, rumble, rattle, clatter, rustle,
roar, drone, patter, clack.
hum, trill, shake; chime, peal, toll; tick, beat,
drum –, din- in the ear.
Adj. rolling etc. *v.*; monotonous etc. (*repeated*),
104; like a bee in a bottle.

408. Resonance.—N. resonance; ring etc. *v.*;
ringing etc. *v.*; tintinnabulation; reflection, reverberation, clangor.
low –, base –, bass –, flat –, grave –, deep
–, pedal- note; bass; *basso*, – *profondo*; bari-,
bary-tone; *contralto*.
V. re-sound, -verberate, -echo; ring, ding,
sing, jingle, gingle, chink, clink; tink, -le; chime;
gurgle etc. 405; plash, guggle, echo, ring in the ear.
Adj. resounding etc. *v.*; resonant, tinnient; tintinnabulary; deep-toned, -sounding, -mouthed;
hollow, sepulchral; gruff etc. (*harsh*) 410.

408a. Non-resonance.—N. thud, thump, dead
sound; non-resonance; muffled drums, cracked
bell; silencer, damper; mute, *sourdine*.
V. sound dead; stop –, damp- the -sound, –
reverberations; deaden, muffle.
Adj. non-resonant, dead, muted, muffled.

409. Sibilation. [Hissing sounds.]—N.
sibilation; hiss etc. *v.*; sternutation; high note etc.
410.
goose, serpent, snake.
V. hiss, buzz, whiz, rustle; fizz, -le, sizzle,
swish; wheeze, whistle, snuffle; squash; sneeze.
Adj. sibilant; hissing etc. *v.*; wheezy.

410. Stridor. [Harsh sounds.]—N. creak etc.
v.; creaking etc. *v.*; discord etc. 414; stridor; harshness, roughness, sharpness etc. *adj.*; cacophony.
acute –, high- note; *soprano*, treble, tenor, *alto*,
falsetto; *voce di testa*; shriek, cry etc. 411.
piccolo, fife, penny -whistle, – trumpet.
V. creak, grate, jar, burr, pipe, twang, jangle,
clank, clink; scream etc. (*cry*) 411; yelp etc.
(*animal sound*) 412; buzz etc. (*hiss*) 409.
set the teeth on edge, écorcher les orielles; pierce
–, split- the -ears, – head; offend –, grate upon
–, jar upon- the ear.
Adj. creaking etc. *v.*; strident, stridulous, harsh,

coarse, hoarse, horrisonous, raucous, metallic, rough, gruff, grum, sepulchral.

sharp, high, acute, shrill, high-pitched; trumpet-toned; piercing, ear-piercing; cracked; discordant etc. 414; cacophonous.

411. Cry.—**N.** cry etc. *v.*; voice etc. (*human*) 580; bark etc. (*animal*) 412.

vociferation, outcry, hullaballoo, chorus, clamor, hue and cry, plaint; lungs; stentor.

V. cry, roar, shout, bawl, brawl, halloo, halloa, hail, hoop, whoop, yell, bellow, howl, scream, screech, screak, shriek, shrill, squeak, squeal, squall, whine, whinny, pule, pipe, yaup.

cheer, hurrah; hoot; grumble, maon, groan.

snore, snort; grunt, etc. (*animal sounds*) 412.

vociferate; raise –, lift up- the voice; call –, sing –, cry- out; exclaim; rend the air; thunder –, shout- at the -top of one's voice, – pitch of one's breath; s'*égosiller*; strain the -throat, – voice, – lungs; give a -cry etc.

Adj. crying etc. *v.*; clam-ant, -orous; vociferous; stentorian etc. (*loud*) 404; open-mouthed.

412. Ululation. [Animal sounds.]—**N.** cry etc. *v.*; crying etc. *v.*; ululation, latration, belling; reboation; call, note; bark, howl, yelp; twittering, woodnote; insect cry, fritinancy, drone; screech; cuckoo.

V. cry, ululate, howl, roar, bellow, blare, rebellow, bark, yelp; bay, – the moon; yap, growl, yarr, yawl, snarl, howl; grunt, -le; snort, squeak; neigh, bray; mew, mewl; purr, caterwaul, pule; bleat, low, moo; troat, croak, crow, screech, caw, coo, gobble, quack, cackle, gaggle, guggle; chuck, -le; cluck; clack; cheep, chirp, chirrup, twitter, sing, cuckoo; pout, wail, hum, buzz; hiss, blatter; hoot.

Adj. crying etc. *v.*; blatant, latrant; re-, mugient; deep-, full-mouthed.

Adv. in full cry.

413. Melody. Concord.—**N.** melody, rhythym, measure; rhyme etc. (*poetry*) 597.

pitch, *timbre*, intonation, tone, overtone.

scale, gamut; diapason; diatonic –, chromatic –, enharmonic- scale; key, clef, chords.

modulation, temperament, syncope, syncopation, preparation, suspension, resolution.

staff, stave, line, space, brace; bar, rest; *appogiato*, *-tura*; acciaccatura, shake, *arpeggio*.

note, musical note, notes of a sclae; sharp, flat, natural; high note etc. (*shrillness*) 410; low note etc. 408; interval; semitone; second, third, fourth etc.; diatessaron.

breve, semibreve, minim, crotchet, quaver; semidemisemi- quaver; sustained note, drone, burden.

tonic; key-, leading-, fundamental-, note; supertonic, mediant, dominant; sub-mediant, -dominant; organ-, pedal-point; octave, tetrachord; major –, minor- -mode, – scale, – key; Doric mode, passage, phrase.

concord, harmony; unison, -ance; chime, homophony; euphon-y, -ism; tonality; consonance; concent; part.

orchestration; harmonization, – phrasing.

[Science of harmony] harmon-y, -ics; thorough-fundamental- bass; counterpoint; faburden.

piece of music etc. 415; composer, harmonist, contrapuntist.

V. be -harmonious etc. *adj.*; harmonize, chime, symphonize, transpose; put in tune, tune, accord, string; score, arrange, orchestrate.

Adj. harmoni-ous, -cal; in -concord etc. *n.*, – tune, – concert; unisonant, concentual, symphonizing, isotonic, homophonous, assonant, consonant.

measured, rhythmical, diatonic, chromatic, enharmonic.

melodious, musical; tuneful, tunable; sweet, dulcet, canorous; mell-ow, -ifluous; soft; clear, – as a bell; silvery; euphon-ious, -ic, -ical; symphonious; enchanting etc. (*pleasure-giving*) 829; fine-, full-, silver-toned.

Adv. harmoniously etc. *adj.*

414. Discord.—**N.** discord, -ance; dissonance, cacaphony, caterwauling; harshness etc. 410; consecutive fifths.

[Confused sounds] Babel, pandemonium; Dutch –, cat's- concert; marrow-bones and cleavers.

V. be -discordant etc. *adj.* '; jar etc. (*sound harshly*) 410.

Adj. discordant; dis-, ab-sonant; out of tune, tuneless; un-musical, -tunable; un-, im-melodious; un-, in-harmonious; sing-song; cacophonous; jarring, harsh etc. 410.

415. Music.—**N.** music, classical –, modern –, descriptive- music; concert, recital; strain, tune, air, *motif*; melody etc. 413; *aria, arietta*; piece of music, *sonata; rond-o, -eau; pastorale, cavatina, roulade, fantasia, toccata, concerto*, overture, symphony, symphonic poem, tone poem, prelude, voluntary, *intermezzo*, variations, *cadenza*; cadence; fugue, canon, serenade, *nocturne, notturno*, rhapsody, romance, *aubade*, dithyramb; opera, operetta; oratorio; composition, movement, stave.

instrumental music; full-, orchestral- score; minstrelsy, tweedledum and tweedledee, band, orchestra etc. 416; concerted piece, *potpourri*, medley, *capriccio*, incidental music; improvisation; peal.

vocal music, vocalism; chaunt, chant; psalm, -ody; hymn; song etc. (*poem*) 597; canticle, canzonet, *cantata, bravura, coloratura*; lay, ballad, ditty, carol, barcarolle, pastoral, recitative, *recitativo, solfeggio*, tonic sol-fa.

Lydian measures; slow -music, – movement; *adagio* etc. *adv.*; minuet; siren strains, soft music, lullaby; *berceuse*, cradle song, dump; dirge etc. (*lament*) 839; pibroch; martial music, march, funeral-, dead- march; dance 'music; waltz etc. (*dance*) 840; rag-time, syncopation, jazz.

solo, duet, *duo, trio*; quartet; quintet, sextet, septet; part song, descant, glee, madrigal, catch, round, chorus, *chorale*; antiphon, -y; accompaniment, second –, alto –, tenor –, bass-part; score, thorough bass; counterpoint.

composer etc. 413; musician etc. 416.

V. compose, perform etc. 416; attune.

Adj. musical; instrumental, orchestral, vocal, choral, lyric, operatic; harmonious etc. 413.

Adv. adagio; largo, larghetto, andan-te, -tino; alla capella; maestoso, moderato; allegr-o, -etto; spiritoso, vivace, veloce; prest-o, -issimo; pian-o, -issimo, fort-e, -issimo, sforzando; con brio; capriccioso; scherz-o, -ando; legato, sostenuto, staccato, crescendo, diminuendo, rallentando, affettuoso, arioso; parlante, cantabile; obbligato; pizzacato, tremolo, vibrato.

416. Musician. [Performance of Music.]—**N.** musician, artiste, virtuoso, performer, player, minstrel; bard etc. (poet) 597; instrumental-, organ-, accompan-, pian-, violin-, flaut-, harp-ist; harper, fiddler, fifer, trumpeter, piper, drummer; catgut scraper.

band, orchestra, waits.

vocal-, melod-ist; singer, warbler; songst-, chaunt-er, -ress; diva, cantatrice, coloratura, soprano, mezzo-soprano, alto, contralto, tenor, baritone, bass, basso, -profundo.

choir, quire, chorister; chorus, — singer; choral society, festival, eisteddfod.

nightingale, philomel, thrush; siren; Orpheus, Apollo, the Muses, Erato, Euterpe, Terpsichore; tuneful -nine, — quire.

composer etc. 413.

performance, virtuosity, execution, touch, expression, solmization.

V. play, pipe, strike —, tune-up, sweep the chords, tickle —, paw- the ivories, vamp, tweedle, fiddle; strike the lyre, beat the drum; blow —, sound —, wind- the horn; grind the organ; touch the -guitar etc. (instruments) 417; thrum, strum, twang, drum, beat —, keep- time, conduct.

execute, perform; accompany; sing —, play- a second; compose, write music, set to music, arrange, harmonize, orchestrate.

sing, chaunt, chant, hum, warble, carol, chirp, chirrup, lilt, purl, quaver, trill, shake, twitter, whistle; sol-fa; intone.

have -an ear for music, — a musical ear, — a correct ear, — absolute pitch.

Adj. playing etc. v.; musical, lyric.

Adv. adagio, andante etc. (music) 415.

417. Musical Instruments.—N. musical instruments; band; string-, brass-, drum and fife-, military-, bugle-, German-, dance-, jazz-band; orchestra, string quartet; orchestration, orchestrelle.

[Stringed instruments] mono-, poly-chord; harp, lyre, lute, archlute, thearbo; mandol-a, -in, -ine; guitar; ukulele; psaltery, zither; bandore, cither, -n; gittern, rebeck, bandurria, banjo, zither banjo, balalaika, samisen; plectrum.

viol, -in, Cremona, Stradivarius; fiddle; kit; vielle, viola, — d'amore, — di gamba; tenor, violoncello, cello; bass, bass-, bass-viol; double-bass, contrabasso, violone, hurdy-gurdy; strings, catgut; bow, fiddlestick.

piano, -forte; grand —, concert grand —, baby —, upright —, cottage- piano; pianino, pianette; harpsi-, clavi-, clari-, mani-chord; clavier, spinet, virginals; dulcimer, cymbalo; Eolian harp; piano-

organ, -player, electric piano, player-piano, pianola.

[Wind instruments] organ, church —, pipe —, American- organ; harmoni-um, -phon; accordion, seraphina, concertina; melodeon; barrel- organ; humming top.

flute, fife, piccolo, flageolet, penny-whistle, reed instrument; clari-net, -onet; bass clarionet; saxophone; basset horn, corno di bassetto; musette, shawm, oboe, hautboy, cor Anglais, corno Inglese, bassoon, double bassoon, contrafagotto; bag-, union-pipes; ocarina, Pandean pipes; calliope; sirene, pipe, pitch-pipe; sourdet; whistle, catcall.

horn, bugle, key bugle, cornet, cornet-à-pistons, cornopean, clarion, trumpet, trombone, ophicleide, serpent; English-, French-, bugle-, sax-, flugel-, alt-, helicon-, post-horn; sackbut, euphonium, bombardon, tuba, bass tuba.

[Vibrating surfaces] cymbal, bell, gong, peal of bells, carillon; tambour, -ine; drum, tom-tom, tabor, -ret, -ourine, -orin; sistrum, grand caisse, bass-, big-, side-, kettle-drum; tympani; war drums; tymbal, timbrel, castanet, bones; musical-glasses, -stones; harmonica, sounding— board, rattle; gramophone, phonograph.

[Vibrating bars] reed, tuning-fork, triangle, Jew's harp, musical box, harmonicon, xylophone, marimba, celeste.

sord-ine, -et; sourd-ine, -et; mute.

418. Hearing. [Sense of sound.]—**N.** hearing etc. v.; audition, auscultation; eavesdropping; audibility; acoustics etc. 402.

acute —, nice —, delicate —, quick —, sharp —, correct —, musical -ear; ear for music.

ear, auricle, lug, acoustic organs, auditory apparatus, ear-drum, tympanum; ear-, speaking-trumpet, megaphone; telephone, radiophone, stethoscope, phonograph, gramophone, microphone.

hearer, auditor, listener, eavesdropper; audi-tory, -ence.

V. hear, overhear; hark, -en; list, -en; give —, lend —, bend- an ear; give attention; catch a sound, prick up one's ears; give -a hearing, — audience -to.

hang upon the lips of, be all ear, listen with both ears, monitor.

become audible; meet —, fall upon —, catch —, reach- the ear; be heard; ring in the ear etc. (resound) 408.

Adj. hearing etc. v.; auditory, auricular, aural, auditive, acoustic.

Adv. arrectis auribis.

Int. hark, — ye!.hear! list, -en! Oyez! attention! lend me your ears!

419. Deafness.—N. deafness, hardness of hearing, surdity; inaudibility.

V. be -deaf etc. adj.; have no ear; shut —, stop —. close- one's ears; turn a deaf ear to.

render deaf, stun, deafen.

Adj. deaf, earless, surd; hard —, dull- of hearing; deaf-mute, stunned, deafened; stone deaf; deaf as -a post, — an adder, — a beetle, — a trunk-maker.

inaudible etc. 405; out of hearing.

420. Light.—N. light, ray, beam, stream, gleam, streak, pencil; sun-, moon-beam; dawn, aurora.

day; sunshine; light of -day, – heaven; sun etc. (*luminary*) 432, day-, broad day-, noontide- light; noon-tide, -day; glare.

glow etc. *v.*; afterglow, sunset; glimmering etc. *v.*; glint; play –, flood- of light; phosphorescence, flush, halo, glory, nimbus, aureole, *aureola*.

spark, *scintilla*; *facula*; sparkling etc. *v.*; emication, scintillation, flash, blaze, coruscation, fulguration; flame etc. (*fire*) 382; lightning, *ignis fatuus*, etc. (*luminary*) 423, radio-activity.

luster, sheen, shimmer, reflection; gloss, tinsel, spangle, brightness, brilliancy, splendor; ef-, re-fulgence; ful-gor, -gidity; dazzlement, resplendence, transplendency; luminousness etc. *adj.*; luminosity; lucidity; renitency; radi-ance, -ation; irradiation, illumination, phosphorescence, luminescence.

radiation, radiant heat, infra-red rays, visible radiation, ultra-violet –, actinic- rays, actinism; X –, Roentgen- rays; phot-, heli-ography; optical instruments etc. 445.

[Science of light] optics; photo-logy, -metry; di-, cat-optrics.

[Distribution of light] *chiaroscuro*, *clair-obscur*, clear obscure, breadth, light and shade, black and white, tonality, half-tone, mezzotint:

reflection, refraction, dispersion, double refraction, polarization, diffraction, interference.

illuminant etc. 423.

V. shine, glow, glitter, phosphoresce; glis-ter, -ten; twinkle, gleam; flare, – up; glare, beam, shimmer, glimmer, flicker, sparkle, scintillate, coruscate, flash, fulgurate, blaze; be -bright etc. *adj.*; reflect light, daze, dazzle, bedazzle, raidate, shoot out beams.

clear up, brighten.

lighten, enlighten; light, – up; irradiate, shine upon; give –, hang out- a light; cast –, throw –, shed- -luster, – light- upon; illum-e, -ine, -inate; relume, strike a light; kindle etc. (*set fire to*) 384.

Adj. shining etc. *v.*; lumin-ous, -iferous; luc-id, -ent, -ulent, -ific, -iferous; illuminating, light, -some; bright, vivid, splendent, nitid, lustrous, shiny, brilliant, beamy, scintillant, radiant, lambent; sheen, -y; glossy, burnished, glassy, sunny, orient, meridian; noon-day, -tide; cloudless, clear; unclouded, -obscured.

garish; re-, tran-splendent; re-, effulgent; ful-gid, -gent; relucent, splendid, blazing, in a blaze, ablaze, rutilant, meteoric, phosphorescent; aglow.

bright as silver; light –, bright- as -day, – noonday, – the sun at noonday.

optical, actinic; photo-genic, -graphic; heliographic, radioactive.

421. Darkness.—N. darkness etc. *adj.*; blackness etc. (*dark color*) 431; obscurity, gloom, murk; dusk etc. (*dimness*) 422;, tenebrosity, umbrageousness.

Cimmerian –, Stygian –, Egyptian- darkness; night; midnight; dead of –, witching time of-night; blind man's holiday; darkness -visible; – that can be felt; palpable, obscure; Erebus.

shade, shadow, umbra, penumbra; sciagraphy; *silhouette*; radiograph, skiagraph.

obscuration; ad-, ob-umbration; obtenebration, offuscation, caligation; extinction; eclipse, total eclipse; gathering of the clouds.

shading; distribution of shade; *chiaroscuro* etc. (*light*) 420.

noctivagation, noctograph, noctuary.

obscurantist.

V. be -dark etc. *adj.*

darken, obscure, shade; dim; tone down, lower; over-cast, -shadow; cloud, eclipse; ob-, of-fuscate; ob-, ad-umbrate, cast into the shade; be-cloud, -dim, -darken; cast –, throw –, spread- a -shade, – shadow, – gloom.

extinguish; put –, blow –, snuff- out; doubt.

Adj. dark, -some, -ling; obscure, tenebrous, tenebrious, sombrous, pitch dark, pitchy, caliginous; black etc. (*in color*) 431.

sunless, lightless etc. (*see* sun, light etc. 423); somber, dusky; unilluminated etc. (*see* illuminate etc. 420); nocturnal; dingy, lurid, gloomy; murk-y, -some; shady, umbrageous; overcast etc. (*dim*) 422; cloudy etc. (*opaque*) 426; darkened etc. *v.*

dark as -pitch, – a pit, – Erebus.

benighted; noctivag-ant, -ous.

Adv. in the -dark, – shade; at night.

422. Dimness.—N. dimness etc. *adj.*; darkness etc. 421; paleness etc. (*light color*) 429.

half-light, *demi-jour*; partial -shadow, – eclipse; shadow of a shade; glimmer, -ing; nebulosity; cloud etc. 353; eclipse.

aurora, dusk, twilight, gloaming, blind man's holiday; break of day, daybreak, dawn.

moon-light, -beam, -shine; star- owl's-, candle-, rush-, fire-light; farthing candle.

V. be -,grow- -dim etc. *adj.*; flicker, twinkle, glimmer; loom, lower; fade; darken; pale, – its ineffectual fire.

render -dim etc. *adj.*; dim, bedim, obscure.

Adj. dim, dull, lack-luster, dingy, darkish, shorn of its beams; dark 421.

faint, shadowed forth; glassy; bleary; cloudy; misty etc. (*opaque*) 426; muggy, fuliginous; nebulous, -ar; obnubilated, overcast, crepuscular, twilight, muddy, lurid, leaden, dun, dirty; looming etc. *v.*

pale etc. (*colorless*) 429; confused etc. (*invisible*) 447.

423. Luminary. [Source of light.]—N. luminary; light etc. 420; flame etc. (*fire*) 382.

spark, *scintilla*; phosphorescence.

sun, orb of day, day star, Phoebus, Apollo, Helios, Phaethon, Hyperion, Ra, Aurora; star, orb, meteor; falling –, shooting- star; blazing –, dog-star; Sirius, canicula, Aldebaran; morning star, Lucifer, Phosphor, evening star; Hesperus, Venus, planet, moon etc. 318; constellation, galaxy; northern light, *aurora -borealis*, – *australis*, zodiacal light; mock sun, parhelion.

lightning; fork –, sheet –, summer- lightning, St. Elmo's fire; phosphorus; *ignis fatuus*; Jack o' – Friar's- lantern; Will o' the wisp, fire-drake, *Fata Morgana*.

glow-worm, fire-fly.

radium, luminous paint.

[Artificial light] gas; gas –, lime –, electric –, head –, search –, spot –, flash –, flood –, footlight; lamp, oil –, gas –, arc –, incandescent-lamp; flare; lant-ern, -horn; dark lantern, bull's eye, projector; candle, *bougie*, tallow –, wax- candle; dip, farthing dip; taper, rush-light; oil etc. (*grease*) 356; wick, burner; Argand, moderator, duplex; torch, *flambeau*, link, brand; cresset; gase-, chande-, electro-lier; candelabrum, *girandole*, sconce, luster, candle-stick.

firework, fizgig; pyrotechnics; Roman candle, Very light, star shell, parachute light; rocket, lighthouse etc. (*signal*) 550.

V. illuminate etc. (*light*) 420.

Adj. self-luminous, incandescent; phosphor-ic, - escent; luminescent, fluorescent, radiant etc. (*light*) 420.

424. Shade.—N. shade; awning etc. (*cover*) 223; parasol, sunshade, umbrella; screen, curtain, shutter, blind, gauze, veil, mantle, mask; cloud, mist, gathering of clouds; smoke screen; smoked glasses, colored spectacles; blinkers, blinders.

umbrage, glade; shadow etc. 421.

V. draw a curtain; put up –, close- a shutter; veil etc. *v.*; cast a shadow etc. (*darken*) 421; screen, obstruct the view.

Adj. shady, umbrageous, bowery.

425. Transparency.—N. transparen-ce, -cy; translucen-ce, -cy; diaphaneity; luc-, pelluc-, limp-idity.

transparent medium, glass, crystal, mica; lymph, water.

v. be -transparent etc. *adj.*; transmit light.

Adj. transparent, pellucid, lucid, diaphanous; trans-, tra-lucent; limpid, clear, serene, crystalline, clear as crystal, vitreous, transpicuous, glassy, hyaline.

426. Opacity.—N. opacity; opaqueness etc. *adj.*

film; cloud etc. 353.

V. be -opaque etc. *adj.*; obstruct the passage of light; ob-, of-fuscate.

Adj. opaque, impervious to light.

dim etc. 422; turbid, thick, muddy, opacous, ob-fuscated, fuliginous, cloudy, hazy, foggy, vaporous, nubiferous, muggy.

smoky, fumid, murky, dirty.

427. Semitransparency.—N. semitrans-parency, opalescence, milkiness, pearliness; gauze, muslin; film; mist etc. (*cloud*) 353; frosted glass.

Adj. semi-transparent, -pellucid, -diaphanous, - opacous, -opaque; opal-escent, -ine; pearly, milky, frosted, mat; misty.

428. Color.—N. color, hue, tint, tinge, dye, complexion, shade, tincture, cast, livery, coloration, chromatism, glow, flush; tone, key.

pure –, positive –, primary –, primitive –, complementary- color; three primaries; spectrum, chromatic dispersion; broken –, secondary –, tertiary- color.

local color, coloring, keeping, tone, value, aerial perspective.

[Science of color] chromatics, spectrum analysis; prism, spectroscope.

pigment, coloring matter, paint, dye, wash, distemper, stain; medium; mordant; oil-paint etc. (*painting*) 556.

V. color, dye, tinge, stain, tint, tinct, tone, paint, wash, ingrain, grain, illuminate, emblazon, imbue; paint etc. (*fine art*) 556; daub.

Adj. colored etc. *v.*; colorific, tingent, tinctorial; chromatic, prismatic; full-, high-, deep-colored; doubly-dyed; polychromatic.

bright, vivid, intense, deep; fresh, unfaded; rich, gorgeous; highly colored; gay; variegated etc. 440.

gaudy, florid; garish; showy, flaunting, flashy; raw, crude; glaring, flaring; discordant, inharmonious.

mellow, harmonious, pearly, sweet, delicate, tender, refined.

429. Achromatism. [Absence of color.]—**N.** achromatism; de-, dis-coloration; pall-or, -idity; paleness etc. *adj.*; etiolation; neutral tint, monochrome, black-and-white.

V. lose -color etc. 428; fade, fly, go; become - colorless etc. *adj.*; turn pale, pale, whiten.

deprive of color, decolorize, bleach, tarnish, achromatize, blanch, etiolate, wash out, tone down.

Adj. uncolored etc. (*see* color etc. 428); colorless, achromatic, hueless, pale, pallid; pale-, tallow-faced; faint, dull, cold, muddy, leaden, dun, wan, sallow, dead, dingy, ashy, ashen, ghastly, cadaverous, glassy, lack-luster; discolored etc. *v.* light-colored, fair, *blond*; white etc. 430.

pale as -death, – ashes, – a witch, – a ghost, – a corpse.

430. Whiteness.—N. whiteness etc. *adj.*; argent.

albification, albescence, albinism, etiolation.

snow, paper, chalk, milk, lily, ivory, silver, alabaster; white lead, chinese –, flake –, ivory –, zinc- white, white-wash, -ning, whiting.

V. be -white etc. *adj.*

render -white etc. *adj.*; whiten- bleach, blanch, etiolate, whitewash, silver, frost.

Adj. white; milky, milk-, snow-white; snowy, niveous, candid, chalky; hoar, -y; frosted, silvery; argent, -ine; canescent.

whitish, creamy, pearly, ivory, fair, *blond*, ash-blond, platinum blond; blanched etc. *v.*; high in tone, light.

white as -a sheet, – driven snow, – a lily, – silver; like -ivory etc. *n.*

431. Blackness.—N. blackness etc. *adj.*; darkness etc. (*want of light*) 421; swarthness, lividity, dark color, tone, color; *chiaroscuro* etc. 420.

nigrification, infuscation, denigration.

jet, ink, ebony, coal, pitch, soot, smudge, charcoal, sloe, raven, crow; black.

[Pigments] lamp –, ivory –, blue-black; writing –, printing –, printer's –, Indian- ink.

V. be -black etc. *adj.*

render -black etc. *adj.*; blacken, infuscate, denigrate; blot, -ch; smutch; smirch; darken etc. 421.

Adj. black, sable, swarthy, somber, dark, inky, ebon, atramentous, jetty; coal-, jet-black; fuliginous, pitchy, sooty, swart, dusky, dingy, murky, low-toned, low in tone; of the deepest dye.

black as -jet etc. *n.*, – my hat, – a shoe, – a tinker's pot, – November, – thunder, – midnight; nocturnal etc. (*dark*) 421; nigrescent; gray etc. 432; obscure etc. 421.

Adv. in mourning.

432. Gray.—**N.** gray etc. *adj.*; neutral tint, silver, pepper and salt, *chiaroscuro, grisaille*, grayness.

[Pigments] Payne's gray; black etc. 431.

Adj. gray, grey; steel –, iron- gray, dun, drab, dingy, leaden, livid, somber, sad, pearly; silver, -y, -ed; ash-en, -y; ciner-eous, -itious; grizzl-y, -ed; dove-, slate-, stone-, mouse-, ash-colored; mole; cool.

433. Brown.—**N.** brown etc. *adj.*

[Pigments] bister, ocher, sepia, Vandyke brown.

Adj. brown, adust, bay, dapple, auburn, chestnut, nutbrown, cinnamon, hazel, fawn, puce, *écru*, russet, tawny, fuscous, chocolate, maroon, foxy, tan, brunette, whitey-brown; snuff-, liver-colored; brown as -a berry, – mahogany; reddish brown; copper-, rust- colored; henna, bronze, khaki; russet, roan, sorrel.

sub-burnt; tanned etc. *v.*

V. render -brown etc. *adj.*; tan, embrown, bronze.

434. Redness.—**N.** red, scarlet, vermilion, cardinal, Post Office, red, carmine, crimson, pink, lake, *cerise*, cherry red, maroon, carnation, *couleur de rose, rose du Barry*; magenta, damask; flesh -color, – tint; color; fresh –, high- color; warmth; gules.

ruby, garnet, carbuncle; rose; rust, iron-mold.

[Dyes and pigments] cinnabar, cochineal; fuchsine; ruddle, madder, redlead; light –, Venetian- red; red ink, annotto.

redness etc. *adj.*; rub-escence, -icundity, -ification; erubescence, blush.

V. be –, become- -red etc. *adj.*; blush, flush, color up, mantle, redden.

render- red etc. *adj.*; redden, rouge; rub-ify, -ricate; incarnadine; ruddle.

Adj. red etc. *n.*; -dish; rufous, ruddy, florid, incarnadine, sanguine, bloody, gory; ros-y, -eate; blowz-y, -ed; brunt; rubi-cund, -form; lurid, stammel, blood-red; russet, murrey, carroty, sorrel, lateritious.

rose-, ruby-, cherry-, claret-, wine-, plum-,

flame-, flesh-, peach-, salmon-, brick-, brickdust-colored, reddish brown etc. 433.

red as -fire, – blood, – scarlet, – a turkeycock, – a lobster; warm, hot; foxy.

435. Greenness.—**N.** green etc. *adj.*; blue and yellow; vert.

emerald, verd antique, verdigris, malachite, beryl, aquamarine, reseda.

[Pigments] *terre verte*, verditer, bice, chlorophyl.

greenness, verdure, verdancy; viridity, -escence.

Adj. green, verdant; glaucous, olive; porraceous; green as grass.

emerald –, pea –, grass –, apple –, sea –, olive –, bottle –, leaf- green.

greenish; vir-ent, -escent.

436. Yellowness.—**N.** yellow etc. *adj.*; or.

[Pigments] gamboge; cadmium –, chrome –, Indian –, lemon- yellow; orpiment, yellow ocher, Claude tint, aureolin.

crocus, saffron, topaz, gold.

jaundice; London fog; yellowness etc. *adj.*

Adj. yellow, aureate, gold, golden, gilt, gilded, flavous, citrine, fallow; fulv-ous, -id; sallow, luteous, fawny, creamy, sandy; xanth-ic, -ous; jaundiced.

gold-, citron-, saffron-, lemon-, sulphur-, amber-, straw-, primrose-, cream-colored; flazen, yellowish, buff.

yellow as a -quince, – guinea, – crow's foot.

437. Purple.—**N.** purple etc. *adj.*; blue and red, bishop's purple; aniline dyes, gridelin, amethyst; purpure.

livid-ness, -ity.

V. empurple.

Adj. purple, violet, plum-colored, lavender, lilac, puce, *mauve*; livid.

438. Blueness.—**N.** blue etc. *adj.*; garter-blue; watchet.

[Pigments] ultramarine, smalt, cobalt, cyanogen; Prussian –, syenite- blue; bice, indigo, woad.

lapis lazuli, sapphire, turquoise.

blue-, bluish-ness; bloom

Adj. blue, azure, cerulean; sky-blue, -colored, -dyed; navy-blue, aquamarine, electric blue, royal blue, cyanic; bluish; atmospheric, retiring; cold.

439. Orange.—**N.** orange, red and yellow; gold; or; flame etc. color, *adj.*

[Pigments] ochre, Mars orange, cadmium.

V. gild, warm.

Adj. orange; ocherous; orange-, gold-, flame-, copper-, brass-, apricot-colored; warm, hot, glowing.

440. Variegation.—N. variegation; di-, trichromism; iridescence, irisation, play of colors, polychrome, maculation, spottiness, striae.

spectrum, rainbow, iris, tulip, peacock, chameleon, butterfly, tortoiseshell; mackerel, – sky; zebra, leopard, mother-of-pearl, nacre, opal, marble, batik.

check, plaid, tartan, patchwork; mar-, parquetry; mosiac, *tesserae*, tesselation, chess-board, checkers, chequers; harlequin; Joseph's coat; tricolor; patches, bands, stripes, spots etc of color.
V. be -variegated etc. *adj.*; variegate, stripe, streak, checker, chequer; be-, speckle, fleck; be-, sprinkle; stipple, maculate, dot, bespot; tattoo, inlay, tesselate, damascene; embroider, braid, quilt.
Adj. variegated etc. *v.*; many-colored, -hued; divers-, parti-colored; di-, poly-chromatic; bi-, tri-, versi-color; of all -the colors of the rainbow, – manner of colors; kaleidoscopic.

iridescent; opal-ine, -escent; prismatic, nacreous, pearly, shot, *gorge de pigeon, chatoyant,* irisated.

pied, piebald, skewbald; motley; mottled, marbled; pepper and salt, paned, dappled, clouded, cymophanous.

mosiac, tesselated, chequered, plaid; tortoiseshell etc. *n.*

spott-ed, -y; punctuated, powdered; speckled etc. *v.*; freckled, fleabitten, studded; fleck-ed, -ered; striated, barred, veined; brind-ed, -led; tabby; watered; grizzled; listed; embroidered etc. *v.*; daedal.

441. Vision.—N. vision, sight, optics, eye-sight.

view, look, espial, glance, ken, *coup d'oeil*; glimpse, peep, glint; gaze, stare, leer; perlustration, contemplation; conspect-ion, -uity; regard, survey; in-, intro-spection; *reconnaissance*, speculation, watch, espionage, *espionnage*, autopsy; ocular - inspection, – demonstration; sight-seeing.

macrography, micrography.

point of view; view-, stand- point; gazebo, loop-hole, *belvedere*, watchtower.

field of view; theater, amphitheater, arena, vista, horizon; commanding –, bird's eye –, panoramic- view; periscope.

visual organ, organ of vision; eye; naked –, unassisted- eye; eye-ball, retina, pupil, iris, cornea, white; optics, orbs; saucer –, goggle –, gooseberry-eyes.

short sight etc. 443; clear –, sharp –, quick –, eagle –, piercing-, –, penetrating- -sight, – glance, – eye; perspicacity, discernment; catopsis.

eagle, hawk; cat, lynx; Argus.

evil eye; basilisk, cockatrice.

spectacles, telescope etc. 445.

V. see, behold, discern, perceive, have in sight, descry, sight, make out, discover, distinguish, recognize, spy, espy, ken; get –, have –, catch- a -sight, – glimpse- of; command of view of; witness, contemplate, speculate; cast –, set- the eyes on; be a -spectator etc. 444- of; look on etc. (*be present*) 186; see sights etc. (*curiosity*) 445; see at a glance etc. (*intelligence*) 498.

look, view, eye; lift up the eyes, open one's eye; look -at, – on, – upon, – over, – about one, – round; survey, scan, inspect; run the eye -over, – through; reconnoiter, glance -round, – on, – over; turn –, bend- one's looks upon; direct the

eyes to, turn the eyes on, cast a glance, make eyes at.

observe etc. (*attend to*) 457; watch etc. (*care*) 459; see with one's own eyes; watch for etc. (*expect*) 507; peek, peep, peer, pry, take a peep; play at bo-peep.

look -full in the face, – hard at, – intently; strain one's eyes; fix –, rivet- the eyes upon; stare, gaze; pore over, gloat -over, – on; leer, ogle, glare; goggle; cock the eye, squint, gloat, look askance; give the glad eye.

Adj. seeing etc. *v.*; visual, ocular, -al; ophthalmic.

far-, clear-sighted etc. *h.*; eagle-, hawk-, lynx-, keen-, Argus-eyed.

visible etc. 446.

Adv. visibly etc. 446; in sight of, with one's eyes open.

at -sight, – first sight, – a glance, – the first blush; *primâ facie*.

Int. look! etc. (*attention*) 457.

Phr. the scales falling from one's eyes.

442. Blindness.—N. blindness, anopsia, cecity, excecation, *amaurosis*, cataract, ablepsy, prestriction; dim-sightedness etc. 443.

V. be -blind etc. *adj.*; not see; lose sight of; have the eyes bandaged; grope in the dark.

not look; close –, shut –, turn away –, avert-the eyes; look another way; wink etc. (*limited vision*) 443; shut the eyes –, be blind- to; wink –, blink- at.

render -blind etc. *adj.*; blind, -fold; hoodwink, dazzle; put one's eyes out; throw dust into one's eyes; *jeter de la poudre aux yeux*; screen from sight etc. (*hide*) 528.

Adj. blind; eye-, sight-, vision-less; dark; stone-, sand-, stark-blind; undiscerning; dim-sighted etc. 443.

blind as -a bat, – a buzzard, – a beetle, – a mole, – an owl; wall-eyed.

blinded etc. *v.*

Adv. blind-ly, -fold; darkly.

443. Dim-sightedness. [Imperfect vision.] [Fallacies of vision.]—**N.** dim –, dull –, half –, short –, near –, long –, double –, astigmatic –, failing- sight; dim etc -sightedness; snow blindness; purblindness, lippitude; my-, presby-opia; confusion of vision; astigmatism; nystagmus; color-blindness, dichromism, chromato-pseudo-blepsis, Daltonism; nyctalopy; *strabismus*, strabism, squint, cast in the eye, swivel eye, goggle eyes; obliquity of vision.

winking etc. *v.*; nictitation; blinkard, albino.

dizziness, swimming, scotomy; cataract; ophthalmia.

[Limitation of vision] eye shade, blinker, blinder; screen etc. (*hider*) 530.

[Fallacies of vision] *deceptio visûs*; refraction, distortion, illusion, false light, *anamorphosis*, virtual image, *spectrum, mirage*, looming, phasma; phant-asm, -asma, -om; vision; specter, apparition, ghost; *ignis fatuus* etc. (*luminary*) 423; specter of the Brocken; magic mirror; magic lantern etc. (*show*) 448; mirror, lens etc. (*instrument*) 445.

V. be -dim-sighted etc. **⋆.**; see double; have a - mote in the eye, — mist before the eyes, — film over the eyes; see through a -prism, — glass darkly; wink, blink, nictitate; squint; look ask-ant, -ance; screw up the eyes, glare, glower.

dazzle, glare, blur, swim, loom.

Adj. dim-sighted etc. *n.*; my-, presby-opic; astigmatic; moon-, mope-, blear-, goggle-, gooseberry-, one-eyed; blind of one eye, monoculous; half-, pur-, color-blind; dichromatic. blind as a bat etc. (*blind*) 442; winking etc. *v.*

444. Spectator.—N. spectator, beholder, observer, inspector, viewer, looker-on, onlooker, witness, eye-witness, bystander, passer by; sight-seer.

spy, scout; sentinel etc. (*warning*) 668.

v. witness, behold etc. (*see*) 441; look on etc. (*be present*) 186.

445. Optical Instruments.—N. optical instruments; lens, meniscus, magnifier, reading —, burning- glass; micro-, mega-, teino-scope; spectacles, glasses, barnacles, goggles, giglamps, eyeglass, *pince-nez*, monocle; periscopic lens; telescope, glass, lorgnette, binocular; spy-, opera-, field-glass, periscope, range finder.

mirror, reflector, speculum; looking-, pier-, cheval-, hand-glass.

prism; camera, *camera-lucida, -obscura*; projector, stereopticon, magic lantern etc. (*show*) 448; chro-, thau-matrope; stereo-, pseudo-, poly-, kaleido-scope.

photo-, opto-, erio-, actino-, luci-, radio-, spectro-meter; polari-, polemo-, spectro-scope, diffraction grating.

optics, optician, optometry, optometrist; microscop-y, -ist; photometry, photography; photographer.

446. Visibility.—N. visibility, perceptibility; conspicuousness, distinctness etc. *adj.*; conspicuity; appearance etc. 448; exposure; manifestation etc. 525; ocular -proof, — evidence, — demonstration; field of view etc. (*vision*) 441.

V. be —, become- -visible etc. *adj.*; appear, emerge, open to the view; meet —, catch- the eye; present —, show —, manifest —, produce —, discover —, reveal —, expose —, betray- itself; stand -forth, — out; show; arise; peep —, peer —, crop- out; start —; spring —, show —, turn —, crop- up; glimmer, glitter, glow, loom; glare; burst forth, scintillate; burst upon the -view, — sight; heave in sight; come -in sight, — into view, — out, — forth, — forward; see the light of day; break through the clouds; make its appearance, show its face, materialize, appear to one's eyes, come upon the stage, enter; float before the eyes, speak for itself. etc. (*manifest*) 525; attract the attention etc. 457; reappear; live in a glass house.

expose to view etc. 525.

Adj. visible, perceptible, perceivable, discernible, apparent; in -view, — full view, — sight; exposed to view, *en évidence*; unclouded.

obvious etc. (*manifest*) 525; plain, clear,

distinct, definite; well-defined, -marked; in focus; recognizable, palpable, autoptical; glaring, staring, conspicuous; stereoscopic; in -bold, — strong, — high- relief.

periscopic, panoramic.

before —, under- one's eyes; before one, *à vue d'oeil*, in one's eye, *oculis subjecta fidelibus.*

Adv. visibly etc. *adj.*; in sight of; before one's eyes etc. *adj.*; *veluti in speculum.*

447. Invisibility.—N. invisibility, nonappearance, imperceptibility; indistinctness etc. *adj.*; mystery, delitescence.

concealment etc. 528; latency etc. 526.

V. be -invisible etc. *adj.*; be hidden etc. (*hide*) 528; lurk etc. (*lie hidden*) 526; escape notice.

render -invisible etc. *adj.*; conceal etc. 528; put out of sight.

not see etc. (*be blind*) 442; lose sight of.

Adj. invisible, imperceptible; un-, in-discernible; un-, non-apparent; out of —, not in- sight; *à perte de vue*; behind the -scenes, — curtain; view-, sightless; in-, un-conspicuous; unseen etc. (*see* see etc. 441); covert etc. (*latent*) 526; eclipsed, under an eclipse.

dim etc. (*faint*) 422; mysterious, dark, obscure, confused; indistin-ct, -guishable; shadowy, indefinite, unde/ined; ill-defined, -marked; blurred, fuzzy, out of focus; misty etc. (*opaque*) 426; veiled etc. (*concealed*) 528; delitescent.

448. Appearance.—N. appearance, phenomenon, sight, spectacle, show, premonstration, scene, species, view, *coup d'oeil*; look-out, out-look, prospect, vista, perspective, bird's-eye view, scenery, landscape, picture, *tableau*; display, exposure, *mise en scène*; scenery, *décor*; rising of the curtain.

phant-asm, -om etc. (*fallacy of vision*) 443.

pageant, *spectacle*; peep-, raree-, gallanty-show; *ombres chinoises*; projector, optical —, magic-lantern, phantasmagoria, dissolving views; cinema, -tograph; bio-scope, -graph; moving pictures, movies, film, screen etc.; pan-, di-, cosm-, georama; *coup — , jeu- de théâtre*; pageantry etc. (*ostentation*) 882; insignia etc. (*indication*) 550.

aspect, phase, *phasis*, seeming; shape etc. (*form*) 240; guise, look, complexion, color, image, mien, air, cast, carriage, port, demeanor; presence, expression, first blush, face of the thing; point of view, light.

lineament, feature, trait, lines; out-line, -side; contour, *silhouette*, face, countenance, physiognomy, visage, phiz, mug, cast of countenance, profile, *tournure*, cut of one's jib, metoposcopy; outside etc. 220.

V. appear; be —, become- visible etc. 446; seem, look, show; present —, wear —, carry —, have —, bear —, exhibit —, take —, take on —, assume- the -appearance, — semblance- of; look like; cut a figure, figure; present to the view; show etc. (*make manifest*) 525.

Adj. apparent, seeming, ostensible; on view.

Adv. apparently; to all -seeming, — appearance; ostensibly, seemingly, as it seems, on the face of it, *primâ facie*; at the first blush, at first sight; in the eyes of; to the eye.

449. Disappearance.—N. disappearance, evanescence, eclipse, occultation.

departure etc. 293; exit, vanishing point; dissolving views.

V. disappear, vanish, dissolve, fade, melt away, pass, go, avaunt; be -gone etc. *adj.*; leave -no trace, — 'not a rack behind;' go off the stage etc. (*depart*) 293; suffer —, undergo- an eclipse; be lost to —, retire from- -sight, — view.

lose sight of.

efface etc. 552.

Adj. disappearing etc. *v.*; evanescent; missing, lost; lost to -sight, — view; gone; *spurlos versenki.*

Int. vanish! disappear! avaunt! etc. (*ejection*) 297.

450. Intellect.—N. intellect, mind, understanding, reason, thinking principle; rationality; cogitative —, cognitive —, intellectual- faculties; faculties, senses, consciousness, observation, percipience, apperception, mentality, intelligence, intellection, intuition, association of ideas, instinct, flair, conception, judgment, wits, parts, capacity, intellectuality, reasoning power, brains, genius; wit etc. 498; ability etc. (*skill*) 698; wisdom etc. 498.

soul, spirit, ghost, inner man, heart, breast, bosom, *penetralia mentis, divina particula aurae,* heart's core; ego, psyche, pneuma, subconsciousness, subconscious, subliminal self; dual personality.

organ —, seat- of thought; *sensorium*, sensory, brain, gray matter; head, -piece; pate, noddle, skull, scull, *pericranium, cerebrum, cranium,* brain-pan, -box; sconce, upper story.

[Science of mind] metaphysics; psychics, psycho-logy, -metry, -genesis, -analysis, -physics, psychi-atry, -cal research, thought reading etc. 992; ideology; mental —, moral- philosophy; philosophy of the mind; pneumat-, phren-ology; no —, craniology, -scopy.

ideal-ity, -ism; transcendental-, spiritual-ism; immateriality etc. 317.

metaphysician, psychologist etc.

V. note, notice, mark; take -notice, — cognizance- of; be -aware, — conscious- of; realize; appreciate; ruminate etc. (*think*) 451; fancy etc. (*imagine*) 515; conceive, reason, understand.

Adj. [Relating to intellect] intellectual, mental, rational, subjective, metaphysical, nooscopic, spiritual; ghostly; psych-ical, -ological; cerebral. immaterial etc. 317; endowed with reason.

- **Adv.** *in petto.*

450a. Absence or want **of Intellect.—N.** absence —, want- of -intellect etc. 450; imbecility etc. 499; brutality; brute -instinct, — force.

Adj. unendowed with reason.

451. Thought.—N. thought; exercitation —, exercise- of the intellect; reflection, cogitation, consideration, meditation, study, lucubration, speculation, deliberation, pondering; head-, brainwork; cerebration; mentation, deep reflection, close study, application etc. (*attention*) 457.

abstract thought, abstraction, contemplation, musing; brown study etc. (*inattention*) 458; reverie, Platonism; depth of thought, workings of the mind, thoughts, inmost thoughts; self-counsel, communing, -consultation.

association —, succession —, flow —, train —, current- of -thought, — ideas.

after —, mature- thought; reconsideration, second thoughts; retrospection etc. (*memory*) 505; excogitation; examination etc. (*inquiry*) 461; invention etc. (*imagination*) 515.

thoughtfulness etc. *adj.*

V. think, reflect, reason, cogitate, excogitate, consider, deliberate; bestow -thought, — consideration- upon; speculate, contemplate, meditate, ponder, muse, dream, ruminate; brood —, conover; animadvert, study; bend—, apply- the mind etc. (*attend*) 457; digest, discuss, hammer at, weigh, perpend; realize, appreciate; fancy etc. (*imagine*) 515; trow.

take into consideration; take counsel etc. (*be advised*) 695; commune with —, bethink- oneself; collect one's thoughts; revolve —, turn over —, run over- in the mind; chew the cud —, sleep- upon; take counsel of —, advise with- one's pillow.

rack —, ransack —, crack —, beat —, cudgelone's brains; set one's -brain, — wits- to work.

harbor —, entertain —, cherish —, nurture- an idea etc. 453; take into one's head; bear in mind; reconsider.

occur; present —, suggest- itself; come —, getinto one's head; strike one, flit across the view, come uppermost, run in one's head; enter —, pass in —, cross —, flash on —, flash across —, float in —, fasten itself on —, be uppermost in —, occupy- the mind; have in one's mind.

make an impression; sink —, penetrate- into the mind; engross the thoughts.

Adj. thinking etc. *v.*; thoughtful, pensive, meditative, reflective, cogitative, museful, wistful, contemplative, speculative, deliberative, studious, sedate, introspective, Platonic, philosophical.

lost —, engrossed —, rapt —, absorbed- in thought etc. (*inattentive*) 458; deep musing etc. (*intent*) 457.

in the mind, under consideration, in contemplation.

Adv. all things considered; taking everything into account.

Phr. the mind being on the stretch; the -mind, — head- -turning, — running- upon.

452. Incogitancy. [Absence or want of thought.]**—N.** incogitancy, vacancy, inunderstanding; inanity, fatuity etc. 499; thoughtlessness etc. (*inattention*) 458.

V. not -think etc. 451; not think of; dismiss from the -mind, — thoughts etc. 451.

indulge in reverie etc. (*be inattentive*) 458.

put away thought; unbend —, relax —, divert- the mind.

Adj. vacant, unintellectual, unideal, unoccupied, unthinking, inconsiderate, thoughtless; absent etc. (*inattentive*) 458; diverted; irrational etc. 499; narrow-minded etc. 481.

un-thought of, -dreamt of, -considered; off one's mind; incogitable, not to be thought of, inconceivable.

453. Idea. [Object of thought.]—**N.** idea, notion, conception, thought, apprehension, impression, perception, image, sentiment, reflection, observation, consideration; abstract idea, principle; archetype.

view etc. (*opinion*) 484; theory etc. 514; conceit, fancy; phantasy etc. (*imagination*) 515.

point of view etc. (*aspect*) 448; field of view.

454. Topic. [Subject of thought.]—**N.** subject of –, material for- thought; food for the mind, mental *pabulum*.

subject, -matter; matter, theme, topic, what it is about, *thesis*, text, business, affair, matter in hand, argument; motion, resolution; head, chapter; case, point; proposition, theorem; field of inquiry; moot point, problem, etc. (*question*) 461.

V. float –, pass- in the mind etc. 451.

Adj. thought of; uppermost in the mind; *in petto*.

Adv. under -discussion, – consideration, – advisement; in -question, – the mind; on -foot, – the carpet, – the *tapis*; before the house, relative to etc. 9.

455. Curiosity. [The desire of knowledge.]—**N.** interest, thirst for knowledge; curi-osity, -ousness; inquiring mind; inquisitiveness.

sight-seer, quidnunc, newsmonger, Paul Pry, peeping Tom, eavesdropper; gossip etc. (*news*) 532; questioner, *enfant terrible*.

V. be -curious etc. *adj.*; take an interest in, stare, gape; prick up the ears, see sights, lionize; pry, speer; dig up.

Adj. curious, inquisitive, burning with curiosity, overcurious, nosey; inquiring etc. 461; prying; inquisitorial; agape etc. (*expectant*) 507; attentive etc. 457.

Phr. what's the matter? what next?

456. Incuriosity. [Absence of curiosity.]—**N.** incuriosity; incuriousness etc. *adj.*; *insouciance* etc. 866; indifference, apathy.

V. be -incurious etc. *adj.*; have no -curiosity etc. 455; take no interest in etc. 823; mind one's own business.

Adj. incurious, uninquisitive, uninterested, indifferent, bored; impassive etc. 823.

457. Attention.—**N.** attention; mindfulness etc. *adj.*; intent-ness, -iveness; thought etc. 451; adverten-ce, -cy; observ-ance, -ation; consideration, reflection, perpension; heed; particularity; notice, regard etc. *v.*; circumspection etc. (*care*) 459; study, scrutiny, once-over; in-, intro-spection; revision, -al.

active –, diligent –, exclusive –, minute –, close –, intense –, deep –, profound –, abstract –, labored –, deliberate- -thought, – attention, – application, – study.

minuteness, attention to detail etc. 459.
absorption of mind etc. (*abstraction*) 458.
indication, calling attention to etc. *v.*

V. be -attentive etc. *adj.*; attend, advert to, observe, look, see, view, remark, notice, regard, take notice, mark; give –, pay- -attention, – heedto; listen in, incline –, lend- an ear to; trouble one's head about; give a thought –, animadvert- to; occupy oneself with; contemplate etc. (*think of*) 451; look -at, – to, – after, – into, – over; see to; turn –, bend –, apply –, direct –, give- the - mind, – eye, – attention- to; have -an eye to, – in one's eye; bear in mind; take into -account, – consideration; keep in -sight, – view; have regard to, heed, mind, take cognizance of, be engaged in, entertain, recognize; make –, take- note of; note.

examine cursorily; glance -at, – upon, – over; cast –, pass- the eyes over; run over, turn over the leaves, dip into, perstringe; skim etc. (*neglect*) 460; take a cursory view of.

examine, – closely, – intently; scan, scrutinize, consider; give –, bend- one's mind to; overhaul, revise, pore over; inspect, review, pass under review; take stock of; fix –, rivet –, focus –, devote- the - eye, – mind, – thoughts, – attention- on *or* to; hear –, think- out; mind one's business.

revert –, hark back- to; watch etc. (*expect*) 507, (*take care of*) 459; hearken –, listen- to; prick up the ears; have –, keep- the eyes open; come to the point.

meet with attention; fall under one's -notice, – observation; be -under consideration etc. (*topic*) 454.

catch –, strike- the eye; attract notice; catch –, awaken –, wake –, invite –, solicit –, attract –, claim –, excite –, engage –, occupy –, strike –, arrest –, fix –, engross –, absorb –, rivet-the- attention, – mind, – thoughts; be -present to, – uppermost in- the mind.

bring under one's notice; point -out, – to, – at, – the finger at; lay the finger on, indigitate, indicate; direct –, call- attention to; show; put a mark etc. (*sign*) 550- upon; call soldiers to 'attention;' bring forward etc. (*make manifest*) 525.

Adj. attentive, mindful, heedful, observant, regardful; alive –, awake- to, alert; observing etc. *v.*; taken up –, occupied- with; engaged –, engrossed –, interested –, wrapped- in; absorbed, rapt; breathless; pre-occupied etc. (*inattentive*) 458; watchful etc. (*careful*) 459; intent on, openeyed, breathless, undistracted, upon the stretch; on the watch etc. (*expectant*) 507.

steadfast.

Int. see! look, – here, – out, – alive, – you, – to it! mark! lo! behold! soho! hark, – ye! mind ! halloo! observe! lo and hehold!, attention! *nota bene*;N.B.; *.†* ; I'd have you to know; notice! take notice! O yes! *Oyez!*

Phr. this is –, these are- to give notice.

458. Inattention.—**N.** in-attention, – consideration; inconsiderateness etc. *adj.*; oversight; inadverten-ce, -cy; non-observance, disregard.

supineness etc. (*inactivity*) 683; *étourderie*; want of thought; heedlessness etc. (*neglect*) 460; *insouciance* etc. (*indifference*) 866.

abstraction; absence −, absorption- of mind; preoccupation, distraction, reverie, brown study, deep musing, fit of abstraction, woolgathering.

V. be -inattentive etc. *adj.*; overlook, disregard; pass by etc. (*neglect*) 460; not -observe etc. 457; think little of.

close −, shut- one's eyes to; wink at; pay no attention to; dismiss −, discard −, discharge- from one's -thoughts, − mind; drop the subject, think no more of; set −, turn −, put- aside; turn -away from, − one's attention from, − a deaf ear to, − one's back upon.

abstract oneself, dream, indulge in reverie.

escape -notice, − attention; come in at one ear and go out at the other; forget etc. (*have no remembrance*) 506.

call off −, draw off −, call away −, divert −, distract- the -attention, − thoughts, − mind; put out of one's head; dis-concert, -compose; put out, confuse, perplex, bewilder, fluster, muddle, dazzle; throw a sop to Cerberus.

Adj. inattentive; un-observant, -mindful, -heeding, -discerning; inadvertent; mind-, regard-, respect-less; listless etc. (*indifferent*) 866; blind, deaf; flighty, hand over head; cur-, percur-sory; giddy-, scatter-, hare-brained; unreflecting, *écervelé*, inconsiderate, off-hand, thoughtless, dizzy, muzzy, brainsick; giddy, − as a goose; wild, harum-scarum, ranipole, high-flying; heed-, careless etc. (*neglectful*) 460.

absent, absent-minded, abstracted, *distrait*; lost; lost −, wrapped- in thought, woolgathering; rapt, in the clouds, bemused; dreaming −, musing- on other things; pre-occupied; engrossed etc. (*attentive*) 457; in a -reverie etc. *n.*; off one's guard etc. (*inexpectant*) 508; napping; dreamy.

disconcerted, put out etc. *v.*; rattled.

Adv. inattentively, inadvertently etc. *adj.*; per incuriam, sub silentio.

Int. stand -at ease, − easy!

Phr. the attention wanders; one's wits gone a -woolgathering, − bird's nesting; it never entered into one's head; the mind running on other things; one's thoughts being elsewhere; had it been a bear it would have bitten you.

459. Care. [Vigilance.]—**N.** care, solicitude, heed; heedfulness etc. *adj.*; scruple etc. (*conscientiousness*) 939.

watchfulness etc. *adj.*; vigilance, *surveillance*, eyes of Argus, watch, vigil, look out, watch and ward, *l'oeil du maître*.

alertness etc. (*activity*) 682; attention etc. 457; prudence etc., circumspection etc. (*caution*) 864; forethought etc. 510; precaution etc. (*preparation*) 673; tidiness etc. (*order*) 58, (*cleanliness*) 652; accuracy etc. (*exactness*) 494; minuteness, attention to detail; meticulousness, nicety, circumstantiality.

V. be -careful etc. *adj.*; reck; take care etc. (*be cautious*) 864; pay attention to etc. 457; take care of; look −, see- -to, − after; keep -an eye, − a sharp eye- upon; keep -watch, − watch and ward; mount guard, set watch, watch; keep in -sight, − view; chaperon, play gooseberry; mind, − one's business.

look -sharp, − about one; look with one's own eyes; keep a -good, − sharp- look-out; have all one's -wits, − eyes- about one; watch for etc. (*ex-*

pect) 507; stand to; keep one's eyes −, have the eyes −, sleep with one eye- open.

take precautions etc. 673; protect etc. (*render safe*) 664.

do one's best etc. 682; mind one's Ps and Qs, speak by the card, pick one's steps.

Adj. care-, regard-, heed-ful; taking care etc. *v.*; particular; prudent etc. (*cautious*) 864; considerate; thoughtful etc. (*deliberative*) 451; provident etc. (*prepared*) 673; alert etc. (*active*) 682; sure-footed.

guarded, on one's guard; on the -qui vive, − alert, − watch, − look-out; awake, broad awake, vigilant; watch-, wake-, wist-ful; Argus-, lynx-eyed; wide awake etc. (*intelligent*) 498; on the watch for etc. (*expectant*) 507.

tidy etc. (*orderly*) 58, (*clean*) 652; accurate etc. (*exact*) 494; scrupulous etc. (*conscientious*) 939; cavendo tutus etc. (*safe*) 664.

Adv. carefully etc. *adj.*; with care, gingerly.

Phr. quis custodiet ipsos custodes?

460. Neglect.—**N.** neglect; carelessness etc. *adj.*; trifling etc. *v.*; negligence; omission, laches, default; remissness, slackness, procrastination; supineness etc. (*inactivity*) 683; inattention etc. 458; nonchalance etc. (*insensibility*) 823; imprudence, recklessness etc. 863; slovenliness etc. (*disorder*) 59; (*dirt*) 653; improvidence etc. 674; non-completion etc. 730; inexactness etc. (*error*) 495.

paraleipsis [in rhetoric].

trifler, slacker, waster, waiter on Providence; Micawber.

V. be -negligent etc. *adj.*; take no care of etc. (take care of etc. 459); neglect; let -slip, − go; lay −, set −, cast −, put- aside; keep −, leave- out of sight; lose sight of.

overlook, disregard; pass -over, − by; let pass; blink; wink −, connive- at; gloss over; take no -note, − notice, − thought, − account- of; pay no regard to; *laisser aller*; allow to lie on the table.

scamp; trifle, fribble; do by halves; skimp; cut; slight etc. (*despise*) 930; play − trifle- with; slur; skim, − the surface; *effleurer*; take a cursory view of etc. 457.

slur −, slip −, skip −, jump- over; pretermit, miss, skip, jump, omit, give the go-by to, push aside, throw into the background, shelve, sink; ignore, shut one's eyes to, refuse to hear, turn a deaf ear to; leave out of one's calculation; not -attend to etc. 457, − mind; not trouble -oneself, − one's head- -with, − about; forget etc. 506; be caught napping etc. (*not expect*) 508; leave a loose thread; let the grass grow under one's feet.

render -neglectful etc. *adj.*; put −, throw- off one's guard.

Adj. neglecting etc. *v.*; unmindful, negligent, neglectful; heedless, careless, thoughtless; perfunctory, remiss, slack.

inconsiderate; un-, in-circumspect; off one's guard; un-wary, -watchful, -guarded; offhand.

supine etc. (*inactive*) 683; inattentive etc 458; insouciant etc. (*indifferent*) 823; imprudent, reckless etc. 863; slovenly etc. (*disorderly*) 59, (*dirty*) 653; inexact etc. (*erroneous*) 495; improvident etc. 674.

neglected etc. *v.*; un-heeded, -cared for, -

perceived, -seen, -observed, -noticed, -noted, -marked, -attended to, -thought of, -regarded, -remarked, -missed; shunted, shelved.

un-examined, -studied, -searched, -scanned, -weighed, -sifted, -explored.

Adv. negligently etc. *adj.*; hand over head, anyhow; in an unguarded moment etc. (*unexpectedly*) 508; *per incuriam.*

Int. never mind, no matter, let it pass; it will be all the same a hundred years hence.

461. Inquiry. [Subject of Inquiry. Question.]—**N.** inquiry; request etc. 765; search, research, quest; pursuit etc. 622.

examination, review, scrutiny, investigation, indagation; per-quisition, -scrutation, -vestigation; inqu-est, -isition; exploration; *exploitation*, ventilation.

sifting; calculation, analysis, dissection, resolution, induction; Baconian method.

strict —, close —, searching —, exhaustive-inquiry; narrow —, strict- search; study etc. (*consideration*) 451.

scire facias, ad referendum; trial.

questioning etc. *v.*; interroga-tion, -tory; third degree; interpellation; challenge, examination, cross-examination, catechism; feeler, Socratic method, zetetic philosophy; leading question; discussion etc. (*reasoning*) 476; questionnaire, questionary.

reconnoitering, *reconnaissance*; prying etc. *v.*; espionage, *espionnage*; domiciliary visit, peep behind the curtain; lantern of Diogenes.

question, query, problem, *desideratum*, point to be solved, porism; subject —, field- of -inquiry, — controversy; point —, matter- in dispute; moot-point; issue, question at issue; bone of contention etc. (*discord*) 713; plain —, fair —, open- question; enigma etc. (*secret*) 533; knotty point etc. (*difficulty*) 704; *quod-libet*; threshold of an inquiry.

inquirer, investigator, experimenter, inquisitor, inspector, querist, examiner, catechist; scrut-ator, -ineer; analyst; quidnunc etc. (*curiosity*) 455.

V. make -inquiry etc. *n.*; inquire, seek, search, frisk, speer, look -for, — about for, — out for; scan, reconnoiter, explore, sound, rummage, ransack, pry, peer, look round; look —, go- -over, — through; spy, over-haul.

scratch the head, slap the forehead.

look —, peer —, pry- into every hole and corner; look behind the scenes; trace up; hunt —, fish —, dig —, ferret- out; unearth; leave no stone unturned.

seek a -clue, — clew; hunt, track, trail, shadow, mouse, dodge, trace; follow the -trail, — scent; pursue etc. 622; beat up one's quarters; fish for; feel for etc. (*experiment*) 463.

investigate; take up —, institute —, pursue —, follow up —, conduct —, carry on —, prosecute- -an inquiry etc. *n.*; look -at, — into; pre-examine; discuss, canvass, agitate.

examine, study, consider, calculate; dip —, dive —, delve —, go deep- into; make sure of, probe, sound, fathom; probe to the -bottom, — quick; scrutinize, analyze, anatomize, dissect, parse, resolve, sift, winnow; view —, try- in all its phases; thresh out.

bring in question, subject to examination; put to

the proof etc. (*experiment*) 463; audit, tax, pass in review; take into consideration etc. (*think over*) 451; take counsel etc. 695.

ask, question, demand; put —, pop —, propose —, propound —, moot —, start —, raise —, stir —, suggest —, put forth —, ventilate —, grapple with —, go into- a question.

put to the question, interrogate, catechize, pump, grill; cross-question, -examine; dodge; require an answer; pick —, suck- the brains of; feel the pulse. be -in question etc. *adj.*; undergo examination.

Adj. inquiry etc. *v.*; inquisitive etc. (*curious*) 455; requisit-ive, -ory; catechetical, inquisitorial, analytic; in -search, — quest- of; on the look-out for, interrogative, zetetic; all-searching.

un-determined, -tried, -decided; in -question, — dispute, — issue, — course of inquiry; under -discussion, — consideration, — investigation etc. *n.*, *sub judice*, moot, proposed; doubtful etc. (*uncertain*) 475.

Adv. what? why? wherefore? whence? whither? where? *quaere?* how -comes, — happens, — is- it? what is the reason? what's -the matter, — up, in the wind? what on earth? when? who?

462. Answer.—**N.** answer, response, reply, replication, *riposte*, rejoinder, surrejoinder, rebutter, surrebutter, counter-evidence etc. 468, counter-charge, defence, plea; retort, repartee; contradiction etc. 536; rescript, -ion; antiphon, -y; acknowledgment; password; echo.

discovery etc. 480*a*; solution etc. (*explanation*) 522; rationale etc. (*cause*) 153; clue etc. (*indication*) 550.

Oedipus; oracle, etc. 513; return etc. (*record*) 551.

V. answer, respond, reply, rebut, retort, rejoin; give —, return for- answer; acknowledge, echo.

explain etc. (*interpret*) 522; solve etc. (*unriddle*) 522; discover etc. 480*a*; fathom, hunt out etc. (*inquire*) 461; satisfy, set at rest, determine.

Adj. answering etc. *v.*; respon-sive, -dent; oracular; antiphonal; conclusive.

Adv. because etc. (*cause*) 153; on the -scent, — right scent.

Int. *eureka!*

463. Experiment.—**N.** experiment; essay etc. (*attempt*) 675; research etc. (*investigation*) 461; trial, tentative method, *tâtonnement.*

verification, probation, *experimentum crucis*, proof, criterion, diagnostic test, tryout, crucial test, acid test.

crucible, reagent, check, touchstone, pix; assay, ordeal; ring.

empiricism, rule of thumb.

feeler; pilot —, messenger- balloon, *ballon d'essai*; pilot engine; scout; straw to show the wind. speculation, random shot, leap in the dark.

analy-zer, -st; adventurer, explorer, sourdough, prospector; experiment-er, -ist, -alist; assayer.

V. experiment; essay etc. (*endeavor*) 675; try, assay, sample; make -an experiment, — trial of; give a trial to; put upon —, subject to- trial; experiment upon; rehearse; put —, bring —, submit-to the -test, — proof; prove, verify, test, touch, practise upon, try one's strength.

grope; feel —, grope- -for, — one's way; fumble; *tâttonner, aller à tâtons*; put —, throw- out a feeler; send up a pilot balloon; see how the -land lies, — wind blows; consult the barometer; feel the pulse; fish —, bob- for; cast —, beat- about for; angle, trawl, cast one's net, beat the bushes.

venture, try one's fortune etc. (*adventure*) 675; explore etc. (*inquire*) 461.

Adj. experimental; probat-ive, ory, -ionary; analytic, docimastic; tentative; empirical; speculative, tentive.

under probation, on one's trial, on trial, on approval.

464. Comparison.—N. comparison, collation, contrast; identification.

sim-ile, -ilitude; allegory etc. (*metaphor*) 521.

V. compare -to, — with; collate, confront; place side by side etc. (*near*) 197; set —, pit- against one another; contrast balance.

identify, draw a parallel, parallel.

compare notes; institute a comparison; *parva componere magnis.*

Adj. comparative, relative; metaphorical etc. 521.

compared with etc. *v.*; comparable.

Adv. relatively etc. (*relation*) 9; as compared with etc. *v.*

465. Discrimination.—N. discrimination, distinction, differentiation, diagnosis, diorism; nice perception; perception —, appreciation- of difference; acuteness; estimation etc. 466; nicety, refinement; taste etc. 850; *critique*, judgement, tact; insight, discernment etc. (*intelligence*) 498; *nuances.*

V. discriminate, distinguish, differentiate, severalize; separate; draw the line, sift; separate —, winnow- the chaff from the wheat; split hairs.

estimate etc. (*measure*) 466; know -which is which, — one's stuff, — one's way about, — what is what, — 'a hawk from a handsaw.'

take into -account, — consideration; give —, allow- due weight to; weigh carefully.

Adj. discriminating etc. *v.*; dioristic, discriminative, critical, distinctive; nice.

Phr. *il y a fagots et fagots; rem acu tetigisti.*

465a. Indiscrimination.—N. indiscrimination; promiscuity; indistinctness, -ion; uncertainty etc. (*doubt*) 475; obtuseness.

V. not -indiscriminate etc. 465; overlook etc.' (*neglect*) 460- a distinction; con-found, -fuse, jumble; swallow whole.

Adj. indiscriminate, undiscriminating, promiscuous; undistinguish-ed, -able, -ing; unmeasured.

466. Measurement.—N. measurement, admeasurement, mensuration, survey, valuation, appraisment, assessment, assize; estim-ate, -ation; dead reckoning; reckoning etc. (*numeration*) 85; gauging etc. *v.*

metrology, weights and measures, compound arithmetic.

measure, yard measure, standard, rule, foot-rule, chain, tape, staff, compass, callipers; dividers; gage, gauge, planimeter; meter, line, rod, check.

volt, kilowatt, ampere, candle power; horse power; axle load; foot pound.

flood —, high water- mark; Plimsoll mark; index etc. 550.

scale; gradu-ation, -ated scale; nonius; vernier etc. (*minuteness*) 193; pedo (*length*)- 200, sounding line etc. (*depth*) 208, thermo (*heat* etc. 398)-, baro (*air* etc. 338)-, dynamo (*power*)- 276, anemo (*wind* 349)-, gonio (*angle* 244)- meter; landmark etc. (*limit*) 233; balance etc. (*weight*) 310; optical instruments etc. 445.

co-ordinates, ordinate and abscissa, polar co-ordinates, latitude and longitude, declination and right ascension, altitude and azimuth.

geo-, stereo-, hypso-metry; metage; surveying, land surveying; geo-desy, -detics, -desia; ortho-, alti-metry; *cadastre.*

astrolabe, armillary sphere.

land, -surveyor; geometer, topographer, car-tographer, hydrographer.

V. measure, meter, mete; value, assess, rate, appraise, estimate, form as estimate, set a value on; appreciate; standardize.

span, pace, step; apply the -compass etc. *n.*; gauge, plumb, probe, calliper, sound, fathom etc. 208; heave the -log, — lead; weigh etc. 319; survey.

take an average etc. 29; graduate.

Adj. measuring etc. *v.*; metric, -al; measurable; geodetical, cadastral, topographical.

467. Evidence. [on one side]—**N.** evidence; facts, premises, *data, praecognita*, grounds.

indication etc. 550; criterion etc. (*test*) 463.

testi-mony, -fication; attestation; deposition etc. (*affirmation*) 535; examination.

admission etc. (*assent*) 488; authority, warrant, credential, diploma, voucher, certificate, docket; record etc. 551; document, muniments; *pièce justificative*; deed, warranty etc. (*security*) 771; signature, seal etc. (*identification*) 550; exhibit, citation, reference.

witness, indicator; eye-, ear-witness; deponent; sponsor.

oral —, documentary —, hearsay —, external —, extrinsic —, internal —, intrinsic —, circumstantial —, cumulative —, *ex parte* —, presumptive —, collateral —, constructive- evidence; proof etc. (*demonstration*) 478; evidence in chief; finger prints, dactylogram.

secondary evidence; confirmation, corroboration, adminicle, support; ratification etc. (*assent*) 488; authentication, verification; compurgation, wager of law, comprobation.

citation, reference.

V. be -evidence etc. *n.*; evince, show, betoken, tell of; indicate etc. (*denote*) 550; imply, involve, argue, bespeak, breathe.

have —, carry- weight; tell, speak volumes; speak for itself etc. (*manifest*) 525.

rest —, depend- upon; repose on.

bear -witness etc. *n.*; give -evidence etc. *n.*; testify, depose, witness, vouch for; sign, seal, undersign, set one's hand and seal, sign and seal, deliver as one's act and deed, certify, attest; acknowledge etc. (*assent*) 488.

make absolute, confirm, ratify, corroborate, endorse, countersign, support, bear out, vindicate, uphold, warrant.

adduce, attest, cite, quote; refer —, appeal- to; call, — to witness; bring -forward, — into court; allege, plead; produce —, confront- witnesses; collect —, bring together —, rake up- evidence.

have —, make out- a case; establish, circumstantiate, authenticate, substantiate, verify, make good, quote chapter and verse; bring -home to, — to book.

Adj. showing etc. *v.*; evidential, indica-tive, -tory; deducible etc. 478; grounded —, founded —, based- on; first hand, authentic, verifiable; corroborative, confirmatory; significant, conclusive.

Adv. by inference; according to, witness, *a fortiori*; still -more, — less; *raison de plus*; in corroboration etc. *n.* of; *valeat quantum*; under -seal, — one's hand and seal.

468. Counter-evidence. [Evidence on the other side, on the other hand.]—**N.** counter-evidence, evidence on the other -side, — hand; disproof; refutation etc. 479; negation etc. 536; conflicting evidence.

plea etc. 617; vindication etc. 937; counter-protest; *tu quoque* argument; other side —, reverse- of the shield.

V. countervail, oppose; run counter; rebut etc. (*refute*) 479; subvert etc. (*destroy*) 162; check, weaken; contravene; contradict etc. (*deny*) 536; tell another story, turn the -tables, — scale; alter the case; cut both ways; prove a negative.

audire alteram partem.

Adj. countervailing etc. *v.*; contradictory, in rebuttal.

un-attested, -authenticated, -supported by evidence; suppositious, trumped up.

Adv. *per contra*, conversely, on the other hand.

469. Qualification.—**N.** qualification, limitation, modification, coloring.

allowance, grains of allowance, consideration, extenuating circumstances.

condition, proviso, exception; exemption; salvo, saving clause; discount etc. 813.

V. qualify, limit, modify, affect, temper, leaven, give a color to, introduce new conditions.

allow —, make allowance- for; admit exceptions, take into account.

take exception, object.

Adj. qualifying etc. *v.*; conditional; extenuatory; exceptional etc. (*unconformable*) 83.

hypothetical etc. (*supposed*) 514; contingent etc. (*uncertain*) 475.

Adv. provided, — always; if, unless, but, yet; according as; conditionally, admitting, supposing; on the supposition of etc. (*theoretically*) 514; with the understanding, even, although, though, for all that, after all, at all events.

with grains of allowance, *cum grano salis*; *exceptis excipiendis*; wind and weather permitting; if possible etc. 470.

subject to; with this -proviso etc. *n.*

470. Possibility.—**N.** possibility, potentiality; what -may be, — is possible etc. *adj.*; compatibility etc. (*agreement*) 23.

practicability, feasibility; practicableness etc. *adj.*

contingency, chance etc. 156.

V. be -possible etc. *adj.*; stand a chance, have a leg to stand on; admit of, bear.

render -possible etc. *adj.*; put in the way of.

Adj. possible; on the -cards, — dice; *in posse*, within the bounds of possibility, conceivable, credible, imaginable; compatible etc. 23.

practicable, feasible, workable, performable, achievable; within -reach, — measurable distance; accessible, superable, surmountable; at-, obtainable; contingent etc. (*doubtful*) 475.

Adv. possibly, by possibility; perhaps, -chance, -adventure; may be, haply, mayhap.

if possible, wind and weather permitting, God willing, *Deo volente*, D.V.

471. Impossibility.—**N.** impossibility etc. *adj.*; what -cannot, — can never- be; sour grapes; infeasibility, impracticability; hopelessness etc. 859.

V. be -impossible etc. *adj.*; have no chance whatever.

attempt impossibilities; square the circle; discover the -philosopher's stone — elixir of life, — secret of perpetual motion; wash a blackamoor white; skin a flint; make -a silk purse out of a sow's ear, — bricks without straw; have nothing to go upon; weave a rope of sand, build castles in the air, *prendre la lune avec les dents*, extract sunbeams from cucumbers, set the Thames on fire, milk a he-goat into a sieve, catch a weasel asleep, *rompre l'anguille au genou*, be in two places at once.

Adj. impossible; not -possible etc. 470; absurd, contrary to reason; unlikely, at variance with facts; unreasonable etc. 477; incredible etc. 485; beyond the bounds of -reason, — possibility; from which reason recoils; visionary; inconceivable etc. (*improbable*) 473; prodigious etc. (*wonderful*) 870; un-, in-imaginable, unthinkable, not a Chinaman's chance.

impracticable, unachievable; un-, in-feasible; insuperable; un-, in-surmountable; unat-, unobtainable; out of -reach, — the question; not to be -had, — thought of; beyond control; desperate etc. (*hopeless*) 859; incompatible etc. 24; inaccessible, uncomeatable, impassable, impervious, innavigable, inextricable.

out of -, beyond- one's -power, — depth, — reach, — grasp; too much for; *ultra crepidam*.

Phr. the grapes are sour; *non possumus*; *non nostrum tantas componere lites*.

472. Probability.—**N.** probability, likelihood; likeliness etc. *adj.*

vraisemblance, verisimilitude, plausibility;

color, semblance, show of; presumption; presumptive −, circumstantial- evidence; credibility.

reasonable −, fair −, good −, favorable- - chance, − prospect; prospect, well-grounded hope; chance etc. 156.

V. be -probable etc. *adj.*; give −, lend¹- color to; point to; imply etc. (*evidence*) 467; bid fair etc. (*promise*) 511; stand fair for; stand −, run- a good chance.

presume, infer, suppose, take for granted.

think likely, dare say, flatter oneself; expect etc. 507; count upon etc. (*believe*) 484.

Adj. probable, likely, hopeful, to be expected, in a fair way.

plausible, specious, ostensible, colorable, *ben trovato*, well-founded, reasonable, credible, easy of belief, presumable, presumptive, apparent.

Adv. probably etc. *adj.*; belike; in all - probability, − likelihood; very −, most- likely; as likely as not; like enough; ten etc. to one; apparently, seemingly, according to every reasonable expectation; *primâ facie*; to all appearance etc. (*to the eye*) 448.

Phr. the -chances, − odds- are; appearances −, chances- are in favor of; there is reason to -believe, − think, − expect; I dare say; all Lombard Street to a China orange.

473. Improbability.—N. improbability, unlikelihood; unfavorable −, bad −, little −, small −, poor −, scarcely any −, no −, not a ghost of a- chance; bare possibility; long odds; incredibility etc. 485.

V. be -improbable etc. *adj.*; have a -small chance etc. *n.*

Adj. improbable, unlikely, contrary to all reasonable expectation, implausible.

rare etc. (*infrequent*) 137; unheard of, inconceivable; un-, in-imaginable; incredible etc. 485; more than doubtful.

Int. not likely! no fear!

Phr. the chances are against.

474. Certainty.—N. certainty; necessity etc. 601; certitude, certainness, surety, assurance, sureness; dead −, moral- certainty; infallibleness etc. *adj.*; infallibility, reliability.

gospel, scripture, church, pope, court of final appeal; *res judicata*, *ultimatum*.

positiveness; dogmat-ism, -ist, -izer; *doctrinaire*, know-all, bigot, -ry; opinionist, Sir Oracle; *ipse dixit*; zealot.

fact; positive −, matter of- fact; *fait accompli*.

V. be -certain etc. *adj.*; stand to reason.

render -certain etc. *adj.*; in-, en-, as-sure; clinch, make sure; determine, decide, set at rest, 'make assurance double sure;' know etc. (*believe*) 484; dismiss all doubt.

dogmatize, lay down the law.

Adj. certain, sure; assured etc. *v.*; solid, well-founded.

unqualified, absolute, positive, determinate, definite, clear, unequivocal, categorical, unmistakable, decisive, decided, ascertained.

inevitable, unavoidable, ineluctable, avoidless.

unerring, infallible; unchangeable etc. 150; to be depended on, trustworthy, reliable, bound.

un-impeachable, -deniable, -questionable; indisputable, -contestable, -controvertible, - defeasible, -dubitable; irrefutable etc. (*proven*) 478; conclusive, without power of appeal, final.

indubious; without −, beyond a −, without a shade or shadow or- -doubt − question; past dispute; beyond all -question, − dispute; undoubted, -contested, -questioned, -disputed; question-, doubt-less.

bigoted, fanatical, dogmatic, opinionat-ed, -ive, *doctrinaire*.

authoritative, authentic; official.

sure as -fate, − death and taxes, − a gun.

evident, self-evident, axiomatic; clear, − as day, − as the sun at noonday; obvious.

Adv. certainly etc. *adj.*; for certain, certes, sure, no doubt, doubtless, and no mistake, *flagrante delicto*, sure enough, to be sure, of course, as a matter of course, *à coup sur*, to a certainty, undoubtedly; in truth etc. (*truly*) 494; at -any rate, − all events; without fail; *coûte que coûte*; whatever may happen, if the worst come to the worst; come −, happen- what -may; − will; sink or swim; rain or shine.

Phr. *cela va sans dire*; there is -no question, − not a shadow of doubt; the die is cast etc. (*necessity*) 601.

475. Uncertainty.—N. uncertainty, incertitude, doubt; doubtfulness etc. *adj.*; dubi-ety, - tation, -tancy, -ousness.

hesitation, suspense; perplexity, embarrassment, dilemma, quandary, Morton's fork, bewilderment; timidity etc. (*fear*) 860; indecision, vacillation etc. 605; *diaporesis*, indetermination.

vagueness etc. *adj.*; haze, fog; obscurity etc. (*darkness*) 421; ambiguity etc. (*double meaning*) 520; contingency, double contingency, possibility upon a possibility; conjecture; open question etc. (*question*) 461; *onus probandi*; blind bargain, pig in a poke, leap in the dark, something or other; needle in a bottle of hay; roving commission.

fallibility, unreliability, untrustworthiness, precariousness.

V. be -uncertain etc. *adj.*; wonder whether.

lose the -clue, − clew, − scent; miss one's way.

not know -what to make of, etc. (*unintelligibility*) 519, − which way to turn, − whether one stands on one's head or one's heels; float in a sea of doubt, hesitate, flounder; lose -oneself, − one's head, − one's way, wander aimlessly; muddle one's brains.

render -uncertain etc. *adj.*; put out, pose, puzzle, perplex, embarrass; confuse, -found; bewilder, mystify, bother, nonplus, addle the wits, throw off the scent; *ambiguas in vulgus spargere voces*; keep in suspense.

doubt etc. (*disbelieve*) 485; hang −, tremble- in the balance; depend.

Adj. uncertain; casual; random etc. (*aimless*) 621; changeable etc. 149.

doubtful, dubious; indecisive; unsettled, - decided, -determined; in suspense, open to discussion; controvertible; in question etc. (*inquiry*) 461; insecure, unstable.

vague; in-determinate, -definite; ambiguous, equivocal; undefin-ed, -able; confused etc. (in-distinct) 447; mystic, mysterious, veiled, obscure, cryptic, oracular.

perplexing etc. v.; enigmatic, paradoxical; apocryphal, problematical, hypothetical; ex-perimental etc. 463.

fallible, questionable, precarious, slippery, ticklish, debatable, disputable; un-reliable, -trustworthy.

contingent, — on, dependent / on; subject to; dependent on circumstances; occasional; provisional.

unauth-entic, -enticated, -oritative; un-ascertained, confirmed; undemonstrated; un-told, -counted.

in a -state of uncertainty, — cloud, — maze; ignorant etc. 491; on the horns of a dilemma; afraid to say; out of one's reckoning, astray, adrift; as -sea, — fault, — a loss, — one's wit's end, — a nonplus; puzzled etc. v.; lost abroad, désorienté; dis-tracted, -traught.

Adv. pendente lite; sub spe rati.

Phr. Heaven knows; who can tell? who shall decide when doctors disagree?

476. Reasoning.—N. reasoning; ratio-cination, -nalism; dialectics, induction, generalization.

discussion, comment; ventilation; inquiry etc. 461.

argumentation, controversy, debate; polemics, wrangling; contention etc. 720; logomachy; dis-putation, -ceptation; paper war.

art of reasoning, logic.

process —, train —, chain- of reasoning; de-, in-duction; systhesis, analysis.

argument; case, plea, plaidoyer, opening; lemma, proposition, terms, premises, postulate, data, starting point, principle; inference etc. (judgment) 480.

pro-, syllogism; enthymeme, sorites, dilemma, perilepsis, a priori reasoning, reductio ad ab-surdum, horns of a dilemma, argumentum ad hominem, comprehensive argument.

reasoner, logician, dialectician; disputant; contro-ver-sialist, -tist; wrangler, arguer, debater, polemic, casuist, rationalist; scientist.

logical sequence; good case; correct —, just —, sound —, valid —, cogent —, logical —, forcible —, persuasive —, persuasory —, consectary —, con-clusive etc. 478 —, subtle- reasoning; force of argument; strong -point, — argument.

arguments, reasons, pros and cons.

V. reason, argue, discuss, debate, dispute, wrangle; bandy -words, — arguments; chop logic; hold —, carry on- an argument; controvert etc. (deny) 536; canvass; comment —, moralize-upon; consider etc. (examine) 461.

open a -discussion, — case; join —, be at- issue; moot; come to the point; stir —, agitate —, ventilate —, torture- a question; try conclusions; take up a -side, — case.

contend, take one's stand upon, insist, lay stress on; infer etc. 480.

follow from etc. (demonstration) 478.

Adj. rational; reasoning etc. v.; rationalistic; argumentative, controversial, dialectic, polemical; discurs-ory, -ive; disputations.

debatable, controvertible.

logical; in-, de-ductive; synthetic, analytic; relevant etc. 23.

Adv. for, because, hence, whence, seeing that, since, sith, then, thence, so; for -that, — this, — which- reason; for-, inasmuch as; whereas, ex con-cesso, considering, in consideration of; there-, where-fore; consequently, ergo, thus, accordingly; a fortiori.

in -conclusion, — fine; finally, after all, au bout du compte, on the whole, taking one thing with another.

rationally etc. adj.

477. Sophistry. [The absence of reasoning.] **Intuition.** [False or vicious reasoning; show of reason.]—N. intuition, instinct, association; presen-timent; rule of thumb.

sophistry, paralogy, perversion, casuistry, jesuitry, equivocation, evasion, mental reservation; chicane, -ry; quiddit, quiddity; mystification; special pleading; speciousness etc. adj.; nonsense etc. 497; word-, tongue-fence.

false —, vicious- reasoning; petitio principii, ignoratio elenchi; post hoc ergo propter hoc; non sequitur, ignotum per ignotius.

misjudgment etc. 481; false teaching etc. 538.

sophism, solecism, paralogism; quibble, quirk, elenchus, elench, fallacy, quodlibet, subterfuge, subtlety, quillet; inconsistency, antilogy; 'a mockery, a delusion and a snare;' claptrap, mere words; 'lame and impotent conclusion.'

meshes —, cobwebs- of sophistry; flaw in an argument; weak point, bad case.

over-refinement; hair-splitting etc. v.

sophist, casuist, paralogist.

V. judge -intuitively, — by intuition; hazard a proposition, talk at random.

reason -ill, — falsely etc. adj.; paralogize; misjudge etc. 481.

pervert, quibble; equivocate, mystify, evade, elude; gloss over, varnish; misteach etc. 538; mislead etc. (error) 495; cavil, refine, subtilize, split hairs; misrepresent etc. (lie) 544.

beg the question, reason in a circle, cut blocks with a razor, beat about the bush, play fast and loose, blow hot and cold, prove that black is white and white black, travel out of the record, parler à tort et à travers, put oneself out of court, not have a leg to stand on.

Adj. intuitive, instinctive, impulsive; in-dependent of —, anterior to- reason; gratuitous; hazarded; unconnected.

unreasonable, illogical, false, unsound, invalid; unwarranted, not following; inconsequent, -ial; in-consistent, incongruous; abson-ous, -ant; un-scientific; untenable, inconclusive, incorrect; fall-acious, -ible; groundless, unproved.

deceptive, sophistical, sophisticated, casuistical, jesuitical; illus-ive, -ory; specious, hollow, plausible, ad captandum, evasive; irrelevant etc. 10.

weak, feeble, poor, flimsy, loose, vague, irrational; nonsensical etc. (absurd) 497; foolish etc. (imbecile) 499; frivolous, pettifogging, quib-bling; finespun, over-refined.

at the end of one's tether, au bout de son latin.

Adv. intuitively etc. *adj.*; by intuition; illogically etc. *adj.*

Phr. *non constat*; that goes for nothing.

478. Demonstration.—N. demonstration, proof; conclusiveness etc. *adj.*; *apodixis*, probation, comprobation.

logic of facts etc. (*evidence*) 467; *experimentum curcis* etc. (*test*) 463; argument etc. 476; irrefragability.

V. demonstrate, prove, establish, make good; show; evince etc. (*be evidence of*) 467; verify etc. 467; settle the question, reduce to demonstration, set the question at rest.

make out, – a case; prove one's point, have the best of the argument; draw a conclusion etc. (*judge*) 480.

follow, – of course; stand to reason; hold -good, – water.

Adj. demonstra-ting etc. *v.*, -tive, -ble; probative, unanswerable, conclusive; apodictic, -al; irre-sistible, -futable, -fragable, undeniable.

categorical, decisive, crucial.

demonstrated etc. *v.*; proven; unconfuted, - answered, -refuted; evident etc. 474.

deducible, consequential, consectary, inferential, following.

Adv. of course, in consequence, consequently, as a matter of course.

Phr. *probatum est*; there is nothing more to be said, Q.E.D., it must follow.

479. Confutation.—N. con-, re-futation; answer, complete answer; disproof, conviction, redargution, invalidation; expos-ure, -ition; clincher; retort; *reductio ad absurdum*; knock down – , *tu quoque*- argument.

V. con-, re-fute; parry, negative, disprove, redargue, expose, show the fallacy of, rebut, defeat; demolish etc. (*destroy*) 162; over-throw, -turn; scatter to the winds, explode, invalidate; silence; put –, reduce- to silence; clinch -an argument, – a question; give one a set down, stop the mouth, shut up; have, – on the hip; get the better of; confound, convince.

not leave a leg to stand on, cut the ground from under one's feet.

be confuted etc.; fail; expose –, show- one's weak point.

Adj. confut-ing, -ed etc. *v.*; capable of refutation; re-, con-futable.

condemned -on one's own showing, – out of one's own mouth.

Phr. the argument falls to the ground, *cadit quaestio*, it does not hold water, *suo sibi gladio hunc jugulo.*

480. Judgment. [Conclusion.]**—N.** result, conclusion, upshot; deduction, inference, ergotism, illation; corollary, porism; moral.

estimation, valuation, appreciation, judication; di-, ad-judication; arbitr- ament, -ement, -ation; assessment, ponderation.

award, estimate; review, criticism, *critique*, notice, report.

decision, determination, judgment, finding, verdict, sentence, decree, – nisi, – absolute, – interlocutory; dictum; *res judicata*.

plébiscite, referendum, voice, casting vote; vote etc. (*choice*) 609; opinion etc. (*belief*) 484; good judgment etc. (*wisdom*) 498.

judge, jurist, umpire; arbi-ter, -trator; assessor, referee; censor, reviewer, critic; *connoisseur*; commentator etc. 524; inspector, inspecting officer.

V. judge, conclude; come to –, draw –, arrive at- a conclusion; ascertain, determine, make up one's mind.

deduce, derive, gather, collect, draw an inference, make a deduction, weet, ween.

form an estimate, estimate, size up, appreciate, value, count, assess, rate, rank, account; regard, consider, think of; look upon etc. (*believe*) 484.

settle; pass –, give- an opinion; decide, try, pronounce, rule; pass -judgment, – sentence; sentence, doom; find; give –, deliver- judgment; adjud-ge, -icate; arbitrate, award, report; bring in a verdict; make absolute, set a question ar rest; confirm etc. (*assent*) 488.

comment, criticize; review, pass under review etc (*examine*) 457; investigate etc. (*inquire*) 461.

hold the scales, sit in judgment; try –, hear- a cause.

Adj. judging etc. *v.*; judicious etc. (*wise*) 498; determinate, conclusive, censorious, critical etc. 932.

Adv. on the whole, all things considered.

480a. Discovery. [Result of search or inquiry.]**—N.** discovery, invention, detection, disenchantment, disclosure, find, ascertainment, revelation.

trover etc. 775.

V. discover, find, determine, evolve; fix upon; find –, trace –, make –, hunt –, fish –, worm –, ferret –, root-out; fathom; bring –, draw-out; educe, elicit, bring to light, invent; dig –, grub –, fish- up; unearth, disinter.

solve, resolve; un-riddle, -ravel, -lock; pick –, open- the lock; find a -clue, – clew- to; interpret etc. 522; disclose etc. 529.

trace, get at; hit it, have it; lay one's -finger, – hands- upon; spot; get –, arrive- at the -turth etc. 494; put the saddle on the right horse, hit the right nail on the head.

be near the truth, burn; smoke, scent, sniff, smell a rat.

open the eyes to; see -through, – daylight, – in its true colors, – the cloven foot; detect; catch, – tripping.

pitch –, fall –, light –, hit –, stumble –, pop- upon; come across; meet –, fall in- with.

recognize, realize, verify, make certain of, identify.

Int. *eureka!*

481. Misjudgment.—N. misjudgment, obliquity of –, warped- judgment; mis-calculation, -computation, -conception etc. (*error*) 495; hasty conclusion.

prejud-gment, -ication, -ice; foregone conclusion; pre-notion, -vention, -conception, - dilection, -possession, -apprehension; -sumption, - sentiment; fixed –, preconceived- idea; *idée fixe*; *mentis gratissimus error*; fool's paradise.

esprit de corps, party spirit, race –, class-prejudice, partisanship, clannishness, *prestige*.

bias, warp, twist; hobby, fad, whim, craze, quirk, crotchet, partiality, infatuation, blind side, mote in the eye.

one-sided –, partial –, narrow –, confined –, superficial- -views, – ideas,– conceptions, – notions; narrow mind; bigotry etc. (*obstinacy*) 606; *odium theologicum*; pedantry; hypercriticism. *doctrinaire* etc. (*positive*) 474.

V. mis-judge, -estimate, -think, -conjecture, - conceive etc. (*error*) 495; fly in the face of facts; mis-calculate, -reckon, -compute.

overestimate etc. 482; underestimate etc. 483.

pre-, fore-judge; pre-suppose, -sume, -judicate; dogmatize; have a -bias etc. *n.*; have only one idea; *jurare in verba magistri*, run away with the notion; jump –, rush- to a conclusion; look only at one side of the shield; view -with jaundiced eye, – through distorting spectacles; not see beyond one's nose; *dare pondus fumo*; get the wrong sow by the ear etc. (*blunder*) 699.

give a -bias, – twist; bias, warp, twist; pre-judice, -possess.

Adj. misjudging etc. *v.*; ill-judging, wrong-headed; prejudiced, prejudicial, etc. *v.*; jaundiced; short-sighted, pur-blind; partial, one-sided, superficial.

narrow-minded; confined, insular, provincial, parochial, illiberal, intolerant, narrow, besotted, infatuated, fanatical, cracked, warped, *entêté*, positive, dogmatic, dictatorial; conceited; opin-, opini-ative; opinion-ed, -ate, -ative, -ated; self-opinioned, wedded to an opinion, *opinâtre*; bigoted etc. (*obstinate*) 606; crotchety, fussy, impracticable; unreason-able, -ing; stupid etc. 499; credulous etc. 486.

misjudged etc. *v.*

Adv. *ex parte.*

Phr. nothing like leather; the wish the father to the thought.

482. Overestimation.—N. overestimation etc. *v.*; exaggeration etc. 549; vanity etc. 880; optim-, pessim-ism, -ist; megalomania.

much -cry and little wool, – ado about nothing; storm in a teacup; fine talking, rodomontade, gush, hot air, gas, bombast.

egotism etc. 880; boasting etc. 884.

V. over-estimate, -rate, -value, -prize, -weigh, - reckon, -strain, -praise; estimate too highly, attach too much importance to, make mountains of molehills, catch at straws; strain, magnify; exaggerate etc. 549; set too high a value upon; think –, make- -much, – too much- of; outreckon.

extol, – to the skies; make the -most, – best, – worst- of, eulogize, panegyrize, gush, puff, boost; make two bites of a cherry.

have too high an opinion of oneself etc. (*vanity*) 880.

Adj. overestimated etc. *v.*; oversensitive etc.

(*sensibility*) 822; inflated, puffed up, exaggerated etc. 549.

Phr. all his geese are swans; *parturiunt montes*.

483. Underestimation.—N. underestimation; depreciation etc. (*detraction*) 934; pessim-ism, -ist; undervaluing etc. *v.*; modesty etc. 881.

V. under-rate, -estimate, -value, -reckon; depreciate; disparage etc. (*detract*) 934; not do justice to; mis-, dis-prize; ridicule etc. 856; slight etc. (*despise*) 930; neglect etc. 460; slur over, under-state.

make -light, – little, – nothing, – no account-of; minimize, belittle, run down, think nothing of; set -no store by, – at naught; shake off as dewdrops from the lion's mane.

Adj. depreciat-ing, -ed, -ive, -ory, etc. *v.*; un-appreciated, -valued, -prized; pejorative.

484. Belief.—N. belief; credence; credit; assurance; faith, trust, troth, confidence, presumption, sanguine expectation etc. (*hope*) 858; dependence on, reliance on.

persuasion, conviction, convincement, plerophory, self-conviction; certainty etc. 474; opinion, mind, view; conception, thinking; impression etc. (*idea*) 453; surmise etc. 514; conclusion etc. (*judgment*) 480.

tenet, dogma, principle, way of thinking; popular belief etc. (*assent*) 488.

firm –, implicit –, settled –, fixed –, rooted –, deep-rooted –, staunch –, unshaken –, steadfast –, inveterate –, calm –, sober –, dispassionate –, impartial –, well-founded- -belief, – opinion etc.; *uberrima fides*.

system of opinions, school, doctrine, articles, canons; declaration –, profession- of faith; tenets, credenda, creed; thirty-nine articles etc. (*orthodoxy*) 983a; catechism; assent etc. 488; *propaganda* etc. (*teaching*) 537.

credibility etc. (*probability*) 472.

V. believe, credit; give -faith, – credit, – credence- to; see, realize; assume, receive; set down –, take- for; have –, take- it; consider, esteem, presume.

count –, depend –, calculate –, pin one's faith –, reckon –, lean –, build –, rely –, rest- upon; lay one's account for; make sure of.

make oneself easy -about, – on that score; take on -trust, – credit; take for -granted, – -gospel; allow –, attach- some weight to.

know, – for certain; have –, make- no doubt; doubt not; be – rest- -assured etc. *adj.*; persuade –, assure –, satisfy- oneself; make up one's mind.

give one credit for; confide –, believe –, put one's trust- in; place –, repose- implicit confidence in; take -one's word for, – at one's word; place reliance on, rely upon, swear by, regard to.

think, hold; take, – it; opine, be of opinion, conceive, trow, ween, fancy, apprehend; have –, hold –, possess –, entertain –, adopt –, imbibe –, embrace –, get hold of –, hazard –, foster –, nurture –, cherish- -a belief, – an opinion etc. *n.*

view –, consider –, take –, hold –, conceive –, regard –, esteem –, deem –, look upon – account –, set down- as; surmise etc. 514.

get – , take- it into one's head; come round to an opinion; swallow etc. (*credulity*) 486.

cause to -be believed etc. *v.*; satisfy, persuade, have the ear of, gain the confidence of, assure; convince, -vict, -vert; put across, sell; wean, bring round; bring – , put – , win- over; indoctrinate etc. (*teach*) 537; cram down the throat; produce – , carry- conviction; bring – , drive- home to.

go down, find credence, pass current; be - received etc. *v.*, – current etc. *adj.*; possess – , take hold of – , take possession of- the mind.

Adj. believing etc. *v.*; certain, sure, assured, positive, cocksure, satisfied, confident, unhesitating, convinced, secure.

under the impression; impressed – , imbued – , penetrated- with.

confiding, trustful, suspectless; unsusp-ecting, - icious; void of suspicion; credulous etc. 486; wedded to.

believed etc. *v.*; accredited, putative; unsuspected.

worthy of – , deserving of – , commanding- - belief, – confidence; credible, reliable, trusted, trustworthy, to be depended on, undoubted; satisfactory; probable etc. 472; fiduci-al, -ary; persuasive, impressive.

relating to belief, doctrinal.

Adv. in the -opinion, – eyes- of; *me judice*; me-seems, -thinks; to the best of one's belief; I - dare say, – doubt not, – have no doubt, – am sure; in my opinion; sure enough etc. (*certainty*) 474; depend – , rely- upon it; be – , rest- assured; I'll warrant you etc. (*affirmation*) 535.

485. Unbelief. Doubt.—N. un-, dis-, mis-belief; discredit, miscreance; infidelity etc. (*irreligion*) 989; dissent etc. 489; change of - opinion etc. 484; retraction etc. 607.

doubt etc. (*uncertainty*) 475; skepticism, misgiving, demur; dis-, mis-trust; misdoubt, suspicion, jealousy, scruple, qualm; *onus probandi*.

incredib-ility, -leness; incredulity; unbeliever etc. 487.

V. dis-believe, -credit; not -believe etc. 484; misbelieve; refuse to admit etc. (*dissent*) 489; refuse to believe etc. (*incredulity*) 487.

doubt; be -doubtful etc. (*uncertain*) 475; doubt the truth of; be -skeptical as to etc. *adj.*; diffide; dis-, mis-trust; suspect, smoke, scent, smell a rat; have – , harbor – , entertain- -doubts, - suspicions; have one's doubts.

demur, stick at, pause, hesitate, scruple, waver, stop and consider.

hang in -suspense, – doubt.

throw doubt upon, raise a question; bring – , call- in question; question, challenge, query; dispute; deny etc. 536; cavil; cause – , raise – , start – , suggest – , awake- a -doubt, – suspicion; ergotize.

startle, stagger; shake – , stagger- one's faith, – belief.

Adj. unbelieving; incredulous – , skeptical- as to; distrustful – , shy – , suspicious- of; doubting etc. *v.*

doubtful etc. (*uncertain*) 475; disputable; unworthy – , undeserving- of -belief etc. 484; questionable; sus-pect, -picious; open to -suspicion,

– doubt; staggering, hard to believe, incredible, not to be believed, inconceivable.

fallible etc. (*uncertain*) 475; undemonstrable; controvertible etc. (*untrue*) 495.

Adv. *cum grano salis.*

Phr. *fronti nulla fides*; *nimium ne crede colori*; *'timeo Danaos et dona ferentes;' credat Judaeus Apella*; let those believe who may.

486. Credulity.—N. credul-ity, -ousness etc. *adj.*; gull-, cull-ibility; gross credulity, infatuation; self-delusion, -deception; blind reasoning; superstition; one's blind side; bigotry etc. (*obstinacy*) 606; hyper-orthodoxy etc. 984; misjudgment etc. 481.

credulous person etc. (*dupe*) 547.

V. be -credulous etc. *adj.*; *jurare in verba magistri*; follow implicitly; swallow, – whole, gulp down; take on trust; take for -granted, – gospel; run away with -a notion, – an idea; jump – , rush-to a conclusion; think the moon is made of green cheese; take – , grasp- the shadow for the substance; catch at straws.

impose upon etc. (*deceive*) 545.

Adj. credulous, gullible; easily -deceived etc. 545; simple, green, soft, childish, silly, stupid; over-credulous, -confident; infatuated, superstitious; confiding etc. (*believing*) 484.

Phr. the wish the father to the thought; *credo quia impossibile.*

487. Incredulity.—N. incredul-ous-ness, -ity; skepticism, pyrrhonism; want of faith etc. (*irreligion*) 989.

suspiciousness etc. *adj.*; scrupulosity; suspicion etc. (*unbelief*) 485; dissent etc. 489.

unbeliever, skeptic, aporetic; atheist, agnostic, infidel, disbeliever, misbeliever, pyrrhonist etc. 989; heretic etc. (*heterodox*) 984.

v. be -incredulous etc. *adj.*; distrust etc. (*disbelieve*) 485; refuse to believe; shut one's -eyes, – ears- to; turn a deaf ear to; hold aloof; ignore; *nullis jurare in verba magistri.*

Adj. incredulous, skeptical, unbelieving, inconvincible; hard – , shy- of belief; suspicious, scrupulous, distrustful, heterodox etc. 984.

488. Assent.—N. assent, -ment; acquiescence, admission; nod; ac-, con-cord, -cordance; agreement etc. 23; affirm-ance, -ation; recognition, acknowledgment, avowal; confession, – of faith.

unanimity, common consent, *consensus*, acclamation, chorus, *vox populi*; popular – , current- -belief, – opinion; public opinion; concurrence etc. (*of causes*) 178; co-operation etc. (*voluntary*) 709.

ratification, confirmation, corroboration, approval, acceptance, *visa*; indorsement etc. (*record*) 551.

consent etc. (*compliance*) 762.

affirmant, consenter, covenantor, subscriber, endorser, upholder.

V. assent; give – , yield – , not- assent; acquiesce; agree etc. 23; receive, accept, accede, accord, concur, lend oneself to, consent, coincide, reciprocate, go with; be -at one with etc. *adj.*; go along —, chime in —, strike in —, close- with; echo, enter into one's views, agree in opinion; vote —, give one's voice- for; recognize; subscribe —, conform —, defer- to; say -yes, — ditto, — amen; — aye- to.

acknowledge, own, admit, allow, avow, confess; concede etc. (*yield*) 762; come round to; abide by; permit etc. 760.

come to —, arrive at- -an understanding, — terms, — an agreement.

con-, af-firm; ratify, approve, endorse, countersign; visa; corroborate etc. 467.

go —, swim- with the stream, float with the current; be in the fashion, join in the chorus; be in every mouth.

Adj. assenting etc. *v.*; of one -accord, — mind; of the same mind, at one with, agreed, acquiescent, content; willing etc. 602.

un-contradicted, -challenged, -questioned, - controverted.

carried —, agreed- *-nem. con.* etc. *adv.*; unanimous; agreed on all hands, carried by acclamation.

affirmative etc. 535.

Adv. yes, yea, ay, aye, true; good; well; very - well, — true; well and good; granted; *placet*; even —, just- so; to be sure, surely, 'thou hast said;' truly, exactly, precisely, that's just it, indeed, certainly, certes, *ex concesso*; of course, unquestionably, assuredly, no doubt, doubtless, undoubtedly.

be it so; so -be it, — let it be, so mote it be; amen; with all my heart; willingly etc. 602.

with one -consent, — voice, — accord; unanimously, *unā voce*, by common consent, in chorus, to a man, *nem. con.*; *nemine - contradicente, — dissentiente*; without a dissentient voice; as one man, one and all, on all hands.

489. Dissent.—N. dissent; discordance etc. (*disagreement*) 24; difference —, diversity- of opinion.

non-conformity etc. (*heterodoxy*) 984; protestantism, recusancy, schism; disaffection; secession etc. 624; recantation etc. 607.

dissension etc. (*discord*) 713; discontent etc. 832; cavilling.

protest; contradiction etc. (*denial*) 536; non-compliance etc. (*rejection*) 764; disapprobation etc. 932; hartal.

dissent-ient, -er; non-juror, -content; recusant, sectary, schismatic, protestant, non-conformist, separatist, non-co-operator, conscientious objector, passive resister.

V. dissent, demur; call in question etc. (*doubt*) 485; differ in opinion, disagree; say -no etc. 536; refuse -assent, — to admit; cavil, protest, raise one's voice against, make bold to differ; repudiate; contradict etc. (*deny*) 536; agree to differ.

have no notion of, differ *toto caelo*; revolt -at, — from the idea.

shake the head, shrug the shoulders; look - askance, — askant.

secede; recant etc. 607.

Adj. dissenting etc. *v.*; negative etc. 536; diss-ident, -entient; unconsenting etc. (*refusing*) 764;

non-content, -juring; protestant, recusant; unconvinced, -verted.

unavowed, unacknowledged; out of the question. discontented etc. 832; unwilling etc. 603; extorted.

sectarian, denominational, schismatic, heterodox, intolerant.

Adv. no etc. 536; at -variance, — issue- with; under protest; *non placet*.

Int. God forbid! not for the world; not on your life; I beg to differ; I'll be hanged if; never tell me; your humble servant, pardon me; tell that to the marines.

Phr. many men many minds; *quot homines tot sententiae*; *tant s'en faut*; *il s'en faut bien*.

490. Knowledge.—N. knowledge; cogn-izance, -ition, -oscence; acquaintance, experience, ken, privity, insight, familiarity; com-, ap-prehension; recognition; appreciation etc. (*judgment*) 480; intuition; consci-ence, -ousness; preception, precognition; acroamatics.

light, enlightenment; glimpse, inkling; side light; glimmer, -ing; dawn; scent, suspicion; impression etc. (*idea*) 453; discovery etc. 480a.

system —, body- of knowledge; science, philosophy, pansophy; theory, Etiology; circle of the sciences; pandect, doctrine, body of doctrine; cy-, ency-clopedia; school etc. (*system of opinions*) 484.

tree of knowledge; republic of letters etc. (*language*) 560.

erudition, learning, lore, scholarship, reading, letters; literature; booklearning, bookishness; biblio-mania, -latry; information, general information; store of -knowledge etc.; education etc. (*teaching*) 537; culture, attainments; acquirements, -sitions; accomplishments, proficiency; practical knowledge etc. (*skill*) 698; higher education, liberal education; dilettantism; rudiments etc. (*beginning*) 66.

deep —, profound —, solid —, accurate —, acroatic —, acroamatic —, vast —, extensive —, encyclopedical- -knowledge, — learning; omniscience, pantology.

march of intellect; progress —, advance- of - science, — learning; schoolmaster abroad.

V. know, ken, scan, wot; wot —, be aware etc. *adj.-* of; ween, weet, trow, have, possess.

conceive; ap-, com-prehend; take, realize, understand, appreciate; fathom, make out; recognize, discern, perceive, see, get a sight of, experience.

know full well; have —, possess- some knowledge of; be -*au courant* etc. *adj.*; have -in one's head, — at one's fingers' ends; know by - heart, — rote; be master of; *connaître le dessous des cartes*, know what's what etc. 698.

see one's way; learn, discover etc. 480a.

come to one's knowledge etc. (*information*) 527.

Adj. knowing etc. *v.*; cognitive; acroamatic.

aware —, cognizant —, conscious- of; acquainted —, made acquainted- with; privy —, no stranger- to; *au -fait, — courant*; in the secret; up —, alive- to; sensible of; behind the -scenes, — curtain; let into; apprized —, informed- of; undeceived.

proficient —, versed —, read —, forward —,

strong –, at home- in; conversant –, familiar-
with.

erudite, instructed, learned, lettered, educated;
high-brow; well-conned, -informed, -read, -
grounded, -educated; enlightened, shrewd, in-
sightful, *savant*, blue, bookish, scholastic, solid,
profound, deep-read, book-learned; accomplished
etc. (*skilful*) 698; omniscient; self-taught, -
educated.
    known etc. *v.*; ascertained, well-known,
recognized, received, notorious, noted; proverbial;
familiar, – as household words, to every
schoolboy; hackneyed, trite, commonplace.
    knowable, cogn-oscible, -izable.
    Adv. to –, to the best of- one's knowledge.
    Phr. one's eyes being opened etc. (*disclosure*)
529.

491. Ignorance.—N. ignorance, nescience,
tabula rasa, crass ignorance, *ignorance crasse*;
unacquaintance; unconsciousness etc. *adj.*; dark-,
blind-ness; incomprehension, inexperience, simplicity.
    unknown quantities, *x, y, z*.
    sealed book, *terra incognita*, virgin soil, unex-
plored ground; dark ages.
    [Imperfect knowledge] smattering, super-
ficiality, half-learning, sciolism, glimmering;
bewilderment etc. (*uncertainty*) 475; incapacity.
    [Affectation of knowledge] pedantry; charlatan-
ry, -ism.
    V. be -ignorant etc. *adj.*; not -know etc. 490;
know -not, – not what, – nothing of; have no -
idea, – notion, – conception; not have the
remotest idea; not know chalk from cheese.
    ignore, be blind to; keep in ignorance etc. (*con-
ceal*) 528.
    see through a glass darkly; have a -film over the
eyes, – glimmering etc. *n.*; wonder whether; not
know what to make of etc. (*unintelligibility*) 519;
not pretend –, not take upon oneself- to say.
    Adj. ignorant, nescient; un-knowing, -aware, -
acquainted, -apprized, -witting, -weeting, -
conscious; wit-, weet-less; a stranger to; un-
conversant.
    un-informed, -cultivated, -versed, -instructed, -
taught, -initiated, -tutored, -schooled, -guided, -
enlightened; Philistine; behind the age.
    shallow, superficial, green, rude, empty, half-
learned, illiterate; un-read, -informed, -educated, -
learned, -lettered, -bookish; empty-headed;
lowbrow; pedantic.
    in the dark; be-nighted, -lated; blind-ed, -fold;
hoodwinked; misinformed; *au bout de son latin*, at
the end of his tether; at fault; at sea etc. (*uncertain*)
475; caught tripping.
    un-known, -apprehended, -explained, -
ascertained, -investigated, -explored, -heard of, -
perceived; concealed etc. 528; novel.
    Adv. ignorantly etc. *adj.*; unawares;- for -
anything, – aught- one knows; not that one knows.
    Int. God –, Heaven –, the Lord –, nobody-
knows.
    Phr. a little learning is a dangerous thing.

492. Scholar.—N. scholar, *connoissuer*,
savant, pundit, schoolman, professor, graduate,

wrangler, moonshee; academ-ician, -ist; fellow,
don, post graduate, advanced student; master –,
bachelor- of arts; doctor, licentiate, gownsman;
philo-sopher, -math; scientist, clerk; soph, -ist, -
ister; linguist, classicist; glosso-, etymo-, philologist;
philologer; lexico-, glosso-grapher; scholiast, commentator. annotator, grammarian; *littérateur*,
literati, dilettanti, illuminati; Mezzofanti, admirable Crichton, Maecenas.
    book-worm, *helluo librorum*, biblio-phile, -
maniac; blue-stocking, *bas-bleu*; big-wig, learned
Theban.
    learned –, literary- man; *homo multarum
literarum*; man of -learning, – letters, –
education; high-brow, intelligentsia.
    antiquar-ian, -y; archeologist; sage etc. (*wise
man*) 500.
    pendant, *doctrinaire*; pedagogue, Dr. Pangloss;
pantologist.
    teacher etc. 540; schoolboy etc. (*learner*) 541.
    Adj. learned etc. 490; brought up at the feet of
Gamaliel.

493. Ignoramus.—N. ignoramus, illiterate,
moron, dunce, numskull; wooden spoon; no
scholar.
    sciolist, smatterer, dabbler, half-scholar;
charlatan; wiseacre.
    novice, griffin; greenhorn etc. (*dupe*) 547; tyro
etc. (*learner*) 541.
    lubber etc. (*bungler*) 701; fool etc. 501; pedant
etc. 492.
    Adj. bookless, shallow, simple, dense, dumb,
thick, dull, ignorant etc. 491.

494. Truth. [Object of knowledge.]—N. fact,
reality etc. (*existence*) 1; plain matter of fact;
nature etc. (*principle*) 5; truth, verity; gospel; orthodoxy etc. 983*a*; authenticity; veracity etc. 543.
    accuracy, exactitude; exact-, precise-ness etc.
adj.; precision, delicacy; rigor, mathematical
precision, punctuality; clockwork precision etc.
(*regularity*) 80.
    orthology; *ipsissima verba*; letter of the law,
realism.
    plain –, honest –, sober –, naked –,
unalloyed –, unqualified –, stern –, exact –, in-
trinsic- truth; *nuda veritas*; the very thing; not an -
illusion etc. 495; real Simon Pure; unvarnished
tale; the truth, the whole truth and nothing but the
truth; just the thing.
    V. be -true etc. *adj.*, – the case; stand the test;
have the true ring; hold -good, – true, – water;
conform to- rule.
    render –, prove- -true etc. *adj.*; substantiate etc.
(*evidence*) 467.
    get at the truth etc. (*discover*) 480*a*.
    Adj. real, actual etc. (*existing*) 1; veritable, true;
certain etc. 474; substantially –, categorically-
true etc; true -to the letter; – to life, – to scale, –
the facts, – as gospel; unimpeachable; veracious
etc. 543; unre-, uncon-futed; un-ideal -imagined;
realistic.
    exact, accurate, definite, precise, well defined,
just, right, correct, strict, severe; close etc. (*similar*)
17; literal; rigid, rigorous; scrupulous etc. (*con-*

scientious) 939; religiously exact, punctual,
mathematical, scientific; faithful, constant,
unerring; curious, particular, punctilious,
meticulous, nice, delicate, fine.

genuine, authentic, legitimate, pukka; orthodox
etc. 983*a*; official, *ex officio.*

pure, natural, sound, sterling; un-sophisticated, -
adulterated, -varnished, -colored; in its true colors.

well-grounded, -founded; solid, substantial,
tangible, valid; undis-torted, -guised; un-affected, -
exaggerated, -romantic, -flattering.

Adv. truly etc.*adj.*; verily, indeed, in reality; as
a matter of fact; beyond -doubt, – question; with
truth etc. (*veracity*) 543; certainly etc. (*certain*)
474; actually etc. (*existence*) 1; in effect etc.
(*intrinsically*) 5.

exactly etc. *adj.* ; *ad amussim*; *verbatim*, – *et
literatim*; word for word, literally, *literatim*,
totidem verbis, *sic*, to the letter, chapter and verse,
ipsissimis verbis; *ad unguem*; to an inch; to a -
nicety, – hair, – tittle, – turn, – T; *au pied de
la lettre*; neither more nor less; in -every respect,
– all respects; *sous tous les rapports*; at -any rate,
– all events; strictly speaking.

Phr. the -truth, – fact- is; *rem acu tetigisti.*

495. Error.—N. error, fallacy; misconception,
-apprehension, -understanding; inexactness etc.
adj.; laxity; misconstruction etc. (*misinterpretation*) 523; miscomputation etc.
(*misjudgment*) 481; *non-sequitur* etc. 477;
misstatement, -report; anachronism; malapropism.

mistake; miss, fault, blunder, boner, bloomer,
howler, *quid pro quo*, cross purposes, oversight,
misprint, *erratum*, *corrigendum*, slip, blot, flaw,
loose thread; trip, stumble etc. (*failure*) 732; botchery etc. (*want of skill*) 699; slip of the -tongue,
– pen; *lapsus -linguae*, – *calami*, clerical error;
bull etc. (*absurdity*) 497.

il-, de-lusion; false -impression, – idea; bubble;
self-deceit, -deception; warped notion; mists of
error; superstition, exploded notion.

heresy etc. (*heterodoxy*) 984; hallucination etc.
(*insanity*) 503; false light etc. (*fallacy of vision*)
443; dream etc. (*fancy*) 515; fable etc. (*untruth*)
546; bias etc. (*misjudgment*) 481; misleading etc.
v.

V. be -erroneous etc. *adj.*

cause error; mis-lead, -guide; lead -astray, –
into error; beguile, misinform etc. (*misteach*) 538;
delude; give a false -impression, – idea; falsify,
garble, misstate; deceive etc. 545; lie etc. 544.

err; be -in error etc. *adj.*; – mistaken etc. *v.*; be
deceived etc. (*duped*) 547; mistake, receive a false
impression, deceive oneself; fall into –, lie under
–, labor under- -an error etc. *n.*; be in the wrong,
blunder; mis-apprehend, -conceive, -understand, -
reckon, -count, -calculate etc. (*misjudge*) 481.

play –, be- at cross purposes etc. (*misinterpret*)
523.

trip, stumble; lose oneself etc. (*uncertainty*) 475;
go astray; fail etc. 732; take the wrong sow by the
ear etc. (*mismanage*) 699; put the saddle on the
wrong horse; reckon without one's host; take the
shadow for the substance etc. (*credulity*) 486;
dream etc. (*imagine*) 515.

Adj. erroneous, untrue, false, devoid of truth,
fallacious, faulty, apocryphal, unreal, ungrounded,

groundless; unsubstantial etc. 4; heretical etc.
(*heterodox*) 984; unsound; illogical etc. 477;
wrong.

in-, un-exact; in-accurate, -correct; indefinite etc.
(*uncertain*) 475.

illus-ive, -ory; delusive; mock; ideal etc.
(*imaginary*) 515; spurious etc. 545; deceitful etc.
544; perverted.

controvertible, unsustain-able, -ed; unauthen-
ticated, untrustworthy.

exploded, refuted, discarded.

in –, under an- error etc. *n.*; mistaken etc. *v.*;
tripping etc. *v.*; out, – in one's reckoning;
aberrant; beside –, wide of the- -mark, – truth;
astray etc. (*at fault*) 475; on -a false, – the wrong-
scent; in the wrong box; at cross purposes, all in the
wrong, all abroad, at sea.

Adv. more or less.

496. Maxim.—N. maxim, aphorism; apo-,
apoph-thegm; *dictum*, saying, gnome, adage, saw,
proverb, epigram; sentence, *mot*, motto, word, by-
word, precept, moral, phylactery, *protasis*,
brocard.

axiom, postulate, theorem, *scholium*, truism.

reflection etc. (*idea*) 453; conclusion etc.
(*judgment*) 480; golden rule etc. (*precept*) 697;
principle, *principia*; profession of faith etc. (*belief*)
484; formula.

wise –, sage –, received –, admitted –,
recognized- maxim etc.; true –, common –,
hackneyed –, trite –, commonplace- saying etc.

Adj. aphoristic, proverbial, phylacteric;
axiomatic, gnomic.

Adv. as -the saying is, – they say.

497. Absurdity.—N. absurd-ity, -ness etc. *adj.*;
imbecility etc. 499; alogy, nonsense, paradox, inconsistency; stultiloqu-y, -ence, futility.

blunder, muddle, bull; Irish-, Hibernic-ism; slipslop; anti climax; bathos; sophism etc. 477.

farce, burlesque, *galimatias*, *amphigouri*, rhapsody; farrago etc. (*disorder*) 59; extravagance,
romance; sciomachy.

joke, catch, sell, pun, verbal quibble, macaronic;
jargon, fustian, twaddle etc. (*no meaning*) 517;
exaggeration etc. 549; moonshine, stuff; mare's
nest.

vagary, tomfoolery, mummery, monkey trick,
practical joke, *boutade*, *escapade*.

V. play the fool etc. 499; stultify, blunder, muddle; joke; talk nonsense, *parler à tort et à travers*;
battre la campagne; be -absurd etc. *adj.*

Adj. absurd, nonsensical, preposterous,
egregious, senseless, farcical, inconsistent,
ridiculous, extravagant, quibbling, futile;
macaronic, punning, paradoxical.

foolish etc. 499; sophistical etc. 477; unmeaning
etc. 517; without rhyme or reason; fantastic.

Int. fiddle-de-dee! pish! pish and tush! pho! stuff
and nonsense! rubbish! !rot! bosh! in the name of
the Prophet—figs!

Phr. *credat Judaeus Apella*; tell it to the
marines.

498. Intelligence. Wisdom.—N. intelligence,
capacity, comprehension, understanding, intellect

etc. 450; nous, parts, sagacity, mother wit, wit, *esprit*, gumption, quick parts, grasp of intellect; acuteness etc. *adj.*; acumen, subtlety, penetration; perspica-cy, -city; discernment; long-headedness, due sense of, good judgment; discrimination etc. 465; craftiness, cunning etc. 702; refinement etc. (*taste*) 850.

head, brains, gray matter, headpiece, upper story, long head; eagle -eye, – glance; eye of a - lynx, – hawk.

wisdom, sapience, sense; good –, common –, plain –, horse- sense; clear thinking; rationality, reason; reasonableness etc. *adj.*; judgment; solidity, depth, profundity, caliber; enlarged views; reach –, compass- of thought; enlargement of mind.

genius, inspiration, *geist*, fire of genius, heaven-born genius, soul; talent etc. (*aptitude*) 698.

[Wisdom in action] prudence etc. 864; vigilance etc. 459; tact etc. 698; foresight etc. 510; sobriety, self-possession, *aplomb*, ballast, mental -poise, – balance.

a bright thought, inspiration, brainwave, not a bad idea.

V. be -intelligent etc. *adj.*; have all one's wits about one; understand etc. (*intelligible*) 518; catch –, take in- an idea; take a -joke, – hint.

see -through, – at a glance, – with half an eye, – far into, – through a millstone; penetrate; discern etc. (*descry*) 441; foresee etc. 510.

discriminate etc. 465; know what's what etc. 698; listen to reason.

Adj. [Applied to persons] intelligent, quick of apprehension, keen, acute, alive, brainy, awake, bright, quick, sharp; quick-, keen-, clear-, sharp- - eyed, -sighted, -witted; wide awake; canny, shrewd, astute; clear-headed; far-sighted etc. 510; discerning, perspicacious, penetrating, piercing; argute nimble-, needle-witted; sharp as a needle; alive to etc. (*cognizant*) 490; clever etc. (*apt*) 698; arch etc. (*cunning*) 702; *pas si bête*; acute etc. 682.

wise, sage, sapient, sagacious, reasonable, rational, sound, in one's right mind, sensible, *abnormis sapiens*, judicious, strong-minded.

un-prejudiced, -biassed, -bigoted, -prepossessed; un-dazzled, -perplexed; of unwarped judgment, impartial, equitable, fair, broad-minded.

cool; cool-, long-, hard-, strong-headed; long-sighted, calculating, thoughtful, reflecting; solid, deep, profound.

oracular; heaven-directed, -born.

prudent etc. (*cautious*) 864; sober, staid, solid; considerate, politic, wise in one's generation; watchful etc. 459; provident etc. (*prepared*) 673; in advance of one's age; wise as -a serpent, – Solomon, – Solon.

[Applied to actions] wise, sensible, reasonable, judicious; well-judged, -advised; prudent, politic; expedient etc. 646.

499. Imbecility. Folly.—N. want of -intelligence etc. 498, – intellect etc. 450; shallow-, silli-, foolish-ness etc. *adj.*; imbecility, incapacity, vacancy of mind, poverty of intellect, clouded perception, poor head, apartments to let; stup-, stolidity; hebetude, dull understanding, meanest capacity; short-sightedness; incompetence etc. (*unskilfulness*) 699.

one's weak side; bias etc. 481; infatuation etc. (*insanity*) 503.

simplicity, puerility, babyhood; dotage, anility, second childishness, senile dementia, fatuity; idiocy, -tism; driveling.

folly, frivolity, desipience, irrationality, trifling, ineptitude, nugacity, inconsistency, lip-wisdom, conceit; sophistry etc. 477; giddiness etc. (*inattention*) 458; eccentricity etc. 503; extravagance etc. (*absurdity*) 497; rashness etc. 863.

act of folly etc. 699.

V. be -imbecile etc. *adj.*; have no -brains, – sense etc. 498.

trifle, drivel, *radoter*, dote; ramble etc. (*madness*) 503; play the -fool, – monkey, – goat, take leave of one's senses; not see an inch beyond one's nose; stultify oneself etc. 699; talk nonsense etc. 497.

Adj. [Applied to persons] un-intelligent, -intellectual, -reasoning; mind-, wit-, reason-, brain-less; having no -head etc. 498; not -bright etc. 498; inapprehensible.

weak-, addle-, puzzle-, blunder-, muddle-, muddy-, pig-, beetle-, maggotty-, gross-headed; beef-, fat- -witted, -headed.

weak, feeble-minded; dull-, shallow-, rattle-, lack-brained; half-, nit-, short-, dull-, blunt-witted; shallow-, clod-, addle-pated; dim-, short-sighted; thick-skulled; weak in the upper story.

shallow, *borné*, weak, wanting, soft, nutty, sappy, spoony; dull, – as a beetle; stupid, heavy, insulse, obtuse, blunt, stolid, doltish, asinine; inapt etc. 699; prosaic etc. 843.

child-ish, -like; infant-ine, -ile; baby-, bab-ish; puerile; anile; simple etc. (*credulous*) 486.

fatuous, idiotic, imbecile, moronic, driveling; blatant, babbling; vacant; sottish; bewildered etc. 475.

blockish, unteachable; Boeot-ian, -ic; bovine; un-gifted, -discerning, -enlightened, -wise, -philosophical; apish.

foolish, silly, senseless, irrational, insensate, non-sensical, inept; maudlin.

narrow-minded etc. 481; bigoted etc. (*obstinate*) 606; giddy etc. (*thoughtless*) 458; rash etc. 863; eccentric etc. (*crazed*) 503.

[Applied to actions] foolish, unwise, indiscreet, injudicious, improper, unreasonable, without reason, ridiculous, silly, stupid, asinine; ill-imagined, -advised, -judged, -devised; inconsistent, irrational, unphilosophical; extravagant etc. (*nonsensical*) 497; sleeveless, idle, useless etc. 645; inexpedient etc. 647; frivolous etc. (*trivial*) 643; absurd etc. 497.

Phr. *Davis sum non Oedipus.*

500. Sage.—N. sage, wise man; pundit; master -mind, – spirit of the age; longhead, thinker, philosopher.

authority, oracle, mentor, luminary, shining light, *esprit fort*, *magnus Apollo*, Solon, Solomon, Nestor, Magi, 'second Daniel.'

man of learning etc. 492; expert etc. 700; wizard etc. 994.

[Ironically] wiseacre, bigwig.

Adj. wise, learned; authoritative, oracular; erudite etc. 490; venerable, reverenced, revered, *emeritus*.

501. Fool.—N. fool, idiot, tomfool, wiseacre, simpleton, Simple Simon, nit-wit, witling, dizzard, donkey, ass; ninny, -hammer; moron, dolt, booby, Tom Noddy, looby, hoddy-doddy, noddy, nonny, noodle, nizy, owl; goose, -cap; *imbécile*; gaby, *radoteur*, nincompoop, *badaud*, zany; trifler, babbler; pretty fellow; natural, *niais*.

child, baby, infant, innocent, milksop, sop.

oaf, lout, loon, lown, dullard, doodle, calf, colt, buzzard, block, put, stick, stock, numps, tony.

bull-, dunder-, addle-, block-, dull-, logger-, jolt-, jolter-, beetle-, gross-, thick-, giddy-head; num-, thick- skull; lack-, shallow-brain; half-, lack-wit; dunder-pate; fat-head, poor stick.

sawney, gowk; clod, -hopper; clod-, clot-poll, pate; bull-calf; men of Boeotia, wise men of Gotham.

un sot à triple étage, sot; jobbernowl, changeling, mooncalf, *gobemouche*.

dotard, driveller; old -fogey, – woman; crone, grandmother.

greenhorn etc. (*dupe*) 547; dunce etc. (*ignoramus*) 493; lubber etc. (*bungler*) 701; madman etc. 504.

one who -will not set the Thames on fire, – did not invent gunpowder; *qui n'a pas inventé la poudre*; no conjuror.

502. Sanity.—N. sanity; soundness etc. *adj.*; rationality, normality, sobriety, lucidity, lucid interval; senses, sober senses, sound mind, *mens sana*.

V. be -sane etc. *adj.*; retain one's senses, – reason.

become -sane etc. *adj.*; come to one's senses, sober down.

render -sane etc. *adj.*; bring to one's senses, sober.

Adj. sane, rational, reasonable, *compos mentis*, of sound mind; sound, -minded.

self-possessed; sober, -minded.

in one's -sober senses, – right mind; in possession of one's faculties.

Adv. sanely etc. *adj.*

503. Insanity.—N. disordered -reason, – intellect; diseased –, unsound –, abnormal- mind; derangement, unsoundness.

insanity, lunacy; madness etc. *adj.*; mania, *rabies*, *furor*, mental aliénation, paranoia, aberration; *amentia*, dementation, -tia, -cy; *dementia praecox*; *morosis*, idiocy, phrenitis, frenzy, raving, incoherence, wandering, delirium, calenture of the brain, delusion, hallucination; lycanthropy, brain storm, *delirium tremens*, D.T.'s.

vertigo, dizziness, swimming; sunstroke, *coup de soleil*, siriasis.

fanatisism, infatuation, craze; oddity, eccentricity, twist, monomania; klepto-, dipso-mania; hypochondriasis etc. (*low spirits*) 837; *melancholia*, hysteria.

screw –, tile –, slate- loose; bee in one's bonnet, rats in the upper story.

dotage etc. (*imbecility*) 499.

V. be –, become- -insane etc. *adj.*; lose one's senses, – reason, – faculties, – wits; go –, run-

mad, run amuck; rave, dote, ramble, wander; drivel etc. (*be imbecile*) 499; have a -screw loose etc. *n.*, – devil; *avoir le diable au corps*; lose one's head etc. (*be uncertain*) 475.

derange, render – , drive- -mad etc. *adj.*; madden, dementate, addle the wits, derange the head, infatuate, befool; turn -the brain, – one's head.

Adj. insane, mad, lunatic; crazy, crazed, *aliéné*, *non compos mentis*; not right, cracked, touched; bereft of reason; unhinged, deranged, unsettled in one's mind; insensate, reasonless, beside oneself, demented, daft; phren-, fren-zied, -etic; possessed, – with a devil; far gone, maddened, moonstruck; shatterpated; barmy; mad-, scatter-, shatter-, crack-brained, off one's head; bug-house, *loco*.

maniacal; manic, manic-depressive; delirious, light-headed, incoherent, rambling, doting, wandering; frantic, raving, stark staring mad, amok, amuck.

corybantic, dithyrambic; rabid, giddy, vertiginous, dizzy, wild, haggard, mazed; flighty; distracted, -aught; bewildered etc. (*uncertain*) 475.

mad as a -March hare, – hatter; of -unsound mind etc. *n.* touched –, wrong –, not right- in one's -head, – mind, – wits, – upper story; out of one's -mind, – senses, – wits; not in one's right mind.

fanatical, infatuated, odd, eccentric; hypp-ed, -ish.

imbecile, silly etc. 499.

Adv. like one possessed.

Phr. the mind having lost its balance; the reason under a cloud; *tête -exaltée, -montée*.

504. Madman—N. madman, lunatic, maniac, bedlamite, candidate for Bedlam, raver, madcap; energumen; paranoiac; auto-, mono-, pyro-, megalo-, dipso-, klepto-maniac; hypochondriac etc. (low spirit) 837.

dreamer etc. 515; rhapsodist, seer, high-flier, enthusiast, crank, eccentric, nut, fanatic, *fanatico*; *exalté*; knight errant, Don Quixote.

idiot etc. 501.

505. Memory.—N. memory, remembrance; reten-tion, -tiveness; tenacity; *veteris vestigia flammae*; tablets of the memory; readiness.

reminiscence, recognition, recurrence, recollection, rememoration; retrospect, -ion; after-thought.

suggestion etc. (*information*) 527; prompting etc. *v.*; hint, reminder, token of remembrance, *memento*, *souvenir*, keepsake, relic, *memorandum*; remembrancer, flapper; memorial etc. (*record*) 551; commemoration etc. (*celebration*) 883.

things to be remembered, *memorabilia*.

art of – , artificial- memory; *memoria technica*; mnemo-nics, -technics; phrenotypics; Mnemosyne; memorandum-, note-, engagement-, prompt-book.

retentive – , tenacious – , green – , trustworthy –, capacious –, faithful –, correct –, exact –, ready –, prompt- memory.

V. remember, mind; retain the -memory, – remembrance- of; keep in view.

have – , hold – , bear – , carry – , keep – , retain- in *or* in the -thoughts, – mind, – memory, – remembrance; be in – , live in , remain in – , dwell in –, haunt –, impress- one's -memory, – thoughts, – mind.

   sink in the mind; run in the head; not be able to get it out of one's head; be deeply impressed with; rankle etc. (*revenge*) 919.

   recur to the mind; flash -on the mind, – across the memory.

   recognize, recollect, bethink oneself, recall, call up, conjure up, retrace; look –, trace- -back, – backwards; think –, look back- upon; review; call –, recall –, bring- to mind; remembrance; carry one's thoughts back; rake up the past.

   suggest etc.'(*inform*) 527; prompt; put –, keep-in mind; remind; fan the embers; call –, summon –, rip- up; renew; *infandum renovare dolorem*; task –, tax –, jog –, flap –, refresh –, rub up –, awaken- the memory; pull by the sleeve; bring back the memory, put in remembrance, memorialize.

   get –, have –, learn –, know –, say –, repeat- by -heart, – rote; drive –, get- into -one's head; say one's lesson; repeat, – as a parrot; have at one's finger's ends.

   commit to memory; memorize; con, – over; fix –, rivet –, imprint –, impress –, stamp –, grave –, engrave –, store –, treasure up –, bottle up –, embalm –, enshrine- in the memory; load –, store –, stuff –, burden- the memory with.

   redeem from oblivion; keep the memory -alive, – green; *tangere ulcus*; keep up the memory of; commemorate etc. (*celebrate*) 883.

   make a note of etc. (*record*) 551.

   Adj. remember-ing, -ed etc. *v.*; mindful, reminiscential; retained in the memory etc. *v.*; pent up in one's memory; fresh; green, – in remembrance, still vivid; unforgotten, present to the mind; within one's -memory etc. *n.*; indelible; not to be forgotten, unforgettable, enduring; uppermost in one's thoughts; memorable etc. (*important*) 642.

   Adv. by -heart, – rote; without book, *memoriter*.

   in memory of; *in memoriam*; suggestive.

   Phr. *manet altâ mente repostum*; *forsan et haec olim meminisse juvabit*.

   506. Oblivion.—N. oblivion; forgetfulness etc. *adj.*; obliteration etc. 552, of –, insensibility etc. 823 to- the past.

   short –, treacherous –, loose –, slippery –, failing- memory; decay –, failure –, lapse- of memory; memory like a sieve; waters of -Lethe, – oblivion, *amnesia*.

   pardon, acquittal, amnesty, oblivion; absolution.

   V. forget; be -forgetful etc. *adj.*; fall –, sink-into oblivion; have -a short memory etc. *n.* – no head.

   forget one's own name, have on the tip of one's tongue, come in at one ear and go out at the other.

   slip –, escape –, fade from –, die away from-the memory; lose, – sight of.

   unlearn; efface etc. 552 –, discharge- from the memory; consign to -oblivion, – the tomb of the Capulets; think no more of etc. (*turn the attention from*) 458; cast behind one's back, wean one's thoughts from; let bygones be bygones etc. (*forgive*) 918.

   Adj. forgotten etc. *v.*; unremembered, past recollection, bygone, out of mind; buried –, sunk-in oblivion; clean forgotten; gone out of one's -head, – recollection.

   forgetful, oblivious, mindless, heedless, Lethean; insensible etc. 823- to the past.

   Phr. *non mi ricordo*; the memory -failing, – deserting one, – being at (*or* in) fault.

   507. Expectation.—N. expect-ation, -ance, -ancy; anticipation, reckoning, calculation; contingency; foresight etc. 510.

   contemplation, prospection, look out; prospect, perspective, horizon, vista; destiny etc. 152.

   suspense, waiting, abeyance; curiosity etc. 455; anxious –, ardent –, eager –, breathless –, sanguine- expectation; torment of Tantalus.

   presumption, hope etc. 858; trust. etc. (*belief*) 484; prognostication, auspices etc. (*prediction*) 511.

   V. expect; look -for, – out for, – forward to; hope for, anticipate; have in -prospect, – contemplation; keep in view; contemplate, promise oneself; not -wonder etc. 870 -at, – if.

   wait –, tarry –, lie in wait –, watch –, bargain- for; keep a -good, – sharp- look-out for; await; stand at 'attention,' abide, bide one's –, mark- time, watch.

   foresee etc. 510; prepare for etc. 673; forestall etc. (*be early*) 132; count upon etc. (*believe in*) 484; think likely etc. (*probability*) 472; make one's mouth water.

   lead one to expect etc. (*predict*) 511; have in store for etc. (*destiny*) 152.

   prick up one's ears, hold one's breath.

   Adj. expentant; expecting etc. *v.*; in-'-expectation etc. *n.*; on the watch etc. (*vigilant*) 459; open -eyed, -mouthed; agape, gaping, all agog; on -tenterhooks, – tiptoe, – the tiptoe of expectation; *aux aguets*; ready; curious etc. 455; looking forward to; prepared for; on the rack.

   expected etc. *v.*; long expected, foreseen; in prospect etc. *n.*; prospective; in -one's eye, – view, – the horizon; impending etc. (*destiny*) 152.

   Adv. expectantly; in the event of; on the watch etc. *adj.*; with -breathless expectation etc. *n.*; – bated breath, – eyes, – ears strained; *arrectis auribus*; on edge.

   Phr. we shall see; *nous verrons*.

   508. Inexpectation.—N. in-, non-expectation; false expectation etc. (*disappointment*) 509; miscalculation etc. 481; unforeseen contingency, the unforeseen, the unexpected.

   surprise, sudden burst, thunderclap, blow, shock; bolt out of the blue; eye-opener; wonder etc. 870.

   V. not -expect etc. 507; be taken by surprise; start; miscalculate etc. 481; not bargain for; come –, fall- upon.

   be -unexpected etc. *adj.*; come -unawares etc. *adv.*; turn up, pop, drop from the clouds; come –, burst –, flash –, bounce –, steal –, creep- upon one; come –, burst- like a thunder-clap; -bolt; take –, catch- -by surprise, – unawares, – napping. pounce –, spring a mine- upon.

   surprise, startle, take aback, electrify, stun, stagger, take away one's breath, throw off one's guard; astonish etc. (*strike with wonder*) 870.

Adj. non-expectant; surprised etc. *v.*; unwarned, -aware; off one's guard; inattentive etc. 458.

un-expected, -anticipated, -prepared for, -looked for, -foreseen, -hoped for; dropped from the clouds; beyond – , contrary to – , against- expectation; out of one's reckoning; unheard of etc. (*exceptional*) 83; startling; sudden etc. (*instantaneous*) 113.

Adv. abruptly, unexpectedly, plump, pop, *à l'improviste*, unawares; without -notice, – warning, – saying 'by your leave;' like a -thief in the night, – thunderbolt; in an unguarded moment; suddenly etc. (*instantaneously*) 113.

Int. heyday! etc. (*wonder*) 870.

Phr. little did one -think, – expect; nobody would ever -suppose, – think, – expect; who would have thought?'

509. Disappointment. [Failure of expectation.]—**N.** disappointment, disillusionment; blighted hope, balk; blow; slip 'twixt cup and lip; non-fulfilment of one's hopes; sad – , bitter- disappointment; trick of fortune; afterclap; false – , vain- expectation; miscalculation etc. 481; fool's paradise; much cry and little wool.

V. be disappointed; look -blank, – blue; look – , stand- -aghast etc. (*wonder*) 870; find to one's cost; laugh on the wrong side of one's mouth; find one a false prophet.

disappoint; crush – , dash – , balk – , disappoint – , blight – , falsify – , defeat – , not realize- one's -hope, – expectation; balk, jilt, bilk; play one -false, – a trick; dash the cup from the lips; tantalize; dumb-found, -founder; disillusion, -ize; dissatisfy, disgruntle.

Adj. disappointed etc. *v.*; disconcerted, aghast; out of one's reckoning; disgruntled.

Phr. the mountain brought forth a mouse; *nascitur ridiculus mus*; *parturiunt montes*; *diis aliter visum*, the bubble burst; one's countenance falling.

510. Foresight.—N. foresight, prospicience, prevision, longsightedness; anticipation; providence etc. (*preparation*) 673.

fore-thought, -cast; pre-deliberation, -surmise; foregone conclusion etc. (*prejudgment*) 481; prudence etc. (*caution*) 864.

foreknowledge; *prognosis*; pre-cognition, - science, -notion, -sentiment; second sight; sagacity etc. (*intelligence*) 498.

prospect etc. (*expectation*) 507; foretaste; prospectus etc. (*plan*) 626.

V. foresee; look -forwards to, – ahead, –, beyond; scent from afar; feel in one's bones; look – , pry – , peep into the future.

see one's way; see how the -land !ies, – wind blows, – cat jumps.

anticipate; expect etc. 507; be beforehand etc. (*early*) 132; predict etc. 511; fore-know, -judge, -cast; surmise; have an eye to the -future, – main chance; *respicere finem*; keep a sharp look-out etc. (*vigilance*) 459; forewarn etc. 668.

Adj. foreseeing etc. *v.*; prescient; anticipatory; far-seeing, -sighted; sagacious etc. (*intelligent*) 498; weather-wise; provident etc. (*prepared*) 673; prospective etc. 507.

Adv. against the time when.

511. Prediction.—N. prediction, announcement; program, programme etc. (*plan*) 626; premonition etc. (*warning*) 668; *prognosis*, prophecy, vaticination, Mantology, prognostication, premonstration, augur-y, -ation; a-ha-riolation; fore-, a-boding; bode-, abode-ment; omin-ation, -ousness; auspices, forecast; sign, presage, prognostic; omen etc. 512; horoscope, nativity; sooth, -saying; fortune-telling; divination; crystal gazing, necromancy etc. 992; prophet etc. 512.

[Divination by the stars] astrology, horoscopy, astromancy, judicial astrology.*

[Place of prediction] *adytum*.

prefigur-ation, -ement; prototype, type.

V. predict, prognosticate, prophesy, vaticinate, divine, foretell, soothsay, augurate, tell fortunes; cast a -horoscope, – nativity; advise; forewarn etc. 668.

presage, augur, bode; a-, fore-bode, -cast; fore-, be-token; pre-figure, -show; portend; fore-show, -shadow, shadow forth, typify, ominate, signify, point to, precurse.

usher in, herald, premise, announce; lower.

hold out – , raise – , excite- -expectation, – hope; bid fair, promise, lead one to expect; be the -precursor etc. 64.

Adj. predicting etc. *v.*; predictive, prophetic, fatidical, vaticinal, oracular, Sibylline, haruspical, weatherwise.

ominous, presageful, portentous; augur-ous, -al, -ial; auspici-al, -ous; prescious, monitory, extispicious, premonitory, precursory, significant of, pregnant with, big with the fate of.

Phr. 'coming events cast their shadows before.'

*The following terms, expressive of different forms of divination, have been collected from various sources, and are here given as a curious illustration of bygone superstitions:

Divination *by oracles*, Theomancy; *by the Bible*, Bibliomancy; *by ghosts*, Psychomancy; *by spirits seen in a magic lens*, Cristallomantia; *by shadows or manes*, Sciomancy; *by appearances in the air*, Aeromancy, Chaomancy, *by the stars at birth*, Genethliacs; *by meteors*, Meteoromancy; *by winds*, Austromancy; *by sacrificial appearances*, Aruspicy (*or* Haruspicy), Hieromancy, Hieroscopy; *by the entrails of animals sacrificed*, Hieromancy; *by the entrails of a human sacrifice*, Anthropomancy; *by the entrails of fishes*, Ichthyomancy; *by sacrificial fire*, Pyromancy; *by red-hot iron*, Sideromancy; *by smoke from the alter*, Capnomancy; *by mice*, Myomancy; *by birds*, Orniscopy, Ornithomancy; *by a cock picking up grains*, Alectryomancy (or Alectoromancy); *by fishes*, Ophiomancy; *by herbs*, Botanomancy; *by water*, Hydromancy; *by fountains*, Pegomancy; *by a wand*, Rhabdomancy; *by dough of cakes*, Crithomancy; *by meal*, Aleuromancy, Alphitomancy; *by salt*, Halomancy; *by dice*, Cleromancy; *by arrows*, Belomancy; *by a balanced hatchet*, Axinomancy; *by a balanced sieve*, Coscinomancy; *by a suspended ring*, Dactyliomancy; *by dots made at random on paper*, Geomancy; *by precious stones*, Lithomancy; *by pebbles*, Pessomancy; *by pebbles drawn from a heap*, Psephomancy; *by mirrors*, Catoptromancy; *by writings in ashes*, Tephramancy; *by dreams*, Oneiromancy; *by the hand*, Palmistry, Chiromancy; *by nails reflecting the sun's rays*, Onychomancy; *by finger rings*, Dactylomancy; *by numbers*, Arithmancy; *by drawing lots*, Sortilege; *by passages in books*, Stichomancy; *by the letters forming the name of the person*, Onomancy, Nomancy; *by the features.* Anthroposcopy; *by the mode of laughing.* Geloscopy; *by ventriloquism.* Gastromancy; *by walking in a circle.* Gyromancy; *by dropping melted wax into water.* Ceromancy: *by currents.* Bletonism.

512. Omen.—N. omen, portent, presage, prognostic, augury, auspice; sigh etc. (*indication*) 550; herald, forerunner, harbinger etc. (*precursor*) 64.

bird of ill omen, signs of the times; gathering clouds; warning etc. 668.

prefigurement etc. 511.

513. Oracle.—N. oracle; prophet, -ess; seer, soothsayer, augur, fortune-teller, palmist, medium, clairvoyant, crystal gazer, witch, geomancer, *aruspex*; a-, ha-ruspice; Sibyl; Python, -ess; Pythia; Pythian −, Delphian- oracle; Monitor, Sphinx, Tiresias, Cassandra, Sibylline leaves; Zadkiel, Old Moore; sorcerer etc. 994; interpreter etc. 524.

514. Supposition.—N. supposition, assumption, postulation, condition, pre-supposition, hypothesis, postulate, *postulatum*, theory, *data*; pro-, position; *thesis*, theorem; proposal etc. (*plan*) 626.

bare −, vague −, loose- -supposition, − suggestion; conceit; conjecture; guess, − work; rough guess, shot; conjecturality; surmise, suspicion, inkling, suggestion, suggestiveness, association of ideas, hint; presumption etc. (*belief*) 484; divination, speculation.

theorist, speculator, doctrinarian, hypothesist.

V. suppose, conjecture, surmise, suspect, guess, divine; theorize; pre-sume, -surmise, -suppose; assume, fancy, wis, take it; give a guess, speculate, believe, dare say, take it into one's head, take for granted.

put forth; pro-pound, -pose; moot; hypothesize; start, put a case, submit, move, make a motion; hazard −, throw out −, put forward- a - suggestion, − conjecture.

allude to, suggest, hint, put it into one's head.

suggest itself etc. (*thought*) 451; run in the head etc. (*memory*) 505; marvel −, wonder- -if, − whether.

Adj. supposing etc. *v.*; given, mooted, postulatory; assumed etc. *v.*; supposit-ive, -itious; gratuitous, speculative, conjectural, hypothetical, suppositional, theoretical, academic, supposable, presumptive, putative.

suggestive, allusive, stimulating.

Adv. if, − so be; an; on the -supposition etc. *n.*; *ex hypothesi*; in -case, − the event of; *quasi*, as if, provided; perhaps etc. (*by possibility*) 470; for aught one knows.

515. Imagination.—N. imagination; originality; invention; fancy; inspiration; *verve*; empathy.

warm −, heated −, excited −, sanguine −, ardent −, fiery −, boiling −, wild −, bold −,

daring −, playful −, lively −, fertile- - imagination, − fancy.

'mind's eye;' 'such stuff as dreams are made of.'

ideal-ity, -ism; romanticism, utopianism, castlebuilding; dreaming; frenzy; ecs-, ex-tasy; calenture etc. (*delirium*) 503; reverie, brown study, trance; somnambulism.

conception, *vorstellung*, ercogitation, 'a fine frenzy,' poetic frenzy, divine afflatus; cloud-, dream-land; flight −, fumes- of fancy; 'thick-coming fancies;' creation −, coinage- of the brain; imagery, word painting.

conceit, maggot, figment, myth, dream, vision, shadow, chimera; phan-tasm, -tasy; fantasy, fancy; whim, -sey; vagary, rhapsody, romance, *extravaganza*; air-drawn dagger, bugbear, nightmare; flying Dutchman, great sea-serpent, man in the moon, castle in the air, *château en Espagne*; Utopia, Atlantis, happy valley, millennium, fairy land; land of Prester John, kingdom of Micomicon; work of fiction etc. (*novel*) 594; poetry etc. 597; drama etc. 599; Arabian nights; *le pot au lait*; dream of Alnaschar etc. (*hope*) 858; day − golden- dream

illusion etc. (*error*) 495; phantom etc. (*fallacy of vision*) 443; *Fata Morgana* etc. (*ignis fatuus*) 423; vapor etc. (*cloud*) 353; stretch of the imagination etc. (*exaggeration*) 549.

idealist, romanticist, visionary; mopus; romancer, dreamer; somnambulist; rhapsodist etc. (*fanatic*) 504.

V. imagine, fancy, conceive; ideal-, real-ize; dream, − of; 'give to airy nothing a local habitation and a name.'

create, originate, devise, invent, coin, fabricate; improvise, strike out something new.

set one's wits to work; strain −, crack- one's invention; rack −, ransack −, cudgel- one's brains; excogitate.

give -play, − the reins, − a loose- to the - imagination, − fancy; empathize; indulge in reverie.

conjure up a vision; fancy −, represent −, picture −, figure- to oneself; envisage.

float the mind; suggest itself etc. (*thought*) 451.

Adj. imagined etc. *v.*; *ben trovato*; air-drawn, - built.

imagin-ing etc. *v.*, -ative; original, inventive, creative, fertile, productive; ingenious.

romantic, high-flown, flighty, extravagant, fanatic, enthusiastic, Utopian, Quixotic; preposterous, rhapsodical.

ideal, unreal; in the clouds, *in nubibus*; unsubstantial etc. 4; illusory etc. (*fallacious*) 495; fictitious, theoretical, hypothetical.

fabulous, legendary; myth-ic, -ological; chimerical; imagin-, vision-ary; notional; fan-cy, - ciful, -tastic, -tastical; whimsical; fairy, -like.

dreamy, entranced, vaporous.

516. Meaning. [Idea to be conveyed.] [Thing signified.]**—N.** meaning; signific-ation, -ance; sense, expression; im-, pur-port; drift, tenor, implication, connotation, essence, force, spirit bearing, coloring; scope.

matter; subject, -matter; argument, text, sum and substance; gist etc. 5.

general –, broad –, substantial – colloquial –, literal –, plain –, simple –, accepted –, natural –, unstrained –, true etc. (*exact*) 494 –, honest etc. 543 –, *primâ facie* etc. (*manifest*) 525– meaning.

literality; literal interpretation; after acceptation; allusion etc. (*latency*) 526; suggestion etc. (*information*) 527; synonym; figure of speech etc. 521; acceptation etc. (*interpretation*) 522.

V. mean, signify, express, connote, denote; im-, pur-port; convey, imply, breathe, indicate, bespeak, bear a sense; tell –, speak- of; touch on; point –, allude- to; drive at; involve etc. (*latency*) 526; delcare etc. (*affirm*) 535.

understand by etc. (*interpret*) 522.

Adj. meaning etc. *v*.; expressive, suggestive, meaningful, allusive; signific-ant, -ative, -atory; pithy; full of –, pregnant with- meaning.

declaratory etc. 535; intelligible etc. 518; literal, metaphrastic; synonymous; tantamount etc. (*equivalent*) 27; implied etc. (*latent*) 526; explicit etc. 525; literal etc. 562.

Adv. to that effect; that is to say etc. (*being interpreted*) 522.

literally; evidently, from the context.

517. Unmeaningness. [Absence of meaning.]—**N.** unmeaningness etc. *adj*.; scrabble, scribble, scrawl, daub, (*painting*), strumming (*music*).

empty sound, dead letter, *vox et praeterea nihil*; 'a tale told by an idiot, full of sound and fury, signifying nothing;' 'sounding brass and a tinkling cymbal.'

nonsense, jargon, gibberish, jabber, mere words, hocus-pocus, fustian, rant, bombast, balderdash, palaver, patter, flummery, *verbiage*, babble, *bavardage*, *baragouin*, platitude, *niaiserie*; inanity; rigmarole, rodomontade; truism; *nugae canorae*; twaddle, twattle, fudge, trash; stuff, – and nonsense; bosh, rubbish, rot, drivel, moonshine, wish-wash, fiddle-faddle, flapdoodle; absurdity etc. 497; vagueness etc. (*unintelligibility*) 519.

V. mean nothing; be -unmeaning etc. *adj*.; twaddle, quibble, rant, gabble, scrabble etc. *n*.

Adj. unmeaning; meaning-, sense-less; nonsensical; void of -sense etc. 516.

in-, un-expressive; vacant, fatuous; not significant; insignificant,.

trashy, washy, inane, vague, trumpery, trivial, fiddle-faddle, twaddling, quibbling.

unmeant, not expressed; tacit etc. (*latent*) 526.

inexpressible, undefinable, incommunicable.

Int. rubbish! etc. 497.

518. Intelligibility.—**N.** intelligibility, clearness, clarity, explicitness etc. *adj*.; lucidity, perspicuity; legibility, plain speaking etc. (*manifestation*) 525; precision etc. 494; a word to the wise.

V. be -intelligible etc. *adj*.; speak -for itself, – volumes; tell its own tale, lie on the surface.

render -intelligible etc. *adj*.; popularize, simplify, clear up; elucidate etc. (*explain*) 522.

understand, comprehend; take, – in; catch, grasp, recognize, follow, collect, master, make out;

see -with half an eye, – daylight, – one's way; enter into the ideas of; come to an understanding.

Adj. intelligible; clear, – as -day, – crystal, – noonday; lucid; per-, tran-spicuous; luminous, transparent; comprehensible.

easily understood, easy to understand, for the million, -intelligible to the meanest capacity, popularized.

plain, distinct, explicit, clear-cút; positive; definite etc. (*precise*) 494.

graphic, vivid, telling; expressive etc. (*meaning*) 516; illustrative etc. (*explanatory*) 522.

un-ambiguous, -equivocal, -mistakable etc. (*manifest*) 525, -confused; legible, recognizable; obvious etc. 525.

Adv. in plain -terms, – words, – English.

Phr. he that runs may read etc. (*manifest*) 525.

519. Unintelligibility.—**N.** unintelligibility, incomprehensibility, imperspicuity; in-conceivableness, vagueness etc. *adj*.; obscurity; ambiguity etc. 520; doubtful meaning; uncertainty etc. 475; perplexity etc. (*confusion*) 59; spinosity; *obscurum per obscurius*; mystification etc. (*concealment*) 528; latency etc. 526; transcendentalism.

paradox; enigma, riddle etc. (*secret*) 533; *dignus vindice nodus*; sealed book; steganography, freemasonry.

pons asinorum, asses' bridge; double –, high-Dutch, Greek, Hebrew; jargon etc. (*unmeaning*). 517.

obscurantist.

V. be -unintelligible etc. *adj*.; require -explanation etc. 522; have a doubtful meaning, pass comprehension.

render -unintelligible etc. *adj*.; conceal etc. 528; darken etc. 421; confuse etc. (*derange*) 61; perplex etc. (*bewilder*) 475.

not -understand etc. 518; lose, – the clue; miss; not know what to make of, be able to make nothing of, give it up; not be able to -account for, – make either head or tail of; be at sea etc. (*uncertain*) 475; wonder etc. 870; see through a glass darkly etc. (*ignorance*) 491.

not understand one another; play at cross purposes etc. (*misinterpret*) 523.

Adj. un-intelligible, -accountable, -decipherable, -discoverable, -knowable, -fathomable; in-cognizable, -explicable, -scrutable; inap-, incomprehensible; insol-vable, -uble; impenetrable.

illegible, indecipherable, as Greek to one, unexplained, paradoxical; enigmatic, -al; puzzling, baffling.

obscure, dark, muddy, clear as mud, seen through a mist, dim, nebulous, shrouded in mystery; undiscernible etc. (*invisible*) 447; misty etc. (*opaque*) 426; hidden etc. 528; latent etc. 526.

indefinite etc. (*indistinct*) 447; perplexed etc. (*confused*) 59; undetermined, vague, loose, ambiguous; mysterious; mystic, -al; transcendental; oc\ cult, recondite, esoteric, abstruse, crabbed.

incon-ceivable, -ceptible; searchless; above –, beyond –, past- comprehension; beyond one's depth; unconceived.

inexpressible, undefinable, incommunicable, unutterable, ineffable, unpronounceable.

520. Equivocalness. [Having a double sense.]—N. equivocalness etc. *adj.*; double - meaning etc. 516; ambiguity, *double entendre*, pun, paragram, *calembour*, quibble, *équivoque*, anagram; conundrum etc. (*riddle*) 533; word-play etc. (*wit*) 842; homonym, -y; amphibo-ly, -logy; ambiloquy.

Sphinx, Delphic oracle.

equivocation etc. (*duplicity*) 544; white lie, mental reservation etc. (*concealment*) 528.

V. be -equivocal etc. *adj.*; have two -meanings etc. 516; equivocate etc. (*palter*) 544.

Adj. equivocal, ambiguous, amphibolous, homonymous; double-tongued etc. (*lying*) 544.

521. Metaphor.—N. figure of speech; *façon de parler*, way of speaking, colloquialism.

phrase etc. 566; figure, trope, metaphor, tralatition, metonymy, enallage, *catachresis*, synecdoche, autonomasia; irony, satire, figurativeness etc. *adj.*; image, -ry; *metalepsis*, type, anagoge, simile, personification, *prosopopaeia*, allegory, apologue, parable, fable; allusion, adumbration; application; euphemism; euphuism.

V. employ -metaphor etc. *n.*; personify, allegorize, adumbrate, shadow forth, apply, allude -, refer- to.

Adj. metaphorical etc. *n.*; figurative, catachrestical, typical, tralatitious, parabolic, allegorical, allusive, anagogical; ironical; colloquial.

Adv. so to -speak, - say, - express oneself; as it were.

Phr. *mutato nomine de te fabula nattatur.*

522. Interpretation.—N. interpretation, definition; explan-, explic-ation; solution, answer; rationale; plain -, simple -, strict- interpretation; meaning etc. 516.

translation; rend-ering, -ition; reddition; literal -, free- translation; key, crib; secret; clew etc. (*indication*) 550; Rosetta stone.

exegesis; ex-pounding, -position; Hermeneutics; comment, -ary; inference etc. (*deduction*) 480; illustration, exemplification; gloss, annotation, *scholium*, note; e-, di-lucidation; enucleation; *éclaircissement, mot de l'énigme.*

symptomat-, semei-ology; metoposcopy, physiognomy; diagnosis, prognosis; paleography etc. (*philology*) 560.

accept-ion, -ation, -ance; light, reading, lection, construction, version.

equivalent, - meaning etc. 516; synonym; para-, meta-phrase; convertible terms, apposition; dictionary etc. 562; polyglot.

V. interpret, explain, define, construe, translate, render; do -, turn- into; transfuse the sense of.

find out etc. 480a- -the meaning etc. 516- of; read; spell -, figure -, make- out; decipher, decode, unravel, disentangle, puzzle out; find the key of, enucleate, resolve, solve; read between the lines.

account for; find -, tell- the cause etc. 153- of; throw -, shed- -light, - new light, - a fresh light- upon; clear up, elucidate.

illustrate, exemplify; unfold, expound, comment upon, annotate; popularize etc. (*render intelligible*) 518.

take -, understand -, receive -, accept- in a particular sense; understand by, put a construction on, be given to understand.

Adj. explanatory, expository; explica-tive, -tory; exegetical; hermeneutic, interpretive, illustrative, elucidative, annotative, scholiastic.

polyglot; literal; para-, meta-phrastic; cosignificative, synonymous; equivalent etc. 27.

Adv. in -explanation etc. *n.*; that is to say, *id est, videlicet*, to wit, namely, in other words.

literally, strictly speaking; in -plain, - plainer- - terms, - words, - English; more simply.

523. Misinterpretation.—N. misinterpretation, -apprehension, -understanding, - acceptation, -construction, -application; *catachresis*; cross -reading, - purposes; mistake etc. 495.

misrepresentation, perversion, exaggeration etc. 549; false -coloring - construction; abuse of terms; parody, travesty; falsification etc. (*lying*) 544.

V. mis-interpret, -apprehend, -understand, - conceive, -judge, -doubt, -spell, -translate, - construe, -apply; mistake etc. 495.

misrepresent, pervert; garble etc. (*falsify*) 544; distort; detort; travesty, play upon words; stretch -, strain -, wrest- the -sense, - meaning; explain away; put a -bad, - false- construction on; give a false coloring, look through -rose colored -, - dark - spectacles.

be -, play- at cross purposes.

Adj. misinterpreted etc. *v.*; untranslat-ed, -able.

Adv. at cross purposes.

524. Interpreter.—N. interpreter, translator, ex-positor, -pounder, -ponent, -plainer; demonstrator.

scholiast, commentator, annotator; meta-, paraphrast.

spokesman, speaker, mouthpiece, prolocutor; diplomat etc. 758.

guide, courier, dragoman, *valet de place, cicerone*, showman; oneirocritic; Oedipus; oracle etc. 513.

525. Manifestation.—N. manifestation; unfolding; plainness etc. *adj.*; plain speaking; expression; showing etc. *v.*; exposition, demonstration, *séance*; exhibition, production; display, showing off etc. 882; premonstration. [Thing shown] exhibit, show.

indication etc. (*calling attention to*) 457; publicity etc. 531; disclosure etc. 529; openness etc. (*honesty*) 543, (*artlessness*) 703; *épachement*, prominence.

V. make -, render -manifest etc. *adj.*; bring - forth, - forward, - to the front, - into view; give notice, express; represent, set forth, exhibit; show,

– up; expose; produce; hold up – , expose- to view; set – , place – , lay- before -one, – one's eyes; tell to one's face; trot out, put through one's paces, unfold, show off, show forth, unveil, bring to light, display, demonstrate, unroll; lay open; draw – , bring- out; bring out in strong relief; call – , bring- into notice; hold up the mirror; wear one's heart upon his sleeve; show one's -face, – colors; manifest oneself; speak out; make no -mystery, – secret- of; unfurl the flag; proclaim etc. (*publish*) 531.

indicate etc. (*direct attention to*) 457; disclose etc. 529; elicit etc. 480*a*; interpret etc. 522.

be -manifest etc. *adj.*; appear etc. (*be visible*) 446; transpire etc. (*be disclosed*) 529; speak for itself, stand to reason; stare one in the face; loom large, appear on the horizon, rear its head; give -token, – sign, – indication of; tell its own tale etc. (*intelligible*) 518; go without saying.

Adj. manifest, apparent; salient, striking, demonstrative, prominent, in the foreground, notable, pronounced.

flagrant; notorious etc. (*public*) 531; arrant; stark staring; unshaded, glaring.

defin-ed, -ite; distinct, conspicuous etc. (*visible*) 446; obvious, evident, incontestable, unmistakable, not to be mistaken, plain, clear, palpable, self-evident, autoptical; intelligible etc. 518; clear as -day, – daylight, – noonday; plain as -a pikestaff, – the sun at noonday, – the nose on one's face, – the way to the parish church.

ostensible; open, – as day; overt, patent, express, explicit; naked, bare, literal, downright, undisguised, exoteric.

unreserved; frank, plain spoken etc. (*artless*) 703; barefaced, brazen, bold, shameless, daring, flaunting, loud.

manifested etc. *v.*; disclosed etc. 529; expressible, capable of being shown, producible; in-, un-concealable.

Adv. manifestly, openly etc. *adj.*; before one's eyes, under one's nose, to one's face, face to face, above board, *cartes sur table*, on the stage, in plain sight, in open court, in the open, – streets; at the cross roads; in market overt; in the face of -day, – heaven; in -broad – , open- daylight; without reserve; at first blush, *primâ facie*, on the face of; in set terms.

Phr. *cela saute aux yeux*; he that runs may read; you can see it with half an eye; it needs no ghost to tell us; the meaning lies on the surface; *cela va sans dire*; *res ipsa loquitur*.

526. Latency.—N. latency, inexpression; hidden – , occult- meaning; occultness, occultism, mysticism, mystery, cabala, symbolism, anagoge; silence etc. (*taciturnity*) 585; concealment etc. 528; more than meets the -eye, – ear; Delphic oracle; *les dessous des cartes*, undercurrent.

allusion, insinuation, implication; innuendo etc. 527; adumbration; 'something rotten in the state of Denmark.'

snake in the grass etc. (*pitfall*) 667; secret etc. 533.

darkness, invisibility, imperceptibility.

latent influence, power behind the throne; friend at court, wire puller.

V. be -latent etc. *adj.*; lurk, smoulder, underlie,

make no sign; escape -observation, – detection, – recognition; lie hid etc. 528.

laugh in one's sleeve; keep back etc. (*conceal*) 528.

involve, imply, implicate, connote, import, understand, allude to, infer, leave an inference; symbolize; whisper etc. (*conceal*) 528.

Adj. latent; lurking etc. *v.*; secret etc. 528; occult, symbolic, mystic; implied etc. *v.*; dormant.

un-apparent, -known, -seen etc. 441; in the background; invisible etc. 447; indiscoverable, dark; impenetrable etc. (*unintelligible*) 519; unspied, -suspected.

un-said, -written, -published, -breathed, -talked of, -told etc. 527, -sung, -exposed, -proclaimed, -disclosed etc. 529, -pronounced, -mentioned, -expressed; not expressed, tacit.

un-developed, -solved, -explained, -traced, -discovered etc. 480*a*, -tracked, -explored, – invented.

indirect, crooked, inferential; by -inference, – implication; implicit; constructive; allusive, covert, muffled; steganographic; under-stood, -hand, -ground; concealed etc. 528; delitescent.

Adv. by a side wind; *sub silentio*; in the background; behind -the scenes, – one's back, – the veil; below the surface; on the tip of one's tongue; secretly etc. 528; between the lines; by a mutual understanding.

Phr. 'thereby hangs a tale.' 'that is another story.'

527. Information.—N. information, enlightenment, acquaintance, knowledge etc. 490; publicity etc. 531.

communication, intimation; not-ice, -ification; e-an-nunciation; announcement; representation; round robin, presentment.

case, estimate, specification, report, advice, monition; news etc. 532; return etc. (*record*) 551; account etc. (*description*) 594; statement etc. (*affirmation*) 535.

mention; acquainting etc. *v.*; instruction etc. (*teaching*) 537; outpouring; intercommunication, communicativeness.

informant, authority, teller, announcer, annunciator, harbinger, herald, intelligencer, commentator, columnist, reporter, exponent, mouthpiece; informer, keek, eavesdropper, delator, detective, sleuth; *mouchard*, spy, stool pigeon, newsmonger; messenger etc. 534; *amicus curiae*.

valet de place, *cicerone*, pilot, guide; guide-, hand-book; *vade mecum*; manual; map, plan, chart, gazetteer; itinerary etc. (*journey*) 266.

hint, suggestion, 'wrinkle, innuendo, inkling, whisper, passing word, word in the ear, subaudition, cue, by-play; gesture etc. (*indication*) 550; gentle – broad- hint; *verbum sapienti*; word to the wise; insinuation etc. (*latency*) 526.

V. tell; inform, – of; acquaint, – with; impart, – to; make acquainted with, bring to the ears of, apprise, advise, enlighten, awaken.

let fall, mention, express, intimate, represent, communicate, make known; publish etc 531; notify, signify, specify, convey the knowledge of.

let one – , have one to- know; serve notice, give one to understand; give notice; set – , lay – , put-before; point out, put into one's head; put one in possession of; instruct etc. (*teach*) 537; direct the attention to etc. 457.

an-nounce, -nunciate; report. – progress; bring –, send –, leave –, write- word; tele-graph, -phone; ring –, call- up; wire; retail, render an account; give an account etc. (*describe*) 594; state etc. (*affirm*) 535.

disclose etc. 529; show cause; explain etc. (*interpret*) 522.

hint; give an inkling of; give –, drop –, throw out- a hint; insinuate; allude –, make allusion- to; glance at; tip off, tip the wink etc. (*indicate*) 550; suggest, prompt, give the cue, breathe; whisper, – in the ear.

give a bit of one's mind; tell one plainly, – once for all; speak volumes.

un-deceive, -beguile; set right, correct, open the eyes of, disabuse.

be -informed of etc.; know etc. 490; learn etc. 539; get scent of, gather from; awaken –, open one's eyes- to; become -alive, – awake- to; keep posted; hear, overhear, understand.

come to one's -ears, – knowledge; reach one's ears.

Adj. informed etc. *v.*; *communiqué*; reported etc. *v.*; published etc. 531; advisory.

expressive etc. 516; explicit etc. (*open*) 525, (*clear*) 518; plain-spoken etc. (*artless*) 703.

declara-, nuncupa-, exposi-tory; declarative, enunciative, communicat-ive, -ory; oral.

Adv. from information received; according to - rumor, – report; in the air; from what one can gather.

Phr. a little bird told me.

528. Concealment.—N. concealment; hiding etc. *v.*; occultation, mystification.

seal of secrecy; screen etc. 530; disguise etc. 530; masquerade; masked battery; hiding place etc. 530; cipher, code, crypt-, stegan-ography; invisible –, sympathetic- ink; palimpsest; freemasonry.

stealth, -iness; obreption; slyness etc. (*cunning*) 702.

latit-ancy, -ation; seclusion etc. 893; privacy, secrecy, secretness; *incognita.*

reticence; reserve; mental –, reservation, aside; *arrière pensée*, suppression, evasion, white lie, misprision; silence etc. (*taciturnity*) 585; suppression of truth etc. 544; underhand dealing; close-, secretive-ness etc. *adj.*; mystery.

latency etc. 526; snake in the grass; secret etc. 533.

V. conceal, hide, secrete, stow away, put out of sight; lock –, seal –, bottle- up.

cover, screen, cloak, veil, shroud; screen from - sight, – observation; draw the veil; draw –, close- the curtain; curtain, shade, eclipse, throw a veil over; be-cloud, -fog, -mask; mask, disguise; ensconce, muffle, smother; whisper.

keep -from, – back, – to oneself; keep -snug, – close, – secret, – dark; bury; sink, suppress; keep -from, – out of- -view, – sight; keep in –, throw into- the -shade, – background; cover up one's tracks; stifle, hush up, withhold, reserve; fence with a question; ignore etc. 460.

code, codify, use a cipher.

keep -a secret, – one's own counsel; hold one's

tongue etc. (*silence*) 585; make no sign, not let it go further; not breathe a -word, – syllable- about; not let the right hand know what the left is doing; hide one's light under a bushel, bury one's talent in a napkin.

keep –, leave- in -the dark, – ignorance; blind, – the eyes; blindfold, hoodwink, mystify; puzzle etc. (*render uncertain*) 475; bamboozle etc. (*deceive*) 545.

be -concealed etc. *v.*; suffer an eclipse; retire from sight, couch; hide oneself; lie -hid, – in ambush, – low, – *perdu*, – snug, – close; seclude oneself etc. 893; lurk, sneak, skulk; slink, pussyfoot, prowl; steal -into, – out of, – by, – along; play at -bopeep, – hind and seek; hide in holes and corners.

Adj. concealed etc. *v.*; hidden; veiled, secret, recondite, mystic, cabalistic, occult, dark; cryptic, -al, private, privy, *in petto*, auricular, clandestine, close, inviolate.

behind a -screen etc. 530; under -cover, – an eclipse; in -ambush, – hiding, – disguise; in a - cloud, – fog, – mist, – haze, – dark corner; in the -shade, – dark; clouded, wrapt in clouds; invisible etc. 447; buried, underground, *perdu*; incommunicado; secluded etc. 893.

un-disclosed etc. 529; -told etc. 527; covert etc. (*latent*) 526; mysterious etc. (*unintelligible*) 519.

irrevealable, inviolable; confidential; esoteric; not ot be spoken of.

obreptitious, furtive, stealthy, feline; skulking etc. *v.*; surreptitious, underhand, hole and corner; sly etc. (*cunning*) 702; secretive, evasive, noncommittal, reserved, reticent, uncommunicative, buttoned up; close, – as wax; taciturn etc. 585.

Adv. secretly etc. *adj.*; in -secret, – private, – one's sleeve, – holes and corners; in the dark etc. *adj.*

januis clausis, with closed doors, *a huis clos*; hugger-mugger, *à la dérobée*; under the -cloak of, – rose, – table; *sub rosâ, en tapinois*, in the background, aside, on the sly, with bated breath, *sotto voce*, in a whisper, without beat of drum, *à la sourdine.*

in –, strict- confidence; confidentially etc. *adj.*; between -ourselves, – you and me; *entre nous, inter nos*, under the seal of secrecy; in -code, – cipher.

underhand, by stealth, like a thief in the night; stealthily etc. *adj.*; behind -the scenes, – the curtain, – one's back, – a screen etc. 530; *incognito; in camerâ.*

Phr. it -must, – will- go no further; 'tell it not in Gath,' nobody the wiser.

529. Disclosure.—N. disclosure; retection; unveiling etc. *v.*; deterration, revealment, revelation; divulgence, expos-ition, -ure; *exposé*; whole truth; tell-tale etc. (*news*) 532.

acknowledgment, avowal; confession, -al; shrift. bursting of a bubble; *dénouement.*

V. dis-close, -cover, -mask; draw –, draw aside –, lift –, raise –, lift up –, remove –, tear- the -veil, – curtain; un-mask, -veil, -fold, -cover, -seal, -kennel; take off –, break- the seal; lay -open, – bare; expose; open, – up; bare, bring to light; evidence; make -clear, – evident, – manifest; evince.

divulge, reveal, break; let into the secret; reveal the secrets of the prison-house; tell etc. (*inform*) 527; breathe, utter, blab, peach; let -out, – fall, – drop, – the cat out of the bag; betray; tell tales, – out of school; come out with; give -vent, – utterance- to; open the lips, blurt out, vent, whisper about; speak out etc. (*make manifest*) 525; make public etc. 531; unriddle etc. (*find out*) 480a; split; blow the gaff; break the news.

acknowledge, allow, concede, grant, admit, own, confess, avow, throw off all disguise, turn inside out, make a clean breast; show one's -hand, – cards; unburden –, disburden- one's -mind, – conscience, – heart; open –, lay bare –, tell a piece of- one's mind; unbosom oneself, own to the soft impeachment; say –, speak- the truth; turn - King's, – Queen's, – States's- evidence.

raise –, drop –, lift –, remove –, throw off- the mask; expose; debunk; lay open; un-deceive, - beguile; disabuse, set right, correct, open the eyes of; *désillusionner*.

be -disclosed etc.; transpire, come to light; come in sight etc. (*be visible*) 446; become known, escape the lips; come –, ooze –, creep –, leak –, peep –, crop- out; show its -face, – colors; discover etc. itself; break through the clouds, flash on the mind.

Adj. disclosed etc. *v.*

Int. out with it!

Phr. the murder is out; a light breaks in upon one; the scales fall from one's eyes; the eyes are opened.

530. Ambush. [Means of concealment.]—**N.** hiding-place; secret -place, drawer; recess, hole, funk hole, holes and corners; closet, crypt, *adytum*, abditory, *oubliette*, safe, – deposit.

am-bush, -buscade; stalking horse; lurking-hole, -place; secret path, backstairs; retreat etc. (*refuge*) 666.

screen, cover, shade, blinder; veil, curtain, blind, *purdah*, cloak, cloud.

mask, vizor, visor, disguise, masquerade dress, domino; *camouflage*.

pitfall etc. (*source of danger*) 667; trap etc. (*snare*) 545.

v. ambush, ambuscade, lie in ambush etc. (*hide oneself*) 528; lie in wait for; set a trap for etc. (*deceive*) 545.

Adv. *aux aguets*.

531. Publication.—**N.** publication; public - announcement etc. 527; promulgation, propagation, proclamation, pronouncement, encylical, *pronunciamento*; circulation, indiction, edition, imprint, impression, printing; hue and cry.

publicity, notoriety, currency, flagrancy, cry, *bruit*; *vox populi*; report etc. (*news*) 532.

the Press, fourth estate, public press, newspaper, periodical, journal, gazette; house organ, trade publication, tabloid, daily, weekly, monthly, quarterly, annual, magazine, monograph, book; review; news sheet, special edition, supplement, feature, rotogravure, comic strips; leaflet, pamphlet; telegraphy; publisher etc. *v.*

circular, – letter; manifesto, advertisement,

puff, placard, bill, *affiche*, broadside, poster; notice etc. 527; program.

V. publish; make -public, – known etc. (*information*) 527; speak – , talk- of; broach, utter; put forward; circulate, propagate, promulgate; spread –, abroad; rumor, diffuse, disseminate, evulgate; put –, give –, send- forth; emit, edit, get out; issue; cover, report; bring –, lay –, drag- before the public; give -out, – to the world; put –, bandy –, hawk –, buzz –, whisper –, bruit –, blaze- about; drag into the -open day, – limelight; voice.

proclaim, herald, blazon; blaze –, noise- abroad; sound a trumpet; trumpet –, thunder- forth; give tongue; announce with -beat of drum, – flourish of trumpets; proclaim -from the housetops, – at Charing Cross, at the cross roads; declare, declaim.

advertise, placard; post, – up; *afficher*, publish in the Gazette, send round the crier.

raise a -cry, – hue and cry, – report; set news afloat.

telegraph, cable, wireless, broadcast.

be -published etc; be –, become- public etc. *adj.*; come out; go –, fly –, buzz –, blow- about; get -about, – abroad, – afloat, – wind; find vent; see the light; go forth, take air, acquire currency, pass current; go -the rounds, – the round of the newspapers, – through the length and breadth of the land; *virum volitare per ora*; pass from mouth to mouth; spread; run –, spread- like wildfire.

Adj. published etc. *v.*; current etc. (*news*) 532; in circulation, public; notorious; flagrant, arrant; open etc. 525; trumpet-tongued; encyclical, promulgatory; exoteric.

Adv. publicly etc. *adj.*; in open court, with open doors; in the limelight.

Int. *Oyez!* O yes! notice!

Phr. notice is hereby given; this is –, these are- to give notice.

532. News.—**N.** news; information etc. 527; piece –, budget- of -news, – information; report, story, yarn, copy, filler, intelligence, tidings; stop press news.

word, advice, *aviso*, message; dis-, des-patch; telegram, cable, wireless telegram, radio-gram, marconi-gram, communication, errand, embassy; *bulletin*.

microphone; public address system, P.A.; walkie talkie, radio -telephone, -phone.

radio, wireless (Eng.), high fidelity, hi fi, radio set, transistor, receiver; speaker, loudspeaker, amplifier, tweeter, woofer; transmitter, broadcaster; AM –, FM –, short wave – transmitter; radio station, studio, control room, network, hookup, circuit; frequency, kilocycles, megacycles; band, channel, modulation, amplification; broadcast, program, newscast, network show, commerical announcement, serial, sound effects; signature, station – identification, – break; radio listener, audiophile.

television, TV, video, color television; television –, live – broadcast, telecast, TV show; televising, telecasting, transmission, television channel, video, audio, beam, reception, image, test pattern; rain, snow, ghost; television –, TV – station, mobile unit, TVmobile, transmitter, televisor, boost, camera; set, monitor, tube, screen.

rumor, hearsay, *on dit*, flying rumor, news stirring, cry, buzz, *bruit*, fame; talk, *ouï-dire*, scandal, eavesdropping; town –, table- talk; tittle-tattle; *canard*, topic of the day, idea afloat.

fresh –, stirring –, old – stale- news; glad tidings; old –, stale- story.

narrator etc. (*describe*) 594; news-, scandal-monger; tale-bearer; tell-tale, gossip, tattler, busy-body, chatterer; informer.

broad-, news-, sports-caster; commentator, announcer, master of ceremonies, M.C., programmer, sound man, radioman, ham, radioperator.

television technician, TV man, cameraman, soundman.

V. transpire etc. (*be disclosed*) 529; rumor etc. (*publish*) 531.

broadcast, radio, transmit, send, release, beam; sign – on, – off; go on –, go off – the air, monitor; listen –, tune – in.

tele-vise, -cast; color cast.

Adj. many-tongued; rumored; publicly –, currently- -rumored, – reported; rife, current, floating, afloat, going about, in circulation, in everyone's mouth, all over the town.

Adv. as the story -goes, – runs; as they say, it is said.

533. Secret.—N. secret; dead –, profound-secret; *arcanum*, mystery; latency etc. 526; Asian mystery; sealed book, secrets of the prison-house; *le dessous des cartes*.

enigma, riddle, puzzle, nut to crack, conundrum, charade, rebus, logogriph; mono-, ana-gram; acrostic, cross-word puzzle; Sphinx; *crux criticorum*.

maze, labyrinth, Hyrcynian wood.

problem etc. (*question*) 461; paradox etc. (*difficulty*) 704; unintelligibility etc. 519; *terra incognita* etc. (*ignorance*) 491.

Adj. secret etc. (*concealed*) 528.

534. Messenger.—N. messenger, envoy, emissary, legate; nuncio, internuncio; intermediary; ambassador etc. (*diplomatist*) 758.

marshal, flag-bearer, herald, crier, trumpeter, bellman, pursuivant, *parlementaire*, *apparitor*.

courier, runner, dawk, *estafette*; Hermes, Mercury, Iris, Ariel.

postman, letter carrier, telegraph boy, messenger boy, district messenger; despatch rider, commissionaire, erand-boy.

mail; post, -office; letter-bag; mail -boat, – train, – coach, – van, aerial mail; tele-graph, -phone; cable, wire; carrier-pigeon; wireless telegraph, -phone; radiotele-graph, -phone.

journalist, newspaperman, reporter; gentleman –, representative- of the press; sob sister; penny-a-liner; special –, war –, own- correspondent; spy, scout; informer etc. 527.

535. Affirmation.—N. affirm-ance, -ation; statement, allegation, assertion, predication, declaration, word, averment.

asseveration, adjuration, swearing, oath, affidavit; deposition etc. (*record*) 551; avouchment, assurance; protest, -ation; profession; acknowledgment etc. (*assent*) 488; pledge.

vote, voice, suffrage, ballot.

remark, observation; position etc. (*proposition*) 514; saying, *dictum*, sentence, *ipse dixit*.

emphasis, positiveness, peremptoriness; dogmatism etc. (*certainty*) 474; dogmatist etc. 887.

V. assert; make -an assertion etc. *n*.; have one's say; say, affirm, predicate, declare, state, represent; protest, profess.

put -forth, – forward; advance, allege, propose, propound, enunciate, enounce, broach, set forth, hold out, maintain, contend, pronounce, pretend.

depose, depone, aver, avow, avouch, asseverate, swear; make –, take one's- oath; make –, swear –, put in- an affidavit; take one's Bible oath, kiss the book, vow, *vitam impendere vero*; swear till -one is black in the face, – all's blue; be sworn, call Heaven to witness; vouch, warrant, certify, assure, swear by bell, book and candle.

swear by etc. (*believe*) 484; insist –, take one's stand- upon; emphasize, lay stress on; assert -roundly, – positively; lay down, – the law; raise one's voice, dogmatize, have the last word; rap out; repeat; re-assert, -affirm.

announce etc. (*information*) 527; acknowledge etc. (*assent*) 488; attest etc. (*evidence*) 467; adjure etc. (*put to one's oath*) 768.

Adj. asserting etc. *v.*; declaratory, predicatory, pronunciative, affirmative, *soi-disant*; positive; certain etc. 474; express, explicit etc. (*patent*) 525; absolute, emphatic, flat, broad, round, pointed, marked, distinct, decided, confident, assertive, insistent, trenchant, dogmatic, definitive, formal, solemn, categorical, peremptory; unretracted; predicable, affirmable.

Adv. affirmatively etc. *adj.*; in the affirmative. with emphasis, *ex cathedrâ*, without fear of contradiction.

I must say, indeed, i' faith, let me tell you, why, give me leave to say, marry, you may be sure, I'd have you to know; upon my -word, – honor; by my troth, egad, I assure you; by -jingo, – Jove, – George, – etc.; troth, seriously, sadly; in –, in sober- -sadness, – truth, – earnest; of a truth, truly, pardi, perdy; in all conscience, upon oath; be assured etc. (*belief*) 484; yes etc. (*assent*) 488; I'll -warrant, – warrant you, – engage, – answer for it, – be bound, – venture to say, – take my oath; in fact, as a matter of fact, forsooth, joking apart; so help me God; not to mince the matter.

Phr. quoth he; *dixi*.

536. Negation.—N. ne-, abne-gation; denial; dis-avowal, -claimer; abjuration; contra-diction, -vention; recusation, protest; rebuttal; recusancy etc. (*dissent*) 489; flat –, emphatic- -contradiction, – denial; *démenti*.

qualification etc. 469; repudiation etc. 610; retraction etc. 607; confutation etc. 479; refusal etc. 764; prohibition etc. 761.

V. deny; contra-dict, -vene; controvert, give denial to, gainsay, negative, shake the head.

dis-own, -affirm, -claim, -avow; recant etc. 607; revoke etc. (*abrogate*) 756.

dispute, impugn, traverse, rebut, join issue upon; bring –, call- in question etc. (*doubt*) 485.

deny -flatly, – peremptorily, – emphatically, – absolutely, – wholly, – entirely; give the lie to, belie.

repudiate etc. 610; set aside, ignore etc. 460; rebut etc. (*confute*) 479; qualify etc. 469; refuse etc. 764.

Adj. denying etc. *v.*; denied etc. *v.*; contradictory; negat-ive, -ory; revocatory; recusant etc. (*dissenting*) 489; at issue upon.

Adv. no, nay, not, nowise; not a -bit, – whit, – jot; not -at all, – in the least, – so; no such thing; nothing of the -kind, – sort; quite the contrary, *tout au contraire*, far from it; *tant s'en faut*; on no account, in no respect; by -no, – no manner of-means; negatively.

phr. there never was a greater mistake; I know better; *non haec in foedera*.

537. Teaching.—**N.** teaching etc. *v.*; instruction; edification; education; pedagogy; tuition; tutor-, tutel-age; direction, guidance.

qualification, preparation; train-, school-ing etc. *v.*; discipline; exer-cise, -citation; drill, practice.

persuasion, proselytism, propagandism, *propaganda*; in-doctrination, -culcation, oculation.

explanation etc. (*interpretation*) 522; lesson, lecture, sermon, homily; apologue, parable; discourse, prelection, preachment, disquisition.

exercise, task;' *curriculum*; course, – of study; grammar, three R's, initiation, A.B.C. etc. (*beginning*) 66.

elementary –, primary –, secondary –, grammar school –, high school –, college –, university –, technical –, liberal –, classical –, religious –, denominational –, moral –, secular-education; technical –, vocational- training; university extension lectures; propaedeutics, moral tuition; evening classes, correspondence course.

physical education, gymnastics, calisthenics, eurythmics; *sloyd*.

V. teach, instruct, edify, school, tutor; cram, prime, coach; enlighten etc. (*inform*) 527.

in-culcate, -doctrinate, -oculate, -fuse, -stil, -fix, -graft, -filtrate; im-bue, -pregnate, -plant; graft, sow the seeds of, disseminate, propagandize.

give an idea of; put -up to, – in the way of; set right.

sharpen the wits, enlarge the mind; give new ideas, open the eyes, bring forward, 'teach the young idea how to shoot;' improve etc. 658.

expound etc. (*interpret*) 522; lecture; prelect; read –, give- a -lesson, – lecture, – sermon, – discourse; hold forth, preach; sermon-, moral-ize; point a moral.

train, discipline; bring up, – to; educate, form, ground, prepare, qualify, drill, exercise, practice, habituate, familiarize with, nurture, dry-nurse, breed, rear, take in hand; break, – in; tame; pre-instruct; initiate; inure etc. (*habituate*) 613.

put to nurse, send to school.

direct, guide; direct attention to etc. (*attention*) 457; impress upon the -mind, – memory; beat into, – the head; convince etc. (*belief*) 484.

Adj. teaching etc. *v.*; taught etc. *v.*; educational;

scholastic, academic, doctrinal; disciplinal; instructive, didactic, hortative, pedagogic, tutorial.

Phr. the schoolmaster abroad.

538. Misteaching—**N.** mis-teaching, -information, -intelligence, -guidance, -direction, -persuasion, -instruction, -leading etc. *v.*; perversion, false teaching; sophistry etc. 477; college of Laputa; the blind leading the blind.

V. mis-inform, -teach, -direct, -guide, -instruct, -correct; pervert; put on a false –, throw off the-scent; deceive etc. 545; mislead etc. (*error*) 495; misrepresent; lie etc. 544; *ambiguas in vulgum spargere voces*, preach to the wise, teach one's grandmother to suck eggs.

render unintelligible etc. 519; bewilder etc. (*uncertainty*) 475; mystify etc. (*conceal*) 528; unteach.

Adj. misteaching etc. *v.*; unedifying.

Phr. *piscem natare doces.*

539. Learning.—**N.** learning; acquisition of -knowledge etc. 490, – skill etc. 698; acquirement, attainment; edification; scholarship, erudition; lore; information; self-instruction; study, reading, perusal; inquiry etc. 461.

ap-, prenticeship; pupil-age, -arity; tutelage, novitiate, matriculation.

docility etc. (*willingness*) 602; aptitude etc. 698.

V. learn; acquire –, gain –, receive –, take in –, drink in –, imbibe –, pick up –, gather –, get –, obtain –, collect –, glean- -knowledge, – information, – learning.

acquaint oneself with, master; make oneself -master of, – acquainted with; grind, cram; get –, coach- up; learn by -heart, – rote.

read, spell, peruse; con –, pore -, thumb- over; wade through; dip into; run the eye -over, – through; turn over the leaves.

study; be -studious etc. *adj.*; consume the midnight oil, mind one's book.

go to -school, – college, – the university; serve -an (or one's) apprenticeship, – one's time; learn one's trade; be -informed etc. 527; be -taught etc. 537.

Adj. studious; schol-astic, -arly; teachable; docile etc. (*willing*) 602; apt etc. 698; industrious etc. 682; learned erudite.

Adv. at one's books; *in statu pupillari* etc. (*learner*) 541.

540. Teacher.—**N.** teacher, trainer, instructor, institutor, master, tutor, don, director, Corypheus, dry nurse, coach, grinder, crammer; governor, bear-leader; governess, duenna; disciplinarian.

professor, lecturer, reader, prelector, prolocutor, preacher; Boanerges; pastor etc. (*clergy*) 996; schoolmaster, dominie, usher, pedagogue, abecedarian; schoolmistress, dame, monitor, proctor, pupil-teacher.

expositor etc. 524; preceptor, guide; mentor etc. (*adviser*) 695; pioneer, apostle, missionary, propagandist, moonshee; example etc. (*model for imitation*) 22.

professorship etc. (*school*) 542.

tutelage etc. (*teaching*) 537.

Adj. professorial, tutorial etc. 537.

541. Learner.—N. learner, scholar, student, *alumnus, élève,* pupil; ap-, prentice; articled clerk; school-boy, -girl, beginner, tyro, abecedarian, alphabetarian.

recruit, novice, neophyte, tenderfoot, inceptor, *débutant*, catechumen, probationer; undergraduate; freshman, frosh; sophomore, junior, senior; junior –, senior- soph; sophister, questionist, fellow-, commoner, pensioner, exhibitioner, sizar, scholar, fellow, advanced –, post graduate –, research- student.

class, form, grade, standard, remove; pupilage etc. *(learning)* 539.

disciple, follower, apostle, proselyte; fellow student, school-mate, -fellow, class mate, condisciple.

Adj. *in statu pupillari,* in leading strings, sophomoric.

542. School.—N. school, academy, university, *alma mater,* college, seminary, Lyceum; instit-ute, -ution, *conservatoire; palaestra, gymnasium.*

day –, boarding –, public –, preparatory –, elementary –, primary –, nursery –, dame's –, grammar –, Board –, County –, Council –, parochial –, denominational –, Sunday –, religious –, collegiate –, secondary –, continuation –, night –, correspondence –, secretarial –, military –, law –, medical –, business –, technical- school; technical –, training- college; Polytechnic; training ship; *Kindergarten,* nursery, *crèche,* reformatory.

pulpit, desk, reading desk, ambo, class-, lecture-room, theater, amphitheater, forum, stage, rostrum, platform, hustings, tribune.

school –, horn –, text-book; grammar, primer, abecedary, rudiments, manual, *vade mecum,* Lindley, Murray, Cocker.

professor-, lecture-, reader-ship; chair; schoolmaster etc. 540.

School Board, Council of Education; *propaganda.*

Adj. scholastic, academic, collegiate; educational.

Adv. *ex cathedrâ.*

543. Veracity.—N. veracity; truthfulness, frankness etc. *adj.;* truth, sooth, sincerity, candor, honesty, fidelity; plain dealing, *bona fides;* love of truth; probity etc. 939; ingenuousness etc. *(artlessness)* 703.

the truth the whole truth and nothing but the truth; honest –, sober- truth etc. *(fact)* 494; unvarnished tale; light of truth.

V. speak –, tell- the truth; speak by the card; paint in its –, show oneself in ones -true colors; make a clean breast etc. *(disclose)* 529; speak one's mind etc. *(be blunt)* 703; not -lie etc. 544, – deceive etc. 545.

Adj. truthful, true; ver-acious, -edical; scrupulous etc. *(honorable)* 939; sincere, candid, frank, open, straightforward, unreserved; open-, true-, simple- hearted; honest, trustworthy; undissembling etc. (dissemble etc. 544); guileless, pure; unperjured, ture blue, as good as one's word;

unaffected, unfeigned, *bonâ fide;* outspoken, ingenuous etc. *(artless)* 703; undisguised etc. *(real)* 494.

Adv. truly etc. *(really)* 494; on oath; in plain words etc. 703; in –, with –, of a –, in good –, very- truth; as the -dial to the sun, – needle to the pole; honor bright; troth; in good -sooth, – earnest; unfeignedly, with no nonsense, in sooth, sooth to say, *bonâ fide, in foro conscientiae;* without equivocation; *cartes sur table,* from the bottom of one's heart; by my troth etc. *(affirmation)* 535.

544. Falsehood.—N. false-hood, -ness; fals-ity, -ification; misrepresentation; deception etc. 545; untruth etc. 546; guile; bad faith; lying etc. *v.;* misrepresentation; mendacity, perjury, false swearing; forgery, invention, fabrication; subreption; covin.

perversion –, suppression- of truth; *suppressio veri;* perversion, distortion, false coloring; exaggeration etc. 549; prevarication, equivocation, shuffling, fencing, evasion, fraud; *suggestio falsi* etc. *(lie)* 546; mystification etc. *(concealment)* 528; simulation etc. *(imitation)* 19; dis-simulation, -sembling; deceit.

sham; pretence, pretending, malingering.

lip-homage, – service; mouth honor; hollowness; mere -show, – outside, eye-wash, window dressing; duplicity, double dealing, insincerity, hypocrisy, cant, humbug, casuistry; jesuit-ism, -ry; pharisaism; Machiavelism, 'organized hypocrisy;' crocodile tears, mealy-mouthedness, quackery; charlatan-ism, -ry; gammon; bun-kum, -come; flam, ban, flim-flam, cajolery, flattery; Judas kiss; perfidy etc. *(bad faith)* 940; *il volto sciolto i pensieri stretti.*

unfairness etc. *(dishonesty)* 940; artfulness etc. *(cunning)* 702; misstatement etc. *(error)* 495.

V. be -false etc. *adj.,* – a liar etc. 548; speak - falsely etc. *adv.;* tell a -lie etc. 546; lie, fib; lie like a trooper; swear falsely, forswear, perjure oneself, bear false witness.

mis-state, -quote, -cite, -report, -represent; belie, falsify, pervert, distort; put a false construction upon etc. *(misinterpret)* 523.

prevaricate, equivocate. quibble; palter, – to the understanding; *répondre en Normand;* trim, shuffle, fence, mince the truth, beat about the bush, blow hot and cold, play fast and loose.

garble, gloss over, disguise, give a color to; give –, put- a -gloss, – false coloring- upon; color, varnish, cook, dress up, embroider; varnish right and puzzle wrong, exaggerate etc. 549.

invent, fabricate; trump –, get- up; forge, hatch, concoct; romance etc. *(imagine)* 515; cry 'wolf!'

dis-semble, -simulate; feign, assume, put on, pretend, make believe; play -falsé, – a double game; coquet; act –, play- a part; affect etc. 855; simulate, pass off for; counterfeit, fake, sham, make a show of; malinger; swing the lead; say the grapes are sour.

cant, play the hypocrite, sham Abraham, *faire pattes de velours,* put on the mask, clean the outside of the platter, lie like a conjuror; hang out –, hold out –, sail under- false colors; 'commend the poisoned chalice to the lips;' *ambiguas in vulgus spargere voces;* deceive etc. 545.

Adj. false, deceitful, mendacious, unveracious,

fraudulent, untruthful, dishonest; faith-, truth-, troth-less; un-fair, -candid; evasive; un-, disingenuous; hollow, insincere, Parthis mendacior; forsworn.

canting; hypocrit-, jesuit-, pharisa-ical; tartuffish; Machiavelian; double-tongued, -faced, -handed, -minded, -hearted, -dealing; two-faced, bare-faced; Janus-faced; smooth-faced, -spoken, -tongued; plausible; mealy-mouthed; affected etc. 855.

collus-ive; -ory; artful etc. (cunning) 702; perfidious etc. 940, spurious etc. (deceptive) 545; untrue etc. 546; falsified etc. v.; covinous.

Adv. falsely etc. adj.; à la Tartufe, with a double tongue; out of whole cloth; slily etc. (cunning) 702.

545. Deception.—N. deception; falseness etc. 544; untruth etc. 546; impos-ition, -ture; fraud, deceit, guile; fraudulen-ce, -cy; covin; knavery etc. (cunning) 702; misrepresentation etc. (falsehood) 544.

delusion, gullery, bluff, spoof, blague; juggl-ing, -ery; sleight of hand, legerdemain; presti-giation, -digitation; magic etc. 992; conjur-ing, -ation; hocus pocus, jockeyship; trickery, coggery, hanky-panky, chicanery, pettifogging, sharp practice; supercherie, cozenage, circumvention, ingannation; collusion; treachery etc. 940; practical joke.

trick, cheat, wile, ruse, blind, feint, plant, bubble fetch, catch, chicane, juggle, reach, hocus, bite; thimble-rig, card-sharping, artful dodge, machination, swindle, hoax; tricks upon travellers; confidence trick; strategem etc. (artifice) 702; theft etc. 791.

snare, trap, pitfall, decoy, gin; sprin-ge, -gle; noose, hook; bait, decoy-duck, tub to the whale, baited trap, guet-à-pens; cobweb, net, meshes, toils, mouse-trap, bird-lime; ambush etc. 530; trapdoor, sliding panel, false bottom; spring-net, -gun; mask, -ed battery; mine; booby trap.

Cornish hug; wolf in sheep's clothing etc. (deceiver) 548; disguise, -ment; false colors, masquerade, mummery, borrowed plumes; pattes de velours.

mockery etc. (imitation) 19; copy etc. 21; counterfeit, sham, brummagem, make-believe, forgery, fraud, fake; lie etc. 546; 'a mockery, a delusion, and a snare,' hollow mockery.

whited -, painted- sepulcher; tinsel, paste, false jewelry, scagliola, ormolu, German silver, Britannia metal, paint; jerry building; man of straw.

illusion etc. (error) 495; ignis fatuus etc. 423; mirage etc. 443.

V. deceive, take in; defraud, cheat, jockey, do, cozen, diddle, nab, gyp, chouse, double cross, play one false, bilk, cully, jilt, bite, pluck, swindle, victimize; abuse; mystify; blind one's eyes; blindfold, hoodwink, spoof, bluff; throw dust into the eyes, 'keep the word of promise to the ear and break it to the hope,' 'draw a herring across the trail.'

impose -, practice -, play -, put -, palm -, foist- upon; snatch a verdict.

circumvent, overreach; out-reach, -wit, maneuvre; steal a march upon, give the go-by to, leave in the lurch.

set -, lay- a -trap, - snare- for; bait the hook, forlay, spread the toils, lime; decoy, waylay, lure,

beguile, delude, inveigle; tra-, tre-pan; kidnap; let-, hook-in; trick; en-, in-trap, -snare, entoil, benet; nick, springe; catch, - in a trap; sniggle, entangle, illaqueate, hocus, practice on one's credulity, dupe, gull, hoax, fool, befool, bamboozle; hum, -bug; gammon, stuff up, dope, sell; play a -trick, - practical joke- upon one; balk, trip up, throw a tub to a whale; fool to the top of one's bent, send on -a wild goose chase, - a fool's errand; make -game, - a fool, - an April fool, - an ass- of; trifle with, cajole, flatter; come over etc. (influence) 615; gild the pill, make things pleasant, divert, put a good face upon; dissemble etc. 544.

cog, - the dice, play with marked cards; live by one's wits, play at hide and seek; obtain money under false pretences etc. (steal) 791; conjure, juggle, practice chicanery; gerrymander.

play -, palm -, foist -, fob- off.

lie etc. 544; misinform etc. 538; mislead etc. (error) 495; betray etc. 940; be -deceived etc. 547.

Adj. deceived etc. v.; deceiving etc. v.; cunning etc. 702; prestigi-ous, -atory; decept-ive, -ious; deceitful, covinous; delus-ive, -ory; illus-ive, -ory; elusive, insidious, ad captandum vulgus.

untrue etc. 546; mock, sham, make-believe, counterfeit, faked, pseudo, spurious, so-called; pretended, feigned, trumped up, bogus, scamped, fraudulent, tricky, factitious, artificial, bastard; surreptitious, illegitimate, contraband, adulterated, sophisticated; unsound, rotten at the core; colorable; disguised; meretricious; tinsel, pinchbeck, plated; catch-penny; Brummagem; simulated etc. 544.

Adv. under -false colors, -- the garb of, - cover of; over the left.

Phr. fronti nulla fides.

546. Untruth.—N. untruth, falsehood, lie, story, thing that is not, fib, bounce, crammer, taradiddle, whopper.

forgery, fabrication, invention; mis-statement, -representation; perversion, falsification, gloss, suggestio falsi; exaggeration etc. 549.

fiction; fable, nursery tale; romance etc. (imagination) 515; untrue -, false -, trumped up- -story, - statement; thing devised by the enemy; canard; shave, sell, hum, yarn, traveler's tale, Canterbury tale, cock and bull story, fairy tale, clap-trap.

myth, moonshine, bosh, all my eye, -and Betty Martin, mare's nest, farce.

irony; half truth, white lie, pious fraud; mental reservation etc. (concealment) 528.

pretence, pretext; false -plea etc. 617; subterfuge, evasion, shift, shuffle, make-believe; sham etc. (deception) 545.

profession, empty words; Judas kiss etc. (hypocrisy) 544; disguise etc. (mask) 530.

V. have a false meaning; not ring true.

pretend, sham, feign, counterfeit, make believe.

Adj. untrue, false, trumped up; void of -, without- foundation; far from the truth, false as dicer's oaths; unfounded, ben trovato, invented, fabulous, fabricated, forged; fict-, fact-, supposit-, surrept-itious; e-, il-lusory; ironical; satirical; evasive; soi-disant etc. (misnamed) 565.

Phr. se non e vero e ben trovato.

547. Dupe.—N. dupe, gull, gudgeon, *gobemouche*, cull, cully, victim, sucker, pigeon, April fool; laughing stock etc. 857; Cyclops, simple Simon, flat, mug, greenhorn; fool etc. 501; puppet, cat's paw.

V. be -deceived etc. 545, – the dupe of; fall into a trap; swallow –, nibble at- the bait; bite; catch a Tartar.

Adj. credulous etc. 486; mistaken etc. (*error*) 495.

548. Deceiver.—N. deceiver etc. (deceive etc. 545); dissembler, hypocrite; sophist, Pharisee, Jesuit, Mawworm, Pecksniff, Joseph Surface, Tartufe, Janus; serpent, snake in the grass, cockatrice, Juaas, wolf in sheep's clothing; Molly Maguire; jilt; shuffler.

liar etc. (lie etc. 544; story-teller, perjurer, false-witness, *mentuer à triple étage*, Scapin.

imposter, pretender, capper, decoy, fraud, *soi-disant*, humbug; adventurer; Cagliostro, Fernam Mendez Pinto; ass in lion's skin etc. (*bungler*) 701; actor etc. (*stage player*) 599.

quack, *charlatan*, mountebank, saltimbanco, *saltimbanque*, empiric, quacksalver, medicaster.

conjuror, juggler, magician, necromancer, trickster, prestidigitator, medium, jockey; crimp; decoy-duck, stool pigeon; rogue, knave, cheat; swindler etc. (*thief*) 792; jobber.

549. Exaggeration.—N. exaggeration; expansion etc. 194; hyperbole, stretch, strain, coloring; high coloring, caricature, *caricatura*; extravagance etc. (*nonsense*) 497; Baron Munchausen; men in buckram, yarn, fringe, embroidery, traveler's tale; Pelion upon Ossa.

storm in a teacup; much ado about nothing etc. (*over-estimation*) 482; puffery etc. (*boasting*) 884; rant etc. (*turgescence*) 577.

figure of speech, *façon de parler*; stretch of - fancy, – the imagination; flight of fancy etc. (*imagination*) 515.

false coloring etc. (*falsehood*) 544; aggravation etc. 835.

V. exaggerate, magnify, pile up, aggravate; amplify etc. (*expand*) 194; overestimate etc. 482; hyperbolize; over-charge, -state, -draw, -lay, -shoot the mark, -praise; make -much, – the most- of; strain, – a point; stretch, – a point; go great lengths; spin a long yarn; draw –, shoot with- a long-bow; deal in the marvelous.

out -Herod Herod, run riot, talk at random. heighten, overcolor; color -highly, – too highly; embroider, *broder*; flourish; color etc. (*misrepresent*) 544; puff etc. (*boast*) 884.

Adj. exaggerated etc. *v.*; overwrought; bombastic etc. (*magniloquent*) 577; hyperbolical, on stilts; fabulous, extravagant, preposterous, egregious, *outré*, high-flying.

Adv. hyperbolically etc. *adj.*

550. Indication.—N. indication; symbol-ism, -ization; semeio-logy, -tics; sign of the times.

lineament, feature, *trait*, characteristic, trick,

diagnostic; divining-rod; cloven hoof; footfall; means of recognition; earmark.

sign, symbol; ind-ex, -ice, -icator; point, -er; marker; exponent, note, token, symptom.

type, figure, emblem, cipher, device; representation etc. 554; epigraph, motto, posy.

gest-ure, -iculation; pantomime; wink, glance, leer; nod, shrug, beck; touch, nudge; grip; dactylo-logy, -nomy; freemasonry, telegraphy, chirology, by-play, dumb-show; cue; hint etc. 527; clue, clew, key, scent, tract etc. 551.

signal, -post; rocket, blue light; watch-fire, - tower; telegraph, semaphore, flag-staff; cresset, fiery cross; calumet; heliograph, signal-, flash-lamp; radar, radar signal, pulse –, microwave –, radar; tracing, blips, pips.

mark, line, stroke, dash, score, stripe, streak, scratch, tick, dot, point, notch, nick, blaze; asterisk, red letter, Italics, heavy type, inverted commas, quotation marks, sublineation, underlining, jotting; print; impr-int, -ess, ession; note, annotation, mark of exclamation.

[For identification] badge, criterion; countercheck, -mark, -sign, -foil, duplicate, tally; label, tab, ticket, stub, billet, letter, counter, *tessera*, card, bill, check; witness, voucher; stamp; *cachet*; trade –, Hall- mark; broad arrow; signature; address –, visiting- card; *carte de visite*; credentials etc. (*evidence*) 467; passport, identity book; attestation; hand, – writing, sign-manual; cipher; monogram, – mark, seal, sigil, signet; autograph, - y, paraph, brand; superscription; in-, en-dorsement; title, heading, rubric, docket; *mot -de passe*, – du guet; *passe-parole*; shibboleth; watch-, catch-, password; open *sesame*.

insignia, banner, -et, -ol; bandrol; flag, colors, streamer, standard, eagle, labarum, oriflamb, *oriflamme*; figure-head; ensign; pen-non, -nant, - dant; burgee, blue Peter, jack, ancient, gonfalon, union-jack; tricolor, stars and stripes; bunting.

hearldry, crest; coat of –, arms; armorial bearings, hatchment; e-, scutcheon; shield, supporters; livery, uniform; cockade, *epaulette*, brassard, chevron; garland, chaplet, love-knot, fillet, favor.

[Of locality] beacon, cairn, post, staff, flagstaff, hand, pointer, vane, cock, weathercock; guide-, hand-, finger-, directing-, sign-post; pillars of Hercules, pharos, signal fire; land-, sea-mark; lighthouse, balize; pole-, load-, lode-star; cynosure, guide; address, direction, name; sign, -board.

[Of the future] warning etc. 668; omen etc. 512; prefigurement etc. 511. [Of the past] trace record etc. 551. [Of danger] warning etc. 668; alarm etc. 669. [Of authority] scepter etc. 747. [Of triumph] trophy etc. 733. [Of quantity] gauge etc. 466. [Of distance] mile-stone, -post. [Of disgrace] brand, fool's cap, stigma, mark of Cain. [For detection] check, tell-tale; test etc. (*experiment*) 463.

notification etc. (*information*) 527; advertisement etc. (*publication*) 531.

word of command, call; bugle-, trumpet-call; reveille, taps; bell, alarum, cry; battle –, rallying-cry.

church, bell, angelus, sacring bell; muezzin.

exposition etc. (*explanation*) -522; proof etc. (*evidence*) 463; pattern etc. (*prototype*) 22.

V. indicate; be the -sign etc. *n.*- of; denote,

betoken; argue, testify etc. (*evidence*) 467; bear the
-impress etc. *n.*- of; con-note, -notate.
   represent, stand for; typify etc. (*prefigure*) 511;
symbolize.
   put -an indication, — a mark, — etc. *n.*; note,
mark, tick, blaze, stamp, earmark; set one's seal
upon; label, ticket, docket; dot, spot, score, dash,
trace, chalk; print; im-print, -press,· surprint;
engrave, stereotype, electrotype.
   signal, transmit, send, radiate, beam, deflect,
echo, bounce back, return.
   make a -sign etc. *n.*; signalize; give —, hang out-
a signal; beck, -on; gesture; not; wink, glance, leer,
nudge, shrug, tip the wink; gesticulate; raise —,
hold up- the-finger, — hand; saw the air, suit the
action to the word.
   wave —, unfurl —, hoist —, hang out- a banner
etc. *n.*; wave -the hand, — a kerchief; give the cue
etc. (*inform*) 527; show one's colors; give —,
sound- an alarm; beat the drum, sound the trumpets, raise a cry.
   sign, seal, attest etc. (*evidence*) 467; underline
etc. (*give importance to*) 642; call attention to etc.
(*attention*) 457; give notice etc. (*inform*) 527.
   Adj. indicat-ing etc. *v.*; -ive, -ory; de-, con-
notative; diacritical, representative, typical, symbolic, pantomimic, pathognomonic, symptomatic,
ominous, characteristic, demonstrative, diagnostic,
exponential, emblematic, armorial; individual etc.
(*special*) 79.
   known —, recognizable- by; indicated etc. *v.*;
pointed, marked.
   [Capable of being denoted] denotable; indelible.
   Adv. in token of; symbolically etc. *adj.*; in
dumb show.
   Phr. *ecce signum*; *ex ungue leonem*, *ex pede
Herculem.*

551. Record.—**N.** trace, vestige, relic, remains;
scar, *cicatrix*; foot-step, -mark, -print; track, mark,
wake, trail, spoor, scent, *piste.*
   monument, hatchment, escutcheon, slab, tablet,
trophy, achievement; obelisk, pillar, column,
monolith, cromlech, dolmen; memorial; *memento*
etc. (*memory*) 505; testimonial, medal, ribbon, order; commemoration etc. (*celebration*) 883.
   record, note, minute; *dossier*; register, -try; census, roll etc. (*list*) 86; cartulary, diptych,
Domesday book; entry, memorandum, indorsement, inscription, copy, duplicate, docket;
notch etc. (*mark*) 550; muniment, deed etc.
(*security*) 771; document; deposition, *procèsverbal*; affidavit; certificate etc. (*evidence*) 467.
   note-, memorandum-, pocket-, commonplace-
book; portfolio; scoring-board, -sheet; bulletin
board; card index, file; pigeon-holes, *excerpta, adversaria*, jottings, dottings.
   gazette, -er; newspaper, magazine etc. 531;
alman-ac, -ack; calendar, ephemeris, noctuary,
diary, log, journal, account-, cash-, day-book,
ledger.
   archive, scroll, state-paper, Congressional
Record, return, blue-book; statistics etc. 86;
compte rendu; Acts —, Transactions —,
Proceedings- of; Hansard's Debates; chronicle, annals; legend; history, biography etc. 594.
   registration; en-, in-rolment; tabulation; entry,

booking; signature etc. (*identification*) 550; recorder etc. 553; journalism.
   drawing, photograph etc. 554; phonograph —,
gramophone- record; music roll.
   V. record; put —, place- upon record; go on
record; chronicle, calendar, hand down to
posterity; keep up the memory of etc. (*remember*)
505; commemorate etc. (*celebrate*) 883; report
etc. (*inform*) 527; commit to —, reduce. to-
writing; put —, set down- -in writing, — in black
and white; put —, jot —, take —, write —, note
—, set-down; note, minute, put on paper; take —,
make- a -note, — minute, — memorandum; make
a return.
   mark etc. (*indicate*) 550; sign etc. (*attest*) 467.
   enter, book; post, — up; insert, make an entry
of; mark —, tick- off; register, list, docket, enroll,
inscroll; file etc. (*store*) 636.
   Adv. on record.

552. Obliteration. [Suppression of sign.]—**N.**
obliteration; erasure, rasure; effacement; interference; cancel, -lation; cassation; cir-
cumduction; deletion, blot; *tabula rasa.*
   V. efface, obliterate, erase, rase, expunge, cancel; blot —, take —, rub —, scratch —, strike —,
wipe —, wash —, sponge- out; wipe —, rub- off;
wipe away; deface, render illegible; draw the pen
through, apply the sponge.
   interfere, jam, black-, block-out; clutter, screen.
   be -effaced etc.; leave no -trace etc. 449; 'leave
not a rack behind.'
   Adj. obliterated etc. *v.*; out of print; printless;
leaving no trace; intestate; un-recorded, -registered,
-written.
   Int. *dele*; out with it!

553. Recorder.—**N.** recorder, notary, clerk;
regis-trar, -trary, -ter; prothonotary; amanuensis,
secretary, scribe, stenographer, remembrancer,
book-keeper, *custos rotulorum*, Master of the
Rolls.
   annalist;.histori-an, -ographer; chronicler, journalist, reporter, columnist; biographer etc.
(*narrator*) 594; antiquary etc. (*antiquity*) 122;
.memorialist.
   draughtsman etc. 559; engraver 558;
photographer, cinematographer, camera man.
   Recording instrument, recorder, camera,
phonograph, gramophone, dictaphone,
telegraphone, telautograph, printing telegraph, tape
recorder, ticker, time recorder, cash register, turn-
stile, speedometer, voting machine, seismograph,
radar, oscilloscope, teletypewriter, pari-mutuel,
photostat.

554. Representation.—**N.** ·represent-ation, -
ment; imitation etc. 19; illustration, delineation,
depictment, portrayal; imagery, portraiture,
iconography; design, -ing; art, fine arts; painting
etc. 556; sculpture etc. 557; engraving etc. 558;
photography, radiography, skiagraphy.
   person-ation, -ification; impersonation; drama
etc. 599.

picture, drawing, sketch, draught, draft; tracing; copy etc. 21; photo-, helio-graph; daguerreo-, talbo-, calo-, helio-type; cabinet, *carte-de-visite,* snapshot; X-ray photograph; radio-gram, -graph, skia-graph, -gram.

image, likeness, icon, portrait; striking –, speaking- likeness; very image; effigy, fac-simile.

figure, – head; puppet, doll, *figurine,* aglet, manikin, lay-figure, model, *marionnette, fantoccini,* bust; waxwork, statue, -tte, automaton, Robot.

hieroglyphic, anaglyph; dia-, mono-gram, graph.

map, plan, chart; ground plan, projection, elevation; ichno-, carto-graphy; atlas; outline, scheme; view etc. (*painting*) 556.

artist, draughtsman etc. 559.

V. represent, delineate; depict, -ure; portray; picture; take –, catch- a likeness etc. *n.*; hit off, photograph, daguerreotype; figure; shadow -forth, – out; adumbrate; body forth; describe etc. 594; trace, copy; mold.

dress up; illustrate, symbolize.

paint etc. 556; carve etc. 557; engrave etc. 558.

person-ate, -ify; impersonate; assume a character; pose as; act; play etc. (*drama*) 599; mimic etc. (*imitate*) 19; hold the mirror up to nature.

Adj. represent-ing etc. *v.,* -ative; illustrative; represented etc. *v.*; imitative, figurative.

like etc.. 17; graphic etc. (*descriptive*) 594.

555. Misrepresentation.—N. misrepresentation, distortion, exaggeration; daubing etc. *v.*; bad likeness, daub, sign-painting; scratch, caricature; *anamorphosis.*

V. misrepresent, distort, overdraw, travesty, parody, burlesque, exaggerate, caricature, daub.

Adj. misrepresented etc. *v.*

556. Painting.—N. painting; depicting; drawing etc. *v.*; design; perspective, skiagraphy; *chiaroscuro* etc. (*light*) 420; composition; treatment, values, atmosphere, tone, technique.

historical –, portrait –, miniature –, landscape –, marine –, flower –, scene- painting; scenography.

school, style; the grand style, high art, *genre,* portraiture; ornamental art etc. 847.

mono-, poly-chrome; *grisaille.*

pallet, palette; easel; brush, pencil, stump; blacklead, charcoal, crayons, chalk, pastel; paint etc. (*coloring matter*) 428; water-, body-, oil-color; oils, oil-paint; varnish etc. 356a; *gouache,* tempera, distemper, fresco, water-glass; enamel; encaustic painting; *graffito, gesso;* mosiac; tapestry.

picture, painting, piece, *tableau,* canvas; oil etc.-painting; fresco, cartoon; easel –, cabinet- picture; drawing, draught, draft; pencil etc. –, watercolor-drawing; sketch; outline; study.

portrait etc. (*representation*) 554; whole –; full –, half- length; kitcat, head; miniature, shade, *silhouette;* profile.

landscape, sea-piece, -scape; view, scene, prospect; interior; bird's- eye view; pan-, di-orama; still life.

picture –, art- gallery; *studio, atelier.*

V. paint, design, limn, draw, sketch, pencil, scratch, shade, stipple, hatch, dash off, chalk out, square up; color, dead-color, wash, varnish; draw in -pencil etc. *n.*; paint in -oils etc. *n.*; stencil; depict etc. (*represent*) 554.

Adj. painted etc. *v.*; pictorial, graphic, picturesque, decorative; classical, romantic, pre-Raphaelite, modern, cubist, futurist, vorticist.

pencil, oil etc. *n.*

Adv. in -pencil etc. *n.*

Phr. *fecit, delineavit.*

557. Sculpture.—N. sculpture, insculpture; carving etc. *v.*; statuary, ceramics, plastic arts.

high –, low –, bas- relief; relievo; *basso-, alto-, mezzo-relievo; intaglio,* anaglyph; medal, -lion; *cameo.*

marble, bronze, *terra cotta;* ceramic ware, pottery, porcelain, china, earthenware, faïence, enamel, *cloisonné.*

statue etc. (*image*) 554; cast etc. (*copy*) 21; glyptotheca.

V. sculpture, carve, cut, chisel, model, mold; cast.

Adj. sculptured etc. *v.*; in relief, anaglyptic, ceroplastic, ceramic; parian; marble etc. *n.*

558. Engraving.—N. engraving, chalcography; line –, mezzotint –, stipple –, chalk- engraving; dry-point, bur; etching, aquatinta; plate –, copper-plate –, steel –, wood-, process-, photo-engraving; xylo-, ligno-, glypto-, cero-, litho-, chromolitho-, photolitho-, zinco-, glypho- -graphy, -graph.

impression, print, engraving, plate; steel-, copper-plate; etching; mezzo-, aqua-, litho-tint; cut, woodcut, block; stereo-, grapho-, auto-, helio-type; half-tone; *photogravure, rotogravure.*

graver, *burin,* etching-point, style; plate, stone, wood-block, negative; die, punch, stamp.

printing; plate –, copper-plate –, intaglio –, anastatic –, lithographic –, color –, three color-printing; type-printing etc. 591.

illustr-, illumin-ation; *vignette,* initial letter, *cul de lampe,* tail-piece.

V. engrave, grave, stipple, scrape, etch; bite, – in; lithograph etc. *n.*; print.

Adj. insculptured; engraved etc. *v.*

Phr. *sculpsit, imprimit.*

559. Artist.—N. artist; painter, limner, drawer, sketcher, delineator; cartoon-, caricatur-ist, designer, engraver; draughtsman; copyist; enameller, -list.

historical –, landscape –, genre –, marine –, flower –, portrait –, miniature –, scene –, sign-painter; engraver; Apelles; sculptor, carver, chaser, modeller, lapidary, *figuriste,* statuary; Phidias, Praxiteles; Royal Academician.

photographer, retoucher.

560. Language.—N. language; phraseology etc. 569; speech etc. 582; tongue, lingo, vernacular, slang; mother — , vulgar — , native- tongue; household words; King's *or* Queen's English; idiom; dialect etc. 563.

volapuk, esperanto, ido, occidental, Ro.

confusion of tongues, Babel, *pasigraphie*; pantomime etc. (*signs*) 550; *onomatopaeia.*

phil-, gloss-, glott-ology; linguistics, chrestomathy; paleo-logy; -graphy; comparative grammar.

literature, letters, polite literature, *belles lettres,* muses, humanities, *literae humaniores,* republic of letters, dead languages, classics; genius of a language; scholarship etc. (*knowledge*) 490.

linguist etc. (*scholar*) 492.

V. speak, say, express by words etc. 566.

Adj. lingu-al, -istic; dialectic; vernacular, current, colloquial, slangy; bilingual, polyglot; literary.

561. Letter.—N. letter; character; hieroglyphic etc. (*writing*) 590; type etc. (*printing*) 591; capitals; majus-, minus-cule; alphabet, ABC, abecedary, christcross row, chrisscross row.

consonant, vowel, diphthong; mute, surd; sonant, liquid, labial, dental, palatal, gutteral.

syllable; mono-, dis-, poly-syllable; affix, prefix, suffix.

spelling, orthography; phon-ography, -etic spelling; ana-, meta-grammatism.

cipher, monogram, anagram; double — acrostic.

V. spell.

Adj. literal; alphabetical, abecedarian; syllabic; uncial etc. (*writing*) 590; phonetic, voiced, mute etc. *n.*

562. Word.—N. word, term, vocable; name etc. 564; phrase etc. 566; root, etymon; derivative; part of speech etc. (*grammar*) 567.

dictionary, vocabulary, word book, lexicon, index, glossary, thesaurus, *gradus, delectus,* concordance.

etymology, lexicology, derivation; phonology, orthoepy; gloss-, termin-, orism-ology; paleology etc. (*philology*) 560; comparative philology.

lexicograph-er, -y;, glossographer etc. (*scholar*) 492; etymologist; logolept.

verbosity, verbiage, loquacity etc. 584.

Adj. verbal, literal; titular, nominal. [Similarly derived] conjugate, paraonymous; derivative.

Adv. verbally etc. *adj.*; *verbatim* etc. (*exactly*) 494.

563. Neology.—N. neolo-gy; -gism; newfangled expression; barbarism; caconym; archaism, black letter, monkish Latin; corruption; missaying, antiphrasis.

paronomasia, play upon words; wordplay etc. (*wit*) 842; *double-entente* etc. (*ambiguity*) 520; palindrome, paragram, clinch; abuse of -language, — terms.

dialect, brogue, *patois,* provincialism, broken English, *lingua franca*; Brit-, Gall-, Scott-, Hibernicism; American-ism; Gipsy lingo, Romany, pidgin English.

dog Latin, macaronics, gibberish, confusion of tongues, Babel; jargon.

colloquialism etc. (*figure of speech*) 521; byword; technicality, lingo, slang, cant, *argot*, St. Giles's Greek, thieves' Latin, peddler's French, flash tongue, Billingsgate, Wall Street slang.

pseudonym etc. (*misnomer*) 565; Mr. So-and-so; what d'ye call 'em, what's his name; thingum-my, -bob; *je ne sais quoi.*

neologist, coiner of words.

V. coin words.

Adj. neologic, -al; rare; archaic; obsolete etc. (*old*) 124; colloquial, dialectic, slang, cant.

564. Nomenclature.—N. nomenclature; naming etc. *v.*; nuncupation, nomination, baptism; orismology; *onomatopaeia*; antonomasia.

name; appella-tion, -tive; designation; title; head, -ing, caption; denomination; by-name, epithet.

style, proper name; prae-, ag-, cog-nomen; patronymic, surname; cognomination; compellation, description; empty -title, — name; handle to one's name; namesake, eponym.

synonym, antonym.

term, expression, noun; by-word; convertible terms etc. 522; technical term; cant etc. 563.

V. name, call, term, denominate, designate, style, entitle, intitule, clepe, dub, christen, baptize, nickname, characterize, specify, define, distinguish by the name of; label etc. (*mark*) 550.

be -called etc. *v.*; take — , bear — , go (*or* be known) by — , go (*or* pass) under — , rejoice in- the name of.

Adj. named etc. *v.*; hight, yclept, known as; what one may -well, — fairly, — properly, — fitly-call.

nuncupa-tory, -tive; cognominal, titular, nominal; orismological.

565. Misnomer.—N. misnomer; *lucus a non lucendo*; Mrs. Malaprop; what d'ye call 'em etc. (*neologism*) 563.

nickname, *sobriquet,* by-name, handle, moniker; assumed -name, — title; *alias; nom de -guerre, — plume, — theâtre*; pseudonym, pen name, stage name.

V. mis-name, -call, - term; nickname; assume -a name, — an alias.

Adj. misnamed etc. *v.*; pseudonymous; *soidisant*; self-called, -styled, -christened; so-called; nameless, anonymous; without a — , having no-name; innominate, unnamed.

Adv. in no sense.

566. Phrase.—N. phrase, expression, set phrase; sentence, paragraph; figure of speech etc. 521; idi-om, -otism; turn of expression.

paraphrase etc. (*synonym*) 522; periphrase etc. (*circumlocution*) 573; motto etc. (*proverb*) 496. phraseology etc. 569.

V. express, phrase; word, – it; give -words, – expression- to; voice; arrange in –, clothe in –, put into –, express by- words; couch in terms; find words to express; speak by the card.

Adj. expressed etc. *v.*; idiomatic.

Adv. in -round, – set, – good, set- terms; in set phrases.

567. Grammar.—N. grammar, accidence, syntax, *praxis*, analysis, paradigm, punctuation; parts of speech, inflexion, case, declension, conjugation; *jus et norma loquendi*; Lindley Murray etc. (*school-book*) 542; correct style; philology etc. (*language*) 560.

V. parse, analyze; decline, conjugate; punctuate.

Adj. grammatical; syntactic; inflexional.

568. Solecism.—N. solecism; bad –, false –, faulty- grammar; slip, error; slip of the -pen, – tongue; *lapsus calami-*, – *linguae*; *faux pas*; slipslop; bull.

V. use -bad, – faulty- grammar; solecize, commit a solecism; murder the -King's, – Queen's- English; break Priscian's head.

Adj. ungrammatical; in-correct, -accurate; faulty, improper, incongruous, abnormal.

569. Style.—N. style, diction, phraseology, wording; manner, strain; composition; mode of expression, choice of words, literary power, ready pen, pen of a ready writer; command of language etc. (*eloquence*) 582; authorship; *la morgue littéraire*.

V. express by words etc. 566; write.

570. Perspicuity.—N. perspicuity etc. (*intelligibility*) 518; plain speaking etc. (*manifestation*) 525; defin-iteness, -ition; exactness etc. 494; perspicuousness, logical acuteness.

Adj. lucid etc. (*intelligible*) 518; explicit etc. (*manifest*) 525; exact etc. 494.

571. Obscurity.—N. obscurity etc. (*unintelligibility*) 519; involution; hard words; ambiguity etc. 520; vagueness etc. 475, inexactness etc. 495; what d'ye call 'em etc. (*neologism*) 563; cloudiness, confusion.

Adj. obscure etc. *n.*; crabbed; involved, confused.

572. Conciseness.—N. conciseness etc. *adj.*; brevity, 'the soul of wit,' laconism; Tacitus; ellipsis; syncope; abridgment etc. (*shortening*) 201; compression etc. 195; epitome etc. 596; monostitch; portmanteau word, telescope word, protogram.

V. be -concise etc. *adj.*; condense etc. 195; abridge etc. 201; abstract etc. 596; come to the point.

Adj. concise, brief, short, terse, close; to the point, exact; neat, compact, condensed, pointed; laconic, curt, pithy, trenchant, summary; pregnant; compendious etc. (*compendium*) 596; succinct; elliptical, epigrammatic, crisp, sententious.

Adv. concisely etc. *adj.*; briefly, summarily; in - brief, – short, – a word, – few words, – a nutshell; for shortness sake; to -come to the point, – make a long story short, – cut the matter short, – be brief; it comes to this, the long and short of it is.

573. Diffuseness.—N. diffuseness etc. *adj.*; amplification etc. *v.*; dilating etc. *v.*; verbosity, *verbiage*, wordiness, cloud of words, *copia verborum*; flow of words etc. (*loquacity*) 584.

poly-, tauto-, batto-, perisso-logy; pleonasm, exuberance, redundance; thrice-told tale; prolixity; circumlocution, *ambages*; periphra-se, -sis; roundabout phrases; episode; expletive; penny-a-lining; padding, drivel, twaddle, rigmarole; richness etc. 577.

V. be -diffuse etc. *adj.*; run out on, descant, expatiate, enlarge, dilate, amplify, expand, inflate, pad; launch –, branch- out; rant.

maunder, prose; harp upon etc. (*repeat*) 104; dwell on, insist upon.

digress, ramble, *battre la campagne*, beat about the bush, perorate, spin a long yarn, protract; spin –, swell –, draw- out; drivel.

Adj. dif-, pro-fuse; wordy, verbose, largiloquent, copious, exuberant, effusive, pleonastic, lengthy; long, -some, -winded, -spun, -drawn out; diffusive, spun out, protracted, prolix, prosing, maundering; circumlocutory, periphrastic, ambagious, roundabout; digressive; dis-, ex-cursive; rambling, episodic; flatulent, frothy.

Adv. diffusely etc. *adj.*; at large, *in extenso*; about it and about it.

574. Vigor.—N. vigor, power, force; boldness, raciness etc. *adj.*; spirit, point, antithesis, piquancy; *verve*, glow, fire, warmth, ardor, enthusiasm; 'thoughts that breathe and words that burn;' strong language; punch; gravity, sententiousness; elevation, loftiness, sublimity.

eloquence; command of -words, – language.

Adj. vigorous, nervous, powerful, forcible, trenchant, mordant, biting, incisive, impressive; sensational.

spirited, lively, glowing, sparkling, racy, bold, slashing; pungent, *piquant*, full of point, pointed, pithy, antithetical; sententious.

lofty, elevated, sublime, grand, weighty, ponderous; eloquent; vehement, petulant, impassioned; poetic.

Adv. in -glowing, – good set, – no measured- terms.

575. Feebleness.—N. feebleness etc. *adj.*;

Adj. feeble, bald, tame, meager, insipid, nerve-les, jejune, vapid, trashy, cold, frigid, poor, dull, dry, languid; pros-ing, -y, -aic; unvaried, monotonous, weak, frail, washy, wishy-washy, sloppy; sketchy, slight; careless, slovenly, loose, lax; slip-shod, -slop; inexact; dis-jointed, -connected; puerile, childish; flatulent; rambling etc. (*diffuse*) 573.

576. Plainness.—N. plainness etc. *adj.*; simplicity, severity; plain -terms, — English; Saxon English; household words.
V. speak plainly; call a spade 'a spade;' plunge *in medias res*; come to the point.
Adj. plain, simple; un-ornamented, -adorned, -varnished; home-ly, -spun; neat; severe, chaste, pure, Saxon; commonplace, matter of fact, natural, prosaic, sober, unimaginative.
dry, unvaried, monotonous etc. 575.
Adv. in plain -terms, — words, — English, — common parlance; point blank.

577. Ornament.—N. ornament; floridness etc. *adj.*; turg-idity, -escence; altiloquence etc. *adj.*; orotundity; declamation, teratology; well-rounded periods; elegance etc. 578.
inversion, antithesis, alliteration, *paronomasia*; figurativeness etc. (*metaphor*) 521.
flourish; flowers of -speech, — rhetoric; euphuism, -emism.
big-, high-sounding words; macrology, *sesquipedalia verba*, sesquipedalianism; Alexandrine; inflation, pretension; rant, bombast, fustian, bunkum, balderdash, prose run mad; fine writing; Minerva press.
phrasemonger; euph-uist, -emist.
V. ornament, overlay with ornament, overcharge; smell of the lamp.
Adj. ornamented etc. *v.*; beautified etc. 847; ornate, florid, rich, flowery; euph-uistic, -emistic; sonorous; high-, big-sounding; inflated, swelling, tumid; turg-id, -escent; pedantic, pompous, stilted; high-flown, -flowing; sententious, rhetorical, declamatory; grandiose; grand-, magn-, altiloquent; sesquipedal, -ian; Johnsonian, mouthy; bombastic; fustian; frothy, flashy, flaming, flamboyant.
antithetical, alliterative; figurative etc. 521; artificial etc. (*inelegant*) 579.
Adv. ore *rotundo*; with rounded phrase.

578. Elegance.—N. elegance, purity, grace, ease, felicity, distinction, gracefulness, refinement, readiness etc. *adj.*; concinnity, euphony, numerosity, balance, rythym, symmetry, proportion; restraint; good taste, propriety.
well rounded —, well turned —, flowing-periods; the right word in the right place; antithesis etc. 577.
purist, stylist.
V. point an antithesis, round a period.
Adj. elegant, polished, classical, Attic, correct, Ciceronian, artistic; chaste, pure, Saxon, academical.

graceful, easy, readable, fluent, flowing, tripping; unaffected, natural, unlabored; mellifluous; euph-onious, -emistic; rhythmical, balanced, symmetrical.
felicitous, happy, neat; well —, neatly- put, — expressed.

579. Inelegance.—N. inelegance; vulgarity, bad taste; stiffness etc. *adj.*; unlettered Muse; barbarism; slang etc. 563; solecism etc. 568; mannerism etc. (*affectation*) 855; euphuism; fustian etc. 577; cacophony; want of balance; words that - break the teeth, — dislocate the jaw.
V. be -inelegant etc. *adj.*
Adj. inelegant, graceless, ungraceful, unpolished; harsh, abrupt; dry, stiff, cramped, formal, *guindé*; forced, labored, awkward; artificial, mannered, ponderous; turgid etc. 577; affected, euphuistic; barbarous, uncouth, grotesque, rude, crude, halting; vulgar, offensive to ears polite.

580. Voice.—N. voice; vocality; organ, lungs, bellows; good -, fine —, powerful etc. (*loud*) 404 —, musical etc. 413- voice; intonation; tone etc. (*sound*) 402- of voice.
vocalization; cry etc. 411; strain, utterance, prolation; exclam-, ejacul-, vocifer-ation; enunci-, articul-ation; articulate sound; distinctness; clearness, — of articulation; stage whisper; delivery; attack.
accent, -uation; emphasis, stress; broad —, strong —, pure —, native —, foreign- accent; pronunciation.
[Word similarly pronounced] homonym.
orthoepy; euphony etc. (*melody*) 413.
gastri-, ventri-loquism; ventriloquist; polyphonism, -ist.
[Science of voice] phonology etc. (*sound*) 402.
V. sing, speak, utter, breathe, voice; give -utterance, — tongue; cry etc. (*shout*) 411; ejaculate, rap out; vocalize, prolate, articulate, enunciate, enounce, pronounce, accentuate, aspirate, deliver, mouth; emit, murmur, whisper, — in the ear, croon, yodel.
Adj. vocal, phonetic, oral; ejaculatory, articulate, distinct, stertorous; enunciative; accentuated, aspirated; euphonious etc. (*melodious*) 413.

581. Aphony—N. aphony, *aphonia*; dumbness etc. *adj.*; obmutescence; absence —, want- of voice; dysphony; silence etc. (*taciturnity*) 585; raucity; harsh etc. 410 —, unmusical etc. 414- voice; *falsetto*, 'childish treble;' mute, dummy, deaf mute.
V. keep silence etc. 585; speak -low, — softly; whisper etc. (*faintness*) 405.
silence; render -mute, — silent etc. 403; muzzle, muffle, suppress, smother, gag, strike dumb, dumbfound, -founder; drown the voice, put to silence, stop one's mouth, cut one short.
stick in the throat.
Adj. aphon-ous, -ic, dumb, mute; deaf-mute, —

and dumb; mum; tongue-tied; breath-, tongue-, voice-, speech-, word-less; mute as a ;fish, – stock-fish, – mackerel; silent etc. (*taciturn*) 585; muzzled; in-articulate, -audible.

croaking, raucous, hoarse, husky, dry, hollow, sepulchral, hoarse as a raven.

Adv. with -bated breath, – the finger on the lips; *sotto voce*; in a -low tone, – cracked voice, – broken voice; in an aside.

Phr. *vox faucibus haesit.*

582. Speech.—N. speech, faculty of speech; locution, talk, parlance, verbal intercourse, prolation, oral communication, word of mouth, *parole*, palaver, prattle; effusion.

oration, recitation, delivery, say, address, speech, lecture, harangue, sermon, *tirade*, screed, formal speech, salutatory, peroration; prelection; speechifying; soliloquy etc. 589; allocution etc. 586; interlocution etc. 588.

oratory; elo-cution, -quence; rhetoric, declamation; grandi-, multi-loquence; burst of eloquence; facundity; talkativeness; flow –, command- of -words, – language; *copia verborum*; power of speech, gift of the gab; *usus loquendi.*

speaker etc. *v.*; spokesman, pro-, inter-locutor; mouthpiece, Hermes; ora-tor, -trix, -tress; Demosthenes, Cicero; rhetorician; stump –, platform- orator, tub-thumper; elocutionist; speechmaker, patterer, *improvisatore.*

V. speak, – of; say, utter, pronounce, deliver, give utterance to; utter –, pour- forth; breathe, let fall, come out with; rap –, blurt- out; have on one's lips; have at the -end, – tip- of one's tongue.

break silence; open one's -lips, – mouth; lift –, raise- one's voice; give –, wag the- tongue; talk, outspeak; put in a word or two.

hold forth; make –, deliver- -a speech etc. *n.*; speechify, harangue, declaim, stump, flourish, spout, rant, recite, lecture, preach, sermonize, discourse, be on one's legs; have – , say- one's say; expatiate etc. (*speak at length*) 573; speak one's mind.

soliloquize etc. 589; tell etc. (*inform*) 527; speak to etc. 586; talk together etc. 588.

be -eloquent etc. *adj.*; have -a tongue in one's head, – the gift of the gab etc. *n.*

pass –, escape- one's lips; fall from the ͡lips, – mouth.

Adj. speaking etc., spoken etc. *v.*; oral, lingual, phonetic, not written, unwritten, outspoken; elo-quent, -cutionary; oral-, rhetorical; declamatory; grandiloquent etc. 577; talkative etc. 584.

Adv. orally etc. *adj.*; by word of mouth, *viva voce*, from the lips of.

Phr. quoth –, said- he etc.

583. Stammering. [Imperfect Speech.]—N. inarticulateness; stammering etc. *v.*; hesitation etc. *v.*; impediment in one's speech; aphasia, titubancy, traulism; whisper etc. (*faint sound*) 405; lisp, drawl, tardiloquence; nasal -tone, – accent; twang; *falsetto* etc. (*want of voice*) 581; broken -voice, – accents, – sentences.

brogue etc. 563; slip of the tongue, *lapsus linguae.*

V. stammer, stutter, hesitate, falter, hammer; balbu-tiate, -cinate; haw, hum and haw, be unable to put two words together.

mumble, mutter; maund, -er; whisper etc. 405; mince, lisp; jabber, gabble, gibber; sp-, spl-utter; muffle, mump; drawl, mouth; croak; speak -thick, – through the nose; snuffle, clip one's words; murder the -language, – King's (*or* Queen's) English; mis-pronounce, -say.

Adj. stammering etc. *v.*; inarticulate, guttural, nasal; tremulous.

Adv. *sotto voce* etc. (*faintly*) 405.

584. Loquacity.—N. loquac-ity, -iousness; talkativeness etc. *adj.*; garrulity; multiloquence, much speaking, effusion, wordiness.

jaw; gab, -ble; jabber, chatter; prate, prattle, cackle, clack; twaddle, trattle, rattle; *caquet, -terie*; blabber, *bavardage*, bibble-babble, gibble-gabble; small talk etc. (*converse*) 588.

fluency, flippancy, volubility, flowing tongue; flow, – of words; *flux de -bouche, – mots, – paroles*; *copia verborum, cacoëthes loquendi*; verbosity etc. (*diffuseness*) 573; gift of the gab etc. (*eloquence*) 582.

talker; chatter-er, -box; babbler etc. *v.*; rattle; ranter; sermonizer, proser, driveller; wind bag; gossip etc. (*converse*) 588; magpie, jay, parrot, poll, Babel; *moulin à paroles.*

V. be -loquacious etc. *adj.*; talk glibly, pour forth, patter; prate, palaver, prose, chatter, prattle, clack, jabber, jaw; rattle, – on; twaddle, twattle; babble, gabble; out-talk; talk oneself -out of breath, – hoarse; maunder, gush, blatter; talk a donkey's hind leg off; expatiate etc. (*speak at length*) 573; gossip etc. (*converse*) 588; din in the ears etc. (*repeat*) 104; talk -at random, – nonsense etc. 497; be hoarse with talking.

Adj. loquacious, talkative, conversational, garrulous, linguacious, multiloquous; chattering etc. *v.*; chatty etc. (*sociable*) 892; declamatory etc. 582; open-mouthed.

fluent, voluble, glib, flippant; long-tongued, -winded etc. (*diffuse*) 573.

Adv. trippingly on the tongue; glibly etc. *adj.*

Phr. the tongue running -fast, – loose, – on wheels.

585. Taciturnity.—N. silence, muteness, obmutescence; taciturnity, pauciloquy, costiveness, curtness; reserve, reticence etc. (*concealment*) 528; *aposiopesis.*

man of few words.

V. be -silent etc. *adj.*; keep silence; hold one's -tongue, – peace, – jaw; not speak etc. 582; say nothing; seal –, close –, put a padlock on- the -lips, – mouth; put a bridle on one's tongue; keep one's tongue between one's teeth; make no sign, not let a word escape one; keep a secret etc. 528; not have a word to say; lay –, place- the finger on the lips; render mute etc. 581.

stick in one's throat.

Adj. silent, mute, mum; silent as -a post, – a stone, – the grave etc. (*still*) 403; dumb etc. 581.

taciturn, sparing of words; close, – mouthed, –

tongued; laconic, costive, inconversable, curt; reserved; reticent etc. (*concealing*) 528.
Inf. tush! silence! mum! hush! *chut!* hist! tut! etc. 403.

586. Allocution.—**N.** allocution, alloquy, address; speech etc. 582; apostrophe, interpellation, appeal, invocation, salutation; word in the ear. [Feigned dialogue] dialogism.
platform etc. 542; audience etc. (*interview*) 588.
V. speak to, address, accost, make up to, apostrophize, appeal to, invoke; hail, salute; call to, halloo.
take -aside, − by the button, button-hole; talk to in private.
lecture etc. (*make a speech*) 582.
Int. soho! halloo! hey! hist! hi!

587. Response etc.; *see* Answer 462

588. Interlocution.—**N.** interlocution; collocution, colloquy, converse, conversation, confabulation, talk, discourse, verbal intercourse; communion, oral communication, commerce; dia-, duo-, tria-logue.
causerie, chat, chit-chat; small −, table −, teatable −, town −, village −, idle- talk; tattle, gossip, tittle-tattle; babble, -ment; *tripotage*, cackle, prittle-prattle, *on dit*; talk of the -town, − village.
conference, parley, interview, audience, *pourparler*; *tête-à-tête*; reception, *conversazione*; congress etc. (*council*) 696; pow-wow.
hall of audience, *durbar*, coliseum, assembly hall, auditorium.
palaver, debate, logomachy, war of words, controversy.
talker, gossip, tattler; Paul Pry; tabby; chatterer etc. (*loquacity*) 584; interlocutor etc. (*spokesman*) 582; conversation-ist, -alist; dialogist.
'the feast of reason and the flow of soul;' *mollia tempora fandi*.
V. talk together, converse, confabulate; hold −, carry on −, join in −, engage in- a conversation; put in a word; shine in conversation; bandy words; parley; palaver; chat, gossip, tattle; prate etc. (*loquacity*) 584.
discourse −, confer −, commune −, commerce- with; hold -converse, − conference, − intercourse; talk it over; be closeted with; talk with one -in private, − tête-à-tête.
Adj. conversing etc. *v.*; interlocutory; conversational, -able; discursive, -coursive; chatty etc. (*sociable*) 892; colloquial, *tête-à-tête*, confabulatory.

589. Soliloquy.—**N.** soliloquy, monologue, apostrophe.
solilo-quist, -quizer, monologist.

V. soliloquize; say −, talk- to oneself; say aside, think aloud, apostrophize.
Adj. soliloquizing etc. *v.*
Adv. aside.

590. Writing.—**N.** writing etc. *v.*; chiro-, stelo-, cero-graphy, graphology; stylography; pen-craft, -script, -manship; quill-driving; typewriting.
writing, manuscript, MS., *literae scriptae*; these presents.
stroke −, dash- of the pen; *coup de plume*; line; pen and ink.
letter etc. 561; uncial writing, cuneiform character, arrow-head, Ogham, Runes, futhorc; hieroglyphic, hieratic, demotic; script; contraction.
short-hand; steno-, brachy-, tachy-graphy; secret writing, writing in cipher; crypt-, stegan-ography; phono-, pasi-, poly-, logo-graphy.
copy; tran-, re-script; draft, rough −, fair- copy; handwriting; signature, sign-manual; auto-, mono-, holo-graph; hand, fist; mark.
calligraphy; good −, running −, flowing −, cursive −, legible −, copperplate −, round −, bold-hand.
cacography, *griffonage*, *barbouillage*; bad −, cramped −, crabbed −, illegible- hand; scribble etc. *v.*; *pattes de mouche*; ill-formed letters; pot-hooks and hangers.
stationery, pen, quill, goose-quill, reed; stylographic-, fountain-pen; pencil, style, stylus; paper, foolscap, parchment, vellum, papyrus, pad, tablet, block, note book, slate, marble, pillar, table, black board.
ink-bottle, -pot, -stand, -well, -horn; typewriter.
transcription etc. (*copy*) 21; inscription etc. (*record*) 551; superscription etc. (*indication*) 550.
composition, authorship; *cacoethes scribendi*.
writer, scribe, amanuensis, scrivener, secretary, clerk, penman, copyist, transcriber, quill-driver; writer for the press etc. '(*author*) 593.
shorthand writer, stenographer; typewriter, typist.
V. write, pen; copy, engross; write out, − fair; transcribe; scribble, scrawl, scrabble, scratch; interline; stain paper; write down etc. (*record*) 551; sign etc. (*attest*) 467; take down, − in shorthand; typewrite, type.
compose, indite, draw up, redact, draft, formulate; dictate; inscribe, throw on paper, dash off; concoct.
take -up the pen, − pen in hand; shed −, spill −, dip one's pen in- ink.
Adj. writing etc. *v.*; written etc. *v.*; in -writing, − black and white; under one's hand.
uncial, Runic, cuneiform, hieroglyphical etc. *n.*
Adv. *currente calamo*; pen in hand.

591. Printing.—**N.** printing; block −, type-printing, lino-, mono-type; plate printing etc. (*engraving*) 558; the press etc. (*publication*) 531; composition.
print, letterpress, text, matter, standing type; context, note, page, column; over-running; head-, foot-line, title.
typography; stereo-, electro-, apro-type; type,

black letter, heavy type, font, fount; pi, pie; capitals etc. (*letters*) 561; diamond, pearl, nonpareil, minion, brevier, bourgeois, long primer, small pica, pica, english, great primer.

folio etc. (*book*) 593; copy, impression, pull, proof, galley –, author's –, page- proof, revise. printer, compositor, reader; printer's devil.

V. print; compose; put –, go- to press; pass –, see- through the press; publish etc. 531; bring out; appear in –, rush into- print.

Adj. printed etc. *v.*; in type; typographical etc. *n.*

592. Correspondence.—N. correspondence, letter, epistle, note, *billet*, post-, letter-card, missive, circular, form letter; favor, *billet-doux*; des-, dis-patch; *bulletin*, communication etc. 532; these presents; rescript, -ion; post etc. (*messenger*) 534; letter writer, correspondent.

V. correspond, – with; write –, send a letter-to; keep up a correspondence; drop a line to; despatch; communicate with; circularize.

Adj. epistolary.

593. Book.—N. book, -let; writing, work, volume, tome, opuscule; tract, -ate; *livret*; *brochure*, *libretto*, handbook, treatise, text-book, codex, manual, pamphlet, monograph, enchiridion, circular, publication; book of poems; novel; chap-book.

part, issue, number, *livraison*; album, portfolio; periodical, serial, magazine, *ephemeris*, annual, journal.

paper, bill, sheet, broadsheet, screed; leaf, -let; fly-leaf, page; quire, ream.

chapter, section, head, article, paragraph, passage, clause, supplement, appendix; *feuilleton*. folio, quarto, octavo; duo-, sexto-, octo-decimo.

en-, cyclopedia, dictionary, lexicon, thesaurus, concordance, anthology, bibliography; compilation, compendium, catalogue etc. 86; library, bibliotheca; the press etc. (*publication*) 531.

writer, author, *littérateur*, essayist, journalist, publicist; scribe, penman, war –, special –, correspondent; pen, scribbler, the scribbling race; ghost, hack, literary hack, Grub-street writer; writer for –, gentlemen of –, representative of- the press; reporter, penny-a-liner; editor, sub-editor; playwright etc. 599; poet etc. 597.

bookseller, publisher; biblio-pole, -polist, - grapher; librarian; book -collector, – worm.

book -shop, – club, circulating –, lending –, public- library; publishing house.

knowledge of books, bibliography; book-learning etc. (*knowledge*) 490.

594. Description.—N. description, account, statement, report; *exposé* etc. (*disclosure*) 529; specification, particulars, scenario, plot; state –, summary- of facts; brief etc. (*abstract*) 596; return etc. (*record*) 551; *catalogue raisonné* etc. (*list*) 86; guide-book etc. (*information*) 527.

delineation etc. (*representation*) 554; sketch, vignette; monograph; minute –, detailed –, particular –, circumstantial –, graphic- account; narration, recital, rehearsal, relation.

histori-, chron-ography; historic Muse, Clio; history; bi-, autobi-ography; necrology, obituary. narrative, history; memoir, memorials; annals etc. (*chronicle*) 551; tradition, legend, saga, epic, epos, story, tale, historiette; personal narrative, journal, letters, life, adventures, fortunes, experiences, confessions; anecdote, ana, *trait*.

work of -fiction, short story, novelette, novel, romance, penny dreadful, shilling, shocker, Minerva press; fairy –, nursery- tale; fable, allegory, parable, apologue.

relator etc. *v.*; *raconteur*; historian etc. (*recorder*) 553; biographer, fabulist, novelist, story teller, romancer, teller of tales, spinner of yarns, anecdotist.

V. describe; set forth etc. (*state*) 535; draw a picture, picture; portray etc. (*represent*) 554; characterize, particularize; narrate, relate, recite, recount, sum up, run over, recapitulate, rehearse, fight one's battles over again.

unfold etc. (*disclose*) 529- a tale; tell; give –, render- an account of; report, make a report, draw up a statement.

detail; enter into –, descend to- -particulars, –details.

Adj. descriptive, graphic, narrative, epic, suggestive, well-drawn; historic; auto-, biographical, realistic, expository, tradition-al, -ary; legendary; fabulous, mythical; anecdotic, storied; described etc. *v.*

595. Dissertation.—N. dissertation, treatise, essay; *thesis*, theme; tract, -ate, -ation, excursus; discourse, memoir, disquisition, lecture, sermon, homily, pandect.

commentary, review, *critique*, criticism, article; lead-er, -ing article, editorial; argument, running commentary.

investigation etc. (*inquiry*) 461; study etc. (*consideration*) 451; discussion etc. (*reasoning*) 476; exposition etc. (*explanation*) 522.

commentator, critic, essayist, pamphleteer; publicist, reviewer, leader writer, editor, annotator.

V. dissert –, descant –, write –, touch- upon a subject; dissertate; treat of –, take up –, ventilate –, discuss –, deal with –, go into –, canvass –, handle –, do justice to- a subject; comment, criticize, interpret-etc. 522.

Adj. dis-cursive, -coursive; disquisitional, disquisitionary; expository, critical.

596. Compendium.—N. compend, -ium; abstract, *précis*, epitome, *multum in parvo*, analysis, pandect, digest, sum and substance, brief, abridgment, summary, *aperçu*, draft, minute, note; synopsis, textbook, *conspectus*, outlines, syllabus, contents, heads, prospectus.

album; scrap –, note –, memorandum –, commonplace- book; extracts, *excerpta*, cuttings; fugitive -pieces, – writings; *spicilegium*, flowers, anthology, miscellany, *collectanea, analecta*; compilation.

recapitulation, *résumé*, review.

abbrevia-tion, -ture; contraction; shortening etc. 201; compression etc. 195.

V. abridge, abstract, epitomize, summarize; make –, prepare –, draw –, compile- an abstract etc. *n.*

recapitulate, review, skim, run over, sum up. abbreviate etc. (*shorten*) 201; condense etc. (*compress*) 195; compile etc. (*collect*) 72; edit, blue pencil.

Adj. compendious, synoptic, analectic, analytical; abridged etc. *v.*

Adv. in -short, – epitome, – substance, – few words.

Phr. it lies in a nutshell.

597. Poetry.—N. poetry, poetics, poesy, Muse, Calliope, tuneful Nine, Parnassus, Helicon, Pierides, Pierian spring, afflatus, inspiration.

versification, rhyming, making verses; prosody, scansion, orthometry.

poem; epic, – poem; epopee, *epopaea*, ode, epode, idyl, lyric, éclogue, pastoral, bucolic, georgic, dithyramb, anacreontic, sonnet, roundelay, *rondel, rondoletto, rondeau, rondo*, triolet; madrigal, canzonet, *cento*, monody, elegy, palinode; rhapsody.

dramatic –, lyric- poetry; opera; posy, anthology.

song, ballad, lay; love –, drinking –, war –, folk –, sea- song; lullaby; music etc. 415; nursery rhymes.

[Bad poetry] doggerel, Hudibrastic verse, prose run mad; macaronics; macaronic –, leonineverse; runes.

canto, stanza, distich, verse, line, couplet, triplet, quatrain, sestet; *strophe, antistrophe*, refrain, chorus, burden.

verse, rhyme, assonance, crambo, meter, measure, foot, numbers, strain, rhythm; accentuation etc. (*voice*) 580; iambus, dactyl, spondee, trochee, anapaest etc.; hex-, pent-ameter; Alexandrine; blank verse, alliteration.

elegiacs etc. *adj.*; elegiac etc. *adj.* -verse, – meter, – poetry.

poet, – laureate; laureate; minor poet, bard, lyrist, scald, troubadour, *trouvère*; mistrel; minne-, meister-singer; *improvisatore*; versifier, sonneteer; ballad monger; rhym-er, -ist, -ester; poetaster.

V. poetize, sing, versify, make verses, rhyme, scan.

Adj. poetic, -al; lyric, -al; tuneful; epic; dithyrambic etc. *n.*; metrical; a-, catalectic; elegiac, iambic, trochaic, spondaic, anapest; Ionic, Sapphic, Alcaic, Pindaric.

598. Prose.—N. prose, – writer, pros-aism, - aist, -er.

V. prose, write prose.

write -prose, – in prose.

Adj. pros-y, -aic; unpoetical.

rhymeless, unrhymed, in prose, not in verse.

599. Drama.—N. drama, the -drama, – stage,

– theater, – play; theatricals, dramaturgy, histrionic art, buskin, sock, *cothurnus*, Melpomene and Thalia, Thespis.

play, stage-play, piece, five-act play, tragedy, comedy, opera, comic opera, *vaudeville, comedietta, lever de rideau*, curtain raiser, interlude, afterpiece, exode, farce, *divertissement, extravaganza*, burletta, harlequinade, pantomime, mimodrama, burlesque, *opéra bouffe*, musical comedy, review, revue, intimate revue, variety, cabaret entertainment, *ballet, spectacle*, masque, *drame, comédie drame*; melo-drama, -drame; *comédie larmoyante*, emotional drama, sensation drama, tragi-, farcical-comedy; mono-drame, - logue; duologue; trilogy; charade, *proverbe*; mystery, miracle –, morality-, play.

act, scene, *tableau*; in-, intro-duction; pro-, epilogue, curtain; *libretto*, book, script.

performance, representation, show, *mise en scène*, stagery, *jeu de théâtre*, stage-craft; acting; gesture etc. 550; impersonation etc. 554; stage business, gag, patter, buffoonery.

theater; play-, opera-house; house; music hall; *cabaret*; amphitheater, circus, hippodrome; puppet-show, *fantoccini*; *marionnettes*, Punch and Judy.

cinema, -tograph-, picture –, theater, the pictures, the movies, the talkies.

auditory, *auditorium*, front of the house, stalls, boxes, balcony, dress –, upper- -circle, – boxes, amphitheater, pit, gallery; *foyer*; greenroom; dressing rooms, *coulisses*.

flat; drop, – scene; wing, screen, side-scene; transformation scene, curtain, act-drop, safety –, fire- curtain; *proscenium*, forestage.

stage, revolving stage, scene, the boards; star –, grave –, trap, mezzanine floor; flies; gridiron, floats, battens, footlights; lime –, spot –, flood –, bunch-lights; scenery, set, *décor*; orchestra.

theatrical -costume, – properties, props.

part, *rôle*, character, cast, *dramatis personae*; *répertoire.*

actor, player; stage –, strolling- player; old –, stager, performer; mime, -r; *artiste*; com-, tragedian, straight man; *tragédienne*, Thespian, Roscius, star.

pantomimist, clown, harlequin, *buffo*, buffoon, *farceur, grimacier*, pantaloon, columbine; *Pierrot, Pierrette*; punch, -inello; *pulcinell-o, -a*; mute, *figurante*, general utility; super, -numerary, extra.

mummer, guiser, guisard, gysart. masque.

mountebank, Jack Pudding; tumbler, posturemaster, acrobat, equilibrist, juggler, contortionist; *danseuse, ballerina*, ballet -dancer, – girl; *coryphée; bayadère, geisha*; chorus -singer, – girl.

company; first tragedian, *prima donna*; lead, leading lady, protagonist; *jeune premier*; juvenile lead, *débutant, -e*; light –, genteel –, low- -comedy, – comedian; *soubrette*, walking gentleman, *amoroso*, heavy, heavy father, *ingénue, jeune veuve, commère, compère.*

property man, *costumier*, machinist, stage hand, electrician, prompter, call-boy; director, manager; stage –, acting –, business- manager; *entrepreneur, impresario*, producer, press agent dramatic -author, – writer; play-writer, -wright; dramatist, mimographer; dramatic critic.

V. act, play, perform; stage, produce, put on the stage; personate etc. 554; mimic etc. (*imitate*) 19; enact; play –, act –, go through –, perform- a part; rehearse, spout, gag, rant; 'strut and fret one's hour upon a stage;' tread the -stage, – boards; come out;, star.

Adj. dramatic; theatric, -al; scenic, histrionic, anctorial, comic, tragic, buskined, farcical, tragi-comic, melodramatic, operatic; stagey spectacular; stagestruck.

Adv. on the -stage, – boards; before -the floats, – an audience; in the limelight, behind the footlights; behind the scenes.

600. Will.—N. will, volition, conation, velleity; will and pleasure, free-will; freedom etc. 748; discretion; choice, inclination, intent, purpose, option etc. (*choice*) 609; voluntariness; spontane-ity, -ousness; originality.

pleasure, wish, desire, mind; frame of mind etc. (*inclination*) 602; intention etc. 620; predeter-mination etc. 611; self-control etc. determination etc. (*resolution*) 604; will-power.

V. will, list; see – , think- -fit; determine etc. (*resolve*) 604; settle etc. (*choose*) 609; volunteer.

have a will of one's own; do what one chooses etc. (*freedom*) 748; have it all one's own way; have one's -will, – own way.

use – , exercise- one's discretion; take -upon oneself, – one's own course, – the law into one's own hands; do -of one's own accord, – upon one's own -responsibility, – authority; take the bit between one's teeth; take responsibility; originate etc. (*cause*) 153.

Adj. voluntary, volitive, volitional, wilful; free etc. 748; optional; discretion-al, -ary; volitient; dictatorial.

minded etc. (*willing*) 602; prepense etc. (*predetermined*) 611; intended etc. 620; autocratic; unbidden etc. (bid etc. 741); spontaneous; original etc. (*causal*) 153.

Adv. voluntarily etc. *adj.*; at -will, – pleasure; *à -volonté*, – *discretion*; *al piacere*; *ad -libitum*, – *arbitrium*; as -one thinks proper, – it seems good to.

of one's own -accord, – free will; *proprio -*, *suo -*, *ex mero- motu*; out of one's own head; by choice etc. 609; purposely etc. (*intentionally*) 620; deliberately etc. 611.

Phr. *stet pro ratione voluntas*; *sic volo sic jubeo*.

601. Necessity.—N. involuntariness; instinct, blind –, natural- impulse; inborn –, innate-proclivity; the force of circumstances.

necessi-ty, -tation, necessarianism; obligation; compulsion etc. 744; subjection etc. 749; stern –, hard –, dire –, imperious –, inexorable –, iron –, adverse- -necessity, – fate; what must be.

desti-ny, -nation; fatality, fate, *kismet*, doom, foredoom, election, predestination; pre-, foreordination; lot, fortune; fatalism, determinism; inevitableness etc. *adj.*; spell etc. 993.

star, -s; planet, -s; astral influence; sky, Fates, Norns, *Parcae*, Sisters three, Clotho, Lachesis, Atropos; book of fate; God's will, will of Heaven; wheel of Fortune, Ides of March, Hobson's choice.

last -shift, – resort; *dernier ressort*; *pis aller*

etc. (*substitute*).147; necessaries etc. (*requirement*) 630.

necess-arian, -itarian; fatalist, determinist; automaton.

V. lie under a necessity; be -fated, – doomed, – destined etc., – in for, – under the necessity of; have no -choice, – alternative; be- obliged –, forced –, driven –, one's -fate etc. *n.*- to; be -pushed to the wall, – driven into a corner, – unable to help, – drawn irresistibly.

destine, doom, foredoom, devote; pre-destine, -ordain; cast a spell etc. 992; necessitate; compel etc. 744.

Adj. necessary; needful etc. (*requisite*) 630. fated; destined etc. *v.*; fateful; elect; spell-bound. compulsory etc. (*compel*) 744; uncontrollable, inevitable, unavoidable, irréstible, irrevocable, inexorable, binding; avoid-, resist-less; written in the book of fate.

involuntary, instinctive, automatic, blind, mechanical; un-conscious, -witting, -thinking; unintentional etc. (*undesigned*) 621; impulsive etc. 612.

Adv. necessarily etc. *adv.*; of -necessity, – course; *ex necessitate rei*; needs must; perforce etc. 744; *nolens volens*; will he nil he, willy nilly, *bon gré mal gré*, willing or unwilling, *coûte que coûte*, forcefully.

faute de mieux; by stress of; if need be.

Phr. it cannot be helped; there is no- help for, – helping- it; it -will, – must, – must needs- be, – be so, – have its way; the die is cast; *jacta est alea*; *che sarà sarà*; 'it is written;' one's- days are numbered, – fate is sealed; *Fata obstant*; *diis aliter visum*.

602. Willingness.—N. willingness, voluntariness etc. *adj.*; willing mind, heart.

disposition, inclination, leaning, *animus*; frame of mind, humor, mood, vein; bent etc. (*turn of mind*) 820; *penchant* etc. (*desire*) 865; aptitude etc. 698.

doc-ility, -ibleness, tractability; persuasi-bleness, -bility;. pliability etc. (*softness*) 324.

geniality, cordiality; goodwill; alacrity, readiness, earnestness, forwardness, enthusiasm; zeal, eagerness etc. (*desire*) 865.

assent etc. 488; compliance etc. 762; pleasure etc. (*will*) 600.

labor of love, self-appointed task; volunteer, -ing, gratuitous service; unpaid worker, amateur.

V. be -willing etc. *adj.*; incline, lean to, mind, propend; had as lief; lend –, give –, turn- a willing ear; have -a, – half a, – a great- mind to; hold –, cling- to; desire etc. 865.

see –, think- -good, – fit, – proper; acquiescence etc. (*assent*) 488; comply with etc. 762.

swallow –, nibble at- the bait; gorge the hook; swallow hook, line and sinker; have –, make- no scruple of; make no bones of; jump –, catch- at; meet half way; volunteer, offer oneself etc. 763.

Adj. willing, minded, fain, disposed, inclined, favorable, favorably- minded, -inclined, -disposed; nothing loth; in the -vein, – mood, – humor, – mind.

ready, forward, enthusiastic, earnest, eager; bent upon etc. (*desirous*) 865; predisposed, propense.

docile; persua-dable, -sible; suasible, easily persuaded, facile, easy-going; amenable; tractable etc.
(*pliant*) 324; genial, gracious, cordial, hearty; content etc. (*assenting*) 488.

voluntary, gratuitous, spontaneous; unasked etc.
(ask etc. 765); unforced etc. (*free*) 748.

Adv. willing etc. *adj.*; fain, freely, as lief, heart
and soul; with -pleasure, – all one's heart, – open
arms; with -good, – right good- will; *de bonne
volonté, ex animo; con amore,* heart in hand,
nothing loth, without reluctance, of one's own accord, graciously, with a good grace, without demur.

à la bonne heure; by all -means, – manner of
means; to one's heart's content; yes etc. (*assent*)
488.

Int. 'sure, -ly! of course!

603. Unwillingness.—N. unwillingness etc.
adj.; indispos-ition, -edness; disinclination, aver-
sation, aversion; nolleity, nolition; renitence; reluctance; indifference etc. 866; backwardness etc.
adj.; slowness etc. 275; want of -alacrity, –
readiness; indocility etc. (*obstinacy*) 606.

scrupul-ousness, -osity; qualms of conscience,
delicacy, demur, scruple, qualm, shrinking, recoil;
hesitation etc. (*irresolution*) 605; fastidiousness
etc. 868.

averseness etc. (*dislike*) 867; dissent etc. 489;
refusal etc. 764.

slacker, scrimshanker, *embusqué,* unwilling
worker, forced labor.

V. be -unwilling etc. *adj.*; nill; dislike etc. 867;
grudge, begrudge; not be able to find it in one's
heart to, not have the stomach to.

demur, stick at, scruple, stickle; hang fire, run
rusty, slack, shirk, scamp, give up, fight shy of, not
pull fair; recoil, shrink, swerve; hesitate etc. 605;
avoid etc. 623.

oppose etc. 708; dissent etc. 489; refuse etc.
764.

Adj. unwilling; not in the vein, loth, shy of,
disinclined, indisposed, averse, reluctant, not content; adverse etc. (*opposed*) 708; laggard, back-
ward, remiss, slack, slow to; renitent; indifferent
etc. 866; scrupulous; squeamish etc. (*fastidious*)
868; repugnant etc. (*dislike*) 867; rest-jff, -ive;
demurring etc. *v.*; unconsenting etc. (*refusing*)
764; involuntary etc. 601; grudging, irreconcilable.

Adv. unwilling etc. *adj.*; grudgingly, with a
heavy heart; with -á bad, – an ill- grace; against
–, sore against- -one's wishes, – one's will, – the
grain; *invitâ Minervâ; à contre coeur; malgré soi;*
in spite of -one's teeth, – oneself; *nolens volens*
etc. (*necessity*) 601; perforce etc. 744; under
protest; no etc. 536; not for the world, far be it
from me; not if I can help it; if I must I must.

604. Resolution.—N. determination, will; iron
–, unconquerable-' will; will of one's own,
decision, resolution, backbone, grit; strength of -
mind, – will; resolve etc. (*intent*) 620; *intransigeance;* firmness etc. (*stability*) 150; energy,
manliness, vigor; game, pluck; resoluteness etc.
(*courage*) 861; zeal etc. 682; *aplomb*; desperation;
devot-ion, -edness.

mastery over self; self-control, -command, -

mastery, -possession, -reliance, -government, -
restraint, -conquest, -denial; moral -courage, –
strength, – fiber; perseverance etc. 604*a*; tenacity;
obstinacy etc. 606; bull-dog; British lion.

V. have -determination etc. *n.*; know one's own
mind; be -resolved etc. *adj.*; make up one's mind,
will resolve, determine; decide etc. (*judgment*)
480; form –, come to- a -determination, –
resolution, – resolve; conclude, fix, seal, determine once for all, bring to a crisis, drive matters to
an extremity; take a decisive step etc. (*choice*) 609;
take upon oneself etc. (*undertake*) 676.

devote oneself –, give oneself up- to; throw
away the scabbard, kick down the ladder, nail
one's colors to the mast, set one's back against the
wall, set one's teeth, put one's foot down, burn
one's bridges, take one's stand; stand firm etc.
(*stability*) 150; steel oneself; stand no nonsense,
not listen to the voice of the charmer.

buckle to; put –, lay –, set- one's shoulder to
the wheel; put one's heart into; run the gantlet,
make a dash at, take the bull by the horns; beard
the lion in his den; rush –, plunge- *in medias res;*
go in for; insist upon, make a point of; set one's
heart, – mind- upon.

stick at nothing; make short work of etc. (*activity*) 682; not stick at trifles; go -all lengths, –
the whole hog; persist etc. (*persevere*) 604*a*; go
down with colors flying, die game; go through fire
and water, ride in the whirlwind and direct the
storm.

Adj. resolved etc. *v.* determined; strong-willed, -
minded; resolute etc. (*brave*) 861; self-possessed,
plucky, tenacious; decided, definitive, peremptory;
un-hesitating, -flinching, -shrinking; firm, cast iron,
indomitable, game to the backbone; inexorable,
relentless, not to be -shaken, – put down; *tenax
propositi;* inflexible etc. (*hard*) 323; obstinate etc.
606; steady etc. (*persevering*) 604*a*; unbending,
unyielding, irrevocable; firm as a rock; grim.

earnest, serious; set –, bent –, intent- upon.
steeled –, proof- against; *in utrumque paratus.*

Adv. resolutely etc. *adj.*; in –, in good- earnest;
seriously, joking apart, earnestly, heart and soul; on
one's metal; manfully, like a man, with a high
hand; with a strong hand etc. (*exertion*) 686.

at any -rate, – risk, – hazard, – price, –
cost, – sacrifice; at all -hazards, – risks, –
events; cost what it may; *coûte que coûte; à tort et
à travers;* once for all; neck or nothing; rain or
shine; with colors nailed to the mast.

Phr. *spes sibi quisque.*

604a. Perseverance. —N. perseverance; continuance etc. (*inaction*) 143; permanence etc. (*absence of change*) 141; firmness etc. (*stability*) 150.

constancy, steadiness; singleness –, tenacity- of
purpose; persistence, plodding, patience; sedulity
etc. (*industry*) 682; pertina-cy, -city, -ciousness;
iteration etc. 104.

bottom, game, pluck, stamina, backbone, grit;
indefatiga-bility, -bleness; bulldog courage.

V. persevere, persist; hold -on, – out; die in the
last ditch, be in at the death; stick –, cling –,
adhere- to ; stick to one's text, keep on; keep to –,
maintain- one's -course, – ground; bear –, keep
–, hold-up; plod; stick to work etc. (*work*) 686;

continue etc. 143; follow up; die -in harness, – at one's post.

Adj. persevering, constant; stead-y, -fast; un-deviating, -wavering, -faltering, -swerving, - flinching, -sleeping, -flagging, -drooping; steady as time; uninter-, un-remitting; plodding; industrious etc. 682; strenuous etc. 686; pertinacious; persist-ing, -ent.

solid, sturdy, staunch, stanch, ture to oneself; un-changeable etc. 150; unconquerable etc. (*strong*) 159; indomitable, game to the last, indefatigable, untiring, unwearied, never tiring.

Adv. through -evil report and good report, – thick and thin, – fire and water; *per fas et nefas*; without fail, sink or swim, at any price, *vogue la galère*; in sickness and in health.

Phr. never say die; *vestigia nulla retrorsum.*

605. Irresolution.—N. irresolution, infirmity of purpose, indecision; in-, un-determination, loss of will power; unsettlement; uncertainty etc. 475; demur, suspense; hesi-tating etc. *v.*, -tation, -tancy; vacillation; ambivalence; changeableness etc. 149; fluctuation; alternation etc. (*oscillation*) 314; caprice etc. 608; lukewarmness.

fickleness, levity, *légèreté*; pliancy etc. (*softness*) 324; weakness; timidity etc. 860; cowardice etc. 862; half measures.

waverer, ass between two bundles of hay; shut-tlecock, butterfly; timeserver, opportunist, turn coat.

V. be -irresolute etc. *adj.*; hang –, keep- in suspense; heave '*ad referendum*;' think twice about, pause; dawdle etc. (*inactivity*) 683; remain neuter; dilly dally. hesitate, boggle, hover, wobble, shilly-shally, hum and haw, demur, not know one's own mind; debate, balance; dally –, coquet- with; will and will not, *chasser-balancer*; go half-way, compromise, make a compromise; be thrown off one's balance, stagger like a drunken man; be afraid etc. 860; let 'I dare not' wait upon 'I would;' falter, waver.

vacillate etc. 149; change etc. 140; retract etc. 607; fluctuate; alternate etc. (*oscillate*) 314; keep off and on, play fast and loose; blow hot and cold etc. (*caprice*) 608.

shuffle, palter, blink; trim.

Adj. irresolute, infirm of purpose, double-minded, half-hearted; un-decided, -resolved, - determined; drifting; shilly-shally; fidgety, tremulous; wobbly; hesitating etc. *v.*; off one's balance; at a loss etc. (*uncertain*) 475.

vacillating etc. *v.*; unsteady etc. (*changeable*) 149; unsteadfast, fickle, unreliable, irresponsible, unstable, without ballast; capricious etc. 608; volatile, frothy; light, -some, -minded; giddy; fast and loose.

weak, feeble-minded, frail; timid etc. 860; cowardly etc. 862; facile; pliant etc. (*soft*) 324; unable to say 'no,' easy-going.

revocable, reversible.

Adv. irresolutely etc. *adj.*; irresolvedly; in faltering accents; off and on; from pillar to post; see-saw etc. 314.

Int. 'how happy could I be with either!'

606. Obstinacy.—N. obstinateness etc. *adj.*; obstinacy, tenacity; perseverance etc. 604*a*; im-

movability; old school; inflexibility etc. (*hardness*) 323; obdur-acy, -ation; dogged resolution; resolution etc. 604; ruling passion; blind side.

self-will, contumacy, perversity; pervica-cy, -city; indocility.

bigotry, intolerance, dogmatism; opinia-try, - tiveness; fixed idea etc.; intractibility, in-corrigibility; (*prejudgment*) 481; fanaticism, zealotry, infatuation, monománia, opinionativeness.

mule; opin-ionist, -ionatist, -iator, -ator; stickler, dogmatist, die-hard, bitter-ender; bigot; zealot, en-thusiast, fanatic.

V. be -obstinate etc. *adj.*; stickle, take no denial, fly in the face of facts; opinionate, be wedded to an opinion, hug a belief; have one's own way etc. (*will*) 600; persist etc. (*persevere*) 604*a*; have –, insist on having- the last word.

die -hard, – fighting, fight -against destiny, – to the last ditch; not yield an inch, stand out.

Adj. obstinate, tenacious, stubborn, obdurate, case-hardened; inflexible etc. (*hard*) 323; im-movable, not to be moved; inert etc. 172; un-changeable etc. 150; inexorable etc. (*determined*) 604; mulish, obstinate as a mule, pig-headed.

dogged; sullen, sulky; un-moved, -influenced, - affected.

wilful, self-willed, perverse; res-ty, -tive, -tiff; pervicacious, wayward, refractory, unruly; head-y, -strong; *entete*; contumacious; cross-grained.

arbitrary, dogmatic, opinionated, positive, bigoted; prejudiced etc. 481; prepossessed, in-fatuated; stiff-backed, -necked, -hearted; hard-mouthed, hidebound; unyielding; im-pervious, - practicable, -persuasible; unpersuadable; in-, un-tractable; incorrigible, deaf to advice, impervious to reason; crotchety etc. 608.

Adv. obstinately etc. *adj.*

Phr. *non possumus*; no surrender.

607. Tergiversation.—N. change of -mind, – intention, – purpose; afterthought.

tergiversation, recantation; palinode, -ody; renunciation; abjur-ation, -ement; defection etc. (*relinquishment*) 624; going over etc. *v.*; apostasy; retract-ion, -ation; withdrawal, disavowal etc. (*negation*) 536; revo-cation, -kement; reversal; repentance etc. 950; *redintegratio amoris.*

coquetry, flirtation; vacillation etc. 605; back-sliding, recidivation.

turn-coat, -tippet; rat, apostate, renegade, mugwump; con-, per-vert; proselyte, deserter; backslider, recidivist; black leg.

time-server, -pleaser; timist, Vicar of Bray, trim-mer, ambidexter; weathercock etc. (*changeable*) 149; Janus.

V. change one's -mind, – intention, – purpose, – note; abjure, renounce; withdraw from etc. (*relinquish*) 624; wheel –, turn –, veer- round; turn a pirouette; go over –; pass –, change –, skip- from one side to another; go to the right about; box the compass, shift one's ground, go upon another tack; back down, crawl, crawfish.

apostatize, change sides, go over, rat; recant, retract; revoke; rescind etc. (*abrogate*) 756; recall, forswear, abjure, unsay; come -over, – round- to an opinion.

draw in one's horns, eat one's words; eat –

swallow- the leek; swerve, flinch, back out of, retrace one's steps, think better of it; come back –, return- to one's first love; turn over a new leaf etc. (*repent*) 950;

trim, shuffle, play fast and loose, blow hot and cold, coquet, flirt, hold with the hare but run with the hounds; straddle; *nager entre deux eaux*; wait to see how the -cat jumps, – wind blows.

Adj. changeful etc. 149; irresolute etc. 605; ductile, slippery as an eel, trimming, ambidextrous, timeserving; coquetting etc. *v.*

revocatory, reactionary.

Phr. 'a change came o'er the spirit of my dream.'

608. Caprice.—**N.** caprice, fancy, humor; whim, -sey, -wham; crotchet, *capriccio*, quirk, freak, maggot, fad, vagary, prank, fit, flim-flam, *escapade*, *boutade*, wild-goose chase; capriciousness etc. *adj.*; kink.

V. be -capricious etc. *adj.*; have a maggot in the brain; take it into one's head, strain at a gnat and swallow a camel; blow hot and cold; play -fast and loose, – fantastic tricks.

Adj. capricious; erratic, eccentric, fitful, hysterical; full of -whims etc. *n.*; maggoty; inconsistent, fanciful, fantastic, whimsical, crotchety, particular, humorsome, freakish, skittish, wanton, wayward; contrary; captious; arbitrary; unrestrained, undisciplined; not amenable to reason; uncomfortable etc. 83; penny wise and pound foolish; fickle etc. (*irresolute*) 605; frivolous, sleeveless, giddy, volatile.

Adv. by fits and starts, without rhyme or reason, at one's own sweet will.

Phr. *nil fuit unquam six impar sibi*; the deuce is in him.

609. Choice.—**N.** choice, option; discretion etc. (*volition*) 600; preoption; alternative; dilemma; *ambarras de choix*; adoption, co-optation; novation; decision etc. (*judgment*) 480.

election, poll, ballot, vote, voice, suffrage, plumper, cumulative vote; *plebiscitum*, *plébiscite*, *vox populi*; *referendum*, electioneering; voting etc. *v.*; franchise; ballot box; slate, ticket.

selection, excerption, gleaning, eclecticism; *excerpta*, gleanings, cuttings, scissors and paste; pick etc. (*best*) 650.

preference, prelation; predilection etc. (*desire*) 865.

V. offer for one's choice, set before; hold out –, present –, offer- the alternative; put to the vote.

use –, exercise –, one's- discretion, – option; adopt, take up, embrace, espouse; choose, elect, co-opt; take –, make- one's choice; make choice of, fix upon.

vote, poll, hold up one's hand; divide.

settle; decide etc. (*adjudge*) 480; list etc. (*will*) 600; make up one's mind etc. (*resolve*) 604.

select; pick, – and choose; pick –, single- out, excerpt; cull, glean, winnow; sift –, separate –, winnow- the chaff from the wheat; pick up, pitch upon; pick one's way; indulge one's fancy.

set apart, reserve, mark out for; mark etc. 550.

prefer; have -rather, – as lief; fancy etc. (*desire*) 865; be persuaded etc. 615.

take a -decided, – decisive- step; commit oneself to a course; pass –, cross- the Rubicon; cast in one's lot with; take for better or for worse.

Adj. optional; co-optative; discretional etc. (*voluntary*) 600; on approval.

eclectic; choosing etc. *v.*; preferential; chosen etc. *v.*; choice etc. (*good*) 648.

Adv. optionally etc. *adj.*; at pleasure etc. (*will*) 600; either, – the one or the other; or; at the option of; whether or not; once for all; for one's money.

by -choice, – preference; in preference; rather, before.

609a. Absence of Choice.—**N.** no –, Hobson's- choice; first come, first served; necessity etc. 601; not a pin to choose etc. (*equality*) 27; any, the first that comes.

neutrality, indifference; indecision etc. (*irresolution*) 605.

V. be -neutral etc. *adj.*; have no choice; waive, not vote; abstain –, refrain- from voting; leave undecided; make a virtue of necessity.

Adj. neu-tral, -ter; indifferent; undecided etc. (*irresolute*) 605.

Adv. either etc. (*choice*) 609.

610. Rejection.—**N.** rejection, repudiation, exclusion; declination; refusal etc. 764.

V. reject; set –, lay- aside; give up; decline etc. (*refuse*) 764; exclude, except, eliminate; pluck, spin; cast.

repudiate, scout, set at naught; fling –, cast –, thrown –, toss- -to the winds, – to the dogs, – overboard, – away; send to the right about; disclaim etc. (*deny*) 536; discard etc. (*eject*) 297, (*have done with*) 678.

Adj. rejected etc. *v.*; reject-aneous, -itious; not -chosen etc. 609, – to be thought of; out of the question.

Adv. neither, – the one nor the other; no etc. 536.

Phr. *non haec in foedera.*

611. Predetermination.—**N.** premeditation, -deliberation, -determination, -destination; foreordination; foregone conclusion; *parti pris*; resolve, propendency; intention etc. 620; project etc. 626.

V. pre-determine, -destine, -meditate, -resolve, -concert; foreordain; resolve beforehand.

Adj. pre-pense, -meditated etc. *v.*, -designed; advised, studied, designed, calculated; aforethought; intended etc. 620; foregone.

well-laid, -devised, -weighed; maturely considered; cut and dried; cunning.

Adv. advisedly etc. *adj.*; with premeditation, deliberately, all things considered, with eyes open, in cold blood; intentionally etc. 620.

612. Impulse.—**N.** impulse, sudden thought; *impromptu*, improvisation; inspiration, hunch, flash, spurt.

improvisatore, *improvisatrice*, improviser, extemporizer; creature of impulse.
V. flash on the mind.
say what comes uppermost; improvise, extemporize; rise to the occasion; spurt.
Adj. extemporaneous, impulsive, indeliberate; improvis-ed, -ate, -atory; un-, unpre-meditated; *improvisé*; unprompted, -guided; natural, unguarded; spontaneous etc. (*voluntary*) 600; instinctive etc. 601.
Adv. extem-pore, -poraneously; offhand, *impromptu, à l'improviste*; improviso; on the spur of the -moment, – occasion.

613. Habit.—N. habit, -ude; assuetude, - faction; wont; run, way.
common –, general –, natural –, ordinary –, habitual- -course, – run, – state- of things; matter of course; beaten -path, – track, – ground.
prescription, custom, use, usage, immemorial usage, practice; tradition; prevalence, observance; conventionalism, -ity; mode, fashion, vogue; *etiquette* etc. (*gentility*) 852; order of the day, cry; conformity etc. 82.
habitué, addict.
one's old way, old school, consuetude, *veteris vestigia flammae; laudator temporis acti.*
rule, standing order, precedent, routine; red-tape, -tapism; pipe-clay; rut, groove.
cacoëthes; bad –, confirmed –, inveterate –, intrinsic etc. 5- habit; addiction, trick.
training etc. (*education*) 537; seasoning, hardening, inurement; radication; second nature, acclimatization; knack etc. (*skill*) 698.
V. be -wont etc. *adj.*
fall into a custom etc. (*conform to*) 82; tread –, follow- the beaten -track, – path; *stare super antiquas vias*; move in a rut, run on in a groove, go round like a horse in a mill, go on in the old job-trot way.
habituate, inure, harden, season, caseharden; accustom, familiarize; naturalize, acclimatize; keep one's hand in; train etc. (*educate*) 537.
get into the -way, – knack- of; learn etc. 539; cling –, adhere- to; repeat etc. 104; acquire –, contract –, fall into- a -habit, – trick; addict oneself –, take- to; accustom oneself to.
be -habitual etc. *adj.*; prevail; come into use, become a habit, take root; gain –, grow- upon one.
Adj. habitual; ac-, customary; prescriptive; accustomed etc. *v.*; traditional; of -daily, – every-day- occurrence; wonted, usual, general, ordinary, common, frequent, every-day, household, jog-trot; well-trodden, -known; familiar, vernacular, trite, commonplace, banal, bromidic, conventional, regular, set, stock, officinal, established, stereotyped; pre-vailing, -valent; current, received, acknowledged, recognized, accredited; of course, admitted, understood.
conformable etc. 82; according to -use, – custom, – routine; in -vogue, – fashion; fashionable etc. (*genteel*) 852.
wont; used – given – addicted –, attuned –, habituated etc. *v.*- to; in the habit of; *habitué*; at home in etc. (*skilful*) 698; seasoned; permeated –, imbued- with; devoted –, wedded- to; never free from.

hackneyed, fixed, rooted, deep-rooted, ingrafted, permanent, inveterate, besetting; naturalized; ingrained etc. (*intrinsic*) 5.
Adv. habitually etc. *adj.*; always etc. (*uniformly*) 16.
as -usual, – is one's wont, – things go, – the world goes, – the sparks fly upwards; *more -suo, – solito.*
as a rule, for the most part; generally etc. *adj.*; most often, – frequently.
Phr. *cela s'entend.*

614. Desuetude.—N. desuetude, disusage; disuse etc. 678; want of -habit, – practice; inusitation; newness to; new brooms.
infraction of usage etc. (*unconformity*) 83; non-prevalence; 'a custom more honored in the breach than the observance.'
V. be -unaccustomed etc. *adj.*; leave off –, cast off –, break off –, wean oneself of –, violate –, break through –, infringe- -a habit, – a custom, – a usage; break one's fetters; disuse etc. 678; wear off.
Adj. un-accustomed, -used, -wonted, -seasoned, -inured, -habituated, -trained; new; green etc. (*unskilled*) 699; fresh, original, unhackneyed.
unusual etc. (*unconformable*) 83; unconventional, non-observant; disused etc. 678.
Adv. just for once.

615. Motive.—N. motive, springs of action.
reason, ground, call, principle; mainspring, *primum mobile*, key-stone; the why and the wherefore; *pro* and *con*, reason why; secret –, ulterior- motive, *arrière-pensée*; intention etc. 620.
inducement, consideration; attraction etc. 288; loadstone; magnet, -ism, -ic force; allect-ation, -ive; temptation, enticement, *agacerie*, allurement, witchery; bewitch-ment, -ery; charm; spell etc. 993; fascination, blandishment, cajolery; seduc-tion, - ement; honeyed words, voice of the tempter, son of the Sirens; forbidden fruit, golden apple.
persuasi-bility, -bleness; attractability; impress-, suscept-ibility; softness; persuas-, attract-iveness; tantalization.
influence, prompting, dictate, instance; impuls-e, -ion; incit-ement, -ation; press, instigation; provocation etc. (*excitation of feeling*) 824; inspiration; per-, suasion; encouragement, advocacy; exhortation, advice etc. 695; solicitation etc. (*request*) 765; lobbying.
incentive, stimulus, spur, fillip, whip, goad, rowel, provocative, whet, dram.
bribe, lure; decoy, – duck; bait, trail of a red herring; bribery and corruption; sop, – for Cerberus.
prompter, tempter; seduc-er, -tor; suggester, coaxer, wheedler; instigator, firebrand, incendiary; Siren, Circe; *agent provocateur*; lobbyist.
V. induce, move; draw, – on; bring in its train, give an -impulse etc. *n.*- to; inspire; put up to, prompt, call up; attract, beckon.
stimulate etc. (*excite*) 824; spirit up, inspirit; a-, rouse; ecphorize; animate, incite, provoke, instigate. set on, actuate; act –, work –, operate-

upon; encourage; pat –, clap- on the -back, – shoulder.

influence, weigh with, bias, sway, incline, dispose, predispose, turn the scale, inoculate; lead, – by the nose; have –, exercise- influence- -with, – over, – upon; go –, come- round one; turn the head, magnetize.

persuade; prevail -with, – upon; overcome, carry; bring -round, – to one's senses; draw –, win –, gain –, come –, talk- over; procure, enlist, engage; invite, court.

tempt, seduce, overpersuade, entice, allure, captivate, fascinate, intrigue, bewitch, carry away, charm, conciliate, wheedle, coax, lure, suggest; inveigle; tantalize; cajole etc. (deceive) 545.

tamper with, bribe, suborn, grease the palm, bait with a silver hook, gild the pill, make things pleasant, put a sop into the pan, throw a sop to, bait the hook.

enforce, force; impel etc. (push) 276; propel etc. 284; whip, lash, goad, spur, prick, urge; egg –, hound –, hurry- on; drag etc. 285; exhort; advise etc. 695; call upon etc.; press etc. (request) 765; advocate.

set -an example, – the fashion; keep in countenance; back up.

be -persuaded etc.; yield to temptation, come round; concede etc. (consent) 762; obey a call; follow -advice, – the bent, – the dictates of; act · on principle.

Adj. impulsive, motive; suas-, persuas-, hortative, -ory; protreptical; inviting, tempting etc. v.; seductive, attractive, irresistible; fascinating etc. (pleasing) 829; provocative etc. (exciting) 824.

induced etc. v.; disposed; persuadable etc. (docile) 602; spellbound; instinct –, smitten- with; inspired etc. v.- by.

Adv. because, therefore etc. (cause) 155; from - this, – that- motive; for -this, – that- reason; for; by reason –, for the sake –, on the score –, on account- of; out of, from, as, forasmuch as.

for all the world; on principle.

615a. Absence of Motive.—N. absence of motive; caprice etc. 608; chance etc. (absence of design) 621.

V. have no motive; scruple etc. (be unwilling) 603.

Adj. without rhyme or reason; aimless etc. (chance) 621.

Adv. capriciously; out of mere caprice.

616. Dissuasion.—N. dissuasion, dehortation, expostulation, remonstrance; deprecation etc. 766.

discouragement, damper, wet blanket; warning.

cohibition etc. (restraint) 751; curb etc. (means of restraint) 752; check etc. (hindrance) 706.

reluctance etc. (unwillingness) 603; contraindication.

V. dissuade, dehort, cry out against, remonstrate, expostulate, warn, contraindicate.

disincline, indispose, shake, stagger; dispirit; discourage, -hearten, -enchant; deter; hold –, keep-back etc. (restrain) 751; render -averse etc. 603;

repel; turn aside etc. (deviation) 279; wean from; act as a drag etc. (hinder) 706; throw cold water on, damp, cool, chill, blunt, calm, quiet, quench; deprecate etc. 766.

Adj. dissuading etc. v.; dissuasive; dehortatory, expostulatory; monit-ive, -ory.

dissuaded etc. v.; uninduced etc. (induce etc. 615); unpersuadable etc. (obstinate) 606; averse etc. (unwilling) 603; repugnant etc. (dislike) 867.

617. Plea. [Ostensible motive, ground, or reason assigned.]—**N.** plea, pretext; allegation, advocation; ostensible -motive, – ground, – reason; excuse etc. (vindication) 937; color; gloss, guise.

loop-, starting-hole; how to creep out of, salvo, come off.

handle, peg to hang on room, locus standi; stalking horse, cheval de bataille, cue.

pretence etc. (untruth) 546; put off, subterfuge, dust thrown in the eyes; blind; moonshine; mere –, shallow- pretext; lame -excuse, – apology, tale to a whale; flase plea, sour grapes; makeshift, shift, white lie; special pleading etc. (sophistry) 477; soft sawder etc. (flattery) 933.

V. plead, allege; shelter oneself under the plea of; excuse etc. (vindicate) 937; gloss over; lend a color to; furnish a -handle etc. n.; make a -pretext, – handle- of; use as a plea etc. n.; take one's stand upon, make capital out of; pretend etc. (lie) 544.

Adj. ostensible etc. (manifest) 525; excusing; alleged, apologetic; pretended etc. 545.

Adv. ostensibly; under -color, – the plea, – the pretence- of.

618. Good.—N. good, benefit, advantage; improvement etc. 658; interest, service, behoof, behalf; weal; main chance, summum bonum, common weal; ·consummation devoutly to be wished;· gain, boot; profit, harvest.

boon etc. (gift) 784; good turn; blessing, benison; world of good; piece of good -luck, – fortune; nuts, prize, windfall, godsend, waif, treasure trove.

good fortune etc. (prosperity) 734; happiness etc. 827.

[Source of good] goodness etc. 648; utility etc. 644; remedy etc. 662; pleasure-giving etc. 829.

Adj. commendable etc. 931; useful etc. 644; good etc., beneficial etc. 648.

V. benefit, profit, advantage, serve, help, avail; do good to, gain, prosper, flourish.

Adv. well, aright, satisfactorily, favorably, not amiss; all for the best; to one's -advantage etc. n.; in one's -favor, – interest- n.

Phr. so far so good.

619. Evil.—N. evil, ill, harm, hurt, mischief, nuisance; machinations of the devil, Pandora's box, ills that flesh is heir to.

blow, buffet, stroke, scratch, bruise, wound, gash, mutilation; mortal -blow, – wound; im-

medicabile vulnus; damage, loss etc. (*deterioration*) 659.

disadvantage, prejudice, drawback.

disaster, accident, casualty; mishap etc. (*misfortune*) 735; bad job, devil to pay; calamity, bale, woe, catastrophe, tragedy; ruin etc. (*destruction*) 162; adversity etc. 735.

mental suffering etc. 828. [Evil spirit] demon etc. 980. [Cause of evil] bane etc. 663. [Production of evil] badness etc. 649; painfulness etc. 830; evil doer etc. 913.

outrage, wrong, injury, foul play; bad –, ill-turn; disservice; spoliation etc. 791; grievance, crying evil.

V. be in trouble etc. (*adversity*) 735; harm, injure, hurt, do disservice to.

Adj. disastrous, bad etc. 649; awry, out of joint; disadvantageous, injurious, harmful.

Adv. amiss, wrong, ill, to one's cost.

620. Intention.—N. intent, -ion, -ionality; purpose; *quo animo*; project etc. 626; undertaking etc. 676; predetermination etc. 611; design, ambition.

contemplation, mind, *animus*, view, purview, proposal; study; look out.

final cause; *raison d'être*; *cui bono*; object, aim, end; 'the be all and the end all;' drift etc. (*meaning*) 516; tendency etc. 176; destination, mark, point, butt, goal, target, bull's-eye, quintain; prey, quarry, game.

decision, determination, resolve; set –, settled-purpose; *ultimatum*; resolution etc. 604; wish etc. 865; *arrière-pensée*; motive etc. 615.

[Study of final causes] teleology.

V. intend, purpose, design, mean; have to; propose to oneself; harbor a design; have in -view, – contemplation, – one's eye, – *petto*; have an eye to.

bid –, labor- for; be –, aspire –, endeavour-after; be –, aim –, drive –, point –, level- at; take aim; set before oneself; study to.

take upon oneself etc. (*undertake*) 676; take into one's head; meditate, contemplate; think –, dream –, talk- of; premeditate etc. 611; compass, calculate; dest-ine, -inate, propose.

project etc. (*plan*) 626; have a mind to etc. (*be willing*) 602; desire etc. 865; pursue etc. 622.

Adj. intended etc. *v.*; intentional, advised, express, determinate; prepense etc. 611; bound for; intending etc. *v.*; minded, disposed, inclined; bent upon etc. (*earnest*) 604; at stake, on the -anvil, – *tapis*; in -view; – prospect, – the breast of; *in petto*; teleological.

Adv. intentionally etc. *adj.*; advisedly, wittingly, knowingly, designedly, purposely, on purpose, by design, studiously, pointedly; with -intent etc. *n.*; deliberately etc. (*with premeditation*) 611; with one's eyes open, in cold blood.

for; with -a view, – an eye- to; in order -to, – that; to the end –, with the intent- that; for the purpose –, with the view –, in contemplation –, on account- of.

in pursuance of, pursuant to; *quo animo*; to all intents and purposes.

621. Chance.†[Absence of purpose in the succession of events.]—**N.** chance etc. 156; lot, fate

etc. (*necessity*) 601; luck; good luck etc. (*good*) 618; bad luck etc. 735; wheel of fortune; mascot; swastika.

speculation, venture, stake, flutter, flier, gamble, game of chance; mere –, random- shot; blind bargain, leap in the dark; pig in a poke etc. (*uncertainty*) 475; fluke, pot-luck.

drawing lots; sorti-legy, -tion; *. sortes, – Virgilianae*; *rouge et noir*, hazard, *roulette*, pitch and toss, chuck-farthing, cup-tossing, heads or tails, cross and pile, wager; bet, -ting; risk, stake, plunge; gambling; the turf.

stock exchange, bourse, board of trade, curb exchange.

gaming-, gambling-, betting-house; hell; betting ring, totalizator; dice, – box; dicer; gambler, -ester, plunger, stock operator, manipulator, punter; man of the turf; adventurer, speculator; bookmaker, layer, backer.

V. chance etc. (*hap*) 156; stand a chance etc. (*be possible*) 470.

toss up; cast –, draw- lots; leave –, trust- -to chance, – to the chapter of accidents; tempt fortune; chance it, take one's chance; run –, incur –, encounter- the -risk, – chance; stand the hazard of the die.

speculate, try one's luck, set on a cast, raffle, put into a lottery, buy a pig in a poke, shuffle the cards.

risk, venture, hazard, stake; lay, – a wager; make a bet, wager, bet, gamble; game, play for; play at chuck-farthing.

Adj. fortuitous etc. 156; unintentional, -ded; accidental; not meant; un-designed, -purposed; unpremeditated etc. 612; never thought of.

indiscriminate, promiscuous; undirected, random; aim-, drift-, design-, purpose-, cause-less; without purpose.

possible etc. 470.

Adv. casually etc. 156; unintentionally etc. *adj.*; unwittingly.

en passant, by the way, incidentally; as it may happen; at -random, – a venture, – haphazard; as luck would have it, by -chance, – good fortune; un-, -luckily.

† See note on 156.

622. Pursuit. [Purpose in action.]—**N.** pursuit; pursuing etc. *v.*; prosecution; pursuance; enterprise etc. (*undertaking*) 676; business etc. 625; adventure etc. (*essay*) 675; quest etc. (*search*) 461; scramble, hue and cry, game; hobby.

chase, hunt, *battue*, race, steeplechase, hunting, coursing; ven-ation, -ery; fox-chase; sport, -ing; shooting, angling, fishing, hawking.

pursuer; hunt-er, -sman; sportsman, Nimrod, the field; hound etc. 366.

V. pursue, prosecute, follow; run –, make –, be –; hunt – prowl- after; shadow; carry on etc. (*do*) 680; engage in etc. (*undertake*) 676; set about etc. (*begin*) 66; endeavor etc. 675; court etc. (*request*) 765; seek etc. (*search*) 461; aim at etc. (*intention*) 620; follow the trail etc. (*trace*) 461; fish for etc. (*experiment*) 463; press on etc. (*haste*) 684; run a race etc. (*velocity*) 274.

chase, give chase, course, dog, hunt, hound, stalk; tread –, follow- on the heels of etc. (*sequence*) 281.

rush upon; rush headlong etc. (*violence*) 173;

ride — , run- full tilt at; make a leap — , jump — , snatch- at; run down; start game.

tread a path; take — , hold- a course; shape — , direct — , bend- one's -steps, — course; play a game; fight — , elbow- one's way; follow up; take - to, — up; go in for; ride one's hobby.

Adj. pursuing etc. *v.*; in quest of etc. (*inquiry*) 461; in -pursuit, — full cry, — hot pursuit; on the scent.

Adv. in pursuance of etc. (*intention*) 620; after.

Int. tally-ho! yoicks! so-ho!

623. Avoidance. [Absence of pursuit.]—N. abst-ention, -inence; forbearance; refraining etc. *v.*; inaction etc. 681; neutrality.

avoidance, evasion, elusion; seclusion etc. 893. avolation, flight; escape etc. 671; retreat etc. 287; recoil etc. 277; departure etc. 293; rejection etc. 610.

shirker etc. *v.*; slacker; truant; fugitive, refugee; runa-way, -gate; renegade; deserter.

V. abstain, refrain, spare, not attempt; not do etc. 681; maintain the even tenor of one's way.

eschew, keep from, let alone, have nothing to do with; keep — , stand — , hold- -aloof, — off; take no part in, have no hand in.

avoid, shun; steer — , keep- clear of; fight shy of; keep -one's, — at a respectful- distance; keep — , get- out of the way; evade, elude, turn away from; set one's face against etc. (*oppose*) 708; deny oneself.

shrink; hang — , hold — , draw- back; recoil etc. 277; retire etc. (*recede*) 287; flinch, blink, blench, shy, shirk, dodge, parry, make way for, give place to.

beat a retreat; turn -tail, — one's back; take to one's heels; run, -away, — for one's life; cut and run; be off, — like a shot; fly, flee; fly — , flee — , run away- from; take — , take to- flight; desert, elope; make — , scamper — , sneak — , shuffle — , sheer- off; break — , burst — , tear oneself — , slip — , slink — , steal- -away, — away from; skip cable, part company, turn on one's heel; sneak out of, play truant, give one the go by, give leg bail, take French leave, slope, decamp, flit, bolt, abscond, levant, skedaddle, absquatulate, cut one's stick, walk one's chalks, show a light pair of heels, make oneself scarce; escape etc. 671; go away etc. (*depart*) 293; abandon etc. 624; reject etc. 610.

lead one a -dance, — a merry chase, — pretty dance; throw off the scent, play at hide and seek.

Adj. unsought, unattempted; avoiding etc. *v.*; neutral; shy of etc. (*unwilling*) 603; elusive, evasive, distant; fugitive, runaway; shy, wild.

Adj. lest, in order to avoid.

Int. forbear! keep — , hands- off! *sauve qui peut!* devil take the hindmost.

624. Relinquishment.—N. relinquish-, abandon-ment; desertion, defection, secession, withdrawal; cave of Adullam; *nolle prosequi.*

discontinuance etc. (*cessation*) 142; renunciation etc. (*recantation*) 607; abrogation etc. 756; resignation etc. (*retirement*) 757; desuetude etc. 614; cession etc. (*of property*) 782.

V. relinquish, give up, abandon, desert, forsake, leave in the lurch; depart — , secede — , withdraw-from; back — out of, — down from, leave, go back on one's word, quit, take leave of, bid a long farewell; vacate etc. (*resign*) 757.

renounce etc. (*abjure*) 607; forego, have done with, drop; write off; disuse etc. 678; discard etc. 782; wash one's hands of; drop all idea of; *nolle-pros.*; lose interest in.

break — , leave- off; desist; stop etc. (*cease*) 142; hold — , stay- one's hand; quit one's hold; give over, shut up shop.

throw up the -game, — cards; give up the -point, — argument; pass to the order of the day, move the previous question, table the motion.

Adj. unpursued; relinquished etc. *v.*; relinquishing etc. *v.*

Int. avast etc.! (*stop*) 142.

625. Business.—N. business, occupation, employment; pursuit etc. 622; what one is doing-, — about; affair, concern, matter, case, undertaking.

matter in hand, irons in the fire; thing to do, *agendum*, task, work, job, chore, errand, transaction, commission, mission, charge, care; duty etc. 926.

part, *rôle*, cue; province, function, look-out, department, capacity, sphere, orb, field, line; walk, — of life; beat, round, routine; race, career.

office, place, post, incumbency, living situation, appointment, billet, berth, employ; service etc. (*servitude*) 749; engagement; undertaking etc. 676.

vocation, calling, profession, *métier*, cloth, faculty; industry, art; industrial arts; craft, mystery, handicraft; trade etc. (*commerce*) 794.

exercise; work etc. (*action*) 680; avocation; press of business etc. (*activity*) 682.

V. pass — , employ — , spend- one's time in; employ oneself -in, — upon; occupy — , concern-oneself with; make it one's -business etc. *n.*; undertake etc. 676; enter a profession; betake oneself to, turn one's hand to; have to do with etc. (*do*) 680.

drive a trade; carry on — , do — , transact- -business, — a trade etc. *n.*; keep a shop; ply one's task, — trade; labor in one's vocation; pursue the even tenor of one's way; attend to -business, — one's work.

officiate, serve, act; act — , play- one's part; do duty; serve — , discharge — , perform- the -office, — duties, — functions- of; hold — , fill- -an office, — a place, — a situation; hold a portfolio.

be -about, — doing, — engaged in, — employed in, — occupied with, — at work on; have one's hands in, have in hand; have on one's -hands, — shoulders; bear the burden; have one's hands full etc. (*activity*) 682.

be -in the hands of, — on the stocks, — on the anvil; pass through one's hands.

Adj. business-like; work-a-day; professional; official, functional; busy etc. (*actively employed*) 682; on — , in- -hand; — one's hands; afoot; on -foot, — the anvil; going on; acting.

Adv. in the course of business, all in a day's work; professionally etc. *adj.*

626. Plan.—N. plan, scheme, design, project; propos-al, -ition; suggestion; resolution, motion;

precaution etc. (*provision*) 673; deep-laid etc. (*premeditated*) 611- plan etc.; racket.

system etc. (*order*) 58; organization etc. (*arrangement*) 60; germ etc. (*cause*) 153; Five Year Plan.

sketch, skeleton, outline, draught, draft, *ébauche*, *brouillon*; rough-cast, – draft, – draught, – copy; proof, revise.

forecast, *programme*, prospectus, scenario; *carte du pays*; card; bill, protocol; order of the day, list of agenda, *memorandum*; bill of fare etc. (*food*) 298; base of operations; platform, plank.

rôle; policy etc. (*line of conduct*) 692.

contrivance, invention, expedient, receipt, nostrum, artifice, device, gadget; stratagem etc. (*cunning*) 702; trick etc. (*deception*) 545; alternative, loophole, shift etc. (*substitute*) 147; last shift etc. (*necessity*) 601.

measure, step; stroke, – of policy; master stroke; trump-, court-card; *chaval de bataille*, great gun; *coup*, – *d'état*; clever –, bold –, good- -move, – hit, – stroke; bright -thought, – idea, great idea.

intrigue, cabal, plot, frame-up, conspiracy, complot, machination; under-, counter-plot.

schem-ist, -atist; strategist, machinator, schemer; projector, author, builder, artist, promoter, designer etc. *v.*; conspirator; *intrigant* etc. (*cunning*) 702.

V. plan, scheme, design, frame, contrive, project, forecast, sketch; conceive, devise, invent etc. (*imagine*) 515; set one's wits to work etc. 515; spring a project; fall –, hit- upon; strike –, chalk –, cut –, lay –, map-out; lay down a plan; shape –, mark- out a course; predetermine etc. 611; concert, preconcert, preestablish; prepare etc. 673; hatch, – a plot; concoct; take -steps, – measures.

cast, recast, systematize, organize; arrange etc. 60; digest, mature.

plot; counter-plot, -mine; dig a mine; lay a train; intrigue etc. (*cunning*) 702.

Adj. planned etc. *v.*; strategic, -al; planning etc. *v.*; in course of preparation etc. 673; under consideration; on the *-tapis*, – carpet, – table.

627. Method. [Path.]—**N.** method, way, manner, wise, gait, form, mole, fashion, tone, guise; *modus operandi*; procedure etc. (*line of conduct*) 692.

path, road, route, course; line of -way, – road; trajectory, orbit, track, beat, tack.

steps; stair, -case; flight of stairs, ladder, stile.

bridge, viaduct, gauntry, pontoon, stepping stone, plank, gangway, catwalk, drawbridge; pass, ford, ferry, tunnel, subway, elevated; pipe etc. 260.

door; gateway etc. (*opening*) 260; channel, passage, avenue, means of access, approach, perron, adit, entrance; artery, lane, alley, aisle, lobby, corridor, cloister; back- door, -stairs; secret passage; covert-way.

road-, path-, stair-way; thoroughfare; highway, pike, turnpike, trail, parkway, *boulevard*; turnpike –, royal –, coach- road; broad –, King's –, Queen's- highway; beaten -track, – path; horse –, bridle- road, – track, – path; pathway; walk, *trottoir*, foot-path, pavement, flags, side-walk; by –, cross- -road, – path, – way; cut; short -cut

etc. (*mid-course*) 628; *carrefour*; private –, occupation- road; highways and byways; rail-, tramroad, -way; funicular, ropeway, causeway; defile, cutting; canal etc. (*conduit*) 350; street etc. (*abode*) 189.

Adv. how; in what -way, – manner; by what mode; so, in this way, after this fashion, on these lines.

one way or another, anyhow; somehow or other etc. (*instrumentality*) 631; by way of; *viâ*; in transitu etc. 270; on the high road to.

Phr. hae tibi erunt artes.

628. Mid-course.—**N.** middle-, mid-course; moderation, mean etc. 29; middle etc. 68; *juste milieu*, *mezzo termine*, golden mean, *aurea mediocritas*.

straight etc. (*direct*) 278 -course, – path; short –, cross- cut; short- circuit; great circle sailing.

neutrality; half –, half and half- measures; compromise.

V. keep in –, steer –, preserve- -a middle, – an even- course; go straight etc. (*direct*) 278.

go half way, compromise, make a compromise.

Adj. neutral, average, even, impartial, moderate, straight etc. (*direct*) 278.

629. Circuit.—**N.** circuit, round-about way, digression, divagation, *détour*, circum-ambience, - ambulation, bendibus, *ambages*, loop; winding etc. (*circuition*) 311; zigzag etc. (*deviation*) 279.

V. perform –, make- a circuit; go -round about, – out of one's way; make a *détour*; meander etc. (*deviate*) 27; circumambulate.

lead a pretty dance; beat about, – the bush; make two bites of a cherry.

adj. circuitous, indirect, round-about; zig-zag etc. (*deviating*) 279; circum-ambient, -ambulatory.

Adv. by -a side wind, – an indirect course; in a roundabout way; from pillar to post.

630. Requirement.—**N.** requirement, need, wants, necessities; necessaries, – of life; stress, exigency, pinch, *sine quâ non*, matter of necessity; case of -need, – life or death.

needfulness, essentiality, necessity; in-dispensability, urgency, prerequisite.

requisition etc. (*request*) 765, (*exaction*) 741; run upon; demand –, call- for.

desideratum etc. (*desire*) 865; want etc. (*deficiency*) 640.

charge, claim, command, injunction, requisition, mandate, order, *ultimatum*:

V. require, need, want, have occasion for, entail; not be able to -do without, – dispense with; prerequire.

render necessary, necessitate, create a necessity for, call for, put in requisition; make a requisition etc. (*ask for*) 765, (*demand*) 741.

stand in need of; lack etc. 640; desiderate; desire etc. 865; be -necessary etc. *adj.*

Adj. required etc. *v.*; requisite, needful,

necessary, imperative, essential, indispensable, prerequisite; called for; in -demand, – request. urgent, exigent, pressing, instant, crying, absorbing.

in want of; destitute of etc. 640.

Adv. *ex necessitate rei* etc. (*necessarily*) 601; of –, out of stern- necessity; at a pinch.

Phr. there is no time to lose; it cannot be - spared, – dispensed with.

631. Instrumentality.—N. instrumentality; aid etc. 707; subservien-ce, -cy; mediation, intervention, -mediacy, medium, inter-medium, -mediary, vehicle, hand; agency etc. 170.

minister, handmaid, servant, slave, maid, valet; midwife, *accoucheur*, obstetrician; go-between; cat's paw; stepping-stone.

key; master –, pass –, latch- key; 'open seseme;' passport, *passe partout*, safe-conduct; influence.

instrument etc. 633; expedient etc. (*plan*) 626; means etc. 632.

V. subserve, minister, tend, mediate, intervene; come –, go- between, interpose; pull the strings; be -instrumental etc. *adj.*; pander to.

Adj. instrumental; useful etc. 644; ministerial, subservient, mediatorial; inter-mediate, -vening; conducive.

Adv. through, by, *per*; where-, there-, here-by; by the -agency etc. 170- of; by dint of; by –, in- virtue of; through the -medium etc. *n.*- of; along with; on the shoulders of; by means of etc. 632; by –, with- -the aid etc. (*assistance*) 707- of.

per fas et nefas, by fair means or foul; somehow, – or other; by hook or by crook.

632. Means.—N. means, resources, revenue, wherewithal, ways and means, income; capital etc. (*money*) 800; stock in trade etc. 636; provision etc. 637; a shot in the locker; appliances etc. (*machinery*) 633; means and appliances; conveniences; cards to play; expendients etc. (*measures*) 626; two strings to one's bow; sheet anchor etc. (*safety*) 666; aid etc. 707; medium etc. 631.

V. find –, have –, possess- means etc. *n.*; provide the wherewithal.

Adj. instrumental etc. 631; mechanical etc. 633.

Adv. by means of, with; by -what, – all, – any, – some- means; where-, here-, there-with; wherewithal.

how etc. (*in what manner*) 627; through etc. (*by the instrumentality of*) 631; with –, by- the aid etc. (*assistance*) 707- of; by the -agency etc. 170- of.

633. Instrument.—N. machinery, mechanism, engineering.

instrument, organ, tool, implement, utensil, contrivance, machine, motor, engine, lathe, gin, mill, pump.

gear; tack-le, -ling, trice, rigging, gear, apparatus, appliances; plant, *matériel*; harness, trap-

pings, fittings, accouterments; equip-ment, -age; appointments, furniture, upholstery; chattels; paraphernalia etc. (*belongings*) 780; *impedimenta*.

mechanical powers; lever, -age; mechanical advantage; crow, -bar; handspike, gavelock, jemmy, arm, limb, wing; oar, paddle; pulley, sheave; parbuckle; wheel and axle; wheel-, clock-work; wheels within wheels; pinion, gear wheel, spur –, bevel-gearing, chains, belting, crank, winch, capstan, windlass, crane, derrick, hoist, lift etc. 307; cam; pedal; wheel etc. (*rotation*) 312; inclined plane; wedge; screw; jack; spring, mainspring.

handle, hilt, haft, shaft, heft, shank, blade, trigger, tiller, helm, treadle, key; turnscrew, screwdriver, spanner, wrench.

hammer etc. (*impulse*) 276; edge tool etc. (*cut*) 253; borer etc. 262; vice, teeth etc. (*hold*) 781; nail, rope etc. (*join*) 45; peg etc. (*hang*) 214; support etc. 215; spoon etc. (*vehicle*) 272; arms etc. 727; oar etc. (*navigation*) 267.

Adj. instrumental etc. 631; mechanical, machinal, automatic, self-acting; brachial.

634. Substitute.—N. substitute etc. 147; deputy etc. 759; proxy, alternative, understudy.

635. Materials.—N. material, raw material, stuff, stock, staple; building materials, bricks and mortar; metal; stone; clay, brick; crockery etc. 384; compo, -sition; reinforced –, ferro-, concrete; cement; wood, ore, timber; gravel, cobbles, macadam,*asphalt, tarmac.

materials; supplies, munition, fuel, grist, household stuff; *pabulum* etc. (*food*) 298; ammunition etc. (*arms*) 727; contingents; relay, reinforcement; baggage etc. (*personal property*) 780; means etc. 632.

Adj. raw etc. (*unprepared*) 674; wooden etc. *n.*

636. Store.—N. stock, fund, mine, vein, lode, quarry; spring; fount, -ain; well, -spring; milch-cow.

stock in trade, supply; heap etc. (*collection*) 72; treasure; reserve, *corps de réserve*, reserve fund, nest-egg, savings, *bonne bouche*.

crop, harvest, mow, vintage; yield, product, gleanings.

store, accumulation, hoard, rick, stack; lumber; relay etc. (*provision*) 637.

store-house, -room, -closet; depository, *dépôt*, cache, safe deposit, vault, pantechnicon, repository, -servatory, -pertory; *repertorium*; promptuary, warehouse, *entrepôt*, magazine, dump, buttery, larder, pantry, panary, lanary, still-room, spence; crib, garner, granary, silo, barn; bunker; thesaurus; bank etc. (*treasury*) 802; armoury; arsenal; dock; gallery, museum, library, conservatory, hot-house; manag-ery, -erie, aquarium, zoological gardens.

reservoir, cistern, tank, sump, pond, mill-pond; gasometer.

budget, quiver, bandolier, portfolio; coffer etc. (*receptacle*) 191.

conservation; storing etc. *v.*; storage.
dictionary etc. 562; list etc. 86.

V. store; put –, lay –, set- by; stow away; set
–, lay- apart; store –, hoard –, treasure –, lay
–, heap –, put –, garner –, save- up; *cache*; accumulate, amass, hoard, fund, garner, save, bank.

conserve, reserve; keep –, hold- back; husband,
– one's resources.

deposit; stow, stack, load, dump; harvest; heap,
collect etc. 72; lay -in, – down, – by, store etc.
adj.; keep, file [papers] lay in etc. (*provide*) 637;
preserve etc. 670; put by for a rainy day.

Adj. stored etc. *v.*; in -store, – reserve, – ordinary; spare, supernumerary.

637. Provision.—N. provision, supply; grist, –
to the mill; subvention etc. (*aid*) 707; resources etc.
(*means*) 632.

provising etc. *v.*; purveyance; reinforcement;
commissary, commissariat.

rations; iron –, emergency- rations; provender
etc. (*food*) 298; *viaticum*; ensilage.

caterer, purveyor, commissary, quartermaster,
steward, housekeeper, manciple, feeder, batman,
victualler, storekeeper, grocer, provision merchant,
green-, grocer, *comprador*, *restaurateur*; sutler etc.
(*merchant*) 797; innkeeper, publican, confectioner,
baker, butcher, wine merchant, vintner.

V. provide; make -provision, – due provision
for; lay in, – a stock, – a store.

sup-ply, -peditate; furnish; find, – one in; arm.

cater, victual, provision, purvey, forage; beat up
for; stock, – with; make good, replenish; fill, –
up; recruit, feed, ration.

have in -store, – reserve; keep, – by one, – on
foot; have to fall back upon; store etc. 636; provide
against a rainy day etc. (*economy*) 817.

638. Waste.—N. consumption, expenditure,
exhaustion; dispersion etc. 73; ebb; leakage etc.
(*exudation*) 295; loss etc. 776; wear and tear;
waste; prodigality etc. 818; misuse etc. 679;
wasting etc. *v.*; rubbish etc. (*useless*) 645.

mountain in labor.

v. spend, expend, use, consume, swallow up,
exhaust, deplete; impoverish; spill, drain, empty;
disperse etc. 73.

cast –, throw –, fling –, fritter- away; burn the
candle at both ends, waste; squander etc. 818.

'waste its sweetness on the desert air;' cast -one's
bread upon the waters, – pearls before swine; employ a steam engine to crack a nut, waste powder
and shot, break a butterfly on a wheel; labor in
vain etc. (*useless*) 645; cut a whetstone with a
razor, pour water into a sieve; tilt at windmills.

leak etc. (*run out*) 295; run to waste; ebb; melt
away, run dry, dry up.

Adj. wasted etc. *v.*; at a low ebb.

wasteful etc. (*prodigal*) 818; penny wise and
pound foolish.

Phr. *magno conatu magnas nugas; le jeu n'en
vaut pas la chandelle.*

639. Sufficiency.—N. sufficiency, adequacy,
enough, withal, *quantum sufficit*, satisfaction, competence; no less.

mediocrity etc. (*average*) 29.

fill; fullness etc (*completeness*) 52; plen-itude, -
ty; abundance; copiousness etc. *adj.*; amplitude,
galore, lots, profusion; full measure; 'good measure
pressed down, shaken together and running over.'

luxuriance etc. (*fertility*) 168; affluence etc.
(*wealth*) 803; fat of the land; 'a land flowing with
milk and honey;' cornucopia; horn of -plenty, –
Amalthaea; mine etc. (*stock*) 636.

outpouring; flood etc. (*great quantity*) 31; tide
etc. (*river*) 348; repletion etc. (*reduncance*) 641;
satiety etc. 869; rich man etc. 803.

V. be -sufficient etc. *adj.*; suffice, do, just do,
satisfy, pass muster; have -enough etc. *n.*; eat –,
drink –, have- one's fill; roll –, swim- in; wallow
in etc. (*superabundance*) 641.

abound, exuberate, teem, flow, stream, rain,
shower down; pour, – in; swarm; bristle with.

render -sufficient etc. *adj.*; replenish etc. (*fill*)
52.

Adj. sufficient, enough, adequate, up to the
mark, commensurate, competent, satisfactory,
valid, tangible.

measured; moderate etc. (*temperate*) 953.

full etc. (*complete*) 52; ample, plen-ty, -tiful, -
teous; plenty as blackberries; copious, abundant;
abounding etc. *v.*; replete, enough and to spare,
flush; choke-full; well-stocked, -provided; liberal;
unstint-ed, -ing; stintless; without stint; un-sparing,
-measured; lavish etc. 641; wholesale.

rich, luxuriant etc. (*fertile*) 168; affluent etc.
(*wealthy*) 803; wantless; big with etc. (*pregnant*)
161.

un-exhausted, -wasted; exhaustless,
inexhaustible.

Adv. sufficiently, amply etc. *adj.*; full; in -
abundance etc. *n.*; with no sparing hand; to one's
heart's content, *ad libitum*, without stint.

Phr. cut and come again.

640. Insufficiency.—N. insufficiency;
inadequa-cy, -teness; incompetence etc. (*impotence*) 158; deficiency etc. (*incompleteness*) 53;
imperfection etc. 651; shortcoming etc. 304;
paucity; stint; scantiness etc. (*smallness*) 32; none
to spare; bare subsistence.

scarcity, dearth; want, need, lack, poverty,
exigency; inanition, starvation, famine, drought.

dole, pittance, mite; short -allowance, – commons; half-rations; banyan –, fast- day, Lent.

emptiness, poorness etc. *adj.*; depletion,
vacancy, flaccidity; ebb-tide; low water; 'a beggarly
account of empty boxes;' indigence etc. (*poverty*)
804; insolvency etc. (*non-payment*) 808; poor man
etc. 804; bankrupt etc. 808.

V. be -insufficient etc. *adj.*; not -suffice etc. 639;
come short of etc. 304; run dry.

want, lack, need, require; *caret*; be in want etc.
(*poor*) 804; live from hand to mouth.

render- insufficient etc. *adj.*; drain of resources;
impoverish etc. (*waste*) 638; stint etc. (*begrudge*)
819; put on short -commons, – allowance.

do -insufficiently etc. *adv.*; scotch the snake.

Adj. insufficient, inadequate; too -little etc. 32;
not -enough etc. 639; unequal to; incompetent etc.
(*impotent*) 158; 'weighed in the balance and found
wanting;' perfunctory etc. (*neglect*) 460; deficient

etc. (*incomplete*) 53; wanting etc. *v.*; imperfect etc. 651; ill-furnished, -provided, -stored, -off.

slack, at a low ebb; empty, vacant, bare; short –, out –, destitute –, devoid –, bereft etc. 789 –, denuded- of; dry, drained.

un -provided, -supplied, -furnished; un-replenished, -fed; un-stored, -treasured; empty-handed.

meager, poor, thin, scrimp, sparing, spare, stint-ed, stunted; skimpy; starv-ed, -eling; half-starved, emaciated, famine-stricken, famished, underfed, undernourished; jejune.

scant etc. (*small*) 32; scarce; not to be had, – for love or money, – at any price; scurvy; stingy etc. 819; at the end of one's tether; without - resources etc. 632; in want etc. (*poor*) 804; in debt etc. 806.

Adv. insufficiently etc. *adj.*; in default –, for want- of; failing.

641. Redundance.—N. redundance; too - much, – many; superabundance, -fluity, -fluence, -saturation; nimiety, transcendency, exuberance, profuseness; profusion etc. (*plenty*) 639; repletion, enough in all conscience, *satis superque*, lion's share; more than -enough etc. 639; plethora, engorgement, congestion, load, surfeit, sickener; turgescence etc. (*expansion*) 194; over-dose, - measure, -supply, -flow; inundation etc. (*water*) 348; avalanche.

accumulation etc. (*store*) 636; heap etc. 72; drug, – in the market; glut; crowd; burden.

excess; sur-, over-plus, epact; margin; remainder etc. 40; duplicate; surplusage; expletive; work of –, supererogation; bonus, bonanza.

luxury; intemperance etc. 954; extravagance etc. (*prodigality*) 818; exorbitance, lavishment.

pleonasm etc. (*diffuseness*) 573; too many irons in the fire; embarassment of riches; money to burn.

V. super-, over-abound; know no bounds, swarm; meet one at every turn; creep –, bristle-with; overflow; run –, flow –, well –, brim-over; run riot; over-run, -stock, -lay, -charge, -dose, - feed, -burden, -load, -do, -whelm, -shoot the mark etc. (*go beyond*) 303; surcharge, supersaturate, gorge, glut, load, drench, whelm, inundate, deluge, flood; drug, – the market.

choke, cloy, accloy, suffocate; pile up, lay it on, – with a trowel, lay on thick; impregnate with; lavish etc. (*squander*) 818.

send –, carry- coals to Newcastle, – owls to Athens; teach one's grandmother to suck eggs; *pisces natare docere*; kill the slain, 'gild refined gold,' 'paint the lily;' butter one's bread on both sides, put butter upon bacon; employ a steam-engine to crack a nut etc. (*waste*) 638.

exaggerate etc. 549; wallow in; roll in etc. (*plenty*) 639; remain on one's hands, hang heavy on hand, go a begging.

Adj. redundant; too -much, – many; exuberant, inordinate, superabundant, excessive, overmuch, replete, profuse, lavish; prodigal etc. 818; exor-bitant; overweening; extravagant; overcharged etc. *v.*; supersaturated, drenched, overflowing; running -over, – to waste, – down.

crammed –, filled- to overflowing; gorged, stuff-ed, ready to burst; dropsical, turgid, plethoric, full-blooded; obese etc. 194; voluminous.

superfluous, unnecessary, needless, super-vacaneous, uncalled for, to spare, in excess; over and above etc. (*remainder*) 40; *de trop*; adscititious etc. (*additional*) 37; supernumerary etc. (*reserve*) 636; on one's hands, spare, duplicate, supererogatory, expletive; *un peu fort*.

Adj. over, too, over and above; over –, too-much; too far; without –, beyond – out of-measure; with ... to spare; over head and ears; up to one's eyes, – ears; *extra*; beyond the mark etc. (*transcursion*) 303; over one's head.

Phr. It never rains but it pours.

642. Importance.—N. importance, consequence, moment, prominence, consideration, mark, materialness.

import, significance, concern; emphasis, interest. greatness etc. 31; superiority etc. 33; notability etc. (*repute*) 873; weight etc. (*influence*) 175; value etc. (*goodness*) 648; usefulness etc. 644.

gravity, seriousness, solemnity; no -joke, – laughing matter; pressure, urgency, stress; matter of life and death.

memorabilia, notablia, great doings; red-letter day.

great -thing, – point; main chance, 'the be all and end all,' cardinal point, outstanding feature; substance, gist etc. (*essence*) 5; sum and substance, *gravamen*, head and front; important –, principal –, prominent –, essential- part; half the battle; *sine quâ non*; breath of one's nostrils etc. (*life*) 359; cream, salt, core, kernel, heart, nucleus; key, - note, -stone; corner stone; trumpcard etc. (*device*) 626; salient points.

top-sawyer, first fiddle, *prima donna*, chief, big-wig; triton among the minnows.

V. be -important etc. *adj.*, – somebody, – something; import, signify, matter, be an object; carry weight etc. (*influence*) 175; make a figure etc. (*repute*) 873; be in the ascendant, come to the front, lead the way, take the lead, play first fiddle, throw all else into the shade; lie at the root of; deserve –, merit –, be worthy- -of notice, – regard, – consideration.

attach –, ascribe –, give- importance etc. *n.-* to; value, care for; set store -upon, – by; mark etc. 550; mark with a white stone, underline; write –, put –, print- in -italics, – capitals, – large letters, – large type, – letters of gold; accentuate, em-phasize, lay stress on.

make -a fuss, – a stir, – a piece of work, – much ado- about; make -of, – much of.

Adj. important; of -importance etc. *n.*; momen-tous, material; to the point; not to be -overlooked, – despised, – sneezed at; egregious; weighty etc. (*influential*) 175; of note etc. (*repute*) 873; notable, prominent, salient, signal; memorable, remarkable; worthy of -remark, – notice; never to be forgotten; stirring, eventful.

grave, serious, earnest, noble, grand, solemn, im-pressive, commanding, imposing.

urgent, pressing, critical, instant.

paramount, essential, vital, all-absorbing, radical, cardinal, chief, main, prime, primary, prin-cipal, leading, capital, foremost, overruling; of vital etc. importance.

in the front rank, first-rate, A1; superior etc. 33; considerable etc. (*great*) 31; marked etc. *v.*; rare etc. 137.

significant, telling, trenchant, emphatic, pregnant; *tanti.*

Adv. materially etc. *adj.*; in the main; above all, *par excellence*, to crown all.

643. Unimportance.—N. unimportance, insignificance, nothingness, immateriality.

triviality, trivia, fribble, levity, frivolity; paltriness etc. *adj.*; poverty; smallness etc. 32; vanity etc. (*uselessness*) 645; matter of - indifference etc. 866; no object; side issue.

nothing, − to signify, − worth speaking of, − particular, − to boast of, − to speak of; small −, no great −, trifling etc. *adj.*-matter; mere -joke, − nothing; hardly −, scarcely- anything; nonentity, cipher, figurehead; no great shakes, *peu de chose*; child's play; small beer.

toy, plaything, popgun, paper pellet, gimcrack, geegaw, bauble, trinket, *bagatelle*, kickshaw, knicknack, whim-wham, trifle, 'trifles light as air.'

trumpery, trash, rubbish, stuff, *fatras*, frippery; 'leather or prunello;' chaff, drug, froth, bubble, smoke, cobweb; weed; refuse etc. (*inutility*) 645; scum etc. (*dirt*) 653.

joke, jest, snap of the fingers; fudge etc. (*unmeaning*) 517; fiddlestick, − end; pack of nonsense, mere farce.

straw, pin, fig, continental, button, rush; bulrush, feather, halfpenny, farthing, brass farthing, doit, peppercorn, jot, rap, pinch of snuff, old song.

minutiae, details, minor details, small fry; dust in the balance, feather in the scale, drop in the ocean, flea-bite, molehill; fingle-fangle.

nine days' wonder, *ridiculus mus*; flash in the pan etc. (*impotence*) 158; much ado about nothing etc. (*overestimation*) 482; storm in a teacup.

V. be -unimportant etc. *adj.*; not -matter etc. 642; go for −, matter −, signify- -little, − nothing. − little or nothing; not matter a -straw etc. *n.*

make light of etc. (*underestimate*) 483; catch at straws etc. (*overestimate*) 482.

Adj. unimportant; of -little, − small, − no- - account, − importance etc. 642; immaterial; un-, non-essential; not vital; irrelevant, incidental, indifferent.

subordinate etc. (*inferior*) 34; *médiocre* etc. (*average*) 29; passable, fair, respectable, tolerable, commonplace; uneventful, mere, common; ordinary etc. (*habitual*) 613; inconsiderable, so-so, insignificant, inappreciable, nugatory.

trifling, trivial; slight, slender, light, flimsy, frothy, idle; puerile etc. (*foolish*) 499; airy, shallow; weak etc. 160; powerless etc. 158; frivolous, petty, niggling; pid-, ped-dling; fribble, inane, ridiculous, farcical; fini-cal, -kin; fiddle-faddle, namby-pamby, wishy-washy, milk and water.

poor, paltry, pitiful; contemptible etc. (*contempt*) 930; sorry, mean, meager, shabby, miserable, wretched, vile, scrubby, scrannel, weedy, niggardly, scurvy, putid, beggarly, worthless, twopenny-half penny, cheap, trashy, catchpenny, gimcrack, trumpery, one-horse; toy.

not worth -the pains, − while, − mentioning, − speaking of, − a thought, − a curse, − a straw, − rap etc. *n.*; beneath −, unworthy of- -notice, −

regard, − consideration, − contempt; *de lanâ caprinâ*; vain etc. (*useless*) 645.

Adv. slightly etc. *adj.*; rather, somewhat, pretty well, fairly well, tolerably.

for aught one cares.

Int. no matter! pish! tush! tut! pshaw! pugh! pooh, -pooh! fudge! bosh! humbug! fiddle-stick, − end! fiddlededee! never mind! *n'importe!* what - signifies, − matter, − boots it, − of that, −'s the odds! a fig for! stuff ! nonsense! stuff and nonsense!

Phr. *magno conatu magnas nugas*; *le jeu n'en vaut pas la chandelle*; it -matters not, − does not signify; it is of no -consequence, − importance.

644. Utility.—N. utility; usefulness etc. *adj.*; efficacy, efficiency, adequacy; service, use, stead, avail; help etc. (*aid*) 707; applicability etc. *adj.*; subservience etc. (*instrumentality*) 631; function etc. (*business*) 625; value; worth etc. (*goodness*) 648; money's worth; productiveness etc. 168; *cui bono* etc. (*intention*) 620; utilization etc. (*use*) 677; step in the right direction.

common weal, public good; utilitarianism etc. (*philanthropy*) 910.

V. be -useful etc. *adj.*; avail, serve; subserve etc. (*be instrumental to*) 631; conduce etc. (*tend*) 176; answer −, serve- -one's turn, − a purpose.

act a part etc. (*action*) 680; perform −, discharge- -a function etc. 625; do −, render- -a service, − good service, − yeoman's service; bestead, stand one in good stead; be the making of; help etc. 707.

bear fruit etc. (*produce*) 161; bring grist to the mill; profit, remunerate; benefit etc. (*do good*) 648.

find one's -account, − advantage- in; reap the benefit of etc. (*be better for*) 658.

render useful etc. (*use*) 677.

Adj. useful; of -use etc. *n.*; serviceable, usable, proficuous, good for; subservient etc. (*instrumental*) 631; conducive etc. (*tending*) 176; subsidiary etc. (*helping*) 707.

advantageous etc. (*beneficial*) 648; profitable, gainful, remunerative, worth one's salt; in-, valuable; prolific etc. (*productive*) 168.

adequate; ef-ficient, -ficacious; effect-ive, -ual; practicable, expedient etc. 646.

applicable, available, ready, handy, at hand, tangible; commodious, adaptable; of all work.

Adv. usefully etc. *adj.*; *pro bono publico*.

645. Inutility.—N. inutility; uselessness etc. *adj.*; inefficacy, futility, inep-, inap-titude; unsubservience; inadequacy etc. (*insufficiency*) 640; inefficiency etc. (*incompetence*) 158; unskilfulness etc. 699; disservice; unfruitfulness etc. (*unproductiveness*) 169; labor -in vain, − lost, − of Sisyphus; lost -trouble, − labor; work of Penelope; sleeveless errand, wild goose chase, mere farce.

tautology etc. (*repetition*) 104; supererogation etc. (*redundance*) 641.

vanitas vanitatum, vanity, inanity, worthlessness, nugacity; triviality etc. (*unimportance*) 643.

caput mortuum, waste paper, dead letter; blunt tool.

litter, rubbish, lumber, odds and ends, cast-off clothes; button-top; shoddy; rags, orts, trash, refuse, sweepings, scourings, off-scourings, dross, slag, waste, rubble, dottle, drast, *débris*; stubble, leavings; broken meat; dregs etc. (*dirt*) 653; weeds, tares; rubbish heap, dust hole; *rudera*, deads. *fruges consumere natus* etc. (*drone*) 683.

V. be -useless etc. *adj.*; go a begging etc. (*redundant*) 641; fail etc. 732.

seek –, strive- after impossibilities; use vain efforts, labor in vain, roll the stone of Sisyphus, beat the air, lash the waves; *battre l'eau avec un bâton*, *donner un coup d'épée dans l'eau*, fish in the air, milk the ram, drop a bucket into an empty well, sow the sand; bay the moon; preach –, speak- to the winds; whistle jigs to a milestone; kick against the pricks, *se battre contre des moulins*; lock the stable door when the steed is stolen etc. (*too late*) 135; hold a farthing candle to the sun; cast pearls before swine etc. (*waste*) 638; carry coals to Newcastle etc. (*redundance*) 641; wash a blackamoor white etc. (*impossible*) 471.

render -useless etc. *adj.*; dis-mantle, -mast, -mount, -qualify, -able; unrig; cripple, lame etc. (*injure*) 659; spike guns, clip the wings; put out of gear.

Adj. useless, inutile, inefficacious, futile, unavailing, bootless; inoperative etc. 158; inadequate etc. (*insufficient*) 640; in-, un- subservient; inept, inefficient etc. (*impotent*) 158; of no -avail etc. (*use*) 644; ineffectual etc. (*failure*) 732; incompetent etc. (*unskilful*) 699; 'stale, flat and unprofitable;' superfluous etc. (*redundant*) 641; dispensable; thrown away etc. (*wasted*) 638; abortive etc. (*immature*) 674.

worth-, value-less; unsaleable; not worth a straw etc. (*trifling*) 643; dear at any price.

vain, empty, inane; gain-, profit-, fruit-less; unserviceable, -profitable; ill-spent; unproductive etc. 169; *hors de combat*; barren, sterile, impotent, unproductive; effete, past work etc. (*impaired*) 659; obsolete etc. (*old*) 124; fit for the -dust-hole, – wastepaper basket; good for nothing; of no earthly use; not worth -having, – powder and shot; leading to no end, uncalled for; un-necessary, - needed, superfluous.

Adv. uselessly etc. *adj.*; to -little, – no, – little or no- purpose.

Int. *cui bono?* what's the good!

646. Expedience. [Specific subservience.]—**N.** expedien-ce, -cy; desirableness, -bility etc. *adj.*; fitness etc. (*agreement*) 23; utility etc. 644; propriety; advantage; opportunism, pragmatism.

high time etc. (*occasion*) 134.

V. be -expedient etc. *adj.*; suit etc. (*agree*) 23; befit; suit –, befit- the -time, – season, – occasion.

conform etc. 82.

Adj. expedient; desir-, advis-, accept-able; convenient; worth while, meet; fit, -ting; due, proper, eligible, seemly, becoming; befitting etc. *v.*; opportune etc. (*in season*) 134; *in loco*; suitable etc. (*accordant*) 23; applicable etc. (*useful*) 644; practical, effective, pragmatical; suitable, handy.

Adv. in the right place; conveniently etc. *adj.*; in the nick of time.

Phr. *operae pretium est*.

647. Inexpedience.—**N.** enexpedien-ce, -cy; undesira-bleness, -bility etc. *adj.*; discommodity, impropriety; unfitness etc. (*disagreement*) 24; inutility etc. 645; inconvenience, inadvisability; disadvantage.

V. be -inexpedient etc. *adj.*; come amiss etc. (*disagree*) 24; embarrass etc. (*hinder*) 706; put to inconvenience; pay too dear for one's whistle.

Adj. inexpedient, undesirable; un-, in-advisable; objectionable; troublesome, in-apt, -eligible, - admissable, -convenient; in-, dis-commodious; disadvantageous; inappropriate, unsuitable, unfit etc. (*inconsonant*) 24.

ill-contrived, -advised; unsatsifactory; unprofitable etc., unsubservient etc. (*useless*) 645; inopportune etc. (*unseasonable*) 135; out of –, in the wrong- place; improper, unseemly.

clumsy, awkward; cum-brous, -bersome; lumbering, unwieldy, hulky; unmanageable etc. (*impracticable*) 704; impedient (*in the way*) 706.

unnecessary etc. (*redundant*) 641.

Phr. it will never do.

648. Goodness. [Capability of producing good. Good qualities.]—**N.** goodness etc. *adj.*; excellence, merit; virtue etc. 944; value, worth, price.

super-excellence, -eminence; superiority etc. 33; perfection etc. 650; *coup de maître*; master-piece, *chef d'oeuvre*, prime, flower, cream, *élite*, pick, A1, none such, *nonpareil*, *crème de la crème*, flower of the flock, cock of the roost, salt of the earth; champion.

tid-bit; gem, – of the first water; *bijou*, precious stone, jewel, pearl, diamond, ruby, brilliant, treasure; good thing; *rara avis*, one in a thousand.

beneficence etc. 906; good man etc. 948.

V. be -beneficial etc. *adj.*; produce –, do- - good etc. 618; profit etc. (*be of use*) 644; benefit; confer a -benefit etc. 618.

be the making of, do a world of good, make a man of.

produce a good effect; do a good turn, confer an obligation; improve etc. 658.

do no harm, break no bones.

be -good etc. *adj.*; excel, transcend etc. (*be superior*) 33; bear away the bell.

stand the -proof, – test; pass -muster, – an examination.

challenge comparison, vie, emulate, rival.

Adj. harm-, hurt-less; unobnoxious; in-nocuous, -nocent, -offensive.

beneficial, valuable, of value; serviceable etc. (*useful*) 644; advantageous, profitable, edifying; salutzry etc. (*healthful*) 656.

favorable; propitious etc. (*hopegiving*) 858; fair.

good, – as gold; excellent; better; superior etc. 33; above par; nice, fine; genuine etc. (*true*) 494.

best, choice, select, picked, elect, eximious, *recherché*, rare, priceless; unpara-goned, -lleled etc. (*supreme*) 33; superlatively etc. 33- good; super-fine, -excellent; bonzer; of the first water; first-rate, -class; high-wrought; exquisite, very best, crack, prime, tip-top, gilt-edged, capital, cardinal; standard etc. (*perfect*) 650; inimitable.

admirable, estimable; praiseworthy etc. (*approve*) 931; pleasing etc. 829; *couleur de rose*, precious, of great price; costly etc. (*dear*) 814; worth -its weight in gold, – a Jew's eye, – a king's ransom; matchless, peerless, invaluable, inestimable, precious as the apple of the eye.

tolerable etc. (not very good) 651; up to the mark, un-exceptionable, -objectionable; satisfactory, tidy.

in -good, – fair- condition; fresh; unspoiled; sound etc. (perfect) 650.

Adv. beneficially etc. adj.; well etc. 618.

649. Badness. [Capability of producing evil. Bad qualities.]—**N.** hurtfulness etc. adj.; virulence.

evil doer etc. 913; bane etc. 663; plague-spot etc. (insalubrity) 657; evil star, ill wind; snake in the grass, skeleton in the closet; amari aliquid, thorn in the side; Jonah, jinx, hoodoo.

malignity; malevolence etc. 907; tender mercies [ironically].

ill-treatment, annoyance, molestation, abuse, oppression, persecution, outrage; misusage etc. 679; injury etc. (damage) 659.

badness etc. adj.; peccancy, abomination; painfulness etc. 830; pestilence etc. (disease) 655; guilt etc. 947; depravity etc. 945.

V. be -hurtful etc. adj.; cause –, produce –, inflict –, work –, do- evil etc. 619; damnify, endamage, hurt, harm, scathe; injure etc. (damage) 659; pain etc. 830.

wrong, aggrieve, oppress, persecute; trample –, tread –, bear hard –, put-upon; overburden; weigh -down, – heavy on; victimize; run down; molest etc. 830.

maltreat, abuse; ill-use, -treat; thwart, buffet, bruise, scratch, maul; smite etc. (scourge) 972; do -violence, – harm, – a mischief; stab, pierce, outrage.

do –, make- mischief; bring –, get- into trouble.

destroy etc. 162.

Adj. hurt-, harm-, scath-, bane-, bale-ful; injurious, deleterious, detrimental, noxious, pernicious, mischievous, full of mischief, mischief-making, malefic; malignant, nocuous, noisome; prejudicial; dis-serviceable, advantageous; wide-wasting.

unlucky, sinister; obnoxious, untoward, disastrous.

oppressive, burdensome, onerous; malign etc. (malevolent) 907.

corrupting etc. (corrupt etc. 659) virulent, venomous, envenomed, corrosive; poisonous etc. (morbific) 657; deadly etc. (killing) 361; destructive etc. (destroying) 162; inauspicious etc. 859.

bad, ill, arrant, as bad bad can be, dreadful; horrid, -rible; dire; rank, peccant, foul, fulsome; rotten, – at the core.

vile, base, villainous; mean etc. (paltry) 643; injured etc., deteriorated etc. 659; unsatisfactory, exception, -able, indifferent; below par etc. (imperfect) 651; ill-contrived, -conditioned; wretched, sad, grievous, deplorable, lamentable; piti-ful, -able, woeful etc. (painful) 830.

evil, wrong; depraved etc. 945; shocking; reprehensible etc. (disapprove) 932.

hateful, – as a toad; abominable, detestable, execrable, cursed, accursed, confounded; damn-ed, -able; infernal; diabolic etc. (malevolent) 907.

inadvisable etc. (inexpedient) 647; unprofitable etc. (useless) 645; incompetent etc. (unskilful) 699; irremediable etc. (hopeless) 859.

Adv. badly etc. adj.; wrong, ill; to one's cost; where the shoe pinches.

Phr. bad is the best; the worst come to the worst.

650. Perfection.—**N.** perfection; perfectness etc. adj.; indefectibility; inpecc-ancy, -ability.

pink, beau idéal, phoenix, paragon; pink –, acme- of perfection; ne plus ultra; summit etc. 210.

cygne noir; philosopher's stone; chrysolite, Koh-i-noor, black tulip.

model, standard, pattern, mirror, admirable Crichton; trump; very prince of.

master-piece, -stroke, super-excellence etc. (goodness) 648; transcendence etc. (superiority) 33.

V. be -perfect etc. adj.; transcend etc. (be supreme) 33.

bring to perfection, perfect, ripen, mature; consummate, complete etc. 729; put in trim etc. (prepare) 673; put the finishing touch to.

Adj. perfect, faultless, ideal; indefective, -ficient. -fectible; immaculate, spotless, impeccable; free from -imperfection etc. 651; un-blemished, -injured etc. 659; sound, – as a roach; in perfect condition; scathless, intact, harmless; seaworthy etc. (safe) 644; right as a trivet; in seipso totus teres atque rotundus; consummate etc. (complete) 52; finished etc. 729; complete in itself.

best etc. (good) 648; model, standard; inimitable, unparagoned, unparalleled etc. (supreme) 33; superhuman, divine; beyond all praise etc. (approbation) 931; sans peur et sans reproche.

Adj. to perfection, to the limit; perfectly etc. adj.; ad unguem; clean, – as a whistle.

651. Imperfection.—**N.** imperfection; imperfectness etc. adj.; deficiency; inadequacy etc. (insufficiency) 640; peccancy etc. (badness) 649; immaturity etc. 674.

fault, defect, weak point; screw loose; rift within the lute; fly in the ointment; flaw etc. (break) 70; gap etc. 198; twist etc. 243; taint, attainder; bar sinister, hole in one's coat; blemish etc. 848; weakness etc. 160; half-blood, touch of the tar brush; shortcoming etc. 304; drawback; seamy side.

mediocrity; no great -shakes, – catch; not much to boast of.

V. be -imperfect etc. adj.; have a -defect etc. n.; lie under a disadvantage; spring a leak.

not –, barely- pass muster; fall short etc. 304.

Adj. imperfect; not -perfect etc. 650; de-ficient, -fective; faulty, unsound, mutilated, tainted; out of -order, – tune; cracked, leaky; sprung; warped etc. (distort) 243; lame; injured etc. (deteriorated) 659; peccant etc. (bad) 649; frail etc. (weak) 160; inadequate etc. (insufficient) 640; crude etc. (unprepared) 674; incomplete etc. 53; found wanting; below par; shorthanded; below –, under- its full -strength, – complement.

indifferent, middling, ordinary, mediocre; average etc. 29; so-so; *così-così*, milk and water; tolerable, fair, passable; pretty -well, – good; rather –, moderately- good; good –, well-enough; decent; not -bad, – amiss; inobjectionable, admissable, bearable, only better than nothing.

secondary, inferior; second-rate, -best, one-horse.

Adv. almost etc.; to a limited extent, rather etc. 32; pretty, moderately; only; considering, all things considered, enough.

Phr. *surgit amari aliquid.*

652. Cleanness.—**N.** cleanness etc. *adj.*; purity; cleaning etc. *v.*; purification, defecation etc. *v.*; purgation, lustration; de-, abs-tersion; epuration, mundation, ablution, lavation, colature; disinfection etc. *v.*; drain-, sewerage.

lavatory, bath, -room; swimming pool, natatorium; public baths; hot –, cold –, Turkish –, Swedish –, Russian – vapor- bath; *hammam*, laundry, washhouse; washerwoman, laundress, laundryman; scavenger, cleaner, sweeper, goodie; crossing sweeper, white wings, dustman, sweep.

brush; broom, besom, carpet-sweeper, vacuum-cleaner, mop, squilgee, rake, shovel, sieve, riddle, screen, filter; scraper, strigil.

napkin, *serviette*, cloth, table-, carving-cloth, table-linen, napery, maukin, handkerchief, towel, sudary; doyley, doily, duster, sponge, mop, swab.

cover, drugget, mat, doormat.

soap, wash, lotion, detergent, cathartic, purgative; purifier etc. *v.*; dentifrice, tooth-powder, -paste; mouth wash; disinfectant.

V. be –, render- clean etc. *adj.*

clean, -se; mundify, rinse, wring, flush, full, wipe, mop, sponge, scour, swab, scrub, holystone, brush up.

wash, shampoo, lave, launder, buck; abs-, deterge; clear, purify; de-purate, -spumate, -fecate; purge, expurgate; Bowdlerize; elutriate, lixiviate, edulcorate, clarify, refine, rack; fil-ter, -trate; drain, strain.

disinfect, sterilize, pasteurize, fumigate, ventilate, deodorize; whitewash.

sift, winnow, screen, riddle, pick, weed, comb, rake, brush, sweep.

rout –, clear –, sweep etc.- out; make a clean sweep of.

Adj. clean, -ly; pure; immaculate; spot-, stain-taint-less; without a stain, un-stained, -spotted, - soiled, -sullied, -tainted, -infected, -adulterated; aseptic; sweet, – as a nut.

neat, spruce, tidy, trim, gimp, clean as a new penny, like a cat in pattens; cleaned etc. *v.*; kempt.

Adv. neatly etc. *adj.*; clean as a whistle.

653. Uncleanness.—**N.** uncleanness etc. *adj.*; impurity; immundi-ty, -city; impurity etc. [of mind] 961.

defilement, contamination etc. *v.*; defedation; soil-ure, -iness; abomination; leaven; taint, -ure; fetor etc. 401.

decay; putre-scence, -faction; corruption; mold, must, mildew, dry-rot, *mucor*, rubigo, caries.

slovenry; slovenliness etc. *adj.*; squalor.

dowdy, drab, slut, malkin, slattern, sloven, slammerkin, scrub, draggletail, mudlark, dustman, sweep; beast.

dirt, filth, soil, slop; dust, cobweb, flue; smoke, soot, smudge, smut, grime, raff.

sordes, dregs, grounds, lees; sedi-, settle-ment; heel-tap; dross, -iness; mother, precipitate, *scoria*, ashes, cinders, recrement, slag; scum, froth.

hog-wash, swill, ditch-, dish-, bilge-water; rinsings, cheese-parings; sweepings etc. (*useless refuse*) 645; off-, out-scourings; off-scum; *caput mortuum*, *residuum*, sprue, feculence, clinker, draff; scurf, -iness; *exuviae*, morphew; fur, -fur; dandruff; tartar.

riffraff; vermin, louse, cootie, flea, bug.

mud, mire, quagmire, *alluvium*, silt, sludge, slime, slush, slosh.

spawn, offal, garbage, carrion; *excreta* etc. 299; slough, peccant humor; pus, matter, suppuration, *lienteria*; *feces*, excrement, ordure, dung; sew-, sewer-age; muck, coprolite; guano, manure, compost.

dunghill, *coluvies*, mixen, midden, bog, laystall, sink, w.c., water-, earth-closet, latrine, privy, jakes, John's, cess, -pool; sump, sough, *cloaca*, drain, sewer, common sewer; Cloacina; dust-hole.

sty, pig-sty, lair, den, Augean stable, sink of corruption; slum, rookery.

V. be –, become- unclean etc. *adj.*; rot, putrefy, fester, rankle, reek; stink etc. 401; mold, -er; go - bad etc. *adj.*

render -unclean etc. *adj.*; dirt, -y; soil, smoke, tarnish, slaver, spot, smear, daub, blot, blur, smudge, smutch, smirch; d-, dr-abble, -aggle; spatter, slubber; be-smear etc.; -mire, -slime, -grime, - foul; splash, stain, distain, maculate, sully, pollute, defile, debase, contaminate, taint, leaven; corrupt etc. (*injure*) 659; cover with -dust etc. *n.*; drabble in the mud.

wallow in the mire; slob-, slab-ber.

Adj. unclean, dirty, filthy, grimy; soiled etc. *v.*; not to be handled with kid gloves; dusty, snuffy, smutty, sooty, smoky; thick, turbid, dreggy; slimy; uncleanly, slovenly, untidy, sluttish, dowdy, slatternly, draggletailed; un-combed, -kempt, -scoured, -swept, -wiped, -washed, -strained, -purified; squalid.

nasty, coarse, foul, impure, offensive, abominable, beastly, reeky, reechy; fetid etc. 401.

moldy, lentiginous, musty, mildewed, rusty, moth-eaten, mucid, rancid, bad, gone bad, touched, fusty, reasty, rotten, corrupt, tainted, high, fly-blown, maggoty; putr-id, -escent, -efied; purulent, carious, peccant, fec-al, -ulent; stercoraceous, excrementitious; scurfy, impetiginous; gory, bloody; rotting etc. *v.*; rotten as -a pear, - cheese.

crapulous etc. (*intemperate*) 954; gross etc. (*impure in mind*) 961.

654. Health.—**N.** health, sanity; soundness etc. *adj.*; vigor; good –, perfect –, excellent –, rude –, robust- health; bloom, *mens sana in còrpore sanò*; Hygeia; incorrupti-on, -bility; good state –, clean bill- of health, eupepsia.

V. be in health etc. *adj.*; bloom, flourish.

keep -body and soul together, – on one's legs; enjoy -good, – a good state of - health; have a clean bill of health.

return to health; recover etc. 660; get better etc.
(*improve*) 658; take a -new, – fresh- lease of life;
convalesce, be convalescent, recruit; restore to
health; cure etc. (*restore*) 660.

Adj. health-y, -ful; in -health etc. *n.*; well,
sound, strong, fit, hearty, hale, fresh, blooming,
green, whole; florid, flush, hardy, stanch, staunch,
brave, robust, vigorous, weather-proof; convalescent.

un-scathed, -injured, -maimed, -marred, -
tainted; sound of wind and limb, safe and sound;
without a scratch.

on one's legs; sound as a -roach, – bell; fresh as
-a daisy, – a rose, – April; picture of health; bursting with health; fit as a fiddle; hearty as a buck;
in -fine, – high- feather; in -good case, – full
bloom; in fine fettle; pretty bobbish, tolerably well,
as well as can be expected.

sanitary etc. (*health-giving*) 656; sanatory etc.
(*remedial*) 662.

655. Disease.*—N. disease, illness, sickness
etc. *adj.*; ailing etc. *v.*; 'the ills that flesh is heir to;'
morb-idity, -osity; infirmity, ailment, indisposition;
complaint, disorder, malady; distemper, -ature.

visitation, attack, seizure, stroke, fit, epilepsy,
apoplexy, shock, shell-shock.

delicacy, loss of health, valetudinarianism, in-
validism, cachexy; *cachexia*, atrophy, *marasmus*;
indigestion, *dyspepsia*; decay etc. (*deterioration*)
659; malnutrition, decline, consumption, palsy,
paralysis, prostration; occupational diseases.

taint, pollution, infection, contagion, septicity,
septicaemia, blood poisoning, pyaemia, epi-, endemic; murrain, plague, pestilence, virus, pox.

sore, ulcer, abscess, fester, boil; pimple etc.
(*swelling*) 250; carbuncle, gathering, whitlow, imposthume, peccant humor, issue; rot, canker, cancer, *carcinoma*, *caries*, mortification, corruption,
gangrene, *sphacelus*, leprosy, eruption, rash,
breaking out, venereal disease.

fever, calenture; inflammation.

fatal etc. (*hopeless*) 859- -disease etc.; dangerous
illness, galloping consumption, churchyard cough;
general breaking up, break up of the system.

[Disease of the mind] neurasthenia; idiocy etc.
499; insanity etc. 503.

martyr to disease; cripple; 'the halt, the lame
and the blind;' valetudinar-y, -ian; invalid, patient,
case; sick-room, -chamber, hospital etc. 662.

[Science of disease] path-, eti-, nos-ology,
therapeutics, diagnosis, prognosis.

V. be -ill etc. *adj.*; ail, suffer, labor under, be affected with, complain of; droop, flag, languish,
halt; sicken, peak, pine, waste away, fail, lose
strength; gasp.

keep one's bed; feign sickness etc. (*falsehood*)
544; malinger.

lay -by, – up; take –, catch- -a disease etc. *n.*,
– an infection; be stricken by; break out.

Adj. diseased; ailing etc. *v.*; ill, – of; taken ill,
seized with; indisposed, unwell, sick, squeamish,
poorly, seedy; affected –, afflicted- with illness;
laid up, confined, bed-ridden, invalided, in
hospital, on the sick list; out of -health, – sorts;
valetudinary.

un-sound, -healthy; sickly, morbose, healthless,

infirm, chlorotic, unbraced, drooping, flagging,
lame, halt, crippled, halting.

morbid, tainted, vitiated, peccant, contaminated,
poisoned, septic, tabid, mangy, leprous, cankered;
rotten, – to, – at- the core; withered, palsied,
paralytic, tuberculous; dyspeptic.

touched in the wind, broken-winded, spavined,
gasping; *hors de combat* etc. (*useless*) 645.

weak-ly, -ened etc. (*weak*) 160; decrepit;
decayed etc. (*deteriorated*) 659; incurable etc.
(*hopeless*) 859; in declining health; cranky; in a
bad way, in danger, prostrate; moribund etc.
(*death*) 360.

morbific, epidemic etc. 657.

*Extended lists of different diseases are beyond the scope of
this work.

656. Salubrity.—N. salubrity, salubriousness;
healthiness etc. *adj.*

fine -air, – climate; eudiometer.

[Preservation of health]   *hygiène*;
valetudinarian, -ism, preventorium, sanitarian;
sanitarium, *sanitorium*, immunity.

V. be -salubrious etc. *adj.*; agree with, be good
for; assimilate etc. 23.

Adj. salu-brious, -tary, -tiferous, wholesome;
health-y, -ful; sanitary, prophylactic, benign,
bracing, tonic, invigorating, good for, nutritious,
hyg-eian, -ienic.

in-noxious, -nocuous, -nocent; harmless, unin-
jurious, uninfectious; immune.

sanative etc. (*remedial*) 662; restorative etc.
(*reinstate*) 660; useful etc. 644.

657. Insalubrity.—N. insalubrity,
unhealthiness etc. *adj.*; non-naturals; plague spot;
malaria etc. (*poison*) 663; death in the pot, contagion.

Adj. insalubrious; un-healthy, -wholesome;
noxious, noisome, foul; morbi-fic, -ferous;
mephitic, septic, azotic, deleterious; pesti-lent, -
ferous, -lential; virulent, venomous, envenomed,
poisonous, toxic, narcotic.

contagious, infectious, catching, taking, communicable, epidemic, zymotic, sporadic, endemic,
pandemic, epizoötic.

innutritious, indigestible, ungenial; uncongenial
etc. (*disagreeing*) 24.

deadly etc. (*killing*) 361.

658. Improvement.—N. improvement; a-,
melioration; betterment; mend, amendment, emendation; mending etc. *v.*; advancement; advance etc.
(*progress*) 282; ascent etc. 305; promotion, preferment; elevation etc. 307; increase etc. 35.

cultiv-, civiliz-ation; menticulture, culture,
march of intellect; eugenics, euthenics, meliorism,
telesis.

reform, -ation; revision, radical reform; second
thoughts, correction, *limae labor*, refinement,
elaboration; purification etc. 652; repair etc.
(*restoration*) 660; recovery etc. 660.

revise; revised –, new- edition.

reformer, radical, progressive.
V. improve; be −, become −, get- better; mend, amend.
advance etc. (*progress*) 282; ascend etc. 305; increase etc. 35; fructify, ripen, mature; pick up, come about, rally, take a favorable turn; turn -over a new leaf, − the corner; raise one's head, sow one's wild oats; recover etc. 660.
be -better etc. *adj.*, − improved by; turn to - right, − good, − best- account; profit by, reap the benefit of; make -good use of, − capital out of; place to good account; take advantage of.
render better, improve, emend, make over, better; a-, meliorate; correct.
improve −, refine- upon; rectify; enrich, mellow, elaborate, fatten.
promote, cultivate, advance, forward, enhance; bring -forward, − on; foster etc. 707; invigorate etc. (*strengthen*) 159.
touch −, rub −, brush −, furbish −, bolster −, vamp −, brighten −, warm- up; polish, cook, make the most of, set off to advantage; prune; repair etc. (*restore*) 660; put in order etc. (*arrange*) 60.
review, revise, edit, redact; make -corrections, − improvements etc. *n.*; doctor etc. (*remedy*) 662; purify etc. 652.
relieve, refresh, revive, infuse new blood into, recruit, re-invigorate, renew, revivify, freshen; build -afresh, − anew; uplift, inspire.
re-form, -model, -organize; new model, civilize.
view in a new light, think better of, appeal from Philip drunk to Philip sober.
palliate, mitigate; lessen etc. 36- an evil.
Adj. improving etc. *v.*; progressive, improved etc. *v.*; better, − off, − for; all the better for; better advised.
reform-, emend-atory; reparatory etc. (*restorative*) 660; remedial etc. 662.
corrigible, improvable, curable, accultural.
Adv. on -consideration, − reconsideration, − second thoughts, − better advice; *ad melius inquirendum*; on the -mend, − up grade.

659. Deterioration.—N. deterioration, debasement; want, ebb; recession etc. 287; retrogradation etc. 283; decrease etc. 36.
degenera-cy, -tion, -teness; degradation; depravation, -ement; depravity etc. 945; demoralization, retrogression.
impairment, inquination, injury, damage, loss, detriment, delaceration, outrage, havoc, inroad, ravage, scath; perversion, prostitution, vitiation, discoloration, oxidation, pollution, defedation, poisoning, venenation, leaven, contamination, canker, corruption, adulteration, alloy.
decl-ine, -ension, -ination; decadence, -cy; falling off etc. *v.*; caducity, decrepitude, senility.
decay, dilapidation, ravages of time, wear and tear; cor-, e-rosion; mouldi-, rotten-ness; moth and rust, dry-rot, blight, marasmus, atrophy, collapse; disorganization; *délabrement* etc. (*destruction*) 162.
wreck, mere wreck, honeycomb, *magni nominis umbra*.
V. be −, become- -worse, − deteriorated etc. *adj.*; have seen better days, deteriorate, degenerate,

fall off; wane etc. (*decrease*) 36; ebb; retrograde etc. 283; decline, droop; go down etc. (*sink*) 306; go -downhill, − on from bad to worse, − farther and fare worse; jump out of the frying pan into the fire.
run to -seed, − waste; swale, sweal; lapse, be the worse for; break, − down; spring a leak, crack, start; shrivel etc. (*contract*) 195; fade, go off, wither, molder, rot, rankle, decay, go bad; go to − fall into- decay; 'fall into the sear and yellow leaf,' rust, crumble, shake; totter, − to its fall; perish etc. 162; die etc. 360.
[Render less good] deteriorate; weaken etc. 160; put back; taint, infect, contaminate, poison, empoison, envenom, canker; corrupt, exulcerate, pollute, vitiate, inquinate; de-, em-base; denaturalize, leaven; de-flower, -bauch, -file, - prave, -grade; stain etc. (*dirt*) 653; discolor; alloy, adulterate, sophisticate, tamper with, prejudice.
pervert, prostitute, demoralize, brutalize; render vicious etc. 945; compromise.
embitter, ex-, acerbate, aggravate.
injure, impair, labefy, damage, harm, hurt, shend, scathe, spoil, mar, despoil, dilapidate, waste; overrun; ravage; pillage etc. 791.
wound, stab, pierce, maim, lame, surbate, cripple, hough, hamstring, hit between the wind and water, scotch, mangle, mutilate, disfigure, blemish, deface, warp.
blight, rot; cor-, e-rode, eat away; wear -away, − out; gnaw, − at the root of; sap, mine, undermine, shake, sap the foundations of, break up; dis-organize, -mantle, -mast; destroy etc. 162.
damnify etc. (*aggrieve*) 649; do one's worst; knock down; deal a blow to; play -havoc, − sad havoc, − the mischief, − the deuce, − the very devil- -with, − among; decimate.
Adj. unimproved etc. (improve etc. 658); deteriorated etc. *v.*; altered, − for the worse; injured etc. *v.*; sprung; withering, spoiling, etc. *v.*; on the -wane, − decline; tabid; degenerate; worse the −, all the- worse for; out of -repair, − tune; imperfect etc. 651; the worse for wear; battered; weather-ed, -beaten; stale, *passé*, shaken, dilapidated, frayed, faded, wilted, shabby, second-hand, second-rate, threadbare; worn, − to- -a thread, − a shadow, − the stump, rags; reduced, − to a skeleton, skeletonized; far gone.
decayed etc. *v.*; moth-, worn-eaten; mildewed, rusty, moldy, spotted, seedy, time-worn, moss-grown; discolored; effete, wasted, crumbling, moldering, rotten, cankered, blighted, tainted; depraved etc. (*vicious*) 945; decrep-id, -it; broken down; done, − for, − up; worn out, used up; fit for the -dust-hole, − wastepaper basket; past work etc. (*useless*) 645.
at a low ebb, in a bad way, on one's last legs, washed -up; − out; undermined, deciduous; nodding to its fall etc. (*destruction*) 162; tottering etc. (*dangerous*) 665; past cure etc. (*hopeless*) 859; fatigued etc. 688; backward, retrograde etc. (*retrogressive*) 283; deleterious etc. 649; behind the times.
Adv. on the down grade; beyond hope.
Phr. out of the frying pan into the fire; *aegrescit medendo*.

660. Restoration.—N. restor-ation, -al; re-instatement, -placement, -habilitation, establishment, -construction; reporduction etc. 163; re-novation, -newal; reviv-al, -escence; refreshment etc. 689; re-suscitation, -animation, -vivification, -viction; Phoenix; reorganization.

renaissance, renascence, rebirth, second youth, rejuvenation, rejuvenescence, new birth; regeneration, -cy, -teness; palingenesis, reconversion, resurgence, resurrection.

redress, retrieval, reclamation, recovery; convalescence; resumption, résumption.

recurrence etc. (repetition) 104; réchauffé, rifacimento.

cure, recure, sanation; healing etc. v.; redintegration; rectification, instauration.

repair, reparation, mending; recruiting etc. v.; cicatrization; disinfection; tinkering.

reaction; redemption etc. (deliverance) 672; restitution etc. 790; relief etc. 834.

mender, repairer, renewer; tinker, cobbler; doctor etc. 662; vis medicatrix etc. (remedy) 662. curableness.

V. return to the original state; recover, rally, revive; come -to, − round, − to oneself; pull through, weather the storm, be oneself again; get -well, − round, − the better of, − over, − about; rise from -one's ashes, − the grave; resurge, resurrect; survive etc. (outlive) 110; resume, reappear; come to, − life again; live −, rise- again; relive.

heal, skin over, cicatrize; right itself.

restore, put back, place in statu quo; re-instate, -place, -seat, -habilitate, -establish, -estate, -install.

re-construct, -build, -organize, -constitute; reconvert; re-new, -novate; recondition; regenerate; rejuvenate.

re-deem, -claim, -cover, -trieve; rescue etc. (deliver) 672.

redress, recure; cure, heal, remedy, doctor, physic, medicate; break of; bring round, set on one's legs.

re-suscitate, -vive, -animate, -vivify, -call to life; reproduce etc. 163; warm up; reinvigorate, refresh etc. 689.

redintegrate, make whole; recoup etc. 790; make -good, − all square; rectify; put −, set- -right, − to rights, − straight; set up, correct; put in order etc. (arrange) 60; refit, recruit; fill up, − the ranks; reinforce.

repair, mend; put in -repair, − thorough repair, − complete repair; retouch, botch, vamp, tinker, doctor, cobble; do −, patch −, plaster −, vamp-up; darn, fine-draw, heel-piece; stop a gap, stanch, staunch, caulk, calk, careen, splice, bind up wounds.

Adj. restored etc. v.; redivivus, convalescent; in a fair way; none the worse; rejuvenated, renascent.

restoring etc. v.; restorative, recuperative; sana-, repara-tive, -tory; curative, remedial.

restor-, recover-, san-, remedi-, retriev-, cur-able.

Adv. in statu qho; as you were.

Phr. revenons à nos moutons.

661. Relapse.—N. relapse, lapse; falling back etc. v.; retrogradation etc. (retrogression) 283; deterioration etc. 659.

[Return to, or recurrence of a bad state] backsliding, recidivation, recrudescence.

V. relapse, lapse; fall −, slide −, sink- back; have a relapse; return; retrograde etc. 283; recidivate; fall off etc. 659- again.

662. Remedy.—N. remedy, help, redress; antidote, anti-toxin, -biotic; anti-, counter-poison, prophylactic, antiseptic, germicide, bactericide, corrective, restorative, stimulant, pick-me-up, tonic; sedative etc. 174; palliative; febrifuge; alterant, ative; specific; emetic, carminative; narcotic etc. adj.; Nepenthe, Mithridate.

cure; radical −, perfect −, certain- cure; sovereign remedy.

physic, medicine, patent medicine, Galenicals, simples, drug, wonder −, miracle − drugs; potion, draught, dose, pill, bolus, lozenge, tablet, tabloid, capsule; electuary; linct-us, -ure; medicament.

nostrum, receipt, recipe, prescription; catholicon, panacea, elixir, elixir vitae, philosopher's stone; balm, balsam, cordial, theriac, ptisan.

salve, ointment, cerate, oil, lenitive, lotion, cosmetic; plaster; epithem, embrocation, liniment, cataplasm, sinapism, arquebusade, traumatic, vulnerary, pepastic, poultice, collyrium, depilatory.

compress, pledget; bandage etc. (support) 215.

treatment, medical treatment, regimen; diet-ary, -etics; vis medicatrix, − naturae; médicine expectante; seton, blood-letting, bleeding, venesection, phlebotomy, cupping, leeches; operation, surgical operation; tonsillectomy, appendectomy; injection, electrolysis, massage.

pharma-cy, -cology, -ceutics; acology; materia medica, pharmacopoeia, therapeutics, therapy, posology, pathology etc. 655; home-, hetero-, all-, hydr-opathy; cold water −, open air- cure; dietetics; sur-, chirur-gery, osteopathy; healing art, leechcraft, practice of medicine; ortho-paedy, -praxy; dentistry, midwifery, obstetrics, gynecology.

faith -cure, − healing, Christian science; psycho-therapy, -analysis, psychiatry.

hospital, infirmary, clinic; pest-, lazar-house; lazaretto, lazaret; lock hospital; maison de santé; ambulance; dispensary; sanatorium, sanitarium; spa, baths, pump-room, well; hospice; Red Cross; nursing home; asylum.

doctor, physician, surgeon; medical −, general-practitioner, consultant, specialist; medical attendant; medical student, medico; chemist, apothecary, pharmacopolist, druggist; leech; Aesculapius, Hippocrates, Galen; accoucheur, gynecologist, midwife, oculist, aurist, dentist; operator; osteopath, bonesetter; nurse, monthly nurse, sister; dresser; masseur, masseuse.

V. apply a -remedy etc. n.; doctor, dose, physic, nurse, minister to, attend, dress the wounds, plaster, bandage, poultice; heal, cure, work a cure, kill or cure, remedy, stay (disease), snatch from the jaws of death; prevent etc. 706; relieve etc. 834; palliate etc. 658; restore etc. 660; drench with physic; consult, operate, extract, deliver; bleed, cup, let blood, transfuse; electrolyse; psycho-analyse.

Adj. remedial; restorative etc. 660; corrective, palliative, healing; sana-tory, -tive; prophylactic; salutiferous etc. (salutary) 656; medic-al, -inal; therapeutic, surgical, chirurgical, orthopedic, epulotic, paregoric, tonic, corroborant, analeptic, balsamic, anodyne, hypnotic, neurotic, narcotic, sedative, lenitive, demulcent, emollient; depuratory; deter-sive, -gent; abstersive, disinfectant, febrifugal, alternative; traumatic, vulnerary.

dietetic, alimentary; nutrit-ious, -ive; peptic; alexi-pharmic, -teric; remedi-, cur-able.

663. Bane. —**N.** bane, curse, thorn in the -side, -flesh, bugbear, *bête noire*; evil etc. 619; hurtfulness etc. (*badness*) 649; painfulness etc. (*cause of pain*) 830; scourge etc. (*punishment*) 975; *damnosa hereditas*; white elephant.

sting, fang, thorn, tang, bramble, briar, nettle.

poison, leaven, virus, venom; intoxicant; arsenic, Prussic acid, antimony, tartar emetic, strychnine, nicotine, cyanide of potassium, corrosive sublimate; curare; hyoscine etc.; poison-, mustard-, tear-gas; carbon di-, mon-oxide; ptomaine poisoning, botulism; miasm, mephitis, malaria, azote, sewer gas; pest, stench etc. 401.

rust, worm, moth, moth and rust, fungus, mildew; dry-rot; canker, -worm; cancer; torpedo; viper etc. (*evil-doer*) 913; demon etc. 980.

hemlock, hellebore, nightshade, *belladonna*, henbane, aconite; Upas tree.

drugs, dope, opium, morphia, morphine, cocaine, heroin, hashish, bhang.

[*Science of poisons*] Toxicology.

Adj. baneful etc. (*bad*) 649; poisonous etc. (*unwholesome*) 657.

664. Safety. —**N.** safety, security, impregnability; invulnera-bility, -bleness etc. *adj.*; danger -past, − over; storm blown over; coast clear; escape etc. 671; means of escape, safety-valve; safeguard, palladium, sheet anchor, rock, tower of strength.

guardian-, ward-, warden-ship; tutelage, custody, safe keeping; preservation etc. 670; protection, auspices.

safe-conduct, escort, convoy; guard, sheild etc. (*defense*) 717; guardian angel, tutelary -god, − deity, − saint; *genius loci.*

protector, guardian; ward-en, -er; preserver, custodian, *duenna chaperon*, third person.

watch-, ban-dog; Cerberus; watch-, patrol-, police-man, constable, peeler, bobby, copper, cop, bull, flat-foot, detective, armed guard; sentinel, sentry, scout etc. (*warning*) 668; garrison; guard-ship.

[Means of safety] refuge etc., anchor etc. 666; precaution etc. (*preparation*) 673; quarantine, *cordon sanitaire*. [Sense of security] confidence etc. 858.

V. be -safe etc. *adj.*; keep one's head above water, tide over, save one's bacon; ride out −, weather- the storm; light upon one's feet; bear a charmed life; escape etc. 671; possess nine lives.

make −, render- -safe etc. *adj.*; protect, watch over; take care of etc. (*care*) 459; preserve etc. 670; cover, screen, shelter, shroud, flank, ward; guard etc. (*defend*) 717; secure etc. (*restrain*) 751; intrench, fence round etc. (*circumscribe*) 229; house, nestle, ensconce; take charge of.

escort, convoy; garrison; watch, mount guard, patrol, scout, spy.

make assurance double sure etc. (*caution*) 864; take up a loose thread; take precautions etc. (*prepare for*) 673; take in a reef; double reef top-sails.

seek safety; take −, find- shelter etc. 666; run into port.

Adj. safe, secure, sure; in -safety, − security; have an anchor to windward; on the safe side; under the -shield of, − shade of, − wing of, − shadow of one's wing; under -cover, − lock and key; out of -danger, − the meshes, − harm's way; in -harbor, − port; on sure ground, at anchor, high and dry, above water, on *terra firma*; un-threatened, -molested; protected etc. *v.*; cavendo tutus; panoplied etc. (*defended*) 717.

snug, sea-, air-worthy; weather-, water-, fire-, bomb-proof.

defensible, tenable, proof against, invulnerable; un-assailable, -attackable; im-pregnable, -perdible; founded on a rock; inexpugnable.

safe and sound etc. (*preserved*) 670; harmless; scathless etc. (*perfect*) 650; unhazarded; not -dangerous etc. 665.

protecting etc. *v.*; guardian, tutelary; per-servative etc. 670; trustworthy etc. 939.

Adv. *ex abundanti cautela*; with impunity.

Phr. all's well; all clear; *salva res est*; *suave mari magno*; safety first.

665. Danger. —**N.** danger, peril, insecurity, jeopardy, risk, hazard, venture, precariousness, slipperiness; instability etc. 149; defenselessness etc. *adj.*

exposure etc. (*liability*) 177; vulnerability; vulnerable point, heel of Achilles; forlorn hope etc. (*hopelessness*) 859.

[Dangerous course] leap in the dark etc. (*rashness*) 863; road to ruin, *facilis descensus Averni*, hair-breadth escape.

cause for alarm; source of danger etc. 667. [Approach of danger] rock −, breakers- ahead; storm brewing; clouds -in the horizon, − gathering; warning etc. 668; alarm etc. 669. [Sense of danger] apprehension etc. 860.

V. be -in danger etc. *adj.*; be exposed to −, run into −, incur −, encounter- danger etc. *n.*; run a risk; lay oneself open to etc. (*liability*) 177; lean on −, trust to- a broken reed; feel the ground sliding from under one, have to run for it; have the -chances, − odds- against one.

hang by a thread, totter; tremble on the -verge, − brink; sleep − stand -on a volcano; sit on a barrel of gunpowder, live in a glass house.

bring −, place −, put- in -danger etc. *n.*; endanger, expose to danger, imperil; jeopard, -ize, compromise; sail too near the wind etc. (*rash*) 863; put one's head in the lion's mouth.

adventure, risk, hazard, venture, stake, set at hazard; run the gauntlet etc. (*dare*) 861; engage in a forlorn hope.

threaten etc. 909- danger; run one hard; lay a trap for etc. (*deceive*) 545.

Adj. in -danger etc. *n.*; endangered etc. *v.*; fraught with danger; danger-, hazard-, peril-. parl-, pericul-ous; unsafe, unprotected etc. (safe, protect etc. 664); insecure, untrustworthy, unreliable; built upon sand, on a sandy basis.

defence-, fence-, guard-, harbor-less; unshielded; vulnerable, expugnable, unsheltered, exposed; open to etc. (*liable*) 177.

aux abois, at bay; on -the wrong side of the wall, – a lee shore, – the rocks.

at stake, in question; precarious, aleatory, critical, ticklish; slip-pery, -py; hanging by a thread etc. *v.*; with a halter round one's neck; between - the hammer and the anvil, – Scylla and Charybdis, – two fires; on the -edge, – brink, – verge of a- -precipice, – volcano; in the lion's den, on slippery ground, under fire; not out of the wood.

un-warned, -admonished, -advised; unprepared etc. 674; off one's guard etc. (*inexpectant*) 508.

tottering; un-stable, -steady; shaky, top-heavy, tumble-down, ramshackle, crumbling, waterlogged; help-, guide-less; in a bad way; reduced to – , at- the last extremity; trembling in the balance; nodding to its fall etc. (*destruction*) 162.

threatening etc. 909; ominous, ill-omened; alarming etc. (*fear*) 860; explosive; poisonous etc. 657.

adventurous etc. (*rash*) 863, (*bold*) 861.

Int. stop! look out! beware! take care!

Phr. *incidit in Scyllam qui vult vitare Charybdim; nam tua res agitur paries dum proximus ardet.*

666. Refuge. [Means of safety.]—**N.** refuge, sanctuary, retreat, fastness; stronghold, keep, last resort; ward; prison etc. 752; asylum, ark, home, almshouse, refuge for the destitute; hiding-place etc. (*ambush*) 530; *sanctum sanctorum* etc. (*privacy*) 893.

roadstead, anchorage; breakwater, mole, port, haven; harbor, – of refuge; sea-port; pier, jetty, embankment, quay.

covert, shelter, abri, screen, lee-wall, wing, shield, umbrella; splash-, dash-board, mudguard.

wall etc. (*inclosure*) 232; fort etc. (*defence*) 717.

anchor, kedge; grap-nel, -pling iron; sheet-, mushroom-anchor, main-stay; support etc. 215; check etc. 706; ballast.

jury-mast; vent-peg; safety -valve, – lamp; lightning conductor.

means of escape etc. (*escape*) 671; life-boat, swimming belt, cork jacket; life preserver, breeches buoy; parachute, plank, stepping-stone.

safeguard etc. (*protection*) 664.

V. seek – , take – , find- refuge etc. *n.*; seek – , find- safety etc. 664; throw oneself into the arms of; claim sanctuary; take to the -hills, – woods; make port, reach shelter, bar – , bolt – , lock -the door, – gete; let the portcullis down; raise the drawbridge.

667. Pitfall. [Source of danger.]—**N.** rocks, reefs, coral reef, sunken rocks, snags; sands, quicksands, Goodwin sands, sandy foundation; slippery ground; breakers, shoals, shallows, bank, shelf, flat, lee shore, iron-bound coast; rock – . breakers- ahead; derelict.

precipice; abyss, chasm, pit, crevasse; maelstrom, whirlpool, eddy, vortex, rapids, current, bore, tidal wave; storm, squall, hurricane, whirlwind; volcano;

ambush etc. 530; pitfall, trap-door; trap etc. (*snare*) 545.

sword of Damocles; wolf at the door, snake in the grass, viper in one's bosom, death in the pot; latency etc. 526.

ugly customer, dangerous person, *le chat qui dort*; firebrand, hornet's nest.

Phr. *latet anguis in herbâ*; *proximus ardet Ucalegon.*

668. Warning.—**N.** warning, caution, *caveat*; notice etc. (*information*) 527; premoni-tion, - shment; prediction etc. 511; contraindication; symptom; lesson, dehortation; admonition, monition; alarm etc. 669.

handwriting on the wall, *tekel upharsin*, yellow flag; fog-signal, -horn; siren; monitor, warning voice, Cassandra, signs of the times, Mother Carey's chickens, stormy petrel, bird of ill omen, gathering clouds, clouds in the horizon, cloud no bigger than a man's hand, death-watch.

watch-tower, beacon, signal-post; light-house etc. (*indication of locality*) 550.

sent-inel, -ry; watch, -man; watch and ward; watch-, ban-, house-dog; patrol, vedette, picket, bivouac, scout, spy, spial; advanced – , rear-guard, lookout, flagman.

cautiousness etc. 864.

V. warn, caution; fore-, pre-warn; ad-, pre-monish; give -notice, – warning; menace etc. (*threaten*) 909; put on one's guard; sound the alarm etc. 669; croak.

beware, ware; take -warning, – heed at one's peril; watch out for; keep watch and ward etc. (*care*) 459.

Adj. warning etc. *v.*; premonitory, monitory, cautionary; admonitory, -tive; ominous, threatening, lowering, minatory, symptomatic.

warned etc. *v.*; on one's guard etc. (*careful*) 459; (*cautious*) 864.

Adv. *in terrorem* etc. (*threat*) 909.

Int. beware! ware! take care! mind! – take care- what you are about; mind! look out!

Phr. *ne reveillez pas le chat qui dort*; *foenum habet in cornu.*

669. Alarm. [Indication of danger.]—**N.** alarm; alarum, larum, alarm bell, tocsin, *alerte*; beat of drum, sound of trumpet, note of alarm, hue and cry, signal of distress, S.O.S.; blue-lights; war-cry, -whoop; warning etc. 668; fog-signal, -horn; siren; yellow flag; danger signal; red -light, – flag; fire -bell, – alarm; burglar alarm, police whistle, watchman's rattle.

false alarm, cry of wolf; bug-bear, -aboo.

V. give – , raise – , sound – , beat- the *or* an -alarm etc. *n.*; alarm; warn etc. 668; ring the tocsin; *battre la générale*; cry wolf.

Adj. alarming etc. *v.*

Int. *sauve qui peut! qui vive?* who goes there?

670. Preservation.—**N.** preservation; safe keeping; conservation etc. (*storage*) 636; maintenance, upkeep, support, sustentation, con-

servatism; *vis conservatrix*; salvation etc. (*deliverance*) 672; drying etc. *v.*
[Means of preservation] prophylaxis; preserv-er, -ative; canned goods; cold pack; hygi-astics, -antics; cover, durgget; *cordon sanitaire.*
[Superstitious remedies] charm etc. 993.
V. preserve, maintain, keep, sustain, support; keep -up, – alive; not willingly let die; shore –, bank- up; nurse; save, rescue; be –, make- safe etc. 664; take care of/ etc. (*care*) 459; guard etc. (*defend*) 717.
stare super antiquas vias; hold one's own; hold –, stand- -one's ground etc. (*resist*) 719.
embalm, dry, cure, smoke, salt, pickle, season, kyanize, bottle, pot, tin, can; husband etc. (*store*) 636.
Adj. preserving etc. *v.*; conservative; prophylatic; preserva-tory, -tive; hygienic.
preserved etc. *v.*; un-impaired, -broken, -injured, -hurt, -singed, -marred; safe, – and sound; intact, with a whole skin, without a scratch.
Phr. *nolumus leges Angliae mutari.*

671. Escape.—N. escape, scape; avolation, elopment, flight, get-away; evasion etc. (*avoidance*) 623; retreat; narrow –, hairbreadth- escape; close –, near- shave; come off, impunity.
[Means of escape] loophole etc. (*opening*) 260; path etc. 627; secret -door, – passage; refuge etc. 666; vent, – peg; safety-valve; drawbridge, fire-escape.
reprieve etc. (*deliverance*) 672; liberation etc. 750.
refugee etc. (*fugitive*) 623.
V. escape, scape; make –, effect –, make good- one's escape, make a get-away; get -off, – clear off, – well out of; *échapper belle*, save one's bacon; weather the storm etc. (*safe*) 664; escape scot-free.
elude etc., make off etc. (*avoid*) 623; march off etc. (*go away*) 293; give one the slip; slip through the -hands, – fingers; slip the collar, wriggle out of; break -loose, – from prison; break –, slip –, get- away; find -vent, – a hole to creep out of.
Adj. escap-ing, -ed etc. *v.*; stolen away, fled.
Phr. the bird has flown.

672. Deliverance.—N. deliverance, ex-trication, rescue; repriev-e, -al; respite; ransom; liberation etc. 750; truce, armistice; redemption, salvation; riddance; gaol delivery; exemption, day of grace; redeemableness.
V. deliver, extricate, rescue, save, redeem, ran-som, free, -liberate, release, set free, redeem, eman-cipate; bring -off, – through; *tirer d'affaire*, get the wheel out of the rut; snatch from the jaws of death, come to the rescue; rid; retrieve etc. (*restore*) 660; be –, get- rid of.
Adj. saved etc. *v.*; extric-, redeem-, rescu-able.
Phr. to the rescue!

673. Preparation.—N. preparation; providing etc. *v.*; provi-sion, -dence; anticipation etc. (*foresight*) 510; precaution, -concertation,

disposition; forecast etc. (*plan*) 626; rehearsal, not of preparation.
[Putting in order] arrangement etc. 60; clearance; adjustment etc. 23; tuning; equipment, outfit, accoutrement, armament, array.
ripening etc. *v.*; maturation, evolution; elaboration, concoction, digestion; gestation, hatch-ing, incubation, sitting.
groundwork, datum, first stone, cradle, stepping-stone; foundation, scaffold etc. (*support*) 215; scaf-folding, *échafaudage.*
[Preparation -of men] training etc. (*education*) 537; inurement etc. (*habit*) 613; novitiate; [– of food] cook-ing, -ery; brewing, culinary art; [– of the soil] till-, plough-, sow-ing; semination, cultivation.
[State of being prepared] prepared-, readi-,ripe-mellow-ness; maturity; *un impromptu fait à loisir*
[Preparer] preparer, teacher, coach, trainer, pioneer; *avant-courrier*, -*coureur*; sappers and miners, paver, navvy; packer, stevedore; warm-ingpan; precursor etc. 64.
V. prepare; get –, make- ready; make preparations, settle preliminaries, get up, sound the note of preparation; address oneself to.
set –, put- in order etc. (*arrange*) 60; forecast etc. (*plan*) 626; prepare –, plough –, dress- the ground; till –, cultivate- the soil; predispose, sow the seed, lay a train, dig a mine; lay –, fix- the - foundations, – basis, -groundwork; dig the foun-dations, erect the scaffolding; lay the first stone etc. (*begin*) 66.
rough-hew; cut out work; block –, hammer-out; lick into shape etc. (*form*) 240.
elaborate, mature, ripen, mellow, season, bring to maturity; nurture etc.
(*aid*) 707; hatch, cook, brew; temper; anneal, smelt; dry, cure etc. 670.
equip, arm, man; fit-out, -up; furnish, rig, dress, garnish, betrim, accouter, array, fettle, fledge; dress –, furbish –, brush –, vamp- up; refurbish; sharp-en one's tools, trim one's foils, set, prime, attune; whet the -knife, – sword; wind –, screw- up; ad-just etc. (*fit*) 27; put in- trim, – train, – gear, – working order, – tune, – a groove for, – har-ness; pack, stow away, store.
train etc. (*teach*) 537; inure etc. (*habituate*) 613; breed; prepare etc.- for; rehearse; make provision for; take -steps, – measures, – precautions; provide, – against; beat up for recruits; open the door to etc. (*facilitate*) 705.
set one's·house in order, make all snug; clear - decks, – for action; close one's ranks;·shuffle the cards.
prepare oneself; serve an apprenticeship etc. (*learn*) 539; lay oneself out for, get into harness, gird up one's loins, buckle on one's armor, *reculer pour mieux sauter*, prime and load, shoulder arms, get the steam up, put the horses to.
guard –, make sure- against; forearm, make sure, prepare for the evil day, have a rod in pickle, provide against a rainy day, feather one's nest; lay in provisions etc. 637; make investments; keep on foot.
be -prepared, – ready etc. *adj.*; hold oneself in readiness, watch and pray, keep one's powder dry; lie in wait for etc. (*expect*) 507; anticipate etc. (*foresee*) 510; *principiis obstare*; *veniente oc-currere morbo.*
Adj. preparing etc. *v.*; in -preparation, – course

of preparation, – agitation, – embryo, – hand, – train; afoot, afloat; on -foot, – the stocks, – the anvil; under consideration etc. (*plan*) 626; brewing, hatching, forthcoming, brooding; in -store for, – reserve.

precautionary, provident; prepara-tive, -tory; provisional, inchoate, under revision; preliminary etc. (*precedent*) 62.

prepared etc. *v.*; in readiness; ready, – to one's hand, – made, cut and dried; ready for use, reach me down; made to one's hand, handy, on the table, made to order; in gear; in working -order, – gear; snug; in practice.

ripe, mature, mellow; practiced etc. (*skillet*) 698; labored, elaborate, highly-wrought, smelling of the lamp, worked up.

in -full feather, – best bib and tucker; in –, at-harness; in – the saddle, – arms, – battle array, – war paint; up in arms; armed -at all points, – to the teeth, – *cap-à-pie*; sword in hand; booted and spurred.

in utrumque – , *semper- paratus*; on the alert etc. (*vigilant*) 459; at one's post.

Adv. in -preparation, – anticipation of; afoot, astir, abroad; abroach.

674. Non-preparation.—N. non-, absence of – , want of- preparation; unpreparedness; in-culture, inconcoction, improvidence.

immaturity, crudity; rawness etc. *adj.*; abortion; disqualification.

[Absence of art] nature, state of nature; virgin soil, unweeded garden; rough diamond, neglect etc. 460.

rough copy etc. (*plan*) 626; germ etc. 153; raw material etc. 635.

improvisation etc. (*impulse*) 612.

V. be -unprepared etc. *adj.*; want – , lack-preparation; lie fallow; *s'embarquer sans biscuits*; live from hand to mouth.

[Render unprepared] dismantle etc. (*render useless*) 645; undress etc. 226.

extemporize, improvise.

surprise, pay a surprise visit, take by surprise, drop in upon, take unawares; take pot-luck.

Adv. un-prepared etc. prepare etc. 673] without -preparation etc. 673; incomplete etc. 53; rudimen-tal, embryonic, abortive; immature, unripe, raw, green, crude; coarse; rough, -cast, -hewn; in the rough; un-hewn, -formed, -fashioned, -wrought, -labored, -blown, -cooked, -boiled, -concocted, -cut, -polished.

callow, un-hatched, -fledged, -nurtured, -licked, -taught, -educated, -cultivated, -trained, -tutored, -drilled, -exercised; precocious, premature; un-, in-digested; un-mellowed, -seasoned, -leavened.

fallow; un-sown, -tilled; natural, in a state of na-ture; undressed; in dishabille, *en déshabille, en négligé*.

un-, dis-qualified; unfitted; ill-digested; un-begun, -ready, -arranged, -organized, -furnished, -provided, -equipped, -trimmed; out of -gear, – or-der; dismantled etc. *v.*

shiftless, improvident, unthrifty, thoughtless, unguarded; happy-go-lucky; caught napping etc. (*inexpectant*) 508; unpremeditated etc. 612.

Adv. extempore etc. 612.

675. Essay.—N. essay, trial, endeavor, aim, at-tempt; venture, adventure, speculation, *coup d'essai, début*; probation etc. (*experiment*) 463.

V. try, essay; experiment etc. 463; endeavor, strive; tempt, tackle, take on, attempt, make an at-tempt; venture, adventure, speculate, take one's chance, tempt fortune; try one's -fortune, – luck, – hand; use one's endeavor; feel – , grope – , pick- one's way.

try hard, push, make a bold push, use one's best endeavor; do one's best etc. (*exertion*) 686.

Adj. essaying etc. *v.*; experimental etc. 463; tentative, empirical, probationary.

Adv. experimentally etc. *adj.*; on trial, at a ven-ture; by rule of thumb.

if one may be so bold.

676. Undertaking.—N. undertaking, compact etc. 769; engagement etc. (*promise*) 768; enter-, em-prise; venture etc. 675; pilgrimage; matter in hand etc. (*business*) 625; move; first move etc. (*beginning*) 66.

V. undertake; engage – , embark- in; launch –, plunge- into; volunteer; apprentice oneself to; engage etc. (*promise*) 768; contract etc. 769; take upon -oneself, – one's shoulders; devote oneself to etc. (*determination*) 604.

take -up, – in hand; tackle; set – , go- about; set – , fall- -to, – to work; launch forth; set up shop; put in -hand, – execution; set forward; break the neck of a business, be in for; put one's hand to; betake oneself to, turn one's hand to, go to do; begin etc. 66; broach, institute, etc. (*originate*) 153; put – , lay- one's -hand to the plough, – shoulder to the wheel.

have in hand etc. (*business*) 625; have many irons in the fire etc. (*activity*) 682.

Adj. undertaking etc. *v.*; on the anvil etc. 625; adventurous, venturesome.

Int. here goes!

677. Use.—N. use; employ, -ment; exer-cise, -citation; appli-cation, -ance; adhibition, disposal; consumption; agency etc. (*physical*) 170; usufruct; usefulness etc. 644; recourse, resort, avail, pragmatism.

[Conversion to use] utilization, service, wear.

[Way of using] usage.

V. use, make use of, employ, put to use; apply, put in -action, – operation, – practice; set -in motion, – to work.

ply, work, wield, handle, manipulate; play, – off; exert, exercise, practice, avail oneself of, profit by; resort – , have recourse – , recur – , take – , betake oneself- to; take -up with, – advantage of; lay one's hands on, try.

render useful etc. 644; mold; turn to -account, – use; convert to use, utilize, administer; work up; call – , bring- into play; put into requisition; call – , draw- forth; press – , enlist- into the service; bring to bear upon, devote, dedicate, consecrate, apply, adhibit, dispose of; make a -handle, – cat's paw- of.

fall beak upon, make a shift with; make the -most, – best- of.

use – , swallow- up; consume, absorb, expend; tax, task, wear, put to task.

Adj. in use; used etc. *v.*; well-worn, -trodden. useful etc. 644; subservient etc. (*instrumental*) 631; utilitarian; pragmatical.

678. Disuse.—N. forbearance, abstinence; disuse; relinquishment etc. 782; desuetude etc. (*want of habit*) 614.

V. not use; do without, dispense with, let alone, not touch, forbear, abstain, spare, waive, neglect; keep back, reserve.

lay -up, – by, – on the shelf, – up in a napkin; shelve; set –, put –, lay- aside; disuse, leave off, have done with; supersede; discard etc. (*eject*) 297; dismiss, give warning.

throw aside etc. (*relinquish*) 782; make away with etc. (*destroy*) 162; cast –, heave –, throw-overboard; cast to the -dogs, – winds; dismantle etc. (*render useless*) 645.

lie –, remain- unemployed etc. *adj.*

Adj. not used etc. *v.*; un-employed, -applied, -disposed of, -spent, -exercised, -touched, -trodden, -essayed, -gathered, -culled; uncalled for, not required.

disused etc. *v.*; done with; run down, used up, cast off.

679. Misuse.—N. mis-use, -usage, - employment, -application, -appropriation.

abuse, profanation, prostitution, desecration; waste etc. 638.

V. mis-use, -employ, -apply, -appropriate. desecrate, abuse, profane, prostitute; waste etc. 638; over-task, -tax, -work; squander etc. 818.

cut a whetstone with a razor, employ a steam-engine to crack a nut; catch at a straw.

Adj. misused etc. *v.*

680. Action.—N. action, performance; doing etc. *v.*; perpetration; exercise, -citation; movement, operation, evolution, work; labor etc. (*exertion*) 686; *praxis*, execution; procedure etc. (*conduct*) 692; handicraft; business etc. 625; agency etc. (*power at work*) 170.

deed, act, overt act, stitch, touch, gest; transaction, job, doings, dealings, proceeding, measure, step, maneuver, bout, passage, move, stroke, blow; *coup*, – *de main*, – *d'état*; *tour de force* etc. (*display*) 882; feat, exploit, stunt; achievement etc. (*completion*) 729; handiwork, workmanship, crafts-manship; manufacture; stroke of policy etc. (*plan*) 626.

actor etc. (*doer*) 690.

V. do, perform, execute; achieve etc. (*complete*) 729; transact, enact; commit, perpetrate; inflict; exercise, prosecute, carry on, work, practice, play.

employ oneself, ply one's task; officiate, have in hand etc. (*business*) 625; labor etc. 686; be at work; pursue a course; shape one's course etc. (*conduct*) 692.

act, operate; take -action, – steps; strike a blow, lift a finger, stretch forth one's hand; take in hand etc. (*undertake*) 676; put oneself in motion; put in practice; carry into execution etc. (*complete*) 729; act upon.

be -an actor etc. 690; take –, act –, play –, perform- a part in; participate in; have a -hand in, – finger in the pie; have to do with; be a -party to, – participator in; bear –, lend- a hand; pull an oar, run in a race; mix oneself up with etc. (*meddle*) 682.

be in action; come into operation etc. (*power at work*) 170.

Adj. doing etc. *v.*; acting; in action; in harness; on duty; at work; in operation etc. 170; up to one's ears in work, in the midst of things.

Adv. in the -act, – midst of, – thick of; red-handed, *in' flagrante delicto*; while one's hand is in.

681. Inaction.—N. inaction, passiveness, ab-stinence from action; non-interference; Fabian –, conservative- policy; neglect etc. 460; stagnation, vegetation; loafing.

inactivity etc. 683; rest etc. (*repose*) 687; quiescence etc. 265; want of – , in- occupation; unemployment; idle hours, time hanging on one's hands, *dolce far niente*; sinecure.

V. not -do, – act, – attempt; be -inactive etc. 683; abstain from doing, do nothing, hold, spare; not -stir, – move, – lift- a -finger, – foot, – peg; fold one's -arms, –, hands; leave –, let- alone; let -be, – pass, – things take their course, – it have its way, – well alone; *quieta non movere*; *stare super antiquas vias*; rest and be thankful, live and let live; lie –, rest- upon one's oars; *laisser -aller*, – *faire*; stand aloof; refrain etc. (*avoid*) 623; keep oneself from doing; remit –, relax- one's efforts; desist etc. (*relinquish*) 624; stop etc. (*cease*) 142; pause etc. (*be quiet*) 265.

wait, lie in wait, bide one's time, take time, tide it over.

cool –, kick- one's heels; loaf, while away the -time, – tedious hours; pass –, fill –, beguile- the time; talk against time; waste time etc. (*inactive*) 683.

lie -by, – on the shelf, – in ordinary, – idle, – to, – fallow; keep quiet, slug; have nothing to do, whistle for want of thought; twiddle one's thumbs.

undo, do away with; take -down, – to pieces; destroy etc. 162.

Adj. not doing etc. *v.*; not done etc. *v.*; undone; passive; un-occupied, -employed; out of -employ, – work, – a job; fallow; *désoeuvré*.

Adv. *re infectâ*, at a stand, *les bras croisés*, with folded arms; with the hands -in the pockets, – behind one's back; *pour passer le temps*.

Int. so let it be! stop! etc. 142; hands off!

Phr. nothing doing; *cunctando restituit rem*.

682. Activity.—N. activity; briskness, liveliness etc. *adj.*; animation, life, vivacity, spirit, verve, dash, energy, go.

nimbleness, agility; smartness, quickness etc. *adj.*; velocity etc. 274; alacrity, promptitude; des-, dis-patch; expedition; haste etc. 684; punctuality etc. (*early*) 132.

eagerness, zeal, ardor, *perfervidum ingenium*, *empressement*, earnestness, intentness; *abandon*; vigor etc. (*physical energy*) 171; devotion etc. (*resolution*) 604; exertion etc. 686.

industry, assiduity; assiduousness etc. *adj.*; sedulity; laboriousness; drudgery etc. (*labor*) 686; painstaking, diligence; perseverance etc. 604*a*; indefatigation; habits of business.

vigilance etc. 459; wakefulness; sleep-, restlessness; *pervigilium, insomnia*; racketing.

movement, bustle, hustle, stir, fuss, ado, bother, pottering; fidget, -iness; flurry etc. (*haste*) 684.

officiousness; dabbling, meddling; inter-ference, -position, -meddling, butting in, intrusiveness; tampering with, intrigue.

press of business, no sinecure, plenty to do, many irons in the fire, great doings, busy hum of men, battle of life, thick of -things, – the action; the madding corwd.

housewife, busy bee; new brooms; sharp fellow, blade; hustler, devotee, enthusiast, fan, zealot, fanatic; meddler, intermeddler, intriguer, busybody, kibitzer, pickthank.

V. be -active etc. *adj.*; busy oneself in; stir, -about, – one's stumps; bestir –, rouse- oneself; speed, hasten, peg away, lay about one, bustle, fuss; raise –, kick up- a dust; push; make a -push, – fuss, – stir; go ahead, push forward; flight –, elbow- one's way; make progress etc. 282; toil etc. (*labor*) 686; drudge, plod, persist etc. (*persevere*) 604*a*; keep -up the ball, – the pot boiling.

look sharp; have all one's eyes about one etc. (*vigilance*) 459; rise, arouse oneself, get up early, hustle, push; be about, keep moving, steal a march, kill two birds with one stone; seize the opportunity etc. 134; lose no time, not lose a moment, make the most of one's time, not suffer the grass to grow under one's feet, improve the shining hour, make short work of; dash off; make haste etc. 684; do one's best, take pains etc. (*exert oneself*) 686; do –, work- wonders.

have -many irons in the fire, – one's hands full, – much on one's hands; have other -things to do, – fish to fry; be busy; not have a moment -to spare, – that one can call one's own.

have one's fling, run the round of; go all lengths, stick at nothing, run riot.

outdo; over-do, -act, -lay, -shoot the mark; make a toil of a pleasure.

have a hand in etc. (*act in*) 680; take an active part, put in one's oar, have a finger in the pie, mix oneself up with, trouble one's head about, intrigue; agitate.

tamper with, meddle, moil; inter-meddle, -fere, -pose; obtrude; poke –, thrust- one's nose in, butt in.

Adj. active; brisk, – as a lark, – as a bee; lively, animated, vivacious; alive, – and kicking; frisky, spirited, stirring.

nimble, – as a squirrel; agile; light-, nimble-footed; featly, tripping.

quick, prompt, yare, instant, ready, alert, spry, sharp, smart, slick, go-ahead; fast etc. (*swift*) 274; quick as a lamplighter, expeditious; awake, broad awake; wide awake etc. (*intelligent*) 498.

forward, eager, ardent, strenuous, zealous, enterprising, pushing, in earnest; resolute etc. 604.

industrious, assiduous, diligent, sedulous, notable, painstaking; intent etc. (*attention*) 457; indefatigable etc. (*persevering*) 604*a*; unwearied; unsleeping, sleepless, never tired; plodding, hardworking etc. 686; business-like, workaday.

bustling; restless, – as a hyena; fussy, fidgety, pottering; busy, – as a hen with one chicken.

working, laboring, at work, on duty, in harness; up in arms; on one's legs, at call; up and -doing, – stirring.

busy, occupied; hard at -work, – it; up to one's ears in, full of business, busy as a bee.

meddling etc. *v.*; meddlesome, pushing, officious, overofficious, *intrigant*.

astir, stirring; a-going, -foot; on foot; in full swing; eventful; on the alert etc. (*vigilant*) 459.

Adv. actively etc. *adj.*; with -life and spirit, – might and main etc. 686, – haste etc. 684, – wings; full tilt, *in mediis rebus*.

Int. be –, look- -alive, – sharp! move –, push-on! keep moving! go ahead! stir your stumps! *age quod agis!*

Phr. *carpe diem* etc. (*opportunity*) 134; *nulla dies sine lineâ*; *nec mora nec requies*; no sooner said than done etc. (*early*) 132; catch a weasel asleep.

683. Inactivity.—N. inactivity; inaction etc. 681; inertness etc. 172; obstinacy etc. 606.

lull etc. (*cessation*) 142; quiescence etc. 265; rust, -iness.

idle-, remiss-ness etc. *adj.*; sloth, indolence, indiligence; otiosity, dawdling etc. *v.*

dullness etc. *adj.*; languor; segni-ty, -tude; lentor; sluggishness etc. (*slowness*) 275; procrastination etc. (*delay*) 133; torp-or, -idity, -escence; stupor etc. (*insensibility*) 823; somnolence; drowsiness etc. *adj.*; nodding etc. *v.*; oscitation, -ancy; pandiculation, hypnotism, lethargy; heaviness, heavy eye-lids, sand in the eyes.

sleep, slumber; sound –, heavy –, balmy-sleep; Morpheus, dreamland; coma, trance, catalepsy, hypnosis, *ecstasis*, dream, hibernation, nap, doze, snooze, *siesta*, wink of sleep, forty winks, snore; Hypnology.

dull work; pottering; relaxation etc. (*loosening*) 47; Castle of Indolence.

[Cause of inactivity] lullaby, *berceuse*; anesthetic, sedative etc. 174; torpedo.

idler, drone, droil, dawdle, mopus; do-little, *fainéant*, dummy, sleeping partner; afternoon farmer; truant etc. (*runaway*) 623; lounger, *lazzarone*, floater, loafer, tramp, beggar, cadger; lubber, -bard; slow-coach etc. (*slow*) 275; opium –, lotus- eater; slug; lag-, slug-gard, lie-abed; slumberer, dormouse, marmot; waiter on Providence, *fruges consumere natus*.

V. be -inactive etc. *adj.*; do nothing etc. 681; move slowly etc. 275; let the grass grow under one's feet; take one's time, dawdle, poke, drawl, droil, lag, hang back, slouch; loll, -op; lounge, loaf, loiter; go to sleep over; sleep at one's post; *ne battre que d'une aile*.

take -it easy, – things as they come; lead an easy life, vegetate, swim with the stream, eat the bread of idleness; loll in the lap of -luxury, – indolence; waste –, consume –, kill –, lose time; burn daylight, waste the precious hours.

idle –, trifle –, fritter –, fool- away time; spend –, take- time in; ped-, pid-dle; potter, putter, dabble, faddle, fribble, fiddle-faddle; dally, dilly-dally.

sleep, slumber, be asleep; hibernate; oversleep; sleep like a -top, – log, – dormouse; sleep -soundly, – heavily; doze, drowze, snooze, nap; take a -nap etc. *n.*; dream; snore; settle –, go –, go off- to sleep; drop off; fall – , drop- asleep; close – , seal up- -the -eyes, – eyelids; weigh down the eyelids; get sleepy, nod, yawn; go to bed, turn in. languish, expend itself, flag, hang fire; relax. render -idle etc. *adj.*; sluggardize; mitigate etc. 174.

Adj. inactive; motionless etc. 265; unoccupied etc. (*doing nothing*) 681.

indolent, lazy, slothful, idle, otiose, lusk, remiss, slack, inert, torpid, sluggish, languid, supine, heavy, dull, leaden, lumpish; exanimate, soulless; listless; dron-y, -ish; lazy as Ludlam's dog.

dilatory, laggard; lagging etc. *v.*; slow etc. 275; rusty, flagging; lackadaisical, maudlin, fiddle-faddle; pottering etc. *v.*; shilly-shally etc. (*irresolute*) 605.

sleeping etc. *v.*; alseep; fast – , dead – , sound-alseep; in a sound sleep; sound as a top, dormant, comatose; in the -arms, – lap- of Morpheus.

sleep-y, -ful; dozy, drowsy, somnolent, tor-pescent; lethargic, -al; heavy, – with sleep; nap-ping; somni-fic, -ferous; sopor-ous, -ific, -iferous; hypnotic; balmy, dreamy; un-, una-wakened. sedative etc. 174.

Adv. inactively etc. *adj.*; at leisure etc. 685.

Phr. the eyes begin to draw straws.

684. Haste.—**N.** haste, urgency; des-, dis-patch; acceleration, spurt, spirt, forced march, rush, dash; velocity etc. 274; precipit-ancy, -ation, -ousness etc. *adj.*; impetuosity; *brusquerie*; hurry, scurry, scuttle drive, scramble, push, hustle, bustle, fuss, fidget, flurry, flutter, splutter.

V. haste, hasten; make -haste, – a dash etc. *n.*; hurry – , dash – , whip – , push – , press- -on, – forward; hurry, skurry, scuttle along, bundle on, dart to and fro, bustle, flutter, scramble; plunge, – headlong; run, race, speed; dash off; rush etc. (*violence*) 173.

bestir oneself etc. (*be active*) 682; lose -no time, – not a moment, – not an instant; make short work of; make the best of one's -time, – way.

be -precipitate etc. *adj.*; jump at; be in -haste, – a hurry etc. *n.*; have -no time, – not a moment- - to lose, – to spare; work -under pressure, – against time.

quicken etc. 274; accelerate, expedite, put on, precipitate, urge, whip, spur, flog, goad.

Adj. hasty, hurried, *brusque*; scrambling, cur-sory, precipitate, headlong, furious, boisterous, im-petuous, hot-headed; feverish, fussy; pushing.

in -haste, – a hurry etc. *n.*; in -hot, – all- haste; breathless, pressed for time, hard pressed, urgent.

Adv. with -haste, – all haste, – breathless speed; in haste etc. *adj.*; apace etc. (*swiftly*) 274; amain; all at once etc. (*instantaneously*) 113; at short notice etc., immediately etc. (*early*) 132; posthaste; by -express, – telegraph, – wire. – wireless, – air mail.

hastily, precipitately etc. *adj.*; helter-skelter, hurry-skurry, holusbolus; slap-dash, -bang; full-tilt, -drive; heels over head, head and shoulders, headlong, *à corps perdu.*

by -fits and starts, – spurts; hop, skip and jump.

Phr. *sauve qui peut*, devil take the hindmost; no time to be lost; no sooner said than done etc. (*early*) 132; a word and a blow.

Int. hurry up! look alive! get a move on! buck up! double march! rush! urgent!

685. Leisure.—**N.** leisure; spare -time, – hours, – moments; vacant hour; time, – to spare, – on one's hands; holiday etc. (*rest*) 687; *otium cum dignitate*, ease.

V. have -leisure etc. *n.*; take one's -time, – leisure, – ease; repose etc. 687; move slowly etc. 275; while away the time etc. (*inaction*) 681; be -master of one's time, – an idle man; *desipere in loco.*

Adj. leisurely; slow etc. 275; deliberate, quiet, calm, undisturbed; at -leisure, – one's ease, – a loose end.

Phr. time hanging heavy on one's hands.

686. Exertion.—**N.** exertion, effort, strain, tug, pull, stress, force, pressure, throw, stretch, struggle, spell, spurt, spirt; stroke – , stitch- of work.

'a stong pull, a long pull and a pull all together;' dead lift; heft; gymnastics, sports; exer-cise, -citation; wear and tear; ado; toil and trouble; uphill – , hard – , warm- work; harvest time.

labor, work, toil, travail, manual labor, sweat of one's brow, swink, operoseness, drudgery, slavery, fagging, hammering; *limae labor.*

trouble, pains, duty; resolution etc. 604; energy etc. (*physical*) 171.

V. exert oneself; exert – , tax- one's energies; use exertion.

labor, work, toil, moil, sweat, fag, drudge, slave, drag a lengthened chain, wade through, strive, strain; make – , stretch- a long arm; pull, tug, ply; ply – , tug at- the oar; do the work; take the laboring oar.

bestir oneself (*be active*) 682; take trouble, trouble oneself.

work hard; rough it; put forth -one's strength, – a strong arm; fall to work, bend the bow; buckle to, set one's shoulder to the wheel etc. (*resolution*) 604; work like a -Briton, – horse, – carthorse, – galley-slave, – coalheaver; labor – , work-day and night; redouble one's efforts; do double duty; work double -hours, – tides; sit up, burn the -midnight oil, – candle at both ends; stick to etc. (*persevere*) 604a; work – , fight- one's way; lay about one, hammer at.

take pains; do one's -best, – level best, – ut-most; do -the best one can, – all one can, – all in one's power, – as much as in one lies, – what lies in one's power; use one's -best, – utmost- en-deavor; try one's -best, – utmost; play one's best card; put one's -best, – right- leg foremost; have one's whole soul in one's work, put all one's strength into, strain every nerve; spare no -efforts, – pains; go all lengths; go through fire and water etc. (*resolution*) 604; move heaven and earth, leave no stone unturned.

Adj. laboring etc. *v.*

laborious, operose, elaborate; strained; toil-, trouble-, burden-, weari-some; uphill; herculean; gymnastic, athletic, palestric.

hardworking, painstaking, strenuous, energetic. hard at work, on the stretch.

Adv. laboriously etc. *adj.*; lustily; with -might and main, – all one's might, – a strong hand, – sledge-hammer, – much ado; to the best of one's abilities, *totis viribus, vi et armis, manibus pedibusque*, tooth and nail, *unguibus et rostro*,

hammer and tongs, heart and soul; through thick
and thin etc. (*perseverance*) 604a.

by the sweat of one's brow, *suo Marte*.

687. Repose.—N. repose, rest, silken repose;
sleep etc. 683.

relaxation, breathing time; halt, pause etc.
(*cessation*) 142; respite.

day of rest, *dies non*, Sabbath, Lord's day,
holiday, red-letter day, vacation, recess.

V. repose; rest, – and be thankful; take -rest, –
one's ease.

relax, unbend, slacken; take breath etc. (*refresh*)
689; rest upon one's oars; pause etc. (*cease*) 142;
stay one's hand.

lie down; recline, – on a bed of down, – on an
easy chair; go to -rest, – bed, – sleep etc. 683.

take a holiday, shut up shop; lie fallow etc.
(*inaction*) 681.

Adj. reposing etc. *v.*; unstrained.

Adv. at rest.

688. Fatigue.—N. fatigue; weariness etc. 841;
yawning, drowsiness etc. 683; lassitude, tiredness,
fatigation, exhaustion; sweat.

anhelation, shortness of breath, panting; faintness; collapse, prostration, swoon, fainting,
deliquium, syncope, lipothymy.

V. be -fatigued etc. *adj.*; yawn etc. (*get sleepy*)
683; droop, sink, flag; lose -breath, – wind; gasp,
pant, puff, blow, drop, swoon, faint, succumb.

fatigue, tire, weary, bore, irk, fag, jade, harass,
exhaust, knock up, wear out, prostrate.

tax, task, strain; over-task, -work, -burden, -tax,
strain.

Adj. fatigued etc. *v.*; weary etc. 841; drowsy etc.
683; drooping etc. *v.*; haggard; toil-, way-worn;
footsore, surbated, weatherbeaten; faint; done –,
used –, knock- up; exhausted, prostrate, spent;
over-tired, -spent, -fatigued; forspent; unre-freshed,
stored.

worn, – out; battered, shattered, pulled down,
seedy, altered.

breath-, wind-less; short of –, out of -breath, –
wind; blown, puffing and blowing; short-breathed;
anhelous; broken-, short-winded.

ready to drop, more dead than alive, dog -tired;
– weary, walked off one's legs, tired to death, on
one's last legs, played out, *hors de combat*.

fatiguing etc. *v.*; tire-, irk-, weari-some; weary;
trying.

689. Refreshment.—N. bracing etc. *v.*;
recovery of -strength etc. 159; restoration, revival
etc. 660; repair, refection, refocillation, refreshment, regalement, bait; relief etc. 834.

V. brace etc. (*strengthen*) 159; reinvigorate; air,
freshen up, refresh, recruit; repair etc. (*restore*)
660; fan, revocillate.

breathe, respire; draw –, take –, gather –,
take a long –, regain –, recover- breath; get better, raise one's head; recover –, regain –, renew-
one's strength etc. 159; perk up.

come to oneself etc. (*revive*) 660; feel like a
giant refreshed.

Adj. refreshing etc. *v.*; recuperative etc. 660.

refreshed etc. *v.*; un-tired, -wearied.

690. Agent.—N. doer, actor, agent, performer,
perpetrator, operator; execu-tor, -trix; practitioner,
worker, stager.

bee, ant, working bee, laboring oar, shaft horse,
servant –, maid- of all work, general servant, factotum.

workman, artisan; crafts-, handicrafts-man;
mechanic, operative; working –, laboring- man;
hewers of wood and drawers of water, laborer,
navvy; hand, man, day laborer, journeyman, hack;
mere -tool etc. 633; porter, docker, stevedore,
beast of burden, drudge, fag.

maker, artificer, artist, wright, manufacturer,
architect, contractor, builder, mason, bricklayer,
smith, forger, Vulcan; black-, tin-smith; carpenter;
ganger, platelayer.

machinist, mechanician, engineer, electrician,
plumber, gasfitter etc.

semp-, sem-, seam-stress; needle-, char-, work-
woman; tailor, cordwainer.

minister etc. (*instrument*) 631; servant etc. 746;
representative etc. (*commissioner*) 758; (*deputy*)
759.

co-worker, fellow-worker, party to, participator
in, co-operator, colleague, associate, collaborator,
particeps criminis, dramatis personae; personnel.

Phrs. *'quorum pars magna fui.'*

691. Workshop.—N. work-shop, -house;
laboratory; manufactory, mill, factory, armory, arsenal, mint, forge, loom; cabinet, *studio, bureau,
atelier* hive, – of industry; nursery; hot-house, -
bed; kitchen, kitchenette; dock, -yard; slip, yard,
wharf; found-ry, -ery; furnace; vineyard, orchard,
farm, kitchen garden.

melting pot, crucible, alembic, caldron, mortar,
matrix.

692. Conduct.—N. dealing, transaction etc.
(*action*) 680; business etc. 625.

tactics, game, policy, polity; general-, statesman-
, seaman-ship; strate-gy, -gics; plan etc. 626.

husbandry; house-keeping, -wifery; stewardship;
ménage; regimen, *régime*; econom-y, -ics; political
economy; management; government etc. (*direction*) 693.

execution, manipulation, treatment, campaign,
career, life, course, walk, race.

conduct; behavior; de-, com-portment; carriage,
maintien, demeanor, guise, bearing, manner, mien,
air, observance.

course –, line- of -conduct, – action, –
proceeding; *rôle*; process, ways, practice,
procedure, *modus operandi*; method etc., path etc.
627.

V. transact, execute; des-, dis-patch; proceed
with, discharge; carry -on, – through, – out, –
into effect; work out; go –, get- through; enact; put
into practice; officiate etc. 625.

behave −, comport −, demean −, carry −, bear −, conduct −, acquit- oneself.

run a race, lead a life, play a game; take −, adopt- a course; steer −, shape- one's course; play one's- part, − cards; shift for oneself; paddle one's own canoe.

conduct; manage etc. (*direct*) 693.

deal −, have to do- with; treat, handle a case; take -steps, − measures.

Adj. conducting etc. *v.*; strategical, business-like, practical, economic, executive.

693. Direction.—N. direction; manage-ment, -ry; government, gubernation, conduct, legislation, regulation, guidance; steer-, pilot-age; reins, − of government; helm, rudder, controls, joy stick, needle, compass, binnacle; guiding −, load −, lode −, pole- star; cynosure.

super-vision, -intendence; *surveillance*, oversight; eye of the master; control, charge, auspices; board of control etc. (*council*) 696; command etc. (*authority*) 737.

premier-, senator-ship; director etc. 694; chair, seat, portfolio.

statesmanship; state-, king-craft.

minis-try, -tration; administration; steward-, proctor-ship; agency.

V. direct, manage, govern, conduct; order, prescribe, cut out work for; head, lead; lead −, show- the way; take the lead, lead on; regulate, guide, steer, pilot; take −, be at- the helm; have −, handle −, hold −, take- the reins, handle the ribbons; drive, tool; tackle.

super-intend, -vise; overlook, control, keep in order, look after, see to, oversee, legislate for; ad-minister, ministrate; patronize; have the -care, − charge- of; have −, take- the direction; pull the -strings, − wires; rule etc. (*command*) 737; have −, hold- -office, − the portfolio; preside, − at the board; take −, occupy −, be in- the chair; pull the stroke oar.

Adj. directing etc. *v.*; executive, supervisory, hegemonic.

Adv. at the -helm, − head of, in charge of; un-der the auspices of.

694. Director.—N. director, manager, gover-nor, rector, comptroller; super-intendent, -visor; intendant; over-seer, -looker; foreman, boss, straw boss; supercargo, husband, inspector, visitor, ranger, surveyor, aedile, moderator, monitor, task-master; master etc. 745; leader, ringleader, demagogue, corypheus, conductor, fugleman, precentor, bellwether, agitator.

guiding star etc. (*guidance*) 693; adviser etc. 695; guide etc. (*information*) 527; pilot; helms-man; steers-man, -mate; man at the wheel; wire-puller.

driver, whip, Jehu, charioteer; coach-, car-, cab-man, jarvey; postilion, *vetturino*, muleteer, team-ster; whipper in; engineer, engine driver, motor-man, *chauffeur.*

head, − man; principal, president, speaker; chair, -man; captain etc. (*master*) 745; superior; dean; mayor etc. (*civil authority*) 745; vice-

president, prime minister, premier, vizier, grand vizier; dictator.

officer, functionary, minister, official, red-tapist, bureaucrat; man −, Jack- in office; office-bearer; person in authority etc. 745.

statesman, strategist, legislator, lawgiver, politi-cian, administrator, statist, statemonger; Minos, Draco; arbiter etc. (*judge*) 967; king maker, power behind the throne.

board etc, (*council*) 696.

secretary, − of state; Reis Effendi; vicar etc. (*deputy*) 759; steward; factor; agent etc. 758; bailiff, middleman; ganger, clerk of. works; land-reeve; factotum, major-domo, seneschal, house-keeper, shepherd, *croupier*; proctor, procurator, curator, librarian.

Adv. *ex officio.*

695. Advice.—N. advice, counsel, adhortation; word to the wise; suggestion, submonition, recom-mendation, advocacy, consultation.

exhortation etc. (*persuasion*) 615; expostulation etc. (*dissuasion*) 616; admonition etc. (*warning*) 668; guidance etc. (*direction*) 693.

instruction, charge, injunction.

adviser, prompter; counsel, -lor; monitor, men-tor, Nestor, *magnus Apollo*, senator; teacher etc. 540.

guide, manual, chart etc. (*information*) 527.

physician, leech, archiater; arbiter etc. (*judge*) 967.

refer-ence, -ment; consultation, conference, parley, *pourparler* etc. 696.

V. advise, counsel; give -advice, − counsel, − a piece of advice; suggest, prompt, submonish, recommend, prescribe, advocate; exhort etc. (*per-suade*) 615.

enjoin, enforce, charge, instruct, call; call upon, etc. (*request*) 765; dictate.

expostulate etc. (*dissuade*) 616; admonish etc. (*warn*) 668.

advise with; lay heads −, consult- together; compare notes; hold a council, deliberate, be closeted with.

confer, consult, refer to, call in; take −, follow-advice; follow implicitly; be advised by, have at one's elbow, take one's cue from.

Adj. recommendatory; hortative etc. (*per-suasive*) 615; dehortatory etc. (*dissuasive*) 616; ad-monitory etc. (*warning*) 668; consultative.

Int. go to!

696. Council.—N. council, committee, sub-committee, *comitia*, court, chamber, cabinet, board, bench, staff; consultation.

senate, *senatus*, parliament, house, − of Lords, − Peers, − Commons, legislature, legislative assembly, federal council, chamber of deputies, directory, *reichsrath, rigsdag, cortes,* storthing, witenagemote, *junta,* divan, *musnud, sanhedrim,* Amphictyonic council; *duma,* zemstvo, soviet, *cheka, ogpu; Dail Eireann;* caput, consistory, chapter, syndicate; court of appeal etc. (*tribunal*) 966; board of -control, − works; vestry; county −, borough −, district −, parish −, town- council, local board.

cabinet –, privy- council, royal commission; cockpit, convocation, synod, congress, congregation, convention, diet, states-general, aulic council.

League of Nations, assembly, *caucus*, conclave, *clique*, conventicle; meeting, sitting, *séance*, conference, session, hearing, palaver, *pourparler*, *durbar*, pow-wow, house; *quorum*.

senator; member, – of parliament; councilor, M.P., representative of the people.

Adj. senatorial, curule, parliamentary.

697. Precept.—N. precept, direction, instruction, charge; prescript, -ion; *recipe*, receipt; golden rule; maxim etc. 496.

commandment, rule, ruling, canon, law, code, *corpus juris*, *lex scripta*, common –, unwritten –, canon- law; the Ten Commandments; act, statute, convention, rubric, stage direction, regulation; form, -ula, -ulary; technicality; nice point.

order etc. (*command*) 741.

698. Skill.—N. skill, skilfulness, address; dexter-ity, -ousness; adroitness, expertness etc. *adj* ; proficiency, competence, craft, callidity, facility, knack, trick, sleight; master-y, -ship; excellence, panurgy; ambidext-erity, -rousness; sleight of hand etc. (*deception*) 545.

sea-, air-, marks-, horse-manship; tight-, rope-ancing.

accomplish-, acquire-, attain-ment; art, science; techn-icality, -ology, -ique; practical –, technical-nowledge; technocracy; finish, technic.

knowledge of the world, world wisdom, *savoir-vire*; tact; mother wit etc. (*sagacity*) 498; iscretion etc. (*caution*) 864; *finesse*; craftiness etc. (*cunning*) 702; management etc. (*conduct*) 692; *rs celare artem*; self-help.

cleverness, talent, ability, ingenuity, capacity, arts, talents, faculty, endowment, *forte*, turn, gift, genius, flair, feeling; intelligence etc. 498; sharp-ess, readiness etc. (*activity*) 682; invention etc. 15; apt-ness, -itude; turn –, capacity –, genius-or; felicity, capability, *curiosa felicitas*, ualification, habilitation.

proficient etc. 700.

masterpiece, *coup de maître*, *chef- d'oeuvre*, *tour de force*; good stroke etc. (*plan*) 626.

V. be -skilful etc. *adj* ; excel in, be master of; have – a turn for etc. *n*.

know -what's what, – a hawk from a handsaw, - what one is about, – on which side one's bread s buttered, – what's o'clock, – a thing or two; have cut one's -eye, – wisdom- teeth.

see -one's way, – where the wind lies, – which vay the wind blows; have -all one's-wits about one, – one's hand in; *savoir vivre*; *scire quid valeant numeri quid ferre recusent*

look after the main chance; cut one's coat according to one's cloth; live by one's wits; exercise one's discretion, feather the oar, sail near the wind; stoop to conquer etc. (*cunning*) 702; play one's -cards well, – best card; hit the right nail on the head, put the saddle on the right horse.

take advantage of, make the most of; profit by etc. (*use*) 677; make a hit etc. (*succeed*) 731; make a virtue of necessity; make hay while the sun shines etc. (*occasion*) 134.

Adj. skilful, dexterous, adroit, expert, apt, slick, handy, quick, deft, ready, resourceful, gain; smart etc. (*active*) 682; proficient, good at, up to, at home in, master of, a good hand. at, *au fait*, thoroughbred, masterly, crack, accomplished; conversant etc. (*knowing*) 490.

experienced, practiced, skilled; up –, well up-in; in -practice, – proper cue; competent, efficient, qualified, capable, fitted, fit for, up to the mark, trained, initiated, prepared, primed, finished.

clever, able, ingenious, felicitous, gifted, talented, endowed, cute, inventive etc. 515; shrewd, sharp etc. (*intelligent*) 498; cunning etc. 702; alive to, up to snuff, not to be caught with chaff; discreet.

neat-handed, fine-fingered, ambidextrous, sure-footed; cut out –, fitted- for.

technical, artistic, scientific, daedalian, ship-shape; workman-, business-, statesman-like.

Adv. skilfully etc. *adj* ; well etc. 618; artistically; with -skill, – consummate skill; *secundum artem*, *suo Marte*; to the best of one's abilities etc. (*exertion*) 686; like a machine.

699. Unskillfulness.—N. unskillfulness etc. *adj* ; want of -skill etc. 698; incompeten-ce, -cy; inability, -felicity, -dexterity, -experience; clumsiness; disqualification, unproficiency; quackery.

folly, stupidity etc. 499; indiscretion etc. (*rashness*) 863; thoughtlessness etc. (*inattention*) 458, (*neglect*) 460.

mis-management, -conduct; impolicy; malad-ministration; mis-rule, -government, -application, - direction, -feasance.

absence of rule, rule of thumb; bungling etc. *v* ; failure etc. 732; screw loose; too many cooks.

blunder etc. (*mistake*) 495; *étourderie*, *gaucherie*, act of folly, *balourdise*; botch, -ery; bad job, sad work.

sprat sent out to catch a whale, much ado about nothing, wildgoose chase.

bungler etc. 701; fool etc. 501.

layman, amateur.

V. be -unskillful etc. *adj*; not see an inch beyond one's nose; blunder, bungle, boggle, fumble, muff, botch, bitch, flounder, loppet, stumble, trip; hobble etc. 275; put one's foot in it; make a -mess, – hash, – sad work- of; overshoot the mark.

play -tricks with, – Puck; mismanage, -conduct, -direct, -apply, -send.

stultify –, make a fool of –, commit- oneself; act foolishly; play the fool; put oneself out of court; lose one's -head, – cunning.

begin at the wrong end; do things by halves etc. (*not complete*) 730, make two bites of a cherry; play at cross purposes; strain at a gnat and swallow a camel etc. (*caprice*) 608; put the cart before the horse; lock the stable door when the horse is stolen etc. (*too late*) 135.

not know -what one is about, – one's own interest, – on which side one's bread is buttered; stand in one's own light, quarrel with one's bread and butter, throw a stone in one's own garden, kill the goose which lays the golden eggs, pay dear for one's whistle, cut one's own throat, burn one's fingers; knock –, run- one's head against a stone wall; fall into a trap, catch a Tartar, bring. the house about one's ears; have too many -eggs in one basket (*imprudent*) 863, – irons in the fire.

mistake etc. 495; take the shadow for the substance etc.

(*credulity*) 486; be in the wrong box, aim at a pigeon and kill a crow; take –, get- the wrong sow by the ear, – the dirty end of the stick; put -the saddle on the wrong horse, – a square peg into a round hole, – new wine into old bottles.

cut a whetstone with a razor; hold a farthing candle to the sun etc. (*useless*) 645; fight with –, grasp at- a shadow; catch at straws, lean on a broken reed, reckon without one's host, pursue a wildgoose chase; go on a fool's –, sleeveless-errand; go further and fare worse; loose –, miss-one's way; fail etc. 732.

Adj. un-skillful etc. 698; unskilled, inexpert; bungling etc. *v.*; awkward, clumsy, unhandy, lub-berly, *gauche, maladroit*; left-, heavy-handed; slovenly, slatternly; gawky.

adrift, at fault.

in-, un-apt; inhabile; un-tractable, -teachable; giddy etc. (*inattentive*) 458; inconsiderate etc. (*neglectful*) 460; stupid etc. 499; inactive etc. 683; incompetent; un-, dis-, ill-qualified; unfit; quackish; raw, green, inexperienced, rusty, out of practice.

un-accustomed, -used, -trained etc. 537; - initiated, -conversant etc. (*ignorant*) 491; shiftless; unbusinesslike, unpractical; unstatesmanlike.

un-, ill-, mis-advised; ill-devised, -imagined, - judged, -contrived, -conducted; un-, mis-guided; misconducted, foolish, wild; infelicitous; penny wise and pound foolish etc. (*inconsistent*) 608.

Phr. one's fingers being all thumbs; the right hand forgets its cunning.

il se noyerait dans une goutte d'eau.

incidit in Scyllam qui vult vitare Charybdim; *out of the frying pan into the fire.*

700. Proficient.—N. proficient, expert, adept, dab; *connoisseur* etc. (*scholar*) 492; master, -hand; top-sawyer, *prima donna*, first fiddle, *chef de cuisine*; protagonist; past master; profess-or, -ional, specialist.

picked man; medalist, prizeman.

veteran; old -stager, – campaigner, – soldier. – file, – hand; man of -business, – the world.

nice –, good –, clean- hand; practised –, ex-perienced- -eye, – hand; marksman; good –, dead –, crack- shot; rope-dancer, funambulist, acrobat, contortionist; cunning man; conjuror etc. (*deceiver*) 548; wizard etc. 994.

genius; master-mind, – head, – spirit.

cunning –, sharp -blade, – fellow; jobber; cracksman etc. (*thief*) 792; politician, tactician, diplomat, -ist, strategist.

pantologist, admirable Crichton, Jack of all trades; prodigy of learning; walking encyclopedia; mine of information.

701. Bungler.—N. bungler; blunderer, -head; marplot, fumbler, lubber, lout, oaf, duffer, stick, clown; bad –, poor- -hand, – shot; butter-fingers.

no conjuror, flat, muff, slow coach, looby, lub-ber, swab; clod, yokel, hick, awkward squad, novice, greenhorn, jaywalker, *blanc-bec*.

land lubber; fresh water –, fair weather- sailor; horse-marine; fish out of water, ass in lion's skin, jackdaw in peacock's feathers; quack etc. (*deceiver*) 548; Lord of Misrule.

sloven, slattern, trapes,

Phr. *il n'a pas inventé la poudre*; he will never set the Thames on fire.

702. Cunning.—N. cunning, craft; cun-ningness, craftiness etc. *adj.*; subtlety, artificiality; maneuvring etc. *v.*; temporization; circumvention.

chicane, -ry; sharp practice, knavery, jugglery; concealment etc. 528; nigger in the woodpile; guile, duplicity etc. (*falsehood*) 544; foul play.

diplomacy, politics; Machiavellism; jobbery, back-stairs influence, gerrymandering.

art, -ifice; device, machination; plot etc. (*plan*) 626; maneuver, stratagem, dodge, artful dodge, wile; trick, -ery etc. (*deception*) 545; *ruse, – de guerre, finesse*, side-blow, thin end of the wedge, shift, go by, subterfuge, evasion; white lie etc. (*untruth*) 546; juggle, *tour de force*; tricks -of the trade, – upon travelers; imposture, deception; *ex-pie-glerie*, net, trap etc. 545.

Ulysses, Machiavel, sly boots, fox, reynard; Scotch-, Yorkshire-man; Jew, Yankee; intriguer, *intrigant*, schemer, trickster.

V. be -cunning etc. *adj.*; have cut one's eye-teeth; contrive etc. (*plan*) 626; live by one's wits; maneuver; intrigue, gerrymander, *finesse*, double, temporize, stoop to conquer, *reculer pour mieux sauter*, circumvent, steal a march upon; overreach etc. 545; throw off one's guard; surprise etc. 508; outdo, get the better of, snatch from under one's nose; snatch a verdict; waylay, undermine, in-troduce the thin end of the wedge; play -a deep game, – tricks with; have an axe to grind; am-biguas in vulgum spargere voces*; flatter, make things pleasant.

Adj. cunning, crafty, artful; skilful etc. 698; sub-tle, feline, vulpine; cunning as a -fox, – serpent; deep, – laid; profound; designing, contriving; in-triguing etc. *v.*; strategic, diplomatic, politic, Machiavellian; time-serving; artificial; trick-y, -sy; wily, sly, slim, insidious, stealthy, foxy; underhand etc. (*hidden*) 528; subdolous; deceitful etc. 545; double-tongued, -faced; shifty; crooked; arch, pawky, shrewd, acute; sharp, – as a needle; canny, astute, leery, knowing, up to snuff, too clever by half, not to be caught with chaff.

Adv. cunningly etc. *adj.*; slily, on the sly, by a side wind.

Phr. diamond cut diamond.

703. Artlessness.—N. artlessness etc. *adj.*; nature, simplicity; innocence etc. 946; *bonhomie, naiveté, abandon*, candor, sincerity; singleness of - purpose, – heart; honesty etc. 939; plain speaking; *épanchement.*

rough diamond, matter of fact man; *le palais de vérité; enfant terrible.*

V. be -artless etc. *adj.*; look one in the face; wear one's heart upon his sleeve for daws to peck at; think aloud; speak -out. – one's mind; be free with one, call a spade a spade.

Adj. artless, natural. pure, native, simple, plain, martificial, untutored, unsophisticated, *ingenu*, unaffected, *naive*; sincere, frank; open, – as day; candid, ingenuous, guileless, unsuspicious, childlike; honest etc. 939; innocent etc. 946; Arcadian; undesigning, straightforward; unreserved, unvarnished, above-board; simple-, single-minded; frank-, open-, single-, simple-hearted; open and above-board.

free-, plain-, out-spoken; blunt, downright, direct, matter of fact, unpoetical; unflattering.

Adv. in plain -words. – English; without mincing the matter; not to mince the matter etc. (*affirmation*) 535.

Phr. *Davus sum non Oedipus; liberavi animam meam.*

704. Difficulty.—N. difficulty; hardness etc. *adj.*; impracticability etc. (*impossibility*) 471; tough –, hard –, uphill- work; hard –, Herculean –, Augean- task; task of Sisyphus, Sisyphean labor, tough job, teaser, rasper, dead lift.

dilemma, embarrassment; perplexity etc. (*uncertainty*) 475; involvement; intricacy; entanglement etc. 59; cross fire; awkwardness, delicacy, ticklish card to play, deadlock, knot, Gordian knot, *dignus vindice nodus*, net, meshes, maze; coil etc. (*convolution*) 248; crooked path.

nice –, delicate –, subtle –, knotty-point; vexed question, *vexata quaestio*, poser; puzzle etc. (*riddle*) 533; paradox; hard –, nut to crack; bone to pick, *crux, pons asinorum*, where the shoe pinches.

nonplus, quandary, strait, pass, pinch, pretty pass, stress, brunt; critical situation, crisis; trial, rub, emergency, exigency, scramble.

scrape, hobble, slough, quagmire, hot water, hornet's nest; sea – , peck- of troubles; pretty kettle of fish; pickle, stew, *imbroglio*, mess, muddle, botch, fuss, bustle, ado; false position; set fast, stand; dead -lock, – set; fix, horns of a dilemma, *cul de sac*; hitch; stumbling block etc. (*hindrance*) 706.

V. be -difficult etc. *adj.*; run one hard, go against the grain, try one's patience, put one out; put to one's -shifts, – wit's end; go hard with – , try- one; pose, perplex etc. (*uncertain*) 475; bother, nonplus, gravel, bring to a dead lock; be -impossible etc. 471; be in the way of etc. (*hinder*) 706.

meet with – , labor under – , get into – , plunge into – , struggle with – , contend with – , grapple with- difficulties; labor under a disadvantage; be -in difficulty etc. *adj.*

fish in troubled waters, buffet the waves, swim against the stream, scud under bare poles.

have -much ado with, – a hard time of it; come to the -push. – pinch; bear the brunt.

grope in the dark, lose one's way, weave a tangled web, walk among eggs.

get into a -scrape etc. *n.*; bring a hornet's nest about one's ears; be put to one's shifts; flounder, boggle, struggle; not know which way to turn etc. (*uncertain*) 475; get -tangled up, – wound up; *perdre son latin*; stick - at, – in the mud. – fast; come to a -stand, – dead lock; hold the wolf by the ears.

render -difficult etc. *adj.*; encumber, embarrass, ravel, entangle; put a spoke in the wheel etc. (*hinder*) 706; lead a pretty dance.

Adj. difficult, not easy, hard, tough; trouble-, toil-, irk-some; operose, laborious, onerous, arduous, Herculean, formidable; sooner – , more easily- said than done; difficult – , hard- to deal with; ill-conditioned, crabbed; not -to be handled with kid gloves. – made with rosewater.

awkward, unwieldy, unmanageable; intractable, stubborn etc. (*obstinate*) 606; perverse, refractory, plaguy, trying, thorny, rugged; knot-ted, -ty; invious; path-, track-less; labyrinthine etc. (*convoluted*) 248; intricate, complicated etc. (*tangled*) 59; impracticable etc. (*impossible*) 471; not -feasible etc. 470; desperate etc. (*hopeless*) 859.

embarrassing, perplexing etc. (*uncertain*) 475; delicate, ticklish, critical; beset with – , full of – , surrounded by – , entangled by – , encompassed with- difficulties.

under a difficulty; in -difficulty, – hot water, – the suds. – a cleft stick, – a fix, – the wrong box, – a scrape etc. *n.*; – deep water, – a fine pickle; *in extremis*; between -two stools, – Scylla and Charybdis; surronded by -shoals, – breakers, – quicksands; at cross purposes; not out of the wood.

reduced to straits; hard – , sorely- pressed; run hard; pinched, put to it, straitened; hard -up, – put to it, – set; put to one's shifts; puzzled, at a loss etc. (*uncertain*) 475; at -the end of one's tether, – one's wit's end. – a nonplus, – a standstill; graveled, nonplussed, stranded, aground; stuck – , set- fast; up a tree, at bay, *aux abois*, driven -into a corner, – from post to pillar, – to extremity, – to one's wit's end. – to the wall; *au bout de son latin*; out of one's -depth, – reckoning; put – , thrown -out.

accomplished with difficulty; hard-fought, -earned.

Adv. with -difficulty, – much ado; hardly etc. *adj.*; uphill; against the -stream, – grain; *à rebours*; *invitâ Minervâ*; in the teeth of; at – , upon- a pinch; at long odds.

Phr. ay there's the rub; *hic labor hoc opus*; things are come to a pretty pass.

705. Facility.—N. facility, ease; easiness etc. *adj.*; capability; feasibility etc. (*practicability*) 470; flexibility, pliancy etc. 324; smoothness etc. 255; convenience.

plain – , smooth – , straight- sailing; mere child's play, holiday task.

smooth water, fair wind; smooth – royal- road; clear -coast, – stage; *tabula rasa; full play* etc. (*freedom*) 748.

disen-cumbrance, -tanglement; deoppilation; permission etc. 760.

V. be -easy etc. *adj.*; go on – , run- smoothly; have -full play etc. *n.*; go – , run- on all fours; obey the helm, work well.

flow – , swim – , drift – , go- with the- -stream, – tide; see one's way; have -it all one's own way, – the game in one's own hands; walk over the course, win -at a canter, – hands down; make -light of, – nothing of; be at home in etc. (*skilful*) 698.

render -easy etc. *adj.*; facilitate, smooth, ease; popularize; lighten, – the labor; free, clear; disencumber, -embarrass, -entangle, -engage; deobstruct, unclog, extricate, unravel; untie –, cut- the knot; disburden, unload, exonerate, emancipate, free from, deoppilate; humor etc. (*aid*) 707; lubricate etc. 332; relieve etc. 834.

leave -a hole to creep out of, – a loophole, – the matter open; give -the reins to, – full play, – full swing; make way for; open the -door to, – way; prepare –, smooth –, clear- the -ground, – way, – path, – road; pave the way, bridge over; permit etc. 760.

Adj. easy, facile; feasible etc. (*practicable*) 470; easily -managed, – accomplished; within reach, accessible, easy of access, for the million, open to.

manageable, wieldy; towardly, tractable; submissive; yielding, ductile; pliant etc. (*soft*) 324; glib, slippery; smooth etc. 255; on -friction wheels, – velvet; convenient.

un-, dis-burdened, -encumbered, -embarrassed; exonerated; un-loaded, -obstructed, -trammeled, -impeded, -restrained etc. (*free*) 748; at ease, light. at – , quite at- home; in -one's element, – smooth water.

Adv. easily etc. *adj.*; readily, smoothly, swimmingly, *ad lib.*, on easy terms, single-handed.

Phr. touch and go.

Int. all clear!

706. Hindrance.—N. prevention, preclusion, obstruction, stoppage; prohibition; inter-ruption, -ception, -clusion; hindrance, impedition; retardment, -ation; constriction; embarrassment, oppilation; coarctation, stricture, restriction; anchor etc. 666; restraint etc. 751 & 752; inhibition etc. 761; blockade etc. (*closure*) 261; picketing.

inter-ference, -position; obtrusion; discouragement, -countenance, -approval, approbation; opposition etc. 708.

impedimen`, let, obstacle, obstruction, knot, knag; check, hitch, *contretemps, impasse*, screw loose, grit in the oil.

bar, stile, barrier; turn-stile, -pike; gate, portcullis; bulwark, parapet, barricade etc. (*defence*) 717; wall, dead wall, breakwater, groyne; bulkhead, block, buffer; stopper etc. 263; boom, dam, weir, burrock.

drawback, objection; stumbling-block, -stone; lion in the path; snag; snags and sawyers.

en-, in-cumbrance; clog, skid, shoe, spoke; brake, drag, – chain, – weight; stay, stop; preventive, prophylactic; contraception; load, burden, fardel, *onus*, millstone round one's neck, *impedimenta*; dead weight; lumber, pack; nightmare, Ephialtes, incubus, old man of the sea; remora.

difficulty etc. 704; insuperable etc. 471- obstacle; estoppel; ill wind; head wind etc. (*opposition*) 708; trammel, tether etc. (*means of restraint*) 752; hold back, counterpoise; damper, wet blanket, hinderer, marplot, kill-joy, dog in the manger, interloper; trail of a red herring; opponent etc. 710.

V. hinder, impede, impedite, embarrass.

keep –, stave –, ward- off; picket; obviate; a-, ante-vert; turn aside, draw off, prevent, forefend, nip in the bud; retard, slacken, check, let; counteract, -check; preclude, debar, foreclose, estop;

inhibit etc. 761; shackle etc. (*restrain*) 751; restrict, restrain, cohibit.

obstruct, filibuster, stop, stay, bar, bolt, lock; block, – up; belay, barricade; block –, stop- the way; dam up etc. (*close*) 261; put on the -brake etc. *n.*; scotch –, lock –, put a spoke in- the wheel; put a stop to. 142; traverse, contravene; inter-rupt, -cept; oppose etc. 708; hedge -in, – round; cut off; interclude.

inter-pose, -fere, -meddle etc. 682.

cramp, hamper; clog, – the wheels; cumber; en-in-cumber; handicap; choke; saddle –, load-with; overload, lay; lumber, trammel, tie one's hands, put to inconvenience; in-, discommode; discompose; hustle, drive into a corner; choke off. run –, fall- foul of; cross the path of, break in upon.

thwart, frustrate, disconcert, balk, foil, baffle, snub, override, circumvent; defeat etc. 731; spike guns etc. (*render useless*) 645; spoil, mar, clip the wings of; cripple etc. (*injure*) 659; put an extinguisher on; damp; dishearten etc. (*dissuade*) 616; discountenance, throw cold water on, spoil sport; lay –, throw- a wet blanket on; cut the ground from under one, take the wind out of one's sails, undermine; be –, stand- in the way of; act as a drag; hang like a millstone round one's neck.

Adj. hindering etc. *v.*; obstr-uctive, -uent; impedi-tive, -ent; intercipient; prophylactic etc. (*remedial*) 662.

in the way of, unfavorable; onerous, burdensome; cumb-rous, -ersome; obtrusive.

hindered etc. *v.*; wind-bound, water-logged, heavy laden; hard pressed.

unassisted etc. (*see* assist etc. 707); single-handed, alone; deserted etc. 624.

707. Aid.—N. aid, -ance; assistance, help, opitulation, succor; support, lift, advance, furtherance, promotion; coadjuvancy etc. (*co-operation*) 709.

patronage, championship, countenance, favor, interest, advocacy, auspices.

sustentation, subvention, subsidy, bounty, alimentation, nutrition, nourishment, maintenance; manna in the wilderness; food etc. 298; means etc. 632.

ministr-y, -ation; subministration; accomodation.

relief, rescue; help at a dead lift; supernatural aid; *deus ex machinâ*.

supplies, reinforcements, succors, contingents, recruits; support etc. (*physical*) 215; adjunct, ally etc. (*helper*) 711.

V. aid, assist, help, succor, lend one's aid; come to the aid of; contribute, subscribe to; bring –, give –, furnish –, afford –, supply- -aid etc. *n.*; render assistance; give –, stretch –, lend –, bear –, hold out- a -hand, – helping hand; give one a -lift, – cast, – turn; take -by the hand, – in tow; help a lame dog over a stile, lend wings to.

relieve, rescue; set -up, – agoing, – on one's legs; bear –, pull- through; give new life to, be the making of; reinforce, recruit; set –, put –, push-forward; give -a lift, – a shove, – an impulse- to; promote, further, forward, advance; speed, expedite, quicken, hasten.

support, sustain, uphold, prop, hold up, bolster.

cradle, nourish; nurture, nurse, dry nurse, suckle, put out to nurse; manure, cultivate, force; foster; cherish, foment; feed –, fan- the flame.

serve; do service to, tender to, pander to; ad-, sub-, minister to; tend, attend, wait on; take care of etc. 459; entertain; smooth the bed of death.

oblige, accomodate, consult the wishes of; humor, cheer, encourage.

second, stand by; back, – up; pay the piper, abet; work –, make interest –, stick up –, take up the cudgels- for; take up –, espouse –, adopt- the cause of; advocate, beat up for recruits, press into the service; squire, give moral support to, keep in countenance, countenance, patronize; lend - oneself, – one's countenance- to; smile –, shine- upon; favor, befriend, take up, take in hand, enlist under the banners of; side with etc. (*co-operate*) 709.

be of use to; subserve etc. (*instrument*) 631; benefit etc. 648; render a service etc. (*utility*) 644; conduce etc. (*tend*) 176.

Adj. aiding etc. *v* ; auxiliary, adjuvant, helpful; coadjuvant etc. 709; subservient, ministrant, ancillary, accessory, subsidiary.

at one's beck; friendly, amicable, favorable, propitious, well-disposed; neighborly; obliging etc. (*benevolent*) 906.

Adv. with –, by- -the aid etc. *n*.- of; on –, in- behalf of; in -aid, – the service, – the name, – favor, – furtherance- of; on account of; for the sake of, on the part of; *non obstante*.

Int. help! save us! to the rescue! S.O.S.!

708. Opposition.—N. opposition, antagonism, oppug-nancy, -nation; impugnation; contravention; counteraction etc. 179; counterplot.

cross-fire, under-current, head-wind.

clashing, collision, conflict, lack of harmony, contest.

competition, two of a trade, rivalry, emulation, race; war to the knife.

absence of -aid etc. 707; resistance etc. 719; restraint etc. 751; hindrance etc. 706.

V. oppose, conteract, run counter to; withstand etc. (*resist*) 719; control etc. (*restrain*) 751; hinder etc. 706; antagonize, oppugn, fly in the face of, go dead against, kick against, fall foul of; set –, pit- against; face, confront, cope with; make a -stand, – dead set- against; set -oneself, one's face- against; protest –, vote –, raise one's voice- against; disfavor, turn one's back upon; set at naught, slap in the face, slam the door in one's face.

be –, play- at cross purposes; counter-work, - mine; thwart, overthwart.

stem, breast, encounter; stem –, breast- the - tide, – current, – flood; buffet the waves; beat up –, make head- against; grapple with; kick against the pricks etc. (*resist*) 719; contend etc. 720 –, do battle etc. (*warfare*) 722- -with, – against.

contra-dict, -vene; belie; go –, run –, beat –, militate- against; come in conflict with.

emulate etc. (*compete*) 720; rival, spoil one's trade.

Adj. oppos-ing, -ed etc. *v* ; adverse, antagonistic; ambivalent; contrary etc. 14; at variance etc. 24; at issue, at war with; in opposition; 'agin the Government.'

un-favorable, -friendly; hostile, inimical, cross, unpropitious.

in hostile array, front to front, with crossed bayonets, at daggers drawn; up in arms; resistant etc. 791.

competitive, emulous.

Adv. against, *versus*, counter to, in conflict with, at cross purposes.

against the -grain, – current, – stream, – wind, – tide; with a headwind; with the wind - ahead, – in one's teeth.

in spite, in despite, in defiance; in the -way, – teeth, – face- of; across; a-, over-thwart; where the shoe pinches.

though etc. 30; even; *quand même*; *per contra*.

Phr. *nitor in adversum*.

709. Co-operation.—N. co-operation; coadjuvancy, -tancy; coagency, coefficiency; concert, concurrence, complicity, participation; union etc. 43; amalgamation, combination etc. 48; collusion.

association, alliance, colleagueship, jointstock, copartnership, trust, cartel, pool, ring, combine, interlocking directorate; confederation etc. (*party*) 712; federation, coalition, fusion; a long pull, a strong pull and a pull all together; log-rolling, freemasonry.

unanimity etc. (*assent*) 488; *esprit de corps*, party spirit; clan-, partisan-ship; reciprocity, concord etc. 714.

V. co-operate, co-adjute, concur; conduce etc. 178; combine, cartelize, unite one's efforts; keep –, draw –, pull –, club –, hang –, hold –, league –, band –, be banded- together; stand –, put- shoulder to shoulder; act in concert, join forces, fraternize, cling to one another, conspire, concert, lay one's heads together; confederate, be in league with; collude, understand one another, play into the hands of, hunt in couples.

side –, take side –, go along –, go hand in hand –, join hands –, make common cause –, strike in –, unite –, join –, mix oneself up –, take part –, play along –, cast in one's lot- with; join –, enter into- partnership with; rally round, follow the lead of; come to, pass over to, come into the views of; be –, row –, sail- in the same boat; sail on the same tack.

be a party to, lend oneself to; participate; have a -hand in, – finger in the pie; take –, bear- part in; second etc. (*aid*) 707; take the part of, play the game of; espouse a -cause, – quarrel.

Adj. co-operating etc. *v* ; in -co-operation etc. *n*., – league etc. (*party*) 712; coadju-vant, -tant; hand and glove with.

favorable etc. 707- to; un-opposed etc. 708.

Adj. as one man etc. (*unanimously*) 488; shoulder to shoulder; in co-operation with.

710. Opponent.—N. opponent, antagonist, adversary; adverse party, opposition; enemy etc. 891; assailant.

oppositionist, obstructive; obscurantist; brawler, wrangler, brangler, disputant, extremist, irreconcilable; diehard, bitter-ender.

malcontent; Jacobin, Fenian etc. 742; demagogue, reactionist.

passive resister, conscientious objector.

rival, competitor, contestant.

711. Auxiliary.—N. auxiliary; recruit; assistant; adju-vant, -tant; adjunct; help, er, -mate, -ing hand; midwife; colleague, partner, mate, *confrère*, co-operator; coadju-tor, -trix; collaborator.

ally; friend etc. 890; confidant, *fidus Achates*, pal, chum, buddy, *alter ego*.

confederate; ac-, complice; accessory, – after the fact; *particeps criminis*.

aide-de-camp. secretary, clerk, associate, marshal; right-hand; candle-, bottle-holder; hand-maid; servant etc. 746; puppet, cat's-paw; stooge, dependent, creature, jackal; tool, *âme damnée*; satellite, adherent, parasite.

votary, disciple; secta-rian, -ry; seconder, backer, upholder, supporter, abettor, advocate, partisan, champion, patron, friend at court, mediator.

friend in need, Jack at a pinch, *deus ex machinâ*, guardian angel, fairy godmother; special providence, tutelary genius.

712. Party.—N. party, faction, side, denomination, class, communion, set, crowd, crew, band, horde, posse, phalanx; regiment etc. 726; family, clan etc. 166.

Tories, Conservatives, Unionists, Whigs, Liberals, Radicals, Labour party, Socialists, Communists etc.; Republicans, Democrats, Farmer-Labor; *Fascisti*, Revolutionaries etc. 742.

community, body, fellowship, sodality, solidarity; con-, fraternity; sorority; brother-, sisterhood.

Freemasons, Knights Templars, Odd Fellows, Ku Klux Klan etx.

knot, gang, *clique*, ring, circle; *coterie*, club, *casino*.

corporation, corporate body, guild; establishment, company, copartnership, firm, house, joint concern, joint-stock company, trust, investment trust, combine etc. 709.

society, association; instit-ute, -ution; union; trade-union; league, syndicate, alliance, *Verein, Bund, Zollverein*, combination; league –, alliance- offensive and defensive; coalition; federation; confedera -tion, -cy; junto, cabal, *camarilla, camorra, brigue*; freemasonry; party spirit etc. (*co-operation*) 709.

staff; cast, *dramatis personae*.

V. unite, join; club together etc. (*co-operate*) 709; cement –, form- a party etc. *n.*; associate etc. (*assemble*) 72.

Adj. in -league, – partnership, – alliance etc. *n.*

bonded –, banded –, linked etc. (*joined*) 43- together; embattled; confederated, federative, joint, corporate, leagued, fraternal, masonic, cliquish.

Adv. hand in hand, side by side, shoulder to shoulder, *en masse*, in the same boat.

713. Discord.—N. disagreement etc. 24; discord, -accord, -sidence, -sonance; jar, clash, shock; jarring, jostling etc. ӎ; screw loose.

variance, difference, dissension, misunderstanding, cross purposes, odds, *brouillerie*; division, split, rupture, disruption, division in the camp, house divided against itself, rift within the lute; disunion, breach; schism etc. (*dissent*) 489; feud, faction.

quarrel, dispute, rippet, spat, tiff, *tracasserie*, squabble, altercation, words, high words; wrangling etc. ӎ ; jangle, brabble cross questions and crooked answers, snip-snap; family jars.

polemics; litigation; strife etc. (*contention*) 720; warfare etc. 722; outbreak, open rupture; breaking off of negotiations, recall of ambassadors; declaration of war.

broil, brawl, row, racket, hubbub, rixation; embroilment, embranglement, *imbroglio, fracas*, breach of the peace, piece of work, scrimmage, rumpus; breeze, squall; riot, disturbance etc. (*disorder*) 59; commotion etc. (*agitation*) 315; bear garden, Donnybrook Fair.

subject of dispute, ground of quarrel, battle ground, disputed point; bone -of contention, – to pick; apple of discord, *casus belli*; question at issue etc. (*subject of inquiry*) 461; vexed question, *vexata quaestio*, brand of discord.

troublous times; cat-and-dog life; contentiousness etc. *adj.* ; enmity etc. 889; hate etc. 898; Kilkenny cats; disputant etc. 710; strange bedfellows.

V. be -discordant etc. *adj.* ; disagree, come amiss etc. 24; clash, jar, jostle, pull different ways, conflict, have no measures with, misunderstand one another; live like cat and dog; differ; dissent etc. 489; have a -bone to pick, – crow to pluck- with.

fall out, quarrel, dispute; litigate; controvert etc. (*deny*) 536; squabble, wrangle, jangle, brangle, bicker, nag; spar etc. (*contend*) 720; have -words etc. *n.* with; fall foul of.

split; break –, break squares –, part company- with; declare war, try conclusions; join –, put in- issue; pick a quarrel, fasten a quarrel on; sow –, stir up- -dissension etc. *n.*; embroil, estrange, entangle, disunite, widen the breach; set -at odds, – together by the ears; set –, pit- against; rub up the wrong way.

get into hot water, fish in troubled waters, brawl; kick up a -row, – dust; turn the house out of window.

Adj. discordant; disagreeing etc. ӎ ; out of tune, dissonant, inharmonious, harsh, grating, jangling, ajar, on bad terms; dissentient etc. 489; inconsistent, contradictory, incongruous, discrepant; un- reconciled, -pacified.

quarrelsome, unpacific; gladiatorial, controversial, polemic, disputatious; factious; liti-gious, -gant; pettifogging.

at odds, at loggerheads, at daggers drawn, at variance, at issue, at cross purposes, at sixes and sevens, at feud, at high words; up in arms, together by the ears, in hot water, embroiled.

torn, disunited.

Phr. *quot homines tot sententiae*; no love lost between them, *non nostrum tantas componere lites*.

714. Concord.—N. concord, accord, harmony, symphony, homology; aggreement etc. 23; sympathy etc. (*love*) 897; response; union, unison, unity; bonds of harmony; peace etc. 721; unanimity etc. (*assent*) 488; league etc. 712; happy family.

rapprochement; réunion; amity etc. (*friendship*) 888; reciprocity; alliance, *entente cordiale*, good understanding, conciliation, arbitration, peacemaker etc. 724.

V. agree etc. 23; accord, harmonize with; fraternize; be -concordant etc. *adj*. ; go hand in hand; blend –, tone in- with; run parallel etc. (*concur*) 178; understand one another; pull together etc. (*co-operate*) 709; put up one's horses together, sing in chorus.

side –, sympathize –, go –, chime in –, fall in- with; come round; be pacified etc. 723; assent etc. 488; enter into the -ideas, – feelings- of; reciprocate.

hurler avec les loups; go –, swim- with the stream.

pour oil on troubled waters, keep in good humor, render accordant, put in tune; come to an understanding, meet half-way; keep the –, remain at- peace.

Adj. concordant, congenial; agreeing etc. *v.*; in-accord etc. *n.*; harmonious, united, cemented; banded together etc. 712; allied; friendly etc. 888; fraternal; conciliatory; at one with; of one mind etc. (*assent*) 488.

at peace, in still water; tranquil etc. (*pacific*) 721.

Adv. with one voice etc. (*assent*) 488; in concert with, hand in hand; on one's side, unanimously.

715. Defiance.—N. defiance; daring etc. ℣ ; dare, challenge, *cartel*; threat etc. 909; war-cry, - whoop.

V. defy, dare, beard; brave etc. (*courage*) 861; bid defiance to; set at -defiance, – naught; hurl defiance at; dance the war dance; snap the fingers at, laugh to scorn; disobey etc. 742.

show -fight, – one's teeth, – a bold front; bluster, look big, stand akimbo; double – , shake-the fist; threaten etc 909.

challenge, call out; throw –, fling- down the -gauntlet, – gage, – glove.

Adj. defiant; defying etc. ℣ ; with arms akimbo; rebellious, insolent; reckless, greatly daring.

Adv. in -defiance, – the teeth- of; under one's very nose.

Int. do your worst! come if you dare! come on! marry come up! hoity toity!

Phr. *noli me tangere*; *nemo me impune lacessit*.

716. Attack.—N. attack; assault, – and battery; onset, onslaught, charge.

aggression, drive, offence; incursion, inroad; invasion; irruption; outbreak; *estrapade*, *ruade*; *coup de main*, sally, *sortie*, *camisade*, raid, foray; run -at, – against; dead set at.

storm, -ing; boarding, *escalade*; siege, investment, obsession, bombardment, cannonade; air raid.

fire, volley; platoon –, file –, rapid-fire; *fusillade*; sharp-shooting, sniping; broadside; raking –, cross –, machine gun- fire; – volley of grapeshot, *feu d'enfer*; salvo.

cut, thrust, lunge, pass, *passado*, *carte* and tierce, home thrust, *coup de pied*; kick, punch, etc. (*impulse*) 276.

battue, razzia, Jacquerie, dragonnade; devastation etc. 162.

assailant, aggressor, invader.

base of operations, point of attack.

V. attack, assault, assail; set –, fall- upon; charge, impugn, break a lance with, enter the lists.

assume –, take- the offensive; be –, become- the aggressor; strike the first blow, fire the first shot, throw the first stone at; lift a hand –, draw the sword- against; take up the cudgels; advance –, march- against; march upon, invade, harry; come on, show fight.

strike at, poke at, thrust at; aim –, deal- a blow at; give –, fetch- one a -blow, – kick; have a -cut, – shot, – fling, – shy- at; be down –, pounce- upon; fall foul of, pitch into, launch out against; bait, slap on the face; make a -thrust, – pass, – set, – dead set- at; dunt; bear down upon.

close with, come to close quarters, bring to bay.

ride full tilt against; let fly at, dash at, run a tilt at, rush at, tilt at, run at, fly at, hawk at, have at, let out at; make a -dash, – rush at; attack tooth and nail; strike home; drive –, press- one hard; be hard upon, run down, strike at the root of.

lay about one, run amuck.

fire -upon, – at, – a shot at; shoot at, pop at, level at, let off a gun at; open fire, pepper, bombard, shell, pour a broadside into; fire -a volley, – red-hot shot; spring a mine.

throw -a stone, – stones- at; stone, lapidate, pelt; hurl -at, – against, – at the head- of.

beset, besiege, beleaguer; lay siege to, invest, open the trenches, plant a battery, sap, mine; storm, board, scale the walls.

cut and thrust, bayonet, butt; kick, strike etc. (*impulse*) 276; whip etc. (*punish*) 972.

Adj. attacking etc. *v.*; aggressive, offensive, obsidional.

up in arms; on the warpath; over the top.

Adv. on the offensive.

Int. 'up and at them!'

717. Defense.—N. defense, protection, guard, ward; shielding etc. *v.*; propugnation; preservation etc. 670; guardianship.

self-defense, -preservation; resistance etc. 719.

safeguard etc. (*safety*) 664; screen etc. (*shelter*) 666, (*concealment*) 530; barrage; fortification; muni-tion, -ment; bulwark, fosse, moat, ditch, intrenchment, trench, dugout, gas mask; dike, dyke; parapet, parados, sunk fence, embankment, mound, mole, bank; earth- field-work, gabions; fence, wall, dead wall, contravallation; paling etc. (*inclosure*) 232; palisade, haha, stockade, *stoccado*, *laager*, *sangar*; barri-er, -cade; boom; portcullis, *chevaux de frise*; aba-, abat-, abba-tis; *vallum*, circumvallation, battlement, rampart, scarp; e-, counter-scarp; glacis, casemate.

mine, countermine.

buttress, abutment; shore etc. (*support*) 215.

breastwork, *banquette*, curtain, mantlet, bastion, demilune, redan, ravelin; advanced –, horn –, out- work, lunette; barb-acan, -ican; redoubt; fort-elage, -alice; lines; coast defense.

loop-hole, machicolation; sally-port, postern gate.

hold, stronghold, fastness; asylum etc. (*refuge*) 666; keep, donjon, fortress, citadel; capitol, castle; tower, – of strength; fort, barracoon, pah, sconce, martello tower, peel-house, block-house, rath; wooden walls; turret, barbette.

buffer, corner-stone, fender, apron, mask, gauntlet, thimble, carapace, armor, shield, buckler; target, targe, aegis, breastplate, cuirass, plastron, habergeon, mail, coat of mail, brigandine, hauberk, lorication, helmet, helm, basinet, sallet, salade, heaume, morion, murrion, armet, cabaset, vizor, casquetel, siege-cap, head-piece, casque, steel helmet, tin hat; *pickelhaube*, csako; shako etc. (*dress*) 225; bearskin; panoply; truncheon etc. (*weapon*) 727.

garrison, picket, piquet; defender, protector; guardian etc. (*safety*) 664; trabant, body guard, champion; knight-errant, Paladin; propugner.

V. defend, forfend, fend; shield, screen, shroud; fence round etc. (*circumscribe*) 229; fence, intrench; guard etc. (*keep safe*) 664; guard against; take care of etc. (*vigilance*) 459; bear harmless; keep –, ward –, beat- off; hinder etc. 706.

parry, repel, propugn, put to flight; give a warm reception to [*ironical*]; hold –, keep- at -bay, – arm's length.

stand –, act- on the defensive; show fight; maintain –, stand- one's ground; stand by; hold one's own; bear –, stand- the brunt; fall back upon, hold, stand in the gap.

Adj. defending etc. *v.*; defensive; mural; armed, – at all points, – cap-à-pie, – to the teeth; panoplied; accoutred, harnessed; iron-plated, -clad; loop-holed, castellated, machicolated; casemated; defended etc. *v.*; proof against, bomb-, bullet-proof; protective.

Adv. defensively; on the -defense, – defensive; in defense; at bay, *pro aris et focis*.

Int. no surrender! *il ne passeront pas!*

Phr. defense not defiance.

---

718. Retaliation.—N. retaliation, reprisal, retort; counter-stroke, -blast, -plot, -project; retribution, *lex talionis*; reciprocation etc. (*reciprocity*) 12.

requital, desert, tit for tat, give and take, blow for blow, *quid pro quo*, a Roland for an Oliver, measure for measure, an eye for an eye, diamond cut diamond, the biter bit, a game at which two can play; boomerang.

recrimination etc. (*accusation*) 938; revenge etc. 919; compensation etc. 30; reaction etc. (*recoil*) 277.

V. retaliate, retort, turn upon; pay -off, – back; pay in -one's own, – the same- coin; cap; reciprocate etc. 148; turn the tables upon, return the compliment; give -a *quid pro quo* etc. *n.*, – as much as one takes; give and take, exchange -blows, – fisticuffs; be -quits, – even- with; pay off old scores.

serve one right, be hoist on one's own petard, throw a stone in one's own garden, cathch a Tartar.

Adj. retaliating etc. *v.*; retalia-tory, -tive; retributive, recriminatory, reciprocal.

Adv.. in retaliation; *en revanche*.

Phr. *mutato nomine de te fabula narratur; par pari refero; tu quoque*; you're another; *suo sibi gladio hunc jugulo*.

---

719. Resistance.—N. resistance, stand, front, oppugnation; opposition etc. 708; renitence, reluctation, recalcitration, recalcitrance; repugnance; kicking etc. *v.*

repulse, rebuff.

insurrection etc. (*disobedience*) 742; strike; turn –, lock –, barring- out; *levée en masse*, *Jacquerie*; riot etc. (*disorder*) 59.

V. resist; not -submit etc. 725; repugn, reluctate, withstand; stand up –, strive –, bear up –, be proof –, make head- against; stand, – firm, – one's ground, – the brunt of, – out; hold -one's ground, – one's own, – out.

breast the -wave, – current; stem the -tide, – torrent; face, confront, grapple with; show a bold front etc. (*courage*) 861; present a front; make a –, take one's- stand.

kick, – against; recalcitrate, kick against the pricks; oppose etc. 708; fly in the face of; lift the hand against etc. (*attack*) 716; rise up in arms etc. (*war*) 722; strike, turn out; draw up a round robin etc. (*remonstrate*) 932; revolt etc. (*disobey*) 742; make a riot.

prendre le mors aux dents; take the bit between the teeth; sell one's life dearly, die hard, keep at bay; repel, repulse.

Adj. resisting etc. *v.*; resist-ive, -ant; refractory etc. (*disobedient*) 742; recalcitrant, re-nitent, - pulsive, -pellant; up in arms.

proof against; unconquerable etc. (*strong*) 159; stubborn, unconquered; indomitable etc. (*persevering*) 604*a*; unyielding etc. (*obstinate*) 606.

Int. hands off! keep off!

---

720. Contention.—N. contention, strife; contest, -ation; struggle; belligerency; opposition etc. 708.

controversy, polemics; debate etc. (*discussion*) 476; war of words, logomachy, litigation; paper war, ink slinging; high words etc. (*quarrel*) 713; sparring etc. *v.*

competition, rivalry, corrival-ry, -ship; agonism, *concours*, match, race, horse-racing, heat, steeple chase, point-to-point race, handicap; boat race, regatta; field-day; sham fight, Derby day; turf, sporting, bull-fight, tauromachy, *gymkhana*, rodeo, Olympiad.

wrestling, *ju-jitsu*, pugilism; boxing, fisticuffs, spar, mill, set-to, scrap, round, bout, event; prize-fighting; quarter-staff, single stick; gladiatorship, gymnastics; athletic-s, – sports; games of skill etc. 840.

shindy; *fracas* etc. (*discord*) 713; clash of arms; tussle, scuffle, broil, fray; affray, -ment; velitation; col-, luctation; brabble, *brique*, scramble, *mêlée*, scrimmage, stramash, bush-fighting.

free –, stand up –, hand to hand –, running-fight.

conflict, skirmish; ren-, en-counter; *rencontre*, collision, affair, brush, fight; battle, – royal; combat, action, engagement, joust, tournament; tilt, - ing; tourney, list; pitched battle, guerilla warfare.

death-struggle, struggle for life or death, Armageddon; hard knocks, sharp contest, tug of war.

naval -engagement, – battle; *naumachia*, sea-fight.

duel, -lo; single combat, monomachy, satisfaction, *passage d'armes,* passage of arms, affair of honor; triangular duel; hostile meeting, digladiation; appeal to arms etc. (*warfare*) 722.

deeds –, feats- of arms; pugnacity; combativeness etc. *adj.*; bone of contention etc. 713.

V. contend; contest, strive, struggle, scramble, wrestle; spar, square; exchange -blows, – fisticuffs; scrap, mix with, fib, justle, tussle, tilt, box, stave, fence; skirmish; fight etc. (*war*) 722; wrangle etc. (*quarrel*) 713.

contend etc. –, grapple –, engage –, close –, buckle –, bandy –, try conclusions –, have a brush etc. *n.*. –, tilt- with; encounter, fall foul of, pitch into, clapperclaw, run a tilt at; oppose etc. 708; reluct.

join issue, come to blows, be at loggerheads, setto, come to the scratch, exchange shots, measure swords, meet hand to hand; take up the -cudgels, – glove, – gauntlet; enter the lists; couch one's lance; give satisfaction; appeal to arms etc. (*warfare*) 722.

lay about one; break the peace.

compete –, cope –, vie –, race- with; outvie, emulate, rival; run a race; contend etc. –, stipulate –, stickle- for; insist upon, make a point of.

Adj. contending etc. *v.*; together by the ears, at loggerheads, at war, at issue.

competitive, rival; belligerent; contentious, combative, bellicose, unpeaceful; warlike etc. 722; quarrelsome etc. 901; pugnacious; pugilistic, gladiatorial; palestric, -al.

Phr. *a verbis ad verbera*; a word and a blow.

721. Peace.—N. peace; amity etc. (*friendship*) 888; harmony etc. (*concord*) 714; tranquility etc. (*quiescence*) 265; truce etc. (*pacification*) 723; pacificism; pipe –, calumet- of peace.

piping time of peace, quiet life; neutrality.

V. be at peace; keep the peace etc. (*concord*) 714; make peace etc. 723.

Adj. pacific; peace-able, -ful; calm, tranquil, untroubled, halcyon; bloodless; neutral.

Phr. the storm blown over; the lion lies down with the lamb.

722. Warfare.—N. warfare; fighting etc. *v.*; hostilities; war, arms, the sword; Mars, Bellona, grim visaged war, *horrida bella*, Armageddon.

appeal to -arms, – the sword; ordeal –, wager-of battle; *ultima ratio regum*, arbitrament of the sword.

battle array, campaign, crusade, expedition; mobilization; state of siege; battle-field etc. (*arena*) 728; warpath.

art of war, tactics, strategy, castrametation; general-, soldier-ship; aerial –, submarine –, naval –, chemical-, atomic-, guerilla- warfare; military evolutions, ballistics, gunnery; chivalry; poison gas; gun-powder, shot, – and shell.

battle, tug of war etc. (*contention*) 720; service, campaigning, active service, tented field; fiery cross, trumpet, clarion, bugle, pibroch, slogan; war-cry, -whoop; battle cry, beat of drum, rappel, tom-tom; word of command; pass-, watch-word.

war to the -death, – knife; *guerre à -mort, – outrance*; open –, internecine –, civil- war.

V. arm; raise –, mobilize- troops; raise up in arms; take up the cudgels etc. 720; take up –, fly to –, appeal to- -arms, – the sword; draw –, unsheathe- the sword; dig up the hatchet; go to –, declare –, wage –, let slip the dogs of- war; cry havoc; kindle –, light- the torch of war; raise one's banner, send round the fiery cross; hoist the black flag; throw –, fling- away the scabbard; enrol, enlist, join up; take the field; take the law into one's own hands; do –, give –, join –, engage in –, go to- battle; flesh one's sword; set to, fall to, engage, measure swords with, draw the trigger, cross swords; come to -blows, – close quarters; fight; combat; contend etc. 720; battle –, break a lance- with.

serve; see –, be on- -service, – active service; campaign; wield the sword, shoulder a musket, smell powder, be under the fire; spill –, imbrue the hands in- blood; be on the warpath.

carry on -war, – hostilities; keep the field; fight the good fight; go over the top; cut one's way through; fight -it out, – like devils, – one's way, – hand to hand; sell one's life dearly.

Adj. conten-ding, -tious etc. 720; armed, – to the teeth, – cap-à-pie; sword in hand; in –, under –, up in- arms; at war with; bristling with arms; in -battle array, – open arms, – the field; embattled.

unpacific, unpeaceful; belligerent, combative, armigerous, bellicose, martial, warlike; mili-tary, -tant; soldier-like, -ly; chivalrous; strategical, internecine.

Adv. *flagrante bello*, in the -thick of the fray, – cannon's mouth; at the -swords's point, – point of the bayonet.

Int. *vae victis!* to arms! to your tents O Israel!

Phr. the battle rages.

723. Pacification.—N. pacification, conciliation; reconcil-iation, -ement; shaking of hands, accomodation, arrangement, adjustment; terms, compromise; amnesty, deed of release.

peace-offering; olive-branch; overtures; pipe –, calumet –, preliminaries- of peace.

truce, armistice; suspension of -arms, – hostilities; breathing-time; convention; *modus vivendi*; flag of truce, white flag, *parlementaire, cartel.*

hollow truce, *pax in bello*; drawn battle.

V. pacify, tranquilize, compose; allay etc. (*moderate*) 174; reconcile, propitiate, placate, conciliate, meet half-way, hold out the olive-branch, heal the breach, make peace, restore harmony, bring to terms.

settle –, arrange –, accommodate- -matters, – differences; set straight; make up a quarrel, *tantas componere lites*; come to -an understanding, – terms; bridge over, hush up; make -it, – matters-up; shake hands.

raise a siege; put up –, sheathe- the sword; bury the hatchet, lay down one's arms, turn swords into ploughshares; smoke the calumet of peace, close the temple of Janus; keep the peace etc. (*concord*) 714; be -pacified etc.; come round.

Adj. conciliatory, pacificatory; composing etc *v.*; pacified etc. *v.*

Phr. *requiescat in pace.*

724. Mediation.—N. media-tion, -torship, -tization; inter-vention, -position, -ference, - meddling, -cession; parley, negotiation, arbitration; flag of truce etc. 723; good offices, peace -offering; diploma-tics, -cy; compromise etc. 774.

mediator, intercessor, peacemaker, make-peace, negotiator, go-between; diplomatist etc. (con-signee) 758; moderator, propitiator, umpire, arbitrator.

V. media-te, -tize; inter-cede, -pose, -fere, -vene; step in, negotiate; meet half-way; arbitrate; *magnas componere lites.*

Adj. mediatory, propitiatory, diplomatic.

725. Submission.—N. submission, yielding, acquiescence, compliance; non-resistance; obedience etc. 743; submissiveness, deference.

surrender, cession, capitulation, resignation.

obeisance, homage, kneeling, genuflexion, courtesy, curtsy, *salaam, kowtow,* prostration.

V. succumb, submit, yield, bend, resign, defer to, accede.

lay down – , deliver up- one's arms; hand over one's sword; lower – , haul down – , strike- one's flag, – colors; deliver the keys of the city.

surrender, – at discretion; cede, capitulate, come to terms, retreat, beat a retreat; draw in one's horns etc. (*humility*) 879; give -way, – ground, – in, – up; cave in; suffer judgment by default; bend, – to one's yoke, – before the storm; reel back; bend – , knuckle- -down, – to, – under; knock under.

humble oneself; eat -dirt, – the leek, – humble pie; bite – , lick- the dust; be – , fall- at one's feet; craven; crouch before, throw oneself at the feet of; swallow the -leek, – pill; kiss the rod; turn the other cheek; *avaler des couleuvres,* gulp down.

obey etc. 743; kneel to, bow to, pay homage to, cringe to, truckle to; bend the -neck, – knee; kneel, fall on one's knees, bow submission, courtesy, curtsy, *kowtow;* make obeisance.

pocket the affront; make -the best of, – a virtue of necessity; grin and abide, shrug the shoulders, resign oneself; submit with a good grace etc. (*bear with*) 826.

Adj. surrendering etc. *v.*; submissive, resigned, crouching; down-trodden; down on one's marrow bones; on one's bended knee; weak-kneed, un-, non-resisting; pliant etc. (*soft*) 324; undefended. untenable, indefensible; humble etc. 879.

Phr. have it your own way; it can't be helped; amen etc. (*assent*) 488.

726. Combatant.—N. combatant; disputant, controversialist, polemic, litigant, belligerent; competitor, rival, corrival; fighter, assailant, aggressor; champion, Paladin; moss-trooper; swashbuckler, fire-eater, duellist, bully, bludgeon-man, rough, fighter, fighting-man, prize-fighter, pugilist, pug, boxer, bruiser, the fancy, gladiator, athlete, wrestler; fighting-, game-cock; swordsman, *sabreur.*

warrior, soldier, Amazon, man-at-arms, armigerent; campaigner, veteran; red-coat, military man, *rajpoot,* brave.

armed force, troops, soldiery, military, forces, sabaoth, the army, standing army, regulars, the line, troops of the line, militia, territorials, yeomanry, volunteers, trainband, fencible; auxiliary – , reserve- forces; reserves, *posse comitatus,* national guard, *gendarme,* beefeater; guards, -man; yeoman of the guard, life guards, household troops.

janissary; myrmidon; Mama-, Mame-luke; spahee, *spahi,* Cossack, Croat, Pandour; irregular, free lance, *franc-tireur, bashi-bazouk, guerilla, condottiere;* mercenary.

levy, draught, commando; *Land-wehr, -sturm;* conscript, recruit, rookie, cadet, raw levies.

private, – soldier; Tommy Atkins, rank and file, peon, trooper, doughboy, sepoy, *askari, legionnaire,* legionary, food for powder, cannon fodder; officer etc. (*commander*) 745; subaltern, ensign, shave-tail, standard bearer, non-com; spear-pike-man; halberdier, lancer; musketeer, carabineer, rifleman, sharpshooter, yager, skirmisher; grenadier, fusileer; archer, bowman.

horse and foot; horse – , foot- soldier; cavalry, horse, artillery, horse – , field – , heavy – , mountain- artillery, infantry, light horse, *voltigeur, Uhlan,* mounted rifles, dragoon, hussar, trooper; light – , heavy- dragoon; heavy; *cuirassier;* gunner, cannoneer, bombardier, artillery-man, matross; sapper, – and miner; engineer; light infantry, rifles, *chasseur, zouave;* military train, supply and transport, coolie.

army, – corps, *corps d'armée,* host, division, column, wing, detachment, *escadrille,* garrison, flying column, brigade, regiment, *corps,* battalion, squadron, company, platoon, battery, subdivision, section, squad; piquet, picket, guard, rank, file; legion, phalanx, cohort; cloud of skirmishers; impi.

war-horse, charger, *destrier.*

armored -train, – car; tank.

marine, man of war's man etc. (*sailor*) 269; navy, first line of defense, wooden walls; naval forces, fleet, flotilla, armada, squadron.

man-of-war, warship; H.M.S., U.S.S.; capital ship; line-of-battle ship, battle ship; super-, dreadnought, battle – , armored – , protected – light-cruiser; scout, flotilla leader; destroyer, torpedo boat; submarine, submersible, U-boat; submarine chaser, eagle boat, mystery ship, Q-boat; mine-layer, -sweeper; ship of the line, iron-clad, turret-ship, ram, Monitor, floating battery; first-rate, frigate, sloop of war, corvette, gunboat, bomb-vessel, fire-boat; flag ship, guard ship, cruiser; air-plane carrier; privateer; tender; depôt – , parent-ship; store – , troop- ship; transport, catamaran.

aircraft etc. 273; air force, scout, fighter, bomber, troop carrier, aerial patrol, seaplane, flying boat, torpedo plane; airship, Zeppelin; rigid – , semi-rigid – , non-rigid- airship; dirigible – , free – , captive – , kite – , observation- balloon.

anti-aircraft guns, searchlights, sound locators; catapult.

727. Arms.—N. arm, -s; weapon, deadly weapon; arma-ment, -ture; panoply, stand of arms; armor etc. (*defense*) 717; armory etc. (*store*) 636.

ammunition; powder, – and shot; explosive; propellant; gun-powder, -cotton; dynam-, melin-cord-, lydd-ite; trinitrotoluene, T.N.T., ammonal; cartridge; ball cartridge, *cartouche,* fire-ball; dud;

black Marie; 'villainous saltpeter;' poison —, mustard —, lachrymatory —, tear- gas.

sword, saber, broadsword, cutlass, falchion, scimitar, cimeter, brand, whinyard, bilbo, glaive, glave, rapier, skean, Toledo, Ferrara, tuck, claymore, creese, kris, *kukri*, dagger, dirk, hanger, poniard, stiletto, stylet, dudgeon, bayonet; sword-bayonet, -stick; side arms, foil, blade, steel; axe, bill; pole-, battle-axe; gisarm, halberd, partisan, tomahawk, bowie-knife; at-, att-, yat-aghan; yatachan; good —, trusty —, naked- sword; cold —, naked-steel.

club, mace, truncheon, staff, bludgeon, cudgel, life-preserver, shillelagh, sprig; hand-, quarter-staff; bat, cane, stick, knuckle-duster, sand bag.

gun, piece; fire-arms; artillery, ordnance; siege —, battering-train; park, battery; cannon, gun of position, heavy —, siege —, field —, mountain —, anti-aircraft —, breech loading —, quick firing-gun; field piece, mortar, trench mortar; mine —, flame- -thrower, napalm; howitzer, carronade, culverin, basilisk; falconet jingal, swivel, *pederero, bouche à feu*; smooth bore, rifled cannon; Armstrong —, Lancaster —, Paixhan —, Whitworth —, Parrott —, Krupp —, Gatling —, Maxim —, Vickers —, Hotchkiss —, Lewis —, machine- gun; tommy gun, Thompson's submachine gun; *mitrailleu-r, -se*; pompom; blow pipe.

small arms; musket, -ry, firelock, flintlock, fowling-piece, shot gun, rifle, *fusil*, caliver, carbine, blunderbuss, musketoon, Brown Bess, matchlock, harquebuss, *arquebuse*, haguebut; petronel; smallbore; breech-, muzzle-loader; Minie —, Enfield —, Westly Richards —, Snider —, Springfield —, Martini-Henry —, Lee-Metford —, Lee-Enfield —, Mauser —, Mannlicher —, magazine —, repeating- rifle; needle-gun, *chassepot*; pis-tol, -et; revolver, automatic pistol, automatic; wind-, air-gun; flame —, gas- projector.

bow, cross-bow, arbalest, balister, catapult, sling; battering-ram etc. (*impulse*) 276; gunnery; ballistics etc. (*propulsion*) 284.

missile, bolt, projectile, shot, pellet, ball; grape; grape —, canister —, bar —, cannon —, langrel —, langrage —, round —, chain- shot; explosive; incendiary —, expanding —, soft-nosed —, dum-dum- bullet; slug, stone, brickbat; hand —, rifle-grenade; high explosive —, incendiary —, stink-, A-, H-, atomic —, hydrogen — bomb; petard, torpedo, carcass, rocket; congreve, — rocket; shrapnel, *mitraille*; thunderbolt; mine, land mine, infernal machine.

pike, lance, spear, spontoon, javelin, assagai, throwing stick —, dart, djerrid, arrow, reed, shaft, bolt, boomerang, harpoon, gaff.

728. Arena.—N. arena, field, platform; scene of action, theater; walk, course; hustings; stage, boards etc. (*playhouse*) 599; amphitheater; Coli-, Colos-seum; Flavian amphitheater, hippodrome, circus, race-course, track, *stadium, corso*, turf, cockpit, bear-garden, play-ground, playing fields, *gymnasium, palaestra*, ring, lists; tilt-yard, -ing ground; *Campus Martius, Champ de Mars*; aerodrome, airport, air base, flying field.

theater —, seat- of war; battle-field, -ground; field of -battle, — slaughter; no man's land; Aceldama, camp; the enemy's camp; trysting- place etc. (*place of meeting*) 74.

729. Completion.—N. completion; accomplish-, achieve-, fulfil-ment; performance, execution; des-, dis-patch; consummation, culmination, climax; finish, conclusion, effectuation; close etc. (*end*) 67; terminus etc. (*arrival*) 292; winding up; *finale, dénouement*, catastrophe, issue, upshot, result; final —, last —, crowning —, finishing- -touch, — stroke; last finish, *coup de grâce*; crowning of the edifice; coping-, keystone; missing link etc. 53; superstructure, *ne plus ultra*, work done, *fait accompli*. elaboration; finality; completeness etc. 52.

V. effect, -uate; accomplish, achieve, compass, consummate, hammer out; bring to -maturity, — perfection; perfect, complete; elaborate.

do, execute, make; go —, get- through; work out, enact; bring -about, — to bear, — to pass, — through, — to a head.

des-, dis-patch; knock —, finish —, polish- off; make short work of; dispose of, set at rest; perform, discharge, fulfil, realize; put in -practice, — force; carry -out, — into effect, — into execution; make good; be as good as one's word.

do thoroughly, not do by halves, go the whole hog; drive home; be in at the death etc. (*persevere*) 604*a*; carry through, play out, exhaust, deliver the goods, fill the bill.

finish, bring to a close etc. (*end*) 67; wind up, stamp, clinch, seal, set the seal on, put the seal to; give the -final touch etc. *n*. to; put the -last, — finishing- hand to; crown, — all; cap.

ripen, culminate; come to a -head, — crisis; come to its end; die -a natural death, — of old age; run -its course, — one's race; touch —, reach —, attain- the goal; reach etc. (*arrive*) 292; get in the harvest.

Adj. completing, final; conclu-ding, -sive; crowning etc, *v.*; exhaustive, complete, mature, perfect, consummate.

done, completed etc. *v.*; done for, sped, wrought out; highly wrought etc. (*preparation*) 673; thorough etc. 52; ripe etc. (*ready*) 673.

Adv. completely etc. (*thoroughly*) 52; to crown all, out of hand.

Phr. the race is run; *actum est; finis coronat opus; consummatum est; c'en est fait*; it is all over; the game is played out, the bubble has burst.

730. Non-Completion.—N. non-completion, -fulfilment; shortcoming etc. 304; incompleteness etc. 53; drawn -battle, — game; work of Penelope, task of Sisyphus.

non-performance, inexecution; neglect etc. 460.

V. not -complete etc. 729; leave -unfinished etc. *adj.*, — undone; neglect etc. 460; let -alone, — slip; lose sight of.

fall short of etc. 304; do things by halves; scotch the snake, not kill it; hang fire; be slow to; collapse etc. 304.

Adj. not completed etc. *v.*; incomplete etc. 53; uncompleted, unfinished; unaccomplished; unperformed, unexecuted; sketchy, addle.

in progress, in hand; going on, proceeding; on one's hands; on the fire; on the stocks; in preparation; lacking the finishing touch.

Adv. *re infectâ*.

731. Success.—N. success, -fulness; speed; advance etc. (*progress*) 282.

trump card; hit, stroke; lucky −, fortunate −, good- -hit, − stroke; bold −, master- stroke; *coup de maître*, checkmate; half the battle, prize; profit etc. (*acquisition*) 775; best seller.

continued success; good fortune etc. (*prosperity*) 734; time well spent.

advantage over; edge; upper-, whiphand; ascendancy, mastery; expugnation, conquest, victory, subdual; subjugation etc. (*subjection*) 749.

triumph etc. (*exultation*) 884; proficiency etc. (*skill*) 698; conqueror, victor, winner, champion; master of the -situation, − position.

V. succeed; be -successful etc. *adj.*; gain one's - end, − ends; crown with success.

gain −, attain −, carry −, secure −, win- -a point, − an object; put over; make a go of; manage to, contrive to; accomplish etc. (*effect, complete*) 729; do −, work- wonders.

come off -well, − successfully, − with flying colors; make short work of; take −, carry- by storm; bear away the bell; win -one's spurs, − the battle; win −, carry −, gain- the -day, − prize, − palm; climb on the bandwagon; have -the best of it, − it all one's own way, − the game in one's own hands, − the ball at one's feet, − one on the hip; walk over the course; carry all before one, remain in possession of the field; score a success, win hands down.

speed; make progress etc. (*advance*) 282; win −, make −, work −, find- one's way; strive to some purpose; prosper etc. 734; drive a roaring trade; make profit etc. (*acquire*) 775; reap −, gather- the -fruits, − benefit of, − harvest; make one's fortune, get in the harvest, turn to good account; turn to account etc. (*use*) 677.

triumph, be triumphant; gain −, obtain- -a victory, − an advantage; chain victory to one's car.

surmount −, overcome −, get over- -a difficulty, − an obstacle etc. 706; *se tirer d'affaire*; make head against; stem the -torrent, − tide, − current; weather -the storm, − a point; turn a corner, keep one's head above water, tide over; master; get −, have −, gain- the -better of, − best of, − upper hand, − ascendancy, − whip hand, − start of; distance; surpass etc. (*superiority*) 33.

defeat, conquer, vanquish, discomfit; over-come, throw, -power, -master, -match, -set, -ride, -reach; out-wit, -do, -flank, -maneuver, -general, -vote; take the wind out of one's adversary's sails; beat, − hollow; rout, lick, drub, floor, worst; put -down, − to flight, − to the rout, − *hors de combat*; − out of court.

silence, quell, nonsuit, checkmate, upset, confound, nonplus, trump; baffle etc. (*hinder*) 706; circumvent, elude; trip up − the heels of; drive - into a corner, − to the wall; run hard, put one's nose out of joint.*

settle, do for; break the -neck of, − back of; capsize, sink, shipwreck, drown, swamp; subdue; subjugate etc. (*subject*) 749; reduce; make the enemy bite the dust; victimize, roll in the dust, trample under foot, put an extinguisher upon.

answer, − the purpose; avail, prevail, take effect, do, turn out well, work well, take, tell, bear fruit; hit -it, − the mark, − the right nail on the head; nick it; turn up trumps, make a hit; find one's account in.

Adj. succeeding etc. *v.*; successful; prosperous

etc. 734; triumphant; flushed −, crowned- with success; victorious; set up; in the ascendant; unbeaten etc. (*see* beat etc. *v.*); well-spent; felicitous, effective, in full swing.

Adv. successfully etc. *adj.*; with flying colors, in triumph, swimmingly; *à merveille*, beyond all hope; to some −, good- purpose; to one's heart's content.

Phr. *veni vidi vici*, the day being one's own, one's star in the ascendant; *omne tulit punctum*.

732. Failure.—N. failure; non-success, -fulfilment; dead failure, successlessness; abortion, miscarriage; *brutum fulmen* etc. 158; labor in vain etc. (*inutility*) 645; no go; inefficacy; inefficaciousness etc. *adj.*; vain −, ineffectual −, abortive- -attempt, − efforts; flash in the pan, 'lame and impotent conclusion;' frustration; slip 'twixt cup and lip etc. (*disappointment*) 509.

blunder etc. (*mistake*) 495; fault, omission, miss, oversight, slip, trip, stumble, claudication, footfall; false −, wrong- step; *faux pas*, titubation, *bévue*, *faute*, lurch; botchery etc. (*want of skill*) 699; scrape, jam, mess, muddle, foozle, *fiasco*, breakdown.

mishap etc. (*misfortune*) 735; split, collapse, smash, blow, explosion.

repulse, rebuff, defeat, rout, overthrow, discomfiture; beating, drubbing; *quietus*, nonsuit, subjugation; check-, fool's-mate.

fall, downfall, ruin, perdition; wreck etc. (*destruction*) 162; death-blow; bankruptcy etc. (*non-payment*) 808.

losing game, *affaire flambée*.

victim, prey; bankrupt.

V. fail; be -unsuccessful etc. *adj.*; not -succeed etc. 731; make -vain efforts etc. *n.*; do −, labor −, toil- in vain; lose one's labor, take nothing by one's motion; bring to naught, make nothing of; wash a blackamoor white etc. (*impossible*) 471; roll the stone of Sisyphus etc. (*useless*) 645; do by halves etc. (*not complete*) 730; lose ground etc. (*recede*) 283; flunk; fall short of etc. 304.

miss, − one's aim, − the mark, − one's footing, − stays; slip, trip, stumble; make a -slip etc. *n.*, − blunder etc. 495, − mess of, − botch of; bitch it, miscarry, abort, go up like a rocket and come down like the stick, reckon without one's host; get the wrong sow by the ear etc. (*blunder, mismanage*) 699.

limp, halt, hobble, titubate; fall, tumble; lose one's balance; fall -to the ground, − between two stools; flounder, falter, stick in the mud, run aground, split upon a rock; run −, knock −, dash- one's head against a stone wall; break one's back; break down, sink, drown, founder, have the ground cut from under one; get into -trouble, − a mess, − a scrape; come to grief etc. (*adversity*) 735; go to - the wall, − the dogs, − pot; lick −, bite- the dust; be -defeated etc. 731; have the worst of it, lose the day, come off second best, lose; fall a prey to; succumb etc. (*submit*) 725; not have a leg to stand on.

come to nothing, end in smoke; fall -to the ground, − through, − dead, − still-born, − flat; slip through one's fingers; hang −, miss- fire; flash in the pan, collapse; topple down etc. (*descent*) 305; go to wrack and ruin etc. (*destruction*) 162.

go amiss, go wrong, go cross, go hard with, go on a wrong tack; go on −, come off −, turn out

—, work- ill; take -a wrong, — an ugly- turn; gang agley.

be all -over with, — up with; explode; dash one's hopes etc. (*disappoint*) 509; defeat the purpose; upset the apple cart; sow the wind and reap the whirlwind, jump out of the frying pan into the fire.

Adj. unsuccessful, successless; failing, tripping etc. *v.*; at fault; unfortunate etc. 735.

abortive, addle, still-born; fruitless, sterile, bootless; ineffect-ual, -ive; inefficient etc. (*impotent*) 158; inefficacious; lame, hobbling, *décousu*; insufficient etc. 640; unavailing etc. (*useless*) 645; of no effect.

aground, grounded, swamped, stranded, cast away, wrecked, foundered, capsized, shipwrecked, non-suited; foiled; defeated etc. 731; struck —, borne —. broken- down; down-trodden; over-borne, -whelmed; all up with; beaten to a frazzle.

lost, undone, ruined, broken; bankrupt etc. (*not paying*) 808; played out; done -up, — for; dead beat, ruined root and branch, *flambé*, knocked on the head; destroyed etc. 162.

frustrated, thwarted, crossed, unhinged, disconcerted, dashed; thrown -off one's balance, — on one's back, — on one's beam ends; unhorsed, in a sorry plight; hard hit.

stultified, befooled, dished, hoist on one's own petard, victimized, sacrificed.

wide of the mark etc. (*error*) 495; out of one's reckoning etc. (*inexpectation*) 508; left in the lurch; thrown away etc. (*wasted*) 638; unattained; uncompleted etc. 730.

Adv. unsuccessfully etc. *adj.*; to little or no purpose, in vain, *re infectâ*.

Phr. the bubble has burst, the game is up, all is lost; the devil to pay; *parturiunt montes* etc. (*disappointment*) 509.

733. Trophy.—N. trophy; medal, prize, palm; ribbon, blue ribbon, *cordon bleu*; citation; cup, laurel, -s; bays, crown, chaplet, wreath, civic crown; Victoria Cross, V.C., *Croix de Guerre*, Iron Cross; Distinguished Service Cross, Medal of Honor, Congressional Medal; insignia etc. 550; feather in one's cap etc. (*honor*) 873; decoration etc. 877; garland, triumphal arch.

triumph etc. (*celebration*) 883; flying colors etc. (*show*) 882.

monumentum aere perennius.

734. Prosperity.—N. prosperity, welfare, well-being; affluence etc. (*wealth*) 803; success etc. 731; thrift, roaring trade; chicken in every pot, the full dinner paid; good —, smiles of- fortune; blessings, godsend.

luck; good —, run of- luck; sunshine; fair - weather, — wind; palmy —, bright —, halcyon-days; piping times, tide, flood, high tide.

Saturnia regna, Saturnian age; golden -time, — age; bed of roses; fat of the land, milk and honey, loaves and fishes, fleshpots of Egypt.

made man, lucky dog, *enfant fâté*, spoiled child of fortune.

upstart, *parvenu, nouveau riche*, profiteer, skip-jack, mushroom.

V. prosper, thrive, flourish; be -prosperous etc. *adj.*; drive a roaring trade; go on -well, — smoothly, — swimmingly; sail before the wind, swim with the tide; run -smooth, — smoothly, — on all fours.

rise —, get on- in the world; work —, make-one's way; look up; lift —, raise- one's head, make one's -fortune, — pile, feather one's nest.

flower, blow, blossom, bloom, fructify, bear fruit, fatten, batten.

keep oneself afloat; keep —, hóld- one's head above water; light —, fall- on one's -legs, — feet; drop into a good thing; bear a charmed life; bask in the sunshine; have a -good, — fine- time of it; have a run, — of luck; have the -good fortune etc. *n.* to; take a favorable turn; live -on the fat of the land, — in clover.

Adj. prosperous; thriving etc. *v.*; in a fair way, buoyant; well -off, — to do, — to do in the world; set up, at one's ease; rich etc. 803; in good case; in -full, — high- feather; fortunate, lucky, in luck; born -with a silver spoon in one's mouth, — under a lucky star; on the sunny side of the hedge.

auspicious, propitious, providential.

palmy, halcyon; agreeable etc. 829; *couleur de rose.*

Adv. prosperously etc. *adj.*; swimmingly; as good luck would have it; beyond all -expectation, — hope, — one's wildest dreams.

Phr. one's star in the ascendant, all for the best, one's course runs smooth.

735. Adversity.—N. adversity, çvil etc. 619; failure etc. 732; bad —, ill —, evil —, adverse —, hard- -fortune, — hap, — luck, — lot; frowns of fortune; evil -dispensation, — star, — genius; ups and downs of !ife, broken fortunes; hard -case, — lines, — life; sea —, peck- of troubles; hell upon earth; slough of despond; jinx.

trouble, humiliation, hardship, curse, blight, blast, load, pressure.

pressure of the times, iron age, evil day, time out of joint; hard —, bad —, sad- times; rainy day, cloud, dark cloud, gathering clouds, ill wind; visitation, infliction; affliction etc. (*painfulness*) 830; bitter -pill, — cup; care, trial; the sport of fortune.

mis-hap, -chance, -adventure, -fortune; disaster, calamity, catastrophe; accident, casualty, cross, reverse, check, *contretemps*, rub, pinch, setback.

losing game; falling etc. *v.*; fall, down-fall, come-down; ruin-ation; -ousness; undoing; extremity; ruin etc. (*destruction*) 162.

V. be -ill off etc. *adj.*; go hard with; fall on evil, — days; go on ill; not -prosper etc. 734.

go -downhill, — to rack and ruin etc. (*destruction*) 162, — to the dogs; fall, — from one's high estate; decay, sink, decline, go down in the world; have seen better days; bring down one's grey hairs with sorrow to the grave; come to grief; be all - over, — up- with; bring a -wasp's, — hornet's- nest about one's ears.

Adj. unfortunate, unblest, unhappy, unlucky; im-, un-prosperous; luck-, hap-less; out of luck; in trouble, in a bad way, in an evil plight; under a cloud; clouded; ill —, badly- off; in adverse cir-cumstances; poor etc. 804; behindhand, down in the world, decayed, undone; on the road to ruin, on its last legs, on the wane; in one's utmost need.

planet-struck, devoted; born -under an evil star, − with a wooden ladle in one's mouth; ill-fated, -starred, -omened; inconspicuous, ominous, doomed, unpropitious.

adverse, untoward; disastrous, calamitous, ruinous, dire, deplorable.

Adv. if the worst come to the worst, as ill luck would have it, from bad to worse, out of the frying pan into the fire.

Phr. one's star is on the wane; one's luck -turns, − fails; the game is up, one's doom is sealed, the ground crumbles under one's feet, *sic transit gloria mundi, tant va la cruche à l'eau qu'à la fin elle se casse.*

---

736. Mediocrity.—N. moderate − , average-circumstances; respectability; middle classes, *bourgeoisie*; mediocrity; golden mean etc. (*midcourse*) 628, (*moderation*) 174.

V. jog on; go − , get on- -fairly, − quietly, − peaceably, − tolerably, − respectably; steer a middle course etc. 628.

Adj. middling, so-so, fair, medium, moderate, mediocre, second-, third- etc. -rate.

---

737. Authority.—N. authority; influence, patronage, power, preponderance, credit, *prestige*, prerogative, jurisdiction; right etc. (*title*) 924.

divine right, dynastic rights, authoritativeness; absolut-eness, -ism; despotism, tyranny; *jus nocendi.*

command, empire, sway, rule; domin-ion, -ation; sovereignty, supremacy, suzerainty; lord-, head-ship; chiefdom; seignior-y, -ity, hegemony, patriarchate, patriarchy; master-y, -ship, -dom; government etc. (*direction*) 693; dictation, control.

hold, grasp; grip, -e; reach; iron sway etc. (*severity*) 739; fangs, clutches, talons; rod of empire etc. (*scepter*) 747.

reign, regnancy, *régime*, dynasty; director-, dictator-ship; protector-ate, -ship; caliphate, pashalic, electorate; presiden-cy, -tship; administration; pro-, consulship; prefecture; seneschalship; magistra-ture, -cy; raj.

empire; monarchy; king-hood, -ship; royalty, regality, autocracy, monocracy, arist-archy, - ocracy; oligarchy, democracy, demogogy; republic, -anism, federalism; socialism, collectivism; communism, bolshevism, syndicalism; mob law, mobocracy, ochlocracy, ergatocracy; *vox populi, imperium in imperio*; bureaucracy; beadle-, bumble-dom; stratocracy; martial law, military -power, − government; feodality, feudal system, feudalism.

Thearchy, diarchy; du-, tri-, heter-archy; du-, tri-umvirate; auto-cracy, -nomy; limited monarchy; constitutional -government, − monarchy; home rule, autonomy; self-government, -determination; representative government; Soviet government.

gyn-archy, -ocracy, -aeocracy; petticoat government, matriarchate, matriarchy.

[Vicarious authority] commission etc. 755; deputy etc. 759; permission etc. 760.

country, state, realm, commonwealth, canton,

---

constituency, toparchy, municipality, polity, body politic, *posse comitatus.*

person in authority etc. (*master*) 745; judicature etc. 965; cabinet etc. (*council*) 696; usurper; seat of -government, − authority; head-quarters.

[Acquisition of authority] accession; installation etc. 755; usurpation.

V. authorize etc. (*permit*) 760; warrant etc. (*right*) 924; dictate etc. (*order*) 741; have − , hold −, possess − , exercise − , exert − , wield- -authority etc. *n.*

be -at the head of etc. *adj.*; hold − , be in − , fill an- office; hold − , occupy- a post; be -master etc. 745.

rule, sway, command, control, administer; govern etc. (*direct*) 693; lead, preside over, reign; possess − , be seated on − , occupy- the throne; sway − , wield- the scepter; wear the crown.

have − , get- the -upper, − whip- hand; gain a hold upon, preponderance, dominate, boss, rule the roost; over-ride, -rule, -awe; lord it over, hold in hand, keep under, make a puppet of, lead by the nose, hold in the hollow of one's hand, turn round one's little finger, bend to one's will, hold one's own, wear the breeches; have -the ball at one's feet, − it all one's own way, − the game in one's own hand, − on the hip, − under one's thumb; be master of the situation; take the lead, play first fiddle, set the fashion; give the law to; carry with a high hand; lay down the law; 'ride in the whirlwind and direct the storm;' rule with a rod of iron etc. (*severity*) 739.

ascend − , mount- the throne, take the reins, − into one's hand; assume -authority etc. *n.*, − the reins of government; take − , assume the- command.

be -governed by, − in the power of; be under - the rule of, − the domination of.

Adj. ruling etc. *v.*; regnant, at the head, dominant, paramount, supreme, predominant, preponderant, in the ascendant, influential; gubernatorial; imperious; authoritative, executive, administrative, clothed with authority, official, *ex officio*, ministerial, bureaucratic, departmental, imperative, peremptory, overruling, absolute; hegemonic, -al; arbitrary; compulsory etc. 744; stringent.

regal, sovereign; royal, -ist; monarchical, kingly; imperial, -istic; princely; feudal; aristo-, auto-cratic; oligarchic etc. *n.*; democratic, republican, dynastic.

at one's command; in one's -power, − grasp; under control; authorized etc. (*due*) 924.

Adv. in the name of, by the authority of, *de par le Roi*, in virtue of; under the auspices of, in the hands of.

at one's pleasure; by a -dash, − stroke- of the pen; *ex mero motu; ex cathedrâ.*

Phr. the grey mare the better horse; 'every inch a king.'

---

738. Laxity. [Absence of authority.]—**N.** laxity; lax-, loose-, slack-ness; toleration etc. (*lenity*) 740; freedom etc. 748.

anarchy, interregnum; relaxation; loosening etc. *v.*; remission; dead letter, *brutum fulmen*, misrule; license, licentiousness; insubordination etc. (*disobedience*) 742; lynch law etc. (*illegality*) 964; nihilism.

[Deprivation of power.] dethronement, deposition, usurpation, abdication.
V. be -lax etc. *adj* ; *laisser -faire*, – *aller*; hold a loose rein; give -the reins to, – rope enough, – a loose to; tolerate; relax; misrule.

go beyond the length of one's tether; have one's - swing, – fling; act without -instructions, – authority; act on one's own responsibility, usurp authority.

dethrone, depose; abdicate.
Adj. lax, loose; slack; remiss etc. (*careless*) 460; weak.

relaxed; licensed; reinless, unbridled; anarchical; unauthorized etc. (*unwarranted*) 925.

739. Severity.—N. severity; strictness, formalism, harshness etc. *adj.*; rigor, stringency, austerity; inclemency etc. (*pitilessness*) 914*a*; arrogance etc. 885.

arbitrary power; absolut-, despot-ism; dictatorship, autocracy, tyranny, domineering, oppression; assumption, usurpation; inquisition, reign of terror, martial law; iron -heel, – rule, – hand, – sway; tight grasp; brute -force, – strength; coercion etc. 744; strong –, tight- hand.

hard -lines, – measure; tender mercies [ironical.]; sharp practice; bureaucracy, réd tape; pipe-clay, officialism.

tyrant, disciplinarian, martinet, stickler, formalist, bashaw, despot, hard master, Draco, oppressor, inquisitor, extortioner, harpy, vulture, bird of prey.
V. be -severe etc. *adj.*

assume, usurp, arrogate, take liberties; domineer, bully etc. 885; tyrannize, inflict, wreak, stretch a point, put on the screw; be hard upon; bear –, lay- a heavy hand on; be –, come- down upon; illtreat; deal-hardly with, – hard measure to; rule with a rod of iron, chastise with scorpions; dye with blood; oppress, override; trample –, tread- -down, – upon, – under foot; crush under an iron heel, ride roughshod over; rivet the yoke; hold –, keep- a tight hand; force down the throat; coerce etc. 744; give no quarter etc. (*pitiless*) 914*a*.

Adj. severe; strict, hard, harsh, dour, rigid, stiff, stern, rigorous, uncompromising, exacting, exigent, *exigeant*, inexorable, inflexible, obdurate, austere, relentless, Spartan, Draconian, stringent, strait-laced, puritanical, prudish, searching, unsparing, ironhanded, hard-headed, peremptory, absolute, positive, arbitrary, imperative; coercive etc. 744; tyrannical, despotic, masterful, extortionate, grinding, withering, oppressive, inquisitorial; inclement etc. (*ruthless*) 914*a*; cruel etc. (*malevolent*) 907; haughty, arrogant etc. 885.

Adv. severely etc. *adj.*; with a -high, – strong, – tight, – heavy-hand.

at the point of the -sword, – bayonet.
Phr. *Delirant reges plectuntur Achivi.*

740. Leniency.—N. leni-ency, -ence, -ty; moderation etc. 174; toler-ance, -ation; mildness, gentleness; favor; indulgen-ce, -cy; clemency, mercy, forbearance, quarter; compassion etc. 914.

V. be -lenient etc. *adj.*; tolerate, bear with; *parcere subjectis*, give quarter.

indulge, allow one to have his own way, spoil.
Adj. lenient; mild, – as milk; gentle, soft; tolerant, indulgent, easy-going; clement etc. (*compassionate*) 914; forbearing; complaisant, longsuffering.

741. Command.—N. command, order, ordinance, act, *fiat*, bidding, *dictum*, hest, behest, call, beck, nod.

des-, dis-patch; message, direction, injunction, charge, instructions; appointment, fixture.

demand, exaction, imposition, requisition, claim, reclamation, revendication; *ultimatum* etc. (*terms*) 770; request etc. 765; requirement.

dictation; dict-, mand-ate; *caveat*, decree, decree -nisi, – absolute, *senatus consultum*; precept; pre-, re-script; writ, ordination, bull, edict, decretal, dispensation, prescription, brevet, placet, ukase, *firman*, hatti-sheriff, warrant, passport, *mittimus*, *mandamus*, summons, subpoena, *nisi prius*, interpellation, citation; word, – of command; *mot d'ordre*; bugle –, trumpet- call; beat of drum, tattoo; order of the day; enactment etc. (*law*) 963; *plébiscite* etc. (*choice*) 609.

V. command, order, decree, enact, ordain, dictate, direct, give orders.

prescribe, set, appoint, mark out; set –, prescribe –, impose- a task; set to work, put in requisition etc. 926.

bid, enjoin, charge, call upon, instruct; require, – at the hands of; exact, impose, tax, task; demand; insist on etc. (*compel*) 744.

claim, lay claim to, revendicate, reclaim.

cite, summon; call –, send- for; subpoena; beckon.

issue a command; make –, issue –, promulgate- -a requisition, – a decree, – an order etc. *n.*; give the -word of command, – word, – signal; call to order; give –, lay down- the law; assume the command etc. (*authority*) 737; remand.

be -ordered etc.; receive an order etc. *n.*
Adj. commanding etc. *v.*; authoritative etc. 737; decret-ory, -ive, -al; imperative, jussive, decisive, final.

Adv. in a commanding tone; by a -stroke, – dash- of the pen; by order, at beat of drum, on the first summons; at the word of command.

Phr. -the decree is gone forth; *sic volo sic jubeo; le Roi le veut.*

742. Disobedience.—N. disobedience, insubordination, contumacy; infraction, -fringement; violation, non-compliance; non-observance etc. 773.

revolt, rebellion, mutiny, outbreak, rising, uprising, putsch, insurrection, *émeute*; riot, tumult etc. (*disorder*) 59; strike etc. (*resistance*) 719; barring out; defiance etc. 715.

mutinousness etc. *adj.*; mutineering; sedition, treason; high –, petty –, misprison of- treason; *premunire*; *lèse- majesté*; violation of law etc. 964; defection, secession, revolution, *sabotage*, bolshevism, *Sinn Fein.*

insurgent, mutineer, rebel, revolter, rioter, traitor, *carbonaro*, *sansculottes*, red republican, communist, Fenian, chartist, *frondeur*; seceder, runagate, brawler, anarchist, demagogue; suffragette; Spartacus, Masaniello, Wat Tyler, Jack Cade; bolshevist, bolshevik, maximalist, ringleader.

V. disobey, violate, infringe; shirk; set at defiance etc. (*defy*) 715; set authority at naught, run riot, fly in the face of, bolt, take the law into one's own hands; kick over the traces.

turn –, run- restive; champ the bit; strike etc. (*resist*) 719; rise, – in arms; secede; mutiny, rebel.

Adj. disobedient; uncompl-ying, -iant; unsubmissive; unruly, ungovernable; insubordinate, impatient of control; rest-iff, -ive; refractory, contumacious; recusant etc. (*refuse*) 764; recalcitrant; resisting etc. 719; lawless, mutinous, seditious, insurgent, riotous, revolutionary.

disobeyed, unobeyed; unbidden.

743. Obedience.—N. obedience; observance etc. 772; compliance; submission etc. 725; subjection etc. 749; non-resistance; passiveness, passivity, resignation.

allegiance, loyalty, fealty, homage, deference, devotion, fidelity, constancy.

submiss-ness, -iveness; ductility etc. (*softness*) 324; obsequiousness etc. (*servility*) 886.

V. be -obedient etc. *adj.*, obey, bear obedience to; submit etc. 725; comply, answer the helm, come at one's call; do -one's bidding, – what one is told, – suit and service; attend to orders, serve - devotedly, –, loyally, – faithfully.

follow, – the lead of, – to the world's end; serve etc. 746; play second fiddle.

Adj. obedient; compl-ying, -iant; law-abiding, loyal, faithful, leal, devoted; at one's -call, – command, – orders, – beck and call; under - beck and call, – control.

restrainable; resigned, passive; submissive etc. 725; henpecked; pliant etc. (*soft*) 324.

unresist-ed, -ing.

Adv. obediently etc. *adj.*; in compliance with, in obedience to.

Phr. to hear is to obey; as –, if- you please; at your service.

744. Compulsion.—N. compulsion, coercion, coaction, constraint, eminent domain, duress, enforcement, press, conscription.

force; brute –, main –, physical- force; the sword, *ultima ratio*; club –, mob –, lynch- law; *argumentum baculinum*, *le droit du plus fort*, martial law.

restraint etc. 751; necessity etc. 601; *force majeure*; Hobson's choice; the spur of necessity.

V. compel, force, make, drive, coerce, constrain, enforce, necessitate, oblige.

force upon, press; cram –, thrust –, force-down the throat; say it must be done, make a point of, insist upon, take no denial; put down, dragoon.

extort, wring from; put –, turn- on the screw; drag into; bind, – over; pin –, tie- down; require, tax, put in force; commandeer; restrain etc. 751.

Adj. compelling etc. *v.*; coercive, coactive; inexorable etc. 739; compuls-ory, -atory; obligatory, stringent, peremptory, binding.

forcible, not to be trifled with; irresistible etc. 601; compelled etc. *v.*; fain to.

Adv. by -force etc. *n.*, – force of arms; on compulsion, perforce; *vi et armis*, under the lash; at the point of the -sword, – bayonet; forcibly; by a strong arm.

under protest, in spite of one's teeth; against one's will etc. 603; *nolens volens* etc. (*of necessity*) 601; by stress of -circumstances, – weather; under press of; *de rigueur*.

745. Master.—N. master, *padrone*; lord, – paramount; command-er, -ant; captain; chief, -tain; *sahib*, sirdar, sachem, sheik, head, senior, governor, *duce*, ruler, dictator; leader etc. (*director*) 694.

lord of the ascendant; cock of the -walk, – roost; grey mare; mistress.

potentate; liege, – lord; suzerain, sovereign, monarch, autocrat, despot, tyrant, oligarch, overlord.

crowned head, emperor, king, anointed king, majesty, *imperator*, protector, president, stadtholder, judge.

caesar, kaiser, czar, sultan, grand Turk, caliph, imaum, shah, padishah, sophi, mogul, great mogul, khan, cham; lama, tycoon, mikado, inca, cazique; donm; vaivode; wai-, way-wode; landamman; seyyid, cacique.

prince, duke etc. (*nobility*) 875; arch-duke, doge, elector; seignior; mar-, land-grave; rajah, emir, nizam, nawab, negus.

empress, queen, sultana, czarina, princess, infanta, duchess, margravine, begum, maharani.

regent, viceroy, exarch, palatine, khedive, hospodar, beglerbeg, three-tailed bashaw, pasha, pashaw, bashaw, bey, beg, dey, scherif, tetrarch, satrap, mandarin, subhadar, nabob, maharajah; burgrave; laird etc. (*proprietor*) 779; High Commissioner.

the -authorities, – powers that be, – government; staff, *état major*, aga, official, man in office, person in authority.

[Naval authorities] admiral, -ty, – of the fleet; rear-, vice-, port-admiral; senior-, naval officer, S.N.O., commodore, captain, commander, lieutenant-commander, lieutenant, sub-lieutenant, midshipman, warrant –, petty- officer, leading seaman; skipper, mate, master.

[Military authorities] marshal, field-marshal, *maréchal*; general, -issimo; commander-in-chief, *seraskier*, *hetman*; lieutenant-, major-general; commandant; colonel, lieutenant-colonel, major, captain, centurion, skipper, lieutenant, second-lieutenant, officer, staff-officer, *aide de camp*, brigadier, brigade-major, adjutant, *jemidar*, ensign, cornet, cadet, subaltern, warrant officer, quartermaster, noncommissioned officer, N.C.O.; sergeant, -major; top-sergeant, color sergeant; corporal, -major; lance-, acting-corporal; drum major; shavetail.

[Air authorities] air -marshal, – commodore; group captain, squadron leader, wing commander, flight lieutenant, flying –, pilot- officer.

[Civil authorities] judge etc. 967; mayor, -alty; prefect, chancellor, archon, provost, magistrate, syndic; alcalde, alcaid; burgomaster, *corregidor*, seneschal, alderman, warden, constable, portreeve; lord mayor, sheriff; officer etc. (*executive*) 965.

746. Servant.—N. subject, liegeman; servant, retainer, follower, henchman, servitor, domestic, menial, help, lady help, *employé, attaché*; official. retinue, suite, *cortège*, staff, court.

attendant, squire, usher, page, buttons, donzel, footboy; dog robber; train-, cup-bearer; waiter, busboy, tapster, butler, livery servant, lackey, footman, flunkey, valet, *valet de chambre*; boots; scout, gyp; equerry, groom; jockey, hostler, ostler, tiger, orderly, messenger, cad, gillie, caddie; *wallah*; journeyman, herdsman, swineherd.

bailiff, castellan, seneschal, chamberlain, major-domo, groom of the chambers.

secretary; under −, assistant- secretary; clerk; clerical staff, stenographer, subsidiary; agent etc. 758; subaltern; under-ling, -strapper; man.

maid, -servant, waitress; handmaid; *confidente*, lady's maid, abigail, *soubrette*; nurse, *bonne, ayah*; nurse-, nursery-, house-, parlor-, waiting-, chamber-, kitchen-, scullery-, between −, laundry −, dairy-maid; *femme −, fille- de chambre*; camarista; *chef de cuisine, cordon bleu*, cook, scullion, Cinderella; maid −, servant- of all work, tweeny, general servant, girl, slavey; laundress, bed-maker, goodie, char-woman etc. (*worker*) 690.

serf, vassal, slave, negro, helot; bondsman, -woman; bondslave; *âme damnée, odalisque*, ryot, *adscriptus glebae*; vill-ain, -ein; bead-, bede-sman; sizar; pension-er, -ary; client; dependant, -ent; hanger on, stooge, satellite; parasite etc. (*servility*) 886; led captain; *protégé*, ward, hireling, mercenary, puppet, creature.

badge of slavery; bonds etc. 752.

V. serve; minister to, wait −, attend −, dance attendance −, pin oneself- upon; squire, tend, hang on the sleeve of, char, do for; fag; valet.

Adj. in the train of; in one's -pay, − employ; at one's call etc. (*obedient*) 743; in bonds.

747. Scepter. [Insignia of authority.]**—N.** scepter, regalia, rod of empire, sword of state, mace, *fasces*, wand; staff, − of office; *bâton*, truncheon; flag etc. (*insignia*) 550; ensign −, emblem −, badge −, insignia- of authority, rank marks, brassard, badge, sash; cocked −, brass- hat.

epaulette, aiguilette, crown, star, eagle, bar, double bar, pip, stripe, chevron, curl, ring, anchor, shoulder-strap, tab.

throne, chair, musnud, divan, dais, woolsack.

toga, pall, mantle, robes of state, ermine, purple.

crown, coronet, diadem, tiara, triple crown, miter, crozier, cardinal's hat etc.; cap of maintenance; decoration; title etc. 877; portfolio.

key, signet, seals, talisman; helm; reins etc. (*means of restraint*) 752.

748. Freedom.—N. freedom, liberty, independence; license etc. (*permission*) 760; facility etc. 705.

scope, range, latitude, play; free −, full- -play, − scope; free stage and no favor; swing, full swing, elbow-room, margin, rope, wide berth; Liberty Hall.

franchise, denization; free −, freed-, liveryman; denizen.

autonomy, self-government, homerule, self-determination, liberalism, free trade; non-interference etc. 706.

immunity, exemption; emancipation etc. (*liberation*) 750; en-, af-franchisement; rights, privileges.

free land, freehold; allodium; frankalmoigne, mortmain.

independent, free-lance, -thinker, -trader.

V. be -free etc. *adj.*; have -scope etc. *n.*, − the run of, − one's own way, − a will of one's own, − one's fling; do what one -likes, − wishes, − pleases, − chooses; go at large, feel at home, paddle one's own canoe; stand on one's -legs, − rights; shift for oneself.

take a liberty; make -free with, − oneself quite at home; use a freedom; take -leave, − French leave.

set free etc. (*liberate*) 750; give the reins to etc. (*permit*) 760; allow −, give- scope etc. *n.* to; give a horse his head.

make free of; give the -freedom of, − franchise; en-, af-franchise.

laisser -faire, − aller; live and let live; leave to oneself; leave −, let- alone; mind one's own business.

Adj. free, − as air; out of harness, independent, at large, loose, scot free; left -alone, − to oneself.

in full swing; uncaught, unconstrained, unbuttoned, unconfined, unrestrained, unchecked, unprevented, unhindered, unobstructed, unbound, uncontrolled, untrammeled.

unsubject, ungoverned, unenslaved, unenthralled, unchained, unshackled, unfettered, unreined, unbridled, uncurbed, unmuzzled, unimpeded.

unrestricted, unlimited, unconditional; absolute; discretionary etc. (*optional*) 600.

unassailed, unforced, uncompelled.

unbiassed, unprejudiced, uninfluenced, spontaneous.

free and easy; at −, at one's- ease; *dégagé*, quite at home; wanton, rampant, irrepressible, unvanquished.

exempt; freed etc. 750; freeborn; autonomous, freehold, allodial; *gratis* etc. 815.

unclaimed, going a begging.

Adv. freely etc. *adj.*; *ad libitum* etc. (*at will*) 600.

749. Subjection.—N. subjection; depend-ence, -ance, -ency; subordination; thrall, thraldom, enthralment, subjugation, bondage, serfdom; feudal- -ism, -ity; vassalage, villenage; slavery, enslavement, involuntary servitude.

service; servi-tude, -torship; tendence, employ, tutelage, clientship; liability etc. 177; constraint etc. 751; oppression etc. (*severity*) 739; yoke etc. (*means of restraint*) submission etc. 725; obedience etc. 743.

V. be -subject etc. *adj.*; be −, lie- at the mercy of; depend −, lean −, hang- upon; fall -a prey to, − under; play second- fiddle.

be a -mere machine, − puppet, − football; not dare to say one's soul is his own; drag a chain. serve etc. 746; obey etc. 743; submit etc. 725.

break in, tame; subject, subjugate; master etc. 731; tread -down, − under foot; weigh down; drag at one's chariot wheels; reduce to -subjection, −

slavery; en-, in-, be-thral; enslave, lead captive; take into custody etc. (*restrain*) 751; rule etc. 737; drive into a corner, hold at the sword's point; keep under; hold in -bondage, – leading strings, – swaddling clothes.

Adj. subject, dependent, subordinate; feud-al, -atory; in subjection to, under control; in -leading strings, – harness; subjected, enslaved etc. *v.*; constrained etc. 751; subservient, servile, fawning, slavish, obsequious, cringing; down-trodden; overborne, -whelmed; under the lash, on the hip, led by the nose, henpecked; the -puppet, – sport, – plaything- of; under one's -orders, – command, – thumb; like dirt under one's feet; a slave to; at the mercy of; in the -power, – hands, – clutches- of; at the feet of; at one's beck and call etc. (*obedient*) 743; liable etc. 177; parasitical; stipendiary.

Adv. under.

750. Liberation.—N.
liberation, disengagement, release, disenthrallment, enlargement, emancipation; af-, en-franchisement; manumission; discharge, dismissal.

deliverance etc. 672; redemption, extrication, acquittance, absolution; acquittal etc. 970; escape etc. 671.

V. liberate, free; set -free, – clear, – at liberty; render free, emancipate, release; en-, af-franchise; manumit; enlarge; dis-band, -charge, -miss, - enthral; let -go, – loose, – out, – slip; cast –, turn- adrift; deliver etc. 672; absolve etc. (*acquit*) 970; reprieve.

unfetter etc. 751; untie etc. 44; loose etc. (*disjoin*) 44; loosen, relax; un-bolt, -bar, -close, -cork, -clog, -hand, -bind, -latch, -chain, -harness; dis-engage, -entangle; clear, extricate, unloose.

gain –, obtain –, acquire- one's -liberty etc. 748; get -rid, – clear- of; deliver oneself- from; shake off the yoke, slip the collar; break -loose, – prison; tear asunder one's bonds, cast off trammels; escape etc. 671.

Adj. at -liberty, – large, free, liberated etc. *v.*; out of harness etc. 748; adrift.

Int. unhand me! let me go!

751. Restraint.—N.
restraint; hindrance etc. 706; coercion etc. (*compulsion*) 744; cohibition, constraint, repression; discipline, control, self-restraint etc. 604.

confinement; durance, duress; im-, prisonment; incarceration, coarctation, entombment, mancipation, durance vile, thrall, -dom, limbo, captivity; blockade; quarantine; detention.

arrest, -ation; custody, keep, care; charge, ward, restringency.

curb etc. (*means of restraint*) 752; *lettres de cachet*.

limitation, restriction, protection, monopoly; prohibition etc. 761; economic pressure.

prisoner etc. 754.

V. restrain, check; put –, lay- under restraint; en-, in-, be-thral; restrict; debar etc. (*hinder*) 706; constrain; coerce etc. (*compel*) 744; curb, control; hold –, keep- -back, – from, – in, – in check, – within bounds; hold in -leash, – leading strings; withhold.

keep under; repress, suppress; smother; pull in, rein in; hold, – fast; keep a tight hand on; prohibit etc. 761; in-, co-hibit.

enchain; fasten etc. (*join*) 43; fetter, shackle; en-, trammel; bridle, muzzle, gag, pinion, manacle, handcuff, tie one's hands, hobble, bind hand and foot; swathe, swaddle; pin –, peg- down; tether, picket; tie, – up, – down; secure; forge fetters.

confine; shut –, clap –, lock –, box –, mew –, bottle –, cork –, seal –, button- up; shut –, hem –, bolt –, wall –, rail- in; impound, pen, coop; enclose etc. (*circumscribe*) 229; cage; in-, en-cage; close the door upon, cloister; imprison, immure; incarcerate, entomb; clap –, lay- under hatches; put in -irons, – a strait waistcoat; throw –, cast- into prison; put into bilboes.

arrest; take -up, – charge of, – into custody; take –, make- -prisoner, – captive; captivate; lead -captive, – into captivity; send –, commit- to prison; commit; give in -charge, – custody; subjugate etc. 749.

Adj. re-, con-strained; imprisoned etc. *v.*; pent up; jammed in, wedged in; under -restraint, – lock and key, – hatches; serving –, doing- time; in swaddling clothes; on *parole*; in custody etc. (*prisoner*) 754; cohibitive; coactive etc. (*compulsory*) 744.

stiff, restringent, straitlaced, hide-bound.

ice-, wind-, weather-bound; 'cabined, cribbed, confined;' in Lob's pound, laid by the heels.

Adv. in captivity, under arrest, behind the bars, in -prison, – jail, – durance vile.

752. Prison. [Means of restraint.]—N.
prison, -house; jail, gaol, cage, coop, den, death house, condemned –, cell; stronghold, fortress, keep, donjon, dungeon, *Bastille*, *oubliette*, bridewell, house of correction, hulks, tool-booth, panopticon, penitentiary, guard-room, clink, can, stir, tronk, jug, lock-up, hold; round –, watch – , station –, sponging-house; station; house of detention, black hole, pen, fold, pound; enclosure etc. 232; penal settlement; chain gang; debtors' prison; reformatory; federal penitentiary, state prison; criminal lunatic asylum; bilboes, stocks, limbo, quod.

Dartmoor, Newgate, Fleet, Marshalsea; King's (or Queen's) Bench; Sing Sing, Dannemora.

bond; strap, bandage, splint, tourniquet; irons, pinion, gyve, fetter, shackle, trammel, manacle, handcuff, bracelets, darbies, strait waistcoat, strait-jacket.

yoke, collar, halter, harness; muzzle, gag, bit, brake, curb, snaffle, bridle; rein, -s; ribbons, lines, bearing-rein; martingale, leading string; tether, picket, band, guy, chain; cord etc. (*fastening*) 45.

bolt, bar, lock, padlock, rail, wall; paling, palisade; fence; barrier, barricade.

brake, drag etc. (*hindrance*) 706.

753. Keeper.—N.
keeper, custodian, *custos*, ranger, warder, jailer, gaoler, turnkey, castellan, guard; watch, -dog, -man; Charley; sen-try, -tinel; watch and ward; *concierge*, coast-guard, *guarda costa*, gamekeeper.

escort, body guard, convoy.

protector, governor, duenna; guardian; governess etc. (*teacher*) 540; nurse, *bonne*, *ayah*, *amah*.

754. Prisoner.—N. prisoner, captive, *détenu*, close prisoner.

jail-bird, ticket-of-leave man.

V. stand committed; be -imprisoned etc. 751.

Adj. imprisoned etc. 751; in -prison, – quod, – durance vile, – limbo, – custody, – charge, – chains; under -lock and key, – hatches; on *parole*; detained at his Majesty's pleasure.

755. Commission. [Vicarious authority.]—**N.** commission, delegation; con-, as-signment; procuration; deputation, legation, mission, embassy; agency, agentship; power of attorney, proxy; clerkship.

errand, charge, *brevet*, diploma, *exequatur*, permit etc. (*permission*) 760.

appointment, nomination, return; charter; ordination; installation, inauguration, investiture; accession, coronation, enthronement.

vicegerency; regency, regentship.

viceroy etc. 745; consignee etc. 758; deputy etc. 759.

V. commission, delegate, depute; consign, assign; charge; in-, en-trust; turn over to; commit, – to the hands of; authorize etc. (*permit*) 760.

put in commission, accredit, engage, hire, bespeak, appoint, name, nominate, return, ordain; install, induct, inaugurate, invest, crown; en-roll, -list.

employ, empower; give power of attorney to; set –, place- over; send out.

be commissioned, be accredited; represent, stand for; stand in the -stead, – place, – shoes- of.

Adj. commissioned etc. *v.*

Adv. *per procuratione.*

756. Abrogation.—N. abrogation, annulment, nullification; cancelling etc. *v.*; cancel; revo-cation, -kement; repeal, rescission, defeasance.

. dismissal, *congé*, demission; depos-al, -ition; sack, dethronement; disestablish-, disendow-ment; deconsecration.

aboli-tion, -shment; dissolution.

- counter-order, -mand; repudiation, retractation; recantation etc. (*tergiversation*) 607.

V. abrogate, annul, cancel; destroy etc. 162; abolish; revoke, repeal, rescind, reverse, retract, recall; over-rule, -ride; set aside; disannul, dissolve, quash, nullify, declare null and void; dis-establish, -endow; deconsecrate.

disclaim etc. (*deny*) 536; ignore, repudiate; recant etc. 607; divest oneself, break off.

counter-mand, -order; do away with; sweep –, brush- away; throw -overboard, – to the dogs; scatter to the winds, cast behind.

dismiss, discard; cast –, turn- -off, – out, – adrift, – out of doors, – aside, – away; send -off, – away, – about one's business; discharge, get rid of, fire out, fire etc. (*eject*) 297; jilt.

cashier; break; oust; set down, unseat, -saddle; un-, de-, disen-throne; depose, uncrown; unfrock, strike off the roll; dis-bar, -bench.

be -abrogated etc.; receive its quietus.

Adj. abrogated etc. *v.*; *functus officio.*

Int. get along with you! begone! go about your business! away with!

757. Resignation.—N. resignation, retirement, abdication, renunciation, abjuration, disclaimer, abandonment, relinquishment.

V. resign; give –, throw- up; lay down, throw up the cards, wash one's hands of, abjure, renounce, forego, disclaim, abandon, relinquish, retract, demit; deny etc. 536.

abrogate etc. 756; desert etc. (*relinquish*) 624; get rid of etc. 782.

abdicate; vacate, – one's seat; accept the stewardship of the Chiltern Hundreds; retire; tender –, send in –, hand in- one's resignation.

Adj. abdicant, renunciatory etc. *v.*

Phr. 'Othello's occupation's gone.'

758. Consignee.—N. consignee, trustee, nominee, committee.

delegate; commiss-ary, -ioner; emissary, envoy, commissionaire; messenger etc. 534.

diplomatist, diplomat, *corps diplomatique*, embassy; am-, em-bassador; representative, resident, consul, legate, nuncio, internuncio, *chargé d' affaires, attaché.*

vicegerent etc. (*deputy*) 759; plenipotentiary.

functionary, placeman, curator; treasurer etc. 801; agent, factor, bailiff, steward, clerk, secretary, attorney, solicitor, proctor, broker, underwriter, commission agent, auctioneer, one's man of business; factotum etc. (*director*) 694; caretaker.

negotiator, go between; middleman; under agent, *employé*; servant etc. 746.

salesman; commercial, – traveler; bagman, *commis-voyageur*, touter.

newspaper –, own –, war –, special-correspondent; reporter.

759. Deputy.—N. deputy, substitute, vice, proxy, *locum tenens*, delegate, representative, next friend, surrogate, secondary.

regent, vicegerent, vizier, minister, vicar; premier etc. (*director*) 694; chancellor, prefect, provost, warden, lieutenant, archon, consul, proconsul; viceroy etc. (*governor*) 745; commissioner etc. 758; plenipotentiary, *alter ego.*

team, eight, eleven; champion.

V. be -deputy etc. *n.*; stand –, appear –, hold a brief –, answer- for; represent; stand –, walk- in the shoes of; stand in the stead of.

substitute, ablegate, accredit; commission, empower, delegate etc. 755.

Adj. acting; vice, -regal; accredited to.

Adv. in behalf of, by proxy.

760. Permission.—N. permission, leave; allow-, suffer-ance; toler-ance, -ation; liberty, law, license, concession, grace; indulgence etc. (*lenity*) 740; favor, dispensation, exemption, release; connivance; vouchsafement.

authorization, warranty, accordance, admission.

permit, warrant, *brevet*, precept, sanction, authority, *firman*; pass, -port; furlough, license, *carte blanche*, ticket of leave; grant, charter, patent.

V. permit; give -permission etc. *n.*, – power;

let, allow, admit; suffer, bear with, tolerate, recognize; concede etc. 762; accord, vouchsafe, favor, humor, gratify, indulge, stretch a point; wink at, connive at; shut one's eyes to.

grant, empower, charter, enfranchise, privilege, confer a privilege, license, authorize, warrant; sanction; entrust etc. (*commission*) 755.

give -*carte blanche*, – the reins to, – scope to etc. (*freedom*) 748; leave -alone, – it to one, – the door open; open the -door to, – floodgates; give a loose to.

let off; absolve etc. (*acquit*) 970; release, exonerate, dispense with.

ask –, beg –, request- -leave, – permission.

Adj. permitting etc. *v.*; permissive, indulgent; permitted etc. *v.*; patent, chartered, permissible, allowable, lawful, legitimate, legal; legalized etc. (*law*) 963; licit; unforbid, -den; unconditional.

Adv. permissibly; by –, with –, on- -leave etc. *n.*; *speciali gratiâ*; under favor of; *pace*; *ad libitum* etc. (*freely*) 748, (*at will*) 600; by all means etc. (*willingly*) 602; yes etc. (*assent*) 488.

761. Prohibition.—N. pro-, in-hibition; *veto*, disallowance; interdict, -ion; injunction; embargo, ban, *verboten*, taboo, proscription; *index expurgatorius*; restriction etc. (*restraint*) 751; hindrance etc. 706; forbidden fruit.

V. pro-, in-hibit; forbid, put one's *veto* upon, disallow; bar; debar etc. (*hinder*) 706, forefend.

keep -in, – within bounds; restrain etc. 751; cohibit, withhold, limit, circumscribe, clip the wings of, restrict, narrow; interdict, taboo; put –, place- under -an interdiction, – the ban; proscribe, censor; exclude, shut out; shut –, bolt –, show- the door; warn off; dash the cup from one's lips; forbid the banns.

Adj. prohibit-ive, -ory; interdictive; proscriptive; restrictive, exclusive; forbidding etc. *v.*

prohibited etc. *v.*; not -permitted etc. 760; unlicensed, contraband, under the ban of; illegal etc. 964; unauthorized, not to be thought of.

Adv. on no account etc. (*no*) 536.

Int. forbid it heaven! etc. (*deprecation*) 766. hands –, keep- off! hold! stop! avast!

Phr. that will never do.

762. Consent.—N. consent; assent etc. 488; acquiescence; approval etc. 931; compliance, agreement, concession; yield-ance, -ingness; accession, acknowledgment, acceptance, agnition.

settlement, ratification, confirmation, ad-justment.

permit etc. (*permission*) 760; promise etc. 768.

V. consent; assent etc. 488; yield assent, admit, allow, concede, grant, yield; come -over, – round; give in to, acknowledge, agnize, give consent, comply with, acquiesce, agree to, fall in with, accede, accept, embrace an offer, close with, take at one's word, have no objection.

satisfy, meet one's wishes, settle, come to terms etc. 488; not -refuse etc. 764; turn a willing ear etc. (*willingness*) 602; jump at; deign, vouchsafe; promise etc. 768.

Adj. consenting etc. *v.*; agreeable, compliant; agreed etc. (*assent*) 488; unconditional.

Adv. yes etc. (*assent*) 488; by all means etc. (*willingly*) 602; if –, as- you please; be it so, so be it, well and good, of course.

763. Offer.—N. offer, proffer, presentation, tender, bid, overture; propos-al, -ition; motion, invitation; candidature; offering etc. (*gift*) 784.

V. offer, proffer, present, tender; bid; propose, move; make -a motion, – advances; start; invite, hold out, place- at one's disposal, – in one's way, put forward.

hawk about; offer for sale etc. 796; press etc. (*request*) 765; lay at one's feet.

offer –, present- oneself; volunteer, come forward, be a candidate; stand –, bid- for; seek; be at one's service; go a begging; bribe etc. (*give*) 784.

Adj. offer-ing, -ed etc. *v.*; in the market, for sale, to let, disengaged, on hire.

764. Refusal.—N. refusal, rejection; non-, in-compliance; denial; declining etc. *v.*; declension; peremptory –, flat –, point blank- refusal; repulse, rebuff; discountenance.

recusancy, renunciation, abnegation, negation, protest, disclaimer; dissent etc. 489; revocation etc. 756.

V. refuse, reject, deny, decline; nill, negative; refuse –, withhold- one's assent; shake the head; close the -hand, – purse; grudge, begrudge, be slow to, hang fire.

be deaf to; turn -a deaf ear to, – one's back upon; set one's face against, discountenance, not hear of, have nothing to do with, wash one's hands of, stand aloof, forswear, set aside, cast behind one; not yield an inch etc. (*obstinacy*) 606.

resist, cross; not -grant etc. 762; repel, repulse; shut –, slam- the door in one's face; rebuff; send -back, – to the right about, – away with a flea in the ear; deny oneself, not be at home to; discard etc. (*repudiate*) 610; rescind etc. (*revoke*) 756; disclaim, protest; dissent etc. 489.

Adj. refusing etc. *v.*; rest-ive, -iff; recusant; uncomplying, noncompliant, unconsenting, uncomplaisant, protestant; not willing to hear of, deaf to.

refused etc. *v.*; ungranted, out of the question, not to be thought of, impossible.

Adv. no etc. 536; on no account, not for the world; no thank you.

Phr. *non possumus*; [ironically] your humble servant; *bien obligé*.

765. Request.—N. requ-est, -isition; claim etc. (*demand*) 741; petition, suit, prayer; begging letter, round-robin.

motion, overture, application, canvass, address, appeal, apostrophe; imprecation; rogation; proposal, proposition.

orison etc. (*worship*) 990; incantation etc. (*spell*) 993.

mendicancy; asking, panhandling, begging etc. *v.*; postulation, solicitation, invitation, entreaty, importunity, supplication, instance, impetration, imploration, obsecration, obtestation, invocation, interpellation.

V. request, ask; beg, crave, sue, pray, petition, solicit, invite, pop the question, make bold to ask; beg -leave, – a boon; apply to, call to, put to; call -upon, – for; make –, address –, prefer –, put up- a -request, – prayer, – petition; make - application, – a requisition; ask –, trouble- one for; claim etc. (*demand*) 741; offer up prayers etc. (*worship*) 990; whistle for.

beg hard, entreat, beseech, plead, supplicate, implore, apostrophize; conjure, adjure; obtest; cry to, kneel to, appeal to; invoke, evoke; impetrate, imprecate, ply, press, urge, beset, importune, dun, tax, clamor for; cry -aloud, – for help; fall on one's knees; throw oneself at the feet of; come down on one's marrow-bones.

beg from door to door, send the hat round, go a begging; mendicate, mump, cadge, panhandle, beg one's bread.

dance attendance on, besiege, knock at the door. bespeak, canvass, tout, make interest, court; seek, bid for etc. (*offer*) 763; publish the banns.

Adj. requesting etc. *v.*; precatory; suppli-ant, -cant, -catory; invoc-, imprec-, rog-atory; postulant, mendicant.

importunate, clamorous, urgent; solicitous; cap in hand; on one's -knees, – bended knees, – marrow-bones.

Adv. prithee, do, please, pray; be so good as, be good enough; have the goodness, vouchsafe, will you, I pray thee, if you please.

Int. for -God's, – heaven's, – goodness', – mercy's- sake.

766. Deprecation. [Negative request.]—**N.** deprecation, expostulation; remonstrance; intercession, mediation.

V. deprecate, protest, expostulate, enter a protest, intercede for.

Adj. deprecatory, expostulatory, intercessory, mediatorial.

deprecated, protested.

un-, unbe-sought; unasked etc: (*see* ask etc. 765).

Int. cry you mercy! God forbid! forbid it Heaven! Heaven -forefend, – forbid! far be it from! hands off! etc. (*prohibition*) 761.

767. Petitioner.—**N.** petitioner, solicitor, applicant; suppli-ant, -cant; suitor, candidate, claimant, postulant, aspirant, competitor, bidder; place –, pot- hunter; prizer.

beggar, mendicant, mumper, sturdy beggar, cadger, panhandler.

canvasser, barker, touter etc. 768.

sycophant, parasite etc. 886.

768. Promise.—**N.** promise, undertaking, word, troth, plight, pledge, *parole*, word of honor, vow; oath etc. (*affirmation*) 535; profession, assurance, warranty, guarantee, insurance, obligation; contract etc. 769.

engagement, pre-engagement; affiance; betroth, -al, -ment; marriage -compact, – vow.

V. promise; give a -promise etc. *n.*; undertake, engage; make –, form- an engagement; enter - into, – on- an engagement; bind –, tie –, pledge –, commit –, take upon- oneself; vow; swear etc. (*affirm*) 535; give –, pass –, pledge –, plight-one's -word, – honor, – credit, – troth; betroth, plight faith; take the vows.

assure, warrant, guarantee, vouch for, avouch, covenant etc. 769; attest etc. (*bear witness*) 467.

hold out an expectation; contract an obligation; become -bound to, – sponsor for; answer –, be answerable- for; secure; give security etc. 771; underwrite.

adjure, administer an oath, put to one's oath, swear a witness.

Adj. promising etc. *v.*; promissory; votive; under hand and seal; upon -oath, – affirmation.

promised etc. *v.*; affianced, pledged, bound; committed, compromised; in for it.

Adv. as one's head shall answer for; upon my honor.

Phr. in for a penny, in for a pound.

768a. Release from engagement.—**N.** release etc. (*liberation*) 750.

Adj. absolute; unconditional etc. (*free*) 748.

769. Compact.—**N.** compact, contract, agreement, bargain, deal, transaction; affidation; pact, -ion; bond, covenant, indenture.

stipulation, settlement, convention; compromise, *cartel*.

protocol, treaty, *concordat, Zollverein, Sonderbund*, charter, *Magna Charta*, Pragmatic Sanction.

negotiation etc. (*bargaining*) 794; diplomacy etc. (*mediation*) 724; negotiator etc. (*agent*) 758.

ratification, completion, signature, seal, sigil, signet.

V. contract, covenant, agree for, engage etc. (*promise*) 768.

treat, negotiate, stipulate, make terms; bargain etc. (*barter*) 794.

make –, strike- a bargain; come to -terms, – an understanding; compromise etc. 774; set at rest; close, – with; conclude, complete, settle; confirm, ratify, clench, subscribe, underwrite; en-, in-dorse; put the seal to; sign, seal etc. (*attest*) 467; indent.

take one at one's word, bargain by inch of candle.

Adj. contractual, agreed etc. *v.*; conventional; under hand and seal; signed, sealed and delivered.

Phr. *caveat emptor.*

770. Conditions.—**N.** conditions, terms; articles, – of agreement.

clauses, provisions; proviso etc. (*qualification*) 469; covenant, stipulation, obligation, *ultimatum, sine quâ non; casus foederis.*

V. make –, come to- -terms etc. (*contract*) 769; make it a condition, stipulate, insist upon, make a point of; bind, tie up.

Adj. conditional, provisional, guarded, fenced, hedged in.

Adv. conditionally etc. (*with qualification*) 469; provisionally, *pro re natâ*; on condition; with a reservation.

771. Security.—N. security; guaran-ty, -tee; gage, waranty, bond, tie, pledge, plight, mortgage, debenture, hypothecation, bill of sale, lien, pignus, pawn, pignoration; real security; bottomry; collateral, vadium.

stake, deposit, earnest, handsel, caution.

promissory note; bill, – of exchange; I.O.U.: personal security, covenant, specialty; *parole* etc. (*promise*) 768.

acceptance, indorsement, signature, execution, stamp, seal.

spon-sor, -sion, -sorship; surety, bail; main-pernor, hostage.

recognizance; deed –, covenant- of indemnity.

authentication, verfication, warrant, certificate, voucher, docket, doquet; record etc. 551; probate, attested copy.

receipt; ac-, quittance; discharge, release.

muniment, title-deed, instrument; deed, – poll; assurance, insurance, indenture; charter etc. (*compact*) 769; charter-poll; paper, parchment, settlement, will, testament, last will and testament, codicil.

V. give -security, – bail, – substantial bail; go bail; pawn, impawn, hock, spout, mortgage, hypothecate, impignorate.

guarantee, warrant, assure; accept, indorse, underwrite, insure.

execute, stamp; sign, seal etc. (*evidence*) 467.

let, set; grant –, take –, hold- a lease; hold in pledge; lend on security etc. 787.

Adj. secure, -ed; pledged etc. *v.*; in pawn, on deposit.

772. Observance.—N. observance, performance, compliance; obedience, etc. 743; fulfilment, satisfaction, discharge; acquit-tance, - tal.

adhesion, acknowledgment; fidelity etc. (*probity*) 939; exact etc. 494- observance.

V. observe, comply with, respect, acknowledge, abide by; cling to, adhere to, be faithful to, act up to; meet, fulfil; carry -out, – into execution; execute, perform, keep, satisfy, discharge; do one's office.

perform –, fulfill –, discharge –, acquit oneself of- an obligation; make good; make good –, keep- one's -word, – promise; redeem one's pledge; keep faith with, stand to one's engagement.

Adj. observant, faithful, true, loyal; honorable etc. 939; true as the -dial to the sun, – needle to the pole; punct-ual, -ilious; meticulous; literal etc. (*exact*) 494; as good as one's word.

Adv. faithfully etc. *adj.*

773. Non-observance.—N. non-observance etc. 772; evasion, inobservance, failure, omission, neglect, laches, laxity, informality.

infringement, infraction; violation, transgression.

retractation, repudiation, nullification; protest; forfeiture.

lawlessness; disobedience etc. 742; bad faith etc. 940.

V. fail, neglect, omit, elude, evade, give the go by to, cut, set aside, ignore; shut –, close- one's eyes to, avoid.

infringe, transgress, pirate, violate, break, trample under foot, do violence to, drive a coach and six through.

discard, protest, repudiate, fling to the winds, set at naught, nullify, declare null and void; cancel etc. (*wipe off*) 552.

retract, go back from, be off, forfeit, go from one's word, palter; stretch –, strain- a point.

Adj. violating etc. *v.*; lawless, transgressive; elusive, evasive; lax, casual; non-observant.

unfulfilled etc. (*see* fulfil etc. 772).

774. Compromise.—N. com-promise, - mutation, -position; middle term, *mezzo termine*; compensation etc. 30; adjustment, mutual concession.

V. com-promise, -mute, -pound; take the mean; split the difference, meet one half way, give and take; come to terms etc. (*contract*) 769; submit to –, abide by- arbitration; patch up, bridge over, fix up, arrange; adjust, – differences; agree; make -the best of, – a virtue of necessity; take the will for the deed.

775. Acquisition.—N. acquisition; gaining etc. *v.*; obtainment; procur-ation, -ement; purchase, descent, inheritance; gift etc. 784.

recovery, retrieval, revendication, replevin; redemption, salvage, trover; find, *trouvaille*, foundling.

gain, thrift; money-making, -grubbing; lucre, filthy lucre, loaves and fishes, the main -chance, pelf; emolument etc. 973; wealth etc. 803.

profit, earnings, winnings, innings, clean-up, pickings, perquisite, net profit; income etc. (*receipt*) 810; pro-ceeds, -duce, -duct; out-come, - put; return, fruit, crop, harvest, tilth; second crop, aftermath; benefit etc. (*good*) 618.

sweepstakes, trick, prize, pool.

[Fraudulent acquisition] subreption; theft, stealing etc. 791.

V. acquire, get, gain, win, earn, obtain, procure, gather, annex; collect etc. 72; pick, – up; glean, take etc. 789.

find; come –, pitch –, light- upon; scrape -up, – together; get in, reap and carry, net, bag, sack, bring home, secure, come across, derive, draw, get in the harvest.

profit; make –, draw- profit; turn to -profit, – account; make -capital out of, – money by; obtain a return, reap the fruits of; reap –, gain- an advantage; turn -a penny, – an honest penny; make the pot boil, bring grist to the mill; make –; coin –, raise- money; raise -funds, – the wind; fill one's pocket etc. (*wealth*) 803.

treasure up etc. (*store*) 636; realize, clear; produce etc. 161; take etc. 789.

get back, recover, regain, retrieve, revendicate, replevy, redeem, come by one's own.

come -by, − in for; receive etc. 785; inherit;
step into, − a fortune, − the shoes of; succeed to.
get -hold of, − between one's finger and thumb,
− into one's hand, − at; take −, come into −,
enter into- possession.
be -profitable etc. *adj.*; pay, answer.
accrue etc. (*be received*) 785.
Adj. acquir-ing, -ed etc. *v.*; acquisitive; productive, profitable, advantageous, gainful,
remunerative, paying, lucrative.

776. Loss.—N. loss; de-, perdition; forfeiture,
lapse.
privation, bereavement; deprivation etc.
(*dispossession*) 789; riddance.
V. lose; incur −, experience −, meet with- a
loss; miss; mislay, let slip, allow to slip through the
fingers, squander; be without etc. (*exempt*) 777a;
forfeit.
get rid of etc. 782; waste etc. 638.
be lost, lapse.
Adj. losing etc. *v.*; not having etc. 777a.
shorn of, deprived of; denuded, bereaved, bereft,
minus, cut off; dispossessed etc. 789; rid of, quit of;
out of pocket.
lost etc. *v.*; long lost; irretrievable etc. (*hopeless*)
859; irredentist; off one's hands.
Int. farewell to! adieu to! good riddance!

777. Possession.—N. possession, seisin; owner-
ship etc. 780; occupancy; hold, -ing; tenure,
tenancy, feodality, dependency; villenage; socage,
chivalry, knight service.
exclusive possession, impropriation, monopoly,
corner; retention etc. 781; pre-possession, -
occupancy; nine points of the law.
future possession, heritage, inheritance, heirship,
reversion, fee, seigniority, feud, fief.
bird in hand, *uti possidetis*, *chose* in possession.
V. possess, have, hold, occupy, enjoy; be -
possessed of etc. *adj.*; have -in hand etc. *adj.*; own
etc. 780; command.
inherit; come -to, − in for.
engross, monopolize, forestall, regrate, im-
propriate, have all to oneself, corner; have a firm
hold of etc. (*retain*) 781; get into one's hand etc.
(*acquire*) 775.
belong to, appertain to, pertain to; be -in one's
possession- etc. *adj.*; vest in.
Adj. possessing etc. *v.*; worth; possessed of,
seized of, master of, in possession of; endowed −,
blest −, instinct −, fraught −, laden −, charged
−, instilled −, with.
possessed etc. *v.*; on hand, by one; in hand, in
store, in stock; in one's -hands, − grasp, −
possession; at one's -command, − disposal; one's
own etc. (*property*) 780.
unsold, unshared.

777a. Exemption.—N. exemption; exception,
immunity, privilege, release etc. 927a; absence etc.
187.
V. not -have etc. 777; be -without etc. *adj.*

Adj. exempt from, devoid of, without, unpossessed of, unblest with, immune from.
not -having etc. 777; unpossessed; untenanted
etc. (*vacant*) 187; without an owner.
unobtained, unacquired.

778. Participation. [Joint possession.]—N.
participation; co-, joint-tenancy; possession −,
tenancy- in common; joint −, common- stock; co-,
partnership; communion; community of -
possessions, − goods; communalism, communism,
socialism, collectivism; co-operation etc. 709;
profit sharing.
snacks, co-portion, picnic, hotchpotch; co-
heirship, -parceny, -parcenary; gavelkind.
participator, sharer; co-, partner; shareholder;
co-, joint-tenant; tenants in common; co-heir, -
parcener.
communist, socialist.
V. par-ticipate, -take; share, − in; come in for a
share; go -shares, − snacks, − halves; share and
share alike.
have −, possess −, be seized- -in common, −
as joint tenants etc. *n.*
join in; have a hand in etc. (*co-operate*) 709.
Adj. partaking etc. *v.*; communistic, socialistic,
co-operative, profit sharing.
Adv. share and share alike.

779. Possessor.—N. possessor, holder; occupant, -ier; tenant; person −, man- -in possession etc.
777; renter, lodger, lessee, under-lessee; zemindar,
ryot; tenant -on sufferance, − at will, − from year
to year, − for years, − for life.
owner; propriet-or; -ress, -ary; impropriator,
master, mistress, lord.
land-holder, -owner, -lord, -lady; lord -of the
manor, − paramount; heritor, laird, vavasor,
landed gentry, mesne lord.
cestui-que-trust, beneficiary, mortgagor.
grantee, feoffee, relessee, devisee; legat-ee, -ary.
trustee; holder etc.- of the legal estate; mortgagee.
right −, rightful- owner.
[Future possessor] heir, − apparent; −
presumptive; heiress; inherit-or, -ress, -rix; reversioner, remainder-man.

780. Property.—N. property, possession, *suum
cuique, meum et tuum.*
owner-, proprietor, lord-ship; seignority; empire
etc. (*dominion*) 737.
interest, stake, estate, right, title, claim, demand,
holding; tenure etc. (*possession*) 777; vested −,
contingent −, beneficial −, equitable- interest;
use, trust, benefit; legal −, equitable- estate; seisin.
absolute interest, paramount estate, freehold; fee,
− simple, − tail; estate -in fee, − in tail, − tail;
estate in tail -male, − female, − general.
limitation, term, lease, settlement, strict settlement, particular estate; estate -for life, − for
years, − *pur autre vie*; remainder, reversion, ex-
pectancy, possibility.

dower, dowry, *dot*, jointure, marriage portion, appanage, inheritance, heritage, patrimony, alimony; legacy etc. (*gift*) 784.

assets, belongings, means, resources, circumstances; wealth etc. 803; money etc. 800; what one -is worth, – will cut up for; estate and effects.

landed –, real- -estate, – property; realty; land, -s; subdivision; plot, site; tenements; hereditaments; corporeal –, incorporeal- hereditaments; acres; ground etc. (*earth*) 342; acquest; messuage.

territory, state, kingdom, principality, realm, empire, protectorate, margravate, dependancy, colony, sphere of influence, mandate.

manor, honor, domain, demesne; farm, ranch, plantation, *hacienda*; allodium etc. (*free*) 748; fieff, feoff, feud, zemindary, dependency.

free-, copy-, lease-holds; chattels real; fixtures, plant, heirloom easement; folkland; right of - common, – user.

personal -property, – estate, – effects; personalty, chattels, goods, effects, movables; stock, – in trade; things, traps, rattle-traps, paraphernalia; equipage etc. 633.

parcels, appurtenances.

impedimenta; lug-, bag-gage; bag and baggage; pelf; cargo, lading.

rent-roll; income etc. (*receipts*) 810.

patent, copyright; *chose* in action; credit etc. 805; debt etc. 806.

V. possess etc. 777; be the -possessor etc. 779- of own; have for one's own, – very own; come in for, inherit; enfeoff.

savor of the realty.

be one's own -property etc. *n.*; belong to; ap-, pertain to.

Adj. one's own; landed, predial, manorial, allodial, seignorial; free-, copy-, lease-hold; feu-, feo-dal; hereditary, entailed, personal.

Adv. to one's -credit, – account; to the good.

to one and -his heirs for ever, – the heirs of his body, – his heirs and assigns, – his executors, administrators and assigns.

781. Retention.—N. retention; retaining etc. *v.*; keep, detention, custody; tenacity, firm hold, grasp, gripe, grip, iron grip.

fangs, teeth, claws, talons, nail, hook, tentacle, *tenaculum*; bond etc. (*vinculum*) 45.

clutches, tongs, forceps, pincers, nippers, pliers, tweezers, vise.

paw, hand, finger, wrist, fist, neaf, neif.

bird in hand; captive etc. 754.

V. retain, keep; hold, – fast, – tight, – one's own, – one's ground; clinch, clench, clutch, grasp, gripe, hug, have a firm hold of.

secure, withold, detain; hold – , keepback; keep close; husband etc. (*store*) 636; reserve; have – , keep- in stock etc. (*possess*) 777; enfail, tie up, settle.

Adj. retaining etc. *v.*; retentive, tenacious.

unforfeited, undeprived, undisposed, uncommunicated.

incommunicable, inalienable; in mortmain; in strict settlement.

Phr. *uti possidetis.*

782. Relinquishment.—N. relinquishment, abandonment etc. (*of a course*) 624; renunciation,

expropriation, dereliction; cession, surrender, dispensation; resignation etc. 757; riddance.

derelict etc. *adj.*; jetsam; waif, foundling, orphan.

v. relinquish, give up, surrender, yield, cede; let -go, – slip; spare, drop, resign, forego, renounce, abjure, abandon, expropriate, give away, dispose of, part with; lay -aside, – apart, – down, – on the shelf etc. (*disuse*) 678; set – , put- aside; make away with, cast behind; discard, cast off, dismiss; maroon.

give -notice to quit, – warning; supersede; be – , get- -rid of, – quit of; eject etc. 297.

rid – , disburden – , divest – , dispossess-oneself of; wash one's hands of; divorce, desert; disinherit, cut off.

cast – , throw – , pitch – , fling- -away, – aside, – overboard, – to the dogs; cast – , throw – , sweep- to the winds; put – , turn – , sweep-away; jettison.

quit one's hold.

Adj. relinquished etc. *v.*; cast off, derelict; unowned, unappropriated, unculled; left etc. (*residuary*) 40; divorced; disinherited.

Int. away with!

783. Transfer.—N. transfer, conveyance, assignment, alienation, abalienation; demise, limitation; conveyancing; transmission etc. (*transference*) 270; enfeoffment, bargain and sale, lease and release; exchange etc. (*interchange*) 148; barter etc. 794; substitution etc. 147.

succession, reversion; shifting -use, – trust; devolution.

V. transfer, convey; alien, -ate; assign; grant etc. (*confer*) 784; consign; make – , hand- over; pass, hand, transmit, negotiate; hand down; exchange etc. (*interchange*) 148.

change -hands, – from one to another; devolve, succeed; come into possession etc. (*acquire*) 775; take over.

abalienate; disinherit; dispossess etc. 789; substitute etc. 147.

Adj. alienable, negotiable, transferable, reversional.

Phr. estate coming into possession.

784. Giving.—N. giving etc. *v.*; bestowal, donation; present-ation, -ment; accordance; con-, cession; delivery, consignment, dispensation, communication, endowment; invest-ment, -iture; award.

almsgiving, charity, liberality, generosity; philanthropy etc. 910.

[Thing given] gift, donation, present, *cadeau*; fairing; free gift, boon, favor, benefaction, grant, offering, oblation, sacrifice, immolation.

grace, act of grace, *bonus, bonanza.*

allowance, contribution, subscription, subsidy, tribute, subvention.

bequest, legacy, devise, will, dotation, appanage; dowry; voluntary -settlement, – conveyance etc. 783; amortization.

alms, largess, bounty, dole, sportule, donative, help, oblation, offertory, Peter's pence, *honorarium*, gratuity, Maundy money, Christmas box, Easter offering, vail, tip, *douceur*, drink money, *pourboire, trinkgeld, backsheesh*; fee etc. (*recompense*) 973; consideration.

bribe, bait, ground-bait; peace-offering, handsel.

giver, grantor etc. *v*.; donor, feoffer, settlor; almoner; testator; investor, subscriber, contributor; fairy godmother; Santa Claus, benefactor etc. 816.

V. deliver, hand, pass, put into the hands of; hand –, make –, deliver –, pass –, turn- over.

present, give away, dispense, dispose of; give –, deal –, dole –, mete –, fork –, shell –, squeeze- out.

pay etc. 807; render, impart, communicate.

concede, cede, yield, part with, shed cast; spend etc. 809.

give, bestow, confer, grant, accord, award, assign.

entrust, consign, vest in.

make a present; allow, contribute, subscribe, donate, furnish its quota.

invest, endow, settle upon; bequesth, leave, devise.

furnish, supply, help; ad-, minister to; afford, spare; accommodate –, indulge –, favor- with; shower down upon; lavish, pour on, thrust upon; tip, bribe; tickle –, grease- the palm; offer etc. 763; sacrifice, immolate.

Adj. giving etc. *v.*; given etc. *v.*; allow-ed, -able; concessional; communicable; charitable, eleemosynary, sportulary, tributary; *gratis* etc. 815.

785. Receiving.—N. receiving etc. *v.*; acquisition etc. 775; reception etc. (*introduction*) 296; suscipiency, acceptance, admission.

re-, ac-cipient; assignee, devisee; lega-tee, -tary; grantee, feoffee, donee, relessee, lessee.

sportulary, stipendiary; beneficiary; pension-er, -ary; almsman.

income etc. (*receipt*) 810.

v. receive; take etc. 789; acquire etc. 775; admit.

take in, catch, touch; pocket; put into one's pocket, – purse; accept; take off one's hands.

be received; come -in, – to hand; pass –, fall into one's hand; go into one's pocket; fall to one's -lot, – share; come –, fall- to one; accrue; have - given etc. 784 to one.

Adj. receiving etc. *v.*; re-, suscipient.

received etc. *v.*; given etc. 784; second-hand.

not given, unbestowed etc. (*see* give, bestow etc. 784).

786. Apportionment.—N. apportion-, allot-, consign-, assign-, appoint-ment; appropriation; dispensation, -tribution; allocation, division, deal; repartition; administration.

dividend, portion, contingent, share, allotment, lot, cut, split, measure, dose; dole, meed, pittance; *quantum*, ration; ratio, proportion, quota, *modicum*, mess, allowance.

V. apportion, divide; cut, split, divvy; distribute, administer, dispense; billet, allot, detail, cast, share, mete; portion –, parcel –, dole- out; deal, carve.

partition, assign, appropriate, appoint.

come in for one's share etc. (*participate*) 778.

Adj. apportioning etc. *v.*; respective.

Adv. respectively, each to each.

787. Lending.—N. lending etc. *v.*; loan, advance, accommodation, feneration; mortgage etc. (*security*) 771; investment.

mont de piété, pawnshop, hock shop, spout, my uncle's.

lender, pawnbroker, money lender, usurer, Jew, Shylock.

V. lend, advance, loan, accommodate with; lend on security; pawn etc. (*security*) 771.

intrust, invest; place –, put- out to interest; sink, risk.

let, demise, lease, set, under-, sub-let.

Adj. lending etc. *v.*; lent etc. *v.*; unborrowed etc. (*see* borrowed etc. 788).

Adv. in advance; on -loan, – security.

788. Borrowing.—N. borrowing, pledging, pawning.

borrowed plumes; plagiarism etc. (*thieving*) 791.

replevin.

V. borrow, desume; pawn.

hire, rent, farm; take a -lease, – demise; take –, hire- by the -hour, – mile, – year etc.

raise –, take up- money; float bonds; raise the wind; fly a kite, borrow of Peter to pay Paul; run into debt etc. (*debt*) 806.

make use of, plagiarize, pirate.

replevy.

789. Taking.—N. taking etc. *v.*; reception etc. (*taking in*) 296; deglutition etc. (*taking food*) 298; appropriation, prehension, prensation; capture, caption; ap-, de-prehension; abreption, seizure; abduction, -lation; subtraction etc. (*subduction*) 38; abstraction, ademption.

dispossession; depriv-ation, -ement; bereavement; divestment; disherison; distraint, distress, sequestration, confiscation, attachment, execution; eviction etc. 297.

rapacity, extortion, vampirism, predacity, blood-sucking; theft etc. 791.

resumption; repris-e, -al; recovery etc. 775.

clutch, swoop, wrench; grip etc. (*retention*) 781; haul, take, catch; scramble.

taker, captor, capturer; vampire; extortioner.

V. take, catch, hook, nab, bag, sack, pocket, put into one's pocket, scrounge; receive; accept.

reap, crop, cull, pluck; gather etc. (*get*) 775; draw.

ap-, im-propriate; assume, possess oneself of; take possession of; commandeer; lay –, clap- one's hands on; help oneself to; make free with, dip one's hands into; lay under contribution; intercept; scramble for; deprive of.

take –, carry –, bear- -away, – off; abstract; hurry off –, run away- with; abduct; steal etc. 791; ravish; seize; pounce –, spring- upon; swoop -to, – down upon; take by -storm, – assault; snatch, reave.

snap up, nip up, whip up, catch up; kidnap, crimp, capture, lay violent hands on.

get –, lay –, take –, catch –, lay fast –, take firm- hold of; lay by the heels, take prisoner; fasten upon, grip, grapple, embrace, gripe, clasp, grab, clutch, collar, throttle, take by the throat, claw, clinch, clench, make sure of.

catch at, jump at, make a grab at, snap at, snatch at; reach, make a long arm, stretch forth one's hand.

take -from, – away from; deduct . etc. 38; retrench etc. (*curtail*) 201; dispossess, ease one of, snatch from one's grasp; tear –, tear away –, wrench –, wrest –, wring- from; extort; deprive of, bereave; disinherit, cut off with a shilling.

oust etc. (*eject*) 297; divest; levy, distrain, confiscate; sequest-er, -rate, accroach; usurp; despoil, strip, fleece, shear, displume, impoverish, eat out of house and home; drain, – to the dregs; gut, dry, exhaust, swallow up; absorb etc. (*suck in*) 296; draw off; suck, – like a leech, – the blood of.

retake, resume; recover etc. 775.

Adj. taking etc. *v.*; privative, prehensile; pred-aceous, -al, -atory, -atorial; rap-acious, -torial; ravenous; parasitic; all-devouring, -engulfing.

bereft etc. 776.

Adv. at one fell swoop.

Phr. give an inch and take an ell.

790. Restitution.—N. restitution, return; ren-, red-dition; reinstatement, restoration; reinvestment, recuperation; repatriation; rehabilitation etc. (*reconstruction*) 660; reparation, atonement, indemnity, compensation, recompense.

release, replevin, redemption; recovery etc. (*getting back*) 775; remitter, reversion.

V. return, restore; recondition; give –, carry – bring- back; render, – up; give up; let go, unclutch; dis-, re-gorge; regurgitate; recoup, reimburse, repay, indemnify, reinvest, remit, rehabilitate; repair etc. (*make good*) 660.

redeem, recover etc. (*get back*) 775; take back again; revest, revert.

Adj. restoring etc. *v.*; recuperative etc. 660; in full restitution, to compensate for.

Phr. *suum cuique.*

791. Stealing.—N. stealing etc. *v.*; theft, thievery, robbery, latrociny, direption; abstraction, appropriation; plagiar-y, -ism; rape, kidnapping, depredation; raid, hold up.

spoliation, plunder, pillage; sack, -age; rapine, *brigandage*, highway robbery, foray, *razzia*; blackmail; piracy, privateering, buccaneering; filibustering, -ism; burglary; house-breaking; cattle-stealing, -rustling, -lifting.

peculation, embezzlement; fraud etc. 545; larceny, petty larceny, pilfering, shop-lifting.

thievishness, rapacity, kleptomania, Alsatia; den of -Cacus, – thieves.

license to plunder, letters of marque.

V. steal, thieve, rob, purloin, pilfer, filch, lift, prig, bag, nim, crib, cabbage, palm; abstract; appropriate, plagiarize.

convey away, carry off, abduct, kidnap, shanghai, impress, crimp; make –, walk –, run-off with; run away with; spirit away; seize etc. (*lay violent hands on*) 789.

plunder, pillage, rifle, sack, loot, ransack, spoil, spoliate, despoil, strip, sweep, gut, forage, levy black-mail, pirate, pickeer, maraud, lift cattle, rustle, poach, smuggle, run.

stick –, hold- up.

swindle, peculate, embezzle; sponge, mulct, rook, bilk, pluck, pigeon, skin, fleece, diddle; defraud etc. 545; obtain under false pretences; live by one's wits

rob –, borrow of- Peter to Paul; set a thief to catch a thief.

disregard the distinction between *meum* and *tuum*.

Adj. thieving etc. *v.*; thievish, light-fingered; furacious, -tive; piratical; pred-aceous, -al, -atory, -atorial; raptorial etc. (*rapacious*) 789.

stolen etc. *v.*

Phr. *sic vos non vobis.*

792. Thief.—N. thief, robber, *homo trium literarum*, pilferer, rifler, filcher, plagiarist.

spoiler, depredator, pillager, marauder; harpy, shark, land-shark, falcon, moss-trooper, bushranger, Bedouin, brigand, freebooter, bandit, thug, dacoit, pirate, corsair, viking, Paul Jones; buccan-eer, -ier; piqu-, pick-eerer; rover, ranger, privateer, filibuster; rapparee, wrecker, picaroon; smuggler, poacher, plunderer; racketeer.

highwayman, Dick Turpin, Claude Duval, Macheath, knight of the road, footpad, sturdy beggar; abductor, kidnapper.

cut-, pick-purse; pick-pocket, light-fingered gentry; sharper; card-, skittle-sharper; crook; thimblerigger; rook, Greek, blackleg, leg, welsher, defaulter; Autolycus, Cacus, Barabbas, Jeremy Diddler, Robert Macaire, artful dodger, trickster; swell mob, *chevalier d'industrie*; shop-lifter.

swindler, peculator; forger, coiner, counterfeiter, shoful; fence, receiver of stolen goods, duffer; smasher.

burglar, housebreaker; cracks-, mags-man; Bill Sikes, Jack Sheppard, Jonathan Wild, Raffles, cat burglar.

793. Booty.—N. booty, spoil, plunder, price, loot, graft, swag, pickings, boodle; *spolia opima*, prey; blackmail; stolen goods.

Adj. looting etc. *n.*; manubial, spoliative.

794. Barter.—N. barter, exchange, scorse, truck system; interchange etc. 148.

a Roland for an Oliver; *quid pro quo*; commutation, -position.

trade, commerce, mercature, buying and selling, bargain and sale; traffic, business, nundination, custom, shopping; commercial enterprise, speculation, jobbing, stock-jobbing, *agiotage*, brokery, arbitrage.

dealing, transaction, negotiation, bargain.

free trade.

V. barter, exchange, truck, scorse, swop; interchange etc. 148; commutate etc. (*substitute*) 147; compound for.

trade, traffic, buy and sell, give and take, nundinate; carry on –, ply –, drive- a trade; be in -

business, — the city; keep a shop, deal in, employ one's capital in.

trade —, deal —, have dealings- with; transact —, do- business with; open —, keep- an account with.

bargain; drive —, make- a bargain; negotiate, bid for; dicker, haggle, higgle; chaffer, huckster, cheapen, beat down; stickle, — for; out-, underbid; ask, charge; strike a bargain etc. (*contract*) 769.

speculate, give a sprat to catch a herring; buy in the cheapest and sell in the dearest market; rig the market.

Adj. commercial, mercantile, trading; interchangeable, marketable, staple, in the market, for sale.

wholesale, retail.

Adv. across the counter; on 'change.

795. Purchase.—N. purchase, emption; buying, purchasing, shopping; pre-emption, refusal.

coemption, bribery; slave trade.

buyer, purchaser, *emptor*, vendee; patron, employer, client, customer, *clientèle*.

V. buy, purchase, invest in, procure; rent etc. (*hire*) 788; repurchase, buy in.

keep in one's pay, bribe, suborn; pay etc. 807; spend etc. 809. .

make —, complete- a purchase; buy over the counter; pay cash for.

shop, market, go a shopping.

Adj. purchased etc. *v.*

Phr. *caveat emptor.*

796. Sale.—N. sale, vent, disposal; auction, roup, Dutch auction; custom etc. (*traffic*) 794.

vendi-bility, -bleness.

seller, salesman; peddler, smous; vender, vendor, consignor; merchant etc. 797; auctioneer.

V. sell, vend, dispose of, effect a sale; sell -over the counter, — by auction etc. *n.*; dispense, retail; deal in etc. 794; sell -off, — out; turn into money; realize; bring -to, — under- the hammer; put up to auction; auction, offer —, put up- for sale; hawk, peddle, bring to market; offer etc. 763; undersell; dump, unload.

let; mortgage etc. (*security*) 771.

Adj. under the hammer, in the market, for sale.

saleable, marketable, vendible, in demand, having a ready sale; unsaleable etc., unpurchased, unbought; on one's hands.

797. Merchant.—N. merchant, trader, dealer, monger, chandler, salesman; changer; regrater; shop-keeper, -man; trades-man, -people, -folk.

retailer; chapman, hawker, huckster, higgler; peddler, smous, pedlar, *colporteur*, cadger, Autolycus; sutler, *vivandière*; coster-man, -monger; market woman; cheap jack; caterer etc. 637; tallyman.

money-broker, -changer, -lender; stock-broker, -jobber; cambist, usurer, moneyer, banker.

jobber; broker etc. (*agent*) 758; buyer etc. 795; seller etc. 796.

concern; firm etc. (*partnership*) 712.

798. Merchandise.—N. merchandise, ware, commodity, effects, goods, article, stock, produce, staple commodity; stock in trade etc. (*store*) 636; cargo etc. (*contents*) 190.

799. Mart.—N. mart; market, -place, *forum*; fair, bazaar, staple; stock —, exchange; 'change, *bourse*, Wall Street, Rialto, hall, guildhall; toll-booth, custom-house; Tattersalls.

shop, stall, booth; wharf; office, chambers, counting-house, *bureau*; coun-, comp-ter.

ware-house, -room; *dépôt*, interposit, *entrepôt*, *emporium*, establishment; store etc. 636.

open market, market-overt.

800. Money.—N. money -matters, — market; finance; accounts etc. 811; funds, treasure; capital, stock; assets etc. (*property*) 780; wealth etc. 803; supplies, ways and means, wherewithal, sinews of war, almighty dollar, needful, cash.

sum, amount; balance, -sheet; sum total; proceeds etc. (*receipts*) 810.

currency, circulating medium, specie; coin, — of the realm; piece, hard cash, dollar, sterling coin; pounds, shillings and pence; L s. d., guineas; pocket, breeches pocket, purse; money in hand; the best, ready, — money; filthy lucre, shekels, roll, jack, rhino, blunt, dust, bawbees, brass, dibs, dough, mopus, tin, salt, chink, oof, spondulics, pile, wads.

precious metals, gold, silver, copper, nickel; bullion, bar, ingot, nugget.

petty cash; pocket-, pin-money; small —, change; small coin, loose cash; doit, stiver, rap, mite, farthing, *sou*, penny, shilling, bob, tanner, tester, groat, guinea, ducat; *rouleau*; *wampum*; good —, round —, lump- sum; power —, mint —; tons- of money; plum, lac of rupees, millions, money-bags, miser's hoard, stocking, mine of wealth etc. 803.

[Science of coins] numismatics, chrysology.

paper-money; money —, postal —, Post Office-order; note, — of hand; bank —, treasury- note; Bradbury; promissory note; I.O.U, bond; bill, — of exchange; draft, check, order, warrant, *coupon*, debenture, exchequer bill, *assignat*, greenback, gold —, silver- certificate.

copper, nickel, dime, quarter, two bits, half a dollar, dollar, buck, simoleon, fiver, tenner, a twenty, a sawbuck, a century, a grand; eagle, double eagle.

gold standard, bimetallism, fiat money; rate of —, exchange; in-, de-flation.

remittance etc. (*payment*) 807; credit etc. 805; liability etc. 806; solvency etc. 803.

draw-er, -ee; oblig-or, -ee; moneyer, coiner, counterfeiter, forger.

false —, bad- money; base —, counterfeit- coin, flash note, slip, kite; Bank of Elegance.

argumentum ad crumenam.

V. amount to, come to, mount up to; touch the pocket; draw, — upon; endorse etc. (*security*) 771; issue, utter, circulate; discount etc. 813.

forge, counterfeit, coin, circulate —, pass- bad money.

Adj. monetary, pecuniary, crumenal, fiscal, financial, sumptuary, numismatical; sterling; solvent etc. 803.

801. Treasurer.—N. treasurer; bursar, -y; purser, purse-bearer; cash-keeper, banker; depositary; questor, receiver, steward, trustee, chartered –, accountant; Accountant-General, almoner, liquidator, paymaster, cashier, teller; cambist; money-changer etc. (*merchant*) 797.

financier, Chancellor of the Exchequer, minister of finance; Secretary of the Treasury, Director of the Budget, Controller of Currency.

802. Treasury.—N. treasury, bank, exchequer, almonry, fisc, hanaper, bursary; safe; strong-box, - hold, -room; coffer; chest etc. (*receptacle*) 191; depository etc. 636; till, -er; cash-box, -register, purse, pocketbook, wallet; money-bag, -belt, -box, *porte-monnaie*.

purse-strings; pocket, breeches pocket.

sinking fund; stocks; government –, public –, parliamentary- -stocks, – funds, – securities, bonds; gild-edged securities; Consols, Liberty bonds, government bonds, *crédit mobilier*.

803. Wealth.—N. wealth, riches, fortune, handsome fortune, opulence, affluence; good –, easy- circumstances; independence; competence etc., (*sufficiency*) 639; solvency, soundness, solidity.

provision, livelihood, maintenance; alimony, dowry; means, resources, substance; property etc. 780; command of money.

income etc. 810; capital, money; round sum etc. (*treasure*) 800; mint of money, mine of wealth, El Dorado, Pactolus, Golconda, Potosi, *bonanza*; philosopher's stone.

long –, full –, well lined –, heavy- purse; purse of Fortunatus.

pelf, Mammon, lucre, filthy lucre; loaves and fishes; fleshpots of Egypt.

rich –, moneyed –, warm- man; man of substance; capitalist, millionaire, Nabob, Croesus, Midas, Plutus, Dives, Timon of Athens; Timo-, Pluto-cracy; Danaë.

V. be -rich etc. *adj.*; roll –, wallow- in -wealth, – riches; have money to burn.

afford, well afford; command -money, – a sum; make both ends meet, hold one's head above water.

become -rich etc. *adj.*; fill one's -pocket etc. (*treasury*) 802; feather one's nest, clean up –, make- a fortune; make money etc. (*acquire*) 775. enrich, imburse.

worship -Mammon, – the golden calf.

Adj. wealthy, rich, affluent, opulent, monied, worth -a great deal, – much; well -to do, – off; warm; well –, provided for.

made of money; rich as Croesus; rolling in - riches, – wealth.

flush, – of -cash, – money, – tin; in -funds, – cash, – full feather; solvent, solid, sound, pecunious, out of debt, all straight; able to pay 20s in the L.

Phr. one's ship coming in.

804. Poverty.—N. poverty, indigence, penury, pauperism, destitution, want; need, -iness; lack,

necessity, privation, distress, difficulties, wolf at the door.

bad –, poor –, needy –, embarrassed –, reduced –, straitened- circumstances; slender –, narrow- means; straits; hand to mouth existence, *res angusta domi*, low water, impecuniosity.

beggary; mendi-cancy, -city; broken –, loss of-fortune; insolvency etc. (*non-payment*) 808.

empty -purse, – pocket; light purse; beggarly account of empty boxes.

poor man, pauper, mendicant, mumper, beggar, starveling; *pauvre diable*.

V. be -poor etc. *adj.*; want, lack, starve, live from hand to mouth, have seen better days, go down in the world, be on one's uppers, come upon the parish; go to -the dogs, – wrack and ruin; not have a -penny etc. (*money*) 800, – shot in one's locker; beg one's bread; *tirer le diable par la queue*; run into debt etc. (*debt*) 806.

render -poor etc. *adj.*; impoverish; reduce, – to poverty; pauperize, fleece, ruin, bring to the parish.

Adj. poor, indigent; poverty-striken; badly –, poorly –, ill- off; poor as -a rat, – a church mouse, – Job's turkey, – Job; fortune-, dower-, money-, penni-less; unportioned, unmoneyed; impecunious; broke, flat; out –, short- of -money, – cash; without –, not worth- a rap etc. (*money*) 800; *qui n'a pas le sou*, out of pocket, hard up; out at -elbows, – heels; seedy, bare-footed; beggar-ly, - ed; destitute; fleeced, strapped, stripped; bereft, bereaved; reduced.

in -want etc. *n.*; needy, necessitous, distressed, pinched, straitened; put to one's -shifts, – last shifts; unable to -keep the wolf from the door, – make both ends meet; embarrassed, under hatches; involved etc. (*in debt*) 806; insolvent etc. (*not paying*) 808.

Adv. in *formâ pauperis.*

Phr. *zonam perdidit.*

805. Credit.—N. credit, trust, tick, score, tally, account.

letter of credit, circular note; duplicate; mortgage, lien, debenture, paper credit, floating capital; draft; securities.

creditor, lender, lessor, mortgagee; dun; usurer.

V. keep –, run up- an account with; entrust, credit, accredit.

place to one's -credit, – account; give –, take-credit; fly a kite.

Adj. credit-ing, -ed; accredited.

Adv. on -credit etc. *n.*; to the -account, – credit- of.

806. Debt.—N. debt, obligation, liability, indebtment, debit, score.

arrears, deferred payment, deficit, default; insolvency etc. (*non-payment*) 808; bad debt.

interest; usance, usury; premium; floating -debt, – capital.

debtor, debitor; mortgagor; defaulter etc. 808; borrower.

V. be -in debt etc. *adj.*; owe; incur –, contract- a debt etc. *n.*; run up -a bill, – a score, – an account; go on tick, put on the cuff; borrow etc. 788; run –, get- into debt; outrun the constable.

answer –, go bail- for; back one's note.

Adj. indebted; liable, chargeable, answerable for.

in -debt, – embarrassed circumstances, – difficulties; incumbered, involved; involved –, plunged –, deep –, over head and ears- in debt; deeply involved; fast tied up; insolvent etc. (*not paying*) 808; *minus*, out of pocket.

unpaid; unrequieted, unrewarded; owing, due, in arrear, outstanding.

807. Payment.—N. pay-, defray-ment; discharge; ac-, quittance; settlement, clearance, liquidation, satisfaction, reckoning, arrangement.

acknowledgment, release; receipt, – in full, – in full of all demands; voucher.

repayment, reimbursement, retribution; pay etc. (*reward*) 973; money paid etc. (*expenditure*) 809.

ready money etc. (*cash*) 800; stake, remittance, instalment.

payer, liquidator etc. 801.

V., pay, defray, make payment; pay -down, – on the nail, – ready money, – at sight, – in advance; cash, honor a bill, acknowledge; redeem; pay in kind.

pay one's -way, – shot, – footing;' pay -the piper, – sauce for all, – costs; do the needful; come across; shell –, fork- out; come down with, – the dust; tickle –, grease- the palm; expend etc. 809; put –, lay- down.

discharge, settle, quit, acquit oneself of; account –, reckon –, settle –, be even –, be quits- with; strike a balance; settle –, balance –, square- accounts with; quit scores; foot the bill; wipe –, clear- off old scores; satisfy; pay in full; satisfy –, pay in full of- all demands; clear, liquidate; pay - up, – old debts.

disgorge, make repayment; repay, refund, reimburse, retribute; make compensation etc. 30.

Adj. paying etc., paid etc. *v.*; owing nothing, out of debt, all straight, clear of -debt, – encumbrance; unowed, never indebted.

Adv. to the tune of; on the nail; money –, cash-down; cash on delivery.

808. Non-payment.—N. non-payment; default, defalcation; protest, repudiation; application of the sponge; whitewashing.

insolvency, bankruptcy, failure; overdraft, overdrawn account; insufficiency etc. 640; run upon a bank.

waste paper bonds; dishonored –, protested- bills; bogus cheque.

bankrupt, insolvent debtor, lame duck, man of straw, welsher, stag, defaulter, absconder, levanter.

V. non -pay etc. 807; fail, break, stop payment; become -insolvent, – bankrupt; be gazetted.

protest, dishonor, repudiate, nullify.

pay under protest; button up one's pockets, draw the purse strings; apply the sponge; pay over the left shoulder, get whitewashed; swindle etc. 791; run up bills, fly kites.

Adj. not paying; in debt etc. 806; behindhand, in arrear; beggared etc. (*poor*) 804; unable to make both ends meet; *minus*; worse than nothing.

insolvent, bankrupt, in the gazette, gazetted, ruined.

unpaid etc. (*outstanding*) 806; *gratis* etc. 815; unremunerated.

809. Expenditure.—N. expenditure, money going out; out-goings, -lay; expenses, disbursement; prime cost etc. (*price*) 812; circulation; run upon a bank.

[Money paid] payment etc. 807; pay etc. (*remuneration*) 973; bribe etc. 973; fee, footing, garnish; subsidy; tribute, Peter's pence; contingent, quota; donation etc. 784.

pay in advance, earnest, handsel, deposit, instalment.

investment; purchase etc. 795.

V. expend, spend; run –, get- through; pay, disburse; open –, loose –, untie- the purse strings; lay –, shell –, fork- out; bleed; make up a sum, invest, sink money.

fee etc. (*reward*) 973; pay one's way etc. (*pay*) 807; subscribe etc. (*give*) 784; subsidize, bribe.

Adj. expend-ing, -ed etc. *v.*; sumptuary, liberal etc. 816; openhanded, lavish etc. 818; extensive etc. 814.

810. Receipt—N. receipt, accountable –, conditional –, binding –, return- receipt; value received, money coming in; income, incomings, innings, revenue, return, proceeds; gross receipts, net profit; earnings etc. (*gain*) 775.

rent, – roll; rent-al, -age; rack-rent.

premium, *bonus*; sweepstakes, tontine, prize, drawing.

pension, annuity; jointure etc. (*property*) 780; alimony, pittance; emolument etc. (*remuneration*) 973.

V. receive etc. 785; take money; draw –, derive- from; get, be in receipt of, acquire etc. 775; take etc. 789.

bring in, yield, afford, pay, return; accrue etc. (*be received from*) 785.

Adj. receiv-ing, -ed etc. *v.*; profitable etc. (*gainful*) 775.

811. Accounts.—N. accounts, accompts; commercial –, monetary- arithmetic; statistics etc. (*numeration*) 85; money matters, finance, budget, bill, score, reckoning, account.

books, account book, ledger; day –, cash –, pass- book; journal; debtor and creditor –, cash –, petty cash –, running- account; account-current; balance, – sheet; *compte rendu*, account settled.

book-keeping, audit; double –, single- entry; reckoning etc. 85.

chartered –, certified public –, accountant; auditor, actuary, bookkeeper; financier etc. 801; accounting party.

V. keep accounts, enter, post, book, credit, debit, carry over; take stock; balance –, make up –, square –, settle –, wind up –, cast up –, add up –, tot' up- accounts; make accounts square.

bring to book, audit, tax, surcharge and falsify; falsify –, garble –, cook ∟, doctor- an account.

Adj. monetary etc. 800; account-able, -ing; statistical.

812. Price.—N. price, amount, cost, expense, prime cost, charge, figure, demand, damage, fare, hire; wages etc. (*remuneration*) 973.

dues, duty, toll, tax, impost, cess, sess, tallage, levy, capitation-, poll-, income-, sur-, sales-, super-tax; gabel, *gabelle*; gavel, *octroi*, custom, tariff, excise, assessment, taxation, benevolence, tithe, tenths, exactment, ransom, salvage; broker-, wharf-, lighter-, ton-, freight-age.

worth, rate, value, valuation, appraisement, money's worth, par value; penny etc. -worth; price current, market price, quotation; what it will -fetch etc. *v.*

bill etc. (*account*) 811; shot.

V. bear −, set −, fix- a price; appraise, assess, price, charge, demand, ask, require, exact, run up; distrain; run up a bill etc. (*debt*) 806; have one's price; liquidate.

amount to, come to, mount up to; stand one in, fetch, sell for, cost, bring in, yield, afford.

Adj. priced etc. *v.*; to the tune of, *ad valorem*; mercenary, venal.

Phr. no penny, no paternoster; *point d'argent, point de Suisse*, no longer pipe, no longer dance, no song, no supper.

one may have it for.

813. Discount.—N. discount, abatement, concession, reduction, depreciation, allowance, qualification, set off, drawback, poundage, *agio*, percentage; rebate, -ment; backwardation, contango; salvage; tare and tret.

V. discount, bate; a-, re-bate; deduct, reduce, mark down, take off, allow, give, make allowance; tax, depreciate.

Adj. discounting etc. *v.*

Adv. at a discount, below par.

814. Dearness.—N. dearness etc. *adj.*; high −, famine −, fancy- price; overcharge; extravagance; exorbitance, extortion; heavy pull upon the purse; Pyrrhic victory.

V. be -dear etc. *adj.*; cost -much, − a pretty penny; rise in price, look up.

overcharge, bleed, fleece, skin, extort.

pay -too much, − through the nose, −, too dear for one's whistle.

Adj. dear; high, -priced; of great price, expensive, costly, precious, worth a Jew's eye, dear bought; unreasonable, extravagant, exorbitant, extortionate; at a premium; not to be had, − for love or money; beyond −, above- price; priceless, of priceless value.

Adv. dear, -ly; at great −, heavy- cost; *à grands frais*.

Phr. prices looking up; *le jeu ne vaut pas la chandelle*.

815. Cheapness.—N. cheapness, low price; depreciation; bargain; good penny etc.- worth, *bon marché*.

[Absence of charge] gratuity; free -quarters, − seats, − admission, − warren; pass, Annie Oakley; run of one's teeth; nominal price, peppercorn rent; labor of love.

drug in the market.

V. be -cheap etc. *adj.*; cost little; come down −, fall- in price.

buy for -a mere nothing, − an old song; have one's money's worth; cheapen, beat down.

Adj. cheap; low, − priced; moderate, reasonable; in-, un-expensive; well −, worth the money; *magnifique et pas cher*; good −, cheap- at the price; dirt −, dog- cheap; cheap, -as dirt, − and nasty; catchpenny.

reduced, marked down, half-price, depreciated, unsaleable.

gratuitous, *gratis*, free, for love, − nothing; cost-expense-less; without charge, not charged, untaxed; scot −, shot −, rent- free; free of -cost, − expense; honorary, unbought, unpaid, complimentary.

Adv. for a mere song; at -cost price, − prime cost, − a reduction, − a bargain; on the cheap.

816. Liberality.—N. liberality, generosity, munificence; bount-y, -eousness, -ifulness; hospitality; charity etc. (*beneficence*) 906.

benefactor, free giver, Lady Bountiful.

V. be -liberal etc. *adj.*; spend −, bleed- freely; shower down upon; open one's purse strings etc. (*disburse*) 809; spare no expense, give -with both hands, − *carte blanche*.

Adj. liberal, free, generous; charitable etc. (*beneficent*) 906; hospitable; bount-iful, -eous; handsome; unsparing, ungrudging; open-, free-, full-handed; open-, large-, free-hearted; munificent, princely, unstinting.

overpaid.

Adv. liberally, ungrudgingly, with open hand.

817. Economy.—N. economy, frugality; thrift, -iness; prudence, care, husbandry, good housewifery, savingness, retrenchment.

savings; prevention of waste, save-all; cheese parings and candle ends; parsimony etc. 819.

V. be -economical etc. *adj.*; economize, save; retrench; cut- down expenses, − one's coat according to one's cloth, make both ends meet, keep within compass, meet one's expenses, pay one's way; keep one's head above water; husband etc. (*lay by*) 636; save −, invest- money; put out to interest; provide −, save- -for, − against- a rainy day; feather one's nest; look after the main chance.

Adj. economical, frugal, careful, thrifty, saving, chary, spare, sparing; parsimonious etc. 819.

underpaid.

Adv. sparingly etc. *adj.*; *ne quid nimis*.

818. Prodigality.—N. prodi-gality, -gence; un-thriftiness, waste, -fulness; profus-ion, -eness; extravagance; squandering etc. *v.*; lavishness; malver-sation.

prodigal; spend-, waste-thrift; losel, play-boy, spender, squanderer, locust.

V. be -prodigal etc. *adj.*; squander, lavish, sow broadcast; pour forth like water; pay through the nose etc. (*dear*) 814; spill, waste, dissipate, exhaust, drain, eat out of house and home, overdraw, outrun the constable; run -out, − through; misspend; throw -good money after bad, − the helve after the hatchet; burn the candle at both ends; make ducks and drakes of one's money;

squander one's substance, spend money like water; fool −, potter −, muddle −, fritter −, throwaway one's money; pour water into a sieve, kill the goose that lays the golden eggs; *manger son blé en herbe*.

Adj. prodigal, profuse, thriftless, unthrifty, improvident, wasteful, losel, extravagant, lavish, dissipated, over liberal; full-handed etc. (*liberal*) 816.

penny wise and pound foolish.

Adv. with an unsparing hand; money burning one's pocket; recklessly profuse.

Int. hang the expense!

819. Parsimony.—N. parsimony, parcity; parsimoniousness, stinginess etc. *adj.*; stint; illiberality, avarice, tenacity, avidity, rapacity, extortion, venality, cupidity; selfishness etc. 943; *auri sacra fames*.

miser, niggard, churl, screw, tightwad, skinflint, crib, codger, muckworm, money-grubber, pinchfist, scrimp, lickpenny, hunks, curmudgeon, *Harpagon*, Silas Marner, harpy, extortioner, Jew, usurer.

V. be -parsimonious etc. *adj.*; grudge, begrudge, stint, skimp, pinch, gripe, screw, dole out, hold back, withhold, starve, famish, live upon nothing, skin a flint.

drive a -bargain, − hard bargain; cheapen, beat down; stop one hole in a sieve; have an itching palm, grasp, grab.

Adj. parsimonious, penurious, stingy, miserly, mean, shabby, peddling, scrubby, pennywise, near, niggardly, frugal to excess; close; fast-, close-, strait-handed; close-, hard-, tight-fisted; tight, sparing; chary, grudging, griping etc. *v.*; illiberal, ungenerous, churlish, hidebound, sordid, mercenary, venal, covetous, usurious, avaricious, greedy, extortionate, rapacious.

Adv. with a sparing hand.

820. Affections.—N. affections, character, qualities, disposition, nature, spirit, tone; temper, - ament; *diathesis*, idiosyncrasy; cast −, habit −, frame- of -mind, − soul; predilection, turn; natural −, turn of mind; bent, bias, predisposition, proneness, proclivity; propen-sity, -sedness, -sion, - dency; vein, humor, mood, grain, mettle; sympathy etc. (*love*) 897.

soul, heart, breast, bosom, inner man; heart's - core, − strings, − blood; heart of hearts, *penetralia mentis*; secret and inmost recesses of the −, cockles of one's- heart; inmost -heart, − soul; back-bone.

passion, pervading spirit; ruling −, master-passion; *furore*; fulness of the heart, heyday of the blood, flesh and blood, flow of soul, force of character.

V. have −, possess- -affections etc. *n.*; be of a - character etc. *n.*; be -affected etc. *adj.*; breathe.

Adj. affected, characterized, formed, molded, cast; at-, tempered; framed; pre-, disposed; prone, inclined; having a -bias etc. *n.*; tinctured −, imbued −, penetrated −, eaten up- with.

inborn, inbred, ingrained, in the grain, congenital, inherent, bred in the bone; deep-rooted, ineffaceable, inveterate; pathoscopic.

Adv. in one's -heart etc. *n.*; at heart; heart and soul etc. 821; in the -vein, − mood.

821. Feeling.—N. feeling; suffering etc. *v.*; durance, tolerance, sufferance, supportance, experience, response; sympathy etc. (*love*) 897; impression, inspiration, affection, sensation, emotion, pathos, deep sense.

fire, warmth, glow, unction, *gusto*, vehemence; ferv-or, -ency; heartiness, cordiality; earnestness, eagerness; *empressment*, ardor, zeal, passion, enthusiasm, *verve*, *furore*, fanaticism; excitation of feeling etc. 824; fulness of the heart etc. (*disposition*) 820; passion etc. (*state of excitability*) 825; ecstasy etc. (*pleasure*) 827.

blush, suffusion, flush; hectic; tingling, thrill, kick, turn, shock; agitation etc. (*irregular motion*) 315; quiver, heaving, flutter, flurry, fluster, twitter, tremor; throb, -bing; pulsation, palpitation, painting; trepid-, perturb-ation; ruffle, hurry of spirits, pother, stew, ferment.

V. feel; receive an -impression etc. *n.*; be - impressed with etc. *adj.*; entertain −, harbor −, cherish- -feeling etc. *n.*

respond; catch the -flame, − infection; enter the spirit of.

bear, suffer, support, sustain, endure, brook, thole, aby; abide etc. (*be composed*) 826; experience etc. (*meet with*) 151; taste, prove; labor −, smart- under; bear the brunt of, brave, stand.

swell, glow, warm, flush, blush, change color, mantle; turn -color, − pale, − red, − black in the face; blench; crimson, whiten, pale, tingle, thrill, heave, pant, throb, palpitate, go pit-a-pat, tremble, quiver, flutter, twitter; stagger, reel; shake etc. 315; be -agitated, − excited etc. 824; look -blue, − black; wince, draw a deep breath.

impress etc. (*excite the feelings*) 824.

Adj. feeling etc. *v.*; sentient; sensuous; sensorial, -y; emo-tive, -tional; of −, with- feeling etc. *n.*

warm, quick, lively, smart, strong, sharp, acute, cutting, piercing, incisive; keen, − as a razor; trenchant, pungent, racy, *piquant*, poignant, caustic.

impressive, deep, profound, indelible; deep-, home-, heart-felt; swelling, soul-stirring, deep-mouthed, heart-expanding, electric, thrilling, rapturous, ecstatic.

earnest, wistful, eager, breathless; fer-vent, -vid; gushing, passionate, warmhearted, hearty, cordial, sincere, zealous, enthusiastic, glowing, ardent, burning, red-hot, fiery, flaming; boiling, − over.

pervading, penetrating, absorbing; rabid, raving feverish, fanatical, hysterical; impetuous etc. (*excitable*) 825; overmastering.

impressed −, moved −, touched −, affected −, penetrated −, seized −, imbued etc. 820- with; devoured by; wrought up etc. (*excited*) 824; struck all of a heap; rapt; in a -quiver etc. *n.*; enraptured etc. 829.

Adv. heart and soul, from the bottom of one's heart, *ab imo pectore*, *de profundis*, at heart, *con amore*, heartily, devoutly, over head and ears.

Phr. the heart -big, − full, − swelling, − beating, − pulsating, − throbbing, − thumping, − beating high, − melting, − overflowing, − bursting, − breaking.

822. Sensibility.—N. sensi-bility, -bleness, - tiveness; moral sensibility; impress-, affect-ibility; suscepti-bleness, -bility, -vity; mobility; viva-city, - ciousness; tender-, soft-ness; sentimental-ity, -ism. excitability etc. 825; fastidiousness etc. 868; physical sensibility etc. 375.

sore -point, — place; where the shoe pinches.
V. be -sensible etc. *adj.*; have a -tender, —
warm, — sensitive- heart.
  take to —, treasure up in the- heart; shrink.
'die of a rose in aromatic pain;' touch to the
quick.
  Adj. sensi-ble, -tive; impressi-ble, -onable;
suscepti-ve, -ble; 'alive to, impassion-able, -ed;
gushing; warm-, tender-, soft-hearted; tender —, as
a chicken; soft, sentimental, romantic; enthusiastic,
highflying, spirited, mettlesome, vivacious, lively,
expressive, mobile, tremblingly alive; excitable etc.
825; over-sensitive, without skin, thin-skinned;
fastidious etc. 868.
  Adv. sensibly etc. *adj.*; to the -quick, — inmost
core.

823. Insensibility.—N. insensi-bility, -bleness;
moral insensibility; inertness, *inertia, vis inertiae*;
impassi-bility, -bleness; inappetency, apathy,
phlegm, dulness, hebetude, supineness, lukewarmness, insusceptibility, unimpressibility.
  cold -fit, — blood, — heart; cold-, cool-ness;
frigidity, *sang-froid*; stoicism, imperturbation etc.
(*inexcitability*) 826; *nonchalance*, unconcern, dry
eyes; *insouciance* etc. (*indifference*) 866;
recklessness etc. 863; callousness; heart of stone,
stock and stone, marble, deadness.
  torp-or, -idity; obstupefaction, lethargy, coma,
trance; sleep etc. 683; suspended animation; stup-
or, -efaction; paralysis, palsy; numbness etc.
(*physical insensibility*) 376.
  neutrality; quietism, vegetation.
  V. be -insensible etc. *adj.*; have a rhinoceros
hide; show -insensibility etc *n.*; not -mind, — care,
— be affected by; have no desire for etc. 866; have
—, feel —, take- no interest in; *nil admirari*; not care
a -straw etc. (*unimportance*) 643 for; disregard etc.
(*neglect*) 460; set at naught etc. (*make light of*)
483; turn a deaf ear to etc. (*inattention*) 458;
vegetate.
  render -insensible, — callous; blunt, obtund,
numb, benumb, paralyze, chloroform, deaden,
hebetate, stun, stupefy; brut-ify, -alize.
  inure; harden, — the heart; steel, case-harden,
sear.
  Adj. insensible, unconscious; impassi-ve, -ble;
blind to, deaf to, dead to; un-, in-susceptible; unim-
press-ionable, -ible; passion-, spirit-, heart-, soulless; unfeeling, unmoral.
  apathetic; leuco-, phlegmatic; dull, frigid; cold, -
blooded, -hearted; unemotional; cold as charity;
flat, obtuse, inert, supine, sluggish, torpid; sleepy
etc. (*inactive*) 683; languid, half-hearted, tame;
numb, -ed; comatose; anesthetic etc. 376;
stupefied, chloroformed, palsy-stricken.
  indifferent, lukewarm; Laodicean; careless.mind-
less, regardless; inattentive etc. 458; neglectful
etc. 460; disregarding.
  unconcerned, *nonchalant, pococurante, insouciant, sans souci*; unambitious etc. 866.
  un-affected, -ruffled, -impressed, -inspired, -
excited, -moved, -stirred, -touched, -shocked, -
struck; unblushing etc. (*shameless*) 885;
unanimated; vegetative.
  callous, thick-skinned, pachydermatous, impervious; hard, -ened; inured, case-hardened;
steeled —, proof- against; imperturbable etc. (*inexcitable*) 826; unfelt.

  Adv. insensibly etc. *adj.*; *aequo animo*; without
being -moved, — touched, — impressed; in cold
blood; with -dry eyes, — withers unwrung.
  Phr. never mind; it is of no consequence etc.
(*unimportant*) 643; it cannot be helped; nothing
coming amiss; it is all -the same, — one- to.

824. Excitation.—N. excitation of feeling;
mental —, excitement; suscitation, galvanism,
stimulation, piquancy, provocation inspiration,
calling forth, infection; interest, animation,
agitation, perturbation; subjugation, fascination,
intoxication; en-, ravishment; entrancement, high
pressure.
  unction, impressiveness etc. *adj.*; emotional appeal; melodrama; psychological moment, crisis;
sensationalism.
  trail of temper, *casus belli*; irritation etc. (*anger*)
900; passion etc. (*state of excitability*) 825; thrill
etc. (*feeling*) 821; repression of feeling etc. 826.
  V. excite, affect, touch, move, impress, strike, interest, intrigue, animate, inspire, impassion, smite,
infect; stir —, fire —, warm- the blood; set astir; a-,
wake; a-, waken; call forth; e-, pro-voke; raise up,
summon up, call up, wake up, blow up, get up,
light up; raise; get up steam, rouse, arouse, stir, fire,
kindle, enkindle, apply the torch, set on fire, inflame, illuminate.
  stimulate; ex-, suscitate; inspirit; spirit up, stir up,
work up; infuse life into, five new life to; bring —,
introduce- new blood; quicken; sharpen, whet;
work upon etc. (*incite*) 615; hurry on, give a fillip,
put on one's mettle.
  fan the -fire, — flame; blow the coals, stir the
embers; fan, — into a flame; foster, heat, warm,
foment, raise to a fever heat; keep -up, — the pot
boiling; revive, rekindle; rake up, rip up.
  stir —, play on —, come home to- the feelings;
touch -a string, — a chord, — the soul, — the
heart; go to one's heart, penetrate, pierce, go
through one, touch to the quick, open the wound;
possess —, pervade —, penetrate —, imbrue —,
absorb —, affect —, disturb- the soul.
  absorb, rivet the attention; sink into the -mind,
— heart; prey on the mind; intoxicate; over-whelm,
-power; *bouleverser*, upset, turn one's head.
  fascinate; enrapture etc. (*give pleasure*) 829.
  agitate, perturb, ruffle, fluster, flutter, shake,
disturb, faze, startle, shock, stagger; give one a -
shock, — turn; strike -dumb, — all of a heap; stun,
astound, electrify, galvanize, petrify.
  irritate, sting; cut, — to the -heart, — quick; try
one's temper; fool to the top of one's bent, pique;
infuriate, madden, make one's blood boil; lash into
fury etc. (*wrath*) 900.
  be -excited etc. *adj.*; flash up, flare up; catch the
infection; thrill etc. (*feel*) 821; mantle; work
oneself up; seethe, boil, simmer, foam, fume,
flame, rage, rave; run mad etc. (*passion*) 825.
  Adj. excited etc. *v.*; wrought up, on the *qui vive*,
astir, sparkling; in a -quiver etc. 821, — fever, —
ferment, — blaze, — state of excitement; in
hysterics; black in the face, over-wrought; hot, red-
hot, flushed, feverish; all -of a twitter, — of a flutter, — of a dither, — in a pucker; with -quivering
lips, — tears in one's eyes.
  flaming; boiling, — over; ebullient, seething;
foaming, — at the mouth; fuming, raging, carried
away by passion, wild, raving, frantic, mad, dis-

tracted, distraught, beside oneself, out of one's wits,
amuck, ready to burst, *bouleversé*, demoniacal.
lost, *eperdu*, tempest-tossed; haggard; ready to
sink.

stung to the quick, up, on one's high ropes.
exciting etc. *v.*; impressive, warm, glowing, fervid, swelling, imposing, spirit-stirring, thrilling;
high-wrought; soul-stirring, -subduing; heart-
swelling, -thrilling; agonizing etc. (*painful*) 830;
telling, sensational, melodramatic, hysterical; over-
powering, -whelming; more than flesh and blood
can bear.

piquant etc. (*pungent*) 392; spicy, appetizing,
provocative, *provaquant*, tantalizing.

Adv. till one is black in the face.

Phr. the heart, -beating high, — going pit-a-pat,
— leaping into one's mouth; the blood -being up,
— boiling in one's veins; the eye -glistening. — 'in
a fine frenzy rolling;' the head turned.

825. Excitability. [Excess of sensitiveness.] — **N.** excitability, impetuosity,
vehemence; boisterousness etc. *adj.*; turbulence;
impatience, intolerance, non-endurance; irritability
etc. (*irascibility*) 901; itching etc. (*desire*) 865;
wincing; disquiet, -ude; restlessness; fidge-ts, -
tiness; agitation etc. (*irregular motion*) 315.

trepidation, perturbation, ruffle, hurry, -skurry,
fuss, flurry; fluster, flutter; pother, stew, ferment;
whirl; thrill etc. (*feeling*) 821; state —, fever- of excitement; transport.

passion, excitement, flush, heat; fever, -heat; fire,
flame, fume, blood boiling; tumult; effervescence,
ebullition; boiling, — over; whiff, gust, storm, tempest; scene, breaking out, burst, fit, paroxysm, explosion; out-break, -burst; agony.

violence etc. 173; fierceness etc. *adj.*; rage, fury,
furor, *furore*, desperation, madness, distraction,
raving, delirium, brain storm; frenzy, hysterics; intoxication; tearing —, raging- passion, towering
rage; anger etc. 900.

fascination, infatuation, fanaticism; Quixot-ism, -
ry; *tête montée*.

V. be -impatient etc. *adj.*; not be able to -bear
etc. 826; bear ill, wince, chafe, champ the bit; be in
a -stew etc. *n.*; be out of all patience, fidget, fuss,
not have a wink of sleep; toss, — on one's pillow.

lose one's temper etc. 900; break —, burst —,
fly- out; go —, fly- -off, — off the handle, — off at
a tangent; explode; flare up, flame up, fire up, burst
into a flame, take fire, fire, burn; boil, — over;
foam, fume, rage, rave, rant, tear; go —, run- -
wild, — mad; go into hysterics; run -riot, —
amuck; *battre la campagne*, *faire le diable à
quatre*, play the deuce; raise -Cain, — the devil.

Adj. excitable, easily excited, in an excitable
state; high strung; irritable etc. (*irascible*) 901; impatient, intolerant.

feverish, febrile, hysterical; delirious, mad,
moody, maggoty-headed.

unquiet, mercurial, electric, galvanic, hasty,
hurried, restless, fidgety, fussy; chafing etc. *v.*

startlish, mettlesome, high mettled, skittish.

vehement, demonstrative, violent, wild, furious,
fierce, fiery, hot-headed, mad-cap.

over-zealous, enthusiastic, impassioned,
fanatical; rabid etc. (*eager*) 865.

rampant, clamorous, uproarious, turbulent, tempestuous, tumultuary, boisterous.

impulsive, impetuous, passionate; uncontroll-ed,
-able; ungovernable, irrepressible, stanchless, inextinguishable, burning, simmering, volcanic, ready
to burst forth.

excit-ed, -ing etc. 824.

Int. pish! pshaw!

Phr. *noli me tangere*.

826. Inexcitability. [Absence of excitability,
or of excitement.] — **N.** inexcit- imperturb-, inirrit-
ability; even temper, tranquil mind, dispassion;
tolerance, toleration, patience.

passiveness etc. (*physical inertness*) 172; hebetude, -ation; impassibility etc. (*insensibility*) 823;
stupefaction.

coolness, calmness etc. *adj.*; composure,
placidity, indisturbance, imperturbation, *sang-
froid*, tranquility, serenity; quiet, -ude; peace of
mind, mental calmness.

staidness etc. *adj.*; gravity, sobriety, Quakerism;
philosophy, equanimity, stoicism, command of
temper; self-possession, -control, -command, -
restraint; presence of mind.

submission etc. 725; resignation; suffer-, support-
, endur-, long-suffer-, forbear-ance; longanimity;
fortitude; patience -of Job, — 'on a monument,' —
'sovereign o'er transmuted ill;' moderation;
repression —, subjugation- of feeling; restraint etc.
751.

tranquilization etc. (*moderation*) 174.

V. be -composed etc. *adj.*

laisser -faire, — *aller*; take things -easily, — as
they come; take it easy, run on, live and let live;
take -easily, — cooly, — in good part; *aequam
serva e mentem*.

bear, — well, — the brunt; go through, support,
endure, brave, disregard.

tolerate, suffer, stand, bide, abide, aby; bear —,
put up —, abide- with; acquiesce; submit etc.
(*yield*) 725; submit with a good grace; resign —,
reconcile- oneself to; brook, digest, eat, swallow,
pocket, stomach; make -light of, — the best of, — a
virtue of necessity; put a good face on, keep one's
countenance; carry -on, — through; check etc.
751- oneself.

compose, appease etc. (*moderate*) 174;
propitiate; repress etc. (*restrain*) 751; render insensible etc. 823; overcome —, allay —, repress-
one's -excitability etc. 825; master one's feelings.

make -oneself, — one's mind- easy; set one's
mind at -ease, — rest.

calm —, cool- down; thaw, grow cool.

be -borne, — endured; go down.

Adj. in-, un-excitable; imperturbable; un-
susceptible etc. (*insensible*) 823; un-, dispassionate; cold-blooded, inirritable; enduring etc.
v.; stoical, Platonic, philosophic, staid, stayed;
sober, — minded; grave; sober —, grave- as a
judge; sedate, demure, cool-, level-headed; steady.

easy-going, peaceful, placid, calm; quiet, — as a
mouse; tranquil, serene; cool, — as -a cucumber,
— custard; undemonstrative.

temperate etc. (*moderate*) 174; composed,
collected; un-excited, -stirred, -ruffled, -disturbed, -
perturbed, -impassioned; unoffended; unresisting.

meek, tolerant; patient, — as Job; submissive
etc. 725; tame; content, resigned, chastened, sub-
dued, lamblike; gentle, — as a lamb; *suaviter in
modo*; mild, — as mother's milk; soft as pep-

permint; armed with patience, bearing with,
clement, forbearant, long-suffering.

Adv. 'like patience on a monument smiling at
grief;' *aequo animo*, in cold blood etc. 823; more
in sorrow than in anger.

Int. patience! and shuffle the cards.

827. Pleasure.—N. pleasure, gratification, enjoyment, fruition; ob-, de-lectation; relish, zest;
gusto etc. (*physical pleasure*) 377; satisfaction etc.
(*content*) 831; complacency.

well-being; good etc. 618; snugness, comfort,
ease; cushion etc. 215; *sans souci*, mind at ease.

joy, gladness, delight, glee, cheer, sunshine;
cheerfulness etc. 836.

treat, refreshment; frolic, fun, lark, gambol,
merry-making; amusement etc. 840; luxury etc.
377; hedonism.

mens sana in corpore sano.

happiness, felicity, bliss; beati-tude, -fication; enchantment, transport, rapture, ravishment, ecstasy;
summum bonum; paradise, elysium etc. (*heaven*)
981; third —, seventh- heaven; unalloyed -
happiness etc.

honeymoon; palmy —, halcyon- days; golden -
age, — time; *Saturnia regna*, Eden, Arcadia,
happy valley, Agapemone; Cockaigne.

V. be pleased etc. 829; feel —, experience-
pleasure etc. *n.*; joy; enjoy —, hug- oneself; be in -
clover etc. 377, — elysium etc. 981; tread on enchanted ground; fall —, go- into raptures.

feel at home, breathe freely, bask in the sunshine.

be -pleased etc. 829- with; receive —, derive-
pleasure etc. *n.*- from; take -pleasure etc. *n.*- in;
delight in, rejoice in, indulge in, luxuriate in; gloat
over etc. (*physical pleasure*) 377; enjoy, relish,
like; love etc. 897; take -to, — a fancy to; have a
liking for; enter into the spirit of.

take in good part.

treat oneself to, solace oneself with.

Adj. pleased etc. 829; not sorry; glad, -some;
pleased as Punch.

happy, blest, blessed, blissful, beatified; happy as
-a king, — the day is long; thrice happy, *ter
quaterque beatus*; enjoying etc. *v.*; joyful etc. (*in
spirits*) 836; hedonic.

in -a blissful state, — paradise etc. 981; — raptures, — ecstasies, — a transport of delight.

comfortable etc. (*physical pleasure*) 377; at
ease; content etc. 831; *sans souci*, in clover.

overjoyed, entranced, enchanted; enraptured;
en-, rapt; transported; fascinated, captivated;
with a joyful face, — sparkling eyes.

pleasing etc. 829; ecstatic, beat-ic, -ific; painless,
unalloyed, without alloy, cloudless.

Adv. happily etc. *adj.*; with pleasure etc.
(*willingly*) 60; with -glee etc. *n.*

phr. one's heart leaping with joy.

828. Pain.—N. mental suffering, pain, dolor;
suffer-ing, -ance; ache, smart etc. (*physical pain*)
378; passion.

displeasure, dissatisfaction, discomfort, discomposure, disquiet; *malaise*; inquietude, uneasiness,
vexation of spirit; taking; discontent etc. 832.

dejection etc. 837; weariness etc. 841.

annoyance, irritation, worry, infliction,
visitation; plague, bore; bother, -ation; stew,
vexation, mortification, chagrin, *esclandre*;
mauvais quart d'heure.

care, anxiety, solicitude, trouble, trial, ordeal,
fiery ordeal, shock, blow, cark, dole, fret, burden,
load.

concern, grief, sorrow, distress, affliction, woe,
bitterness, gloom, heartache; heavy —, aching —,
bleeding —, broken- heart; heavy affliction,
gnawing grief; unhappiness, infelicity, misery,
tribulation, wretchedness, desolation; despair etc.
859; extremity, prostration, depth of misery.

nightmare, *ephialtes*, incubus.

anguish, agony; throe, tor-ture, -ment;
crucifixion, martyrdom; pang, twinge, stab; the
rack, the stake; purgatory etc. (*hell*) 982.

hell upon earth; iron age, reign of terror; slough
of despond etc. (*adversity*) 735; peck —, sea- of
troubles; ills that flesh is heir to etc. (*evil*) 619;
miseries of human life; unkindest cut of all.

sufferer, victim, prey, martyr, object of compassion, wretch, shorn lamb.

V. feel —, suffer —, experience —, undergo —,
bear —, endure- pain etc. *n.*; smart, ache etc.
(*physical pain*) 378; suffer, bleed, ail; be the victim
of; bear — take up- the cross.

labor under afflictions; quaff the bitter cup, have
a bad time of it; fall on evil days etc. (*adversity*)
735; go hard with, come to grief, fall a sacrifice to,
drain the cup of misery to the dregs, sup full of
horrors.

sit on thorns, be on pins and needles, wince, fret,
chafe, worry oneself, be in a taking, fret and fume,
take -on, — to heart.

grieve; mourn etc. (*lament*) 839; yearn, repine,
pine, droop, languish, sink; give way; despair etc.
859; break one's heart; weigh upon the heart etc.
(*inflict pain*) 830.

Adj. in —, in a state of —, full of- pain etc. *n.*;
suffering etc. *v.*; pained, afflicted, worried,
displeased etc. 830; aching, griped, sore etc.
(*physical pain*) 378; on the rack; in limbo; between hawk and buzzard.

un-comfortable, -easy; ill at ease; in a -taking, —
way; disturbed; discontented etc. 832; out of
humor etc. 901*a*; weary etc. 841.

heavy laden, stricken, crushed, a prey to, victimized, ill-used.

unfortunate etc. (*hapless*) 735; to be pitied,
doomed, devoted, accursed, undone, lost, stranded.

unhappy, infelicitous, poor, wretched, miserable,
woe-begone; cheerless etc. (*dejected*) 837;
careworn.

concerned, sorry; sorrow-ing, -ful; cut up,
chagrined, horrified, horror-stricken; in —,
plunged in —, a prey to- grief etc. *n.*; in tears etc.
(*lamenting*) 839; steeped to the lips in misery;
heart-stricken, -broken, -scalded; broken-hearted;
in despair etc. 859.

Phr. 'the iron entered into our soul;' *haeret
lateri lethalis arundo;* one's heart bleeding.

829. Pleasurableness. [Capability of giving
pleasure; cause or source of pleasure.]—N.
pleasurable-, pleasant-, agreeable-ness etc. *adj.*;
pleasure giving, jocundity, delectability;
amusement etc. 840.

attraction etc. (*motive*) 615; attractiveness, -

ability; invitingness etc. *adj.*; charm, fascination, captivation, enchantment, witchery, seduction, winsomeness, winning ways, amenity, amiability, sweetness.

loveliness etc. (*beauty*) 845; sunny –, bright-side; sweets etc. (*sugar*) 396; goodness etc. 648; manna in the wilderness, land flowing with milk and honey.

treat; regale etc. (*physical pleasure*) 377; dainty; tit-, tid-bit; nuts, *sauce piquante.*

V. cause –, produce –, create –, give –, afford –, procure –, offer –, present –, yield-pleasure etc. 827.

please, charm, delight; gladden etc. (*make cheerful*) 836; take, captivate, fascinate; enchant, entrance, enrapture, transport, bewitch; en-, ravish.

bless, beatify; satisfy; gratify –, desire etc. 865; slake, satiate, quench; indulge, humor, flatter, tickle; tickle the palate etc. (*savory*) 394; regale, refresh; enliven; treat; amuse etc. 840; take –, tickle –, hit- one's fancy; meet one's wishes; win –, gladden –, rejoice –, warm the cockles of- the heart; do one's heart good.

attract, allure etc. (*move*) 615; stimulate etc. (*excite*) 824; interest, intrigue.

make things pleasant, popularize, gild the pill, sweeten.

Adj. causing pleasure etc. *v.*; pleasure-giving; pleas-ing, -ant, -urable; agreeable, cushy; grat-eful, -ifying; leef, lief, acceptable; welcome, – as the roses in May; welcomed; favorite; to one's -taste, – mind, – liking, – heart's content; satisfactory etc. (*good*) 648.

refreshing; comfortable; cordial; genial; glad, -some; sweet, delectable, nice, dainty; delic-ate, -ious; dulcet; luscious etc. 396; palatable etc. 394; luxurious, voluptuous; sensual etc. 377.

attractive etc. 615; inviting, prepossessing, engaging; win-ning, -some; taking, fascinating, captivating, killing; seduc-ing, -tive; alluring, enticing; appetizing etc. (*exciting*) 824; cheering etc. 836; bewitching; interesting, absorbing, enchanting, entrancing, enravishing.

charming; delightful, felicitous, exquisite; lovely etc. (*beautiful*) 845; ravishing, rapturous; heartfelt, thrilling, ecstatic; beat-ic, -ific; seraphic; empyrean; elysian etc. (*heavenly*) 981.

palmy, halcyon, Saturnian.
Phr. *decies repetita placebit.*

830. Painfulness. [Capability of giving pain; cause or source of pain.]—**N.** painfulness etc. *adj.*; trouble, care etc. (*pain*) 828; trial; af-, in-fliction; cross, blow, stroke, burden, load, curse; bitter -pill, – draught, – cup; waters of bitterness.

annoyance, grievance, nuisance, vexation, mortification, sickener; bore, bother, pother, hot water, sea of troubles, hornet's nest, plague, pest.

cancer, ulcer, sting, thorn; canker etc. (*bane*) 663; scorpion etc. (*evil-doer*) 913; dagger etc. (*arms*) 727; scourge etc. (*instrument of punishment*) 975; carking –, canker worm of- care.

mishap, misfortune etc. (*adversity*) 735; *désagrément, esclandre*, rub.

source of -irritation, – annoyance; wound, sore subject, skeleton in the closet; thorn in -the flesh, – one's side; where the shoe pinches, gall and wormwood.

sorry sight, heavy news, provocation; affront etc. 929; head and front of one's offending.

infestation, molestation; malignity etc. (*malevolence*) 907.

V. cause –, occasion –, give –, bring –, induce –, produce –, create –, inflict- pain etc. 828; pain, hurt, wound.

pinch, prick, gripe etc. (*physical pain*) 378; pierce, lancinate, cut.

hurt –, wound –, grate upon –, jar upon- the feelings; wring –, pierce –, lacerate –, break –, rend- the heart; make the heart bleed; tear –, rend- the heart-strings; draw tears from the eyes.

sadden; make -unhappy etc. 828; plunge into sorrow, grieve, fash, afflict, distress; cut -up. – to the heart.

displease, annoy, incommode, discommode, discompose, trouble, disquiet, disturb, thwart, cross, perplex, molest, tease, rag, tire, irk, vex, mortify, wherret, worry, plague, bother, pester, bore, pother, harass, harry, badger, heckle, bait, beset, infest, persecute, importune, be troublesome.

wring, harrow, torment, torture; put to the -rack, – question; break on the wheel, rack, scarify; cruci-ate, -fy; convulse, agonize; barb the dart; plant a -dagger in the breast, – thron in one's side.

irritate, provoke, sting, nettle, try the patience, pique, fret, rile, tweak the nose, chafe, gall; sting –, wound –, cut- to the quick; aggrieve, affront, enchafe, enrage, ruffle, sour the temper; give offence etc. (*resentment*) 900.

maltreat, bite, snap at, assail, bully; smite etc. (*punish*) 972.

sicken, disgust, revolt, nauseate, disenchant, repel, offend, shock, stink in the nostrils; go against –, turn- the stomach; make one sick, set the teeth on edge; go against the grain, grate on the ear; stick in one's -throat, – gizzard; rankle, gnaw, corrode, horrify, appal, freeze the blood; chill the spine; make the -flesh creep, – hair stand on end; make the blood -curdle, – run cold; make one shudder.

haunt, – the memory; weigh –, prey- on the -heart, – mind, – spirits; bring one's grey hairs with sorrow to the grave; add a nail to one's coffin.

Adj. causing pain, hurting etc. *v.*; hurtful etc. (*bad*) 649; painful; dolor-ific, -ous; unpleasant; un-, dis-pleasing; disagreeable, unpalatable, bitter, distasteful; uninviting; unwelcome; undesir-able, -ed; obnoxious; unacceptable, unpopular, thankless.

unsatisfactory, untoward, unlucky, uncomfortable.

distressing; afflict-ing, -ive; joy-, cheer-, comfort-less; dismal, disheartening; depress-ing, -ive; dreary, melancholy, grievous, piteous; woeful, rueful, mournful, deplorable, pitiable, lamentable; sad, affecting, touching, pathetic.

irritating, provoking, stinging, annoying, aggravating, mortifying, galling; unaccommodating, invidious, vexatious; trouble-, tire-, irk-, weari-some; plagu-ing, -y; awkward.

importunate; teas-, pester-, bother-, harass-, worry-, torment-, cark-ing.

in-toler-, -suffer-, -support-able; un-bear-, -endur-able; past bearing; not to be -borne, – endured; more than flesh and blood can bear; enough to -drive one mad, – provoke a saint, – make a parson swear, – try the patience of Job.

shocking, terrific, grim, appalling, crushing; dreadful, fearful, frightful; thrilling, tremendous, dire; heart-breaking, -rending, -wounding, -corroding, -sickening; harrowing, rending.

odious, hateful, execrable, repulsive, repellent, abhorrent; horri-d, -ble, -fic, -fying; offensive; nause-ous, -ating; disgust-, sicken-, revolt-ing; nasty; loath-some, -ful; fulsome; vile etc. (*bad*) 649; hideous etc. 846.

sharp, acute, sore, severe, grave, hard, harsh, cruel, biting, acrimonious, caustic; cutting, corroding, consuming, racking, excruciating, searching, searing, grinding, grating, agonizing; envenomed.

ruinous, disastrous, calamitous, tragical; desolating, withering; burdensome, onerous, oppressive; cumb-rous, -ersome.
Adv. painfully etc. *adj.*; with -pain etc. 828; deuced.
Int. *hinc illae lachrymae!* woe is me!
Phr. *surgit amari aliquid*; the place being too hot to hold one; the iron entering the soul.

831. Content.—N. content, -ment, -edness; complacency, satisfaction, entire satisfaction, ease, heart's ease, peace of mind; serenity etc. 826; cheerfulness etc. 836; ray of comfort; comfort etc. (*well-being*) 827.

re-, conciliation; resignation etc. (*patience*) 826. waiter on Providence.
V. be -content etc. *adj.*; rest -satisfied, – and be thankful; take the good the gods provide, let well alone, feel oneself at home, hug oneself, lay the flattering unction to one's soul.

take -up with, – in good part; assent etc. 488; be reconciled to, make one's peace with; get over it; take -heart, – comfort; put up with etc. (*bear*) 826.

render -content etc. *adj.*; set at ease, comfort; set one's -heart, – mind- at -ease, – rest; speak peace; conciliate, reconcile, win over, propitiate, disarm, beguile; content, satisfy; gratify etc. 829.
be -tolerated etc. 826; go down, – with; do.
Adj. content, -ed; satisfied etc. *v.*; at -ease, – one's ease, – home; with the mind at ease, *sans souci, sine curâ*, easy-going, not particular; conciliatory; unrepining, of good comfort; resigned etc. (*patient*) 826; cheerful etc. 836.

un-afflicted, -vexed, -molested, -plagued; serene etc. 826; at rest; snug, comfortable; in one's element.
satisfactory, satisfying, ample, sufficient, adequate, tolerable.
Adv. to one's heart's content; *à la bonne heure*; all for the best.
Int. amen etc. (*assent*) 488; very well, so much the better, well and good; it –, that- will do; it cannot be helped.
Phr. nothing comes amiss.

832. Discontent.—N. discontent, -ment; dissatisfaction; dissent etc. 489; labor unrest.

disappointment, mortification; cold comfort; regret etc. 833; repining, taking on etc. *v.*; inquietude, vexation of spirit, soreness; heart-burning, -grief; querulousness etc. (*lamentation*) 839; hypercriticism.

malcontent, grumbler, growler, croaker, *laudator temporis acti*; censurer, complainer, faultfinder, murmurer, Adullamite, Diehard, Bitterender.
the Opposition, cave of Adullam, indignation meeting, 'winter of our discontent.'
V. be -discontented etc. *adj.*; quarrel with one's bread and butter; repine; regret etc. 833; wish one at the bottom of the Red Sea; take -on, – to heart; shrug the shoulders; make a wry –, pull a long-face; knit one's brows; look -blue, – black, – black as thunder, – blank, – glum.

take -in bad part, – ill; fret, chafe, make a piece of work; grumble, croak, grouse; lament etc. 839.
cause -discontent. etc. *n.*; dissatisfy, disappoint, mortify, put out, disconcert; cut up; dishearten.
Adj. discontented; dissatisfied etc. *v.*; unsatisfied, ungratified; dissident; dissentient etc. 489; malcontent, exigent, exacting, hypercritical.
repining etc. *v.*; regretful etc. 833; down in the mouth etc. (*dejected*) 837.
in -high dudgeon, – a fume, – the sulks, – the dumps, – bad humor; glum, sulky; sour, – as a crab; soured, sore; out of -humor, – temper.
disappointing etc. *v.*; unsatisfactory.
Int. so much the worse!
Phr. that –, it- will never do.

833. Regret.—N. regret, repining; home sickness, nostalgia; *mal –, maladie- du pays*; lamentation etc. 839; contrition, compunction, penitence etc. 950.
bitterness, heart-burning.
laudator temporis acti etc. (*discontent*) 832.
V. regret, deplore; bewail etc. (*lament*) 839; repine, cast a longing lingering look behind; rue, – the day; repent etc. 950; *infandum renovare dolorem*.
prey –, weigh –, have a weight- on the mind; leave an aching void.
Adj. regretting etc. *v.*; regretful; home-sick.
regretted etc. *v.*; much to be regretted, regrettable; lamentable etc. (*bad*) 649.
Int. what a pity! hang it!
Phr. 'tis -pity, – too true.

834. Relief.—N. relief; deliverance; refreshment etc. 689; easement, softening, alleviation, mitigation, palliation etc. 174; soothing, lullaby; cradle song, *berceuse*.
solace, consolation, comfort, encouragement.
lenitive, restorative etc. (*remedy*) 662; poultice etc. *v.*; cushion etc. 215; crumb of comfort, balm in Gilead; aspirin.
V. relieve, ease, alleviate, mitigate, palliate, soothe, addulce; salve; soften, – down; foment, stupe, poultice; assuage, allay.
cheer, comfort, console; encourage, bear up, pat on the back, give comfort, set at ease; enliven, gladden –, cheer- the heart.
remedy; cure etc. (*restore*) 660; refresh; pour - balm into, – oil on.
smoothe the ruffled brow of care, temper the wind to the shorn lamb, lay the flattering unction to one's soul.
disburden etc. (*free*) 705; take off a load of care.
be relieved; breathe more freely, draw a long breath; take comfort; dry –, wipe- the -tears, – eyes.

Adj. relieving etc. *v.*;` consolatory, soothing; assua-ging, -sive; bal-my, -samic; lenitive, palliative; anodyne etc. (*remedial*) 662; curative etc. 660.

---

835. Aggravation.—N. aggravation, heightening; exacerbation; exasperation; overestimation etc. 482; exaggeration etc. 549.

V. aggravate, render worse, heighten, embitter, sour; ex-, acerbate; exasperate, envenom; tease, provoke, enrage.

add fuel to the -fire, — flame; fan the flame etc. (*excite*) 824; go from bad to worse etc. (*deteriorate*) 659.

Adj. aggravated etc. *v.*; worse, unrelieved; aggravable; aggravating etc. *v.*

Adv. out of the frying pan into the fire, from bad to worse, worse and worse.

Int. so much the worse!

---

836. Cheerfulness.—N. cheerfulness etc. *adj.*; geniality, gaiety, *l'allegro*, cheer, good humor, spirits; high —, animal —, flow of- spirits; glee, high glee, light heart; sunshine of the -mind, — breast; *gaieté de coeur, bon naturel.*

liveliness etc. *adj.*; life, alacrity, vivacity, animation, *allégresse*; jocundity, joviality, jollity; levity; jocularity etc. (*wit*) 842.

mirth, merriment, hilarity, exhilaration; laughter etc. 838; merry-making etc. (*amusement*) 840; heyday, rejoicing etc. 838; marriage bells.

nepenthe, Euphrosyne.

optimism etc. (*hopefulness*) 858; self-complacency.

V. be -cheerful etc. *adj.*; have the mind at ease, smile, put a good face upon, keep up one's spirits; view -the bright side of the picture, — things en couleur de rose; *ridentem dicere verum*, cheer up, brighten up, light up, bear up; chirp, take heart, cast away care, drive dull care away, perk up.

rejoice etc. 838; carol, chirrup, lilt; frisk, rollick, give a loose to mirth.

cheer, enliven, elate, exhilarate, gladden, inspirit, animate, raise the spirits, inspire; put in good humor; cheer —, rejoice- the heart; delight etc. (*give pleasure*) 829.

Adj. cheerful; happy etc. 827; cheer-y, -ly; of good cheer, smiling; blithe; in —, in good- spirits; in high -spirits, — feather; happy as -the day is long, — a king; gay, — as a lark; *allegro*; light, -some, -hearted; buoyant, *débonnaire*, bright, free and easy, airy; janty, jaunty, canty; spright-ly, -ful; spry; spirit-ed, -ful; lively; animated, breezy, vivacious; brisk, — as a bee; sparkling; sportive; full of -play, — spirit; all alive.

sunny, palmy; hopeful etc. 858.

merry, — as a -cricket, — grig, — marriage bell; joyful, joyous, jocund, jovial; jolly, — as a thrush, — as a sandboy; blithesome; glee-ful, -some; hilarious, rattling.

winsome, bonny, hearty, buxom.

play-ful, -some; *folâtre*, playful as a kitten, tricksy, frisky, frolicsome; gamesome; jocose, jocular, waggish; mirth-, laughter-loving; mirthful, rollicking.

elate, -d; exulting, jubilant, flushed; rejoicing etc. 838; cock-a-hoop.

---

cheering, inspiriting, exhilarating; cardiac, -al; pleasing etc. 829; flourishing, halcyon.

Adv. cheerfully etc. *adj.*

Int. never say die! come! cheer up! hurrah! etc. 838; 'hence loathed melancholy!' begone dull care! away with melancholy!

---

837. Dejection.—N. dejection; dejectedness etc. *adj.*; depression, prostration; lowness —, depression- of spirits; weight —, oppression —, damp- on the spirits; low —, bad —, drooping —, depressed- spirits; heart sinking; heaviness —, failure- of heart.

heaviness etc. *adj.*; infestivity, gloom; weariness etc. 841; *taedium vitae*, disgust of life; *mal du pays* etc. (*regret*) 833.

melancholy; sadness etc. *adj.*; *il penseroso, melancholia*, dismals, mumps, mopes, lachrymals, dumps, blues, blue devils, doldrums, vapors, megrims, spleen, horrors, hypochondriasis, pessimism; despondency, slough of Despond; disconsolateness etc. *adj.*; hope deferred, blank despondency.

prostration, — of soul; broken heart; despair etc. 859; cave of -despair, — Trophonius.

demureness etc. *adj.*; gravity, solemnity; long —, grave- face.

hypochondriac, seek-sorrow, self-tormentor, *heautontimorumenos*, *malade imaginaire, médecin tant pis*; croaker, pessimist; mope, mopus.

[Cause of dejection] affliction etc. 830; sorry sight; *memento mori*; damper, wet blanket, Job's comforter; death's head, skeleton at the feast.

V. be -dejected etc. *adj.*; grieve; mourn etc. (*lament*) 839; take on, give way, lose heart, despond, droop, sink.

lower, look down-ast, frown, pout; hang down the head; pull —, make- a long face; laugh on the wrong side of the mouth; grin a ghastly smile; look -blue, — like a drowned man; lay —, take- to heart.

mope, brood over; fret; sulk; pine, — away; yearn; repine etc. (*regret*) 833; despair etc. 859.

refrain from laughter, keep one's countenance; be —, look- grave etc. *adj.*; repress a smile, keep a straight face.

depress; dis-courage, -hearten; dis-pirit; damp, dull, deject, lower, sink, dash, knock down, un-man, prostrate, break one's heart; frown upon; cast a -gloom, — shade- on; sadden; damp —, dash —, wither- one's hopes; weigh —, lie heavy —, prey-on the -mind, — spirits; damp —, depress- the spirits.

Adj. cheer-, joy-, spirit-less; uncheer-ful, -y; unlively; unhappy etc. 828; melancholy, dismal, somber, dark, gloomy, adust, *triste*, clouded, murky, lowering, frowning, lugubrious, Acherontic, funereal, mournful, lamentable, dreadful.

dreary, flat; dull, — as -a beetle; — ditchwater; depressing etc. *v.*

'melancholy as a gib cat;' oppressed with —; a prey to- melancholy; down-cast, -hearted; down -in the mouth, — on one's luck; heavy-hearted; in the -dumps, — suds, — sulks, — doldrums; in doleful dumps, in bad humor; sullen; mumpish, dumpish; mopish, moping; moody, glum; sulky etc. (*discontented*) 832; out of -sorts, — humor, — heart, — spirits; ill at ease, low-spirited, in low spirits, a cup too low; weary etc. 841; dis-couraged, -heartened; desponding; chop-, jaw-, crest-fallen.

sad, pensive, *penseroso*, tristful; dole-some, -ful; woebegone, lachrymose, in tears, melancholic, hypped, hypochondriacal, bilious, jaundiced, atrabilious, saturnine, splenetic; lackadaisical.

serious, sedate, staid, stayed; grave, – as -a judge, – an undertaker, – a mustard pot; sober, solemn, demure; grim; grim-faced, -visaged; rueful, wan, long-faced.

disconsolate; un-, in-consolable; forlorn, comfortless, desolate, *désolé*, sick at heart; soul-, heart-sick; *au désepoir*; in despair etc. 859; lost.

overcome; broken-, borne-, bowed-down; heart-stricken etc. (*mental suffering*) 828; cut up, dashed, sunk; unnerved, unmanned; down-fallen, -trodden; broken-hearted; care-worn.

Adv. with -a long face, – tears in one's eyes; sadly etc. *adj.*

Phr. the countenance falling; the heart -failing, – sinking within- one.

838. Rejoicing. [Expression of pleasure.] —**N.** rejoicing, exultation, triumph, jubilation, heyday, flush, revelling; merry-making etc. (*amusement*) 840; jubilee etc. (*celebration*) 883; *paean, Te Deum* etc. (*thanksgiving*) 990; congratulation etc. 896; applause etc. 971.

smile, simper, smirk, grin; broad –, sardonic-grin.

laughter, giggle, titter, crow, cheer, chuckle, snicker, snigger, shout; Homeric laughter, horse – hearty- laugh; guffaw; burst –, fit –, shout –, roar –, peal- of laughter; cachinnation.

risibility; derision etc. 856.

Momus; Democritus the Abderite; rollicker; Laughter holding both his sides.

V. rejoice; thank –, bless-' one's stars; congratulate –, hug- oneself; rub –, clap- one's hands; smack the lips, fling up one's cap; dance, skip, caleer; sing, carol, chirrup, chirp; hurrah; cry for –, leap with- joy; exult etc. (*boast*) 884; triumph; hold jubilee etc. (*celebrate*) 883; make merry etc. (*sport*) 840; sing a paean of joy.

smile, simper, smirk; grin, – like a Cheshire cat; mock, laugh in one's sleeve; laugh, – outright; giggle, titter, snigger, crow, smicker, chuckle, snicker, cackle; burst -out, – into a fit of laughter; shout, split, roar.

shake –, split –, hold both- one's sides; roar –, die- with laughter.

raise laughter etc. (*amuse*) 840.

Adj. rejoicing etc. *v.*; jubilant, exultant, triumphant; flushed, elated; laughing etc. *v.*; risible; ready to -burst, – split, – die with laughter; convulsed with laughter.

laughable etc. (*ludicrous*) 853.

Int. hip, hip, -hurrah! huzza! aha! hail! tolderolloll! tra-la la! Heaven be praised! *io triumphe! tant mieux!* so much the better.

Phr. the heart leaping with joy.

839. Lamentation. [Expression of pain.] —**N.** lament, -ation; wail, complaint, plaint, murmur, mutter, grumble, groan, moan, whine, whimper, sob, sigh, suspiration, heaving, deep sigh.

cry etc. (*vociferation*) 411; scream, howl; out-cry, wail of woe, frown, scowl.

tear; weeping etc. *v.*; flood of tears, fit of crying, lachrymation, melting mood, weeping and gnashing of teeth.

plaintiveness etc. *adj.*; languishment; condolence etc. 915.

mourning, weeds, willow, cypress, crêpe, crape, deep mourning; sackcloth and ashes; knell etc. 363; dump, deathsong, dirge, coronach, keen, *nenia*, requiem, elegy, *epicedium*; threne; mon-, thren-ody; jeremiad; ululation.

mourner, professional mourner, keener; grumbler etc. (*discontent*) 832; Niobe; Heraclitus.

V. lament, mourn, deplore, grieve, weep over; be-wail, -moan; keen; condole with etc. 915; fret etc. (*suffer*) 828; wear –, go into –, put on-mourning; wear -the willow, – sackcloth and ashes; *infandum renovare dolorem* etc. (*regret*) 833; give sorrow words.

sigh; give –, heave –, fetch- a sigh; 'waft a sigh from Indus to the pole;' sigh 'like furnace;' wail, cry, weep, sob, greet, blubber, pipe, snivel, bib-ber, whimper, pule; pipe one's eye; drop –, shed- -tears, – a tear; melt –, burst- into tears; *fondre en larmes*; cry -oneself blind, – one's eyes out.

scream etc. (*cry out*) 411; mew etc. (*animal sounds*) 412; groan, moan, whine, yammer; roar; roar –, bellow- like a bull; cry out lustily, rend the air, yell.

frown, scowl, make a wry face, grimace, gnash one's teeth, wring one's hands, tear one's hair, beat one's breast, roll on the ground, burst with grief.

complain, murmur, mutter, grumble, growl, clamor, make a fuss about, croak, grunt, maunder; deprecate etc. (*disapprove*) 932.

cry out before one is hurt, complain without cause.

Adj. lamenting etc. *v.*; in mourning, in sack-cloth and ashes; crying, sorrowing, -ful etc. (*unhappy*) 828; mourn-, tear-ful; lachrymose; plaint-ive, -ful, quer-ulous, -imonious; in the melting mood.

in tears, with tears in one's eyes; with -moistened, – watery- eyes; bathed –, dissolved-in tears; 'like Niobe all tears.'

elagiac, epicedial, threnetic.

Adv. *de profundis; les larmes aux yeux.*

Int. heigh-ho! alas! alack! O dear! ah –, woe is-me! lackadaisy! well –, lack –, alack- a day! well-a-way! alas the day! *O tempora! O mores!* what a pity! *miserabile dictu!* O lud lud! too true!

Phr. tears -standing in, – starting from- the eyes; eyes -suffused, – swimming, – brimming –, over- flowing with tears.

840. Amusement.—**N.** amuse-, entertain-ment; diver-sion, -tissement; reaction, relaxation, solace; pastime, *passetemps*, sport; labor of love; pleasure etc. 827.

fun, frolic, merriment, whoopee, jollity; jovial-ity, -ness; heyday; laughter etc. 838; jocos-ity, - eness; droll-, buffoon-, tomfool-ery; mummery, masquing, pleasantry; wit etc. 842; quip, quirk.

play; game, – at romps; gambol, romp, prank, antic, rig, lark, spree, skylarking, vagary, trick, monkey trick, *gambade, fredaine, escapade, échappée*, bout, *espièglerie*; practical joke etc. (*ridicule*) 856.

dance; round –, square –, solo –, step –, tap –, clog –, skirt –, sand –, folk –, morris-dance, *pas seul*, step, turn, *chassé*, cut, shuffle, double shuffle; hop, reel, rigadoon, saraband, hornpipe, bolero, fandango, pavan, tarantella, minuet, waltz, polka; galop, -ade; Schottische, *pas de quatre*, Boston, one-, two-step, rumba, tango, maxixe, fox-, turkey-trot, shimmy, ragtime, cakewalk, jazz, blues, Charleston; jig, breakdown, fling, strathspey; *allemande*; gavot, -te; mazurka, morisco; quadrille, lancers, country dance, *cotillon*, polonaise, Sir Roger de Coverley, Swedish dance; *ballet* etc. (*drama*) 599; ball; *bal*, – *masqué*, – *costumé*; masquerade, fancy dress ball; *thé dansant*; Terpsichore, choreography, Russian ballet, classical dancing; eurythmics; nautch dance, *danse du ventre*, cancan.

festivity, merry-making; party etc. (*social gathering*) 892; *fête*, festival, gala, *ridotto*; revel-s, -ry, -ling; carnival, brawl, saturnalia, high jinks; feast, banquet etc. (*food*) 298; regale, *symposium*, wassail; carous-e, -al; jollification, junket, wake, pic-nic, *fête champêtre*, garden party, gymkhana, regatta, track meet, field day, jamboree, treat.

round of pleasures, dissipation, a short life and a merry one, racketing, holiday making, high jinks. rejoicing etc. 838; jubilee etc. (*celebration*) 883.

bonfire, fireworks, *feu-de-joie*, rocket, catherine wheel, roman candle etc.

holiday; gala – , red letter – , play- day; high days and holidays; high – , Bank- holiday; May – , Derby- day; Saint – , Easter – ; Whit- Monday; King's birthday, Empire Day; *mi-carême*; Bairam; wayzgoose, bean feast, beano.

place of amusement, theater etc. 599; concert-, ball-, assembly-room; music-hall, cinema, movies, talkies, vaudeville; hippodrome, circus, rodeo; *casino, kursaal*; winter garden; park, pleasance, arbor; garden etc. 371; pleasure-, play-, cricket-, football-, polo-, croquet-, archery-, hunting-ground; golf links, race course, stadium, gridiron, bowl, speedway, racing track, ring; gymnasium, swimming pool; shooting gallery; tennis-, racket-court; bowling-green, -alley; croquet-lawn, rink, skating rink; roller-coaster, roundabout, carousel, merry-go-round; swing; *montagne russe*; switchback, scenic railway etc.

game, – of -chance, – skill; athletic sports, gymnastics; fencing; archery, rifle-shooting; tournament, pugilism etc. (*contention*) 720; sporting etc. 622; horse-racing, the turf; aquatics etc. 267; skating, roller skating; ski-running, -joring, -jumping, bobsleighing, luging, tobogganing, winter sports; sliding; cricket, tennis, lawn – , table – , deck-tennis, rackets, fives, squash, ping pong, trap bat and ball, battledore and shuttlecock, badminton, *la grâce*; pall mall, tip-cat, croquet, golf, curling, hockey, basketball, soccer, football, Rugby, Association, *pallone*, polo; tent-pegging, tilting at the ring, quintain, greasy pole; quoits, *discus*; throwing the hammer, putting the -weight, – shot, tossing the caber; knurr and spell; leap-frog; hop, skip and jump; French and English, tug of war; blind man's buff, hunt the slipper, hide-and-seek, kiss in the ring; snapdragon; cross questions and crooked answers; jig-saw puzzle; rounders, base-ball, *la crosse* etc.; angling; swimming, diving, water-polo.

billiards, pool, pyramids, snooker, bagatelle; bowls, skittles, ninepins, kail, American bowls.

cards; bridge, auction, contract, whist, rubber; round game, coon-can, loo, cribbage, *bésique*, pinocle, euchre, drole, *écarté*, skat, picquet, all-fours, quadrille, ombre, reverse, Pope Joan, commit; bo-, boa-ston; *vingt-et-un*; *quinze*, thirty-one, put-and-take, speculation, connections, brag, cassino, lottery, commerce, snip-snap-snorem, lift smoke, blind hookey, Polish bank, poker, banker; faro; Earl of Coventry, Napoleon, nap, patience, pairs; old maid, fright, beggar-my-neighbor; *baccarat*, *chemin de fer*, *monté*, *roulette*.

chess, draughts, backgammon, dominoes, checkers, mah jong, merelles, nine men's morris, go-bang, solitaire; game of – , fox and-goose; lotto; etc.

morra; gambling etc. (*chance*) 621.

toy, plaything, bauble; doll etc. (*puppet*) 554; teetotum; knick-knack etc. (*trifle*) 643; magic lantern etc. (*show*) 448; peep-, puppet-, raree-, gallanty-show; marionettes, Punch and Judy; toy-shop; 'quips and cranks and wanton wiles, nods and becks and wreathed smiles.'

sportsman, gamester, gambler etc. 621; reveler, master of the -ceremonies, – revels; *arbiter elegantiarum*.

V. amuse, entertain, divert, eliven; tickle; – the fancy; titillate, raise a smile, put in good humor; cause – , create – , occasion – , raise – , excite – , produce – , convulse with- laughter; set the table in a roar, be the death of one.

recreate, solace, cheer, rejoice; please etc. 829; interest; treat, regale.

amuse oneself; game; play, – a game, – pranks, – tricks; sport, disport, toy, wanton, revel, junket, feast, carouse, banquet, make merry; drown care; drive dull care away; frolic, gambol, frisk, romp; caper; dance etc. (*leap*) 309; keep up the ball; run a rig, sow one's wild oats, have one's fling, paint the town red, take one's pleasure; see life; *desipere in loco*, play the fool.

make – , keep- holiday; go a Maying.

while away – , beguile- the time; kill time, dally.

Adj. amusing, entertaining, diverting etc. *v.*; recreative, lusory; pleasant etc. (*pleasing*) 829; laughable etc. (*ludicrous*) 853; witty etc. 842; festive, -al; jovial, jolly, jocund, roguish, rompish; sporting; playful – as a kitten; sportive, ludibrious.

amused etc. *v.*; 'pleased with a feather, tickled with a straw.'

Adv. 'on the light fantastic toe,' at play, in sport.

Int. *vive la bagatelle! vogue la galère!*

Phr. *Deus nobis haec otia fecit; dum vivimus vivamus.*

841. Weariness.—N. weariness, defatigation, boredom, *ennui*; lassitude etc. (*fatigue*) 688; drowsiness etc. 683.

disgust, nausea, loathing, sickness, satiety etc. 869; *taedium vitae* etc. (*dejection*) 837.

wearisome-, tedious-ness etc. *adj.*; dull work, tedium, monotony, twice told tale.

bore, button-hole, proser, wet blanket; heavy hours, 'the enemy' [time].

V. weary; tire etc. (*fatigue*) 688; bore; bore – weary – , tire- -to death, – out of one's life, – out of all patience; set – , send- to sleep.

pall, sicken, nauseate, disgust.

harp on the same string; drag its -slow, – weary-length along.

never hear the last of; be -tired etc. *adj.* -of, – with; yawn; died with *ennui*.

Adj. wearying etc. *v.*; wearing; weari-, tire-, irksome; uninteresting, stupid, bald, devoid of interest, dry, monotonous, dull, arid, tedious, humdrum, mortal, flat; pros-y, -ing; slow; soporific, somniferous, dormitive.

disgusting etc. *v.*; unenjoyed.

weary; tired etc. *v.*; drowsy etc. (*sleepy*) 683; uninterested, flagging, used up, worn out, *blasé*, life-weary, weary of life; sick of.

Adv. wearily etc. *adj.*; *usque ad nauseam.*

Phr. time hanging heavily on one's hands; *toujours perdrix*; *crambe repetita.*

842. Wit.—N. wit, -tiness; attic -wit, – salt; atticism; salt, *esprit*, point, fancy, whim, humor, drollery, pleasantry.

farce, buffoonery, fooling, tomfoolery; harlequinade etc. 599; broad -farce, – humor; fun, *espièglerie*; *vis comica.*

jocularity; jocos-ity, -eness; facetiousness; waggery, -ishness; whimsicality, comicality etc. 853.

smartness, ready wit, banter, *badinage*, *persiflage*, retort, repartee, *quid pro quo*; ridicule etc. 856.

facetiae, quips and cranks; jest, joke, capital joke; standing -jest, – joke; conceit, quip, quirk, crank, quiddity, *concetto*, *plaisanterie*, brilliant idea; merry –, bright –, happy- thought; sally; flash, – of wit, – of merriment; scintillation; *mot*, – *pour rire*; witticism, smart saying, *bon mot*, *jeu d'esprit*, epigram; jest book; dry joke, *quodlibet*, cream of the jest.

word-play, *jeu de mots*; play -of, – upon-words; pun, -ning; *double entente* etc. (*ambiguity*) 520; quibble, verbal quibble; conundrum etc. (*riddle*) 533; anagram, acrostic, double acrostic, *nugae canorae*, trifling, idle conceit, *turlupinade.*

old joke, Joe Miller, chestnut, hoary-headed jest.

V. joke, jest, cut jokes; crack a joke; perpetrate a -joke, – pun; make -fun of, – merry with; set the table in a roar etc. (*amuse*) 840; scintillate.

retort, flash back; banter etc. (*ridicule*) 856; *ridentem dicere verum*; joke at one's expense.

Adj. witty, attic, salty; quick-, nimble-witted; keen, clever, smart, brilliant, pungent, jocular, jocose, funny, waggish, facetious, whimsical, humorous, gilbertian; playful etc. 840; merry and wise; pleasant, sprightly, *spirituel*, sparkling, epigrammatic, full of point, *ben trovato*; comic etc. 853.

Adv. in joke, in jest, in sport, in play.

843. Dullness.—N. dullness, heaviness, flatness; infestivity etc. 837; stupidity etc. 499; want of originality, dearth of ideas.

prose, matter of fact; heavy book, *conte à dormir debout*; platitude.

V. be -dull etc. *adj.*; prose, platitudinize, take *au sérieux*, be caught napping.

render -dull etc. *adj.*; damp, depress, throw cold water on, lay a wet blanket on; fall flat upon the ear; hang fire.

Adj. dull, – as ditch water; dry, insipid, jejune; unentertaining, uninteresting, unlively,

unimaginative; heavisome, heavy-gaited; insulse; dry as dust; pros-y, -ing, -aic; matter of fact, commonplace, banal, pointless; 'weary, flat, stale and unprofitable.'

stupid, slow, flat, sluggish, ponderous, humdrum, monotonous; melancholic etc. 837; stolid etc. 499; plodding.

Phr. *Davus sum non Oedipus.*

844. Humorist.—N. humorist, wag, wit, reparteeist, epigrammatist, gag man, punster; *bel esprit*, life of the party; wit-snapper, -cracker, -worm; joker, jester, jokesmith, Joe Miller, *drôle de corps*, *gaillard*, spark, *persiffleur*, banterer.

buffoon, *farceur*, merry-andrew, mime, tumbler, acrobat, mountebank, charlatan, posturemaster, harlequin, punch, *pulcinella*, scaramouch, clown; wearer of the -cap and bells, – motley; motley fool; pantaloon, gipsy; jack -pudding, – in the green, – a dandy; zany; mad-cap, pickle-herring, witling, caricaturist, *grimacier.*

845. Beauty.—N. beauty, the beautiful, *le beau ideal*, loveliness.

[Science of the perception of beauty] Callaesthetics.

form, elegance, grace, beauty unadorned; symmetry etc. 242; comeliness, fairness etc. *adj.*; pulchritude, polish, gloss; good -effect, – looks; *belle tournure*; bloom, brilliancy, radiance, splendor, gorgeousness, magnificence; sublimi-ty, -fication.

concinnity, delicacy, refinement; charm, *je ne sais quoi*, style, *chic*, swank.

Venus, – of Milo; Aphrodite, Hebe, the Graces, Peri, Houri, Cupid, Apollo, Hyperion, Adonis, Antinous, Narcissus; Helen of Troy.

peacock, butterfly; flower, flow'ret gay, rose, lily, asphodel; garden; flower of, pink of; *bijou*; jewel etc. (*ornament*) 847; work of art.

pleasurableness etc. 829.

beautifying; landscape gardening; decoration etc. 847; calisthenics.

V. be -beautiful etc. *adj.*; shine, beam, bloom; become one etc. (*accord*) 23; set off, grace, flatter one.

render -beautiful etc. *adj.*; beautify; polish, burnish; gild etc. (*decorate*) 847; set out.

'snatch a grace beyond the reach of art.'

Adj. beaut-iful, -eous; handsome; pretty, lovely, graceful, elegant; delicate, dainty, refined, exquisite; fair, personable, comely, seemly; bonny; good-looking; well-favored, -made, -formed, -proportioned; proper, shapely; symmetrical etc. (*regular*) 242; harmonious etc. (*color*) 428; sightly.

fit to be seen, passable, not amiss.

goodly, dapper, tight, jimp; gimp; janty, jaunty; natty, quaint, trim, tidy, neat, spruce, smart, tricksy.

bright, -eyed; rosy-, cherry-cheeked; rosy, ruddy; blooming, in full bloom.

brilliant, shining; beam-y, -ing; sparkling, swanky, splendid, resplendent, dazzling, glowing; glossy, sleek.

showy, specious, rich, gorgeous, superb, magnificent, grand, fine, sublime, imposing, majestic 873.

artistic, -al; aesthetic; pict-uresque, -orial; *fait à piendre*, paintable; well-composed, -grouped, - varied; curious.

enchanting etc. (*pleasure-giving*) 829; attractive etc. (*inviting*) 615; becoming etc. (*accordant*) 23; ornamental etc. 847.

undeformed, undefaced, unspotted; spotless etc. (*perfect*) 650.

846. Ugliness.—N. ugliness etc. *adj.*; deformity, inelegance; disfigurement etc. (*blemish*) 848; want of symmetry, inconcinnity; distortion etc. 243; squalor etc. (*uncleanness*) 653.

forbidding countenance, vinegar aspect, hanging look, wry face, *'spretae injuria formae.'*

eyesore, object, figure, sight, fright, specter, scarecrow, hag, harridan, satyr, witch, toad, baboon, monster, Caliban, Aesop, *'monstrum horrendum informe ingens cui lumen ademptum.'*

V. be -ugly etc. *adj.*; look ill, grin horribly a ghastly smile, make faces.

render -ugly etc. *adj.*; deface; dis-, de-figure; deform, spoil, distort etc. 243; blemish etc. (*injure*) 659; soil etc. (*render unclean*) 653.

Adj. ugly, – as -sin, – a toad, – a scarecrow, – a dead monkey; plain, bald etc. 226; homely etc. (*unadorned*) 849; ordinary, unornamental, inartistic; unsightly, unseemly, uncomely, unshapely, unlovely; sightless, seemless; not fit to be seen; unbeaut-eous, -iful; beautiless; shapeless etc. (*amorphous*) 241; course; garish, over-decorated etc. 882.

mis-shapen, -proportioned; monstrous; gaunt etc. (*thin*) 203; dumpy etc. (*short*) 201; curtailed of its fair proportions; ill-made, -shaped, -proportioned; crooked etc. (*distorted*) 243; hard-featured, -visaged; ill-, hard-, evil-favored; ill-looking; unprepossessing.

graceless, inelegant; ungraceful, ungainly, uncouth; stiff; rugged, rough, gross, rude, awkward, clumsy, slouching, rickety; gawky; lump-ing, -ish; lumbering; hulk-y, -ing; unwieldy.

squalid, haggard; grim, -faced, -visaged; grisly, ghastly; ghost-, death-like; cadaverous, gruesome.

frightful, hideous, · odious, uncanny, forbidding, repellant, repulsive; horri-d, -ble; shocking etc. (*painful*) 830.

foul etc. (*dirty*) 653; dingy etc. (*colorless*) 429; gaudy etc. (*color*) 428; disfigured etc. *v.*; discolored (*blemished*) etc. 848.

847. Ornament.—N. ornament, -ation, -al art; ornat-ture, -eness; adorn-ment, decoration, embellishment; architecture.

garnish, polish, varnish, French polish, gilding, japanning, lacquer, ormolu, enamel.

cosmetics, rouge, powder, lipstick, lip salve, mascara; manicure, nail polish; permanent –, Marcel –, finger-wave.

pattern, diaper, powdering, panelling, graining, pargeting, inlay, detail; texture etc. 329; richness; tracery, molding, beading, reeding, fillet, listel, strapwork, *coquillage*, flourish, *fleur-de-lis*, arabesque, fret, *anthemion*; egg and -tongue, – dart; *astragal*, zigzag, *acanthus, cartouche*; pilaster etc. (*projection*) 250; cyma, ogee.

em-, broidery, needlework; knitting, crochet, tatting, brocade, *brocatelle*, beads, bugles; galloon, lace, gimp, *guipure*, fringe, trapping, border, edging, insertion, *motif*, trimming; *passementerie*; drapery, hanging, tapestry, arras; millinery, ermine.

wreath, festoon, garland, lei, chaplet, flower, nosegay, *bouquet*, posy, 'daisies pied and violets blue.'

tassle, knot; shoulder-knot, *épaulette*, epaulet, aigulet, *aiguilette*, frog; star, rosette, bow; feather, plume, *panache, aigrette*.

jewel, -ry, -lery; bijoutry; *bijou, -terie*; diadem, tiara; pendant, trinket, locket, necklace, armilla, bracelet, bangle, armlet, anklet, ear-, nose- ring, carcanet, chain, *châtelaine*, albert, brooch, torque.

gem, precious stone; diamond, brilliant, beryl, aquamarine, alexandrite, -cat's eye, emerald, calcedony, chrysoprase, cornelian, jasper, bloodstone, agate, heliotrope; girasol, -e; onyx, plasma; sard, -onyx; garnet, lapis-lazuli, opal, peridot, chrysolite, sapphire, ruby; spinel, -le; balais; oriental –, topaz; turquois, -e; zircon, jacinth, hyacinth, carbuncle, amethyst; moonstone; pearl, coral.

finery, frippery, gewgaw, gimcrack, knick-knack, tinsel, spangle, sequin, *clinquant*, pinch-beck, paste; excess of ornament etc. (*vulgarity*) 851; gaud, pride, ostentation; frills and furbelows.

illustration, illumination, *vignette; fleuron*; head-, tail-piece; *cul-de-lampe*; flowers of rhetoric etc. 577; work of art, article of vertu, *bric-à-brac*, curio, *bibelot*.

V. ornament, embellish, enrich, decorate, adorn, beautify, adonize.

smarten, furbish, polish, gild, varnish, whitewash, enamel, japan, lacquer, paint, grain.

garnish, trim, dizen, bedizen, prink, prank; trick –, fig- out; deck, bedeck, dight, bedight, array; dress, – up, preen, spruce up, titivate; spangle, bespangle, powder; embroider, work; chase, tool, emboss, fret; emblazon, blazon, illuminate; illustrate.

become etc. (*accord with*) 23.

Adj. ornamented, beautified etc. *v.*; ornate, rich, gilt, begilt, tesselated, enamelled, inlaid; festooned; topiary.

smart, gay, tricksy, flowery, glittering; new-gilt, - spangled; fine, – as -a Mayday queen, – fivepence, – a carrot fresh scraped; pranked out, bedight, well-groomed.

in full dress etc. (*fashion*) 852; *en grande - tenue*, – *toilette*; in best bib and tucker, in Sunday best, *endimanché*; dressed to advantage.

showy, flashy, gaudy etc. (*vulgar*) 851; garish; gorgeous.

ornamental, decorative; becoming etc. (*accordant*) 23.

848. Blemish.—N. blemish, disfigurement, deformity; defect etc. (*imperfection*) 651; flaw; injury etc. (*deterioration*) 659, spots on the sun; eyesore.

stain, blot, slur; spot, -tiness; speck, -le; blur, freckle, mole, *macula*, patch, blotch, birthmark, blain, maculation, tarnish, smudge, smear; dirt etc. 653; bruise, black eye, scar, wem; pustule; excrescence, pimple etc. (*protuberance*) 250.

V. disfigure etc. (*injure*) 659; speckle; render ugly etc. 846.

Adj. pitted. freckled. discolored. bloodshot. bruised. disfigured; stained etc. *n.*; imperfect etc. 651; injured etc. (*deteriorated*) 659.

849. Simplicity.—**N.** simplicity; plain-, homeli-ness; undress, nudity, nakedness, beauty unadorned, chastity, chasteness.
V. be -simple etc. *adj.*
render -simple etc. *adj.*; simplify, chasten, strip of ornament.
Adj. simple, plain; home-ly, -spun; ordinary, household.
natural, unaffected; free from -affectation, – ornament; *simplex munditiis*; *sans façon, en déshabillé*, nude. naked.
chaste, inornate, severe.
un-adorned, -ornamented, -decked, -garnished, -arranged, -trimmed, -varnished.
bald, flat, dull, blank.

850. Taste. [Good taste.]—**N.** taste; good –, refined –, cultivated- taste; delicacy, refinement, fine feeling, gust, *gusto*, tact, *finesse*; nicety etc. (*discrimination*) 465; polish, elegance, grace.
virtu; dilettanteism, virtuosity; fine art; cul-ture, -ivation.
[Science of taste] esthetics.
man of -taste etc.; *connoisseur*, judge, critic, *conoscente, virtuoso, amateur, dilettante*, Aristarchus, Corinthian, *arbiter elegantarum*, stagirite, euphemist.
'caviar to the general.'
V. appreciate, judge, criticize, discriminate etc. 465.
Adj. in good taste; tasteful, tasty; unaffected, pure, chaste, classical, attic; cultivated, refined; dainty; esthetic, artistic; elegant etc. 578; euphemistic.
to one's -taste, – mind; after one's fancy; *comme il faut*; *tiré à quatre épingles*.
Adv. elegantly etc. *adj.*
Phr. *nihil tetigit quod non ornavit.*

851. Vulgarity. [Bad taste.]—**N.** vulgar-ity, -ism; barbar-, Vandal-, Gothic-ism; *mauvais goût*, bad taste; Babbittry; *gaucherie*, awkwardness, want of tact; ill-breeding etc. (*discourtesy*) 895; ungentlemanly behavior.
coarseness etc. *adj.*; indecorum, misbehavior.
low-, homeli-ness; low life, *mauvais ton*, rusticity; boorishness etc. *adj.*; brutality; rowdy-, ruffian-, blackguard-ism; ribaldry; slang etc. (*neology*) 563.
bad joke, *mauvaise plaisanterie.*
[Excell of ornament] gaudi-, tawdri-ness; false ornament; finery, frippery, trickery, tinsel, gewgaw, *clinquant.*
rough diamond, tomboy, hoyden, cub, unlicked cub; clown etc. (*commonalty*) 876; Hun, Goth, Vandal, Boeotian; vulgarian; snob, cad, bounder, gent; *parvenu* etc. 876; frump, dowdy; slattern etc. 653.
V. be -vulgar etc. *adj.*; misbehave; talk –, smell of the- shop.
Adj. in bad taste, vulgar, unrefined, gutter.
coarse, indecorus, ribald, gross; unseemly, un-

beseeming, unpresentable; *contra bonos mores*; ungraceful etc. (*ugly*) 846.
dowdy, slovenly etc. (*dirty*) 653; ungenteel, shabby genteel; low etc. (*plebeian*) 876;uncourtly; uncivil etc. (*discourteous*) 895; ill-bred, -mannered; underbred; ungentleman-ly, -like; unladylike, unfeminine; wild, – as an unbacked colt.
unkempt, uncombed, untamed, unlicked, unpolished, uncouth, plebeian; incondite; heavy, rude, awkward; home-ly, -spun, -bred; provincial, hick, countrified, rustic, uncultivated, freshwater; boorish, clownish; savage, brutish, blackguard; rowdy, snobbish; barbar-ous, -ic; Gothic, unclassical, doggerel, heathenish, tramontane, outlandish; Bohemian.
obsolete etc. (*antiquated*) 124; unfashionable, old-fashioned, out of date; new-fangled etc. (*unfamiliar*) 83; fantastic, odd etc. (*ridiculous*) 853.
particular; affected etc. 855; meretricious; extravagant, monstrous, horrid; shocking etc. (*painful*) 830.
gaudy, tawdry, bedizened, tricked out, gingerbread; obtrusive, flaunting, loud, flashy, garish, showy.

852. Fashion.—**N.** fashion, style, *ton, bon ton*, society; good –, polite- society; drawing room, civilized life, civilization, town, *beau monde*, high life, court; world; fashionable –, gay- world; Vanity Fair; show etc. (*ostentation*) 822.
manners, breeding etc. (*politeness*) 894; air, demeanor etc. (*appearance*) 448; *savoir faire*; gentlemanliness, gentility, decorum, propriety, *bienséance*; conventions –, dictates- of society; Mrs. Grundy; convention, -ality; punctilio; form, -ality; etiquette, point of etiquette; custom etc. 613; mode, vogue, style, go; rage etc. (*desire*) 865; prevailing taste, *dernier cri*, dress etc. 225.
man –, woman- of -fashion, – the world; height –, pink –, star –, glass –, leader- of fashion; *arbiter elegantiarum* etc. (*taste*) 850; upper ten thousand etc. (*nobility*) 875; *élite* etc. (*distinction*) 873.
V. be -fashionable etc. *adj.*, – the rage etc. *n.*; have a run, pass current.
follow –, conform to –, fall in with- the fashion etc. *n.*; go with the stream etc. (*conform*) 82; *savoir -vivre, – faire*; keep up appearances, behave oneself.
set the –, bring into- fashion; give a tone to –, cut a figure in- society, rub shoulders with nobility, keep one's carriage.
Adj. fashionable; in -fashion etc. *n.*; *à la mode, comme il faut*; admitted –, admissible- in -society etc. *n.*; presentable, decorous, punctilious, conventional etc. (*customary*) 613; genteel; well-bred, -mannered, -behaved, -spoken; gentleman-like, -ly; ladylike; civil, polite etc. (*courteous*) 894.
polished, refined, thoroughbred, courtly; *distingué*, aristocratic, unembarrassed, poised, *dégagé*; ja-, jau-nty; dashing, fast, showy, high toned, toney.
modish, stylish, in the latest style, *recherché*; new-fangled etc. (*unfamiliar*) 83.
in -court, – full, – evening- dress; *en grande tenue* etc. (*ornament*) 847.
Adv. fashionably etc. *adj.*; for fashion's sake.

853. Ridiculousness.—N. ridiculousness etc. *adj.*; comical-, odd-ity etc. *adj.*; extravagance, drollery.

farce, comedy; burlesque etc. (*ridicule*) 856; buffoonery etc. (*fun*) 840; frippery; doggerel verses; Irish bull, Hibernianism, Hibernicism; Spoonerism; absurdity etc. 497; bombast etc. (*unmeaning*) 517; anticlimax, bathos; monstrosity etc. (*unconformity*) 83; laughing stock etc. 857.

V. be -ridiculous etc. *adj.*; pass from the sublime to the ridiculous; make one laugh; play the fool, make a fool of oneself, commit an absurdity.

play a joke on, make a -fool of, – sucker of, – monkey of.

Adj. ridiculous, ludicrous; comic, -al; droll, funny, laughable, *pour rire*, grotesque, farcical, odd; whimsical, – as a dancing bear; fanciful, fantastic, queer, rum, quizzical, waggish, quaint, *bizarre*; eccentric etc. (*unconformable*) 83; strange, outlandish, out of the way, *baroque*, *rocaille*, rococo; awkward etc. (*ugly*) 846.

absurd, extravagant, *outré*, monstrous, preposterous, bombastic, inflated, stilted, burlesque, mock heroic.

drollish; serio-, tragic-comic; gimcrack, contemptible etc. (*unimportant*) 643; doggerel; ironical etc. (*derisive*) 856; risible.

Phr. *'risum teneatis amici?' rideret Heraclitus.*

854. Fop.—N. fop, fine gentleman; swell; dand-y, -iprat; exquisite, coxcomb, toff, beau, macaroni, blade, blood, buck, man about town, fast man; fribble, jemmy, spark, popinjay, puppy, prig, *petit maître*; jacka-napes, -dandy; man milliner; Jemmy Jessamy, carpet-knight, masher, Dundreary, Johnnie, dude.

belle, fine lady, *coquette*, flirt.

855. Affectation.—N. affectation; affectedness etc. *adj.*; acting a part etc. *v.*; pretence etc. (*falsehood*) 544; (*ostentation*) 882; boasting etc. 884.

charlatanism, quakery, shallow profundity, humbug, pretension, airs, pedantry, purism, precisianism, euphuism, prunes and prisms; teratology etc. (*altiloquence*) 577.

mannerism, *simagrée*, grimace.

conceit, foppery, dandyism, man millinery, coxcombry, puppyism.

stiffness, formality, buckram; prudery, demureness, coquetry, mock modesty, *minauderie*, sentimentalism; *mauvaise honte*, false shame.

affector, performer, actor; pedant, pedagogue, *doctrinaire*, purist, euphuist, mannerist; shoneen; *grimacier*; lump of affectation, *précieuse ridicule*, *bas bleu*, blue stocking, poetaster; prig, hypocrite; charlatan etc. (*deceiver*) 548; *petit maître* etc. (*fop*) 854; flatterer etc. 935; *coquette*, prude, puritan; precisian, formalist.

V. affect, act a part, put on; give oneself airs etc. (*arrogance*) 885; boast etc. 884; coquet; simper, mince, attitudinize, strike a pose, pose; flirt a fan; over-act, -play, -do.

Adj. affected, full of affectation, pretentious, pedantic, stilted, stagey, theatrical, big-sounding, *ad captandum*, canting, insincere.

not natural, unnatural; self-conscious; *maniéré*; artificial; over-wrought, -done, -acted; euphuistic etc. 577.

stiff, starch, formal, prim, smug, demure, *tiré à. quatre épingles*, quakerish, puritanical, prudish, pragmatical, priggish, conceited, coxcomical, foppish, dandified; fini-cal, -kin, -cky, mincing, simpering, namby-pamby, sentimental, languishing.

856. Ridicule.—N. ridicule, derision; sardonic -smile, – grin; irrision; snigger; scoffing etc. (*disrespect*) 929; mockery, quiz, banter, irony, *persiflage*, raillery, chaff, *badinage*; quizzing etc. *v.*

squib, satire, skit, quip, quib, grin.

parody, burlesque, travesty; farce etc. (*drama*) 599; caricature, take-off.

buffoonery etc. (*fun*) 840; practical joke, horseplay.

V. ridicule, deride; laugh at, grin at, smile at; snigger; laugh in one's sleeve; banter, rally, chaff, joke, twit, quiz, poke fun at, jolly, roast, rag; fleer; play –, play tricks- upon; fool, – to the top of one's bent; show up.

satirize, parody, caricature, burlesque, travesty.

turn into ridicule; make merry with; make -fun, – game, – a fool, – an April fool- of; rally; scoff etc. (*disrespect*) 929.

raise a laugh etc. (*amuse*) 840; play the fool, make a fool of oneself.

be ridiculous etc. 853.

Adj. deris-ory, -ive; mock; sarcastic, ironical, quizzical, burlesque, Hudibrastic; scurrilous etc. (*disrespectful*) 929.

Adv. in -ridicule etc. *n.*

857. Laughing-stock. [Object and cause of ridicule.]**—N.** laughing-, jesting-, gazing-stock; butt, game, fair game; April fool etc. (*dupe*) 547.

original, oddity; queer –, odd- fish; quiz, square toes; old –, fogey *or* fogy..

monkey; buffoon etc. (*jester*) 844; pantomimist etc. (*actor*) 599.

jest etc. (*wit*) 842.

858. Hope.—N. hope, -s; desire etc. 865; fervent hope, sanguine expectation, trust, confidence, reliance; faith etc. (*belief*) 484; affiance, assurance; secur-eness, -ity; reassurance.

good -omen, – auspices; promise; well-grounded hopes; good –, bright- .prospect; clear sky.

as-, pre-sumption; anticipation etc. (*expectation*) 507.

hopefulness, buoyancy, optimism, enthusiasm, heart of grace, aspiration; optimist, utop-ian, -ist; Pollyanna.

castles in the air, *châteaux en Espagne*, hope chest, *le pot au lait*, Utopia, millennium; day –, golden- dream; dream of Alnaschar; airy hopes, fool's paradise; *mirage* etc. (*fallacies of vision*) 443; fond hope.

beam –, ray –, gleam –, glimmer –, dawn –, flash –, star- of hope; cheer; bit of blue sky, silver lining of the cloud, bottom of Pandora's box, balm in Gilead.

anchor, sheet-anchor, main-stay; staff etc. (*support*) 215; heaven etc. 981.

V. hope, trust, confide, rely on, put one's trust in, lean upon; pin one's -hope, – faith- upon etc. (*believe*) 484.

feel –, entertain –, harbor –, indulge –, cherish –, feed –, foster –, nourish –, encourage –, cling to –, live in- hope etc. *n.*; see land; feel –, rest- -assured, – confident etc. *adj.*

presume; promise oneself; expect etc. (*look forward to*) 507.

hope for etc. (*desire*) 865; anticipate.

be -hopeful etc. *adj.*; look on the bright side of, view on the sunny side, make the best of it, hope for the best; put -a good, – a bold, – the best-face upon; keep one's spirits up; take heart, – of grace; be of good -heart, – cheer; flatter oneself, lay the flattering unction to one's soul.

catch at a straw, hope against hope, count one's chickens before they are hatched.

give –, inspire –, raise –, hold out- hope etc. *n.*; raise expectations; encourage, hearten, cheer, assure, reassure, buoy up, embolden; promise, bid fair, augur well, be in a fair way, look up, flatter, tell a flattering tale.

Adj. hoping etc. *v.*; in -hopes etc. *n.*; hopeful, confident; secure etc. (*certain*) 484; sanguine, in good heart, buoyed up, buoyant, elated, flushed, exultant, enthusiastic; utopian.

unsus-pecting, -picious; fearless, free –, exempt from- -fear, – suspicion, – distrust, – despair; undespairing, self-reliant.

probable, on the high road to; within sight of - shore, – land; promising, propitious; of –, full of- promise; of good omen; auspicious, *de bon augure*; reassuring; encouraging, cheering, inspiriting, looking up, bright, roseate, *couleur de rose*, rose-colored.

Adv. hopefully etc. *adj.*

Phr. *nil desperandum*; never say die, *dum spiro spero*, *latet scintillula forsan*, all is for the best, *spero meliora*; the wish being father to the thought; 'hope told a flattering tale;' *rusticus expectat dum defluat amnis*.

859. Hopelessness. [Absence, want, or loss of hope.]—**N.** hopelessness etc. *adj.*; despair, desperation; despondency etc. (*dejection*) 837; pessimism.

hope deferred, dashed hopes; vain expectation etc. (*disappointment*) 509.

airy hopes etc. 858; forlorn hope; bad -job, – business; *enfant perdu*; gloomy –, black spots in the- horizon; slough of Despond, cave of Despair. Job's comforter; bird of -bad, – ill-omen.

V. despair; lose –, give up –, abandon –, relinquish- -all hope, – the hope of; give -up, – over; yield to despair; falter; despond etc. (*be dejected*) 837; *jeter le manche après la cognée*.

inspire –, drive to- despair etc. *n.*; disconcert; dash –, crush –, shatter –, destroy- one's hopes; hope against hope.

Adj. hopeless, desperate, despairing, in despair, *au désespoir*, forlorn; inconsolable etc. (*dejected*) 837; broken-hearted.

out of the question, not to be thought of; im-practicable etc. 471; past -hope, – cure, – mending, – recall; at one's last gasp etc. (*death*) 360; given -up, – over.

incurable, cureless, immedicable, remediless, beyond remedy; incorrigible; irre-parable, - mediable, -coverable, -versible, -trievable, - claimable, -deemable, -vocable; ruined, undone; immitigable.

unpromising, unpropitious; inauspicious, ill-omened, threatening, clouded over, lowering, ominous.

Phr. *'lasciate ogni speranza voi ch' entrate;'* its days are numbered; the worst come to the worst.

860. Fear.—**N.** fear, timidity, diffidence, want of confidence; apprehensive-, fearful-ness etc. *adj.*; solicitude, anxiety, care, apprehension, misgiving; mistrust etc. (*doubt*) 485; suspicion, qualm; hesitation etc. (*irresolution*) 605.

nervous-, restless-ness etc. *adj.*; in-, dis-quietude; flutter, trepidation, fear and trembling, perturbation, tremor, quivering, shaking, trembling, throbbing heart, palpitation, ague fit, cold sweat; abject fear etc. (*cowardice*) 862; mortal funk, heart-sinking, despondency; despair etc. 859.

fright; affright, -ment; alarm, pavor, dread, awe, terror, horror, dismay, consternation, panic, scare, stampede [of horses].

intimidation, terrorism, reign of terror.

[Object of fear] bug-bear, -aboo; scarecrow; hobgoblin etc. (*demon*) 980; daymare, nightmare, Gorgon, Medusa, mormo, ogre, Hurlothrumbo, raw head and bloody bones, fee faw fum, *bête noire*, *enfant terrible*.

alarmist etc. (*coward*) 862.

V. fear, stand in awe of; be -afraid etc. *adj.*; have -qualms etc. *n.*; apprehend, sit upon thorns, eye askance; distrust etc. (*disbelieve*) 485.

hesitate etc. (*be irresolute*) 605; falter, funk, cower, crouch; skulk etc. (*cowardice*) 862; let 'I dare not' wait upon 'I would;' take -fright, – alarm; start, wince, flinch, shy, shrink; fly etc. (*avoid*) 623.

tremble, shake; shiver, – in one's shoes; shudder, flutter; shake –, tremble- -like an aspen leaf, – all over; quake, quaver, quiver, quail; get the wind up.

grow –, turn- pale; blench, stand aghast; not dare to say one's soul is one's own.

inspire –, excite- -fear, – awe; raise apprehensions; give –, raise –, sound- an alarm; alarm, startle, scare, cry 'wolf,' disquiet, dismay; fright, -en; affright, terrify; astound; frighten from one's propriety; frighten out of one's -wits, – senses, – seven senses; awe; strike -all of a heap, – an awe into, – terror; harrow up the soul, appal, unman, petrify, horrify.

make one's -flesh creep, – hair stand on end, – blood run cold, – teeth chatter; chill one's spine; take away –, stop- one's breath; make one - tremble etc.

haunt, obsess, beset; prey –, weigh- on the mind.

put in -fear, – bodily fear; terrorize, intimidate, cow, daunt, over-awe, abash, deter, discourage; browbeat, bully; threaten etc. 909.

Adj. fearing etc. *v.*; frightened etc. *v.*; in -fear, – a fright etc. *n.*; haunted with the -fear etc. *n.- of.*

afraid, fearful; tim-id, -orous; nervous, diffident, coy, faint-hearted, tremulous, shaky, afraid of one's shadow, apprehensive, restless, fidgety; more frightened than hurt.

aghast; awe-, horror-, terror-, panic- -struck, -stricken; frightened to death, white as a sheet; pale, – as -death, – ashes, – a ghost; breathless, in hysterics.

inspiring fear etc. *v.*; alarming; formidable, redoubtable; perilous etc. *(danger)* 665; portentous; fear-ful, -some; dread, -ful; fell; dire, -ful; shocking; terri-ble, -fic; tremendous; horri-d, -ble, -fic; ghastly; awful, awe-inspiring, eerie, weird; revolting etc. *(painful)* 830.

Adv. *in terrorem.*

Int. 'angels and ministers of grace defend us!'

Phr. *ante tubam trepidat; horresco referens,* one's heart failing one, *obstupui steteruntque comae et vox faucibus haesit.*

861. Courage. [Absence of fear.]—**N.** courage, bravery, valor; resolute-, bold-ness etc. *adj.*; spirit, daring, gallantry, intrepidity; contempt –, defiance- of danger; derring-do; audacity; rashness etc. 863; dash; defiance etc. 715; confidence, self-reliance.

man-liness, -hood; nerve, pluck, mettle, game; heart, – of grace; spunk, gameness, grit, face, virtue, hardihood, fortitude; firmness etc. *(stability)* 150; heart of oak; bottom, backbone etc. *(perseverance)* 604*a*.

resolution etc. *(determination)* 604; tenacity, bull-dog courage.

prowess, heroism, chivalry.

exploit, feat, achievement; heroic -deed, – act; bold stroke.

man, – of mettle; hero, demigod, paladin, heroine, Amazon, Hector, Joan of Arc; lion, tiger, panther, bulldog; game-, fighting-cock; bully, fire-eater etc. 863; dare-devil.

V. be -courageous etc. *adj.*; dare, venture, make bold; face –, front –, affront –, confront –, brave –, defy –, despise –, mock- danger; look in the face; look -full, – boldly, – danger- in the face; face; meet, – in front; brave, beard; defy etc. 715.

take –, muster –, summon up –, pluck up-courage; nerve oneself, take heart; take –, pluck up- heart of grace; hold up one's head, screw one's courage to the sticking place; come -to, – up to-the scratch; stand, – to one's guns, – fire, – against; bear up – against; hold out etc. *(persevere)* 604*a*.

put a bold face upon; show –, present- a bold front, face the music; envisage; show fight.

bell the cat, take the bull by the horns, beard the lion in his den, march up to the cannon's mouth, go through fire and water, run the gauntlet, go over the top.

give –, infuse –, inspire- courage; reassure, encourage, embolden, inspirit, cheer, hearten, nerve, put upon one's mettle, rally, raise a rallying cry; pat on the back, make a man of, keep in countenance.

Adj. courageous, brave; val-iant, -orous; gallant, intrepid; spirit-ed, -ful; high-spirited, -mettled; mettlesome, game, plucky; man-ly, -ful; resolute; stout, -hearted; iron-, lion-hearted; heart of oak; Penthesilean.

bold, – spirited; daring, audacious; fear-, daunt-, dread-, awe-less; un-daunted, -appalled, -dismayed, -awed, -blenched, -abashed, -alarmed, -flinching, -shrinking, -blenching; apprehensive; confident, self-reliant; bold as -a lion, – brass.

enterprising, adventurous; ventur-ous, -esome; dashing, chivalrous; söldierly etc. *(warlike)* 722; heroic.

fierce, savage; pugnacious etc. *(bellicose)* 720.

strong-minded, hardy, doughty; firm etc. *(stable)* 150; determined etc. *(resolved)* 604; dogged, indomitable etc. *(persevering)* 604*a*.

up to, – the scratch; upon one's mettle; reassured etc. *v.*; unfeared, undreaded.

Phr. one's blood being up.

862. Cowardice. [Excess of fear.]—**N.** cowardice, pusillanimity; cowardliness etc. *adj.*; timidity, effeminacy.

poltroonery, baseness; dastard-ness, -y; abject fear, funk; Dutch courage; fear etc. 860; white feather, faint heart.

coward, poltroon, dastard, sneak, recreant; shy –, dunghill- cock; coistril, milksop, white-liver, nidget, cur, craven, one that cannot say 'Boo' to a goose; Bob Acres, Jerry Sneak.

alarm-, terror-, pessim-ist; runagate etc. *(fugitive)* 623; shirker.

V. quail etc. *(fear)* 860; be -cowardly etc. *adj.*, – a coward etc. *n.*; funk; cower, skulk, sneak; flinch, shy, fight shy, slink, turn tail; run away etc. *(avoid)* 623; show the white feather, have cold feet, show a yellow streak.

Adj. coward, -ly; fearful, shy; tim-id, -orous; skittish; poor-spirited, spirit-less, soft, effeminate.

weak-minded;- infirm of purpose etc. 605; weak-, faint-, chicken-, lily-, pigeon-hearted; yellow; white-, lily-, milk-livered; milksop, smock-faced; unable to say 'Boo' to a goose.

dastard, -ly; base, craven, sneaking, dunghill, recreant; unwar-, unsoldier-like.

'in face a lion but in 'heart a deer.'

unmanned; frightened etc. 860.

Int. *sauve qui peut!* devil take the hindmost!

Adv. in fear and trembling, in fear of one's life, in a blue funk.

Phr. *ante tubam trepidat,* one's courage oozing out.

863. Rashness.—**N.** rashness etc. *adj.*; temerity, want of caution, imprudence, indiscretion; over-confidence, presumption, audacity.

precipit-ancy, -ation; impetuosity; levity; foolhardi-hood, -ness; heed-, thought-lessness etc. *(inattention)* 458; carelessness etc. *(neglect)* 460; desperation; Quixotism, knight-errantry; fire-eating.

gam-ing, -bling; blind bargain, leap in the dark, fool's paradise; too many eggs in one basket.

desperado, rashling, mad-cap, dare-devil, Hotspur, fire-eater, bully, *bravo,* Hector, scapegrace, *enfant perdu;* Don Quixote, knight-errant, Icarus; adventurer; gam-bler, -ester; dynamitard.

V. be -rash etc. *adj.*; stick at nothing, play a desperate game; run into danger etc. 665; play with -fire, – edge tools.

carry too much sail, sail too near the wind, ride at single anchor, go out of one's depth.

take a leap in the dark, buy a pig in a poke.

donner tête baissée; knock one's head against a wall etc. (*be unskilful*) 699; rush on destruction; kick against the pricks, tempt Providence, go on a forlorn hope.

count one's chickens before they are hatched; reckon without one's host; catch at straws; trust to −, lean on- a broken reed.

Adj. rash, incautious, indiscreet, injudicious; imprudent, improvident, temerarious; uncalculating; heedless; careless etc. (*neglectful*) 460; without ballast, heels over head; giddy etc. (*inattentive*) 458; wanton, reckless, wild, madcap; desperate, devil-may-care.

hot-blooded, -headed, -brained; head-long, -strong; break-neck; fool-hardy; harebrained; precipitate, impulsive.

over-confident, -weening; ventur-esome, -ous; adventurous, Quixotic; fire-eating, cavalier; free-and-easy.

off one's guard etc. (*inexpectant*) 508.

Adv. post haste, *à corps perdu*, hand over head, *tête baissée*, head- foremost; happen what may.

Phr. neck or nothing, the devil being in one.

864. Caution.—N. caution; cautiousness etc. *adj.*; discretion, prudence, cautel, heed, circumspection, calculation, deliberation; safety first. foresight etc. 510; vigilance etc. 459; warning etc. 668.

coolness etc. *adj.*; self-possession, -command; presence of mind, *sang froid*; well-regulated mind; worldly wisdom, Fabian policy.

V. be -cautious etc. *adj.*; take -care, − heed, − good care; have a care; mind, − what one is about; be on one's guard etc. (*keep watch*) 459; make assurance double sure; ca' canny.

bespeak etc. (*be early*) 132.

think twice, look before one leaps, keep one's weather eye open, count the cost, look to the main chance, cut one's coat according to one's cloth; feel one's -ground, − way; see how the land lies etc. (*foresight*) 510; wait to see how the cat jumps; bridle one's tongue; *reculer pour mieux sauter* etc. (*prepare*) 673; let well alone, let sleeping dogs lie, *ne pas réveiller le chat qui dort*.

keep out of -harm's way, − troubled waters; keep at a respectful distance, stand aloof; keep −, be- on the safe side.

husband one's resources etc. 636.

caution etc. (*warn*) 668.

Adj. cautious, wary, guarded; on one's guard etc. (*watchful*) 459; *cavendo tutus*; *in medio tutissimus*.

care-, heed-ful; cautelous, stealthy, chary, shy of, circumspect, prudent, canny, safe, non-committal, discreet, politic; sure-footed etc. (*skilful*) 698.

unenterprising, unadventurous, cool, steady, self-possessed; over-cautious.

suspicious, leery, vigilant.

Adv. cautiously, gingerly etc. *adj.*

Int. have a care! look out! *cave canem!*

Phr. *timeo Danaos*; *festina lente*.

865. Desire.—N. desire, wish, fancy, fantasy; want, need, exigency.

mind, inclination, leaning, bent, *animus*, partiality, *penchant*, predilection; propensity etc. 820; willingness etc. 602; liking, love, fondness, relish.

longing, hankering; solicitude, anxiety; yearning, coveting; aspiration, ambition, vaulting ambition; eagerness, zeal, ardor, *empressement*, breathless impatience, over-anxiety; solicitude, impetuosity etc. 825.

appet-ite, -ition, -ence, -ency; sharp appetite, keenness, hunger, stomach, twist; thirst, -iness; drouth, mouth-watering; itch, -ing; prurience, *cacoëthes*, cupidity, lust, concupiscence.

edge of -appetite, − hunger; torment of Tantalus; sweet −, lickerish- tooth; itching palm; longing −, wistful −, sheep's-eye.

avidity; greed, -iness; covetous-, ravenous-ness etc. *adj.*; grasping, craving, canine appetite, rapacity; voracity etc. (*gluttony*) 957.

passion, rage, *furore*, mania, *manie*; inextinguishable desire; dips-, klept-, mon-omania.

[Person desiring] desirer, lover, *amateur*, votary, devotee, aspirant, solicitant, candidate; cormorant etc. 957; sycophant.

[Object of desire] *desideratum*; want etc. (*requirement*) 630; 'consumation devoutly to be wished;' attraction, magnet, allurement, fancy, temptation, seduction, lure, fascination, *prestige*, height of one's ambition, idol; whim, -sey; maggot; hobby, -horse.

Fortunatus' cap, wishing cap, love potion.

V. desire; wish, − for; be -desirous etc. *adj.*; have a -longing etc. *n.*; hope etc. 858.

care for, affect, like, list; take to, cling to, take a fancy to; fancy; prefer etc. (*choose*) 609.

have -an eye, − a mind- to; find it in one's heart etc. (*be willing*) 602; have a fancy for, set one's eyes upon; cast a sheep's eye −, look sweet- upon; take into one's head, have a heart, be bent upon; set one's -cap at, − heart upon; mind upon; covet.

want, miss, need, lack, desiderate, feel the want of; would fain -have, − do; would be glad of.

be -hungry etc. *adj.*; have a good appetite, play a good knife and fork; hunger −, thirst −, crave −, lust −, itch −, hanker −, run mad- after; raven −, die- for; burn to.

desiderate; sigh −, cry −, gape −, gasp −, pine −, pant −, languish −, yearn −, long −, be on thorns −, hope- for; aspire after; catch at, grasp at, jump at.

woo, court, solicit; fish −, spell −, whistle −, put up- for; ogle.

cause −, create −, raise −, excite −, provoke-desire; whet the appetite; appetize, titillate, allure, attract, take one's fancy, tempt; hold out -temptation, − allurement; tantalize, make one's mouth water, *faire venir l'eau à la bouche*.

gratify desire etc. (*give pleasure*) 829.

Adj. desirous; desiring etc. *v.*; orectic, appetitive; inclined etc. (*willing*) 602; partial to; fain, wishful, optative; anxious, wistful, curious; at a loss for, sedulous, solicitous.

craving, hungry, sharp-set, peckish, ravening, with an empty stomach, esurient, lickerish, thirsty, athirst, parched with thirst, pinched with hunger, famished, dry, drouthy; hungry as a -hunter, − hawk, − horse, − church mouse.

greedy, − as a hog; over-eager, voracious; ravenous, − as a wolf; open-mouthed, covetous, rapacious, grasping, extortionate, exacting, sordid, *alieni appetens*; insati-able, -ate; unquenchable, quenchless; omnivorous.

unsatisfied, unsated, unslaked.

eager, avid, keen; burning, fervent, ardent; agog; all agog; breathless; impatient etc. (*impetuous*) 825; bent –, intent –, set- -on, – upon; mad after, *enragé*, rabid, dying for, devoured by desire.

aspiring, ambitious, vaulting, sky-aspiring.

desirable; popular; desired etc. *v.*; in demand; pleasing etc. (*giving pleasure*) 829; appeti-zing, -ble; tantalizing.

Adv. wistfully etc. *adj.*; fain.

Int. would -that, – it were! O for! *esto perpetua!* if only!

Phr. the wish being the father to the thought; *sua cuique voluptas*; *hoc erat in votis*, the mouth watering, the fingers itching; *aut Caesar aut nullus*.

866. Indifference.—N. indifference, neutrality; coldness etc. *adj.*; unconcern, *insouciance, nonchalance*; want of -interest, – earnestness; anorexy, inappetency; apathy etc. (*insensibility*) 823; supineness etc. (*inactivity*) 683; disdain etc. 930; recklessness etc. 863; inattention etc. 458.

V. be -indifferent etc. *adj.*; stand neuter; take no interest in etc. (*insensibility*) 823; have no -desire etc. 865, – taste, – relish- for; not care for; care nothing -for, – about; not care a -straw etc. (*unimportance*) 643 -about, – for; not mind.

set at naught etc. (*make light of*) 483; spurn etc. (*disdain*) 930.

Adj. indifferent, cold, frigid, lukewarm; cool, – as a cucumber; unconcerned, *insouciant*, phlegmatic, *pococurante*, easy-going, devil-may-care, careless, listless, lackadaisical, feckless; half-hearted; un-ambitious, -aspiring, -desirous, - solicitous, -attracted.

un-attractive, -alluring, -desired, -desirable, - cared for, -wished, -valued, all one to.

insipid etc. 391; vain.

Adv. for aught one cares.

Int. never mind.

867. Dislike.—N. dis-like, -taste, -relish, - inclination, -placency.

reluctance; backwardness etc. (*unwillingness*) 603.

repugnance, disgust, queasiness, turn, nausea, loathing; avers-eness, -ation, -ion; abomination, antipathy, abhorrence, horror; mortal –, rooted- - antipathy, – horror; hatred, detestation; hate etc. 898; animosity etc. 900; hydrophobia.

sickener; gall and wormwood etc. (*unsavory*) 395; shuddering, cold sweat.

V. dis-, mis-like, -relish; mind, object to; have rather not, not care for; have –, conceive –, entertain –, take- -a dislike, – an aversion- to; have no -taste, – stomach- for.

shun, avoid etc. 623; eschew; withdraw –, shrink –, recoil- from; not be able to -bear, – abide, – endure; shrug the shoulders at, shudder at, turn up the nose at, look askance at; make a - mouth, – wry face, – grimace; make faces.

loathe, nauseate, abominate, detest, abhor; hate etc. 898; take amiss etc. 900; have enough of etc. (*be satiated*) 869.

cause –, excite- dislike; disincline, repel, sicken; make –, render- sick; turn one's stomach, nauseate, wamble, disgust, shock, stink in the nostrils; go against the -grain, – stomach; stick in the throat; make one's blood run cold etc. (*give pain*) 830; pall.

Adj. disliking etc. *v.*; averse to, loth, adverse; shy of, sick of, out of conceit with; disinclined; heart-, dog-sick; queasy.

disliked etc. *v.*; uncared for, unpopular; out of favor; repulsive, repugnant, repellent; abhorrent, insufferable, fulsome, nauseous; loath-some, -ful; offensive; disgusting etc. *v.*; disagreeable etc. (*painful*) 830; unsavory etc. 395.

Adv. *usque ad nauseam*.

Int. faugh! foh! ugh!

868. Fastidiousness.—N. fastidiousness etc. *adj.*; nicety, meticulosity, hypercriticism, difficulty in being pleased, *friandise*, epicurism, *omnia suspendens naso*.

discrimination, discernment, good taste, perspicacity.

epicure, gourmet.

[Excess of delicacy] prudery, prudishness, primness.

V. be -fastidious etc. *adj.*; split hairs, discriminate, have a sweet tooth.

mince the matter; turn up one's nose at etc. (*disdain*) 930; look a gift horse in the mouth, see spots on the sun.

Adj. fastidious, meticulous, exacting, nice, delicate, *délicat*, finical, finicky, difficult, dainty, lickerish, squeamish, thin-skinned; s-, queasy; hard –, difficult- to please; querulous, particular, over-particular, straitlaced, prudish, prim, scrupulous; censorious etc. 932; hypercritical, discriminating, discerning, perspicacious.

Phr. *noli me tangere*.

869. Satiety.—N. satiety, satisfaction, saturation, repletion, glut, surfeit; weariness etc. 841.

spoiled child; *enfant gâté*; too much of a good thing, *toujours perdrix*; *crambe repetita*.

V. sate, satiate, satisfy, saturate; cloy, quench, slake, pall, glut, gorge, surfeit; bore etc. (*weary*) 841; tire etc. (*fatigue*) 688; spoil.

have -enough of, – quite enough of, – one's fill, – too much of; be -satiated etc. *adj.*

Adj. satiated etc. *v.*; overgorged; *blasé*, used up, sick of, heart-sick.

Int. enough! hold! *eheu jam satis!*

870. Wonder.—N. wonder, marvel; astonish-, amaze-, wonder-, bewilder-ment; amazedness etc. *adj.*; admiration, awe; stup-or, -efaction; stound, fascination; sensation; surprise etc. (*inexpectation*) 508; cynosure.

note of admiration; thaumaturgy etc. (*sorcery*) 992.

V. wonder, marvel, admire; be -surprised etc. *adj.*; start; stare; open –, rub –, turn up- one's eyes; gloar; gape, open one's mouth, hold one's breath; look –, stand- -aghast, – agog; look blank etc. (*disappointment*) 509; *tomber des nues*; not believe one's -eyes, – ears, – senses.

not be able to account for etc. (*unintelligible*) 519; not know whether one stands on one's head or one's heels.

surprise, astonish, amaze, astound; dumbfound, - er; startle, dazzle; strike, – with -wonder, – awe; electrify; stun, stupefy, petrify, confound, bewilder, flabbergast; stagger, throw on one's beam ends, fascinate, turn the head, take away one's breath, strike dumb; make one's -hair stand on end, – tongue cleave to the roof of one's mouth; make one stare.

take by surprise etc. (*be unexpected*) 508.

be -wonderful etc. *adj.*; beggar –, baffle-description; stagger belief.

Adj. surprised etc. *v.*; aghast, all agog, breathless, agape; open-mouthed; awe-, thunder-, moon-, planet-struck; spell-bound; lost in - amazement, – wonder, – astonishment; struck all of a heap, unable to believe one's senses, like a duck in thunder.

wonderful, wondrous; surprising etc. *v.*; unexpected etc. 508; unheard of; mysterious etc. (*inexplicable*) 519; miraculous; *foudroyant*.

in-describable, -expressible, -effable; un-utterable, -speakable.

monstrous, prodigious, stupendous, marvelous; in-conceivable, -credible; in-, un-imaginable; strange etc. (*uncommon*) 83; passing strange.

striking etc. *v.*; over-whelming; wonder-working.

Adv. wonderfully etc. *adj.*; fearfully; for a –, in the name of- wonder; strange to say; *mirabile - dictu*, – visu; to one's great surprise.

with -wonder etc. *n.*, – gaping mouth, – open eyes, – upturned eyes; eyes starting out of one's head.

Int. lo, – and behold! O! hey-day! halloo! what! indeed! really! surely! humph! h∘m! good -lack, – heavens, – gracious! – lord! by jove! gad so! well a day! dear me! only think! lack-a-daisy! my -stars, – goodness! gracious goodness! goodness gracious! mercy on us! heavens and earth! God bless me! bless -us, – my heart! odzookens! *O gemini!* adzooks! hoity-toity! strong! Heaven save –, bless-the mark! can such things be! zounds! 'sdeath! what -on earth, – in the world! who would have thought it! etc. (*inexpectation*) 508; fancy! did you ever? you don't say so! what do you say to that! how now! where am I? well I'm blowed! etc.

Phr. *vox faucibus haesit*; one's hair standing on end.

871. Expectance. [Absence of wonder.]—**N.** expectan-ce, -cy etc. (*expectation*) 507; calmness, composure, tranquillity, serenity, coolness, imperturbability etc. 826.

nine days' wonder.

V. expect etc. 507; not -be surprised, – wonder etc. 870; *nil admirari*, make nothing of.

Adj. expecting etc. *v.*; unamazed, astonished at nothing; *blasé* etc. (*weary*) 841; unimaginative, calm, serene, imperturbable etc. 826; expected etc. *v.*; foreseen.

common, ordinary etc. (*habitual*) 613.

Int. no wonder; of course; why not?

872. Prodigy.—**N.** prodigy, phenomenon; wonder, -ment; genius, marvel, miracle; freak, monster

etc. (*unconformity*) 83; curiosity, lion, infant prodigy, sight, spectacle; *jeu –, coup- de théâtre*; gazing-stock; sign; portent etc. 512.

bursting of a -shell, – bomb; volcanic eruption, peal of thunder; thunder-clap, -bolt.

what no words can paint; wonders of the world; *annus mirabilis*; *dignus vindice nodus*.

873. Repute.—**N.** distinction, mark, name, figure; repute, reputation, character; good –, high-repute; note, notability, notoriety, *éclat*, 'the bubble reputation,' vogue, celebrity; fame, famousness; renown; populairty, *aura popularis*; esteem, approval, approbation etc. 931; credit, *succès d'estime, prestige*, talk of the town; name to conjure with.

glory; honor; luster etc. (*light*) 420; illustriouness etc. *adj.*

account, regard, respect; reputableness etc. *adj.*; respectability etc. (*probity*) 939; good -name, – report; fair name.

dignity; stateliness etc. *adj.*; solemnity, grandeur, splendor, nobility, majesty, sublimity.

rank, standing, brevet rank, precedence, *pas*, station, place, *status*; position, – in society; order, degree, *locus standi*, caste, condition.

greatness etc. *adj.*; eminence; height etc. 206; importance etc. 642; pre-, super-eminence; high mightiness, primacy; top of the -ladder, – tree.

elevation; ascent etc. 305; super-, ex-altation; dignification, aggrandizement.

dedication, consecration, enthronement, canonization, apotheosis, deification, celebration, enshrinement, glorification.

hero, man of mark, great card, celebrity, worthy, lion, *rara avis*, notability, somebody; man of rank etc. (*nobleman*) 875; pillar of the -state, – society, – church.

chief etc. (*master*) 745; first fiddle etc. (*proficient*) 700; scholar etc. 492; cynosure, mirror; flower, pink, pearl; paragon etc. (*perfection*) 650; choice and master spirits of the age; *élite*; star, sun, constellation, galaxy.

ornament, honor, feather in one's cap, halo, aureole, nimbus; halo –, blaze- of glory; blushing honors; laurels etc. (*trophy*) 733.

memory, posthumous fame, niche in the temple of fame; immor-tality, -tal name; *magni nominis umbra*.

V. be conscious of glory; be proud of etc. (*pride*) 878; exult etc. (*boast*) 884; be vain of etc. (*vanity*) 880.

be -distinguished etc. *adj.*; shine etc. (*light*) 420; shine forth, figure; make –, cut- a -figure, – dash, – splash.

rival, surpass; out-shine, -rival, -vie, -jump; emulate, vie with, eclipse; throw –, cast- into the shade; overshadow.

live, flourish, glitter, scintillate, flaunt; gain –, acquire- honor etc. *n.*; play first fiddle etc. (*be of importance*) 642; bear the -palm, – bell; lead the way; take -precedence, – the wall of; gain –, win- -laurels, – spurs, – golden opinions etc. (*approbation*) 931; graduate, take one's degree, pass one's examination, win a -scholarship, – fellowship.

make -a, – some- -noise, – noise in the world; leave one's mark, exalt one's horn, star, have a run, be run after; enjoy popularity, come -into vogue, – to the front; raise one's head.

enthrone, signalize, immortalize, deify, exalt to the skies; hand one's name down to posterity.

consecrate; dedicate to, devote to; enshrine, inscribe, blazon, lionize, blow the trumpet, crown with laurel.

confer −, reflect- honor etc. *n.* on; shed a luster on; redound to one's honor, ennoble.

give −, do −, pay −, render- honor to; honor, accredit, pay regard to, dignify, glorify; sing praises to etc. (*approve*) 931; look up to; exalt, aggrandize, elevate, nobilitate.

Adj. distinguished, *distingué*, noted; of -note etc. *n.*; honored etc. *v.*; popular; fashionable etc. 852.

in good odor; in −, in high- favor; reput-, respect-, credit-able.

remarkable etc. (*important*) 642; notable, notorious; celebrated, renowned, in every one's mouth, talked of; fam-ous, -ed; far-famed; conspicuous, to the front; foremost; in the -front rank, − ascendant.

imperishable, deathless, immortal, never fading, *aere perennius*; time-honored.

illustrious, glorious, splendid, brilliant, radiant; bright etc. 420; full-blown; honorific.

eminent, prominent; high etc. 206; in the zenith; at the -head of, − top of the tree; peerless, of the first water; superior etc. 33; super-, pre-eminent.

great, dignified, proud, noble, honorable, worshipful, lordly, grand, stately, august, princely, imposing, solemn, transcendent, majestic, sacred, sublime, heaven-born, heroic, *sans peur et sans reproche*; sacrosanct.

Int. hail! all hail! *ave! viva! vive!* long life to! glory −, honor- be to!

Phr. one's name -being in every mouth, − living for ever; *sic itur ad astra, fama volat, aut Caesar aut nullus*; not to know him argues oneself unknown; none but himself could be his parallel, *palmam qui meruit ferat.*

874. Disrepute.—**N.** disrepute, discredit; ill-, bad- -repute, -name, -odor, -favor; disapprobation etc. 932; in-gloriousness, derogation; a-, debasement; abjectness etc. *adj.*; degradation, dedecoration; 'a long farewell to all one's greatness;' odium, obloquy, opprobrium, ignominy.

dishonor, disgrace; shame, humiliation; scandal, baseness, vileness; perfidy, turpitude etc. (*improbity*) 940; infamy.

tarnish, taint, defilement, pollution.

stain, blot, spot, blur, stigma, brand, reproach, imputation, slur.

crying −, burning- shame; *scandalum magnatum*, badge of infamy, blot in one's escutcheon; bend −, bar- sinister; champain, point champain; by- word of reproach; Ichabod.

argumentum ad verecundiam; sense of shame etc. 879.

V. be -inglorious etc. *adj.*; incur -disgrace etc. *n.*; have −, earn- a bad name; put -−, wear- a halter round one's neck; disgrace −, expose- oneself.

play second fiddle; lose caste; pale one's ineffectual fire; recede into the shade; fall from one's high estate; keep in the background etc. (*modesty*) 881; be conscious of disgrace etc. (*humility*) 879; look -blue, − foolish, − like a fool; cut a -poor,

− sorry- figure; laugh on the wrong side of the mouth; make a sorry face, go away with a flea in one's ear, slink away.

cause -shame etc. *n.*; shame, disgrace, put to shame, dishonor; throw −, cast −, fling −, reflect- dishonor etc. *n.* upon; be a -reproach etc. *n.* to; derogate from.

tarnish, stain, blot, sully, taint; discredit, degrade, debase, defile; beggar; expel .etc. (*punish*) 972.

impute shame to, brand, post, stigmatize, vilify, defame, slur, cast a slur upon, hold up to shame, send to Coventry; tread −, trample- under foot; show up, drag through the mire, heap dirt upon; reprehend etc. 932.

bring low, put down, snub; take down a peg, − lower, − or two.

obscure, eclipse, outshine, take the shine out of; throw −, cast- into the shade; overshadow; leave −, put- in the background; push into a corner, put one's nose out of joint; put out, − of countenance.

upset, throw off one's center; discompose, disconcert; put to the blush etc. (*humble*) 879.

Adj. disgraced etc. *v.*; blown upon; shorn of -its beams, − one' glory; overcome, down-trodden; loaded with -shame etc. *n.*; in -bad repute etc. *n.*; out of -repute, − favor, − fashion, − countenance; at a discount; under -a cloud, − an eclipse; unable to show one's face; in the -shade, − background; out at elbows, down in the world, down and out.

inglorious; nameless, renownless, obscure, unknown to fame; un-noticed, -noted, -honored, -glorified.

shameful; dis-graceful, -creditable, -reputable; despicable; questionable; unbecoming, unworthy; derogatory; degrading, humiliating, *infra dignitatem*, dedecorous, scandalous, infamous, too bad, unmentionable; ribald, opprobrious; arrant, shocking, outrageous, notorious, shady.

ignominious, scrubby, dirty, abject, vile, beggarly, pitiful, low, mean, shabby, base etc. (*dishonorable*) 940.

Adv. to one's shame be it spoken.

Int. fie! shame! for shame! *proh pudor! O tempora! O mores!* ough! *sic transit gloria mundi.*

875. Nobility.—**N.** nobility, rank, condition, distinction, optimacy, blood, *pur sang*, birth, high descent, order; quality, gentility; blue blood of Castile; *ancien régime.*

high life, *haut monde*; upper -classes, − ten thousand; *élite*, aristocracy, great folks; fashionable world etc. (*fashion*) 852; salariat.

peer, -age; house of -lords, − peers; lords, − temporal and spiritual; *noblesse*; baronage, knightage; noble, -man; lord, -ling; grandee, *magnifico, hidalgo*; don, -ship; aristocrat, swell, three-tailed bashaw; gentleman, squire, squireen, patrician, laureate.

gentry, gentlefolk; squirarchy, better sort, *magnates, primates, optimates.*

king etc. (*master*) 745; prince, crown prince, *Dauphin*; duke; marquis, -ate; earl, viscount, baron, thane, banneret; baronet, -cy; knight, -hood; count, armiger, laird; sig-, seig-nior; esquire, boyar, margrave, vavasor, sheik, emir, ameer, scherif, pasha, effendi, sahib.

queen etc. 745; princess, begum, duchess, marchioness; countess etc.; lady, dame.

personage –, man- of -distinction, – mark, –
rank; nota-bles, -bilities; celebrity, big-wig,
magnate, great man, star; *magni nominis umbra*;
'every inch a king;' grand Panjandrum
V. be -noble etc. *adj.*
Adj. noble, exalted; of -rank etc. *n.*; princely,
titled, patrician, aristocratic; high-, well-born; of
gentle blood; genteel, *comme il faut*, gentlemanlike, courtly etc. (*fashionable*) 852; highly
respectable.
Adv. in high quarters.

876. Commonalty.—N. commonalty,
democracy; obscruity; low -condition, – life, –
society, – company; *bourgeoisie*; mass of -the
people, – society; Brown, Jones, and Robinson;
Tom, Dick, and Harry; lower –, humbler- -
classes, – orders; vulgar –, common- herd; rank
and file, *hoc genus omne*; the -many, – general,
– crowd, – people, – populace, – multitude,
– million, – masses, – mobility, – peasantry;
king Mob; proletariat, *fruges consumere nati*,
great unwashed; man in the street
mob; rabble, – rout; chaff, rout, horde,
canaille; scum –, *residuum* –, dregs- of -the
people, – society; swinish multitude, *faex populi*;
profanum –, *ignobile- vulgus*; vermin, riff-raff,
tag-rag and bobtail; small fry.
commoner, one of the people, democrat,
plebeian, republican, proletary, *prolétaire*,
roturier, Mr. Snooks, *bourgeois*, *épicier*,
Philistine, cockney; *grisette*, *demi-monde*.
peasant, countryman, boor, carle, churl; vill-ain,
-ein; serf, kern, tyke, tike, chuff, ryot, fellah; long-
shoreman; swain, clown, hind; clod, -hopper; hobnail, yokel, hick, rube, cider squeezer, bog-trotter,
bumpkin; ploughman, -boy; rustic, chawbacon,
tiller of the soil; hewers of wood and drawers of
water, groundling; gaffer, loon, put, cub, Tony
Lumpkin, looby, lout, under-ling; *gamin*, guttersnipe, street arab, mudlark; rough, rowdy, ruffian, roughneck; pot-wallopper, slubberdegullion;
vulgar –, low- fellow; cad, curmudgeon.
upstart, *parvenu*, *nouveau-riche*, skipjack;
nobody, – one knows; *hesterni quirites*,
pessoribus orti; *bourgeois gentilhomme*, *novus
homo*, snob, gent, mushroom, no one knows who,
adventurer; man of straw.
beggar, panhandler, gaberlunzie, muckworm,
mudlark, *sans-culotte*, raff, tatterdemalion, caitiff,
ragamuffin, Pariah, outcast of society, tramp, weary
Willie, bum, vagabond, *chiffonaier*, rag-picker,
Cinderella, cinderwench; scrub, jade; boots,
gossoon.
Goth, Vandal, Hottentot, savage, barbarian,
Yahoo; unlicked cub, rough diamond.
barbar-ousness, -ism; Boeotia.
V. be -ignoble etc. *adj.*, – nobody etc. *n.*
Adj. ignoble, common, mean, low, base, vile,
sorry, scrubby, beggarly, below par; no great shakes
etc. (*unimportant*) 643; home-ly, -spun; vulgar,
low-minded; snobbish, *parvenu*.
plebeian, proletarian; of -low, – mean- -
parentage, – origin, extraction; low-, base-, earth-
born, low bred; mushroom, dunghill, risen from
the ranks; unknown to fame, obscure, untitled.

rustic, uncivilized; lout-, boor-, clown-, churl-,
brut-, raff-ish; rude, unlicked, unpolished.
barbar-ous, -ian, -ic, -esque; cockney, born
within sound of Bow bells.
underling, menial, servile, subaltern.
Adv. below the salt.

877. Title.—N. title, honor; knighthood etc.
(*nobility*) 875.
royal –, serene- highness, excellency, grace;
lordship, worship, Rt. Hon., rever-ence, -end;
esquire, sir; madam, *madame*; master, mistress,
Mr., Mrs., *signor*, *señor*, *Mein Herr*, *mynheer*;
your –, his- honor; handle to one's name.
decoration, laurel, palm, wreath, garland, bays,
medal, ribbon, riband, blue ribbon, *cordon*, cross,
crown, coronet, star, garter; feather, – in one's
cap; chevron, epaulet, *épaulette*, colors, cockade;
livery; order, arms, armorial bearings, shield,
scutcheon, crest, reward etc. 973.

878. Pride.—N. dignity, self-respect, *mens sibi
conscia recti*.
pride; haughtiness etc. *adj.*; high notions,
hauteur; vainglory, crest; arrogance etc. (*assumption*) 885; pomposity etc. 882.
proud man, highflier; fine -gentleman, – lady;
grande dame.
V. be -proud etc. *adj.*; put a good face on; look
one in the face; stalk abroad, perk oneself up;
presume, swagger, strut; rear –, lift up –, hold
up- one's head; hold one's head high, look big, take
the wall, 'bear like the Turk no rival near the
throne,' carry with a high hand; ride the –, mount
on one's- high horse; set one's back up, bridle, toss
the head; give oneself airs etc. (*assume*) 885; boast
etc. 884.
pride oneself on; glory in, take pride in; pique
–, plume –, hug- oneself; stand upon, be proud
of; put a good face on; not -hide one's light under a
bushel, – put one's talent in a napkin; not think
small beer of oneself etc. (*vanity*) 880.
Adj. dignified; stately; proud, -crested; lordly,
baronial; lofty-minded; high-souled, -minded, -
mettled, -handed, -plumed, -flown, -toned.
haughty, paughty, insolent, lofty, high, mighty,
swollen, puffed up, flushed, blown; vain-glorious;
purse-proud, fine; proud as -a peacock, Lucifer;
bloated with pride.
supercilious, disdainful, bumptious, magisterial,
imperious; high-handed, – and mighty; overweening, consequential; arrogant etc. 885; unblushing etc. 880.
stiff, -necked; starch; perked –, stuck- up; in
buckram, straitlaced; prim etc. (*affected*) 855.
on one's -high horses, – tight ropes, – high
ropes; on stilts; *en grand seigneur*.
Adv. with head erect, with one's nose in the air.
Phr. *odi profanum vulgus et arceo*.

879. Humility.—N. hum-ility, -bleness; meek-,
low-ness; lowli-ness, -hood; abasement, self-
abasement, -effacement; submission etc. 725;
resignation.

condescension; affability etc. (*courtesy*) 894. modesty etc. 881; verecundity, blush, suffusion, confusion; sense of -shame, — disgrace; humiliation, mortification; let —, set- down.

V. be -humble etc. *adj.*; deign, vouchsafe, condescend; humble —, demean- oneself; stoop, — to conquer; carry coals; submit etc. 725; submit with a good grace etc. (*brook*) 826; yield the palm.

lower one's -tone, — note; sing small, draw in one's horns, sober down; hide one's -face, — diminished head; not dare to show one's face, take shame to oneself, not have a word to say for oneself; feel —, be conscious of- -shame, — disgrace; drink the cup of humiliation to the dregs; eat -humble pie, — one's words, — dirt; be humiliated, receive a snub.

blush -for, — up to the eyes; redden, change color; color up; hang one's head, look foolish, feel small.

render humble; humble, humiliate; let —, set —, take —, tread —, frown- down; snub, abash, abase, make one sing small, strike dumb; teach one -his distance, — his place; take down a peg, — lower; throw —, cast- into the shade etc. 874; stare —, put- out of countenance; put to the blush; confuse, ashame, mortify, disgrace, crush; send away with a flea in one's ear.

get a set down.

Adj. humble, lowly, meek; modest etc. 881; humble-, sober-minded; unoffended; submissive etc. 725; servile etc. 886.

condescending; affable etc. (*courteous*) 894.

humbled etc. *v.*; bowed down, resigned; abashed, ashamed, dashed; out of countenance; down in the mouth; down on one's -knees, — marrow-bones; humbled in the dust, brow-beaten; chap-, crest-fallen; dumbfoundered, flabbergasted, struck all of a heap.

shorn of one's glory etc. (*disrepute*) 874.

Adv. with downcast eyes, — bated breath, — bended knee; on all fours, on one's feet.

under correction, with due deference.

Phr. I am your -obedient, — very humble- servant; my service to you.

880. Vanity.—N. vanity; conceit, -edness; self-conceit, -complacency, -confidence, -sufficiency, -esteem, -love, -approbation, -praise, -glorification, -laudation, -gratulation, -applause, -admiration; *amour-propre*; selfishness etc. 943.

airs, pretensions, mannerism; egotism; prigg-ism, -ishness; coxcombery, gaudery, vainglory, elation; pride etc. 878; ostentation etc. 882; assurance etc. 885.

vox et praeterea nihil; cheval de bataille.

ego-ist, -tist; peacock, coxcomb etc. 854; Sir Oracle etc. 887.

V. be -vain etc. *adj.*, — vain of; pique oneself etc. (*pride*) 878; lay the flattering unction to one's soul.

have -too high, — an overweening- opinion of -oneself, — one's talents; blind oneself as to one's own merit; not think -small beer, — *vin ordinaire*-of oneself; put oneself forward; fish for compliments; give oneself airs etc. (*assume*) 885; boast etc. 884.

render -vain etc. *adj.*; inspire with -vanity etc. *n.*; inflate, puff up, turn up, turn one's head.

Adj. vain, — as a peacock; conceited, assured, overweening, pert, forward, perky; vain-glorious, high-flown; ostentatious etc. 882; puffed up, inflated, flushed.

self-satisfied, -confident, -sufficient, -flattering, -admiring, -applauding, -glorious, -opinionated; *entêté* etc. (*wrong-headed*) 481; wise in one's own conceit, pragmatical, overwise, pretentious, priggish; egotistic, -al; *soi-disant* etc. (*boastful*) 884; arrogant etc. 885.

un-abashed, -blushing; un-constrained, -ceremonious; free and easy.

Adv. vainly etc. *adj.*

Phr. how we apples swim!

881. Modesty.—N. modesty; humility etc. 879; diffidence, timidity; retiring disposition, unobtrusiveness, bashfulness etc. *adj.*; *mauvaise honte*; blush, -ing; verecundity; self-knowledge.

reserve, constraint; demureness etc. *adj.*; blushing honors.

V. be -modest etc. *adj.*; retire, reserve oneself; give way to; draw in one's horns etc. 879; hide one's face.

keep -private, — in the background, — one's distance; pursue the noiseless tenor of one's way, 'do good by stealth and blush to find it fame,' hide one's light under a bushel, cast a sheep's eye.

Adj. modest, diffident; humble etc. 879; timid, timorous, bashful; shy, nervous, skittish, coy, sheepish, shamefaced, blushing, over-modest.

unpreten-ding, -tious; un-obtrusive, -assuming, -ostentatious, -boastful, -aspiring; poor in spirit.

out of countenance etc. (*humbled*) 879.

reserved, constrained, demure.

Adv. humbly etc. *adj.*; quietly, privately; without -ceremony, — beat of the drum; *sans facon.*

882. Ostentation.—N. ostentation, display, show, flourish, parade, *étalage*, pomp, array, state, solemnity; dash, splash, glitter, strut, swank, side, swagger, pomposity; preten-se, -sions; showing off; fuss.

magnificence, splendor; *coup d'oeil*; grand doings.

coup de théâter; stage -effect, — trick; clap-trap; *mise en scène; tour de force; chic.*

demonstration, flying colors; tomfoolery; flourish of trumpets etc. (*celebration*) 883; pageant, -ry; spectacle, exhibition, procession; turn —, set- out; grand function; *fête*, gala, field-day, review, march past, promenade, insubstantial pageant.

dress; court —, full —, evening —, ball —, fancy- dress; tailoring, millinery, man-millinery, frippery; foppery, equipage.

ceremon-y, -ial; ritual; form, -ality; etiquette; punct-o, -ilio, -ilious-ness; starched-, stateli-ness. mummery, solemn mockery, mouth honor. attitudinarian; fop etc. 854.

V. be -ostentatious etc. *adj.*; come —, put oneself- forward; attract attention, star it.

make —, cut- a -figure, — dash, — splash; strut, blow one's own trumpet; figure, — away; make a show, — display; glitter.

show -off, — one's paces; parade, march past;

display, exhibit, put forward, hold up; trot –, hang- out; sport, brandish, blazon forth; dangle, – before the eyes.

cry up etc. (*praise*) 931; *prôner*, flaunt, emblazon, prink, set off, mount, have framed and glazed.

put a good, – smiling- face upon; clean the outside of the platter etc. (*disguise*) 544.

Adj. ostentatious, showy, dashing, pretentious ja-, jau-nty; grand, pompous, palatial; high sounding; turgid etc. (*big-sounding*) 577; garish, gorgeous; gaudy, – as a -peacock, – butterfly, – tulip; flaunting, flashing, flaming, glittering; gay etc. (*ornate*) 847; colorful.

splendid, magnificent, sumptuous.

theatrical, dramatic, spectacular, scenic, ceremonial, ritual, -istic.

solemn, stately, majestic, formal, stiff, ceremonious, punctilious, starch-ed, -y.

en grande tenue, in best bib and tucker, in Sunday best, *endimanché*.

Adv. with -flourish of trumpet, – beat of drum, – flying colors, – a brass band.

ad captandum vulgus.

883. Celebration.—**N.** celebration, solemnization, jubilee, diamond jubilee, commemoration, ovation, paean, triumph, jubilation.

triumphal arch, bonfire, salute; salvo, – of artillery; *feu de joie*, flourish of trumpets, *fanfare*, colors flying, illuminations, fireworks.

inauguration, installation, presentation; *début*, coming out, birthday anniversary, bi-, ter-, centenary; silver –, golden –, diamond- wedding, - day; coronation; Lord Mayor's show; harvest home, red letter day, festival; trophy etc. 733; *Te Deum* etc. (*thanksgiving*) 990; tete etc. 882; holiday etc. 840.

V. celebrate, keep, signalize, do honor to, commemorate, solemnize, hallow, mark with a red letter, hold high festival, maffick.

pledge, drink to, toast, hob and nob.

inaugurate, install, instate, induct, chair.

rejoice etc. 838; kill the fatted calf, hold jubilee, roast an ox, fire a salute.

Adj. celebrating etc. *v.*; commemorative, celebrated, immortal.

Adv. in -honor, – commemoration, – celebration of.

Int. hail! all hail! *io -paean, – triumphe!* 'see the conquering hero comes!'

884. Boasting.—**N.** boasting etc. *v.*; boast, vaunt, crake; preten-ce, -sions; puff, -ery; flourish, *fanfaronnade*; gasconade; bluff, swank, brag, - gardism; bravado, bunkum, Buncombe; high-falutin; jact-itation, -ancy; bounce, rant, bluster; venditation, vaporing, rodomontade, bombast, fine talking, tall talk, magniloquence, teratology, heroics; jingoism, Chauvinism; exaggeration etc. 549; gas, hot air.

vanity etc. 880; *vox et praeterea nihil*; much cry and little wool, *brutum fulmen*.

exultation; glorification; flourish of trumpets; triumph etc. 883.

boaster; bragg-art, -adocio; hot air merchant;

Gascon, *fanfaron*, pretender, fourflusher, *soi-disant*; windbag, blowhard, bluffer; chauvinist; blusterer etc. 887; charlatan, jack-pudding, trumpeter; puppy etc. (*fop*) 854.

V. boast, make a boast of, brag, vaunt, puff, show off, flourish, crake, crack, trumpet, strut, swagger, vapor, bluff; draw the long bow.

exult, crow over, neigh, chuckle, triumph; glory, gloat, jubilate; throw up one's cap; talk big, *se faire valoir, faire claquer son fouet*, take merit to oneself, make a merit of, sing *Io triumphe*, holloa before one is out of the wood.

Adj. boasting etc. *v.*; magniloquent, flaming, Thrasonic, stilted, gasconading, braggart, boastful, pretentious, *soi-disant*; vain-glorious etc. (*conceited*) 880.

elate, -d; jubilant, triumphant, exultant; in high feather; flushed, – with victory; cock-a-hoop; on stilts.

vaunted etc. *v.*

Adv. vauntingly etc. *adj.*; with a brass band.

Phr. 'let the galled jade wince.'

885. Insolence. [Undue assumption of superiority.]—**N.** insolence; haughtiness etc. *adj.*; arrogance, airs; overbearance, brashness, bumptiousness, contumely, disdain; domineering etc. *v.*; tyranny etc. 739.

impertinence; cheek, nerve, sauce; sauciness etc. *adj.*; flippancy, dicacity, petulance, procacity, bluster; swagger, -ing etc. *v.*; bounce; terrorism; jingoism, chauvinism.

as-, pre-sumption; beggar on horseback; usurpation.

impudence, assurance, audacity, self-assertion, hardihood, front, face, brass; shamelessness etc. *adj.*; effrontery, hardened front, face of brass.

assumption of infallibility.

malapert, saucebox etc. (*blusterer*) 887.

V. be -insolent etc. *adj.*; bluster, vapor, swagger, swell, give oneself airs; snap one's fingers, kick up a dust; swear etc. (*affirm*) 535; rap out oaths; roister.

arrogate; as-, pre-sume; make -bold, – free; take a liberty, give an inch and take an ell.

domineer, bully, dictate, hector; lord it over, bulldoze; *traiter de haut, regarder de haut en bas*; exact; snub, huff, beard, fly in the face of; put to the blush; bear –, beat- down; browbeat, intimidate; trample –, tread- -down, – under foot; dragoon, ride roughshod over, terrorize.

out-face, -look, -stare, -brazen, -brave; stare out of countenance; brazen out; lay down the law; teach one's grandmother to suck eggs; assume a lofty bearing; talk –, look- big; put on big looks, act the *grand seigneur*; mount –, ride- the high horse; toss the head, carry with a high hand.

tempt Providence, want snuffing.

Adj. insolent, haughty, arrogant, imperious, magisterial, dictatorial, arbitrary; high-handed, high and mighty; contumelious, supercilious, overbearing, intolerant, domineering; overweening, high-flown.

flippant, pert, cavalier, saucy, forward, impertinent, fresh, malapert.

precocious, assuming, would-be, bumptious.

bluff; brazen-, browed-faced, shameless, aweless, unblushing, unabashed; bold-, bare-faced; dead – lost- to shame.

impudent, audacious, presumptuous, free and easy, devil-may-care, rollicking; janty, jaunty; roistering, blustering, hectoring, swaggering, vaporing; thrasonic, fire-eating, 'full of sound and fury.'

Adv. insolently, with a high hand; *ex cathedrâ*.

Phr. one's bark being worse than his bite.

886. Servility.—N. servility; slavery etc. (*subjection*) 749; obsequiousness etc. *adj.*; subserviency; abasement; pros-tration, -ternation; genuflexion etc. (*worship*) 990; fawning etc. *v.*; tuft-hunting, time-serving, flunkeyism; sycophancy etc. (*flattery*) 933; humility etc. 879.

sycophant, parasite, yes-man; toad, -y, -eater; tuft-hunter; snob, flunkey, lap-dog, spaniel, lickspittle, smell-feast, *Graeculus esuriens*, hanger on, stooge, *cavaliere servente*, led captain, carpet knight; time-server, fortune-hunter, Vicar of Bray, Sir Pertinax Mac Sycophant, pick-thank; flatterer etc. 935; doer of dirty work; *âme damnée*, tool; reptile; slave etc. (*servant*) 746; courtier; sponge, jackal; truckler.

V. cringe, bow, stoop, kneel, bend the knee; fall on one's knees, prostrate oneself; worship etc. 990.

sneak, crawl, crouch, cower, truckle to, grovel, fawn, toady, lick the feet of, kiss the hem of one's garment.

pay court to; feed –, fatten –, batten- on; dance attendance on, pin oneself upon, hang on the sleeve of, *avaler des couleuvres*, keep time to, fetch and carry, do the dirty work of.

go with the stream, follow the crowd, worship the rising sun, hold with the hare and run with the hounds.

Adj. servile, obsequious; supple, – as a glove; soapy, oily, pliant, cringing, fawning, slavish, groveling, sniveling, mealy-mouthed; beggarly, sycophantic, parasitical; abject, prostrate, down on one's marrow-bones; base, mean, sneaking; crouching etc. *v.*

Adv. hat –, cap- in hand.

887. Blusterer.—N. bluster-, swagger-, vapor-, roister-, brawl-er; brazen-face; *fanfaron*; braggart etc. (*boaster*) 884; bully, terrorist, rough, roughneck; hooligan, hoodlum, larrikin, ruffian; Mohock, -hawk; drawcansir, swashbuckler, Captain Boabdil, Sir Lucius O'Trigger, Thraso, Pistol, Parolles, Bombastes Furioso, Hector, Chrononhotonthologos; jingo; desperado, dare-devil, fire-eater; fury etc. (*violent person*) 173; rowdy.

puppy etc. (*fop*) 854; prig; Sir Oracle, dogmatist, *doctrinaire*, stump orator, jack-in-office; saucebox, malapert, jackanapes, minx; bantam-cock.

888. Friendship.—N. friendship, amity; friendliness etc. *adj.*; brotherhood, fraternity, sodality, confraternity, sorosis, sisterhood; harmony etc. (*concord*) 714; peace etc. 721.

firm –, staunch –, intimate –, familiar –, bosom –, cordial –, tried –, devoted –, lasting –, fast –, sincere –, warm –, ardent- friendship.

cordiality, fraternization, *entente cordiale*, good

understanding, *rapprochement*, sympathy, fellow-feeling, response, welcomeness; *camaraderie*.

affection etc. (*love*) 897; favoritism; goodwill etc. (*benovolence*) 906; partiality.

acquaintance, familiarity, intimacy, intercourse, fellowship, knowledge of; introduction.

V. be -friendly etc. *adj.*, – friends etc. 890; – acquainted with etc. *adj.*; know; have the ear of; keep- company with etc. (*sociality*) 892; hold communication –, have dealings –, sympathize- with; have a leaning to; bear good will etc. (*benevolence*) 906; love etc. 897; make much of; befriend etc. (*aid*) 707; introduce to.

set one's horses together; hold out –, extend the right hand of -friendship, – fellowship; become -friendly etc. *adj.*; make -friends etc. 890 with; break the ice, be introduced to; make –, pick –, scrape- acquaintance with; get into favor, gain the friendship of.

shake hands with, fraternize, embrace; receive with open arms, throw oneself into the arms of; meet half way, take in good part.

Adj. friendly, amic-able, -al; well affected, unhostile, neighborly, brotherly, fraternal, sisterly, sympathetic, harmonious, hearty, cordial, warm-hearted, devoted.

friends –, well –, at home –, hand in hand-with; on -good, – friendly, – amicable, – cordial, – familiar, – intimate- -terms, – footing; on -speaking, – visiting- terms; in one's good - graces, – books.

acquainted, familiar, intimate, thick, hand and glove, hail fellow well met, free and easy; welcome.

Adv. amicably etc. *adj.*; with open arms; *sans cérémonie*; arm in arm.

889. Enmity.—N. enmity, hostility; un-friendliness etc. *adj.*; discord etc. 713.

alienation, estrangement; dislike etc. 867; hate etc. 898; antagonism.

heartburning; animosity etc. 900; malevolence etc. 907.

V. be -inimical etc. *adj.*; keep –, hold- at arm's length; be at loggerheads; bear malice etc. 907; fall out; take umbrage etc. 900; harden the heart, alienate, estrange.

Adj. inimical, unfriendly, hostile; at -enmity, – variance, – swords points, – daggers drawn, – open war with; up in arms against; in bad odor with.

on bad –, not on speaking- terms; cool; cold, -hearted; estranged, alienated, disaffected, irreconcilable.

890. Friend.—N. friend, – of one's bosom, intimate acquaintance, neighbor, well-wisher; *alter ego*; best –, bosom –, fast- friend; *amicus usque ad aras*; *fidus Achates*; *persona grata*.

favorer, *fautor*, patron, backer, Maecenas; tutelary saint, good genius, advocate, partisan, sympathizer; ally; friend in need etc. (*auxiliary*) 711.

associate, compeer, comrade, mate, companion, *confrère*, *camarade*, *confidante*, colleague; old –, crony; side-kick; chum, buddy, bunkie, roommate, pal; play-fellow, -mate; classmate, schoolfellow; bed-fellow, -mate; maid of honor.

compatriot; fellow – , countryman, – towns-man.

shop-, ship-. mess-mate; fellow – , boon – , pot-companion; co-partner.

Arcades ambo, Pylades and Orestes, Castor and Pollux, Nisus and Euryalus, Damon and Pythias, *par nobile fratrum*.

host, Amphitryon, Boniface; guest, visitor, frequenter, *habitué*; *protégé*.

891. Enemy.—N. enemy; antagonist, foeman; open – , bitter- enemy; opponent etc. 710; back friend.

public enemy, enemy to society, traitor, anar-chist etc. 743.

Phr. every hand being against one.

892. Sociality.—N. soci-ality, -ability, -ableness etc. *adj.*; social intercourse; consociation; inter-course, -community; consort-, companion-, fellow-, comrade-ship; clubbism; *esprit de corps*.

conviviality; good -fellowship, – company, *camaraderie*; joviality, jollity, *savoir -vivre*, festivity, festive board, merry-making; loving cup; hospitality, heartiness; cheer.

welcome, -ness; greeting; hearty – , warm – , welcome- reception; urbanity etc. (*courtesy*) 894; intimacy, familiarity.

good – , jolly- fellow, good mixer, Rotarian; *bon enfant*.

social – , family- circle; circle of acquaintance, *coterie*, society, company.

social -gathering, – *réunion*; assembly etc. (*assemblage*) 72; party, entertainment, reception, *levée*, at home, *conversazione*, *soirée*, *matinée*, evening – , morning – , afternoon – , garden – , dinner – , tea – , cocktail- party; symposium, sing-song; kettle-, drum; *partie carrée*, dish of tea, *ridotto*, rout, housewarming; ball, prom, hop, dance, *thé dansant*; festival etc. (*amusement*) 840; wedding breakfast; 'the feast of reason and the flow of soul.'

visit, -ing; round of visits; call, morning call; in-terview etc. (*interlocution*) 588; assignation; tryst, -ing place; appointment.

club etc. (*association*) 712.

V. bé -sociable etc. *adj.*; know; be -acquainted etc. *adj.*; associate – , sort – , keep company – , walk hand in hand -with; eat off the same trencher, club together, consort, bear one company, join; make acquaintance with etc. (*friendship*) 888; make advances, fraternize, embrace; in-tercommunicate.

be – , feel – , make oneself- at home with; make free with; crack a bottle with; take pot luck with, receive hospitality, live at free quarters.

visit, pay a visit; interchange -visits, – cards; call -at, – upon; leave a card; drop in, look in; look one up, beat up one's quarters.

entertain; give a -party etc. *n.*; be at home, see one's friends, hang out, keep open house, do the honors; receive, – with open arms; welcome; give a warm reception etc. *n.* to; kill the fatted calf.

Adj. sociable, companionable, clubbable, clubby, conversable, cosy, cosey, chatty, con-versational; homiletical.

convivial; fest-ive, -al; jovial, jolly, hospitable. welcome, – as the roses in May; *fêté*, en-tertained.

free and easy, hail fellow well met, familiar, on visiting terms, acquainted.

social, neighborly; international, cosmopolitan, gregarious.

Adv. *en famille*, in the family circle; *sans - facon, – cérémonie*, arm in arm.

893. Seclusion. Exclusion.—N. seclusion, privacy; retirement; concealment; reclusion, recess; snugness etc. *adj.*; delitescence; rustication, *rus in urbe*; solitude; solitariness etc. (*singleness*) 87; isolation; loneliness etc. *adj.*; estrangement from the world, anchoritism, voluntary exile; aloofness.

cell, hermitage; convent etc. 1000; *sanctum sanctorum*; study, library, den; hide-out.

depopulation, desertion, desolation; wilderness etc. (*unproductive*) 169; howling wilderness; rot-ten borough, Old Sarum.

exclusion, excommunication, banishment, exile, ostracism, proscription; cut, – direct; dead cut. inhospit-ality, -ableness etc. *adj.*; un-, dis-sociability; domesticity, Darby and Joan.

recluse, hermit, eremite, cenobite; anchor-et, - ite; Simon Stylites; Troglodyte, Timon of Athens, Santon, *solitaire*, ruralist, disciple of Zim-mermann, closet cynic, Diogenes; outcast, Pariah, casta ᵂʸ outsider, pilgarlic; wastrel, foundling, or-phan.

V. be - , live- secluded etc. *adj.*; keep – , stand – , hold oneself- -aloof, – in the background; keep snug; shut oneself up; deny – , seclude-oneself; creep into a corner, rusticate, *aller planter ses choux*; retire, – from the world; hermetize, take the veil; abandon etc. 624.

cut, – dead; refuse to -associate with, – acknowledge; look cool – , turn one's back – , shut the door- upon; repel, blackball, ex-communicate, exclude, exile, expatriate; banish, outlaw, maroon, ostracize, proscribe, cut off from, send to Coventry, keep at arm's length, draw a cor-don round; boycott, blockade, lay an embargo on, isolate.

depopulate; dis-, un-people.

Adj. secluded, sequestered, retired, delitescent, private, bye; out of the -world, -way; in a back-water; 'the world forgetting by the world forgot.'

snug, domestic, stay-at-home.

unsociable; un-, dis-social; inhospitable, cynical, inconversable, unclubbable, *sauvage*, eremetic. solitary; lone-ly, -some; isolated, single.

excluded, estranged; unfrequented; uninhabit-able, -ed; tenantless; un-tenanted, -occupied; aban-doned; deserted, – in one's utmost need; un-friended; kith-, friend-, home-less; lorn, forlorn, desolate.

un-visited, -introduced, -invited, -welcome; un-der a cloud, left to shift for oneself, derelict, out-cast, outside the gates.

banished etc. *v.*; under an embargo.

Phr. *noli me tangere*.

894. Courtesy.—N. courtesy; respect etc. 928; good -manners, – behavior, – breeding; manners; politeness etc. *adj.*; *bienséance*, urbanity, comity, gentility; gentle – , breeding; polish, presence, cultivation, culture; civili-ty, -zation; amenity, suavity; good -temper, − humor; amiability, easy temper, complacency, soft tongue, mansuetude; condescension etc. (*humility*) 879; affability, complaisance, *prévenance*, amiability, gallantry, chivalry; pink of -politeness, − courtesy.

compliment; fair −, soft −, sweet- words; honeyed phrases, flattering remarks, ceremonial; salutation, reception, presentation, introduction, *accueil*, greeting, recognition; welcome, *abord*, respects, *devoir*, regards, remembrances; kind -regards, − remembrances; love, best love, duty; deference.

obeisance etc. (*reverence*) 928; bow, courtesy, curtsy, scrape, *salaam, kow-tow*, bowing and scraping; kneeling; genuflexion etc. (*worship*) 990; obsequiousness. etc. 886; capping, shaking hands etc. *v*.; grip of the hand, embrace, hug, squeeze, *accolade*, loving cup, *vin d'honneur*, pledge; love token etc. (*endearment*) 902; kiss, buss, salute.

mark of recognition, not; 'nods and becks and wreathed smiles;' valediction etc. 293; condolence etc. 915.

V. be -courteous etc. *adj*.; show -courtesy etc. *n*.

mind one's P's and Q's, behave oneself, be all things to all men, conciliate, speak one fair, take in good part; make −, do- the amiable; look as if butter would not melt in one's mouth; mend one's manners.

receive, do the honors, usher, greet, hail, bid welcome; welcome, − with open arms; shake hands; hold out − press −, squeeze- the hand; bid God speed; speed the parting guest; cheer, serenade.

salute; embrace etc. (*endearment*) 902; kiss, − hands; drink to, pledge, hob and nob; move to, nod to; smile upon.

uncover, cap; touch −, take off- the hat; doff the cap; pull the forelock; present arms; make way for; bow; make one's bow; scrape, curtsy, courtesy; bob a -curtsy, − courtesy; kneel; bow −, bend- the knee; salaam, *kowtow*.

visit, wait upon, present oneself, pay one's respects, pay a visit etc. (*sociability*) 892; dance attendance on etc. (*servility*) 886; pay attentions to; do homage to etc. (*respect*) 928.

prostrate oneself etc. (*worship*) 990.

give −, send- one's duty etc. *n*. to.

render -polite etc. *adj*.; polish, civilize, humanize.

Adj. courteous, polite, civil, mannerly, urbane; well-behaved, -mannered, -bred, -brought up, gently bred, of gentle -breeding, − manners, good-mannered, polished, civilized, cultivated; refined etc. (*taste*) 850; gentlemanlike etc. (*fashion*) 852; gallant, chivalrous, on one's good behavior.

fine −, fair −, soft- spoken; honey-mouthed, -tongued; oily, unctuous, bland, suave; obliging, conciliatory, complaisant, complacent; obsequious etc. 886.

ingratiating, winning; gentle, mild; good-humored, cordial, gracious; amiable, tactful, addressful, affable, genial, friendly, familiar; neighborly.

Adv. courteously etc. *adj*.; with a good grace; with -open, − outstretched- arms; *à bras ouverts*; *suaviter in modo*, in good humor.

Int. hail! welcome! well met! *ave!* all hail! good -day, − morning etc., − morrow! God speed! *pax vobiscum!* may your shadow never be less! *chin-chin!*

895. Discourtesy.—N. discourtesy; ill-breeding; ill −, bad −, ungainly- manners; in-suavity; grouchiness; un-courteousness etc. *adj*., tactlessness; rusticity, inurbanity; illiberality, incivility, displacency.

disrespect etc. 929; procacity, impudence; barbar-ism, -ity; misbehavior, brutality, blackguard--ism, conduct unbecoming a gentleman, *grossièreté, brusquerie*; vulgarity etc. 851.

churlishness etc. *adj*.; spinosity, perversity; moroseness etc. (*sullenness*) 901a.

bad-, ill-temper; sternness etc. *adj*.; austerity; moodishness, captiousness etc. 901; cynicism; tartness etc. *adj*.; acrimony, acerbity, virulence, asperity.

scowl, black looks, frown; short answer, rebuff; hard words, contumely; unparliamentary language, personality.

bear, bruin, brute, grouch, blackguard, beast; unlicked cub; frump, cross-patch; saucebox etc. 887.

V. be -rude etc. *adj*.; insult etc. 929; treat with discourtesy; take a name in vain; make -bold, − free- with; take a liberty; stare out of countenance, ogle, point at, put to the blush.

cut; turn -one's back upon, − on one's heel; give the cold shoulder; keep at -a distance, − arm's length; look -cool, − coldly, − black- upon; show the door to, send away with a flea in the ear.

lose one's temper etc. (*resentment*) 900; sulk etc. 901a; frown, scowl, glower, pout; snap, snarl, growl.

render -rude etc. *adj*.; brut-alize, -ify.

Adj. dis-, un-courteous; uncourtly; ill-bred, -mannered, -behaved, -conditioned, unbred; un-manner-ly, -ed; im-, un-polite; un-polished, -civilized, -genteel; ungentleman-like, -ly; unladylike; blackguard; vulgar etc. 851; dedecorous; foul-mouthed, -spoken; abusive.

un-civil, -gracious, -ceremonious; cool; pert, forward, obtrusive, impudent, rude, saucy, precocious; insolent etc. 885.

repulsive; un-complaisant, -accommodating, -neighborly, -gallant; inaffable; un-gentle, -gainly; rough, rugged, bluff, blunt, gruff; churl-, boor-, bear-ish; brutal, *brusque*; stern, harsh, austere; cavalier.

tart, sour, crabbed, sharp, short, trenchant, sarcastic, crusty, biting, caustic, virulent, bitter, acrimonious, venomous, contumelious; snarling etc., *v*.; surly, − as a bear; perverse; grim, sullen etc. 901a; peevish etc. (*irascible*) 901.

Adv. discourteously etc. *adj*.; with -discourtesy etc. *n*., − a bad grace.

896. Congratulations.—N. con-, gratulation; felicitation; salute etc. 894; condolence etc. 915; compliments of the season; good −, best- wishes.

V. con-, gratulate; felicitate, compliment; give −, wish one- joy; tender −, offer- one's congratulations; wish -many happy returns of the day, − a merry Christmas and a happy new year.

congratulate oneself etc. (*rejoice*) 838.

Adj. con-, gratulatory.

897. Love.—N. love; fondness etc. *adj.*; liking; inclination etc. (*desire*) 865; regard, dilection, admiration, fancy.

affection, sympathy, fellow-felling; tenderness etc. *adj.*; heart, brotherly love; benevolence etc. 906; attachment.

yearning, tender passion, *affaire de coeur*, *amour*, gallantry, passion, flame, devotion, fervor, enthusiasm, transport of love, rapture, enchantment, infatuation, adoration, idolatry.

narcissism, Oedipus complex, Electra complex.

Cupid, Venus, Eros; myrtle; true lover's knot; love -token, — suit, — affair, — tale, — story; the old story, plighted love; courtship etc. 902; *amourette*.

maternal love.

attractiveness, charm; popularity; favorite etc. 899.

lover, suitor, follower, admirer, adorer, wooer, amoret, beau, sweetheart, inamorato, swain, young man, flame, love, truelove; leman, Lothario, gallant, paramor, *amoroso*, *cavaliere servente*, captive, *cicisbeo*; *caro sposo*, Don Juan, sheik, ladies' man, squire of dames, Knave of Hearts.

inamorata, lady-love, idol, darling, duck, Dulcinea, angel, goddess, *cara sposa*; mistress.

betrothed, affianced, *fiancée*.

flirt, *coquette*; amorette; pair of turtle doves; abode of love, *agapemone*.

V. love, like, affect, fancy, care for, take an interest in, be partial to, sympathize with; be -in love etc. *adj.*- with; have —, entertain —, harbor —, cherish- a -love etc. *n.* for; regard, revere; take to, bear love to, be wedded to; set one's affections on; make much of, feast one's eyes on; hold dear, prize, treasure; hug, cling to, cherish, pet, caress etc. 902.

burn; adore, idolize, love to distraction, *aimer eperdument*; dote -on, — upon.

take a fancy to, fall for, be stuck on, look sweet upon; become -enamored etc. *adj.*; fall in love with, lose one's heart; desire etc. 865.

excite love; win —, gain —, secure —, engage- the -love, — affections, — heart; take the fancy of; have a place in —, wind round- the heart; attract, attach, endear, charm, fascinate, captivate, bewitch, seduce, enamor, enrapture, turn the head.

get into favor; ingratiate —, insinuate —, worm- oneself; propitiate, curry favor with, pay one's court to, make a date with, *faire l'aimable*, set one's cap at, flirt, coquet.

Adv. loving etc. *v.*; fond of; taken —, struck- with; smitten, bitten; attached to, wedded to; enamored; charmed etc. *v.*; in love; lovesick; over head and ears in love.

affectionate, tender, sweet upon, sympathetic, loving, fond, amorous, amatory; erotic, uxurious, ardent, passionate, rapturous, devoted, motherly.

loved etc. *v.*; beloved; well —, dearly- beloved; dear, precious, darling, pet, little; favorite, popular.

congenial; to —, after- one's -mind, — taste, — fancy, — own heart.

in one's good -graces etc. (*friendly*) 888; dear as the apple of one's eye, nearest to one's heart.

lovable, adorable; lovely, sweet; attractive, seductive, winning; charming, engaging, interesting, enchanting, captivating, fascinating, intriguing, bewitching; amiable, like an angel, angelic, seraphic.

898. Hate.—N. hate, hatred, vials of hate; Hymn of Hate.

dis-affection, -favor; alienation, estrangement, coolness; enmity etc. 889; animosity etc. 900.

umbrage, pique, grudge; dudgeon, spleen; bitterness, — of feeling; ill —, bad- blood; acrimony; malice etc. 907; implacability etc. (*revenge*) 919.

repugnance etc. (*dislike*) 867; odium, unpopularity; loathing, detestation, antipathy; object of -hatred, — execration; abomination, aversion, *bête noire*; enemy etc. 891; bitter pill; source of annoyance etc. 830.

V. hate, detest, abominate, abhor, loathe; recoil —, shudder- at; shrink from, view with horror., hold in abomination, revolt against, execrate; scowl etc. 895; disrelish etc. (*dislike*) 867.

owe a grudge; bear -spleen, — a grudge, — malice etc. (*malevolence*) 907; conceive an aversion to.

excite —, provoke- hatred etc. *n.*; be -hateful etc. *adj.*; stink in the nostrils; estrange, alienate, repel, set against, sow dissension, set by the ears, envenom, incense, irritate, rile, ruffle, vex; horrify etc. 830.

Adj. hating etc. *v.*; abhorrent; averse from etc. (*disliking*) 867; set against.

bitter etc. (*acrimonious*) 895; implacable etc. (*revengeful*) 919.

un-loved, -beloved, -lamented, -deplored, - mourned, -cared for, -endured, -valued; disliked etc. 867.

crossed in love, forsaken, rejected, love-lorn, jilted.

obnoxious, hateful, odious, abominable, repulsive, offensive, shocking, disgusting etc. (*disagreeable*) 830.

invidious, spiteful; malicious etc. 907.

insulting, irritating, provoking.

[Mutual hate] at -daggers drawn, — swords points; not on speaking terms etc.. (*enmity*) 889.

Phr. no love lost between.

899. Favorite.—N. favorite, pet, cosset, minion, idol, jewel, spoiled child, *enfant gâté*; led captain; crony; fondling; apple of one's eye, man after one's own heart; *persona grata*.

love, dear, darling, duck, honey, jewel; mopsey, moppet; sweetheart etc. (*love*) 897.

general —, universal- favorite; idol of the people; matinée idol, movie —, radio- star.

900. Resentment.—N. resentment, displeasure, animosity, anger, wrath, indignation; vexation, exasperation, bitter resentment, wrathful indignation.

pique, umbrage, huff, miff, soreness, dudgeon, acerbity, virulence, bitterness, acrimony, asperity, spleen, gall; heart-burning, -swelling; rankling.

ill —, bad- -humor, — temper; irascibility etc. 901; ill blood etc. (*hate*) 898; revenge etc. 919.

excitement, irritation; warmth, bile, choler, ire, fume, pucker, dander, ferment, ebullition; towering -passion, — rage, *acharnement*, angry mood, taking, pet, tiff, passion, fit, tantrums.

burst, explosion, paroxysm, storm, rage, fury, desperation; violence etc. 173; fire and fury; vials of wrath; gnashing of teeth, hot blood, high words.

scowl etc. 895; sulks etc. 901a.

[Cause of umbrage] affront, provocation, offence; indignity etc. (*insult*) 929; grudge, crow to pluck, sore subject; red rag to a bull; *casus belli*.

Furies, Erinys, Eumenides, Alecto, Megaera, Tisiphone.

buffet, slap in the face, box on the ear, rap on the knuckles.

V. resent; take -amiss, – ill, – to heart, – offence, – umbrage, – huff, – exception; take in - ill part, – bad part, – dudgeon; *ne pas entendre raillerie*; breathe revenge, cut up rough.

fly –, fall –, get- into a -rage, – passion; bridle –, oristle –, froth –, fire –, flare- up; open –, pour out- the vials of one's wrath.

pout, knit the brow, frown, scowl, lower, snarl, growl, gnarl, gnash, snap; redden, color; look - black, – black as thunder, – daggers; bite one's thumb; show –, grind- one's teeth; champ the bit.

chafe, mantle, fume, kindle, fly out, take fire; boil, – over; boil with -indignation, – rage; rage, storm, foam; vent one's -rage, – spleen; lose one's temper, stand on one's hind legs, stamp the foot, kick up a row, fly off the handle, cut up rough; stamp –, quiver –, swell –, foam- with rage; burst with anger; raise Cain, breathe fire and fury.

have a fling at; bear malice etc. (*revenge*) 919.

cause –, raise- anger; affront, offend; give - offence, – umbrage; anger; hurt the feelings; insult, discompose, fret, ruffle, nettle, heckle, huff, pique; excite etc. 824; irritate, stir the blood, stir up bile; sting, – to the quick; rile, provoke, chafe, wound, incense, inflame, enrage, aggravate, add fuel to the flame, fan into a flame, widen the breach, envenom, embitter, exasperate, infuriate, kindle wrath; stick in one's gizzard; rankle etc. 919.

put out of humor; put one's -monkey, – backup; set –, get- one's back up; raise one's -gorge, – dander, – choler; work up into a passion; make - one's blood boil, – the ears tingle; throw into a ferment, madden, drive one mad; lash into -fury, – madness; fool to the top of one's bent; set by the ears.

bring a hornet's nest about one's ears.

Adj. angry, wrath, irate; ire-, wrath-ful; cross etc. (*irascible*) 901; sulky etc. 901a; bitter, virulent; acrimonious etc. (*discourteous*) etc. 895; violent etc. 173.

warm, burning; boiling, – over; fuming, raging; foaming, – at the mouth; convulsed with rage.

offended etc. *v.*; waxy, *acharné*; wrought, worked up; indignant, hurt, sore, peeved; set against.

fierce, wild, rageful, furious, mad with rage, fiery, infuriate, rabid, savage; relentless etc. 919.

flushed with -anger, – rage; in a -huff, – stew, – fume, – pucker, – passion, – rage, – fury; on one's high ropes, up in arms; in high dudgeon.

Adv. angrily etc. *adj.*; in the height of passion; in the heat of -passion, – the moment.

Phr. one's -blood, – back, – monkey- being up; *fervens difficili bile jecur*; the gorge rising, eyes flashing fire; the blood -rising, – boiling; *haeret lateri lethalis arundo*.

901. Irascibility.—N. irascibility, temper; crossness etc. *adj.*; susceptibility, procacity,

petulance, irritability, tartness, acerbity, protervity; pugnacity etc.' (*contentiousness*) 720.

excitability etc. 825; bad –, fiery –, crooked –, irritable etc. *adj.*- temper; *genus irritabile*, hot blood.

ill humor etc. (*sullenness*) 901a; asperity etc., churlishness etc. (*discourtesy*) 895.

huff etc. (resentment) 900; a word and a blow.

Sir Fretful Plagiary; brabbler, Tartar; shrew, vixen, virago, termagant, dragon, scold, Xanthippe; porcupine; spit-fire; fire-eater etc. (*blusterer*) 887; fury etc. (*violent person*) 173.

V. be -irascible etc. *adj.*; have a -temper etc. *n.*, – devil in one; fire up etc. (*be angry*) 900.

Adj. irascible; bad-, ill-tempered; irritable, susceptible; excitable etc. 825; thin-skinned etc. (*sensitive*) 822; fretful, fidgety; on the fret.

hasty, over-hasty, quick, warm, hot, testy, touchy, techy, tetchy; like -touchwood, – tinder; huffy; pet-tish, -ulant; waspish, snapp-y, -ish, peppery, fiery, passionate, choleric, shrewish, 'sudden and quick in quarrel.'

querulous, captious, mood-y, -ish; quarrelsome, contentious, disputatious; pugnacious etc. (*bellicose*) 720; cantankerous, exceptious; restive etc. (*perverse*) 901a; churlish etc. (*discourteous*) 895.

cross, – as -crabs, – two sticks, – a cat, – a dog, – the tongs; like a bear with a sore head; fractious, peevish, *acariâtre*.

in a bad temper; sulky etc. 901a; angry etc. 900.

resent-ful, -ive; vindictive etc. 919.

Int. pish!

901a. Sullenness.—N. sullenness etc. *adj.*; morosity, spleen; churlishness etc. (*discourtesy*) 895; irascibility etc. 901.

moodiness etc. *adj.*; perversity; obstinacy etc. 606; torvity, spinosity; crabbedness etc. *adj.*

ill –, bad- -temper, – humor; sulks, dudgeon, mumps, doleful dumps, doldrums, fit of the sulks, *bouderie*, black looks, scowl; huff etc. (*resentment*) 900.

V. be -sullen etc. *adj.*; sulk; frown, scowl, lower, glower, grouse, grouch, crab, gloam, pout, have a hang-dog look, glout.

Adj. sullen, sulky; ill-tempered, -humored, - affected, -disposed; in -an ill, – a bad, – a shocking- -temper, – humor; out of -temper, – humor; knaggy, torvous, crusty, crabbed; sore as a boil; surly etc. (*discourteous*) 895.

moody; spleen-ish – -ly; splenetic, cankered.

cross, -grained; perverse, wayward, humorsome; restive; cantankerous, refractory, intractable, exceptious, sinistrous, deaf to reason, unaccommodating, rusty, crust, froward.

dogged etc. (*stubborn*) 606.

grumpy, glum, grim, grum, morose, frumpish; in the -sulks etc. *n.*; out of sorts; scowl-, glower-, growl-ing.

peevish etc. (*irascible*) 901.

902. Endearment. [Expression of affection or love.]—**N.** endearment, caress; blandish-, blandiment; *épanchement*, fondling, billing and cooing, dalliance.

embrace, salute; kiss, buss, smack, osculation,

deosculation; amorous glances; ogle, side glance, sheep's eyes.

courtship, wooing, suit, addresses, the soft impeachment; love-making; an affair; serenading; caterwauling.

flirting etc. *v.*; flirtation, gallantry; coquetry, spooning.

ture lover's knot, plighted love, engagement, bethrothal; love -tale, − token, − letter; *billet-doux*, valentine.

honeymoon; Strephon and Chloe, 'Arry and Arriet.

V. caress, fondle, pet, dandle, nurse; pat, − on the -head, − cheek; chuck under the chin, smile upon, coax, wheedle, cosset, coddle, cocker; make -of, − much of, pamper; cherish, foster, kill with kindness.

clasp, hug, cuddle; fold −, strain- in one's arms; nestle, nuzzle, neck, embrace, kiss, buss, smack, blow a kiss; salute etc. (*courtesy*) 894.

bill and coo, spoon, toy, dally, flirt, coquet; galli-, gala-vant; philander; make love; pay one's - court, − addresses, − attentions- to; serenade; court, woo; set one's cap at; be −, look- sweet upon; ogle, cast sheep's eyes upon; *faire les yeux doux*.

fall in love with, win the affections etc. (*love*) 897; die for.

propose; make −, have- an offer; pop the question; plight one's -troth, − faith; become - engaged, − betrothed.

Adj. caressing etc. *v.*; 'sighing like furnace;' love-sick, spoony.

carressed etc. *v.*

903. Marriage.—N. marriage, matrimony, wedlock, union, intermarriage, *vinculum matrimonii*, nuptial tie, knot.

married state, coverture, bed, cohabitation.

match; betrothment etc. (*promise*) 768; wedding, nuptials, Hymen, bridal; e-, spousals; leading to the altar etc. *v.*; nuptial benediction, *epithalamium*,

torch −, temple- of Hymen; hymeneal altar; honeymoon.

bride, bridegroom;. brides-maid; -man.

best −, grooms-man, page, usher.

married -man, − woman, − couple; neogamist, Benedick, partner, spouse, mate, yokemate; husband, man, consort, baron; old −, good- man; wife of one's bosom; help-meet, -mate, rib, better half, grey mare, old woman, good wife; feme, − coverte; squaw, lady; matron, -age, -hood; man and wife; wedded pair, Darby and Joan.

affinity, soul-mate.

mono-, bi-, di-, deutero-, tri-, poly-gamy; mormonism; poly-andry; Turk, Bluebeard.

unlawful −, left-handed −, companionate −, morganatic −, ill-assorted- marriage; *mésalliance*; *mariage de convenance*; an affair.

match-maker, marriage broker, matrimonial agent.

V. marry, wive, take to oneself -a wife; be - married, − spliced; go −, pair- off; wed, espouse, lead to the hymeneal altar, take 'for better, for worse,' give one's hand to, bestow one's hand upon; remarry; intermarry.

marry, join, handfast; couple etc. (*unite*) 43; tie

the nuptial knot; give -away, − in marriage; affy, affiance; betroth etc. (*promise*) 768; publish − bid- the banns; be asked in church.

Adj. married etc. *v.*; one, − bone and one flesh. marriageable, nubile.

engaged, betrothed, affianced.

matrimonial, marital, conjugal, connubial, wedded; nuptial, hymeneal, spousal, bridal.

Phr. the gray mare the better horse.

904. Celibacy.—N. celibacy, singleness, single blessedness; bachelor-hood, -ship; miso-gamy, -gyny.

virginity, *pueelage*; maiden-hood, -head.

, unmarried man, bachelor, agamist, old bachelor; miso-gamist, -gynist; celibate.

unmarried woman, spinster; maid, -en; virgin, *feme sole*, old maid; bachelor girl; nun etc.

V. live single; keep bachelor hall.

Adj. un-married, -wedded; wife-, spouse-less; single, virgin, celibate.

905. Divorce.—N. divorce, -ment; separation; judicial separation, separate maintenance; *separatio a -mensâ et thoro*, − *vinculo matrimonii*.

widowhood, viduage, viduity, weeds.

widow, -er; relict; dowager; *divorcée*; cuckold.

V. live -separately, − apart; separate, divorce, disespouse, put away; wear the horns.

906. Benevolence.—N. benevolence, Christian charity; God's -love, − grace; good-will; philanthropy etc. 910; unselfishness etc. 942.

good -nature, − feeling, − wishes; kind-, kindli ness etc. *adj.*; lovingkindness, benignity, brotherly love, charity, humanity, fellow-feeling, sympathy; goodness −, warmth- of heart; *bon-homie*; kindheartedness; amiability, milk of human kindness, tenderness; love etc. 897; friendship etc. 888.

toleration, consideration, generosity; mercy etc. (*pity*) 914.

charitableness etc. *adj.*; bounty, alms-giving; good works, beneficence, the luxury of doing good.

acts of kindness, a good turn; good −, kind- - offices, − treatment.

good Samaritan, sympathizer, well-wisher, philanthropist, *bon enfant*; altruist.

V. be -benevolent etc. *adj.*; have one's heart in the right place, bear good will; wish -well, − God speed; view − regard- with an eye of favor; take in good part; take −, feel- an interest in; be −, feel-interested- in; sympathize with, feel for; fraternize etc. (*be friendly*) 888.

enter into the feelings of others, do as you would be done by, meet halfway.

treat well; give comfort, smooth the bed of death; do -good, − a good turn; benefit etc. (*goodness*) 648; render a service, be of use; aid etc. 707.

Adj. benevolent; kind, -ly; wellmeaning; amiable; obliging, accommodating, indulgent, considerate, gracious, complacent, good-humored.

warm-, soft-, kind-, tender-, large-, broad-hearted; merciful etc. 914; philanthropic etc. 910; charitable, beneficent, humane, benign, benignant; bount-eous, -iful etc. 816.

good-, well-natured; spleenless; sympath-izing, -etic; complaisant etc. (*courteous*) 894; kindly, well-meant, -intentioned.

fatherly, motherly, brotherly, sisterly; pat-, mat-, frat-ernal; friendly etc. 888.

Adv. with -a good intention, – the best intentions.

Int. God speed! much good may it do!

907. Malevolence.—N. malevolence; bad intent, -ion; un-, dis-kindness; ill -nature, – will, – blood; bad blood; enmity etc. 889; hate etc. 898; malignity; malice, – aforethought, – prepense; maliciousness etc. *adj.*; spite, despite; resentment etc. 900.

uncharitableness etc. *adj.*; incompassionateness etc. 914*a*; gall, venom, rancor, rankling, virulence, mordacity, acerbity; churlishness etc. (*discourtesy*) 895.

hardness of heart, heart of stone, obduracy; cruelty; cruelness etc. *adj.*; brutality, savagery; ferity, -ocity; barbarity, inhumanity, immanity, truculence, ruffianism; evil eye, cloven -foot, – hoof; Inquisition; torture.

ill –, bad- turn; affront etc. (*disrespect*) 929; outrage, atrocity; ill usage; intolerance, bigotry, persecution; tender mercies [ironical]; 'unkindest cut of all.'

V. be -malevolent etc. *adj.*; bear –, harbor- -spleen, – a grudge, – malice; betray –, show- the cloven foot.

hurt etc. (*physical pain*) 378; annoy etc. 830; injure, harm, wrong; do -harm, – an ill office- to; outrage; disoblige, malign, plant a thorn in the breast.

molest, worry, harass, haunt, harry, bait, tease, throw stones at; play the devil with; hunt down, dragoon, hound; persecute, oppress, grind; maltreat; ill-treat, -use.

wreak one's malice on, do one's worst, break a butterfly on the wheel; dip –, imbrue- one's hands in blood; have no mercy etc. 914*a*.

Adj. male-, unbene-volent; unbenign; ill-disposed, -intentioned, -natured, -conditioned, -contrived; evil-minded, -disposed.

malicious; malign, -ant; rancorous; de-, spiteful; mordacious, caustic, bitter, envenomed, acrimonious, virulent; un-amiable, -charitable; maleficent, venomous, grinding, galling.

harsh, disobliging; un-kind, -friendly, -gracious; treacherous; inofficious; invidious; uncandid; churlish etc. (*uncourteous*) 895; surly, sullen etc. 901*a*.

cold, -blooded, -hearted; hard-, flint-, marble-, stony-hearted; hard of heart, unnatural; ruthless etc. (*unmerciful*) 914*a*; relentless etc. (*revengeful*) 919.

cruel; brut-al, -ish; savage, – as a -bear, – tiger; ferine, feral, ferocious; inhuman; barbarous, fell, untamed, tameless, truculent, incendiary; blood-thirsty etc. (*murderous*) 361; atrocious.

fiend-ish, -like; demoniacal; diabolic, -al; devilish, infernal, hellish, Satanic.

Adv. malevolently etc. *adj.*; with -bad intent etc. *n.*

908. Malediction.—N. malediction, malison, curse, imprecation, denunciation, execration,

anathema, ban, proscription, excommunication, commination, thunders of the Vatican, fulmination, *maranatha*, aspersion, vilification, vituperation, scurrility.

abuse; foul –, bad –, strong –, un-parliamentary- language, Limehouse; Billingsgate, sauce, evil speaking; cursing etc. *v.*; profane swearing, oath.

threat etc. 909; more bark than bite; invective etc. (*disapprobation*) 932.

V. curse, accurse, imprecate, damn, swear at; slang; curse with bell, book and candle; invoke –, call down- curses on the head of; devote to destruction.

execrate, beshrew, scold; anathematize etc. (*censure*) 932; hold up to execration, denounce, proscribe, excommunicate, fulminate, thunder against; threaten etc. 909; curse up hill and down dale.

curse and swear; swear, – like a trooper; fall a cursing, rap out an oath, damn, cuss.

Adj. curs-ing, -ed etc. *v.*; maledictory.

Int. woe to! beshrew! *ruat coelum!* ill –, woe-betide! confusion seize! damn! confound! blast! curse! devil take! hang! out with! a plague –, out-upon! aroynt! *honi soit!*

Phr. *delenda est Carthago.*

909. Threat.—N. threat, menace; defiance·etc. 715; abuse, minacity, intimidation; fulmination;-commination etc. (*curse*) 908; gathering clouds etc. (*warning*) 668.

V. threat, -en; menace; snarl, growl, gnarl, mutter, bark, bully.

defy etc. 715; intimidate etc. 860; keep –, hold up –, hold out- *in terrorem*; shake –, double –, clinch- the fist at; thunder, talk big, fulminate, use big words, bluster, look daggers.

Adj. threatening,, menacing; mina-tory, -cious; comminatory, abusive; *in terrorem*; ominous etc. (*predicting*) 511; defiant etc. 715; under the ban.

Int. *vae victis!* at your peril! do your worst!

910. Philanthropy.—N. philanthropy; altruism, humanit-y, -arianism; universal benevolence; *deliciae humani generis;* cosmopolitanism, utilitarianism, the greatest happiness of the greatest number, social science, sociology.

common weal, public welfare, socialism, communism.

patriotism, civism, nationality, love of country, *amor patriae*, public spirit.

chivalry, knight errantry; generosity etc. 942.

philanthropist, altruist etc. 906; utilitarian, Benthamite, socialist, communist, cosmopolite, citizen of the world, *amicus humani generis*; knight errant; patriot.

Adj. philanthropic, altruistic, humanitarian, utilitarian, cosmopolitan; public-spirited, patriotic; humane, large-hearted etc. (*benevolent*) 906; chival-ric, -rous, generous etc. 942.

Adv. pro -bono publico, – aris et focis.

Phr. *'humani nihil a me alienum puto.'*

911. Misanthropy.—N. misanthropy, incivism; egotism etc. (*selfishness*)· 943; moroseness etc. 901*a*; cynicism; defeatism.

misanthrope, misanthropist, egotist, cynic, man-hater, Timon, Diogenes.

woman-hater, misogynist.

Adj. misanthropic, antisocial, unpatriotic; egotistical etc. (*selfish*) 943; morose etc. 901*a*.

912. Benefactor.—N. benefactor, savior, good genius, tutelary saint, patron, guardian angel, fairy godmother, good Samaritan; *pater patriae*; salt of the earth etc. (*good man*) 948; auxiliary etc. 711.

913. Evil-doer.[*Maleficent being.*]**—N.** evil--doer, – worker; wrong doer etc. 949; mischief maker, marplot; oppressor, tyrant; firebrand, incendiary, pyromaniac, anarchist, destroyer, Hun, Boche, Vandal, iconoclast; communist; terrorist, apache, gunman, gangster, racketeer.

savage, brute, ruffian, barbarian, semi-barbarian, caitiff, desperado; Mo-hock, -hawk; bludgeon man, bully, rough, hooligan, larrikin, dangerous classes, ugly customer; thief etc. 792.

cockatrice, scorpion, hornet; viper, adder; snake, – in the grass; serpent, cobra, asp, rattlesnake, anaconda; canker-, wire-worm; locust, Colorado beetle; torpedo; bane etc. 663.

cannibal; Anthropophag-us, -ist; bloodsucker, vampire, ogre, ghoul, gorilla; vulture; gyr-, ger-falcon.

wild beast, tiger, hyaena, butcher, hangman; cut-throat etc. (*killer*) 361; blood-, sleuth-, hell-hound.

hag, hellhag, beldam, Jezebel.

monster; fiend etc. (*demon*) 980; homicidal maniac, devil incarnate, demon in human shape; Frankenstein's monster.

harpy, siren, vampire; Furies, Eumenides etc. 900.

Attila, scourge of the human race.

Phr. *foenum habet in cornu.*

914. Pity.—N. pity, compassion, commiseration; bowels; – of compassion; condolence etc. 915; sympathy, fellow-feeling, tenderness, yearning, forbearance, humanity, mercy, clemency, exorability; leniency etc. (*lenity*) 740; charity, ruth, long-suffering.

melting mood; *argumentum ad misericordiam*; quarter, grace, *locus poenitentiae.*

sympathizer, champion, partisan.

V. pity; have –, show –, take- pity etc. *n.*; commiserate, compassionate; condole etc. 915; sympathize; feel –, be sorry –, yearn- for; weep, melt, thaw, enter into the feelings of.

forbear, relent, relax, give quarter, wipe the tears, *parcere subjectis*, give a *coup de grâce*, put out of one's misery; be cruel to be kind.

raise –, excite- pity etc. *n.*; touch, soften; melt, – the heart; appeal to one's better feelings; propitiate, disarm.

ask for -mercy etc. *n.*; supplicate etc. (*request*) 765; cry for quarter, beg one's life, kneel, deprecate.

Adj. pitying etc. *v.*; pitiful, compassionate, sympathetic, touched.

merciful, clement, ruthful; humane; humanitarian etc. (*philanthropic*) 910; tender, –

hearted, – as a chicken; soft, – hearted; unhard-ened; lenient etc. 740; exorable, forbearing; melting etc. *v.*; weak.

Int. for pity's sake! mercy! have –, cry you-mercy! God help you! poor -thing, – dear, – fellow! woe betide! *quis talia fando temperet a lachrymis!*

Phr. one's heart bleeding for; *haud ignara mali miseris succurrere disco.*

914a. Pitilessness.—N. pitilessness etc. *adj.*; inclemency; inexorability, hardness of heart; inflexibility; severity etc. 739; malevolence etc. 907.

V. have no –, shut the gates of- mercy etc. 914; give no quarter.

Adj. piti-, merci-, ruth-, bowel-less; unpitying, unmerciful, inclement; in-, un-compassionate; inexorable, inflexible; harsh etc. 739; cruel etc. 907; unrelenting etc. 919.

915. Condolence.—N. condolence; lamentation etc. 839; sympathy, consolation.

V. condole with, console, sympathize etc. 914; share one's misery; feel for; express –, testify- pity; afford –, supply- consolation; lament etc. 839-with; send one's condolences.

916. Gratitude.—N. gratitude, thankfulness, gratefulness, feeling of obligation.

acknowledgement, recognition, thanksgiving, giving thanks.

thanks, praise, benediction; paean; *Te Deum* etc. (*worship*) 990; grace, – before, – after-meat; thank-offering.

requital.

V. be -grateful etc. *adj.*; thank; give –, render –, return –, offer –, tender- thanks etc. *n.*; acknowledge, requite.

feel –, be –, lie- under an obligation; *savoir gré*; not look a gift horse in the mouth; never forget, overflow with gratitude; thank –, bless-one's stars; fall on one's knees.

Adj. grateful, thankful, obliged, beholden, indebted to, under obligation.

Int. thanks! many thanks! gramercy! much obliged! thank you! thank Heaven! Heaven be praised!

917. Ingratitude.—N. ingratitude, thanklessness, oblivion of benefits; unthankfulness. 'benefits forgot;' thankless -task, – office.

V. be -ungrateful etc. *adj.*; forget benefits; look a gift horse in the mouth.

Adj. un-grateful, -mindful, -thankful; thankless, ingrate, wanting in gratitude, insensible of benefits forgotten; un-acknowledged, -thanked, requited, -rewarded; ill-requited.

Int. thank you for nothing! *'et tu Brute!'*

918. Forgiveness.—N. forgiveness, pardon, condonation, grace, remission, absolution, amnesty, oblivion; indulgence; reprieve.

conciliation; reconciliation etc. (*pacification*) 723; propitiation.

excuse, exoneration, quittance, release, indemnity; bill –, act –, covenant –, deed- of indemnity; exculpation etc. (*acquittal*) 970.

longanimity, placability, forbearance; *amantium irae*; *locus poenitentiae*.

V. forgive, – and forget; pardon, condone, think no more of, let bygones be bygones, shake hands; forget an injury, bury the hatchet; clean the slate.

excuse, pass over, overlook; wink at etc. (*neglect*) 460; bear with; allow –, make allowances- for; let one down easily, not be too hard upon, pocket the affront; blot out one's transgression.

let off, remit, absolve, give absolution, reprieve; acquit etc. 970.

beg –, ask –, implore- pardon etc. *n.*; conciliate, propitiate, placate; make up a quarrel etc. (*pacify*) 723; let the wound heal.

Adj. forgiving, placable, conciliatory.

forgiven etc. *v.*; un-resented, -avenged, revenged.

Adv. cry you mercy.

Phr. *veniam petimusque damusque vicissim*; more in sorrow than in anger.

919. Revenge.—N. revenge, -ment; vengeance; avenge-ment, -ance; sweet revenge, *vendetta*, death-feud, eye for an eye, blood for blood, a Roland for an Oliver; retaliation etc. 718; day of reckoning.

rancor, vindictiveness, implacability; malevolence etc. 907; ruthlessness etc. 914*a*.

avenger, vindicator, Nemesis, Eumenides.

V. re-, a-venge; take –, have one's- revenge; breathe -revenge, – vengeance; wreak one's -vengeance, – anger; give no quarter.

have -accounts to settle, – a crow to pluck, – a rod in pickle; pay off old scores.

keep the wound green; harbor -revenge, – vindictive feeling; bear malice; rankle, – in the breast; have at one's mercy.

Adj. revenge-, venge-ful; vindictive, rancorous, pitiless etc. 914*a*; ruthless, rigorous, avenging, retaliative.

unforgiving, unrelenting; inexorable, stony-hearted, implacable; relent-, remorse-less.

aeternum servans sub pectore vulnus; rankling, immitigable.

Phr. *manet -cicatrix,– altâ mente repostum*. revenge is sweet.

920. Jealousy.—N. jealous-y, -ness; jaundiced eye, heartburning; green-eyed monster; yellows; Juno.

V. be -jealous etc. *adj.*; view with -jealousy, – a jealous eye.

Adj. jealous, – as a Barbary pigeon; jaundiced, yellow-eyed, horn-mad.

921. Envy.—N. envy; enviousness etc. *adj.*; rivalry; *jalousie de métier*.

V. envy, covet, lust after, crave, burst with envy, regard with envious eyes.

Adj. envious, invidious, covetous; *alieni appetens*.

922. Right.—N. right; what -ought to, – should- be; fitness etc. *adj.*; *summum jus*.

justice, equity; equitableness etc. *adj.*; propriety; fair play, impartiality, measure for measure, give and take, *lex talionis*, square deal.

Astraea, Nemesis, Themis.

scales of justice, even-handed justice, retributive justice, *suum cuique*; clear stage –, fair field- and no favor; Queensberry rules.

morals etc. (*duty*) 926; law etc. 963; honor etc. (*probity*) 939; virtue etc. 944.

V. be -right etc. *adj.*; stand to reason.

see -justice done, – one righted, – fair play; do justice to; recompense etc. (*reward*) 973; hold the scales even, give and take; serve one right, put the saddle on the right horse; give -every one, – the devil- his due; *audire alteram partem*.

deserve etc. (*be entitled to*) 924.

Adj. right, good; just, reasonable; fit etc. 924; equi-al, -able, -itable; evenhanded, fair, – and square.

legitimate, justifiable, rightful; as it -should, – ought to- be; lawful etc. (*permitted*) 760, (*legal*) 963.

deserved etc. 924.

Adv. rightly etc. *adj.*; in -justice, – equity, – reason.

without -distinction of, – regard to, – respect to- persons; upon even terms.

Int. all right!

923. Wrong.—N. wrong; what -ought not to, – should not- be; *malum in se*; unreasonableness, grievance; shame.

injustice; unfairness etc. *adj.*; iniquity, foul play, partiality, leaning; favor, -itism; nepotism, party spirit, partisanship; undueness etc. 925; unlawfulness etc. 964.

robbing Peter to pay Paul etc. *v.*; the wolf and the lamb; vice etc. 945.

a custom more honored in the breach than the observance.

V. be -wrong etc. *adj.*; cry to heaven for vengeance.

do -wrong etc. *n.*; be -inequitable etc. *adj.*; favor, lean towards; encroach; impose upon; reap where one has not sown; give an inch and take an ell; rob Peter to pay Paul.

Adj. wrong, -ful; bad, too bad; unjust, -fair; in-, un-equitable; unequal, partial, one-sided.

objectionable; un-reasonable, -allowable, -warrantable, -justifiable; not cricket, not playing the game; improper, unfit; unjustified etc. 925; illegal etc. 964; iniquitous, criminal; immoral etc. 945; injurious etc. 649.

in the wrong, – box.

Adv. wrongly etc. *adj.*

Phr. it will not do; this is too bad.

924. Dueness.—N. due, -ness; right, privilege, prerogative, prescription, title, claim, pretension, demand, birthright.

immunity, license, liberty, franchise; vested - interest, – right; licitness.

sanction, authority, warranty, charter; warrant etc. (*permission*) 760; constitution etc. (*law*) 963; tenure; bond etc. (*security*) 771.

deserts, merits, dues.

claimant, appellant; plaintiff etc. 938.

V. be -due etc. *adj.* to, – the due etc. *n.* of; have -right, – title, – claim- to; be entitled to; have a claim upon; belong to etc. (*property*) 780.

deserve, merit, be worthy of, richly deserve.

demand, claim; call upon –, come upon –, appeal to- for; re-vendicate, -claim; exact; insist -on, – upon; challenge; take one's stand, make a point of, require, lay claim to, assert, assume, arrogate, make good; substantiate; vindicate a -claim, – right; make out a case.

give –, confer- a right; sanction, entitle; authorize etc. 760; sanctify, legalize, ordain, prescribe, allot.

give every one his due etc. 922; pay one's dues; have one's -due, – rights; stand upon one's rights.

use a right, assert, enforce, put in force, lay under contribution.

Adj. having a right to etc. *v.*; entitled to; claiming; deserving, meriting, worthy of.

privileged, allowed, sanctioned, warranted, authorized; ordained, prescribed, constitutional, chartered, enfranchised.

prescriptive, presumptive; absolute, indefeasible; un-, in-alienable.

imprescriptible, inviolable, unimpeachable, unchallenged; sacrosanct.

due to, merited, deserved, condign, richly deserved, *emeritus*.

allowable etc. (*permitted*) 760; lawful, licit, legitimate, legal; legalized etc. (*law*) 963.

square, unexceptionable, right; equitable etc. 922; due, *en règle*; fit, -ting; correct, proper, meet, befitting, becoming, seemly; decorous; creditable, up to the mark, right as a trivet; just –, quite- the thing; *selon les règles*.

Adv. duly, *ex officio*, *de jure*; by -right, – divine right; as is -fitting, – proper, – fitting and proper; *jure divino*, *Dei gratiâ*, in the name of.

Phr. *civis Romanus sum*.

925. Undueness. [Absence of right.]—**N.** undueness etc. *adj.*; *malum prohibitum*; impropriety; illegality etc. 964.

falseness etc. *adj.*; emptiness –, invalidity- of title; illegitimacy.

loss of right, disfranchisement, forfeiture.

usurpation, assumption, tort, violation, breach, encroachment, presumption, seizure, stretch, exaction, imposition, lion's share.

usurper, pretender, Carlist; imposter.

V. be -undue etc. *adj.*; not be -due etc. 924.

infringe, encroach, trench on, exact; arrogate, – to oneself; give an inch and take an ell; stretch –, strain- a point; usurp, violate, do violence to; sail under false colors.

dis-franchise, -entitle, -qualify; invalidate.

relax etc. (*be lax*) 738; misbehave etc. (*vice*) 945; misbecome.

Adj. undue; unlawful etc. (*illegal*) 964; unconstitutional, *ultra vires*; illicit; un-authorized, -warranted, -allowed, -sanctioned, -justified; un-, dis-entitled, -qualified; un-privileged, -chartered.

illegitimate, bastard, spurious, false; usurped, tortious.

un-deserved, -merited, -earned; unfulfilled, forfeited, disfranchised.

improper; un-meet, -fit, -befitting, -seemly; un-, mis-becoming; seemless; *contra bonos mores*; not the thing, out of the question, not to be thought of; preposterous, pretentious, would- be.

926. Duty.—**N.** duty, what ought to be done, moral obligation, accountableness, liability, *onus*, responsibility; bounden –, imperative- duty; call, – of duty.

allegiance, fealty, tie; engagement etc. (*promise*) 768; part; function, calling etc. (*business*) 625.

morality, morals, decalogue; case of conscience; conscientiousness etc. (*probity*) 939; conscience, inward monitor, still small voice within, sense of duty, tender conscience.

dueness etc. 924; propriety, fitness, seemliness, amenableness, decorum; the -thing, – proper thing; the -right, – proper- thing to do.

[Science of morals] eth-ics, -ology; deon-, aretology; moral –, ethical-philosophy; casuistry, polity.

observance, fulfilment, discharge, performance, acquittal, satisfaction, redemption; good behavior.

V. be -the duty of, – incumbent etc. *adj.* on, – responsible etc. *adj.*; behoove, become, befit, beseem; belong –, pertain- to; fall to one's lot; devolve on; lie -upon, – on one's head, – at one's door; rest -with, – on the shoulders of.

take upon oneself etc. (*promise*) 768.

be –, become- -bound to, – sponsor for; be responsible for; incur a -responsibility etc. *n.*; be –, stand –, lie- under an obligation; have to answer for, owe it to oneself.

impose a -duty etc. *n.*; enjoin, require, exact; bind, – over; saddle with, prescribe, assign, call upon, look to, oblige.

enter upon –, perform –, observe –, fulfil –, discharge –, adhere to –, acquit oneself of –, satisfy- -a duty, – an obligation; act one's part, redeem one's pledge, do justice to, be at one's post; do duty; do one's duty etc. (*be virtuous*) 944.

be on one's good behavior, mind one's P's and Q's.

Adj. obligatory, binding; imperative, peremptory; stringent etc. (*severe*) 739; behooving etc. *v.*; incumbent –, chargeable- on; under obligation; obliged –, bound –, tied- by; saddled with.

due –, beholden –, bound –, indebted- to; tied down; compromised etc. (*promised*) 768; in duty bound.

amenable, liable, accountable, responsible, answerable.

right, meet etc. (*due*) 924; moral, ethical, casuistical, conscientious, ethological.

Adv. with a safe conscience, as in duty bound, on one's own responsibility, at one's own risk, *suo periculo*; *in foro conscientiae*; *quamdiu se bene gesserit*; at one's post, on duty.

Phr. *dura lex sed lex*.

927. Dereliction of Duty.—**N.** dere; liction of duty; fault etc. (*guilt*) 947- sin etc. (*vice*) 945; non-observance, -performance, -co-operation; neglect, carelessness, laziness, incompetence, eye-service, relaxation, infraction, violation, transgression, failure, evasion, indolence; dead letter.

slacker, loafer, striker, non-co-operator.

V. violate; break, – through; infringe; set - aside, – at naught; trample -on, – under foot; slight, neglect, evade, renounce, forswear, repudiate; wash one's hands of; escape, transgress, fail.

call to account etc. (*disapprobation*) 932.

927a. Exemption.—N. exemption, freedom, irresponsibility, immunity, liberty, license, release, exoneration, excuse, dispensation, absolution, franchise, renunciation, discharge; exculpation etc. 970; *aegrotat.*

V. be -exempt etc. *adj.*

exempt, release, acquit, discharge, quit-claim, remise, remit; free, set at liberty, let off, pass over, spare, excuse, dispense with, give dispensation, license; stretch a point; absolve etc. (*forgive*) 918; exonerate etc. (*exculpate*) 970; save the necessity.

Adj. exempt, free, immune, at liberty, scot free; released etc. *v.*; unbound, unencumbered; irresponsible, unaccountable, not answerable; excusable.

928. Respect.—N. respect, regard, consideration; courtesy etc. 894; attention, deference, reverence, honor, esteem, estimation, veneration, admiration; approbation etc. 931.

homage, fealty, obeisance, genuflexion, kneeling, prostration; obsequiousness etc. 886; salaam, *kowtow*, bow, presenting arms, salute.

respects, regards, duty, *devoirs*, *égards.*

devotion etc. (*piety*) 987.

V. respect, regard; revere, -nce; hold in reverence, honor, venerate, hallow; esteem etc. (*approve of*) 931; think much of; entertain –, bear- respect for; have a high opinion of; look up to, defer to; pay -attention, – respect etc. *n.*- to; do –, render- honor to; do the honors, hail; show courtesy etc. 894; salute, present arms; do –, pay-homage to; pay tribute to; kneel to, bow to, bend the knee to; fall down before, prostrate oneself, kiss the hem of one's garment; worship etc. 990.

keep one's distance, make room, observe due decorum, stand upon ceremony.

command –, inspire- respect; awe, impose, overawe, dazzle.

Adj. respecting etc. *v.*; respectful, deferential, decorous, reverential, obsequious, ceremonious, bare-headed, cap in hand, on one's knees; prostrate etc. (*servile*) 886.

respected etc. *v.*; in high -esteem, – estimation; time-honored, venerable, *emeritus.*

Adv. in deference to; with -all, – due, – the highest- respect; with submission.

saving your -grace, – presence; *salva sit reverentia*; *pace tanti nominis.*

Int. hail! all hail! *esto perpetua!* may your shadow never be less!

929. Disrespect.—N. dis-respect, -esteem, - estimation, -favor, -repute; low estimation; disparagement etc. (*dispraise*) 932; (*detraction*) 934.

irreverence; slight, neglect; *spretae injuria formae*; superciliousness etc. (*contempt*) 930.

vilipendency, contumely, affront, dishonor, insult, indignity, outrage, discourtesy etc. 895; practical joking; scurrility, scoffing, sibilation; ir-, derision; mockery; irony etc. (*ridicule*) 856; sarcasm.

hiss, hoot, gibe, flout, jeer, scoff, gleek, taunt, sneer, quip, fling, wipe, slap in the face.

V. hold in disrespect etc. (*despise*) 930; misprize, disregard, slight, undervalue, depreciate, trifle with, set at naught, pass by, push aside, overlook, turn one's back upon, laugh in one's sleeve; be -disrespectful etc. *adj.*, – discourteous etc. 895; treat with -disrespect etc. *n.*; set down, browbeat.

dishonor, desecrate; insult, affront, outrage.

speak slightingly of; disparage etc. (*dispraise*) 932; vilipend, call names; throw –, fling- dirt; drag through the mud, point at, indulge in personalities; make -mouths, – faces; bite the thumb; take –, pluck- by the beard; toss in a blanket, tar and feather.

have –, hold- in derision; deride, scoff, sneer, laugh at, snigger, ridicule, gibe, mock, jeer, taunt, twit, niggle, gleek, gird, flout, fleer; roast, turn into ridicule; guy, burlesque etc. 856; laugh to scorn etc. (*contempt*) 930; smoke; fool; make -game, – a fool, – an April fool- of; play a practical joke; rag; lead one a dance, run the rig upon, have a fling at, scout, hiss, hoot, mob.

Adj. disrespectful; aweless, irreverent; disparaging etc. 934; insulting etc. *v.*; supercilious etc. (*scornful*) 930; rude, derisive, contemptuous, sarcastic; scurri-le, -lous; contumelious.

un-respected, -worshipped, -envied, -saluted; un-dis-regarded.

Adv. disrespectfully etc. *adj.*

930. Contempt.—N. contempt, disdain, scorn, sovereign contempt; despi-sal, -ciency; vilipendency, contumely; slight, sneer, spurn, by-word.

contemptuousness etc. *adj.*; scornful eye; smile of contempt; derision etc. (*disrespect*) 929.

[State of being despised] despisedness.

V. despise, contemn, scorn, disdain, feel contempt for, view with a scornful eye, disregard, slight, not mind; pass by etc. (*neglect*) 460.

look down upon; hold -cheap, – in contempt, – in disrespect; think -nothing, – small beer- of; make light of; underestimate etc. 483; esteem - slightly, – of small or no account; take no account of, care nothing for; set no store by; not care a -straw etc. (*unimportance*) 643; set at naught, laugh in one's sleeve, snap one's fingers at, shrug one's shoulders, turn up one's nose at, pooh-pooh, damn with faint praise; sneeze –, whistle –, sneer- at; curl up one's lip, toss the head, *traiter de haut*; laugh at etc. (*be disrespectful*) 929.

point the finger of –, hold up to –, laugh to-scorn; scout, hoot, flout, hiss, scoff at.

turn -one's back, – a cold shoulder- upon; tread –, trample- -upon, – under foot; spurn, kick; fling to the winds etc. (*repudiate*) 610; send away with a flea in the ear.

Adj. contemptuous; disdain-, scorn-ful; withering, contumelious, supercilious, cynical, haughty, bumptious, cavalier; derisive.

contemptible, despicable; pitiable; pitiful etc.
(*unimportant*) 643; despised etc. *v.*; down-
trodden; unenvied.

Adv. contemptuously etc. *adj.*

Int. a fig for etc. (*unimportant*) 643; bah! never
mind! away with! hang it! fiddle-de-dee!

931. Approbation.—N. approbation; approval, -ement; sanction, advocacy; nod of approbation;
esteem, estimation, good opinion, golden opinions,
admiration; love etc. 897; appreciation, regard, account, popularity, *kudos*, credit; repute etc. 873.

commendation, praise; laud, -ation; good word;
meed –, tribute- of praise; encomium; eulog-y, -
ium; *éloge*, panegyric; homage, hero worship;
benediction, blessing, benison.

applause, plaudit, clap; clapping, – of hands;
accl-aim, -amation; cheer; paean, hosannah; shout
–, peal –, chorus –, thunders- of -applause etc.
Kentish fire; Prytaneum; blurb.

V. approve; think -good, – much of, – well of,
– highly of; esteem, value, prize; set great store -
by, – on.

do justice to, appreciate; honor, hold in esteem,
look up to, admire; like etc. 897; be in favor of,
wish God speed; hail, – with satisfaction.

stand –, stick- up for; uphold, hold up, countenance, sanction; clap –, pat- on the back; keep
in countenance, endorse, give credit, recommend;
mark with a white -mark, – stone.

commend, praise; be-, laud; compliment, pay a
tribute, bepraise; clap, – the hands; applaud,
cheer, acclaim, acclamate, encore; panegyrize,
eulogize, cry up, *prôner*, puff; extol, – to the
skies; magnify, glorify, exalt, boost, swell, make
much of; flatter etc. 933; bless, give a blessing to;
have –, say- a good word for; speak -well, –
highly, – in high terms- of; sing –, sound –,
chaunt –, resound- the praises of; sing praises to;
cheer –, applaud- to the -echo, – very echo.

redound to the -honor, – praise, – credit- of;
do credit to; deserve -praise etc. *n.*; recommend itself; pass muster.

be -praised etc.; receive honorable mention; be
in -favor, – high favor- with; ring with the praises
of, win golden opinions, gain credit, find favor
with, stand well in the opinion of; *laudari a
laudato viro.*

Adj. approving etc. *v.*; in favor of; lost in admiration.

commendatory, complimentary, benedictory,
laudatory, panegyrical, eulogistic, encomiastic, ac-
clamatory, lavish of praise, uncritical.

approved, praised etc. *v.*; un-censured, -
impeached; popular, in good odor; in high esteem
etc. (*respected*) 928; in –, in high- favor.

deserving –, worthy of- praise etc. *n.*;
praiseworthy, commendable, of estimation; good
etc. 648; meritorious, estimable, creditable,
plausible, unimpeachable; beyond all praise.

Adv. commendably, with credit, to admiration;
well etc. 681; with three times three.

Int. hear, hear! well done! *brav-o!* -*a!* -*i!*
bravissimo! euge! macte virtute! so far so good,
that's right, quite right; *optime!* one cheer more;
may your shadow never be less! *esto perpetua!*
long life to! *viva! enviva!* God speed! *valete et
plaudite! encore! bis!*

Phr. *probatum est.*

932. Disapprobation.—N. disappro-bation, -
val; improbation; dis-esteem, -valuation, -
placency; odium; dislike etc. 867; dissent etc. 489.

dis-praise, -commendation; blame, censure,
obloquy; detraction etc. 934; disparagement,
depreciation; denunciation; condemnation etc.
971; ostracism; boycott; black-list, -ball; *index -
expurgatorius*, – *librorum prohibitorum.*

animadversion, reflection, stricture, objection,
exception, criticism; sardonic -grin, – laugh; sarcasm, insinuation, innuendo; bad –, poor –, left-
handed- compliment.

satire; sneer etc. (*contempt*) 930; taunt etc.
(*disrespect*) 929; cavil, carping, censoriousness;
hypercriticism etc. (*fastidiousness*) 868.

reprehension, remonstrance, expostulation,
reproof, reprobation, admonition, increpation,
reproach; rebuke, reprimand, castigation, jobation,
lecture, curtain lecture, blow up, wigging, dressing,
– down; rating, scolding, trimming; correction, set
down, rap on the knuckles, *coup de bec*, rebuff;
slap, – on the face; home thrust; hit; frown, scowl,
black look.

diatribe; jeremiad; *tirade*, philippic.

clamor, outcry, hue and cry; hiss, -ing; sibilation,
cat-call; execration etc. 908.

chiding, upbraiding etc. *v.*; exprobration, abuse,
vituperation, invective, objurgation, contumely,
personal remarks; hard –, cutting –, bitter-
words.

evil-speaking; bad language etc. 908; personality.

V. disapprove; dislike etc. 867; lament etc. 839;
object to, take exception to; be scandalized at,
think ill of; view with -disfavor, – dark eyes, –
jaundiced eyes; *nil admirari*, disvalue, improbate.

frown upon, look grave; bend –, knit- the
brows; shake the head at, shrug the shoulders; turn
up the nose etc. (*contempt*) 930; look -askance, –
black upon; look with an evil eye; make a wry -
face, – mouth- at; set one's face against.

dis-praise, -commend, -parage; deprecate, speak
ill of, not speak well of, slate, condemn etc. (*find
guilty*) 971.

blame; lay –, cast- blame upon; censure, *fron-
der*, reproach, pass censure on, reprobate, impugn.

remonstrate, expostulate, recriminate.

reprehend, chide, admonish; bring –, call- -to
account, – over the coals, – to order; take to
task, reprove, lecture, bring to book; read a -lesson,
– lecture- to; rebuke, correct.

reprimand, chastise, castigate, lash, blow up,
trounce, trim, *laver la tête*, overhaul; give it one,
– finely; gibbet.

accuse etc. 938; impeach, denounce; hold up to -
reprobation, – execration; expose, brand, gibbet,
stigmatize; show –, pull –, take- up; cry 'shame'
upon; be outspoken; raise a hue and cry against.

execrate etc. 908; exprobrate, speak daggers,
vituperate; abuse, –, like a pickpocket; scold, rate,
objurgate, upbraid, fall foul of; jaw; rail, – at, – in
good set terms; bark at; anathematize, call names;
call by -hard, – ugly- names; a-, re-vile; vili-fy, -
pend; bespatter; backbite; clapperclaw; rave –,
thunder –, fulminate- against; load with
reproaches; lash with the tongue.

exclaim –, protest –, inveigh –, declaim –,
cry out –, raise one's voice- against.

decry; cry –, run –, frown- down; clamor, hiss,

hoot, mob, ostracize; draw up –, sing- a round robin; black-ball, -list.

animadvert –, reflect- upon; glance at; cast -reflection, – reproach, – a slur- upon; insinuate, damn with faint praise; 'hint a fault and hesitate dislike;' not to be able to say much for.

scoff at, point at; twit, taunt etc. (*disrespect*) 929; sneer at etc. (*despise*) 230; satirize, lampoon; defame etc. (*detract*) 934; depreciate, find fault with, criticize, cut up; pull –, pick- to pieces; take exception; cavil; peck –, nibble –, carp- at; be -censorious etc. *adj.*; pick -holes, – a hole, – a hole in one's coat; make a fuss about.

take –, set- down; snub, snap one up, give a rap on the knuckles; throw a stone -at, – in one's garden; have a -fling, – snap- at; have words with, pluck a crow with; give one a -wipe, – lick with the rough side of the tongue.

incur blame, excite disapprobation, scandalize, shock, revolt; get a bad name, forfeit one's good opinion, be under a cloud, come under the ferule, bring a hornet's nest about one's ears.

take blame, stand corrected; have to answer for.

Adj. disapproving etc. *v.*; scandalized.

disparaging, condemnatory, damnatory, denunciatory, reproachful, abusive, objurgatory, clamorous, vituperative; defamatory etc. 934.

satirical, sarcastic, sardonic, cynical, dry, sharp, cutting, biting, severe, virulent, withering, trenchant, hard upon; censorious, critical, captious, carping, hypercritical; fastidious etc. 868; sparing of –, grudging- praise.

disapproved, chid etc. *v.*; in bad odor, blown upon, unapproved; unblest; at a discount, exploded; weighed in the balance and found wanting.

blameworthy, reprehensible etc. (*guilt*) 947; to –, worthy of- blame, answerable, uncommendable, exceptionable, not to be thought of, bad etc. 649; vicious etc. 945.

un-lamented, -bewailed, -pitied.

Adv. with a wry face; reproachfully etc. *adj.*

Int. it is too bad! it -won't, – will never- do! marry come up! Oh! come! 'sdeath!

forbid it Heaven! God –, Heaven- forbid! out –, fie- upon it! away with! tut! *O tempora! O mores!* shame! fie, – for shame! out on you!

tell it not in Gath! ·

933. Flattery.—N. flattery, adulation, gloze; bland-ishment, -iloquence; cajolery; fawning, wheedling etc. *v.*; captation, coquetry, sycophancy, obsequiousness, flunkeyism, toad-eating, tuft-hunting; snobbishness.

incense, honeyed words, flummery; bun-kum, -combe; blarney, *placebo*, butter; soft -soap, – sawder; rose water.

voice of the charmer, mouth honor; lip-homage; euphemism; unctuousness etc. *adj.*

V. flatter, praise to the skies, puff; wheedle, cajole, glaver, coax; fawn, –, upon; humor, gloze, soothe, pet, coquet, slaver, butter; be-spatter, -slubber, -plaster, -slaver; lay it on thick, overpraise; earwig, cog, collogue; truckle –, pander *or* pandar –, pay court- to; court; creep into the good graces of; curry favor with, hang on the sleeve of; fool to the top of one's bent; lick the dust.

lay the flattering unction to one's soul, gild the pill, make things pleasant.

overestimate etc. 482; exaggerate etc. 549.

Adj. flattering etc. *v.*; adulatory; mealy-, honey-mouthed; honeyed; smooth, – tongued; soapy, oily, unctuous, blandiloquent, specious; fine-, fairspoken; plausible, servile, sycophantic, fulsome; courtier-ly, -like.

Adv. ad captandum.

934. Detraction.—N. detraction, disparagement, depreciation, vilification, obloquy, scurrility, scandal, defamation, aspersion, traducement, slander, calumny, obtrectation, evil-speaking, backbiting, *scandalum magnatum*.

personality, libel, squib, lampoon, skit, pasquinade; *chronique scandaleuse*.

sarcasm, cynicism; criticism (*disapprobation*) 932; invective etc. 932; envenomed tongue; *spretae injuria formae*.

detractor etc. 936.

V. detract, derogate, decry, depreciate, disparage; run –, cry- down; minimize, make light of; belittle, sneer at etc. (*contemn*) 930; criticize, pull to pieces, pick a hole in one's coat, asperse, cast aspersions, blow upon, bespatter, blacken; vilify, -pend; avile; give a dog a bad name, brand, malign, backbite, libel, lampoon, traduce, slander, defame, calumniate, bear false witness against; speak ill of behind one's back.

'damn with faint praise, assent with civil leer; and without sneering, others teach to sneer.'

fling dirt etc. (*disrespect*) 929; anathematize etc. 932; dip the pen in gall, view in a bad light.

Adj. detracting etc. *v.*; defamatory, detractory, derogatory; disparaging, libellous; scurril-e, -ous; abusive; foul-spoken, -tongued, -mouthed; slanderous; calumni-ous, -atory; sar-castic, -donic; satirical, cynical.

935. Flatterer.—N. flatterer, adulator; eulogist, -phemist; optimist, encomiast, *laudator*, whitewasher, booster.

toad-y, -eater; sycophant, courtier, pickthank, Sir Pertinax MacSycophant; *flâneur*, *prôneur*; puffer, touter, *claqueur*; claw-back, ear-wig, doer of dirty work; parasite, hanger on etc. (*servility*) 886.

936. Detractor.—N. detractor, reprover; censor, -urer; cynic, critic, caviller, carper, word-catcher.

defamer, backbiter, slanderer, knocker, Sir Benjamin Backbite, lampooner, satirist, traducer, libeller, calumniator, dearest foe, dawplucker, Thersites; Zoilus; good-natured –, candid- friend [satirically]; reviler, vituperator, castigator; shrew etc. 901.

disapprover, *laudator temporis acti*.

937. Vindication.—N. vindication, justification, warrant; exoneration, exculpation; acquittal etc. 970; whitewashing.

extenuation; pallia-tion, -tive; softening, mitigation.

reply, defense; recrimination etc. 938.

apology, gloss, varnish; plea etc. 617; salvo; ex-

cuse, extenuating circumstances; allowance, – to be made; *locus poenitentiae.*
apologist, vindicator, justifier; defendant etc. 938.
justifiable charge, true bill.
V. justify, warrant; be an -excuse etc. *n.*- for; lend a color, furnish a handle; vindicate; ex-, disculpate; acquit etc. 970; clear, set right, exonerate, whitewash.
extenuate, palliate, excuse, soften, apologize, varnish, slur, gloze; put a -gloss, – good face-upon; mince; gloss over, bolster up, help a lame dog over a stile.
advocate. defend, plead one's cause; stand –, stick –, speak- up for; contend –, speak- for; bear out, keep in countenance, support; plead etc. 617; say in defense; plead ignorance; confess and avoid, propugn, put in a good word for.
take the will for the deed, make allowance for, do justice to; give -one, – the Devil- his due.
make good; prove -the truth of, – one's case; be justified by the event.
Adj. vindicat-ed, -ing etc. *v.*; vindicat-ive, -ory; palliative; exculpatory; apologetic.
excusable, defensible, pardonable; veni-al, -able; specious, plausible, justifiable.
Phr. *'honi soit qui mal y pense.'*

938. Accusation.—N. accusation, charge, imputation, slur, inculpation, exprobration, delation; crimination; in-, ac-, re-crimination; *tu quoque* argument; invective etc. 932.
de-nunciation, -nouncement; libel, challenge, citation, arraignment; im-, ap-peachment; indictment, bill of indictment, true bill; lawsuit etc. 969; condemnation etc. 971.
gravamen of a charge, head and front of one's offending, *argumentum ad hominem*; scandal etc. (*detraction*) 934; *scandalum magnatum.*
accuser, prosecutor, plaintiff, complainant, petitioner; relator, informer; appellant.
accused, defendant, prisoner, panel, co-, respondent; litigant.
V. accuse, charge, tax, impute, twit, taunt with, reproach.
brand with reproach; stigmatize, slur; cast a -stone at, – slur on; incriminate; inculpate, implicate; call to account etc. (*censure*) 932; take to-blame, – task; put in the black book.
inform against, indict, denounce, arraign; im-, ap-peach; have up, show up, pull up, challenge, cite, lodge a complaint; prosecute, bring an action against etc. 969.
charge –, saddle- with; lay to one's -door, – charge; lay the blame on, bring home to; cast –, throw- in one's teeth; cast the first stone at.
have –, keep- a rod in pickle for; have a crow to pluck with.
trump up a charge.
Adj. accusing etc. *v.*; accusat-ory, -ive; imputative, denunciatory; re-, criminatory.
accused etc. *v.*; suspected; under -suspicion, – a cloud, – *surveillance*; in -custody, – detention; in the -lock up, – watch house, – house of detention.
accusable, imputable; in-defensible, -excusable; un-pardonable, -justifiable; vicious etc. 945.
Int. look at home; *tu quoque* etc. (*retaliation*) 718.

939. Probity.—N. probity, integrity, rectitude; uprightness etc. *adj.*; honesty, faith; honor; good faith, *bona fides*; purity, clean hands.
fairness etc. *adj.*; fair play, justice, equity, impartiality. principle; grace.
constancy; faithfulness etc. *adj.*; fidelity, loyalty; incorrupt-ion, -ibility.
trustworthiness etc. *adj.*; truth, candor, singleness of heart; veracity etc. 543; tender conscience etc. (*sense of duty*) 926.
punctil-iousness, -io; delicacy, nicety; scrupulosity, -ousness etc. *adj.*; scruple; point, – of honor; punctuality.
dignity etc. (*repute*) 873; respectability, -bleness etc. *adj.*; gentleman; man of -honor, – his word; *fidus Achates, preux chevalier*; *galantuomo*; truepenny, trump, brick; true Briton, white man, sportsman.
court of honor, a fair field and no favor; *argumentum ad verecundiam.*
V. be -honorable etc. *adj.*; deal -honorably, – squarely, – impartially, – fairly; speak the truth etc. (*veracity*) 543; tell the truth and shame the devil, *vitam impendere vero*; show a proper spirit, make a point of; do one's duty etc. 944; play the game.
redeem one's pledge etc. 926; keep –, be as good as- one's -promise, – word; keep faith with, not fail.
give and take, *audire alteram partem*, give the devil his due, put the saddle on the right horse.
redound to one's honor.
Adj. upright; honest, – as daylight; veracious etc. 543; virtuous etc. 944; honorable; fair, right, just, equitable, impartial, even-handed, square; fair –, open- and aboveboard.
constant, – as the northern star; faithful, loyal, staunch; true, – blue, – to one's colors, – to the core, – as the needle to the pole; true-hearted, trust-y, -worthy; as good as one's word, to be depended on, incorruptible.
manly, straightforward etc. (*ingenuous*) 703; frank, candid, open-hearted.
conscientious, tender-conscienced, right-minded; high-principled, -minded; scrupulous, religious, strict; nice, punctilious, correct, punctual; respect-, reput-able; gentlemanlike.
inviol-able, -ate; un-violated, -broken, -betrayed; un-bought, -bribed.
innocent etc. 946; pure; stainless; un-stained, -tarnished, -sullied, -tainted, -perjured; uncorrupt, -ed; unde-filed, -praved, -bauched; *integer vitae scelerisque purus*; *justus et tenax propositi.*
chivalrous, jealous of honor, *sans peur et sans reproche*; high-spirited.
supra-mundane, unworldly, overscrupulous.
Adv. honorably etc. *adj.*; *bona fide*; on the square, in good faith, honor bright, *foro conscientiae*, with clean hands; by fair means.

940. Improbity.—N. improbity; dishon-esty, -our; deviation from rectitude; disgrace etc. (*disrepute*) 874; fraud etc. (*deception*) 545; lying etc. 544; bad –, Punic- faith; *mala* –, *Punica, fides*; infidelity; faithlessness etc. *adj.*; Judas kiss, betrayal; scrap of paper.
breach of -promise, – trust, – faith; prodition, disloyalty, divided allegiance, treason, high

treason; apostacy etc. (*tergiversation*) 607; non-observance etc. 773.

shabbiness etc. *adj.*; villainy; baseness etc. *adj.*; abjection, debasement, turpitude, moral turpitude, laxity, trimming, shuffling.

perfidy; perfidiousness etc. *adj.*; treachery, double-dealing; unfairness etc. *adj.*; knavery, roguery, rascality, foul-play; jobb-ing, -ery; Tammany, graft; venality, nepotism; corruption, job, shuffle, fishy transaction, barratry; sharp practice, heads I win, tails you lose; mouth-honor etc. (*flattery*) 933.

V. be -dishonest etc. *adj.*; play false; break one's -word, — faith, — promise; jilt, betray, forswear; shuffle etc. (*lie*) 544; live by one's wits, sail near the wind; play with marked cards.

disgrace —, dishonor —, demean —, degrade-oneself; derogate, stoop, grovel, sneak, lose caste; sell oneself, go over to the enemy; seal one's infamy.

Adj. dishon-est, -orable; un-conscientious, -scrupulous; fraudulent etc. 545; knavish; disgraceful etc. (*disreputable*) 874; wicked etc. 945.

false-hearted, disingenuous; unfair, one-sided; double, -tongued, -faced; time-serving, crooked, tortuous, insidious, Machiavellian, dark, slippery; questionable; fishy; perfidious, treacherous, perjured.

infamous, arrant, foul, base, vile, low, ignominious, blackguard:

contemptible, abject, mean, shabby, little, paltry, dirty, scurvy, scabby, sneaking, groveling, scrubby, rascally, pettifogging; beneath one; not cricket.

low-minded, -thoughted; base-minded.

undignified, indign; unbe-coming, -seeming, fitting; de-rogatory, -grading; *infra dignitatem*; ungentleman-ly, -like; un-knightly, -chivalric, -manly, -handsome; recreant, inglorious.

corrupt, venal; debased, mongrel.

faithless, of bad faith, false, unfaithful, disloyal; untrustworthy; trust-, troth-less; lost to shame, dead to honor.

Adv. dishonestly etc. *adj.*; *malâ fide*, like a thief in the night, by crooked paths; by foul means.

Int. *O tempora! O mores!*

941. Knave.—**N.** knave, rogue, villain; Seapin, rascal; Lazarillo de Tormes; bad man etc. 949; blackguard etc. 949.

traitor, betrayer, arch-traitor, conspirator, stool pigeon, Judas, Catiline; reptile, serpent, snake in the grass, wolf in sheep's clothing, sneak, Jerry Sneak, tell-tale, squealer, mischief-maker, trimmer; renegade etc. (*tergiversation*) 607; truant, recreant; sycophant etc. (*servility*) 886.

942. Disinterestedness.—**N.** disinterestedness etc. *adj.*; generosity; liberal-ity, -ism; altruism; benevolence etc. 906; elevation, loftiness of purpose, exaltation, magnanimity; chival-ry, -rous spirit; heroism, sublimity.

self-denial, -abnegation, -effacement, -sacrifice, -immolation, -control etc. (*resolution*) 604; stoicism, devotion, martyrdom, *suttee*.

labor of love.

V. be -disinterested etc. *adj.*; make a sacrifice, lay one's head on the block; put oneself in the place of others, do as one would be done by, do unto others as we would men should do unto us.

Adj. disinterested; unselfish; self-denying, -sacrificing, -devoted; generous.

handsome, liberal, noble; noble-, high-minded; princely, great, high, elevated, lofty, exalted, spirited, stoical, magnanimous; great-, large-hearted, chivalrous, heroic, sublime.

un-bought, -bribed; uncorrupted etc. (*upright*) 939.

943. Selfishness.—**N.** selfishness etc. *adj.*; self-love, -indulgence, -worship, -interest; ego-tism, -ism; egocentrism, narcissism; *amour propre* etc. (*vanity*) 880; nepotism.

worldliness etc. *adj.*; world wisdom.

illiberality; meanness etc. *adj.*

time-server; tuft-, fortune-hunter; self-seeker; jobber, worldling; egotist, egoist, monopolist, nepotist, profiteer; temporizer, trimmer; dog in the manger, charity that begins at home.

V. be -selfish etc. *adj.*; please —, indulge —, coddle- oneself; consult one's own -wishes, —pleasure; look after one's own interest; feather one's nest; take care of number one, have an eye to the main chance, know on which side one's bread is buttered; give an inch and take an ell; wangle.

Adj. selfish; self-seeking, -indulgent, -interested; wrapt up —, centered- in self; egotistic, -al; egoistical; egocentric.

illiberal, mean, ungenerous, narrowminded; mercenary, venal; covetous etc. 819.

unspiritual; earthly, -minded; mundane; worldly, -minded, -wise; time-serving.

interested; *alieni appetens sui profusus*.

Adv. ungenerously etc. *adj.*; to gain some private ends; from selfish —, interested- motives.

Phr. *après nous le déluge.*

944. Virtue.—**N.** virtue; virtuousness etc. *adj.*; morality; moral rectitude; integrity etc. (*probity*) 939; nobleness etc. 873.

morals; ethics etc. (*duty*) 926; cardinal virtues.

merit, worth, desert, excellence, credit; self-control etc. (*resolution*) 604; self-denial etc. (*temperance*) 953.

well-doing; good -actions, — behavior; discharge —, fulfilment —, performance- of duty; well spent life; innocence etc. 946.

V. be -virtuous etc. *adj.*; practice -virtue etc. *n.*; do —, fulfil —, perform —, discharge- one's duty; redeem one's pledge etc. 926; act well, — one's part; fight the good fight; acquit oneself well; command —, master- one's passions; keep -straight, — in the right path.

set -an, — a good- example; be on one's -good, — best- behavior.

Adj. virtuous, good; innocent etc. 946; meritorious, deserving, worthy, desertful, correct; dut-iful, -eous; moral; right, -eous, -minded; well-intentioned, creditable, laudable, commendable, praiseworthy; above —, beyond- all praise; excellent, admirable; sterling, pure, noble.

exemplary; match-, peer-less; saint-ly, -like; heaven-born, angelic, seraphic, godlike.

Adv. virtuously etc. *adj.*; *e merito.*

945. Vice.—N. vice; evil-doing. – courses;
wrong doing; wickedness, viciousness etc. *adj.*;
iniquity, peccability, demerit; sin, Adam; old – of-
fending- Adam.

immorality, impropriety, indecorum, scandal,
laxity, looseness of morals; want of -principle, –
ballast; obliquity, backsliding, infamy,
demoralization, pravity, depravity, pollution; hardness of heart; brutality etc. (*malevolence*) 907;
corruption etc. (*debasement*) 659; knavery etc.
(*improbity*) 940; profligacy; lust etc. 961;
flagrancy, atrocity; cannibalism.

infirmity; weakness etc. *adj.*; weakness of the
flesh, frailty, imperfection; error; weak side; foible;
fail-ing, -ure; crying – , besetting- sin; defect,
deficiency, shortcoming; cloven foot.

lowest dregs of vice, sink of iniquity, Alsatian
den; *gusto picaresco.*

fault, crime; criminality etc. (*guilt*) 947.

sinner etc. 949.

V. be -vicious etc. *adj.*; sin, commit sin, do
amiss, err, transgress; misdemean – , forget – ,
misconduct- oneself; mis-do, -behave; fall, lapse,
slip, trip, offend, trespass; deviate from the -line of
duty, – path of virtue etc. 944; take a wrong
course, go astray; hug a -sin, – fault; sow one's
wild oats.

render -vicious etc. *adj.*; demoralize, brutalize;
corrupt etc. (*degrade*) 659.

Adj.* vicious; sinful; sinning etc. *v.*; wicked,
iniquitous, bad, immoral, unrighteous, wrong,
criminal; naughty, incorrect; undut-eous, -iful.

unprincipled, lawless, disorderly, *contra bonos
mores*, indecorous, unseemly, improper; dissolute,
profligate, scampish; unworthy; worth-, desert-less;
disgraceful, recreant; reprehensible, blameworthy,
uncommendable; dis-creditable, -reputable.

base, sinister, scurvy, foul, gross, vile, black,
grave, facinorous, felonious, nefarious, shameful,
scandalous, infamous, villainous, of a deep dye,
heinous, flag-rant, -itious; atrocious, incarnate, accursed.

Mephistophelian, satanic, diabolic, hellish, infernal, stygian, fiend-ish, -like, hell-born,
demoniacal, devilish.

mis-created, -begotten; demoralized, corrupt,
depraved.

evil-minded, -disposed; ill-conditioned;
malevolent etc. 907; heart-, grace-, shame-, virtue-
less; abandoned, lost to virtue; unconscionable;
sunk – , lost – , deep – , steeped- in iniquity.

incorrigible, irreclaimable, obdurate, reprobate,
past praying for; culpable, reprehensible etc.
(*guilty*) 947.

unjustifiable; in-defensible, -excusable; inexpiable, unpardonable, irremissible.

weak, frail, lax, infirm, imperfect, indiscreet;
demoralizing, degrading.

Adv. wrong; sinfully etc. *adj.*; without excuse.

Int. *O tempora! O mores!*

*Most of these adjectives are applicable both to the act and
to the agent.

946. Innocence.—N. innocence; guiltlessness
etc. *adj.*; incorruption, impeccability.

clean hands, clear conscience, *mens sibi conscia
recti.*

innocent, new born babe, lamb, dove.

V. be -innocent etc. *adj.*; *nil conscire sibi nullâ
pallescere culpâ.*

acquit etc. 970; exculpate etc. (*vindicate*) 937.

Adj. innocent, not guilty, unguilty; guilt-, fault-,
sin-, stain-, blood-, spot-less; clear, immaculate;
rectus in curiâ; un-spotted, -blemished, -erring; undefiled etc. 939; unhardened, Saturnian; Arcadian
etc. (*artless*) 703.

in-, un-culpable; unblam-ed, -able; blameless,
inerrable, above suspicion; irrepr-oachable, -
ovable, -ehensible; un-exceptionable, -
objectionable, -impeachable; salvable; venial etc.
937.

harmless; in-offensive, -noxious, -nocuous; dove-
, lamb-like; pure, harmless as doves; innocent as -a
lamb, – the babe unborn; more sinned against
than sinning.

virtuous etc. 944; un-reproved, -impeached, -
reproached.

Adv. innocently etc. *adj.*; with clean hands; with
a -clear, – safe- conscience.

947. Guilt.—N. guilt, -iness; culpability;
crimin-ality, -ousness; deviation from rectitude etc.
(*improbity*) 940; sinfulness etc. (*vice*) 945; peccability.

mis-conduct, -behavior, -doing, -deed; malprac-
tice, fault, sin, error, transgression; dereliction,
delinquency; indiscretion, lapse, slip, trip, *faux
pas, peccadillo*; flaw, blot, omission; fail-ing, -ure.

offence, trespass; mis-demeanor, -feasance, -
prision, tort; mal-efaction, -feasance, -versation;
crime, felony.

enormity, atrocity, outrage; deadly – , mortal
– , unpardonable- sin; died without a name.

corpus delicti.

Adj. guilty, to blame, culpable, peccable, in
fault, censurable, reprehensible, blameworthy, uncommendable, illaudable; weighed in the balance
and found wanting; exceptionable, objectionable.

Adv. *in flagrante delicto*; red-handed, in the
very act.

948. Good Man.—N. good man, worthy.

good woman, goddess, *madonna*, virgin.

model, paragon etc. (*perfection*) 650; good
example; hero, demigod, seraph, angel; innocent
etc. 946; saint etc. (*piety*) 987; benefactor etc. 912;
philanthropist etc. 910; Aristides.

brick, trump, rough diamond, ugly duckling.

salt of the earth; one in ten thousand; one of the
best.

Phr. *si sic omnes!*

949. Bad Man.—N. bad man, wrongdoer,
worker of iniquity; evil-doer etc. 913; sinner; the -
wicked etc. 945; bad example.

rascal, scoundrel, villain, miscreant, caitiff;
wretch, reptile, viper, serpent, cockatrice, basilisk,
urchin; tiger, monster; devil etc. (*demon*) 980;
devil incarnate; demon in human shape, Nana
Sahib; hell-hound, -cat; rake-hell.

bad woman, jade, Jezebel, adultress, etc. 962.

scamp, scapegrace, rip, runagate, ne'er-do-well,
reprobate, *roué*, rake; limb; one who has sold him-

self to the devil, fallen angel, *âme damnée*, *vaurien*, *mauvais sujet*, loose fish, sad, dog; lost −, black-sheep; castaway, recreant, defaulter; prodigal etc. 818; libertine etc. 962.

rough, rowdy, ugly customer, ruffian, hoodlum, bully; Jonathan Wild; hangman; incendiary; thief etc. 792; murderer etc. 361.

culprit, delinquent, criminal, melefactor, misdemeanant; felon; convict, jail-bird, ticket-of-leave man; outlaw.

blackguard, *polisson*, loafer, sneak; raps-, rascallion; cullion, mean wretch, varlet, kern, *âme-de-boue*, *drôle*; cur, dog, hound, whelp, mongrel; lown, loon, runnion, outcast, vagabond; rogue etc. (*knave*) 941; scum of the earth, riff-raff; *Arcades ambo*.

Int. sirrah!

950. Penitence.—N. penitence, contrition, compunction, repentance, remorse; regret etc. 833.

self-reproach, -reproof, -accusation, -condemnation, -humiliation; stings −, pangs −, qualms −, prickings −, twinge −, twitch −, touch −, voice- of conscience; compunctious visitings of nature.

acknowledgment, confession etc. (*disclosure*) 529; apology etc. 952; recantation etc. 607; penance etc. 952; resipiscence.

awakened conscience, deathbed repentance, *locus poenitentiae*, stool of repentance, cutty stool.

penitent, Magdalen, prodigal son, returned prodigal, a sadder and wiser man.

V. repent, be sorry for; be -penitent etc. *adj.*; rue; regret etc. 833; think better of; recant etc. 607; knock under etc. (*submit*) 725; plead guilty; sing -*miserere*, − *de profundis*; cry *peccavi*; own oneself in the wrong; acknowledge, confess etc. (*disclose*) 529; humble oneself; beg pardon etc. (*apologize*) 952; turn over a new leaf, put on the new man, turn from sin; reclaim; repent in sackcloth and ashes etc. (*do penance*) 952; learn by experience.

Adj. penitent; repenting etc. *v.*; repentant, contrite; conscience-smitten, -stricken; self-accusing, -convicted.

penitenti-al, -ary; chastened, reclaimed; not hardened; un-hardened.

Adv. *meâ culpâ*.

Phr. *peccavi*; *erubuit*; *salva res est*; *vous l'avez voulu, Georges Dandin*.

951. Impenitence.—N. impenitence, irrepentance, recusance.

hardness of heart, seared conscience, induration, obduracy.

V. be -impenitent etc. *adj.*; steel −, harden- the heart; die -game, − and make no sign.

Adj. impenitent uncontrite, obdurate; hard, -ened; seared, recusant; unrepentant; relent-, remorse-, grace-, shrift-less.

lost, incorrigible, irreclaimable.

unre-claimed, -formed; unrepented, unatoned.

952. Atonement.—N. atonement, reparation; compromise, composition; compensation etc. 30; quittance, quits; indemni-ty, -fication; expiation,

redemption, reclamation, conciliation, propitiation.

amends, apology, *amende honorable*, satisfaction; peace −, sin −, burnt- offering; scapegoat, sacrifice.

penance, fasting, maceration, sackcloth and ashes, white sheet, shrift, flagellation, lustration; purga-tion, -tory.

V. atone, − for; expiate; propitiate; make -amends, − good; reclaim, redeem, repair, ransom, absolve, purge, shrive, do penance, stand in a white sheet, repent in sackcloth and ashes.

set one's house in order, wipe off old scores, make matters up; pay the -forfeit, − penalty.

apologize, beg pardon, express regret, *faire amende honorable*, give satisfaction; come −, fall-down on one's -knees, − marrow bones.

Adj. propitiatory, expiatory; sacrific, -ial, -atory; piacul-ar, -ous. .

953. Temperance.—N. temperance, moderation, sobriety, soberness.

forbearance, abnegation; self-denial, -restraint, -control etc. (*resolution*) 604.

frugality; vegetarianism, teetotalism, total abstinence, prohibition; abst-inence, -emiousness, asceticism etc. 955; system of -Pythagoras, − Cornaro; Pythagorism, Stoicism.

vegetarian; Pythagorean, gymnosophist; teetotaler etc. 958; abstainer.

V. be -temperate etc. *adj.*; abstain, forbear, refrain, deny oneself, spare; know when one has had enough; take the pledge; look not upon the wine when it is red.

Adj. temperate, moderate, sober, frugal, sparing; abst-emious, -inent; within compass; measured etc. (*sufficient*) 639.

Pythagorean; vegetarian; teetotal, pussy-foot.

954. Intemperance.—N. intemperance; sensuality, animalism, carnality; pleasure; effeminacy, silkiness; luxur-y, -iousness; lap of -pleasure, − luxury.

indulgence; high-, free- living, in-abstinence, self-indulgence; voluptuousness etc. *adj.*; epicurism, -eanism; sybaritism.

dissipation; licentiousness etc. *adj.*; debauchery; crapulence.

revel-s, -ry; debauch, carousal, jollification, drinking bout, wassail, Saturnalia, orgies; excess, too much; intoxication etc. 959.

Circean cup; drug habit etc. 663.

V. be -intemperate etc. *adj.*; indulge, exceed; live -well, − high, − on the fat of the land; give a loose to -indulgence etc. *n.*; dine not wisely but too well; wallow in -voluptuousness etc. *n.*; plunge into dissipation.

revel, rake, live hard, run riot, sow one's wild oats; slake one's -appetite, − thirst; swill; pamper.

Adj. intemperate, inabstinent, intoxicated etc. 958; sensual, self-indulgent; voluptuous, luxurious, licentious, wild, dissolute, rakish, fast, debauched.

brutish, crapulous, swinish, piggish, hoggish, bestial.

Paphian, Epicurean, Sybaritical; bred −, nursed- in the lap of luxury; indulged, pampered, full-fed.

954a. Sensualist.—N. Sybarite, voluptuary, Sardanapalus, man of pleasure, carpet knight; epicure, -an; *gourm-et, -and;* gormandizer, gutling, glutton, pig, hog; votary – , swine- of Epicurus; sensualist; Heliogabalus; free – , hard- liver; libertine etc. 962; hedonist.

955. Asceticism.—N. asceticism, puritanism, sabbatarianism; cynicism, austerity; total abstinence.

mortification, maceration, sackcloth and ashes, flagellation; penance etc. 952; fasting etc. 956; martyrdom.

ascetic; anchor-et, -ite; martyr; *Heautontimorumenos*; hermit etc. (*recluse*) 893; puritan, sabbatarian, cynic.

Adj. ascetic, austere, puritanical; cynical; over-religious.

956. Fasting.—N. fasting; exrophagy; famishment, starvation; banting.

fast, *jour maigre*; fast .– , banyan-day; Lent, quadragesima; Rama-dan, -zan; spare – , meager-diet; lenten -diet, – entertainment; *soupe maigre,* short -rations, – commons; Barmecide feast; hunger strike.

V. fast, starve, clem, famish, perish with hunger; dine with Duke Humphrey; make two bites of a cherry.

Adj. lenten, quadragesimal; unfed; starved etc. *v.*; half-starved; fasting etc. *v.*; hungry etc. 865.

957. Gluttony.—N. gluttony; greed; greediness etc. *adj.*; voracity.

epicurism; good – , high- living; edacity, gulosity, crapulence; gutt-, guzz-ling; over-indulgence.

good cheer, blow out; feast etc. (*food*) 298; gastronomy.

epicure, *bon vivant, gourmand*; glutton, cormorant, hog, belly-god, Apicius, gastronome, gormandizer.

V. gormandize, gorge; over-gorge, -eat- oneself; engorge, eat one's fill, cram, stuff, stodge, glut, satiate; gutt-le, guzz-le; bolt, devour, gobble up; gulp etc. (*swallow food*) 298; raven, eat out of house and home.

have the stomach of an ostrich; play a good knife and fork etc. (*appetite*) 865.

Adj. gluttonous, greedy; gormandizing etc. *v.*; edacious, omnivorous, crapulent, swinish, voracious, devouring.

pampered; over-fed, -gorged.

958. Sobriety.—N. sobriety; teetotalism, temperance etc. 953.

water-drinker; teetotal-er, -ist; abstainer, Good Templar, Rechabite, band of hope; prohibitionist, pussyfoot.

V. take the pledge.

Adj. sober, – as a judge; dry, on the water wagon.

959. Drunkenness.—N. drunkenness etc. *adj.*; intemperance; drinking etc. *v.*; inebri-ety, -ation; ebri-ety, -osity; befuddlement; insobriety; intoxication; temulency, bibacity, wine-bibbing; compotation; deep potations, bacchanals, *bacchanalia,* libations.

oino-, dipso-mania; *delirium tremens*, d.t., alcohol, -ism.

drink; alcoholic drinks, alcohol, booze; gin, blue ruin, grog, brandy, port wine; punch, -bowl; cup, rosy wine, flowing bowl; drop, – too much; dram; beer, wine, spirits etc. (*beverage*) 298; cocktail, nip, peg; stirrup cup.

drunkard, sot, toper, tippler, bibber, wine-bibber; hard – , gin – , dram- drinker; soak, soaker, sponge, tun; love-, toss-pot; thirsty soul, reveller, carouser; Bacchanal, -ian; Bacch-al, -ante; devotee to Bacchus, dipsomaniac.

V. get – , be- drunk etc. *adj.*; see double; take a -drop, – glass- too much; drink, tipple, tope, booze, bouse, guzzle, swill, soak, sot, lush, bib, swig, carouse; sacrifice at the shrine of Bacchus; take to drinking; drink -hard, – deep, – like a fish; have one's swill, drain the cup, splice the main brace, take a hair of the dog that bit you.

liquor, – up; wet one's whistle, take a whet; lift one's elbow; crack a – , pass the- bottle; toss of etc. (*drink up*) 298; go to the -ale, – public house.

make one-drunk etc. *adj.*; inebriate, fuddle, fuzzle, get into one's head.

Adj. drunk, tipsy; intoxicated; inebri-ous, -ate, -ated; in one's cups; in a state of -intoxication etc. *n.*; temulent, -ive; fuddled, mellow, cut, boosy, fou, fresh, merry, elevated, squiffy; plastered, befuddled; sozzled; flush, -ed; flustered, disguised, groggy, beery, topheavy; potvaliant, glorious; potulent; over-come, -taken; whittled, screwed, tight, primed, oiled, corned, raddled, sewed up, lushy, nappy, muddled, muzzy, bosky, obfuscated, maudlin; crapulous, dead – , blind- drunk.

inter pocula; in – , the worse for- liquor, having had a drop too much, half seas over, three sheets in the wind; under the table, blind to the world, one over the eight.

drunk as -a piper, – a fiddler, – a lord, – Chloe, – an owl, – David's sow, – a wheelbarrow.

drunken, bibacious, bibulous, sottish; given – , addicted- to -drink, – the bottle; toping etc. *v.*; wet.

Phr. *nunc est bibendum.*

960. Purity.—N. purity; decency, decorum, delicacy; continence, chastity, honesty, virtue, modesty, shame; pudicity, *pucelage*, virginity.

vestal, virgin, Joseph, Hippolytus; Lucretia, Diana; prude.

Adj. pure, undefiled, modest, delicate, decent, decorous; *virginibus puerisque*; chaste, continent, virtuous, honest, Platonic.

961. Impurity.—N. impurity; uncleanness etc. (*filth*) 653; immodesty; grossness etc. *adj.*; indelicacy, indecency; impudicity; obscenity, ribaldry, smut, bawdry, *double entendre, équivoque*; Aretinism; pornography.

concupiscence, lust, carnality, flesh, salacity; pruriency, lechery, lasciviency, lubricity, lewdness.

incontinence, intrigue, *faux pas*; *amour*, *-ette*; gallantry; dabauchery. libertinism, *libertinage*, fornication; *liaison*; wenching, venery, dissipation.

seduction; defloration, defilement, abuse, violation, rape; incest.

social evil, harlotry, stupration, whoredom, concubinage, cuckoldom, adultery, advoutry, *crim. con.*; free love.

seraglio, harem, zenana; brothel, bagnio, stew, bawdy-house, *lupanar*, house of ill fame, *bordel*, kip.

V. be -impure etc. *adj.*; intrigue; debauch, defile, assault, attack, seduce; prostitute; abuse, violate, deflower; commit -adultery etc. *n.*

Adj. impure; unclean etc. (*dirty*) 653; not to be mentioned to ears polite; immodest, shameless; indecorous, -delicate, -decent; loose, suggestive. *risqué*, coarse, gross, broad, free, equivocal, smutty, fulsome, ribald, obscene, bawdy, pornographic.

concupiscent, prurient, lickerish, rampant, lustful; carnal, -minded; lewd, lascivious, lecherous, libidinous, erotic, ruttish, salacious; Paphian, voluptuous; incestuous.

· unchaste, light, wanton, licentious, adulterous, debauched, dissolute; of -loose character, – easy virtue; frail, gay, riggish, incontinent, meretricious, rakish, gallant, dissipated; no better than she should be; on the -town, – streets, – *pavé*, – loose.

adulterous, incestuous, bestial.

962. Libertine.—N. libertine; voluptuary etc. 954*a*; rake, debauchee, loose fish, rip, rake-hell, fast man; *intrigant*, gallant, seducer, fornicator, lecher, satyr, goat, whoremonger, *paillard*, adulterer, gay deceiver, Lothario, Don Juan, Bluebeard.

adulteress, advoutress, courtesan, prostitute, strumpet, tart, hustler, chippy, broad, harlot, whore, punk, *fille de joie*; woman, – of the town; street-walker, Cyprian, miss, piece; frail sisterhood, fallen woman; demirep, wench, trollop, trull, baggage, hussy, drab, bitch, jade, skit, rig, quean, mopsy, slut, minx, harridan; woman -of easy virtue etc. (*unchaste*) 961; wanton, fornicatress; Jezebel, Messalina, Delilah, Thaïs, Phryne, Aspasia, Lais, *lorette*, *cocotte*, *petite dame*, *grisette*; *demi-monde*; white slave.

concubine, mistress, fancy woman, kept woman, doxy, *chère amie*, *bona roba*.

pimp; pand-er, -ar; bawd, *conciliatrix*, procuress, mackerel; wittol.

963. Legality.—N. legality; legitima-cy, teness, legitimization.

legislature; law, code, *corpus juris*, constitution, pandect, charter, act, enactment, statute, rule; canon etc. (*precept*) 697; ordinance, institution, regulation; by-, bye-law, rescript; decree etc. (*order*) 741; *ordonnance*; standing order; *plébiscite* etc. (*choice*) 609.

legal process; form, -ula, -ality; rite; arm of the law; *habeas corpus*.

[Science of law] jurisprudence, nomology; legislation, codification.

equity, common law; *lex* –, *lex nonscripta*, unwritten law; law of nations, international law, *jus gentium*; *jus civile*; civil –, criminal –, canon –, statute –, ecclesiastical- law; *lex mercatoria*. constitutional-ism, -ity; justice etc. 922.

V. legalize, legitimize; enact, ordain; decree etc. (*order*) 741; pass a law; legislate; codify, formulate; authorize.

Adj. legal, legitimate; according to law; vested, constitutional, chartered, legalized; lawful etc. (*permitted*) 760; statut-able, -ory; legislat-orial, -ive.

Adv. legally etc. *adj.*; in the eye of the law; *de jure*.

964. Illegality. [Absence or violation of law.]—**N.** lawlessness; breach –, violation- of law; disobedience etc. 742; unconformity etc. 83.

arbitrariness etc. *adj.*; antinomy, violence, brute force, despotism, outlawry.

mob –, lynch –, club –, Lydford –, martial –, drumhead- law; *coup d'état*; *le droit du plus fort*; *argumentum baculinum*.

illegality, informality, unlawfulness, illegitimacy, bar sinister.

trover and conversion; smuggling, boot-legging, rum-running, poaching; simony.

speakeasy, speakie, blind pig.

V. offend against –, violate- the law; set the law at defiance, ride rough-shod over, drive a coach and six through a statute; make the law a dead letter, take the law into one's own hands.

smuggle, run, poach.

Adj. illegal; prohibited etc. 761; not allowed, unlawful, illegitimate, illicit, contraband, actionable.

unchartered, unconstitutional; unwarrant-ed, -able; unauthorized; informal, unofficial; in-, extra-judicial.

lawless, arbitrary; despotic, -al; summary, irresponsible; un-answerable, -accountable.

null and void; a dead letter.

Adv. illegally etc. *adj.*; with a high hand, in violation of law.

965. Jurisdiction. [Executive.]—**N.** jurisdiction, judicature, administration of justice, soc; executive, commission of the peace; magistracy etc. (*authority*) 737.

judge etc. 967; tribunal etc. 966; municipality, corporation, bailiwick, shrievalty; lord lieutenant; lord –, mayor, city manager, alderman etc. 745; sheriff, bailie, shrieve, chief –, constable; police, – force; constabulary, bumbledom.

officer; proctor, high –, commissioner; bailiff, tipstaff, bum-bailiff, catchpoll, beadle; police-man, -constable, -sergeant; *sbirro*, *alguazil*, *gendarme*, kavass, *lictor*, macebearer, *huissier*, bedel.

press-gang; exciseman, gauger; custom-house officer, *douanier*.

coroner, edile, aedile, portreeve, paritor; *posse comitatus*.

V. judge, sit in judgment.

Adj. executive, administrative, municipal;

inquisitorial, causidical; judic-atory, -iary, -ial; juridical.

Adv. *coram judice.*

---

966. Tribunal.—N. tribunal, court, board, bench, judicatory, curia; court of -justice, – law, – arbitration; inquisition; guild.

justice –, judgment –, mercy- seat; woolsack; bar, – of justice; dock; forum, hustings, *bureau*, drum-head; jury-, witness-box.

senate-house, town-hall, theater; House of - Lords, – Commons.

assize, eyre; ward-, burgh-mote; superior courts of Westminister; court of -record, – oyer and terminer, – assize, – appeal – error; High court of -Judicature, – Appeal; Judicial Committee of the Privy Council; Star-Chamber; Court of -Chancery, – King's *or* Queen's Bench, – Exchequer, – Common Pleas, – Probate, – Arches, – Admiralty, – Criminal Appeal; Lords Justices' –, Rolls –, Vice Chancellor's –, Stannary –, Divorce –, Palatine –, ecclesiastical –, county –, police- court; sessions; quarter –, pettysessions; court -leet, – baron, – of pie poudre, – of common council; board of green cloth.

court-martial; drum-head court-martial; *durbar*, divan; Areopagus; *rota.*

Adj. judicial etc. 965; appellate; curial.

---

967. Judge.—N. judge; justi-ce, -ciar, -ciary; chancellor; justice –, judge- of assize; recorder, common serjeant; puisne –, assistant –, county court- judge; conservator –, justice- of the peace, J.P.; court etc. (*tribunal*) 966; grand –, petty –, coroner's- jury; panel, juror, juryman; twelve men in a box; magistrate, police magistrate, stipendiary, the great unpaid, beak; his -worship, – honor, – lordship; deemster, moderator.

Lord -Chancellor, – Justice; Master of the Rolls, Vice-Chancellor; Lord Chief -Justice, – Baron; Mr. Justice; Baron, – of the Exchequer.

jurat, assessor; arbi-ter, -trator; umpire; refer-ee, -endary; revising barrister; domesman; censor etc. (*critic*) 480; official –, receiver.

archon, tribune, praetor, *ephor*, syndic, *podestà*, mullah, ulema, mufti, cadi, kadi; Rhadamanthus.

litigant etc. (*accusation*) 938.

V. adjudge etc. (*determine*) 480; try a -case, – prisoner.

Adj. judicial etc. 965.

Phr. 'a Daniel come to judgment.'

---

968. Lawyer.—N. lawyer, jurist, legist, civilian, pundit, publicist, juisconsult, legal adviser, advocate; barrister, – at law; counsel, -lor; King's *or* Queen's counsel; K.C.; Q.C.; silk gown, leader; junior, – counsel; stuff gown, serjeant-at-law; bencher, tubman; judge etc. 967.

bar, legal profession, gentleman of the long robe; junior –, outer –, inner- bar; Inns of Court; equity draftsman, conveyancer, pleader, special pleader.

solicitor, attorney, proctor; notary, – public; scrivener, cursitor; writer, – to the signet; S.S.C.; limb of the law; pettifogger.

V. practice -at, – within- the bar; plead; call – to called- -to, – within- the bar; take silk.

Adj. learned in the law; at the bar; forensic.

---

969. Lawsuit.—N. lawsuit, suit, action, cause, petition; litigation; dispute etc. 713.

citation, arraignment, prosecution, impeachment; accusation etc. 938; presentment, true bill, indictment.

apprehension, arrest; committal; imprisonment etc. (*restraint*) 751.

writ, summons, subpoena, *latitat*, *nisi prius*; *habeas corpus.*

pleadings; declaration, bill, claim; *procèsverbal*, bill of right, information, *corpus delicti*; affidavit, state of facts; answer, replication, plea, demurrer, rebutter, rejoinder; surre-butter, - joinder.

suitor, party to a suit; litigant etc. 938; libellant.

hearing, trial; verdict etc. (*judgment*) 480; appeal, – motion; writ of error; *certiorari*.

case, decision, precedent, ruling; decided case, reports.

V. go to –, appeal to the- law; bring to -justice, – trial, – the bar; put on trial, pull up; accuse etc. 938; prefer –, file- a claim etc. *n.*; take the law of, inform against.

serve with a writ, cite, apprehend, arraign, sue, prosecute, bring an action against, indict, impeach, attach, distrain, commit; arrest; summon, -s; give in charge etc. (*restrain*) 751.

empanel a jury, implead, join issue; close the pleadings; set down for hearing.

try, hear a cause; sit in judgment; adjudicate etc. 480.

Adj. litigious etc. (*quarrelsome*) 713; *qui tam*; *coram* –, *sub- judice.*

Adv. *pendente lite.*

Phr. *adhuc sub judice lis 'est.*

---

970. Acquittal.—N. acquit-tal, -ment; clearance, exculpation, exoneration; discharge etc. (*release*) 750; *quietus*, absolution, compurgation, reprieve, respite; pardon etc. (*forgiveness*) 918.

[Exemption from punishment] impunity, immunity.

V. acquit, exculpate, exonerate, clear; absolve, whitewash, assoil, discharge, release; liberate etc. 750.

reprieve, respite; pardon etc. (*forgive*) 918; let off, – scot free.

Adj. acquitted etc. *v.*; un-condemned, punished, -chastised; recommended to mercy.

---

971. Condemnation.—N. condemnation, conviction, proscription, damnation; death warrant; penalty etc. 974.

attain-der, -ture, -tment.

V. condemn, convict, cast, bring home to, find guilty, damn, doom, sign the death warrant, sentence, pass sentence on, attaint, confiscate, proscribe, sequestrate; non-suit.

disapprove etc. 932; accuse etc. 938.

stand condemned.

Adj. condem-, dam-natory; condemned etc. *v.*; non-suited etc. (*failure*) 732; self-convicted.

Phr. *mutato nomine de te fabula narratur.*

972. Punishment.—N. punishment, punition; chast-isement, -ening; correction, castigation.

discipline, infliction, trial; judgment; penalty etc. 974; retribution; thunderbolt, Nemesis; requital etc. (*reward*) 973; penology; retributive justice.

lash, scaffold etc. (*instrument of punishment*) 975; imprisonment etc. (*restraint*) 751; chain gang; transportation, banishment, expulsion, deportation, exile, involuntary exile, ostracism; penal servitude, hard labor; galleys etc. 975; beating etc. *v.*; flagellation, fustigation, gantlet, *strappado*, *estrapade*, *bastinado*, *argumentum baculinum*, stick law, rap on the knuckles, box on the ear; blow etc. (*impulse*) 276; stripe, cuff, kick, buffet, pummel; slap, – in the face; wipe, douse; *coup de grâce*; torture; rack; picket, -ing; *dragonnade*; capital punishment, extreme penalty; execution; hanging etc. *v.*; de-capitation, -collation; garrot-te, -to; electrocution, lethal chamber; crucifixion, impalement; martyrdom, *auto-da-fé*; *noyade*; *hara-kiri*, happy despatch.

V. punish; chast-ise, -en; castigate, correct, inflict punishment, administer correction, deal retributive justice.

visit upon, pay; pay –, serve- out; settle with, get even with, get one's own back; do for; make short work of, give a lesson to, strafe, serve one right, make an example of; have a rod in pickle for; give it one.

strike etc. 276; deal a blow to, administer the lash, smite; slap, – the face; smack, cuff, box the ears, spank, thwack, thump, beat, lay on, swinge, buffet; thresh, thrash, pummel, drub, leather, trounce, baste, belabor; lace, – one's jacket; dress, give a -dressing, – down; trim, warm, wipe, tund, cob, bang, strap, comb, lash, lick, larrup, whallop, whop, flog, scourge, whip, birch, cane, give the stick, switch, flagellate, horsewhip, *bastinado*, towel, rub down with an oaken towel, rib roast, dust one's jacket, fustigate, pitch into, lay about one, beat black and blue; beat to a -mummy, – jelly; give a black eye; hit on the head; sandbag, keelhaul.

execute; bring to the -block, – gallows; behead; de-capitate, -collate; guillotine; hang, turn off, gibbet, bowstring, hang, draw and quarter; shoot; decimate; burn; electrocute; break ,on the wheel, crucify; em-, im-pale; flay; lynch; put to death.

torture; put -on, – to- the rack; picket.

banish, exile; trans-, de-port; expel, ostracize; rusticate; drum out; dismiss, -bar, -bench; strike off the roll, unfrock; post.

suffer, – for, – punishment; be -flogged, – hanged etc.; come to the gallows, dance upon nothing, die in one's shoes, be rightly served.

Adj. punishing etc. *v.*; penal; puni-tory, -tive; inflictive, castigatory; punished etc. *v.*

Int. *à la lanterne!*

973. Reward.—N. reward, recompense, remuneration, prize, meed, guerdon, reguerdon; indemni-ty, -fication, price; quittance; compensation; reparation, *ersatz*, assythment, redress; retribution, reckoning, acknowledgment, requital, amends, sop; atonement; consideration, return, *quid pro quo*; salvage, perquisite; vail etc. (*donation*) 784; *douceur*, bribe, bait, baksheesh,

tip; hush-, smart-money; black-mail; carcelage; *solatium*.

allowance, salary, stipend, wages; pay, -ment; emolument; tribute; batta, shot, scot; premium, fee, *honorarium*; hire.

crown etc. (*decoration of honor*) 877.

V. re-ward, -compense, -pay, -quite; re-munerate; compensate; fee, tip, bribe; pay one's footing etc. (*pay*) 807; make amends, indemnify, atone; satisfy, acknowledge.

get for one's pains, reap the fruits of.

Adj. remunerat-ive, -ory; munerary, compensatory, retributive, reparatory.

974. Penalty.—N. penalty; retribution etc. (*punishment*) 972; pain, pains and penalties; *peine forte et dure*; penance etc. (*atonement*) 952; the devil to pay.

fine, mulct, amercement; forfeit, -ure; escheat, damages, deodand, sequestration, confiscation, *premunire*.

V. penalize, fine, mulct, amerce, sconce, confiscate; sequest-rate, -er; escheat; estreat, forfeit.

975. Scourge. [Instrument of punishment.]**—N.** scourge, rod, cane, stick; ra-, rat-tan; birch, – rod; rod in pickle; switch, ferule, cudgel, truncheon; rubber hose.

whip, lash, strap, thong, cowhide, knout; cat, – o'-nine-tails, *sjambok*, quirt; rope's end.

pillory, stocks, whipping-post; cuck-, duck-ing stool; brank; triangle, wooden horse, maiden, thumbscrew, boot, rack, wheel, iron heel; treadmill, crank, galleys.

scaffold; block, axe, *guillotine*; stake; cross; gallows, gibbet, Tyburn tree; drop, noose, rope, halter, bowstring; electric chair, lethal chamber.

house of correction etc. (*prison*) 752.

gaol-, jail-er; executioner; hang-, heads-man; Jack Ketch; lyncher.

976. Deity.—N. Deity, Divinity; God-head, -ship; Omnipotence, Providence.

[Quality of being divine] divin-eness, -ity.

God, Lord, Jehovah, *Deus*; The -Almighty, – Supreme Being, – First Cause; *Ens Entium*; Author –, Creator- of all things; Author of our being; The -Infinite, – Eternal; The All-powerfull, -wise, -merciful, -holy; The Omni-potent, -scient.

[Attributes and perfections] infinite -power, – wisdom, – goodness, – justice, – truth, – love, – mercy; omni-potence, -science, -presence; unity, immutability, holiness, glory, majesty, sovereignty, infinity, eternity.

The -Trinity, – Holy Trinity, – Trinity in Unity, – Triune God; Three in One and One in Three.

God the Father; The -Maker, – Creator, – Preserver.

[Functions] creation, preservation, divine government; The-ocracy, -archy; providence; ways –, dealings –, dispensations –, visitations- of Providence.

God the Son, Jesus, Christ; The -Messiah, – Anointed, – Savior, – Redeemer, – Mediator,

– Intercessor, – Advocate, – Judge; The Son of - God, – Man, – David; The Only Begotten; The Lamb of God, The Word; Em-, Im-manuel; The - King of Kings and Lord of Lords, – King of Glory, – Prince of Peace, – Good Shepherd, – Way, – Truth, – Life, – Bread of Life, – Light of the World; The -Lord our, – Sun of- Righteousness.

The -Incarnation, – Hypostatic Union, – Word made Flesh.

[Functions] salvation, redemption, atonement, propitiation, mediation, intercession, judgment.

God the Holy Ghost, The Holy Spirit, Paraclete; The -Comforter, – Consoler, – Spirit of Truth, – Dove.

[Functions] inspiration, unction, regeneration, sanctification, consolation.

eon, aeon, special providence, *Deus ex machinâ; Avatar.*

V. create, uphold, preserve, govern etc.

atone, redeem, save, propitiate, mediate etc.

predestinate, elect, call, ordain, bless, justify, sanctify, glorify etc.

Adj. almighty, holy, hallowed, sacred, divine, heavenly, celestial; messianic; sacrosanct; all-powerful, -wise, -seeing, -knowing; omnipotent, omniscient; supreme.

super-human, -natural; ghostly, spiritual, hyper-physical, unearthly; the-istic, -ocratic, deistic; anointed.

Adv. *jure divino,* by divine right; *Deo volente,* D.V.

977. Angel. [Beneficent spirits.]—**N.** angel, archangel; heavenly host, choir invisible, host of heaven, sons of God; Michael, Gabriel etc.; seraph, -im; cherub, -im; ministering spirit, morning star; saint, *Madonna;* Our Lady, the Blessed Virgin, the Virgin Mary.

Adj. angelic, seraphic, cherubic.

978. Satan. [Maleficent spirits.]—**N.** Satan, the Devil, Lucifer, Ahrimanes, Belial; Sammael, Zamiel, Beelzebub, the Prince of the Devils; Mephistopheles, his satanic majesty.

the tempter; the evil -one, – spirit; the -author of evil, – wicked one, – old Serpent; the Prince of -darkness, – this world, – the power of the air; the -foul, – arch- fiend; the devil incarnate; the - common enemy, – angel of the bottomless pit; Abaddon, Apollyon, Mammon.

fallen agnels, unclean spirits, devils; the -rulers, – powers- of darkness; inhabitants of Pandemonium; demon etc. 980.

diabolism; devil-ism, -ship, -dom, -ry, -worship; *diablerie;* satanism, manicheism; the cloven foot; black magic etc. 992.

Adj. satanic, diabolic, devilish, infernal, hell-born.

979. Jupiter.—**N.** god, -dess; heathen gods and goddesses; Pantheon; Jupiter, Jove, Zeus, Apollo, Mars, Mercury, Neptune, Vulcan, Bacchus, Pluto, Saturn, Cupid, Eros, Pan; Juno, Ceres, Proserpina, Dina, Minerva, Pallas, Athenae, Venus, Aphrodite, Vesta; The Fates etc. 601.

Allah, Brahma, Vishnu, Siva, Shiva, Krishna, Juggernaut, Buddha; Ra, Isis, Osiris; Belus, Bel, Baal, Asteroth etc.; Thor, Odin; Mumbo Jumbo; good –, tutelary- genius; demiurge, familiar, – spirit; Sibyl; fairy, fay; sylph, -id; Ariel, peri, nymph, nereid, dryad, oread, sea-maid, Banshee, Benshie, Ormuzd; Oberon, Titania, Mab, hamadryad, naiad, mermaid, kelpie, Ondine, nix, nixie, sprite; denizens of the air; pixy etc. (*bad spirit*) 980.

mythology; heathen –, fairy- mythology; Lemprière, folklore.

Adj. fairy-, sylph-like; sylphic.

980. Demon.—**N.** demon, -ry, -ism, -ology; evil genius, fiend, familiar, – spirit; devil; bad –, unclean- spirit; cacodemon, incubus, Frankenstein's monster, succubus and succuba, Titan, Shedim, Mephistopheles, Asmodeus, Moloch, Belial, Ahriman, fury, The Furies etc. 900; harpy; Friar Rush.

vampire, ghoul; af-, ef-freet; afrite; ogre, -ss; gnome, gin, djinn, imp, deev, *lamia;* bo-gie, -gle; nis, kobold, flibbertigibbet, fairy, brownie, pixy, elf, dwarf, urchin, Puck, Robin Goodfellow; lepre-, cluri-chaune; troll, dwerger, sprite, oaf, changeling, bad fairy, nixe, pigwidgeon, Will-o'-the-wisp; Erl King.

[Supernatural appearance] ghost, specter, apparition, genie, spirit, shade, shadow, vision, phantom etc. 443; materialization (*spiritualism*) 992; hob-, goblin; wraith, spook, werwolf, boggart, banshee, *loup-garou, lemures;* evil eye.

nisse, necks; mer-man, -maid, -folk; siren, Lorelei; satyr, faun.

Adj. supernatural, weird, uncanny, unearthly, spectral; ghost-ly, -like; elf-in, -like; fiend-ish, -like; impish, demoniacal; haunted.

981. Heaven.—**N.** heaven; kingdom of - heaven, – God; heavenly kingdom; throne –, presence- of God; inheritance of the saints in light.

Paradise, Eden, abode of the blessed; Holy City, New Jerusalem; celestial bliss, glory.

[Mythological -heaven] Olympus; [– paradise] Elysium, Elysian fields, Arcadia, bowers of bliss, garden of the Hesperides, Islands of the Blessed; happy hunting-ground; third –, seventh-heaven; Valhalla (Scandinavian); Nirvana (Buddhist).

future state, eternity, eternal life, life after death, eternal home, resurrection, translation; resuscitation etc. 660; apotheosis, deification.

Adj. heavenly, celestial, supernal, unearthly, from on high, paradisiacal, beatific, elysian, Olympian, Arcadian.

982. Hell.—**N.** hell, bottomless pit, place of torment; habitation of fallen angels; Pandemonium, Abaddon, Domdaniel.

hell fire; everlasting -fire, – torment; lake of fire and brimstone; fire that is never quenched, worm that never dies.

purgatory, limbo, gehenna, abyss.

[Mythological hell] Tartarus, Hades, Avernus, Styx, Stygian creek, pit of Acheron, Cocytus,

Phlegethon, Lethe; infernal regions, *inferno*, shades below, realms of Pluto.

Pluto, Rhadamanthus, Erebus, Charon, Cerberus; Tophet.

Adj. hellish, infernal, stygian.

---

983. Theology. [Religious Knowledge.]—**N.** Theology (natural and revealed); Theo-gony, -sophy; Divinity; Hagio-logy, -graphy; Caucasian mystery; monotheism; religion; religious - persuasion, – sect, – denomination; cult; creed etc. (*belief*) 484; articles –, declaration –, profession –, confession- of faith.

theolog-ue, -ian; divine, schoolman, canonist, monotheist.

Adj. theological, religious; canonical; denominational; sectarian etc. 984.

983a. Orthodoxy.—N. orthodoxy; strictness, soundness, religious truth, true faith; truth etc. 494.

Christian-ity, -ism; Catholic-ism, -ity; 'the faith once delivered to the saints;' hyperorthodoxy etc. 984; iconoclasm.

the Holy –, the Orthodox- Church; Catholic –, Universal –, Apostolic –, Established- Church; temple of the Holy Ghost; Church –, body –, members –, disciples –, followers- of Christ; Christian, – community; true believer; canonist etc. (*theologian*) 983; Christendom, collective body of Christians, the Church Militant.

canons etc. (*belief*) 484; thirty-nine articles; Apostles' –, Nicene –, Athanasian- Creed; Church Catechism; textuary.

Adj. orthodox, sound, literal, strict, faithful, catholic, schismless, Christian, evangelical, scriptural, divine, monotheistic; true etc. 494.

---

984. Heterodoxy. [Sectarianism.]—**N.** heterodoxy; error etc. 495; false doctrine, heresy, schism; schismantic-ism, -alness; recusancy, backsliding, apostasy; atheism etc. (*irreligion*) 989.

bigotry etc. (*obstinacy*) 606; fanaticism, iconoclasm; hyperorthodoxy, precisianism, bibliolatry, hagiolatry, sabbatarianism, puritanism; idolatry etc. 991; superstition etc. (*credulity*) 486; dissent etc. 489.

sectar-ism, -ianism; nonconformity; secularism; syncretism, religious sects; the clash of creeds.

protestant-, advent-, Arian-, Erastian-, Calvin-, quaker-, method-, anabapt-, Pusey-, tractarian-, ritual-, Origen-, Sabellian-, Socinian-, De-, The-, mon-, material-, positiv-, latitudinairan-ism etc.

High –, Low –, Broad –, Free- Church; ultramontanism; monasticism; pap-ism, -istry; papacy; Anglican-, Catholic-, Roman-ism; popery, Scarlet Lady, Church of Rome, Greek Church; Christian Science, The Church of Christ Scientist.

pagan-, heathen-, ethic-ism; mythology; animism; poly-, di-, tri-, pan-theism; dualism; heathendom.

Juda-, Gentil-, Mahometan-, Islam-, Turc-, Brahmin-, Hindoo-, Buddh-, Lama-, Confucian-, Shinto-, Sabian-, Gnostic- Soofee-, Hylothe-, Mormon-ism.

Theosophy; Spiritualism, Occultism.

---

heretic, antichrist; pagan, heathen; pai-, pay-nim; *giaour*; gentile; pan-, poly-theist; idolator; misbeliever, apostate, backslider.

bigot etc. (*obstinacy*) 606; fanatic, dervish, abdal, iconoclast.

latitudinarian, limitarian, Deist, Theist, Unitarian; positivist, materialist; agnostic, sceptic etc. 989.

schismatic; sectar-y, -ian, -ist; seceder, separatist, recusant, dissenter; non-conformist, -juror; Huguenot, Protestant; orthodox dissenter, Congregationalist, Independent; Episcopalian, Presbyterian; Lutheran, Calvinist, Quaker, Methodist, Weslayan; Ana-, Baptist; Dunker; Mormon, Latter-day Saint, Irvingite, Sandemanian, Glassite, Erastian; Sub-, Supra-lapsarian; Gentoo, Antinomian, Swedenborgian, Adventist, Plymouth Brother; Theosophist etc.

Catholic, Roman Catholic, Romanist, papist, ultramontane; Old Catholic, tractarian, Anglican, Puseyite, ritualist; Puritan.

Jew, Hebrew, Rabbist; Mahometan, Mohammedan, Mussulman, Moslem, Islamite, Osmanli; Brahm-in, -an; Parsee, Sofi, Soofee; Buddhist; Zoroastrian, Magi, Gymnosophist, fire-worshipper, Sabian, Gnostic, Sadducee, Rosicrucian etc.

Adj. heterodox, heretical; un-orthodox, scriptural, -canonical; antiscriptural, apocryphal; un-, anti-christian; schismatic, recusant, iconoclastic; sectarian; dis-senting, -sident; secular etc. (*lay*) 997.

pagan; heathen, -ish; ethnic, -al; gentile, painim; pan-, poly-theistic; agnostic, sceptic.

Judaical, Mohammedan, Moslem, Brahminical, Buddhist etc. *n.*; Romish, Protestant etc. *n.*

bigoted etc. (*prejudiced*) 481; (*obstinate*) 606; superstitious etc. (*credulous*) 486; fanatical; idolatrous etc. 991; visionary etc. (*imaginative*) 515.

---

985. Revelation.—N. revelation, inspiration, *afflatus*.

Word, – of God; Scripture; the -Scriptures, – Bible, – Book of Books; Holy -Writ, – Scriptures; inspired writings, Gospel.

Old Testament, Septuagint, Vulgate, Pentateuch; Octateuch; the -Law, – Jewish Law, – Prophets; major –, minor- Prophets; Hagio-grapha, -logy; Hierographa; Apocrypha.

New Testament; Gospels, Evangelists, Acts, Epistles, Apocalypse, Revelations.

Talmud; Mishna, Masorah.

prophet etc. (*seer*) 513; evangelist, apostle, disciple, saint; the –, the Apostolical- fathers; Holy Men of old, inspired -writers, – penmen.

Adj. scriptural, biblical, sacred, prophetic; evangel-ical, -istic; apostolic, -al; inspired, theopneustic, apocalyptic, ecclesiastical, canonical, textuary.

---

986. Pseudo-Revelation.—N. the -Koran, – Alcoran; Ly-king, Shaster, Vedas, Zendavesta, Vedidad, Purana, Edda; Go-, Gau-tama; Book of Mormon.

[False prophets and religious founders] Buddha, Zoroaster, Zerdhusht, Confucius, Mahomet.

[Idols] golden calf etc. 991; Baal, Moloch, Dagon.

987. Piety.—N. piety, religion, theism, faith; religiousness, holiness etc. *adj.*; saintship; religionism; sanctimony etc. (*assumed piety*) 988; reverence etc. (*respect*) 928; humility, veneration, devotion; prostration etc. (*worship*) 990; grace, unction, edification; sancti-ty, -tude; consecration.

spiritual existence, odor of sanctity, beauty of holiness.

theopathy, beatification, adoption, regeneration, conversion, justification, sanctification, salvation, inspiration, bread of life; Body and Blood of Christ.

believer, convert, theist, Christian, devotee, pietist; the -good, – righteous, – just, – believing. – elect; Saint, *Madonna*.

the children of -God, – the kingdom, – light.

V. be -pious etc. *adj.*; have -faith etc. *n.*; believe, receive Christ; revere etc. 928; worship etc. 950; be -converted etc.

convert, edify, sanctify, hallow, keep holy, beatify, regenerate, inspire, consecrate, enshrine.

Adj. pious, religious, devout, devoted, reverent, godly, heavenly minded, humble; pure, – in heart; holy, spiritual, pietistic; saint-ly, -like; seraphic, sacred, solemn.

believing, faithful, Christian, Catholic.

elected, adopted, justified, sanctified, regenerated, inspired, consecrated, converted, unearthly, not of the earth.

988. Impiety.—N. impiety; sin etc. 945; irreverence; profan-eness etc. *adj.*, -ity, -ation; blasphemy, desecration, sacrilege; scoffing etc. *v.*

[Assumed piety] hypocrisy etc. (*falsehood*) 544; pietism, cant, pious fraud; lip-devotion, -service, -reverence; mis-devotion, formalism, austerity; sanctimon-y, -iousness etc. *adj.*; pharisaism, precisianism; sabbat-ism, -arianism; *odium theologicum*, sacerdotalism; bigotry etc. (*obstinacy*) 606, (*prejudice*) 481.

hardening, backsliding, declension, perversion, reprobation apostacy, recusancy.

sinner etc. 949; scoffer, blasphemer; sacrilegist; worldling; hypocrite etc. (*dissembler*) 548; Scribes and Pharisees; Tartufe, Maw-worm.

bigot; saint [ironically] ; Pharisee, sabbatarian, formalist, methodist, puritan, pietist, precisian; religionist, devotee, ranter, fanatic, wowser.

the -wicked, – evil, – unjust, – reprobate; son of -men, – Belial, – the wicked one; children of darkness.

V. be -impious etc. *adj.*; profane, desecrate, blaspheme, revile, scoff; swear etc. (*malediction*) 908; commit sacrilege.

snuffle; turn up the whites of the eyes; idolize.

Adj. impious; irreligious etc. 989; desecrating etc. *v.*; profane, irreverent, sacrilegious, blasphemous.

un-hallowed, -sanctified, -regenerate; hardened, perverted, reprobate.

hypocritical etc. (*false*) 544; canting, pietistical, sanctimonious, unctuous, pharisaical, over-righteous, righteous over much

bigoted, fanatical etc. 481 and 606; priest-ridden.

Adv. under the -mask, – cloak, – pretence, – form, – guise- of religion.

989. Irreligion.—N. irreligion, indevotion; ungodliness etc. *adj.*; laxity, quietism, apathy, indifference, passivity.

scepticism, doubt; un-, dis-belief; incredul-ity, -ousness etc. *adj.*; want of -faith, – belief; pyrrhonism; doubt etc. 485; agnosticism.

atheism, deism; hylotheism; materialism; positivism; nihilism.

infidelity, freethinking, antichristianity, rationalism.

atheist, anti-christian, sceptic, unbeliever, deist, infidel, pyrrhonist; *giaour*, heathen, alien, gentile, Nazarene; *esprit fort*, freethinker, latitudinarian, rationalist; materialist, positivist, nihilist, agnostic.

V. be -irreligious etc. *adj.*; disbelieve, lack faith; doubt, question etc. 485.

dechristianize; serve Mammon, love darkness better than light.

Adj. irreligious; in-, un-devout; devout-, god-, grace-less; un-godly, -holy, -sanctified, -hallowed; atheistic, without God.

sceptical, free-thinking; un-believing, -converted; incredulous, faithless, lacking faith; deistical; un-, anti-christian.

worldly, mundane, earthly, carnal, unspiritual; worldly etc.- minded.

Adv. irreligiously etc. *adj.*

990. Worship.—N. worship, adoration, devotion, aspiration, latria, homage, service, humiliation; kneeling, genuflexion, prostration.

prayer, invocation, supplication, rogation, intercession, orison, holy breathing; petition etc. (*request*) 765; collect, litany, Lord's prayer, paternoster, *Ave Maria*, rosary; bead-roll; latria, dulia, hyperdulia, vigils; revival; cult.

thanksgiving; giving –, returning- thanks; grace, praise, glorification, benediction, doxology, hosanna; h-, allelujah; *Te Deum, non nobis Domine, nunc dimittis*; paean.

psalm, -ody; hymn, plainsong, chant, chaunt, response, anthem, motet; antiphon, -y.

oblation, sacrifice, incense, libation; burnt –, votive –, thank-offering; offertory, collection.

discipline; self-discipline, -examination, -denial; fasting.

divine services office, duty; morning prayer; mass, matins, evensong, vespers, compline; holy day etc. (*rites*) 998.

worshipper, congregation, communicant, celebrant.

V. worship, lift up the heart, aspire; revere etc. 928; adore, do service, pay homage; humble oneself, kneel; bow –, bend- the knee; fall -down, – on one's knees; prostrate oneself, bow down and worship, recite the rosary.

pray, invoke, supplicate; put –, offer- up -prayers, – petitions; beseech etc. (*ask*) 765; say one's prayers, tell one's beads;

return –, give- thanks; say grace, bless, praise, laud, glorify, magnify, sing praises; give benediction, lead the choir, intone, chant, sing.

propitiate, offer sacrifice, fast, deny oneself; vow, offer vows, give alms.

work out one's salvation; go to church; attend -service, – mass; communicate etc. (*rite*) 998.

Adj. worshipping etc. *v.*; devout, devotional, reverent, pure, solemn; fervid etc. (*heartfelt*) 821.

Int. h-, allelujah! hosanna! glory be to God! O Lord! pray God that! God -grant, – bless, – save, – forbid! *sursum corda.*

991. Idolatry.—N. idol-atry, -ism; demon-ism, -olatry; idol –, demon –, devil –, fire- worship; zoolatry, fetishism, Mari-, Bibli-, ecclesi-, heliolatry.

deification, apotheosis, canonization; hero worship.

sacrifices, hecatomb, holocaust; human sacrifices, immolation, mactation, infanticide, self-immolation, *suttee.*

idol, golden calf, graven image, fetish, *avatar,* Juggernaut, joss, *lares et penates;* Baal etc. 986. idolator etc. *n.*

V. worship -idols, – pictures, – relics; put on a pedestal, bow down to, prostrate oneself before, make sacrifice to; deify, canonize, idolize.

Adj. idolatrous.

992. Sorcery.—N. sorcery; superstition; occult -art, – sciences; black –, magic; the black art, necromancy, theurgy, thaumaturgy; demon-ology, - omy, -ship; *diablerie,* bedevilment; witch-craft, - ery; glamor; fetis-hism, -ism; ghost dance; hoodoo, voodoo; Shamanism [Esquimaux], vampirism; conjuration; bewitchery, exorcism, enchantment, incantation, obsession, possession, mysticism, second sight, mesmerism, animal magnetism; od –, odylic- force; electro-biology, *clairvoyance;* spiritualism, spirit-rapping, table-turning; thought reading, telepathy, thought transference, automatic writing, *planchette,* ouija board; crystal gazing; spirit manifestation, materialization, astral body, ectoplasm etc.

divination etc. (*prediction*) 511; sortilege, ordeal, *sortes Virgiliance;* hocus-pocus etc. (*deception*) 545; oracle etc. 513.

V. practice -sorcery etc. *n.*; cast a -horoscope, – nativity; conjure, exorcise, charm, enchant; bewitch, -devil; overlook, look on with the evil eye; entrance, mesmerize, magnetize; fascinate etc. (*influence*) 615; taboo; wave a wand; rub the -ring, – lamp; cast a spell; call up spirits, – from the vasty deep; raise spirits from the dead; raise –, lay-ghosts; command genii.

Adj. magic, -al; mystic, weird, cabalistic, talismanic, phylacteric, incantatory; charmed etc. *v.*

993. Spell.—N. spell, charm, incantation, exorcism, weird, cabala, exsufflation, cantrap, runes, abracadabra, hocus-pocus, open *sesame,* counter-charm, Ephesian letters, bell, book and candle, Mumbo-jumbo, evil-eye, fee-faw-fum.

talisman, amulet, periapt, telesm, phylactery, philter, wish-bone, merry-thought, mascot, scarab, swastika; fetish; *agnus Dei.*

wand, caduceus, rod, divining rod, lamp of Aladdin, magic carpet, seven-league boots; magic ring; wishing –, Fortunatus's- cap.

994. Sorcerer.—N. sorcerer, magician; thaumat-, the-urgist; conjuror, necromancer, seer,

wizard, witch; fairy etc. 980; *lamia,* hag, warlock, charmer, exorcist, voodoo, mage, diviner, dowser; cunning –, , medicine- man, witch doctor; Shaman, figure-flinger, ecstatica, medium, *clair-voyant,* mesmerist, hypnotist; *deus ex machinâ;* astrologer; soothsayer etc. 513.

Katerfelto, Cagliostro, Merlin, Comus, Mesmer, Rosicrucian; Hecate, Circe, Lilith, siren, weird sisters; witch of Endor.

995. Churchdom.—N. church, -dom; ministry, apostleship, priesthood, prelacy, hierarchy, church government, christendom, pale of the church.

clerical-, sacerdotal-, episcopalian-, ultramontan-ism; Theocracy; ecclesiolog-y, -ist; priestcraft, *odium theologicum.*

monach-ism, -y; monasticism, monkhood.

[Ecclesiastical offices and dignities] pontificate; primacy, archbishopric, archiepiscopacy; prelacy; bishop-ric, -dom; episcop-ate, -acy; see, diocese; deanery, stall; canon-ry, -icate; prebend, -aryship; benefice, incumbency, glebe, advowson, living, cure, – of souls; rectorship; vicar-iate, -ship; pastor-ate, -ship; deacon-ry, -ship; -curacy; chaplain, -cy, -ship; cardinal-ate, -ship; abbacy, presbytery.

holy orders, ordination, institution, consecration, induction, reading in, preferment, translation, presentation.

popedom, papacy; the -Vatican, – apostolic see, – see of Rome; religious sects etc. 984.

council etc. 696; conclave, college of cardinals, convocation, synod, consistory, chapter, vestry, presbytery; sanhedrim, *congé d'élire;* ecclesiastical courts, consistorial court, court of Arches.

V. call, ordain, induct, prefer, translate, consecrate, present, elect, bestow.

take -orders, – the veil, – vows.

Adj. ecclesi-astical, -ological; clerical, sacerdotal, priestly, prelatical, pastoral, ministerial, capitular, theocratic; hierarchical, archiepiscopal; episcopal, -ian; canonical; mon-astic, -achal; monkish; abbati-al, -cal; pontifical, papal, apostolic; untramontane, priest-ridden.

996. Clergy.—N. clergy, clericals, ministry, priesthood, presbytery, the cloth, the pulpit.

clergyman, divine, ecclesiastic, churchman, priest, presbyter, hierophant, pastor, shepherd, minister, clerk in holy orders; father, – in Christ; *padre, abbé, curé;* patriarch; reverend; black coat; confessor; sky pilot.

dignitaries of the church; ecclesi-, hier-arch; eminence, reverence, elder, primate, metropolitan, archimandrite, archbishop, bishop, prelate, diocesan, suffragan, dean, subdean, archdeacon, prebendary, canon, rural dean, rector, parson, vicar, perpetual curate, residentiary, beneficiary, incumbent, chaplain, curate, – in charge; deacon, -ess; preacher; lay reader, lecturer; capitular; missionary, propagandist, Jesuit, revivalist, field preacher.

churchwarden, sidesman, clerk, precentor, choir; almoner, *suisse,* verger, beadle, sexton, sacristan; acol-yth, -othyst, -yte; thurifer; chorister, choir boy.

[Roman Catholic priesthood] Pope, *Papa,* Holy

Father, pontiff, high priest, cardinal; ancient –, flamen; confessor, penitentiary; spiritual director.

cenobite, conventual, abbot, prior, monk, friar, lay brother, beadsman, mendicant, pilgrim, palmer; canon-regular, -secular; Jesuit, Franciscan, Friars minor, Minorites; Observant, Capuchin, Dominican, Carmelite; Augustinian; Gilbertine; Austin-, Black-, White-, Grey-, Crossed-, Crutched- Friars; Bonhomme, Carthusian, Benedictine, Cistercian, Trappist, Cluniac, Premonstratensian, Maturine; Templar, Hospitaller.

abb-, prior-, canon-ess; mother superior; *religieuse*, nun, sister, *beguine*, novice, postulant.

[Under the Jewish dispensation] prophet, priest, high priest, Levite; Rabbi, -n; scribe.

[Mohammedan etc.] mullah, ulema, imauam, sheik; so-fi, -phi; mufti, hadji, muezzin, dervish; fakir, -quir; brahmin, gooroo, druid, bonze, santon, abdal, Lama, talapoin, caloyer etc.

V. take orders etc. 995.

Adj. the – , the very – , the Right- Reverend; ordained, in orders, called to the ministry.

997. Laity.—N. laity, flock, fold, congregation, assembly, brethren, people.

temporality, secularization.

layman, civilian; parishioner, catechumen; secularist.

V. secularize.

Adj. secular, lay, laical, civil, temporal, profane.

998. Rite.—N. rite; ceremon-y, -ial; ordinance, observance, function, duty; form, -ulary; solemnity, sacrament; incantation etc. (*spell*) 993; service, psalmody etc. (*worship*) 990; liturgies.

ministration; preach-ing, -ment; predication, sermon, homily, exhortation, lecture, discourse, pastoral.

baptism, christening, chrism; immersion; baptismal regeneration; font; circumcision.

confirmation; imposition – , laying on- of hands; churching, purification, ordination etc. (*churchdom*) 995; excommunication.

Eucharist, Lord's supper, communion; the – , the holy- sacrament; celebration, high celebration; *missa cantata*; offertory; introit; consecration; con-, tran-substantiation; real presence; elements, bread and wine; mass; high –, low –, dry- mass.

matrimony etc. 903; burial etc. 363; visitation of the sick.

seven sacraments, impanation, extreme unction, last rites, *viaticum*, invocation of saints, canonization, transfiguration, auricular confession; fasting; maceration, flagellation, sackcloth and ashes; penance etc. (*atonement*) 952; absolution; telling of beads, reciting the rosary, processional; thurification, incense, holy water, aspersion.

relics, rosary, beads, reliquary, host, cross, rood, crucifix, pax, pix, pyx, *agnus Dei*, censer, thurible, patera, urceole; chalice, patten, Holy Grail, sangrail; seven-branch candle stick, monstrance, sacring bell.

ritual, rubric, canon, ordinal; liturgy, prayerbook, book of common prayer, pietas, euchology,

litany, lectionary; missal, breviary, mass-book, bead-roll.

psalter; psalm – , hymn- book; hymn-al, -ology; psalmody.

ritual-, ceremonial-ism; sabbat-ism, -arianism; ritualist, sabbatarian.

holyday, feast, fast; Sabbath, Passover, Pentecost; Advent, Christmas, Noel, Epiphany, Lent, Shrove Tuesday, Ash Wednesday, Maundy Thursday; Passion – , Holy- week; Good Friday, Easter, Ascension Day, Whitsuntide; Trinity Sunday, Corpus Christi; All-Saints' – , – Souls'- Day; Candle-, Lam-, Martin-, Michael-mas; hogmanay; Ramadan, -zan; Bairam etc. etc.

V. perform service, do duty, minister, officiate, baptize, dip, sprinkle; confirm, lay hands on; give – , administer – , take – , receive – , attend – , partake of- the -sacrament, – communion; communicate; celebrate mass; administer – , receive- extreme unction; anele, shrive, absolve, confess; do penance; genuflect; cross oneself, make the sign of the cross.

excommunicate, ban with bell, book and candle.

preach, sermonize, predicate, lecture.

Adj. ritual, -istic; ceremonial, liturgic; baptismal, eucharistical; paschal.

999. Canonicals.—N. canonicals, vestments; robe, gown, Geneva gown, frock, pallium, surplice, cassock, dalmatic, scapulary, cope, scarf, tunicle, chasuble, alb, *alba*, stole; fan-on, -nel; tonsure, cowl, hood; calo-te, -tte; bands; capouch, amice, orarium, ephod; apron, lawn sleeves, pontificals; pall; miter, tiara, triple crown; shovel – , cardinal's- hat; biretta; crosier; pastoral staff; costume etc. 225.

1000. Temple.—N. place of worship; house of -God, – prayer.

temple, cathedral, minister, church, kirk, chapel, meeting-house, bethel, tabernacle, conventicle, *basilica*, fane, holy place, chantry, oratory.

synagogue; mosque; marabout; pantheon; pagoda; joss-house; dagobah, tope; kiosk.

parsonage, rectory, vicarage, manse, deanery, glebe, church house; Vatican; bishop's palace; Lambeth.

altar, shrine, sanctuary, Holy of Holies, *sanctum sanctorum*, sacrarium, -isty; communion – , holy – , Lord's- table; table of the Lord; pyx; baptistery, font; piscina, stoup; aumbry; sedile; reredos; rood-loft, – screen; jube.

chancel, quire, choir, nave, aisle, transept, lady chapel, vestry, crypt, cloisters, porch; triforum, clerestory, churchyard, *golgotha*, calvary, Easter sepulcher; stall, pew, sitting; pulpit, ambo, lectern, reading-desk, confessional, prothesis, credence, baldachin, *baldacchino*; jesse, apse, belfry; chapter-house; presbytery.

monastery, priory, abbey, friary, convent, nunnery, cloister.

Adj. claustral, cloistered; monast-ic, -erial; conventual.

INDEX

The numbers refer to the headings under which the words or phrases occur. When the same word or phrase may be used in various senses, the several headings under which it, or its synonyms, will be found, according to those meanings, are indicated by the words printed in Italics. These words in Italics are not intended to explain the meaning of the word or phrase to which they are annexed, but only to assist in the required reference.

When the word given in the Index is itself the title or heading of a category, the number of reference is printed in blacker type, thus: **abode 189**.

abundanti cautelâ,
ex – 664
abuse *deceive* 545
ill-treat 649
misuse 679
malediction 908
threat 909
upbraid 932
violate 961
– of *language* 563
– of *terms* 523
abusive 895, 934
abut *near* 197 *touch*
199, 215
abutment 717
aby *remain* 141
endure 821, 826
abysmal *deep* 208
abyss *space* 180
depth 208
interval 198
danger 667
hell 982
A.C. 106
academic
teaching 537, 542
theory 514
academical
style 578
academicals
225 *robes*
academician 492
Royal – 559
academy 542
acanthus 847
a capite ad calcem
52
acariâtre 901
acarpous 169
acatalectic 597
acaudal 38
accede 488, 725, 762
accelerate
early 132
stimulate 173
velocity 274
hasten 684
accension 384
accent *sound* 402
tone of voice 580
rhythm 597
accentuate 642
accentuated 580
accept *assent* 488
consent 762
receive 785
take 789
acceptable 646,·829
acceptance 771
acceptation 522
acception 522
access 286
easy of – 705
means of – 627
accessible 470, 705
accession
adjunct 39
increase 35
addition 37
- to *office* 737, 755
consent 762
accessory
extrinsic 6
additive 37
adjunct 39
accompanying 88
aid 707
auxiliary 711

acciaccatura 413
accidence 567
accident *event* 151
chance 156
disaster 619
misfortune 735
fatal – 361
accidental
extrinsic 6
fortuitous 156
undesigned 621
accidents,
trust to the chap-
ter of – 621
accipient 785
acclamation
assent 488
approbation 931
acclimatize 370, 613
acclivity 217
accloy 641
accolade 894
accommodate
suit 23
adjust 27
aid 707
reconcile 723
give 784
lend 787
– oneself to 82
accommodation
space 180
accommodating
kind 906
accompaniment
adjunct 39
coexistence 88
musical 415
accompany
add 37
coexist 88
concur 120
music 416
accompli, fait – 729
accomplice 711
accomplish
execute 161
complete 729
succeed 731
accomplishment
490, 698
accompts 811
accord
uniform 16
agree 23
music 413
assent 488
concord 714
grant 760
give 784
of one's own – 602
according
- as *qualification*
469
– to *evidence* 467
– to *circumstances*
8
– to *law* 963
– to *rule*
conformably 82
– *rumor* 527
accordingly
logically 476
accordion 417
accost 586
accoucheur 631, 662
accouchement 161
account *list* 86

adjudge 480
description 594
credit 805
money - 811
fame 873
approbation 931
call to – 932
find one's – in
useful 644
success 731
make no – of 483,
930
not – for 519
on – of *motive* 615
behalf 707
on no – 536
send to one's – 361
take into – 457,
469
small – 643
to one's – 780
turn to –
improve 658
use 677
success 731
gain 775
– as *deem* 484
– *book* 551
– for 155, 522
– with 794, 807
accountable
liable 177
debit 811
duty 926
accountant 301, 811
certified public –
811
accounts 811
accouple 43
accoutered
armed 717
accouterment
dress 225
appliance 633
equipment 673
accoy 174
accredit
commission 755,
759
money 805
honor 873
accredited 484, 613
– to 755, 759
accretion 35, 46
accrimination 938
accroach 789
accrue *add* 37
result 154
acquire 775
be received 785,
810
accubation 213
accueil 894
accultural 35
accumbent 213
accumulate
collect 72
store 636
redundance 641
accurate 494
– *knowledge* 490
accurse 908
accursed
disastrous 649
undone 828
vicious 945
accusation 938
accuse

disapprove 932
charge 938
lawsuit 969
accustom 613
ace *small* 32
unit 87
within an – 197
aceldama *kill* 361
arena 728
acephalous 59
acerbate 659, 835
acerbity
acrimony 395
sourness 397
rudeness 895
spleen 900, 901
malevolence 907
acervate 72
acetous 397
acetylene 388
acharné 900
Achates, fidus –
890, 939
ache *physical* 378
mental 828
Acheron
pit of – 982
Acherontic
moribund 360
gloomy 837
achievable 470
achieve *end* 67
produce 161
do 680
accomplish 729
achievement 551,
861
Achilles, heel of –
vulnerable 665
achromatism 429
acicular 253
acid 397
acid test 463
acknowledge
answer 462
assent 488
disclose 529
avow 535
consent 762
observe 772
pay 807
thank 916
repent 950
reward 973
acknowledged
custom 613
acme 210
– of perfection 650
Acology 662
acolyte 996
acomous 226
aconite 663
acoustic 418
– organs 418
acoustics 402
acquaint
– oneself with 539
– with 527
acquaintance
knowledge 490
information 527
friend 890
make – with 888
acquiesce
assent 488
willing 488
consent 762
tolerate 826

acquire
develop 161
get 775
receive 785
– a habit 613
– learning 539
acquirement
knowledge 490
learning 539
talent 698
receipt 810
acquisition
knowledge 490
gain 775
acquit
liberate 750
exempt 927a
vindicate 937
innocent 946
absolve 970
acquit oneself
behave 692
– of a debt 807
– of a duty 926
– of an obligation
772
acquittal 506, 970
acquittance 771
acres *space* 180
land 342
property 780
Acres, Bob 862
acrid 392, 395
acridity 171
acrimony
physical 171
caustic 830
discourtesy 895
hatred 898
anger 900
malevolence 907
acroamatism 490
acrobat
strength 159
actor 599
proficient 700
mountebank 844
Acropolis 210
across 219, 708
acrostic 533, 561,
842
act *imitate* 19
physical 170
- of a play 599
personate 599
voluntary 680
statute 697
in the – 680, 947
– a part *feign* 544
– one's part 625,
926
– upon
physical 170
mental 615
take steps 680
– up to 772
– well one's part
944
– without author-
ity 738
acting *deputy* 759
actinic 420
actinometer 445
action *physical* 170
voluntary 680
battle 720
law 969
line of – 692

put in – 677
suit the – to the
  word 550
thick of the – 682
activate 171
actionable 964
active *physical* 171
  voluntary 682
  – service 722
  – thought 457
activity 682
actor
  impostor 548
  player 599
  agent 690
  affectation 855
Acts *record* 551
  Apostolic 985
actual *existing* 1
  present 118
  real 494
actuary 85, 811
actuate 176, 615
actum est 729
acu tetigisti, rem
  465, 494
acuity 253
aculeated 253
acumen 498
acuminated 253
acupuncture 260
acustics 402
acute *energetic* 171
  physically violent
  173
  pointed 253
  physically sensible
  375
  musical tone 410
  perspicacious 498
  cunning 702
  strong feeling 821
  morally painful
  830
  – angle 244
  – ear 418
  – note 410
acutely 31
acuteness 465
ad
  – eundem 27
  – hominem 79
  – infinitum 105
  – instar 82
  – interim 106
  – lib 705
  – rem 23
A.D. 106
adage 496
adagio *music* 415
  slow 275
Adam *sin* 945
  – 's apple 250
adamant,159, 323
adapt 23, 27
  – oneself to 82
adaptable
  conformable 82
  useful 644
add *increase* 35
  join 37
  numerically 85
  – up 811
addendum 39
adder 913
addict *habit* 613
adding machine 85
additament 39

addition
  extrinsical 6
  increase 35
  adjunction 37
  thing added 39
  arithmetical 85
addle *barren* 169
  incomplete 730
  abortive 732
  – the wits, 475, 503
addlehead 501
addleheaded 499
address
  residence 189
  direction 550
  speech 582
  speak to 586
  skill 698
  request 765
  – oneself to 673
addresses
  courtship 902
addressful 894
adduce
  bring to 288
  evidence 467
addulce 834
ademption 789
adenoid 250
adenology 329
adept 700
adequate *power* 157
  sufficient 639
  for a purpose 644
adhere *stick* 46
  – to 604a, 613
  – to an obligation
  772
  – to a duty 926
adherent
  follower 711
adhesive, 46, 327,
  352
adhibit 677
adhortation 695
adieu *departure* 293
  loss 776
adipocere 356
adipose 355
adit *orifice* 260
  conduit 350
  passage 627
adjacent 197
adjection 37
adjective 39
adjoin 197, 199
adjourn 133
adjudge 480
adjudicate 480
adjunct
  thing added 39
  accompaniment 88
  aid 707
  auxiliary 711
adjuration 535, 536
adjure 765, 768
adjust *adapt* 23
  equalize 27
  order 58
  prepare 673
  settle 723, 762
  – differences 774
adjutage 260, 350
adjutant
  auxiliary 711
  military 745
adjuvant *helping*
  707

auxiliary 711
admeasurement
  466
adminicle 467
administer
  utilize 677
  conduct 693
  exercise authority
  737
  distribute 786
  – correction 972
  – oath 768
  – sacrament 998
  – to aid 707
  give 784
administration of
  justice 965
administrative 737,
  965
administrator 694
admirable 648, 744
admiral 745
Admiralty, court of
  – 966
admirari, nil – 871,
  932
admiration
  wonder 870
  love 897
  respect 928
  approval 931
admired *disorder* 59
admirer 897
admissible
  relevant 23
  receivable 296
  tolerable 651
  – in society 852
admit
  composition 54
  include 76
  let in 296
  assent 488
  acknowledge 529
  permit 760
  concede 762
  accept 785
  – exceptions 469
  – of 470
admitted
  customary 613
  – maxim &c. 496
admixture 41
admonish
  warn 668
  advise 695
  reprove 932
ado *activity* 682
  exertion 686
  difficulty 704
  make much –
  about 542
  much – about
  nothing
  overestimate 482
  unimportant 643
  unskilful 699
adolescence 131
Adonis 845
adonize 847
adopt
  naturalize 184
  choose 609
  – a cause *aid* 707
  – a course 692
  – an opinion 484
adoption
  religious 987

adore 897, 990
adorn 847
adown 207
adrift *unrelated* 10
  disjoined 44
  dispersed 73
  uncertain 475
  unapt 699
  free 750
  go – *deviate* 279
  turn – *disperse* 73
  liberate 750
  dismiss 756
adroit 698
adscititious
  extrinsic 6
  added 37
  redundant 641
adscriptus glebae
  746
adulation 933
adulator 935
Adullam, cave of
  624, 832
Adullamite 832
adult 131
adulterate *mix* 41
  deteriorate 659
adulterated 545
adulterer 962
adultery 961
adumbrate
  darkness 421
  allegorize 521
  represent 554
adumbration
  semblance 21
  allusion 526
aduncity 244, 245
adust
  color 433
  gloomy 837
adustion 384
advance *increase* 35
  course 109
  progress 282
  assert 535
  improve 658
  aid 707
  succeed 731
  lend 787
  in – *precedence* 62
  front 234
  precession 280
  in – of 33
  in – of one's age
  498
  – against 716
  – of learning &c.
  490
advanced 282
  – in life 128
  – guard 234
  – student 541
  – work 717
advances, make –
  offer 763
  social 892
advantage
  superiority 33
  influence 175
  good 618
  expedience 646
  mechanical – 633
  dressed to – 847
  find one's – in 644
  gain an – 775
  set off to – 658

take – of 677, 698
  – over *success* 731
advantageous
  beneficial 648
  profitable 775
advene 37
advent
  futurity 121
  event 151
  approach 286
  arrival 292
Advent 998
adventism 984
adventitious 6, 156
adventive 156
adventure *event* 151
  chance 156
  pursuit 622
  danger 665
  trial 675
  the great – 360
adventurer
  traveler 268
  deceiver 548
  experimenter 463
  gambler 621
  rash 863
  ignoble 876
adventures 594
adventurous
  undertaking 676
  bold 861
  rash 863
adversaria 551
adversary 710
adverse
  contrary 14
  opposed 708
  unprosperous 735
  disliking 867
  – party 710
adversity 735
advert 457
advertise 531
advice *notice* 527
  news 532
  counsel 695
advisable 646
advise *predict* 511
  inform 527
  counsel 695
  – with one's pillow
  451
advised *predeter-*
  mined 611
  intended 620
  better – 658
adviser 540, 695
advocacy 931
advocate
  prompt 615
  recommend 695
  aid 707
  auxiliary 711
  friend 890
  vindicate 937
  counsellor 968
Advocate, the – 976
advocation 617
advoutress 962
advoutry 961
advowson 995
adynamic 160
adytum *room* 191
  prediction 511
  secret place 530
adze 253
adzooks 870

aedile 965
aegis 717
aegrescit medendo 659
aegrotat 927a
aeolian 349
— harp 417
aequam servare mentem 826
aequo animo 823 826
aerate 334, 353
aere perennius 873
aerial 273
elevated 206
flying 267
gas 334
air 338
— navigation 267
— navigator 269
— mail 534
— patrol 726
— perspective 428
— warfare 722
aerie 189
aerify 334
aerodonetics 267
aerodrome 728
aerodynamics 267, 334, 349
aerolite 318
aerology 338
aeromancy 511
aeromechanics 267
aerometer 338
aeronaut 269
aeronautical 273
aeronautics 267, 338
aeroplane 273
aerostat balloon 273
aerostatics 267, 334
aerostation 338
aery 317
Aesculapius 662
Aesop 846
aesthetic
sensibility 375
beauty 845
taste 850
aestival 125
aeternum servans sub pectore vulnus 919
afar 196
affable 879, 894
affair event 151
topic 454
business 625
battle 720
love 902, 903
— of honour 720
affaires, charge d' — 758
affaire de coeur 897
affect relate to 9
tend to 176
qualify 469
feign 544
touch 824
desire 865
love 897
affectation 855
affected with
feeling 821
disease 655

affectibility 822
affecting 830
affection 821, 897
affections 820
affettuoso 415
affiance 768, 858
affianced 897, 903
affiche 531
affidation 769
affidavit
affirmation 535
record 551
lawsuit 969
affiliation
relation 9
kindred 11
attribution 155
affine 11
affinitive 9
affinity 9, 17
male 905
affirmation 535, 488
affix add 37
sequel 39
fasten 43
letter 561
afflation 349
afflatus 349, 597, 985
afflict 830
— with illness 655
affliction pain 828
infliction 830
adversity 735
affluence
sufficiency 639
prosperity 734
wealth 803
affluent river 348
afflux 286
afford supply 784
wealth 803
yield 810
sell for 812
— aid &c. 707
afforestation 371
affranchise
make free of 748
liberate 750
affray 720
affreet 980
affriction 331
affright 860
affront molest 830
provocation 900
insult 929
— danger 861
affuse 337
afield 186
afire 382
afloat extant 1
unstable 149
going on 151
ship 273
navigation 267
ocean 341
news 532
preparing 673
keep oneself — 734
set — publish 531
afoot on hand 625
preparing 673
astir 682
afore 116
aforementioned 116
aforesaid
preceding 62
repeated 104

prior 116
aforethought 611
aforetime 116
afraid 860
be — irresolute 605
— to say uncertain 475
afresh 104, 123
Afric heat 382
Afrikander 57
afrite 980
aft 235
after in order 63
in time 117
too late 135
rear 235
pursuit 622
be — intention 620
pursuit 622
go — follow 281
— all for all that 30
qualification 469
on the whole 476
— time 133
after acceptation 516
after-age 124
after-clap 509
after-crop 65, 168
after-dinner 117
after-glow 40, 65, 420
after-growth 65
after-life 152
aftermath
sequel 65
fertile 168
profit 775
aftermost 235
afternoon 126
— farmer 683
after-part 65, 235
after-piece 599
after-taste 65, 390
after-thought
thought 451
memory 505
change of mind 607
after-time 121
afterwards 117
age 745
agacerie 615
again 90, 104
— and again 136
come — periodic 138
fall off — 661
live — 660
against
counteraction 179
anteposition 237
provision 673
voluntary opposition 708
chances — 473
declaim — 932
false witness — 934
go — 708
set — actively 898
set one's face 764, 932
stand up — resist 719
raise &c. one's voice — 489
— one's will 744
— one's expectation 508

— the grain difficult 704
painful 830
dislike 867
— the stream 704
— the time when 510
— or e's will 744
— one's wishes 603
agamist 904
agape open 260
curious 455
expectant 507
wonder 870
Agapemone 827, 897
agate 847
age time 106
period 108
long time 110
era 114
present time 118
oldness 124
advanced life 128
of — 131
from age to — 112
age quod agis! 682
agency
physical 170
instrumentality 631
means 632
employment 677
voluntary action 680
direction 693
commission 755
agenda 625, 626
agent physical 153
intermediary 228
voluntary 690
consignee 759
— provocateur 615
agentship 755
ages: for — 110
— ago 122
agglomerate 46, 72
agglutinate 46
aggrandize
in degree 35
in bulk 194
honor 873
aggravate
increase 35
vehemence 173
exaggerate 549
render worse 659
distress 835
exasperate 900
aggravating 830
aggravation 835
aggregate 50, 72, 84
aggregation 46
aggression 716
aggressor 726
aggrieve 649, 830
aggroup 72
aghast
disappointed 509
fear 860
wonder 870
agile 274, 682
agio 813
agiotage 794
agitate move 315
inquire 461
activity 682
excite the feelings

824
— a question 476
agitation [see agitate]
changeableness 149
energy 171
motion 315
in — preparing 673
agitator leader 694
aglet 554
agley, gang — 732
aglow 382, 420
agnate 11
agnition 762
agnomen 564
agnostic 487
agnosticism 984, 989
agnus Dei 993, 998
ago 122
not long — 123
agog expectant 507
desire 865
wonder 870
agoing 682
set — 707
agonism 720
agonizing 824, 830
agony 378, 828
— of death 360
— of excitement 825
agrarian 371
agree accord 23
concur 178
assent 488
concord 714
consent 762
compact 769
compromise 774
— in opinion 488
— with salubrity 656
agreeable
comfortable 82
physically 377
mentally 829
agreeably to 82
agreement 23 [see agree]
compact 769
agrestic 371
agriculture 371
agronomy 371
aground fixed 150
in difficulty 704
failure 732
ague-fit 860
aguets, aux —
expectation 507
ambush 530
aguish cold 383
ah me! 839
aha! rejoicing 838
ahead 234, 280
go — progression 282
shoot — transcursion 303
activity 682
rock — 665, 667
Ahrimanes 987, 980
aid 707, 906
by the — of 631, 632
aide-de-camp 711, 745

aidless 160
aigrette 847
aiguille 253
aiguillette 747, 847
aigulet 847
ail 655, 828
aileron 267, 273
ailment 655
aim 278, 620, 675
 – a blow at 716
aimable 894
 faire l' – 897
aimer éperdument
 897
aimless *without*
 motive 615a
 chance 621
air *unsubstantial* 4
 broach 66
 lightness 320
 gas 334
 atmospheric **338**
 wind 349
 tune 415
 appearance 448
 refresh 689
 demeanor 692
 fashionable 852
 beat the – 645
 fill the – 404
 fine – *salubrity* 656
 fish in the – 645
 fowls of the – 366
 in the – 527
 rend the – 404
 take – 531
air-balloon 273
air base 728
air-commodore 745
aircraft 273, 726
air-drawn 515
airdrome 273
air-force 726
air-gun 727
airing 266
air-mail 273
airman 269
airmanship 698
air-marshal 745
air-passage 351
air-pipe **351**
airport 273, 292,
 728
air-pump 349
air-raid 716
airs *affectation* 855
 pride 878
 vanity 880
 arrogance 885
air-shaft 351
air service 267
airship 273, 726
air-tight 261
airways 267
airworthy 273, 664
airy [*see* air]
 windy 349
 unimportant 643
 gay 836
 – hopes 858, 859
 give to – nothing
 a local habita-
 tion &c. 515
aisle *passage* 260
 way 627
 in a church 1000
ait 346
ajar *open* 260

discordant 713
ajee 217
ajutage 260, 350
akimbo *angular* 244
 stand – 715
akin *related* 9
 consanguineous 11
 similar 17
al fresco 220
alabaster *white* 430
alack! 839
alacrity *willing* 602
 active 682
 cheerful 836
Aladdin's lamp 993
alar 267
alarm *warning* 668
 notice of danger
 669
 fear 860
 cause for – 665
 give an – *indicate*
 550
alarmist 862
alarum 114, 550, 669
alas! 839
alate 267
alb 999
albeit 30
albert
 chain 847
albification 430
albinescence 430
albinism 430
albino 443
album 593, 596
albumen
 semi-liquid 352
 protein 357
Alcaic 597
alcaid 745
alcalde 745
alcazar 189
alchemy 144
alcohol 995
Alcoran 986
alcove 191, 252
Aldebaran 423
alderman 745
ale 298
alea, jacta est – 601
aleatory 665
Alecto 173
alectromancy 511
alehouse 189
 go to the – 959
alembic
 conversion 144
 vessel 191
 furnace 386
 laboratory 691
alentours 197
alert *watchful* 457,
 459
 active 682
alerte 669
aleuromancy 511
Alexandrine
 ornate style 577
 verse 597
alexandrite 848
alexipharmic 662
alexiteric 662
algebra 85
algid 383
algology 369
algorithm 85
alguazil 965

alias
 otherwise 18
 pseudonym 565
alibi 187
alien *irrelevant* 10
 foreign 57
 transfer 783
 gentile 989
alienable 783
alienate
 transfer 783
 estrange 44, 889
 set against 898
alienation
 mental – 503
alieni appetens
 grasping 865
 envious 921
 selfish 943
alienism 54
align 278
alight *stop* 265
 arrive 292
 descend 306
 on fire 382
alike 17
 share and share –
 778
aliment *food* 298
alimentary 662
 – *canal* 350
alimentation
 aid 707
alimony
 property 780
 provision 803
 income 810
aliquot 51, 84
aliter visum, diis –
 601
alive
 living 359
 intelligent 498
 active 682
 cheerful 836
 be – *with* 102
 keep – *continue*
 143
 keep the memory
 – 505
 look – 684
 – to *attention* 457
 cognizant 490
 informed 527
 able 698
 sensible 822
alkahest 335
all *whole* 50
 complete 52
 generality 78
 – *absorbing* 642
 in – *ages* 112
 – *aboard* 495
 – *agog* 865
 – in all 50
 – *along* 106
 – *along* of 154
 – *but* 32
 – *colors* 440
 – *considered* 451,
 480
 – *day* long 110
 – *devouring* 190
 in – *directions* 278
 – *engrossing* 190
 at – *events com-
 pensation* 30
 qualification 469

true 494
 resolve 604
 – fours *easy* 705
 cards 840
 – in good *time* 152
 – hail! *welcome* 292
 honor to 873
 celebration 883
 courtesy 894
 – hands *everybody*
 78
 on – hands 488
 – of a dither 824
 – of a heap 72
 – *knowing* 976
 – manner of *differ-
 ence* 15
 multiform 81
 with – one's might
 686
 – at once 113
 – one 27, 866
 – out 52
 – over *end* 67
 universal 78
 destruction 162
 space 180
 at – points 52
 – in one's power
 686
 – *powerful
 mighty* 159
 God 976
 in – quarters 180
 with – *respect* 928
 in – *respects* 52,
 494
 – right! 922
 – Saints' day 998
 – *searching* 461
 – *seeing* 976
 on – *sides* 227
 – sorts *diverse* 16a
 mixed 41
 multiform 81
 – *talk* 4
 – things to all
 men 894
 – the time 106
 at – *times* 136
 – *together* 50
 – *ways* 243, 279
 – *wise* 976
 – the world and
 his wife 78
 of – *work
 useful* 644
 maid – 746
Allah 979 ·
allay
 moderate 174
 pacify 723
 relieve 834
 – *excitability* 826
allective 615
allege *evidence* 467
 assert 535
 plea 617
allegiance 743, 926
allegory 464, 521,
 594
allegro *music* 415
 cheerful 836
allelujah 990
allemande 840
all-embracing 76
alleviate 174, 834
alley *court* 189

passage 26
 way 627
alliance *relation* 9
 kindred 11
 *physical co-opera-
 tion* 178
 *voluntary co-oper-
 ation* 709
 party 712
 union 714
allied to *like* 17
alligation 43
align 278
alliteration
 similarity 17
 style in writing
 577
 poetry 597
allocation 60, 786
allocution **586**
allodium *free* 748
 property 780
allopathy 662
alloquy 586
allot *arrange* 60
 distribute 786
 due 924
allow *assent* 488
 admit 529
 permit 760
 consent 762
 give 784
 – to have one's
 own way 740
allowable 760, 924
allowance
 qualification 469
 gift 784
 allotment 786
 discount 813
 salary 973
 with grains of –
 485
 make – for *forgive*
 918
 vindicate 937
alloy *mixture* 41
 combination 48
 debase 659
allude *hint* 514
 mean 516
 refer to 521
 latent 526
 inform 527
allure *move* 615
 create desire 865
alluring 829
allusive
 relative 9
alluvial *level* 213
 land 342
 plain 344
alluvium
 deposit 40
 land 342
 soil 653
ally *combine* 48
 auxiliary 711
 friend 891
alma mater 542
almanac
 list 86
 chronometry 114
 record 551
almighty 157
Almighty, the – 976
almoner
 treasurer 801

arctic *northern* 237
  cold 383
arctics 225
arcuation 245
ardent *fiery* 382
  eager 682
  feeling 821
  loving 897
  – expectation 507
  – imagination 515
ardet, proximus –
  665, 667
ardor *vigor* 574
  activity 821
  feeling 821
  desire 865
arduous 704
area 181, 182
arefaction 340
arena *space* 180
  region 181
  field of view 441
  field of battle 728
arenaceous 330
areola 247
areolar 219
areometer 321
Areopagus 966
arête 253
aretinism 961
aretology 926
Argand lamp 423
argent 430
argillaceous 324
argosy 273
argot 563
argonaut 269
argue *evidence* 467
  reason 476
  indicate 550
  dissectation 595
argument *disagree-
  ment* 24
  topic 454
  discussion 476
  meaning 516
  have the best of
  an – 478
argumentum
  – baculinum
  compel 744
  lawless 964
  punish 972
  – ad crumenam
  800
  – ad hominem
  reasoning 476
  accuse 938
  – ad verecundiam
  939
Argus-eyed 441, 459
argute 498
aria 415
arianism 984
arid 340
  unproductive 169
  uninteresting 841
Ariel *courier* 268
  swift 274
  messenger 534
  spirit 979
arietation 276
arietta 415
aright *well* 618
Ariman [see Ahri-
  manes]
ariolation 511
arioso 415

aris et focis, pro –
  defence 717
  philanthropy 910
arise *exist* 1
  begin 66
  happen 151
  mount 305
  appear 446
  – from 154
Aristarchus 850
Aristides
  good man 948
aristocracy
  power 737
  fashion 852
  nobility 875
ἄριστον μέτρον 628
Arithmancy 511
arithmetic 85
ark *abode* 189
  asylum 666
arm *part* 51
  power 157
  instrument 633
  provide 637
  prepare 673
  war 722
  weapon 727
  make a long – 200
  – chair 215
  – in arm
  together 88
  friends 888
  sociable 892
  – of the law 963
  – of the sea 343
armada 726
Armageddon 720,
  722
armament 673, 727
armed 717
  – at all points 673
  – force 726
  – guard 664
armet 717
armful 25
armiger 875
armigerent 726
armigerous 722
armilla 247, 847
armillary sphere
  466
armipotent 157
armistice
  cessation 142
  respite 672
  pacification 723
armless 158
armlet *ring* 247
  gulf 343
  ornament 847
armor *cover* 223
  defence 717
  arms 727
  buckle on one's –
  673
  – plated 223
armored
  – car 726
  – cruiser 726
  – train 726
armorial bearings
  550, 877
armory *store* 636
  workshop 691
arm's length
  at – 196
  keep at –

  repel 289
  defence 717
  enmity 889
  seclusion 893
  discourtesy 895
arms 727 [see arm]
  heraldry 550
  war 722
  honors 877
  clash of – 720
  deeds of – 720
  with folded – 681
  in – *infant* 129
  throw oneself into
  the – of 666, 880
  under – 722
  up in – *active* 682
  discord 713
  résistance 719
  resentment 900
  enmity 889
Armstrong gun 727
army *collection* 72
  multitude 102
  troops 726
aroma 400
around 227
  lie – 220
arouse *move* 615
  excite 824
  – oneself 682
aroynt *begone* 297
  malediction 908
arquebusade 662
arquebuse 727
arraign 938, 969
arrange
  set in order 60
  plan 626
  compromise 774
  – with creditors
  807
  – itself 58
arrange – matters
  pacify 723
  – music 413, 416
  – in a series 69
  – under 76
arrangement 23, 60
  [see arrange]
  order 58
  temporary – 111
arrant *identical* 31
  manifest 525
  notorious 531
  bad 649
  disreputable 874
  base 940
arras 847
array *order* 58, 60
  series 69
  assemblage 72
  multitude 102
  dress 225
  prepare 673
  adorn 847
  ostentation 882
  battle – 722
arrear, in – 53, 808
arrears *debt* 806
arrectis auribus
  hear 418
  expect 507
arrest *stop* 142
  restrain 751
  in law 969
  – the attention 457
arrière-pensée

  after-thought 65
  mental reservation
  528
  motive 615
  set purpose 620
arrival 292
arrive *happen* 151
  reach 292
  complete 729
  – at a conclusion
  480
  – at the truth 480a
arrogant *severe* 739
  proud 878
  insolent 885
arrogate 885, 924
  – to oneself
  undue 925
arrondissement 181
arrosion 331
arrow *swift* 274
  missile 284
  arms 727
  broad – 550
arrow-head
  form 253
  writing 590
'Arry and 'Arriet
  902
ars celare artem
  698
arsenal *store* 636
  workshop 661
arsenic 663
arson 384
art *representation*
  554
  business 625
  skill 698
  cunning 702
  fine – 850
  work of – 845, 847
  – gallery 556
artery 350, 627
artes, hae tibi
  erunt – 627
artesian well 343
artful 544, 702
  – dodge 545, 702
article *thing* 3
  part 51
  matter 316
  chapter 593
  review 595
  goods 798
articled clerk 541
articles
  thirty-nine – 983a
  – of agreement
  770
  – of faith 484, 983
articulate 366
articulation
  junction 43
  speech 580
articulo, in –
  transient 111
  dying 360
artifice 626, 702
artificer 690
artificial
  fictitious 545
  cunning 702
  affected 855
  – language 579
artillery
  explosion 404
  arms 727

artilleryman 726
artisan 690
artist *painter* &c.
  559
  contriver 626
  agent 690
artiste *music* 416
  drama 599
artistic *skilful* 698
  beautiful 845
  taste 850
  – language 578
artlessness 703
aruspex 513
aruspicy 511
arundo, haeret
  lateri lethalis –
  828
as *motive* 615
  – broad as long 27
  – can be 52
  – good as 27
  – if similar 17
  suppose 514
  – little as may be
  32
  – it may be
  circumstance 8
  event 151
  chance 156
  – much again 90
  – soon as 120
  – they say 496, 532
  – things are 7
  – things go 151,
  613
  – to 9
  – usual 82
  – it were 17, 521
  – you were 141,
  283
  – well as 37
  – the world wags
  151
ascend *be great* 31
  increase 35
  rise 305
  improve 658
ascendancy
  power 157
  influence 175
  success 731
ascendant
  lord of the – 745
  in the –
  influence 175
  important 642
  success 731
  authority 737
  repute 873
  one's star in the –
  prosperity 734
ascension
  [see ascend]
  calefaction 384
  – Day 998
ascent
  [see ascend]
  gradient 217
  rise 305
  glory 873
ascertain *fix* 150
  determine 480
ascertained 474,
  490
ascertainment 480a
asceticism 955
ascititious

attract – 882
call to – 457
call – to 550
give – 418
pay –s to 894
pay one's –s to 902
attenuate
  decrease 36
  weaken 158
  reduce 195
  rarefy 322
attenuated 203
attest
  bear testimony 467
  affirm 535
  adjure 768
attested copy 771
attic simple 42
  garret 191
  summit 210
  style 578
  wit 842
  taste 850
Attila 913
attire 225
attitude
  circumstance 8
  situation 183
  posture 240
attitudinarian 882
attitudinize 855
attollent 307
attorney
  consignee 758
  at law 968
  power of – 755
attract
  bring towards 288
  induce 615
  allure 865
  excite love 897
  – the attention 457
  visible 446
attraction
  [see attract]
  natural power 157
  bring towards 288
attractive
  [see attract]
  pleasing 829
  beautiful 845
attrahent 288
attribute
  speciality 79
  accompaniment 88
  power 157
  –s of the Deity 976
  – to 155
attribution 155
attrite 330
attrition 330, 331
attroupement 72
attune music 415
  prepare 673
attuned to
  habit 613
attunement 23
auburn 433
A.U.C. 106
auction 796, 840
auctioneer 758, 796
auctorial 599
audacity
  courage 861

rashness 863
insolence 885
audible 402
become – 418
scarcely – 405
audience
  hearing 418
  conversation 588
  before an – 599
audire alteram
  partem
  counter-evidence 468
  right 922
  justice 939
audit
  numeration 85
  examination 461
  accounts 811
auditive 418
auditor
  hearer 418
  accountant 811
auditorium 189, 588
auditory
  sound 402
  hearing 418
  theater 599
  – apparatus 418
au fait 698
au fond 5
auf wiedersehen 293
Augean
  – stable 653
  – task 704
auger 262
aught 51
for – one cares
  unimportant 643
  indifferent 866
for – one knows
  ignorance 491
  conjecture 514
augment
  increase 35
  thing added 39
  expand 194
augur 513
  – well 858
augurate 511
augury 512
august 873
Augustinian 996
auk 366
auld lang syne 122
aulic council 696
aumbry 1000
aunt 11
aura wind 349
  sensation 380
aurea mediocritas 628
aureate 436
aureola 420
aureole 420, 873
aureolin 436
auribus, arrectis – 418
auricular hearing 418
  clandestine 528
  – confession 998
auri sacra fames 819
aurist 662
aurora
  dawn 125

light 420, 423
twilight 422
– australes 423
– borealis 423
Auroral 236
ausculation 418
auspice omen 512
auspices
  influence 175
  prediction 511
  protection 664
  direction 693
  aid 707
  under the – of 693, 737
auspicious
  opportune 134
  prosperous 734
  hopeful 858
austerity
  harsh taste 395
  severe 739
  discourteous 895
  ascetic 955
  pietism 988
austral 237
austromancy 511
authentic 467
  certain 474
  true 494
authentication
  evidence 467
  security 771
author 164, 593
  projector 626
  dramatic – 599
  – of our being 976
  – of evil 978
  – 's proof 591
authoritative 474, 741
authority
  testimony 467
  sage 500
  informant 527
  power 737
  permission 760
  right 924
  ensign of – 747
  person in – 745
  do upon one's own – 600
authorized due 924
  legalized 963
authorship
  production 161
  style 569
  writing 590
autobiography 594
autocar 272
autochthonous 188
autocracy 737, 739
autocrat 745
autocratic 600, 737
auto-da-fe 384, 972
autograph 550, 590
Autolycus thief 792
  pedlar 797
automaniac 504
automatic 601, 633
– pistol 727
– writing 992
automaton 554, 601
automobile 272
automobilist 268
automotive 266
autonomasia 521
autonomy 737, 748

autopsy
  post-mortem 363
  vision 441
autoptical 446, 535
autotype 558
autumn 126
auxiliary 711
  additional 34
  helpful 707
  – forces 726
avail benefit 618
  useful 644
  succeed 731
  of no – 645
  – oneself of 677
avalanche fall 306
  snow 383
  redundance 641
avaler les couleu-
  vres 725, 886
avant-courier 64, 673
avant-propos 64
avarice 819
avast! stop 142, 265
  desist 624
  forbid 761
avatar change 140
  deity 976
  idol 991
avaunt! 297, 449
ave! honor 873
  courtesy 894
Ave maria 990
avenge 919
avenue
  plantation 371
  way 627
aver 535
average mean 29, 628
  médiocre 651
  – circumstances 736
  take an – 466
Averni, facilis de-
  scensus – 217, 665
Avernus 982
averruncate 297, 301
aversion unwilling-
  ness 603
  dislike 867
  hate 898
avert 706
  – the eyes 442
aviary 370
aviation 267
aviator 269
avidity avarice 819
  desire 865
airette 272
avile 932, 934
avion 273
aviso 532
avocation 625
avoidance 623
avoidless 474, 601
avoirdupois 319
avolation 623, 671
avouch 535, 768
avow assent 488
  disclose 529
  assert 535
avulsion 44, 301
avuncular 11
await future 121

be kept waiting 133
impend 152
expect 507
awake attentive 457
  careful 459
  intelligent 498
  active 682
  – to life immortal 360
awaken inform 527
  excite 824
  – the attention 457
  – the memory 505
award adjudge 480
  give 784
aware 490
away 187, 196
  break – 623
  fly – 293
  move – 287
  take – from 789
  get &c. – 671
  throw &c. –
  eject 297
  reject 610
  waste 638
  relinquish 782
  – from unrelated 10
  – with! 930, 932
  do – with undo 681
  abrogate 756
awe fear 860
  wonder 870
  respect 928
aweless fearless 861
  insolent 885
  disrespectful 329
awful 31, 860
  – silence 403
awhile 111
awkward
  inelegant 579
  inexpedient 647
  unskilful 699
  difficult 704
  painful 830
  ugly 846
  vulgar 851
  ridiculous 853
  – squad 701
awl 262
awn 253
awning 223, 424
awry oblique 217
  distorted 243
  evil 619
axe edge tool 253
  impulse 276
  weapon 727
  for beheading 975
  have an – to grind 702
Axinomancy 511
axiom 496
axiomatic 474
axis support 215
  center 222
  rotation 312
axle 312
  wheel and – 633
axle load 466
axletree 215
ay 488
ayah 746, 753
aye ever 112
  yes 488
azimuth

horizontal 213
direction 278
measurement 466
– circle 212
azoic 358
azote 663
azotic 657
azure 438
azygous single 87

B

Baal 979, 986
Babbittry 851
babble rivulet 348
faint sound 405
unmeaning 517
talk 584, 588
babbler 501
babbling
foolish 499
babe 129
innocent as the –
unborn 946
Babel confusion 59
discord 414
tongues 560
jargon 563
loquacity 584
baboon 846
baby infant 129
fool 501
– linen 225
babyhood 127
babyish 499
baccarat 840
bacchanals 959
Bacchus 979
drink 959
bachelor 904
– of arts 492
– girl 374
bacillus 193
back rear 235
shoulder 250
aid 707
behind one's –
latent 526
hidden 528
come – 292
give – 790
fall – relapse 661
go – 283
go – from retract
773
have at one's – 215
hold – avoid 623
keep – reserve 636
look – 505
on one's – impo-
tent 158
horizontal 213
failure 732
pat on the –
incite 615
encourage 861
approve 931
pay – retaliate 718
put – deteriorate
659
restore 660
send – 764
take – again 790
carry one's
thoughts – 505
some time – 122
spring – 277
trace – 505

turn – 283
turn one's – 283
turn one's – upon
repel 289
inattention 458
avoid 623
oppose 508
seclusion 893
discourtesy 895
disrespect 929
contempt 930
set one's – against
the wall 604
– to back 235
– down 283
– one's note 806
– out retire 283
change sides 607
relinquish 624
– pedal 273
– up support 215
influence 615
aid 707
put one's – up
anger 900
set one's – up
pride 878
backbite 932, 934
backbiter 936
backbone
intrinsic 5
energy 171
frame 215
center 222
resolution 604
persevere 604a
soul 820
game to the – 604
back door 627
back down 607
backer 711
back-fire 406
back friend 891
backgammon 840
background
distance 196
rear 235
in the –
latent 526
ignoble 874
keep in the –
hide 528
modest 881
seclusion 893
put one in the –
874
throw into the –
460
backsheesh 784,
973
backside 235
backslider 607
backsliding
regression 283
tergiversation 607
relapse 661
vice 945
heterodox 984
impiety 988
backstairs
ambush 530
way 627
– influence 702
backward
tardy 133
regression 283
unwilling 603
deteriorate 659

backwardation 813
backwards 283
bend – 325
– and forwards
interchange 148
oscillation 314
backwater 275, 283
in a – 893
backwoodsman
inhabitant 188
agriculture 371
bacon
butter upon – 641
save one's – 664,
671
Baconian method
461
bacteria 193
bactericide 660
baculinum, argu-
mentum –
compel 744
lawless 964
punish 972
bad 649
unclean 653
wrong 923
– blood 898, 907
go – 653, 659
– business 859
– case 477
– chance 473
put a – construc-
tion on 523
– debt 806
– fairy 980
– faith 940
– grace 895
– habit 613
– hand 701
– humor
discontent 832
dejection 837
anger 900
sullen 901a
not a – idea 498
– intent 907
– job evil 619
botch 699
hopeless 859
– joke 851
– language 908
view in a – light
934
– luck &c. 735
– man 949
– money 800
– name 932, 934
in – odor 889
take in – part 832,
900
– repute 874
– smell 401
– spirit 980
– spirits 837
– taste 579, 851
– temper 900, 901,
901a
on – terms 713,
889
– time of it 828
– turn 619, 907
in a – way
disease 655
worse 659
danger 665
adversity 735
– woman 949

from – to worse
aggravation 835
badaud 501
badge 550
– of authority 747
– of infamy 874
– of slavery 746
badger 830
– dog 366
badinage 842, 856
badly off
adversity 735
poor 804
badminton 840
badness 649
Baedeker 266
baffle hinder 706
defeat 731
– description
unconformable 83
wonder 870
baffling
puzzling 519
bag put up 184
receptacle 191
protrude 250
acquire 775
take 789
steal 791
– and baggage 780
bagatelle
trivial 643
pastime 840
baggage 270
minx 129
materials 635
property 780
hussy 962
baggy 47
bagman 758
bagnio 961
bagpipes 417
bah! 930
bail 771
go – 806
leg – 623
bailie 965
bailiff
director 694
servant 746
factor 758
officer 965
bailiwick
region 181
jurisdiction 965
Bairam
holiday 840
rite 998
bairn 129
bait attraction 288
food 298
trap 545
lure 615
refresh 689
attack 716
bribe 784
harass 830
swallow the – 547
bake 384
bakehouse 386
baker 637
baker's dozen 98
baking heat 382
bal 840
balais 847
balaclava helmet
225
balance equal 27

mean 29
compensate 30
remainder 40
numeration 85
weigh 319
compare 464
style 578
hesitate 605
money 800
accounts 811
in the – 475
the mind losing its
– 503
off one's –
irresolute 605
fail 732
want of – 579
– accounts with
pay 807
balanced 150, 242
balbucinate 583
balbutiate 583
balcony 250
theater 599
bald bare 226
style 575
uninteresting 841
ugly 846
plain 849
baldachin 223, 1000
balderdash 517, 577
baldric 230, 247
bale bundle 72
load 190
ladle 270
evil 619
– out 297
baleful 649
balister 727
balize 550
balk disappoint 509
deceive 545
hinder 706
Balkanize 713
ball globe 249
missile 284
shot 727
dance 840
party 892
– at one's feet 731,
737
keep up the – 143,
682
ballad 415, 597
– monger 597
ballast
compensation 30
weight 319
wisdom 498
safety 666
–without – rash 863
vicious 945
ballerina 599
ballet 599, 840
ballet-dancer 599
ballistics
projectiles 284
war 722
arms 727
ballon d'essai 463
balloon 273, 726
balloonist 269
balloonry 267
ballot 535, 609
ball-room 840
balm moderate 174
fragrance 400
remedy 662

ask 765
- one's bread 765
  poor 804
- leave 760
- one's life 914
- pardon 952
- the question 477
beget 161
begetter 164, 166
beggar idler 683
  petitioner 767
  poor 804
  degrade 874
  low person 876
  sturdy - 792
- description 83,
  870
- my neighbor
  840
- on horseback 885
beggared
  bankrupt 808
beggarly mean 643
  vile 874
  vulgar 876
  servile 886
- account of
  empty boxes
  640, 804
begging
go a -
  too much 641
  useless 645
  offered 763
  free 748
- letter 765
begilt 847
begin 66
- again 104
beginner 541
beginning 66
begird 227, 229
beglerbeg 745
begone
  depart 293
  ejection 297
  abrogate 756
- dull care 836
Begotten, the only
  - 976
begrime 653
begrudge
  unwilling 603
  refuse 764
  stingy 819
beguile mislead 495
  deceive 545
  reconcile 831
- the time
  inaction 681
  amusement 840
beguine 996
begum 745, 875
behalf 618, 707
in - of 759
behave oneself
  conduct 692
  fashion 852
  courtesy 894
behavior 692
on one's good -
  894, 944
behead 361, 972
behemoth 192
behest 741
behind
  in order 63
  in space 235

sequence 281
- the age 124, 491
- one's back 187
speak ill of - one's
  back 934
- the bars 751
- the scenes
  cause 153
  unseen 447
  cognizant 490
  latent 526
  hidden 528
  playhouse 599
- time 133
behindhand
  late 133
  shortcoming 304
  adversity 735
  insolvent 808
behold 441, 457
beholden 916, 926
beholder 444
behoof 618
behoove 926
being 1, 3
  created - 366
  human - 372
  time - 106
Bel 979
belabor 276, 972
belated late 133
  ignorant 491
belaud 931
belay join 43
  restrain 706
belch 297
beldam 130, 913
beldame 173
beleaguer 716
bel esprit 844
belfry 206, 1000
Belial 978, 980
sons of - 988
belie deny 536
  falsify 544
  contradict 708
belief 484, 983
  easy of - 472
  hug a - 606
believe
  [see belief]
  suppose 514
  reason to - 472
- who may 485
  not - one's senses
  870
believer
  religious 987
  true - 983a
belike 472
belittle
  decrease 36
  underestimate 482
  disparage 934
bell 417, 550
  alarm - 669
  bear away the -
  goodness 648
  success 731
  repute 873
  church - 350
  cracked - 408a
  passing - 363
- book and candle
  swear 535
  curse 908
  spell 993
  rite 998

- the cat 861
- shape 249, 252
belladonna 663
belle 374, 854
a la - étoile 220,
  845
belles-lettres 560
belli, casus - 824
bellicose 720, 722
bellied 250
belligerent
  contentious 720
  warlike 722
  combatant 726
belling 412
bellman 354
bello, flagrante -
  722
Bellona 722
bellow loud 404
  cry 411
  animal cry 412
  wail 839
bellows 349, 580
bells, peal of - 407
bellwether 64, 694
belly receptacle 191
  inside 221
  convex 250
-ful 52, 639
- god 957
- timber 298
belomancy 511
belong to related 9
  component 56
  included 76
  attribute 157
  property 777, 780
  duty 926
beloved 897
below 207
  here - 318
- the mark 32
- par 34, 207
  bad 649
  indifferent 651
  discount 813
  ignoble 876
- its full strength
  651
- stairs 207
belt outline 230
  ring 247
  strait 343
  swimming - 666
belting 633
Belus 979
belvedere 441
bemask 528
bemingle 41
bemire 653
bemoan 839
bemused 458
bench support 215
  council 696
  tribunal 966
Bench, King's -
  752
bencher 968
bend oblique 217
  angle 244
  curve 245
  incline 278
  deviate 279
  depression 308
  circuit 311
  give 324
  submit 725

- backwards 235
- the bow 686
- the brows 932
- one's course 27
- the knee
  bow down 308
  submit 725
  humble 879
  servile 886
  courtesy 894
  respect 928
  worship 990
- one's looks upon
  441
- the mind 457
- over 250
- to rules &c. 82
- sinister 874
- one's steps 622
- to tend 176
- towards 278
- to one's will 737
beneath 207
- one 940
- notice 643
Benedick 903
Benedictine 996
benediction
  gratitude 916
  approval 931
  worship 990
  nuptial - 903
benefaction 784
benefactor 816, 912
benefice 995
beneficent 906
beneficial 648
- interest 780
beneficiary
  possessor 779
  receiver 785
  clergy 996
benefit good 618
  use 644
  do good 648
  aid 707
  acquisition 775
  property 780
  benevolence 906
  reap the - of 131
benefits forgot 917
bene gesserit,
  quamdiu se -
  926
benet 545
benevolence
  tax 812
  love 897
  kindness 906
  universal - 910
Bengal heat 382
benighted
  dark 421
  ignorant 491
benign 656, 906
benignant 906
benison 618, 931
Benjamin's mess
  33, 50
Benshie 979
bent tendency 176
  angle 244
  turn of mind 820
  desire 865
  fool to the top of
  one's - 856
- on willing 602
  resolved 604

intention 620
  desirous 865
Benthamite 910
ben trovato
  likely 472
  imagination 515
  untruth 546
  wit 842
benumb
  insensible 376
  cold 385
  deaden affections
  823
beplaster 933
bepraise 931
bequest 270
  gift 784
bereavement
  death 360
  loss 776
  take away 789
bereft poor 804
- of life 360
- of reason 503
béret 225
berg, ice - 383
bergamot 400
berlin 272
berth lodging 189
  bed 215
  office 625
beryl green 435
  jewel 847
beseech 765, 990
beseem 926
berserk 173, 503
beset surround 227
  follow 281
  attack 716
  entreat 705
  annoy 830
  haunt 860
- with difficulties
  704
besetting 78, 613
- sin 945
beshrew 908
beside except 83
  near 197
  alongside 236
- the mark 10, 495
- oneself 503, 824
besides 37
besiege
  surround 227
  attack 716
  solicit 765
bésique 840
besmear 233, 653
besom 652
besotted 481
bespangle 847
bespatter dirt 653
  disapprove 932
  flatter 933
  detract 934
bespeak early 132
  evidence 467
  indicate 516
  engage 755
  ask for 765 -
bespeckle 440
bespot 440
besprinkle 41, 440
best 648, 650

all for the –
 good 618
 prosper 734
 content 831
 hope 858
bad is the – 649
do one's –
 care 459
 try 675
 activity 682
 exertion 686
have the – of it 731
make the – of it
 over-estimate 482
 use 677
 submit 725
 compromise 774
 take easily 826
 hope 858
the – 800
to the – of one's
 belief 484
– bib and tucker
 prepared 673
 ornament 847
 ostentation 882
– friends 890
– intentions 906
– man 903
– part 31, 50
– seller 731
make the – of
 one's time 684
bestead 644
bestial 954, 961
bestir oneself
 activity 682
 haste 684
 exertion 686
bestow 784
– one's hand 903
– thought 451
bestraddle 215
bestrew 73
bestride 206, 215
bet 621
betake oneself to
 journey 266
 business 625
 use 677
bête, pas si – 498
bête noire bane 663
 fear 860
 hate 898
bethel 1000
bethink 451, 505
bethral 749, 751
betide 151
betimes 132
betoken
 evidence 467
 predict 511
 indicate 550
betray disclose 529
 deceive 545
 dishonor 940
– itself visible 446
betrayer 941
betrim 673
betroth 768, 903
betrothed 897
better good 648
 improve 658
 appeal to one's –
 feelings 914
get – health 654
 improve 658
 refreshment 689

restoration 660
get the – of, 479,
 702, 731
think – of 658, 950
seen – days
 deteriorate 659
 adversity 735
 poor 804
– half 903
only – than noth-
 ing 651
– sort 875
for – for worse
 choice 609
 marriage 903
between 228
– cup and lip 111
far – 198
lie – 228
– the lines 526
vibrate – two ex-
 tremes 149
– ourselves 528
– two fires 665
– maid 746
betwixt 228
bevel 217
– gearing 653
bever 298
beverage 298
bévue 732
bevy 72, 102
bewail regret 833
 lament 839
beware 665, 668
bewilder
 put out 458
 uncertainty 475
 astonish 870
bewitch
 fascinate 615
 please 829
 excite love 897
 exorcise 992
bey 745
beyond superior 33
 distance 196
 go – 303
– compare 31, 33
– control 471
– one's depth 208,
 519
– expression 31
– one's grasp 471
– hope 731, 534
– the mark 303,
 641
– measure 641
– possibility 471
– praise
 perfect 650
 approbation 931
 virtue 944
– price 814
– question 474, 494
– reason 471
– remedy 859
– seas 57
bezel 217
bhang 663
bias influence 175
 tendency 176
 slope 217
 prepossession 481
 disposition 820
bib pinafore 225
 drink 959
bibber weep 839

tope 959
bibble-babble 584
bibelot 847
bibendum, nunc
 est – 959
Bible 895
– oath 535
biblioclasm 162
bibliography 593
bibliolatry
 learning 490
 heterodoxy 984
 idolatry 991
bibliomancy 511
bibliomania 490
bibliomaniac 492
bibliophile 492
bibliopole 593
bibliotheca 593
bibulous 298, 959
bicameral 90
bicapital 90
bice 435, 438
bicentenary 98,
 138, 883
bicker flutter 315
 quarrel 713
bicolor 440
biconjugate 91
bicuspid 91
bicycle 272
bid order 741
 offer 763
– the banns 903
– defiance 715
– fair tend 176
 probable 472
 promise 511
 hope 858
– a long farewell
 624
– for intend 620
 offer 763
 request 765
 bargain 794
bidder 767
bide wait 133
 remain 141
 take coolly 806
– one's time 133
 watch 507
 inactive 681
bidet 271
biennial
 periodic 138
 plant 367
bienséance 852, 894
bier 363
bifacial 90
bifarious 90
bifid 91
bifold 90
biform 90
bifurcate 91, 244
big in degree 31
 in size 192
 wide 194
 look – defy 715
 proud 878
 insolent 885
 talk – 885, 909
– sounding
 loud 404
 words 577
 affected 855
– swollen 194
– with ≈1
– with the fate of

511
bigamy 903
biggin 191
bight 343
bigot positive 474
 prejudice 481
 obstinate 606
 heterodox 984
 impious 988
bigotry 907
bigwig scholar 492
 sage 500
 nobility 875
bijou goodness 648
 beauty 845
 ornament 847
bilander 273
bilateral 90, 236
bilbao 727
bilboes 752
 put into – 751
bile 900
bilge base 211
 convex 250
 yawn 260
– water 653
bilious 837
bilingual 560
bilk
 disappoint 509
 cheat 545
 steal 791
bill list 86
 hatchet 253
 placard 531
 ticket 550
 paper 593
 plan 626
 weapon 727
 money order 800
 money account
 811
 charge 812
 in law 969
 true – 969
– and coo 902
– of exchange 771
– of fare food 298
 plan 626
– of indictment
 938
–s of mortality 360
– of sale 771
billet locate 184
 ticket 550
 apportion 786
billet epistle 592
– doux 902
billfold 191
billhook 253
billiard – ball 249
– room 191
– table flat 213
billiards 840
Billingsgate 563,
 908
billion 98
billow sea 348
 river 341
billy-cock 225
billy-goat 373
bimetallism 800
bin 191
binary 89
bind connect 43
 cover 223
 compel 744
 condition 770

obligation 926
– hand and foot
 751
– oneself 768
– over 744
– up wounds 660
binding 681, 744
bine 367
binnacle 693
binocular 445
binomial 89
biogenesis 161
biograph 448
biography 594
biology 357, 359
bioscope 448
biota 357
biparous 89
bipartite 44, 91
biplane 273
biplicity 89
biquadrate 96
birch flog 972
– rod 975
bird 366
 kill two –s with
 one stone 682
–'s eye view 441,
 448
–s of a feather 17
the – has flown
 187, 671
– in hand 777, 781
– of ill omen
 omen 512
 warning 668
 hopeless 859
– of passage 268
– of prey 739
 a little – told me
 527
birdcage 370
birdlime glue 45
 trap 545
biretta 999
birth beginning 66
 production 161
 paternity 166
 nobility 875
– place 153
– right 924
birthday 138, 883
– suit 226
birthmark 848
bis repeat 104
 approval 931
biscuits, s'embar-
 quer sans – 674
bise 349
bisection 68, 91
bishop punch 298
 clergy 996
–'s palace 1000
–'s purple 437
bishopric 995
bisque 33
bissextile 138
bister 433
bistoury 253
bisulcate 259
bit
 small quantity 32
 part 51
 interval 106
 curb 752
 just a – 26
– by bit
 by degrees 26

unexpected 508
disappointment 509
evil 619
action 680
get wind 688
failure 732
prosper 734
pain 828, 830
come to -s 720, 722
deal a - at 716
deal a - to 972
death - 360, 361
- for blow 718
- one's brains out 361
- the coals 824
- down 162
- the fire 384
- the gaff 529
- hole 351
- the horn 416
- hot and cold
lie 544
irresolute 605
tergiversation 607
caprice 608
- a kiss 902
- off *disperse* 73
- out *food* 298
darken 421
gorge 957
- over *past* 122
- pipe 349, 727
- the trumpet 873
- one's own trumpet 882
- up *destroy* 162
eruption 173
inflate 194
wind 349
excite 824
objurgate 932, 934
blower 349
blowhard 884
blown [see blow]
fatigued 688
proud 878
storm - over 664, 721
- upon 874, 932
blow-out 406
blowzy *swollen* 194
red 434
blubber *fat* 356
cry 839
Blucher boot 225
bludgeon 727
- man 726, 913
blue *sky* 338
color 438
learned 490
bit of - hope 858
look -
disappointed 509
feeling 821
discontent 832
disrepute 874
out of the - 508
swear till all's - 535
true - 543, 939
- book 86, 551
- blood 875
- devils 837
- jacket 269
- light 550, 669

- pencil 174, 596
- moon 110
- Peter 293, 550
- and red 437
- ribbon 733, 877
- ruin 959
- stocking
scholar 492
affectation 855
- and yellow 435
Bluebeard
marriage 903
libertine 962
blueness 438
blues 837, 840
bluff *violent* 173
high cliff 206
blunt 254
deceive 545
boasting 884
insolent 885
discourteous 895
blunder *error* 495
absurdity 497
awkward 699
failure 732
- upon 156
blunderbuss 727
blunderhead 701
blunderheaded 499
blunt *weaken* 160
inert 172
moderate v. 174
obtuse 254
benumb 376
damp v. 616
plain-spoken 703
cash 800
deaden 823
discourteous 895
- tool 645
- witted 499
bluntness 254
blur
imperfect vision 443
dirt 653
blemish 848
stigma 874
blurb 931
blurred
invisible 447
blurt out 529, 582
blush *flush* 382
redden 434
feel 821
humbled 879
modest 881
at first - see 441
appear 448
manifest 525
put to the -
humble 897
browbeat 885
discourtesy 895
blushing honors 873, 881
bluster *violent* 173
defiant 715
boasting 884
insolent 885
threaten 909
blusterer 887
blustering [see bluster]
windy 349
Bo to a goose, not say - 862

boa 225
boanerges 540
boar 366, 373
board *layer* 204
support 215
food 298
hard 323
council 696
attack 716
tribunal 966
festive - 892
go by the - 158, 162
go on - 293
on - 186, 273
preside at the - 693
- of trade 621
- school 542
boarding-house 189
boarder 188
boards 599, 728
boast 884
not much to - of 651
boasting 884
boaston 840
boat 273
in the same - 88
- race 720
boating 267
boatman 269
boatswain 269
bob *depress* 308
leap 309
oscillate 314
agitate 315
money 800
- a curtsy 894
- for *fish* 463
Bobadil, Captain - 887
bobbed
hair 53
bobbin 312
bobbing *fuel* 388
bobbish 654
bobby *police* 664
bobsleigh 272
bobsleighing 840
bobtailed 53
bocage 367
bocca, per amusare la - 304
Boche 913
boddice 225
bode 511
bodega 189
bodily
substantially 3
wholly 50
material 316
- enjoyment 377
- fear 860
- pain 378
bodkin
go between 228
perforator 262
body *substance* 3
whole 50
assemblage 72
frame 215
matter 316
party 712
in a - together 88
- and blood of Christ 987
- clothes 225

- color 556
- of doctrine 490
- forth 554
- guard 717, 753
- of knowledge 490
- politic
mankind 372
authority 737
keep - and soul together 654
- of water 438
Boeotian *rustic* 371
stupid 499
fool 501
vulgar 851
ignoble 876
Boer 371
bog 345, 653
- trotter 876
boggart 980
boggle *hesitate* 605
awkward 699
difficulty 704
bogie 980
truck 272
bogle 980
bogus 545
Bohemian
unconventional 83
nomad 268
ungenteel 851
boil *violence* 173
effervesce 315
bubble 353
heat 382, 384
ulceration 655
excitement 824, 825
anger 900
- down 195
boiler 386
boisterous
violent 173
hasty 684
excitable 825
bold *prominent* 250
unreserved 525
vigorous 574
brave 861
make - with 895
show a - front 715, 861
- faced 885
- push *essay* 675
- relief *visible* 446
- stroke *plan* 626
success 731
bole 50
bolero 840
bollard 45
bolshevik 144, 146
bolshevist 737, 742
bolster *support* 215
repair 658
aid 707
- up *vindicate* 937
bolt *sift* 42
fasten 43
fastening 45
close 261
move rapidly 274
propel 284
run away 623
escape 671
hindrance 706
shaft 727
disobey 742

shackle 752
thunder - 872
- the door 761
- food 298, 957
- in 751
- upright 212
bolthead 191
bolus *mouthful* 298
remedy 662
bomb 404, 727
- proof 664, 717
- vessel 726
bombard 716
bombardier 726
bombardon 417
bombast
unmeaning 517
magniloquence 577
ridiculous 853
boasting 884
exaggeration 549
Bombastes Furioso 887
bomber
aeroplane 726
bombilation 404
bon de - augure 858
- enfant *social* 892
kindly 906
- gré mal gré 601
- marché 815
- mot 842
- naturel 836
- ton 852
- vivant 957
- voyage 293
bona - fides
veracity 543
probity 939
- roba 962
bonanza 641, 784
wealth 803
bonbon 396
bond *relation* 9
tie 45
compact 769
security 771
money 800
right 924
- of union 9, 45
government - 802
Liberty - 802
bondage 749
bonded together 712
bonds [see bond]
fetters 752
funds 802
in - service 746
tear asunder one's - 750
- of harmony 714
bondsman 746
bone *strength* 159
dense 321
hard 323
bred in the - 5
feel it in one's - 510
- of contention 713, 720
one - and one flesh 903
- to pick *difficulty* 704
discord 713

708
bar 189
buffo 599
buffoon *actor* 599
humorist 844
butt 857
buffoonery 840, 842
bug 653
bugaboo 669, 860
bugbear
imaginary 155
bane 663
alarm 669
fear 860
buggy 272
bugle
instrument 417
war-cry 722
ornament 847
– *call* 550, 741
build *construct* 161
form 240
– *anew* 658
– *upon a rock* 150
– *up compose* 54
– *upon belief* 484
builder 626, 690
building *material* 635
buildings 189
built on *basis* 211
bulb 249, 250
bulge 250
bulk 50, 192
– *large* 31
bulkhead 228, 706
bull *animal* 366
male 373
error 495
absurdity 497
solecism 568
police 664
ordinance 741
– *in a china shop* 59
like a – *at a gate* 173
take the – *by the horns* 604, 861
Bull, John – 188
bullcalf 501
bulldog *animal* 366
pluck 604, 604a
courage 861
bulldoze 885
bullet *ball* 249
arms 727
missile 284
bulletin 532, 592
– *board* 551
bullfight 720
bullhead 501
bullion 800
bullseye *centre* 222
lantern 423
aim 620
bully *fighter* 726
maltreat 830
frighten 860
courage 861
rashness 863
bluster 885
blusterer 887
threaten 909
evil doer 913
bad man 949
bulrush
worthless 643

bulwark 706, 717
bum 876
bumbailiff 965
bumbledom 737, 965
bumboat 273
bump 250, 276
– *off* 361
bumper 52
bumpkin 876
bumptious
proud 878
insolent 885
contemptuous 930
bun 298
bunch *collection* 72
protuberance 250
– *light* 599
bunchbacked 243
Buncombe
[*see* bunkum]
Bund 712
bundle *packet* 72
go 266
– *on* 275, 684
– *out* 297
bung 263
– *up* 261
bungalow 189
bungle 59, 699
bungler 701
bunion 259
bunk 186, 215
bunker 181
bunkie 890
bunkum *lie* 544
style 577
boast 884
flattery 933
bunting 550
buoy *raise* 307
float 320
hope 858
buoyant
floating 305
light 320
elastic 325
prosperous 734
cheerful 836
hopeful 858
bur *clinging* 46
sharp 253
rough 256
in engraving 558
burden *lading* 190
weight 319
melody 413
poetry 597
too much 641
clog 706
oppress 828
care 830
– *the memory* 505
– *of a song repetition* 104
burdensome
[*see* burden]
hurtful 649
laboring 686
bureau *chest* 191
office 691
shop 799
tribunal 960
bureaucracy 737
bureaucrat 694
burgee 550
burgeon
[*see* bourgeon]

burgess 188
burgh 189
burgher 188
burghmote 966
burglar 792
– *alarm* 669
burglary 791
burgomaster 745
burgrave 745
burial 363
buried *deep* 208
imbedded 229
hidden 528
– *in a napkin* 460
– *in oblivion* 506
burin 558
burke 361
burlesque
imitation 19
travesty 21
absurdity 497
misrepresent 555
drama 599
comic 853
ridicule 856
burletta 599
burly 192
burn *near* 197
rivulet 348
hot 382
consume 384
near the truth 480a
excited 825
love 897
punish 972
– *the candle at both ends*
waste 638
exertion 686
prodigal 818
– *daylight* 683
– *one's bridges* 604
– *one's fingers* 699
– *in* 384
– *out* 385
– *to* 865
burner 423
burning [*see* burn]
passion 821
angry 900
– *glass* 445
– *with curiosity* 455
– *pain* 378
– *shame* 874
burnish *polish* 255
shine 420
beautify 845
burnous 225
burnt [*see* burn]
red 434
– *offering* 952, 990
burr 410
burrock 706
burrow *lodge* 184
excavate 252
bursar 801
bursary 802
burst *disjoin* 44
instantaneous 113
explosion 173
brittle 328
sound 406
paroxysm 825
bubble –
disclosure 529
all over 729

ready to –
replete 641
excited 824
– *of anger* 900
– *away* 623
– *of eloquence* 582
– *of envy* 921
– *into a flame* 825
– *forth begin* 66
expand 194
be seen 446
–*ing with health* 654
– *with grief* 839
– *in* 294
– *of laughter* 838
– *out* 295
– *upon arrive* 292
unexpected 508
– *into tears* 839
burthen
[*see* burden]
bury *enclose* 229
inter 363
conceal 528
– *the hatchet* 918
– *one's talent* 528
busboy 746
busby 225
bush *branch* 51
jungle 344
shrub 367
beat about the –
629
bushel *much* 31
multitude 102
receptacle 191
size 192
hid under a – 460
not hide light un-
der a – 878
bush-fighting 720
bushing 224
bushranger 792
bushy 256
business *event* 151
topic 454
occupation 625
commerce 794
full of – 682
man of –
proficient 700
consignee 758
mind one's –
incurious 456
attentive 457
careful 459
let alone 748
send about one's –
297
stage – 599
business-like
orderly 58
business 625
active 682
practical 692
skilful 698
buskin *dress* 225
drama 599
buss *boat* 273
courtesy 894
endearment 902
bust 554
bustle *energy* 171
dress 225
agitation 315
activity 682
haste 684

difficulty 704
bustling
[*see* bustle]
eventful 151
busy 682
busybody 532, 682·
but
on the other hand 30
except 83
limit 233
qualifying 469
– *now* 118
butcher *kill* 361
provisions 637
evil-doer 913
butler 746
butt *cask* 191
push 276
aim 620
attack 716
laughing-stock 857
– *in* 294, 682
– *end* 67
butte 206
butter 357
flattery 933
– *bread on both sides* 641
– *not melt in mouth* 894
buttered *side*
know – *skill* 698
selfish 943
not know – 699
butter-fingers 701
butterfly
variegated 440
fickle 605
beauty 845
gaudy 882
break – *on wheel*
waste 638
spite 907
butter-scotch 396
buttery 636
buttock 235
button *fasten* 43
fastening 45
little 193
hanging 214
knob 250
trifle 643
take by the – 586
– *hole* 586
– *up close* 261
restrain 751
– *up one's pockets* 808
buttoned-up
reserved 528
buttonholder 841
buttons *page* 746
button-top
useless 645
buttress
strengthen 159
support 215
defence 717
butyraceous 355
buxom 836
buy 795
– *a pig in a poke* 621
– *and sell* 794
buzz *hiss* 409
insect cry 412

publish 531
news 532
buzzard *fool* 501
blind as a – 442
between hawk
and –
agitation 315
worry 315
by *alongside* 236
instrumental 631
go – *pass* 303
– air mail 684
– and by 121, 132
– the card 82
– the hour &c.
hire 788
– itself 87
– means of 632
– no means 32
have – one 637,
777
– my troth &c. 535
– the way
à propos 9
beside the purpose
10
parenthetical 134
– wire 684
– wireless 684
bye *departure* 293
sequestered 893
bygone 122, 506
let –s be bygones
918
by-law 963
by-name 565
by-path 279
by-play 527, 550
byre 189
byssus 256
bystander 197, 444
byway 627
by-word
maxim 496
cant term 563, 564
reproach 574
contempt 930

C

C 3 160
cab 272
cabal *plan* 626
confederacy 712
cabala 526, 993
cabalistic 528, 992
cabaret 599
cabasset 717
cabbage 791
caber, tossing the –
840
cabin 189, 191
cabined, cribbed,
confined 751
cabinet
photograph 554
receptacle 191
workshop 691
council 696
– *picture* 556
cabin plane 273
cable 45, 205
news 531, 532
slip – 623
telegraphic – 534
cabman 268, 694
caboose 386

cabriolet 272
cacation 299
cache 636
cachet 530
lettre de – 751
cachexy 160, 655
cachinnation 838
cacique 745
cackle *of geese* 412
chatter 584
talk 588
laugh 838
cacodemon 980
cacoëthes 613, 865
– *loquendi* 584
– *scribendi* 590
cacography 590
caconym 563
cacophony
stridor 410
discord 414
style 579
Cacus 792
den of – 791
cad *servant* 746
vulgar 851
plebeian 876
cadastre 86, 466
cadaverous
corpse 362
pale 429
hideous 846
caddie 746
caddy 191
cadeau 784
cadence *pace* 264
fall 306
sound 402
music 415
cadenza 415
cadet *junior* 129
soldier 726
officer 745
cadge 765
cadger *idler* 683
beggar 767
huckster 797
cadi 967
cadit quaestio 479
cadmium 439
cadre 726
caduceus 993
caducity
fugacity 111
age 128
impotence 158
decay 659
Caesar 745
aut – aut nullus
ambition 865
fame 873
caesura
disjunction 44
discontinuity 70
cessation 142
interval 198
caetera desunt 53
caeteris paribus 27
café 189
cafeteria 189
caftan 225
cage *receptacle* 191
restrain 751
prison 752
Cagliostro 548, 994
cahotage 59, 315
Cain 361
mark of – 550

raise – 825
caique 273
cairn 363, 550
caisse
grand – 417
caisson 191
caitiff *churl* 876
ruffian 913
villain 949
cajolery
imposition 544,
545
persuasion 615
flattery 933
cake *stick* 46
food 298
consolidate 321
sweet 396
– *walk* 840
calabash 191
calamity *evil* 619
adversity 735
suffering 830
calamo, currente –
590
calash *cap* 225
vehicle 272
calcedony 847
calcine 384
calcitrate 276
calculate
reckon 85
investigate 461
expect 507
intend 620
– *upon* 484
calculated
tending 176
premeditated 611
calculation
[*see* calculate]
caution 864
calculating [*ditto*]
prudent 498
– *machine* 85
calculus 85
caldron
convert 144
vessel 191
heat 386
laboratory 691
calèche 272
caleer 838
calefaction 384
calembour 520
calendar *list* 86
chronicle 114
record 551
calender 255
calenture 503, 655
calf *young* 129
give birth 161
leather 223
animals 366
fool 501
golden – 986, 991
Caliban 846
caliber *degree* 26
size 192
breadth 202
opening 260
*intellectual
capacity* 498
calibrate 26
calidarium 356
calidity 382
caliginous 421
caliph 745

caliphate 737
calisthenics
training 537
beauty 845
caliver 727
calk 660
call *cry* 412
signal 550
name 564
motive 615
visit 892
sanctify 976
ordain 995
at one's – 682, 743
within – 197
– to account 932
– – attention to 457
– to the bar 968
– into being 161
– of duty 926
– for *require* 630
order 741
ask 765
– forth
resort to 677
excite 824
– in *advice* 695
– to mind 505
– to the ministry
996
– names 929, 932
– into notice 525
– off the attention
458
– to order 741
– out *cry* 411
challenge 715
– over *number* 85
– into play 677
– in question 485
– the roll 85
– up 527
– up spirits 992
– to 586
– up *recollect* 505
motive 615
excite 824
– upon
demand 741
request 765
visit 892
duty 924, 926
– to witness 467
callæsthetics 845
callant 129
call-boy
theatre 599
called, so – 545
callidity 698
calligraphy 590
calling
business 625
Calliope 417, 597
callipers 466
callosity 323
callous 376, 823
callow *young* 127
infant 129
bare 226
unprepared 674
calm *physical* 174
quiet 265
dissuade 616
leisure 685
peace 721
moral 826
unamazed 871
– *belief* &c. 484

– before a storm
145
calmative 174
caloric 382
calorimeter 389
calote 999
calotype 556
caloyer 996
calumet *token* 550
– of peace 721, 723
calumniator 936
calumny 934
calvary 1000
Calvinism 984
calyx 191
cam 633
camarade 890
camaraderie 888,
892
camarilla 712
camarista 746
camber 250
cambist 797, 801
camboose 386
camel 271
swallow a – 608,
694
cameo *convex* 250
sculpture 557
camera 445, 553
in – 528
– *lucida* 445
– *obscura* 445
camerated 191
camilla 274
camisade 716
camisole 225
camorra 712
camouflage 530
camp *locate* 184
abode 189
military 728
– bed 215
– stool 215
campagna 180, 344
campaign 692, 722
campaigner 726
campaigning 266
campaniform 249,
252
campanile 206
campestrian 344
Campus Martius
728
can *power* 157
mug 191
preserve 670
jail 752
best one – 686
– it be! 870
canaille 876
canal *opening* 260
conduit 350
way 627
– boat 273
canard 532, 546
canary 366
cancan
dance 840
cancel
compensate 30
neutralize 179
obliterate 552
abrogate 756
repudiate 773
cancelled 219
cancelli 191
cancer *disease* 655

bane 663
painful 830
candelabrum 423
candent 382
candid *white* 430
sincere 543
ingenuous 703
honorable 939
candidate 767, 865
candidature 763
candle 423
bargain by inch of
– 769
burn – at both
ends 686
not fit to hold a –
to 34
– ends 40, 817
– holder 711
– light 126, 422
– power 466
– stick 423, 998
hold – to sun 645
Candlemas 998
candor
veracity 543
artlessness 705
honor 939
candy *dense* 321
sweet 396
cane *weapon* 727
punish 972
scourge 975
canescent 430
Canicula 423
canicular 382
caniculated 259
canine 366
– appetite 865
canister 191
canker *disease* 655
deterioration 659
bane 663
pain 830
canned goods 670
cannel coal 388
cankered
sullen 901a
cankerworm 663
evil-doer 913
care 830
cannibal 913
cannibalism 945
cannon
collision 276
loud 404
arms 727
– fodder 726
–'s mouth *war* 722
courage 861
cannonade 716
cannonball 249, 274
cannoneer 726
cannot 271
cannular 260
canny 498, 702
ca' – 864
canoe 273
paddle one's own
– 748
canon *rule* 80
ravine 198
music 415
belief 484
precept 697
priest 996
rite 998
– law 697

canonical
regular 82
inspired 985
ecclesiastical 995
canonicals 999
canonist 983
canonization
repute 873
deification 991
rite 998
canonry 995
canopy 223
– of heaven 318
canorous 413
cant *oblique* 217
jerk 276
hypocrisy 544
neology 563
impiety 988
cantabile 415
cantankerous 901,
901a
cantata 415
missa – 998
cantatrice 416
canteen 189, 191
canter 266, 274
win at a – 705
canterbury
receptacle 191
Canterbury tale
546
cantharides 171
canticle 415
cantilever 215
canting 855
cantle 51
cantlet 32, 51
canto 597
canton 181, 737
cantonment 184,
189
cantrap 993
canty 836
canvas *sail* 267
picture 556
under press of –
274
canvass
investigate 461
discuss 476
dissert 595
solicit 765
canvasser 767
canyon 350
canzonet 415, 597
caoutchouc 325
cap *be superior* 33
height 206
summit 210
cover 223
hat 225
retaliate 718
complete 929
salute 894
fling up one's –
838
Fortunatus's – 993
set one's – at 897,
902
– and bells 844
– fits 23
– in hand
request 765
servile 886
respect 928
– of maintenance
747

capability
endowment 5
power 157
skill 698
facility 705
capacious *space* 180
– memory 505
capacity
endowment 5
power 157
space 180
size 192
intellect 450
wisdom 498
office 625
talent 698
cap-à-pie
complete 52
armed –
prepared 673
defence 717
war 722
caparison 225
cape *height* 206
cloak 225
projection 250
capella, alla – 415
caper *leap* 309
dance 840
capful *quantity* 25
small 32
– of wind 349
capillament 205
capillary
hairlike 205
thin 203
capital *city* 189
top 201
letter 561
important 642
excellent 648
money 800
wealth 803
make – out of
pretext 617
acquire 775
print in –s 642
– messuage 189
– punishment 972
ship 726
capitalist 803
capitation 85
– tax 812
capitol 189, 717
capitular 995, 996
capitulate 725
capnomancy 511
capon 373
caponize 38, 158
capote 225
capouch 999
capper 548
capriccio *music* 415
whim 608
caprice 608
out of – 615a
capricious
irregular 139
changeable 149
irresolute 605
whimsical 608
capriole 309
capsize 218, 731
capsized 732
capstan 307, 633
capstone 210
capsular 252
capsule *vessel* 190

tunicle 223
medicine 662
captain 269, 745
captandum, ad –
sophistry 477
deception 545
affectation 855
ostentation 882
flattery 933
captation 933
captious
capricious 608
irascible 901
censorious 932
caption
taking 789
beginning 66
heading 564
captivate
induce 615
restrain 751
please 829
captivated 827
captivating 829, 897
captive
prisoner 754
adorer 897
lead – 749
make – 751
– balloon 273
captivity 751
capture 789
Capuchin 996
caput 696
– mortuum 645,
653
caquet 584
car 272
carabineer 726
carack 273
caracole 309
caracoler 266
carafe 191
caramel 396
carambole 276
carapace 717
cara sposa 897
carat 309
caravan 266, 272
caravansary 189
caravel 273
carbine 727
carbohydrates 298
carbon 388
– dioxide 663
– monoxide 663
carbonaro 742
carbonization 384
carboy 191
carbuncle *red* 434
abscess 655
jewel 847
carcanet 847
carcass
structure 329
corpse 362
bomb 727
carcelage 973
carcinoma 655
card *unravel* 60
ticket 550
plan 626
address – 550
by the – 82
great – 873
house of –s 328
leave a – 892
on the –s 152, 177,

470
play one's – 692
play one's best –
686
play one's –s well
698
playing –s 840
shuffle the –s
begin again 66
change 140
chance 621
prepare 673
speak by the –
care 459
veracity 543
phrase 566
throw up the –s
757
ticklish – 704
trump – 626
– index 60, 86, 551
–s to play 632
cardcase 191
cardiac 836
cardigan 225
cardinal *intrinsic* 5
dress 225
red 434
important 642
excellent 648
priest 995, 996
–'s hat 747
– points 278
– virtues 944
cardioid 245
card-sharper 792
card-sharping 545
care *attention* 459
business 625
adversity 735
custody 751
economy 817
pain 828
fear 860
for aught one –s
643, 866
desire 865
love 897
careen *slope* 217
repair 660
career 625, 692
careless
inattentive 458
neglectful 460,
927
feeble 575
insensible 823
indifferent 866
caress 897, 902
caret *incomplete* 53
want 640
careworn 828, 837
cargo 270
large quantity 31
contents 190
property 780
goods 798
– boat 273
caricature
likeness 19
copy 21

circumfluent
lie round 227
move round 311
circumforaneous
traveling 266
circuition 311
circumfuse 73
circumgyration 312
circumjacence **227**
circumlocution 573
circumnavigate
navigation 267
circuition 311
circumrotation 312
circumscribe
surround 229
limit 233, 761
circumscription **229**
circumspection
attention 457
care 459
caution 459
circumstance
phase 8
event 151
circumstances
property 780
bad – 804
depend on – 475
good – 803
under the – 8
circumstantial 8
– account 594
– evidence 467
probability 472
circumstantiality
459
circumstantiate 467
circumvallation
enclosure 229,
232
defence 717
line of – 233
circumvent
environ 227
move round 311
cheat 545
cunning 702
hinder 706
defeat 731
circumvest 225
circumvolution
winding 248
rotation 312
circus
buildings 189
drama 599
arena 728
amusement 840
cirrus 353
cistern
receptacle 191
store 636
Cistercian 996
cit 188
citadel 717
citation 467, 733
cite
quote as example
82
as evidence 467
summon 741
accuse 938
arraign 969
cithern 417
citizen 188
– of the world 910
citriculture 371

citrine 436
city 189
in the – 794
city manager 965
civet 400
civic 372
civil *courteous* 894
laity 997
– authorities 745
– crown 733
– law 963
– war 722
civilian *lawyer* 968
layman 997
civilization
improvement 658
fashion 852
courtesy 894
civilized life 852
civism 910
clack *clatter* 407
animal cry 412
talkative 584
clad 225
claim *requisition*
630
demand 741
property 780
right 924
lawsuit 969
– the attention
457
claimant
petitioner 767
right 924
clair-obscur 420
clairvoyance 992
clairvoyant 513, 994
clamant 411
clamber 305
clammy 352
clamor *cry* 411
wail 839
– against 932
– for 765
clamorous
[*see* clamor]
loud 404
excitable 825
clamp *fasten* 43
fastening 45
clan *race* 11
class 75
family 166
party 712
clandestine 528
clangor 404
clank 410
clannishness 481
clanship 709
clap *explosion* 406
applaud 931
thunder –
prodigy 872
– the hands
rejoice 838
– on 31
– on the shoulder
615
– together 43
– up *imprison* 751
clapperclaw
contention 720
censure 932
claptrap
pretence 546
display 882
claquer 935

faire – son fouet
884
clarence 272
claret color 434
clarify 652
clarinet 417
clarion *music* 417
war 722
clarity 518
clash *disagree* 24
cross 179
concussion 276
sound 406
oppose 708
discord 713
– of arms 720
clasp *fasten* 43
fastening 45
stick 46
come close 197
belt 230
embrace 902
class *arrange* 60
category **75**
learners 541
party 712
– prejudice 481
– room 542
classic *old* 124
symmetry 242
classical
elegant writing
578
taste 850
– art 556
– dancing 840
– education 537
– music 415
classicist 492
classics 560
classify 60
classmate 890
clatter 404, 407
claudication
slowness 275
failure 732
clause *part* 51
passage 593
condition 770
clausis, januis –
528
claustral 110
clavate 250
clavichord 417
clavier 417
claw *hook* 781
grasp 789
– back 935
clay *soft* 324
earth 342
corpse 362
material 635
– pipe 392
clay-cold 383
claymore 727
clean
entirely 52
perfect 650
unstained 652
– bill of health 654
– breast
disclose 529
– forgotten 506
– hand
proficient 700
with – hands
honesty 939
innocence 946

– out *empty* 297
– shaven 226
– sweep
revolution 146
destruction 162
clean-up 775
clear *simple* 42
sound 413
light 420
transparent 425
visible 446
certain 474
intelligible 518
manifest 525
easy 705
liberate 750
profit 775
vindicate 937
innocent 946
acquit 975
all – 664, 705
coast – 664
get – off 671
keep – of 623
make – 529
– for action
prepare 673
– articulation 580
– conscience 946
– the course 302
– cut 518
– the ground
facilitate 705
– of *distant* 196
– off *pay* 807
– out *empty* 297
clean 652
– sighted
vision 441
shrewd 498
– sky *hope* 858
– stage
occasion 134
easy 705
right 922
– thinking 498
– the throat 297
– up *light* 420
intelligible 518
interpret 522
clearheaded 498
clear-obscure 420
cleat 45
cleavage
cutting 44
structure 329
cleave *sunder* 44
adhere 46
bisect 91
cleaver 253
cledge 342
clef 413
cleft *divided* 44
bisected 91
chink 198
in a – stick
difficulty 704
clem 956
clement
lenient 740
long-suffering
826
compassionate
914
clench *compact* 769
retain 781
take 789
clepe 564

clepsydra 114
clerestory 191, 1000
clergy 996
clerical 995, 996
– error 495
– staff 746
clerk *scholar* 492
recorder 553
writer 590
helper 711
servant 746
agent 758
clergy 996
articled – 541
– in holy orders
995
– of works 694
clerkship
commission 755
cleromancy 511
clever
intelligent 498
skilful 698
smart 842
too – by half 702
clew *ball* 249
interpretation 522
indication 550
seek a – 461
click 406
client
dependant 746
customer 795
clientship
subjection 749
cliff *height* 206
vertical 212
steep 217
land 342
climacteric 128
climate *region* 181
weather 338
fine – 656
climatology 338
climax
supremacy 33
summit 210
culmination 729
climb 305
– on the band-
wagon 731
clime 181
clinal 217
clinch *fasten* 43
close 261
certify 474
pun 563
complete 729
clutch 781
snatch 789
– an argument 47
– the fist at 909
clincher 479
cling *adhere* 46
– to *near* 197
willing 602
persevere 604a
habit 613
observe 772
desire 865
love 897
– to hope 858
– to one another
709
clinic 662
clink
resonance 408
stridor 410

- of thought 498
compassion 914
  object of – 828
compatible
  consentaneous 23
  possible 470
compatriot
  inhabitant 188
  friend 890
compeer *equal* 27 _
  friend 890
compel 744
compellation 564
compendency 43
compendious 201
compendium 596
  book 593
compensate
  make up for 30
  requite 973
compensation 30
compère 599
competence
  power 157
  sufficiency 639
  skill 698
  wealth 803
competition
  opposition 708
  contention 720
competitor
  opponent 710
  combatant 726
  candidate 767
compilation
  collect 72
  book 593
  compendium 596
compile 54
complacent
  pleased 827
  content 831
  courteous 894
  kind 906
complain 839
complainant 938
complaint
  illness 655
  murmur 839
  lodge a – 938
  – *without cause*
    839
complaisant
  lenient 740
  courteous 894
  kind 906
complement
  adjunct 39
  remainder 40
  part 52
  arithmetic 84
complementary
  correlation 12
  colour 428
complete
  entire 52
  accomplish 729
  compact 769
  – *answer* 479
  – *circle* 311
  in a – *degree* 31
completeness 52
completion 729
complex 59
complexion
  state 7
  color 428
  appearance 448

compliance
  conformity 82
  obedience 743
  consent 762
  observance 772
complicate
  derange 61
complicated
  disorder 59
  convolution 248
complice 711
complicity 709
compliment
  courtesy 894, 896
  praise 931
  poor – 932
  –s *of season* 896
complimentary
  free 815
complot 626
comply [*see* compli-
    ance]
compo *coating* 223
  material 635
component 56
componere lites
    723, 724
comport
  – *oneself* 692
  – *with* 23
compos mentis 502
compose
  make up 54, 56
  produce 161
  moderate 174
  music 416
  write 590
  printing 591
  pacify 723
  assuage 826
composed
  self-possessed 826
composer
  music 413
composite 41
composition 54
  [*see* compose]
  combination 48
  piece of music 415
  picture 556
  style 569
  writing 590
  building material
    635
  compromise 774
  barter 794
  atonement 952
compositor
  printer 591
compost 653
composure 826, 871
compotation 959
compote 298
compound
  mix 41
  combination 48
  limited space 182
  enclosure 232
  compromise 774
  – *arithmetic* 466
  – *for substitute* 147
  barter 794
comprador 637
comprehend
  compose 54
  include 76
  know 490
  understand 518

comprehension [*see*
    comprehend]
  intelligence 498
comprehensive 76
  complete 50
  general 78
  wide 192
  – *argument* 476
compress
  contract 195
  curtail 201
  condense 321
  remedy 662
compressible 322
comprise 76
comprobation
  evidence 467
  demonstration 478
compromise
  dally with 605
  mid-course 628
  taint 659
  danger 665
  pacify 723
  compact 769
  compound 774
  atone 952
compromised
  promised 768
compter 799
compte rendu
  record 551
  accounts 811
comptroller 694
compulsion 744
compunction 833,
    950
compurgation
  evidence 467
  acquittal 970
compute 85
comrade 890
comradeship 892
con *think* 451
  get by heart 505
  learn 539
conation 600
conatu magnas
  nugas, magno –
  waste 638
  unimportance 643
conatus 176
concamerate 245
concatenation
  junction 43
  continuity 69
concavity 252
conceal
  invisible 447
  hide 528
  cunning 702
concealment 528,
    893
concede
  assent 488
  admit 529
  permit 760
  consent 762
  give 784
conceit *idea* 453
  folly 499
  supposition 514
  imagination 515
  wit 842
  affectation 855
  vanity 880
conceited
  dogmatic 481

conceivable 470
conceive *begin* 66
  beget 161
  teem 168
  believe 484
  understand 490
  imagine 515
  plan 626
concent 413
concentrate
  assemble 72
  centrality 222
  converge 290
concentric 216, 222
conception
  [*see* conceive]
  intellect 450
  idea 453
concern
  relation 9
  event 151
  business 625
  importance 642
  firm 797
  grief 828
  – *oneself with* 625
concert
  agreement 23
  synchronism 120
  music 415
  act in – 709
  in – *musical* 413
  concord 714
  – *measures* 626
concertina 417
concerto 415
concert-room 840
concession
  permission 760
  consent 762
  compromise 774
  giving 784
  discount 813
concesso, ex –
  reasoning 476
  assent 488
concetto 842
conchoid 245
conchology 223
concierge 163, 753
conciliate
  talk over 615
  pacify 723
  satisfy 831
  courtesy 894
  atonement 952
conciliatory [*see*
    conciliate]
  concord 714
  forgiving 918
conciliatrix 962
concinnity
  agreement 23
  style 578
  beauty 845
conciseness 572
concision 201
conclave
  assembly 72
  council 696
  church 995
conclude
  end 67
  infer 480
  resolve 604
  complete 729
  compact 769
conclusion

[*see* conclude]
  sequel 65
  germination 161
  judgment 480
  try –s 476
  forgone – 611
  hasty – 481
conclusive
  [*see* conclude]
  answer 462
  evidence 467
  certain 474
  proof 478
  – *reasoning* 476
concoct *lie* 544
  write 590
  plan 626
  prepare 673
concomitant
  accompany 88
  same time 120
  concurrent 178
concord *agree* 23
  music 413
  assent 488
  harmony 714
concordance 562
  book 593
concordant 173
concordat 769
concordia discors
    24, 59
concours 720
concourse
  assemblage 72
  convergence 290
concremation 384
concrete *existent* 3
  mass 46
  definite 79
  density 321
  hardness 323
  materials 635
concubinage 961
concubine 926
concupiscence 865,
    961
concur
  co-exist 120
  causation 178
  converge 290
  assent 488
  concert 709
concurrence 178,
    216
concussion 276
condemnation 932,
    971
condemned cell 752
condense
  compress 195
  dense 321
condensed
  concise 572
condescend 879
condign 924
condiment 393
condisciple 541
condition *state* 7
  modification 469
  supposition 514
  term 770
  repute 873
  rank 875
  in – *plump* 192
  in good – 648
  on – 770
  in perfect – 650

idea 453
attention 457
qualification 469
inducement 615
importance 642
gift 784
benevolence 906
respect 928
requital 973
deserve – 642
in – of
  compensation 30
  reasoning 476
on – 658
take into –
  thought 451
  attention 457
under –
  topic 454
  inquiry 461
  plan 626
considered, all
  things –
  collectively 50
  judgment 480
  premeditation 611
  imperfection 651
consign
  transfer 270
  commission 755
  property 783
  give 784
  – to the flames 384
  – to oblivion 506
  – to the tomb 363
consignee 758
consignor 796
consignment
  commission 755
  gift 784
  apportionment 786
consilience 178
consist
  – in 1
  – of 54
consistence
  density 321
consistency
  uniformity 16
  agreement 23
consistently with 82
consistory
  council 696
  church 995
consolation
  relief 834
  condole 915
  religious 976
console
  table 215
Consoler
  the – 976
consolidate
  unite 46, 48
  condense 321
consols 802
consommé 298
consonant
  agreeing 23
  musical 413
  letter 561
consort
  accompany 88
  associate 892
  spouse 903
  – with 23

consortium 23
consortship 892
conspection 441
conspectus 596
conspicuous
  visible 446
  famous 873
conspiracy 626
conspirator 626
  traitor 941
conspire
  concur 178
  co-operate 709
constable
  policeman 664
  governor 745
  officer 965
constant
  fixed 5
  uniform 16
  continuous 69
  regular 80
  continual 112
  frequent 136
  regular 138
  immutable 150
  exact 494
  persevering 604a
  obey 743
  faithful 939
  – flow 69
constellation
  stars 318
  luminary 423
  glory 873
consternation 860
constipation
  closure 261
  density 321
constituency 181, 737
constituent 51, 56
constitute
  compose 54, 56
  produce 161
constitution
  nature 5
  state 7
  composition 54
  structure 329
  charter 924
  law 963
constitutional
  walk 226
  – government 737
constrain
  compel 744
  restrain 751
  abash 881
constraint 195
constrict 195, 706
constringe 195
construct 161
construction 161
  form 240
  structure 329
  meaning 522
  put a false – upon 523
constructive
  latent 526
  – evidence 467
constructor 164
construe 522
consubstantiation 998
consuetude 618
consul 758, 759

consulship 737
consult 695
  – one's pillow 133
  – one's own wishes 943
  – the wishes of 707
consultant 662
consultation 695, 696
consume
  destroy 162
  waste 638
  use 677
  – away 36
  – time
  time 106
  inactivity 683
**consumere natus,
  fruges** – 683
consuming 830
consummate
  great 31
  complete 52
  completed 729
  – skill 698
consummation
  end 67
  completion 729
  – devoutly to be wished
  good 618
  desire 865
consumption [*see* consume]
  decrease 36
  shrinking 195
  disease 655
contact 199
  come in –
  arrive 292
contagion
  transfer 270
  disease 655
  unhealthy 657
contain
  be composed of 54
  include 76
container 191
contaminate
  soil 653
  spoil 659
contaminated
  diseased 655
contango 133, 813
contemn 930
contemper 174
contemplate
  view 441
  think 451
  expect 507
  purpose 620
contemporary 120
contemporation 174
contempt 930
  – of danger 861
contemptible
  unimportant 643
  dishonorable 940
contend
  reason 476
  assert 535
  fight 720
  – with difficulties 704
  – for
  vindicate 937
content
  assenting 488

willing 602
  calm 826
  satisfied **831**
  to one's heart's –
  sufficient 639
  success 731
contention 720
contentious 901
contents
  ingredients 56
  list 86
  components 190
  synopsis 596
conterminate
  end 67
  limit 233
conterminous 199
contesseration 72
contest 709, 720
contestant 710
context 591
  from the – 516
contexture 329
contiguity 199
continence 960
continent
  land 342
continental 643
contingency
  event 151
  uncertainty 475
  expectation 507
contingent
  conditional 8
  casual 156
  liable 177
  possible 470
  uncertain 475
  supply 635
  aid 707
  allotted 786
  donation 809
  unforeseen 508
  – duration 108a
  – interest 780
continual
  perpetual 112
  frequent 136
continuance 143
continuation
  adjunct 39
  sequence 63
  sequel 65
  – school 542
continue
  endure 106, 110
  persist 143
continued 69
  – success 731
continuity 69
  uniformity 16
contortion
  distortion 243
  convolution 248
contortionist 599, 700
contour
  outline 230
  appearance 448
contra 14
  per – 708
  – bonos mores
  vulgar 851
  improper 925
  vice 945
contraband
  deceitful 545
  prohibited 761

illicit 964
contrabasso 417
contraception 706
contract
  shrink 195
  narrow 203
  promise 768
  bargain 769
  bridge 840
  – a debt 806
  – a habit 613
  – an obligation 768
contractility 195
contraction 195
  short-hand 590
  compendium 596
contractor 690
contradict
  contrary 14
  answer 462
  dissent 489
  deny 536
  oppose 708
contradictory
  disagreement 24
  evidence 468
  discord 713
contradistinction 15
contraindicate
  dissuade 616
  warning 668
contraire, tout au – 536
contralto 408, 416
contraposition
  inversion 218
  reversion 237
contrapuntist 413
contrariety 14
contrary
  opposite 14
  antagonistic 179
  captious 608
  opposing 708
  quite the – 536
  – to expectation
  improbable 473
  unexpected 508
  – to reason 471
contrast
  contrariety 14
  difference 15
  comparison 464
contravallation 717
contravene
  contrary 14
  counterevidence 468
  deny 536
  hinder 706
  oppose 708
contre cœur, à – 603
contre-coup 277
contretemps
  ill-timed 135
  hindrance 706
  misfortune 735
contribute
  cause 153
  tend 176
  concur 178
  aid 707
  give 784
contribution 784
  lay under – 789, 924

contrition
  abrasion 331
  regret 833
  penitence 950
contrivance 633
contrive
  produce 161
  plan 626
  – to succeed in 731
contriving
  cunning 702
control
  power 157
  influence 175
  regulate 693
  authority 737
  restrain 751
  board of – 696
  under –
  obedience 743
  subjection 749
controller of
  currency 801
controls 273, 693
controversial
  discussion 476
  discordant 713
controversialist
  476, 726
controversy
  disagreement 24
  discussion 476
  debate 588
  contention 720
controvert
  deny 536
controvertible
  uncertain 475
  debatable 476
  untrue 495
contumacy
  obstinacy 606
  disobedience 742
contumely
  arrogance 885
  rudeness 895
  disrespect 929
  scorn 930
  reproach 932
contund 330
contuse 330
conundrum pun
  520
  riddle 533
  wit 842
convalescence 654,
  660
convection 270
convenance
  mariage de – 903
convene 72
conveniences 632
convenient 646, 705
convent 1000
conventicle
  assembly 72
  council 696
  chapel 1000
convention
  agreement 23
  assembly 72
  rule 80
  council 696
  precept 697
  treaty of peace
  723
  compact 769

–s of society 852
conventional 82,
  613
conventual 996,
  1000
convergence 290
convergent 286
conversable
  talk 588
  sociable 892
conversant
  know 490
  skilful 698
conversation 588
conversational
  loquacious 584
  interlocution 588
  sociable 892
conversazione 588,
  892
converse
  reverse 14
  talk 588
conversely 468
conversion 144
  trover and – 964
convert
  change to 140, 144
  opinion 484
  tergiversation 607
  religion 987
  – to use 677
convertible 13, 27
  – terms 522
convexity 250
convey
  transfer 270
  mean 516
  assign 783
  – away 791
  – the knowledge
  of 527
conveyance
  [see convey]
  vehicle 272
conveyancer 968
conveyancing 783
convict
  convince 484
  condemned 949
  condemn 971
convicted, self –
  950
conviction
  confutation 479
  belief 484
  prove guilty 971
convince
  belief 484
  confute 479
  teach 537
convivial 892
convocate 72
convocation
  council 696
  church 995
convoke 72
convolution
  coil 248
  rotation 312
convoy
  accompany 88
  transfer 270
  guard 664
  escort 753
convulse
  derange 61

violent 173
  agitate 315
  bodily pain 378
  mental pain 830
convulsed with
  – laughter 838
  – rage 900
convulsion
  [see convulse]
  disorder 59
  revolution 146
  in –s 325
coo 412
cook heat 384
  falsify 544
  improve 658
  prepare 673
  servant 746
  too many –s 699
  – accounts 811
cool moderate 174
  cold 383
  refrigerate 385
  grey 432
  dissuade 616
  cautious 864
  indifferent 866
  unamazed 871
  unfriendly 889
  discourteous 895
  look – upon
  unsocial 893
  take –ly 826
  – down 826
  – one's heels
  kept waiting 133
  inaction 681
cooler 387
coolheaded
  judicious 498
  unexcitable 826
coolie
  bearer 271
  military 726
coolness
  insensibility 823
  estrangement 898
coon-can 840
coop abode 189
  restrain 751
  prison 752
co-operation
  physical 178
  voluntary 709
  participation 778
co-operator 690, 711
co-optation 609
co-ordinate
  equal 27
  arrange 60
  measure 466
cootie 653
cop 664
copal 356a
coparcener 778
copartner
  accompanying 88
  participator 778
  associate 890
copartnership
  co-operation 709
  party 712
cope equal 27
  oppose 708
  contend 720
  canonicals 999
copia verborum

diffuse 573
  loquacious 584
coping stone
  top 210
  completion 729
copious
  diffuse style 573
  abundant 639
coportion 778
copper money 800
  policeman 664
copper-colored
  433, 439
copper-plate
  engraving 558
  writing 590
coppice 367
coprolite 653
copse 367
copula 45
copulation 43
copy
  imitate 19
  facsimile 21
  prototype 22
  news 532
  record 551
  represent 554
  write 590
  for the press 591
  plan 626
  – book 22
copyhold 780
copyist
  imitator 19
  artist 559
  writer 590
copyright 780
coquet lie 544
  change the mind
  607
  affected 855
  endearment 902
  flattery 933
  – with
  irresolute 605
coquette
  affected 854, 855
  flirt 897
coquillage 847
coracle 273
coral 847
  – reef 667
coram judice
  jurisdiction 965
  lawsuit 969
cor Anglais 417
corbeille 191
corbel 215
cord tie 45
  filament 205
cordage 45
cordated 245
cordial
  pleasure 377
  dram 392
  willing 602
  remedy 662
  feeling 821
  grateful 829
  friendly 888
  courteous 894
cordiform 245
cordite 727
cordon
  inclosure 232
  circularity 247

decoration 877
  – bleu 733, 746
  – sanitaire
  safety 664
  preservation 670
corduroy 259
cordwainer
  shoemaker 225
  artificer 690
core gist 5
  source 153
  center 222
  gist 642
  true to the – 939
coriaceous 327
Corinthian 850
co-rival
  [see corrival]
cork plug 263
  lightness 320
  – jacket 666
  – up close 261
  restrain 751
corking pin 45
corkscrew
  spiral 248
  perforator 262
  circuition 311
cormorant
  desire 865
  gluttony 957
corn
  projection 250
Cornaro 953
cornea 441
corned 959
cornelian 847
corneous 323
corner place 182
  receptacle 191
  angle 244
  monopoly 777
  – creep into a –
  893
  in a dark – 528
  drive into a – 706
  push into a – 874
  rub off –s 82
  – turn a – 311
  turn the – 658
  – stone
  support 215
  importance 642
  defence 717
cornet music 417
  officer 745
cornice 210
corniculate 253
cornification 323
Cornish hug 545
corno 417
cornopean 417
cornucopia 639
cornute
  projecting 250
  sharp 253
corollary
  adjunct 39
  deduction 480
corona 247
coronach 839
coronation
  enthronement 755
  celebration 883
coroner 363, 965
  –'s jury 967
coronet hoop 247

insignia 747
title 877
corporal
  corporeal 316
  officer 745
corporate 43
  – body 712
corporation
  bulk 192
  convex 250
  association 712
  jurisdiction 965
corporeal 3, 316, 364
  – hereditaments 780
corporeity 316
corps assemblage 72
  troops 726
  à – perdu
  haste 684
  rash 863
  – de reserve 636
corpse 362
corpulence 192
corpus 316
  – Christi 998
  – delicti
  quilt 947
  lawsuit 969
  – juris
  precept 697
  law 963
corpuscle
  small 32
  little 193
corradiation
  focus 74
  convergence 290
corral 232, 370
correct
  orderly 58
  true 494
  inform 527
  disclose 529
  improve 658
  repair 660
  due 924
  censure 932
  honorable 939
  virtuous 944
  punish 972
  – ear 416, 418
  – memory 505
  – reasoning 476
  – style
  grammatical 567
  elegant 578
correction
  [see correct]
  house of – 752
  under – 879
corrective 662
corregidor 745
correlation
  relation 9
  reciprocity 12
correspondence
  correlation 12
  similarity 17
  agreement 23
  writing 592
  – course 537
correspondent
  messenger 534
  journalist 593
  consignee 758
corresponding

similar 17
agreeing 23
corridor region 181
  place 191
  passage 627
  – train 272
corrigendum 495
corrigible 658
corrival 726
corrivalry 720
corrivation 348
corroborant 662
corroboration
  evidence 467
  assent 488
corrode burn 384
  erode 659
  afflict 830
corrosive
  [see corrode]
  acrid 171
  destructive 649
  – sublimate 663
corrugate
  derange 61
  constrict 195
  roughen 256
  rumple 258
  furrow 259
corruption
  decomposition 49
  neology 563
  foulness 653
  disease 655
  deterioration 659
  improbity 940
  vice 945
corrupting
  noxious 649
corsage 225
corsair 273, 792
corse 362
corselet 225
corset 225
corso 728
cortège
  adjunct 39
  continuity 69
  accompaniment 88
  journey 266
  suite 746
cortes 696
cortex
  cortical 223
coruscate 420
corvette 273, 726
corybantic 503
coryphée 599
Corypheus
  teacher 540
  director 694
coscinomancy 511
cosey 892
cosignificative 522
cosine 217
cosmetic
  remedy 662
  ornament 847
cosmic 318
cosmogony &c. 318
cosmopolitan
  abode 189
  mankind 372
  philanthropic 910
  sociality 892
cosmorama 448
cosmos 60, 318

Cossack 726
cosset
  darling 899
  caress 902
cost 812
  pay –s 807
  to one's –
  evil 619
  badness 649
  – what it may 604
  – price 815
costermonger 797
costless 815
costly 814
costive
  taciturn 585
costume 225
  theatrical – 599
costumé 225
  bal – 840
costumier 225
  theatrical 599
cosy snug 377
  sociable 892
cot abode 189
  bed 215
cote 189
cotenancy 778
coterie class 75
  junto 712
  society 892
coterminous 120
cothurnus 599
cotillon 840
cottage 189
  – piano 417
cottager 188
cotter 188
cotton 205
  – seed oil 356
couch lie 213
  bed 215
  stoop 308
  lurk 528
  – one's lance 720
  – in terms 566
couchant 213
couci-couci 651
cough 349
  churchyard – 655
couleur de rose
  good 648
  prosperity 734
  view en – 836
coulisses 599
coulter 253
council
  senate 696
  church 995
  hold a – 695
  – of education 542
  – school 542
councillor 696
counsel
  advice 695
  lawyer 968
  keep one's own – 528
  take – think 451
  inquire 461
  be advised 695
count clause 51
  item 79
  compute 85
  estimate 480
  lord 875
  – one's chickens before they are

hatched 858, 863
  – the cost 864
  – upon
  believe 484
  expect 507
  to be –ed on one's fingers 103
countenance
  face 234
  appearance 448
  favor 707
  approve 931
  keep in –
  conform 82
  induce 615
  encourage 861
  vindicate 937
  keep one's –
  brook 826
  not laugh 837
  out of –
  abashed 879
  put out of – 874
  stare out of – 885
  – falling
  disappointment 509
  dejection 837
counter contrary 14
  number 84
  table 215
  stern 235
  token 550
  shop-board 799
  over the –
  barter 794
  buy 795
  sell 796
  run – 179
  – to 708
counteract
  compensate 30
  physically 179
  hinder 706
  voluntarily 708
counteraction 14, 179
counterbalance 30
counterblast
  counteract 179
  retaliate 718
countercharge 462
counterchange
  correlation 12
  interchange 148
countercharm 993
countercheck
  mark 550
  hindrance 706
counterclaim 30
counter-evidence 468
counterfeit
  imitate 19
  copy 21
  simulate 544
  sham 545
  coinage 792
counterfoil 550
countermand 756
countermarch 266, 283
countermark 550
countermine
  plan 626
  oppose 708
countermotion 283

counterorder 756
counterpane 223
counterpart
  match 17
  copy 21
  reverse 237
counterplot
  plan 626
  oppose 708
  retaliate 718
counterpoint 415
counterpoise
  compensate 30
  weight 319
  hinder 706
counter-poison 662
counterpole 14
counter-project 718
counter-protest 468
counter-revolution 146
counterscarp 717
countersign
  evidence 467
  assent 488
  mark 550
counterstroke 718
countervail
  outweigh 28
  compensate 30
  evidence 468
counterwork 708
countess 875
counting-house 799
countless 105
countrified 189
  vulgar 851
country
  region 181
  abode 189
  rural 371
  authority 737
  love of – 910
country-dance 840
countryman
  commonalty 876
  friend 890
county 181
  – seat 189
  – town 189
  – school 542
  – council 696
  – court 966
coup
  instantaneous 113
  action 680
  – de bec
  attack 716
  censure 932
  – d'épée dans l'eau 645
  – d'essai 675
  – d'état
  revolution 146
  plan 626
  action 680
  lawless 964
  – de grâce
  end 67
  death-blow 361
  completion 729
  punishment 972
  – de main
  violence 173
  action 680
  attack 716
  – de maître
  excellent 648

curry-comb 370
curse *bane* 663
  adversity 735
  painful 830
  malediction 908
cursed *bad* 649
cursitor 968
cursive 590
cursory
  transient 111
  inattentive 458
  hasty 684
  take a – view of
    457
  neglect 460
curst 901*a*
curt *short* 201
  concise 572
  taciturn 585
curtail *retrench* 38
  shorten 201
  –ed of its fair pro-
    portions
  distorted 243
  ugly 846
curtain 223
  shade 424
  hide 528, 530
  theatre 599
  fortification 717
  behind the –
    invisible 447
    inquiry 461
    knowledge 490
  close the – 528
  raise the – 529
  rising of the – 448
  – lecture 932
  – raiser 66, 599
curtsy
  stoop 308, 314
  submit 725
  polite 894
curule 696
curvature 245
curvet *leap* 309
  turn 311
  oscillate 314
  agitate 315
curvilinear 245
  – *motion* 311
cushion *pillow* 215
  soft 324
  relief 834
cushy 829
cusp *angle* 244
  sharp 253
cuspidor 191
cuss 908
custard 298
custodes? quis cus-
  todiet – 459
custodian 753
custody *safe* 664
  captive 751
  retention 781
  in – *prisoner* 754
  accused 938
  take into – 751
custom *old* 124
  habit 613
  barter 794
  sale 796
  tax 812
  fashion 852
  – honored in
    breach 614
customary

[*age* custom]
  regular 80
customer 795
custom-house 799
  – officer 965
custos 753
  – *rotulorum* 553
cut *divide* 44
  bit 51
  discontinuity 70
  interval 198
  curtail 201
  layer 204
  form 240
  notch 257
  blow 276
  eject 297
  reap 371
  physical pain 378
  cold 385
  neglect 460
  carve 557
  engraving 558
  road 627
  attack 716
  portion 786
  affect 824
  mental pain 830
  dance step 840
  *decline acquaint-
    ance* 893
  discourtesy 895
  tipsy 959
  – short 628
  unkindest – of all
    pain 828
  malevolence 907
  – across 302
  – adrift 44
  – along 274
  have a – at 716
  – away 274
  – a whetstone with
    a razor
    sophistry 477
    waste 638
    misuse 679
  – both ways 468
  – capers 309
  – according to
    cloth
    economy 817
    caution 864
  – and come again
    repeat 104
    enough 639
  – dead 893
  – direct 893
  – down *destroy* 162
    shorten 201
    fell 308
    kill 361
    – down expenses
      817
  – and dried
    arranged 60
    prepared 673
  – a figure
    appearance 448
    fashion 852
    repute 873
    display 882
  – the first turf 66
  – the ground from
    under one
    confute 479
    hinder 706
  – to the heart 824,

    830
  – ice with
    influence 175
  – of one's jib 448
  – jokes 842
  – the knot 705
  – off *subduct* 38
    disjoin 44
    kill 361
    impede 706
    bereft 776
    secluded 893
  – off with a shil-
    ling 789
  – open 260
  – out *surpass* 33
    stop 142
    substitute 147
    plan 626
  – out for 698
  – out work
    prepare 673
    direct 693
  – to pieces
    destroy 162
    kill 361
  – a poor figure 874
  – to the quick 830
  – up root and
    branch 162
  – up rough 900
  – and run 274
    depart 293
    escape 623
  – short *stop* 142
    destroy 162
    shorten 201
    silence 581
  – one's stick
    depart 283
    avoid 623
  – one's own throat
    699
  – and thrust 716
  – in two 91
  – up *divide* 44
    destroy 162
    pained 828
    give pain 830
    discontented 832
    dejected 837
    censure 932
  – what one will – up
    for 780
  – one's way
    through 302
cutaneous 223
cute 698
cuticle 223
cutlass 727
cutlery 253
cut-purse 792
cutter 273
cut-throat
  killer 361
  evil-doer 913
cutting *sharp* 253
  cold 383
  path 627
  affecting 821
  painful 830
  reproachful 932
cuttings
  excerpta 596
  selections 609
cutty stool 950
cwt. 98, 319
cyanogen 438

cyanide of potas-
  sium *poison* 663
cycle *time* 106
  period 138
  circle 247
  ride 266
  vehicle 272
  – *car* 272
cyclist 268
cycloid 247
cyclometer 200
cyclone
  rotation 312
  wind 349
Cyclopean
  strong 159
  huge 192
cyclopedia
  knowledge 490
  book 593
Cyclops
  monster 83
  mighty 159
  huge 192
  dupe 547
cygne
  chant du – 360
  – noir 650
cylindric 249
cyma 847
cymbal 417
cymbalo 417
cymophanous 440
cynic
  misanthrope 911
  detractor 936
  ascetic 955
  closet – 893
cynical
  contemptuous 930
  censorious 932
  detracting 934
cynicism
  discourtesy 895
  contempt 930
cynosure *sign* 550
  direction 693
  wonder 870
  repute 873
Cynthia of the
  minute 149
cypher [*see* cipher]
cypress
  interment 363
  mourning 839
Cyprian 962
cyst 191
czar 745

D

da capo 104
dab *small* 32
  paint 223
  slap 276
  clever 700
dabble *water* 337
  dirty 653
  meddle 682
  fribble 683
dabbled *wet* 339
dabbler 493
dachshund 366
dacoit 792
dactyl 597
dactylogram 467
dactyliomancy 511

dactylonomy
  numeration 85
  symbol 550
dad 166
daddy 166
dado 211
daedal
  variegated 440
daedalion
  convoluted 248
  artistic 698
daft 503
dagger 727
  look –s *anger* 900
  threat 909
  air drawn – 515
  plant – in breast
    give pain 830
  speak –s 932
  at –s drawn
    opposed 708
    discord 713
    enmity 889
    hate 898
daggle *hang* 214
  dirty 653
dagobah 1000
Dagon 986
daguerreotype
  represent 554
  paint 556
dahabeah 273
Dail Eireann 696
daily
  frequent 136
  periodic 138
  – occurrence
    normal 82
    habitual 613
  – paper 531
dainty *food* 298
  savory 394
  pleasing 829
  delicate 845
  tasty 850
  fastidious 868
dairy 191, 370
  – maid 946
dais *support* 215
  throne 747
daisy
  fresh as a – 654
  – pied 847
dale 252
dally *delay* 133
  irresolute 605
  inactive 683
  amuse 840
  fondle 902
dalmatic 999
Daltonism 443
dam *parent* 166
  close 261
  pond 343
  obstruct 706
damage *evil* 619
  injure, spoil 659
  price 812
damages 974
damascene 440
damask 434
dame
  woman 374
  teacher 540
  lady 875
damn
  malediction 908
  condemn 971

- with faint
   praise 932, 934
damnable 649
damnatory
   disapprove 932
   condemn 971
damnify
   damage 649
   spoil 659
damnosa hereditas
   663
Damocles
   sword of – 667
Damon and
   Pythias 890
damozel 129
damp
   moderate 174
   moist 339
   cold 385
   sound 405
   dissuade 616
   hinder 706
   depress 837
   dull 843
   – the sound 408a
damper 387
damsel
   youth 129
   female 374
Dan to Beersheba
   52, 180
Danaë 803
Danaos, timeo –
   doubt 485
   caution 864
dance
   jump 309
   oscillate 314
   agitate 315
   rejoice 838
   sport 840
   sociality 892
   lead the – 175
   lead one a –
   run away 623
   circuit 629
   difficult 704
   practical joke 929
   St. Vitus' – 315
   – attendance
   waiting 133
   follow 281
   servant 746
   petition 765
   servility 886
   – the back step
      283
   – upon nothing
      972
   – the war dance
      715
dance-band 417
dance-music 415
dander 900
Dandie Dinmont
   366
dandiprat 193
dandle 902
dandruff 653
dandy
   ship 273
   fop 854
dandyism 855
danger 665
   in – liable 177
   source of – 667
   – past 664

– signal 669
dangerous
   [see danger]
   – classes 913
   – illness 655
   – person 667
dangle hang 214
   swing 314
   display 882
dangler 281
Daniel sage 500
   judge 967
dank 339
Dannemora 752
danseuse 599
dapper
   little 193
   elegant 845
dapple 433
dappled 440
darbies
   handcuffs 752
Darby and Joan
   secluded 893
   married 903
dare defy 715
   face danger 861
   – not 860
   – say probable 472
   believe 484
   suppose 514
dare-devil
   courage 861
   rash 863
   bluster 887
daring 861
   unreserved 525
   – imagination 515
dark
   obscure 421
   dim 422
   black 431
   blind 442
   invisible 447
   unintelligible 519
   latent 526
   joyless 837
   insidious 940
   in the –
   ignorant 491
   leap in the –
   experiment 463
   chance 621
   rash 863
   keep – hide 528
   – ages 491
   – cloud 735
   view with – eyes
      932
   – lantern 423
darkly
   see through a
      glass – 443
darkness [see dark]
   421
   children of – 988
   love – better than
      light 989
   powers of – 978
darky 431
darling beloved 897
   favorite 899
darn 660
dart swift 274
   propel 284
   missile 727
   – to and fro 684
Dartmoor 752

Darwinism 357
dash
   small quantity 32
   mix 41
   swift 276
   fling 284
   mark 550
   courage 861
   cut a – repute 873
   display 882
   – at resolution 604
   attack 716
   – board 666
   – cup from lips 761
   – down 308
   – hopes
   disappoint 509
   fail 732
   dejected 837
   despair 859
   – on 274
   – off paint 556
   write 590
   active 682
   haste 684
   – of the pen 590
dashed [see dash]
   humbled 879
dashing
   fashionable 852
   brave 861
   ostentatious 882
dastard 862
data evidence 467
   reasoning 476
   supposition 514
date time 106
   chronology 114
datum 673
daub cover 223
   paint 428
   misrepresent 555
   dirt 653
daughter 167
daunt 860
dauntless 861
Dauphin 875
davenport 191, 215
davit 214
Davus sum non
      Oedipus
   unintelligent 499
   artless 703
   dull 843
Davy Jones' locker
   310
dawdle tardy 133
   slow 275
   inactive 683
dawk 534
dawn
   precursor 64
   begin 66
   priority 116
   morning 125
   light 420
   dim 422
   glimpse 490
dawplucker 936
day
   period 108
   present time 118
   light 410
   all – 110
   clear as –
   certain 474
   intelligible 518
   manifest 525

close of – 126
decline of – 126
denizens of the –
   366
good old –'s 122
have had its – 124
one fine – 119
open as – 703
order of the – 613
red letter – 642
see the light of –
   446
– after day
   diurnal 110
   frequent 136
– by day
   repeatedly 104
   time 106
   periodic 138
– after the fair
   135
–s gone by 122
– of judgment 121
happy as the – is
   long 827, 836
– and night
   frequent 136
labor – and night
   686
–s numbered
   transient 111
   death 360
– one's own 731
– of rest 686
– star 423
– after to-morrow
   121
– before yesterday
   122
–s of week 138
all in – 's work 625
daybed 215
daybook record 551
   accounts 811
daybreak
   morning 125
   dim 422
day-dream
   fancy 515
   hope 858
day-laborer 690
daylight 125, 420
   see – intelligible
      518
   – saving 114
daymare 859
daze 420
dazed 376
dazzle
   light 420
   blind 422, 443
   put out 458
   astonish 870
   awe 928
dazzling
   [see dazzle]
   beautiful 845
de: – die in diem
   time 106
   periodic 138
   – facto 1
   – fond en comble
      52
   – novo 104
   – omnibus rebus
      81
   – profundis 821
deacon 996

deaconry 995
dead complete 52
   inert 172
   colorless 429
   lifeless 360
   insensible 376
   – against
   contrary 14
   oppose 708
   more – than alive
      688
   – asleep 683
   – beat
   powerless 158
   – certainty 474
   – color 556
   – cut 893
   – drunk 959
   – failure 732
   – flat 213
   – heat 27
   – languages 560
   – letter
   impotent 158
   unmeaning 517
   useless 645
   lazily 738
   exempt 927
   illegal 964
   – level 16
   – lift exertion 686
   difficulty 704, 706
   – lock cease 142
   stoppage 265
   – march 363, 415
   – of night
   midnight 126
   dark 421
   – reckoning
   numeration 85
   measurement 466
   – secret 533
   – set against 708
   – set at
   attack 716
   – shot 700
   – silence 403
   – sound 408a
   – stop 142
   – to 823
   – wall
   hindrance 706
   defence 717
   – weight 706
   – water 343
deaden
   weaken 158
   moderate 174
   sound 405
   mute 408a
   benumb 823
dead-house 363
deadlock 142, 704
deadly killing 361
   pernicious 649
   unhealthy 657
   – sin 947
   – weapon 727
deads 645
deaf 419
   inattentive 458
   – to advice 606
   – and dumb 581
   turn – ear to
   neglect 460
   unbelief 487
   refuse 764
   – to reason 901a

distrait 458
distraught 824
distress
  distraint 789
  poverty 804
  affliction 828
  cause pain 830
  signal of − 669
distressingly
  excessively 31
distribute
  arrange 60
  disperse 44, 73
  allot 786
district 181
  − council 696
distrust
  disbelief 485
  fear 860
distrustful 487
disturb
  derange 61
  change 140
  agitate 315
  excite 824
  distress 828, 830
disturbance 59
disunion
  discord 24
  separation 44
  disorder 59
  discord 713
disuse
  desuetude 614
  relinquish 624
  unemploy 678
disused
  old 124
disvalue 932
ditch
  inclosure 232
  trench 259
  water 343
  conduit 350
  defence 717
  to the last − 606
ditch-water 653
ditheism 984
dither 315
dithyramb
  music 415
  poetry 597
dithyrambic 503
ditto 13, 104
  say − to 488
ditty 415
  − box 191
diurnal 138
diuturnity 110
diva 416
divagate 279, 629
divan sofa 215
  council 696
  throne 747
  tribunal 966
divaricate differ 15
  bifurcate 91
  diverge 291
dive swim 267
  fly 267
  plunge 306, 310
  − into inquire 461
divellicate 44
diver 208
divergence
  difference 15
  variation 20a
  disagreement 24

deviation 279
separation 291
divers different 15
  multiform 81
  many 102
  − coloured 440
diverse 15
diversify
  very 20a
  change 140
diversion
  change 140
  deviation 279
  pleasure 377
  amusement 840
diversity
  difference 15
  irregular 16a
  dissimilar 18
  multiform 81
  − of opinion 489
divert turn 279
  deceive 545
  amuse 840
  − the mind 452, 458
divertissement
  diversion 377
  drama 599
  amusement 840
Dives 803
divest denude 226
  take 789
  − oneself of
  abrogate 756
  relinquish 782
divestment 226
divide differ 15
  separate 44
  part 51
  arrange 60
  arithmetic 85
  bisect 91
  vote 609
  apportion 786
dividend part 51
  number 84
  portion 786
divina particula
  aurae 450
divination
  prediction 511
  sorcery 992
divine predict 511
  guess 514
  perfect 650
  of God 976, 983, 983a
  clergyman 996
divine afflatus 515
  − right.
  authority 737
  due 924
  − service 990
diving 840
diving-bell 208
diving-rod 550, 993
Divinity God 976
  theology 983
divisible
  number 84
division
  [see divide]
  part 51
  class 75
  arithmetic 85
  discord 713

military 726
divisor 84
divorce
  separation 44
  relinquish 782
  matrimonial 905
Divorce Court 966
divulge 529
divulsion 44
divvy 786
dixi 535
dizen 847
dizzard 501
dizzy
  dimsighted 443
  confused 458
  vertigo 503
  − height 206
  − round 312
djerrid 727
djinn 980
do fare 7
  suit 23
  produce 161
  cheat 545
  act 680
  complete 729
  succeed 731
  I beg 765
  all one can − 686
  plenty to − 682
  thing to − 625
  − away with
  destroy 162
  eject 297
  abrogate 756
  − battle 722
  − one's bidding 743
  − business 625
  − to death 361
  − as done by 906, 942
  − for destroy 162
  kill 361
  conquer 731
  serve 746
  punish 972
  − good 906
  − harm 907
  − honor 873
  − into
  translate 522
  − justice to 595
  − like 19
  − little 683
  − no harm 648
  − nothing 681
  − nothing but 136
  − one's office 772
  − as others do 82
  − over 223
  − as one pleases 748
  − a service
  useful 644
  aid 707
  − up 660
  have to − with 680, 692
  − without 678
  − the work 686
  − wrong 923
docere, pisces na-
  tare − 641
docile domesticated 370
  learning 539

willing 602
docimastic 463
dock diminish 36
  cut off 38
  port 189
  shorten 201
  edge 231
  store 636
  tribunal 966
docked
  incomplete 53
docker 690
docket
  list 86
  evidence 467
  note 550
  record 551
  security 771
dockyard 691
doctor
  learned man 492
  restore 660
  remedy 662
  after death the −
  135
  − accounts 811
  when −s disagree 475
doctrinaire
  positive 474
  pedant 492
  affectation 855
  blusterer 887
doctrinal 537
doctrinarian 514
doctrine tenet 484
  knowledge 490
document 551
documentary
  evidence 467
dodder 315
doddering 128
dodecahedron 244
dodge change 140
  shift 264
  deviate 279
  oscillate 314
  pursue 461
  avoid 623
  stratagem 702
dodger, artful − 792
dodo 366
  extinct as the −
  122
doe swift 274
  deer 366
  female 374
doer
  originator 164
  agent 690
doff 226
  − the cap 894
dog follow 281
  animal 366
  male 373
  pursue 622
  wretch 949
  cast to the −s
  destroy 162
  reject 610
  disuse 678
  abrogate 756
  relinquish 782
  fire − 386
  go to the −s
  destruction 162
  fail 732
  adversity 735

poverty 804
sea − 269
watch −
  safety 664
  warning 668
  keeper 753
  hair of − that bit you 959
  let sleeping −s lie 141
  − in manger 706, 943
  −tired 686
  −s of war 722
dog-cart 272
dog-cheap 815
dog-days 382
doge 745
dogged
  obstinate 606
  valour 861
  sullen 901a
dogger 273
doggerel
  verse 597
  ridiculous 851, 853
dog-hole 189
dog-Latin 563
dogma tenet 484
  theology 983
dogmatic
  certain 474
  positive 481
  assertion 535
  obstinate 606
dogmatist 887
dog's ear 258
dog robber 746
dog-sick 867
dog-star 423
dog-trot 275
dog-weary 688
doily 852
doing
  up and − 682
  what one is − 625
doings
  events 151
  actions 680
  conduct 692
doit trifle 643
  coin 800
dolce far niente 681
doldrums
  dejection 837
  sulks 901a
dole
  small quantity 32
  scant 640
  give 784
  allot 786
  parsimony 819
  grief 828
doleful 837
  − dumps 901a
doll small 193
  image 554
dollar 800
dolman 225
dolmen 363, 551
dolor
  physical 378
  moral 828
dolorem, infandum
  renovare − 833
dolorous 830
dolphin 341

- the cup of
  misery 828
- into 348
- pipe 249
- of resources 640
drake *male* 373
  fire – 423
dram *drink* 298
  pungent 392
  stimulus 615
- drinking 959
drama 599
dramatic 599
  ostentation 882
- author 599,
- critic 599
- poetry 597
dramatis personæ
  mankind 372
  play 599
  agents 690
  party 712
drapery 225, 847
drast 645
drastic 171
draught
  [*see also* draft]
  depth 208
  traction 285
  drink 298
  stream of air 349
  delineation 554,
  556
  plan 626
  physic 662
  troops 726
- off 73
draughts
  game 840
draughtsman
  artist 559
draw *equality* 27
  compose 54
  pull 285
  delineate 554, 556
- aside 279
- off the attention
  458
- back
  deduction 40a
  regret 283
  avoid 623
- breath
  refresh 689
  feeling 821
- *relief* 834
- a cheque 800
- a curtain 424
- down 153
- forth 677
- from 810
- on futurity 132
- in one's horns
  tergiversation 607
  humility 879
- in 195
- an inference 480
- the line 465
- lots 621
- near *time* 121
  approach 286
- off *eject* 297
  hinder 706
  take 789
- on *time* 121
  event 151
  induce 615
- out

protract 110
late 133
prolong 200
extract 301
discover 480a
exhibit 525
diffuse style 573
- over *induce* 615
- a parallel 9
- the pen through
  552
- a picture 594
- profit 775
- and quarter 972
- the sword
  attack 716
  war 722
- the teeth of 158
- together
  assemble 72
  co-operate 709
- towards 288
- up *order* 58
  stop 265
  write 590
- up a statement
  594
- upon *money* 800
- the veil 528
drawback *evil* 619
  imperfection 651
  hindrance 706
  discount 813
drawbar 45
drawbridge
  way 627
  escape 671
  raise the – 666
drawcansir 887
drawee 800
drawer
  receptacle 191
  artist 559
- of water 690
drawers
  dress 225
drawhead 45
drawing
  delineation 554,
  556
  prize 810
drawing-room
  assembly 72
  room 191
  fashion 852
drawl *prolong* 200
  creep 275
  in speech 583
  sluggish 683
drawn *equated* 27
- battle
- irresistibly 601
  pacification 723
  incomplete 730
dray 272
- horse 271
drayman 268
dread 860
dreadful *great* 31
  bad 649
  dire 830
  depressing 837
  fearful 860
dreadless 861
dreadnought
  warship 726
dream
  unsubstantial 4

error 495
fancy 515
sleep 683
golden – 858
- of *think* 451
  intend 620
- on other things
  458
dreamer
  madman 504
  imaginative 515
dreamy
  unsubstantial 4
  inattentive 458
  sleepy 683
dreary
  monotonous 16
  solitary 87
  melancholy 830,
  837
dredge *collect* 72
  extract 301'
  raise 307
dregs
  remainder 40
  refuse 645
  dirt 653
- of the people 876
- of vice 945
drench *drink* 298
  water 337
  redundance 641
- with physic 662
drencher 248
drenching rain 348
dress
  uniformity 16
  agree 23
  equalize 27
  clothes 225
  prepare 673
  ornament 847
  ostentation 882
  full – 852
- circle 599
- the ground 371
- up *falsehood* 544
  represent 554
- wounds 662
- to advantage
  847
dress-coat 225
dresser
  sideboard 215
  surgeon 662
dressing 932, 972
- room 191, 599
dressing-gown 225
dressmaker 225
dribble 295, 348
driblet 25, 32
drift
  accumulate 72
  distance 196
  motion 264
  flying 267
  float 267
  transfer 270
  direction 278
  deviation 279
  approach 286
  wind 349
  meaning 516
  intention 620
  snow – 383
drifter 273
drifting 605
driftless 621

drill *fabric* 219
  bore 260
  auger 262
  teach 537
  prepare 673
- hall 191
drink
  swallow 296
  liquor 298
  tipple 959
- one's fill
  enough 639
- in *imbibe* 296,
  298
- in learning 539
- to *celebrate* 883
  courtesy 894
drinking-bout 954
drink-money 784
drip 295, 348
dripping *wet* 330
  fat 356
drive *airing* 266
  impel 276
  propel 284
  break in 370
  urge 615
  haste 684
  direct 693
  attack 716
  compel 744
- at *mean* 516
  intend 620
- a bargain
  barter 794
  parsimony 819
- care away 836
- a coach and six
  through 83
- into a corner
  difficult 704
  hinder 706
  defeat 731
  subjection 749
- to despair 859
- matters to an
  extremity 604
- from *repel* 289
- one hard 716
- home 729
- in 300
- to the last 133
- out 297
- trade
  business 625
  barter 794
drivel *slobber* 297
  imbecile 499
  mad 503
  rubbish 517
driveler 501, 584
driver 268
  director 694
driving rain 348
drizzle 348
droil 683
droit du plus fort
  744
drôle *cards* 840
drole 949
- de corps 844
drollery
  amusement 840
  wit 842
  ridiculous 853
dromedary 271
drone *slow* 275
  sound 407, 412,

413
inactive 683
drool 297
droop
  weak 160
- *hang* 214
  sink 306
  disease 655
  decline 659
  flag 688
  sorrow 828
  dejection 837
drop *small quantity*
  32
  discontinue 142
  powerless 158
  bring forth 161
  spherule 249
  emerge 295
  fall 306
  trickle 348
  relinquish 624
  discard 782
  gallows 975
  let – 308
  ready to –
  fatigue 688
- asleep 683
- astern 283
- from the couds
  508
- dead 360
- by drop
  by degrees 26
  in parts 51
- in the bucket 32
- in upon 674
- into a good
  thing 734
- into the grave
  360
- a hint 527
- all idea of 624
- in *arrive* 292
  immerse 300
  sociality 892
- the mask 529
- off *decrease* 36
  die 360
  sleep 683
- in the ocean
  trifling 643
- the subject 458
- too much 959
dropping fire 70
drop-scene 599
dropsical 194, 641
droshki 272
dross
  remainder 40
  slag 384
  trash 643, 645
  dirt 653
drought
  dryness 340
  insufficiency 640
drouth *desire* 865
drove
  assemblage 72
  multitude 102
drover 370
drown
  affusion 337
  kill 361
  ruin 731, 732
- care 840
- the voice 581
drowsy *slow* 275

sleepy 683
weary 841
drub
  defeat 731, 732
  punish 972
drudge *labour* 686
  worker 682, 690
drug
  render insensible
  376
  superfluity 641
  trash 643
  remedy 662
  bane 663
  – *in the market*
  815
drugget
  cover 223
  clean 652
  preserve 670
druggist 662
druid 996
drum
  repeat 104
  cylinder 249
  sound 407
  music 417
  party 892
  beat of –
  signal 550
  alarm 669
  war 722
  command 741
  parade 882
  ear – 418
  muffled –
  funeral 363
  non-resonance
  408a
  – and fife band 417
  – fire 407
  – out 972
drum-head 964,
  966
drum-major 745
drummer 416
drunken 959
  reel like a – man
  315
drunkenness 959
dry *arid* 340
  style 575, 576, 579
  hoarse 581
  scanty 640
  preserve 670
  exhaust 789
  tedious 841
  dull 842
  thirsty 865
  cynical 932
  teetotal 958
  run – 640
  with – eyes 823
  – dock 189
  – joke 842
  – land 342
  – the tears 834
  – up 340, 638
dryad 979
dry-as-dust
  antiquarian 122
  dull 843
dryness 340
dry-nurse
  teach 537
  teacher 540
  aid 707
dry-point 558

dry-rot
  dirt 653
  decay 659
  bane 663
dualism 984
duality 89
duarchy 737
dub 564
dubious 475
ducat 800
duce 745
duchess 745, 875
duchy 181
duck *stoop* 308
  plunge 310
  water 337
  darling 897, 899
  play –s and
  drakes
  recoil 277
  prodigality 818
  – *'s egg*
  zero 101
  – in thunder 870
ducking-stool 975
duckling 127
duck-pond 370
duct 350
ductile
  elastic 323
  flexible 324
  trimming 607
  easy 705
  docile 743
dud 158, 727
dude 854
duds 225
dudgeon
  dagger 727
  discontent 832
  churlishness 895
  hate 898
  anger 900
  sullenness 901a
due
  expedient 646
  owing 806
  proper 924, 926
  give his – to
  right 922
  vindication 937
  fair 939
  in – course 109
  occasion 134
  – respect 928
  – sense of 498
  – time
  soon 132
  – to
  cause and effect
  154, 155
  give – weight 465
duel 720
duelist 726
dueness 924
duenna
  teacher 540
  guardian 664
  keeper 753
dues 812
duet 415
duff 298
duffer
  bungler 701
  smuggler 792
dug 250
dug-out
  old man 130

boat 273
defence 717
duke *ruler* 745
  noble 875
dulce domum 189
dulcet
  sweet 396
  sound 405
  melodious 413
  agreeable 829
dulcify 174, 396
dulcimer 417
Dulcinea 897
dulcorate 396
dulia 990
dull *weak* 160
  inert 172
  moderate 174
  blunt 254
  insensible 376,
  381
  sound 405
  dim 422
  colorless 429
  ignorant 493
  stolid 499
  style 575
  inactive 683
  unapt 699
  callous 823
  dejected 837
  weary 841
  prosing 843
  simple 849
  – of hearing 419
  – sight 443
dullard 501
dullness 843
duly 924
duma 696
dumb 581
  – animal 366
  – show 550
  – waiter 307
  strike –
  ignorant 493
  astonish 870
  humble 879
dumbfounder
  disappoint 509
  silence 581
  astonish 870
  humble 879
dummy
  substitute 147
  impotent 158
  speechless 581
  inactive 683
dump *music* 415
  store 636
  lament 839
  undersell 796
dumpling 298
dumps
  discontent 832
  dejection 837
  sulk 901a
dumpy *little* 193
  short 201
  thick 202
dun *dim* 422
  colorless 429
  grey 432
  importune 765
  creditor 805
dunce
  ignoramus 493
  fool 501

dunderhead 501
dune 206
dung 653
dungeon 752
dunghill
  dirt 653
  cowardly 862
  baseborn 876
  – cock 366
Dunker 984
dunt 716
duo 415
duodecimal 99
duodecimo
  little 193
  book 593
duodenary 98
duologue
  interlocution 588
  drama 599
dupe
  credulous 486
  deceive 545
  deceived **547**
duplex 90, 189
duplicate
  imitate 19
  copy 21
  double 90
  tally 550
  record 551
  redundant 641
  pawn 805
duplication
  imitation 19
  doubling **90**
  repetition 104
duplicature
  fold 258
duplicity
  duality 89
  falsehood 544
dura lex sed lex 926
durable
  long time 110
  stable 150
durance 141, 751
  in – 754
duration 106
  contingent – 108a
  infinite – 112
durbar
  conference 588
  council 696
  tribunal 966
duress
  compulsion 744
  restraint 751
during 106
  – pleasure &c.
  108a
durity 323
dusk
  evening 126
  half-light 422
dusky
  dark 421
  black 431
dust *levity* 320
  powder 330
  corpse 362
  trash 643
  dirt 653
  money 800
  come to –
  die 360
  come down with
  the – 807

humbled in the –
  879'
kick up a – 885
level with the –
  162
lick the –
  submit 725
  fail 732
make to bite the –
  731
turn to –
  deorganized 358
  die 360
  – in the balance
  643
throw – in the
  eyes
  blind 442
  deceive 545
  plead 617
  – one's jacket 972
duster 652
dust-bin, dust-hole
  191, 645
  fit for the –
  useless 645
  dirty 653
  spoilt 659
dustman
  cleaner 652
dust-storm 330
dusty
  powder 330
  dirt 653
Dutch
  double – 519
  high – 519
  – auction 796
  – courage 862
Dutchman, flying
  515
dutiful 944
duty
  business 625
  w.rk 686
  tax 812
  courtesy 894
  obligation **926**
  respect 928
  worship 990
  rite 998
  do one's –
  virtue 944
  on – 680, 682
duumvirate 737
Duval, Claude –
  792
D.V. 470, 976
dwarf
  lessen 36
  small 193
  elf 980
dwell
  reside 186
  abide 265
  – upon
  descant 573
dweller 188
dwelling 184, 189
dwindle *lessen* 36
  shrink 195
dyad 89
dye 428
dying 360
dyke [*see* dike]
dynamic energy
  157
dynamics 276

dynamitard 863
dynamite 727
dynamo 153
dynasty 737
dysentery 299
dyspepsia 655
dysphony 581

E

each 79
 – to each 786
 – other 12
 – in his turn 148
eager
 willing 602
 active 682
 ardent 821
 desirous 865
 – expectation 507
eagle
 standard 550
 money 800
 – boat 726
 – eye *sight* 441
 intelligence 498
 – winged *swift* 274
 insignia 747
eagre 348
ean 161
ear 418
 corn 154
 come to one's –s
  527
 din in the –
  loud 404
  drum 407
 all – 418
 have the – of
  belief 484
  friendship 888
 lend an –
  hear 418
  attend 457
 meet the – 418
 nice – 418
 no – 419
 offend the – 410
 pick up the –s
  attention 457
  expectation 507
 put about one's –s
  308
 quick – 418
 reach one's –s 527
 ring in the – 408
 set by the –s
  discord 713
  hate 898
  resentment 900
 split the –s 404
 together by the –s
  discord 713
  contention 720
 up to one's –s
  redundance 641
  active 680, 682
 willing – 602
 word in the – 586
 – for music 416,
  418
 in at one – out at
  the other
  inattention 458
  forget 506
 not for –s polite
  961

make the –s tingle
 anger 900
 – ache 378
ear-drum 418
earl 875
earless 419
earliness 132
early 132
 get up – 682
earmark 550
earn 775
earnest *willing* 602
 determined 604
 emphatic 642
 pledge 771
 pay in advance
  809
 eager 821
 in –
  affirmation 535
  veracious 543
  strenuous 682
ear-piercing 410
ear-ring 847
ear-shot 197
 out of – 405
ear-splitting 404
earth *ground* 211
 world 318
 land 342
 corpse 362
 what on –
  inquiry 461
  wonder 870
 – closet 653
earthenware
 baked 384
 sculpture 557
earthling 372
earthly 318
 end of one's –
  career 360
 of no – use 645
earthly-minded
  943, 989
earthquake 146,
  173
earthwork 717
earwig *flatter* 933,
  935
ear-witness 467
ease *bodily* 377
 style 578
 leisure 685
 facility 705
 mental 827
 content 831
 at one's –
  prosperous 734
  mind at –
  cheerful 836
 set at – *relief* 834
 take one's – 687
 – off *deviate* 297
 – one of *take* 789
easel *support* 215
 painting 556
 – picture 556
easement
 property 780
 relief 834
easily
 [*see easy*]
 let one down – 918
 – accomplished
  705
 – deceived 486
 – persuaded 602

East 236, 278
Easter *period* 138
 rite 998
 – Monday
  holiday 840
 – offering
  gift 784
 – sepulcher 1000
easy *gentle* 275
 style 578
 facile 705
 make oneself –
  about 484
 take it –
  inactive 683
  inexcitable 826
 – ascent 217
 – of belief 472
 – chair
  support 215
  repose 687
 – circumstances
  803
 – going
  willing 602
  irresolute 605
  lenient 740
  inexcitable 826
  contented 831
  indifferent 866
 – sail
  moderate 174
  slow 275
 – temper 894
 – terms 705
 – to understand
  518
 – virtue 961
eat *food* 298
 tolerate 826
 – dirt 725, 879
 – one's fill
  enough 639
  gorge 957
 – heartily 298
 – one's words 879
 – out of house and
  home *take* 789
 prodigal 818
 gluttony 957
 – of the same
  trencher 892
 – one's words 607
eatables 298
eaten up with 820
eau, battre l' – 645
 faire venir l' – à la
  bouche 865
 mettre de l' – dans
  son vin 174
eaves 250
eavesdropper 455,
  527
eavesdropping 418,
  532
ébauche 626
ebb *decrease* 36
 contract 195
 regress 283
 recede 287
 waste 638
 spoil 659
 low – 36
 low 207
 depression 308
 insufficient 640
 – and flow 314
 – of life 360

ebb-tide *low* 207
 dry 340
ebony 431
ebriety 959
ebullient
 violent 173
 hot 382
 excited 824
ebullition
 energy 171
 violence 173
 agitation 315
 heating 384
 excitation 825
 anger 900
écarté 840
ecce
 – iterum Crispinus
  104
 – signum 550
eccentric 220
 irregular 83
 foolish 499
 crazed 503, 504
 capricious 608
ecchymosis 299
ecclesiastic
 church 995
 clergy 996
ecclesiastical
 canonical 985
 – court 966
 – law 963
ecclesiolatry 991
écrevelé 458
échafaudage 673
échappée 840
échapper belle 671
échelon 279
echo *imitate* 19
 copy 21
 repeat 104
 reflection 277
 resonance 408
 answer 462
 assent 488
 applaud to the –
  931
 awake –es 404
éclaircissement 522
éclat 873
eclectic 609
eclipse *surpass* 33
 disappearance
  449
 hide 528
 outshine 873, 874
 partial – *dim* 422
 total – *dark* 421
 under an –
  invisible 447
  out of repute 874
ecliptic 318
eclogue 597
economic pressure
  751
economy
 order 58
 conduct 692
 frugality 817
 animal – 359
écorcher les oreilles
  410
ecphorize 615
écru 433
ecstasis 683
ecstasy
 frenzy 515

transport 821
 rapture 827
ecstatic 829
ecstatica 994
ectoplasm 992
ectype 21
ecumenical 78
edacity 957
Edda 986
eddy
 whirlpool 348
 current 312
 danger 667
edematous 194, 324
Eden 827
edge *energy* 171
 height 206
 brink 231
 sidle 279
 advantage 731
 cutting – 253
 on – 256, 507
 take the – off 174
 – of hunger 865
 – in 228
 – one's way 282
edge-tools 253
 play with – 863
edgewise 217
edging
 obliquity 217
 border 231
 ornament 847
edible 298
edict 741
edification
 building 161
 teaching 537
 learning 539
 piety 987
edifice 161
edifying *good* 648
edile 965
edit
 publication 531
 condense 596
 revise 658
edition, new – 658
editor 593
educate 537
educated 490
 self – 490
education
 teaching 537
 knowledge 490
 man of – 492
 higher – 490
educational 537,
  542
educe *extract* 301
 discover 480a
educt 40
eduction 40a
edulcorate 396, 652
eel 248
 wriggle like an –
  315
eerie 860
efface
 delete 162
 disappear 449
 obliterate 552
 – from the
  memory 506
effect
 consequence 154
 product 161
 impression 375

complete 729
carry into – 692
with crushing –
  162
in – 5
take – 731
to that – 516
effective
  capable 157
  useful 644
effectuation 729
expedient 646
effects 780, 798
effectual 731
effectually 52
effectuate 729
effeminate
  weak 160
  womenlike 374
  timorous 862
  sensual 954
effeminize 158
effendi 875
effervesce
  energy 171
  violence 173
  agitate 315
  bubble 353
  excited 825
effervescent 338
effete old 128
  weak 160
  useless 645
  spoiled 659
efficacious
  [see efficient]
efficient
  power 157
  agency 170
  utility 644
  skill 698
effigy 21, 554
effleurer skim 267,
  460
efflorescence 330
effluxion of time
  109
effluence egress 295
  flow 348
effluvium 334, 398
efflux 295
efformation 240
effort 686
effreet 980
effrontery 885
effulgence 420
effuse
  pour out 295, 297
  excrete 299
  speech 582
  loquacity 584
effusion of blood
  361
effusive 573
eft 366
eftsoons 117
egad 535
égards 928
egesta 299
egestion 297
egg beginning 66
  cause 153
  food 298
  walk among –s
  704
  too many –s in
  one basket
  unskilful 699

(imprudent 863)
– and dart
  ornament 847
– on 615
egg-shaped 247,
  249
ego intrinsic 5
  speciality 79
  immaterial 317
  non – 6
egocentrism 943
egotism
  vanity 880
  cynicism 911
  selfishness 943
egregious
  exceptional 83
  absurd 497
  exaggerated 549
  important 642
egregiously 31, 33
egress 295
Egyptian darkness
  421
eheu! fugaces
  labuntur anni
  111
eiderdown 223
eidouranion 318
Eiffel tower 206
eight number 98
  boat 273
  representative 759
eisteddfod 72, 416
eighty 98
either choice 609
  happy with – 605
ejaculate
  propel 284
  utter 580
ejection 185, 297
ejecta 299
ejector 349
eke also 37
– out complete 52
  spin out 110
ekka 272
El Dorado 803
elaborate
  improve 658
  prepare 673
  laborious 686
  work out 729
elaine 356
élan 276
elapse 109, 122
elastic fluid 334
elasticity
  power 157
  strength 159
  energy 171
  spring 325
elate cheer 836
  rejoice 838
  hope 858
  vain 880
  boast 884
elbow angle 244
  projection 250
  push 276
  at one's –
  near 197
  advice 695
  lift one's –
  drink 959
  out at –s
  undress 226
  poor 804

disrepute 874
– one's way
  progress 282
  pursuit 622
  active 682
elbow-chair 215
elbow-grease 331
elbow-room 180,
  748
elder older 124
  aged 128
  veteran 130
  clergy 996
elect choose 609
  good 648
  predestinate 976
  pious 987
  clergy 996
election
  numerical 84
  necessity 601
electioneering 609
elector 745
electorate 737
Electra complex
  897
electric
  swift 274
  sensation 821
  excitable 825
  car 272
– blue 438
– chair 974
– light 423
– piano 417
electrician 599, 690
electricity 157, 388
electrify
  unexpected 508
  excite 824
  astonish 870
electro-biology 992
electrocution 972
electrolier 214, 423
electrolyze 49
electro-magnetism
  157
electromobile 272
electron 32
electronics 157
electroplate 223
electrotype 21, 591
electuary 662
eleemosynary 784
elegance
  in style 578
  beauty 845
  taste 859
  Bank of – 800
elegy interment 363
  poetry 597
  lament 839
element
  component 56
  beginning 66
  cause 153
  matter 316
  in one's –
  facility 705
  content 831
  devouring – 382
  out of its – 195
elementary 42
– education 537
– school 542
elements
  Eucharist 998
elench 477

elephant
  large 192
  carrier 271
  white – bane 663
elevated
  tipsy 959
elevation
  height 206
  vertical 212
  raising 307
  plan 554
– of style 574
  improvement 658
  glory 873
– of mind 942
  angular – 244
élève 541
eleven 98
  representative 759
eleventh hour
  evening 126
  late 133
  opportune 134
elf infant 129
  little 193
  imp 980
elicit cause 153
  draw out 301
  discover 480a
  manifest 525
eligible 646
Elijah's mantle 63
eliminant 299
eliminate
  subduct 38
  simplify 42
  exclude 55
  weed 103
  extract 301
  reject 610
elision 44, 201
élite best 648
  distinguished 873
  aristocratic 875
elixation 384
elixir 662
– of life 471
elk 223
ell 200
  take an –
  take 789
  insolence 885
  wrong 923
  undue 925
  selfish 943
ellipse 247
ellipsis shorten 201
  style 572
ellipsoid 247, 249
elocation 185, 270
elocution 582
éloge 931
elongation 196, 200
elopement 623, 671
eloquence 572, 582
else 37
elsewhere 187
elucidate 522
elude
  sophistry 477
  avoid 623
  escape 671
  succeed 731
  palter 773
elusive 545
elusory 546
elutriate 652
elysian 829, 981

Elysium 827, 981
elytron 223
Elzevir. edition 193
emaciation 195,
  203, 640
emanate 151
  go out of 295
  excrete 299
– from 544
emanation 398
emancipate
  facilitate 705
  free 748, 750
emasculate
  impotent 158
embalm
  interment 363
  perfume 400
  preserve 670
– in the memory
  505
embankment
  esplanade 189
  refuge 666
  fence 717
embar 229
embargo
  stoppage 265
  prohibition 761
  exclusion 893
embark
  transfer 270
  depart 293
– in begin 66
  engage in 676
embarquer sans
  biscuits, s' – 674
embarras de
– choix 609
embarrass 641,
  704, 706
embarrassed 804,
  806
embarrassing 475
embase 659
embassy
  errand 532
  commission 755
  consignee 758
embattled
  arranged 60
  leagued 712
  war array 722
embed
  locate 184
  base 215
  enclose 221
  insert 300
embellish 847
embers 384
embezzle 791
embitter
  deteriorate 659
  aggravate 835
  acerbate 900
emblazon
  color 428
  ornament 847
  display 882
emblem 550, 747
embody
  join 43
  combine 48
  form a whole 50
  compose 54
embolden
  hope 858
  encourage 861

embolism 228, 261,
  300
embonpoint 192
embosomed
  lodged 184
  interjacent 228
  circumscribed 229
emboss *convex* 250
  ornament 847
embouchure 260
embowel 297
embrace
  cohere 46
  compose 54
  include 76
  enclose 227
  choose 609
  take 789
  friendship 888
  sociality 892
  courtesy 894
  endearment 902
  – *an offer* 760
embrangle 61
embranglement 713
embrasure 257, 260
embrocation 662
embroider
  variegate 440
  lie 544
  ornament 847
embroidery
  adjunct 39
  exaggeration 549
embroil *derange* 61
  discord 713
embroilment 59
embrown 433
embryo
  beginning 66
  cause 153
  in – *destined* 152
  preparing 673
embryology 357
embryonic 193, 674
embus 293
embusqué 603
emendation 658
emerald *green* 435
  jewel 847
emerge 295, 446
emergency
  circumstance 8
  event 151
  difficulty 704
emeritus 500, 928
emersion 295, 446
emery
  sharpener 253
  – *paper*
  smooth 255
emetic *remedy* 662
émeute 742
emication 420
emigrant 57, 268
emigrate 266, 295
emigré 268, 295
eminence
  height 206
  fame 873
  church dignitary
  996
eminent domain
  744
eminently 33
emir 745, 875
emissary
  messenger 534

consignee 758
emission 297
emit *eject* 297
  publish 531
  voice 580
  – *vapour* 336
Emmanuel 976
emmet 193
emollient 662
emolument
  acquisition 775
  receipt 810
  remuneration 973
emotion 821
  –al *appeal* 824
  –al *drama* 599
empale 260, 972
empanel 86, 969
empathy 515
emperor 745
emphasis 580
emphatic 535, 642
emphatically 31
empierce
  perforate 260
  insert 300
empire 737, 789
  – *day* 840
empiric 548
empirical 463, 675
empiricism 463
emplane 293
employ
  business 625
  use 677
  servitude 749
  commission 755
  in one's – 746
  – one's capital in
  794
  – oneself 680
  – one's time in
  625
employé
  servant 746
  agent 758
employer 795
empoison 659
emporium 799
empower
  power 157
  commission 755
  accredit 759
  permit 760
empress 745
empressement
  activity 682
  emotion 821
  desire 865
emprise 676
emption 795
emptor 795
  caveat – 769
empty *clear* 185
  vacant 187
  deflate 195
  drain 297
  ignorant 491
  waste 638
  deficient 640
  useless 645
  beggarly account
  of – *boxes*
  poverty 804
  – one's glass 298
  – *purse* 804
  – *sound* 517
  – *stomach* 865

– title *name* 564
  undue 925
  – words 546
empty-handed 640
empty-headed 4,
  491
empurple 437
empyrean *sky* 318
  blissful 829
empyreuma 41
empyrosis 384
emulate *imitate* 19
  goodness 648
  rival 708
  compete 720
  glory 873
emulsion 352
emunctory 350
en – bloc 50
  – masse 50
  – passant
  parenthetical 10
  transient 111
  à propos 134
  – rapport 9
  – règle *order* 58
  conformity 82
  – route
  journey 266
  progress 282
enable 157
enact *drama* 599
  action 680
  conduct 692
  complete 729
  order 741
  law 963
enallage 521
enamel *coating* 223
  painting 556
  ornament 847
enameller 559
enamor 897
encage 751
encamp 184, 189
encampment 184
encaustic 556
enceinte
  with child 161
  region 181
  inclosure 232
enchafe 830
enchain 751
enchant *please* 829
enchanted 827
enchanting 845,
  897
enchantment
  sorcery 992
enchase 43, 259
enchiridion 593
enchorial 188
encincture 229
encircle 76, 227,
  311
enclave *close* 181
  boundary 233
enclose 227, 229
enclosure
  region 181
  envelope 232
  fence 752
encomiast 935
encomium 931
encompass 227, 233
  –ed with difficul-
  ties 704
encore 104, 931

encounter
  undergo 151
  clash 276
  meet 292
  withstand 708
  contest 720
  – *danger* 665
  – *risk* 621
encourage
  animate 615
  aid 707
  comfort 834
  hope 858
  embolden 861
encroach
  transcursion 303
  do wrong 923
  infringe 925
encumber 704, 706
encumbrance
  clear of – 807
encyclical 531
encyclopedia 490,
  593
  walking – 700
encyclopedical
  general 78
  – *knowledge* 490
encysted 229
end
  termination 67
  effect 154
  object 620
  at an – 142
  come to its – 729
  one's journey's –
  292
  on – 212
  put an – to
  destroy 162
  kill 361
  begin at the
  wrong – 699
  – one's days 360
  –s of the earth 196
  – to end *space* 180
  touching 199
  length 200
  – of life 360
  – in smoke 732
  – of one's tether
  sophistry 477
  ignorant 491
  insufficient 640
  difficult 704
endamage 649
endanger 665
endear 897
endearment **902**
endeavor
  pursue 622
  attempt 675
  use one's best –
  686
  – after 620
endemic
  special 79
  interior 221
  disease 657
endimanché 847,
  882
endless
  multitudinous
  102
  infinite 105
  perpetual 112
endlessly 16
endlong 200

endocrine 221
endogenous 367
endorse
  evidence 467
  assent 488
  compact 769
  – *a bill* 800
  approve 931
endorsement 550
endosmose 302
endow
  confer power 157
endowed with
  possessed of 777
endowment
  intrinsic 5
  power 157
  talent 698
  gift 784
endrogynous 83
endue 157
endure *time* 106
  last 110
  persist 143
  continue 141
  undergo 151
  feel 821
  submit to 826
  unable to – 867
  – for ever 112
  – *pain* 828
enduring
  indelible 505
endwise 212
enemy *time* 841
  foe 891
  the common – 978
  thing devised by
  the – 546
  – to society 891
energumen 504
energy *power* 157
  strength 159
  physical 171
  resolution 604
  activity 682
enervate 158, 160
enfant, bon – 906
  – gate
  prosperity 734
  satiety 869
  favorite 899
  – perdu
  hopeless 859
  reckless 863
  – terrible
  curiosity 455
  artless 703
  object of fear 860
enfeeble 160
enfeoff 780, 783
Enfield rifle 727
enfilade
  lengthwise 200
  pierce 260
  pass through 302
enfold 229
enforce *urge* 615
  advise 695
  compel 744
  require 924
enfranchise
  free 748
  liberate 750
  permit 760
enfranchised 924
engage
  bespeak 132

expose]
  appearance 448
  – to weather 338
expound
  interpret 522
  teach 537
expounder 524
express
  rapid 274
  squeeze out 301
  mean 516
  declare 525
  inform 527
  journal 531
  intentional 620
  by – *haste* 684
  – train 272
  – by words 566
expressed, well –
  578
expressible 525
expression [*see*
  express]
  musical 416
  aspect 448
  nomenclature 564
  phrase 566
  mode of – 569
  new fangled – 563
expressive
  meaning 516
  sensibility 822
exprobation 932,
  938
expropriation 782
expugnable 665
expugnation 731
expulsion 55 [*see*
  expel]
expunge 162, 552
expurgate 38, 652
expurgatorious,
  index – 761
exquisite
  savory 394
  excellent 648
  pleasurable 829
  beautiful 845
  fop 854
exquisitely 31
exsiccate 340
exsudation 299
exsufflation 993
exsuscitate 824
extant 1
extasy [*see* ecstasy]
extemporaneous
  [*see* extempore]
  transient 111
extempore
  instant 113
  early 132
  occasion 134
  off-hand 612
  unprepared 674
extend
  expand 194
  prolong 200
  – to 196
extended 202
extensibility 324
extensile 324
extension [*see*
  extend] 35, 142,
  180
  – of time 110
extensive 31, 180
  – knowledge 490

extenso, in –
  whole 50
  diffuse 573
extent 26, 180
extenuate
  decrease 36
  weaken 160
  excuse 937
extenuated 203
extenuating cir-
  cumstances
  469, 937
extenuatory 469
exteriority 220
exterminate 162
extermination 301
external 57, 220
  – evidence 467
  – senses 375
extinct
  inexistent 2
  past 122
  destroyed 162
  darkness 421
  become – 4
extincteur 385
extinction of life
  360
extinguish
  destroy 162
  blow out 385
  darken 421
extinguisher 165
  put an – upon
  hinder 706
  defeat 731
extirpate 301
extispicious 511
extol
  over-estimate 482
  praise 931
extort *extract* 301
  compel 744
  despoil 789
extorted
  dissent 489
extortion 814, 819
extortionate 739,
  865
extra 37, 599, 641
  ab – 220
extract
  draw off 297
  take out 301
  quotation 596
  remedy 662
extraction 301
  paternity 166
  – of roots 85
extractor 301
extradition 270, 297
extrajudicial 964
extramundane 317
extramural 220
extraneous
  extrinsic 6
  not related 10
  foreign 57
  outside 220
extraneousness 57
extraordinary
  great 31
  exceptional 83
extraregarding 220
extravagant
  inordinate 31
  violent 173
  absurd 497

  foolish 499
  fanciful 515
  exaggerated 549
  excessive 641
  high-priced 814
  prodigal 818
  vulgar 851
  ridiculous 853
extravagation 303
extravaganza
  fanciful 515
  drama 599
extravasate 295,
  297
extreme
  inordinate 31
  end 67
  – unction 998
extremis, in –
  dying 360
  difficulty 704
extremist 710
extremity *end* 67
  adversity 735
  tribulation 828
  drive matters to
  an – 604
  at the last – 665
extricate
  take out 301
  deliver 672
  facilitate 705
  liberate 750
extrinsicality 6
extrinsic evidence
  467
extrusion 297, 299
exuberant
  – *style* 573
  redundant 639
exudation 295, 299
exulcerate 659
exult 838, 884
exultant 858
exulting 836
exunge 356
exuviae 653
eye *circle* 247
  opening 260
  organ of sight 441
  all my – and
  Betty Martin
  546
  appear to one's
  – 446
  before one's –s
  front 234
  visible 446
  manifest 525
  cast the –s on
  see 441
  cast the –s over
  attend to 457
  catch the – 457
  close the –s
  blind 442
  death 360
  sleep 683
  dry –s 823
  fix the –s on 457
  have an – to
  attention 457
  intention 620
  desire 865
  in one's –
  visible 446
  expectant 507
  in the –s of

appearance 448
  belief 484
  keep an – upon
  459
  look with one's
  own –s 459
  make –'s at 441
  mind's – 515
  with moistened –s
  839
  open the –s to
  480a
  with open –s 870
  set one's –s upon
  865
  shut one's –s to
  inattention 458
  permit 760
  to the –s 448
  under the –s of
  186
  up to one's –s
  641
  have one's –s
  about one 459
  – askance 860
  –s draw straws 683
  an – for an – 718,
  919
  – glistening 824
  in the – of the law
  963
  – of the master
  693
  – of a needle 260
  –s open
  attention 457
  care 459
  intention 620
  –s opened
  disclosure 529
  –s out 442
eye-ball 441
eyebrows 256
eyeglass 445
eyelashes 256
eyeless 442
eyelet 260
eyelid 223
eye-shade 443
eye-sight 441
eyesore 846, 848
eye-teeth
  have cut one's –
  adolescence 131
  skill 698
  cunning 702
eye-wash 544
eye-witness
  spectator 444
  evidence 467
eyot 346
eyre 966
eyry 189

F

Fabian policy
  delay 133
  inaction 681
  caution 864
fable *error* 495
  metaphor 521
  fiction 546   ●
  description 590
fabric *state* 7
  effect 154

texture 329
fabricate ·
  composition 54
  make 161
  invent 515
  falsify 544
fabrication *lie* 546
fabula narratur, de
  te – *retaliate* 718
  condemn 971
fabulist 594
fabulous
  enormous 31
  imaginary 515
  untrue 546
  exaggerated 549
faburden 413
façade 234
face *exterior* 220
  covering 223
  front 234
  aspect 448
  oppose 708
  resist 719
  brave 861
  impudence 885
  change the – of
  146
  fly in the – of
  disobey 742
  put a good – upon
  sham 545
  calm 826
  cheerful 836
  hope 858
  pride 878
  display 882
  vindicate 93
  in the – of
  presence 186
  opposite 708
  look in the –
  see 441
  proud 878
  make –s
  distort 243
  ugly 846
  disrespect 929
  on the – of
  manifest 525
  show –
  present 186
  visible 446
  not show –
  disreputable 874
  bashful 879
  to one's – 525
  wry – 378
  – about 279
  set one's – against
  708
  – of the country
  344
  on the – of the
  earth
  space 180
  world 318
  – to face *front* 234
  contraposition
  237
  manifest 525
  – of the thing
  appearance 448
facet 220
facetiae 842
facetious 842
facia 234
facile *willing* 602

fame *greatness* 31
  news 532
  renown 873
familiar
  known 490
  habitual 613
  sociable 892
  affable 894
  – *spirit* 979, 980
  on – terms 888
familiarize
  teach 537
  habit 613
famille, en – 892
family
  kin 11
  class 75
  ancestors 166
  posterity 167
  party 712
  in the bosom of
    one's – 221
  happy – 714
  – circle 892
  – jars 713
  – likeness 17
  – tie 11
  in the – way 161
famine 640
  – price 814
famine-stricken
  640
famish
  stingy 819
  fasting 956
famished
  insufficient 640
  hungry 865
famous 873
famously 31
fan *blow* 349
  cool 385
  refresh 689
  stimulate 824
  flirt a – 855
  – the embers 505
  – the flame
  violence 173
  heat 384
  aid 707
  excite 824
  – into a flame
  anger 900
  –shaped 194
fanatic
  madman 504
  imaginative 515
  zealot 682
  religious – 988
fanatical
  misjudging 481
  insane 503
  emotional 821
  excitable 825
  heterodox 984
  over-righteous 988
fanaticism 606
fanciful
  imaginative 515
  capricious 608
  ridiculous 853
fancy *think* 451
  idea 453
  believe 484
  suppose 514
  imagine 515
  caprice 608

choice 609
  pugilism 726
  wit 842
  desire 865
  wonder 870
  love 897
  after one's – 850
  indulge one's –
    609
  take a – to
  delight in 827
  desire 865
  take one's –
  please 829
  – dog 366
  – dress 840
  – price 814
  – woman 962
fandango 840
fandi, mollia tem-
  pora – 588
fane 1000
fanfare *loudness*
  404
  celebration 883
fanfaron 887
fanfaronnade 884
fangs *venom* 663
  rule 737
  retention 781
fan-light 260
fan-like 202
fannel 999
fanon 999
fantasia 415
fantastic *odd* 83
  absurd 497
  imaginative 515
  capricious 608
  unfashionable 851
  ridiculous 853
fantasy
  imagination 515
  desire 865
fantoccini 554, 599
faquir 996
far – away 196
  – be it from
  unwilling 603
  deprecation 766
  – between
  disjunction 44
  few 103
  interval 198
  – from it
  unlike 18
  shortcoming 304
  no 536
  – from the truth
    546
  – and near 180
  – off 196
  – and wide 31,
    180, 196
farce
  absurdity 497
  untruth 546
  drama 599
  wit 842
  ridiculous 853
  mere –
  unimportant 643
  useless 645
farceur
  actor 599
  humorist 844
fardel

bundle 72
  hindrance 706
fare *state* 7
  food 298
  price 812
  bill of –
  list 86
farewell
  departure 293
  relinquishment
    624
  loss 776
  – to greatness 874
far-famed 873
far-fetched 10
far-flung 73
far-gone
  much 31
  insane 503
  spoiled 654
farinaceous 330
farm *till* 371
  property 780
  rent 788
farmer 188, 342,
  371
  afternoon – 683
farm-house 189
Farmer-Labor 712
faro 840
farrago 59
farrier 370
farrow
  produce 161
  litter 167
  multitude 102
far-sighted 442, 510
farther 196
  [and see further]
farthing
  quarter 97
  worthless 643
  coin 800
  – candle 422
farthingale 225
fasces 747
fascia 205, 247
fascicle 51
fasciculated 72
fascinate
  influence 615
  excite 824
  please 829
  astonish 870
  love 897
  conjure 992
fascinated
  pleased 827
fascination [see
  fascinate]
  infatuation 825
  desire 870
fascine 72
Fascisti 712
fas et nefas, per –
  604a, 631
fash 830
fashion
  state 7
  form 240
  custom 613
  method 627
  ton 852
  after a –
  middling 32
  after this – 617
  follow the – 82

be in the – 488
  man of – 852
  set the –
  influence 175
  authority 737
  for –'s sake 852
fast *joined* 43
  steadfast 150
  rapid 274
  fashionable 852
  intemperate 954
  not eat 956
  worship 990
  rite 998
  stick – 704
  – asleep 683
  – by 197
  – day 956
  – friend 890
  – and loose
  sophistry 477
  falsehood 544
  irresolute 605
  tergiversation 607
  caprice 608
  – man *fop* 854
  libertine 962
fasten *join* 43
  hang 214
  restrain 751
  – on the mind 451
  – a quarrel upon
    713
  – upon 789
fastening 45
fast-handed 819
fastidious
  censorious 932
fastidiousness 868
fasting
  insufficiency 640
  worship 990
  penance 952
  abstinence 956
fastness
  asylum 666
  defence 717
fat *corpulent* 192
  expansion 194
  unctuous 355
  oleaginous 356
  kill the –ted calf
  celebration 883
  sociality 892
  – in the fire
  disorder 59
  violence 173
  – of the land
  pleasure 377
  enough 639
  prosperity 734
  intemperance 95
fata – Morgana
  occasion 134
  ignis fatuus 423
  – obstant 601
fatal 361
  – disease 655
fatalism 601
fatality 601
fate *end* 67
  necessity 601
  chance 621
  be one's – 156
  sure as – 474
Fates 601, 979
fat-head 501

father *eldest* 128
  paternity 166
  priest 996
  Apostolical –s 985
  gathered to one's
    –s 360
  heavy – 599
  – upon 155
Father, God the –
  976
fatherland 189
fatherless 158
fatherly 906
fathom
  length 200
  investigate 461
  solve 462
  measure 466
  discover 480a
  knowledge 490
fathomless 208
fatidical 511
fatigation 688
fatigue 688
fatras 643
fatten
  expand 194
  improve 658
  prosperous 734
  – on parasite 886
  – upon
  feed 298
fatuity 4, 499
fatuous 517
fat-witted 499
faubourg 227
fauces 231
faucet 252
faugh! 867
fault
  break 70
  error 495
  imperfection 651
  failure 732
  vice 945
  guilt 947
  at –
  uncertain 475
  ignorant 491
  unskilful 699
  find – with 932
faultless 650, 946
faulty 495, 651
faun 980
fauna 366
faut: comme il –
  taste 850
  fashion 852
  il s'en – bien 489
  tant s'en – 536
faute 732
  – de mieux
  substitution 147
  necessity 601
fauteuil 215
fautor 890
faux pas
  error 568
  failure 732
  misconduct 947
  intrigue 961
favor
  resemble 16
  badge 550
  letter 592
  aid 707
  indulgence 740

permit 760
gift 784
partiality 923
appearances in –
of 472
get into –
friendship 888
love 897
in – *repute* 873
approbation 931
in – of
approve 931
under – of 760
view with – 906
– with 784
favorable
occasion 134
willing 602
good 648
aid 707
– *prospect* 472
– to 709
take a – turn
improve 658
prosperity 734
favorably
well 618
favorer 890
favorite
pleasing 829
beloved 897, **899**
favoritism
friendship 888
wrong 923
fawn *color* 433
cringe 749, 886
flatter 993
fay 979
fealty
obedience 743
duty 926
respect 928
fear **860**
fearful
painful 830
timid 862
fearfully 31, 870
fearless *hope* 858
courage 861
fearsome 860
feasible 470, 705
feast *period* 138
repast 298
pleasure 377
revel 840
rite 998
– one's eyes 897
feast of reason
conversation 588
– and flow of soul
sociality 892
feat *action* 680
courage 861
– of arms 720
– of strength 159
feather
class 75
tuft 256
light 320
trifle 643
ornament 847
decoration 877
in full –
prepared 673
prosperous 734
rich 803
hear a – drop 403

in high –
health 654
cheerful 884
pleased with a –
840
– in one's cap
honor 873
decoration 877
– one's nest
prepare 673
prosperity 734
wealth 803
economy 817
selfish 943
– the oar 698
– in the scale 643
feather-bed 324
feathered tribes
366
feathery 256
featly 682
feature
character 5
component 56
form 240
appearance 448
press 531
lineament 550
– in 56
features
face 234
febrifuge 662
febrile 382, 825
fecal 653
feces 299, 653
fecit 556
feckless 866
feculence 653
fecund 168
fecundate 161
federal council 696
– *penitentiary* 752
federalism 737
federation 48, 709,
712
fee *possession* 777
property 780
pay 809
reward 973
feeble *weak* 160
illogical 477
feeble-minded 497,
605
feebleness
style **575**
feed *eat* 298
supply 637
– the flame 707
fee-faw-fum
bugbear 860
spell 993
feel *sense* 375
touch 379
emotion 821
– for *try* 463
benevolence 906
pity 914
condole with 915
– the pulse 461
– the want of 865
– one's way
essay 675
caution 864
feeler 379
inquiry 461
experiment 463
feeling 698, **821**

feet *low* 207
walkers 266
at one's –
near 197
subjection 749
humility 879
fall at one's –
submit 725
fall on one's –
prosper 734
lick the – of
servile 886
light upon one's
safe 664
spring to one's –
307
throw oneself at
the – of
entreat 765
feign 544, 546
feigned 545
feint 545
felicitas, curiosa –
698
felicitate 896
felicitous
agreeing 23
– *style* 578
skilful 698
successful 731
pleasant 829
felicity 827
feline *cat* 366
stealthy 528
cunning 702
fell *destroy* 162
mountain 206
lay flat 21
skin 223
lay low 308
moor 344
dire 860
malevolent 907
fellah 876
felloe 231
fellow *similar* 17
equal 27
companion 88
dual 89
man 373
scholar 492, 541
fellow-commoner
541
fellow-companion
890
fellow-countryman
890
fellow-creature 372
fellow-feeling
friendship 888
love 897
benevolence 906
pity 914
fellowship
partnership 712
distinction 873
friendship 888
companionship
890
good – 892
fellow-student 541
fellow-worker 690
felly 231
felo-de-se 361
felon 949
felonious 945
felony 947

felt *texture* 219
heart– 821
felucca 273
female 374
feme coverte 903
feme sole 904
feminality
weakness 160
woman 374
feminine 374
feminism 374
femme de chambre
746
fen 345
fence *enclose* 232
evade 544
defence 717
fight 720
prison 752
thief 792
– *round* 229
– with a question
528
fenced 770
fenceless 665
fencible 726
fencing 840
feneration 787
fend 717
fender 717
Fenian 710, 742
**fenum habet in
cornu** 668, 913
feodal 780
feodality 737, 777
feoff *property* 780
feoffee 779, 785
feoffer 784
ferae naturae 366
feral 907
ferine 907
ferment
disorder 59
energy 171
violence 173
agitation 315
lightness 320
effervesce 353
emotion 821
excitement 824,
825
anger 900
**fermentation,
acetous** – 397
fern 367
ferocity 173, 907
Ferrara
sword 727
ferret out 461, 480a
ferro-concrete 635
ferrule 223
ferry 270, 627
ferry-boat 273
ferry-man 269
fertile 161, 168
– *imagination* 515
ferule 975
come under the –
932
fervent *hot* 382
desirous 865
– *hope* 858
fervid *hot* 382
heartfelt 821
excited 824
fervour *heat* 382
animation 821
love 897

festal *eating* 298
social 892
fester 653, 655
festina lente 864
festival
music 416
celebration 883
festivity 840, 892
festoon 245, 847
fetch *bring* 270
arrive 292
evasion 545
sell for 812
– one a blow
strike 276
attack 716
– and carry
servile 886
– a sigh 839
fête 840, 882
fêté 892
fetishism 992
fetid 401
fetish 991, 993
fetter 751, 752
fettle 673
state 5
prepare 673
in fine – 159, 654
fetus 129, 153
feu
– *d'enfer* 716
– *de joie*
amusement 840
celebration 883
feud *discord* 713
possess 777
property 780
death – 919
feudal 737, 780
feudatory 749
feuilleton 593
fever *heat* 382
disease 655
excitement 825
feverish *hurry* 684
animated 821
excited 824
few
a – 100
– and far between
70
– *words*
concise 572
taciturn 585
compendium 596
fewness **103**
fey 360
fez 225
fiancée 897
fiasco 732
fiat 741
– *money* 800
fib *falsehood* 544,
546
thump 720
fiber *link* 45
filament 205
moral – 60
fickle 149, 605
fictile 240
fiction *untruth* 546
work of – 594
fictitious 515, 546
fiddle 416, 417
fiddle-de-dee
absurd 497

hell – 982
on – 382
open – *begin* 66
play with – 863
signal – 550
take –
  excitable 825
  angry 900
between two –s
  665
under – 665, 722
  – at 716
  – the blood 824
  – and fury 900
  – the first shot 716
  – of genius 498
  – off 284
  – a salute 883
  – and sword 162
  – up *excite* 825
  anger 900
  – a volley 716
go through – and
  water
  resolution 604
  perseverance 604a
  courage 861
fire-alarm 669
fire-annihilator 385
fire-arms 727
fire-ball *fuel* 388
  arms 727
fire-balloon 273
fire-barrel 388
fire-bell 669
fire-boat 726
fire-brand
  fuel 388
  instigator 615
  dangerous man
  667
  incendiary 913
fire-brigade 385
fire-curtain 599
fire-drake 423
fire-eater
  fighter 726
  blusterer 887
fire-eating
  rashness 863
  insolence 885
fire-engine 348
fire-escape 671
fire-extinguisher
  385
fire-fly 423
fireless cooker 386
fire-light 422
firelock 727
fireman *stoker* 268
  extinguisher 385
fire-place 386
fire-proof 385, 644
fireside 189
firewood 388
firework
  fire 382
  luminary 423
  celebration 883
  amusement 840
fire-worship 991
fire-worshipper 984
firing *fuel* 388
  explosion 406
firkin 191
firm
  junction 43

stable 150
hard 323
resolute 604
partnership 712
merchant 797
brave 861
stand – 719
  – as a rock 604
  – belief 484
  – hold 781
firmament 318
firman 741, 760
first 66
  – blush
  morning 125
  leading 280
  vision 441
  appearance 448
  manifest 525
  – blow 716
  – cause 976
  – that comes 609a
  – fiddle
  importance 642
  proficient 700
  authority 737
  – come first
  served 609a
  – and foremost 66
  – impression 66
  – and last 87
  – line 234
come back to –
  love 607
  – move 66
  – opportunity 132
at – sight 448
  – stage 66
  – stone
  preparation 673
  attack 716
on the – summons
  741
of the – water
  best 648
  repute 873
first-born 124, 128
first-fruits 154
first-hand 20, 467
firstlings 128, 154
first-rate
  important 642
  excellent 648
  man-of-war 726
firth 343
fisc 802
fiscal 800
fish *food* 298
  sport 361, 622
  animal 366
food for –es 362
other – to fry
  ill-timed 135
  busy 682
queer – 857
  – in the air 645
  – for compliments
  880
  – for *seek* 4
  experiment 463
  desire 865
  – hatchery 370
  – out *inquire* 461
  discover 480a
  – in troubled
  waters
  difficult 704

discord 713
  – up *raise* 307
  find 480a
  – out of water
  disagree 24
  unconformable 83
  displaced 185
  bungler 701
fisherman 361
fishery 370
fishing *kill* 361
  pursue 622
fishing-boat 273
fishpond 343, 370
fish-trail 267
fishy *transaction*
  940
fisk 266, 274
fissile 328
fission 44
fissure 44
  chink 198
fist
  handwriting 590
  grip 781
shake the –
  defy 515
  threat 909
fisticuffs 720
fistula 260
fit *state* 7
  agreeing 23
  equal 27
  paroxysm 173
  agitation 315
  caprice 608
  expedient 646
  healthy 654
  disease 655
  excitement 825
  anger 900
  right 922
  due 924
  duty 926
in –s 315
think – 600
  – of abstraction
  458
  – of crying 839
  – for 698
  – out *dress* 225
  prepare 673
  – to be seen 845
by –s and starts
  irregular 59
  discontinuous 70
  agitated 315
  capricious 608
  haste 684
fitful
  irregular 139
  changeable 149
  capricious 608
fittings 633
five 98
  division by – 99
  – act play 599
  – and twenty 98
Five Year Plan 626
fiver 800
fives *game* 840
fix *join* 43
  arrange 60
  establish 150
  place 184
  immovable 265
  solidify 321

resolve 604
  difficulty 704
  – the eyes upon
  441
  – the foundations
  673
  – the memory 505
  – the time 114
  – the thoughts
  457
  – up 774
  – upon *discover*
  480a
  choose 609
fixed *intrinsic* 5
  permanent 141
  stable 150
  quiescent 265
  habitual 613
  – idea 481
  – opinion 484
  – periods 138
fixity 141
fixity of purpose
  141
fixture
  appointment 741
  property 780
fizgig 423
fizz 409
fizzle 353
  – out 304
flabelliform 194
flabbergast 870
  879
flabby 324
flabbiness 324
flaccid *weak* 160
  soft 324
  empty 640
flag *weak* 160
  flat stone 204
  floor 211
  smoothness 255
  slow 275
  leaf 367
  sign 550
  path 627
  infirm 655
  inactive 683
  tired 688
  weary 841
  lower one's – 725
  red – *alarm* 669
  yellow –
  warning 668
  alarm 669
  – man 668
  – ship 726
  – of truce 723
flag-bearer 534
flagellation
  penance 952
  asceticism 955
  flogging 972
  rite 998
flagelliform 205
flageolet 417
flagitious 945
flagon 191
flagrant
  great 31
  manifest 525
  notorious 531
  atrocious 945
flagrante
  – bello 722

  – delicto
  sure enough 474
  act 680
  guilt 947
flagration 384
flagstaff *tall* 206
  signal 550
flail 276
flair 450, 698
flake 204
  snow – 383
  – white 430
flam 544
flambé 732
flambeau 423
flamboyant 577
flame *fire* 382
  light 420
  luminary 423
  passion 824, 825
  love 897
  catch the –
  emotion 821
  consign to the –s
  384
  add fuel to the –
  173
  in –s 382
  – up 825
  –colored
  red 434
  orange 439
flame-projector 527
flamen 996
flaming *violent* 173
  feeling 821
  excited 824
  ostentatious 882
  boasting 884
flâneur 935
flange *support* 215
  rim 231
  projection 250
flank *side* 236
  protect 664
flannel 384
flap *adjunct* 39
  hanging 214
  move to and fro
  315
  – the memory 505
flapdoodle 517
flapper *girl* 129
flapping *loose* 47
flare *violent* 173
  glare 420
  light 423
  – up
  excited 824, 825
  angry 900
flaring *color* 428
flash *instant* 113
  violent 173
  fire 382
  light 420
  eyes – fire 900
  – lamp 550
  – light 423
  – across the mem-
  ory 505
  – on the mind
  thought 451
  disclose 529
  impulse 612
  – note 800
  – in the pan
  unsubstantial 4
  transientness 111

impotent 158
unproductive 169
failure 732
– tongue 563
– up excited 824
– upon
unexpected 508
– of wit 842
flashing
ostentatious 882
flashy
gaudy color 428
style 577
ornament 847
vulgar 851
flask 191
flat inert 172
abode 189
story 191
low 207
horizontal 213
vapid 391
low tone 408
musical note 413
positive 535
dupe 547
back-scene 599
shoal 667
bungler 701
poor 804
insensible 823
dejected 837
weary 841
dull 843
simple 849
fall – 732
– contradiction
536
– iron 255
– refusal 764
flatfoot 664
flatness 251
flatter deceive 545
cunning 702
please 829
grace 845
encourage 858
approbation 931
adulation 933
– oneself
probable 472
hope 858
– the palate 394
flatterer 935
flattering
– remarks 894
– tale
hope 858
– unction to one's
soul
content 831
vain 880
flattery 933
flattery 544, 933
flatulent
gaseous 334
air 338
wind 349
- style 573, 575
flatus 334, 349
flaunt 873, 882
flaunting vulgar 85
gaudy 428
unreserved 525
flautist 416
Flavian amphi-
theater 728

flavor 390
flavoring 393
flavous 436
flaw break 70
crack 198
error 495
imperfection 651
blemish 848
fault 947
– in an argument
477
flaxen 436
flay divest 226
punish 972
flea jumper 309
dirt 653
– in one's ear
repel 289
eject 297
refuse 764
disrepute 874
abashed 879
discourteous 895
contempt 930
flea-bite 643
flea-bitten 440
fleck 32
flecked 440
flection 279
fled escaped 671
fledge 673
fledgling 123
flee avoid 623
fleece tegument 223
strip 789
rob 791
impoverish 804
surcharge 814
fleet ridicule 856
insult 929
fleet ships 273
swift 274
navy 726
Fleet prison 752
fleeting 4, 111
flesh bulk 192
animal 364
mankind 372
carnal 961
gain – 194
ills that – is heir
to evil 619
disease 655
in the – 359
one – 903
way of all – 360
weakness of the –
945
– and blood
substance 3
materiality 316
animality 364
affections 820
make the – creep
pain 830
fear 860
flesh-color 434
flesh-pots 298
– of Egypt 734,
803
fleshly 316
fleur-de-lis 847
fleuron 847
flexible 324, 705
flexion
curvature 245
fold 258

deviation 279
flexuous 248
flexure 245, 258
flibbertigibbet 980
flicker
changing 149
waver 314
flutter 315
light 420
dim 422
flickering 139
flier 621
flies theatre 599
flight flock 102
volitation 267
swiftness 274
departure 293
avoidance 623
escape 671
– lieutenant 745
put to –
propel 284
repel 717
vanquish 731
– of fancy 515
– of stairs 305,
627
– of time 109
flighty inattentive
458
mad 503
fanciful 515
flim-flam 544, 608
flimsy unsubstan-
tial 4
weak 160
rarity 322
soft 324
sophistical 477
trifling 643
flinch swerve 607
avoid 623
fear 860
cowardice 862
fling propel 284
jig 840
jeer 929
have one's –
active 682
laxity 738
freedom 748
amusement 840
– aside 782
have a – at
attack 716
resent 900
disrespect 929
censure 932
– away reject 610
waste 638
relinquish 782
– down 308
– to the winds
destroy 162
not observe 773
flint hard 323
flint-hearted 907
flintlock 727
flip beverage 298
flippant fluent 584
pert 885
flipper paddle 267
flirt propel 284
coquet 607, 854
love 897
endearment 902
– a fan 855

flit elapse 109
changeable 149
move 264
travel 266
swift 274
depart 293
run away 623
flitter
small part 32
changeable 149
flutter 315
flitting 111
float establish 150
navigate 267
boat 273
buoy up 305
lightness 320
before the –s
on the stage 599
– on the air 405
– before the eyes
446
– bonds 788
– in the mind
thought 451
imagination 515
floater 683
floating
[see float]
rumoured 532
– battery 726
– capital 805
– debt 806
– dock 189
flocculent
woolly 256
soft 324
pulverulent 330
flock
assemblage 72
multitude 102
laity 997
–s and herds 366
– together 72
floe ice 383
flog 972
hasten 684
flood much 31
crowd 72
river 348
abundance 639
redundance 641
prosperity 734
stem the – 708
– of light 420
– of tears 839
flood-gate
limit 233
egress 295
conduit 350
open the –s
eject 297
permit 760
flood-light 423,
599
flood-mark 466
flood-tide
increase 35
complete 52
height 206
advance 282
water 337
floor level 204
base 211
horizontal 213
support 215
overthrow 731

ground – 191
flop 315
Flora 369
floral 367
florescence 154
floriculture 371
florid color 428
red 434
– style 577
health 654
florist 371
floss 256
flotilla 273, 726
flotsam and jetsam
73
flounce
trimming 231
jump 309
agitation 315
flounder
change 149
toss 315
uncertain 475
bungle 699
difficulty 704
fail 732
flour 330
flourish
brandish 314, 315
exaggerate 549
language 577
speech 582
prosper 618
healthy 654
prosperous 734
ornament 847
repute 873
display 882
boast 884
– of trumpets
loud 404
cheerfulness 836
publish 531
ostentation 882
celebrate 883
boast 884
flout 929, 936
flow course 109
hang 214
motion 264
stream 348
murmur 405
abundance 639
– from
result 154
– of ideas 451
– in 294
– into river 348
– out 295
– over 641
– of soul
conversation 588
affections 820
cheerful 836
social 892
– with the tide
705
– of time 109
– of words 582,
584
flower essence 5
produce 161
vegetable 367
prosper 734
beauty 845
ornament 847
repute 873

fortunes of
narrative 594
forty 98
– winks 683
forum 799
school 542
tribunal 966
forward *early* 132
transmit 270
advance 282
willing 602
improve 658
active 682
help 707
vain 880
insolent 885
uncourteous 895
bend – 234
come –
in sight 446
offer 763
display 882
look – to 507
move – 282
press – *haste* 684
put – *aid* 507
offer 763
put oneself – 880
set – 676
– *in knowledge* 490
foss 348
fosse
inclosure 232
ditch 259
defence 717
fossil
ancient 124
hard 323
organic 357
dry bones 362
foster *aid* 707
excite 824
caress 902
– a belief 484
fou 959
foudroyant 870
foul
collide 276
bad 649
dirty 653
unhealthy 657
ugly 846
base 940
vicious 945
fall – of
oppose 708
quarrel 713
attack 716
fight 720
censure 932
run – of
impede 706
– fiend 978
– means 940
– language
malediction 908
– odor 401
– play *evil* 619
cunning 702
wrong 923
improbity 940
foul-mouthed 895
foul-spoken 934
found 153, 215
foundation
beginning 66
stability 150

base 211
support 215
lay the –s 673
sandy – 667
shake to its –s 315
founded
well – 472
– *on base* 211
evidence 467
founder
originator 164
sink 310
fail 732
religious –s 986
foundery 691
founding 22
foundling
trover 775
derelict 782
outcast 893
fount *type* 591
fountain
source 153
river 348
store 636
– *head* 210
– *pen* 590
four 95
on all –s 13, 23
horizontal 213
easy 705
prosperous 734
humble 879
– in hand 272
– *score &c.* 98
– *square* 244
– *times* 96
from the – *winds* 278
fourflusher 884
fourfold 96
four-oar 273
four-poster 215
fourth 96, 97
musical 413
– *estate* 531
four-wheeler 272
fowl 366
fowling-piece 727
fox *animal* 366
cunning 702
– *chase* 622
fox-trot 840
foxy *color* 433, 434
cunning 720
foyer 191, 599
fracas
disorder 59
noise 404
discord 713
contention 720
fraction *part* 51
numerical 84
less than one 100a
fractious 901
fracture
disjunction 44
discontinuity 70
fissure 198
fragile 160, 328
fragment
small 32, 193
part 51, 100a
fragrance 400
fragrant *weed* 392
frail *weak* 160
brittle 328

feeble 575
irresolute 605
imperfect 651
failing 945
impure 961
– sisterhood 962
frais, à grands – 481
frame
condition 7
make 161
support 215
border 231
form 240
substance 316
structure 329
contrive 626
cucumber – 371
have –d and
glazed 822
– of mind
inclination 602
disposition 820
frame-up 626
framework
support 215
structure 329
franchise
voting 609
freedom 748
right 924
exemption 927a
Franciscan 996
franc-tireur 726
frangible 160, 328
frank *open* 525
sincere 543
artless 703
honorable 939
frankalmoigne 748
Frankenstein 913, 980
frankincense 400
frantic
violent 173
delirious 503
excited 824
fraternal
brother 11
concord 714
friendly 888
fraternity
[see fraternal]
party 712
fraternize
co-operate 48, 709
agree 714
sympathize 888
associate 892
fratricide 361
Frau 374
fraud
falsehood 544
deception 545
pretender 548
dishonor 940
pious – 988
fraught *full* 52
pregnant 161
possessing 777
– with danger 665
fray *rub* 331
battle 720
in the thick of the – 722
frayed 659
frazzle

beaten to a – 732
freak 608, 872
– of Nature 83
freckle 848
freckled 440
fredaine 840
free
detached 44, 47
unconditional 52
liberate 672
unobstructed 705
at liberty 748, 750
gratis 815
liberal 816
insolent 885
exempt 927a
impure 961
– balloon 273
– and easy
cheerful 836
adventurous 863
vain 880
insolent 885
friendly 888
sociable 892
– fight 720
– from
simple 42
never – from 613
– gift 784
– from imperfection 650
– lance 726
– land 748
– liver 954a
– love 961
make – of 748
– play 170, 748
– quarters
cheap 815
hospitality 892
– space 180
– stage 748
– trade
commerce 794
– translation 522
– will 600
make – with
frank 703
take 789
sociable 892
uncourteous 895
freebooter 792
freeborn 748
freedman 748
freedom 748
free-handed 816
freehold 780
freely
willingly 602
freeman 748
freemasonry
unintelligible 519
secret 528
sign 550
co-operation 709
party 712
free-spoken 703
freethinker 989
freeze
benumb 381
cold 385
– the blood 830
freezing 383
– *mixture* 387
freight *lade* 184
cargo 190

transfer 270
freightage 812
freighter 273
freight train 272
French
peddler's – 563
– and English 840
– horn 417
– leave *avoid* 623
freedom 748
– polish 847
frenetic 503
frenzy
madness 503
imagination 515
excitement 825
frequency 136
frequent
in number 104
in time 136
in space 186
habitual 613
visit 892
fresco *cold* 383
painting 556
al –
out of doors 220
in the air 338
fresh *additional* 37
new 123
flood 348
cold 383
color 428
remembered 505
unaccustomed 614
good 648
healthy 654
impertinent 885
tipsy 959
– breeze 349
– color 434
– news 532
freshen 658, 689
freshet 348
freshman 541
freshwater 851
freshwater sailor 701
fret *suffer* 378
grieve 828
gall 830
discontent 832
sad 837
ornament 847
irritate 900
– and fume 828
fretful 901
fret-work 219
friable 328, 330
friandise 868
friar 996
–'s lantern 423
– Rush 980
Black –s 996
friary 1000
fribble
slur over 460
trifle 643
dawdle 683
fop 854
fricassee 298
frication 331
friction *force* 157
obstacle 179
rubbing 331
on – wheels 705
friend 711, **890**

comic 853
fur *covering* 223
  hair 256
  warm 384
  dirt 653
furacious 791
furbelow 231
furbish
  improve 658
  prepare 673
  adorn 847
furcated 244
furcation 91
furcular 244
furfur 653
furfuraceous 330
Furies *anger* 900
  evil-doers 913
  demons 980
furious *violent* 173
  haste 684
  passion 825
  anger 900
furiously 31
furl 312
furlong 200
furlough 760
furnace 386
  workshop 691
  like a - *hot* 382
  sighing like -
  lament 839
  in love 902
furnish
  provide 637
  prepare 673
  give 784
  - aid 707
  - a handle 617
  - its quota 784
furniture 633
  - van 272
furor
  insanity 503
  passion 825
furore
  emotion 820, 821
  passion 825
  desire 865
furrow 259
further
  added 37
  distant 196
  aid 707
  go - and fare
  worse
  worse 659
  bungle 699
  not let it go - 528
furthermore 37
furtive
  clandestine 528
  stealing 791
furuncle 250
fury *violence* 173
  excitation 825
  anger 900
  demon 980
furze 367
fuscous 433
fuse *join* 43
  combine 48
  heat 382, 384
  torch 388
fuselage 215
fusel oil 356
fusiform 244, 253

fusil 727
fusileer 726
fusillade 361, 716
fusion *union* 48
  heat 384
  co-operation 709
fuss *agitation* 315
  activity 682
  haste 684
  difficulty 704
  excitement 825
  ostentation 882
  kick up a - 173
  make a - about
  importance 642
  lament 839
  disapprove 932
fussy *crotchety* 481
  bustling 682
  excitable 825
fustian
  absurd 497
  unmeaning 517
  - *style* 577, 579
fustigate 972
fusty 124, 401, 653
futhorc 590
futile 497, 645
future 121
  eye to the - 510
  - *possession* 777
  - state
  destiny 152
  heaven 981
futurity 121
fuzzle 959
fuzzy 447

G

gab 284
  gift of the - 582
gabardine 225
gabble 517, 583
gabelle 812
gaberlunzie 876
gabion 717
gable *side* 236
  - *end* 67
Gabriel 977
Gaby 501
gad
  about 266, 268
gadget 626
gad-so 870
gaff 727
gaffer *old* 130
  man 373
  clown 876
gag
  closure 261
  render mute 403, 581
  dramatic 599
  - *muzzle* 751
  imprison 752
gage *measure* 466
  security 771
  throw down the - 715
gaggle 412
gag-man 844
gaieté de cœur 836
gaiety
  [*see gay*] 836
gaillard 844

gain
  increase 35
  advantage 618
  skilful 698
  acquisition 775
  - the confidence of 484
  - credit 931
  - one's ends 731
  - ground
  progress 282
  improve 658
  - head 175
  - laurels 873
  - learning 539
  - over 615
  - a point 731
  - private ends 943
  - the start
  priority 116
  early 132
  - strength 35
  - time
  protract 110
  early 132
  late 133
  - upon
  approach 286
  pass 303
  become a habit 613
  - a victory 731
gainful *useful* 644
gainless 646
gainsay 536
gait 264, 627
gaiter 225
gala 840, 882
galactic circle 318
galantuomo 939
galavant 902
galaxy
  assemblage 72
  multitude 102
  stars 318
  luminary 423
  glory 873
gale 349
Galen 662
galenicals 662
galimatias 497
galipot 191
galopade 840
galore 639
gall *hurt* 378
  bitter 395
  annoy 830
  anger 900
  malevolence 907
  dip the pen in - 934
gallant *brave* 861
  courteous 894
  love 897
  licentious 961, 962
gallantry
  dalliance 902
gallanty-show 448, 840
galled jade wince, let the - 884
galleon 273
gallery *room* 191
  passage 260
  auditory 599
  museum 636

  picture - 556
galley *ship* 273
  punishment 972, 975
  work like a - *slave* 686
  - proof 591
galliass 273
Gallicism 563
galligaskin 225
gallimaufry 41
galliot 273
gallipot 191
gallivant 902
galloon 847
gallop
  pass away 111
  ride 266
  - *scamper* 274
galloping consumption 655
galloway 271
gallows 361, 975
  come to the - 972
galoche 225
galore 102
galvanic
  excitable 825
galvanism 157
galvanize 824
gamache 225
Gamaliel
  brought up at the feet of - 492
gambade *leap* 309
  prank 840
gamble 156
gambado
  gaiter 225
  leap 309
gambit 66
gambling
  chance 621
  rashness 863
gambling-house 621
gamboge 436
gambol 309, 827, 840
game *lame* 160
  food 298
  animal 366
  savory 394
  resolute 604
  persevering 604a
  aim 620
  gamble 612
  pursuit 622
  tactics 692
  amusement 840
  laughing-stock 857
  brave 861
  make - of
  deceive 545
  ridicule 856
  disrespect 929
  play the - 709, 939
  - in one's hands *easy* 705
  succeed 731
  command 737
  - to the last 604a
  - at which two can play 718
  - up 732
game-cock 726, 861

game-keeper 370, 753
gameness 861
gamesome 836
gamester
  chance 621
  play 840
  rash 863
gamin 876
gaming-house 621
gammer *old* 130
  woman 374
gammon 544, 545
gamey 392
gamut 413
gander 373
gang
  assemblage 72
  go 264
  party 712
  - agley 732
ganger 690
gangrene 655
gangster 361, 913
gangway 260, 627
gantlet 972
  run the -
  resolution 604
  dare 861
gaol 752
  - delivery 672
gaoler 753, 975
gap 70, 198, 252
  stand in the - 717
gape *open* 260
  curiosity 455
  wonder 870
  - for *desire* 865
gaping [*see gape*]
  expectant 507
gar 161
garage 191
garb 225
  under the - of 545
garbage 653
garble
  take from 38
  exclude 55
  erroneous 495
  misinterpret 523
  falsify 544
  - accounts 811
garbled
  incomplete 53
garden *grounds* 189
  horticulture 371
  beautiful 845
  botanic - 371
  zoological - 370
  - party 840
gardener 371
gardens *street* 189
Gargantua 192
gargle 337
gargoyle 350
garish
  light 420
  color 428
  ugly 846
  ornament 847
  vulgar 851
  display 882
garland
  circle 247
  sign 550
  trophy 733
  ornament 847

decoration 877
garlic
　condiment 393
　fetid 401
garment 225
garner 636
garnet 847
　red 434
garnish
　addition 39
　prepare 673
　fee 809
　ornament 847
garniture 225
garran 271
garret 191, 210
garrison
　occupant 188
　safety 664
　defence 717
　soldiers 726
garrotte
　render powerless 158
　kill 361
　punishment 972
garrulity 584
garter
　fastening 45
　decoration 877
　- blue 438
garth 181
gas 334
　talk 482
　fuel 388
　boasting 883
　- balloon 273
　- stove 386
　- bomb 727
　- fitter 690
　- mask 717
　- projector 727
gasconade 884
gaseity 334
gaselier 214
gash cut 44
　interval 198
　wound 619
gasification 334, 336
gaskins 225
gas-light 423
gasoline 388
gasometer 636
gasp blow 349
　droop 655
　fatigue 688
　at the last - 360
　- for desire 865
gasper 392
gastriloquism 580
Gastromancy 511
gastronomy 298, 957
gate beginning 66
　inclosure 232
　mouth 260
　barrier 706
　water - 350
　-way way 627
　- keeper 263
gâté, enfant - 734
Gath, tell it not in -
　conceal 528
　disapprove 932
gather collect 72
　expand 194

fold 258
　conclude 480
　acquire 775
　take 789
　- breath 689
　- flesh 194
　- from one
　　information 527
　- fruits 731
gathered
　- to one's fathers 360
gathering
　assemblage 72
　abscess 655
　- clouds dark 421
　shade 424
　omen 512
　danger 665
　warning 668
　adversity 735
gathering-place 74
gauche clumsy 699
gaucherie 699, 851
gaud 847
gaudery 880
gaudy color 428
　vulgar 851
　showy 882
gauge 466
　rain- 348
　wind- 349
gauger 965
gaunt bulky 192
　lean 203
　ugly 846
gauntlet glove 225
　armor 717
　fling down the - 715
　take up the - 720
gauntry 627
Gautama 986
gauze shade 424
　semitransparent 427
gavel 72, 812
gavelkind 778
gavelock 633
gavot 840
gawky
　awkward 699
　ugly 846
　(ridiculous 853)
gay colour 428
　cheerful 836
　adorned 847
　showy 882
　dissipated 961
　- deceiver 962
　- world 852
gaze 441
gazebo 441
gazelle swift 274
gazette
　publication 531
　record 551
　in the -
　bankrupt 808
gazetteer
　list 86
　information 527
　record 551
gazing-stock
　ridiculous 857
　wondrous 872
géant, à pas de -

274
gear clothes 225
　harness 633
　high - 274
　in - 673
　low - 275
　out of -
　disjoin 44
　derange 61
　useless 645
　unprepared 674
　- wheel 633
geese are swans, all his - 482
gehenna 982
geisha 599
Geist 498
gel 352
gelatin 352
gelatinify 352
geld 38, 158
gelding 271, 373
gelid 383
Geloscopy 511
gem 648, 847
geminate 90
Gemini twins 89
　0 - ! 870
gemote 72
gendarme 726, 965
gender 75
genealogy 69, 166
general
　generic 78
　habitual 613
　officer 745
　the -
　commonalty 876
　things in - 151
　- breaking up 655
　- favorite 899
　- information 490
　- meaning 516
　- public 372
　- run 613
　- servant 690, 746
generalissimo 745
generality
　mean 29
　universal 78
generalize 476
generally speaking 613
generalship 692, 722
generate 161, 168
generation
　consanguinity 11
　period 108
　production 161
　mankind 372
　rising - 167
　spontaneous - 161
　wise in one's - 498
generator 164
generic 78
generosity
　giving 784
　liberality 816
　benevolence 906
　disinterestedness 942
genesis
　beginning 66
　production 161
genet 271
Genethliacs 511

genetics 161
Geneva gown 996
genial
　productive 161
　sensuous 377
　warm 382
　willing 602
　delightful 829
　affable 894
geniality 836
geniculated 244
genie 980
genital 161
genitor 166
geniture 161
genius
　intellect 450
　talent 498
　skill 698
　proficient 700
　prodigy 872
　evil - 980
　good -
　friend 898
　benefactor 912
　spirit 979
　tutelary - 711
　- for 698
　- of a language 560
　- loci 664
genre 556, 559
gent 851, 876
genteel 852, 875
　- comedy 599
gentile 984, 989
gentility
　fashion 852
　rank 875
　politeness 894
gentium, jus - 963
gentle moderate 174
　slow 275
　domesticated 370
　faint sound 405
　lenient 740
　meek 826
　courteous 894
　- blood 875
　- breeding 894
　- hint 527
　- as a lamb 174
　- slope 217
gentlefolk 875
gentleman
　male 373
　squire 875
　man of honor 939
　the old - 978
　walking - 599
gentlemanly 852
gently bred 894
Gentoo 984
gentry 875
　landed - 779
genuflexion
　bowing 308
　submission 725
　servility 886
　courtesy 894
　respect 928
　worship 990, 998
genuine 494, 648
genus 75
　- irritabile vatum 597

geodesist 85, 318
geodesy 318, 466
geography 183, 318
geoid 249
geology &c. 358
geomancer 513
geomancy 511
geometry 466
geoponics 371
georama 448
Georgics 371
geotic 318
gerfalcon 913
germ 153
german 11
　- band 417
　- silver 545
germane 23
germicide 662
germinal 153
germinate 161, 194, 365
　- from 154
gerontic 128
gerrymander 545
gesso 556
gest 680
gestation
　propagation 161
　carriage 270
　maturation 673
gesticulate 550
gesture hint 527
　indication 550
get become 144
　beget 161
　acquire 775
　receive 810
　- ahead 35
　- ahead of 33
　- along 282
　- along with you
　　ejection 297
　dismissal 756
　- at 480a
　- away 287
　- back
　retire 283
　regain 775
　- the best of 731
　- better 658
　- down
　swallow 298
　descend 306
　- you gone 297
　- into harness 673
　- by heart 505
　- home 292
　- in collect 72
　gather 775
　- loose 44
　- near 286
　- off depart 293
　escape 671
　- on advance 282
　prosper 734
　- out eject 297
　extract 301
　publish 531
　- over
　recover from 660
　succeed 731
　be content 831
　- over the ground 274
　- for one's pains 973

- ready 673
- rid of 672
- a sight of 441, 490
- through
cnd 67
transact 692
complete 729
expend 809
- to
extend to 196
arrive 292
- together 72
- into trouble 732
- the wind up 860
- up produce 161
ascend 305
raise 307
learn 539
fabricate 544
prepare 673
rise early 682
foment 824
- into the way of 613
get-away 671
gewgaw
trifle 643
ornament 847
vulgar 851
geyser 382, 386
ghastly
pale 429
hideous 846
frightful 860
ghaut 203
ghetto 189
ghost shade 36.`
fallacy of vision 443
soul 450
writer 593
apparition 980
give up the - 360
needs no - to tell us 525
pale as a -
colorless 429
fear 86C
- dance 992
ghost-like
ugly 846
ghostly
intellectual 450
supernatural 976, 980
Ghost, Holy - 976
ghoul 913, 980
ghyll 348
giant
large 192
tall 206
- refreshed
strong 159
refreshed 689
-'s strides
distance 196
swift 294
giaour 984, 989
gibber 583
gibberish 517, 563
gibbet
brand 932
execute 972
gallows 975
gibble-gabble 584
gibbous 249, 250

gib-cat male 373
gibe 929
giblets 298
gibus 225
giddy
inattentive 458
vertiginous 503
irresolute 605
capricious 608
bungling 699
giddy-head 501
giddy-paced 315
gift power 157
talent 698
given 784
- of the gab 582
look a - horse in the mouth
fastidious 868
ungrateful 917
gifted 698
gig 272, 273
gigantic
strong 159
large 192
tall 206
giggle 838
giglamps 445
Gilbertian 842
Gilbertine 996
gild coat 223
color 439
ornament 847
- refined gold 641
- the pill
deceive 545
tempt 615
please 829
flatter 933
Gilead, balm in - 834, 858
Giles's Greek, St. - 563
gill 348
gillie 746
gilt 436, 847
- edged 648
gimbals 312
gimcrack
weak 160
brittle 328
trifling 643
ornament 847
ridiculous 853
gimlet 262
gimp
clean 652
pretty 845
decoration 847
gin trap 545
instrument 633
intoxicating 959
demon 980
gin mill 189
gin palace 189
gingerbread
weak 160
vulgar 851
gingerly 174, 459, 864
gingle 408
gipsy
wanderer 268
wag 844
- lingo 563
giraffe 206
girandole 423

girasol 847
gird bind 43
strengthen 159
surround 227
jeer 929
- up one's loins
brace 159
prepare 673
girder 45, 215
girdle bond 45
encircle 227
circumference 230
circle 247
put a - round the earth 311
girl 129, 374
girlhood 12,
girt 45
girth
bond 45
circumference 230
gisarm 727
gist essence 5
meaning 516
important 642
git, ci - 363
gittern 417
give yield 324
melt 382
bestow 784
discount 813
- away 782, 784
in marriage 903
- back 790
- birth to 161
- with both hands 816
- in charge
restrain 751
- chase 622
- consent 762
- one credit for 484
- in custody 751
- expression to 566
- forth 531
- the go by 623
- a horse his head 748
- in submit 725
- into consent 762
- light 420
- the mind to 457
- notice
inform 527
warn 668
- it one
censure 932
punish 972
- out emit 297
publish 531
bestow 784
- over cease 142
relinquish 624
lose hope 859
- place to
substitute 147
avoid 623
- play to the imagination 515
- points to 27
- quarter 740
- rise to 153
- one the slip 671
- security 771
- and take

reciprocate 12
compensation 30
interchange 148
retaliation 718
compromise 774
barter 794
equity 922
honour 939
- tongue 531
- a turn to 140
- one to understand 527
- up
not understand 519
unwilling 603
reject 610
relinquish 624
submit 725
resign 757
surrender 782
restore 790
hopeless 859
- up the ghost 360
- way weak 160
brittle 328
submit 725
pine 828
despond 837
modest 881
given [see give]
circumstances 8
supposition 514
received 785
- over dying 360
- time 134
- to 613
giving 784
gizzard 191
stick in one's - 900
glabrous 225
glacial 383
glaciate 385
glacier 383
glacis 217, 717
glad 827, 829
give the - eye 441
would be - of 865
- tidings 532
gladden 834, 836
glade hollow 252
opening 260
shade 424
gladiator 726
gladiatorial 361, 713, 720
gladsome 827, 829
Gladstone bag 191
glair 352
glaive 727
glamor 992
glance look 441
sign 550
see at a - 498
- at
take notice of 457
allude to 527
censure 932
- off deviate 279
diverge 291
gland 221
glare light 420
stare 441
imperfect vision 443
visible 446

glaring
[see glare]
great 31
color 428
visible 446
manifest 525
glass vessel 191
smooth 255
brittle 328
transparent 425
lens 445
musical -es 47
see through a -
darkly 491
- of fashion 852
live in a - house
brittle 328
visible 446
danger 665
- too much 959
glass-coach 272
glasshouse 191, 371
Glassite 984
glassy [see glass]
shining 420
colorless 429
glaucous 435
glave 727
glaver 933
glaze 255
gleam small 32
light 420
glean 609, 775
gleanings 636
glebe land 342
ecclesiastical 995
church 1000
glee music 415
satisfaction 827
merriment 836
gleek 929
glen 252
glengarry 225
glib voluble 584
facile 705
glide lapse 109
move 264
travel 266
fly 267
- into conversion 144
glider 273
glimmer
light 420
dim 422
visible 446
slight knowledge 490, 491
glimpse 441, 490
glint 420
glissade 306
glisten 420
glitter
shine 420
appear 446
illustrious 882
glittering
ornament 847
display 882
gloam 901a
gloaming 126, 422
gloar look 441
wonder 970
gloat 884
- on look 441
- over 441
pleasure 377

delight 827
globated 249
globe
 sphere 249
 world 318
 on the face of the
  – 318
 – *trotter* 268
globule 32, 249
glomeration 72
gloom 421, 827, 837
gloomy horizon 859
glorification 884
glorify
 honor 873
 approve 931
 worship 990
glorious
 illustrious 873
 tipsy 959
glory
 light 420
 honor 873
 heaven 981
 King of – 976
 – in 878, 884
 – be to God 990
gloss *smooth* 255
 sheen 420
 interpretation 522
 falsehood 546
 plea 617
 beauty 845
 – of *novelty* 123
 – over
 neglect 460
 sophistry 477
 falsehood 544
 vindicate 937
glossary 86, 562
glossographer 492
glossologist 492
glossology 560, 562
glossy [*see* gloss]
glottology 560
glout 901*a*
glove 225
 take up the – 720
 throw down the –
  715
glow *warm* 382
 shine 420
 appear 446
 color 428
 style 574
 passion 821
glower
 glare 443
 discourteous 895
 sullen 901*a*
glowing
 [*see* glow]
 orange 439
 excited 824
 beautiful 845
 – *terms* 574
glow-worm 423
gloze 933, 937
glucose 396
glue *cement* 45
 cementing 46
 semiliquid 352
glum
 discontented 832
 dejected 837
 sulky 901*a*
glut

redundance 641
satiety 869
gluttony 957
glutinous 352
glutton 954*a*, 957
gluttony 957
glycerine 332, 356
glyphography 558
glyptography 558
glyptotheca 557
gnarl *protuberance* 250
 anger 900
 threat 909
gnarled 256, 321
gnash one's teeth 839, 900
gnat *little* 193
 strain at a – &c.
 caprice 608
gnaw *eat* 298
 rub 331
 injure 659
gnawing
 – *grief* 828, 830
 – *pain* 378
gnome 496, 980
gnomic 496
gnomon 114
Gnostic 984
go
 cease to exist 2
 energy 171, 682
 move 264
 recede 287
 depart 293
 fade 429
 disappear 449
 fashion 852
 come and – 314
 as things – 613
 – about
 turn round 311
 published 531
 undertake 676
 – across 302
 – after
 in time 117
 in motion 281
 – ahead
 energetic 171
 precede 280
 advance 282
 active 682
 – against 708
 – astray 495
 – away 293
 – back 283, 624
 – bad 659
 – bail 771
 – before 280
 – between
 interjacent 228
 instrumental 631
 mediate 631, 724
 – beyond 303
 – by the board
  158
 – about your
 business
 ejection 297
 dismissal 756
 – by
 conform to 82
 elapse 109
 past 122
 outrun 303

subterfuge 702
give the – by to
 neglect 460
 deceive 545
 avoid 623
 not observe 773
 – by the name of
  564
 – deep into 461
 – down *sink* 306
 decline 659
 – down with
 believed 484
 tolerated 826
 content 831
 – farther and fare
  worse 659
 – forth *depart* 293
 publish 531
 – *halves* 91
 – hand in hand
 accompany 88
 same time 120
 – *hard* 704
 – on *ill* 735
 – in 294
 – in for
 resolution 604
 pursuit 622
 – into
 ingress 294
 inquire 461
 dissert 595
 – all lengths
 complete 52
 resolve 604
 exertion 686
 – mad 503
 – near 286
 – no further
 keep secret 528
 – for nothing
 sophistry 477
 unimportant 643
 – off *explode* 173
 depart 293
 die 360
 wither 659
 marry 903
 – on *time* 106
 continue 143
 advance 282
 – on for ever 112
 – one better 303
 – out
 cease 142
 egress 295
 extinct 385
 – out of one's
  head 506
 – over
 passage 302
 explore 461
 apostate 607
 faithless 940
 – to pieces 162
 – on record 551
 – round 311
 – shares 778
 – to sleep 683
 – through
 meet with 151
 pass 302
 explore 461
 perform 599
 conduct 692
 complete 729

endure 826
 – to *extend* 196
 travel 266
 direction 278
 remonstrance 695
 – up 305
 – to *war* 722
 – with
 assent 488
 concord 714
 – with the stream
 conform 82
 servile 886
 – from one's word
  773
goad 615
 hasten 684
goal *end* 67
 reach 292
 object 620
 reach the –
 complete 729
goat *substitute* 147
 jumper 309
 lecher 962
 he – *male* 373
 play the – 499
gob 269
gobang 840
gobbet
 small piece 32
 food 298
gobble *cry* 412
 gormandize 957
 eat 298
gobemouche 501, 547
go-between 758
goblet 191
goblin 980
go-cart 272
GOD 976
 house of – 1000
 kingdom of – 981
 sons of – 977
 –'s acre 363
 – bless me! 870
 – bless you
 farewell 293
 – forbid 766
 –'s grace 906
 – grant 990
 – knows 491
 –'s love 906
 for –'s sake 765
 –'s will 601
 – willing 470
god 979
 household –s 189
 tutelary – 664
goddess *love* 897
 good woman 948
 heathen 979
Godhead 976
godlike 987
godly 944
godsend *good* 618
 prosperity 734
Godspeed
 farewell 293
 hope 858
 courtesy 894
 benevolence 906
 approbation 931
goer *horse* 271
goes [*see* go]
 as one – 270

here – 676
Gog and Magog 192
goggle 441
 – *eyes* 443
goggles 445
going [*see* go]
 general 78
 rumor 532
 – to *happen* 152
 – on
 incomplete 53, 730
 current 151
 transacting 625
goiter 250
Golconda 803
gold *yellow* 436
 orange 439
 money 800
 write in letters
  of – 642
 worth its weight
  in – 648
gold certificate 800
golden [*see* gold]
 – *age*
 prosperity 734
 pleasure 827
 – *apple* 615
 – *calf*
 wealth 803
 idol 985
 idolatry 991
 – *dream*
 imagination 515
 hope 858
 – *mean*
 moderation 174
 mid-course 628
 – *opinions* 931
 – *opportunity* 134
 – *rule*
 precept 697
 – *season of life* 127
 – *wedding* 883
golf 840
Golgotha 363, 1000
Goliath 159, 192
goloshes 225
gondola 273
gondolier 269
gone [*see* go]
 past 122
 absent 187
 dead 360
 – *bad* 653
 – by
 antiquated 124
 – out of one's rec-
  ollection 506
gonfalon 550
gong 417
goniometer 244, 466
good
 complete 52
 palatable 394
 assent 488
 benefit 618
 beneficial 648
 right 922
 virtuous 944
 pious 987
 as – *as* 197
 be *so* – *as* 765
 do – 906

groove
  furrow 259
  habit 613
  in a – 16
  move in a – 82
  put in a – for 673
grope
  feel 379
  experiment 463
  try 675
  in the dark 442, 704
gross
  great 31
  whole 50
  number 98
  ugly 846
  vulgar 851
  vicious 945
  impure 961
  – credulity 486
  – receipts 810
grosshead 501
grossheaded 499
grossièreté 895
grot [see grotto]
grotesque
  odd 83
  distorted 243
  - style 579
  ridiculous 853
grotto
  alcove 191
  hollow 252
grouch 895, 901a
ground
  cause 153
  region 181
  base 211
  lay down 213
  support 215
  coating 223
  land 342
  plain 344
  evidence 467
  teach 537
  motive 615
  plea 617
  above – 359
  down to the – 52
  dress the – 371
  fall to the – 732
  get over the – 274
  go over the – 302
  level with the – 162
  maintain one's –
    persevere 604a
  play– 840
  prepare the – 673
  stand one's –
    defend 717
    resist 719
  – bait 784
  – cut from under one 732
  – floor
    chamber 191
    low 207
    base 211
  – on
    attribute 155
  – plan 554
  – of quarrel 713
  – sliding from under one 665
  – swell

agitation 315
  waves 348
grounded
  stranded 732
  well– 490
  – on *basis* 211
  evidence 467
groundless
  unsubstantial 4
  illogical 477
  erroneous 495
groundling 876
grounds
  dregs 653
groundwork
  precursor 64
  cause 153
  basis 211
  support 215
  preparation 673
group
  marshal 60
  cluster 72
  - captain 745
grouping 60
grouse 852, 901a
grout 45
grove
  street 189
  glade 252
  wood 367
grovel
  below 207
  move slowly 275
  cringe 886
  base 940
grow
  increase 35
  become 144
  expand 194
  – from
    effect 154
  – into 144
  – less 195
  – taller 206
  – together 46
  – up 194
  – upon one 613
grower 164
growl *cry* 412
  complain 839
  discourtesy 895
  anger 900
  threat 909
growler *cab* 272
  discontented 832
  sulky 901a
grown up 131
growth [see grow]
  development 161
  - in size 194
  tumor 250
  vegetation 367
groyne 706
grub
  small animal 193
  food 298
  – up
    eradicate 301
    discover 480a
Grub-street writer 593
grudge
  unwilling 603
  refuse 764
  stingy 819
  hate 898

anger 900
  bear a – 907
  owe a – 898
grudging 603
  – praise 932
gruel 298
gruesome 846
gruff
  harsh sound 410
  discourteous 895
grum
  harsh sound 410
  morose 901a
grumble
  cry 411
  complain 832, 839
grume 321, 354
grumous 321, 354
grumpy 901a
Grundy, Mrs. 852
grunt 412
  complain 839
guano 653
guarantee 768, 771
guard
  traveling 268
  safety 664
  defence 717
  soldier 726
  sentry 753
  advanced – 668
  mount –
    care 459
    safety 664
  off one's –
    inexpectant 508
  throw off one's –
    cunning 702
  on one's –
    careful 459
    cautious 864
  rear – 668
  – against
    prepare 673
    defence 717
  – ship 664, 726
guarda costa 753
guarded
  conditions 770
guardian
  safety 664
  defence 717
  keeper 753
  – angel
    helper 711
    benefactor 912
guardless 665
guard-room 752
gubernation 693
gubernatorial 737
gudgeon 547
guerdon 973
guernsey 225
guerre:
  nom de – 565
  – à outrance &c. 722
guerilla 726
  – warfare 720
guess 514
guesswork 514
guest 890
  paying – 188
guet:
  mot de – 550
  –à-pens 545

guffaw 838
guggle
  gush 348
  bubble 353
  resound 408
  cry 412
guide
  pattern 22
  courier 524
  teach 537
  teacher 540
  indicate 550
  direct 693
  director 694
  advise 695
guide-book 527
guided by, be – 82
guideless 665
guide-post 550
guiding star 693
guild 712, 966
guildhall 799
guile
  deceit 544, 545
  cunning 702
guileless 543, 703
guillotine 972, 975
guilt 947
guiltless 946
guilty:
  find – 971
  plead – 950
guindé 579
guinea 800
guipure 847
guisard 599
guise
  state 7
  dress 225
  appearance 448
  plea 617
  mode 627
  conduct 692
guiser 599
guitar 417
gulch 198
gules 434
gulf
  interval 198
  deep 208
  lake 343
gull 545, 547
gullible 486
gullet *throat* 260
  rivulet 348
gully *gorge* 198
  hollow 252
  opening 260
  conduit 350
gulosity 957
gulp *swallow* 296
  take food 298
  – down
    credulity 486
    submit 725
gum *fastening* 45
  fasten 46
  resin 356a
  – elastic 325
  – tree 367
gumbo 298
gummy 352
gumption 498
gun *report* 406
  weapon 727
  great – 626
  blow great –s 349

sure as a – 474
gunboat 726
gunfire 404
gunman 361
gunner 776
gunnery
  warfare 722
  cannon 727
gunlayer 284
gunpowder
  warfare 722
  ammunition 727
  not invent – 665
  sit on barrel of – 501
gunroom 193
gun-shot 197
gunwale 232
gurge 312, 348
gurgle
  flow 348
  bubble 353
  faint sound 405
  resonance 408
gurgoyle 350
gush
  flow out 295
  flood 348
  exaggeration 482
  talk 584
gushing
  emotional 821
  impressible 822
gusset 43
gust *wind* 349
  physical taste 390
  passion 825
  moral taste 850
gustation 390
gustful 394
gustless 391
gusto [see gust]
  physical pleasure 377
  emotion 821
gut *destroy* 162
  opening 260
  strait 343
  eviscerate 297
  sack 789
  steal 791
gutting 954a
guts *inside* 221
guttapercha 325
gutter *groove* 259
  conduit 350
  vulgarity 851
guttersnipe 876
guttle 957
guttural
  letter 561
  inarticulate 583
guy
  fastening 45, 752
  yellow 373
  disrespect 929
  grotesque 853
guzzle
  gluttony 957
  drunkenness 959
gybe [see jibe]
gymkhana 720, 840
gymnasium 191
  school 542
  arena 728, 840
gymnast 159
gymnastics

training 537
exercise 686
contention 720
sport 840
gymnosophist
  abstainer 953
  sectarian 984
gynander 83
gynarchy 727
gynecaeum 374
gynecology 662
gyniatrics 374
gynics 374
gyp 545, 746
gyre 311
gyrate 312
gyrfalcon 913
gyromancy 511
gyrostat 312
gysart 599
gyve 752

H

habeas corpus 963, 969
haberdasher 225
habergeon 717
habiliment 225
habilitation 698
habit
  essence 5
  coat 225
  custom 613
  want of – 614
  –s of business 682
  – of mind 820
habitant 188
habitat 189
habitation 189
habit-maker 225
habitual
  unvariable 16
  orderly 58
  ordinary 82
  customary 613
habituate 537, 613
habitude
  state 7
  habit 613
habitué 613
hacienda 189, 780
hack *cut* 44
  shorten 201
  horse 271
  writer 594
  worker 690
  literary – 593
hackle 44
hackney-coach 272
hackneyed
  known 490
  trite 496
  habitual 613
Hades 982
Hadji
  traveler 268
  priest 996
hae tibi erunt artes 627
haeret lateri lethalis arundo
  displeasure 828
  anger 900
haft 633

hag *age* 128
  ugly 846
  wretch 913
  witch 994
haggard
  insane 503
  tired 688
  wild 824
  ugly 846
haggis 298
haggle *cut* 44
  chaffer 794
Hagiographa 985
Hagiolatry 984
Hagiology 983, 985
haguebut 727
ha-ha *trench* 198, 719
haik 225
hail *welcome* 292
  ice 383
  call 586
  rejoicing 838
  honor to 873
  celebration 883
  courtesy 894
  salute 928
  approve 931
  –fellow well met
  friendship 888
  sociality 892
hailstone 383
hair *small* 32
  filament 205
  roughness 256
  to a – 494
  –'s breadth
  near 197
  narrow 203
  –breadth escape
  danger 665
  escape 671
  –s on the head
  multitude 102
  make one's –
  stand on end
  distressing 830
  fear 860
  wonder 870
hairless 226
hairy *rough* 256
halberd 727
halberdier 726
halcyon *calm* 174
  peace 721
  prosperous 734
  joyful 827, 829
hale 654
half 91
  – the battle
  important 642
  success 731
  – distance 68
  – a dozen *six* 98
  several 102
  see with –an eye
  intelligent 498
  intelligible 518
  manifest 525
  – a gale 349
  – and half
  equal 27
  mixed 41
  incomplete 53
  – a hundred 98
  – light 422
  – measures

  incomplete 53
  vacillating 605
  mid-course 628
  – moon 245
  – price 815
  – rations 640
  – scholar 493
  – seas over 959
  – sight 443
  – speed
  moderate 174
  slow 275
  – truth 546
half-blind 443
half-blood
  mixture 41
  unconformity 83
  imperfect 651
half-frozen 352
half-hearted
  irresolute 605
  insensible 823
  indifferent 866
half-learned 491
half-melted 352
halfpenny
  trifle 643
half-starved
  insufficient 640
  fasting 956
half-way
  small 32
  middle 68
  between 228
  go – *irresolute* 605
  mid-course 628
  meet –
  willing 602
  compromise 774
half-witted 499, 501
hall *chamber* 189
  receptacle 191
  mart 799
  music – 599
  – of audience 588
  – mark 550
hallelujah 990
halliard 45
halloo *cry* 411
  look here! 457
  call 586
  wonder 870
hallow
  celebrate 883
  respect 928
hallowed 976
hallucination
  error 495
  insanity 503
halo *light* 420
  glory 873
Halomancy 511
halser 45
halt *cease* 142
  weak 160
  rest 265
  go slowly 275
  lame 655
  fail 732
  at the – 265
halter *rope* 45
  restraint 752
  punishment 975
  wear a – 874
  with a – round one's neck 665
halting

style 579
  – place 292
halve [*see* half]
halves
  do by –
  neglect 460
  not complete 730
  not do by – 729
  go – 778
ham *house* 189
hamadryad 979
hammam 386, 652
hamlet 189
hammer
  repeat 104
  knock 276
  stammer 583
  under the –
  auction 796
  between the – and the anvil 665
  – at *think* 451
  work 686
  – out *form* 240
  prepare 673
  complete 729
hammock 215
hamper *basket* 191
  obstruct 706
hamstring 158, 659
hanaper 802
hand
  measure of length 200
  side 236
  transfer 270
  man 372
  organ of touch 379
  indicator 550
  writing 590
  medium 631
  agent 690
  grasp 781
  transfer 783
  at – *future* 121
  destined 152
  near 197
  useful 644
  bad – 590
  bird in – 781
  come to – 292, 785
  fold one's –s 681
  give one's – to
  marry 903
  good –
  writing 590
  skill 698
  proficiency 700
  helping – 707, 711
  hold in – 737
  hold out the – 894
  hold up the –
  vote 609
  in –
  incomplete 53
  business 625
  preparing 673
  not finished 730
  possessed 777
  money 800
  in the –s of
  authority 737
  subjection 749
  lay –s on
  discover 480a
  use 677

take 789
  rite 998
  much on one's –s 682
  on one's –s
  business 625
  redundant 641
  not finished 730
  for sale 796
  on the other – 468
  no – in 623
  poor – 701
  put into one's –s 784
  put one's – to 676
  ready to one's – 673
  shake –s 918
  stretch forth one's – 680
  take by the – 707
  take in –
  teach 537
  undertake 676
  time hanging on one's –s
  inaction 681
  leisure 685
  weary 841
  try one's – 675
  turn one's – 675
  turn one's – to 625
  under one's
  in writing 590
  promise 768
  compact 769
  – back 683
  – cart 272
  – of death 360
  – down
  record 551
  transfer 783
  have one's –s full 682
  – gallop 274
  – glass 445
  – and glove 709, 888
  – in hand
  joined 43
  accompanying 88
  same time 120
  concur 178
  co-operate 709
  party 712
  concord 714
  friend 888
  social 892
  – to hand
  touching 199
  transfer 270
  fight 720, 722
  – over head
  inattention 458
  neglect 460
  reckless 863
  have a – in
  cause 153
  act 680
  co-operate 709
  have one's – in
  skill 698
  keep one's – in 613
  live from – to mouth
  insufficient 640

unprepared 674
poor 804
-s off! *avoid* 623
leave alone 681
prohibition 761
– over
transfer 783
give 784
win –s down 731
with the –s in the pockets 681
hand-bag 191
hand-barrow 272
handbook
travel 266
information 527
book 593
handcuff 751, 752
handfast 903
handful
quantity 25
small 32
few 103
handicap
equalize 27
inferiority 34
encumber 706
race 720
handicraft 625, 680
handicraftsman 690
effect 154
doing 680
handkerchief
clothes 225
cleaner 652
handle
feel, touch 379
name 565
dissert 595
plea 617
instrument 633
use 677
manage 693
furnish a – 937
make a – of 677
– a case 693
– to one's name
name 564
honor 877
handmaid
instrumentality 631
auxiliary 711
servant 746
handpost 550
handsel
begin 66
security 771
gift 784
pay 809
handsome
liberal 816
beautiful 845
disinterested 942
– fortune 803
handspike 633
handstaff 727
handwriting
signature 550
autograph 590
– on the wall
warning 668
handy
near 197
useful 644, 646
ready 673
dexterous 698

hang
pendency 214
kill 361
curse 908
execute 972
– about 133, 197
– back 133, 623
– in the balance 133
– in doubt 485
– fire *late* 133
cease 142
unproductive 169
inert 172
slow 275
reluctance 603
inactive 683
not finish 730
fail 732
refuse 764
dullness 843
– on hand 641
– down the head 837
– over the head 152
– it! *regret* 833
contempt 930
– out a light 420
– upon the lips of 418
– on
accompany 88
– out
display 882
entertain 892
– over
destiny 152
height 206
project 250
– out a signal 550
– on the sleeve of
servant 746
servility 886
flattery 933
– in suspense 605
– by a thread 665
– together
joined 43
cohere 46
concur 178
co-operate 709
– upon
effect 154
dependency 749
hangar 191, 273
hang-dog look 901a
hanged if, I'll be – 489
hanger
weapon 727
suspender 45, 214
pothooks and –s 590
– on
accompaniment 88
servant 746
servile 886
hanging [*see* hang]
elevated 307
ornament 847
– look 846
hangman
evil-doer 913
bad man 949
executioner 97b

hank *tie* 45
hanker 865
hanky-panky 545
Hansard 551
hansom 272
hap 156
haphazard
chance 156, 621
hapless
unfortunate 735
(*miserable* 828)
(*hopeless* 859)
haply
possibly 470
(*by chance* 156)
happen 151
– as it may
chance 621
– what may
certain 474
reckless 863
happening 151
happiness
[*see* happy]
the greatest – of the greatest number 910
happy *fit* 23
opportune 134
style 578
glad 827
cheerful 836
– despatch 972
– go lucky 674
– hunting grounds 981
– returns of the day 896
– thought 842
– valley
imagination 515
delight 827
harangue 582
hara-kiri 972
harass
fatigue 688
vex 830
worry 907
harbinger
precursor 64
omen 512
informant 527
harbor
abode 189
haven 292
refuge 666
cherish 821
natural – 343
– a design 620
in – 664
– an idea 451
– revenge 919
harborless 665
hard *strong* 159
dense 323
physically insensible 376
sour 397
difficult 704
severe 739
morally insensible 823
grievous 830
impenitent 951
blow – 349
go –
difficult 704

failure 732
adversity 735
pain 828
hit – 276
look – at 441
not be too – upon 918
strike –
energy 171
impulse 276
try – 675
work – 686
– at it 682
– bargain 819
– of belief 487
– to believe 485
– by 197
– case 735
– cash 800
– earned 704
– and fast rule 80
– fought 704
– frost 383
– of hearing 419
– heart
malevolent 907
vicious 945
impenitent 951
– hit 732
– knocks 720
– life 735
– lines
adversity 735
severity 739
– liver 954a
– lot 735
– master 739
– measure 739
– names 932
– necessity 601
– nut to crack 704
– to please 868
– pressed
haste 684
difficulty 704
hindrance 706
– put to it 704
– set 704
– tack 298
– task 703
– time 704
– up 704, 804
– upon
attack 715
severe 739
censure 932
– winter 383
– words
obscure 571
rude 895
censure 932
– work 686
– at work 682
harden [*see* hard]
strengthen 159
accustom 613
– the heart
insensible 823
enmity 889
impenitence 951
hardened
impious 988
– front
insolent 885
hardening
habit 613
hard-featured 846

hard-fisted 819
hard-headed 498, 739
hardihood 861, 885
hardly
scarcely 32
deal – with 739
– any *few* 103
– anything
small 32
unimportant 643
– ever 137
hard-mouthed 606
hardness 3?3
– of heart ͵14a
hardship 735
hardy
strong 159
healthy 654
brave 861
hare 274
hold with the –
and run with the hounds
fickle 607
servile 886
hare-brained 458, 863
harem 961
hariolation 511
hark 418, 457
– back 283
harl 205
harlequin
changeable 149
nimble 274
motley 440
pantomimic 599
humorist 844
harlequinade 599
harlot 962
harlotry 961
harm
evil 619
badness 649
malevolence 907
harmattan 349
harmless
impotent 158
good 648
perfect 650
salubrious 656
safe 664
innocent 946
bear – 717
harmonica 417
harmonics 413
harmonist 413
harmonize 178, 416
harmonium 417
harmony
agreement 23
order 58
music 413
color 428
concord 714
peace 721
friendship 888
harness
fasten 43
fastening 45
accouterment 225
yoke 370
instrument 633
restraint 752
in –
prepared 673

high-brow 492
higher 33
highest 210
highfalutin 884
high-flavored 392
high-flier
 madman 504
 proud 878
high-flown
 imaginative 515
 style 577
 proud 878
 vain 880
 insolent 885
high-flying
 inattentive 458
 exaggerated 549
 ostentatious 822
highlands 206
high-low 225
high-mettled
 excitable 825
 brave 861
high-minded
 honorable 939
 magnanimous
  942
highness title 877
high-pitched 410
high-seasoned 392
high-souled 878
high-sounding
 loud 404
 words 577
 display 882
high-spirited 861,
 939
hight 564
high-toned 852
high-water
 completeness 52
 height 206
 crater 337
 – mark
 measure 466
highway 627
 –s and byways
  627
 – robbery 791
highwayman 792
high-wrought
 good 648
 prepared 673
 excited 824
hike 266
hilarity 836
hill height 206
 convexity 250
 ascent 305
 descent 306
 take to the –s 666
 –dwelling 206
hillock 206
hilt 633
hinc illæ lachrymæ
 155
hind back 235
 clown 876
 on one's – legs
 elevation 307
 anger 900
 – quarters 235
hinder 706
hindermost 67, 235
Hindooism 984
hindrance 706
hinge fasten 43

fastening 45
 cause 153
 depend upon 154
 rotate 312
hinny 271
hint reminder 505
 suppose 514
 inform 527
 take a – 498
 – a fault &c. 932
hinterland 235
hip 236
 have on the –
 confute 479
 success 731
 authority 737
 subjection 749
 – hip, hurrah! 838
hipped [see hypped]
hippocentaur 80
Hippocrates 662
hippocratic 360
hippodrome
 drama 599
 arena 728
 amusement 840
hippogriff 83
Hippolytus 960
hippophagy 298
hippopotamus 192
hirdie-girdie 218
hire
 commission 755
 borrowing 788
 price 812
 reward 973
 on – 763
hireling 746
hirsute 256
hispid 256
hiss sound 409
 animal cry 412
 disrespect 929
 contempt 930
 disapprobation
  932
hist! 585, 586
histology 329
historian 553
historic 594
historiette 594
historical:
 – painter 559
 – painting 556
historiographer 553
historiography 594
history past 122
 record 551
 narrative 594
History, Natural –
 357
histrionic 599
hit chance 156
 strike 276
 reach 292
 succeed 731
 censure 932
 (punish 972)
good – 626
 make a – 731
 – one's fancy 829
 – the mark 731
 – off 545
 – upon
 discover 480a
 plan 626
hitch

fasten 43
 knot 45
 stoppage 142
 hang 214
 jerk 315
 harness 370
 difficulty 704
 hindrance 706
 – up 293
hither 278, 292
 come – 286
hitherto 122
hive
 multitude 102
 location 184
 abode 189
 bees 870
 workshop 691
H.M.S. 726
hoar aged 128
 white 430
 – frost 383
hoard 636
hoarse
 husky 405
 harsh 410
 voiceless 581
 talk oneself – 584
hoary [see hoar]
hoax 545
hob support 215
 stove 386
 – and nob
 celebration 883
 courtesy 894
hobble
 limp 275
 awkward 699
 difficulty 704
 fail 732
 shackle 751
 – skirt 225
hobbledehoy 129
hobby
 crotchet 481
 pursuit 622
 desire 865
hobby-horse 272
hobgoblin
 fearful 860
 demon 980
hobo 268
hobnail 876
Hobson's choice
 necessity 601
 no choice 609a
 compulsion 744
hoc genus omne
 876
hock 771
hock shop 787
hockey 840
hockey rink 213
hocus 545
hocus-pocus
 interchange 148
 unmeaning 517
 cheat 545
 conjuration 992
 spell 993
hod
 receptacle 191
 support 215
 vehicle 272
hoddy-doddy 501
hodge-podge 41, 59
hoe 272, 371

hog animal 366
 sensualist 954a
 glutton 957
 (greedy as a – 865
 go the whole – 604
hog's back 206
hogmanay 998
hogshead 191
hog-wash 653
hoist 307
 – the black flag
  722
 – a flag 550
 – on one's own
 petard
 retaliation 718
 failure 732
hoity-toity! 815,
 870
hold cohere 46
 contain 54
 remain 141
 cease 142
 go on 143
 happen 151
 receptacle 191
 cellar 207
 base 211
 support 215
 halt 265
 believe 484
 be passive 681
 defend 717
 power 737
 restrain 751
 prison 752
 prohibit 761
 possess 777
 retain 781
 enough! 869
 have a firm – 781
 have a – upon 175
 gain a – upon 737
 get – of 789
 quit one's – 782
 take – 175
 – aloof
 stay away 187
 distrust 487
 avoid 623
 – an argument
  476
 – authority 737
 – back avoid 623
 store 636
 hinder 706
 restrain 751
 retain 781
 miserly 819
 – one's breath
 wonder 870
 – converse 588
 – a council 695
 – fast 751, 781
 – forth teach 537
 speak 582
 – good 478, 494
 – one's ground
  141
 – in hand 737
 – one's hand
 cease 142
 relinquish 624
 – hard 265
 – up one's head
  861
 – a lease 771

 – a meeting 72
 – off 623
 – office 693
 – on
 continue 141, 143
 persevere 604a
 – out [see below]
 – one's own
 preserve 670
 defend 717
 resist 719
 – oneself in readi-
 ness 673
 – in remembrance
  505
 – both one's sides
  838
 – a situation 625
 – in solution 335
 – to 602
 – together 43, 709
 – one's tongue
  403, 585
 – up [see below]
 – oneself up 307
hold out
 endure 106
 affirm 535
 persevere 604a
 resist 719
 offer 763
 brave 861
 – expectation
 predict 511
 promise 768
 – temptation 865
hold up
 continue 143
 support 215
 not rain 340
 aid 707
 rob 791
 display 882
 extol 931
 – one's hand
 sign 550
 threat 609
 – to execration
 cures 908
 censure 932
 – the mirror 525
 – to scorn 930
 – to shame 874
 – to view 525
holder 779
holdfast 45
holding
 tenancy 777
 property 780
hole place 182
 hovel 189
 receptacle 191
 opening 260
 ambush 530
 – in one's coat 651
 – and corner
 place 182
 peer into – 461
 hiding 528, 530
 – to creep out of
 plea 617
 escape 671
 facility 705
holiday leisure 685
 repose 687
 amusement 840
 – task easy 705

hunt *inquiry* 461
  pursuit 622
  – after 622
  – in couples 709
  – down 907
  – out *inquiry* 461
  discover 480a
  – slipper 840
hunter *horse* 271
  killer 361
  pursuer 622
place &c. – 767
hunting 361, 622
hunting-ground 840
  happy – 981
hurdle 272
hurdy-gurdy 417
hurl 284
  – against 716
  – defiance 715
hurler avec les
  loups 82, 714
Hurlothrumbo 860
hurly-burly 315
hurrah 411, 836,
  838
hurricane 349, 667
  – deck 210
hurry *haste* 684
  excite 825
  – forward 684
  – off with 789
  – on 615
  – of spirits 821
  – up 684
hurst 367
hurt
  physical pain 378
  evil 619
  maltreat 649
  injure 659
  more frightened
    than – 860
  – the feelings
    pain 830
    anger 900
hurtful 649
hurtle 276
hurtless 648
husband
  store 636
  director 694
  spouse 903
husbandman 371
husbandry
  agriculture 371
  conduct 692
  economy 817
hush *moderate* 174
  stop 265
  silence 403
  taciturn 585
  – up
  conceal 528
  pacify 723
hush-money 30,
  973
husk 223, 226
husky *strong* 159
  dry 340
  faint sound 405
  hoarse 581
hussar 726
hussy 962
hustings
  school 542
  arena 728

tribunal 966
hustle
  perturb 61
  push 276
  agitate 315
  activity 682
  hinder 706
hustler 682, 962
hut 189
hutch 189
huzza 838
hyacinth
  jewel 847
hyaline 425
hybrid
  mixture 41
  exception 83
hydra
  monster 83, 366
  productive 168
  – headed 163
hydrant 348, 385
hydraulics 333, 348
hydro-aeroplane
  273
hydrodynamics
  333, 348
hydrography 341
hydrology 333
hydrolysis 49
hydromancy 511
hydromel 396
hydropathy 662
hydrophobia 867
hydroplane 273
hydrostatics 333
hyemal 383
hyena 913
hyetology 348
hygeian 656
hygiantics 670
hygienic 656, 670
hygre 348
hygrometry 339
hyle 316
hylism 316
hylotheism 984,
  989
Hymen 903
hymeneal 903
hymn *song* 415
  worship 990
  – of hate 898
hymn-book 998
hyoscine 663
hypallage 218
hyperbation 218
hyperbola 245
hyperbole 549
hyperborean
  far 196
  cold 383
hypercriticism
  misjudgment 481
  discontent 832
  fastidiousness 868
  censure 932
hyperdulia 990
Hyperion 423, 845
  – to a satyr 14
hyperorthodoxy 984
hyperphysical 976
hypertrophy 194
hyphen 45
hypnology 683
hypnotic
  remedy 662

sleep 683
hypnotize 376
hypocaust 386
hypochondriac
  madman 504
  low spirits 837
hypochondriasis
  837
hypocrisy
  falsehood 544
  religious – 988
hypocrite 548, 855
  play the – 544
hypostasis 1, 3
Hypostatic union *f*
  976
hypothecate 771
hypothenuse 217
hypothesis 514
hypothesize 514
hypothetical 475,
  514
hypped *insane* 503
  dejected 837
hypsometer 206
Hyrcynian wood
  533
hysteria
  insanity 503
hysteric *violent* 173
hysterical
  spasmodic 608
  emotional 821
  excitable 825
hysterics 173
  in – *excited* 824
  frightened 860
hysteron proteron
  218

I

I 79
iambic 597
ibidem 13
Icarus
  navigator 269
  rash 863
  fate of – 306
ice *cold* 383
  refrigerate 385
iceberg 383
ice-bound 383
  restraint 751
ice-chest 385
ice-house 387
ice-yacht 273
Ichabod 874
ichnography 554
ichor 333
ichthyology 368
ichthyomancy 511
ichthyophagous 298
icicle 383
icon 554
iconoclasm 983a,
  984
iconoclast 165, 913
iconography 554
icosahedron 244
id est 522
idea
  small quantity 32
  notion 453
  give an – of 537

ideal *unreal* 2
  completeness 52
  erroneous 495
  imaginary 515
  perfect 650
ideality 450, 515
idée fixe 481
identification
  identity 13
  comparison 464
  discovery 480a
identity 13
  – book 206
Ideology 450
Ides of March 601
idiocrasy
  essence 5
  tendency 176
idiocy 499
idiom 560, 566
idiomatic 79
idiosyncrasy
  essence 5
  speciality 79
  unconformity 83
  tendency 176
  temperament 820
idiot 501
  tale told by an –
    517
idiotic
  foolish 499
idiotism
  folly 499
  phrase 566
idle *foolish* 499
  trivial 643
  slothful 683
  lie – *inaction* 681
  – conceit 842
  – hours 681
  be an – man
  leisure 685
  – talk 588
  – time away 683
idler 683
Ido 560
idol *desire* 865
  favorite 899
  fetich 991
  – of the people
    899
idolater 984
idolatry 897, **991**
idolize *love* 897
  impiety 988
idoneous 23
idyl 597
if *circumstance* 8
  qualification 469
  supposition 514
  – you please 765
  – possible 470
igloo 189
igneous 382
ignis fatuus
  luminary 423
  phantom 443
  ignite 384
ignoble 876
ignominy 874, 940
ignoramus **493**
ignorance **491**
  keep in – 528
  plead – 937
ignoratio elenchi
  477

ignore
  neglect 460
  incredulity 487
  not known 491
  repudiate 756,
    773
ignotum per
  ignotius 477
ilk 13
ill *evil* 619
  badness 649
  sick 655
  go on – *fail* 732
  adversity 735
  look – 846
  take –
  discontent 832
  anger 900
  – betide 908
  – blood *hate* 898
  malevolence 907
  – at ease *pain* 828
  dejection 837
  house of – *fame*
    961
  –s that flesh is
    heir to *evil* 619
  disease 655
  – humor
  anger 900
  sullenness 901a
  – luck 735
  as – luck would
    have it 135
  – off
  insufficient 640
  adversity 735
  poor 804
  do an – office to
    907
  bird of – *omen*
    668
  – repute 874
  – turn *evil* 619
  spiteful 907
  – usage 907
  – will 907
  wind bad 649
  hindrance 706
  adversity 735
ill-adapted 24
ill-advised
  foolish 499
  inexpedient 647
  unskilful 699
ill-affected 901a
illapse
  conversion 144
  ingress 294
illaqueate 545
ill-assorted 24
illation 480
illaudable 947
ill-balanced 28
ill-bred 851, 895
ill-conditioned
  bad 649
  difficult 704
  discourteous 895
  malevolent 907
  vicious 945
ill-conducted 699
ill-contrived
  inexpedient 647
  bad 649
  unskilful 699
  malevolent 907

insert 300
mean 516
imply 526
be of consequence
    642
importance 642
greatness 30
attach – to 642
attach too much
    – to 482
of no – 643
importune 765, 830
impose *order* 741
awe 928
– *upon*
credulity 486
deceive 545
be unjust 923
imposing
important 642
exciting 824
glorious 873
imposition [*see*
    impose]
undue 925
– of hands 998
**impossibile, credo
    quia** – 486
**impossibilities,
    seek after** – 645
impossibility 471
impossible 471
refusal 764
– *quantity*
algebra 84
impost 812
imposthume 655
impostor 548, 925
imposture 545
impotence 158
**impotent conclu-
    sion** 732
impound 791
impoverish
weaken 160
waste 638
despoil 789
render poor 804
impracticable
impossible 471
misjudging 481
obstinate 606
difficult 704
imprecation
prayer 765
curse 908
impregnable 159,
    664
impregnate *mix* 41
combine 48
fecundate 161,
    168
insert 300
teach 537
– *with* 641
impresario 599
imprescriptible 924
impress *cause*
sensation 375
mark 550
compel 791
excite feeling 824
– *upon the mind*
memory 505
teach 537
impressed with
belief 484

feeling 821
impressible
motive 615
sensibility 822
impression
sensation 375
idea 453
belief 484
printing 531
mark 550
engraving 558
print 591
emotion 821
make an –
act 171
thought 451
impressionable
    375, 822
impressive
language 574
important 642
feeling 821, 824
imprimis 66
imprimit 558
imprint
publisher 531
indication 550
– in the memory
    505
imprison
circumscribe 229
restrain 751
punish 972
improbability 473
improbate 932
improbity 940
impromptu 612
– fait à loisir 673
improper
incongruous 24
foolish 499
solecism 568
inexpedient 647
wrong 923
unmeet 925
vicious 945
– *time* 135
impropriate 777,
    789
impropriator 779
improve 658
– the occasion 134
– the shining
    hour 682
– upon 658
improvement 658
improvident
careless 460
not preparing 674
prodigal 818
rash 863
improvisation
music 415
improvisatore
speech 582
poetry 597
impulse 612
improvise
imagination 515
impulse 612
unprepared 674
improviste, à l'–
    508, 612
improvisatrice
    612
imprudent 460, 863
impudent 885, 895

impudicity 961
impugn *deny* 536
attack 716
blame 932
impugnation 708
impuissance 158
impulse *push* **276**
sudden thought
    612
motive 615
blind – 601
creature of – 612
give an – *to*
propel 284
aid 707
impulsive [*see*
    impulse]
intuitive 477
excitable 825
rash 863
impunity *escape* 671
acquittal 970
with – *safely* 664
impurity 653, **961**
imputation
ascribe 155
slur 874
accuse 938
in 221
go – 294
– as much as
relation 9
degree 26
– the circum-
    stances 8
– doors 221
– durancevile 751
– for
– force 1
undertake 676
promise 768
– re 9
– and out 314
–s and outs 182
in: – articulo 111
– extenso *whole* 50
diffuse 573
– jail 751
– limine 66
– loco 23
– medias res 68
– prison 751
– propriâ personâ
    79
– toto 52
– transitu
transient 111
transfer 270
– statu pupillari
    127
– statu quo 141
– vogue 1
inability 158, 699
inabstinent 954
inaccessible 196,
    471
inaccurate 495, 568
inaction 172, **683**
inactivity **683**, 172
inadequate
powerless 158
insufficient 640
useless 645
imperfect 651
inadmissible
incongruous 24
excluded 55

extraneous 57
inexpedient 647
inadvertence 458
inadvisable 647
inaffable 895
inalienable
retention 781
right 924
inamorata 897
inane *void* 4
unmeaning 517
unthinking 452
insufficient 640
trivial 643
useless 645
inanimate 360
– matter 358
inanition 158
inanity [*see* inane]
inappetency 823,
    866
inapplicable 10, 24
inapposite 10, 24
inappreciable 33,
    193
unimportant 643
inapprehensible
stolid 499
unintelligible 519
inappropriate 24,
    647
inapt
incongruous 24
impotent 158
useless 645
inexpedient 647
unskilful 699
inarticulate 581,
    583
inartificial 703
inartistic 846
inasmuch *whereas* 9
however 26
because 476
inattention 458
inaudible
silence 403
faint sound 405
deaf 419
voiceless 581
inaugural
precursor 64
inaugurate
begin 66
cause 153
install 755
celebrate 883
inauspicious
untimely 135
untoward 649
hopeless 859
inbeing 5
inborn, inbred
intrinsic 5
affections 820
– *proclivity* 601
inca 745
incage 751
incalculable 31, 105
incalescence 382
incandescence 382
incandescent 423
incantation
invocation 765
sorcery 992
spell 993
incantatory 992

incapable 158
incapacious 203
incapacitate 158
incapacity
impotence 158
ignorance 491
stupidity 499
incarcerate 751
incarnadine 434
incarnate
intrinsic 5
bodily 316
fleshly 364
vicious 945
devil –
bad man 949
Satan 978
Incarnation 976
incase 223, 229
incautious 863
incendiary
destroy 162
burn 384
influence 615
malevolent 907
evil-doer 913
bad man 949
incense *fuel* 388
fragrant 400
hate 898
anger 900
flatter 933
worship 990
rite 998
incension
burning 384
incentive 615
inception 66
inceptive 153
inceptor 541
incertitude 475
incessant
repeated 104
ceaseless 112
frequent 136
incest 961
inch *small* 32
length 200
by –es 275
to an – 494
not yield an – 606
give an – *and take*
    an ell 789
– *by inch*
by degrees 26
in parts 51
slowly 275
not see an – *be-*
    yond one's nose
    699
inchoation 66, 673
incide 44
incidence 278
incident 151
incidental
extrinsic 6
circumstance 8
irrelative 10
occurring 151
casual 156
liable 177
chance 621
trivial 643
– *music* 415
incinerate 384
incipience 66
incircumspect 460

incision 44, 259
incisive energy 171
  vigor 574
  feeling 821
incisor 253
incite
  exasperate 173
  urge 615
incivility 895
incivism 911
inclasp 229
inclement
  violent 173
  cold 383
  severe 739
  pitiless 914a
inclination
  [see incline]
  will 600
  affection 820
  desire 865
  love 897
incline tendency 176
  slope 217
  direction 278
  willing 602
  induce 615
  – an ear to 457
  – the head 308
inclined
  disposed 620
  – plane 633
inclose
  surround 227
inclosure 232
include
  composition 54
  – in a class 76
inclusion 76
inclusive
  additive 37
  component 56
  class 76
incogitancy 452
incognita, terra –
  491
incognito 528
incognizable 519
incoherence
  physical 47
  mental 503
incombustible 385
income means 632
  profit 775
  property 780
  wealth 803
  receipt 810
  – tax 812
incoming
  ingress 294
  receipt 810
incommensurable
  10
  – quantity 84, 85
incommode 706
  hinder 706
incommunicable
  unmeaning 517
  unintelligible 519
  retention 781
incommunicado
  528
incommutable 150
incomparable 33
incompassionate
  914a
incompatible 24

incompatibility 15
incompetence
  inability 158
  incapacity 499
  unskilful 699
  dereliction 927
incompleteness 53
  non-completion
  730
incompliance 764
incomprehensible
  infinite 105
  unintelligible 519
incomprehension
  491
incompressible 321
inconcealable 525
inconceivable
  unthinkable 452
  impossible 471
  improbable 473
  incredible 485
  unintelligible 519
  wonder 870
inconceptible 519
inconcinnity
  disagreement 24
  ugliness 846
inconclusive 477
inconcoction 674
incondite 851
incongruous
  differing 15
  disagreeing 24
  illogical 477
  ungrammatical
  568
  discordant 713
inconnection 10, 44
inconsequence
  irrelation 10
inconsequential 477
inconsiderable 32,
  643
inconsiderate
  thoughtless 452
  inattentive 458
  neglectful 460
  foolish 699
inconsistent
  contrary 14
  disagreeing 24
  illogical 477
  absurd 497
  foolish 499
  capricious 608
  discord 713
inconsolable 837
inconsonant
  disagreeing 24
  fitful 149
inconspicuous 447
inconstant 149
incontestable 159,
  474, 525
incontiguous 196
incontinent 961
incontinently 132
incontrollable 173
incontrovertible
  150, 474
inconvenience 647
  put to – 706
inconversable 585,
  893
inconvertible 143
inconvincible 487

incorporate 48
  combine 48
  include 76
  materialize 316
incorporation 761
incorporeal 317
  – hereditaments
  780
incorrect
  illogical 477
  erroneous 495
  solecism 568
  vicious 945
incorrigible
  obstinate 606
  hopeless 859
  vicious 945
  impenitent 951
incorruption
  probity 939
  innocence 946
incrassate
  increase 194
  density 321
  – fluids 352
increase
  – in degree 35
  – in number 102
  – in size 194
incredible
  great 31
  impossible 471
  improbable 473
  doubtful 485
  wonderful 870
incredulity 487, 989
increment
  increase 35
  addition 37
  adjunct 39
  expansion 194
increpation 932
incriminate 938
incrust 223, 224
incubate 370
incubation 673
incubus
  hindrance 706
  pain 828
  demon 980
inculcate 6, 537
inculpable 946
inculpate 938
inculture 674
incumbency
  business 625
  churchdom 995
incumbent
  inhabitant 188
  high 206
  weight 319
  duty 926
  clergyman 996
incumber 706
incumbered 806
incunabula 66, 127
incur 177
  – blame 932
  – danger 665
  – a debt 806
  – disgrace 874
  – a loss 776
  – the risk 621
incurable
  ingrained 5
  disease 655
  hopeless 859

incuriam, per –
  458, 460
incuriosity 456
incursion 294, 716
incurvation 245
indagation 461
indebted
  owing 806
  gratitude 916
  duty 926
indecent 961
indeciduous 150
indecipherable 519
indecision 475, 605
indecisive 475
indeclinable 150
indecorous
  vulgar 851
  vicious 945
  impure 961
indeed existing 1
  very 31
  assent 488
  truly 494
  assertion 535
  wonder 870
indefatigable
  persevering 604a
  active 682
indefeasible
  stable 150, 474
  due 924
indefectible 650
indefensible
  powerless 158
  submission 725
  accusable 938
  wrong 945
indeficient 650
indefinite
  great 31
  unspecified 78
  infinite 105
  misty 447
  uncertain 475
  inexact 495
  vague 519
indeliberate 612
indelible stable 150
  memory 505
  mark 550
  feeling 821
indelicate 961
indemnity
  compensation 30
  restitution 790
  forgiveness 918
  atonement 952
  reward 973
  deed of – 771
indenizen 184
indent scollop 248
  list 86
indentation 252,
  257
indenture 769, 771
independence
  irrelation 10
  freedom 748
  wealth 803
Independent 984
indescribable 31,
  870
indesinent 112
indestructible 150
indeterminate
  indefinite 78

chance 156
  uncertain 475
  irresolute 605
indevotion 989
index
  arrangement 60
  exponent 84
  list 86
  sign 550
  words 62
index expurga-
  torius 761, 932
indexterity 699
Indian:
  – file 69
  – rubber 325
  – summer 126
  – weed 392
indicate
  specify 79
  direct attention to
  457
  mean 516
  mark 550
indication 550
indicative
  evidence 467
indict accuse 938
  arraign 969
indiction 108, 531
indifference
  incuriosity 456
  unwillingness 603
  no choice 609a
  insensibility 823
  unconcern 866
  irreligion 989
  matter of – 643
indifferent
  [see indifference]
  unimportant 643
  bad 649
indigence
  insufficiency 640
  poverty 804
indigenous 5, 186
indigested 674
indigestible 657
indigestion 657
indigitate 457
indign 940
indignation 900
  – meeting 832
indignity 900, 929
indigo 438
indiligence 683
indirect
  oblique 217
  devious 279
  latent 526
  circuitous 629
indiscernible 447
indiscerptible
  whole 50
  unity 87
  dense 321
indiscoverable 526
indiscreet 499, 863,
  945
indiscretion
  guilt 947
indiscriminate
  mixed 41
  unarranged 59
  multiform 81
  casual 621
indiscrimination

465a
indispensable 630
indispose
  dissuade 616
indisposed
  unwilling 603
  sick 655
indisputable 474
indissoluble,
  indissolvable
  joined 43
  whole 50
  stable 150
  dense 321
indistinct 447
indistinction 465a
indistinguishable
  identical 13
  invisible 447
indisturbance 265,
  826
indite 590
individual
  whole 50
  special 79
  unity 87
  person 372
indivisible *whole* 50
  dense 321
indocility 158, 606
indoctrinate 537
indolence 683, 927
indomitable
  strong 159
  determined 604
  persevering 604a
  resisting 719
  courage 861
indoor 221
indorse 769, 771
indorsement 550,
  551
indraught 343, 348
indubitable 474
induce *cause* 153
  power 157
  produce 161
  motive 615
induct 883
induction
  inquiry 461
  reasoning 476
  drama 599
  appointment 755
  - of a priest 995
indulge *lenity* 740
  allow 760
  please 829
  intemperance 954
  gluttony 959
  - one's fancy 609
  - in 827
  - oneself 943
  - in reverie
  inattention 458
  fancy 515
  - with give 784
indulgence
  [*see* indulge]
  absolution 918
indulgent *kind* 906
induration
  hardening 323
  impenitence 951
Indus to the pole,
  from – 180
industry 625, 682

hive of – 691
indweller 188
indwelling 5
inebriety 959
inedible 395
ineffable *great* 31
  inexpressible 521
  wonderful 870
ineffaceable 820
ineffectual
  incapable 158
  useless 645
  failing 732
  - attempt 732
  pale its – fire 422
inefficacious
  incapable 158
  useless 645
  failing 732
inefficient 158
inelastic *soft* 324
  - fluid 333
inelasticity **326**
inelegance **579**, 846
ineluctable 474
inept 24, 158, 645
inequality **28**
inequitable 923
ineradicable
  intrinsic 5
  stable 150
inerrable 946
inertia 172
inertness
  physical **172**
  inactive 683
  moral 823
inestimable 648
inevitable 474, 601
inexact
  erroneous 495
  feeble 575
inexcitability **826**
inexcusable
  accusable 938
  vicious 45
inexecution 730
inexhaustible 105,
  639
inexistence **2**
inexorable
  unavoidable 601
  resolved 604
  stern 739
  compelling 744
  pitiless 914a
  revengeful 919
inexpectation **508**
inexpedience **647**
inexpensive 815
inexperience 491,
  699
inexpert 699
inexpiable 945
inexplicable 519
inexpressible
  great 31
  unmeaning 517
  unintelligible 519
  wonderful 870
inexpressibles 225
inexpression
  latency 526
inexpensive 517
inexpugnable 664
inextension **180a**
  littleness 193

immateriality 317
inextinguishable
  stable 150
  strong 159
  excitable 825
  - desire 865
inextricable
  coherent 46
  disorder 59
  impossible 471
infallibility 474
  assumption of –
  885
infamy *shame* 874
  dishonor 940
  vice 945
infancy 66, 127
infandum renovare
  dolorem 505,
  833
infant **129**
  fool 501
  - prodigy 872
Infanta 745
infanticide 361, 991
infantine 129
  foolish 499
infantry 726
infarction 261
infatuation
  misjudgment 481
  credulity 486
  folly 499
  insanity 503
  obstinacy 606
  passion 825
  love 897
infeasible 471
infect *mix with* 41
  contaminate 659
  excite 824
infectă, re –
  shortcoming 304
  non-completion
  730
  failure 732
infection
  transference 270
  disease 655
infectious 270, 657
infecund 169
infelicity
  inexpertness 699
  misery 828
infelicitous 24
infer 472
inference 476, 480
  by – 467
inferential
  demonstrative 478
  latent 526
inferiority
  in degree **34**
  in size 195
  imperfection 651
  personal – 34
infernal *bad* 649
  malevolent 907
  wicked 945
  satanic 978
  - machine 727
  - regions 982
infertility 169
infest 830
infestivity 837, 843
infibulation 43
infidel 487, 989

infidelity
  dishonor 940
  irreligion 989
infiltrate *mix* 41
  intervene 228
  interpenetrate 294
  moisten 337, 339
  teach 537
infiltration
  passage 302
Infinite, the – 976
infinite 105
  - goodness 976
infinitely *great* 31
infinitesimal
  small 32
  little 193
  - calculus 85
infinity **105**
infirm *weak* 160
  disease 655
  vicious 945
  - of purpose 605
infirmary 662
infirmity 241
  [*see* infirm]
infix 537
inflame
  render violent 173
  burn 384
  excite 824
  anger 900
inflamed 382
inflammable 384,
  388
inflammation
  heating 384
  disease 655
inflate *increase* 35
  expand 194
  blow 349
inflated
  overestimation
  482
  style 573, 577
  ridiculous 853
  vain 880
inflation
  [*see* inflate]
  rarefaction 322
  currency 800
inflect 245
inflexible *hard* 323
  resolved 604
  obstinate 606
  stern 739
  inexorable 914a
inflexion
  change 140
  curvature 245
  grammar 567
inflict *act upon* 680
  severity 739
  - evil 649
  - pain
  bodily pain 378
  mental pain 830
  - punishment 972
infliction
  adversity 735
  mental pain 828,
  830
  punishment 972
influence 153
  change 140
  physical – 175
  inducement 615

instrumentality
  631
  authority 737
  absence of – 175a
  sphere of – 780
  make one's – felt
  631
influx 294
infold 232
inform 527
  - against
  accuse 938
  go to law 969
informal 83, 964
informality 773
informant 527
information
  knowledge 490
  communication
  527
  learning 539
  lawsuit 969
  pick up – 539
informer 532
informity 241
infra dignitatem
  874, 940
infraction
  trespass 303
  disobedience 742
  non-observance
  773
  exemption 927
  - of usage &c.
  unconformity 83
  desuetude 614
infrangible
  combined 46
  dense 321
infra-red rays 420
infrequency **137**
infrigidation 385
infringe
  transgress 303
  disobey 742
  not observe 773
  undueness 925
  dereliction 927
  - a law &c. 83
infundibular 252,
  269
infuriate
  violent 173
  excite 824
  anger 900
infuscate 431
infuse *mix* 41
  insert 300
  teach 537
  - courage 861
  - life into 824
  - new blood 658
infusible 321
infusion [*see* infuse]
  liquefaction 335
infusoria 193
ingannation 545
ingathering 72
ingemination 90
ingenerate 5
ingenious 515, 698
ingenite 5
ingenium, per-
  fervidum – 682
ingénu *artless* 703
ingénue *actress* 599
ingenuity 698

inebriation 959
intra, ab – 221
intractable
  obstinate 606
  difficult 704
  sullen 901a
intramural 221
intransient 110
intransigeance 604
intransitive 110
intransmutable
  110, 150
intrap 545
intraregarding 221
intrench 717
– on 303
intrepid 861
intricate
  confused 59
  convoluted 248
  difficult 704
intrigant
  meddlesome 682
  cunning 702
  libertine 962
intrigue *fascinate*
  615, 897
  plot 626
  activity 682
  cunning 702
  excite 824
  interest 829
  licentiousness 961
intrinsic 5
– evidence 467
– habit 613
– truth 494
intrinsicality 5
introception 296
introduce *lead* 62
  interpose 228
  precede 280
  insert 300
– new blood 140
– new conditions
  469
– to 888
introduction
  [see introduce]
  preface 64
  reception 296
  drama 599
  friendship 888
  courtesy 894
introductory
  precursor 64
  beginning 66
  priority 116
introgression 294
introit 998
intromission 228
intromit
  discontinue 142
  receive 296
introspection 441,
  457
introspective 451
introvert 218
intrude
  interfere 24
  inopportune 135
  intervene 228
  enter 294
  encroach 303
intruder 57
intrusiveness 682
intrust 755, 787

intuition *mind* 450
  unreasoning 477
  knowledge 490
intumescence 194,
  250
intwine 43, 243
inunction 223
inundate
  effusion 337
  flow 348
  redundance 641
inunderstanding
  452
inurbanity 895
inure 613, 673
inured
  insensible 823
insuitation 614
inutility 645
invade *ingress* 294
  encroach 303
  attack 716
invalid
  powerless 158
  illogical 477
  diseased 655
  undue 925
invalidate
  disable 158
  weaken 160
  confute 479
invaluable 648
invariable
  intrinsic 5
  uniform 16
  conformable 82
  stable 150
invasion
  ingress 294
  attack 716
invective 932
inveigh 932
inveigle 545, 615
invent
  discover 480a
  imagine 515
  lie 544
  devise 626
invented
  untrue 546
invention 480a
inventive
  skilful 698
inventor 164
inventory 86
inverse 14, 218
inversion
  derangement 61
  change 140
  of position 218
  contraposition
  237
  reversion 145
  language 577
invertebrate 158
invest
  empower 157
  clothe 225
  besiege 227, 716
  commission 755
  give 784
  lend 787
  expend 809
– in *locate* 184
  purchase 795
– money 817
– with *ascribe* 155

investigate 461
investment 225
– trust 712
make –s 673
inveterate *old* 124
  established 150
  inborn 820
– belief 484
– habit 613
invidious
  painful 830
  hatred 898
  spite 907
  envy 921
invigorate
  strengthen 159
invigorating
  healthy 656
invincible 159
inviolable
  secret 528
  right 924
  honor 939
inviolate
  permanent 141
  secret 528
  honorable 939
invious *closed* 261
  pathless 704
invisibility 447
invisible *small* 193
  not to be seen 447
  concealed 526
– ink 528
become – 4
invitâ Minervâ 603,
  704
invite *induce* 615
  offer 763
  ask 765
– the attention
  457
inviting
  [see invite]
  pleasing 829
invoice 86
invoke *address* 586
  implore 765
  pray 990
– curses 908
– saints 998
involucrum 223
involuntary
  necessary 601
  unwilling 603
– servitude 749
involution [see
  involve]
  algebra 85
involve *include* 54
  derange 61
  wrap 225
  evince 467
  mean 516
  latency 526
involved
  disorder 59
  convoluted 248
  obscure style 571
  in debt 806
involvement 704
invulnerable 664
inward *intrinsic* 5
  inside 221
– bound 294
– monitor 926
inweave 219

inwrap 225
inwrought 5
io triumphe! 838,
  883
Ionic 597
iota 32
I. O. U. 771, 800
ipse dixit 474, 535
ipsissima verba 494
ipso facto 1
irae
  amantium — 918
  tantaene animis
  coelestibus – 900
irascibility 901
irate 900
ire 900
iridescent 440
Iris 268, 534
iris 440, 441
Irish Bull 353
Irishism 497
irk 688, 830
irksome
  tiresome 688
  difficult 704
  painful 830
  weary 841
iron *strength* 159
  smooth 255
  hard 323
  resolution 604
rule with a rod of
  – 739
– age *adversity* 735
  pain 828
– cross 733
– gray 432
– grip 159
– gripe 781
– heel 739
– necessity 601
– rule 739
– entering into the
  soul 828, 830
– sway 739
– will 604
iron-bound coast
  land 342
  danger 667
iron-clad
  covering 223
  defence 717
  man of war 726
iron-handed 739
iron-hearted 861
iron-mold 434
irons 752
  fire – 386
  put in – 751
– in the fire
  business 625
  redundance 641
  active 682
  unskilful 699
irony
  figure of speech
  521
  untruth 546
  ridicule 856
irradiate 420
irrational
  number 84
  illogical 477
  silly 499
irreclaimable
  hopeless 859

vicious 945
impenitent 951
irreconcilable
  unrelated 10
  discordant 24
  unwilling 603
  opponent 710
  enmity 889
irrecoverable
  past 122
  hopeless 859
irredeemable 859
irredentist 776
irreducible
  discordant 24
  out of order 59
  unchangeable 150
irrefragable 478
irrefutable 474, 478
irregular
  diverse 16a
  out of order 59
  multiform 81
  against rule 83
– *in recurrence*
  139
  distorted 243
  combatant 726
irregularity 139
irrelation 10
irrelevant
  unrelated 10
  unaccordant 24
  sophistical 477
  unimportant 643
irreligion 989
irremediable
  bad 649
  hopeless 859
  (*spoiled* 659)
irremissible 945
irremovable 150
irreparable
  hopeless 859
irrepentance 951
irreprehensible 946
irrepressible
  violent 173
  free 748
  excitable 825
irreproachable 946
irreprovable 946
irresistible
  strong 159
  demonstration
  478
  necessary 601
irresoluble 150
irresolution 605
irresolvable 87
irresolvedly 605
irrespective 10
irresponsible
  irresolute 605
  exempt 927a
  arbitrary 964
irretrievable
  stable 150
  lost 776
  hopeless 859
irrevealable 528
irreverence 929,
  988
irreversible
  stable 150
  hopeless 859
irrevocable

484
- apart
exclude 55
relinquish 782
- aside
neglect 460
reject 610
disuse 678
give up 782
- on the table 133
- the axe at the
root of tree 162
- bare 529
- before 527
- brother 996
- by store 636
sickness 655
disuse 678
- to one's charge
938
- claim to 924
- in the dust 162
- eggs 161
- at the door of
155
- down [see below]
- at one's feet 763
- figure nonentity 4
model 22
representation
554
- one's finger
upon 480a
- the first stone 66
- the flattering
unction to one's
soul 831, 834
- the foundations
153, 673
- ghosts 992
- hands on
use 677
take 789
rite 998
- under hatches
751
- one's head on
the block 942
- heads together
695, 709
- in eat 298
store 636
provide 637
- on 972
open divest 226
opening 260
show 525
disclose 529
- oneself open to
177
- out
horizontal 213
corpse 363
plan 626
expend 809
- oneself out for
673
- over 133
- reader 996
- under restraint
751
- in ruins 162
- siege to 716
- stress on 642
- to attribute 155
rest 265
- it on thick

cover 223
too much 641
flatter 933
- together 43
- train 626
- up store 636
sickness 655
disuse 678
- waste 162
lay down locate 184
horizontal 213
assert 535
renounce 757
relinquish 782
pay 807
- one's arms
pacification 723
submission 725
- the law
certain 474
assert 535
command 741
insolence 885
- one's life 360
- a plan 626
layer 204
layette 225
layman 699, 997
laystall 653
lazaret 662
lazar-house 662
lazy 683, 927
lazzarone 683
lb. 319
lea land 342
plain 344
leach 335
lead superiority 33
in order 62
pioneer 64
influence 175
tend 176
soundings 208
- in motion 280
heavy 319
rôle 599
induce 615
direct 693
authority 737
heave the - 466
red - 434
take the -
influence 175
importance 642
authority 737
white - 420
- to the altar 903
- astray 495
- captive
subject 749
restraint 751
- a merry chase
623
- the choir 990
- a dance
run away 623
circuit 629
difficulty 704
disrespect 929
- the dance 280
- one to expect
511
- a life 692
- on 693
- to no end 645
- by the nose 737
- off 62

- the way
precedence 62
begin 66
precession 280
importance 642
direction 693
repute 873
leaden dim 422
colorless 429
grey 432
inactive 683
leader
precursor 64
dissertation 595
director 694
counsel 968
- writer 593
leading
beginning 66
important 642
- article 595
- lady 599
- note music 413
- part 175
- question 461
- seaman 745
- strings
childhood 127
child 129
pupil 541
subject 749
restraint 751, 752
leads 223
leaf part 51
layer 204
plant 367
- of a book 593
turn over a new -
658
- green 435
leafless 226
leaflet 531
leafy 256
league length 200
co-operation 709
party 712
- of Nations 696
leak crack 198
dribble 295
waste 638
spring a -
injury 659
- out
disclosure 529
leaky imperfect 651
leal 743
lean thin 203
oblique 217
- on 215
- to shed 191
willing 602
- towards 923
- upon belief 484
subjection 749
hope 858
leaning
tendency 176
willingness 602
desire 865
friendship 888
favoritism 923
leap
sudden change
146
ascent 305
jump 309
-s and bounds 274

make a - at 622
- in the dark
experiment 463
uncertain 475
chance 621
rash 863
- with joy 838
- year 138
leap-frog 840
learn 490, 539
- by experience
950
- by heart 505
learned 490
learner 541
learning 490, **539**
lease property 780
lending 787
grant a - 771
take a new - of
life 654
- and release 783
leasehold 780
leash lie 43
three 92
hold in - 751
least
- in quantity 34
- in size 193
at the - 32
leather skin 223
tough 327
beat 972
nothing like - 481
- bottle 191
- or prunello 643
leave remainder 40
part company 44
relinquish 624
permission 760
bequeathe 784
French - 623
take - depart 293
freedom 748
- alone
inaction 681
freedom 748
permit 760
- the beaten track
83
- to chance 621
- an inference 526
- a loophole 705
- in the lurch
pass 303
decisive 545
- no trace
be no more 2
disappear 449
obliterate 552
- it to one 76
- to oneself 748
- off cease 142
desuetude 614
relinquish 624
disuse 678
- out 55
- out of one's cal-
culation 460
- a place 293
- ad referendum
605
give me - to say
535
- undecided 609a
- undone 730
- a void regret 833

- word 527
leaven
component 56
cause 153
lighten 320
qualify 469
unclean 653
deterioration 659
bane 663
leavings
remainder 40
useless 645
lecher 962
lechery 961
lectern 1000
lection special 79
interpretation 522
lectionary 998
lecture teach 537
speak 582
dissertation 595
censure 932
sermon 998
- room 542
lecturer
teacher 540
preacher 996
lectureship 542
led - captain
follower 746
servile 886
favorite 899
- by the nose 749
ledge height 206
horizontal 213
shelf 215
projection 250
ledger list 86
record 551
accounts 811
lee 236
leech 662, 695
leef 829
leek eat the -
recant 607
submit 725
Lee-Metford
rifle 727
leer stare 441
dumb-show 550
leery 702, 864
lees 653
lee-shore 665, 667
leet, court - 936
lee-wall 666
leeward 236
lee-way space 180
tardy 133
navigation 267
deviation 279
progression 282
shortcoming 304
left residuary 40
sinistral 239
over the - 545
- alone 748
- in the lurch 732
- to shift for one-
self 893
pay over the -
shoulder 808
left-handed
clumsy 699
- compliment 932
- marriage 903
leg support 215
walker 266

debauched 961
lichgate 363
lichen 367
licit 760, 924
lick *lap* 298
  conquer 731
  punish 972
  – the dust 933
  – into shape 240
lickerish
  savory 394
  desirous 865
  fastidious 868
  licentious 961
lickpenny 819
lickspittle 886
lictor 965
lid 223
lie *situation* 183
  presence 186
  recline 213
  falsehood 544
  untruth 546
  give the – to 536
  white – 617
  – abed 683
  – in ambush 528
  – by 681
  – at one's door
    926
  – down *flat* 213
  rest 687
  – f:llow 674
  – hid 528
  – in *be* 1
  give birth 161
  – low 528
  – under a neces-
    sity 601
  – in a nutshell 32
  – on 215
  – over *defer* 133
  destiny 152
  – in one's power
    157
  – at the root of
    153
  – still 265
  – to
    quiescence 265
    inaction 681
  – under 177
  – in wait for
    expect 507
    inaction 681
lief *pleasant* 829
  as – *willing* 602
  choice 609
liege 745
liegeman 746
lien 771, 805
lienteria 653
lieu 182
  in – of 147
lieutenant 745, 759
  lord – 965
life *essence* 5
  events 151
  vitality 359
  biography 594
  activity 682
  conduct 692
  cheerful 836
  animal – 364
  battle of – 682
  come to – 660
  infuse into

excite 824
  put – into 359
  recall to – 660
  see – 840
  support – 359
  take away – 361
  tenant for – 779
  – to come 152
  – after death 981
  – or death
    need 630
    important 642
    contention 720
  – and spirit 682
Life, the 976
life-blood 5, 359
life-boat 273, 666
life-giving 168
lifeguards 726
lifeless 172, 360
lifelike 17
lifelong 110
life-preserver 666,
  727
life-size 192
lifetime 108
life-weary 841
lift *raise* 307
  aid 707
  steal 791
  – cattle 791
  – up the eyes 441
  – a finger 680
  – hand against
    716
  – one's head 734
  – up the heart 990
  – the mask 529
  – the voice
    shout 411
    speak 582
lift-smoke 840
ligament 45
ligation 43
ligature 45
light *state* 7
  small 32
  window 260
  velocity 274
  arrive 292
  descend 306
  levity 320
  kindle 384
  watch 388
  luminosity 420
  luminary 423
  – in *colour* 429
  white 430
  aspect 448
  knowledge 490
  interpretation 522
  unimportant 643
  easy 705
  gay 836
  loose 961
  blue – *signal* 550
  bring to –
    discover 480a
    manifest 525
    disclose 529
  children of – 987
  come to – 529
  false – 443
  foot –s 599
  half – 422
  make – of
    underrate 483

easy 705
  inexcitable 826
  despise 930
  in one's .own – 699
  obstruct ,the – 426
  side – 490
  see the – *life* 359
    publication 531
  transmit – 425
  throw – upon 522
  a – breaks in upon
    one 529
  – under a bushel
    hide 528
    not hide 878
    modesty 881
  – comedy 599
  – cruiser 726
  – fantastic toe 309
  – upon one's feet
    664
  – heart 836
  – of heel 274
  – horse 726
  – infantry 726
  – purse 804
  – and shade 420
  – of truth 543
  – up *illumine* 420
    excite 824
    cheer 836
  – upon *chance* 156
    arrive at 292
    discover 480a
    acquire 775
Light of the World
  976
lighten
  make light 320
  illume 420
  facilitate 705
lighter *boat* 273
lighterage 812
lighterman 269
light-fingered 791,
  792
light-footed 274,
  682
light-headed 503
lighthouse 550
lightless 421
light-minded 605
lightning
  velocity 274
  flash 420
  spark 423
  like greased – 113
lightsome
  luminous 420
  irresolute 605
  cheerful 836
ligneous 367
lignite 388
lignography 558
ligulate 205
like *similar* 17
  relish 394
  enjoy 377, 827
  wish 865
  love 897
  do what one –s
    748
  look – 448
  we shall not look
    upon his – again
    33
  – master like man
    19

– a pin in paper 58
likely 472
  think – 507
likeness 21, 554
  bad – 555
likewise 37
liking 865, 897
  have a – for 827
  to one's – 829
lilac *color* 437
Liliputian 193
Lillith 994
lilt 416, 836
lily *white* 430
  beauty 845
  paint the – 641
lily-livered 862
limæ labor
  improve 658
  toil 686
limature 330, 331
limb *member* 51
  instrument 633
  scamp 949
  – of the law 968
limber 272, 324
limbo *prison* 751,
  752
  pain 828
  purgatory 982
lime *entrap* 545
  – light 423, 531,
    599
Limehouse 908
limine, in – 66
limit *complete* 52
  end 67
  circumscribe 229
  boundary 233
  qualify 469
  restrain 751
  prohibit 761
limitarian 984
limitation [*see*
  limit]
  estate 780, 783
limited
  – in *quantity* 32
  – in *size* 393
  to a – extent
    imperfect 651
limitless 105
limitrophe 197
limn 556
limner 559
limousine 272
limp *weak* 160
  slow 275
  supple 324
  fail 732
limpid 425
lin 343, 348
lincture 662
line *fastening* 45
  continuous 69
  ancestors 166
  descendants 167
  length 200
  no breadth 203
  string 205
  lining 224
  outline 230
  straight 246
  of steamers 273
  direction 278
  music 413
  appearance 448

measure 466
  mark 550
  writing 590
  verse 597
  vocation 625
  army and navy
    726
  boundary – 233
  draw the – 465
  drop a – to 526
  in a –
    continuous 69
    straight 246
  in a – with 278
  read between the
    –s 522
  sounding – 208
  straight – 246
  troops of the – 726
  – of action 692
  – of battle 69
  – of battle ship
    726
  – engraving 558
  – of march 278
  – of road 627
lineage *kindred* 11
  series 69
  ancestry 166
  posterity 167
lineament
  outline 230
  feature 240
  appearance 448
  mark 550
linear
  continuity 69
  pedigree 166
  length 200
linen 225
liner 273
lines
  fortification 717
  hard –
    adversity 735
    severity 739
    reins 752
linger *protract* 110
  delay 133
  loiter 275
lingerie 225
lingo 560, 563
lingua franca 563
linguacious 584
lingual 560, 582
linguist 492
linguistics 560
liniment 356, 662
lining 224
link *relation* 9
  connect 43
  connecting – 45
  part 51
  term 71
  crossing 219
  torch 423
  golf –s 840
  missing – 53, 729
linked together
  party 712
linoleum 223
linotype 591
linseed oil 356
linsey-wolsey 41
linstock 388
lint 223
lintel 215

love *desire* 865
  courtesy 894
  affection **897**
  favorite 899
  abode of – 897
  labor of –
    willing 602
  inexpensive 815
  amusement 840
  disinterested 942
  God's – 906
  make – 902
  no – lost 713
  – affair 897
  – of country 910
  – lock 256
  not for – or money
    640, 814
love-knot *token* 550
love-lorn 898
lovely 845, 897
love-making 902
love-pot 959
love-potion 865
lover [*see* love]
love-sick 897, 902
love-story 897, 902
love-token 897, 902
loving-cup 892, 894
loving-kindness
  906
low *small* 32
  not high 207
  – *sound* 405
  moo 412
  vulgar 851
  disreputable 874
  common 876
  base 940
  bring – 308
  – condition 876
  – comedy 599
  at a – ebb
  small 32
  inferior 34
  depressed 308
  waste 638
  deteriorated 659
  – fellow 876
  – life 851
  – note 408
  – origin 876
  – price 815
  – spirits 837
  – tide 207
  – tone *black* 431
  mutter 581
  – water *low* 207
  dry 340
  insufficient 640
  poor 804
low-born 876
low-brow 491
low-lands 207
low-minded 876,
  940
lower *inferior* 34
  decrease 36
  overhang 214
  depress 308
  dark 421
  dim 422
  predict 511
  sad 837
  irate 900
  sulky 901a
  – one's *flag* 725

– one's note 879
– orders 876
lowering 668, 859
lowly 879
lown 501, 949
lowness [*see* low]
  207
  humility 879
loy 272
loyal *obedient* 743
  observant 772
  honourable 939
lozenge 244, 662
L. s. d. 800
lubbard[*see* lubber]
lubber 683, 701
lubberly 192, 699
lubricant 332
lubrication 255, **332**
lubricity
  slippery 255
  unctuous 355
  impure 961
lucent 420
lucid
  luminous 420
  transparent 425
  intelligible 518
  – *style* 570
  – *interval* 502
lucidus ordo 58
lucifer 388
Lucifer 423, 978
lucimeter 445
luck *chance* 156, 621
  prosperity 734
  good – 858
luckless 735
lucky 134, 731
lucrative 775
lucre 775, 803
Lucretia 960
luctation 720
lucubration 451
luculent 420
lucus a non lucendo
  18, 565
lud! O – 839
ludibrious 840
ludicrous 853
luff 267
lug *pull* 285
  ear 418
luge 272
luggage 270, 780
  – van 272
lugger 273
lugubrious 837
lukewarm
  temperate 382
  irresolute 605
  torpid 823
  indifferent 866
lull *cessation* 142
  mitigate 174
  silence 403
  – to *sleep* 265
lullaby
  moderate 174
  song 415
  verses 597
  inactivity 683
  relief 834
lumbago 378
lumbar 235
lumbar *disorder* 59
  slow 275

store 636
useless 645
hindrance 706
lumbering 647, 846
lumber-room 191
lumbriciform 249
luminary *star* 318
  light **423**
  sage 500
luminescence 420
luminous *light* 420
  intelligible 518
  – *paint* 423
lump *whole* 50
  chief part 51
  amass 72
  mass 192
  projection 250
  weight 319
  density 321
  in the – 50
  – of *affectation*
    855
  – *sum* 800
  – together *join* 43
  combine 48
  assemble 72
lumpish [*see* lump]
  inactive 683
  ugly 846
Luna 318
lunacy 503
lunar 318
  – *caustic* 384
lunatic 503, 504
luncheon 298
lune avec les dents,
  prendre la –
  158, 471
lunette 717
lunge 276, 716
lungs *wind* 349
  loudness 404
  shout 411
  voice 580
luniform &c. 245
lupanar 961
lurch *incline* 217
  sink 306
  oscillation 314
  failure 732
  leave in the –
  outstrip 303
  deceive 545
  relinquish 624
  left in the –
  defeated 732
lure *attraction* 288,
  865
  deceive 545
  entice 615
lurid *dark* 421
  dim 422
  red 434
lurk *unseen* 447
  latent 526
  hidden 528
lurking-place 530
luscious 394, 829
lush *vegetation* 365
  drunkenness 959
lushy 959
lusk 683
lusory 840
lust 865, 961
  – *after* 921
luster

brightness 420
chandelier 423
glory 873
lustily 404, 686
  cry out – 839
lustless 158
lustration 652, 952
lustrum 108
lusty 159, 192
lusus naturæ 80
lute *cement* 45, 46
  guitar 417
luteous 436
Lutheran 984
luxation 44
luxuriant 168, 639
luxuriate in 377,
  827
luxurious
  pleasant 377
  delightful 829
  intemperate 954
luxury
  physical - 377
  redundance 641
  enjoyment 827
  sensuality 954
lycanthropy 503
Lyceum 542
Lydford law 964
Lydian measure
  415
lyddite 727
lying
  decumbent 213
  deceptive 544
  faithless 986
Ly-king 986
lymph *fluid* 333
  water 337
  transparent 425
lymphatic 337
lynch 972
  – *law* 964
lyncher 975
lynching 361
lynx-eyed 441, 498
lyre 417
lyric 415
  – *poetry* 597
lyrist 597

M

Mab 979
macadamize 255,
  635
Macaire, Robert –
  792
macaroni 854
macaronic
  absurdity 497
  neology 563
  verses 597
Macchiavel [*see*
  Machiavelism]
mace
  weapon 727
  scepter 747
mace-bearer 965
maceration
  saturation 337
  atonement 952
  asceticism 955
  rite 998

Macheath 792
Machiavelism
  falsehood 544
  cunning 702
  dishonesty 940
machicolation 257,
  717
machination
  trick 545
  plan 626
  cunning 702
  -s of the devil 619
machinator 626
machine 633
  like a – 698
  – gun 407, 727
  be a mere – 749
machinist
  theatrical - 599
  workman 690
macilent 203
mackerel
  mottled 440
  procuress 962
  – sky 349, 353
mackintosh 225
macrobiotic 110
macrocosm 318
macrography 441
macrology 577
mac Sycophant,
  Sir Pertinax –
  886, 935
mactation 991
macte virtute 931
macula 848
maculate
  unclean 653
maculation 440, 848
mad *insane* 503
  excited 824
  drive one – 900
  go – 825
  – after 865
  – with rage 900
madam 374
mad-brained 503
madcap
  violent 173
  lunatic 504
  excitable 825
  buffoon 844
  rash 863
madder *color* 434
made
  – to one's hand
    673
  – man 734
  – to order 673
madefaction 339
madman **504**
Madonna
  good 948
  angel 977
  pious 987
madrigal *music* 415
  verses 597
Maecenas 492, 890
Maelstrom
  whirl 312
  water 348
  pitfall 667
maestro 415
maffick 883
magazine
  periodical 53
  record 551

serve – 989
mammoth 192
man *adult* 131
　mankind 372
　male **373**
　prepare 673
　workman 690
　servant 746
　courage 861
　husband 903
make a – of 648, 861
Son of – 976
straight – 599
to a – 488
–at-arms 726
one's – of business 758
–'s estate 131
– in office 745
– in the street 876
–of-war 273, 726
–of-war's man 269
– at the wheel 694
– and wife 903
manacle 751, 752
manage 693
– to *succeed* 731
manageable 705
management
　conduct 692
　skill 698
manager
　stage - 599
　director 694
managery 693
manche après la cognée, jeter le – 859
mancible 637
mancipation 751
mandamus 741
mandarin 745
mandate 630, 741
mandible 298
mandolin 417
mandragora 174
mandrel 312
manducation 298
mane 256
man-eater 361
manége 266, 370
manes 362
manet: – altâmente repostum 505
– *cicatrix* 919
maneuver 680, 702
manful *strong* 159
　resolute 604
　brave 861
manger 191
manger:
cela se laisse – 394
– son blé en herbe 818
mangle
　separate 44
　smooth 255
　injure 659
mangled 53
mangy 655
man-hater 911
manhood 131, 861
ania *insanity* 503
desire 865
niac 504
ibus pedibus–

que 686
manic 503
manic-depressive 503
manicure 847
manicheism 978
manichord 417
manie 865
maniéré 855
manifest
　list 86
　visible 446
　obvious 525
　disclose 529
manifestation **525**
manifesto 531
manifold 81, 102
manikin *dwarf* 193
　image 554
maniple 103
manipulate
　handle 379
　use 677
　conduct 692
manipulator 621
mankind **372**
manly
　adolescent 131
　strong 159
　male 373
　brave 861
　honest 939
manna *food* 396
– in the wilderness *aid* 707
　pleasing 829
manner *kind* 75
　style 569
　way 627
　conduct 692
　in a – 32
　by all – of means 536
　by no – of means 602
　to the – born 5
mannered 579
mannerism
　special 79
　unconformity 83
　affectation 855
　vanity 880
mannerly 894
manners 852, 894
manor 780
　lord of the – 779
　– house 189
manorial 780
Mansard roof 223
manse 1000
mansion 189
manslaughter 361
mansuetude 894
mantelpiece 215
mantilla 225
mantle *spread* 194
　dress 225
　foam 353
　shade 424
　redden 434
　robes 747
　flush 821, 824
　anger 900
mantlet *cloak* 225
　defence 717
Mantology 511
manual *guide* 527

schoolbook 542
book 593
advice 695
– *labor* 686
manubial 793
manufactory 691
manufacture 161, 680
manufacturer 690
manumission 750
manure
　agriculture 371
　dirt 653
　aid 707
manuscript 22, 590
many 102
　the – 876
　for – a day 110
　– irons in the fire 682
　– men many minds 489
　– times *repeated* 104
　frequent 136
many-colored 440
many-sided 81, 236
many-tôngued 532
map 234, 527, 554
　– out 626
mar 659, 706
marabou 83
marabout 1000
maranâtha 908
marasmus
　shrinking 195
　atrophy 655
　deterioration 659
maraud 791
marauder 792
marble *ball* 249
　hard 323
　sculpture 557
　tablet 590
　insensible 823
marble 440
marble-hearted 907
march *region* 181
　journey 266
　progression 282
　music 415
　dead – 363
　forced – 684
　on the – 264
　steal a –
　advance 280
　go beyond 303
　deceive 545
　active 682
　cunning 702
　– against 716
　– of events 151
　– of intellect *knowledge* 490
　improvement 658
　– off 293
　– on a point 278
　– past 882
　– of time 109
　– with 199
March, Ides of–601
marches 233
marchioness 875
marcid 203
marconigram 523
marcor 203
mare *horse* 271

female 374
–'s nest 497, 546
–'s tail *wind* 349
　cloud 353
marechal 745
margarine 356
margin *space* 180
　edge 231
　redundance 641
　latitude 748
margravate 780
margrave 745, 875
marimba 417
marine *fleet* 273
　sailor 269
　oceanic 341
　soldier 726
　tell it to the –s 489, 497
　– *painter* 559
　– *painting* 556
mariner **269**
Mariolatry 991
marionnette
　representation 554
　drama 599
　amusement 840
marish 345
marital 903
maritime 267, 341
mark *degree* 26
　term 71
　take cognizance of 450
　attend to 457
　indication 550
　record 551
　writing 590
　object 620
　importance 642
　repute 873
　beyond the – 303
　leave one's – 873
　man of – 873, 875
　near the – 197
　overshoot the – 699
　put a – upon 457
　save the – 870
　up to the –
　enough 639
　good 648
　skill 698
　due 924
　wide of the – 196, 495
　within the – 304
　– down 813
　– off 551
　– out *choose* 609
　plan 626
　command 741
　– of recognition 894
　– with a red letter 883
　– time *chronometry* 114
　halt 265
　wait 507
　– with a white stone 931
marked [see mark]
　great 31
　affirmed 535
　well– 446

in a – degree 31
play with – cards 545
– down 815
marker 550
market *buy* 795
　mart 799
　bring to – 796
　buy in the cheapest &c. – 794
　in the –
　offered 763
　barter 794
　sale 796
　rig the – 794
　– garden 371
　– overt
　manifest 525
　mart 799
　– place *street* 189
　mart 799
　– *price* 812
　– woman 797
marketable 794, 796
marksman 700
marksmanship 698
marl 342
marmalade 396
marmot 683
maroon
　color 433, 434
　abandon 782, 893
marplot
　bungler 701
　obstacle 706
　malicious 913
marque, letters of – 791
marquee 223
marquetry 440
marquis 875
marriage 903
　companionate – 903
　ill-assorted – 904
　– bells 836
　– portion 780
marriageable 131, – 903
marrow *essence* 5
　interior 221
　central 222
　chill to the – 385
marrow-bones, on one's –
　submit 725
　beg 765
　humble 879
　servile 886
　atonement 952
marrowless 158
marry *combine* 48
　assertion 535
　wed 903
　– come up
　defiance 715
　anger 900
　censure 932
Mars 722, 979
　– orange 439
marsh **345**
marshal
　arrange 60
　messenger 534
　auxiliary 711
　officer 745

make love 902
break one's – 360
– and crop
  completely 52
turn out - 297
– of land 342
– and neck 27
– or nothing
  resolute 604
rash 863
neckcloth 225
necklace 247, 847
necks 980
necrology 360, 594
necromancer 548,
  994
necromancy 992
necropsy 363
necroscopic 363
necrosis 49
nectar 394, 396
need necessity 601
  requirement 637
  insufficiency 640
  indigence 804
  desire 865
  friend in – 711
  in one's utmost –
  735
needful
  necessary 601
  requisite 630
  money 800
  do the – pay 807
needle sharp 253
  perforator 262
  compass 693
  as the – to the
  pole
  veracity 543
  observance 772
  honour 939
  – in a bottle of
  hay 475
needle-gun 727
needle-shaped 253
needless 641
needle-witted 498
needlewoman 690
needlework 847
ne'er-do-well 949
nefarious 945
negation 536, 764
negative
  inexisting 2
  contrary 14
  prototype 22
  quantity 84
  confute 479
  deny 536
  photograph 558
  refuse 764
  prove a – 468
neglect 460
  disuse 678
  leave undone 730
  omit 773
  evade 927
  disrespect 929
  – of time 115
négligé 225, 674
negligence 460
negotiable 270
negotiate
  mediate 724
  bargain 769
  transfer 783

traffic 794
negotiations
  breaking off – 713
negotiator 724, 758
negro 431, 746
negus
  drink 298
  king 745
neif 781
neigh cry 412
  boast 884
neighbor 197, 890
neighborhood 183,
  197, 227
neighborly
  aid 707
  friendly 888
  social 892
  courteous 894
neither 610
  – here nor there
  irrelevant 10
  absent 187
  – more nor less
  equal 27
  true 494
  – one thing nor
  another 83
nem. con. 488
Nemesis
  vengeance 919
  justice 922
  punishment 972
nemine contra-
  dicente 488
nemo me impune
  lacessit 715
nenia 839
neogamist 903
neologism 123
neology 563
neophyte 144, 541
neoteric 123
nepenthe 662, 836
nephelogy 353
nephew 11
nepotism
  nephew 11
  wrong 923
  dishonest 940
  selfish 943
Neptune 341
Nereid 341, 979
nerve 159, 861, 885
  exposed – 378
nerveless 158
nervous weak 160
  style 574
  timid 860
  modest 881
nescience 491
nest
  multitude 102
  cradle 153
  lodging 189
  – of boxes 204
nest-egg 636
nestle lodge 186
  safety 664
  endearment 902
nestling 129
Nestor veteran 130
  sage 500
  advice 695
net remainder 40
  receptacle 191
  intersection 219

inclosure 232
snare 545
difficulty 704
gain 775
– profit gain 775
  receipt 810
nether 207
nethermost 211
netting 219
nettle bane 663
  sting 830
  incense 900
network
  disorder 59
  crossing 219
neuralgia 378
neurasthenia 655
neuritis 378
neurology 329
neurotic 662
neuter matter 316
  no choice 609a
  remain –
  irresolute 605
  stand –
  indifferent 866
neutral mean 29
  no choice 609a
  avoidance 623
  – tint
  colorless 429
  grey 432
  peace 721
neutrality
  mid-course 628
  peace 721
  insensibility 823
  indifference 866
neutralize
  compensate 30
  counteract 179
névé 383
never 107
  – say die
  persevere 604a
  cheerful 836
  hope 858
  it will – do
  inexpedient 647
  prohibit 761
  discontent 832
  disapprobation
  932
–dying 112
–ending 112
–fading
  perpetual 112
  glory 873
  – forget 916
  – to be forgotten
  642
  – indebted 807
  – hear the last of
  841
  – mind
  neglect 460
  unimportant 643
  insensible 823
  indifferent 866
  contempt 930
  – more 107
  – a one 4
  – otherwise 16
  – to return 122
  – was seen the
  like 83
  – so 31

– tell me 489
– thought of 621
– tired active 682
– tiring
  persevering 604a
neverness 107
nevertheless 30
new different 18
  additional 37
  novel 123
  unaccustomed 614
  – birth 660
  – blood change 140
  improve 658
  excite 824
  – brooms 614, 682
  – comer 57
  – conditions 469
  – departure 66
  – edition
  repetition 104
  reproduction 163
  improvement 658
  – ideas 537
  turn over a – leaf
  change 140
  repeat 950
  give – life to 707,
  824
  view in a – light
  658
  put on the – man
  950
New Year's Day
  138
newaub 745
new-born 123, 129
Newcastle, carry
  coals to – 641
new-fangled
  unfamiliar 83
  change 140
  neology 563
new-fashioned 123
new-fledged 129
Newfoundland dog
  366
Newgate 752
new-gilt 847
new-model
  convert 144
  revolutionize 146
  improve 658
newness 123
news 532
  – sheet 531
newsmonger
  curious 455
  informant 527
  news 532
newspaper 531, 551
  – correspondent
  758
newspaperman 534
newt 366
next
  following 63
  later 117
  future 121
  near 197
  – friend 759
  – of kin 11
  – to nothing 32
  – world 152
nexus 45
Niagara 348
niais 501

niaiserie 517
nib cut 44
  end 67
  summit 210
  point 253
nibble eat 298
  – at censure 932
  – at the bait
  dupe 547
  willing 602
nice
  savory 394
  discriminative
  465
  exact 494
  good 648
  pleasing 829
  fastidious 868
  honorable 939
  – ear 418
  – hand 700
  – perception 465
  – point 704
nicely
  completely 52
Nicene Creed 983a
nicety 466
niche recess 182
  receptacle 191
  angle 244
  – in the temple of
  fame 873
nicher, se – 184
nick notch 257
  deceive 545
  mark 550
  – it 731
  – of time 124
Nick, Old – 978
nickel
  money 800
nicknack 643
nickname 565
nicotine 392, 663
nictitate 443
nidget 862
nidification 189
nidor 398
nidorous 401
nidus 153, 189
niece 11
niggard 819
nigger 431
  – in the woodpile
  702
niggle mock 929
niggling 643
nigh 197
night 421
  labor day and –
  686
  orb of – 318
  – and day 136
  – school 542
night-cap 225
nightfall 126
nightingale 416
night-gown 225
nightmare
  bodily pain 378
  dream 515
  incubus 706
  mental pain 828
  alarm 860
nightshade 663
nigrescent 431
nigrification 431

numeral 84, 85
numeration **85**
numerator 84
numerical 85
numerose
  many 102
numerous 102
numismatics 800
numps 501
numskull 501
nun 996
nunc dimittis 990
nuncio 534, 758
nuncupation
  naming 564
nuncupatory
  informing 527
nunindation 794
nunnery 1000
nuptials 903
nurse *remedy* 662
  preserve 670
  help 707
  servant 746
  custodian 753
  fondle 902
  put to − 537
nurseling 129
nursery *infancy* 127
  nest 153
  room 191
  garden 371
  school 542
  workshop 691
  − *rhymes* 597
  − *tale* 546, 594
nursing home 493
nurture *feed* 298
  educate 537
  prepare 673
  aid 707
  − a belief 484
  − an idea 451
nut
  − to crack
  fanatic 504
  riddle 533
  difficulty 704
  − oil 365
nut-brown 433
nutmeg 393
nutmeg-grater 330
nuts 618, 829
nutshell *small* 32
  lie in a − 572
  little 193
  compendium 596
nutation 314
nutriment 298
nutrition 707
nutritious *food* 298
  healthy 656
  remedy 662
nutty 499
nuzzle 902
nyctalopy 443
nymph *girl* 129
  woman 374
  mythology 979
  sea − 341
nystagmus 443

O

O! *wonder* 870
  discontent 932

− for *desire* 865
oaf *fool* 501
  bungler 701
  changeling 980
oak *strong* 159
  heart of −
  hard 323
  brave 861
oakum 205
oar *paddle* 267
  oarsman 269
  instrument 633
  laboring − 686
  lie upon one's −s
  681
  ply the −
  navigate 267
  exert 686
  pull an − 680
  put in an − 228,
  682
  rest on one's −
  cease 142
  quiescence 265
  repose 687
  stroke − 693
oarsman 269
oasis *separate* 44
  exceptional 83
  land 342
oast-house 386
oath
  assertion 535
  bad language 908
  on − 543
  rap out −s 885
  upon − 768
oatmeal 298
obbligato 88, 415
obduction 223
obdurate
  obstinate 606
  severe 739
  malevolent 907
  graceless 945
  impenitent 951
obedience **743**
obeisance *bow* 308
  submission 725
  courtesy 894
  reverence 928
obelisk 206, 551
Oberon 979
obese 194
obesity 192
obey 743
  be subject to 749
  − a call 615
  − the helm 705
  − rules 82
obfuscate 421, 426
obfuscated
  drunk 959
obit 360, 363
  post − 360, 363
obiter dictum
  irrelevant 10
  occasion 134
  interjacent 228
obituary 360, 594
object *thing* 3
  matter 316
  take exception 469
  intention 620
  ugly 846
  disapprove 932
  be an −

important 642
  − to *dislike* 867
  − *lesson* 82
objection 706, 932
  no − 762
objectionable
  inexpedient 647
  wrong 923, 947
objective
  extrinsic 6
  material 316
objector
  conscientious −
  710
objurgate 932
oblate 201
  − *spheroid* 249
oblation *gift* 784
  religious - 990
oblectation 827
obligation
  necessity 601
  promise 768
  conditions 770
  debt 806
  confer an − 648
  feeling of − 916
  under an − 916,
  926
oblige *benefit* 707
  compel 744
  duty 926
oblige, bien −
  refusal 764
obliged
  necessity 601
  grateful 916
  duty 926
obligee 800
obliging
  helping 707
  courteous 894
  kind 906
obliquation 279
obliquity
  slope **217**
  vice 945
  − of judgment 481
  − of vision 443
obliteration **552**
  − of the past 506
oblivion **506**
  nothingness 2
  pardon 506
  forgiveness 918
  redeem from − 505
  − of benefits 917
  − of time 115
oblivious 506
oblong 200
  − *spheroid* 249
obloquy
  disrepute 874
  disapprobation
  932
  detraction 934
obmutescence 581,
  585
obnoxious
  pernicious 649
  unpleasing 830
  hateful 898
  − to *liable* 177
obnubilated 422
oboe 417
obreption 528
obscene 653, 961

obscurantist 421,
  519, 710
obscure *dark* 421
  dim 422
  unseen 447
  uncertain 475
  unintelligible 519
  eclipse 874
  ignoble 876
obscurity *style* **571**
obscurum per
  obscurius 519
obsecration 765
obsequies 363
obsequious
  subject 749
  servile 886
  courteous 894
  respectful 928
  flattery 932
observance *rule* 82
  attention 457
  habit 613
  practice 692
  fulfilment **772**
  duty 926
  rite 998
observant
  friar 996
observation
  intellect 450
  idea 453
  attention 457
  assertion 535
  − car 272
observatory 318
observe [*see* observ-
  ance, observa-
  tion]
  remark 535
  − a duty 926
  − rules 82
observer 444
obsess 860, 992
obsession 716
obsidional 716
obsolete *old* 124
  words 563
  effete 645
obstacle 179, 706
obstant, Fata − 601
obstetrician 631
obstetrics 161, 662
obstinacy **606**
  prejudice 481
obstipation 261
obstreperous 173,
  404
obstruct *close* 261
  hinder 706
  − the passage of
  light 426
  − the view 424
obstructive
  opponent 710
obstruent 706
obstupefaction 823
obstupui steterunt-
  que comæ 860
obtain *exist* 1
  prevail 78
  get 775
  − under false
  pretences 791
obtainable 470
obtenebration 421
obtestation 765

obtrectation 934
obtrude
  interfere 228
  insert 300
  meddle 682
obtruncate 201
obtrusion 228, 706
obtrusive
  interfering 228
  vulgar 851
  rude 895
obtund *mitigate* 174
  blunt 254
  deaden 376
  paralyze 823
obturate 261
obturator 263
obtuse *blunt* 253
  insensible 376
  imbecile 499
  dull 823
  − angle 244
obtuseness 456a
obumbrate 421
obverse 234
obviate 706
obvious *visible* 446
  evident 474
  clear 518
  manifest 525
ocarina 417
occasion
  juncture 8
  opportunity **134**
  cause 153
  befit the − 646
  have − for 630
  on the present −
  118
  on the spur of −
  612
occasional 475
occasionally 136
occidental 236, 560
occiput 235
occision 361
occlusion 261
  unintelligible 919
  latent 526
  hidden 528
  − art 992
occultism 984
occultation 449, 528
occupancy 186, 777
occupant 188, 779
occupation
  business 625
  in the − of 188
  − road 627
occupied 682
  − by 188
  − with 457, 625
occupier 188, 779
occupy 186, 777
  − the chair 693
  − oneself with 457,
  625
  − the mind 451,
  457
  − a post 737
  − time 106
occur 1, 151
  − to the mind 451
  − in a place 186
occurrence 151
  of daily − 613
occursion 276

palaver
  unmeaning 517
  speech 582
  loquacity 584
  colloquy 588
  council 696
pale *stake* 45
  region 181
  inclosure 232
  limit 233
  dim 422
  colourless 429
  emotion 821
  frightened 860
  turn –
  lose color 429
  emotion 821
  fear 860
  – of the church
    995
  – its ineffectual
    fire
  dim 422
  out of repute 874
pale-faced 429
paleocrystic 124
paleography
  past 122
  philology 560
paleology *past* 122
  language 160
paleontology 368
paleozoic 124
palestric 686, 720
paletot 225
palette 556
palfrey 271
palimpsest 147, 528
palindrone
  inversion 218
  neology 563
paling 232, 752
palingenesia 163
palingenesis 660
palinode 597
palinody 607
palisade
  wall 212
  defence 717
  prison 752
pall *covering* 223
  mantle 225
  funeral 363
  disgust 395
  insignia 747
  weary 841
  dislike 867
  satiety 869
  canonicals 999
palladium
  safety 664
Pallas 979
pall-bearer 363
pallet *support* 215
  painter's – 556
palliament 225
palliate
  moderate 174
  mind 658
  relieve 834
  extenuate 937
palliative 174
  remedy 662
allid 429
allium 999
ll-mall 840
lone 840

pallor 429
palm
  measure of length
    200
  trophy 733
  steal 791
  laurel 877
  bear the – 873
  grease the –
  induce 615
  give 784
  itching – 865
  win the – 731
  – off, – upon 545
  – tree 367
palmated 257
palmer
  traveller 268
  clergy 996
palmist 513
palmistry 511
palmy
  prosperous 734
  pleasant 829
  – days
  prosperous 734
  pleasure 827
palpable
  material 316
  tactile 379
  obvious 446
  manifest 525
  – *obscure* 421
palpation 379
palpitate
  tremble 315
  color 440
  emotion 821
  fear 860
palsy
  impotence 158
  *physical insensi-
    bility* 376
  disease 655
  *mental insensi-
    bility* 823
palter
  falsehood 544
  shift 605
  elude 773
paltry *small* 32
  unimportant 643
  mean 940
paludal 345
pampas 344
pamper 902, 954,
  957
pamphlet 531, 593
pamphleteer 595
Pan 979
pan 191
panacea 662
panache 256, 847
panama *hat* 225
panary 636
pancake 298
pandar [*see* pander]
Pandean pipes 417
pandect
  knowledge 490
  dissertation 595
  compendium 596
  code 963
pandemonium 59,
  404, 982
  inhabitants of –
    978

pandemic 657
pander *pimp* 962
  – to *instrument*
    631
  help 707
  flatter 933
pandiculation
  expansion 194
  opening 260
  sleepy 683
Pandoor 726
Pandora's box 619
  bottom of 858
paned 440
panegyric 931
panegyrize 482
panel *list* 86
  layer 204
  partition 228
  accused 938
  jury 967
  sliding – 545
panelling 847
pang 378, 828
Pangloss 492
panguid 355
panhandle 765, 767,
  876
panic 860
panier 225
Panjandrum 875
pannel 213
pannikin 191
pannier 191
panoply 717, 727
panopticon 752
panorama 448, 556
panoramic 78, 446
  – *view* 441
pansophy 490
pant *heat* 382
  fatigue 688
  emotion 821
  – for 865
pantaloon
  old man 130
  pantomimist 599
  buffoon 844
pantaloons 225
pantechnicon 272,
  636
pantheism 984
Pantheon 979, 1000
panther 861
pantile 223, 350
pantologist 492, 700
pantology 490
pantomime 550, 599
pantry 191, 636
pants 225
panurgy 698
pap 250, 354
papa *father* 166
Papa *pope* 996
papacy 984, 995
papal 995
paper *cover* 223
  white 430
  writing 590
  book 593
  security 771
  exist only on – 4
  – *credit* 805
  – *money* 800
  – *pellet* 643
  – *war* 476, 720
Paphian 954, 961

papilla 250
papistry 984
papoose 129
pappous 256
papula 250
papulose 250
papyrus 590
par 27
  above – 648
  below – *low* 207
  imperfect 651
  – *excellence* 33
  – *nobile fratrum*
    alike 17
  friends 890
  de – *le roi* 737
  – *parenthèse* 134
  – *pari refero* 718
  – *value* 812
parable
  metaphor 521
  teaching 537
  description 594
parabola *curve* 245
parabolic
  metaphorical 521
paracentesis 297
parachronism 115
parachute
  balloon 273
  means of safety
    666
  – *light* 423
Paraclete 976
parade *procession*
    69, 266
  walk 189
  ostentation 882
paradigm 22, 567
Paradise *bliss* 827
  heaven 981
  in – 827
parados 717
paradox
  absurdity 497
  obscurity 519
  difficulty 704
paradoxical 475,
  519
paraffin 356
paragon
  perfect 650
  glory 873
  good man 948
paragram
  ambiguous 520
  neology 563
paragraph *part* 51
  phrase 566
  article 593
paraleipsis 460
parallax 196
parallel
  similarity 17
  imitate 19
  harmonious 178
  – *position* 216
  symmetry 242
  draw a – 464
  *none but himself
    can be his* – 873
  run – 178
parallelism 216
  agreement 23
parallelogram 244
parallelopiped 244
paralogism 477

paralogize 477
paralysis
  impotence 158
  *physical insensi-
    bility* 376
  disease 655
  *moral insensi-
    bility* 823
paralyze 158, 376,
  823
paramount
  supreme 33
  important 642
  authority 737
  lord – *master* 745
  possessor 779
  – *estate* 780
paramour 897
paranoia 503, 504
parapet 717
paraph 550
paraphernalia
  machinery 633
  belonging 780
paraphrase
  imitation 19
  copy 21
  synonym 522
  phrase 566
paraphrast 524
paraphrastic 19,
  522
parasite *auxiliary*
    711
  servile 886
  flatterer 935
parasitic
  subjection 749
  grasping 789
  servile 886
parasol *covering* 223
  shade 424
paratus:
  in utrumque –
  resolved 604
  ready 673
  semper – 673
parboil 384
parbuckle 633
Parcae 601
parcel *part* 51
  group 72
  part and – 56
  – *out arrange* 60
  allot 786
parcels
  property 780
parcere subjectis
    740, 914
parch *dry* 340
  heat 382
  bake 384
parched with thirst
    865
parchment
  writing 590
  security 771
parcity 819
pardi 535
pardon 506, 918
  beg – 952
  – *me* 489
pardonable 937
pare *cut* 38
  reduce 195
  peel 204
  divest 226

speech 582
– spelling 561
phonics 402
phonograph 417, 418
phonography
 sound 402
 letter 361
 writing 590
phonology 562
Phosphor 423
phosphorescence 420, 423
phosphorus 423
photo-engraving 558
photograph like 17
photographer 559
photography 445
 light 420
 representation 554
photogravure 558
photolysis 49
photometer 445
photosphere 318
photostat 553
phrase part 51
 music 413
 language 566
phrasemonger 577
phraseology 569
phrenetic 503
phrenitis 503
phrenology 450
phrenotypics 505
Phryne 962
phthisozoics 361
phylacteric
 sorcery 992
phylactery
 maxim 496
 spell 993
physic
 cure 660
 remedy 662
physical 316
– education
 material 316
 teaching 537
– force
 strength 159
 compulsion 744
– nature 3
– pleasure 377
– pain 378
– science 316
physician
 remedy 662
 advice 695
Physics 316
physiognomy
 face 234
 appearance 448
 interpret 522
Physiology
 organization 357
 life 359
Vegetable – 369
physique
 strength 159
 animality 364
phytivorous 298
Phytology 369
pi 591
piacere, al – 600
piacular 952

pianino 417
pianissimo 415
pianist 416
piano gentle 174
 music 415
– organ 417
– player 417
pianoforte 417
pianola 417
piazza 189, 191
pibroch music 415
 war 722
pica 591
picaresco, gusto – 945
picaroon 792
piccolo 410, 417
pick axe 253
 eat 298
 select 609
 best 648
 clean 652
 gain 775
– a-back 215
– the brains of 461
– holes
 censure 932, 934
– the lock 480a
– me up 662
– out extract 301
 select 609
– to pieces
 separate 44
 destroy 162
 find fault 932
– a quarrel 713
– one's steps 459
– up learn 539
 get better 658
 gain 775
– one's way 675
pickaninny 129
pickaxe 253
picked 648
– men 700
pickeer 791
pickeerer 792
pickelhaube
 armor 717
picket join 43
 locate 184
 fence 229
 guard 668
 defence 717
 soldiers 726
 restrain 751
 imprison 752
 torture 972
– boat 273
pickings 775, 793
pickle condition 7
 macerate 337
 pungent 392
 condiment 393
 preserve 670
 difficulty 704
 have a rod in – 673
pickle-herring 844
pickpocket 792
 abuse like a – 932
pickthank busy 682
 servile 886
 flatterer 937
picnic food 298
 participation 778
 amusement 840
picquet 840

pictorial
 painting 556
 beauty 845
picture
 appearance 448
 representation 554
 painting 556
 description 594
– to oneself 515
picture-gallery 556
picture-theater 599
picturesque
 painting 556
 beauty 845
piddle dawdle 683
piddling trivial 643
pidgin English 563
pie food 298
 sweet 396
 printing 591
piebald 440
piece adjunct 59
 bit 31
 painting 556
 drama 599
 cannon 727
 coin 800
 courtesan 962
 fall to –s 162
 go to –s 162
 in –s 330
 of a – 42
 pull to –s 162
 give a – of advice 695
– of good fortune 618
– of music 415
– of news 532
– out 52
– together 43
– of work 713
 make a – of work about 642
pièce
– justificative 467
– de résistance 298
piecemeal 51
pied variegated 440
pied de la lettre,
 au – 494
pie-poudre, court of – 966
pier 189, 666
pierce
 perforate 260
 bodily pain 378
 chill 385
 hurt 649
 wound 659
 affect 824
 mental pain 830
– the head 410
– the heart 830
piercer 262
piercing cold 383
 loud 404
 shrill 410
 intelligent 498
 feeling 821
– eye 441
– pain 378
pier-glass 445
Pierian spring 597
pierre fendre, à – 383

Pierrot 599
pietas 998
piété, mont de – 787
pietism 988
pietist 987, 988
piety 987
pig animal 366
 sensual 954a
– in a poke
 uncertain 475
 chance 621
 rash 863
– together 72
pigeon
 dupe 547
 steal 791
 gorge de – 440
pigeon-hearted 862
pigeon-hole 191, 260
piggin 191
piggish 954
pig-headed 499, 606
pigment 428
pigmy 193
pignoration 771
pignus 771
pig-sticking 361
pigsty 653
pigtail 214
pigwidgeon 193, 980
pike hill 206
 sharp 253
 highway 627
 weapon 727
pikeman 726
pikestaff tall 206
 plain 525
pilaster
 support 215
 projection 250
 ornament 847
pile stake 45
 heap 72
 edifice 161
 post 215
 velvet 256
 money 800
 funeral – 363
– up 549, 641
pile-driver 276
pilfer steal 791
pilferer 792
pilgarlic
 outcast 893
pilgrim 268, 996
pilgrimage 266, 676
pill sphere 249
 medicine 662
 bitter – 735
pillage 659, 791
pillager 792
pillar stable 150
 lofty 206
 support 215
 monument 551
 tablet 590
–s of Hercules 550
– of the state &c. 873
from – to post
 transfer 270
 agitation 315
 irresolute 505
 circuit 629

pillion 215
pillory 975
pillow
 support 215
 soft 324
 consult one's –
 temporize 133
 reflect 451
pilot mariner 269
 inform 527
 guide 693
 director 694
pilot-balloon 463
pilot-boat 273
pilot-officer 745
pilot-jacket 225
pilous 256
pimp 962
pimple 250, 848
pin fasten 43
 fastening 45
 locate 184
 sharp 253
 axis 312
 trifle 643
 might hear a –
 drop 403
 point of a – 193
 not a – to choose 27, 609a
– down 744, 751
– one's faith upon 484
– oneself upon 746, 886
pinafore 225
pince-nez 445
pincers 781
pinch emergency 8
 contract 195
 pain 378
 chill 385
 need 630
 difficulty 704
 adversity 735
 grudge 819
 hurt morally 830
 at a – 630, 704
 jack at a – 711
 where the shoe –s 830
– of snuff 643
pinchbeck 545, 847
pinched [see pinch]
 thin 203
 poor 804
– with hunger 865
pinching 383, 819
Pindaric 597
ping-pong 840
pine disease 655
 dejection 837
 suffer in mind 828
– away 837
– for 865
pinery 371
pinguid 355
pin-hole 260
pinion fasten 43
 wing 267
 instrument 633
 restrain 751
 fetter 752
pink notch 257
 pierce 260
 thrust 276

color 434
perfection 650
glory 873
pink of *beauty* 845
 – fashion 852
 – perfection 650
 – politeness 894
pinnace 273
pinnacle 210
pinocle 840
pin-prick 180a
pins *legs* 266
 – and needles
  bodily pain 378
  numb 381
  mental pain 828
pinscher 366
Pinto, Fernam
  Mendez – 548
pioneer
 precursor 64
 leader 234
 teacher 540
 prepare 673
pious 987
 – *fraud* 546, 988
pip 747
pipe *tube* 260
 conduit 350
 vent 351
 tobacco 392
 sound 410
 cry 411
 music 416, 417
 weep 839
no – no dance 812
 – one's eye 839
 – of peace 721,
  723
pipeclay *habit* 613
 strictness 739
piper 416
 pay the – 707, 807
piping – hot 382
 – time 721, 734
pipkin 191
piquant
 pungent 392
 - *style* 574
 impressive 821
piquante, sauce –
  393, 829
pique *fly* 267
 excite 824
 pain 830
 hate 898
 anger 900
 – oneself
  pride 878
piqueerer 792
piquet 717, 726
pirate 773, 791, 792
piroque 273
pirouette 218, 312
 turn a – 607
Pisa, tower of – 217
pis-aller 147
piscatorial 366
pisces natare
 docere 538, 641
pisciculture 370
piscina 350, 1000
pish! *absurd* 497
 trifling 643
 excitable 825
 irascible 901
•iste 551

Pistol 887
pistol 727
pistol-shot 197
piston 263
pit *deep* 208
 hole 252
 opening 260
 extract 301
 grave 363
 theater 599
 danger 667
 bottomless – 982
 – of Acheron 982
 – against 708, 713
 – against one
  another 464
pit-a-pat
 agitation 315
 rattle 407
 feeling 821
 excitation 824
pitch *degree* 26
 term 71
 location 184
 height 206
 summit 210
 erect 212
 throw 284
 descent 306
 depression 308
 reel 314
 resin 356a
 musical - 413
 black 431
 absolute – 416
 – of one's breath
  411
 – *dark* 421
 – into *attack* 716
 contend 720
 punish 972
 – *overboard* 782
 – one's tent 292
 – and *toss* 621
 – upon *reach* 292
 discover 480a
 choose 609
 get 775
pitched battle 720
pitcher 191
pitchfork 273, 284
 rain –s 348
pitch-pipe 417
piteous 830
piteously *much* 31
pitfall 545, 667
pith *gist* 5
 strength 159
 interior 221
 center 222
 meaning 516
 important part
  642
pithless 158
pithy *meaning* 516
 concise 572
 vigorous 574
pitiable *bad* 649
 painful 830
 contemptible 930
pitied, to be – 828
pitiful
 unimportant 643
 bad 649
 disrepute 874
 pity 914
pitiless 914a

revengeful 919
pittance
 quantity 25
 dole 640
 allotment 786
 income 810
pitted 848
pituitous 352
pity 914
 express – 915
 what a –
  regret 833
 lament 839
 for –'s sake 914
pivot *junction* 43
 cause 153
 support 215
 axis 222, 312
pix *box* 191, 998
 assay 463
pixy 980
pizzicato 415
placable 918
placard 531
placate 723, 918
place
 circumstances 8
 order 58
 arrange 60
 term 71
 situation 182, 183
 locate 184
 abode 189
 office 625
 rank 873
 give – to 623
 have – 1
 in – 183
 in – of 147
 make a – for 184
 out of – 185
 take – 151
 – to one's credit
  805
 – itself 58
 – in order 60
 – upon record 551
 – under
  include 76
placebit, decies re-
  petita – 829
placebo 933
place-hunter 767
placeman 758
placet 488, 741
placid 826
placket 260
plagiarism
 imitation 19
 borrowing 788
 theft 791
plagiarist 792
Plagiary, Sir
  Fretful – 901
plagiedral 217
plague *disease* 655
 pain 828
 worry 830
plague-spot 657
plaguy 704, 830
plaid *shawl* 225
 variegation 440
plaidoyer 476
plain
 horizontal 213
 country 344
 obvious 446

meaning 518
 manifest 525
 style 576
 artless 703
 ugly 846
 simple 849
speak –ly 576
tell one –ly 527
 – English 576
 – dealing 543
 – interpretation
  522
 – question 461
 – sailing 705
 – sense 498
 – speaking 525,
  703
 – terms
  intelligible 518
  interpreted 522
  language 576
  – truth 494
  – words 703
plainness 576
plainsong 990
plain-spoken 525,
  703
plaint 411, 839
plaintiff 938
plaintive 839
plaisance
 [see pleasance]
plaisanterie 842
plaister 223
plait 219, 258
plan *itinerary* 266
 information 527
 representation
  554
 scheme 626
 according to – 82
planchette 992
plane *horizontal* 213
 flat 251
 smooth 255
 fly 267
 aeroplane 273
 soar 305
 inclined – 633
planet *world* 318
 luminary 423
 fate 601
planet-struck
 adversity 735
 wonder 870
planimeter 466
planish 255
plank *board* 204
 program 626
 path 627
 safety 666
plant *place* 184
 insert 300
 vegetable 367
 agriculture 371
 trick 545
 tools 633
 property 780
 – a battery 716
 – a dagger in the
  breast 830
 – oneself 184
 – a thorn in the
  side 830
plantation
 location 184
 agriculture 371

estate 780
planter 188
planter ses choux,
 aller – 893
plaque 204
plash *lake* 343
 stream 348
 sound 405, 408
plashy 345
plasm 22
plasma 847
plasmic 240
plaster *cement* 45
 covering 223
 remedy 662
 – up *repair* 660
plastered 959
plastic *alterable* 149
 form 240
 soft 324
 – arts 557
plastron 717
plat *weave* 219
 ground 344
plate *dish* 191
 layer 204
 covering 223
 flat 251
 food 298
 engraving 558
 – layer 690
 – printing 558,
  591
plateau 213, 344
plated 545
platform
 horizontal 213
 support 215
 stage 542
 scheme 626
 arena 728
 – *orator* 582
platinum-blond 430
platitude 517, 843
Platonic
 contemplative 451
 inexcitable 826
 chaste 960
 – bodies 244
Platonism 451
platoon 726
 – fire 716
platter 191
 layer 204
 flat 251
 clean the outside
  of the – 544
plaudit 931
plausible
 probable 472
 sophistical 477
 false 544
 approbation 931
 flattery 933
 vindication 937
play *operation* 170
 influence 175
 scope 180
 oscillation 314
 music 416
 drama 599
 use 677
 action 680
 freedom 748
 amusement 840
 at – 840
 bring into – 677

punctilio 939
at the - of 197
come to the -
special 79
attention 457
reasoning 476
plain language
576
culminating - 210
disputed - 713
from all -s 180
full of - 574
give -s to 27
go straight to
the - 278
in - relative 9
agreeing 23
conformable 82
knotty - 704
make a - of
resolution 604
contention 720
compulsion 744
conditions 770
due 924
honor 939
nice - 697
on the - of 111,
121
to the - 572, 642
-an antithesis 578
- at direction 278
direct attention
457
intend 620
discourtesy 895
disrespect 929
censure 932
- of attack 716
at the - of the
bayonet 173
- of the compass
278
- of convergence
74
- of death 360
- in dispute 461
- of etiquette 852
in - of fact 1
- the finger of
scorn 930
- of honor 939
- of land 250
- a moral 537
- out 155, 457,
527
- to - race 720
at the - of the
sword
violence 173
severity 739
compulsion 744
- to attribute 155
direction 278
probable 472
predict 511
mean 516
- of view 441, 448
point d'appui 215
point-blank
direct 278
plain language
576
refusal 764
point-champain 874
pointed
great 31

sharp 253
affirmation 535
marked 550
concise 572
language 574
pointedly
intention 620
pointer dog 366
indicator 550
pointless 843
poise 27, 319, 852
mental - 498
poison 659, 663
- gas 722, 727
poisoned 655
commend the -
chalice 544
poisonous 657, 665
poke
pocket 191
pig in a -
uncertain 475
chance 621
dawdle 683
rash 863
- at 276, 716
- the fire 384
- fun at 856
- one's nose in
682
- out project 250
poker 386
cards 840
polacca 273
polacre 273
polar 210
cold 383
- co-ordinates 466
polarization 420
polariscope 445
polarity
duality 89
counteraction 179
contraposition
237
pole measure of
length 200
tall 206
summit 210
axis 222
punt 267
rotation 312
greasy - 840
opposite -s 237
from - to pole 180
pole-axe 727
polecat 401
pole-star 550, 693
polemic
discussion 476
discord 713
contention 720
combatant 726
polemoscope 445
police 965
- court 966
- magistrate 967
policeman 664, 965
policy 626, 692
polish smooth 255
rub 331
furbish 658
beauty 845
ornament 847
taste 850
politeness 894
- off finish 729

Polish bank 840
polished
- language 578
fashionable 852
polite 894
polisson 949
polite 894
offensive to ears -
579
- literature 560
- society 852
politic wise 498
cunning 702
cautious 864
body -
mankind 372
government 737
political economy
692
politician
director 694
proficient 700
politics 702
polity conduct 692
authority 737
duty 926
polka 840
poll 85, 609
- tax 812
pollard 193, 201
tree 367
Poll-parrot 584
pollute soil 653
corrupt 659
disgrace 874
pollution
disease 655
vice 945
Pollyanna 858
polo 840
polonaise 840
poltroon 862
polyandry 903
polychord 417
polychromatic 428,
440
polychrome 440,
556
polygamy 903
polygastric 191
polyglot 522, 560
polygon
buildings 189
figure 244
polygraphy 590
polylogy 573
polymorphic 81
polyphonism 580
polypus 250
polyscope 445
polysyllable 561
polytheism 984
pomade 356
pomatum 356
pommel
support 215
round 249
beat 972
Pomona 369
pomp 882
pom-pom 727
pomposity 882
pompous
language 577
poncho 225
pond 343, 636
fish - 370

ponder 451
ponderable 316,
319
ponderation 319,
480
ponderous 319
- style 574, 579
dull 843
pondus fumo, dare
- 481
poniard 727
pons asinorum 519,
704
pontifical 995
pontificals 999
pontificate 995
pontiff 996
pontoon
vehicle 272
boat 273
way 627
pony 271
poodle 366
pooh, pooh!
unimportance 643
contempt 930
pool lake 343
combination 709
prize 775
billiards 840
poop 235
poor weak 160
- reasoning 477
- style 575
insufficient 640
trifling 643
indigent 804
unhappy 828
cut a - figure 874
- hand 701
- head 499
- house 189
- man 804
- in spirit 881
- stick 501
- thing 914
poorly 160, 655
- off 804
poor-spirited 862
pop noise 406
unexpected 508
- at 716
- in ingress 294
insertion 300
- off die 360
- a question 461
- the question
request 765
endearment 902
- upon arrive 292
discover 480a
Pope
infallibility 474
priest 996
Popedom 995
Pope Joan 840
Popery 984
pop-gun trifle 643
popinjay 854
poplar tall 206
poppy sedative 174
populace 876
popular
in demand 865
celebrated 873
favorite 897
approved 931

- opinion 488
popularis, aura -
873
popularize
render intelligible
518
facilitate 705
make pleasant
829
populate 184
population 188, 372
populi, vox -
publication 531
election 609
authority 737
populous
crowded 72
multitude 102
presence 186
porcelain
baked 384
sculpture 557
porch entrance 66
lobby 191
mouth 231
opening 260
church 1000
porcupine 253, 901
pore opening 260
egress 295
conduit 350
- over look 441
apply the mind
457
learn 539
porism 461, 480
pornographic 961
porous 260
porpoise 192
porridge 298
porringer 191
port abode 189
sinistral 239
gait 264
arrival 292
carriage 448
harbor 666
in - 664
make - 666
- admiral 745
- fire 388
- wine 959
portable small 193
transferable 270
light 320
portage 270
portal entrance 66
mouth 231
opening 260
portative 193, 270
portcullis 706, 717
let down the - 666
porte-monnaie 802
portend 511
portent 512
portentous
prophetic 511
fearful 860
porter janitor 263
carrier 271, 690
porterage 270
portfolio case 191
book 593
magazine 636
direction 693
insignia 747
porthole 260

vegetation 367
praise *thanks* 916
 commendation
 931
 worship 990
praiseworthy 931,
 944
prame 273
prance 266, 315
prandial 298
prank *caprice* 608
 amusement 840
 adorn 847
prate 584
prattle 582, 584
pravity 945
praxis
 grammar 567
 action 680
Praxiteles 559
pray 765, 990
prayer 765, 990
 house of – 1000
prayer-book 998
preach *teach* 537
 speak 582
 predication 998
 – to the winds 645
 – to the wise 538
preacher
 teacher 540
 priest 996
preachment 998
preadamite 124,
 130
preamble 64
preapprehension
 481
prebend 995
prebendary 996
precarious
 transient 111
 uncertain 475
 dangerous 665
precatory 765
precaution
 care 459
 expedient 626
 safety 664
 preparation 673
precede
 superior 33
 – *in or ler* 62
 – *in time* 116
 – *in motion* 280
precedence 873
precedent
 [*see* precede]
 prototype 22
 precursor 64
 habit 613
 legal decision 969
follow –s 82
precentor 694, 996
precept *adage* 496
 maxim 697
 order 641
 permit 760
preceptor 540
precession 62, 280
précieuse *ridicule*
 855
precinct *region* 181
 place 182
 environs 227
 boundary 233
precious *great* 31

excellent 648
valuable 814
beloved 897
– *metals* 800
– *stone* 648, 847
precipice
 vertical 212
 slope 217
 dangerous 667
 on the verge of
 a – 665
precipitancy 684,
 863
precipitate
 early 132
 sink 308
 consolidate 321
 refuse 653
 haste 684
 rash 863
 – *oneself* 306
precipitous 217
précis 596
precise *exact* 494
preciosity 578
precisely
 literally 19
 assent 488
precisianism
 affectation 855
 heterodoxy 984
 over-religious 988
preclude 55, 706
precocious
 early 132
 immature 674
 pert 885
 rude 895
precognition
 forethought 490
 knowledge 510
preconceived idea
 481
preconception 481
preconcert 611, 626
preconcertation 673
precursor
 – *in order* 62, **64**
 – *in time* 116
 predict 511
predatory 789, 791
predecessor 64
predeliberation
 510, 611
predella 215
predesigned 611
predestination
 fate 152
 necessity 601
 predetermination
 611
 Deity 976
predetermination
 611
predial
 land 342
 agriculture 371
 manorial 780
predicament 8, 75
predicate
 affirm 535
 preach 998
prediction **511**
predilection
 bias 481
 affection 820
 desire 865

predispose 615, 673
predisposed
 willing 602
predisposition 176,
 820
predominant 175,
 737
predominate 33
pre-eminent 33, 873
pre-emption 795
preen 847
pre-engage 132
pre-engagement
 768
pre-establish 626
pre-examine 461
pre-exist 1, 116
preface 62, 64
prefect 745, 759
prefecture 737
prefer *choose* 609
 – *a claim* 969
 – *a petition* 765
preference 62
preferment
 improvement 658
 ecclesiastical –
 995
prefigure 511
prefix 62, 64
 letter 561
pre-glacial 124
pregnable 158
pregnant
 producing 161
 productive 168
 predicting 511
 – *style* 572
 important 642
 – *with meaning*
 516
prehensile 789
prehension 789
pre-historic 124
pre-instruct 537
prejudge 481
prejudicate 481
prejudice
 misjudge 481
 evil 619
 detriment 659
prejudicial 481, 649
prelacy 995
prelate 996
prelation 609
prelection 537, 582
prelector 540
preliminaries:
 settle – 673
 – *of peace* 723
preliminary 62, 64
prelude 62, 64
 beginning 66
 music 415
premature 132, 674
premeditate 611,
 620
prémices 154
premier 694, 759
 – *pas* 66
premiership 693
premise *prefix* 62
 precede 116
 announce 511
premises
 precursor 64
 prior 116

ground 182
 evidence 467
 logic 476
premium
 debt 805
 receipt 810
 reward 783
 at a – 814
premonish 668
premonitory 511,
 668
Premonstratensian
 996
premonstration
 appearance 448
 prediction 511
 manifestation 525
premunire 742, 974
prendre la balle au
 bond 134
prenotion
 misjudgment 481
 foresight 510
prensation 789
prentice 541
prenticeship 539
preoccupancy
 possession 777
preoccupation
 inattention 458
preoption 609
preordain 152, 601
preparation **673**
 music 413
 instruction 537
 in – 730
 in course of – 626
preparatory
 preceding 62
prepare the way
 facilitate 705
prepared *expectant*
 507
 ready 698
preparing
 destined 152
prepense
 spontaneous 600
 predetermined
 611
 intended 620
 malice – 907
prepollence 157
preponderance
 superiority 33
 influence 175
 dominance 737
prepossessed
 obstinate 606
prepossessing 829
prepossession
 prejudice 481
 possession 777
preposterous
 great 31
 absurd 497
 exaggerated 549
 ridiculous 853
 undue 925
prepotency 157
pre-Raphaelite 122,
 124, 556
pre-require 630
pre-resolve 611
prerogative 737, 924

presage 511, 512
presbyopia 443
presbyter 996
Presbyterian 984
presbytery 995,
 996, 1000
prescience 510
prescious 511
prescribe *direct* 693
 advice 695
 order 741
 entitle 924
 enjoin 926
prescript 697, 741
prescription·
 remedy 662
prescriptive *old* 124
 unchanged 141
 habitual 613
 due 924
presence
 in space **186**
 appearance 448
 breeding 894
 in the – *of*
 near 197
 real – 998
 saving one's – 928
 – *of God* 981
 – *of mind* 826,
 864
presence-chamber
 191
present
 – *in time* 118
 – *in space* 186
 offer 763
 give 784
 church prefer-
 ment 995
 at – 118
 these –s .590, 592
 – *arms* 894, 928
 – *a bold front* 861
 – *a front* 719
 – *itself event* 151
 visible 446
 thought 451
 – *oneself*
 presence 186
 offer 763
 courtesy 894
 – *to the mind*
 457, 505
 – *time* **118**
 instant 113
 – *to the view* 448
presentable 852
presentation 883,
 894
presentiment
 instinct 477
 prejudgment 481
 foresight 510
presently 132
presentment
 information 527
 law proceeding
 969
preservation
 continuance 141
 conservation **670**
 Divine attributes
 976
preserve *sweets* 396
preserver 664
preshow 511

– an inquiry 461
– the tenor of
one's way 625, 881
pursuer 622
pursuit 622
pursuivant 534
pursy 194
purulent 653
purvey 637
purview 620
pus 653
Puseyite 984
push *exigency* 8
impel 276
progress 282
propel 284
essay 675
activity 682
haste 684
come to the – 704
– aside 460, 929
– forward 682, 707
– from 289
– to the last 133
– on *haste* 684
– out *eject* 297
pushing 282, 284, 682
pusillanimity 862
puss 366
play – in the corner 148
pussy-foot 528, 958
pustule 250, 848
put *place* 184
fool 501
cards 840
clown 876
neatly – 576
– across 484
– about
turn back 283
go round 311
publish 531
– aside
exclude 55
inattention 458
neglect 460
disuse 678
– away
- *thought* 452
relinquish 782
divorce 905
– back
turn back 283
deteriorate 659
restore 660
– before 527
– by 636
– a case 82, 514
– in commission 755
– a construction on 522
– on the cuff 806
– down
destroy 162
record 551
conquer 731
compel 744
pay 807
humiliate 874
- an end to
end 67
stop 142
destroy 162

- *oneself* 361
– in force
complete 729
compel 744
– forth
expand 194
suggest 514
publish 531
assert 535
- *a question* 461
- *strength* 686
– forward
suggest 514
publish 531
ostentation 882
– one's hand to 676
– the horses to 673
– in [*see below*]
– to inconvenience 647
– a mark upon 457
– one's nose out of joint 33
– off *late* 133
divest 226
depart 293
plea 617
– on *clothe* 225
deceive 544
hasten 684
affect 855
– out [*see below*]
– on paper 551
– over 484, 731
– a question 461
– right 660
– the saddle on the right horse 155
– the seal to 729, 769
– to [*see below*]
– together *join* 43
combine 48
assemble 161
– one's trust in 484
– up [*see below*]
– upon 545, 649
put in *arrive* 292
insert 300
– an affidavit 535
– hand 676
– one's head 514
– mind 505
– motion 264
– order 60
– the place of 147
– one's pocket 785
– practice 692
– remembrance 505
– shape 60
– trim 60, 673
– the way of 470
– a word 582, 588
put out
destroy 162
outside 220
extinguish 385
darken 421
distract the attention 458
uncertain 475
difficult 704
discontent 832

– of countenance 874
oneself – of court
sophistry 477
bungling 699
– of gear 158
– of one's head 458
– of joint 61
– of one's misery 914
– to nurse 707
– of order 59
put to *attribute* 155
request 765
– the blush 879
– death 361
– the door 261
– it 704
– one's oath 768
– press 591
– the proof 463
– the question 830
– the rack 830
– rights 60
– sea 293
– shame 874
– silence 581
– the sword 361
– task 677
– use 677
– the vote 609
put up *assemble* 72
locate 184
store 636
– to auction 796
– for 865
– a petition ⎱ 765
– a prayer ⎰ 990
– for sale 796
– a shutter 424
– the sword 723
– to 615
– with 147, 826
putative
attributed 155
believed 484
supposed 514
putid 643
putrefy 653
putrescence 49
putrid 653
putsch 742
puttee 225
putter 683
putting the weight 840
putty 45
puzzle *uncertain* 475
conceal 528
enigma 533
– out 522
puzzled 475, 533
puzzle-headed 499
puzzling 519
pyemia 655
pyjamas 225
Pylades and Oréstes 890
pylon 206
pyramid *heap* 72
height 206
point 253
pyramids
billiards 840
pyre 363

pyriform 249
pyrology 282
pyromaniac 384, 504, 913
pyromancy 511
pyrometer 389
pyrotechnics 423
pyrotechny 382
Pyrrhic victory 814
pyrrhonism 487, 989
Pythagorean 953
Pythia *oracle* 513
Python, -ess 513
pyx *vessel* 191, 998
temple 1000

Q

Q-boat 726
Q.C. 968
Q.E.D. 478
quack *cry* 412
imposter 548
quackery
falsehood 544
want of skill 699
affectation 855
quacksalver 548
quad 189
quadragesima 956
quadrangle
four-sided 95
precinct 182
house 189
angular 244
quadrant 244, 247
quadrate with 23
quadratic 95
quadrature
four 95
angle 244
quadrennial 95
quadrible 96
quadrifid 97
quadriga 95, 272
quadrilateral
sides 236
angles 244
quadrille 840
quadripartition 97
quadrisection 97
quadrivalent 95
quadroon 41
quadruped 366
quadruplet 96
quadruplex 96
quadruplication 96
quaere 461
quaff 298
– the bitter cup 828
quaggy 345
quagmire
marsh 345
dirty 653
difficult 704
quail 860, 862
quaint *odd* 83
pretty 845
ridiculous 853
quake *oscillate* 314
shake 315
cold 383
fear 860

quakerish 826, 855
Quakerism 984
qualification
[*see qualify*]
power 157
modification 469
skill 698
discount 813
qualify *change* 140
modify 469
deny 536
teach 537
qualis ab incepto 141
qualities
character 820
quality *nature* 5
power 157
tendency 176
nobility 875
qualm *disbelieve* 485
unwilling 603
fear 860
qualms of conscience 950
quamdiu se bene gesserit 108a
quand même
compensating 30
opposed 708
quandary 475, 704
quantity 25, 31, 102
quantum *amount* 25
allotment 786
– mutatus 140
– sufficit 639
quaquaversum 278
quarantine 664, 751
quarrel 24, 713
– with one's bread and butter
bungling 699
discontent 832
quarrelsome 901
quarry *object* 620
mine 636
quart 97
quarter *cut up* 44
fourth 95
quadrisection 97
period 108
region 181
locate 184
abode 189
side 236
direction 278
forbearance 740
money 800
mercy 914
give – 914
give no –
kill 361
severe 739
pitiless 914a
revenge 919
– of a hundred 98
– upon 184
quarter-day 138
quarter-deck 210
quarterly
periodical 531
quartermaster 637
quartern 95
quarteron 41
quarters *abode* 189
take up one's – 184

radically 31
radication 613
radio 532
radio-active 171
316
radio-activity 420
radio-graph 421,
554
radiogram
wireless 532
X-ray 554
radiometer 420, 445
radiomicrometer
389
radiophone 418
radio star 899
radiotelegraph 534
radiotelephone 534
radium 423
radius 200, 202
radix 153
radoter 499
radoteur 501
raff 653, 876
raffle 156
Raffles
thief 792
raft 273
rafter 215
rag 32
tease 830, 856,
929
ragamuffin 876
rage *violence* 173
influence 175
excitement 824,
825
fashion 852
desire 865
wrath 900
the battle –s 722
ragged 226
ragoût 41, 298
rag-picker 876
rags *clothes* 225
useless 645
do to – 384
tear to – 162
worn to – 659
ragtime 415, 473
raid 716, 791
rail *inclosure* 232
prison 752
– at 932
– in
circumscribe 229
restrain 751
railing 232
raillerie, ne pas en-
tendre – 900
raillery 856
railway 627
– speed 274
– station 292
raiment 225
rain *stream* 348
sufficient 639
– or shine 474,
604
rainbow 440
raincoat 225
rainless 340
rains but it pours,
never – 641
rainy day 735
provide against
a – 673, 817

rainy season 348
raise *increase* 35
produce 161
erect 212
elevate 307
excite 824
– alarm 860
– anger 900
– one's banner
722
– a cry 531
– a dust 682
– expectations 858
– the finger 550
– funds 775
– one's head
improve 658
refresh 689
prosperity 734
repute 873
– ghosts 992
– hope 511
– a hue and cry
against 932
– a laugh 840
– the mask 529
– money 788
– a question 461,
485
– a report 531
– a siege 723
– the spirits 836
– spirits from the
dead 992
– a storm 173
– troops 722
– up 212, 824
– the voice 441
– one's voice 535,
932
– the wind 775,
778
raised *convex* 250
raison:
– d'être 620
– de plus 467
raj 737
rajah 745
rajpoot 726
rake *drag* 285
gardening 371
clean 652
profligate 949
intemperance 954
libertine 962
– out 301
– up *collect* 72
extract 301
recall 505
excite 824
– up evidence 467
rake-hell 949, 962
raking-fire 716
rakish
intemperate 954
licentious 961
rallentando 415
rally *arrange* 60
improve 658
restore 660
ridicule 856
encourage 861
– round *order* 58
co-operate 709
rallying: – cry 550,
861
– point 74

ram *impulse* 276
sheep 366
male 373
man-of-war 726
milk the – 645
– down 261, 321
– in 300
Ramadan 956, 993
ramage 367
ramble *stroll* 266
wander 279
folly 499
delirium 503
digress 573
rambler 269
rambling 139
ramification *part* 51
bisection 91
posterity 167
filament 205
symmetry 242
divergence 291
rammer 263, 276
ramose 242
ramp *slope* 217
climb 305
leap 309
rampage 173
rampant
violent 173
prevalent 175
vertical 212
raised 307
free 748
vehement 825
licentious 961
rampart 717
ramrod 263
ramshackle 665
ranch 780
rancid 401, 653
rancor 907, 919
randan 273
random *casual* 156
carriage 272
uncertain 475
aimless 621
talk at –
sophistry 477
exaggerate 549
loquacity 584
- *experiment* 463
chance 621
range *extent* 26
collocate 60
series 69
term 71
class 75
space 180
distance 196
roam 266
direction 278
stove 386
freedom 748
out– 196
long – 196
within – 197
–finder 200
– itself 58
– under, – with 76
ranger
director 694
keeper 753
thief 792
rank *have place* 1
degree 26
thorough 31

collocate 60
row 69
term 71
vegetation 365
fetid 401
estimate 480
bad 649
soldiers 726
glory 873
nobility 875
marr-of – 875
– and file
continuity 69
soldiers 726
commonalty 876
– marks 745
rankle *unclean* 653
corrupt 659
painful 830
animosity 900
malevolence 907
revenge 919
ranks
fill up the – 660
risen from the –
876
ransack *seek* 461
deliver 672
plunder 791
price 812
atonement 952
– one's brains
451, 515
ransom 672
rant
unmeaning 517
exaggeration 549
diffuse style 573
turgescence 577
speech 582
acting 599
excitement 825
boasting 884
ranter *talker* 584
false piety 988
rantipole 458
rap *blow* 276
sound 406
trifle 643
money 800
not worth a – 804
– on the knuckles
angry 900
censure 932
punish 972
– out *affirm* 535
voice 580
speak 582
– out oaths 885,
908
rapacity
taking 789
stealing 791
avarice 819
greed 865
rape 791, 961
– oil 356
rapid 274
– slope 217
– strides
progress 282
velocity 274
– succession 136
rapids 348
rapier 727
rapine 791
rapparee 792

rappel 722
rapping, spirit –
992
rapport 9
rapports, sous tous
les – 494
rapprochement
714, 888
rapscallion 949
rapt *attention* 457
inattention 458
emotion 821
– in thought 451
raptorial 789, 791
rapture 827, 897
rapturous 827
rara avis
exceptional 83
good 648
famous 873
rare *exceptional* 83
few 103
infrequent 137
light 322
excellent 648
raree show 448, 840
rarefaction 194, 322
rari nantes 103
rarity 322
rasa, tabula – 552
rascal 941, 949
rascality 940
rase *obliterate* 552
rash
skin disease 655
reckless 863
rasher 204
rashness 863
rasp 330, 331
rasper *difficult* 704
rasure 552
rat *recant* 607
smell a –
discover 480a
doubt 485
rataplan 407
rat-a-tat 407
ratchet 253
rate *degree* 26
motion 264
measure 466
estimation 480
price, tax 812
abuse 932
at a great – 274
rath *early* 132
fort 717
rather 32, 643
have – 609
– good 651
have – not 867
ratification
confirm 467
affirm 488
consent 762
compact 769
ratio *relation* 9
degree 26
proportion 84
apportionment
786
ratiocination 476
ration *quantity* 25
food 298
provisions 637
allotment 786
short –s 956

rational
- *quantity* 84
  intellectual 450
  judicious 498
  sane 502
rationale *cause* 153
  attribution 155
  answer 462
  interpretation 322
rationalism 476,
  989
rationalization 60
rats in the upper
  story 503
rattan 975
ratten 158
rattle *noise* 407
  music 417
  prattle 584
  death – 360
  watchman's – 669
  – on 584
rattle-snake 913
rattle-traps 780
rattling 836
  – *pace* 274
raucity 405, 410
raucous *hoarse* 581
ravage 162, 659
ravages of time 659
rave *madness* 503
  excitement 824,
  825
  – against 932
ravel *untwist* 60
  derange 61
  entangle 219
  difficulty 704
ravelin 717
ravelled 59
raven *black* 431
  hoarse 581
  gorge 957
  – for 865
ravening 173, 865
ravenous 789, 865
raver 504
ravine *interval* 198
  narrow 203
  dike 259
  channel 350
raving *mad* 503
  feeling 821
  excitement 824,
  825
ravish *seize* 789
  please 829
ravished
  pleased 827
ravishment 824
raw *immature* 123
  sensitive 378
  cold 383
  color 428
  unprepared 674
  unskilled 699
  – head and bloody
  bones 860
  – levies 726
  – material 635
raw-boned 203
ray 420
  – of comfort 831
rayah 745
rayless 421
raze 162
  – to the ground

308
razor 253
  cut a whetstone
  with a – 638
  misuse 679
  unskilful 699
  keen as a – 821
razzia
  destruction 162
  attack 716
  plunder 791
re, in – 9
reabsorb 296
reach *degree* 26
  equal 27
  distance 196
  fetch 270
  arrive at 292
  river 348
  deceive 545
  grasp 737
  take 789
  within – *near* 197
  possible 470
  – the ear
  hearing 418
  information 527
  – of thought 498
  – to *distance* 196
  length 200
reach-me-down
  673
reaction
  compensation 30
  reversion 145
  counteraction 179
  recoil 277
  restoration 660
reactionary 145,
  607
reactionist 710
read 522, 539
  well – 490
  – a lecture 537
readable 578
reader *teacher* 540
  printer 591
  clergyman 996
readership 542
readily 705
reading
  speciality 79
  knowledge 490
  interpretation 522
  learning 539
  – glass 445
  – in 995
reading-desk 1000
readjust 23, 27
readmit 296
ready
  expecting 507
  willing 602
  useful 644
  prepare 673
  active 682
  skilful 698
  cash 800
  get – 673
  make – 673
  – to burst forth
  825
  – made 673
  – memory 505
  – money 800
  – pen 569
  – to sink 824

– wit 842
reaffirm 535
reagent 463
real *existing* 1
  substantial 3
  – *number* 84
  true 494
  – estate 780
  – property 780
  – security 771
realism 494
realistic 17
realize
  speciality 79
  intellect 450
  think 451
  discover 480a
  believe 484
  conceive 490
  imagine 515
  accomplish 729
  acquire 775
  sell 796
really *wonder* 870
realm *region* 181
  people 372
  government 737
  property 780
realness 1
realty 780
ream 593
reamer 262
reanimate
  reproduce 163
  life 359
  resuscitate 660
reap *shorten* 201
  agriculture 371
  take 789
  – the benefit of
  be better for 658
  – and carry 775
  – the fruits
  succeed 731
  acquire 775
  reward 973
  – where one has
  not sown 923
  – the whirlwind
  product 154
  failure 732
reappear
  repetition 104
  reproduce 163
  visible 446
  restore 660
rear *sequel* 65
  end 67
  bring up 161
  erect 212
  back 235
  elevate 307
  teach 537
  in the – 281
  – its head
  manifest 525
  – one's head
  pride 878
rear-admiral 745
reason *cause* 153
  intellect 450
  thought 451
  argue 476
  wisdom 498
  motive 615
  by – of 615
  feast of – 588

in – *moderate* 174
  right 922
  listen to – 498
  stand to –
  certain 474
  proof 478
  manifest 525
  what's the – ? 461
  without rhyme
  or – 615a
  – in a circle 477
  – why 153, 615
reasonable
  moderate 174
  probable 472
  judicious 498
  sane 502
  cheap 815
  right 922
  – *prospect* 472
reasoner 476
reasoning 476
reasonless 499
reasons 476
reassemble 72
reassert 535
reassure 858, 861
reasty 401, 653
reave 789
rebate
  subtract 38
  decrement 40a
  moderate 174
  discount 813
rebeck 417
rebel 742
rebellion 715
rebellow 412
rebirth 660
reboation 412
rebound 277, 283
rebours, à –
  reversion 145
  regression 283
  difficult 704
rebuff *recoil* 277
  resist 719
  repulse 732
  refuse 764
  discourtesy 895
  censure 932
rebuild 660
rebuke 932
rebus 533
rebut *answer* 462
  counter evidence
  468
  confute 479
  deny 536
rebutter 462, 969
recalcitrant 719,
  742
recalcitrate 277,
  719
recalescence 382
recall
  recollect 505
  recant 607
  cancel 756
  – to life 660
recant *deny* 536
  retract 607
  resign 756
recapitulate
  enumerate 85
  repeat 104
  describe 594

in – *moderate* 174
  right 922
  summarize 596
recast
  revolution 146
  scheme 626
recede 283, 287
  – into the shade
  874
receipt
  scheme 626
  prescription 662
  precept 697
  security 771
  payment 807
  – of money 810
  – in full 807
receive *include* 76
  admit 296
  belief 484
  assent 488
  acquire 775
  take in 785
  take 789
  – *money* 810
  welcome 892, 894
  – Christ 987
received *known* 490
  habitual 613
  – *maxim* 496
receiver
  vessel 191
  treasurer 801
  official – 967
  – of stolen goods
  792
receiving 785
recension 85
recent 122, 123
receptacle 191
reception
  comprehension 54
  inclusion 76
  arrival 292
  ingestion 296
  interview 588
  receiving 785
  welcome 892, 894
  warm – 892
reception-room 191
recess
  receptacle 191
  corner 244
  regression 283
  ambush 530
  vacation 687
  retirement 893
recesses
  interior 221
  secret – of one's
  heart 820
recession
  motion from 287
Rechabite 958
réchauffé *copy* 21
  repetition 104
  food 298
  made hot 384
  restored 660
recherché 648, 852
recidivation
  regression 283
  relapse 607, 661
recipe *remedy* 662
  precept 697
recipient 191, 785
reciprocal 12, 84
reciprocate
  correlation 12

refluence recoil 277
  regress 283
reflux decrease 36
recoil 277
  regress 283
  current 348
refocillate
  strengthen 159
  refresh 689
reform convert 144
  improve 658
reformatory 542,
  752
reformer 658
refound 144
refraction
  deviation 279
  light 420
  fallacy of vision
  443
refractory
  obstinate 606
  difficult 704
  mutinous 742
  ill-tempered 901a
refrain poetry 597
  avoid 623
  do nothing 681
  temperate 953
  – from laughter
  837
  – from voting
  609a
refrain 104
refresh
  strengthen 159
  cool 385
  refit 658
  restore 660
  recruit 689
  relieve 834
  – the memory 505
refreshing 377, 829
refreshment
  food 298
  recruiting 689
  delight 827
refrigeration
  anesthetic 376
  making cold 385
refrigerator 387
reft 44
refuge 666
refugee 268, 623
refulgence 420
refund 807
refurbish 673
refusal 764
  pre-emption 795
refuse remains 40
  useless 645
  not consent 764
  – assent 489
  – to associate with
  893
  – to believe 487
  – to hear 460
refute 479
refuted 495
regain 775
  – breath 689
regal 737
regale feast 298
  physical pleasure
  377
  refresh 689
  pleasing 829

amusement 840
regalia 747
regality 737
regard
  relation 9
  view 441
  attention 457
  judge 480
  credit 873
  love 897
  respect 928
  approbation 931
  have – to 457
  merit – 642
  pay – to
  believe 484
  honor 873
  – as 484
regardful 457, 459
regardless 458, 823
regards 894, 928
regatta 720, 840
regency 755
regenerate
  reproduce 163
  restore 660
  piety 987
regeneration
  divine function
  976
  baptismal – 998
regent 745, 759
regicide 361
régime
  circumstances 8
  conduct 692
  authority 737
  ancien – 875
regimen diet 298
  remedy 662
  conduct 692
regiment 72, 726
regimentals 225
region 181
register
  arrange 60
  list 86
  chronicle 114
  record 551, 553
registrar 553
registration 551
registry 114
règle: en – 924
regnant 175, 737
regni, anno – 106
regorge 790
regrade 283
regrate 777
regrater 797
regression 283
regret 833, 950
  express – 952
regretted, to be –
  833
reguerdon 973
regular
  uniform 16
  complete 52
  order 58
  arrangement 60
  rule 80
  conformity 82
  periodic 138
  symmetric 242
  habitual 613
  by – intervals 58
  – return 138

regulars 726
regulate
  adjust 23
  arrange 60
  direct 693
regulated by
  conformity 82
regulation 697, 963
regurgitate
  return 283
  flow 348
  restore 790
rehabilitate 660,
  790
rehearse
  repeat 104
  try 463
  describe 594
  drama 599
  prepare 673
Reichsrath 696
reign 175, 737
  – of terror 739, 860
reimburse 790, 807
rein 752
  – in 275, 751
reincarnation 163
reindeer 271
re infectâ 304, 681
reinforce
  strengthen 159
  restore 660
  aid 707
reinforced concrete
  635
reinforcement
  addition 37
  adjunct 39
  materials 635
  provision 637
  aid 707
reinless 738
reins [see rein]
  direction 693
  give the – to
  facilitate 705
  lax 738
  permit 760
  hold the – 693
  take the – 737
  give – to the im-
  agination 515
reinstall 660
reinstate 660, 790
reinvest 790
reinvigorate 658,
  689
Reis Effendi 694
reiterate 104
reject
  exclude 55
  eject 297
  refuse 764
rejected
  hateful 898
rejection 610
rejoice exult 838
  amuse 840
  – the heart
  gratify 829
  cheer 836
  – in 827
  – in the name of
  564
rejoicing 838
rejoin assemble 72
  arrive 292

rejoinder
  answer 462
  law pleadings 969
rejuvenescence 660
rekindle
  ignite 384
  excite 824
relapse
  turn back 145,
  283
  fall back 661
relate narrate 594
  – to refer 9
related kin 11
relation 9
  kin 11
  narrative 594
relationship 9
relative 11, 464
  – position
relativity 9
relator
  accuser 938
relax loose 47
  weaken 160
  moderate 174
  slacken speed 275
  soften 324
  inactive 683
  repose 687
  misrule 738
  liberate 750
  relent 914
  – one's efforts 681
  – the mind 452
relaxation
  [see relax]
  amusement 840
  dereliction 927
relaxed weak 160
relay 635, 637
release death 360
  deliverance 672
  liberate 750
  exempt 760
  from engagement
  768a
  security 771
  restore 790
  repay 807
  forgive 918
  exempt 927a
  discharge 970
  deed of – 923
relegate banish 55
  transfer 270
  remove 297
relent moderate 174
  soften 324
  pity 914
relentless
  resolute 604
  severe 739
  wrathful 900
  malevolent 907
  revenge 919
  impenitent 951
relessee
  possessor 779
  receiver 785
relevancy 9, 23
relevé 298
reliable 474
reliance
  confidence 484
  hope 858
relic remainder 40

reminiscence 505
  token 551
relics corpse 362
  sacred 998
relict 40, 905
relief
  prominence 250
  aid 707
  comfort 834
  bas – 250, 557
  in strong – 446,
  525
relieve improve 658
  aid 707
  comfort 834
relievo 250, 557
religieuse 996
religion 983, 987
  under the mask
  of – 988
religionist 988
religious
  honorable 939
  theological 983
  pious 987
  over– 955
  – education 537
  – persuasion 983
  – sects 984
religiously exact
  494
relinquish 757
  – hope 859
  – life 360
  – property 782
  – a purpose 624
recant 607
relinquishment
  624, 782
reliquary 191, 998
reliquiæ 362
relish pleasure 377
  savor 390
  condiment 393
  savory 394
  delight 827
  desire 865
relive 660
relucent 420
reluct 720
reluctance
  dissuasion 616
  unwilling 603
  dislike 867
reluctation 719
relume 384, 420
rely 484, 858
rem acu tetigisti 23
remain be left 40
  endure 106
  long time 110
  continue 141
  be present 186
  stand 265
  – firm 150
  – on one's hands
  641
  – in one's mind
  505
  – neuter 605
  – in possession of
  the field 731
remainder 40
  estate 780
  in – posterior 117
remainder-man 779
remains

remainder 40
  corpse 362
  vestige 551
  organic – 357
remand defer 133
  order 741
remanet 40
remark observe 457
  affirmation 535
  worthy of – 642
remarkable
  great 31
  exceptional 83
  important 642
remarry 903
Rembrandtesque
  160
remediable, reme-
  dial 660, 662
remediless 859
remedy 660, 662
remembrance 505
remembrances 894
rememoration 505
remigration
  regression 283
  arrival 292
  egress 295
remind 505
  that –s me 134
reminiscence 505
remise 927a
remiss
  neglectful 460
  reluctant 603
  idle 683
  lax 738
remission
  cessation 142
  moderation 174
  laxity 738
  forgiveness 918
  exemption 927a
remit
  [see remission]
  – one's efforts 681
remittance 807
remittent
  periodic 138
remitter 790
remnant 40
remodel
  convert 144
  revolutionize 146
  improve 658
remonstrance 615,
  766, 932
remora cohere 46
  hindrance 706
remorse 950
remorseless 919
remote 10, 196
  – age 122
  – cause 153
  – future 121
remotest idea, not
  have – 491
remotion 270
remount 147
remove subduct 38
  term 71
  displace 185
  transfer 270
  recede 287
  depart 293
  dinner 298
  extract 301

school 541
  – the mask 529
removedness
  distance 196
remugient 412
remunerate 973
remunerative 644,
  775
renaissance 660
renascence 660
renascent 163
rencounter
  contact 199
  meeting 292
  fight 720
rend 44
  – the air 404, 411,
  839
  – the heart-strings
  830
render convert 144
  interpret 522
  give 784
  restore 790
  – an account
  inform 527
  describe 594
  – hors de combat 645
  – a service 644
rendering
  covering 223
rendezvous 72, 74
rendition
  interpretation 522
  restore 790
renegade
  convert 144
  turncoat 607
  fugitive 623
  apostate 941
renew twice 90
  repeat 104
  reproduce 163
  recollect 505
  improve 658
  restore 660
  – one's strength
  689
reniform 245
renitence
  counteraction 179
  hardness 323
  elasticity 325
  unwillingness 603
  resistance 719
renitency
  light 420
renounce
  recant 607
  relinquish 624
  resign 757
  abnegate 764
  – property 782
  repudiate 927
renovare dolorem,
  infandum – 833
renovate 160, 660
renovated new 123
renown 873
renownless 874
rent tear 44
  fissure 198
  hire 788
  purchase 795
rental 810
renter 188, 779
rent-free 815

rent-roll 780, 810
rents houses 189
renunciation
  [see renounce]
  exemption 927a
reorganize
  order 60
  convert 144
  improve 658
  restore 660
repair
  mend 658
  make good 660
  refresh 689
  out of – 659
  – to 266
reparation
  [see repair]
  compensation 30
  restitution 790
  atonement 952
  reward 973
repartee 462, 842
reparteeist 844
repartition 786
repass, pass and –
  314
repast 298
repatriation 790
repay 790, 807, 973
repeal 756
repeat imitate 19
  duplication 90
  iterate 104
  reproduce 163
  affirm 535
  – by rote 505
repeated 104, 136
repeater
  watch 114
  fire-arm 727
repel repulse 289
  deter 616
  defend 717
  resist 719
  refuse 764
  give pain 830
  disincline 867
  banish 893
  excite hate 898
repent 950
repercussion 277
répertoire 399
repertory 636
repetend
  arithmetical 84
  iteration 104
repetition 19, 104
repine
  pain 828
  discontent 832
  regret 833
  sad 837
replace
  substitute 147
  locate 184
  restore 660
replenish 52, 637
repletion
  filling 639
  redundance 641
  satiety 869
replevin
  recovery 775
  borrow 788
  restore 790
replica 21

replication
  answer 462
  law pleadings 969
reply 462, 937
répondre en
  Normand 544
report noise 406
  judgment 480
  inform 527
  publish 531
  news 532
  rumor 532
  record 551
  statement 594
  good – 873
  through evil re-
  port and good –
  604a
  – progress 527
reporter
  informant 527
  messenger 534
  recorder 553
  journalist 593,
  758
reports law 969
repose
  quiescence 265
  leisure 685
  rest 687
  – confidence in
  484
  – on support 215
  evidence 467
  – on one's laurels
  142
reposit 184
repository 636
repostum, manet
  alta mente –
  919
repoussé 250
reprehend 932
reprehensible 945,
  947
represent similar 17
  imitate 19
  exhibit 525
  intimate 527
  declare 535
  denote 550
  delineate 554
  commission 755
  deputy 759
  – to oneself 515
representation
  [see represent]
  copy 21
  portrait 554
  drama 599
representative
  typical 79
  commissioner 758
  deputy 759
  – government 737
  – of the people 696
  – of the press
  messenger 534
  writer 593
repress 751
  – one's feelings
  826
  – a smile 837
reprieve
  respite 133, 970
  deliverance 672
  release 750
  pardon 918

reprimand 932
reprint
  copy 21
  repetition 104
  reproduce 183
reprisal
  retaliation 718
  resumption 789
reprise 40a
reproach
  disgrace 874
  blame 932
  accusation 938
reprobate
  disapproved 932
  vicious 945
  bad man 949
  sinner 988
reprobation 932,
  988
reproduce
  imitate 19
  repeat 104
  renovate 163
reproduction [see
  reproduce] 21,
  163
reproductive 163
reproof 932
reprover 936
reptile
  animal 366
  servile 886
  knave 941
  miscreant 949
republic
  country 181
  people 372
  government 737
  – of letters 560
republican
  party 712
  government 737
  commonalty 876
republicanism 737
repudiate
  exclude 55
  deny 489
  reject 610
  abrogate 756
  violate 773
  not pay 808
  evade 927
repugn 719
repugnance
  incongruity 24
  resistance 719
  dislike 867
  hate 898
repulse recoil 277
  repel 289
  resist 719
  failure 732
  refusal 764
repulsion 157, 289
repulsive
  [see repulse]
  unsavory 395
  painful 830
  ugly 846
  disliked 867
  discourteous 895
  hateful 898
repurchase 795
reputable 873, 939
reputation 873
repute 873

beat a – 623
retreating
  concave 252
retrench *subduct* 38
  shorten 201
  lose 789
  economize 817
retribution
  retaliation 718
  payment 807
  punishment 972
  reward 973
retrieve *restore* 660
  acquire 775
retriever *dog* 366
retroaction
  counteraction 179
  recoil 277
  regression 283
retroactive
  past 122
retrocession
  regression 283
  recession 287
retrograde
  moving back 283
  deteriorated 659
  relapsing 661
retrogression
  regression 283
  deterioration 659
  relapse 661
retrospection
  past 122
  thought 451
  memory 505
retroussé 245
retroversion 218
retrude 289
return *list* 86
  repeat 104
  periodic 138
  reverse 145
  recoil 277
  regression 283
  arrival 292
  answer 462
  report 551
  relapse 661
  appoint 755
  profit 775
  restore 790
  proceeds 810
  reward 973
in –
  compensation 30
 – the compliment
  interchange 148
  retaliate 718
 – to the original
  state 660
 –ed *prodigal* 950
 – thanks 916, 990
return game 104
return match 104
reunion *junction* 43
réunion
  assemblage 72
  concord 714
 lieu de – 74
 point de – 74
 social – 892
revamp 140
revanche, en – 718
reveal 529
 – itself 446
reveille 550

réveiller le chat qui
  dort, ne pas –
  668, 864
revel 840, 954
 – in *enjoy* 377
revelation
  disclosure 480a,
  529
  theological 985
Revelations 985
reveller 840
  drunkard 959
revelling 59, 838
revendicate
  claim 741
  acquisition 775
  due 924
revenge **919**
  breathe – 900
revenons à nos
  moutons 283,
  660
revenue 632, 810
reverberate 277,
  408
reverberatory 386
revere *love* 897
  respect 928
  piety 987
reverence *title* 877
  respect 928
  piety 987
  clergy 996
reverenced 500
reverend 877, 996
reverent 987, 990
reverential 928
reverie
  train of thought
  451
  inattention 458
  imagination 515
reversal 218, 607
reverse *contrary* 14
  inversion 218
 – *of a medal* 235
  anteposition 237
  adversity 735
  abrogate 756
  cards 840
 – *of the shield* 468
reverseless 150
reversible 605
reversion
  [*see* reverse]
  posterity 117
  return 145
  possession 777
  property 780
  succession 783
  remitter 790
reversioner 779
revert *repeat* 104
  return 145
  turn back 283
  revest 790
 – to 457
revest 790
revet 223
reviction 660
review *consider* 457
  inquiry 461
  judge 480
  recall 505
  periodical 531
  dissertation 595
  compendium 596

entertainment 599
revise 658
  parade 882
reviewer 480, 595
revile 932, 988
reviler 936
revise *copy* 21
  consider 457
  printing 591
  plan 626
  improve 658
revising barrister
  967
revision, under –
  673
revisit 186
revival
  reproduction 163
  restoration 660
  worship 990
revivalist 996
revive
  reproduce 163
  improve 658
  resuscitate 660
  excite 824
revivify
  reproduce 163
  life 359
  improve 658
  resuscitate 660
revocable 605
revoir, au – 293
revoke 607, 756
revolt *resist* 719
  disobey 742
  shock 830
  disapproval 932
 – against *hate* 898
 – at the idea
  dissent 489
revolting
  painful 830
revolution
  periodicity 138
  change 146
  rotation 312
  disobedience 742
revolutionize 140,
  146
revolve
  [*see* revolution]
 – in the mind 451
revolver 727
revue 599
  intimate – 599
revulsion
  reversion 145
  revolution 146
  inversion 218
  recoil 277
reward **973**
reword 104
Reynard
  animal 366
  cunning 702
rez-de-chaussée
  191, 207
rhabdology 85
rhabdomancy 511
Rhadamanthus
  967, 982
rhapsodical
  irregular 139
  imaginary 515
rhapsodist
  fanatic 504

rhapsody
  discontinuity 70
  music 415
  nonsense 497
  fancy 515
  poetry 597
rhetoric *speech* 582
  flowers of – 577
rheum
  excretion 299
  fluidity 333
  water 337
rhino 800
rhinoceros hide
  376, 823
rhomb 244
rhumb 278
rhyme
  similarity 17
  verse 597
 without – or
  reason
  absurd 497
  caprice 608
  motiveless 615a
rhymeless 598
rhymester 597
rhythm
  periodicity 138
  melody 413
  elegance 578
  verse 597
rhythmical
 – *style* 578
rialto 799
rib *support* 215
  ridge 250
  wife 903
ribald *vulgar* 851
  disreputable 874
  impure 961
riband
  [*see* ribbon]
ribbed 259
ribbon *tie* 45
  filament 205
  record 550
  decoration 877
 –*s reins* 152
 handle the – 693
riboast 972
rich *savory* 394
  color 428
  language 577
  abundant 639
  wealthy 803
  beautiful 845
  ornament 847
 – man 803
riches 803
richesses, embarras
  de – 641, 803
richly *much* 31
 – *deserve* 924
rick 72, 846
rickety *weak* 160
  ugly 846
  imperfect 651
rickshaw 272
ricochet 277
ricordo, non mi –
  506
rid *deliver* 672
 get – of *eject* 297
  liberation 750
  loose 776
  relinquish 782

riddance 672, 776,
  782
 good – 776
riddle *arrange* 60
  sieve 260
  secret 533
  clean 652
ride *get above* 206
  move 266
  break in 370
 – at anchor 265
 – full tilt at 622,
  716
 – hard 274
 – one's hobby 622
 – rough shod
  violence 173
  severity 739
  insolence 885
  illegality 964
 – out the storm
  664
 – and tie
  periodicity 138
  journey 266
 – the whirlwind
  604, 737
rideau, lever de –
  599
ridentem dicere
  verum 836, 842
rider *appendix* 39
  equestrian 268
rideret Heraclitus
  853
ridge *narrow* 203
  height 206
  prominence 250
ridicule **856**, 929
ridiculous
  absurd 497
  foolish 499
  trifling 643
  grotesque 853
ridiculousness **853**
riding *district* 181
  journey 266
ridotto 840, 892
rifacimento 104,
  660
rife *existence* 1
  general 78
  influence 175
riff-raff *dirt* 653
  commonalty 876
  bad folk 949
rifle *musket* 727
  plunder 791
 – shot 406
rifled cannon 727
rifleman 726
rifler 792
rifles 726
rifle-shooting 840
rift 44, 198
 – within the lute
  651, 713
rig *dress* 225
  prepare 673
  frolic 840
  strumpet 962
 – the market 794
 run the – *upon* 929
rigadoon 840
rigging *ropes* 45
  gear 225
  instrument 633

riggish 961
right *dextral* 238
  straight 246
  true 494
  property 780
  just 922
  privilege 924
  duty 926
  honor 939
  virtuous 944
  bill of – 969
  by – 924
  have a – to 924
  set – *inform* 527
  disclose 529
  that's – 931
  – about
   [*see below*]
  – ahead 234
  – angle 212
  – ascension 466
  – away 133
  step in the – direc-
   tion 644
  – hand [*see below*]
  – itself 660
  – and left 180,
   227, 236
  – line 246
  – man in the right
   place 23
  in one's – mind
   498, 502
  hit the – nail on
   the head 480a,
   698
  – owner 779
  keep the – path
   944
  in the – place 646
  – thing to do 926
  – as a trivet 650
  – word in the
   right place 578
right about: to
  the – 283
  go to the – 311,
   607
  send to the –
  eject 297
  reject 610
  refuse 764
  turn to the – 218,
   279
right hand
  power 157
  dextrality 238
  help 711
  not let the – know
   what the left is
   doing 528
  – of friendship 888
righteous 944
  the – 987
  – overmuch 988
Righteousness:
  Lord our – 976
  Sun of – 976
rightful 922
  – owner 779
rightly served, be –
  972
right-minded 939,
  944
rights 748
  put to – 660
  set to – 60

stand on one's –
  748
rigid *regular* 82
  hard 323
  exact 494
  severe 739
rigmarole 517, 573
rigor. 383
  – *mortis* 360
rigorous *exact* 494
  severe 739
  revengeful 919
rigor 494, 739
Rigsdag 696
rigueur
  de – 744
rile *annoy* 830
  hate 898
  anger 900
rilievo *convex* 250
  sculpture 557
rill 348
rim 231
rime *chink* 198
  frost 283
rimer 262
rimple 258
rind 223
ring
  fastening 45
  pendency 214
  circle 247
  loud 404
  resonance 408
  test 463
  combination 709
  clique 712
  arena 728, 840
  badge 747
  rub the – 992
  have the true –
   494
  – the changes
  repeat 104
  change 140
  changeable 149
  – in the ear 408
  in a – fence 229,
   232
  – with the praises
   of 931
  – the tocsin 669
  – up 527
ringleader
  director 694
  mutineer 742
ringlet 247, 256
rink 840
rinse 652
rinsings 653
riot *confusion* 59
  derangement 61
  violence 173
  discord 713
  resist 719
  mutiny 742
  run – *activity* 682
  excitement 825
  intemperance 954
  – in *pleasure* 742
rioter 742
riotous 173
rip 949, 962
  – open 260
  – up *tear* 44
  recall the past 505
  excite 824

Rip van Winkle
  130
riparian 342
ripe 673
  – age *old* 128
ripen *perfect* 650
  improve 658
  prepare 673
  complete 729
  – into 144
rippet 713
riposte 462
ripple *ruffle* 256
  shake 315
  water 348
  murmur 405
ripuarian 342
rire, pour – 853
rise *grow* 35
  begin 66
  slope 217
  progress 282
  ascend 305
  stir 682
  revolt 742
  – again 660
  – in arms 722
  – from 154
  – to the occasion
   612
  – in price 814
  – up *elevation* 307
  – in the world 734
risible 838, 853
rising [*see rise*]
  – of the curtain
   66, 448
  – generation 127,
   167
  – ground
  height 206
  slope 217
  worship the – sun
   886
risk *chance* 621
  danger 665
  invest 787
  at any – 604
risqué 961
rissole 298
risum teneatis
  amici? 853
rite 963, **998**
  funeral – 363
ritornello 64, 104
ritual
  ostentation 882
  rite 998
ritualism 984
rival
  emulate 648
  oppose 708
  opponent 710
  compete 720
  combatant 726
  outshine 873
rivalry *envy* 921
rive 44
rivel 258
river **348**
rivet 43, 45
  – the attention
   457, 824
  – the eyes upon
   441
  – in the memory
   505

– the yoke 739
riveted *firm* 150
rivulet 348
rixation 713
Ro 560
road *street* 189
  direction 278
  way 627
  on the –
  transference 270
  progression 282
  approach 286
  on the high – to
   278
  – to ruin
  destruction 162
  danger 665
  adversity 735
road-book 266
roads *lake* 343
roadstead 154
  abode 189
  refuge 666
roadster 271
roadway 627
roam 266
roan *horse* 271
  color 433
roar *violence* 173
  wind 349
  sound 404, 407
  bellow 411, 412
  laugh 838
  weep 839
roaring *great* 31
  – trade 731, 734
roast *heat* 384
  ridicule 856
  rib – 972
  – and boiled 298
  – an ox 883
rob 354, 791
robber 792
robbery 791
robe 225, 999
robes – of state 747
Robin Goodfellow
  980
Robinson
  say Jack – 132
Robot 554
robust *strong* 159,
  654
roc 83
rocaille 853
rock *firm* 150
  oscillate 314
  hard 323
  land 342
  safety 664
  danger 667
  build on a – 150
  founded on a –
   664
  split upon a – 732
  – ahead 665
  –bound coast 342
  – oil 356
rocket *rapid* 274
  rise 305
  light 423
  ship 273
  signal 550
  arms 727,
  fireworks 840
  go up like a – and
   come down like

the stick 732
rocking-chair 215
rococo 124, 853
rod *support* 215
  measure 466
  scourge 975
  divining 993
  kiss the – 725
  sounding – 208
  – of empire 747
  – in pickle
  prepared 673
  accusation 938
  punishment 972
  scourge 975
rodeo 720, 840
rodomontade
  exaggeration 482
  unmeaning 517
  boast 884
roe 366, 374
Roentgen rays 420
rogation
  request 765
  worship 990
rogue *cheat* 548
  knave 941
  scamp 949
  –'s march 297
roguery 940
roguish
  playful 840
Roi le veut, le –
  741
roister 885
roisterer 887
Roland for an
  Oliver
  retaliation 716
  revenge 719
  barter 794
rôle *drama* 599
  business 625
  plan 626
  conduct 692
roll *list* 86
  fillet 205
  convolution 248
  rotundity 249
  make smooth 255
  move 264
  fly 267
  rotate 312
  rock 314
  flow 384
  sound **407**
  record 551
  money 800
  strike off the –
   756, 972
  – along 312
  – in the dust 731
  – on the ground
   839
  – of honour 86
  – in 639, 641
  – on 109
  – into one 43
  – in riches 803
  – up 312
  – up in 225
  – in wealth 803
roll-call 85
roller *fillet* 45
  round 249
  clothing 255
  rotate 312

schism *dissent* 489
  discord 713
  heterodoxy 984
schismless 983a
schistose 204
scholar 492, 541
scholarly 539
scholarship
  knowledge 490
  learning 539
  distinction 873
scholastic
  knowledge 490
  teaching 537
  learning 539
  school 542
scholiast 496, 522
scholium 496, 522
school
  herd 72
  multitude 102
  system of
   opinions 484
  knowledge 490
  teaching 537
  academy 542
  painting 556
  go to – 539
  send to – 537
schoolboy 129, 541
  familiar to every –
  490
schooldays 127
schoolfellow 541
schoolgirl 129, 541
schoolman 492, 983
schoolmaster 540
  – abroad 490, 537
schoolroom 191
schooner 273
schottische 840
sciatica 378
science 490, 698
scientific *exact* 494
scientist 476, 492
scimitar 727
scintilla *small* 32
  spark 420, 423
scintillate 446, 873
scintillation
  heat 382
  light 420
  wit 842
scintillula forsan,
  latet – 858
sciolism 491
sciolist 493
sciomachy 497
Sciomancy 511
scion *part* 51
  child 129
  posterity 167
scire: – facias 461
  – quid valeant
  humeri 698
scission 44
scissors 253
  – and paste 609
scissure 198
sclerotics 195
scobs 330
scoff *ridicule* 856
  deride 929
  impiety 988
  – at *despise* 930
  censure 932
scold *shrew* 901

malediction 908
  censure 932
scollop 248, 257
sconce *top* 210
  candlestick 423
  brain 450
  defence 717
  mulct 974
scone 298
scoop
  depression 252
  perforator 262
scooter 272
scope *degree* 26
  opportunity 134
  extent 180
  meaning 516
  freedom 748
scorch
  rush 274
  heat 382, 384
scorching
  violent 173
score
  music 60, 415
  count 85
  list 86
  twenty 98
  notch 257
  furrow 259
  mark 550
  success 731
  credit 805
  debt 806
  accounts 811
  on the – of
   relation 9
   motive 615
scores *many* 102
scoria *ash* 384
  dirt 653
scorify 384
scoring board 551
scorn 930
scorpion
  painful 830
  evil-doer 913
  (bane 663)
  chastise with –s
  739
scorse 794
scot *reward* 973
scot free *free* 748
  cheap 815
  exempt 927a
  escape –
   escape 671
  let off – 970
scotch *notch* 257
  injure 659
  – the snake
   maim 158
  insufficient 640
  non-completion
  730
  – the wheel 706
Scotsman
  canny 702
Scotticism 563
scotomy 443
scoundrel 913, 949
scour *run* 274
  rub 331
  clean 652
  – the country 266
  – the plain 274
scourge *bane* 663

painful 830
punish 972
instrument of
  punishment 975
– of the human
  race 913
scourings 645
scout 234
  observer 444
  feeler 463
  messenger 534
  reject 610
  warship 726
  servant 746
  watch 664
  warning 668
  disrespect 929
  disdain 930
  (looker 444)
  (underrate 483)
  (ridicule 856)
scow 273
scowl
  complain 839
  frown 895
  anger 900
  sullen 901a
  disapprobation
  932
scrabble
  unmeaning 517
  scribble 590
scrag 32, 203
scraggy *lean* 193,
  203
  rough 256
scramble
  confusion 59
  climb 305
  pursue 622
  haste 684
  difficulty 704
  contend 720
  seize 789
scranch 330
scrannel 643
scrap 32, 720
  – of *paper* 158, 940
scrap-book 596
scrape *subduct* 38
  reduce 195
  pulverize 330
  abrade 331
  mezzotint 558
  difficulty 704
  mischance 732
  bow 894
  – together
   assemble 72
   acquire 775
scraper 652
scratch *groove* 259
  abrade 331
  mark 550
  daub 555
  draw 556
  write 590
  hurt 619
  wound 649
  come to the –
  720, 861
  mere – 209
  old – 978
  up to the – 861
  without a – 654,
  670
  – the head 461

– out 552
scrawl 590
scrawny 203
screak 411
scream *cry* 411, 839
screech 411, 412
screech owl 412
screed 582, 593
screen *sift* 60
  sieve 260
  shade 424
  cinema 448
  hide 528
  hider 530
  side-scene 599
  clean 562
  safety 664
  shelter 666
  defence 717
  – from sight 442
screw *fasten* 43
  fastening 45
  distort 243
  oar 267
  rotation 312
  instrument 633
  miser 819
  put on the – 739,
  744
  – one's courage to
   the sticking
   place 861
  – loose *insane* 503
  imperfect 651
  unskilful 699
  hindrance 706
  attack 713
  – up *fasten* 43
  strengthen 159
  prepare 673
  – up the eyes 443
screwed
  drunk 959
screw-driver 633
screw-steamer 273
scribble 517, 590
scribbler 593
scribe *recorder* 553
  writer 590, 593
  priest 996
  –s and Pharisees
  988
scribendi, ca-
  coëthes – 580
scrimshanker 603
scrimmage 713, 720
scrimp *short* 201
  insufficient 640
  stingy 819
scrip 191
script 590, 599
scripta, lex – 963
scriptae, literae–590
scriptural 983a
Scripture
  certain 474
  revelation 985
scrivener *writer* 590
  lawyer 968
scroll 86, 551
scrub *rub* 331
  bush 367
  clean 652
  dirty person 653
  commonalty 876
scrubby *small* 193
  trifling 643

stingy 819
disreputable 874
vulgar 876
shabby 940
scruff 235
scruple
  small quantity 32
  weight 319
  doubt 485
  reluctance 603
  probity 939
scrupulous
  careful 459
  incredulous 487
  exact 494
  reluctant 603
  fastidious 868
  punctilious 939
scrutator 461
scrutiny 457, 461
scrutoire 191
scud *sail* 267
  speed 274
  shower 348
  cloud 353
  – under bare.
   poles 704
scuffle 720
scull *row* 267
  brain 450
scull-cap 225
scullery 191
scullion 746
sculpsit 558
sculptor 559
sculpture 240, 557
scum *dirt* 653
  – of the earth 949
  – of society 876
scupper 350
scurf 653
scurrilous
  ridicule 856
  malediction 908
  disrespect 929
  detraction 934
scurry 274, 684
scurvy
  insufficient 640
  unimportant 643
  base 940
  wicked 945
scut 235
scutcheon
  standard 550
  honor 877
scutiform 251
scuttle *destroy* 162
  receptacle 191
  speed 274
  – along *haste* 684
Scylla and Charyb-
  dis, between –
  danger 665
  difficulty 704
Scyllam, incidit
  in – 699
scythe *pointed* 244
  sharp 253
'sdeath! *wonder* 870
  anger 900
  disapprobation
  932
se non e vero e ben
  trovato 546
sea *multitude* 102
  ocean 341

at – 341
uncertain 475
erroneous 495
go to – 293
on the high –s 41
heavy – 315
the seven –s 341
– of doubt 475
– of troubles
difficulty 704
adversity 735
seaboard 342
seafarer 269
seafaring 267, 273
sea-fight 720
sea-girt 346
sea-going 267, 341
sea-green 435
seal
matrix 22
close 261
evidence 467
mark 550
resolve 604
complete 729
compact 769
security 771
break the – 529
under – 769
– the doom of 162
– one's infamy 940
– the lips 585
– of secrecy 528
– up *restrain* 751
sealed:
one's fate is – 601
hermetically – 261
– book
ignorance 491
unintelligible 519
secret 533
sealing-wax 747
seals *insignia* 747
sealskin 223
seam 43
sea-maid 979
sea-man 269
seamanship 692,
698
sea-mark 550
seamless 50
seamstress 225,
690
seamy side 651
séance 525, 696
sea-piece 556
seaplane 273, 736
sea-port 666
sear *dry* 340
burn 384
deaden 823
– and yellow leaf
128, 659
search *inquire* 461
searching
severe 739
painful 830
searchless 519
searchlight 423,
726
seared conscience
951
searing 830
seascape 556
sea-serpent 83
seaside 342
season *mix* 41

time 106
pungent 392
accustom 613
preserve 670
prepare 673
seasonable 23, 134
seasoning 393
seasons 138
seat *place* 183
locate 184
abode 189
support 215
posterior 235
parliament 693
country – 189
judgment – 966
– of government
737
– of war 728
seated, firmly – 150
seaway 180
seaweed 367
seaworthy 273, 604
sebaceous 355
secant 219
secede *dissent* 489
relinquish 624
disobey 742
seceder
heterodox 984
secern 297
seclusion **893**
second
duplication 90
– *of time* 108
instant 113
– *in music* 413,
415
abet 707
play or sing a –
416
– best 651, 732
– childhood 128,
499
– crop 168, 775
– edition 104
play – fiddle
obey 743
subject 749
disrepute 874
– nature 613
– to none 33
one's – self 17
– rate 659
– sight
foresight 510
sorcery 992
– thoughts
sequel 65
thought 451
improvement 658
– youth 660
secondary
inferior 34
following 63
imperfect 651
deputy 759
– education 537
– evidence 467
– school 542
seconder 711
second-hand
imitation 19
old 124
deteriorated 659
received 785
secondly 90

second-rate 651
secret *key* 522
latent 526
hidden 528
riddle **533**
in the – 490
keep a – 585
– motive 615
– passage 627, 671
– place 530
– writing 590
secrétaire 191
secretary
recorder 553
writer 590
director 694
auxiliary 711
servant 746
consignee 758
– of state 694
– of the treasury
801
secrete *excrete* 297
conceal 528
secretion 299
secretive 528
sect 75
religious – 983,
984
sectarian
dissent 489
ally 711
heterodox 984
sectary 489
section *division* 44
part 51
class 75
chapter 593
troops 726
sector *part* 51
circle 247
secula seculorum,
in – 112
secular
centenary 98
periodic 138
laity 997
– education 537
secularism 984
secundum artem
82, 698
secure *fasten* 43
bespeak 132
belief 484
safe 664
restrain 751
engage 768
gain 775
confident 858
– an object 731
securities 802–805
security *safety* 664
pledge **771**
hope 858
lend on – 787
Sedan
disaster 162
sedan chair 272
sedate
thoughtful 451
calm 826
grave 837
sedative 174, 662
sedentary 265
sedge 367
sedile 1000
sediment *dregs* 653

sedimentary 40
sedition 742
seduce *entice* 615
love 897
debauch 961
seducer 962
seduction 829, 865
sedulous 682, 865
see *view* 441
look 457
believe 484
know 490
bishopric 995
we shall – 507
– after 459
– daylight 480a
– double 959
– fit 600, 602
– at a glance 498
– justice done 922
– life 840
– the light
born 359
published 531
– service 722
– sights 455
– through 480a,
498
– to *attention* 457
care 459
direction 693
– one's way
foresight 510
intelligible 518
skill 698
easy 705
seed *small* 32
cause 153
posterity 167
grain 330
run to – *age* 128
lose health 659
sow the – 673
seedling 129
seed-plot 168, 371
seed-time of life
127
seedy *weak* 160
disease 655
deteriorated 659
exhausted 688
needy 804
seeing that 8, 476
seek *inquire* 461
pursue 622
offer 763
request 765
– safety 664
seek-sorrow 837
seel 217
seem 448
as it –s good to
600
seeming 488
seemingly 472
seemless 846, 925
seemliness 926
seemly
expedient 646
handsome 845
due 924
seep 295
seer *veteran* 130.
madman 504
oracle 513
sorcerer 994
see-saw 12, 314

seethe *wet* 339
hot 382
make hot 384
excitement 824
seething caldron
386
segar 392
segment 44, 51
ségnitude 683
s'égosiller 411
segregate
not related 10
separate 44
exclude 55
segregated
incoherent 47
seigneur, grand –
pride 878
insolence 885
seignior 745, 875
seigniority
authority 737
possession 777
property 780
seigniory 737
seine net 232
seisin 777, 780
seismic 314
seismograph 553
seismometer 276,
314
seize 789, 791
– an opportunity
134
seized with
disease 655
feeling 821
seizure 925
sejunction 44
seldom 137
select *choose* 609
good 648
self 13, 79
–abasement 879
–accusing 950
–admiration 880
–applause 880
–appointed task
602
–assertion 885
–called 565
–command 604,
864
–communing 451
–complacency
836, 880
–confidence 880
–conquest 604
–conscious 855
–consultation 451
–contained 52
–control 604
–conviction
belief 484
penitent 950
condemned 971
–counsel 451
–deceit *error* 495
–deception 486
–defence 717
–delusion 486
–denial
disinterested 942
temperance 953
penance 990
–discipline 990
–effacement 879,

942
—esteem 880
—evident 474, 525
—examination 990
—existing 1
—government 748
—help 698
—immolation 991
—indulgence
selfishness 943
intemperance 954
—interest 943
—knowledge 881
—love 943
—luminous 423
—mastery 604
—opinioned 481
—possession
sanity 502
resolution 604
inexcitability 826
caution 864
—praise 880
—preservation 717
—reliance
resolution 604
hope 858
courage 861
—reproach 950
—respect 878
—restraint 953
—sacrifice 942
—satisfied 880
—seeking 943
—styled 565
—sufficient 880
—taught 490
—tormentor 837
—will 606
selfishness 943
self-same 13
sell convince 484
absurdity 497
deception 545
untruth 546
sale 796
– for 812
– one's life dearly
719, 722
– off 796
– oneself 940
– out 796
seller 796
selon les règles 82
selvedge 231
semaphore 550
semblance
similarity 17
imitation 19
copy 21
probability 472
wear the – of
appearance 448
semeiology 522
semeiotics 550
semester 108
semi- 91
semi-barbarian 913
semibreve 413
semicircle 247
semicircular 245
semicolon 142
semi-diaphanous
427
semi-fluid 352
semi-liquidity 352
semi-lunar 245

seminal 153
seminary 542
semination 673
semi-opaque 427
semi-pellucid 427
semiquaver 413
semitone 413
semi-transparency
427
sempervirent 110
sempiternal 112
sempstress 225, 690
senary 98
senate 696
senate-house 966
senator 695, 696
senatorship 693
senatus consultum
741
send 270, 284
– adrift 597
– away
repel 289
eject 297
refuse 764
– for 741
– forth 284, 531
– a letter to 592
– off 284
– out eject 297
– packing 289
commission 755
– word 527
senescence 128
seneschal
director 694
master 745
servant 746
seneschalship 737
senile 128
senility 158, 659
senior age 128
student 541
master 745
seniores priores 62,
380
seniority 124, 128
sennight 108
señor 373, 877
señora 374
sensation
physical sensi-
bility 375
emotion 821
wonder 870
sensational 574,
824
sensation drama
599
sensations of touch
380
sense 498, 516
deep – 821
horse – 498
in no – 565
accept in a par-
ticular – 522
– of duty 926
senseless
insensible 376
absurd 497
foolish 499
unmeaning 517
senses
external - 375
intellect 450
sanity 502

sensibility **375, 822**
sensible
material 316
wise 498
sensitive 375, 822
sensorial 821
sensorium 450
sensual 377, 954
sensualist 954a
sensuous
sensibility 375
pleasure 377
feeling 821
sentence
decision 480
maxim 496
affirmation 535
phrase 566
condemnation 971
sententious 572,
574
sentient 375, 821
sentiment 453
sentimental
sensitive 822
affected 855
sentinel }263
sentry }
guardian 664
watch 668
keeper 753
separate disjoin 44
exclude 55
bisect 91
diverge 291
divorce 905
– the chaff from
the wheat
discriminate 465
select 609
– into elements 49
– maintenance 905
separation 49
separatist 489, 984
sepia 433
seposition 44, 55
sepoy 726
sept kin 11
class 75
clan 166
Septentrional 237
septett 415
septic 655, 657
septicemia 655
septuagenarian 98
Septuagint 985
septum 228
sepulcher 363
whited – 545
sepulchral
interment 363
resonance 408
stridor 410
hoarse 581
sepulture 363
sequacious 63
sequacity soft 324
tenacity 327
sequel 65, 117
sequela 65, 154
sequence
- in order 63
- in time 117
motion 281
logical – 476
sequent 63
sequester 789, 974

sequestered 893
sequestrate
seize 789
condemn 971
confiscate 974
sequin 847
serac 383
seraglio 961
seraph 948, 977
seraphic
blissful 829
virtuous 944
pious 987
seraphina 417
seraskier 745
sere and yellow
leaf 128
serein 339, 348
serenade music 415
compliment 894
endearment 902
serene
pellucid 425
calm 826
content 831
imperturbable 871
– highness 877
serf slave 746
clown 876
serfdom 749
sergeant 745
serial
continuous 69
periodic 183
book 593
seriatim
in order 58
continuously 69
each to each 79
slowly 275
series 69, 84
sérieux, take au –
843
serio-comic 853
serious great 31
resolved 604
important 642
dejected 837
seriously 535
serjeant:
common – 967
-at-law 968
sermon lesson 537
speech 582
dissertation 595
pastoral 998
funeral – 363
sermonizer 584
seroon 72
serosity 333, 337
serpent
tortuous 248
snake 366
hiss 409
wind instrument
417
wise 498
deceiver 548
cunning 702
evil-doer 913
knave 941
demon 949
the old – 978
great sea – 515
serpentine 248
serrated 244, 257
serried 72, 321

serum 333, 337
servant instrumen-
tality 631
help 711
retainer **746**
– of all work 690
serve benefit 618
business 625
utility 644
aid 707
warfare 722
obey 743
servant 746
– an apprentice-
ship 539
– faithfully 743
– loyally 743
– notice 527
– out 972
– one right
retaliation 718
right 922
punish 972
– as a substitute
147
– one's turn 644
– with a writ 969
service good 618
utility 644
use 677
warfare 722
servitude 749
worship 990
rite 998
hold – 363
at one's – 763
press into the –
677
render a – 644,
906
serviceable 644, 648
serviette 652
servile 749, 876, **886**
servitor 746
servitorship 749
servitude 749
penal – 972
sesame, open – 260
watchword 550
spell 993
sesqui- 87
sesquipedalia verba
577
sesquipedalian 200
sess 812
sessile 46
session council 696
sessions law 966
sestet 597
set
condition 7
join 43
coherence 46
group 72
class 75
firm 150
tendency 176
place 184
form 240
sharpen 253
direction 278
go down 306
dense 321
stage 599
habit 613
prepare 673
gang 712

impose 741
lease 771, 787
make a dead – at
716
– about 66, 676
– abroach 73
– one's affections
on 897
– afloat 153, 531
– against
oppose 708
quarrel 713
hate 898
angry 900
– against one
another 464
– agoing
impulse 276
propulsion 284
aid 717
– apart
separate 44
exclude 55
select 609
– aside
displace 185
disregard 458
neglect 460
negative 536
reject 610
disuse 678
annul 756
refuse 764
not observe 773
relinquish 782
dereliction 927
– one's back up
878
– before
inform 527
choice 609
– before oneself
620
– by 636
– one's cap at
897, 902
– on a cast 621
– down [*see below*]
– by the ears 898
– at ease 831
– an example
model 22
motive 615
– the eyes on 441
– one's face
against
oppose 708
refuse 764
disapprove 932
– the fashion
influence 175
authority 737
fashion 852
– fast 704
– on fire
ignite 384
excite 824
– on foot 66
– foot on 294
– forth *show* 525
assert 535
describe 594
– forward 293
– free 750
– going
[*see* – agoing]
one's hand to

467
– one's heart upon
604, 865
– at hazard 665
– in *begin* 66
rain 348
– on its legs 150
– on one's legs 159,
669
– in motion 264,
677
– to music 416
– at naught
make light of 483
reject 610
oppose 708
defy 715
disobey 742
not observe 773
dereliction 927
– no store by 483,
930
– off
compensation 30
depart 293
improve 658
discount 813
adorn 845
display 882
– on 615
– in order 60
– out *arrange* 60
begin 66
depart 293
decorate 845
display 882
– over 755
– phrase 566
– a price 85, 812
– purpose 620
– at rest *end* 67
answer 462
adjudge 480
complete 729
compact 769
– right
inform 527
disclose 529
teach 537
reinstate 660
vindicate 937
– to rights 60
– sail 293
– the seal on 729
– one's seal to 467
– store by 642
– straight 246, 723
– the table in a
roar 840
– one's teeth 604
– terms
manifest 525
phrase 566
style 574
– a trap for 545
– to 720, 722
– in towards 286
– up
printing 54
originate 153
strengthen 159
produce 161
upright 212
raise 307
successful 731
prosperous 734
– up shop 676

– upon
resolved 604
attack 716
desirous 865
– too high a value
upon 482
– watch 459
– one's wits to
work *think* 451
imagine 515
plan 626
– to work
undertake 676
impose 741
set-back 735
set down
record 551
unseat 756
humiliate 879
slight 929
censure 932
give one a –
confute 479
– as 484
– for 484
– a cause for
hearing 969
– to 155
– in writing 551
setaceous 256
seton 662
setose 256
settee 215
setter 366
settle *regulate* 60
establish 150
be located 184
bench 215
come to rest 265
subside 306
kill 361
decide 480
choose 609
vanquish 731
consent 762
compact 769
pay 807
– accounts 807,
811
– down 133
stability 150
moderate 174
locate oneself 184
– into 144
– matters 723
– preliminaries
673
– property 781
– the question 478
– to sleep 683
– upon *give* 784
– with 807, 992
settled [*see* settle]
characteristic 5
ended 67
account – 811
– opinion 484
– purpose 620
settlement [*see*
settle]
location 184
colony 188
dregs 653
compact 769
deed 771
property 780
strict – 781

settler 188
settlor 784
seven 98
–league boots 274,
992
wake the –
sleepers 404
seventy 98
sever 38, 44
several *special* 79
plural 100
many 102
– times 104
severalize 465
severally 44, 79
severalty 44
severance 38
severe
energetic 171
symmetry 242
exact 494
– *style* 576
harsh 739
painful 830
simple 849
critical 932
severely *very* 31
severity **739**
sew 43
sewage 299, 653
sewed up
drunk 959
sewer 350, 653
sewerage 652, 653
sewer-gas 663
sewing-silk 205
sex *kind* 75
women 374
fair – 374
sexagenarian 98,
130
sexagenary 99
sextant 217, 244,
247
sextet 98
sextodecimo 593
sexton 363, 996
sextuple 98
seyyid 745
sforzando 415
shabbiness 34
shabby *trifling* 643
deteriorated 659
stingy 819
mean 874
disgraceful 940
shabby-genteel 851
shack 189
shackle
fastening 45
hinder 706
restrain 751
fetter 752
shade *degree* 26
small quantity 32
manes 362
darkness 421
shadow **424**
color 428
conceal 528
screen 530
paint 556
ghost 980
eye – 443
in the – 528, 874
shadow of a – 32,
422

throw into the –
surpass 303
conceal 528
glory 873
throw all else into
the – 642
thrown into the –
34, 874
under the – of 664
without a – of
doubt 474
shades:
– below 982
– of death 360
– of difference 15
– of evening 422
shading 421
– off 26
shadow
unsubstantial 4
copy 21
small 32
accompaniment
88
thin 203
be behind 235
sequence 281
dark 421
shade 424
pursue 461, 622
dream 515
demon 980
fight with a – 699
follow as a – 281
partial – 422
without a – of
turning 141
worn to a –
thin 203
worse for wear
659
– of coming
events 511
– forth *dim* 422
predict 511
metaphor 521
represent 554
may your – never
be less
courtesy 894
respect 928
approbation 931
take the – for the
substance
credulous 486
mistake 495
unskilful 699
under the – of
one's wing 664
shadowy 4, 447
shady 874
shaft *deep* 208
frame 215
pit 260
missile 284
axis 312
air-pipe 351
handle 633
weapon 727
shaggy 256
shagreen 223
shah 745
shake *totter* 149
weak 160
vibrate 314
agitation 315
shiver 383

trill 407
music 416
dissuade 616
injure 659
impress 821
excited 824
fear 860
- one's faith 485
- hands
pacification 723
friendship 888
courtesy 894
forgive 918
- the head
dissent 489
deny 536
refuse 764
disapprove 932
- off 297
- off the yoke 759
- to pieces 162
- one's sides 838
- up 315
shakedown bed 215
shakes, no great -
643, 651
shako 225, 717
shaky weak 160
in danger 665
fearful 860
shallop 273
shallow
not deep 32, 209
ignorant 491
ignoramus 493
foolish 499
trifling 643
- pretext 617
- profundity 855
shallow-brain 501
shallowness 209
shallow-pated 499
shallows
danger 667
sham imitation 19
falsehood 544
deception 545,
546
- fight 720
shaman 994
shamanism 992
shamble 275, 315
shambles 361
shame
disrepute 874
wrong 923
censure 932
chastity 960
cry - upon 932
false - 855
for - 874
sense of - 879
- the devil 939
to one's - be it
spoken 874
shamefaced 881
shameful
disgraceful 874
profligate 945
shameless
bold 525
impudent 885
profligate 945
indecent 961
shampoo 652
shandredhan 272
shanghai 791

shank support 215
instrument 633
Shanks's mare 266
shanty 189
shape 240, 448
- one's course
direction 278
pursuit 622
conduct 692
- out a course 626
shapeless 241, 846
shapely 242, 845
shard 51
share
part 51
participate 778
allotted portion
786
- and share alike
778
shareholder 778
shark 792
sharp
energetic 171
violent 173
acute 253
sensible 375
pungent 392
- sound 410
musical tone 413
intelligent 498
active 682
clever 698
cunning 702
feeling 821
painful 830
rude 895
censorious 932
look - 459, 682
- appetite 865
- contest 720
- ear 418
- eye 441
- fellow 682, 700
- frost 383
- look-out 459,
507
- pain 378
- practice
cunning 702
severity 739
improbity 940
- set 865
sharpen
[see sharp]
excite 824
- one's tools 673
- one's wits 537
sharpener 253
sharper 792
sharpness 253
sharpshooter 726
sharpshooting 716
Shaster 986
shatter disjoin 44
disperse 73
render powerless
158
destroy 162
shatter-brained 503
shattered 160, 688
shave reduce 195
shorten 201
layer 204
smooth 255
grate 330
lie 546

close - 671
shaved 226
shaving small 32
layer 204
filament 205
shave-tail 726, 745
shawl 225
shawm 417
shay 272
she 374
sheaf 72
shear reduce 195
shorten 201
sheep 370
take 789
shears 253
sheath 191, 223
sheathe 225
moderate 174
- the sword 723
sheathing 223
sheave 633
shed scatter 73
building 189
divest 226
emit 297
give 784
- blood 361
- light upon 420
- a luster on 873
- tears 839
Shedim 980
sheen 420
sheep 366
sheep-dog 366
sheep-fold 232
sheepish 881
sheep's eye, cast a -
desire 865
modest 881
endearment 902
sheer simple 42
complete 52
deviate 279
- off avoid 623
sheet layer 204
covering 223
paper 593
come down in -s
rain 348
white - 952
winding - 363
- of fire 382
- of water 343
sheet-anchor
safety 664, 666
hope 858
sheet-lightning 423
sheik ruler 745, 875
lover 897
priest 996
shelf 215, 667
on the -
powerless 158
disused 678
inaction 681
shell cover 223
coffin 363
bombard 716
bomb 727
-burst 404
-shock 655
- out 784, 807,
809
shellac 356a
shellback 269
shell-fish 366

shelter 664, 666
- oneself under
plea of 617
sheltie 271
shelve defer 133
locate 184
slope 217
neglect 460
disuse 678
shelving beach 217
shend 659
shepherd tender of
sheep 370
director 694
pastor 996
Shepherd, the Good
- 976
shepherd's dog 366
Sheppard, Jack -
792
shere 32
sheriff 745, 965
Shetland pony 271
shew [see show]
shibboleth 550
shield
heraldry 550
safety 664
buckler 666
defend 717
scutcheon 877
look only at one
side of the - 481
reverse of the -
235, 468
under the - of 664
shift change 140
convert 144
substitute 147
changeable 149
chemise 225
move 264
transfer 270
deviate 279
prevaricate 546
plea 617
cunning 702
last - 601
make a - with
147, 677
put to one's -s
704, 804
- one's ground
607
- off defer 133
- for oneself 692,
748
left to - for one-
self 893
- one's quarters
264
- the scene 140
- to and fro 149
shifting [see shift]
transient 111
- sands 149
- trust or use 783
shiftless 674, 699
shillelagh 727
shilling 800
cut off with a -
789
- shocker 594
shilly-shally 605
shimmer 420
shimmy
dance 840

shindy 720
shine light 420
beauty 845
glory 873
take the - out of
874
- in conversation
588
- forth 873
- upon
illumine 420
aid 707
shingle 330
shingled
hair 53
shingles 223
shining [see shine]
- light sage 500
Shintoism 984
shiny 420
ship lade 190
transfer 270
vessel 273
take - 267, 293
one's - coming in
803
- of the line 726
shipboard, on - 273
ship-load 31, 190
shipman 269
shipmate 890
shipment
contents 190
transfer 270
shippen 189
shipping 273
shipshape order 58
conformity 82
skill 698
shipwreck
destruction 162
vanquish 731
failure 732
shire 181
shirk 603, 623, 742
shirker 862
shirt 225
Shiva 979
shive 22, 204
shiver
small piece 32
divide 44
destroy 162
filament 205
shake 315
brittle 328
cold 383
fear 860
go to -s 162
- in one's shoes
860
shivery brittle 328
powdery 330
shoal
assemblage 72
multitude 102
shallow 209
shoals danger 667
surrounded by -
difficulty 704
shoat 366
shock sheaf 72
violence 173
concussion 276
agitation 315
unexpected 508
disease 655

discord 713
affect 821
move 824
pain 828
give pain 830
dislike 867
scandalize 932
shocking bad 649
painful 830
ugly 846
vulgar 851
fearful 860
disreputable 874
hateful 898
in a – temper 901a
shockingly much 31
shod 225
shoddy 645
shoe support 215
dress 225
hindrance 706
stand in the -s of
commission 755
deputy 759
where the –
pinches
badness 649
difficulty 704
opposition 708
sensibility 822
painful 830
shoemaker 225
shofle 272
shoful 792
shog 173
shoneen 855
shoot
offspring 167
expand 194
dart 274
propel 284
kill 361
sprout 365, 367
pain 378
execute 972
teach the young
idea to – 537
– ahead 282
– ahead of 303
– at 716
– out beams 420
– up increase 35
prominent 250
shooting
[see shoot]
chase 622
– pain 378
– star 318, 423
shooting-coat 225
shop 795, 799
keep a – 625, 794
shut up – end 67
cease 142
relinquish 624
rest 687
smell of the – 851
shopkeeper 797
shoplifter 792
shoplifting 791
shopman 797
shopmate 890
shopping 794, 795
shore
support 215
border 231
land 342
buttress 717

hug the – 286
on – 342
– up 215, 670
shoreless 180
shorn cut short 21
deprived 776
– of its beams
422, 874
– lamb 828
short
not long 201
brittle 328
concise 572
uncivil 895
come – of, fall – of
inferior 34
shortcoming 304
insufficient 640
in – 572, 596
– allowance 640
– answer 895
– breath 688
– by 201
– of cash 804
– commons
insufficiency 640
fasting 956
– circuit 279, 628
– cut straight 246
mid-course 628
– distance 197
– life and merry
840
– measure 53
at – notice 111,
132
– of small 32
inferior 34
subtraction 38
incomplete 53
shortcoming 304
insufficient 640
– sea 348
make – work of
destroy 162
active 682
haste 684
complete 729
conquer 731
punish 972
shortage 53
shortcoming
inequality 28
inferiority 34
motion short of
304
non-completion
730
deficiency 945
shorten 201
– sail 275
shorthand 590
short-handed 651
shorthorn 366
short-lived 111
shortly soon 132
shortness 201
for – sake 572.
shorts 225
short-sighted
myopic 443
misjudging 481
foolish 499
short-story 594
short-winded 160,
688
short-witted 499

shot missile 284
report 406
variegated 440
guess 514
war material 722,
727
price 812
reward 973
bad – 701
exchange -s 720
good – 700
have a – at 716
like a – 113
off like a – 623
pistol – 406
random – 463, 621
round – 727
– in the locker 632
not have a – in
one's locker 804
– and shell 722
shot-free 815
shot-gun 727
should be:
no better than
she – 961
what – 922
shoulder
support 215
projection 250
shove 276
broad -ed 159
cold – 289
have on one's -s
625
on the -s of
high 206
elevated 307
instrumentality
631
shrug the -s
[see shrug]
rest on the -s of
926
rub -s with no-
bility 852
take upon one's -s
676
– arms 673
– a musket 722
– to shoulder 709,
712
– to the wheel
604, 676
shoulder-knot 847
shoulder-strap 747
shout
loud 404
cry 411
rejoice 838
shove 276
give a – to
aid 707
shovel
receptacle 191
transfer 270
vehicle 272
fire-iron 386
cleanness 652
put to bed with
a – 363
– away 297
shovel-hat 999
show visible 446
appear 448
draw attention
457

evidence 467
demonstrate 478
manifest 525
entertainment 599
parade 882
dumb – 550
make a – 544
mere – 544
peep– 840
– off 525
– one's cards 529
– cause 527
– one's colors,
550
– one's face
presence 186
manifest 525
disclose 529
– fight defy 715
attack 716
defend 717
brave 861
– forth 525
– in front 303
– one's cards 529
– one's hand 529
– a light pair of
heels 623
– itself 446
– of 17, 472
– off 882, 884
– one's teeth 715
– up visible 446
manifest 525
ridicule 856
degrade 874
censure 932
accuse 938
shower
assemblage 72
rain 348
– bath 386
– down
abundance 639
– down upon 784,
816
showman 524
showy color 428
beauty 845
ornament 847
fashion 852
vulgar 851
ostentatious 882
shrapnel 727
shred 32, 205
shredder 260
shrew 901
shrewd
knowing 490
wise 498
cunning 702
shriek 410, 411
shrievalty 965
shrieve 965
shrift
confession 529
absolution 952
shriftless 951
shrill 410, 411
shrimp 193
shrine 363, 1000
receptacle 191
shrink
decrease 36
shrivel 195
go back 283, 287
unwilling 603

avoid 623
sensitive 822
– from fear 860
dislike 867
hate 898
shrive 952, 998
shrivel 195
shrivelled thin 203
shroud cover 225
funeral 363
hide 528
safety 664
defend 717
–ed in mystery
519
shrouds 45
Shrove Tuesday
998
shrub plant 367
plantation 371
shrug sign 550
– the shoulders
dissent 489
submit 725
discontent 832
dislike 867
contempt 930
disapprobation
932
shrunk 193, 195
shudder cold 383
fear 860
make one –
painful 830
– at aversion 867
hate 898
shuffle mix 41
derange 61
change 140
interchange 148
changeable 149
move slowly 275
agitate 315
falsehood 544
untruth 546
irresolute 605
recant 607
dance 840
improbity 940
– the cards
begin again 66
change 140
chance 621
prepare 673
patience and –
the cards 826
– off run away 623
– off this mortal
coil 360
– on 266
shuffler 548
shun 623, 867
shunt 270, 279
shunted
shelved 460
shut 261
– the door 761
– the door in one's
face 764
– the door upon
893
– one's ears 419,
487
– the eyes 442
– one's eyes to
not attend to 458
neglect 460

smooth *uniform* 16
calm 174
flattery 213, 251
not rough 255
easy 705
– the bed of death 707, 906
– down 174
– over 174
– the ruffled brow of care 834
– sailing 705
– water *easy* 705
– the way 705
smooth-bore 727
smoothly, go on – *prosperous* 734
smoothness 255
smooth-tongued 544, 933
smother
repress 174
kill 361
stifle sound 581
restrain 751
smoulder *inert* 172
burn 382
latent 526
smous 796, 797
smudge 431, 653, 848
smug *affected* 855
smuggle
introduce 228
steal 791
illegal 964
smuggler 792
smut
dirt 653
impurity 961
smutch 431
snack
small quantity 32
food 298
snacks, go – 778
snaffle 752
snag *projection* 250
sharp 253
danger 667
hindrance 706
snail *slow* 275
snake *undulation* 248
serpent 366
hissing 406
miscreant 913
scotch the – 640
– in the grass
hidden 528
deceiver 548
bad 649
source of danger 667
evil-doer 913
knave 941
snake-like
convoluted 248
snap *break* 44
eat 298
brittle 328
noise 406
rude 895
– at *seize* 789
bite 830
censure 932
– of the fingers
trifle 643

– one's fingers at *defy* 715
insolence 885
despise 930
– the thread 70
– up *seize* 789
– one up
censure 932
–shot 554
snap-dragon 840
snappish 901
snare *deception* 545
snarl *growl* 412
rude 895
angry 900
threaten 909
snatch
small quantity 32
seize 789
– at *pursue* 622
seize 789
– a grace beyond the reach of art 845
– from one's grasp 789
– from the jaws of death 662, 672
– from under one's nose 702
– a verdict 545, 702
snatches, by – 70
sneak *hide* 528
coward 862
servile 886
base 940
knave 941
bad man 949
– off, – out of 623
sneer *disparage* 929
contempt 930
blame 932
sneeze *blow* 349
snuffle 409
– at *despise* 930
sneezed at, not to be – 642
snick 32, 51
snicker 838
sniff *blow* 349
odor 398
discovery 480a
sniffle 349
snigger *laugh* 838
ridicule 856
disrespect 929
sniggle 545
snip
small quantity 32
cut 44
short 201
tailor 225
sniping 716
snippet 32
snip-snap 713
snip-snap-snorem 840
snivel *weep* 839
sniveling
servile 886
snob *vulgar* 851
plebeian 876
servile 886
snobbishness
flattery 933
snood

headdress 225
circle 247
snooker 840
Snooks, Mr. – 876
snooze 683
snozzle 250
snore 411, 683
snort 411, 412
snout 250
snow *ship* 273
ice 383
white 430
snow-ball 72
snow-blindness 443
snow-drift 72
snow-shoe 272
snow-storm 383
snub *short* 201
hinder 706
cast a slur 874
humiliate 879
bluster 885
censure 932
snub-nosed 243
snuff *blow* 349
pungent 392
odor 398
up to – 698, 702
go out like the – of a candle 360
– out 162, 421
– up 296, 398
snuff-color 433
snuffing, want – *pert* 885
snuffle *blow* 349
hiss 409
stammer 583
hypocrisy 988
snuffy 653
snug *closed* 261
comfortable 377
safe 664
prepared 673
content 831
secluded 893
keep – 528, 893
make all – 673
snuggery 189
snugness 827
so *similar* 17
very 31
therefore 476
method 627
– be it 488, 762
– far so good 618
– let it be 681
– much the better 831, 838
– much the worse 832, 835
– to speak 17, 521
soak *immerse* 300
water 337
moist 339
drunkenness 959
– up 340
So-and-so, Mr. – *neology* 563
soap *lubricate* 332
oil 356
cleanser 652
soapy *unctuous* 355
servile 886
flattery 933
soar *great* 31
height 206

fly 267
rise 305
sob 839
sober *moderate* 174
wise 498
sane 502
style 576
grave 837
temperate 953
abstinent 958
– down 174, 502
humility 879
in – sadness
affirmation 535
– senses 502
– truth *fact* 494
sober-minded 502
calm 826
humble 879
sobriety 958
sobriquet 565
sob sister 534
so-called 545, 565
soc *jurisdiction* 965
socage 777
soccer 840
sociable
carriage 272
sociality 892
social *mankind* 372
sociable 892
– circle 892
– evil 961
– gathering 892
– science 910
socialism
government 737
participation 778
philanthropy 910
socialist 712
sociality 892
society
mankind 372
party 712
fashion 852
sociality 892
position in – 873
Socinianism 984
sociology 712
sock *hosiery* 225
drama 599
socket 191, 252
socle 215
Socratic method 461
sod 344
beneath the – 363
sodality 712, 888
sodden 339, 384
sofa 215
Sofi 984, 996
soft *stop!* 142
weak 160
moderate 174
smooth 255
not hard 324
moist 339
marsh 345
silence! 403
– *sound* 405
dulcet 413
credulous 486
silly 499
lenient 740
tender 822
timid 862
own to the – *im-*

peachment 529
– *music* 415
– *pedal* 405
– *sawder* 617, 933
– *soap* 356, 933
– *tongue*, – *words* 894
soften [*see* soft]
moderate 174
relieve 834
pity 914
palliate 937
softening of the brain 158
softer sex 374
soft-hearted 914
softling 160
softness 324
persuasibility 615
soft-spoken 894
soggy 339
soho
attention 457
parley 586
hunting 622
soi-disant
asserting 535
pretender 548
misnomer 565
vain 880
boastful 884
soil *region* 18
land 342
dirt 653
deface 846
till the – 371, 673
soirée 892
sojourn 186, 189
sojourner 188
soke 181
solace *relief* 834
recreation 840
– oneself with *pleasure* 827
solar 318
– system 318
– time 114
solatium 973
sold to the devil 949
soldan [*see* sultan]
solder *join* 43
cement 45
cohere 46
soldier 726
soldier-like 722, 861
sole *alone* 87
base 211
support 215
feme – 904
solecism 568
soleil, coup de – *hot* 384
mad 503
solemn
affirmation 535
important 642
grave 837
glorious 873
ostentatious 882
religious 987
worship 990
– *mockery* 882
– *silence* 403
solemnity *rite* 998
solemnization 883
sol-fa 416

solfeggio 415
solicit *induce* 615
  request 765
  desire 865
  – the attention
    457
solicitor *agent* 758
  petitioner 767
  lawyer 968
solicitous 865
solicitude *care* 459
  pain 828
  anxiety 860
  desire 865
solid *complete* 52
  dense 321
  certain 474
  learned 490
  exact 494
  wise 498
  persevering 604a
  solvent 803
  – *angle* 244
solidarity
  party 712
solidify 321
soliloquy **589**
solitaire *game* 840
  hermit 893
solitary) *alone*
solitude)   87
  secluded 893
solmization 416
solo 87, 415
  – *dance* 840
Solomon) *wise*
Solon   ) 498
  sage 500
solstice 125, 126
soluble *fluid* 333
  liquefy 335
solus 87
solution
  liquefaction 335
  answer 462
  explanation 522
  – *of continuity* 70
solve *liquefy* 335
  discover 480a
  unriddle 522
solvent
  liquefier 335
  monied 803
somatics 316
somber *dark* 421
  black 431
  grey 432
  sad 837
sombrero 225
some *indefinite*
  quantity 25
  small quantity 32
  more than one
    100
  –body *person* 372
  important or dis-
    tinguished 642
  in – *degree*
    degree 26
    small 32
  at – *other time* 119
  in – *place* 182
  – ten or a dozen
    102
  – time ago 122
  – time or other
    119

somehow or other
  cause 155
  instrument 631
somersault 218
something *thing* 3
  small degree 32
  matter 316
  – else 15
  – like 17
  – or other 475
sometimes 136
somewhat
  a little 32
  a trifle 643
somewhere 182
  – about 32
somnambulism
  walking 266
  trance 515
somnambulist
  walker 268
  dreamer 515
somniferous
  sleepy 683
  weary 841
somnolence 683
son 167
Son, God the – 976
sonant 402
  letter 561
sonata 415
Sonderbund 769
song *music* 415
  poem 597
  death – 360, 839
  love– 597
  for a mere – 815
  no – no supper 812
  old – 643
songster 416
soniferous 402
sonnet 597
sonneteer 597
sonorous *sound* 402
  loud 404
  language 577
sons of:
  – Belial 988
  – God 977
Soofeeism 984
soon *transient* 111
  future 121
  early 132
  too – for 135
sooner: – or later
  another time 119
  future 121
  – said than done
    704
soot 431, 653
sooth 511
  in good – 543
soothe
  allay 174
  relieve 834
  flatter 933
soothing
  faint sound 405
  – *syrup* 174
soothsay 511
soothsayer 513, 994
soothsaying 511
sop
  small quantity 32
  food 298
  fool 501
  inducement 615

  reward 973
  – to Cerberus 458
  – in the pan 615
soph 492, 541
Sophi 745, 996
sophism 477, 497
sophist *scholar* 492
  dissembler 548
sophister 492
  student 541
sophistical 477
sophisticate *mix* 41
  debase 659
sophisticated
  spurious 545
sophistry **477**
sophomore 541
soporific 683, 841
soporous 683
soprano 410, 416
sorbet 298
sorcerer **994**
sorcery **992**
sordes 653
sordet 417
sordid *stingy* 819
  covetous 865
sordine 417
sore
  bodily pain 378
  disease 655
  mental suffering
    828, 830
  discontent 832
  anger 900
  – as a boil 901a
  – place 822
  – *subject* 830, 900
sorely *very* 31
s'orienter 278
sorites 476
sorority 712
sorrel 433, 434
sorrow 828
  give – words 839
sorry *trifling* 643
  grieved 828
  mean 876
  make a – face 874
  cut a – figure 874
  be – for 750, 914
  in a – plight 732
  – sight 830, 837
sort *degree* 26
  arrange 60
  kind 75
  – *with*
    sociality 892
sortable   )
sortance   )
  agreement 23
sortes
  chance 156, 621
  – Virgilianæ
  sorcery 992
sortie 716
sortilege
  prediction 511
  sorcery 992
sortilegy 621
sortition 621
sorts, out of –
  ill-health 655
  sulky 901a
S.O.S. 669, 707
so-so *small* 32
  trifling 643

  imperfect 651
sostenuto 415
sot *fool* 501
  drunkard 959
sot à triple étage
    501
sotto voce
  faint sound 405
  conceal 528
  voiceless 581
sou *money* 800
  qui n'a pas le –
    804
soubrette 599, 746
sough *conduit* 350
  noise 405
  cloaca 653
soul *essence* 5
  person 372
  intellect 450
  genius 498
  affections 820
  cure of –s 995
  flow of – 588
  not a – 187
  not dare to say
    one's – is his
    own *subjection*
    749
  fear 860
  – of wit 572
  have one's whole
    – in his work
    686
soulless 683, 823
soul-mate 905
soul-sick 837
soul-stirring 821,
    824
sound *great* 31
  conformable 82
  stable 150
  strong 159
  fathom 208
  bay 343
  noise **402**
  investigate 461
  measure 466
  true 494
  wise 498
  sane 502
  good 648
  perfect 650
  healthy 654
  solvent 803
  orthodox 983a
  catch a – 418
  safe and – 654,
    670
  – the alarm
    indication 550
    warning 668
    alarm 669
    fear 860
  – asleep 683
  full of – and fury
    unmeaning 517
    insolent 885
  – the horn 416
  – of limb 654
  – locator 726
  – mind 502
  – the praises of
    931
  – the note of prep-
    aration 673
  – reasoning 476

  – a retreat 283
  – sleep 683
  – a trumpet
    publish 531
    alarm 669
  – of wind 654
sounding: big –
    577
  – brass 517
sounding-board 417
soundings 208
soundless
  unfathomable 208
  silent 403
soup 298, 352
soupçon 32, 41
souplé 298
sour *acid* 397
  discontented 832
  embitter 835
  uncivil 895
  sulky 901
  – grapes
    impossible 471
    excuse 617
  – the temper 830
source *beginning* 66
  cause 153
sourdet 417
sourdine 417
  à la – *noiseless* 405
  concealed 528
sourdough 463
soured 832
sourness **397**
sous tous les
  rapports 52
souse 310, 337
South *direction* 278
  North and –
  opposite 237
Southern
  antipodes 237
  – Cross 318
souvenir 505
sovereign
  superior 33
  all-powerful 159
  authorities 737
  ruler 745
  – contempt 930
  – *remedy* 662
Soviet 696, 737
sow *scatter* 73
  pig 366
  agriculture 371
  female 374
  get the wrong –
    by the ear
    misjudgment 481
    error 495
    mismanage 699
    fail 732
  – broadcast 818
  – dissension 713,
    898
  – the sand 645
  – the seed
    prepare 673
  – the seeds of
    cause 153
    teach 537
  – one's wild oats
    improve 658
    amusement 840
    vice 945
    intemperance 954

sozzled 959
spa *town* 189
sanatorium 662
space *distribute* 60
time 106
extension 180
musical 413
ship 273
celestial –s 318
wide open –'s 180
spaddle 272
spade 272
call a – a spade
plain language
576
straightforward
703
spade-husbandry
371
spahi 726
span *join* 43
link 45
duality 89
time 106
transient 111
distance 196
near 196
length 200
short 201
measure 466
– new 124
spangle *spark* 420
ornament 847
spaniel *dog* 366
servile 886
spanish fly 171
spank *swift* 274
flog 972
spanking *large* 192
– pace 274
spanner 633
spar *beam* 214
quarrel 713
contend 720
spare *extra* 37
small 193
meagre 203
refrain 623
store 636
scanty 640
redundant 641
disuse 678
inaction 681
relinquish 782
give 784
economy 817
exempt 927a
temperate 953
enough and to –
639
not a moment to –
682
to – 641
– diet 956
– no expense 816
– no pains 686
– room 180
– time 685
spared: be –
live 359
it cannot be – 630
sparge 337
spargefaction
scatter 73
wet 337
sparing [see spare]
small 32

economy 817
parsimony 819
temperate 953
with a – hand 819
with no – hand
639
– of praise 932
– of words 585
spark *small* 32
heat 382
light 420
luminary 423
wag 844
fop 854
as the –s fly up-
wards *habit* 613
sparkle
bubble 353
glisten 420
sparkling
vigorous 574
excitement 824
cheerful 836
wit 842
beauty 845
with – eyes 827
sparse 73
sparsity 103
Spartacus 742
spartan 739
spasm
sudden change 146
violence 173
agitation 315
pain 378
spasmodic
discontinuous 70
irregular 139
changeable 149
violent 173
spat 225, 713
spate 348
spathic 204
spatter *dirt* 653
spatterdash 225
spatula 191, 272
spavined 655
spawn *produce* 161
offspring 167
dirt 653
spay 38, 158
speak 560, 580, 582
– one fair 894
– for 937
– ill of 932, 934
– for itself 518,
528
– low 581
– of *meaning* 516
publish 531
speak 582
– out *make*
manifest 525
artless 703
– softly 581
– to 586
– up 411
– up for 937
– volumes 467
– well of 931
speakeasy 189, 964
speaker
interpreter 524
chairman 694
speakie 964
speaking: much –
584

way of – 521
– likeness 554
on – terms 888
speaking-trumpet
418
spear 260, 727
– shaped 253
spearman 726
special 79
– correspondent
593
special pleader 968
special pleading
sophistry 477
speciali gratiâ 760
specialist 662, 700
speciality 79
specialty
security 771
specie 800
species *kind* 75
appearance 448
human – 372
specific *special* 79
remedy 662
– gravity 321
specification 594
specify
particularize 79
tell 527
name 564
specimen 82
specious
probable 472
sophistical 477
beauty 845
flattering 933
pardonable 937
speck 32
speckle 440, 848
spectacle
appearance 448
prodigy 872
show 882
drama 599
spectacles 445
look through rose
colored – 523
spectacular 882
spectator 444
spectral 4, 980
spectre
fallacy of vision
443
ugly 846
ghost 980
spectroscope
light 420
color 428
optical instru-
ment 445
spectrum
color 428
variegation 440
optical illusion
443
speculate
view 441
think 451
suppose 514
chance 621
essay 675
traffic 794
speculation
experiment 463
cards 840
speculative 463, 514

speculum 445
veluti in – 446
sped *completed* 729
speech 582
figure of – 521
parts of – 567
speechify 582
speechless 403, 581
speechmaker 582
speed
velocity 274
activity 682
haste 684
help 707
succeed 731
with breathless –
684
God – 731, 906
speedily *soon* 132
speedometer 200,
274, 553
speedway 840
speer 455, 461
spell *period* 106
influence 175
read 539
letter 561
necessity 601
motive 615
exertion 686
charm 993
cast a – 992
wonder 870
knurr and – 840
– for 865
– out *interpret* 522
spell-bound 601,
615
spence 636
spencer 225
spend *effuse* 297
waste 638
give 784
purchase 795
expend 809
– freely 816
– time 106
– time in 683
– one's time in
625
spender 818
spendthrift 818
spent 160, 688
spermaceti 356
spermatic 168
spermatize 168
spero, dum spiro –
858
spes sibi quisque
604
spew 297
sphacelus 655
sphere *rank* 26
domain 74
space 180
region 181
ball 249
world 318
business 625
– of influence 181,
780
spheroid 249
spherule 249
sphery 318
sphinx *monster* 83
oracle 513
ambiguous 520

riddle 533
spial 668
spice
small quantity 32
mixture 41
pungent 392
condiment 393
spiced 390
spicilegium 72, 596
spick and span 123
spiculate 253
spiculum 253
spicy 400, 824
spigot 263
spike *sharp* 253
pierce 260
plug 263
– guns 158, 645
spikebit 262
spikenard 356
spill *filament* 205
stopper 263
shed 297
splash 348
match 388
waste 638
lavish 818
– blood 722
– and pelt 59
spin *flying* 267
rotate 312
pluck 610
– out *protract* 110
late 133
prolong 200
diffuse style 573
– the wheel 140
– a long yarn 549
spindle 312
spindling 203
spindle-shanks 203
spindle-shaped 253
spindrift 353
spine 222, 253
spinel 847
spinet *copse* 367
harpsichord 417
spinney 367
spinner of yarns
594
spinosity
unintelligible 519
discourtesy 895
sullenness 901a
spinous *prickly* 253
spinster 374, 904
spiracle 351
spiral 248
spire *height* 206
convolution 248
peak 253
soar 305
spirit *essence* 5
immateriality 317
fuel 388
intellect 450
meaning 516
vigorous language
574
activity 682
affections 820
courage 861
ghost 980
bad – 980
keep one's – up
hope 858
with life and – 682

– type 591
– water 343
stand-pipe 348, 385
stand-point 183, 441
Stannary Court 966
stanza 597
staple
  fastening 45
  whole 50
  peg 214
  texture 329
  material 635
  trade 794
  mart 799
  – commodity 798
star luminary 423
  actor 599
  destiny 601
  badge 747
  ornament 847
  glory 873
  noble 875
  decoration 877
  – in the ascendant
  success 731
  prosperity 734
  – of fashion 852
  – it drama 599
  fame 873
  display 882
  – shell 423
  – trap 599
starboard 238
starch stiff 323
  viscid 352
  affected 855
  proud 878
Star Chamber 966
starched
  ostentatious 882
stare look 441
  curiosity 455
  wonder 870
  make one – 870
  – out of counte-
  nance
  humiliate 879
  insolent 885
  discourteous 895
  – one in the face
  destiny 152
  manifest 525
  Death –s one in
  the face 360
stare super anti-
  quas vias
  continue 143
  habit 613
  preservation 670
  inaction 681
star-gazing 318
staring 446
stark very 31
  sheer 32
  complete 52
  hard 323
  – blind 442
  naked 226
stark staring 31
  manifest 525
  – mad 503
starlight 422
starlike
  pointed 253
starry 318
stars [see star]

worlds 318
bless one's – 916
– in the firmament
  multitude 102
– and stripes 550
start begin 66
  sudden change
  146
  arise 151
  impulse 276
  move 284
  depart 293
  leap 309
  unexpected 508
  suggest 514
  crack 659
  offer 763
  fear 860
  wonder 870
  get the –
  precede 280
  success 731
  give a – to 276
  have the –
  prior 116
  early 132
  get before 280
  – afresh 66
  – a doubt 485
  – game 622
  – off 293
  – a question 461
  – up project 250
  arise 305
  appear 446
starting: – hole
  plea 617
  – point
  departure 293
  reasoning 476
  eyes – out of one's
  head 870
startle doubt 485
  unexpected 508
  excite 824
  fear 860
  wonder 870
startling 508
startlish 825
starts, by fits and –
  608
starvation 640, 956
starve cold 383, 385
  poverty 804
  parsimony 819
  fast 956
starveling thin 203
  insufficient 640
  poor 804
state condition 7
  speciality 79
  nation 372
  inform 527
  affirm 535
  government 737
  realm 780
  ostentation 882
  robes of – 747
  secretary of – 694
  – of affairs 151
  –'s evidence 529
  – of facts
  description 594
  lawsuit 969
  – paper 551
  – room 191
  – of siege 722

statecraft 693
stated periods, at –
  138
stately grand 873
  proud 878
  pompous 882
statement 535, 594
statemonger 694
state prison 752
states-general 696
statesman 694
statesmanlike 698
statesmanship 692, 693
static 404
Statics strength 159
  gravity 319
station degree 26
  term 71
  place 182
  situation 183
  locate 184
  rank 873
stationary
  permanent 141
  quiescent 265
stationery 590
station-house 752
statist 694
statistics 85, 86
statu:
  in – pupillari 127
  in – quo 141, 660
statuary 557, 559
statue 554
  still as a – 265
stature 206
status position 8
  terms 71
  situation 183
  repute 873
status quo
  past 122
  unchanged 145
  restoration 660
  – ante bellum 145
statute 697, 963
staunch health 654
  reinstate 660
  honest 939
  – belief 484
stave music 413, 415
  contention 720
  – in concave 252
  hole 260
  – off 133, 706
stay remain 106
  wait 133
  continue 141
  stop 142
  dwell 186
  support 215
  not move 265
  prevent 706
  – away 187
  – one's hand
  cease 142
  relinquish 624
  rest 687
  – at home 893
stayed [sec staid]
stays corset 225
stead 644
  in the – of
  substitution 147
  commission 755

deputy 759
stand one in
  good – 644
steadfast stable 150
  persevering 604a
  – belief 484
  – thought 457
steady uniform 16
  regular 80
  periodic 138
  stable 150
  persevering 604a
  unexcitable 826
  cautious 864
steal 791
  – along 275, 528
  – away 623
  – on the ear 405
  – a march
  prior 116
  early 132
  precede 280
  deceive 545
  active 682
  cunning 702
  – upon one 508
stealing 791
stealth 528
  do good by – &c.
  881
stealthy 528
  cunning 702
  caution 864
steam navigate 267
  gas 334
  vaporize 336
  bubbles 353
  under – 267
  under sail and –
  274
  – car 272
  – up 171
  get the – up 673
steamboat 273
steam-engine to
  crack a nut
  waste 638
  redundance 641
  misuse 679
steamer 273
  – track 343
stearine 356
steed 271
steel strong 159
  sharp 253
  hard 323
  sword 727
  harden the sensi-
  bility 823
  – gray 432
  – the heart 951
  – helmet 717
  – oneself 604
steeled against
  604, 823
steel-engraving 558
steelyard 319
steep height 206
  cliff 212
  slope 217
  soak 337
steeped in
  – iniquity 945
  – misery 828
steeple 206, 253
steeple-chase
  swift 274

pursuit 622
contest 720
steer beast 366
  mate 373
  direct 693
  – clear 279, 623
  – one's course 692
  – for 278
steerage 279, 693
steersman 269, 694
steganographic 526
steganography
  unintelligible 519
  hidden 528
  writing 590
stellar 318
stellated 253
stelography 590
St. Elmo's fire 423
stem origin 153
  ancestor 166
  front 234
  oppose 708
  – to stern 200
  – the tide 142, 719
  – the torrent 731
stench 401
stencil 556
stenographer 553, 746
stenography 590
stentor cry 411
stentorian loud 404
step degree 26
  term 71
  support 215
  motive 264, 266
  measure 466
  expedient 626
  act 680
  dance the back –
  283
  but a – 197
  take a decisive –
  609
  not stir a – 265
  –dance 840
  – forward 282
  – in mediate 724
  –.into acquire 775
  – on be supported
  by 215
  – in the right
  direction 644
  – into the shoes of
  sequence 63
  posteriority 117
  substitution 147
  – short 275
  – by step
  degree 26
  order 58
  seriatim 69
  slowly 275
  – of time 109
steppe 180, 344
stepping-stone
  link 45
  way 627
  instrument 631
  resource 666
  preparation 673
steps way 627
  bend one's –
  travel 266
  direction 278
  flight of – 305

servant 746
enthral 749
- of dispute 713
- to examination 461
- of inquiry 461
- of thought 454
- to 469, 475
subjection 749
subjective
intrinsic 5
immaterial 317
intellectual 450
subjoin 37
subjugate 731, 749
subjugation 732, 824
subjunctive 37
sublapsarian 984
sublation 38
sublevation 307
sub-lieutenant 745
sublimate
elevate 307
lighten 320
vaporize 336
sublime *high* 206
language 574
beauty 845
glory 873
magnanimous 942
from the - to the ridiculous 853
subliminal 317
sublineation 550
sublunary 318
submarine
deep 208
ship 272
warship 726
- chaser 726
- warfare 722
submediant 413
submerge
destroy 162
immerse 300
plunge 310
steep 337
submersible 273, 726
submersion 208
subministration 707
submission 725
obedience 743
submissive
tractable 705
enduring 826
humble 879
submit to arbitration 774
submonish 695
submultiple 84
subordinate
inferior 34
unimportant 643
subject 749
subordination 58
suborn 615, 795
subpoena 741, 969
subreption
falsehood 544
acquisition 775
subrogation 147
subscribe
assent 488

aid 707
agree to 769
give 784
subscript 39, 65
subscription
gift 784
subsequent
- *in order* 63
- *in time* 117
subserviency
servility 886
subservient
instrumental 631
aid 707
subject 749
subside 36, 306
subsidiary *aid* 707
servant 746
subsidy
assistance 707
gift 784
pay 809
subsist *exist* 1
continue 141
live 359
subsistence 298
subsoil 221, 342
substance
existence 1
thing 3
quantity 25
inside 221
matter 316
texture 329
important part 642
wealth 803
in - 596
man of - 803
substantial
existing 1
hypostatic 3
material 316
dense 321
true 494
- meaning 516
substantiality 3
substantially
intrinsically 5
- true 494
substantiate 467, 924
substantive 1, 3
substitute
inferior 34
change 147
means 634
deputy 759
substitution 147
substratum
substance 3
layer 204
base 211
support 215
interior 221
materiality 316
substructure 211
subsultory 315
subsume 54
subtend 237
subterfuge 617
sophistry 477
lie 546
cunning 702
subterranean 208
subtile *light* 320
rare 322

- *texture* 329
subtilize *rarefy* 322
sophistry 477
subtle *slight* 32
light 320
cunning 702
- *point* 704
- *reasoning* 476
subtlety 477, 498
subtraction
subduction 38
arithmetic 85
taking 789
subtrahend 38, 84
suburb *town* 189
near 197
environs 227
subvention
support 215
aid 707
gift 784
subversion 146
subvert *destroy* 162
invert 218
depress 308
subway 627
- train 272
succedaneum 147
succeed *follow* 63
posterior 117
success 731
transfer 783
- to *acquire* 775
succès d'estime 873
success 731
succession
sequence 63
continuity 69
repetition 104
posteriority 117
transfer 783
in quick - 136
in regular - 138
- of ideas 451
- of time 109
successless 732
successor 65, 117
succinct 572
succor 707
succubus 980
succulent
nutritive 298
juicy 333
semiliquid 352
succumb
fatigue 688
yield 725
fail 732
succussion 315
such: - as 17
- being the case 8
- like 17
- a one 372
suchwise 8
suck
draw off 297
drink 298
take 789
- in 296
- the blood of 789
sucker 260, 547
suckle 707
suckling *infant* 129
suction *force* 157
reception 296
sudary 652
sudation 299

sudatory 386
sudden
transient 111
instantaneous 113
soon 132
unexpected 508
- *burst* 508
- *death* 360
- and quick in quarrel 901
- *thought* 612
sudorific 382
suds *froth* 353
in the - 704, 837
sue *demand* 765
go to law 969
suet 356
suffer *physical pain* 378
disease 655
allow 760
feel 821
endure 826
moral pain 828
- for 972
- *punishment* 972
sufferance, tenant on - 779
suffice 639
sufficiency 639
suffix *adjunct* 39
sequence 63
sequel 65
letter 561
suffiation 349
suffocate *kill* 361
excess 641
suffocating 382, 401
suffocation 361
suffragan 996
suffrage 609
suffragette 742
suffusion
mixture 41
feeling 821
blush 879
sugar 396
sugar-loaf 253
suggest *suppose* 514
inform 527
influence 615
advise 695
- itself 451, 515
- a question 461
suggestio falsi 546
suggestion 626, 695
suggestive
reminder 505
significant 516
descriptive 594
bawdy 961
sui generis 83
suicidal 162
suicide *killing* 361
suisse *beadle* 996
Suisse, point d'argent point de - 812
suit *accord* 23
series 69
class 75
clothes 225
expedient 646
petition 765
courtship 902
follow - 19
law- 969

love- 897
- the action to the word 550
- the occasion 646
do - and service 743
suit case 191
suitable 23, 646
- season 134
suite *sequel* 65
series 69
escort 88
retinue 746
- of rooms 189, 191
suitor
petitioner 767
lover 897
lawsuit 969
sulcated 259
sulky *carriage* 272
obstinate 606
discontented 832
dejected 837
sullen 901a
sullen
obstinate 606
gloomy 837
discourteous 895
sulky 901a
sullenness 901a
sully 653, 874
sulphur 388
- colored 436
sultan 745
sultry 382
sum *number* 84
money 800
- and substance
meaning 516
synopsis 596
important part 642
- total 800
- up *reckon* 85
description 594
compendium 596
sumless 105
summation 37, 85
summary
transient 111
early 132
short 201
concise 572
compendious 596
illegal 964
- of facts 594
summer *season* 125
support 215
heat 382
Indian - 125
St. Luke's - 125
St. Martin's - 125
- lightning 423
- time 114
summer-house 191
summerset 218
summit *top* 210
summon 741, 969
- up 505, 824
- up courage 861
summum:
- bonum 618, 827
- jus 922
sump *base* 211
pool 343
slough 345
store 636

active 682
haste 684
ride full – at 622, 716
run a – at 716
– over 218
– up 307
– with 720
tilth 371, 775
tilting at the ring 840
tilt-yard 728
timber *trees* 367
materials 635
timbre 413
timbrel 417
time 106
instant 113
leisure 685
against – 684
at –s 136
behind the –s 124
course of – 109
doing –
imprisonment 752
employ one's – in 625
glass of – 106
in – course 109
early 132
destiny 152
measure – 114
no – instantly 113
soon 132
no – to lose 630, 684
no – to spare 684
ravages of – 659
slow – 275
take – slow 275
inaction 681
inactive 683
true – 113
waste – 683
– and again 104
– has been 122
– being 118
– to come 121
– of day 113
– drawing on 121
– enough 132
– gone by 135
– hanging on one's hands
inaction 681
leisure 685
weariness 841
– immemorial 122
– of life
duration 106
now 118
age 128
– out of mind 122
– to spare 685
– after time 104
– up 111, 134
– was 122
there being –s when 136
timeful 134
time-honored
old 124
repute 873
respected 928
time-keeper 114
time-recorder 553
timeless 135

timelessness 112
timely 132, 134
timeo Danaos 485, 864
timeous 134
time-piece 114
time-pleaser 607
timetable 605
times present 118
events 151
hard – 735
many – 136
– out of number 104
time-serving
tergiversation 607
cunning 702
servility 886
improbity 940
selfishness 943
time-worn old 124
age 128
deteriorated 659
timid fearful 860
cowardly 862
humble 881
timist 607
Timocracy 803
Timon of Athens
wealth 803
seclusion 893
misanthrope 911
timorous [see timid]
tin preserve 670
money 800
– hat 717
tinct 428
tinctorial 428
tincture
small quantity 32
mixture 41
color 428
tinctured
disposition 820
tinder fuel 388
irascible 901
tine 253
tinge
small quantity 32
mix 41
colour 428
tingent 428
tingle pain 378
touch 380
emotion 821
make the ears – 900
tink 408
tinker
repair 660
tinkle
faint sound 405
resonance 408
tinkling cymbal 517
tinnient 408
tinsel glitter 420
sham 545
ornament 847
frippery 851
tinsmith 690
tint 428
tintamarre 404
tintinnabulary 408
tiny 32, 193
– bit 32
tip end 67
summit 210

cover 223
give 784
reward 973
on –toe high 206
expect 507
– off 527
– the wink 550
tip-cat 840
tippet 214, 225
tipple 298, 959
tippler 959
tipstaff 965
tipsy 959
tip-top 210, 648
tirade 582, 932
tire dress 225
fatigue 688
worry 830
weary 841
tiré à quatre épingles 850
tirer d'affaire 672
se – 731
Tiresias 513
tiresome [see tire]
Tisiphone 173, 900
tissue whole 50
assemblage 72
matted 219
texture 329
tit small 193
pony 271
tit for tat 718
Titan 159, 980
Titania 979
titanic 192
titbit 291, 394, 829
tithe tenth 99
tax 812
tithing 181
titillate 840, 865
titillation 377, 380
titivate 847
title
indication 550
name 564
printing 590
right to property 780
distinction 877
right 924
titled 875
title-deed 771
title-page 66
titter 838
tittle 32
to a –494
tittle-tattle 532, 588
titubancy 583
titubate 306, 732
titular 562, 564
tmesis 218
T.N.T. 727
to direction 278
lie – 681
– all intents and purposes 27, 52
– a certain degree 32
– come 121, 152
– the credit of 805
– crown all 33, 642
– do 59
– the end of the chapter 52
– the end of time 112

– and fro 12, 314
– the full 52
– a great extent 31
– the letter 19
– a man 78
– the point 23
– the purpose 23
– a small extent 32
– some extent 26
– be sure 488
– this day 118
– wit 79
toad 649, 846
– under a harrow 378
toad-eater 886, 935
toad-eating
flattery 933
toadstool 367
toady 886
toast roast 384
celebrate 883
tobacco 392
toboggan 272, 840
toby jug 191
toccata 415
tocsin 669
tod 319
to-day 118
toddle 266, 275
toddy 298
toe 211
on the light fantastic 309, 840
toes turn up the – die 360
toff 854
toffee 396
toga 225, 747
assume the – virilis 131
together 88, 120
come – 290
get – 72
hang – 709
lay heads – 695
– with 37, 88
toggery 225
toil
activity 682
exertion 686
– of a pleasure 682
–s trap 545
toilet 225
– water 400
toilette 225
en grande – 847
toilsome 686, 704
toilworn 688
token 550
give – 525
– of remembrance 505
told, do what one is – 743
tolderolloll 838
Toledo 727
tolerable
a little 32
trifling 643
pretty good 648
not perfect 651
satisfactory 831
tolerably, get on – 736
toleration

laxity 738
lenity 740
permission 760
feeling 821
calmness 826
benevolence 906
toll sound 407
tax 812
– the knell 363
tollbooth
prison 752
market 799
tomahawk 727
tomb 363
lay in the – 363
– of the Capulets 506
tombé des nues 83, 870
tombola 156
tomboy 129, 851
tombstone 363
tom-cat 373
tome 593
tomentous 256
tomfool 501
tomfoolery
absurdity 497
amusement 840
wit 842
ostentation 882
Tom Noddy 501
Tommy Atkins 726
tommy-gun 727
to-morrow 121
– and to-morrow 104, 109
tompion 263
tomtit 193
Tom Thumb 193
tom-tom 417, 722
ton weight 319
fashion 852
–s of money 800
tonality 413, 420
tone state 7
strength 159
tendency 176
sound 402
music 413
color 428
blackness 431
painting 556
method 627
disposition 820
give a – to 852
– down
moderate 174
darken 421
discolor 429
– in with 714
– of voice 580
tone poem 415
toney 852
tongs
fire-irons 386
retention 781
tongue
projection 250
taste 390
language 560
bite the – 392
bridle one's – 585
give – 404, 580
hold one's – 403
slip of the – error 495

track *trace* 461
  record 551
  way 627
  cover up one's –s
    528
  in one's –s 113
  racing – 840
  – meet 840
  – racing 728
trackless
  space 180
  difficult 704
  – trolley 272
tract *region* 181
  book 593
  dissertation 595
  – of time 109
tractable
  malleable 324
  willing 602
  easy 705
tractarian 984
tractile
  traction **285**
  soft 324
traction **285**
tractor 271
trade *exchange* 148
  business 625
  traffic 794
  drive a – 625
  learn one's – 539
  tricks of the – 702
  two of a – 708
  – with 794
trader 797
trade-mark 550
tradesman 797
trade-publication
  531
trade-union 712
trade-wind 349
tradition *old* 124
  description 594
  custom 613
traduce 934
traducer 936
traffic 794
tragedian 599
tragedy
  drama 599
  evil 619
tragic *drama* 599
tragical 830
tragi-comedy 599
tragi-comic 853
trail *sequel* 65
  pendent 214
  slow 275
  follow 281
  traction 285
  odor 398
  inquiry 461
  record 551
  highway 627
  follow in the – of
    281
  – of a red herring
    615, 706
train *sequel* 65
  series 69
  pendent 214
  vehicle 272
  sequence 281
  traction 285
  - *animals* 370
  teach 537

accustom 613
prepare 673
bring in its – 615
in – 673
in the – of 281,
  746
lay a – 626, 673
put in – 673
siege – 727
– de luxe 272
– of reasoning 476
– of thought 451
train-band 726
train-bearer 746
train-ferry 272
trained 698
trainer
  - *of horses* 268
  - *of animals* 370
  teacher 540
training
  education 537
  – college 542
train-oil 356
traipse 275
trait *speciality* 79
  appearance 448
  mark 550
  description 594
traitor
  disobedient 742
  knave 941
  enemy 891
trajection 297
trajectory 627
tra-la-la 838
tralatitious 521
tralineate 279
tralucent 425
tram 272
trammel *hinder* 706
  restrain 751
  fetter 752
  cast –s off 750
tramontane
  foreign 57
  distant 196
  wind 349
  outlandish 851
tramp *stroll* 266
  stroller 268
  idler 683
  vagabond 867
  on the – 264
trample
  – in the dust
  destroy 162
  prostrate 308
  – out 162
  – under foot
  vanquish 731
  not observe 773
  disrepute 874
  insolence 885
  dereliction 927
  contempt 930
  – upon 649, 739
tramway 627
trance *insensibility*
  376
  dream 515
  sleep 683
  lethargy 823
tranquil *calm* 174
  quiet 265
  peaceful 721
  calmness 871

– *mind* 826
tranquilize
  moderate 174
  pacify 723
  soothe 826
transact *act* 680
  conduct 692
  – business 625
  – business with
    794
transaction 151,
  625, 680, 769
transactions 551
transalpine 196
transanimation 140
transatlantic 196
transcalency 384
transcend *great* 31
  superior 33
  go beyond 303
transcendency 641
transcendent 33,
  873
transcendental 78,
  519
transcendentalism
  450
transcolate 295
transcribe 19, 590
transcript 21, 590
transcursion **303**
transept 1000
transfer
  copy 21
  displace 185
  - *of things* 270
  - *of property* **783**
transference **270**
transfiguration
  change 140
  divine - 998
transfix 260
transfixed *firm* 150
transform 140
transformation
  scene 599
transfuse 41, 270
  – the sense of 522
transgress
  go beyond 303
  infringe 773
  violate 927
  sin 945
transgression 947
transi de froid 383
transient 111, 149
transientness **111**
transilience 146,
  303
transistor 532
transit
  conversion 144
  motion 264
  transference 270
  - *circle* 244
transit gloria
  mundi, sic –
  735, 874
transition 144, 270
transitional 140
transitory 111
transitu, in –
  transient 111
  journey 266
  transference 270
translate
  interpret 522

promote 955
translator 524
translation
  transference 270
  resurrection 981
translocation 270
translucence 425
transmarine 196
transmigration 140,
  144
transmission
  moving 270
  passage 302
  - *of property* 783
transmit *light* 425
transmogrify 140
transmutation 140,
  144
transom 215
transparency **425**
transparent
  transmitting
    light 425
  obvious 518
transpicuous
  transmitting
    light 425
  obvious 518
transpierce 260
transpire
  evaporate 336
  appear 525
  be disclosed 529
transplace 270
transplant 270
transplendent 420
transpontine 196
transport
  transfer 270
  ship 273
  war vessel 726
  excitement 825
  delight 827
  please 829
  punish 972
  – of love 897
  – plane 273
transpose
  exchange 148
  displace 185
  invert 218
  transfer 270
  - *music* 413
transubstantiation
  change 140
  sacrament 998
transude 295, 302
transume 140
transumption 270
transverse 217, 219
tranter 271
trap *closure* 261
  gig 272
  snare 545
  stage - 599
  pitfall 667
  fall into a – 547,
    699
  lay a - for 545
trap bat and ball
  840
trap-door
  opening 260
  snare 545
  pitfall 667
trapan 545
trapes 701

trappings
  adjunct 39
  clothes 225
  equipment 633
  ornament 847
Trappist 996
traps
  clothes 225
  baggage 780
trash
  unmeaning 517
  trifling 643
  useless 645
trashy – style 575
traulism 583
traumatic 662
travail 161, 686
trave 215
travel 266
  – out of the record
    477
traveler **268**
  bagman 758
  tricks upon –s
    545, 702
  –'s tale 546, 549
traveling bag 191
traverse *move* 266
  pass 302
  negative 536
  obstruct 706
travesty
  imitate 19, 21
  misinterpret 523
  misrepresent 555
  ridicule 856
travis 215
trawl 285, 463
trawler 273
tray 191
treacherous 907,
  940
  – memory 506
treachery 545, 940
treacle 352, 396
tread 264, 266
  – the beaten track
    82, 613
  – the boards 599
  – down 739, 879
  – on the heels of
    281
  – a path 266, 622
  – the stage 599
  – in the steps of 19
  – under foot
  destroy 162
  subjection 749
  disrepute 874
  insolence 885
  contempt 930
  – upon 649
treadle 633
treadmill 975
treason 742, 940
treasure *cherish* 897
  store 636
  goodness 648
  money 800
  – trove 618
  – up in the
    memory 505
treasurer **801**
treasury **802**
  – note 800
treat *physical*
  pleasure 377

marriage 903
unionist 712
union-jack 550
union-pipes 417
unique
  dissimilar 18
  original 20
  exceptional 83
  alone 87
unirritating 174
unison
  agreement 23
  melody 413
  concord 714
unit 51, 87
Unitarian 984
unite *join* 43
  combine 48
  assemble 72
  concur 178
  converge 290
  party 712
  – one's efforts 709
  – in pairs 89
  – with 709
united 46, 714
unity *identity* 14
  uniformity 16
  whole 50
  complete 52
  single 87
  concord 714
  – of time 120
Unity, Trinity in –
  976
universal 78
  – Church 983*a*
  – favourite 899
universality 52
universe 318
university 542
  – education 537
  – extension 537
  go to the – 539
unjust *wrong* 923
  impious 988
unjustifiable
  wrong 923
  inexcusable 938
  wicked 945
unjustified 923
  undue 925
unkempt
  unclean 753
  vulgar 851
unkennel *eject* 297
  disclose 529
unkind 907
  –est cut of all 828
unknightly 940
unknit (44)
unknowable 519
unknowing 491
unknown
  ignorant 491
  latent 526
  – to fame
  inglorious 874
  low-born 876
  – quantities 491
unlabored
  – *style* 578
  unprepared 674
unlace (44)
unlade 297
unladylike
  vulgar 851

rude 895
unlamented
  hated 898
  disapproved 932
unlatch 44, 750
unlawful
  undue 925
  illegal 964
unlearn 506
unlearned 491
unleavened 674
unless
  circumstances 8
  except 83
  qualification 469
unlettered 491
  – Muse 579
unlicensed 761
unlicked
  unprepared 674
  vulgar 851
  clownish 876
  – cub
  youngster 129
  shapeless 241
  unmannerly 895
unlike 18
unlikely 473
unlikeness 15
unlimber 323
unlimited
  great 31
  infinite 105
  free 748
  – *space* 180
unliquefied 321
unlively 837, 843
unload
  displaced 185
  eject 297
  disencumber 705
unlock *unfasten* 44
  discover 480*a*
unlooked for 508
unloose
  unfasten 44
  liberate 750
unloved 898
unlovely 846
unlucky
  inopportune 135
  bad 649
  unfortunate 735
  in pain 830
unmade 2
unmaimed 654
unmake 145
unman
  mutilate 38
  render powerless
  158
  madden 837
  frighten 860
unmanly
  effeminate 374
  dishonorable 940
unmanageable
  unwieldy 647
  perverse 704
unmanned
  dejected 837
  cowardly 862
unmannered 895
unmannerly 895
unmarked 460
unmarred 654, 670
unmarried 904

unmask 529
unmatched
  different 15
  dissimilar 18
  unparalleled 20
unmeaningness 517
unmeant 517
unmeasured
  infinite 105
  undistinguished
  465*a*
  abundant 639
unmeditated 612
unmeet 925
unmellowed 674
unmelodious 414
unmelted 321
unmentionable 874
  –s 225
unmentioned 526
unmerciful 914*a*
unmerited 925
unmethodical 59
unmindful
  inattentive 458
  neglectful 460
  ungrateful 917
unmingled 42
unmissed 460
unmistakable
  certain 474
  intelligible 518
  manifest 525
unmitigable 173
unmitigated
  great 31
  complete 52
  violent 173
unmixed 42
unmolested 664,
  831
unmoneyed 804
unmoral 823
unmourned 898
unmoved
  quiescent 265
  obstinate 606
  insensible 823
unmusical 424
  – voice 581
unmuzzled 748
unnamed 565
unnatural
  exceptional 83
  affected 855
  spiteful 907
unnecessary
  redundant 641
  useless 645
  inexpedient 647
unneeded 645
unneighborly 895
unnerved
  powerless 158
  weak 160
  dejected 837
unnoted } 460
unnoticed } 874
unnumbered 105
unnurtured 674
uno saltu 113
unobeyed 742
unobjectionable
  good 648
  pretty good 651
  innocent 946
unobnoxious 648

unobscured 420
unobservant 458
unobserved 460
unobstructed 705,
  749
unobtainable 471
unobtained 777*a*
unobtrusive 881
unoccupied
  vacant 187
  unthinking 452
  doing nothing 681
  inactive 683
  untenanted 893
unoffended
  enduring 826
  humble 879
unofficial 964
unoften 137
unopened 261
unopposed 709
unorganized 674
  – matter 358
unornamental 846
unornamented
  – *style* 576
  simple 849
unorthodox 984
unostentatious 881
unowed 807
unowned 782
unpacific 713, 722
unpacified 713
unpack
  unfasten 44
  take out 297
unpaid *debt* 806
  honorary 815
  the great –
  magistracy 967
  – worker 602
unpalatable 395,
  830
unparagoned
  supreme 33
  best 648
  perfect 650
unparalleled
  unimitated 20
  supreme 33
  exceptional 83
unpardonable 938,
  945
unparliamentary
  language 895,
  908
unpassable 261
unpassionate 826
unpatriotic 911
unpeaceful 720, 722
unpeople
  emigration 297
  banishment 893
unperceived
  neglected 460
  unknown 491
unperformed 730
unperjured 543,
  939
unperplexed 498
unpersuadable 606
unpersuaded 616
unperturbed 826
unphilosophical 499
unpierced 261
unpin (44)
unpitied 932

unpitying 914*a*
unplaced 185
unplagued 831
unpleasant 830
unpleasing 830
unpoetical 598, 703
unpolished
  rough 256
  inelegant 579
  unprepared 674
  vulgar 851, 876
  rude 895
unpolite 895
unpolluted
  good 648
  perfect 650
unpopular 830, 867
unpopularity 898
unportioned 804
unpossessed 777*a*
unpractical 699
unprecedented 83,
  137
unprejudiced 498,
  748
unpremeditated
  impulsive 612
  undesigned 621
  unprepared 674
unprepared 508,
  674
unprepossessed 498
unprepossessing
  846
unpresentable 851
unpretending 881
unprevented 748
unprincipled 945
unprivileged 925
unprized 483
unproclaimed 526
unproduced 2
unproductive 645
unproductiveness
  169
unproficiency 699
unprofitable
  unproductive 169
  useless 645
  inexpedient 647
  bad 649
unprolific 169
unpromising 859
unprompted 612
unpronounceable
  519
unpronounced 526
unpropitious
  ill-timed 135
  opposed 708
  hopeless 859
unproportioned 24
unprosperous 735
unprotected 665
unproved 477
unprovided
  scanty 640
  unprepared 674
unprovoked (616)
unpublished 526
unpunctual
  tardy 133
  untimely 135
  irregular 139
unpunished 970
unpurchased 796
unpurified 653

cuique – 865
voluptuary 954a, 962
voluptuous
  pleasure 377
  delightful 829
  intemperate 954
  impure 961
volutation 312
volute 248
vomit 297
vomitory 260, 295
voodoo 992, 994
voracious *desire* 865
  glutton 957
vortex *rotation* 312
  agitation 315
  river 348
  danger 667
vorticist 556
votary
  auxiliary 711
  devotee 865
vote 535, 609
  – for 488
voting machine 553
votis, hoc erat in –
  865
votive 768
  – offering 990
vouch *assert* 535
  – for 467
voucher
  evidence 467
  indication 550
  security 771
  payment 807
vouchsafe
  permit 760
  consent 762
  ask 765
  condescend 879
vow *affirmation* 535
  promise 768
  worship 990
  take –s 995
vowel 561
vox:
  – faucibus hæsit
  voiceless 581
  fear 860
  wonder 870
  – populi
  assent 488
  publication 531
  choice 609
  – et praeterea nihil
  unsubstantial 4
  powerless 158
  unmeaning 517
  vain 880
  boasting 884
voyage 267
voyager 268
vraisemblance 472
vue d'oeil, à – 132, 446
Vulcan 690, 979
vulgar *inelegant* 579
  low born 876
  – tongue 560
vulgarian 851
vulgarity
  want of refinement 851
Vulgate 985
vulgus, ignobile –

876
vulnerable 665
vulnerary 662
vulnus:
  æternum servans
  sub pectore – 919
  immedicabile – 619
vulpine 702
vulture 739, 913

W

wabble *slow* 275
  oscillate 314
wad 263
wadding *lining* 224
  stopper 263
  soft 324
waddle 275
wade 267
  – in blood 361
  – through
  learn 539
  exertion 686
waddle 314
wafer *cement* 45
  thin 203
  lamina 204
waft *transfer* 270
  blow 349
wafted, be – 267
wag *oscillate* 314
  agitate 315
  joker 844
  – on *journey* 266
  progression 282
wage war 722
wager 621
  – of battle 722
  – of law 467
wages 973
waggery *wit* 842
waggish 836, 853
waggle 314, 315
wagon 272
wagoner 268
wagonette 272
wagon-load 31
waif 618, 782
waifs and estrays 73, 268
wail 412, 839
wain 272
wainscot 211, 224
waist 203
waistcoat 225
  put in a strait – 751
wait 133, 681
  lie in – for 530
  – for 507
  – impatiently 133
  – on *accompany* 88
  aid 707
  – to see how the wind blows 607
  – upon *serve* 746
  call on 894
waiter *servant* 746
  – on Providence
  neglect 460
  inactive 683
  content 831

waiting 507
  be kept – 133
waiting-maid 746
waitress 746
waits 416
waive *defer* 133
  not choose 609a
  not use 678
waiwode 745
wake *sequel* 65
  rear 235
  funeral 363
  trace 551
  excite 824
  amusement 840
  in the – of 281
  enough to – the dead 404
  – the thoughts 457
  – up 824
wakeful
  careful 459
  active 682
Walhalla 981
walk *region* 181
  lane 189
  move 266
  business 625
  way 627
  conduct 692
  arena 728
  – one's chalks 293, 623
  – the earth 359
  – of life 625
  –ed off one's legs 688
  – off with 791
  – over the course 705, 731
  – in the shoes of 19
walker 268
walking gentleman 599
wall *vertical* 212
  parietes 224
  inclosure 232
  refuge 666
  obstacle 706
  defence 717
  prison 752
  driven to the – 704
  go to the –
  destruction 162
  die 360
  fail 732
  pushed to the – 601
  take the – 873, 878
  wooden –s 726
  –eyed 442
  – in 229, 751
wallah 746
wallet 191
wallop 315
wallow *low* 207
  plunge 310
  rotate 312
  – in 377, 641
  – in the mire 653
  – in riches 803
  – in voluptuousness 954

wallsend 388
Wall-street 799
  – slang 563
waltz 415, 840
wamble
  vacillate 149
  oscillate 314
  dislike 867
wampum 800
wan 429, 837
wand *scepter* 747
  magic 993
  wave a – 992
wander *move* 264
  journey 266
  deviate 279
  delirium 503
  the attention –s 458
wanderer 268
wandering
  exceptional 83
  – Jew 268
wane
  decrease 36
  age 128
  contract 195
  decay 659
  one's star on the – 735
  wax and – 140
wangle 943
want
  inferiority 34
  shortcoming 304
  requirement 630
  insufficiency 640
  poverty 804
  desire 865
wanted 187
wanting
  incomplete 53
  absent 187
  imbecile 499
  found –
  imperfect 651
  disapproval 932
  guilt 947
wantless 639
wanton
  unconformable 83
  capricious 608
  unrestrained 748
  amusement 840
  rash 863
  impure 961
wapentake 181
war 722
  at – 24, 720
  at – with 708, 722
  declare – 713
  man of – 727
  seat of – 728
  – correspondent 534, 593
  – of words 588, 720
warble 416
war-cry *alarm* 669
  defiance 715
  war 722
ward *part* 51
  parish 181
  safety 664
  asylum 666
  dependent 746
  restraint 751

watch and – 459, 753
  – off 706, 717
war-dance 715
warden
  guardian 664
  master 745
  deputy 759
warder
  perforator 262
  porter 263
  guardian 664
  keeper 753
wardmote 966
wardrobe 191, 225
ward-room 191
war-drum 417
wardship 664
ware
  warning 668
  merchandise 798
warehouse 636, 799
warfare 722
  discord 713
war-horse 726
warlike 722
warlock 994
warm
  violent 173
  hot 382
  make hot 384
  red 434
  orange 439
  wealthy 803
  ardent 821
  excited 824
  angry 900
  irascible 901
  flog 972
  – bath 386
  – the blood 824
  – the cockles of the heart 829
  – imagination 515
  – man 803
  – reception
  repel 717
  welcome 892
  – up 658, 660
  – work 686
warm-hearted
  feeling 821
  sensibility 822
  friendship 888
  benevolence 906
warming 384
warming-pan
  locum tenens 147
  heater 386
  preparation 673
warmth
  vigorous language 574
warn *dissuade* 616
  caution 668
  – off 761
warning *omen* 512
  dissuasion 616
  caution 668
  give – *dismiss* 678
  relinquish 782
  – voice *alarm* 666
warp *change* 140
  tend 176
  contract 195
  distort 243
  navigate 267